THE ELGAR COMPANION TO DAVID RICARDO

The Elgar Companion to David Ricardo

Edited by

Heinz D. Kurz

Professor of Economics, University of Graz and Graz Schumpeter Centre, Austria

and

Neri Salvadori

Professor of Economics, University of Pisa, Italy

 Edward **Elgar**
PUBLISHING

Cheltenham, UK • Northampton, MA, USA

Published by
Edward Elgar Publishing Limited
The Lypiatts
15 Lansdown Road
Cheltenham
Glos GL50 2JA
UK

Edward Elgar Publishing, Inc.
William Pratt House
9 Dewey Court
Northampton
Massachusetts 01060
USA

Paperback edition 2017

A catalogue record for this book
is available from the British Library

Library of Congress Control Number: 2014959492

This book is available electronically in the **Elgar**online
Economics subject collection,
DOI 10.4337/9781784715489

MIX
Paper from
responsible sources
FSC
www.fsc.org   FSC® C013056

ISBN 978 1 84844 850 6 (cased)
ISBN 978 1 78471 548 9 (eBook)
ISBN 978 1 78811 087 7 (paperback)

Typeset by Servis Filmsetting Ltd, Stockport, Cheshire
Printed and bound in Great Britain by TJ International Ltd, Padstow

Contents

List of contributors to this volume and their entries

Abraham-Frois, Gilbert, Emeritus Professor, Université Paris Ouest, France
Biaujeaud, Huguette, on Ricardo

Arena, Richard, Professor of Economics, Université Nice Sophia Antipolis, France
Competition

Aspromourgos, Tony, Professor of Economics, University of Sydney, Australia
Ricardo on Adam Smith

Aßländer, Michael S., Professor for Business Ethics, Technische Universität Dresden, Germany
Mill, John Stuart, on Ricardo

Backhouse, Roger E., Professor of the History and Philosophy of Economics, University of Birmingham, UK and Erasmus University Rotterdam, the Netherlands
Blaug, Mark, on Ricardo

Barens, Ingo, Professor of Economics, Technische Universität Darmstadt, Germany
Keynes, John Maynard, on Ricardo

Bellino, Enrico, Associate Professor of Economics, Università Cattolica del Sacro Cuore, Italy
Accumulation of Capital; Pasinetti, Luigi Lodovico, on Ricardo

Bidard, Christian, Emeritus Professor, Université Paris Ouest, France
Land and Rent; Ricardian Dynamics

Blankenburg, Stephanie, Senior Lecturer in Economics, School of Oriental and African Studies, London, UK
Competition

Casarosa, Carlo, Emeritus Professor, Università di Pisa, Italy
Hicks, John R., on Ricardo

Ciccone, Roberto, Professor of Economics, Università degli Studi Roma Tre, Italy
Corn Model

Cremaschi, Sergio, Former Professor of Moral Philosophy at Università degli Studi del Piemonte Orientale 'Amedeo Avogadro' (Alessandria, Novara, Vercelli), Italy
Belsham, Thomas, and Ricardo; Malthus–Ricardo Debate; Mill, James, and Ricardo; Porter, Sarah Ricardo

Dardi, Marco, Professor of Economics, Department of Economics and Business, Università di Firenze, Italy
Marshall, Alfred, on Ricardo

Deleplace, Ghislain, Emeritus Professor of Economics, Université Paris 8 (Laboratoire d'Economie Dionysien), France
Bullionist Controversy; Monetary Theory; Papers on Money and Banking

Dome, Takuo, Professor of History of Economic Thought at Osaka University, Japan
Taxation

Erreygers, Guido, Professor of Economics, Universiteit Antwerpen, Belgium
Land and Rent; Ricardian Dynamics

Faccarello, Gilbert, Professor of Economics, Université Panthéon-Assas, Paris; and Triangle, École Normale Supérieure de Lyon and CNRS, France
Comparative Advantage; Labour Theory of Value

Faucci, Riccardo, Professor of History of Economic Thought, Università di Pisa, Italy
Historical Schools on Ricardo

Fiaschi, Davide, Associate Professor of Economics, Università di Pisa, Italy
Colonies

Fratini, Saverio, Associate Professor, Università degli Studi Roma Tre, Italy
Surplus

Freni, Giuseppe, Professor of Economics, Università degli Studi di Napoli Parthenope, Italy
Mathematical Formulations of Ricardian Economics

Gehrke, Christian, Associate Professor of Economics, Department of Economics and Graz Schumpeter Centre, Karl-Franzens-Universität Graz, Austria
Dmitriev, Vladimir Karpovich, on Ricardo; Hollander, Jacob Harry, on Ricardo; Improvements in Production; Non-English Editions of Ricardo's Works; Ricardo Editions; Say, Jean-Baptiste, and Ricardo; Whewell, William, on Ricardo

Gilibert, Giorgio, Former Professor of Economics, Università degli Studi di Trieste, Italy
Capital and Profits; Revenue

Groenewegen, Peter, Emeritus Professor, School of Economics, University of Sydney, Australia
Trower, Hutches, and Ricardo

Haas, David, PhD student, Department of Economics, Karl-Franzens-Universität Graz; and researcher at the Graz Schumpeter Centre, Karl-Franzens-Universität Graz, Austria
Jevons, William Stanley, on Ricardo

Hagemann, Harald, Professor of Economics, Universität Hohenheim, Germany
General Glut

Heertje, Arnold, Emeritus Professor of Economics and History of Economic Thought, Universiteit van Amsterdam, the Netherlands
Jewish Background; Life and Activities

King, John E., Emeritus Professor, La Trobe University, Australia; and Honorary Professor, Federation University Australia
Kaldor, Nicholas, on Ricardo; Ricardian Socialists

Klausinger, Hansjoerg, Associate Professor of Economics, WU – Wirtschaftsuniversität Wien, Austria
Hayek, Friedrich von, on Ricardo

Kurz, Heinz D., Professor of Economics, Department of Economics and Graz Schumpeter Centre, Karl-Franzens-Universität Graz, Austria
Böhm-Bawerk, Eugen von, on Ricardo; Bortkiewicz, Ladislaus von, on Ricardo; Endogenous Growth; Exhaustible Resources and Mines; Invariable Measure of Value; Limiting and Regulating Principles; Principles of Political Economy, and Taxation; Samuelson, Paul Anthony, on Ricardo; Schumpeter, Joseph Alois, on Ricardo; Sraffa, Piero, on Ricardo; Technical Change; Walras, Marie-Esprit-Léon, on Ricardo

Maneschi, Andrea, Emeritus Professor of Economics, Vanderbilt University, Nashville, Tennessee, USA
Corn Laws; Ricardo's Four Magic Numbers

Marcuzzo, Maria Cristina, Professor of Economics, Università di Roma 'La Sapienza', Italy
Natural Quantity of Money

Meacci, Ferdinando, Professor of Economics, Department of Economics and Management 'Marco Fanno', Università degli Studi di Padova, Italy
Say's Law; Wealth

Milgate, Murray, Fellow and Director of Studies, Queens' College, University of Cambridge, UK
Member of Parliament

Mongiovi, Gary, Professor of Economics, St. John's University, New York, USA
Recent Interpretations; Torrens, Robert, and Ricardo

Moseley, Fred, Professor of Economics, Mount Holyoke College, Massachusetts, USA
Marx, Karl Heinrich, on Ricardo

O'Brien, D.P., Emeritus Professor, Durham University, UK
National Debt

Opocher, Arrigo, Professor of Economics, Department of Economics and Management 'Marco Fanno', Università degli Studi di Padova, Italy
Poor Laws; Population

Palumbo, Antonella, Associate Professor, Università degli Studi Roma Tre, Italy
Demand and Supply

Parrinello, Sergio, Former Professor of Economics, Università degli Studi di Roma 'La Sapienza', Italy
Foreign Trade

Perrotta, Cosimo, Former Professor of History of Economic Thought, Università degli Studi di Lecce (now Università del Salento), Italy
Riches and Value

Pivetti, Massimo, Former Professor of Economics, Università degli Studi di Roma 'La Sapienza', Italy
Rate of Interest

Porta, Pier Luigi, Professor of Economics, Università degli Studi di Milano-Bicocca, Italy
Notes on Malthus

Quadrio Curzio, Alberto, Emeritus Professor, Università Cattolica del Sacro Cuore; and President of the Class of Moral Sciences of the Accademia Nazionale dei Lincei, Italy
Gold

Rizvi, S. Abu Turab, Professor of Economics and Provost, Lafayette College, USA
Exchange Value and Utility

Rosselli, Annalisa, Professor of Economics, Università di Roma Tor Vergata, Italy
Natural Quantity of Money

Rotondi, Claudia, Associate Professor of Development Economics, Università Cattolica del Sacro Cuore, Italy
Gold

Salvadori, Neri, Professor of Economics, Università di Pisa, Italy
Endogenous Growth; Exhaustible Resources and Mines; Invariable Measure of Value; Principles of Political Economy, and Taxation; Samuelson, Paul Anthony, on Ricardo; Sraffa, Piero, on Ricardo; Walras, Marie-Esprit-Léon, on Ricardo

Signorino, Rodolfo, Associate Professor of Economics, Università degli Studi di Palermo, Italy
Colonies; Essay on Profits; Funding System; Natural and Market Prices

Sigot, Nathalie, Professor of Economics, PHARE, Université Paris 1 Panthéon-Sorbonne, France
Bentham, Jeremy, and Ricardo

Smith, Matthew, Senior Lecturer, University of Sydney, Australia
Tooke, Thomas, and Ricardo

Stirati, Antonella, Professor of Economics, Università degli Studi Roma Tre, Italy
Labour and Wages

Sturn, Richard, Associate Professor of Economics, Department of Public Economics and Graz Schumpeter Centre, Karl-Franzens-Universität Graz, Austria
Ricardian Equivalence

Trabucchi, Paolo, University Researcher, Università degli Studi Roma Tre, Italy
Corn Model

Trautwein, Hans-Michael, Professor of International Economics, Carl von Ossietzky Universität Oldenburg, Germany
Wicksell, Knut, on Ricardo

Tubaro, Paola, Reader in Economic Sociology, University of Greenwich, UK
Tozer, John Edward, on Ricardo

Watarai, Katsuyoshi, Professor of Economics, School of Political Science and Economics, Waseda University, Japan
McCulloch, John Ramsay, and Ricardo; Ricardo's Emancipation from Smith's Theory of Prices

Preface

David Ricardo is arguably one of the most important economists ever, whose impact on the profession has been and still is significant. Paul Samuelson once called him 'the economist's economist' because of his detached, sober and scientific approach to economic problems. This approach also earned him the title of an 'abstract and *a priori* theorist', a man 'with his head in the clouds' (John Maynard Keynes). Close scrutiny shows, however, that he was not only familiar with the facts and rules of the financial sector, but had an intimate knowledge of technical progress taking place in agriculture and manufacture at the time. Hence, while Ricardo's reasoning is abstract, he was keen to base it on premises that were in contact with the real world.

Ricardo was a stockjobber – a speculator on the stock exchange – and an extremely successful one at that. On the occasion of the Battle of Waterloo in 1815, which saw the defeat of the Napoleonic troops, he made a huge fortune. He decided to devote most of his time and energy to what he called 'my most favourite subject': political economy. He had come across Adam Smith's *The Wealth of Nations* in 1799 during a stay with his wife in Bath and had immediately fallen in love with the subject. In altogether less than 15 years, and in parallel with many other things he did professionally and as a Member of Parliament, he succeeded in elaborating one of the most impressive *oeuvres* in the history of our subject. It consisted of numerous essays and pamphlets and his magnum opus, *On the Principles of Political Economy, and Taxation*, first published in 1817. A second edition followed in 1819, a third in 1821.

His vast correspondence with people including James Mill, J.R. McCulloch and Thomas Robert Malthus, his Parliamentary speeches, and so on, comprise several volumes in the altogether 11 volumes of *The Works and Correspondence of David Ricardo* (1951–73), edited by Piero Sraffa with the collaboration of Maurice H. Dobb on behalf of the Royal Economic Society. His writings and correspondence deal with basically all themes in political economy, from production to money and trade, from the private sector to the public one, from taxation to public debt. The emphasis in his reflections on economic matters is on the laws regulating the distribution of the product amongst the different classes of society, landlords, workers and capitalists, in the form of rents, wages and profits. In fact, to him, this was the 'principal problem in Political Economy'.

His works gained him immediate recognition and admiration, but also criticisms. The situation did not change much in the course of time. Ricardo's doctrines and propositions were and remained the objects of occasionally heated disputes. The publication of *The Works and Correspondence* with Sraffa's introduction in Volume I, in combination with Sraffa's reformulation of the 'classical standpoint' in *Production of Commodities by Means of Commodities* published in 1960, have reignited the debate about Ricardo's legacy in economics. The deeper reason for this is to be seen in the fact that the classical economists emerge as authors of a theory of value and distribution *in statu nascendi* that is fundamentally different from the one advocated by the later marginalist authors from William Stanley Jevons to Léon Walras and Alfred Marshall. It was an alternative theory, which by giving it a coherent form could no longer be brushed aside due to the teething problems affecting the original formulations in which it was handed down by Adam Smith and Ricardo. Against this background a reassessment of Ricardo's contribution in the light of the more recent developments appears to be well justified.

There are further reasons that may be invoked on behalf of the present volume. After years, if not decades, in which the problem of income distribution was given short shrift in much of economics, it is back on the agenda with a vengeance. The change in the distribution of income and wealth that has taken place in many countries, industrialized and developing, since the last quarter of the twentieth century gave rise to a growing concern by many people, including social scientists and politicians. It suffices to mention the remarkable success of Thomas Piketty's recent book on the topic, *Capital in the Twenty-First Century* (2013). In addition, several recent developments are worth reporting. They concern first and foremost a number of exegetical issues, which have led to important corrections of the picture we have of Ricardo's views. For example, the discovery of hitherto unknown letters by Ricardo throw new light on his monetary theory. His theory of foreign trade has anew been subjected to critical scrutiny and has led to new advances in a highly complex subject matter. Several other examples could be mentioned. Here it suffices to stress the fact that Ricardo, like other great economists, had repeatedly sound intuitions into particular economic problems, but was not yet capable of expressing them in a clear and coherent way: his vision surpassed what he could state using the analytical tools and language at his disposal. A case in point is his remarkable conviction that the 'great questions' of income distribution 'are not essentially connected with the doctrine of value', a point of view that was only corroborated with Sraffa's discovery of the 'standard commodity'.

The gestation period of *The Elgar Companion to David Ricardo* was long, a great deal longer than originally planned. There are many reasons that contribute to explaining the delay of the enterprise, from authors that did not deliver and had to be replaced to the bad health of one of the editors for a longer period of time and the mourning that plagued the other editor. We are very pleased that, despite the difficulties that had to be overcome, we are now able to present the *Companion* to the scientific community. We take this opportunity to thank all contributors for their fine work and the referees we involved in assessing first versions of the entries for helping to improve them. We apologize to those contributors who delivered their work in good time. We are grateful to them and the publisher for their great amount of patience. May this *Companion* contribute to a better understanding of the works of David Ricardo and a flourishing of the ideas contained in them.

HEINZ D. KURZ AND NERI SALVADORI

Note:

In the following the majority of references to Ricardo's works will be to the 11 volumes of *The Works and Correspondence of David Ricardo* (1951–73), edited by Piero Sraffa with the collaboration of Maurice H. Dobb, Cambridge: Cambridge University Press. Passages cited or pages referred to will be indicated in the following way: *Works*, followed by volume number, chapter number and page number (where relevant). For obvious reasons, in the references appended to each entry, Ricardo's *Works* will not be listed again.

Accumulation of Capital

Capital accumulation is a phenomenon that has been widely studied by classical economists. It is a typical characteristic of the economic systems that have undergone the Industrial Revolution. Ricardo devoted an entire chapter of *On the Principles of Political Economy, and Taxation* to this topic (*Works*, I, XXI: 'Effects of Accumulation on Profits and Interests'), and hinted at it in several other sections throughout the book. According to Ricardo, it is the capitalist class that undertakes the accumulation of capital, that saves and invests (almost) all profits to increase their capital stock as long as the rate of profits is positive (or is higher than that minimum level below which capitalists lose any incentive to invest). This process of accumulation has a permanent effect: the fall in the rate of profits and consequently, sooner or later, the end of accumulation, that is, a convergence to a stationary state:

> The natural tendency of profits then is to fall; for, in the progress of society and wealth, the additional quantity of food required is obtained by the sacrifice of more and more labour. This tendency, this gravitation as it were of profits, is happily checked at repeated intervals by the improvements in machinery, connected with the production of necessaries, as well as by discoveries in the science of agriculture which enable us to relinquish a portion of labour before required, and therefore to lower the price of the prime necessary of the labourer. The rise in the price of necessaries and in the wages of labour is however limited; for as soon as wages should be equal (as in the case formerly stated) to 720*l.* [£720], the whole receipts of the farmer, there must be an end of accumulation; for no capital can then yield any profit whatever, and no additional labour can be demanded, and consequently population will have reached its highest point. Long indeed before this period, the very low rate of profits will have arrested all accumulation, and almost the whole produce of the country, after paying the labourers, will be the property of the owners of land and the receivers of tithes and taxes. (*Works*, I, VI: 120–21)

In looking for the 'fundamental' cause of this fall (for an interpretation of the distinction between 'fundamental' or 'permanent' versus 'temporary' causes in Ricardo see Marcuzzo, 2014), Ricardo wants to exclude two possible misleading justifications. First, he criticizes Smith, who explained the tendency for profits to fall as a consequence of competition engendered by the process of capital accumulation:

> The increase of stock, which raises wages, tends to lower profit. When the stocks of many rich merchants are turned into the same trade, their mutual competition naturally tends to lower its profit; and when there is a like increase of stock in all the different trades carried on in the same society, the same competition must produce the same effect in them all. (*WN*, I.iv.2)

This position is incompatible with Ricardo's theory of profits, according to which profits, being a physical surplus, are independent of prices and thus not affected by competition induced price changes. Second, Ricardo excludes that the saturation of final needs may be at the origin of the fall in profits. He establishes this point on Smith's authority:

> Adam Smith has justly observed 'that the desire of food is limited in every man by the narrow capacity of the human stomach, but the desire of the conveniences and ornaments of building, dress, equipage, and household furniture, seems to have no limit or certain boundary.' Nature then has necessarily limited the amount of capital which can at any one time be profitably engaged in agriculture, but she has placed no limits to the amount of capital that may be

employed in procuring 'the conveniences and ornaments' of life. (*Works*, I, XXI: 293, citing *WN*, I.xi.7)

(by the way, it is interesting to note how, in Ricardo's view, economic growth is essentially conceived as a *structural change* process).

The fundamental cause for the fall in profits is found, according to Ricardo, in the increasing difficulty to obtain the necessary additional wage-goods, which must be produced on less and less fertile plots of land as the system grows:

> From the account which has been given of the profits of stock, it will appear, that no accumulation of capital will permanently lower profits, unless there be some permanent cause for the rise of wages. If the funds for the maintenance of labour were doubled, trebled, or quadrupled, there would not long be any difficulty in procuring the requisite number of hands, to be employed by those funds; but owing to the increasing difficulty of making constant additions to the food of the country, funds of the same value would probably not maintain the same quantity of labour. If the necessaries of the workman could be constantly increased with the same facility, there could be no permanent alteration in the rate of profits or wages, to whatever amount capital might be accumulated. (*Works*, I, XXI: 289)

A simple formulation

Ricardo's position on this argument emerges easily from the simple mathematical formulation of the Ricardian theory proposed by Pasinetti (1960) as an extension of Kaldor (1955–56: §I). The main effects of the accumulation process (i.e., the reduction of the rate of profits and the convergence toward a stationary state) can be presented by a one-industry model. Yet, the diffusion of these effects through the other industries of the economy can be better appreciated by the more general model with two industries. In particular, we will refer to the reformulation of Pasinetti's model based on Ricardo's early writings (here presented in the entry Pasinetti, Luigi Lodovico, on Ricardo). One industry produces the wage-goods (for simplicity 'corn'), and the other produces 'gold'. The quantity produced of corn, Q_c, is represented by a differentiable, increasing, and concave function of the number of workers employed in the industry, N_c:

$$Q_c = f(N_c), \tag{1}$$

where $f' > 0$ and $f'' < 0$. $f'(N_c)$ is the quantity of corn produced by an additional worker employed on an additional plot of land. The assumptions on the first and the second derivatives of f entail that each additional worker produces a positive, but decreasing quantity of corn – decreasing returns to scale prevail. This phenomenon gives rise to a differential income that must be paid as rent to the owners of each plot of land, except for the last one, in order of decreasing fertility. Thus, rents are determined by:

$$R = f(N_c) - N_c f'(N_c). \tag{2}$$

Constant returns to scale prevail in the production of gold, whose technology is described by the function:

$$Q_g = \alpha N_g, \tag{3}$$

where Q_g is the quantity of gold produced, N_g is the number of workers employed in the gold industry and α is the (constant) productivity of labour.

Wage theory is summarized by the following four equations:

$$x = \bar{x}, \tag{4}$$

$$W = x(N_c + N_g), \tag{5}$$

$$K = W, \tag{6}$$

$$K = \bar{K}. \tag{7}$$

As corn is at the same time the output and the unique means of production of itself (and of gold) the corn industry is in the condition to calculate its rate of profits in physical terms as a ratio of quantities of corn:

$$\frac{Q_c - R - xN_c}{xN_c} = \frac{f'(N_c) - x}{x}.$$

Competition requires that the rate of profits of the gold industry adapts to the (predetermined) rate of profits of the corn industry:

$$\frac{p_g Q_g - p_c x N_g}{p_c x N_g} = \frac{f'(N_c) - x}{x}, \tag{8}$$

where p_c and p_g are the price of corn and the price of gold respectively. This equalization takes place through a suitable change of the relative price of gold in terms of corn. Thanks to (3) we see that, in equilibrium, we must have:

$$\frac{p_c}{p_g} = \frac{\alpha}{f'(N_c)}. \tag{8'}$$

This is the price of corn expressed in terms of gold – the latter will be used as the numéraire of the system.

Finally, Pasinetti determines the composition of output on the basis of the Ricardian view that landowners spend (the main part of) their rents in gold, while capitalists and workers spend profits and wages in corn. This can be obtained by introducing only the following equation:

$$p_g Q_g = p_c R. \tag{9}$$

We thus have nine equations in nine unknowns: Q_c, Q_g, N_c, N_g, R, W, K, x and p_c/p_g.

The solution of system (1)–(9) can be represented graphically by the diagrams in Figure 1. The left-hand diagram depicts how the distributive variables in the corn industry are determined: once the outputs of the two industries are known, the sectorial employment levels, N_c^* and N_g^*, are determined. Given N_c^*, total production of corn is

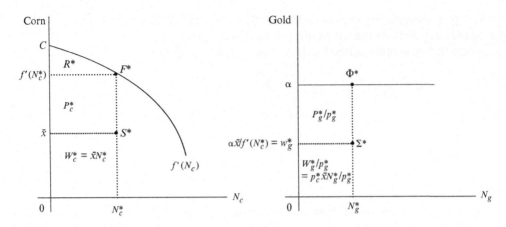

Figure 1   Income distribution in the Ricardian system

represented by area $ON^*_c F^* C$, rents are represented by area R^*, the sum of the differences between the corn obtained from each plot of land and the corn obtained from the least productive cultivated plot. Total wages paid in the corn industry are represented by area $W^*_c = \bar{x} N^*_c$, where $\bar{x}$ is the natural wage. Profits of the corn industry are represented by area P^*_c, that is, the residuum. The rate of profits is the ratio between area P^*_c and area W^*_c or, equivalently, between segments S^*F^* and $N^*_c S^*$, that is:

$$\frac{P^*_c}{W^*_c} = \frac{S^*F^*}{N^*_c S^*} = \frac{f'(N^*_c) - \bar{x}}{\bar{x}}. \tag{10}$$

In the right-hand diagram, referring to the gold industry, magnitudes are represented in terms of gold (in symmetry with the left-hand diagram, where magnitudes appear in terms of corn). Wages and profits of the gold industry, both in terms of gold, are given by areas: $ON^*_g \Sigma^* w^*_g$ and $w^*_g \Sigma^* \Phi^* \alpha$, respectively. It is easy to verify that the ratio between segments $w^*_g \alpha$ and Ow^*_g yields a rate of profits equal to the rate of profits of the corn industry. In fact:

$$\frac{w^*_g \alpha}{Ow^*_g} = \frac{\alpha - \dfrac{\alpha \bar{x}}{f'(N^*_c)}}{\dfrac{\alpha \bar{x}}{f'(N^*_c)}} = \frac{f'(N^*_c) - \bar{x}}{\bar{x}}.$$

Given this situation, the willingness of capitalists to enlarge their capital stock causes them to save and invest in additional means of production both in the production of the wage-good and in the production of the luxury good. The actual division of this investment between the two industries depends on the way in which final demand evolves during the process of accumulation of capital. This is an issue that, at least for classical economists, can hardly be described by means of a univocal or mechanical set of relations (i.e., equations) of the type used to explain rents, profits and the relative price of the two goods. Both the determination of the quantities produced and,

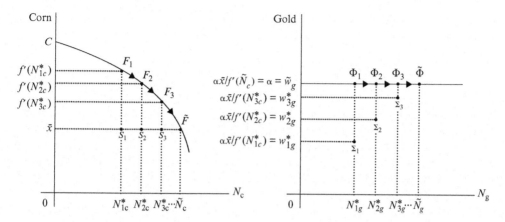

Figure 2   Accumulation of capital

a fortiori, their evolution are issues that involve historical, sociological and habitual elements that no equation is able to incorporate meaningfully. In Garegnani's words these are issues that require an analysis *outside* of the 'core' of the economic system (see Garegnani, 1984).

For our purposes, we can, however, bypass these issues by observing that *any* pattern of evolution of quantities arising in consequence of the accumulation of capital will always entail an increase in the quantity of corn produced, since corn is the means of production of each of the commodities produced in the system. Hence, the presence of positive profits in the solution described by Figure 1 engenders a movement along the arrows in the diagrams represented in Figure 2.

If we first analyse the effects of accumulation of capital, we see an increase in the number of workers employed in the corn industry from N^*_{1c} to N^*_{2c}, N^*_{3c}, and so on. New and less fertile plots of lands are thus being cultivated. Consequently, the amount of corn obtained on the marginal land, $f'(N_c)$, decreases. By a simple inspection of expression (8'), an immediate consequence of this increased difficulty in producing corn entails an increase of the relative price of corn in terms of gold. Moreover, total wages increase from $0N^*_{1c} S_1 \bar{x}$ to $0N^*_{2c} S_2 \bar{x}$, to $0N^*_{3c} S_3 \bar{x}$, and so on, while the wage rate remains fixed at $\bar{x}$ (the constancy of the wage rate will be discussed in depth later in this section). Rents unambiguously increase. Initially, the effect on total profits is ambiguous: they increase for the extension of cultivation, but the profits obtained on each plot of land decrease as they are affected by the reduction of the product obtained on the marginal land. From a certain level of N_c onward, the second effect prevails and total profits of the corn industry decrease. Consider, in fact, the expression of profits of the corn industry, $P_c = Q_c - R - \bar{x}N_c = N_c [f'(N_c) - \bar{x}]$; its derivative with respect to the number of workers employed in the corn industry is $dP_c/dN_c = [f'(N_c) - \bar{x}] + N_c f''(N_c)$; the first addendum is positive and decreasing with respect to N_c, while the second addendum is negative.

The increase of rents induces an increase in the production of gold, hence N_g increases; consequently total wages increase, while profits decrease from a certain point onward – the profits of the gold industry (in terms of gold) are $P_g/p_g = \alpha N_g[1 - \bar{x} f'(N_c)]$. On the basis that any increase of employment in the gold industry requires a corresponding increase of employment in the corn industry (to produce the wage-good for the additional workers of the gold industry), we can assume that $dN_c/dN_g > 0$. Hence:

$$\frac{d(P_g/p_g)}{dN_g} = \alpha\left[1 - \frac{\bar{x}}{f'(N_c)}\right] + \alpha\bar{x}N_g\frac{f''(N_c)}{[f'(N_c)]^2}\frac{dN_c}{dN_g}.$$

The first addendum is positive and decreasing as long as $N_c < \tilde{N}_c$, where $\tilde{N}_c$ is the stationary state employment level for the corn industry, while the second addendum is always negative. When N_c approaches $\tilde{N}_c$, the first addendum of the derivative tends to zero, and thus also and real profits in the gold industry decrease. Moreover, the rate of profits for the whole system, given by the ratios $S_tF_t/N^*_{ct}S_t = \sum_t\Phi_t/N^*_{tg}\sum_t$, with $t = 1, 2,$ ..., always decreases.

   In conclusion, the main consequence of the accumulation of capital is that profits and the rate of profits decrease till they become zero: here both the incentive to accumulate and the source from which to draw additional capital are exhausted. The economy has reached its 'stationary state' – it is in a condition to indefinitely replicate the same productive cycle without expanding or contracting. More realistically, according to Ricardo, the stationary state will be reached before profits completely disappear, that is, when the rate of profits has reached that minimum level that no longer induces capitalists to invest.

   The above analysis makes it clear that the cause of a decrease in profits during the process of accumulation of capital is rooted in the decreasing returns to scale of lands. As is known, in the corn industry this erodes profits in favour of rents (this emerges clearly from the left-hand diagram of Figure 2). But, as corn is the wage-good, this phenomenon extends to the rest of the economy through a higher wage rate expressed in terms of the other commodity(ies): the wage rate remains constant in physical terms at the given level $\bar{x}$, but its value in terms of gold, $(p_c/p_g)\bar{x} = \alpha \cdot \bar{x}/f'(N_c)$, increases as new workers are employed on new (and less fertile) plots of land – the right-hand diagram of Figure 2 depicts this effect very clearly. This reasoning faithfully replicates the description of the effects of accumulation of capital described by Ricardo in the quotation at the end of the introduction above.

The wage rate during the accumulation process
In the above analysis we adopted the simplification of keeping the real wage rate at its natural level, $\bar{x}$. Yet, if we accept the Malthusian principle, the natural wage is that level that keeps the population *unchanged*. This is in contradiction to the increasing need for new labour force to produce the additional quantities of corn and gold. The assumption to keep the wage rate equal to its natural level during the accumulation process can be considered, at first glance, a simplification of analysing the phenomenon of capital accumulation. Actually, Pasinetti (1960) developed a full-fledged analysis of accumulation, by means of a truly dynamic system, in which real wages are endogenously determined. This is done by replacing equation (4) with the following equation:

$$N_c + N_g = \overline{N} \tag{4'}$$

and by adding two differential equations:

$$\frac{dN}{dt} = F(x - \bar{x}) \tag{11}$$

$$\frac{dK}{dt} = G[f'(N_c) - x], \tag{12}$$

where $F(\cdot)$ and $G(\cdot)$ are two sign-preserving functions (a function H is sign preserving if $\text{sgn}[H(x)] = \text{sgn}\,x$). Equations (4′), (6) and (7) lead to a determination of real wages based on the wage-fund theory. In fact, they yield $x = \bar{K}/\bar{N}$. Equation (11) replicates the Malthusian principle: the population increases when the real wage is above its natural level and vice versa; equation (12) entails that new capital is accumulated as long as the rate of profits is positive (it is straightforward to allow for a positive minimum level of the rate of profits below which accumulation stops). Equations (4′) and (7) now come to play the role of the initial conditions of the dynamic system. A formal proof of convergence of the above dynamic model to a stationary solution characterized by:

$$x = \bar{x} \qquad \text{and} \qquad f'(N_c) - \bar{x} = 0$$

is provided in Pasinetti (1960: Appendix). This is the Ricardian 'stationary equilibrium', characterized by a stable population and a null rate of profits.

In connection with the dynamic aspects of Ricardian analysis, a group of contributions presented in the late 1970s and in the 1980s aimed to propose a 'new view' in the Ricardian theories of distribution and growth: the main contributions come from Hicks and Hollander (1977), Casarosa (1978, 1982) and Samuelson (1978). These authors emphasize the role of the 'market' in determining the wage rate during the accumulation process, in contraposition to the 'natural' wage rate, that is the 'subsistence' wage rate, which is considered to prevail only once the stationary state has been reached.

Hicks and Hollander propose determining the market wage rate by means of the apparatus of the demand and supply curves. They consider an economic system where only corn is produced. This can be obtained by setting $N_g = 0$ and considering only equations (1), (2), (4′), (5), (6), (7), (11) and (12); by denoting r as the rate of profits of the system; as $r = [f'(N_c)] - x/x$ we obtain $x = f'(N_c)/(1 + r)$. Hicks and Hollander read this equality in the sense that the wage rate 'is the *discounted* marginal product of labor' (Hicks and Hollander, 1977: 356; original emphasis). They study the dynamics of such a system and prove that the market economy converges toward its stationary state (oscillations for both variables x and N are allowed, unless the elasticity of the marginal productivity curve, $f'(N_c)$, is less than 1 in modulus; ibid.: 353–9).

Casarosa's market wage rate determination is based on the 'wage-fund' theory: the market wage rate is determined by the ratio between the wage fund K and the number of workers N, which is assumed constant in any given period: $x = K/N$. So far, this approach is analogous to that followed by Pasinetti as expressed by our previous equations (4′), (5), (6) and (7). Then Casarosa disregards for a moment the path originated by the initial conditions (4′) and (7) and considers another particular path, characterized by the equality between the rate of capital accumulation and the rate of population growth; he thus replaces equation (4′) with:

$$\frac{1}{K}\frac{dK}{dt} = \frac{1}{N}\frac{dN}{dt}. \qquad (4'')$$

The interest in such a *balanced equilibrium path* (Casarosa, 1982: 233) stems from the fact that, according to Casarosa, it is possible to prove that, given the level of the marginal productivity of 'labour-cum-land', market equilibrium converges towards that path (Casarosa, 1978: §4). Stirati (2011: §5) has emphasized a difficulty on this point: she showed that if the wage rate varies in order to adjust the rate of capital accumulation with the population growth rate, it is not able to adjust the level of capital stock to the level of employment at the same time. According to Casarosa the pleasant consequence of this convergence would have been that 'the market equilibrium is not "disturbed" by the process of economic growth, as long as the marginal productivity of labour does not change' (Casarosa, 1978: 45). A clarification of the assumption of a 'given' level of marginal productivity is in order. Instead of supposing that curve $f'(N_c)$ decreases continuously, Casarosa supposes that the marginal productivity of labour-cum-land decreases stepwise (the quantity of land of each given quality is supposed to be sufficiently large to have pieces of the $f'(N_c)$ curve along which constant returns to scale prevail). The convergence of market dynamics towards the balanced equilibrium path takes place within the limits of each piece.

Finally, Casarosa considers broadening cultivation to less fertile plots of land; the ensuing decrease of marginal productivity of labour-cum-land entails a decrease of the growth rate of capital accumulation, of the wage rate, of the rate of profit, and the convergence to the stationary state (ibid.: §5).

According to Pasinetti:

> [T]here is no incompatibility between the passages from Ricardo's *Works*, quoted at the beginning of Casarosa's paper, and the Pasinetti-Sraffa version of the Ricardian system. I should add something more. If Casarosa's analysis is intended in what I would consider an appropriate way, it itself raises no incompatibility with the Pasinetti-Sraffa version of the Ricardian system. Casarosa concentrates his efforts on defining a particular path of the actual (i.e. market) wage rate, and no objection can be raised to that. In other words I would consider Casarosa's analysis as aimed at depicting in detail one particular dynamic path of the market wage rate that is compatible with Ricardo's theory. (Pasinetti, 1982: 241)

However, Casarosa has aimed to enucleate a tendency towards the balanced growth path for the various paths – considered by Pasinetti – which start from any arbitrary initial condition, as stated in equations (4') and (7).

Nevertheless, in both analyses, the determination of the market wage rate takes the shape of the usual apparatus of demand and supply curves: let $N(t)$ and $K(t)$ be the paths of the population level and the capital stock that are solutions of the dynamic system with initial conditions $N(0) = \overline{N}$ and $K(0) = \overline{K}$. From (5) and (6) we obtain a sort of (decreasing) labour demand curve for each period, $N_c + N_g = K(t)/x(t)$, while the labour supply curve is $N(t)$.

However, there is a weakness in this description of the process of accumulation. The dynamics of capital accumulation and of population are described in the model by two differential equations. But in reality, the speed of adjustment that characterizes these processes is completely different: population dynamics reacts much more slowly to a difference between the 'market' and the natural wage rate than capital dynamics reacts to positive profits. The inadequacy of this procedure is even clearer in Casarosa's analysis, where the convergence towards the balanced growth path is conceived to take place on each given plot of land: the reaction of population size to the difference of the market wage from the natural wage should thus be faster than the speed of exhaustion of the plots of land of a given quality! In general, an analytic specification where the dynamics of population and the dynamics of capital take place in the same time span does not seem appropriate for outlining the fundamental relations of the Ricardian accumulation process. Consider, for example, what would happen in a situation in which the dynamics of capital originates a demand for labour higher than the labour force made available by population dynamics. As no increase of the wage rate is able to 'fuel' the required increase of the labour force in the present period (nor in the subsequent 13–17 years!), the only possible adjustment would be an increase of the wage rate sufficient to dampen the demand of labour until it is adjusted to the existing labour force.

In addition, there is a methodological problem: the choice to determine the market wage rate by a supply and demand apparatus introduces an interdependent link among the relevant variables, which is extraneous to Ricardo's analysis (at least if we follow Sraffa's interpretation):

> The first [property] . . . concerns profits and consists in the fact that the real wage rate and the rate of profit are determined simultaneously from the same group of equations, so that profits do not have the character of a residuum as in the 'accepted version' of the Ricardian theory and in Pasinetti's model. (Casarosa, 1978: 60)

There is, however, an alternative way to investigate the process of accumulation of capital, which can easily be reconciled with the 'surplus approach' (for a general presentation of the surplus approach see Garegnani, 1984; for its connection with the issue of wage determination in the Ricardian accumulation process see Stirati, 2011). This view does not link the determination of the actual wage rate prevailing during the accumulation process to a tendency toward labour market (full employment) equilibrium. Wage determination is a rather complex phenomenon in classical political economy, which cannot be linked by a set of mechanical or deterministic relations with the other variables of the system. The 'normal' wage prevailing in a given period of time is the result of two sets of conditions: (1) historical and institutional circumstances such as customary living standard of workers, the institutional set-up of the country and the bargaining force of the relevant social classes; (2) the current economic conditions, which also include the pace of accumulation, that affect the ratio of the quantities of labour demanded and labour supplied (observe that labour demanded and supplied enter here as given quantities, not as functions of the wage rate, as normally assumed in the traditional approach).

For these reasons, the determination of wages for classical economists is normally separated and developed with different tools from those employed in the analysis of the determination of the rate of profits and of prices. Different levels of abstraction and generality are associated in these stages of analysis: the former is eminently descriptive and based on institutional arguments; the latter is deductive and based on strictly economic arguments.

Thus, as in a specified period of time the normal real wage rate is considered as a given magnitude in the stage of analysis where the rate of profits and relative prices are determined, the same assumption must be adopted when studying the process of accumulation. Obviously, the 'accumulation of capital naturally produces an increased competition among the employers of labour, and a consequent rise in its price' (*Works*, I, IX: 163). This competition will act on *real* wages, but its effect will not be univocal, depending on institutional circumstances. For this reason, the real wage rate prevailing during the accumulation process, x, can be considered as given, even though fixed at a different level, probably higher than the subsistence level. On the other hand, the increased difficulty of production entailed by the extension of cultivation on less and less fertile plots of land, acts by increasing the price of the wage-good (expressed in terms of gold, the numéraire of the system). But this phenomenon will act on *money* wages, that is, on $w = (p_c/p_g)x$. As it is essentially due to technical reasons, it can easily be described by equation $(p_c/p_g)\bar{x} = \alpha\bar{x}/f'(N_c)$.

The analysis developed in previous sections can thus be entirely recovered, simply by reinterpreting symbol $\bar{x}$ as the 'normal' wage prevailing during the accumulation process. This is perfectly compatible with Kaldor's (1955–56) approach, which has sometimes been called the 'fix-wage' approach (see Hicks and Hollander, 1977 or Casarosa, 1982). Probably, according to the interpretation proposed here, the term 'fix wage' is not appropriate. It could be replaced by 'given wage', or 'wage fixed at an institutional level'. Pasinetti (1982) proposes a wider interpretation of the Ricardian notion of 'natural' wage rate, which seems in accordance with the substance of the alternative interpretation proposed here:

> [B]y concentrating all emphasis on the Ricardian notion of *market* wage rate, Casarosa's approach is open to the danger of neglecting – or reducing to irrelevance – the much more fundamental Ricardian notion of a *natural* wage rate. This is in fact the trap into which – it seems to me – Hicks and Hollander (1977) have fallen. In their analysis, the 'natural' wage rate plays no role. To begin with, they confuse it with the 'subsistence wage'; and second, they relegate the latter to play the external role of a boundary 'floor'. All their attention is concentrated on the *market* wage rate. (Pasinetti, 1982: 241; original emphasis)

However, the choice of considering the real wage rate as a given magnitude during the accumulation process seems to be the best way to let emerge the *fundamental effects* of the accumulation process (an increase of money wages, an increase of rents, a decrease of profits and a tendency to the stationary state) and the *fundamental cause* of these effects (the increase of the relative price of the wage-good). Considering the normal real wage as given does not mean that it is assumed that it will not change during this process. There can be several reasons that induce a change of the normal wage rate during the accumulation process: changes of the bargaining positions of capitalists and workers, changes of the institutional set-up of the country, accelerations or decelerations of the accumulation process and so on, which change the proportion between the quantities of labour demanded and supplied. But, as these changes cannot be univocally put in relation with any of the other endogenous variables of the model, it is better to renounce a deterministic explanation of these changes and to take them into account through exogenous changes of parameter $\bar{x}$ (a similar view is expressed by Kurz and Salvadori, 2006: 110–11). The graphs in Figure 2 immediately show how a change in $\bar{x}$ affects the speed of the accumulation process.

Effects of capital accumulation on the labour theory of value of the *Principles*
Until now we have studied the effects of capital accumulation in a simple Ricardian framework that can be traced back to Ricardo's theory of profit of his 'early writings', which, after Sraffa (see his 'Introduction' to Ricardo's *Works* and 1960), can be considered the essential skeleton of Ricardo's approach. As we have seen, in this framework the labour theory of value is obtained as a 'by-product' of the supposition that there exists one commodity (corn) that is at the same time the output and the only input of itself and of the other(s) commodity(ies). Yet, the labour theory of value does not play any relevant role, as the magnitudes necessary to determine the distributive variables of the system can be measured in physical terms. However, in the *Principles*, Ricardo aims to free himself of the very restrictive assumption of a single capital good. Hence, he managed to develop a theory of value independent of income distribution, in order to avoid circular reasoning concerning prices and distribution. To this purpose, he tried to extend the labour theory of value – which Smith confined to the 'early and rude state of society which precedes both the accumulation of stock and the appropriation of land' (*WN*, I.vi.65) – to industrial systems. The productive processes of these systems are characterized by the presence of a set of means of production (capital goods) that assist human labour. Hence, if we want to reduce the price of each commodity to its labour content, we must take into account the labour that has been employed to produce these means of production, that is, indirect labour, in addition to the labour employed to produce the commodity, that is, direct labour (to this matter Ricardo devoted one of the two items of the entry 'ACCUMULATION of capital' of his 'Index' at the end of the *Principles* – the other entry was devoted to the effects on profits and interest; see *Works*, I: 431).

But the emergence of indirect labour is at the origin of all the difficulties met by Ricardo in his extension of the labour theory of value to the generality of cases. Consider two commodities, denoted by indexes c and m. Suppose that wages are still advanced by capitalists. As indirect labour is labour employed to produce the means of production, it is labour erogated *before* the erogation of direct labour to produce the final commodity. Hence, suppose that l_i units of (direct) labour are erogated 1 year before, and λ_i units of (indirect) labour are erogated two years before the obtainment of one unit of commodity i, $i = c, m$. The price equation of the generic commodity i is:

$$p_i = wl_i(1 + r) + w\lambda_i(1 + r)^2, \tag{13}$$

where w is the wage rate and r is the rate of profits. Let $\gamma_i = \lambda_i/l_i$ be the proportion of indirect to direct labour (capital intensity) in the industry of commodity i. As known, it is easy to verify that if capital intensity is uniform between industries c and m:

$$\lambda_c/l_c = \gamma = \lambda_m/l_m \tag{14}$$

then the price of commodity c in equation (13) reduces to $p_c = wl_c(1 + r)[1 + \gamma(1 + r)]$ and the relative price of commodity c in terms of commodity m reduces only to a ratio of labour quantities:

$$\frac{p_c}{p_m} = \frac{l_c}{l_m} = \frac{l_c + \lambda_c}{l_m + \lambda_m}. \tag{15}$$

Equation (15) extends the labour theory of value to the economies where the accumulation of capital has taken place. Yet, it is also immediate to see that there are at least three cases where this extension fails:

(a)   Unequal capital intensity
If (14) does not hold, then the relative price of commodity c in terms of m is:

$$\frac{p_c}{p_m} = \frac{wl_c(1 + r) + w\lambda_c(1 + r)^2}{wl_m(1 + r) + w\lambda_m(1 + r)^2};$$

it clearly depends on labour quantities *and* on income distribution.

(b)   Unequal capital durability
If indirect labour is used to produce fixed capital, that is, a capital good that lasts for more than one period, say T periods, the (constant) depreciation to be imputed to each unit of commodity c and m is a fraction $\delta = 1/T$ of the fixed capital good employed, specific to each industry. In this case, the relative price of commodity c in terms of m becomes:

$$\frac{p_c}{p_m} = \frac{wl_c(1 + r) + w\lambda_c(\delta_c + r)^2}{wl_m(1 + r) + w\lambda_m(\delta_m + r)^2},$$

which does not reduce to (15), even in the case of uniform capital intensity, unless $\delta_c = \delta_m$.

(c)   Unequal rapidity with which circulating capital returns to its employers
If indirect labour is used to produce a circulating capital, which must remain employed for a number of t periods, specific to each industry, the relative price of commodity c in terms of m becomes:

$$\frac{p_c}{p_m} = \frac{wl_c(1 + r) + w\lambda_c(1 + r)^{t_c}}{wl_m(1 + r) + w\lambda_m(1 + r)^{t_m}},$$

which does not reduce to (15), even in the case of uniform capital intensity, unless $t_c = t_m$.

Ricardo was not able to overcome these difficulties satisfactorily. Only the modern developments of classical analysis have provided a wholly general and coherent analysis of the links between prices and income distribution rooted in classical political economy and, in particular, in Ricardo's economics.

ENRICO BELLINO

See also:

Corn Model; Endogeneous Growth; Hicks, John R., on Ricardo; Kaldor, Nicholas, on Ricardo; Mathematical Formulations of Ricardian Economics; Pasinetti, Luigi Lodovico, on Ricardo; Ricardian Dynamics; Technical Change.

References

Casarosa, C. (1978), 'A new formulation of the Ricardian system', *Oxford Economic Papers*, **30**(1), 38–63.

Casarosa, C. (1982), 'The new view of the Ricardian theory of distribution and economic growth', in M. Baranzini (ed.), *Advances in Economic Theory*, Oxford: Basil Blackwell.

Garegnani, P. (1984), 'Value and distribution in the classical economists and Marx', *Oxford Economic Papers*, **36**(2), 291–325.

Hicks, J. and S. Hollander (1977), 'Mr. Ricardo and the moderns', *Quarterly Journal of Economics*, **XCI**(3), 351–69.

Kaldor, N. (1955–56), 'Alternative theories of distribution', *The Review of Economic Studies*, **23**(2), 83–100.

Kurz, H.D. and N. Salvadori (2006), 'Endogenous growth in a stylised "classical" model', in G. Stathakis and G. Vaggi (eds), *Economic Development and Social Change – Historical Roots and Modern Perspectives*, Abingdon, UK and New York: Routledge.

Marcuzzo, C. (2014), 'On the notion of permanent and temporary causes: the legacy of Ricardo', *Journal of the History of Economic Thought*, **36**(4), 421–34.

Pasinetti, L. L. (1960), 'A mathematical formulation of the Ricardian system', *The Review of Economic Studies*, **27**(2), 78–98.

Pasinetti, L.L. (1982), 'A comment on the "new view" of the Ricardian theory', in M. Baranzini (ed.), *Advances in Economic Theory*, Oxford: Basil Blackwell.

Samuelson, P.A. (1978), 'The canonical classical model of political economy', *Journal of Economic Literature*, **16**(4), 1415–34.

Smith, A. ([1776] 1981), *An Inquiry into the Nature and Causes of the Wealth of Nations*, (eds) R.H. Campbell, A.S. Skinner and W.B. Todd, Indianapolis: Liberty Fund.

Sraffa, P. (1960), *Production of Commodities by Means of Commodities. Prelude to a Critique of Economic Theory*, Cambridge: Cambridge University Press.

Stirati, A. (2011), 'Interpretations of the classics – the theory of wages', in R. Ciccone, C. Gehrke and G. Mongiovi (eds), *Sraffa and Modern Economics, Vol. I*, Abingdon and New York: Routledge.

Belsham, Thomas, and Ricardo

Thomas Belsham (1750–1829), formerly a minister of the Independent Church, was appointed in 1789 as Professor of Divinity at the newly formed Unitarian college at Hackney, and after its dissolution in 1796 was first in charge of the New Gravel Pit Chapel at Hackney and then moved to Essex Street Chapel in Central London in 1805 (Webb, 2004).

Unitarianism came into existence as a self-standing body in 1774, when Theophilus Lindsey, a minister who withdrew from the Church of England on anti-Trinitarian grounds, founded a chapel in London at Essex Street. In the same years, Dissenter Joseph Priestley, the philosopher and chemist, founded another Unitarian chapel in Bristol. Other ministers joined the movement, coming mainly from the English Presbyterians. The unifying trait of Unitarianism was a rejection of a view of salvation based on the Trinitarian dogma, including inherited guilt, eternal punishment, vicarious atonement, and the godly nature of Jesus. They were among radicals and reformers at the time of the French Revolution and they campaigned consistently for religious toleration from which they would themselves benefit (Anonymous, 1823a).

Ricardo's 'conversion' to Unitarianism

Until Sraffa's (1951) edition of his *Works*, Ricardo's adhesion to Unitarianism was ignored in the literature. Most sources used then did not mention his conversion to Christianity and even the author of the 'Memoir' avoided any mention of his liaison with what was still perceived as a dangerous sect of radicals (*Works*, X: 39–40; Henderson, 1997: 164). The facts are that, shortly after marriage in 1793, he appears to have become Belsham's 'hearer' at New Gravel Pit Chapel in Hackney from 1794 to 1805, then Robert Aspland's at the same chapel from 1805 to 1812, and again Belsham's at Essex Street Chapel (Anonymous, 1823c). Whether being a 'hearer' meant being a full member of a congregation or rather a fellow traveller or sympathizer is still in doubt. Apparently Ricardo kept his liaison with the Unitarians alive until his death, as proved by the respectful and warm obituary published in *The Monthly Repository*, the Unitarian review (Anonymous, 1823b), following the detailed report of Ricardo's Parliamentary speech for religious toleration in the same issue (Anonymous, 1823c), both of which have been missed by biographers. There is no plausible doubt that can be raised about Ricardo's own sincere interest in religion in spite of the bizarre conjecture that he, being a rational and modern mind, was an obvious atheist, and therefore his conversion to Unitarianism was just a means of acquiring social respectability at the cheapest price (Depoortère, 2002). The answer is that, even if one felt like doing history without evidence, such a conjecture would labour under a fatal logical weakness, namely a need to prove that the choice of joining a radical congregation looked at with suspicion as an alleged hotbed of revolutionaries could be a convenient arrangement for gaining social respectability. Archival sources may yet reveal whether he ever opted for formal affiliation to the Unitarian Congregation or remained forever a 'hearer' or sympathizer, but the evidence suggests that Ricardo was introduced to the ideas of the philosophical tradition deriving from Priestley and Hartley, with which Belsham himself was associated. Needless to say that such ideas had a philosophical character and were just those favoured by Unitarians of the time for contingent reasons not dependent on faith and theology. For sure,

Ricardo never adhered to the established Church – he did not take Holy Communion according to the established rite on his nomination as a High Sheriff of Gloucestershire in 1817 nor did he on entering Parliament (*Works*, X: 42). On his travel on the Continent in 1822 he attended Sunday service on 30 July at the Engelse Kerk in Amsterdam, which is an English-speaking chapel of the Reformed Church of the Netherlands (ibid.: 210). It is true that he was buried in an Anglican cemetery, but this was established practice for Dissenters and even Roman Catholics.

Belsham the philosopher

Belsham taught divinity for several years of his life, and published exegetical studies where he argued that the doctrines of a divine nature of Jesus and a Trinitarian nature of God were completely absent from the original Christian preaching as reflected in New Testament scriptures. Moreover, he lectured on political philosophy, ethics, logic, and other philosophical subjects (Fitzpatrick, 1999). He published, besides sermons, collections of essays and exegetical works, a textbook, *Elements of the Philosophy of the Mind, and of Moral Philosophy. To Which is Prefixed a Compendium of Logic* (1801), in which he drew inspiration mainly from David Hartley and Joseph Priestley while often attacking Dugald Stewart.

   With regard to the method of natural science, he favours separation of scientific terminology and ordinary language (Belsham, 1801: xvi), contends that 'observations of the senses do not teach us the real essence of substances' (ibid.: xxxii) and that the sciences just establish regularities among phenomena. With regard to the social sciences, Belsham argues against Dugald Stewart that 'as moral ideas are equally capable of strict definition with mathematical ideas, demonstration is equally applicable to moral subjects' (ibid.: xlv), and, in some cases at least, explanation of the behaviour of voluntary agents may reach the same degree of precision as 'that with which we foretell the effects of physical causes' (ibid.: lxxxiii), since also in these cases 'the same cause operating in the same circumstances will invariably produce same effects' (ibid.: lxxxii–iii).

   Belsham used to stress the importance of education while recommending 'to select and pursue with particular assiduity two or three branches of science only' (Williams, 1833: 398), and suggesting that these should be chosen among the 'useful' ones, unlike those, for example, metaphysical enquiries, which are 'without the grasp of the human mind' (Belsham, 1826–27, II: 55).

What Ricardo may have learnt from Belsham

Ricardo had recently become Belsham's 'hearer' when he started studying mathematics, geology, mineralogy and chemistry. In his brother's wary wording, he was drawn to these scientific interests by the 'example and instigation of a friend' (*Works*, X: 6). Belsham could have been both a 'friend' who could have encouraged him in such pursuits, and one whose name could have prompted prudence. Belsham was aware of Ricardo's achievements, and he even criticized him on one point – population theory – by writing:

> It is really astonishing that a doctrine so absurd and so contradictory to plain and obvious fact as that of Malthus, should have gained a moment's credit with any person of common understanding. And yet it is wonderful to see what numbers are fascinated with it: among others, my late friend, Mr. Ricardo. He made some use of it in his theory of political

economy, which I could never well understand. ('To Mr. Broadbent', 19 September 1823, in Williams, 1833: 749)

What Ricardo may have learnt from Belsham on methodology is that knowledge of essences is impossible, that causal relations in the real world are under the sway of probability, and accordingly we may try at most to establish connections between a restricted number of basic phenomena, and such explanations should be in terms of 'laws', not 'causes'. This may shed some light on a few matters from Ricardo's debate with Malthus. Ricardo comments on the impossibility of controlling the plurality of causes at work behind any particular effect, suggesting that we should rather stick to simplified ideal cases, the only ones for which we are in a position to establish causal links. He insists on a distinction between the variety of facts and a few general phenomena and on the usefulness of deduction from a restricted number of principles. These claims, albeit arising out of a discussion with another practising economist, and thus reflecting more a kind of reflection on positive practice than mere repetition of philosophical theses, present remarkable similarity with the Priestley-Hartley-Belsham tradition, the main rival to the Scottish tradition (Cremaschi and Dascal, 1996, 1998).

Needless to say, such contextual considerations about the milieu that exerted an intellectual influence on Ricardo at an early stage of his intellectual career have little to do with Ricardo's religious beliefs (Cremaschi and Dascal, 2002). The plain facts are that Ricardo did hear Belsham's weekly instructions for almost three decades. Possible implications for Ricardo scholars are that Ricardo had received some decent, albeit not advanced, education before he met James Mill, that he had been conversant with someone cast among British early nineteenth-century philosophers on a higher level than James Mill himself before he started writing on political economy and before he ever met Mill, Bentham and Malthus (Cremaschi, 2004). This may prompt careful consideration of one more source for Ricardo's methodological ideas, namely the above-mentioned Priestley-Hartley-Belsham tradition, and the suggestion that Ricardo's relationship to James Mill may be seen in a different perspective.

SERGIO CREMASCHI

See also:

Jewish Background; Life and Activities.

References

Anonymous (1823a), 'Parliamentary: Christians' petition against the prosecution of unbelievers', *The Monthly Repository*, **18**(212), August, 485–94.
Anonymous (1823b), 'Obituary', *The Monthly Repository*, **18**(212), August, 551.
Anonymous (1823c), 'Obituary', *Sunday Times*, 14 September 1823, 1.
Belsham, T. (1801), *Elements of the Philosophy of the Mind, and of Moral Philosophy*, London: Johnson.
Belsham, T. (1826–27), *Discourses, Doctrinal and Practical*, 2 vols, London: Hunter.
Cremaschi, S. (2004), 'Ricardo and the Utilitarians', *The European Journal of the History of Economic Thought*, **11**(3), 377–404.
Cremaschi, S. and M. Dascal (1996), 'Malthus and Ricardo on economic methodology', *History of Political Economy*, **28**(3), 475–511.
Cremaschi, S. and M. Dascal (1998), 'Malthus and Ricardo: two styles for economic theory', *Science in Context*, **11**(2), 229–54.
Cremaschi, S. and M. Dascal (2002), 'The Unitarian connection and Ricardo's scientific style', *History of Political Economy*, **34**(2), 505–8.

Depoortère, C. (2002), 'On Ricardo's method: the Unitarian influence examined', *History of Political Economy*, **34**(2), 501–4.

Fitzpatrick, M. (1999), 'Belsham, Thomas', in J.W. Yolton, J.V. Price and J. Stephens (eds), *The Dictionary of Eighteenth-Century British Philosophers, Vol. I*, Bristol: Thoemmes Press, pp. 72–3.

Henderson, J.P. (1997), *The Life and Economics of David Ricardo*, with supplemental chapters by J.B. Davis, Boston, MA: Kluwer.

Webb, R.K. (2004), 'Belsham, Thomas', in H.C.G. Matthew and B. Harrison (eds), *Oxford Dictionary of National Biography, Vol. V*, Oxford: Oxford University Press, pp. 42–3.

Williams, J. (1833), *Memoirs of the Late Reverend Thomas Belsham*, London: printed for the author.

Bentham, Jeremy, and Ricardo

The hypothesis that Bentham's utilitarianism had a strong influence on classical economists, and notably on Ricardo, has long been widely accepted. Stark, for instance, in one of his two articles on Bentham published in *The Economic Journal*, wrote that 'It is not necessary here to furnish concrete proof of the deep indebtedness of Ricardo and his school to Bentham and his philosophy: the identity of outlook is obvious to every reader of the *Principles of Political Economy* or Mill's *Elements*' (1946: 583). For those who doubt, 'concrete proof' has been provided nevertheless – echoing Bentham's alleged statement (reported by Bowring) that '[he] was the spiritual father of Mill and Mill was the spiritual father of Ricardo, so that Ricardo was [his] spiritual grandson' (Bentham, 1838–43, X: 498), the proof is supposed to lie in James Mill's role as a go-between for Bentham and Ricardo. Yet this historical proximity cannot be considered as evidence. Rather, the links between Bentham and Ricardo differ according to whether politics or economics is being considered. In politics, Ricardo has often been presented as a utilitarian; his economic analysis, meanwhile, shows few links with Bentham's. This conventional figure stems from the fact that Mill was supposed to have educated Ricardo in politics: the correspondence between them shows that he acted as a 'schoolmaster' for Ricardo (Mill, Letter to Ricardo dated 9 November 1815, *Works*, VI: 321). Mill himself contributed to this view, stating in a letter to McCulloch, written shortly after Ricardo's death, that the latter 'had hardly a thought or a purpose, respecting either public, or his private affairs, in which [he] was not his confidant and adviser' (*Works*, IX: 390). Concerning economics, Ricardo has been considered to be independent from both Mill and Bentham.

Three characteristics of this debate are worth noting. First, whatever the field – economics or politics – the issue of the relationship between Ricardo and Bentham turns on questions regarding Ricardo's philosophical background. Second, in economics, comparisons between Ricardo and Bentham are rare, almost as if the latter never wrote a book on economics. The reason here may lie in the uneven reputations these authors enjoy within economic theory. But such a comparison allows us to provide some analytical elements that prove the absence of influence between them. Finally, the link between Ricardo and Bentham is usually examined on the assumption that it runs from the latter to the former. Few commentators have raised the question of an influence that went the other way round.

From politics to economics: James Mill as a 'go-between' for Bentham and Ricardo?

James Mill is assumed to have played the same role for both Ricardo and Bentham – namely, he contributed to the diffusion of their ideas. But while his role with regard to

Bentham was circumscribed to what his son, John Stuart Mill, called the 'utilitarian propagandism' (Mill [1873] 1981: 105), he tried to encourage Ricardo to develop his economic theory, for instance writing to him: 'as you are already the best *thinker* on political economy, I am resolved you shall also be the best writer' (Letter of 22 December 1815, *Works*, VI: 340).

James Mill met Bentham in 1808. He seems already to have been familiar with Bentham's writings, and according to Bain (1882: 95–7) he professed himself his disciple. In fact, as underlined by Stimson and Milgate (1993: 901–2; see also Winch, 1966: 4–8), his view that politics must be 'derived from the nature of man' (Mill 1806, quoted in Stimson and Milgate, 1993: 901) came either from utilitarianism or from the Scottish tradition. From the time Bentham met Mill, his utilitarianism became an important doctrine in England and his reputation grew. No doubt this partly resulted from Mill's actions (see, for instance, Halévy [1901–4] 1955: 251): Mill succeeded in getting Bentham's doctrine across, avoiding, for instance, the use of neologisms so common in his writings, and publishing many articles that popularized his principles. Mill's writings also dealt with democracy, liberty of the press and education, these being three important topics for utilitarianism, for which a central focus was on how private interests might converge towards public happiness. These writings were thus considered as the basis for the demands for reform that Radicals introduced in Parliament – demands only very partially addressed by the 1832 Reform Act where neither secret ballots, nor the annual election and universal suffrage were adopted. Nevertheless, the act enabled some democratic progress, such as a rearrangement of seats in the House of Commons from 'rotten boroughs' – those with very tiny populations, so small that voters were susceptible to control – in favour of the industrial boroughs that had sprung up during the Industrial Revolution. It also increased the number of individuals (albeit only males) entitled to vote.

Mill's meeting with Ricardo occurred in 1808 (Winch, 1966: 23) or in 1810 (Henderson and Davies, 1997: 280). As well as encouraging him to publish on economics, Mill urged him to enter Parliament, to which he was elected on 26 February 1819. Mill enrolled him among the 'Philosophical Radicals' – according to Snyder (2006: 277), Ricardo's economic theory, and notably his criticism vis-à-vis the landowning classes, were viewed by Mill 'as being supportive to [their] political program'. This view has recently been challenged, with several commentators underlining Ricardo's originality in this field, and the differences between the two men. Again, no consensus has been reached on this topic, and while Peach (1997: 231) regarded 'Ricardo as a moderate "radical" in the utilitarian tradition of Mill and Bentham', Milgate and Stimson (1991: 17–18) denied any influence of utilitarianism on his political ideas, claiming that he developed, 'independently and . . . before the publication of Mill's *Essay on Government* . . . a quite sophisticated argument for democratic citizenship as a pre-requisite for economic progress'. One of their core arguments is grounded in the issue of the enfranchisement of the working people: 'Ricardo simply held that these individuals were to be represented as a matter of principle. For Mill, it was essential to the argument to show that most of the time, most of the people "continue to be guided by that rank"' (Milgate and Stimson, 2009: 175). A term-by-term comparison between Ricardo's and Bentham's principles does not enable us to reach any definitive conclusion; it only makes it possible to state that both were in favour of secret ballot – Ricardo even quoted Bentham in his speech entitled 'Defence of the Plan of Voting by Ballot' (*Works*, V: 507) – defended the principle of the extension of the franchise, and considered reform of Parliament as requisite for good government. They diverged on the extent of the franchise ('far short of making it universal' for Ricardo; ibid.: 502) and the frequency of elections, but were convinced that controlling how elected representatives behave is needed to prevent them using their 'ability . . . in promoting objects which are mischievous to the [people]' (Letter to Trower on 22 March 1818, *Works*, VII: 261). Here one may recognize Bentham's central theme of 'sinister interest', which may explain why Ricardo is acknowledged to be 'convinced by his arguments' (ibid.).

The literature has also discussed Mill's true role in Ricardo's economics. The starting point was as Ricardo wrote to Maria Edgeworth in 1823: 'I like the formal method, after the manner of Bentham and Mill' (*Works*, IX: 259). The debate about the nature of Ricardo's method in economics shows that other influences were more likely to have been at work (see Depoortère, 2008). Finally, Sraffa's view about the role played by Mill with regard to Ricardo's theory has become dominant: 'it is clear that Mill's contribution to the making of the *Principles* was less than might have been expected from his promises and encouragement. On the theory there is little doubt that his influence was negligible' (*Works*, I: xx).

Ricardo: a utilitarian philosopher?

The literature on the links between Ricardo and Bentham usually only deals with the issue of the influence of utilitarianism on Ricardo – did he adopt that philosophy or not? Answering this question first implies rejecting the view that Ricardo 'had no philosophy at all' (Schumpeter [1954] 1972: 471). Hence, there are three main positions on this issue.

The first position starts by noting that Mill proposed a list of readings in philosophy to Ricardo (see, for instance, his letter to Ricardo on 19 October 1817, *Works*, VII: 194–9). But, as underlined by King, 'most of Ricardo's reading on philosophical issues seems to have come after the publication of his *Principles* in 1817 and was therefore too late to have much influence on the development on his economic thinking' (2013: 33).

The two other positions start from utilitarianism as a philosophy. At that time, utilitarianism took the form that Bentham gave it: he identified two principles, the first being a description of man as a pain-and-pleasure seeker, and the second having a collective flavour by stating the maximization of social happiness as a goal. Consequently, the discussion about the influence of utilitarianism on Ricardo addresses either his conception of individual rationality, or his standard of collective well-being.

Regarding individual rationality, Mitchell has emphasized the role of habit and custom in Ricardo's description of individual behaviour. Each class, Mitchell argued, was characterized by peculiar psychological characteristics: 'Ricardo's capitalists are animated chiefly by a "restless desire" to find the most profitable investments . . . His laborers are creatures ruled by habit and a tropismatic longing to marry' ([1937] 1999: 215). Mitchell concluded that 'Ricardo rested his theory upon a foundation of feelings' (ibid.: 222), and considered him as strongly influenced by utilitarianism. However, some elements in Ricardo's correspondence challenge this conclusion. In a letter to Malthus dated 22 October 1811, he noted his concern that individuals are guided by their personal interest: 'It would be no answer to me to say that men were ignorant of the best and cheapest mode of conducting their business and paying their debts, because *that is a question of fact not science, and might be urged against almost every proposition in Political Economy'* (*Works*, VI: 64; my emphasis). As a consequence, Ricardo renounced any discussion of the consequences of imperfect information. This reflects the difference with Bentham's view, which considered that individuals might be wrong, such that state intervention in economics was necessary.

The debate over his standard of collective well-being starts out with an extract of a letter from Ricardo to Maria Edgeworth, dated 13 December 1822, where he writes 'my motto, after Mr Bentham, is "the greatest happiness to the greatest number"' (*Works*, IX: 239). For Peach (1997: 223), this statement was consistent with Ricardo's 'identification of happiness with the consumption of material output', and proves his adherence to utilitarianism; on the other hand, Milgate and Stimson (1991: 144) consider that 'in defining the standard of material well-being as aggregate production itself, rather than some aggregate of individual utility, [Ricardo] shifted the focus of analysis away from individual utility maximizers'. But what Bentham himself stated shows that neither Peach's nor Milgate and Stimson's distinction should be taken as evidence – although a purely aggregative definition of collective utility was sometimes given by Bentham, he was aware of the problems of such a definition (see Sigot, 2001a) and preferred another approach that implied neither individual utilities nor consumption patterns (see below).

Bentham versus Ricardo: economic analysis
As previously underlined, the debate over the influence of Bentham on Ricardo's economics has been limited to the issue of a possible philosophical influence. As a consequence, the discussion generally centres on liberalism, but one needs to broaden the perspective by taking into account Bentham's own contributions to economics: it is necessary to compare Ricardo's and Bentham's economic analysis on certain key issues in order to identify any possible mutual influence.

Liberalism is often cited as evidence for Ricardo's utilitarianism. This appears, for instance, in Peach (1997: 223) who states that Ricardo's definition of (individual and) collective happiness as material output gave a 'utilitarian basis for his major policy argument in favour of free trade: as the most physically productive economic system, free trade was also (potentially) productive of the greatest happiness of the greatest number'. But such a statement ignores that Bentham underlined the fundamental role of public authorities in economics: to achieve the 'greatest happiness of the greatest number' – in other words, to maximize collective utility – means 'to provide for subsistence; to secure abundance; to befriend equality; to maintain security' (Bentham, 1838–43, I: 302). As a consequence, Bentham considered that the state should intervene whenever security was threatened. Security was understood in its wider sense: it designated the protection of property rights as much as individual reputation, health and so on. Security was a prerequisite for the development of wealth: 'without law', said Bentham, 'there is no security; consequently no abundance, nor even certain subsistence. And the only equality which can exist in such a condition, is the equality of misery' (ibid.: 307). Security belonged to the field of legislation and it was up to the law to guarantee it. As a consequence, the state should provide individuals with, for instance, public hospitals or health insurance (Bentham, 1952–54, II: 119–49. Stabile, 1996: 37, rightly qualified Bentham as 'an early advocate of social insurance'). A bill to set a maximum price for some commodities such as bread or corn, in order to face the risk of famine, was also recommended by him in his *Defence of a Maximum* (1801), in which Bentham declared that he 'never had, nor ever shall have, any horror, sentimental or anarchical, of the hand of government' (Bentham, 1952–54, III: 257–8). On the contrary, Ricardo has been viewed as 'outstandingly the *most*, thoroughgoing advocate of *laissez-faire* among the major British economists' (Hutchison, 1994: 71). Bentham's position vis-à-vis the Poor Laws illustrates this divergence with Ricardo. Contrary with what Cremaschi (2004: 378) has stated, 'Benthamite politicy' was not 'anti-Poor Laws'. More precisely, Bentham advocated radical reform of these laws, and strongly defended the *principles* of social assistance, regarded by some historians as anticipating the welfare state. Although this link with the welfare state is disputed (see Englander, 1998: 87–90), Bentham's conviction that the Poor Laws had to exist is to be contrasted with Ricardo's statement in the *Principles*: 'No scheme for the amendment of the Poor Laws merits the least attention which has not their abolition for its ultimate object' (*Works*, I: 107).

The comparison between Bentham's and Ricardo's economic analysis should now deal with the two main issues considered by classical economics: growth and money.

Concerning growth, the same preoccupation to explain its causes and consequences united classical economists (see, for instance, Barber [1967] 2009: 107). But this did not mean adopting the same growth theory. To put it briefly, Ricardo and Malthus opposed each other regarding whether the growth process was blocked by market or production conditions. Bentham did not adopt such a framework: for him, economic growth was over-determined by political (instead of economic) factors, the wealth and progress of a country depending on its political situation – or, in Bentham's terms, on its degree of security (see Sigot, 2001b). Security played a decisive role for growth via two elements: innovation and incentive to work. Innovation was an engine of progress; it depended on potential profit and rested on a calculation made by the innovator (Bentham, 1952–54, I: 229, 261–4), which was in no way different from that made by any individual regarding the pains and pleasure of any given action. Consequently, the incentive to innovate could not develop if the property of patents were not protected by law. The incentive to work obeyed the same principle: insecurity discouraged individuals from working, since nothing guaranteed they would be able to keep the fruits of their labour. Therefore, they would not seek to accumulate beyond the strict necessities. On the contrary, wealth would develop through the accumulation of luxury goods made possible by the existence of a safe and stable regime.

On the second theme, money, the classical period is generally considered as having given birth to modern analysis. This period saw the development of the Bullionist Controversy, the main issue of which was to explain the depreciation of sterling and the increasing price of gold. Again, Bentham did not participate in this debate: he sought to explain why prices increased, but his interest lay in the fact that inflation might cause bankruptcy. In other words, for Bentham, to prevent inflation was an objective related to confidence – money was a 'promise', whose value depended only on the confidence that people had in it.

As far as the link between Bentham and Ricardo is concerned, the theme of money is of specific interest. There is no evidence that Ricardo and Bentham discussed economic matters together, and Bentham's main economic writings were not available before the publication of his works by Bowring in 1838–43. The only element that truly shows a divergence between them concerns a manuscript by Bentham, entitled 'Sur les prix', upon which Ricardo commented. While translating it into French, Etienne Dumont consulted James Mill to discover his opinion on the manuscript. Although Mill stated that '[he] do[es] not think it will do for publication' (letter to Ricardo, dated 25 December 1810, *Works*, VI: 14), he sent it to Ricardo, who confirmed his opinion: Ricardo advised against publishing the manuscript, because of its 'radical defects', although he also found in it 'very able and just views' (Letter to Mill, dated 1 January 1811, ibid., 14–15). As shown by Deleplace and Sigot (2012: 734), the reason for Ricardo's view was an 'analytical divergence between Bentham and Ricardo on money, the former advocating secure banks, the latter a secure currency': Bentham adopted a microeconomic theory of money, whose focus was on confidence, the primary role of which was 'to grant credit for private activity', while Ricardo held a macroeconomic theory of money, whose focus was on the central bank, the primary role of which was to 'regulate the aggregate quantity of money according to the value of the standard' (ibid.: 759).

Concluding remarks

That Bentham influenced Ricardo in economics is thus doubtful. But was the converse true? Patton raised this question in 1899, and considered that by 'adopting [Ricardo's] ideas, Bentham and James Mill really became his disciples' (quoted by Cremaschi, 2004: 378). There is, however, an important counter-argument to that assertion: Bentham stopped working on economics long before his meeting with Ricardo, and only returned very briefly to this field in 1821, when he adopted some Smithian arguments on international trade (see Sigot, 2001a: 76–7). Even for tactical reasons – such as a weapon for convincing others on the need for reforms – it is doubtful that Bentham accepted theories that were incompatible with his own.

NATHALIE SIGOT

See also:

Exchange Value and Utility; Life and Activities; Mill, James, and Ricardo; Papers on Money and Banking; Poor Laws.

References

Bain, A. (1882), *James Mill: A Biography*, London: Longmans, Green and Co.
Barber, W.J. ([1967] 2009), *A History of Economic Thought*, Middletown, CT: Wesleyan University Press.
Bentham, J. (1838–43), *The Works of Jeremy Bentham, Published under the Superintendence of his Executer, John Bowring*, 11 vols, Edinburgh: Tait.
Bentham, J. (1952–54), *Jeremy Bentham's Economic Writings: Critical Edition Based on His Printed Works and Unprinted Manuscripts by Werner Stark*, 3 vols, London: Allen & Unwin.
Cremaschi, S. (2004), 'Ricardo and the utilitarians', *European Journal of the History of Economic Thought*, **11**(3), 377–403.
Deleplace, G. and N. Sigot (2012), 'Ricardo's critique of Bentham's French manuscript: secure currency versus secure banks', *European Journal of the History of Economic Thought*, **19**(5), 733–64.
Depoortère, C. (2008), 'On Ricardo's method: the Scottish connection considered', *History of Political Economy*, **40**(1), 73–110.
Englander, D. (1998), *Poverty and Poor Law Reform in 19th Century Britain, 1834–1914*, London and New York: Longman.
Halévy, E. ([1901–4] 1955), *The Growth of Philosophical Radicalism*, Boston, MA: Beacon Press.
Henderson, J.P. and J.B. Davis (1997), *The Life and Economics of David Ricardo*, Boston, MA/Dordrecht/London: Kluwer Academic Publishers.
Hutchison, T. (1994), 'James Mill and Ricardian economics', *The Uses and Abuses of Economics*, London and New York: Routledge, pp. 50–83.
King, J.E. (2013), *David Ricardo*, Basingstoke, UK: Palgrave Macmillan.

Milgate, M. and S. Stimson (1991), *Ricardian Politics*, Princeton, NJ: Princeton University Press.
Milgate, M. and S. Stimson (2009), *After Adam Smith: A Century of Transformation in Politics and Political Economy*, Princeton, NJ: Princeton University Press.
Mill, J.S. ([1873] 1981), 'Autobiography', in J.M. Robson and J. Stillinger (eds), *The Collected Works of John Stuart Mill, Vol. I – Autobiography and Literary Essays*, Toronto: University of Toronto Press/London: Routledge and Kegan Paul, pp. 1–290.
Mitchell, W.C. ([1937] 1999), *The Backward Art of Spending Money*, New Brunswick, NJ: Transaction Publishers.
Peach, T. (1997), 'The age of the universal consumer: a reconsideration of Ricardo's politics', *European Journal of the History of Economic Thought*, **4**(2), 217–36.
Schumpeter, J.A. ([1954] 1972), *History of Economic Analysis*, London: George Allen & Unwin.
Sigot, N. (2001a), *Bentham et l'économie. Une histoire d'utilité*, Paris: Economica.
Sigot, N. (2001b), 'Bentham and the classical canon', in E.L. Forget and S. Peart (eds), *Reflections on the Classical Canon in Economics*, London and New York: Routledge, pp. 43–56.
Snyder, L.J. (2006), *Reforming Philosophy: A Victorian Debate on Science and Society*, Chicago, IL: University of Chicago Press.
Stabile, D.R. (1996), *Work and Welfare. The Social Costs of Labor in the History of Economic Thought*, Westport, CT/London: Greenwood Press.
Stark, W. (1946), 'Jeremy Bentham as an economist. II. Bentham's influence', *The Economic Journal*, **56**(224), 583–608.
Stimson, S. and M. Milgate (1993), 'Utility, property, and political participation: James Mill on democratic reform', *American Political Science Review*, **87**(4), 901–11.
Winch, D. (1966), *James Mill: Selected Economic Writings*, Edinburgh and London: Oliver & Boyd.

Biaujeaud, Huguette, on Ricardo*

Biaujeaud's *Essai sur la Théorie Ricardienne de la Valeur* offers an interpretation of Ricardo that is in some respects similar to the work of Sraffa. Her work was originally presented as a doctoral thesis to the Faculty of Law at the University of Paris in December 1933 under the supervision of Gaëtan Pirou. It was published in 1934 and then reprinted by Economica in 1988. This was an absolutely independent investigation; Biaujeaud's contacts with Piero Sraffa, whom she met once (in Paris, when working on her thesis) and Jacob Hollander, took place 'when my work was already very advanced . . . I had submitted to them my ideas and essential conclusions. It seems to me, and I am almost certain, that they accepted them without great controversy.'

Biaujeaud's work passed almost unnoticed in France, despite the preface by Pirou, who also emphasized the significance of her work (Pirou, 1939: 241 and 1948: 21). There were virtually no significant references to this work in France until very much later. Biaujeaud's lack of impact in France is probably due to a lack of diffusion of Ricardian thought in France. Nevertheless, the importance of Biaujeaud's contribution seems incontrovertible. Although only 200 copies of the original work were printed, well-known specialists cited it. Sraffa cited Biaujeaud (*Works*, I: xxxviii*f*). Stigler took note of her work in his 'Ricardo and the 93 per cent labor theory of value' (1958). Mark Blaug included her as the only French author among the twelve references he cited in his article on Ricardo for the *International Encyclopedia of the Social Sciences*. Contemporary specialists such as Roncaglia cited her work in a 1985 conference presentation. But for

---

* This is a revised and shortened version of G. Abraham-Frois (2000), 'Huguette Biaujeaud (c. 1910–1990)' published in *A Biographical Dictionary of Women Economists*, edited by R. W. Dimand, M. A. Dimand and E. L. Forget, Cheltenham: Edward Elgar.

French specialists, this work had taken on the character of a myth, particularly since it was virtually inaccessible until its reissue.

Biaujeaud's book contained a comparative analysis of the three editions of Ricardo's *Principles*, and especially the variations in the important first chapter dedicated to value. She developed an original and interesting position on a 'duality' between value determined as a cost of production and value as determined by labour in Ricardo's theory. But her analysis of the influence of the agricultural sector must also be noted. Sraffa introduces the 'corn model' in his preface to the first volume of Ricardo's *Works*. He argues that in Ricardo's 1815 'Essay on profits' and in his correspondence of 1814 and 1815, the general rate of profit is determined by the rate of profit in agriculture. In his preface, Sraffa recognized that in Ricardo's subsequent work the determining role of agricultural profit is weakened and that there is no longer any trace of it in the *Principles* (*Works*, I: xxxi).

Similarly, Biaujeaud claims that Ricardo 'bases his system on a theory of profits elaborated long before the *Principles* . . . [It emerges] in his 1813 correspondence . . . and blossoms in the Essay' (Biaujeaud [1934] 1988: 64). Moreover, Biaujeaud also notes that 'the general rate of profit is determined by the profit of the farmer. . . . The rate of profit depends on the difficulty of growing wheat, which regulates the rate of wages' (ibid.: 66). Both Sraffa and Biaujeaud note in parallel fashion the limitations of Ricardo's analysis: Sraffa claims that Ricardo never specified the 'rational foundation' by means of which agricultural profits played a determining role (*Works*, I: xxxi). Biaujeaud claims that 'Ricardo, in his first letters, never explains the connection' between agricultural profits and wages (Biaujeaud [1934] 1988: 66). Moreover, Biaujeaud and Sraffa both cite the same letter to Malthus (2 June 1814) as the source of their assertions (ibid.: 65; *Works*, I: xxxii).

According to both authors, there was a 'moment' (a few months, perhaps) when Ricardo seemed to believe that the general rate of profit was determined independently of the values of commodities, by the ratio between the physical quantity of corn produced by the farmer and that necessary for the support of farm labour. A letter to James Mill (30 December 1815), in which Ricardo recognized that he must deal with the problem of value before he could continue, signalled the end of this phase. And here again, both Sraffa and Biaujeaud recognize the progressive movement of Ricardo away from a determining role for corn on the rate of profit, towards a theory based in value (*Works*, I: xxxii; Biaujeaud [1934] 1988: 68, 70, 73).

There seems to be a striking similarity between the interpretations of Huguette Biaujeaud and Piero Sraffa. The analyses of Biaujeaud and Sraffa are, however, not identical; the latter is much more systematic. (In his unpublished papers it becomes clear that Sraffa's ideas on Ricardo were very mature by 1931.)

But Biaujeaud's work attracted Sraffa's attention for another reason (*Works*, I: xxxviii). She examined the changes introduced into the chapter on value in the second and third editions of the *Principles* and, like Sraffa, argued that the theory of value expounded in the third edition did not represent a retreat from a labour theory of value (Biaujeaud [1934] 1988: 39, 154). This view opposed the then widely accepted claims of Jacob Hollander and Edwin Cannan that, in successive editions of the *Principles*, Ricardo had weakened his original argument that embodied labour is the foundation of value. But unlike Sraffa, who held that, in the *Principles*, value is essentially determined by embodied labour, Biaujeaud argued that, from the first edition, value is regulated by cost of production (ibid.: 36–9). Indeed, she claims, there is less an evolution in Ricardo's theory than a continuous strengthening, in which the idea of cost of production becomes more and more precise and the related notion of a measure of value is clarified (ibid.: 154–5).

Biaujeaud's overturning of received opinion becomes even more complete when she argued that, if anything, it is in 'the third edition . . . where Ricardo demonstrates for the first time that value depends on labor' (ibid.: 168). If there is any evolution at all, she argues, it is not away from a labour theory of value, but towards one (ibid.: 103). Biaujeaud notes that Ricardo determined value by cost of production as early as the first edition of the *Principles*. For example, he argued that a general reduction in wages would cause an increase in the prices of those commodities produced with the assistance of fixed capital (ibid.: 70; *Works*, I: xxiii–xxiv). A few pages earlier, Biaujeaud noted that 'to establish these results, which Ricardo recognized were not in accord with received doctrine, he had imagined the extreme case of commodities produced solely by fixed capital and others produced solely by circulating capital, by a machine working without human assistance, or by human work exclusively' (Biaujeaud [1934] 1988: 58).

According to Biaujeaud, this recognition of the difficulty caused by differing capital–labour ratios in the first edition is sufficient to reject the thesis that Ricardo had increasing doubts about the labour theory of value as time passed. In fact, by the second edition, this example was considerably modified, and by the third edition it disappeared entirely, to be replaced by the passage (ibid. 125) that gave birth to George Stigler's notorious 'Ricardo and the 93 per cent labor theory of value' (1958). Stigler distinguished between an analytical labour theory of value, which he claimed not to find in Ricardo, and an empirical labour theory of value, for which he cites textual evidence. But in fact, the 93 per cent labour theory of value exists only because of modifications that appeared in the third edition, as Biaujeaud had noticed at an early time.

Biaujeaud's book is therefore important because it demonstrates that the problem of different capital–labour ratios was present from the first edition of the *Principles*; Ricardo had, from the beginning, a theory of value founded on cost of production. Labour was, by contrast, a 'measure', or means of estimating, value, and this role was essential to the author of the *Principles*. Biaujeaud's position is quite original. On the one hand, she disputes Sraffa's claim by recognizing that the modifications introduced into the third edition of the *Principles* are important (*Works*, I: xxxix–xv). But on the other, she claims that it is not, therefore, necessary to conclude, as did Cannan and Jacob Hollander, that Ricardo weakened his position on the labour theory of value. In fact, she sees in them the point of departure for a deepening of Ricardo's thought (Biaujeaud [1934] 1988: 120–21), but claims that the innovations introduced into the third edition are much less important than the introduction of fixed capital in the first edition. Far from a weakening of Ricardo's recognition of the role of labour, the third edition represents reinforcement or, at least, greater precision.

Many authors have claimed that Ricardo had a theory of value founded on cost of production. Biaujeaud's originality consisted in arguing that 'the labor theory of value and the cost of production theory of value coexisted parallel to one another in Ricardo's thought' (ibid.: 69–70). In fact, she maintains that 'the true interest of the Ricardian system lies in the duality of these two theories' (ibid.: 185).

GILBERT ABRAHAM-FROIS

See also:

Corn Model; Hollander, Jacob Harry, on Ricardo; *Principles of Political Economy, and Taxation*; Sraffa, Piero, on Ricardo.

References

Abraham-Frois, G. (1988), Avant-propos to Biaujeaud.
Biaujeaud, H. (1934), *Essai sur la Théorie de la Valeur*, Paris: Sirey
Biaujeaud, H. (1988), re-edition of Biaujeaud (1934), Paris: Economica.
Cannan, E. ([1929] 1964), *A Review of Economic Theory*, with an introduction by B.A. Corry, New York: Kelley.
Pirou, G. (1939), *Introduction à l'étude de l'Economie Politique*, Paris: Sirey.
Pirou, G. (1948), *La valeur et les prix*, Paris: Sirey.
Stigler, G. J. (1958), 'Ricardo and the 93 per cent labor theory of value', *American Economic Review*, **48**(3): 357–67.

Blaug, Mark, on Ricardo

Mark Blaug became a serious scholar of Ricardo as a graduate student at Columbia University, supervised by George Stigler and Terence Hutchison. (For biographical information see Blaug [1994] 1997a and Backhouse, 2012. This entry draws extensively on Backhouse, 2001 and 2013.) He came to Ricardo having been a committed communist who loved the scholastic, Talmudic nature of the arguments he had found in Marx (see Blaug [1994] 1997a). Though he completely abandoned his youthful Marxism, he never lost his interest in debating issues relating to Marx's system.

Ricardian economics

Blaug's doctoral thesis, which became *Ricardian Economics* (1958), was the result of many hours in the British Library, his drafts being ruthlessly criticized by Stigler. Placing Ricardo's economics in the context of contemporary debates, the book was a significant contribution to economic history. Contrasting his approach with that of Edwin Cannan ([1893] 1967), who had rendered classical economics 'void of sense and logic', he wrote:

> Whether we ought to give the 'ancients' the benefit of historical insight or look down from present heights at their mistakes, in the belief that truth is concentrated in the last increment of economic knowledge, is largely a matter of taste and purpose. Nevertheless, I cannot suppress the conviction that an appraisal of a historical body of doctrine without reference to the conditions under which it was formulated or the contemporary state of analysis out of which it arose soon becomes an uninteresting display of omniscience. (Blaug, 1958: 4)

Thus, where Schumpeter (1954) and Keynes (1936) had seen the heart of the Ricardian system as lying, respectively, in the labour theory of value and Say's Law, and having in mind the interpretation in Sraffa's (1951), 'Introduction' to Ricardo's *Works* (I: xiii–lxii), Blaug saw Ricardian economics as having 'emerged directly and spontaneously out of the great corn laws debate of 1814–16' and hence as centred on the proposition that 'the yield of wheat per acre of land governs the general rate of return on invested capital as well as secular changes in the distributive shares' (1958: 6, 3).

Blaug placed 'Ricardo's system' in the context of a substantial discussion of the period's economic history, itself the fruit of much original research, in which he discussed what was happening to British agriculture at this time, how contemporaries viewed it, the limited and ambiguous data available at the time, and more recent evidence on the importance of wheat in workers' budgets in the early nineteenth century. Blaug presented Ricardo as the master of deductive reasoning whose framing of the main economic problem dominated British economic thinking for decades after his death even if, as was the case, Ricardo's stock fell rapidly in the 1820s.

Over 20 years later, in the preface to the Japanese edition, Blaug ([1980] 1997b: 44–6) listed ten points he believed that he had got right:

1. The optimistic, short-run character of Ricardo's model.
2. Ricardo had an 'empirical' rather than an 'analytical' labour theory of value.
3. Ricardo was concerned with Marxian rather than Keynesian unemployment.
4. Ricardo viewed Malthus's theory of gluts as a fallacious theory of secular stagnation.
5. The sudden eclipse of Malthusian population theory in the 1830s.
6. The reasons why Nassau Senior's *Outline of the Science of Political Economy* (1836) provoked little debate.
7. The failure of Ricardo's followers to test his predictions.
8. The Manchester School's repudiation of Ricardo in favour of Adam Smith.
9. Scepticism about the Marxian view that the 1830s marked a period when classical economics lost vigour.
10. The denunciation of Marx's critique of Ricardo as a muddled forerunner of his own views.

Irrespective of whether one accepts this self-appraisal, when taken together with the economic history content of the book it clearly shows its great scope.

Economic theory in retrospect

The main failings in *Ricardian Economics*, Blaug believed, were that he had failed to address the conceptual problem of how to define and assess Ricardianism, and that, not having the benefit of having read Piero Sraffa's *Production of Commodities by Means of Commodities* (1960) he had failed to make sense of Ricardo's search for an invariable measure of value. This was something he sought to put right in successive editions of his most widely cited book, *Economic Theory in Retrospect* (1962–97). Aimed at students of economics, this book adopted a different approach to history, opening with the bold assertion, 'Criticism implies standards of judgement and my standards are those of modern economic theory' (1962: 1), and its advocacy of the case for absolutism rather than relativism in the history of economic thought. He abandoned the concern to understand why Ricardian economics emerged in favour of a mathematical formulation of Ricardo's system, condensing the historical context to the occasional sentence. Ricardo's contribution to economics was now seen as being much more directly relevant to modern economics:

> [I]f economics is essentially an engine of analysis, a method of thinking rather than a body of substantive results, Ricardo literally invented the technique. His gift for heroic abstraction produced one of the most impressive models, judged by its scope and practical import, in the entire history of economic theory. (Blaug, 1962: 127)

To support this claim, Blaug offered a graphical exposition of Ricardo's theory of distribution and growth, a more technical discussion of value theory, and an algebraic model that shows Ricardo's fundamental theorem to hold in a model with two commodities (corn and gold) as well as in a simple corn model. He used algebra to show that Ricardo's predictions about changes in distributive shares over time depend on his having assumed (implicitly, as a result of his particular numerical examples) very specific functional forms for the production functions.

Economic Theory in Retrospect suggests that Blaug was slow to see the significance of Sraffa's book. It was absent from the first edition (1962), and in the second edition (1968) it was discussed only in a footnote. It was not until the third edition (1978), after he had written his very critical Institute of Economic Affairs pamphlet, *The Cambridge Revolution: Success or Failure?* (1975), that *Production of Commodities* was discussed in the main text. Applying the standards of modern economic theory, as he saw them, to Sraffa's system, he was very critical: Sraffa might have solved a technical problem in Ricardo's theory but the solution he had found had no substantive significance. Unlike the Ricardo he had portrayed in *Ricardian Economics*, who was immersed in contemporary policy problems, Blaug believed that Sraffa had bought logical rigour at the price of empirical relevance.

Later writings
For the last three decades of his life, Blaug's writings on Ricardo were increasingly tied up with his response to those who believed that Sraffa's system offered the basis for a critique of economic theory, something he could never accept. This accounts for his initially describing Samuel Hollander's *The Economics of David Ricardo* (1979), in a review for the *Times Literary Supplement*, as 'a very good book but not the great book on Ricardo that one might have hoped for' (Blaug [1980] 1997c: 346). Hollander, Blaug claimed, 'pour[ed] devastating scorn on the attempt of Sraffians to turn Ricardo into a forerunner of both Marx and Sraffa' (ibid.: 345). However, when Denis O'Brien (1981) published a much more critical review, examining the book far more closely, Blaug endorsed it wholeheartedly. As Blaug became increasingly critical of general equilibrium theory, from which he had been an enthusiast in 1962, he became increasingly hostile to what he saw as Hollander's attempt to force Ricardo into a general equilibrium mould. He was therefore enthusiastic about Terry Peach's *Interpreting Ricardo* (1993), which argued against both Sraffa's and Hollander's readings of Ricardo. Ricardo, he believed, should be seen as a forerunner of neither Marx nor Walras.

Peach's contention that it was important to see Ricardo in the context of his own time echoed the main claim Blaug had made in *Ricardian Economics*. Blaug took up this point repeatedly in the 1990s, arguing that it was important to distinguish between 'historical' and 'rational' reconstructions of Ricardo (or any other economist). The Sraffian and general equilibrium interpretations of Ricardo, Blaug claimed, suffered from the same fault: they offered rational reconstructions whilst claiming that they were historical reconstructions. It was important not to confuse the two (see Blaug, 1999, [1985] 2008, 2009; this is discussed in more detail in Backhouse, 2013). Engaging in several debates with Kurz and Salvadori, who argued that his criticisms were unfounded, his focus was increasingly Sraffa rather than Ricardo.

Conclusion

Blaug was concerned with Ricardo throughout his career – he even named one of his sons after him – but his view of Ricardo reflected his broader evolution as an economist. He had initially pursued a career as an economic historian, *Ricardian Economics* being part of this (see the articles reprinted in Blaug, 1986). Teaching the history of economic thought to economics graduate students at Yale, where the climate was hostile to history, he wrote the lectures out of which *Economic Theory in Retrospect* emerged: that book's absolutist approach was aimed at arousing the interest of students who had no historical proclivities. At this time he was, like many economists, an enthusiast for general equilibrium theory. After moving to Britain he stopped doing historical research, established himself as an applied economist, specializing in the economics of education. He later developed an interest in methodology, becoming increasingly critical of economic theory that was not related to empirical work, and came to be very critical of both general equilibrium theory and Sraffian economics. This evolution of his views as an economist lay beneath the changing emphasis found in his interpretations of Ricardo. Behind all of this lay his aversion to the Marxism of his youth, which may help explain the passion behind his increasingly strong attacks on Sraffian interpretations of Ricardo.

ROGER E. BACKHOUSE

See also:

Kaldor, Nicholas, on Ricardo; Pasinetti, Luigi Lodovico, on Ricardo; Samuelson, Paul Anthony, on Ricardo; Sraffa, Piero, on Ricardo.

References

Backhouse, R.E. (2001), 'Mark Blaug as a historian of economic thought', in S.G. Medema and W.J. Samuels (eds), *Historians of Economics and Economic Thought: The Construction of a Disciplinary Memory*, London: Routledge, pp. 17–39.

Backhouse, R.E. (2012), 'Mark Blaug, 1927–2011', *History of Political Economy*, **44**(4), 567–82.

Backhouse, R.E. (2013), 'Understanding Mark Blaug's attitude towards Sraffian economics', in M. Boumans and M. Klaes (eds), *Mark Blaug: Rebel With Many Causes*, Cheltenham, UK and Northampton, MA: Edward Elgar Publishing, pp. 146–58.

Blaug, M. (1958), *Ricardian Economics*, New Haven, CT: Yale University Press.

Blaug, M. (1962–97), *Economic Theory in Retrospect*, 1st and 2nd editions, Homewood, IL: R.D. Irwin; 3rd to 5th editions, Cambridge, UK: Cambridge University Press.

Blaug, M. (1975), *The Cambridge Revolution: Success or Failure?*, IEA Paperback No. 6, London: Institute of Economic Affairs.

Blaug, M. (1986), *Economic History and the History of Economics*, Brighton, UK: Harvester Press.

Blaug, M. ([1994] 1997a), 'Not only an economist: autobiographical reflections of a historian of economic thought', in M. Blaug, *Not Only an Economist: Recent Essays by Mark Blaug*, Cheltenham, UK and Lyme, NH: Edward Elgar Publishing, pp. 3–25.

Blaug, M. ([1980] 1997b), 'Preface to a Japanese translation of *Ricardian Economics: A Historical Study* (1980)', in M. Blaug, *Not Only an Economist: Recent Essays by Mark Blaug*, Cheltenham, UK and Lyme, NH: Edward Elgar Publishing, pp. 44–50.

Blaug, M. ([1980] 1997c), 'Review of *The Economics of David Ricardo*, by Samuel Hollander', in M. Blaug, *Not Only an Economist: Recent Essays by Mark Blaug*, Cheltenham, UK and Lyme, NH: Edward Elgar Publishing, pp. 344–9.

Blaug, M. (1999), 'Misunderstanding classical economics: the Sraffian interpretation of the surplus approach', *History of Political Economy*, **31**(2), 213–36.

Blaug, M. ([1985] 2008), 'British classical economics', in S.N. Durlauf and L.E. Blume (eds), *The New Palgrave Dictionary of Economics*, 2nd edition, Basingstoke, UK: Palgrave Macmillan.

Blaug, M. (2009), 'The trade-off between rigor and relevance: Sraffian economics as a case in point', *History of Political Economy*, **41**(2), 219–47.

Cannan, E. ([1893] 1967), *A History of the Theories of Production and Distribution from 1776 to 1948*, London: King & Son.
Hollander, S. (1979), *The Economics of David Ricardo*, London: Heinemann Educational.
Keynes, J.M. (1936), *The General Theory of Employment, Interest and Money*, London: Macmillan.
O'Brien, D.P. (1981), 'Ricardian economics and the economics of David Ricardo', *Oxford Economic Papers*, **33**(3), 352–86.
Peach, T. (1993), *Interpreting Ricardo*, Cambridge, UK: Cambridge University Press.
Schumpeter, J.A. (1954), *A History of Economic Analysis*, New York: Oxford University Press.
Sraffa, P. (1960), *Production of Commodities by Means of Commodities*, Cambridge, UK: Cambridge University Press.

Böhm-Bawerk, Eugen von, on Ricardo

Eugen von Böhm-Bawerk (1851–1914) was a major economic theorist and historian of economic thought, elaborating on the 'Austrian' tradition founded by his teacher, Carl Menger (1840–1921). His most important single contribution was his theory of capital and interest, put forward in two parts in *Kapital und Kapitalzins* (*Capital and Interest*). The first part, published in 1884, *History and Critique of Interest Theories*, contains a critical account of the theories of capital and interest since antiquity, whereas the second part, published in 1889, *Positive Theory of Capital*, was devoted to an exposition of his own 'agio' theory of interest. Amongst the Austrian economists, he was the one who dealt most intensively with Ricardo's contributions to the theory of value and distribution (cf. Hennings [1972] 1997). In numerous essays and books he advocated marginal utility theory derived from Menger's work against the classical cost of production theory elaborated by Ricardo – see especially Böhm-Bawerk's controversy with Heinrich Dietzel (Böhm-Bawerk, 1886–87, 1892). Marx's work and the Ricardian elements in it were the focus of attention of Böhm-Bawerk's influential essay 'Karl Marx and the Close of His System' published after the posthumous edition of the third volume of *Capital* by Friedrich Engels in 1894 (see Böhm-Bawerk [1896] 1949). (In the following I draw freely on Kurz, 1998.)

Method

Böhm-Bawerk adopted essentially the same method of the analysis as Adam Smith, Ricardo and Marx, focusing attention on 'long-period positions' of an economic system in conditions of free competition. Any such position is characterized by a general rate of profits, or interest as Böhm-Bawerk preferred to call it, uniform rates of remuneration for all primary factors of production, that is, the services of labour and land, and what the classical economists called 'natural' or 'normal' prices. 'A theorist,' Böhm-Bawerk stressed, fully in accordance with Smith and Ricardo, 'may really venture to abstract from the accidental and temporary fluctuations of the market prices round their normal fixed level' (Böhm-Bawerk [1896] 1949: 87). This involved assuming that the composition of the capital stock of the economy is fully adjusted to the other data of the system. It was with regard to these data, that is, the *content* of the theory, that Böhm-Bawerk differed fundamentally from the classical authors. He set against their 'objective' theory of value and distribution his 'subjective' one, tracing value back to marginal utility rather than labour or cost of production. Scrutiny shows that his theory is a variant of marginalist, or 'neoclassical', analysis.

Böhm-Bawerk was strictly opposed to the method of simultaneous equations to solve the problem of value, as it was advocated, for example, by Léon Walras in his general equilibrium theory, but also in some parts of traditional classical theory (see below) and in modern reformulations of it. To explain prices by means of prices is said to imply 'circular reasoning' and thus a 'deadly sin against all scientific logic'. The right method in economic analysis is said to be the 'causal-genetic method' that traces the phenomena to be explained back to some ultimate source or factor, which itself is beyond further explanation. While Böhm-Bawerk has some sympathy for the classical authors who attempted to locate the source of value in the labour expended in the production of things possessed of the faculty to satisfy human needs and wants, that is, goods, in his view these authors did not get to the bottom of the problem. The 'law of cost', with labour as the common denominator of cost, is said not to be the 'Archimedian point from which the remaining explanation could be supported without itself being in need of some support. It is rather in the midst of an explanation: it explains certain phenomena, but must itself be explained in terms of some other, even more general phenomena.' That law, Böhm-Bawerk contends, is to be complemented by a 'theory of value of productive means or cost goods', which shows 'that this value is itself rooted in marginal utility'. He concludes: 'This is why we cannot consider costs the ultimate cause of the value of the product, but only as a very important and fairly *general intermediate cause*' (Böhm-Bawerk, 1892: 329–30; original emphasis). Böhm-Bawerk thus follows his teacher at the University of Heidelberg, Karl Knies, who in his criticism of Marx's concept of 'abstract labour' had put forward the idea of an 'abstract use value' – use value *in genere*. Economic theory ought to take as its starting point 'the essence of the matter itself'. Böhm-Bawerk explains: 'For, there is no doubt that the *cause and aim* of all human industry is the improvement of our welfare: we derive the attitude of people in regard to goods from the importance these have for their welfare' (Böhm-Bawerk, 1886–87, I: 541; original emphasis).

Value

The above criticism permeates Böhm-Bawerk's entire discussion of classical and especially of Ricardo's value theory (cf. Kurz, 1995: 20–23). The latter is said to offer only a partial explanation of value, which, moreover, is contradictory. It is only partial because it deals exclusively with goods that can be produced and reproduced and turns a blind eye to goods whose quantities cannot be increased. What is called for instead is a theory capable of treating the two classes of goods in terms of a *single* explanatory principle – 'a law of value cast from a single die'. At stake is, in Böhm-Bawerk's words, 'the showdown between the old and the new doctrine' (Böhm-Bawerk, 1892: 321).

With regard to the theory of value of reproducible goods, Böhm-Bawerk discusses what in his view are two variants of the theory of cost – its 'Scylla and Charybdis' – costs determined exclusively by technical conditions, as in the 'socialist labour theory', and costs conceived as a value sum. The first theory has to be rejected because goods that are the product of equal quantities of labour but need different 'expenditures of time or capital' generally have different values due to the different amounts of interest paid in the two cases. This clearly reflects some ideas he encountered in Ricardo. The second notion is taken to be caught in 'circular reasoning', since prices are explained by means of prices. More important, carrying out this reduction one will sooner or later 'come across the most original and most general of all productive means: "labour"' (ibid.: 332). Yet, how is the value of labour to be explained? To trace it back to costs of reproduction would inevitably result in 'circular explanation'. The circularity of the classical argument is said to be clearly visible in Smith and Ricardo's 'reduction' of different kinds of labour to a single kind via the relative wage rates of those different kinds of labour. The fundamental error of the classical authors (and Marx) can be traced back to their giving the wrong answer to the following question: is the value of cost goods and ultimately the value of labour the cause or the effect of the value of the product?

According to Böhm-Bawerk the only way out of the impasse is 'to turn the argument upside down, i.e. to realize that the value of labour is determined from the side of the product' (ibid.: 333). The objection that this involves just another variant of circular reasoning is said to be mistaken, since the values or prices of the products are themselves explained in terms of marginal utilities, that is, magnitudes that are *independent* of prices. Ultimately, the value of labour is said to be determined by the 'marginal utility of labour' (ibid.: 336). Hence the proper solution is to be found in tracing back both prices and costs to a 'third cause' (ibid.: 360) – the marginal utility of products in combination with the scarcity of productive means, including labour. (This leads to the infamous imputation problem, which both Menger and Böhm-Bawerk failed to solve.)

Wages and profits

In Böhm-Bawerk's view the main problem of the theory of distribution is to explain the existence of 'interest' or 'profit' – income received by the capitalist for no other reason than his or her property of capital. The interest paid on capital, Böhm-Bawerk insists, may be compared to a *perpetuum mobile*: it obtains as long as its source, capital, exists. By capital Böhm-Bawerk means a 'complex of produced means of production'. In full agreement with Ricardo he opposes the view that capital is a third original factor of production alongside labour and land; rather, it is a *derived* factor, generated by the services of the other two factors. Böhm-Bawerk subscribes to Adam Smith's view that interest is not a kind of wage of direction or management of the entrepreneur and, in competitive conditions, is proportional to the size of the capital employed. Hence, what is to be explained is a 'uniform rate of return on capital'. This task is said to comprise two problems: first, to illuminate the *origin* of interest, and second, to determine its *size*. Whilst the classical authors, and especially Ricardo, are said to have succeeded at least partly on the second count, they are criticized for having failed on the first.

According to Böhm-Bawerk, the then existing theories of interest can be grouped under six heads: 'colourless theories', 'productivity theories', 'utilization theories', 'abstinence theories', 'labour theories' and 'exploitation theories' (see Kurz, 1994). The first five groups are said to be 'favourable' to interest, whereas the last one is 'inimical' to it. In Böhm-Bawerk's view, Smith's *Wealth of Nations* contains the germs of almost all later theories, especially those tracing interest back to the productivity-enhancing power of capital, to exploitation and to abstinence. However, no coherent doctrine is to be found in the work of the Scotsman, which would go beyond what we find in Anne-Robert-Jacques Turgot.

Böhm-Bawerk calls Ricardo an 'excellent' thinker, 'extremely thorough' and 'brilliant' – a judgement that sits uncomfortably with his qualification of Ricardo's theory of profits as belonging to the 'colourless' theories. By these Böhm-Bawerk means those theories that are 'content with the answers given by Turgot and Smith and leave things at that' (Böhm-Bawerk [1884] reprint 1921: 68). This characterization does not, of course, reprint apply to Ricardo. While he shared with Smith (despite the latter's occasional woolliness) a surplus-based approach to the theory of profits, he corrected grave errors in the Smithian version of it and established the fundamental law of distribution. This law relates to the constraint binding changes in the real wage rate and the general rate of profits, given the system of production in use. In some places Smith seemed to be aware of the inverse relationship between the real wage rate and the rate of profits. Alas, there are other passages in *Wealth of Nations* that blur the picture.

Böhm-Bawerk's criticizes Ricardo for having treated profit and interest as 'self-evident phenomena' that are not in need of any further explanation. This is said to follow from the fact that Ricardo was concerned only with ascertaining the level of the interest rate, but not its origin. The latter, however, is said to be 'theoretically the main question' (ibid.: 76–7). With regard to the factors determining the level he credits Ricardo with major insights: 'Very appealing in terms of their quality and coherence are the views Ricardo develops with respect to the level of capital profits' (ibid.: 78). Yet the dichotomy into origin and level of interest, around which much of Böhm-Bawerk's argument revolves, is a trite one, because the factors that determine the level of the rate of interest at the same time contain the key that explains its origin.

Böhm-Bawerk stresses that in Ricardo rent and profits are determined in a two-stages procedure as 'residuals'. After having ascertained the marginal land on the basis of (1) given gross output levels, (2) given quantities of various qualities of land, (3) given methods of production to cultivate these lands and to produce the various commodities in effectual demand and (4) a given real wage rate, Ricardo shows that (extensive) rents reflect the cost differentials between marginal and intramarginal lands. Simultaneously with the rents of land he determines the competitive rate of profits on marginal land. The 'core' of Ricardo's theory, Böhm-Bawerk rightly stresses, thus consists of an 'explanation of the level of the profits of capital *with the level of the wages of labour*; the latter is the cause, the magnitude of profits is the effect' (ibid.: 80; original emphasis).

Interestingly, while Böhm-Bawerk on the one hand admits that there is an 'iron relationship' (ibid.: 81) tying together wages and profits, he on the other hand insists that wages and profits have to be explained independently of one another, each in terms of its own specific factors. He thus echoes a view we encounter in *The Wealth of Nations*, which Ricardo refuted. Böhm-Bawerk in fact insists: 'the profits of capital do not rest on determinants that are less independent than it can be said of the wages of labour. It is Ricardo's crucial error to have totally ignored these *independent causes*' (ibid.: 82–3; emphasis added). This statement flies in the face of the sound proposition that there is an iron relationship. The causes Böhm-Bawerk has in mind are those contemplated by his three 'Grounds' for interest: (1) 'different circumstances of want and provision' in the present and in the future, (2) the 'under-estimation of the future' and (3) the 'technical superiority of present over future goods' (cf. Böhm-Bawerk [1889] 1959).

The adding-up problem
The problem with Böhm-Bawerk's view is that if wages and profits are to be explained, and their magnitudes to be ascertained, by independent determinants, then in order for the theory to be coherent it must be shown that the independent explanations do not contradict each other. This would be the case if in a given situation the sum total of the claims to the product by workers and capitalists exceeded, or fell short of, the size of the product. In the former case the claimants' demands would more than exhaust the product, whereas in the latter case they would leave an undistributed rest. In the literature this became known as the 'adding-up problem'. Whilst in Ricardo's theory of income distribution in which one type of return (profits) is treated as a residuum it is tautologically true that wages and profits will add up so as to exhaust the product, this is not so in Böhm-Bawerk's case. He would have to show that the positive explanations given for every category of income taken together do imply the exhaustion of the product. Böhm-Bawerk at first does not seem to have been aware of the problem, which was then dealt with by two of the champions of marginal productivity, Philip Wicksteed and Knut Wicksell, who emphasized the importance of the assumption of constant returns to scale in order for Euler's Theorem to hold with regard to homogeneous production functions. (They were in this regard anticipated by Johann Heinrich von Thünen.)

The problem of 'capital'
As regards the denominator in the expression giving the rate of profits (interest), capital, Böhm-Bawerk puts forward the idea that a set of heterogeneous capital goods can be reduced to a 'subsistence fund', denominated in terms of a given number of elementary consumption bundles. The size of the subsistence fund is then taken to decide the 'roundaboutness' of the production process in the economy. Here Böhm-Bawerk uses an idea encountered in Ricardo, who in much of his analysis of the problem of income distribution for simplicity assumed production to consist of a one-way street starting from a quantity of 'unassisted labour' and followed by a temporal sequence of further labour inputs and the associated sequence of intermediate products (capital goods) to final output. In this view the production process is of the flow-input/point-output kind. The larger the subsistence fund, the more roundabout are the processes of production that can be realized, and the more productive is the labour employed. This is the so-called 'superiority of more roundabout processes of production'. In this way Böhm-Bawerk thought to be able to take the amount of social capital in the system as a magnitude that can be given independently of, and prior to, the distribution of income and relative prices. However, his construction cannot generally be sustained (see Sraffa, 1960: §48 and Kurz and Salvadori, 1995: Chapter 14). In Ricardo we find no such construction.

Choice of technique
In his essay 'Karl Marx and the close of his system' ([1896] 1949) and elsewhere, Böhm-Bawerk deals with the choice of technique problem. Marx's 'law of the falling tendency of the rate of profit' and Böhm-Bawerk's case of a transition from a 'production without capital' to ever more 'capitalistic', that is, roundabout and thus superior productions, are special cases of this genus. Starting from a long-period position of the economic system, characterized by a given rate of interest, a given real wage rate and given relative prices, the question is, under what conditions will another (or a new) technique be

adopted and what are the effects of it? Böhm-Bawerk subscribes to the view advocated by Smith, Ricardo and their followers that there will be a shift to another technique if at the given prices this technique allows producers to reap extra profits. Competition will then exert a downward pressure on (some, if not all) prices, thereby gradually wiping out extra profits, and establish a new long-period position. What will be the rate of profit in the new situation?

To this Ricardo had given the fundamentally correct answer that, for a given and constant real wage rate, the rate of profit would be larger (the same), if the new technique included (did not include) at least one method of production by means of which one of the wage goods or some of the means of production needed directly or indirectly in the production of some wage good could be produced at a lower cost. In his 'law of the falling tendency of the rate of profit' Marx had questioned this fundamental insight. While Böhm-Bawerk appears to be inclined to side more with Ricardo than with Marx, there is clear evidence that he never managed to arrive at a clear understanding of the issue. His own conceptualization of the choice of technique problem falls way back behind Ricardo's solution and contains a number of blunders, which are best exposed in his discussion of John Rae's approach to the theory of capital and interest (cf. Böhm-Bawerk [1889] 4th edn 1921: Chapter XI; see also Kurz, 1994: 94–104).

HEINZ D. KURZ

See also:

Capital and Profits; Exchange Value and Utility; Hayek, Friedrich von, on Ricardo; Labour and Wages; Marshall, Alfred, on Ricardo; Marx, Karl Heinrich, on Ricardo; Schumpeter, Joseph Alois, on Ricardo; Wicksell, Knut, on Ricardo.

References

Böhm-Bawerk, E. von ([1884] 1959), *Kapital und Kapitalzins. Erste Abteilung: Geschichte und Kritik der Kapitalzins-Theorien*, Innsbruck: Wagner; translation of 4th edition as *Capital and Interest, Vol. 1*, South Holland, IL: Libertarian Press.

Böhm-Bawerk, E. von (1886–87), 'Grundzüge der Theorie des wirtschaftlichen Güterwerts', *Jahrbücher für Nationalökonomie und Statistik*, two instalments: **47**(1886), 1–82; **48**(1887), 477–541; quoted as I and II.

Böhm-Bawerk, E. von ([1889] 1959), *Kapital und Kapitalzins. Zweite Abteilung: Positive Theorie des Kapitales*, Innsbruck: Wagner; translation of the 4th edition as *Capital and Interest, Vols. 2 and 3*, South Holland, IL: Libertarian Press.

Böhm-Bawerk, E. von (1892), 'Wert, Kosten und Grenznutzen', *Jahrbücher für Nationalökonomie und Statistik*, Third Series, **3**, 321–67.

Böhm-Bawerk, E. von ([1896] 1949), 'Karl Marx and the close of his system', translation of E. von Böhm-Bawerk, 'Zum Abschluß des Marxschen Systems', in O. von Boenigk (ed.) (1896), *Staatswissenschaftliche Arbeiten. Festgaben für Karl Knies*, Berlin: Haering, reprinted in P.M. Sweezy (ed.), *Karl Marx and the Close of His System*, New York: Augustus M. Kelley, pp. 1–118.

Hennings, K.H. ([1972] 1997), *The Austrian Theory of Value and Capital. Studies in the Life and Work of Eugen von Böhm-Bawerk* [based on Hennings's 1972 PhD thesis, Oxford], Cheltenham, UK and Lyme, NH: Edward Elgar Publishing.

Kurz, H.D. (1994), 'Auf der Suche nach dem "erlösenden" Wort: Eugen von Böhm-Bawerk und der Kapitalzins', in B. Schefold et al. (eds), *Vademecum zu einem Klassiker der Theoriegeschichte: Eugen von Böhm-Bawerks 'Geschichte und Kritik der Kapitalzins-Theorien'*, Düsseldorf: Verlag Wirtschaft und Finanzen, pp. 45–110.

Kurz, H.D. (1995), 'Marginalism, classicism and socialism in German-speaking countries, 1871–1932', in I. Steedman (ed.), *Socialism and Marginalism in Economics, 1870–1930*, London and New York: Routledge, pp. 7–86.

Kurz, H.D. (1998), 'Böhm-Bawerk, Eugen von, as an interpreter of the classical economists', in H.D. Kurz and N. Salvadori (eds), *The Elgar Companion to Classical Economics, Vol. 1*, Cheltenham, UK and Lyme, NH: Edward Elgar Publishing, pp. 35–9.

Kurz, H.D. and N. Salvadori (1995), *Theory of Production. A Long-Period Analysis*, Cambridge, UK: Cambridge University Press.
Sraffa, P. (1960), *Production of Commodities by Means of Commodities*, Cambridge, UK: Cambridge University Press.

Bortkiewicz, Ladislaus von, on Ricardo

Ladislaus von Bortkiewicz (1868–1931) of Polish descent was born in Saint Petersburg, where he studied statistics and economics at the University of Saint Petersburg. He first taught statistics at the University of Straßburg (Strasbourg) in Alsace, which after the German-French war in 1872 had been assigned to the German Reich, and was then appointed to the position of Extraordinary Professor of Economics and Statistics at the University of Berlin in 1901, where he stayed until his death in 1931. His published work is wide-ranging, covering statistics, economics, mathematics and physics. Bortkiewicz was well-read in several traditions of economic thought, including classical economics, Karl Marx, Léon Walras and Eugen von Böhm-Bawerk, and he was keen to identify the differences and similarities between them. Therefore, his observations on David Ricardo's contribution are typically embedded in more general discussions and assessments of the development and progress in economic theory. Bortkiewicz's main interest was the theory of value, capital and income distribution. He admired David Ricardo, but also Marx and Walras. His analytic mind was acute and uncompromising. He did not allow sloppy arguments to pass unnoticed and therefore was feared as a 'taskmaster' in the profession. Joseph Schumpeter (1954: 851) severely underestimated his achievements by calling him a 'comma hunter', who 'had no eye for the wider aspects and deeper meanings of a theoretical model'. More to the point, he and Bortkiewicz held fundamentally different views about what the latter dubbed the 'touchstone' of an explanation of interest (i.e., profits).

The 'touchstone' of the theory of profits (and interest)
According to Bortkiewicz there were essentially three approaches to the theory of interest, only one of which met the requirements he postulated:

> I believe that this can be regarded as *the touchstone of such a theory*: whether it is able to show the *general cause of interest* also for the case in which not only *no technical progress*, of whichever type, takes place, but also the length of the periods of production appears to be technically predetermined, so that *no choice* is possible between different methods. (Bortkiewicz, 1906: 970–71; emphasis added)

In other words, interest ought to be explained in conditions of a given system of production and not in the context of a choice of technique problem, as in Böhm-Bawerk's 'Austrian' theory of capital and interest or in John Bates Clark's marginal productivity theory, nor as a fruit of technical progress, as in Schumpeter's 'dynamic theory of profits'. Elsewhere he expounded the implications of his postulate with regard to the theory of value:

> Now my opinion is that in general the value of goods can only depend upon such *technical knowledge as is applied in practice*. But the value of goods remains unaffected by knowledge,

which, on whatever grounds, is not utilized. The result thus obtained can be summed up in the following brief formula: *for [the determination of] the value of goods there come into considera-tion only actual methods of production, and not merely potential ones.* (Bortkiewicz, 1907c: 1299; emphasis added)

Was there a theory that satisfied these requirements? Yes, indeed, and it was David Ricardo's. Bortkiewicz drew the attention to this fact in his treatise 'Wertrechnung und Preisrechnung im Marxschen System' ('Value and Price in the Marxian System'), published in three instalments in 1906–7; only Parts 2 and 3 have been translated into English – see Bortkiewicz ([1906–7] 1952). In his essay Bortkiewicz referred to the work of the Russian mathematical economist Vladimir K. Dmitriev, who in a paper published in Russian in 1898 had formalized Ricardo's approach to the theory of value and distribu-tion (see Dmitriev [1904] 1974). Dmitriev had shown that the rate of profits and relative prices can be determined once 'the technical conditions of production of commodities (including the commodity labour power) are given' (Bortkiewicz [1906–07] 1952, Part 2: 39). Besides the system of production and the real wage rate (i.e., the remuneration of the 'commodity labour power') no other data are needed.

Value and distribution

Bortkiewicz took Dmitriev's formalization as the starting point of his own analysis. And like him he assumed unidirectional production processes of finite duration, that is, one-way avenues starting from what Ricardo had called 'unassisted labour', followed by a series of further labour inputs that, via a number of intermediate products or capital goods, are taken eventually to lead to, or 'mature' as, final outputs. Ricardo had for sim-plicity invoked such 'time-phased' production processes (Samuelson, 1975) and had con-ceived of the prices of commodities as reducible to 'dated quantities of labour' (Sraffa, 1960), with the corresponding dated wage bills discounted forward at the current rate of profits r. Let L_{-1j} be the amount of labour expended during the last year before the com-pletion of one unit of commodity j, L_{-2j} the amount expended two years before, L_{-3j} three years before, and so on. If the process has been started T years ago, and if wages are paid at the beginning of each year (*ante factum*), where w is the real wage rate in terms of some commodity, which also serves as standard of value, then we get the following reduction to dated quantities of labour for the commodity under consideration:

$$p_j = (1 + r)wL_{-1j} + (1 + r)^2wL_{-2j} + (1 + r)^3wL_{-3j} + \ldots + (1 + r)^TwL_{-Tj} \quad (j = 1, 2, \ldots, n)$$

With a given w and a standard fixed as indicated, there are n equations to determine r and the remaining $n - 1$ prices.

Before we continue, the following deserves to be noted. First, while Ricardo was well aware of the fact that commodities are typically produced by means of commodities – for example, corn by means of corn (used as seed and as a means of subsistence) – he variously had recourse to the concept of unidirectional production. Thus, in his two essay fragments on 'Absolute and exchangeable value' written in 1823, he pointed to 'the variety of circumstances under which commodities are actually produced' (*Works*, IV: 368) and spoke of the 'proportions in which immediate labour and accumulated labour enter into different commodities' (ibid.: 379). The basic idea underlying his concept of a 'medium between the extremes' (ibid.: 372) appears to be that commodities can somehow be distinguished in terms of the amount of time that elapses between the beginning of a process and its end. With some circularity of production this idea necessarily breaks down, while with unidirectional processes of production it is applicable in very special cases only. Ricardo did not succeed in grasping fully the implication of the inter-industry relationships for his theory of value and distribution and the sought 'invariable' standard of value. Second, many of the Austrian economists, especially Böhm-Bawerk, based their analyses entirely on the concept of unidirectional production. Third, Bortkiewicz dealt with circular production in a three-sector framework in his famous paper on the 'correction' of Marx's construction in the third volume of *Capital* concerning the so-called problem of the 'transformation' of labour values in prices of production (Bortkiewicz, 1907a and [1907b] 1949). In the rest of his works devoted to a discussion of the contributions of Ricardo and Marx he typically took the two economists to have advocated unidirectional production. This is somewhat ironic, not least because Marx had explicitly criticized Ricardo precisely for this assumption, since it implied that for hypothetically vanishing wages the (maximum) rate of profits was infinite. With a circular flow, as in modern industrial societies, it was, on the contrary, finite and the reduction to dated quantities of labour will never get rid of a 'commodity residue': beside the labour terms there will always be minute fractions of commodities that enter as inputs the next stage of production. Hence Marx rejected the claim of Adam Smith (*WN*, I.vi.11), shared by Ricardo, that the price of every commodity 'either immediately or ultimately' resolves itself entirely into wages and profits (setting aside the problem of land). The presence at each stage of production of what Marx called 'constant capital' (produced means of production) implied an upper limit to the rise in the rate of profits.

Bortkiewicz then used the unidirectional framework to extend the analysis from the case of circulating capital only, which we just discussed, to (1) the problem of a choice of technique, (2) fixed capital and (3) scarce natural resources that are non-exhaustible (land). As regards the first problem, with several alternative ways to produce a given commodity we get as many reduction equations as there are alternatives. Obviously, and flukes apart, different methods of production do not support the same rate of profits r, given the real wage rate. Bortkiewicz corroborated Ricardo's finding that in competitive conditions the method will be chosen that minimizes unit costs. If the method that does so is at the same time a method employed directly or indirectly in the production of wage goods, its adoption will entail an increase in the general rate of profits. Otherwise it will only lead to a reduction in the price of the commodity in the production of which the new method is used (and possibly in the prices of commodities in whose production the commodity enters as a means of production).

The second part of Bortkiewicz's 1906–7 essay extends Dmitriev's formalization to cover more general cases, especially the case of fixed capital. Ricardo had defined fixed capital in the following way: 'According as capital is rapidly perishable, and requires to be frequently reproduced, or is of slow consumption, it is classed under the heads of circulating, or of fixed capital' (*Works*, I: 52). However, he did not spend much time on the particular difficulties the presence of durable instruments of production involves in the theory of value and distribution. Without much ado he rather assumed that the problem can be dealt with in terms of annuities. As a highly successful stockjobber – a speculator on the stock market – Ricardo was, of course, familiar with the annuity formula and put it to productive use in his theory of value and distribution.

Bortkiewicz ([1906–7] 1952, Part 2: 27–32) credits Ricardo with having integrated fixed capital in his theory of value and distribution in a satisfactory way. He then formalizes Ricardo's approach, which implicitly deals with the case of constant efficiency of a machine. Assume that a (new) machine can be used for n years and the price of the brand new item is given by p_{m0}. At the end of the t-th year of its employment the price, that is, its book value, is p_{mt}, $t = 1, 2, \ldots, n$. At the end of its life the price is taken to be equal to zero. (This means that it has neither a scrap value nor incurs disposal costs.) The difference between the prices of the machine in two consecutive years is obviously equal to the machine's depreciation. Now the price of the product, which is produced with the help of the machine, is independent of the age of the machine. This implies that the yearly charge in terms of profits and depreciation – the *annuity* – must be constant across the entire life of the machine. Let z be the charge, then the following equations hold true:

$$z = rp_{m0} + p_{m0} - p_{m1}$$

$$z = rp_{m1} + p_{m1} - p_{m2}$$

$$\ldots\ldots\ldots\ldots\ldots\ldots\ldots$$

$$z = rp_{m(n-1)} + p_{m(n-1)}.$$

Multiplying the i-th equation by $(1 + r)^{-i}$, $i = 1, 2, \ldots, n$, and adding the equations, all terms on the right-hand side except p_{m0} cancel out and one gets:

$$p_{m0} = \frac{z}{1 + r} + \frac{z}{(1 + r)^2} + \ldots + \frac{z}{(1 + r)^n}.$$

Solving the sum of this geometric series for the annual charge on the machine z one gets:

$$z = p_{m0} \frac{r(1 + r)^n}{(1 + r)^n - 1}.$$

The constant annuity represents that part of the price of a commodity as a share of the price of the brand new durable instrument of production employed that is due to the presence of the instrument in production. Compared to Ricardo's treatment of fixed capital, Bortkiewicz observed, Marx's was inferior and did not constitute progress in economic theory.

Bortkiewicz published two papers devoted to the treatment of land in the theory of value and distribution. In both papers the attention focuses on the theories of rent of the German economist Karl Rodbertus on the one hand and Marx on the other, and on whether these theories involved any progress with respect to Ricardo's theory (Bortkiewicz, 1910–11 and 1919). In Volume III of *Capital*, Marx had criticized Ricardo for having missed the concept of 'absolute rent', that is, rent obtained by the proprietor of 'marginal' land. Absolute rent emerges, because the competitive process is said to be imperfect and thus fails to channel surplus value produced in agriculture, which is taken to exhibit a lower organic composition of capital than manufacturing, away from it in an amount necessary to bring about a uniform rate of profit. Some of the non-redistributed surplus value is said to allow the proprietors of marginal land to pocket a rent. Marx located the deeper reason for Ricardo's inability to see this in his failure to distinguish between constant and variable capital. Ricardo is therefore also accused of having missed an important element at work in the transformation (or lack thereof) of (labour) values in prices of production.

Against this criticism two observations are apposite. First, as Bortkiewicz stressed, Ricardo did not advocate the view that some 'law of value', in Marx's sense, holds true for the economy as a whole (see also Kurz and Salvadori, 2013). Second, without free competition across all sectors of the economy the results would, of course, differ from those obtained with free competition. There is nothing surprising here, as the classical theory of differential profit and wages rates, originating with Smith and adopted by Ricardo, shows (see *Works*, I, I: §II). As Bortkiewicz demonstrates, Ricardo's theory of rent emerges largely unscathed (see also Gehrke, 2012). Its substance stands up to criticism, but certain formulations Ricardo used turn out to be misleading or untenable and more general formulations of the theory are possible.

Marx vs Ricardo: analytical progress or regress?

A main concern of Bortkiewicz (1906–7) was to assess whether Marx's theory implied progress or regress relative to Ricardo's. Bortkiewicz saw Ricardo to be the superior theorist, with a single exception: the explanation of the 'source of profits'. In the third part of his essay Marx is said to have had the illuminating idea of building a scheme in which while commodities exchange according to labour values there is surplus value and thus profits. In this way Marx was able to refute both the vulgar idea that profits are the result of raising prices above their values and the proposition that profits are a payment for the 'productive services' of capital. Marx was able to show conclusively that profits reflect 'unpaid labour' and thus exploitation and imply a 'deduction' from the produce of labour, as Adam Smith had argued. As regards the relationship between labour values and prices of production, Bortkiewicz ([1906–7] 1952: 54, 56) concluded:

> The relations of value-calculation and price-calculation have . . . a completely mathematical character, and the inadequacy of Marx's treatment of this problem reflects the meagreness of his mathematical abilities . . . [N]ot only can the reciprocal relationships of prices, wages and the rate of profit be reduced to their correct mathematical expression without the need to start with magnitudes of value and surplus value, but the latter magnitudes do not even appear in the calculation, if one employs exact formulas.

HEINZ D. KURZ

See also:

Dmitriev, Vladimir Karpovich, on Ricardo; Labour Theory of Value; Marx, Karl Heinrich, on Ricardo; Technical Change.

References

Bortkiewicz, L. von (1906), 'Der Kardinalfehler der Böhm-Bawerkschen Zinstheorie', *Schmollers Jahrbuch*, **30**, 943–72.

Bortkiewicz, L. von (1906–7), 'Wertrechnung und Preisrechnung im Marxschen System', three parts, *Archiv für Sozialwissenschaft und Sozialpolitik*, **23**: 1–50; **25**: 10–51 and 445–88.

Bortkiewicz, L. von ([1906–7] 1952), 'Value and price in the Marxian system', English translation of Parts 2 and 3 of Bortkiewicz (1906–7), *International Economic Papers*, **2**, 5–60.

Bortkiewicz, L. von (1907a), 'Zur Berichtigung der grundlegenden theoretischen Konstruktion von Marx im 3. Band des *Kapital*', *Jahrbücher für Nationalökonomie und Statistik*, **34**, 319–35.

Bortkiewicz, L. von ([1907b] 1949), 'On the correction of Marx's fundamental theoretical construction in the "third volume of *Capital*"', English translation of Bortkiewicz (1907a), in E. von Böhm-Bawerk, *Karl Marx and the Close of His System*, (ed.) P.M. Sweezy, New York: A.M. Kelley, pp. 199–221.

Bortkiewicz, L. von (1907c), 'Zur Zinstheorie. II. Entgegnung', *Schmollers Jahrbuch*, **31**, 1288–307.

Bortkiewicz, L. von (1910–11), 'Die Rodbertus'sche Grundrententheorie und die Marx'sche Lehre von der absoluten Grundrente', *Archiv für die Geschichte des Sozialismus und der Arbeiterbewegung*, **1**, 1–14 and 391–434.

Bortkiewicz, L. von (1919), 'Zu den Grundrententheorien von Rodbertus und Marx', *Archiv für die Geschichte des Sozialismus und der Arbeiterbewegung*, **8**, 248–57.

Dmitriev, V.K. ([1904] 1974), *Economic Essays on Value, Competition and Utility*, (ed.) D.M. Nuti, Cambridge, UK: Cambridge University Press; English translation of a collection of Dmitriev's essays published in Russian in 1904; Dmitriev's essay on Ricardo's theory of value was originally published in 1898.

Gehrke, C. (2012), 'Marx's critique of Ricardo's theory of rent: a re-assessment', in C. Gehrke, N. Salvadori, I. Steedman and R. Sturn (eds), *Classical Political Economy and Modern Theory: Essays in Honour of Heinz Kurz*, London: Routledge, pp. 51–84.

Kurz, H.D. and N. Salvadori (2013), 'On the "vexata questio of value": Ricardo, Marx and Sraffa', in L. Taylor, A. Rezai and T. Michl (eds), *Social Fairness and Economics. Economic Essays in the Spirit of Duncan Foley*, London: Routledge, pp. 213–27.

Samuelson, P.A. (1975), 'Trade pattern reversals in time-phased Ricardian systems and intertemporal efficiency', *Journal of International Economics*, **5**(4), 309–63.

Schumpeter, J.A. (1954), *History of Economic Analysis*, New York: Oxford University Press.

Smith, A. ([1776] 1981), *An Inquiry into the Nature and Causes of the Wealth of Nations*, (eds) R.H. Campbell, A.S. Skinner and W.B. Todd, Indianapolis: Liberty Fund.

Sraffa, P. (1960), *Production of Commodities by Means of Commodities*, Cambridge, UK: Cambridge University Press.

Bullionist Controversy

The name 'Bullionist Controversy' was coined after the *Bullion Report* issued in 1810 by a House of Commons Committee. The report gave rise to a flurry of pamphlets and published letters, and, in accordance with the name given later to the controversy, their authors were categorized as 'Bullionists' – those in favour of the report – and 'Anti-Bullionists' – those against it. The classic studies on the Bullionist Controversy are in Viner (1937) and Fetter (1965). Also useful are the 'Note on the Bullion Essays' and the 'Notes on the evidence on the resumption of cash payments', that Sraffa wrote in 1951 and 1952, respectively (*Works*, III: 3–12; V: 350–70), Laidler (1987), Arnon (2011), and for factual information Feaveryear (1931) and Clapham (1944).

The questions raised by the report originated in the suspension of the convertibility of Bank of England notes in 1797 and had been already discussed as early as 1800. They would remain on the agenda until convertibility at pre-1797 parity was resumed in 1821. Therefore the 'Bullionist Controversy' is usually considered as covering the whole period from 1797 to 1821. Following the editor of Ricardo's *Works and Correspondence*, Piero Sraffa, I will use the other name 'Bullion Controversy' to describe the debates having occurred immediately around the *Bullion Report*, that is, from 1809 to 1811.

The Bullionist Controversy has been for many commentators the most important debate in the history of monetary thought of all time. For Viner (1937: 120), 'The germs at least of most of the current monetary theories are to be found in it', and for Hayek (1939: 37), it 'may still be regarded as the greatest of all monetary debates'. Summing up the controversy, Laidler (1987: 293) concludes that 'it is hard to think of any other episode in the history of monetary economics when so much was accomplished in so short a period'.

If the questions debated during the Bullionist Controversy and the answers given to them had a long-lasting importance, the opposition between Bullionists and Anti-Bullionists was nevertheless framed in terms of the practical problems of the time. Two of them were central in the controversy. First there was the question of prolonging the suspension of convertibility or not. During the first and second rounds of the controversy – in 1800–4 and 1809–11 respectively – this question traced a dividing line between the two camps: the Bullionists answered in the negative and the Anti-Bullionists in the positive. During the third round – in 1819–21 – that question lost its importance, the great majority of the participants to the controversy favouring the resumption of convertibility. The dividing line then shifted to the question of the conditions in which this resumption should occur. The second practical problem central to the controversy also boiled down to a question: should the Bank of England (BoE hereafter) be blamed for the bad state of the currency? Again, during the first and second rounds the dividing line was clear-cut: the Bullionists answered in the positive and the Anti-Bullionists in the negative. This opposition remained during the third round; the only difference being that the context of the first two rounds was inflationist, while that of the third was deflationist.

The positions held on these two practical problems – the advisability or not of the suspension of convertibility and the defence or critique of the BoE – thus give an indication of the camp to which a particular author belongs. The changing conditions from one round to another and the fact that these problems interrelated with other practical ones and several theoretical issues, make, however, the cartography of the Bullionist Controversy more complex.

The questions raised during the Bullionist Controversy

A sentence introduced by Ricardo in the second edition of his *Principles of Political Economy, and Taxation* sums up the central issue of the Bullionist Controversy:

> It will scarcely be believed fifty years hence, that Bank [of England] directors and ministers gravely contended in our times, both in parliament, and before committees of parliament, that the issues of notes by the Bank of England, unchecked by any power in the holders of such notes, to demand in exchange either specie, or bullion, had not, nor could have any effect on the prices of commodities, bullion, or foreign exchanges. (*Works*, I: 353–4)

The BoE and the uncompromising Anti-Bullionists maintained that the high price of bullion and the low exchange rate of the pound could *never* be produced by the excess of BoE notes. Ricardo and the uncompromising Bullionists maintained that they were *always* produced by such an overissue. The Bullionist Controversy was then bounded by these two extreme positions, most of the participants staying in the middle and arguing that, in principle, the high price of bullion and the low exchange rate of the pound could be explained by an excess note issue *and* other causes as well. They bent to a Bullionist position when they considered that, in the circumstances of the time, the former factor was mainly operative, and to an Anti-Bullionist position when they denied that and stressed other causes.

The Bullionist Controversy was not then a steady and recurrent fight between two organized and permanent camps, because the emergence of its central issue implied relations with other secondary questions to be settled, and this left ample room for various, if not shifting or contradictory, opinions. However, on two particular occasions, when it was necessary to legislate on the monetary system, this variety of opinions did not preclude a clear-cut outcome. In 1811, the House of Commons rejected the report prepared by its Bullion Committee, which made a diagnosis and proposed remedies focusing on the necessity to regulate the note issue in view of resuming convertibility. That rejection was clearly a victory for the Anti-Bullionists. In 1821, Parliament decided on the restoration of the pre-1797 monetary system, including note convertibility into specie at the old parity and absence of any note-issuing rule. The Bullionists-versus-Anti-Bullionists dividing line, manufactured under inconvertibility, no longer applied to the outcome of this debate on a regime with convertibility, although it still did in its uncompromising variant, which referred to both convertibility and inconvertibility: in 1821 as in 1811, the Bank of England won the field over Ricardo.

If the complexity of the interrelations between the central issue of the Bullionist Controversy – the role of note issuing in monetary disequilibrium – and other questions somewhat obscures the historical account of the debates, it also explains the lasting theoretical influence of that controversy, because its analysis framed later monetary theory and policy. Before going through the successive rounds of the controversy, it may therefore be useful to delineate the interrelations between the various questions then debated.

The first question was: what was the exact state of the currency? Three tests were available: the rise in commodity prices, the high price of gold bullion and the low exchange rate of the pound. Each one raised specific difficulties. Assessing the rise in commodity prices implied first to distinguish between factors operating on all commodities and others specific to particular industries, and second to distinguish among the general factors between the real and monetary causes of variation. Bullionists usually maintained that the rise in prices was mostly general and had a monetary origin, while Anti-Bullionists insisted more on real factors – general (e.g., war conditions) or specific (e.g., agricultural conditions).

The high price of gold bullion was considered by Bullionists as signalling a depreciation of the currency, since gold was the de facto monetary standard. By 'high' they meant a market price of bullion above the mint price of coined gold (£3 17s 10½d per ounce of standard gold). The Anti-Bullionists objected that, convertibility having been suspended, gold was no longer the monetary standard, so that its price was not an indicator of the state of the currency. For them, bullion was a commodity like any other, and its high price could be explained by real factors affecting the supply of and the demand for it, such as changes in the world production of the metal, demand on the Continent, and domestic demand for hoarding purposes or for export (in the latter case, one had to look at the state of the foreign balance).

The low exchange rate of the pound first raised a difficulty of measurement. By 'low' everybody meant below the metallic par of exchange with the foreign currency considered. In contrast with the price of coined gold, which was legally fixed (and could be used as the reference to ascertain the 'high' price of gold bullion), there was no legal par of exchange and the benchmark with which to compare the observed exchange rate had to be computed on the basis of the metal weight contained in domestic and foreign coins. Technical difficulties then appeared: foreign coins might be debased, bear a seignorage or have a fluctuating relation with the foreign money quoted on the exchange market (such as the 'mark banco' of Hamburg). Moreover, the metal used as monetary standard might differ (London was on a de facto gold standard, Hamburg on a silver standard, Paris on gold and silver). A significant part of the literature during the Bullionist Controversy was devoted to sorting out whether and by how much the exchange rate was 'low'. This was not only important to assessing the state of the foreign balance but also to explaining it. For Bullionists, a high price of bullion and a low exchange rate were two sides of the same coin, which reflected a depreciation of the currency; the divergence with a normal situation was then expected to be of the same order of magnitude with both indicators. For Anti-Bullionists, the two indicators had to be treated separately, since each one reflected the operation of specific factors; a significant difference between the measures of bullion being high and the exchange rate being low strengthened their position.

When, leaving aside commodity prices, attention could be concentrated on the high price of gold bullion considered as a monetary indicator and on the appropriately measured low exchange rate, some further steps were still needed to approach the central issue of the controversy. If the high price of bullion reflected the degraded state of the currency, then which currency? The Bullionists insisted that the depreciation concerned BoE notes, and they disqualified any influence of other circulating mediums: specie (which was not degraded, and would soon completely disappear from domestic circulation), country bank notes (whose quantity was ultimately regulated by BoE issues) or credit instruments (which were not part of the currency). These disqualified elements were, of course, debated. As for the low exchange rate, its monetary interpretation by the Bullionists gave rise to the Anti-Bullionist objection that real factors provided the explanation, such as bad harvests in Britain (leading to abnormal food imports) and/or war transfers.

Finally, one could get to the central issue. If note issuing by the BoE was suspected of being responsible for the depreciation of the currency, how did this occur? The Bullionists put forward two complementary elements. On the one hand, the check on overissue imposed by convertibility – notes issued in excess would return back to the BoE and drain its reserves, forcing it to contract the issues – had disappeared in 1797, freeing the BoE from any constraint. On the other hand, the BoE had not adopted the only note-issuing rule that could have prevented an overissue under inconvertibility, that is, watching the price of bullion and the exchange rate. The answer of the BoE and of the Anti-Bullionists who supported it was also twofold. On the one hand, there were plenty of examples, before and since 1797, of an expansion of the note issue being concomitant to a decline in the price of bullion and/or an improvement of the exchange rate, or the symmetrical situation, so that the alleged monetary indicators had to be explained by other factors, mainly the foreign balance. On the other hand, an overissue was impossible as long as – which was the practice claimed by the BoE – notes were issued by discounting good commercial paper generated by actual activity – what would be later called the Real Bills Doctrine. If too many notes had been issued, it could then only be at the request of the government, for which the BoE was not to blame.

Not many participants in the Bullionist Controversy were able to grasp the interrelations between all these questions and to weave them into a consistent whole. Two figures emerge from that difficult exercise: Henry Thornton (1760–1815) and David Ricardo (1772–1823). Before studying its three successive rounds, it is necessary to briefly describe the situation when the Bullionist Controversy started.

The institutional and theoretical context at the start of the controversy

In 1694 the Bank of England had been created as a device to salvage public finance: being a joint-stock company it allowed raising funds to be lent to the Crown. Its secondary role was to become important: it could issue bank notes not only against bullion but also by discounting commercial bills; these notes were convertible into full-bodied coins. This innovation, coupled with the monopoly of note issue in the London area and the prohibition of any other joint-stock banking in England, made the BoE acquire a prominent position in the English monetary system in the second half of the eighteenth century.

This system was three-tiered. Country banks issued notes outside the London area by receiving gold or discounting bills. To guarantee the convertibility of their notes they kept gold reserves deposited (at interest) in London banks or in the BoE vaults. The second tier was composed of London banks, whose business was to receive deposits, operate transfers and discount bills for coins or BoE notes – but not for notes of their own, because of the monopoly of the BoE on note issuing in the London area. The gold reserves required by the activity of these banks were also kept at the BoE, which was the third tier of the system. Two consequences resulted from this institutional network. First, since London was the centre for foreign payments, any demand for bullion generated by them (in case of a negative foreign balance) was translated into an 'external drain' of BoE metallic reserves, when it became more beneficial to obtain gold from the BoE through conversion of its notes than in the bullion market. Second, any demand for gold coins originating in the domestic monetary system ended up in an 'internal drain' of BoE metallic reserves. Not only was the BoE supposed to provide on demand the metallic currency for which its notes were considered as substitutes, but, in times of emergency, it was also supposed to provide, thanks to enlarged note issuing, the liquidity that was urgently needed (lending of last resort).

The problem was that this increasingly pivotal role of the BoE was not accompanied by a corresponding consciousness of that role by its governors and directors, who were more interested in the security of their own establishment than by the needs of the monetary and financial system as a whole, and consequently reacted to a gold drain and/or a financial panic by contracting instead of enlarging their issues. This counterproductive behaviour was observed during the crisis of 1793, when, although the exchanges were favourable – preventing any 'external drain' – the outbreak of the war with France led to a financial panic that degenerated into a high demand for guineas and BoE notes. The BoE reacted by refusing to discount even good paper further, intensifying the panic.

A new alarm occurred in 1795 after two years of war, with an explosive cocktail of financial transfers to the Continent, bad harvests in England and expanded government borrowing from the BoE. This combination of external circumstances and domestic expansion of credit would pave the way for the later controversy between those who would explain the monetary crisis by external factors and those who would blame an overissue of notes. The BoE responded again to the pressure on its reserves by a proportional rationing of its discounts, and again this behaviour started a wave of bank and commercial failures all over the country. In February 1797, rumours of a French invasion provoked another panic that led to a run on some country banks. Because of the structure of the banking system outlined above, the BoE experienced a heavy drain of its reserves, which was seen as threatening the existence of that central institution. On 26 February, a Council convened by Prime Minister William Pitt ordered the BoE to suspend cash payments of its notes; this order was confirmed by the Bank Restriction Act passed on 3 May and was to remain in force till 24 June. Extended by further Acts of Parliament, this unprecedented inconvertibility situation would last until 1821, that is, way after the troubled times – the Revolutionary and later Napoleonic Wars with France – which were directly or indirectly held responsible for it.

What monetary theory were observers equipped with when the Bullionist Controversy started? Breaking with the mercantilist tradition, it was mainly inherited from Hume's vision of an automatic adjustment mechanism of the aggregate quantity of money, which ensured the stability of its value. As described by Hume, the so-called price-specie flow mechanism applied to a pure metallic monetary system in the following way. Suppose that for any reason the quantity of money increases in a greater proportion than output. The quantity theory of money predicts that the value of money will fall, and this will be reflected in increased money prices of all commodities produced nationally. At the ruling exchange rate, these commodities will become dearer than foreign ones, and the balance of trade will sooner or later become negative, depressing the exchange rate until it reaches the bullion export point. Then gold and silver coins will be exported or melted into bullion for export, and this will decrease the domestic quantity of money, reversing the movements of prices and consequently the balance of trade, until the initial situation is restored: 'All water, wherever it communicates, remains always at a level' (Hume, [1752] 1985: 312).

This hydraulic conception introduced interdependence between the domestic value of money (inversely related to its quantity) and its external one (determined by the balance of trade). Because of this interdependence, the same stabilizing mechanism, which relied on a quantity adjustment of domestic monetary circulation and a price adjustment of exports and imports, operated in any circumstance, whether exorbitant or common, and for whatever cause of disequilibrium, domestic (e.g., an abnormal increase or decline in the quantity of money) or external (e.g., a sudden negative or positive foreign balance). Hume's approach had been fundamentally left unchanged by Adam Smith, who had simply extended it to a mixed monetary system in which metallic specie and convertible bank notes circulated side by side. Now an abnormally great quantity of money could result from banks issuing an excess quantity of notes (overissue), but, if the notes were convertible, bullion exports would again correct the excess; these exports would now be fuelled by converting notes at the banks of issue rather than by gathering coins in domestic circulation. If the banks were sound – that is, if they kept enough metallic reserves – the adjustment mechanism operated as in Hume, the only change being that the aggregate quantity of money was reduced in its note component.

The 1797 crisis showed that, even if the banks of issue were sound, the adjustment mechanism could be at fault and require a radical and undesired change in the monetary system: the suspension of convertibility, which degenerated into an enduring fall in the value of the currency. This was a denial of the Hume-Smith vision and pressed for new debates.

The first round: from the shaping of the Bullionist and Anti-Bullionist positions to the ambivalence of Thornton's *Paper Credit of Great Britain*

Considering the novelty of inconvertibility in England and the negative evaluation of previous foreign experiments, such as the system of *assignats* in Revolutionary France, one would have expected the 1797 Bank Restriction Act to generate immediate debates, but Sir Francis Baring's *Observations* in favour of the suspension (see below) had no opponents. The main reason was that at first there were no adverse consequences of suspension. It was only in 1800 that the general price increase and the decline of the exchange rate led to the expression of diverging opinions. This was the first round of the Bullionist Controversy, which, considered from the point of view of analytical achievement, culminated with the publication in 1802 of Henry Thornton's *Paper Credit of Great Britain*.

In 1797, Sir Francis Baring had stressed the pivotal role of the BoE in the English banking system, especially when a run on country banks became contagious and jeopardized the system as a whole (see Baring, 1797). In such a case, the responsibility of the BoE was to be the '*dernier resort*' (last resort) in the money market. Baring was confident in the directors of the BoE for having performed that role in an appropriate way during the crisis of 1793–97. He nevertheless considered that the suspension of convertibility – which he found justified – called for improvements in the monetary system, such as the BoE notes becoming legal tender and their issue being regulated. Baring's positions in 1797 were thus a mix of what would later be Anti-Bullionist – the defence of the suspension and of the BoE – and Bullionist – the necessity for guidelines for Bank directors' behaviour. This ambivalence was an illustration of the absence of controversy at the time.

The beginning of the Bullionist Controversy is generally associated with Walter Boyd's *Letter to the Right Honourable William Pitt*, published in February 1801. According to Boyd, the crucial point was that, having been released from the obligation to reimburse its notes in specie, the BoE in its search for profits had increased the circulation of its notes by 30 per cent, hence the amount of the circulating medium since country banks' issues and London banks' deposits were limited by the availability of BoE notes. This overissue was responsible for the depreciation of the currency, which manifested itself in a general increase in prices. Although the exchanges resulted from various causes, it was likely that they had turned against the pound because of this excess circulation. The reason was that, while under convertibility the BoE was compelled to restrict its issues when it suffered an external drain, under inconvertibility it did not face such a drain and continued increasing its issues, fuelling the domestic depreciation and the deterioration of the exchanges. The solution to the bad state of the currency was thus to dispense with the forced paper money that had been implemented since 1797 and to return to the discipline in the note-issuing behaviour of the BoE that had prevailed under convertibility.

In response, Baring (1801) recognized that the circulation of BoE notes had increased by 30 per cent in four years, but maintained that this by itself could not have produced the observed general price increase and unfavourable exchanges, which were the consequences of the war not of BoE notes being issued in excess. He availed himself of the authority of Adam Smith and affirmed that notes issued by discounting bills on good security could not be in excess. The fact that Smith had considered a competitive banking system (like the Scottish one) under convertibility should have raised doubts about the relevance of that Real Bills Doctrine in a centralized system (like the English one) under inconvertibility, but this was nevertheless a widespread opinion that would be long-lived.

This opposition of views between Boyd and Baring (for more details, see Arnon, 2011) thus reflected what would later be the dividing line between Bullionists and Anti-Bullionists. The analytical foundations of the controversy were, however, lacking. King (1803) stated that the depreciation of the currency should not be judged by the general increase in prices but by two 'tests', valid under convertibility and inconvertibility: the positive difference between the market price of the standard in bullion and its legal price in coin, and the decline in the exchange rate. Ricardo later praised this position (*Works*, III: 51). Another author contributed to the first round of the Bullionist Controversy on the Bullionist side by introducing a statement that would have great importance at the beginning of the second round, especially in Ricardo's writings. Wheatley (1803) stated that the unfavourable exchanges could have only one cause – excess of notes – contrary to common opinion that recognized the possibility of other causes besides this one. Following Viner (1937: 106), commentators thus usually label Wheatley as an 'extreme Bullionist' – a qualifier also given to Ricardo for the same reason.

Both King and Wheatley wrote their pamphlets as a critique of a book published in 1802, whose author – Henry Thornton – outstripped all participants in the first round of the Bullionist Controversy. The publication in 1802 of Henry Thornton's *An Enquiry into the Nature and Effects of the Paper Credit of Great Britain* marked a breakthrough on the questions raised since the beginning of the Bullionist Controversy. In contrast with the Hume-Smith vision that was the reference for the previous participants to the debates, according to which the same adjustment mechanism applied in any circumstance, Thornton made a distinction between various cases, which required different analyses. An external shock, which disturbed foreign economic relations, was different from a domestic one, due to a defect in the workings of the monetary system. Moreover, one should separate normal times, in which adjustments operated mechanically, and special circumstances, which might justify active interventions.

Two main sources of monetary instability may be distinguished in Thornton, and each one requires an appropriate treatment. One is an exogenous disequilibrium, originating domestically (e.g., a bad harvest), in foreign relations (e.g., a war) or at either level (e.g., a panic, provoked by a mistrust in a local bank or a fear of invasion). The problem is then to avoid a cumulative instability, and to minimize the effects of the shock until new exogenous circumstances make it disappear. Active interventions are then required: 'To understand how to provide against this pressure, and how to encounter it, is a great part of the wisdom of a commercial state' (Thornton [1802] 1939: 143). Two elements point to the right direction, one internal and the other external. First, a contraction of the domestic circulation should be avoided because it would impair the capacity of the exporting industries to restore the balance of trade when better times return. As a consequence, 'the bank ought to avoid too contracted an issue of bank notes' (ibid.: 153), even though its gold reserves are diminishing because of the distress, and precisely to compensate the shortage of liquidity induced by the export of the metallic currency. Second, the depressive impact on the exchange of a trade deficit or transfers abroad may be counteracted by capital inflows generated by foreign speculators who anticipate the return of the sterling to its previous parity and want to acquire positions in that currency while it is temporarily weak. The importance of that speculation – hence of the brake it puts on the decline of the exchange and the export of gold – depends on two factors: the interest-rate differential between England and abroad (which is affected by the legislation on the maximum rate of interest) and the length of the period anticipated by foreigners for the return to parity. Here lies the foundation of uncovered interest parity, which is part of the modern common knowledge in international finance.

A completely different situation arises when the disequilibrium is endogenous to the domestic monetary system, for example in the case of an excess supply of bank notes. Now the threat to monetary stability is no longer an exogenous shock beyond the control of a 'commercial state', whose 'wisdom' may only help to *react* to it. The aim is at improving the monetary system, in order to *prevent* the endogenous depreciation from appearing. The solution has then to be found elsewhere, and again two elements may help, one internal, the other external. First, in a system where the volume of bank notes issued was endogenously driven by the demand for them, which depended itself on the difference between the expected return on investment and the interest rate at which one could borrow from the bank, overissue might be avoided if the BoE was allowed to increase its discount rate as much as necessary (which required repealing the Usury Laws), and was strongly induced to do so (which justified a controlled monopoly of issue). Second, by reducing the metallic circulation, the export of gold compensated the excess quantity of bank notes; hence it was a factor of monetary stabilization, *unless* the Bank increased its issues at the same time. Although the absolute level of these issues was impossible to determine, the excess of the market price of bullion over the mint price provided a criterion for their required variation: they should be reduced whenever this divergence became abnormal.

An analytical conclusion emerged from the distinction between exogenous and endogenous sources of monetary instability. If both cases called for the repeal of the legislation imposing a maximum interest rate, they differed diametrically about the expected behaviour of the BoE: an exogenous shock might require expanding the issue (lending of last resort), while an endogenous fall in the value of money required contracting it.

This sophisticated analysis would allow Thornton to adapt his diagnosis and remedies to changing circumstances, without facing contradiction. In 1802, his analysis of the crisis of 1797 insisted on exogenous causes (bad harvests, war transfers), which had generated an adverse foreign balance: the causality ran from an external fall in the value of money (a decline in the exchange rate) to a domestic one (the increase in the market price of gold bullion). Instead of having contracted its note issue – precipitating the crisis – the BoE should have increased it and raised its discount rate to attract foreign capital, until unfavourable circumstances had disappeared. By contrast, as a co-author of the *Bullion Report* in 1810, Thornton would blame the BoE for having overissued in times of inconvertibility: the causality now ran from a domestic fall in the value of money to an external one, and the remedy was a contraction of the note issue and the resumption of convertibility (see below).

Thanks to its theoretical foundations, Thornton's *Paper Credit* thus made Bullionist and Anti-Bullionist arguments coexist. In contrast with the Bullionists Boyd, King and Wheatley, Thornton did not blame the BoE for having taken advantage of inconvertibility and issued in excess; he explained the bad state of the currency by external factors having generated an adverse foreign balance. His analysis of the effects of 'a comparison of the rate of interest taken at the bank with the current rate of mercantile profit' (ibid.:

254) nevertheless contained a powerful critique of what would long be a distinctive mark of Anti-Bullionism: the Real Bills Doctrine, according to which notes could never be in excess as long as they were issued by discounting bills generated by current production. Thornton pointed out that the supply of bills – hence the demand for notes – was not driven by the volume of goods under production but by the difference between the expected rate of return on the money borrowed and the actual discount rate at which the BoE monetized the bills – a point that would be emphasized by Wicksell nearly a century later when dealing with the relation between the natural rate of interest and the money rate of interest. If this difference was large – a circumstance fostered by the legal maximum of 5 per cent imposed on the discount rate – the fact that the BoE only lent on good-quality bills could not prevent the issuing of notes from being in excess, by comparison with what was required by the level of current production. This excess then pushed the market price of bullion upwards. Under convertibility, arbitrage triggered by the positive difference between the market price of gold bullion and the legal price at which the BoE was compelled to give specie for its notes led to a drain of its metallic reserves that forced the BoE to reduce its issues, thus correcting the excess. But this check on overissue disappeared under inconvertibility, and the depreciation of the currency then had no limit. This argument was consistent with a Bullionist approach.

This ambivalence of Thornton's *Paper Credit* contrasts with the tradition started by Hayek (1939) that considered that his later co-authorship of the *Bullion Report* marked an evolution towards a growing concern for 'the dangers of a paper currency' (Hayek, 1939: 56) and the necessity of a return to convertibility. The theoretical possibility of overissue was already present in *Paper Credit*, and Thornton would have no difficulty later basing on it his understanding of the situation discussed during the second round of the Bullionist Controversy. This ambivalence is also at odds with the opposite and more recent view expressed in Arnon (2011), according to which Thornton remained faithful to the same line: the defence of an inconvertible monetary system. As will be shown in the next section, there is one Thornton indeed and it is all based on *Paper Credit*, but this book provides a unified theoretical foundation for both the defence of lending of last resort and the restriction of the note issue, under both convertibility and inconvertibility. The two speeches delivered by Thornton in 1811 and defending the *Bullion Report* are an illustration of that consistency. Thornton thus provides a link between the first and second rounds of the Bullionist Controversy.

The second round: the 'Bullion Controversy'
After a five-year remission the fall in the value of the pound resumed in 1809, to reach 20 per cent in March 1810. This was the time of the 'Bullion Controversy', marked in 1810 by the *Bullion Report* that explained the fall in the value of the pound by the excess issue of BoE notes and suggested contraction of the issue and return to convertibility as remedies. This suggestion was rejected by Parliament, and the matter remained unsettled, although the fall in the value of the pound intensified (with a maximum of 50 per cent in November 1813).

The Bullion Controversy – the second round that marked the climax of the Bullionist Controversy – introduced a new character to our drama: David Ricardo. Not only was it the first time that Ricardo appeared in print but also his letter published in the *Morning Chronicle* of 29 August 1809 initiated the debate.

After two more letters to the *Morning Chronicle* Ricardo expanded his views in his first book, published on 3 January 1810. The title of this pamphlet – *The High Price of Bullion, a Proof of the Depreciation of Bank Notes* (*Works*, III: 47–99) – summed up Ricardo's main argument: the BoE note was depreciated, as proved by the high price of gold bullion and the low exchange rate of the pound, and this depreciation was entirely due to its excess issue. On 1 February, Francis Horner delivered a speech before the House of Commons drawing attention to the necessity of inquiring about these phenomena. On 19 February, a committee composed of 22 members of the House of Commons was appointed, and until May it took evidence from numerous specialists. Its report was co-authored by Francis Horner, William Huskisson and Henry Thornton; it stressed the excess note issue by the BoE and recommended the resumption of note convertibility within two years. The *Bullion Report* was laid before the House of Commons on 8 June 1810. Its publication on 13 August 1810 initiated three favourable new letters from Ricardo to the *Morning Chronicle*, and many pamphlets, either supporting the report – such as William Huskisson's – or attacking it – such as Charles Bosanquet's, criticized by Ricardo. In February 1811 Robert Malthus published an article in the *Edinburgh Review* discussing six of these pamphlets (Malthus, 1811). In April a fourth edition of Ricardo's *High Price* was published, with an 'Appendix' containing observations on Malthus's article and an outline of a plan for note convertibility into bullion instead of specie (*Works*, III: 99–127).

It took Francis Horner nearly one year to obtain a debate on the *Bullion Report* in a plenary session of the House. The resolutions discussed from 6 to 15 May 1811 summed up the Bullionist and Anti-Bullionist positions. Horner moved 16 resolutions embodying the conclusions of the report; two of them were particularly important. The 14th stated a note-issuing rule to be applied as long as inconvertibility was maintained:

> During the continuance of the suspension of Cash Payments, it is the duty of the Directors of the Bank of England to advert to the state of the Foreign Exchanges, as well as to the price of Bullion, with a view to regulate the amount of their Issues. (In Cannan [1919] 1969, Part 2: 9)

Horner's 16th resolution introduced a complete change of view from what had been repeated by the successive Restriction Acts, because the resumption of convertibility would now occur after two years whether the war was at an end or not.

Another Member of Parliament, Nicholas Vansittart, moved 17 counter-resolutions. The third rejected the idea that the BoE note was depreciated. Consequently, the high price of bullion and the low exchange of the pound were entirely to be explained by the adverse foreign balance, as stated by the 15th counter-resolution. Vansittart's 17th counter-resolution repeated the term fixed by the last Restriction Act for the resumption of convertibility, that is, 'six months after the conclusion of a Definitive Treaty of Peace' (ibid.: 19).

Horner's 15 first resolutions were rejected by the 226 Members of the House by a majority of two-thirds, the last one (on the resumption of convertibility) by a majority of four-fifths. This negative vote was confirmed by the adoption of Vansittart's counter-resolutions by a majority of two-thirds. This was a defeat for the Bullionists, both on the diagnosis – the depreciation of the BoE note due to its overissue – and the remedies – the note-issuing rule and the resumption of convertibility. Eight more years would be needed to resurrect the debate in Parliament.

Before moving to that third round of the Bullionist Controversy, we should pay attention to the arguments of the two major authoritative figures supporting the *Bullion Report*, Henry Thornton and David Ricardo. In spite of their defeat in 1811, they would have a lasting influence on monetary theory and policy.

Thornton delivered two speeches during the 1811 debate in Parliament, one supporting Horner's resolutions, the other criticizing Vansittart's counter-resolutions. At the beginning of the first, Thornton underlined that 'the main point at this moment in issue' was not the resumption of cash payments but the note-issuing rule to be adopted by the BoE:

> That main point was, not whether the Bank should open at any particular time, or any change be made as to the law in this respect, which would be a second consideration; but whether with a view to facilitate such opening if it should be prescribed, or with a view to secure the due maintenance of our standard during the long continuance of the restriction of cash payments, if the continuance should be deemed advisable, it was or was not expedient that the Bank should regulate the issues of its paper with a reference to the price of Bullion, and the state of the Exchanges. The Bank and the Bullion Committee were at variance on this leading and essential point. (Thornton, 1811: 327)

As testified by this quotation, the note-issuing rule advocated by Thornton should apply in convertibility and inconvertibility as well, and in both cases implied the rejection of discretionary monetary policies.

In his second speech, Thornton refuted the interpretation of Locke given by the Governor of the BoE, according to which the export of bullion was *always* a consequence of an adverse balance of trade, a circumstance on which the BoE could have no influence. Thornton underlined that 'Mr. Locke, therefore, refers to either of two causes the disappearance of coin' (ibid.: 352), the other cause being that 'two kinds of circulating medium, if of different value, cannot long continue to pass interchangeably' (ibid.), a principle that also applied to the coexistence of specie and depreciated bank notes and pointed to the responsibility of the BoE – whose excess issue was the cause of that depreciation – in the export of bullion. The contraction of the note issue was then the appropriate remedy, as it should already have been in 1802, contrary to what Thornton maintained at the time – an 'error to which he himself had once inclined' (ibid.: 353). This 'error' was to have believed that the export of gold could correct the exchange, a correction made impossible in the circumstances of the time because of the want of exportable specie in domestic circulation. It was then a factual 'error', not a theoretical one.

To conclude on Thornton, the nature of the monetary system – convertibility or inconvertibility – does not seem to be the right key to evaluate the consistency of his positions in 1802 and 1811. In both rounds of the Bullionist Controversy, the question of the return to convertibility was for Thornton of secondary importance. Central in his positions was his analysis of the causes of and remedies to monetary disequilibrium. As to the former, Thornton affirmed that they might be two, exogenous or endogenous to the monetary system, and as to the latter he advocated discretion or the note-issuing rule, according to the particular cause of disequilibrium.

The new actor who emerged in the Bullion Controversy – David Ricardo – opposed the first statement: for him there could be only one cause of monetary disequilibrium – excess issue. For general reasons he thus defended the same note-issuing rule as the one advocated by Thornton in the circumstances of the time – a contraction motivated by the high price of bullion and the low exchange rate of the pound. Hence both authors converged in the defence of the *Bullion Report*. Ricardo's position is analysed in detail in the entry 'Papers on Money and Banking' of the present volume.

The third round: towards the resumption of convertibility
After the end of the war in 1815, a monetary reform took place in England in 1816 with the legal adoption of the gold standard. Until then England was legally on a bimetallic standard (gold and silver), although the golden guinea had been de facto the reference in domestic payments since the 1717 reform. The 1816 reform introduced a new golden coin (the sovereign) and made silver coins a token currency. The return to convertibility seemed still hazardous. In *Proposals for an Economical and Secure Currency* (*Works*, IV: 49–141), Ricardo nevertheless published the same year a plan for a new monetary system, along the lines sketched in 1811. This Ingot Plan had two main aspects: on the one hand BoE notes were to be convertible into bullion and no longer into specie; on the other hand, the note issue should be regulated by the BoE according to the observed market price of bullion, the quantity of notes being expanded when this price was below the legal price at which notes could be obtained from the Bank against bullion, and contracted when this price was higher than the legal price at which bullion could be obtained from the Bank against notes.

The debates on the monetary system resumed in early 1819, two secret committees, one in the House of Commons and one in the House of Lords, being appointed. They took evidence from 24 witnesses and issued their final reports on 6 and 7 May. On 26 May 1819, the House of Commons adopted the nine resolutions embodied in the report of its committee.

Four main interrelated questions were raised during these debates. First, should bank notes be made convertible again or should inconvertibility be prolonged? Second, if the resumption of note convertibility was decided, should it be into gold only or into gold and silver? Third, at which level should the legal price of the standard be fixed, the pre-1797 one or a higher one, to account for the past depreciation of the pound? And fourth, should notes be made convertible again into specie, or, according to Ricardo's Ingot Plan, into bullion?

Only a small minority defended the maintenance of inconvertibility. As seen above, the debate between Bullionists and Anti-Bullionists at the time of the *Bullion Report* had been about the timing of the resumption, not its desirability. For example, Nicholas Vansittart, who in 1811 had defended the maintenance of the suspension until six months after the end of the war, was now, as Chancellor of the Exchequer, in favour of the resumption, more than three years having elapsed since Waterloo. The main impetus for advocating the maintenance of inconvertibility came from the disruptions provoked by the return to a peacetime economy. The two main sectors that suffered from that movement were those that had benefited from the war: agriculture, where high prices of the products had been sustained by the reduction of imports generated by the impediments to transportation by sea, and metalworking industries, which had boomed with the needs of the war. Since these post-war adjustments occurred simultaneously with the general deflation and the consequent contraction of the note issue, the blame was put on money by interests vested in these sectors. The Birmingham School, so designated after the city that was the centre of metalworking industries, was mainly represented by Thomas Attwood, who would develop until the 1840s a doctrine favourable to the management of an inconvertible currency, and his brother Matthias Attwood, who opposed the resumption in Parliament. The question of whether Thomas Attwood anticipated modern analysis of inconvertible money or was simply a crude inflationist has been much debated in the literature (see Fetter, 1965).

On the question of the standard, the majority was also in favour of a single one, most of the discussion being on whether it should be gold *or* silver. For example, Ricardo had favoured silver in his 1816 *Proposals* because of its use as standard by most foreign countries, but he changed his view in favour of gold in 1819 because of the effects of machinery on the value of silver. The double standard (gold *and* silver) was, however, supported by one of the most powerful financiers in Europe, Alexander Baring (the second son of Sir Francis Baring). Before both committees he defended resumption at pre-war parity and Ricardo's convertibility into bullion, but he dissented on the standard. Baring's suggestion of a double standard had, however, no echo in the final reports of the committees. With general deflation spreading, Baring resurrected it in 1821, linking now his double-standard proposal with an argument in favour of devaluation. But again he did not succeed.

The debate on the parity between the pound and gold was about deflation or devaluation. The first option aimed at re-establishing the monetary system as it was before 1797, the only difference being the substitution of a de jure to a de facto gold standard. But, in the eyes of its advocates, it implied the fulfilment of two conditions: a contraction of note circulation, in order to bring the market price of gold bullion down to the pre-war mint price of £3 17s 10½d per ounce standard; and the reconstitution of the gold reserves of the BoE to respond to any possible drain on them. Both conditions were liable to increase the difficulties of a return to peacetime economy, the former by creating liquidity crunches, the latter by exerting an upward pressure on the value of gold in terms of commodities (because of the demand by the BoE), hence aggravating deflation. The second option (devaluation) was symmetrical to the first: the resumption of convertibility was made easier because a higher mint price implied less contraction of the note circulation and lower reserves of the BoE, but this option hurt the interests of the creditors by diminishing the value of debts in terms of gold. The outcome thus depended on the balance of power between creditors and debtors, the BoE being on the creditor side. This conflict of interest was, however, softened by the fact that the post-war stagnation in trade and the consequent general fall of prices had reduced the demand for BoE notes hence their quantity in circulation. The amount of further deflation needed to resume convertibility at pre-war parity was consequently smaller and made acceptable. The position held by Ricardo on this question was an illustration of the pragmatism with which this question was approached.

Ricardo was all the more inclined to neglect the deflationary consequences of resumption at pre-war parity since he himself advocated a plan that, by increasing the security of the monetary system, reduced the need for gold reserves held by the BoE, hence the upward pressure on the relative value of gold. This plan raised the last question debated, that of the kind of note convertibility, into specie (as before 1797) or into bullion (as in Ricardo's Ingot Plan). The House of Commons adopted the obligation for the BoE to deliver standard bullion for its notes. A calendar was set to implement a gradual return to note convertibility at decreasing rates – it started on 1 February 1820, to end on 1 May 1821 at the pre-1797 parity. Although the return to convertibility into coin was announced for 1 May 1823, this three-year implementation of convertibility into bullion – with the prospect that, if it worked, it could be made permanent – was a success for Ricardo, which, however, did not last. As early as 1 May 1821, when pre-war parity was restored, the BoE was given the choice to pay its notes in coin or in bullion; this amounted to dropping Ricardo's Ingot Plan.

After the resumption of cash payments there were still debates about its responsibility in the deflation observed in the following years, but the monetary system retained the main characteristics of the pre-1797 system: on the one hand a mixed circulation of coins issued by the mint and notes convertible into gold coins and issued by the BoE or country banks; on the other hand a pivotal position of the BoE in the system, although not associated with any explicit rule or doctrine related to its note-issuing behaviour. The 1825 monetary crisis shook confidence in that system but nearly 20 more years would elapse before another monetary controversy, this time between the Currency School and the Banking School, led to the Bank Charter Act of 1844, which settled an institutional framework for the gold-standard monetary system and associated central-banking rules that would remain operative in Britain until World War I.

GHISLAIN DELEPLACE

See also:

Gold; Monetary Theory; Natural Quantity of Money; Papers on Money and Banking; Rate of Interest.

References

Arnon, A. (2011), *Monetary Theory and Policy from Hume and Smith to Wicksell*, Cambridge, UK: Cambridge University Press.

Baring, F. (1797), *Observations on the Establishment of the Bank of England and on the Paper Circulation of the Country*, London: Sewell, Cornhill and Debrett.

Baring, F. (1801), *Observations on the Publication of Walter Boyd*, London: Sewell, Cornhill and Debrett.

Boyd, W. (1801), *Letter to the Right Honourable William Pitt on the Influence of the Stoppage of Issues in Specie at the Bank of England, on the Prices of Provisions and Other Commodities*, London: J. Wright.

Cannan, E. (ed.) ([1919] 1969), *The Paper Pound of 1797–1821. The Bullion Report 8th June 1810*, London: King & Son; reprint of the 1925 2nd edition, London: Frank Cass & Co.

Clapham, J. (1944), *The Bank of England*, Cambridge, UK: Cambridge University Press.

Feaveryear, A. (1931), *The Pound Sterling. A History of English Money*, Oxford: Clarendon Press.

Fetter, F.W. (1965), *Development of British Monetary Orthodoxy 1797–1875*, Cambridge, MA: Harvard University Press.

Hayek, F.A. von (1939), 'Introduction' in H. Thornton (1802 [1939]), *An Enquiry into the Nature and Effects of the Paper Credit of Great Britain*, London: George Allen and Unwin, pp. 11–63.

Hume, D. ([1752] 1985), 'Political discourses: of the balance of trade', in E.F. Miller (ed.), *David Hume: Essays, Moral, Political, and Literary*, Indianapolis: Liberty Fund.

King, P. (1803), *Thoughts on the Restriction of Payments in Specie at the Banks of England and Ireland*, London: Cadell and Davies.

Laidler, D. (1987), 'Bullionist Controversy', in J. Eatwell, M. Milgate and P. Newman (eds), *The New Palgrave Dictionary of Economics, Vol. I*, London: Macmillan, pp. 289–94.

Malthus, T.R. (1811), 'Depreciation of paper currency', *The Edinburgh Review*, **17**, February, 340–72.

Thornton, H. ([1802] 1939), *An Enquiry into the Nature and Effects of the Paper Credit of Great Britain*, London: George Allen and Unwin; reprint: Fairfield, NJ: A.M. Kelley, 1991.

Thornton, H. (1811), 'Two speeches of Mr. Henry Thornton on the Bullion Report', in H. Thornton (1802 [1939]), *An Enquiry into the Nature and Effects of the Paper Credit of Great Britain*, London: George Allen and Unwin, pp. 327–61.

Viner, J. (1937), *Studies in the Theory of International Trade*, New York: Harper.

Wheatley, J. (1803), *Remarks on Currency and Commerce*, London: Cadell and Davies.

Capital and Profits

In his *History of Economic Analysis*, Schumpeter blames Ricardo for a serious methodological flaw, namely that of indulging in what he called the 'Ricardian Vice' – in
Schumpeter's own words, the habit 'of piling a heavy load of practical conclusions
upon a tenuous groundwork' (Schumpeter, 1954: 1171), that is, of deriving strong
factual statements from disputable abstract models. Now, Schumpeter died in 1950; his
History was published in 1954; in 1951–72, Sraffa published his monumental, and long
awaited, critical edition of the Ricardian *Works*. If Schumpeter could have profited
from this edition, and in particular of the four volumes of *Correspondence*, he would
certainly have discarded his charge. Indeed, it is quite clear that Ricardo did not show
any interest at all in models, at least in the modern meaning of the word, and that, on
the contrary, he was primarily interested in standing on what he considered the actual
facts. Nevertheless, in the present exposition, I will act, at least initially, 'as if' Ricardo
was really addicted to this pernicious 'vice'. In other words, I will list a series of abstract
models corresponding to the various Ricardian conclusions. Needless to say, Ricardo
never adopted these models. The exposition will represent an unusual revisitation of the
famous 'Introduction' to Ricardo by Sraffa.

The corn model
Let us begin with a very first model, that is, the corn model. I intend here the representation of an economy in which only one commodity, namely corn, is produced by corn. To
use a schematic notation:

$$O \rightarrow O$$

In this economy corn enters production as seed and as a source of energy (food) and corn
is harvested at the end of a suitable period (say, one year). Clearly, the corn produced
and the corn consumed do not consist of the same physical corn. Time has elapsed in
between. The production process has a natural direction – it can (and has to) be repeated,
but cannot be reversed. We can go from the seed to the crop, but we cannot reverse the
process from the crop to the seed. Of course, we can use part of the crop as seed, but this
marks the beginning of a new production process.

Similarly, the crop is expected to surpass the seed. The difference between the
output and the input represents the net product (or surplus) of the economy. A positive net product grants that the system of production is vital and the economy is able
to reproduce itself year after year. The production process presents itself here in a
crystal clear form: it is a perfectly circular process, where a net product of corn is
obtained thanks to a suitable advance of corn. The ratio between the net product and
the corn advanced is a physical ratio (the rate of surplus) and is the strategic variable that summarizes in one single number the 'productivity' of the whole economic
system. In this extreme form, this model has never been adopted by any economist,
but, considered as a pre-analytic vision, it is common to the whole classical political
economy.

The corn theory of profits

Until now, apparently there was no room for people in our model, in spite of the obvious fact that people (at least as workers) are a necessary condition for production. In reality, in this one-commodity world, people can surface *sub specie* of commodities, in the form of corn quantities.

To use a schematic notation:

$$\dagger + \bigcirc \rightarrow \bigcirc$$

The transformation of the worker into a quantity of food (corn) is quite straightforward, and has often been performed. The worker can indeed be considered as a machine that converts into labour the energy supplied by a certain quantity of corn, his or her subsistence.

The representation of a person as a taker of a part of the surplus is more problematic. Each person can appropriate a portion of the net product, but we need to know in whose name this appropriation happens. If the right is based on labour performed, we have a surplus wage (exceeding the subsistence level). The subsistence wage is obviously paid in advance, and conversely, the surplus wage is supposed to be paid ex post. The rationale for this is that the subsistence wage is a necessary advance to start the production process, while the surplus wage is a share of the final crop. If the right is based on the anticipation of the stock of corn necessary to start the production process, the reward takes the form of profit.

The legacy of the previous corn model is a surplus ratio measured in physical terms. In the present model, the surplus wage rate w consists in a quantity of corn per unit of labour performed. The profit rate r consists in a quantity of corn per unit of corn advanced. The profit rate is again a physical rate, that is, a percentage.

Until now we have implicitly assumed that the unit utilized to measure corn corresponds to the standard commonly in use (say: one bushel). But we are free to fix the unit at our convenience, and from now on we will choose the net product as the unit. With the same freedom enjoyed in fixing the net product as the unit of corn, we can fix the total quantity of labour yearly performed in the economy as the unit of labour. In this way, the surplus wage is bound to oscillate between 0 and 1 (when wage absorbs the whole surplus).

We are now able to draw a remarkable conclusion: a simple inverse relation relates the surplus wage w to the profit rate. When $w = 1$ the rate of profits is 0 and when $w = 0$ the rate of profits reaches its maximum level, called R, equal to the surplus rate. In conclusion, the corn capital in our model is equal to $1/R$.

Until now, we have considered only one method for producing corn. If, on the other hand, we suppose that corn can be grown on lands of different quality employing equal quantities of capital and labour, or, alternatively, by using successive portions of labour and capital applied on the same land, the picture changes. Assuming that there could not be two different profit rates in the different methods of producing corn (with a 'law' of, or tendency towards, a uniform profit rate) then a land rent arises. 'Rent is in all cases a portion of the profits previously obtained on the land. It is never a new creation of revenue, but always a part of a revenue already created' (*Works*, I: 18). The rent rate consists of a quantity of corn per unit of land farmed.

The production model corresponding to the corn theory of profits was first envisaged by William Petty in 1662: 'First then, suppose there be in a Territory a thousand people, let these people be supposed sufficient to Till this whole Territory as to the Husbandry of Corn, which we will suppose to contain all necessaries of life, as in the Lords Prayer we suppose the word Bread doth' (Petty [1899] 1964: 89). Petty's idea is also recalled by Marshall (1895: 509n) and once again by Sraffa (1925: 324n; English translation, 1998: 325n). But, though Lord Kaldor (1955–56), and many others after him, used the model in his famous exposition of the Ricardian theory of distribution, Ricardo never adopted this model.

The corn-ratio theory of profits

We now enter into a two-commodity world. Corn is produced by means of labour and corn, while a manufactured commodity is produced by means of itself, corn and labour. In schematic terms:

$$\dagger + \bigcirc \rightarrow \bigcirc$$

$$\dagger + \bigcirc + \square \rightarrow \square$$

The model relies on one fundamental assumption: that wages consist uniquely of corn. Agriculture therefore constitutes a sort of 'core' of the whole economy, allowing the determination once again of the rate of profits in physical terms. The condition that there could not be two different profit rates in manufacture and agriculture (the 'law' of a uniform profit rate) forces the rate of profits outside agriculture to adjust to the agricultural one, and this has to proceed via a change in the relative price of the manufactured commodity with regard to corn.

We are now forced to abandon our initial fiction. The corn-ratio theory of profits cannot properly be intended as a model. It is not an abstract construction from which a factual conclusion is derived. On the contrary, it is a fundamental conviction, for which we are seeking the necessary logical basis. As far as Ricardo is concerned, the starting point is his famous principle that 'it is the profits of the farmer which regulate the profits of all other trades' (*Works*, VI: 104). The rational foundation of this principle:

> which is never explicitly stated by Ricardo in any of his extant letters or papers, is that in agriculture the same commodity, namely corn, forms both the capital (conceived as composed of the subsistence necessary for the workers) and the product; so that the determination of profits by the difference between total product and capital advanced, and also the determination of the ratio of this profit to capital, is done directly between quantities of corn without any question of valuation. It is obvious that only one trade can be in the special position of not employing the products of other trades while all the other trades must employ *its* products as capital. (Sraffa, in *Works*, I: xxxi)

This argument, although never stated by Ricardo in any of his extant letters and papers, must have been formulated 'either in his lost "papers on the profit of Capital" of March [actually February – see Vianello, 2010: 31)] 1814 or in his conversation' (ibid.). This conviction is based on a letter dated 5 August 1814, where Malthus objects to Ricardo that:

[i]n no case of production, is the produce exactly of the same nature as the capital advanced. Consequently we can never properly refer to a material rate of produce ... It is not the particular profits or rate of produce upon the land which determines the general profits of stock and the interest of money. (*Works*, VI: 117–8)

Now, this objection of Malthus could make sense only with reference to some lost formulation of the argument attributed by Sraffa to Ricardo. It is indeed hard to conceive of a more convincing conclusion, especially if we take account of the fact that the supposed Ricardian assumption, far from being extravagant – as remarked by Vianello (2010) – had been previously advanced by such an authority as Adam Smith. According to the latter, 'corn or whatever else is the common and favourite vegetable food of the people, constitutes, in every civilized country, the principal part of the subsistence of the labourer' (*WN*, I.ix.e.29). Nevertheless, the Sraffian attribution to Ricardo of the corn-ratio theory has been endlessly disputed.

The labour theory of value
Corn is again produced by means of corn and a manufactured commodity, while the manufactured commodity is produced by means of itself and corn.

In schematic terms:

$$\unicode{x1F6B6} + \bigcirc + \square \rightarrow \bigcirc$$

$$\unicode{x1F6B6} + \bigcirc + \square \rightarrow \square$$

The model relies on one fundamental assumption: that both inputs and outputs show the same physical composition. The only reasonable justification for this peculiar property is that inputs and outputs are uniquely devoted to wage consumption. Therefore, the model depiction can assume a simpler form:

$$\unicode{x1F6B6} \rightarrow \unicode{x1F6B6}$$

And once again, we can measure the rate of profits in physical terms. It is now labour, instead of corn, that appears on both sides of the accounts: as a result, the rate of profits is no longer determined by the ratio of the corn produced to the corn used up in production, but, instead, by the ratio of the total labour of the country to the labour required to produce the necessaries for that labour. In the words of Ricardo: profits depend upon the 'proportion of the annual labour of the country [which] is devoted to the support of the labourers' (*Works*, I: 48–9).

The attribution to Ricardo of the 'Ricardian' theory of value is bewildering. *Strictu sensu*, Ricardo adopts the theory only in the first edition (out of three) of the *Principles*. This recognition has also prompted some commentators to speak, rather trivially, of a '93% theory of value' (Stigler, 1958). Once again, the clue to understanding the Ricardian process of reasoning, a process that is not particularly straightforward, is offered in Sraffa's 'Introduction'. Let us begin with the very first lines of the *Principles*: 'The produce of the earth – all that is derived from its surface by the united application of labour, machinery and capital is divided among three classes of the community ... To determine the laws which regulate this distribution, is the principal problem in Political

Economy' (*Works*, I: 5). This rightly famous *incipit* places distribution of national income among wages, profits and rents at the origin of the whole economic theory. The fundamental legacy of the corn theory of profits, filtered by the Ricardian adoption of the corn-ratio theory of profits, is that distribution consists of the physical division of the surplus among the three competing classes. If any type of return is determined residually, it is tautologically true that the various incomes are added up so as to exhaust the net product. This conclusion, which is typically Ricardian, is clearly incompatible with any theory, which, providing an autonomous explanation for the various types of return, cannot assume the exhaustion of the product.

Now, this last approach is distinctive of the theory of distribution previously advanced by Adam Smith. Indeed, according to Smith, 'wages, profit and rent, are the three original sources . . . of all exchangeable value' and therefore the natural price varies 'with the natural rate of each of its component parts'. Therefore 'as soon as stock has accumulated in the hands of particular persons' and 'as soon as the land of any country has all become private property' the price of commodities is arrived at by a process of *adding up* the wages, profit and rent (*WN*, I.vi.48–49). In conclusion, a rise in wages generated by a rise in the price of corn has the effect of raising the price of all commodities.

In this way, the problem of distribution has ceased to be a purely physical problem in the field of value theory. 'It has been thought that the price of corn regulates the prices of all other things' – Ricardo observes in his pamphlet *Essay on Profits* – and 'this appears to me to be a mistake' (*Works*, IV: 21). Specifically, according to Ricardo, this is Smith's 'original error respecting value' (*Works*, VI: 100). 'I know I shall be soon stopped by the word price', Ricardo concludes in his essay (*Works*, IV: 19). As Marx was to observe: 'The natural price of commodities is supposed to be calculated and discovered by adding together the natural prices of wages, profit and rent. It is one of Ricardo's chief merits that he put an end to this confusion' (Marx, 1956, III: 8). This is the reason why the first edition of Ricardo's *Principles* opens with a section on value. And the heading of this section declares 'The value of a commodity, or the quantity of any other commodity for which it will exchange, depends on the relative quantity of labour which is necessary for its production, and not on the greater or less compensation which is paid for that labour' (*Works*, I: 11).

As Ricardo rapidly recognized, inputs and outputs cannot be properly considered as consisting of wage-goods only (second edition) and that his value theory had consequently to be modified. In the third edition he recognized that the exchangeable value does not depend 'solely' upon the quantity of labour invested in a commodity, but only 'almost exclusively'. Edwin Cannan (1929) considered this modification as a true 'retreat' on the theme of value from the first edition to the third edition. And this alleged retreat gave origin to the Ricardian '93% theory of value', an unfortunate expression indeed.

It is important to notice that the whole controversy is primarily about the theory of distribution. The theory of value represents only an instrumental issue. When Ricardo discovers in the letter to Malthus dated 14 October 1816 'the effect which the rise of wages produces on the price of those commodities which are produced by the aid of machinery and fixed capital' (*Works*, VII: 82) he considers this 'curious effect' an argument *against* Smith's adding-up theory of distribution rather than as an argument in favour of the abandonment of his own labour theory of value.

Production of commodities by means of commodities

Again, corn is produced by means of corn and a manufactured commodity, while the manufactured commodity is produced by means of itself and corn:

$$\text{⦙} + \bigcirc + \square \rightarrow \bigcirc$$

$$\text{⦙} + \bigcirc + \square \rightarrow \square$$

No restrictive assumptions are made about the composition of inputs and output. As a consequence, we can no longer measure the rate of profits in physical terms. Let us consider the simple arithmetic of the example offered by Sraffa (1960, §5). Points **A** and **B** in the figure stand for the total input and output vectors, respectively. Their respective composition is given by:

$$\mathbf{A} = (280, 12) + (120, 8)$$

$$\mathbf{B} = (575, 0) + (0, 20)$$

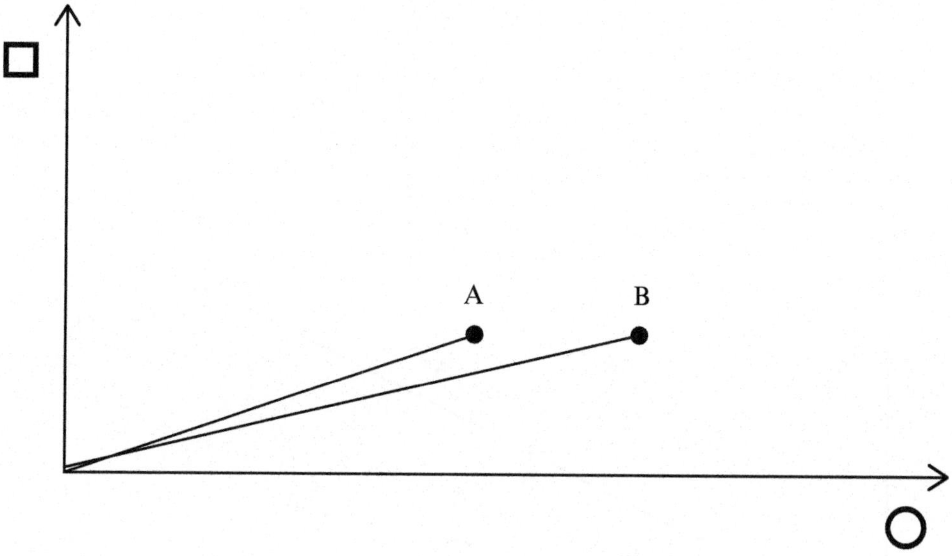

Figure 3

where 20 units of manufactured commodities correspond to 400 units of corn when advanced and to 575 units when produced.

In order to draw the accounts of our economy, we need to align with the origin the two fundamental vectors of inputs and outputs. The traditional way used to achieve this result consists in giving different weights to the two commodities. If, in the example, corn receives a unit weight, the weight p attributed to one unit of manufactured commodity can be considered as its relative price in terms of corn, a price that renders one unit of manufactured commodity equivalent to a certain amount of corn. So both inputs and outputs can be accounted for on the horizontal axis.

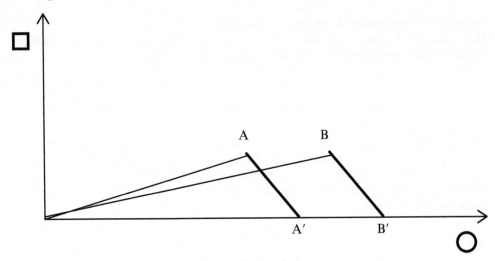

Figure 4

If we add the condition that the profit rate be uniform in the two industries, it can be proved that there is only one relative price of manufactured commodity in terms of corn ($p = 15$) that can perform the task, and we can eventually read the profit rate on the horizontal axis: $r = \mathbf{A'B'}/\mathbf{OA'} = 25\%$.

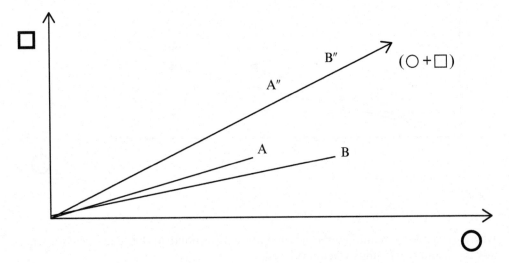

Figure 5

However, there is a possible alternative procedure. We can give different weights to the two industries. For example, we can give unit weight to the corn industry and a different weight to the iron industry: in our example, it is convenient, starting from unity, to increase the weight of the iron industry smoothly. This means that the vector **OB** rotates smoothly westwards (and lengthens). In the meanwhile, vector **OA** cannot stay where it is: it also has to rotate (and lengthen). In our example, it will rotate westward, but at a lesser speed in comparison with the outputs vector (this is granted by the trivial condition that in the two industries' gross production is greater than their self-consumption).

In conclusion, sooner or later, the two vectors, of outputs and inputs, are bound to find a common slope, and we can discover our new three points, **O**, **A'** and **B'** perfectly aligned. In our example, the result will be reached, giving the weight of 3/2 to the iron industry. 'The rate of profits in the Standard system thus appears as a ratio between quantities of commodities irrespective of their prices' (Sraffa, 1960: §29).

A remarkable symmetry is worth noticing. Thanks to the relative weight (price) given to a unit of manufactured commodity, we can visualize the profit rate on the horizontal axis as a ratio between the wheat equivalent of net outputs and the wheat equivalent of inputs. Of course, the quantity **OB'** of corn is *not* actually produced. On the other hand, thanks to the relative weight given to the manufacture, we have identified an industry that is structurally equivalent to the two original industries taken together. Let us call this new invented industry the industry of a 'standard commodity', in which a commodity (a basket of corn and manufactured commodity, whose composition is given by the slope of the vector **OB'**) is produced by itself. Now the profit rate can be visualized as a ratio between the standard net output and the corresponding standard input. Of course, the standard industry is *not* actually in use.

The standard industry is structurally equivalent to the two original industries in the sense that the relations between inputs and output in the two industries (relations that determine the relative price and the common profit rate) are the same for production **OB** and for production **OB'**. Therefore, we can simply read the rate of profit (and of surplus) as the ratio of **A'B'** to **OA'**. The rate of profits thus determined is independent of the relative price. Indeed, the price can be calculated separately, and appears as the exchange ratio, which is 'necessary' (1) for the replacement of the productive stocks by the industries and (2) for granting a *known* common profit rate to the two industries.

The computational burden implied by the two procedures is presumably the same, but this is *not* the point. The picture of the economy is definitely different in the two cases. According to the first procedure, the relative price and the profit rate are simultaneously determined and they appear interdependent. Following the second procedure, we discover that the rate of profits is given before and independently of the relative price. In fact, it comes out in its true nature – as a physical index of the vitality of the system. The relative price has the purely passive role of allowing the necessary exchanges granting the replacement of productive stocks with a given uniform profit rate for the two industries.

Ricardo's final years, between the publication of the third edition of the *Principles* and his premature death in 1823, were entirely devoted to the search for what has been called 'the chimera of an invariable standard of value' (Cannan, 1929: 174). That this search was not the search of a chimera, but a perfectly reasonable research programme is shown by a simple consideration. The rate of profits appears to Ricardo as a physical rate by construction. The increasing difficulty in its measurement, as the value theory is increasing in sophistication, can only be attributed to the measure unit actually in use.

The adoption of the labour theory of value corresponds to an obvious solution. With each commodity being produced by an invariable quantity of labour, we can adopt the net product – a basket composed by corn and manufactures according to the weights 1 and 1. With the corn-ratio theory of profits, the desired net product is composed by the two commodities according to the weights 1 and 0. The weight 0 points to the manufactured commodity as a non basic-commodity, though 'it should perhaps be stated that it was only when the Standard system and the distinction between basics and non-basics had emerged in the course of the present investigation that the above interpretation of Ricardo's theory suggested itself as a natural consequence' (Sraffa, 1960, Appendix D: §1). When we eventually arrive at the general case represented by Sraffa's numerical example, the standard commodity becomes the net product, where the two commodities receive the respective weights of 1 and 3/2. 'The conception of a standard measure of value as a medium between two extremes . . . [also] belongs to Ricardo', Sraffa observes (ibid.: §3).

Surprisingly enough, Joan Robinson's enthusiastic adoption of what she called the Ricardian corn theory of profits was coupled by a much less enthusiastic, to say the least, appreciation of Sraffa's quest for an invariable measure of value. 'For me the Sraffa revolution dates from 1951, the *Introduction* to Ricardo's *Principles*, not from 1960. The thought experiment is simple and robust – the corn model' (Robinson, 1979: 2). 'The definition of the standard commodity takes up a great part of Sraffa's argument but personally I have never found it worth the candle' (Robinson, 1985: 163). 'When you read *Absolute Value and Exchangeable Value* you get the funny feeling. What does this remind me of? And then you say: Of course – Volume I of *Capital* (though two prose styles could not be more different)' (Robinson, 1973: 250).

R.M. Goodwin takes an almost contradictory attitude. 'In this manner Sraffa solved Ricardo's problem of an invariant measure of value', Goodwin recognizes. But 'embodied labour is not an invariant measure of value, independent of the rate of profit'. We have to turn, remembering the original corn model, to a 'generalized corn industry' (Goodwin, 1987: 45).

GIORGIO GILIBERT

See also:

Accumulation of Capital; Corn Model; Labour and Wages; Land and Rent; Limiting and Regulating Principles; Revenue; Surplus.

References

Cannan, E. (1929), *A Review of Economic Theory*, London: P.S. King & Son.
Goodwin, R.M. (1987), *The Dynamics of a Capitalist Economy*, Cambridge, UK: Polity Press.
Kaldor, N. (1955–56), 'Alternative theories of distribution', *The Review of Economic Studies*, **XXIII**(2), 83–100.
Marshall, A. ([1895] 1961), *Principles of Economics, Vol II*, 3rd edition, (ed.) C.W. Guillebaud, London: Macmillan.
Marx, K. (1956), *Theories of Surplus – Value, Part I*, Moscow: Foreign Languages Publishing House.
Petty, W. ([1899] 1964), *Economic Writings, Vol. II*, New York: Kelley.
Robinson, J. (1973), *Collected Economic Papers, Vol. IV*, Oxford: Blackwell.
Robinson, J. (1979), 'Misunderstandings in the theory of production', *Greek Economic Review*, 1(1), 1–7.
Robinson, J. (1985), 'The theory of normal prices and reconstruction of economic theory' [originally titled: 'Spring cleaning'], in G.R. Feiwel (ed.), *Issues in Contemporary Macroeconomics and Distribution*, London: Macmillan.
Schumpeter, J.A. (1954), *History of Economic Analysis*, London: Allen & Unwin.
Smith, A. ([1776] 1976), *An Inquiry into the Nature and Causes of the Wealth of Nations*, in *The Glasgow Edition of the Works and Correspondence of Adam Smith*, (eds) R.H. Campbell, A.S. Skinner and W.B. Todd, Oxford: Clarendon Press.

Sraffa, P. ([1925] 1998), 'Sulle relazioni fra costo e quantità prodotta', *Annali di economia*, **II**, 1. English translation in L.L. Pasinetti (ed.) (1998), *Italian Economic Papers*, **III**, 323–63; reprinted in H.D. Kurz and N. Salvadori (eds) (2003), *The Legacy of Piero Sraffa*, Cheltenham, UK and Northampton, MA: Edward Elgar Publishing.
Sraffa, P. (1960), *Production of Commodities by Means of Commodities*, Cambridge, UK: Cambridge University Press.
Stigler, G.J. (1958), 'Ricardo and the 93% theory of value', *The American Economic Review*, **48**(3), 357–67.
Vianello, F. (2010), 'The Smithian origin of Ricardo's corn-ratio theory of profits: a suggested interpretation', in G. Bonifati and A. Simonazzi (eds), *Il ritorno dell'economia politica*, Rome: Donzelli.

Colonies

Unlike Adam Smith, David Ricardo was not particularly interested in lengthy discussions of possible motives for establishing new colonies and contented himself with devoting just the short Chapter 25 of his *Principles of Political Economy, and Taxation* to colonial trade. Yet, within the latter it is possible to detect (at least) three main analytical arguments related to the colonial issue: (1) colonies as a source of new fertile land and therefore as a viable solution to the problem of decreasing returns on domestic land; (2) colonies as possible outlet markets able to absorb domestic excess supply; and, finally, (3) the effects of trade restrictions between a colony and its mother country. In what follows we briefly discuss these three issues.

Colonies as a source of new fertile land

As is well-known, the rates of growth of capital and labour are determined within the Ricardian model: entrepreneurs increase their capital stock as long as the market rate of profits is above the minimum necessary to induce capital accumulation, while workers expand their families as long as the market rate of wages is above its natural or subsistence rate (Pasinetti, 1960). By the same token, limits to growth are also endogenous in classical economics. Classical economists detect and discuss a number of different reasons why the rate of profits and the rate of capital accumulation may eventually decline and lead to a stationary state. According to Mosselmans (1999), the classical environment induces a perspective focusing on reproduction and internal scarcity, that is, scarcity provoked by ill-advised human actions. Within Ricardo's framework, scarcity is *apparently* provoked by the lack of fertile land, that is, by an objective, non-human factor, but the *real* culprits of Ricardian scarcity are restrictions on the free import of cheap foreign corn in England in the aftermath of Napoleonic Wars.

From this standpoint, the classical authors' emphasis on the limits to growth deriving from the availability of fertile land makes the classical analysis of growth in the newly settled regions particularly illuminating. In fact, as noted by Winch:

> [T]he classical writers were more interested in using the example of new countries to illustrate their analysis of the problems faced by mature economies than in presenting a detailed picture of the actual position of new countries. New countries possess the ideal conditions for growth simply because they are free from the problems posed by diminishing returns in agriculture. (Winch, 1965: 92)

In Ricardo's economics, the pace of economic growth and the related dynamics of the distributive variables depend on supply-side factors, namely the production conditions in the wage-goods sector of the economy. Assuming that the natural or subsistence wage bundle is made up almost exclusively of agricultural products (corn), agriculture turns out to be the crucial sector of the economy and the ratio of (fertile) land to labour the crucial element shaping the growth perspectives of the economy. In Chapter 5, 'Of Wages', Ricardo claims that 'the productive powers of labour are generally greatest when there is an abundance of fertile land' (*Works*, I: 98). In Chapter 6, 'On Profits', he writes:

> [I]n all countries, and all times, profits depend on the quantity of labour requisite to provide necessaries for the labourers, on that land or with that capital which yields no rent. The effects then of accumulation will be different in different countries, and will depend chiefly on the fertility of the land. (*Works*, I: 126)

In the same vein, in an often-quoted letter to Malthus, Ricardo writes:

> [E]very accumulation is attended with increased difficulty in obtaining food, unless it is accompanied with improvements in agriculture; in which case it has no tendency to diminish profits. If there were no increased difficulty, profits would never fall, because there are no other limits to the profitable production of manufactures but the rise of wages. If with every accumulation of capital we could tack a piece of fertile land to our Island, profits would never fall. (*Works*, VI: 162)

Thus, in Ricardo's view, the discovery of new fertile lands plays the same role as technological innovation in agriculture: in both cases the fall of the rate of profits due to a rising cost of production of corn engendered by the accumulation of capital and the growth of labouring population is delayed. Accordingly, the economic conditions for a sustained growth are likely to occur in newly settled regions where the ratio of (fertile) land to labour is usually very high:

> On the first settling of a country, in which there is an abundance of rich and fertile land, a very small proportion of which is required to be cultivated for the support of the actual population, or indeed can be cultivated with the capital which the population can command, there will be no rent; for no one would pay for the use of land, when there was an abundant quantity not yet appropriated, and, therefore, at the disposal of whosoever might choose to cultivate it. (*Works*, I: 69)

> In new settlements, where the arts and knowledge of countries far advanced in refinement are introduced, it is probable that capital has a tendency to increase faster than mankind: and if the deficiency of labourers were not supplied by more populous countries, this tendency would very much raise the price of labour. (Ibid.: 98)

But initial optimism is soon replaced by long-run pessimism. For Ricardo, the Malthusian law of population and the objective limitation of fertile lands will eventually impede growth:

> In proportion as these countries become populous, and land of a worse quality is taken into cultivation, the tendency to an increase of capital diminishes . . . Although, then, it is probable, that under the most favourable circumstances, the power of production is still greater than that of population, it will not long continue so; for the land being limited in quantity, and differing in quality, with every increased portion of capital employed on it, there will be a decreased rate of production, whilst the power of population continues always the same. (Ibid.)

Thus, the process of growth in newly settled regions will inevitably be akin to that of mature economies. In short, the analysis of growth in newly settled regions does not shake Ricardo's belief that the pace of growth in every closed economy basically depends on supply-side factors (such as the availability of fertile lands and the rate of growth of population), given the state of technological knowledge.

Colonies as outlet markets for domestic excess supply

The same supply-side bias underlines Ricardo's rejection of the Smithian 'vent for surplus' doctrine (see Elmslie, 1998). According to Adam Smith, foreign trade in general and colonial trade in particular, by increasing the extent of the market, (1) helps further the process of division and specialization of labour, thus enhancing domestic labour productivity, and (2) counteracts the fall of the rate of profits by opening new outlet markets for domestic excess supply (Winch, 1963). While Ricardo was not oblivious of Smith's productivity argument (Sai-Wing Ho, 1998), the 'vent for surplus' argument was entirely alien to his economic thought. In Chapter 21, 'Effects of Accumulation on Profits and Interest', Ricardo got rid of the Smithian 'competition of capitals' explanation of the fall of the rate of profits by having recourse to Say's argument that 'there is no amount of capital which may not be employed in a country because demand is only limited by production' (*Works*, I: 290). Accordingly, to Ricardo only supply-side factors determine the rate of profits and the rate of capital accumulation in the long run:

> [T]here is no limit to demand – no limit to the employment of capital while it yields any profit, and . . . however abundant capital may become, there is no other adequate reason for a fall of profit but a rise of wages, and further it may be added, that the only adequate and permanent cause for the rise of wages is the increasing difficulty of providing food and necessaries for the increasing number of workmen. (Ibid.: 296)

As a consequence, foreign trade may affect the domestic rate of profits only to the extent that it makes cheaper those commodities generally consumed by workers living in the importing country (Maneschi, 1992):

> It has been my endeavour to shew throughout this work, that the rate of profits can never be increased but by a fall in wages, and that there can be no permanent fall of wages but in consequence of a fall of the necessaries on which wages are expended. If, therefore, by the extension of foreign trade . . . the food and necessaries of the labourer can be brought to market at a reduced price, profits will rise . . . Foreign trade . . . has no tendency to raise the profits of stock, unless the commodities imported be of that description on which the wages of labour are expended. (*Works*, I: 132–3)

Obviously, the same applies to the trade relationship between a colony and its mother country. As Ricardo made clear since his pamphlet *Essay on the Influence of a Low Price of Corn on the Profits of Stock* (1815), colonies can only offer an alternative allocation for domestic capital in search of a rate of profits higher than the one that can be earned in the mother country because of the restriction to the import of cheap foreign corn (see also Kittrell, 1965):

> [The decline in profits is the] effect of a constantly accumulating capital, in a country which refused to import foreign and cheaper corn. But after profits have much fallen, accumulation will be checked, and capital will be exported to be employed in those countries where food is

cheap and profits high. All European colonies have been established with the capital of the mother countries, and have thereby checked accumulation. (*Works*, IV: 16)

In short, Ricardo's rejection of the Smithian 'vent for surplus' doctrine implies the rejection of the view that colonies may turn out to be a crucial element within a policy of demand-led domestic growth.

Trade restrictions between a colony and its mother country

Ricardo agreed with Smith on the negative effects of trade restrictions suffered by a colony to the benefit of its mother country. They both considered free trade as conducive to the best allocation of economic resources at the world economy level:

> Adam Smith, in his observations on colonial trade, has shewn, most satisfactorily, the advantages of a free trade, and the injustice suffered by colonies, in being prevented by their mother countries, from selling their produce at the dearest market, and buying their manufactures and stores at the cheapest. He has shewn, that by permitting every country freely to exchange the produce of its industry when and where it pleases, the best distribution of the labour of the world will be effected, and the greatest abundance of the necessaries and enjoyments of human life will be secured. (*Works*, I: 338)

Yet, though the conclusions are the same, the economic models supporting them are different (what follows is but an attempt to provide a rational reconstruction of the argument developed in Chapter 25 of the *Principles* consistent with Ricardo's overall economic analysis). In Smith's economics the extent of the market is the crucial factor regulating the process of division and specialization of labour and thus affecting the growth of labour productivity and hence the growth of wealth. As a consequence, any restriction to free trade, by curtailing the extent of the world market, entails short-run welfare losses (prices of consumption goods are higher) and long-run efficiency losses (labour productivity stagnates). By contrast, in Ricardo's economics the high (and rising) price of commodities making up workers' natural consumption basket is the basic permanent obstacle to capital accumulation. A corollary of Ricardo's comparative cost analysis is that any restriction to free trade entails an inefficient international allocation of capital, thus leading to a higher domestic price of wage-goods in the long run. Ricardo acknowledged that, in the short run, a few domestic entrepreneurs may pocket monopoly profits generated by the trade restrictions in the exchange with colonies (see *Works*, I: 339–40). Nonetheless, in the long run, such a monopoly does not entail any real advantage for the mother country economy since 'the monopoly of the colony trade will change, and often prejudicially, the direction of capital . . . there will be a worse distribution of the general capital and industry, and, therefore, less will be produced (ibid.: 345–6). Thus, the argument used by Ricardo in Chapter 25, 'On Colonial Trade', to highlight the economic waste resulting from trade restrictions between colonies and the mother country appears to be fully integrated with his own general theory of economic growth: the local monopoly profits from trade restrictions turn out to be a purely monetary phenomenon, eventually eroded by the worsening of the production conditions in the wage-goods sector of the mother country, and thus are definitely not to be considered as a growth-enhancing factor.

DAVIDE FIASCHI AND RODOLFO SIGNORINO

See also:

Accumulation of Capital; Foreign Trade; Land and Rent.

References

Elmslie, B.T. (1998), 'Vent for surplus', in H.D. Kurz and N. Salvadori (eds), *The Elgar Companion to Classical Economics. Vol. II: L–Z*, Cheltenham, UK and Lyme, NH: Edward Elgar Publishing, pp. 504–6.

Kittrell, E.R. (1965), 'The development of the theory of colonization in English classical political economy', *The Southern Economic Journal*, **31**(3), 189–206.

Maneschi, A. (1992), 'Ricardo's international trade theory: beyond the comparative cost example', *The Cambridge Journal of Economics*, **16**(4), 421–37.

Mosselmans, B. (1999), 'Reproduction and scarcity: the population mechanism in classicism and in the "Jevonian revolution"', *The European Journal of the History of Economic Thought*, **6**(1), 34–57.

Pasinetti, L.L. (1960), 'A mathematical formulation of the Ricardian system', *The Review of Economic Studies*, **27**(2), 78–98.

Sai-Wing Ho, P. (1998), 'Foreign trade', in H.D. Kurz and N. Salvadori (eds), *The Elgar Companion to Classical Economics, Volume I: A–K*, Cheltenham, UK and Lyme, NH: Edward Elgar Publishing, pp. 308–12.

Winch, D. (1963), 'Classical economics and the case for colonizations', *Economica*, **30**(120), 387–99.

Winch, D. (1965), *Classical Political Economy and Colonies*, Cambridge, MA: Harvard University Press.

Comparative Advantage

If there is at least one thing that modern economists associate with the name of Ricardo, it is the principle of comparative advantage, which today still forms the basis of the major part of the theories of international trade. It is supposed to explain the direction of the flows of trade between countries and determine the gains each country gets from its participation in international exchanges. It also forms a powerful argument in favour of free trade between nations. This principle is supposed to have been clearly stated for the first time in a few paragraphs of Chapter 7, 'On Foreign Trade' (*Works*, I: 134–6), of Ricardo's *Principles of Political Economy, and Taxation* – a chapter that, unlike the first in particular, remained unchanged from the first edition of the book in 1817 to the third in 1821. While, curiously enough, these paragraphs have most of the time been considered separately from the rest of the *Principles*, as a kind of short parenthesis in Ricardo's writings, they nevertheless have never ceased to be examined and debated, and this created some confusion. A clear understanding of the principle thus requires going back to the texts and answering some simple questions (Faccarello, 2015). How was it stated? How was it interpreted? Is it really a kind of foreign body in Ricardo's theory or are some links to be found with the author's other ideas? As some questions of authorship and vocabulary have been debated among scholars, they will also have to be briefly alluded to.

A statement of the principle of comparative advantage

Towards the beginning of the seventh chapter of the *Principles*, Ricardo introduces an exchange between two countries, England and Portugal, which can produce two commodities: cloth and wine. England exports cloth to – and imports wine from – Portugal, and Portugal exports wine and imports cloth (*Works*, I: 134–5). A specific exchange ratio is supposed to take place between these two countries: *a* units of Portuguese wine are exchanged for *b* units of English cloth. It is also stated that, had each country to

Table 1   The 'four magic numbers' in Ricardo's text

	a units of Wine	b units of Cloth
Portugal	80	90
England	120	100

produce these very quantities of both commodities, Portugal would employ 80 and 90 units of labour respectively to produce *a* units of wine and *b* units of cloth, while England would need respectively 120 and 100 units of labour to produce them. According to the labour theory of value, these numbers, in each country, are also the respective values of the quantities produced. The costs of production, actual and potential – the 'four magic numbers' as Samuelson (1969) called them – are summarized in Table 1.

In spite of the fact that Portugal has an absolute advantage – that is, smaller real costs – in the production of both commodities, and England no absolute advantage at all in any commodity, Ricardo supposes that this exchange is nevertheless possible and actually happens. This is because, Ricardo states, each country has a greater relative facility of production in one commodity – wine is relatively less expensive to produce than cloth in Portugal, and cloth relatively less expensive to produce than wine in England.

What happens here between nations is the same as what happens between two individuals. Adapting an example from the *Wealth of Nations* in which Smith presents the advantages of a division of labour between a tailor and a shoemaker (*WN*, IV.ii.456–57) before generalizing the case to countries, Ricardo reports the case of two men making shoes and hats, one of them having a greater productivity in both productions but being, however, relatively more productive in making shoes than hats (*Works*, I: 136n). In this case, he stresses, it is in the interest of the first to specialize in shoes and buy hats from the second, the reverse being advantageous to the second. It is the same in the interest of countries, as in the case of individuals, not to attempt to produce everything at home but instead to specialize in some production and to exchange. The direction of trade and specialization is thus given by the comparison of the relative costs of production of the commodities in the two countries.

These relative costs can be expressed through ratios. These ratios cannot formally be found in Ricardo. They are advanced by James Mill in the first edition of *Elements of Political Economy* (1821: 88) – who also, in the second and third editions, sometimes spoke of 'the purchasing power of one commodity with respect to another' in each country (1824: 118; 1826: 124). In the above example, the relative costs of production of *a* units of wine and *b* units of cloth are $80/90 \approx 0,9$ in Portugal and $120/100 = 1.2$ in England. The relative cost of the production of wine is smaller in Portugal, and the relative cost of cloth – the inverse ratio – is smaller in England. Hence the rule: a country exports the commodity that is produced there with the lower relative cost – this is what is called its 'comparative advantage' – and imports the other one. Of course, the exchange of commodities in which each country has an absolute advantage is just a special case of this rule.

Ricardo also stresses an important aspect of this analysis. In the above exchange between England and Portugal the product of 80 units of Portuguese labour is exchanged for the product of 100 units of English labour. In international trade the labour theory of value thus does not seem to determine the relative prices of commodities contrary to what happens in domestic exchanges (*Works*, I: 133). Why is it so? Because, Ricardo states, of the relative international immobility of capital and labour, which stands in strong contrast to their domestic mobility (ibid.: 135–6).

The gains from trade and specialization

According to Ricardo such an exchange between England and Portugal is not only possible but profitable to both countries – and apparently possible because profitable. For each country, the gains from trade are immediately determined: they consist in the difference between the cost of production – here the units of labour – the country would have spent in the home production of the quantity of foreign commodity it imports and the cost of the quantity of the home commodity it exports in exchange. Portugal's gains from trade are thus of ten units of labour – Portugal gives a units of wine, the product of 80 units of labour, for b units of cloth for the home production of which it would have spent 90 units. And England's gains from trade are determined in a similar way: they consist in 20 units of labour. Both countries can employ the units of labour they save in the production of more wine or cloth or any other commodity, and, while the gains from trade are not equal on both sides, both countries can nevertheless enjoy a greater amount of use values. In Ricardo's view the advantage that each country gets from free foreign trade is precisely this: a better allocation and accumulation of capital and an increase in the quantities of use values at its disposal. International trade never influences the rate of profits directly – the influence can only be indirect, for example when the importation of cheap corn from abroad reduces the cultivation of pieces of land of worse quality at home, lowers the ground rent and favours profits in consequence.

There is no doubt that Ricardo's point of view is in line with what was called – a bit hastily – 'the eighteenth-century rule' (Viner, 1937: 440) for international trade. What are to be compared, the rule states, are not the real costs of production of a given commodity at home and abroad (as in the absolute advantage approach) but the domestic real costs of the imported and the exported commodities. It is thus advantageous to import a foreign commodity in exchange for a good domestically produced at a smaller real cost than the production at home of the imported commodity would entail. Ricardo, however, adds an important statement: this trade is beneficial to the country even if the imported commodity could have been produced at home at a smaller cost than it is produced abroad. Portugal imports cloth from England though this cloth, the real cost of which is 100 units of labour in England, could have been produced for 90 units at home. Ricardo's innovation is thus of importance. It shows that any country can participate in international exchanges and benefit from them whatever the level of its costs. During two centuries, this statement has been used as a powerful argument in favour of free trade.

With regard to specialization, Ricardo generally supposes that, when constant returns to scale prevail and there is no great difference in size between countries, international trade results in a complete specialization of countries. He recognizes, however, that there could be cases of partial specialization, for example when one of the commodities traded – for example, corn – is produced with an increasing difficulty of production.

Authorship and vocabulary

The very fact that the considerations on the principle of comparative advantage take up little space in Ricardo's long and complex chapter on foreign trade – and, moreover, seems not to be referred to in the rest of the book and in Ricardo's other writings – led some commentators to doubt that it was formulated by Ricardo himself. The question of its 'paternity' was thus debated. Some authors advanced the view that the merit of the first statement of the principle of comparative advantage should go to Robert Torrens – who himself claimed priority (Torrens, 1826: vii). To support this opinion, some passages excerpted from *The Economists Refuted* (Torrens, 1808: 37) and the first edition of the *Essay on the External Corn Trade* (Torrens, 1815: 263) are quoted. Some other scholars, however, were inclined to put forward another candidate – James Mill – and noted that some prefiguration of the principle was contained in his *Commerce Defended* (J. Mill, 1808: 108). Some even supposed that Mill himself, whose role in assisting Ricardo to publish his magnum opus is well known, added the principle in Ricardo's book.

But while it is true that the three editions of his *Elements of Political Economy* (1821, 1824, 1826) greatly contributed to the debates around the principle and made it widely known, James Mill's paternity can certainly be discarded once we realize that he himself attributed the novelty of the analysis to his friend (J. Mill to Ricardo, 18 November 1816, in *Works*, VI: 99) and that a reference to an exchange of wine and cloth between England and Portugal – a feature of Ricardo's celebrated example – can already be found in Ricardo's 'Notes on Bentham' written in 1810–11 (*Works*, III: 330). As for Torrens's claim, it must be noted that it relies on a few paragraphs that, in the writings from which they are excerpted (Torrens, 1808, 1815), are only incidental remarks and do not form a theoretical principle underlying the analysis. Moreover, Torrens later once implicitly recanted his claims. There is thus no doubt today that Ricardo's pages are the first full and clear statement of the doctrine (on this intricate story see, for example, Maneschi, 1998, Ruffin, 2002, 2005 and Aldrich, 2004).

Parallel to these attributional debates and linked to them, the question arose of the origin of the phrase 'comparative advantage' to designate a principle for foreign trade. The words 'comparative' or 'comparatively' are extensively used by Ricardo to mean 'relative' – for example, when he writes of the 'comparative value' or 'comparative quantity' of commodities. The phrase 'comparative advantage' itself is, however, not to be found in Chapter 7 on foreign trade but appears incidentally once, in the context of an open economy in Chapter 29, 'On Sudden Changes in the Channels of Trade' (*Works*, I: 263). 'Comparative disadvantage' is also used once, in Chapter 9, 'Taxes on Raw Produce' (ibid.: 172). On the cost side of the question, and in relation with international trade, the phrases 'comparative difficulty of production' and 'comparative facility [of] production' are employed (ibid.: 343 and 374 respectively).

James Mill, in his *Elements of Political Economy*, also writes of 'comparative facility' of production (Mill, 1821: 84) and clearly contrasts 'greater absolute' to 'greater relative, facility' of production (ibid., 87). He also speaks of 'peculiar advantages' to mean comparative advantage (ibid., 84). It was Torrens who, in the third and fourth editions of his *Essay on the External Corn Trade* (1826, 1827), started to clearly designate the doctrine with the phrases 'comparative advantage' or 'disadvantage' (1826: vii) on the one hand, and 'comparative costs' (1827: 401) on the other. John Stuart Mill, in his essay 'Of the laws of interchange between nations, and the distribution of the gains of commerce among the countries of the commercial world' in the *Unsettled Questions* collection uses the phrase 'comparative cost(s)' (J.S. Mill [1829–30] 1967:

233, 235–6, 254) and, to speak of comparative advantage, writes of a commodity in which the 'advantage is least' or the 'advantage is greatest' (ibid.: 233). In the subsequent literature, both comparative advantage and comparative costs were used interchangeably.

The traditional view: a different statement of the principle of comparative advantage
The above presentation of the principle of comparative advantage is not the one almost universally accepted since almost two centuries. It is relatively new and, while forming until now a kind of minority view, it is gaining ground rapidly because it is more faithful to Ricardo's writings. It is basically due to Sraffa (1930) and was several decades later adopted by Ruffin (2002) and Maneschi (2004). It challenges the traditional interpretation.

The tradition – still to be found in the textbooks of history of economic thought or international economics – was first expressed by James Mill in the three editions of his *Elements of Political Economy* (1821, 1824, 1826) and in his article 'Colony' (1825) written for a supplement to the *Encyclopaedia Britannica*. It was subsequently powerfully restated by John Stuart Mill in his 1829–30 essay written a few years after Ricardo's death and published later in 1844 in *Essays on Some Unsettled Questions of Political Economy*. This approach was developed afterwards by generations of neoclassical economists (on this history see, for example, Viner, 1937 and Maneschi, 1998). It went unquestioned and oriented all the debates until recently. While at first sight the differences between the two interpretations seem to consist in details of trifling importance, they lead in fact to widely diverging approaches.

According to James and John Stuart Mill's approach, and while the analysis is again conducted in real terms, the 'four magic numbers' are interpreted as the technical coefficients prevailing in the production processes in the two countries – and consequently as the labour values of one unit of each commodity in each country. Hence the following modified table, in which the countries are first considered in autarky (Table 2).

Once the countries open to foreign trade, international exchanges ensue following the indication given by the relative pre-trade costs. Except in the unlikely case where no trade is possible because of identical relative costs in both countries – a case considered by James Mill – it is asserted that any country can participate in international exchanges and benefit from them.

The difference with the first interpretation given above seems to be minor. However, the developments give a totally different flavour to the ensuing analysis and results. Ricardo's statement of the principle started with an actual exchange between England and Portugal. The relative price of the two commodities was given – a units of wine = b units of cloth – and the gains from trade for each country immediately determined in terms of saved resources. Once, however, the 'magic numbers' are interpreted as

Table 2   The 'four magic numbers' according to J. and J.S. Mill

	One unit of wine	One unit of cloth
Portugal	80	90
England	120	100

technical coefficients, the questions of the determination of the quantities exchanged between the two countries and of the exchange ratio at which trade is realized are still to be answered and, from this point of view, Ricardo's approach is allegedly incomplete. The possible benefits – if any – each country gets from foreign trade also depend on the answers given to these questions. This is the reason why, in his 1829–30 essay, John Stuart Mill, considering different price elasticities of the countries' demands for imports, introduced the reciprocal demands in the picture. The demand for imports of each country is supposed to depend on the possible barter ratios between the commodities and, once the reciprocal demands are known, the international equilibrium relative price can be determined – and so are the benefits accruing to each nation. The international equilibrium rate must lie within the interval bounded by the countries' relative autarky prices of the commodities, and the more this rate is close to (different from) a country's relative autarky price, the smaller (the greater) is this country's gain from trade – this gain being nil when the two coincide. J.S. Mill was thus pioneering a now well-established tradition in the field.

Some pending questions
It is, however, to be noted that, while more faithful to Ricardo's text, the above first interpretation of the principle of comparative advantage tells only part of the story and leaves some important problems unsolved. As a matter of fact, sticking as it does to Ricardo's always-quoted few paragraphs excerpted from Chapter 7 of the *Principles*, it cannot avoid some difficulties (for a more detailed analysis see Faccarello, 2015).

A first difficulty ensues from the fact that the initial exchange ratio – that is, *a* Portuguese wine = *b* English cloth – is taken for granted. But this relative price is assumed, not explained. With regard to prices, Ricardo in these paragraphs simply stresses that in foreign trade the theory of labour value does not apply because of the relative immobility of capital and labour. The question thus remains of how this ratio is determined.

A second difficulty arises when we note that the benefits countries get from foreign trade are assessed at the macroeconomic level. The principle of comparative advantage tells us that it is in the interest of each country to exchange and points out both the direction of trade and its global benefits. But the countries are not themselves the agents of trade: they do not decide to import and export such and such commodity with the view of obtaining a global benefit in terms of capital allocation and enjoyment of use values. Economies are market based and only the individual agents, acting in markets according to their own private interests, decide what to do. In this perspective the principle of comparative advantage is seemingly of no use to them and does not explain why they engage in trade.

Finally, a third difficulty arises if we realize that, in the famous Chapter 7 of the *Principles* devoted to foreign trade, the developments mainly deal with money prices and money flows between countries: is it possible to ignore this fact and to isolate the above-quoted example – expressed in real terms and generally interpreted as a barter between the two countries – from the rest of the chapter?

These three main difficulties are of course linked together. We noted how the traditional approach solved the first problem: is the solution different here? With regard to the second and third questions, they remain apparently unanswered in both interpretations.

A monetary theory of foreign trade

As a matter of fact, and even if this is not obvious as long as we focus our attention on the four magic numbers, Ricardo bases his views on foreign trade on an analysis of the behaviour of individual agents in markets, in the context of a monetary regime in which gold is the standard of money, is freely traded domestically and abroad, and where bank-notes are convertible in gold on demand – that is, an ideal gold standard. The analysis is slightly different in a regime of inconvertibility. Moreover, his theoretical approach also entails a version of the quantity theory of money and a Humean-like specie-flow mechanism, both being essential for his theory of international trade – we disregard here the questions linked to the existence of bounties, taxes, and so on. New research is currently emerging on these essential aspects of Ricardo's thought, but it is possible to give some hints along the following lines.

Ricardo's developments are based on a simple idea: merchants engage in trade – be it domestic or foreign – only if it is profitable for them to do so. They buy and sell commodities considering their money prices and they trade if they have a reasonable expectation to sell them dearer than they bought them, with transportation costs included in the computation (*Works*, I: 138, 170). Thus, merchants do not barter but, at their individual level, calculate in monetary terms. When they buy abroad and import, they settle the transaction with a bill of exchange they buy in a specialized market, and they receive such a bill when they export commodities. In the exchange of wine and cloth between England and Portugal, this means that English merchants import wine if and only if the price of wine is higher in England than in Portugal – what seems intuitively the case owing to the costs of production – but also that English merchants export cloth if and only if cloth is dearer in Portugal than in England (ibid.: 137) – what seems counterintuitive in this specific case. Ricardo gives an example where the price of one unit of wine is respectively £50 in England and £45 in Portugal, and that of one unit of cloth is £45 in England and £50 in Portugal (ibid.: 138).

These prices are, of course, gold prices, expressed in terms of convertible – at its mint price – pounds sterling. Note also that the inequalities between the prices of wine and cloth in the two countries respect the inequality, stated above, between the cost ratios in the different countries. But the very notion of a comparative advantage somewhat vanishes at the micro level – it is of no use in decisions to trade – and, in this perspective, it is understandable that Ricardo did not refer repeatedly to it in his writings. As for the celebrated 'gains from trade', stated at the macro level, they can be considered as the unintended consequence of the actions of agents in the market, whose only purpose is their own individual monetary gain.

But why can such a trade of cloth between England and Portugal happen? This is because, Ricardo states, gold does not have necessarily the same value in different countries (ibid.: 142–3). The monetary units of nations are defined by specific weights of gold, and currencies are convertible into each other at the rate given by the mint prices. But if gold does not have the same market value – its exchange ratio with such or such commodity – everywhere, gold prices of commodities will generally be higher, all other things being equal, where this market value is lower, and lower where it is higher. Commodities produced in exactly the same conditions in terms of labour value will thus not have the same gold price, and it can happen that, like cloth in Ricardo's example, a commodity having the least labour value can have a higher price than the same commodity with a superior labour value. This – and not the alleged international relative immobility of capital and labour – is the explanation why, between countries, the exchange ratios between commodities might not be determined by the labour theory of value.

This state of things indicates the direction of the flows of trade and the respective specialization of countries in the usual cases. This also determines the prices at which the transactions are made. Contrary to J.S. Mill's approach, Ricardo's reasoning is straightforward: if competition prevails in markets, the price of an imported commodity is simply the price that prevails in the exporting country augmented by the costs of transportation, insurance and so on (ibid.: 340–41, 374–5).

Now why and when does gold not have the same market value in different countries? Let us start from a situation of equilibrium that Ricardo significantly refers to with both phrases 'equilibrium of money' (ibid.: 141–42, 145) and 'trade of barter' (ibid.: 137, 140). Suppose a strict international immobility of capital and labour: the balance of payment is thus reduced to the balance of trade. Equilibrium is defined as the situation when there is no (net) flow of gold between countries: it is a monetary equilibrium in Hume's sense – gold is divided between the different countries according to the natural needs of trade. It is also the situation when, in modern parlance, the balance of trade equilibrates.

This state of things is, of course, hypothetical: many destabilizing shocks can throw a country out of equilibrium. How and with which consequence? A destabilizing shock is by definition one that will disturb in the end, one way or another, the optimal division of gold between nations and provoke a change in the market value of gold in the country, thus generating modifications in the gold prices and international flows of commodities. In this process the comparative advantage of a country might change, temporarily or in a more lasting way.

A bad harvest, for example, will suddenly make the quantity of money 'redundant' because there are fewer commodities to circulate. Prices will rise in consequence, and gold flows out of the country because it becomes one of the cheapest commodities. Consequently the market value of gold will rise and money prices fall until the situation equilibrates: in this process, during the period of disequilibrium, the comparative advantage of a country might change, but for a time only, until the next harvest. Imagine, however, with Ricardo, some technical improvement in the production of one commodity, wine in England, for example (ibid.: 137). Also in this case equilibrium is disrupted: because of the fall of the price of wine, money will again become 'super-abundant' in the country, with the same initial consequences as before. But here the situation is a lasting one and the comparative advantage – and thus the flows of international trade – of the country might be durably modified, with the final attainment of another 'equilibrium of money' or 'trade of barter'.

GILBERT FACCARELLO

See also:

Competition; Foreign Trade; Monetary Theory; Ricardo's Four Magic Numbers.

References

Aldrich, J. (2004), 'The discovery of comparative advantage', *Journal of the History of Economic Thought*, **26**(3), 379–99.

Faccarello, G. (2015), 'Autopsy of a text: being an enquiry concerning Mr Ricardo's principles of international trade', *The European Journal of the History of Economic Thought* (forthcoming).

Maneschi, A. (1998), *Comparative Advantage in International Trade. A Historical Perspective*, Cheltenham, UK and Lyme, NH: Edward Elgar Publishing.

Maneschi, A. (2004), 'The true meaning of Ricardo's four magic numbers', *Journal of International Economics*, **62**(2), 433–43.

Mill, J. (1808), *Commerce Defended*, London: Baldwin.

Mill, J. ([1821], 1824, 1826), *Elements of Political Economy*, London: Baldwin, Cradock and Joy; 2nd edition, 1926, London: Baldwin, Cradock and Joy; 3rd edition, 1926, revised and corrected, 1844, London: Henry G. Bohn.

Mill, J. (1825), 'Colony', *Supplement to Encyclopaedia Britannica*, London: J. Innes.

Mill, J.S. ([1829–30] 1967), 'Of the laws of interchange between nations, and the distribution of the gains of commerce among the countries of the commercial world', in *Essays on Some Unsettled Questions of Political Economy*, 1844, London: John W. Parker, pp. 1–46; in *Collected Works of John Stuart Mill, Vol. IV: Essays on Economics and Society, 1824–1845*, Toronto: University of Toronto Press, pp. 232–61.

Ruffin, R. (2002), 'David Ricardo's discovery of comparative advantage', *History of Political Economy*, **34**(4), 727–48.

Ruffin, R. (2005), 'Debunking a myth: Torrens on comparative advantage', *History of Political Economy*, **37**(4), 711–22.

Samuelson, P.A. (1969), 'The way of an economist', in P. Samuelson (ed.), *International Economic Relations. Proceedings of the Third Congress of the International Economic Association*, London: Macmillan, pp. 1–11.

Smith, A. ([1776] 1976), *An Inquiry into the Nature and Causes of the Wealth of Nations*, in *The Glasgow Edition of the Works and Correspondence of Adam Smith*, (eds) R.H. Campbell, A.S. Skinner and W.B. Todd, Oxford: Clarendon Press.

Sraffa, P. (1930), 'An alleged correction of Ricardo', *The Quarterly Journal of Economics*, **44**(3), 539–45.

Torrens, R. (1808), *The Economists Refuted*, London: Oddy.

Torrens, R. (1815), *Essay on the External Corn Trade*, London: Hatchard.

Torrens, R. (1826), *Essay on the External Corn Trade*, 3rd edition, London: Longman, Rees, Orme, Brown, & Green.

Torrens, R. (1827), *Essay on the External Corn Trade*, 4th edition, London: Longman, Rees, Orme, Brown, & Green.

Viner, J. (1937), *Studies in the Theory of International Trade*, New York: Harper & Brothers.

Competition

The Ricardian notion of competition and markets is situated within the wider framework of an economic system of the production, distribution and exchange 'of such commodities only as can be increased in quantity by the exertion of human industry' (*Works*, I: 12). These are the only commodities 'on the production of which competition operates without restraint' (ibid.), that is, 'free competition' prevails. There are, however, two other cases in which competition is present but does not have the same economic meaning. The first concerns situations in which increases in the supply of goods are constrained by factors other than the exertion of human industry or the attempt to reduce the 'difficulty of production'. The second case arises from the conditions of compatibility between international trade on the one hand, and the operation of competition at national levels on the other. This entry discusses these three forms of competition: free competition without restraint, 'monopoly' or restrained competition and international competition.

Free competition without restraint: a starting point
For the case of free competition without restraint, it is necessary to draw a clear distinction between production, distribution and exchange activities. 'Production' not only refers to the application of human industry in the different sectors of the economic

system to ensure the reproduction of commodities, of wage earners and of capital stock and its owners, it also creates a global 'net produce' or 'revenue' (see *Works*, I: XXVI). The concept of national income or surplus implies that production must be analysed as a whole, taking account of the complete set of industries that generate the net product. According to Ricardo, the system of production is therefore clearly inter-industrial: in a system of free competition, in order to increase the level of human activity and to reduce the difficulty of production, capital owners in any given industry *can* invest their accumulated capital or increase the number of the workers they employ, but they can *also* transfer capital or labour from other (national or foreign) industries if necessary:

> By far the greatest part of those goods which are the object of desire are procured by labour; and they may be multiplied, not in one country alone, but in many, almost without any assignable limit if we are disposed to bestow the labour necessary to obtain them. (Ibid.: 12)

Income distribution also plays its role in the characterization of competition in Ricardian economics. Distribution does not depend on productivity but on the existence of social classes that, as industries, can only be defined in relation to the global economy and its national surplus. The 'proportions allotted' to rent, profit and wages are different for every specific 'stage of society' (ibid.: 5), and depend on factors such as the fertility of the soil, the level of capital accumulation, the state of technology and population size. Therefore, the Ricardian conception of income distribution also excludes a view of competition mainly based on intra-sectoral relations between firms. It specifically requires the consideration of the socioeconomic rules that govern the distribution of the national produce between profits and wages. The emphasis on such rules, which shape competition between owners of capital, is what sets Ricardo's theory of competition apart from later approaches that focus exclusively on the economic productivity of factors of production.

Finally, the analysis of exchange activities addresses issues arising from the relationship between income variables and constraints on production due to the size of the surplus and relative prices. These activities reflect the interaction of supply and demand and, therefore, the process of convergence of market towards natural prices that plays a central role in the Ricardian mechanism of competition.

This distinction between production, distribution and exchange activities is essential to fully grasp the Ricardian concept and mechanisms of free competition, and is sufficient to differentiate this clearly from another later approach to competition: in this later approach, competition is basically defined from the vantage point of a self-contained notion of a pure exchange economy in which market exchanges, production and income distribution are all conceptualized as extended forms of bilateral or multilateral barter. Ricardo explicitly rejects this view in his notes on Malthus's *Principles of Political Economy*:

> In all that Mr M. has yet said about exchangeable value, it appears to depend a great deal on the wants of mankind, and the relative estimation in which they hold commodities. This would be true if men from various countries were to meet in a fair, with a variety of productions, and each with a separate commodity, undisturbed by the competition of any other seller. Commodities, under such circumstances, would be bought and sold according to the relative wants of those attending the fair – but when the wants of society are well known, when there are hundreds of competitors who are willing to satisfy those wants, on the condition only that

they shall have the known and usual profits, there can be no such rule for regulating the value of commodities.

In such a fair as I have supposed, a man might be willing to give a pound of gold, for a pound of iron, knowing the use of the latter metal; but when competition freely operated, he could not give that value for iron, and why? Because iron would infallibly sink to its cost of production – cost of production being the pivot about which all market price moves. (*Works*, II: 24–25n)

Moreover, and as already mentioned, for Ricardo, production, distribution and exchange activities must be understood within a framework of general economic inter-dependencies, not within a given industry only or from a partial equilibrium point of view. This also applies to the concept of free competition.

The nature of free competition without restraint

A more detailed account of the Ricardian concept of free competition without restraint starts with the opening pages of Ricardo's *Principles*. As mentioned, free competition without restraint refers to those industries in which the only 'assignable limit' (*Works*, I: 12) to the increase of production is the 'difficulty of production' or 'the exertion of human industry'. In other words, this case concerns freely reproducible commodities, and it is the predominant form of competition. Even though the 'difficulty of pro-duction' clearly does represent an 'assignable limit', at any one moment in time, it is, however, never insuperable.

As long as human beings are prepared to expend ingenuity and effort, such difficulties can be addressed and overcome. In this scenario, the price of a commodity is propor-tional to the difficulties encountered, and thus equal to its natural level. Obviously, the natural rate of profit is directly linked to this natural level of prices, reflecting the opera-tion of free competition without restraint in the various industries. Barriers of entry, whether these arise from natural scarcity, the nature of specific goods or the interference of private or public power, cannot interfere with the 'only assignable limit' of the 'dif-ficulty of production', or discourage motivated owners of capital to invest in an industry with a higher rate of profit than the one they have current business in. Quite the contrary, owners of capital are always driven by the desire to achieve higher rates of profit, relative to those prevailing in their own industry:

No one accumulates but with a view to make his accumulation productive, and it is only when so employed that it operates on profits. Without a motive there could be no accumulation . . . The farmer and the manufacturer can no more live without profit, than the labourer without wages. Their motive for accumulation will diminish with every diminution of profit, and will cease altogether when their profits are so low as not afford them an adequate compensation for their trouble, and the risk which they must necessarily encounter in employing their capital productively. (Ibid.: 122)

Ricardo here does not refer to subjective drivers of capital accumulation that would reflect patterns or determinants of individual behaviours, such as means–end optimiza-tion. Rather, the motives of capital accumulation are governed by the social norms that characterize and, to an extent, define different social classes. Yet again, for Ricardo, the economic system is thus not a self-contained system of barter, but a socially embedded system that comprises distinct, yet interdependent, activities and mechanisms of produc-tion, income distribution and exchange. This view of profits and profit motives can also be found in Ricardo's *Essay on Profits* where he refers to the 'usual and ordinary rate of profits' (*Works*, IV: 10–12).

For a better understanding of the Ricardian notion of competitive mechanisms, it is also useful to consider cases in which market prices deviate from natural prices in some industries of the national economic system, or more specifically, 'accidental and temporary deviations of the actual or market price of commodities from this, their primary and natural price' (*Works*, I: 88), such as demand shocks due to 'the caprice of taste, or a change in the amount of population' (ibid.), 'a change of fashion' (ibid.: 90), 'sudden changes in the channels of trade' (see *Works*, I: XIX) or, more generally to 'any other cause which should suddenly and unexpectedly increase the demand or diminish the supply of' a given commodity (ibid.: 119). In such cases, market prices, and therefore actual sectoral rates of profit, will deviate from natural prices, and therefore the natural and uniform rate of profit. In consequence:

> [C]apital is either encouraged to enter into, or is warned to depart from the particular employment in which the variation has taken place. Whilst every man is free to employ his capital where he pleases, he will naturally seek for it that employment which is the more advantageous . . . This restless desire on the part of all employers of stock, to quit a less profitable for a more advantageous business, has a strong tendency to equalize the rate of profits of all. (Ibid.: 88)

As is well known, Ricardo, however, also noted – differently from Adam Smith – that 'it is perhaps very difficult to trace the steps by which' (ibid.: 89) this equalization is achieved. Real transfers of capital, implying an absolute change of sectoral capital employment are rather rare (ibid.). Help will come from 'bankers' and from the 'monied class', that is, 'a number of men . . . engaged in no trade, but [living] on the interest of their money, which is employed in discounting bills, or in loans to the more industrious part of the community' (ibid.). Faced, in their own current industry, with a market price below the natural price, owners of capital driven by the restless desire to increase their profits, will lay off a part of their workforce and reduce their demand for loans or bills destined to fund their capital investment in this industry. If, by contrast, the market price in their industry rises, they will employ more workers and increase their borrowing to banks and the monied class. Ricardo, however, also warns:

> [I]t is to be understood that I am speaking of profits generally. I have already remarked that the market price of a commodity may exceed its natural or necessary price, as it may be produced in less abundance than the new demand for it requires. This, however, is but a temporary effect. The high profits on capital employed in producing that commodity will naturally attract capital to that trade; and as soon as the requisite funds are supplied, and the quantity of the commodity is duly increased, its price will fall, and the profits of the trade will conform to the general level. (Ibid.: 119)

This remark is particularly useful to summarize core aspects of the Ricardian notion of competitive mechanisms: first and regarding the role played by credit, the uniformization of rates of profit relies on the use of 'funds', and not only on that of direct transfers of capital. Second, Ricardian competition is firmly placed within a system of general economic interdependencies. It is fundamentally inter-sectoral, not only intra-sectoral. It concerns activities of production (increase or decrease of sectoral quantities of commodity), distribution (rates of profit) as well as exchange (supply and demand, market prices). Third, there remained, of course, ample space for further elaboration, in regard, for example, to assumptions about the nature of returns to scale, the behaviour of owners of capital, their speed of reaction to changes in demand, and of the determinants or nature of the latter. Since Ricardo did not analyse these (and other) issues more explicitly, the efficacy and efficiency of the process of market prices gravitating towards natural prices was left unresolved.

Exceptional cases of competition without restraint
Competition without restraint also concerns labour:

> The market price of labour is the price which is really paid for it, from the natural operation of the proportion of the supply to demand; labour is dear when it is scarce, and cheap when it is plentiful. However much the market price of labour may deviate from its natural price, it has, like commodities, a tendency to conform to it. (*Works*, I: 94)

This said, the production of labour is not, strictly speaking, subject to the 'difficulty of production'. From this point of view, labour is not a commodity in the same sense as wheat or iron. Wages are not only a price, but also a distributive variable, as are profits. In his explanation of the level and evolution of wages, Ricardo thus feels obliged to include both economic considerations of the supply of and demand for labour (wages being a market and a natural price) as well as social and demographic considerations (wages also being a distributional variable embedded in, and reflective of, the wider workings of society and the role of social norms):

> It is when the market price of labour exceeds its natural price, that the condition of the labourer is flourishing and happy, that he has it in his power to command a greater proportion of the necessaries and enjoyments of life, and therefore to rear a healthy and numerous family. When, however, by the encouragement which high wages give to the increase of population, the number of labourer is increased, wages again fall to their natural price, and indeed from a re-action sometimes fall below it. (Ibid.)

Ricardo then also considers the reverse case in which 'the market price of labour is below its natural price' (ibid.). In this case, poverty and the deterioration of the condition of wage earners reduce the supply of labour and restore the level of the natural wage (ibid.). Thus, while Ricardo appears to argue that his conception of competition without restraint applies to labour just as much as to any other commodities, the natural price of labour does not primarily depend on its difficulty of production but on demographic as well as social influences:

> It is not to be understood that the natural price of labour, estimated even in food and necessaries, is absolutely fixed and constant. It varies at different times in the same country, and very materially differs in different countries. It essentially depends on the habits and customs of the people. (Ibid.: 96–7)

Labour, therefore, provides a first exception from Ricardo's conception of competition without restraint. The social embeddedness of wages limits the validity of this notion, and Ricardo's use of the term 'natural' is clearly different from its wider use in the context of the production of conventional commodities. Even so, this conceptual difference only goes so far. It certainly does not extend to any notion of social welfare, a position exemplified by Ricardo's strong opposition to the Poor Laws, in reference to his analysis of wage formation:

> These then are the laws by which wages are regulated, and by which happiness of far the greatest part of every community is governed. Like all other contracts, wages should be left to the fair and free competition of the market, and should never be controlled by the interference of the legislature. (Ibid.: 105)

Another exception from competition without restraint is the regulation of the rate of interest. For Ricardo, the rate of interest is 'ultimately and permanently governed by the rate of profit' (ibid.: 297). This does not, however, mean the rate of interest is subject to competition without restraint, through the process of the uniformization of the rate of profit, since, for Ricardo, the rate of interest 'is however subject to temporary variations from other causes' (ibid.). These causes are twofold. First, such temporary variations derive from changes in the quantity and value of money. Second, they can result from 'the alteration in the proportion of supply to demand, although there should not be either greater facility or difficulty of production' (ibid.). That is, given the motives of owners of capital to engage in capital transfers, their demand for loans from bankers and the monied class will vary. While there is a tendency of the rate of interest to converge on the natural rate of profit through a competitive process of supply and demand, this process does not depend on any direct influence of the concept of difficulty of production.

Monopoly or restrained competition
A much bigger exception to competition without restraint are goods whose value is primarily determined by factors other than the 'difficulty of production' alone. Ricardo describes this case at the start of the *Principles*:

> There are some commodities, the value of which is determined by their scarcity alone. No labour can increase the quantity of such goods, and therefore their value cannot be lowered by an increased supply. Some rare statues and pictures, scarce books and coins, wines of peculiar qualities, which can be made only from grapes grown on a particular soil, of which there is a limited quantity, are all of this description. Their value is wholly independent of the quantity of labour originally necessary to produce them, and varies with the varying wealth and inclinations of those who are desirous to possess them. (Ibid.: 12)

The price of such commodities only depends on the relative wealth of the potential buyers and, given this, on demand and supply relations. The level of 'the exertion of human industry' is not essential and the 'difficulty of production' as a constraint on production is vastly overshadowed by the fixity of supply. While competition continues to play a role, there are no natural prices or natural rates of profit. Fixity of supply is now a real barrier to entry, and competition takes the form of intra-sectoral competition. The world of competition without restraint is far apart and removed from this scenario, which is much closer to the example of the fair Ricardo picked up on and criticized in Malthus's *Principles of Political Economy*.

Ricardo also likens the case of scarce commodities to that of a 'monopoly'. As with many other classical authors (Arena, 1992) monopoly here is understood as restrained competition. Thus, Ricardo refers to 'peculiar wines which are produced in very limited quantity' or 'those works of art, which, from their excellence or rarity, have acquired a fanciful value' (*Works*, I: 250), and defines commodities subject to monopoly conditions as those whose supply cannot possibly be increased to the extent that 'therefore the competition is wholly on one side – amongst the buyers' (ibid.: 249). In such cases, the set monopoly price will not be determined by the cost of production (ibid.: 250). For Ricardo, natural resources and raw materials are not included in this category, since there is at least some role for the 'difficulty of production' to constitute the more relevant 'assigned limit' to production. Different from truly scarce commodities, 'there is competition among the sellers, as well as amongst the buyers' (ibid.) in raw materials industries. Thus, Ricardo does not define monopoly in terms of the number or uniqueness of suppliers, but rather in terms of the nature of supply conditions, and their potential responsiveness to the application of human ingenuity and effort. Monopoly therefore is a case of restrained competition. As such, it is subject only to the law of demand and supply since the cost of production here exerts no relevant influence on price formation and the way in which competition functions.

International competition

Ricardo is very clear that the 'same rule which regulates the relative value of commodities in one country, does not regulate the relative value of the commodities exchanged between two or more countries' (ibid.: 133). In a national context, 'it is perhaps very difficult to trace the steps by which this change [of the 'restless desire on the part of all employers of stock, to quit a less profitable for a more advantageous business'] is effected' (ibid.: 88–9). As discussed, there may be relevant temporary as well as more permanent exceptions to competition without restraint. Ultimately, therefore, the tendency to a uniform rate of profit(s) may be a theoretical norm that describes core features of capitalism, rather than a commonplace empirical reality. Be this as it may, international economic (trade) relations are not governed by the same concept of competition without restraint that is at least very relevant in a domestic context:

> If the profits of capital employed in Yorkshire should exceed those of capital employed in London, capital would speedily move from London to Yorkshire, and an equality of profits would be effected; but if in consequence of the diminished rate of production in the lands of England, from the increase of capital and production, wages should rise, and profits fall, it would not follow that capital and population would necessarily move from England to Holland, or Spain, or Russia, where profits might be higher. (Ibid.: 134)

The reason is that Ricardo considers capital to be largely immobile across borders. Without barriers to the free flow of capital across borders, the labour theory of value would apply globally as well nationally, with only transportation costs (or 'the additional quantity of labour required to convey them [the commodities] to the various markets where they were to be sold'; ibid.: 136) to be added to nationally determined natural prices. These barriers to the free cross-border flow of capital are not a matter of government regulation, but of habit and risk-averseness in the presence of high uncertainty:

> Experience, however, shews, that the fancied or real insecurity of capital, when not under the immediate control of its owner, together with the natural disinclination which every man has to quit the country of his birth and connexions, and intrust himself with all his habits fixed, to a strange government and new laws, check the emigration of capital. These feelings, which I

should be sorry to see weakened, induce most men of property to be satisfied with a low rate of profits in their own country, rather than seek a more advantageous employment for their wealth in foreign nations. (Ibid.: 137)

In modern terms, for Ricardo, outward foreign direct investment is unlikely to replace exports, due to very low, if any (fancied or real) internalization and locational advantages abroad. In consequence, while absolute advantage prevails at home, comparative advantage governs international trade relations under conditions of free competition, or should do so, if global gains from international trade are to be maximized.

For Ricardo's well-known argument in favour of the principle of comparative advantage (see Parrinello on 'Foreign Trade' in this volume for detail) to hold, in a two country – two goods (2 × 2) – model, he requires an additional assumption, namely that Hume's price-specie flow mechanism works: for it to be possible for lower-productivity English cloth, requiring, say, 100 labour hours to produce a given amount of cloth, to be exchanged in international markets for higher-productivity Portuguese cloth, requiring, say, 80 labour hours to produce the same amount (and quality) of cloth – an exchange that could not take place within national boundaries – it is necessary for there to be a universal specie currency system. If, say, gold coins, are the internationally accepted means of payment, the production of these takes place in a third country, is subject to the labour theory of value in the gold-producing industry, and free trade policies govern the economic relations between Portugal and England, England will initially run up a trade deficit with Portugal in the cloth trade. This will put downward pressure on money supply in England, and upward pressure in Portugal, as gold coins flow from England to Portugal. Accepting the quantity theory of money (as Ricardo did in this context) – the level of (market) prices in terms of gold is determined by the quantity of gold relative to commodities in any given country – market prices and money wages will fall in England and rise in Portugal, to the extent that cross-border trade in cloth becomes comparatively advantageous for England. In other words, it is the assumption of money neutrality that translates comparative advantage into cross-border (market price) competitiveness.

Ricardo is also well aware that international competition (or competitiveness) is a concept heavily subject to state intervention at national level, and that there is a close relationship between the efficacy of competition without restraints at national level and international economic relations. For one, Ricardo's well-known advocacy of the repeal of the Corn Laws in Britain highlights his understanding of the dynamic, rather than purely static, advantages of international trade and competition: in a world in which industrial profits are squeezed between subsistence wages and rising rents on land (due to a combination of political, demographic and technological factors), the abolition of trade barriers for cheap food (corn) imports can help to improve the future prospects of national industrial or capitalist development and accumulation, governed by the principle of absolute advantage and the labour theory of value. Free trade is not a policy to advocate global optimal resource allocation, but a policy that facilitates capital accumulation in a national context (in this case Britain in the first half of the nineteenth century), given the workings of competition without restraint within borders, and within the capitalist sector of British society at the time.

Ricardo also clearly rejects Adam Smith's theory of the vent-for-surplus (*Works*, I: 293–300), the idea, that is, that the division of labour (or climbing up the technological ladder) is driven by the expansion of export markets. In Ricardo's view, Adam Smith's notion of vent-for-surplus, or limitless demand, ignores the fact that profit expectations are continuously tempered by government interventions, with 'a fair and free market rate of interest' (ibid.: 296–7) never coming to bear upon the economy, even though this is ultimately governed by the rate of profit, in a national context. This may be down to 'mistaken notions of policy' (ibid.: 296), even if the consequent regulations are often evaded (ibid.: 297), but the bottom line is, for Ricardo, that government interferences will invalidate export-driven growth as a dynamic principle of the explanation of international trade relative to that of comparative advantage. What prevails, in Ricardo, is the national policy perspective and context, not the logical expansion of comparative advantage to the global level.

Clearly, Ricardo's conceptualization of international economic relations and competition is, by now, outdated. Not only does this remain focused on merchandise trade (as opposed to foreign direct investment) but neither is there any place for the role of international credit money. International competition is a matter of money price competition in the presence of the price-specie flow mechanism. While Ricardo highlights potential dynamic, as well as static advantages, from free trade policy, these remain limited to low-cost imports in specific historical circumstances. Further dynamic increasing returns to scale from export promotion are not acknowledged, and even denied, but Ricardo certainly makes it clear that international economic relations, in his time, are relations of exchange, not production implemented at a global level. Today, this makes Ricardo's ideas on international competition and its ruling principles effectively redundant, since we have reached a stage in which global or internationally organized production under private control is becoming a reality, and the difference Ricardo made between national and international systems of capitalist production no longer applies, or only to a very much lessened extent.

RICHARD ARENA AND STEPHANIE BLANKENBURG

See also:

Comparative Advantage; Demand and Supply; Exchange Value and Utility; Natural and Market Prices; Ricardo's Four Magic Numbers.

Reference

Arena, R. (1992), 'Libre-concurrence et concurrence entravée: trois exemples historiques', *Cahiers d'Economie Politique*, **20**(20–21), 77–99.

Corn Laws

> It is to be hoped that we shall, even in the present Session of Parliament, get rid of many
> of these injurious laws; a better spirit of legislation appears likely to prevail in the present
> day; and that absurd jealousy which influenced our forefathers, will give way to the pleasing
> conviction, that we can never, by freedom of commerce, promote the welfare of other
> countries without also promoting our own.
> (Ricardo, 'On Protection to Agriculture', in *Works*, IV: 252)

Many authors ascribe to the Corn Laws that prevailed in Britain after 1815 a central importance in David Ricardo's formulation of the classical system of economic thought that he expounded in the *Principles of Political Economy, and Taxation* and used to project the likely pattern of British economic development. The purpose of this entry is to examine Ricardo's analysis of the likely effects of the Corn Laws contained in the pamphlet *On Protection to Agriculture* (1822) where he discussed them in great detail. The Corn Law adopted by Parliament in 1815 prohibited the importation of corn (wheat) when its domestic price was below 80s per quarter, and allowed it when the price was 80s or above. Similar laws governed the import of oats and barley. Owing to abundant crops, the 1815 Corn Law did not have the desired effect (from the viewpoint of landlords and farmers) of maintaining a high price of corn, which fell from 74s per quarter in 1814 to 66s in 1815, 56s in 1821 and 45s in 1822. This precipitated a crisis in the agricultural sector that led in 1822 to a revision of the Corn Law with the reintroduction of a sliding scale (see Boyer, 2006).

While there are numerous references to 'corn' throughout Ricardo's *Principles*, his own index surprisingly contains no entry on the Corn Laws. Without citing these laws specifically, Ricardo analyses at length the untoward effects of taxes and duties on corn on the British economy, such as the failure to use resources according to comparative advantage, the stunting of economic growth and the adverse pattern of income distribution among landlords, capitalists and workers. In Chapter 19 of the *Principles* Ricardo refers indirectly to the Corn Laws in an extensive quotation from John R. McCulloch's article 'Corn Laws and Trade' in the supplement of Volume III of the *Encyclopaedia Britannica*. In a footnote introduced in the second edition of the *Principles* at McCulloch's own behest, Ricardo expresses his appreciation for the 'excellent suggestions and observations' found in this article (*Works*, I: 267).

Ricardo's own analysis of the Corn Laws and their impact is found mainly in his pamphlet *On Protection to Agriculture*, and in his correspondence and Parliamentary speeches. Regarding the genesis of this pamphlet, G. de Vivo (1987: 185) writes, 'The years 1821 and 1822 were a period of severe distress in agriculture, and in both years a Committee on Agriculture was appointed by the Commons. Ricardo served on both of them, and a by-product of this was a pamphlet *On Protection to Agriculture* (April 1822).' Regarding proposals designed to alleviate the depression in agriculture, 'By all odds the best pamphlet published was Ricardo's *On Protection to Agriculture*. It was a systematic treatise on the fragmentary ideas expressed in his speeches in the Commons. Its significance lies in the influence that it had on future anti-Corn Law agitation' (Barnes, 1930: 175). Whereas some observers had ascribed the problems affecting agriculture in Britain to causes such as the insufficient protection that this sector enjoyed after the end of the Napoleonic Wars, the value of the British pound as a consequence of Prime Minister Robert Peel's bill 'for restoring the ancient standard' (Ricardo's expression for resuming cash payments in gold), and an unduly harsh tax burden, Ricardo offers a simple explanation for 'the distressed state of our agriculture': the low price of corn was due to an excess of supply over demand, for which the Corn Laws were primarily responsible, as well as large corn imports from Ireland. Moreover, increased supplies of corn cause a larger relative decline in its price due to inelastic demand, so that their overall value declines (*Works*, IV: 219–21).

As Ricardo states in the Introduction to his pamphlet:

It is to the present corn-law that much of the distress is to be attributed, and I hope to make it appear, that the occupation of a farmer will be exposed to continual hazard, and will be placed under peculiar disadvantages, as compared with all other occupations, while any system of restriction on the importation of foreign corn is continued, which shall have the effect of keeping the price of corn in this country habitually and considerably above the prices of other countries. (Ibid.: 209)

Ricardo cites three adverse consequences that follow when the price of corn in Britain exceeds that in other countries:

Besides the impolicy of devoting a greater portion of our labour to the production of food than would otherwise be necessary, thereby diminishing the sum of our enjoyments and the power of saving, by lowering profits, we offer an irresistible temptation to capitalists to quit this country, that they may take their capitals to places where wages are low and profits high. (Ibid.: 237)

The three harmful effects of the Corn Laws are (1) forgoing the gains from trading a commodity produced with comparative advantage in favour of growing the import commodity, food, inefficiently on home soil, (2) the consequent reductions of profits, the saving rate and the rate of capital accumulation and (3) the movement of investment funds from Britain to other countries. These will be discussed in turn, and followed by an additional injury they cause and a spurious allegation in their favour that Ricardo identifies and rejects in his pamphlet.

Loss of comparative advantage and of the related gains from trade
In order to highlight the advantages of free trade, economists can proceed either directly as Ricardo did in Chapter 7 and other chapters of his *Principles*, or indirectly by considering the other side of the coin and analysing the adverse consequences of protection, as Ricardo did in his 1822 pamphlet. Thus, in the *Principles* Ricardo stressed two gains from trade:

It is quite as important to the happiness of mankind, that our enjoyments should be increased by the better distribution of labour, by each country producing those commodities for which by its situation, its climate, and its other natural or artificial advantages, it is adapted, and by their exchanging them for the commodities of other countries, as that they should be augmented by a rise in the rate of profits. (*Works*, I: 132)

By a 'better distribution of labour' Ricardo intends a reallocation of the labour force in line with the country's comparative advantage. In his 1822 pamphlet, on the other hand, he points to the harmful consequences of protection in agriculture, where a high price of corn induces farmers to grow it on land of inferior quality or subject to diminishing returns to labour so that corn is no longer competitive with that grown abroad. Protectionism prevents Britain from exploiting its comparative advantage in manufacturing and hence leads to an inferior allocation of resources:

It appears then that, in the progress of society, when no importation takes place, we are obliged constantly to have recourse to worse soils to feed an augmenting population, and with every step of our progress the price of corn must rise, and with such rise, the rent of the better land which had been previously cultivated, will necessarily be increased. A higher price becomes necessary to compensate for the smaller quantity which is obtained; but this higher price must never be considered as a good – it would not have existed if the same return had been obtained with less labour – it would not have existed if, by the application of labour to manufactures, *we had indirectly obtained the corn by the exportation of those manufactures in exchange for corn.* A high price, if the effect of a high cost, is an evil, and not a good; the price is high, because a great deal of labour is bestowed in obtaining the corn. If only a little labour was bestowed upon it, more of the labour of the country, which constitutes its only real source of wealth, would have been at its disposal to procure other enjoyments which are desirable. (*Works*, IV: 212–13; emphasis added)

In this passage Ricardo makes a point that anticipates that found in present-day texts of international trade: that trade is an *indirect* method of production, whereby certain commodities can be obtained more cheaply by importing them in exchange for exports than producing them directly. This outcome is consistent with what Jacob Viner refers to as the 'eighteenth-century rule' for gains from trade, which stipulates that 'it pays to import commodities from abroad whenever they can be obtained in exchange for exports at a smaller real cost than their production at home would entail' (Viner, 1937: 440). Ricardo had resorted to this 'rule' in his well-known paragraphs of Chapter 7 of the *Principles* where he discusses the gains from trade when England and Portugal trade cloth for wine, given by the smaller amount of labour that each country would use in its export sector to produce the commodities exchanged for imports as compared to the amount required to produce the imported commodities directly. He uses the rule again in Section VII of his 1822 pamphlet when he argues that England can obtain more corn when its labour produces manufactures that can be traded for corn. Using the personal pronoun 'I', Ricardo even provides a numerical estimate of the resulting gains from trade, equivalent to the losses from protection:

I can produce a quantity of cloth which affords me a remunerating price at sixty pounds, which I can sell to a foreign country, if I will lay out the proceeds in the purchase of thirty quarters of wheat at two pounds per quarter, but I am refused permission to do so, and am obliged, by the operation of a law, to employ the capital which yielded me sixty pounds in cloth, in raising fifteen quarters of wheat at four pounds per quarter. (*Works*, IV: 247)

He thus quantifies the gains from trade as the additional consumption of 15 quarters of wheat made possible through the export of cloth instead of using the same amount of labour to produce corn under autarky. This is an alternative version of Viner's eighteenth-century rule, which measures the gains from trade by the saving of labour when a given consumption of import commodities is obtained indirectly via exports rather than through direct production.

Without citing Adam Smith, Ricardo elaborates on the gains from trade along lines similar to those employed by Smith in Chapter 2, Book 4 of the *Wealth of Nations*, resorting to *reductio ad absurdum* to show the fallacy in his opponents' reasoning. According to Ricardo, consistency demands that those who advocate growing corn at home should also insist that 'we should cultivate beet-root and make our own sugar' and 'erect hot-houses, and raise our own grapes for the purpose of making wine, and protect the maker of wine by the same course of policy. Either the doctrine is untenable in the case of corn, or it is to be justified in all other cases' (ibid.: 248).

Ricardo dismisses the argument that, because capital was applied to the land in the past, it would be wasted if Britain were now 'rather to import cheap corn from abroad than grow it at a dear price at home'. After asking two rhetorical questions he offers a countervailing argument similar to one he had already used in the *Principles* in response to those who bemoan sunk costs:

> Is it not then in the highest degree absurd, first to pass a law under the operation of which the necessity is created of cultivating poor lands, and then having so cultivated them at a great expense, make that additional expense the ground for refusing ever to purchase corn from those who can afford to produce it at a cheaper price? That some capital would be lost cannot be disputed, but is the possession or preservation of capital the end, or the means? The means, undoubtedly. What we want is an abundance of commodities, and if it could be proved that by the sacrifice of a part of our capital we should augment the annual produce of those objects which contribute to our enjoyment and happiness, we ought not, I should think, to repine at the loss of a part of our capital. (Ibid.: 247–9)

A lower rate of profits and hence lower savings and capital accumulation

The higher cost incurred when a given amount of labour and capital produces a smaller output of corn must be compensated for by an increase in its price that causes wages to rise and profits to fall:

> Corn being one of the chief articles on which the wages of labour are expended, its value, to a great degree, regulates wages. There is no other way of keeping profits up but by keeping wages down. In this view of the law of profits, it will at once be seen how important it is that so essential a necessary as corn, which so powerfully affects wages, should be at a low price; and how injurious it must be to the community generally, that, by prohibitions against importation, we should be driven to the cultivation of our poorer lands to feed our augmenting population. (*Works*, IV: 236–7)

In one of the few such references in his writings, Ricardo relates low profits to the looming possibility of a 'stationary state' in a country subject to the Corn Laws, in contrast to the 'prosperity and happiness' that characterizes a 'rapidly progressive state' where such laws do not prevail. He also decries the redistribution of income in favour of the landlord class entailed by these laws:

> A low rate of interest is a symptom of a great accumulation of capital; but it is also a symptom of a low rate of profits, and of an advancement to a stationary state; at which the wealth and resources of a country will not admit of increase. As all savings are made from profits, as a country is most happy when it is in a rapidly progressive state, profits and interest cannot be too high. It would be a poor consolation indeed to a country for low profits and low interest, that landlords were enabled to raise money on mortgage with diminished sacrifices. Nothing contributes so much to the prosperity and happiness of a country as high profits. (Ibid.: 234–5)

Capital flight

In the *Principles* Ricardo contrasts the mobility of capital among different parts of England to its relative immobility between countries, and asserts:

> [I]f in consequence of the diminished rate of production in the lands of England, from the increase of capital and population, wages should rise, and profits fall, it would not follow that capital and population would necessarily move from England to Holland, or Spain, or Russia, where profits might be higher. (*Works*, I: 134)

However, in his pamphlet *Essay on Profits* Ricardo had already warned of the possibility of capital moving out of Britain: 'It cannot be doubted, that low profits, which are the inevitable effects of a really high price of corn, tend to draw capital abroad: this consideration ought therefore to be a powerful reason to prevent us from restricting importation' (*Works*, IV: 16). In the *Principles* he also expresses concern over the possibility of capital leaving the country due to 'the amount of taxes, and the increased price of labour' to which it is subject, as a result of which:

> [I]t becomes the interest of every contributor to withdraw his shoulder from the burthen, and to shift this payment from himself to another; and the temptation to remove himself and his capital to another country, where he will be exempted from such burthens, becomes at last irresistible, and overcomes the natural reluctance which every man feels to quit the place of his birth, and the scene of his early associations. (*Works*, I: 247–8)

In Chapter 31 'On Machinery' introduced into the third edition of the *Principles* in 1821, one year before the publication of *On Protection to Agriculture*, Ricardo voices similar concerns over capital being 'carried abroad' because of unwise legislation. After noting that the adoption of machinery may deteriorate the condition of workers if the addition to fixed capital comes at the expense of circulating capital, Ricardo was unequivocal in insisting that public policy should foster improvements in machinery. If the government were to prevent these improvements in order to alleviate their impact on labour, England's economic position would suffer since other countries would adopt them instead and end up exporting the commodities in question:

> The employment of machinery could never be safely discouraged in a State, for if a capital is not allowed to get the greatest net revenue that the use of machinery will afford here, it will be carried abroad, and this must be a much more serious discouragement to the demand for labour, than the most extensive employment of machinery. By investing part of a capital in improved machinery, there will be a diminution in the progressive demand for labour; by exporting it to another country, the demand will be wholly annihilated. (Ibid.: 396–7)

In the passage quoted above from his pamphlet, Ricardo again refers to the 'irresistible temptation to capitalists to quit this country, that they may take their capitals to places where wages are low and profits high', and strengthens his critique of the Corn Laws by adding the possibility of capital flight to the previous two effects of the Corn Laws. Not only do they lower the saving rate, but also the rate of capital accumulation is further lowered if investment moves overseas to take advantage of higher interest rates. As Winch (1965: 76) points out: 'The possibility of loss of capital to other countries was used by Ricardo and his followers as a specter to frighten opponents of their policy proposals: both the Corn Laws, and the burden of taxation caused by the National Debt were depicted as reasons for capital export.'

Enhanced fluctuations in the price of corn and their impact on corn imports

A fourth adverse consequence of maintaining the price of corn in England at a higher level than in other countries is that it is liable to fluctuate more, adding uncertainty to the operations of farmers, landlords and traders. Ricardo stresses that landlords and farmers are harmed by these fluctuations, and that landlords would prefer a lower but less unstable price of corn even if this entails a decline in rental income.

This is an issue that Ricardo did not consider in the *Principles* but examines at some length in Section VII of his pamphlet. He notes that a fixed duty on the import of corn of 40s, as recommended by Webb Hall, would mean, in case of an abundant crop, that its price would have to fall by the same amount before corn could be exported. But the same problem results from Britain's Corn Laws, which prevent the importation of wheat until the price rises to 80s. The Corn Laws have another detrimental effect from which the fixed duty is exempt. Since, as a result of a high price of corn, British ports would be kept open to duty-free imports for three months, traders would have the incentive to import an enormous quantity of corn to the ruin of the home growers. This is a dynamic consequence of protectionism that is not captured by static reasoning of the type economists often use to illustrate its detrimental effects.

The spurious danger of dependence upon foreign grain
In the Conclusion of his 1822 pamphlet, Ricardo disposes of yet another objection raised by opponents to the repeal of the Corn Laws:

> Before I conclude, it will be proper to notice an objection which is frequently made against freedom of trade in corn, viz., the dependence in which it would place us for an essential article of subsistence on foreign countries. This objection is founded on the supposition that we should be importers of a considerable portion of the quantity which we annually consume. (*Works*, IV: 264–5)

Ricardo counters this objection with the dynamic argument that the foreign price of corn would not remain unchanged in the face of large British imports, but would in fact have to rise in accordance with the law of diminishing returns to labour in the exporting countries. This price increase would be reflected in the British price and lead to greater output in Britain and hence to smaller imports. More importantly, even if this objection did not apply, Ricardo poses the question:

> [W]hat danger should we incur from our dependence, as it is called, on foreign countries for a considerable portion of our food? If our demand was constant and uniform, which, under such a system, it would undoubtedly be, a considerable quantity of corn must be grown abroad expressly for our market. It would be more the interest, if possible, of the countries so growing corn for our use, to oppose no obstacles to its reaching us, than it would be ours to receive it. (Ibid.: 264–6)

It is difficult to come up with a more telling illustration of the international interdependence fostered by international trade, and the mutual advantage of participating countries in ensuring stable trade relations in the face of political arguments that may be voiced against them.

Ricardo's proposal for a gradual reduction of agricultural protection
In the same Conclusion, Ricardo puts on his Member of Parliament hat and suggests a policy designed to appeal to other MPs of gradual reduction of agricultural protection leading to 'a substantially free trade in corn'. He proposes 'to give the monopoly of the home-market to the British grower till corn reaches seventy shillings per quarter'. At that point he suggests levying a duty of 20s on the import of corn in order to prevent unlimited imports of corn when British ports are open. The 20s duty would be reduced by 1s

every year until it reaches 10s, and a drawback of 7s per quarter allowed on exports of wheat when supplies are plentiful. Ricardo grants that even the lowest 10s duty would still be 'too high as a countervailing duty for the peculiar taxes which are imposed on the corn grower . . . but I would rather err on the side of a liberal allowance than of a scanty one' (*Works*, IV: 263–6).

Terry Peach (1993: 101) calls Ricardo's 'advocacy of this package . . . very much an exercise in *realpolitik*'. In a letter to McCulloch of 8 February 1822, Ricardo wrote 'I have no hope of good measures being adopted, the landlords are too powerful in the House of Commons to give us any hope that they will relinquish the tax which they have in fact contrived to impose on the rest of the community' (Peach, 1993: 100). Ricardo's recommendations for a reform of the Corn Laws contained in his 1822 pamphlet and his Parliamentary speeches were in the end rejected by the Commons with only 25 votes in favour.

ANDREA MANESCHI

See also:

Comparative Advantage; *Essay on Profits*; Foreign Trade; Malthus–Ricardo Debate; Ricardo's Four Magic Numbers.

References

Barnes, D.G. (1930), *A History of the English Corn Laws from 1660–1846*, New York: F.S. Crofts & Co.
Boyer, G.R. (2006), 'Corn Laws', in J.J. McCusker (ed.), *History of World Trade since 1450, Vol. 1*, Farmington Hills, MI: Thomson Gale, pp. 160–63.
de Vivo, G. (1987), 'Ricardo, David (1772–1823)', in J. Eatwell, M. Milgate and P. Newman (eds), *The New Palgrave Dictionary of Economics, Vol. 4*, London: Macmillan, pp. 183–98.
Peach, T. (1993), *Interpreting Ricardo*, Cambridge, UK: Cambridge University Press.
Viner, J. (1937), *Studies in the Theory of International Trade*, New York: Harper.
Winch, D. (1965), *Classical Political Economy and Colonies*, Cambridge, MA: Harvard University Press.

Corn Model

The logic of the argument in Sraffa's reconstruction

It has been observed by Sraffa (*Works*, I: xxxi) that the principle that appears to guide Ricardo in the surviving letters of 1814 and the early months of 1815 as well as in the *Essay on Profits* (published in the February of that year) is that 'it is the profits of the farmer that regulate the profits of all other trades' (Ricardo to Trower, 8 March 1814, *Works*, VI: 104). The most relevant conclusion Ricardo derives from this principle concerns the effect exercised on the general rate of profits by the extension of cultivation to less fertile or more distant land attendant upon capital accumulation or the imposition of restrictions on the importation of corn. According to the views held by Ricardo during the period under consideration, if the operation of decreasing returns in agriculture is not counteracted by improvements in husbandry, this extension of cultivation causes a fall in the rate of profit in agriculture and *hence* a fall in the general rate of profit.

The principle was a new one for Ricardo, who had previously adhered to the Smithian 'competition-of-capitals' explanation of the rate of profit (*Works*, III: 92) and first began to move in this direction during the summer of 1813 (see Ricardo's letters to Malthus of 10 and 17 August 1813, *Works*, VI: 93–5; see also Sraffa, *Works*, IV: 3 and VI: xxi).

Malthus, who continued to adhere to the Smithian view, constantly opposed Ricardo's conclusions by claiming, in Ricardo's words, that 'the profits of the farmer no more regulate the profits of other trades, than the profits of other trades regulate the profits of the farmer' (Ricardo to Trower, 8 March 1814, *Works*, VI: 104). Ricardo himself later abandoned the principle of the determining role of agricultural profits, which does not reappear in the *Principles* (1817–21) and thus constitutes the distinctive feature of his early theory of profits.

Neither in the *Essay* nor in other extant papers or correspondence does Ricardo specify the grounds on which his principle rests. According to Sraffa, the 'rational foundation' Ricardo implicitly relied on was as follows:

[In] agriculture the same commodity, namely corn, forms both the capital (conceived as composed of the subsistence necessary for workers) and the product; so that the determination of profit by the difference between total product and capital advanced, and also the determination of the ratio of this profit to the capital, is done directly between quantities of corn without any question of valuation. It is obvious that only one trade can be in the special position of not employing the products of other trades while all the others must employ *its* product as capital. It follows that if there is to be a uniform rate of profit in all trades it is the exchangeable values of the products of *other* trades relatively to their own capitals (*i.e.* relatively to corn) that must be adjusted so as to yield the same rate of profit as has been established in the growing of corn; since in the latter no value changes can alter the ratio of product to capital, both consisting of the same commodity. (*Works*, I: xxxi; emphasis in the original)

It is to designate this reconstruction of Ricardo's early theory of profits that, since the middle of the 1960s, the expression 'corn model' has been increasingly used. The expression replaces the one originally employed by Sraffa (*Works*, I: xlix; cf. xxxiii): 'corn-ratio theory of profits'.

As stated above, no explicit argument along 'corn-ratio' lines is to be found in Ricardo's extant letters or papers. In his Introduction to the *Principles*, Sraffa (ibid.: xxxi) surmises that Ricardo may have put forward such argument 'either in his lost "papers on the profits of Capital" of March 1814' (the main conclusions of which he tried to summarize in the letter to Trower quoted above) 'or in conversation', and reports the following objection by Malthus as a revealing echo of Ricardo's own formulation of the issue:

In no case of production, is the produce exactly of the same nature as the capital advanced. Consequently we can never properly refer to a material rate of produce . . . It is not the particular profits or rate of produce upon the land which determines the general profits of stock and the interest of money. (Malthus to Ricardo, 5 August 1814, *Works*, VI: 117–18)

Besides supporting the conjecture that Ricardo may have explicitly formulated a 'corn-ratio' argument, Malthus's objection is evidence of his perception that such an argument represented the inner structure of Ricardo's reasoning. 'The nearest that Ricardo comes to an explicit statement' of the rational foundation of his reasoning is, according to Sraffa (*Works*, I: xxxii), in the following 'striking passage': 'The rate of profits and of interest must depend on the proportion of production to the consumption necessary to such production' (Ricardo to Malthus, 26 June 1814, *Works*, VI: 108). What is 'striking' here is the fact that the two magnitudes are compared with no suggestion that a process of evaluation would be needed for this purpose. The 'corn-ratio' reasoning implicit in Ricardo's early theory of profits is also reflected, Sraffa adds, in the numerical examples of the *Essay on Profits*, where both capital and product are expressed in corn, so that the profit rate is calculated without reference to prices, and it is precisely this procedure that is the target of Malthus's objections to the *Essay*. (Further indirect evidence in favour of Sraffa's reconstruction put forward by Langer, 1982 and de Vivo, 1985 concerns Torrens's explicit use of 'corn-ratio' reasoning at a time when he was under the influence of Ricardo's *Essay*.)

Two basic assumptions

As clarified by Sraffa's passage reported above, Ricardo's 'agricultural' theory of profits appears to entail two basic assumptions: (1) the wage rate consists of a given quantity of corn; (2) in all industries, wages are the only capital advanced. The first assumption finds an explanation in the idea, a staple of classical political economy, that the real wage is generally kept at the subsistence level by the prevailing social and economic conditions. Although subsistence was conceived as including customary elements, Ricardo regarded the wage basket – at least in the *Essay on Profits* and in writings of the period under consideration – as consisting largely of food and therefore of the products of agriculture, of which 'corn' is taken as representative. As regards Ricardo's implicit neglect of any sort of capital other than wages in the determination of the rate of profit, it seems reasonable to suppose that he erroneously believed capital to be ultimately reducible to advanced wages alone on the basis of Smith's (in itself correct) reduction of the price of any commodity to the sum of wages, profits and rent paid in the various stages of the production process (see Garegnani, 1984: 300n). He was indeed to adopt this view of capital in the theory of profits of the later *Principles* at the level of the economy as a whole. In Ricardo's 'corn' theory of profits, such a 'vertically integrated' concept of capital obviously implies the notion of an 'enlarged' agricultural sector including the production of industrial goods used as direct or indirect inputs of agriculture. On the other hand, Ricardo's primary interest during the period under consideration in changes in the rate of profit deriving particularly from the extension of cultivation is what can explain his exclusive consideration of changes in the productivity of labour *directly* employed in agriculture, implicitly taking as invariant the production conditions of any commodity other than corn.

It should be noted that by the time Ricardo published the *Essay on Profits*, both the above-mentioned assumptions had come under attack from Malthus. On reading Ricardo's *Essay*, Malthus commented that 'the real capital of the farmer . . . does not consist merely in raw produce, but in ploughs wagons threshing machines &c: and in the tea sugar clothes &c: &c: used by his labourers' (Malthus to Horner, 14 March 1815, *Works*, VI: 187; see Malthus's letter to Ricardo of 12 March 1815, ibid.: 185, for a similar argument). It seems probable, however, that at least in an initial stage of the discussion Malthus perceived the first assumption (namely that the wage rate consists of a given quantity of corn) as the cornerstone of Ricardo's argument (see Sraffa, *Works*, I: xxxii, where 'the simplification that wages consist only of corn' is said to have been 'under frequent attack from Malthus'). Taken by itself, Malthus's objection in the letter to Ricardo of 5 August 1814 quoted above ('in no case of production, is the produce exactly of the same nature as the capital advanced') could, of course, refer equally well to Ricardo's neglect of capital components other than wages or of goods other than corn in the wage basket. As pointed out by Vianello (2011: 251–2), however, the conclusion Malthus draws in the same letter is that the extension of cultivation to inferior land would be compatible with an increased rate of profit (as entailed by the explanation of profits in terms of the 'scarcity of capital' that Malthus was putting forward there in opposition to Ricardo) on account of the possible 'slight fall in the real price of labour . . . or what comes to the same thing, *a rise in the price of produce without a proportionate rise of labour*' (Malthus to Ricardo, 5 August 1814, *Works*, VI: 118; our emphasis; for a similar argument, see Malthus's letter to Ricardo of 6 July 1814, ibid.: 111; for Malthus's own explanation of the rate of profits, see below).

Further confirmation that this conclusion was based on the price effect due to the presence of goods other than corn in the wage basket is provided, Vianello adds, by the fact that, in that same period, in opposition to Adam Smith's view that the increase in the average price of corn caused by a bounty on corn exports (through less severe price falls in the years of plenty) would not encourage further tillage because '[t]he money price of labour, and of every thing that is the produce either of land or labour, must necessarily . . . rise . . . in proportion to the money price of corn' (*WN*, IV.v.a.14), Malthus pointed out that '[t]he expenditure of the labouring classes of society . . . by no means consists wholly in food, and still less, of course, in mere bread or grain' (Malthus [1814] 1986: 89). (Vianello, 2011, suggests that Smith's still influential treatment of the effects of a bounty on the exportation of corn, with its implicit notion of a wage basket consisting of corn only, may have furnished Ricardo with the 'building blocks' of his 'corn-ratio' theory of profits.)

A coherent application of the surplus approach to distribution

A very important aspect of the 'corn-ratio' theory of profits is that it represents a first coherent application, albeit under fairly restrictive assumptions, of the explanation of profits and rent based on the notion of a physical surplus. It was indeed by means of this theoretical construction that Ricardo prevented his analysis from being clouded by the veil of the relations between distributive shares and prices, which he was not prepared to address until the later *Principles*. He thus succeeded in not losing sight of the fact that the above-mentioned classes of income stem from a 'non-price' source, namely the capacity of the economy to produce an excess of output over and above the reproduction requirements (including workers' subsistence). And the concept of profits and rent as competing shares of the material surplus allowed Ricardo to state that, however prices may change, those incomes must be inversely related either to one another or to wages. For example, with regard to the relation between profits and rent, 'Rent then is in all cases a portion of the profits previously obtained on the land. It is never a new creation of revenue, but always part of a revenue already created' (*Works*, IV: 18). Ricardo could then oppose his rigorous conclusion of a threefold trade-off among profits, rent and wages to confused views such as those epitomized by Malthus, according to which changes in prices made it possible for profits and rent to move in the same direction with real wages remaining unvaried (see, for example, Malthus to Ricardo, 5 August 1814, *Works*, VI: 117).

Together with the theoretical aspect concerning the approach to the distribution of the product, the 'corn-ratio' theory of profits provides an application of a further, methodological feature of the classical conceptual framework. We refer to the separation, which is peculiar to this approach, into distinct analytical stages of the determination of distribution and relative prices on the one hand and the determination of outputs on the other. Within the classical framework, while the relations connecting distributive variables and prices display, for given levels of output and the associated methods of production, an absolutely general character and are hence conceivable in an abstract form (such as that of mathematical functions), the mutual influences between levels of production and distributive variables may indeed operate through various channels whose direction and relative importance cannot be ascertained in the abstract. Once this feature of the classical framework is taken into account, it becomes clear why the classical authors did not find it natural to attempt a simultaneous determination of outputs, distribution and prices of the kind found in the later neoclassical theories, and why they 'instinctively' proceeded in their analyses of the general principles of value and distribution under the implicit assumption of given levels of output (on this point see Garegnani, 2002: 243–6). By virtue of the general character attributed to them, the relations worked out under this assumption were then used as analytical scaffolding for the study of the wider set of reciprocal influences amongst outputs, distribution and prices that could operate in any concrete situation under the specific conditions characterizing it.

It might appear, however, that with regard to the influence on distribution and prices that the level of output is able to have through its impact on the conditions of production, the analytical separation we have just talked about is not to be found in Ricardo's letters of 1814 and in the *Essay on Profits*. One of the general conclusions Ricardo draws there is indeed that because of the need to extend cultivation to inferior land, a lower rate of profit and a higher price of corn will necessarily be associated with increased production of the latter. Closer examination shows, however, that there is really no contradiction between this element of Ricardo's early theory of profits and the separate determination of distribution and outputs that characterizes the classical method of analysis. *Ceteris paribus*, the extension of cultivation to inferior land, with the consequent worsening of the conditions of production that affect the profit rate, is a necessary consequence of the increase in agricultural output and therefore enters coherently into what Ricardo sees as the general principles of profit determination. On the other hand, changes in the level of output may also affect the conditions of production through the possible action of increasing returns to scale, that is, by making it profitable to adopt different types of capital equipment, inducing improvements in the organization of labour, and so on. Whether and to what extent the latter counteracting influences actually do operate is, however, something that cannot be assessed in the abstract, and therefore with the same degree of generality, as the necessary worsening of the relevant conditions of production due to the expansion of tillage to inferior land. We can thus understand why the latter effect of changes in agricultural output is fully considered by Ricardo in his theory of profits, while he does not take into account the former category of influences, with respect to which the determination of the profit rate is therefore still kept separate from the study of output changes. Ricardo thus admits in the initial part of the *Essay* that despite the depressive effect of the expansion of agricultural production on profits, '[p]rofits might . . . increase because improvements might take place in agriculture, or in the implements of husbandry', and he includes the improvements just mentioned among the circumstances which 'may retard . . . the *natural* effects of the progress of wealth', that is, the fall in profits (*Works*, IV: 11; our emphasis).

On some different interpretations of Ricardo's early theory of profits – Samuel Hollander
As we have seen, the interpretation of Ricardo's early theory of profits suggested by
Sraffa can be summarized in the following two propositions. First, the determining role
of agricultural profits is the principle that guides Ricardo after his abandonment of
the Smithian 'competition-of-capitals' explanation of the rate of profit in the summer
of 1813 and up to the more mature theory of value and distribution presented in the
Principles. Second, the 'rational foundation' of this principle lies in a 'corn-ratio' reasoning. Opposing views must therefore either claim (1) that Ricardo did not maintain
in some significant sense that the rate of profit in agriculture determines the general
rate of profits, or, if this is admitted, (2) that Ricardo reached this particular conclusion
along different lines from those suggested by Sraffa. We shall now present and discuss
the primary aspects of the interpretations put forward by Samuel Hollander (1973, 1979;
further specifications in 1975, 1983) and Terry Peach (1993), which have given rise to
particularly lively debate and in which, as we shall see, one can respectively find the positions (1) and (2) just mentioned. This will enable us to discuss some aspects of Ricardo's
early theory of profits that have been left aside so far, particularly in connection with his
treatment of prices.

   According to Hollander, in determining the trend of the general profit rate, Ricardo
never assigned an analytically relevant role to the rate of profit in agriculture. While
acknowledging the existence of 'formal' statements in this direction made by Ricardo
in 1814 and 1815 (Hollander, 1975: 189; 1979: 124, 145), Hollander claims that in this
period Ricardo already held the view that Hollander believes was subsequently to play
a central role in the *Principles*, that is, that 'variations in the money-wage rate, in consequence of changing prices of wage-goods, will be accompanied by inverse movements
in the general rate of profit' (Hollander, 1973: 260). More precisely, Hollander contends
first that in 1814 and 1815 Ricardo generally conceived the wage basket as including
non-food goods (that Ricardo did not consider capital components other than wages
when determining the rate of profit is on the other hand acknowledged by Hollander,
1979: 162) and, second, that it was by focusing on changes in the level of money wages
due to variations in the money price of wage-goods that, in this period, Ricardo was able
to see that the general rate of profit varies in the same direction as productivity in the
wage-goods sector. Hollander adds that this view, which he describes as the 'weak' (i.e.,
less restrictive) version of Ricardo's theory, is sometimes – and notably both at the beginning of 1814 and in the *Essay on Profits* – replaced by a 'strong' (more restrictive) version
where, for the sake of simplicity or to strengthen his argument, Ricardo assumes that
the wage basket consists of corn alone and where it is therefore changes in agricultural
productivity alone that determine changes in the general rate of profit (for the distinction between the two versions of the theory, see Hollander, 1973: 275; for the 'strong'
version at the beginning of 1814 and in the *Essay*, see Hollander, 1975: 190). And it is as
a shorthand representation of the latter version of the theory – in which, even though the
wage basket consists exclusively of corn, agricultural productivity is still seen affecting
the general rate of profits through its influence on the price of corn and hence on the level
of money wages – that Ricardo's assertions about a special role for agricultural profits
should, in Hollander's opinion, be understood.

   As regards this point, it is not clear why, in the alleged 'strong' version of his theory,
Ricardo should have preferred to use the expression 'profits of the farmer' in order to

designate agricultural productivity as the exclusive circumstance in the determination of the general rate of profits (Garegnani, 1982: 68; see Hollander, 1983: 171 for a passage in which the 'translation' of one expression into the other is allegedly performed by Ricardo, and the reply in Garegnani, 1983: 177) nor why Malthus should have insisted on opposing Ricardo on these grounds (see, for example, Malthus's letters to Ricardo of 5 August 1814, *Works*, VI: 118; 23 November 1814, ibid.: 153; 2 April 1815, ibid.: 207). More generally, that is, with respect to both the 'strong' and the 'weak' versions of the theory attributed to Ricardo, on Hollander's reconstruction Ricardo should have had some kind of argument that – without constituting a fully developed theory of value (by means of which Ricardo would have been able to reach definite conclusions about the general rate of profit) – could nonetheless lead him to maintain that increases in the money price of corn, and hence in the money level of wages, are not entirely passed on in the form of increases in the money prices of other commodities; for, in the absence of such an argument, Ricardo's supposed reasoning in terms of money wages would clearly be indeterminate.

What we find in the period under examination with respect to prices is, however, Ricardo's initial adherence to the then generally accepted view, derived as we have seen from the authority of Adam Smith, according to which an increase in the money price of corn causes an increase in the money prices of all other commodities (see Ricardo's letter to Malthus of 26 June 1814, *Works*, VI: 108; see also Ricardo's 1810 *Notes on Bentham*, *Works*, III: 270). It was not until August 1814 – at least a year after his abandonment of the Smithian 'competition-of-capitals' explanation of the rate of profits and several months after the first systematic exposition of his new theory in the lost 'papers on the profits of Capital' – that Ricardo stated that in his opinion, and contrary to the strict Smithian view, the money price of commodities would increase in a lesser proportion than the money price of corn (Ricardo to Malthus, 11 August 1814, *Works*, VI: 120; the idea is already implied in a passage in Ricardo's letter to Malthus of 25 July 1814, ibid.: 115).

Hollander initially admitted that the lack of a positive argument explaining *why* the money price of manufactures should rise less than the money price of corn ought to be seen as a 'serious stumbling block' (1973: 265; on this point see also 1979: 131) for Ricardo allegedly reasoning in terms of money wages. He subsequently suggested, however, that in his letter of 11 August Ricardo may have relied on the 'reduced demand for manufactures', which would accompany the increase in the money price of corn '[to constrain] the rise in manufacturing prices behind the increase in money wage costs' (Hollander, 1983: 171). This interpretation does not, however, appear tenable on close examination of the relevant texts. It is true that the less than proportional increase in the money price of manufactures is presented by Ricardo in his letter to Malthus of 11 August hand in hand with a reduction in the demand for these goods. Ricardo's mention of demand does not, however, play any positive role in limiting the rise of manufacture prices below the rise of wages and rather appears to be a buffer against the specific form of Malthus's objection to his theory of profits in the letter to which Ricardo is replying.

As we have seen, all through their discussion during the spring and summer of 1814, Malthus objected that an increase in the price of corn due to restrictions on its importation would entail a rise in the profit rate. This would happen, Malthus claimed, because by reducing the amount of labour that the same amount of money capital would be able to command, the rise in the price of corn would reduce aggregate production, while, he added, aggregate demand would *not* generally fall in the same proportion (the proportion between supply and demand for commodities in general being the manifestation of the 'abundance or scarcity of capital', which Malthus believed to be the ultimate determinant of the profit rate; *Works*, VI: 117). In his letter of 5 August 1814 Malthus gave an instance of his theory (which by its nature concerned the aggregates of production and demand) for the hypothetical case of a cotton or wool capitalist who, 'be[ing] obliged to pay more for the labour he employs . . . will not be able to work up the same quantity of goods with his capital; the goods will in consequence rise in price, and his profits, from the general scarcity of capital, will be increased' (ibid.). While acknowledging the reduction in the production of manufactures as a consequence of the extension of cultivation, in his letter of 11 August 1814 Ricardo denies that the rate of profit can be generally raised through that channel, and argues that the contraction in the production of manufactures is necessarily accompanied by a contraction of demand to the same extent except in the event of people spending part of their capital. As the latter case can occur, if at all, only temporarily ('for a short period capital and produce may diminish faster than demand – yet in the long run effective demand cannot augment or continue stationary with a diminishing capital', ibid.: 120), Ricardo concludes that the reduction in the production of manufactures would not prevent the manufacturing profit rate from being pushed downwards in line with the fall of the agricultural profit rate occasioned – as Ricardo reiterates in the same letter – by the extension of cultivation. As a result, he points out, the rise in manufacture prices would be less than proportional, compared to the rise in wages induced by the higher price of corn (Ricardo to Malthus, 11 August 1814, ibid.). It thus appears to be the adjustment to the fall of the profit rate in agriculture, arrived at independently of price changes, that Ricardo regards as keeping the rise in manufacture prices below the increase in wages (Garegnani, 1982: 72–3). Demand is not involved in the argument other than to repeat that it cannot exceed aggregate production, in the attempt to clear up Malthus's analytically opaque allegation about prices and profits based on the opposite belief.

According to Sraffa (*Works*, I: xxx; cf. xxxiii), an initial step in Ricardo's thinking towards a general explanation of prices (independent of the role of demand envisaged by Hollander) can be detected in those 'fragmentary elements [of a new theory of value]' to be found in the *Essay on Profits*, where it is stated that the relative prices of commodities vary with changes in the 'difficulties of their production' (Ricardo, *Works*, IV: 19). As a result of this, Ricardo abandons any residual adherence to Smith's view of the direct influence of the money price of corn on the money prices of other commodities. In the *Essay*, the constancy of the prices of commodities, in the face of a rise in corn, replaces the less than proportional increase by which he had previously combined the received opinion about money prices and the fall in the profit rate (see *Works*, IV: 21n, where the view that 'the price of corn regulates the price of all other things' is dismissed as 'a mistake').

The tentative character of this new argument is revealed, however, by the fact that neither in the *Essay* nor in the post-*Essay* correspondence does Ricardo feel so confident of his new explanation of prices to abandon the 'agricultural' form of his theory of profits and rest the whole weight of his explanation of profits on a theory of value. As today we can clearly see, the fundamental limitation of a theory of prices based on the 'difficulties of production' lies in the fact that the effects on relative prices of changes in the methods of production are not independent of the effects on the general rate of profit produced by those very changes. Therefore, it would be hardly surprising if Ricardo, though with his still primitive understanding of the relation between prices and profits, was not ready to take the 'difficulty-of-production' explanation of prices as a reliable alternative to the 'corn-ratio' reasoning, as a support for his theory of profits. In actual fact, a sign of this uneasiness emerges quite clearly in the oscillation of Ricardo's position in the post-*Essay* correspondence. Once he had accepted Malthus's objection about the multi-commodity composition of the farmer's capital, the attempt to apply that kind of price determination leads Ricardo to admit that what happens to the rate of profit in agriculture in the event of an extension of cultivation remains wholly indeterminate (see the letter to Malthus of 17 April 1815, *Works*, VI: 213–14, where Ricardo points at the fact that the result depends on whether the rise in the relative price of corn is such as to offset the worsening in the conditions of production). In fact, unlike a fall in the corn prices of manufactures conceived as the mere reflection of a known fall in the profit rate (which, as we have seen, was Ricardo's position in the pre-*Essay* correspondence), a fall due to an autonomous cause, such as the worsening in the production conditions of corn, might seem capable of reversing the very fall in the profit rate in agriculture, thus providing Malthus's argument with a force it did not previously possess. While occasionally opposing to Malthus the inconsistency between a rise of the rate of profit in agriculture procured by a fall in the corn price of manufactures, and the decrease that that fall would cause in the manufacturing profit rate (see, for example, the letter to Malthus of 17 April 1815, ibid.: 213), Ricardo had to acknowledge that his tentative determination of prices entailed 'a labyrinth of difficulties', entreating Malthus to give his 'simple doctrine fair consideration', as 'it accounts for all the phenomena in an easy, natural manner' (ibid.: 214; on the whole question see Garegnani, 1982: 76–7).

The whole phase in the development of Ricardo's ideas starting with the post-*Essay* correspondence should indeed be seen as the 'transition' (Sraffa, *Works*, I: xxxiv) between Ricardo's 'primitive "agricultural" theory of profits' and his more mature general theory in the *Principles*, the 'turning point' in this transition being located by Sraffa as late as December 1815, when Ricardo wrote, 'I know I shall be soon stopped by the word price' (Ricardo to Mill, 30 December 1815, *Works*, VI: 348).

Hollander's objections to Sraffa

Alongside his own interpretation of Ricardo's early theory of profits, Hollander objects to the evidence put forward in support of Sraffa's reconstruction. In this section we provide an outline of Hollander's stances in this respect, as well as of some of the reactions they have stimulated.

Hollander (1973: 265–7; cf. 1979: 127–8) dismisses as irrelevant Malthus's statement to the effect that 'in no case of production, is the produce exactly of the same nature as the capital advanced' – which Sraffa (*Works*, I: xxxi) presents as 'no doubt an echo of Ricardo's own formulation . . . never stated [by him] in any of his extant letters and papers' – and claims that in his letter of 5 August 1814 Malthus was merely replying to a *single* letter in which Ricardo *had* made recourse to a 'corn calculation' (Ricardo to Malthus, 25 July 1814, *Works*, VI: 114–5). In his comment on Hollander, however, Garegnani (1982: 71) points out that Ricardo's 'corn calculation' in that letter does *not* entail homogeneity between capital and product in agriculture, as it allows for a less than proportional increase in the corn-value of capital in relation to a given rise in the price of corn, which rules out any possibility of Malthus's objection referring to that letter in particular. With regard to the well known table in the *Essay*, Hollander (1973: 274) contends that since Ricardo refers to capital as being valued in corn, the latter acts there merely as the numéraire. This claim has been challenged by Eatwell (1975: 185n) and Garegnani (1982: 73), who both point out that Ricardo does not revalue capital on inframarginal land as the price of corn increases in consequence of the extension of cultivation to inferior land. Concerning the 'striking passage' in Ricardo's letter to Malthus of 26 June 1814 ('the proportion of production to the consumption necessary to such production'), Hollander (1973: 262) claims that the same letter contains an explanation of the expression in terms of the inverse relationship between money wages and the general rate of profits; in contrast with this interpretation, Garegnani (1982: 72) offers a reading of the passage indicated by Hollander that is instead compatible with Sraffa's interpretation.

Finally, Ricardo's post-*Essay* correspondence is taken by Hollander (1975: 188, 193 and 199) as additional evidence in favour of *his* reconstruction, on the grounds that in those letters Ricardo has recourse to 'price calculations', while against Sraffa's interpretation of such crude 'price calculations' as a sign of the 'transition between the *Essay* and the *Principles*' (Sraffa, *Works*, I: xxxiv), Hollander claims, as we have seen above, that this transition never occurred. (For Hollander's view of the additional evidence in favour of Sraffa's reconstruction put forward by Langer and de Vivo, see Hollander, 1995, and the reply in de Vivo, 1996).

On some different interpretations of Ricardo's early theory of profits – Terry Peach
Unlike Hollander, Peach acknowledges the existence of a special role for the profits of the farmer in his reconstruction of Ricardo's early theory of profits. While he (1993: 3, 57, 86; cf. 1998: 599 and 2002: 386) believes that an important distinction must be drawn between an otherwise unspecified 'regulatory' role for the rate of profit in agriculture, which should be ascribed to Ricardo but that would be of little analytical relevance, and a more precise 'determining' role, which would on the contrary be alien to Ricardo's thinking, it is his opinion that prior to the *Principles*, in Ricardo's analysis 'there was something "special" about agriculture, since it was the agricultural rate to which other rates supposedly conformed' (Peach, 1993: 86). Peach maintains, however, that Ricardo did not reach this conclusion through a 'corn-ratio' reasoning. It therefore appears that, despite Peach's formal opposition to the principle of a determining role of agricultural profits, what he actually opposes is the *second* of the two propositions in which we have summarized Sraffa's reconstruction of Ricardo's early theory of profits.

Peach's own reconstruction mainly rests on the *Essay on Profits* rather than on the previous correspondence. In actual fact, Peach implicitly introduces a break in Ricardo's reasoning the moment he suggests that in the pre-*Essay* correspondence Ricardo conjectured the direction of the change in the agricultural rate of profit in isolation from the rest of the economic system without relying on any assumption under which this would be rigorously possible, whereas such an assumption would be present, at least implicitly, in the *Essay* (on this point, see, for example, Peach, 1993: 57, where he doubts whether *any* 'logically sound "rational foundation"' can be found behind Ricardo's initial expositions of his new theory such as the one contained in his letter to Trower of 8 March 1814).

According to Peach, Ricardo constantly reasoned both in the pre-*Essay* correspondence and in the *Essay* in terms of a wage basket comprising non-food items and an agricultural capital including components other than wages. He claims, however, that in the pre-*Essay* correspondence Ricardo drew from Smith's view of the relation between the price of corn and the price of other commodities, that the latter would change 'in the same direction, if not quite to the same extent' (Peach, 1993: 67) as the former; and that in this idea Ricardo found sufficient grounds for playing down the possible effect of changes in relative prices, thus being satisfied with being 'roughly' (ibid.; cf. 86) able to study changes in the agricultural rate of profit by looking exclusively at the worsening of the conditions of production due to the extension of cultivation. In the *Essay*, instead, Ricardo would have proceeded on the 'tacit assumption' (ibid.: 71) that the money prices of all commodities, including corn, remain constant after the extension of cultivation to inferior land, thus basing his analysis on the condition of strictly constant relative prices. (Note that Peach, 1984, had previously suggested that in the pre-*Essay* correspondence Ricardo would have taken the Smithian view concerning money prices as implying the proportional increase in the money price of commodities in the face of a given increase in the money price of corn, thus providing an interpretation of Ricardo's early theory of profits in terms of constant relative prices that covered the *entire* period between the summer of 1813 and the first months of 1815. The idea re-emerges in Peach, 1993: 76–9, where it remains, however, completely unrelated to the idea of a 'roughly' isolated agricultural sector Peach advances as his main interpretation, and should therefore be considered abandoned by Peach himself.)

The idea of constant prices in the *Essay* is, however, clearly contradicted (Kurz, 1994: 414) by Ricardo's theory of value in terms of the 'difficulty of production', which, as we have seen, is tentatively introduced there, and indeed by the very terms of the debate on the effects of restrictions on the importation of corn to which the *Essay* was written as a contribution. The major difficulty in Peach's reconstruction lies, however, in the fact that while the assumption of constant relative prices would on the one hand have enabled Ricardo to determine the fall in the agricultural rate of profit attendant upon the extension of cultivation in isolation from the rest of the economy, it would have made it impossible on the other for the decreased rate to be transmitted to the rest of the economic system (de Vivo, 1994: 39; Mongiovi, 1994: 256; cf. Prendergast, 1986: 1101 for the same objection directed at Peach's interpretation of the *Essay* in 1984). According to Peach, however, it was only in a later and apparently quite separate stage of his reasoning that Ricardo went on to consider this question. It was only 'at this juncture', Peach (1993: 72) claims, 'that he announced his new rudimentary theory of exchange value' implying the rise in the relative price of corn as cultivation is extended. Moreover, on this view, it did not occur to Ricardo that the conclusions regarding the agricultural rate of profit that he had supposedly drawn previously on the 'tacit assumption' of constant relative prices might need to be reconsidered once the assumption was dropped. 'That this should have been overlooked' Peach (ibid.: 74) comments, 'may reflect the *Essay*'s hasty composition'. The explanation is hardly compatible, however, with the fact that Ricardo is known to have produced his new theory of profits at least one year before the composition of the *Essay* and had since been constantly engaged in discussing Malthus's objections to it. The inconsistency appears therefore to lie in Peach's reconstruction rather than in Ricardo's reasoning.

As for the evidence adduced in support of Sraffa's reconstruction, Peach's position is the following. Peach (ibid.: 62) argues that when observing that 'in no case of production, is the produce exactly of the same nature as the capital advanced' Malthus was in fact abandoning 'the capital-product homogeneity assumption, introduced by *him* in the letter of 6 July 1814' (original emphasis). Peach is here referring to the same 'corn-calculation' Hollander (1973: 266) had found in Ricardo's letter to Malthus of 25 July 1814 (*Works*, VI: 114–5), and that, according to him, would have represented the single letter to which Malthus was replying with his statement. As Peach notes, Ricardo's 'corn-calculation' was in fact introduced by Malthus in his previous letter (ibid.: 111). Since, however, both for Malthus and for Ricardo that 'calculation' admitted for a less than proportional increase in the corn value of capital attending a given rise in the price of corn, it cannot be advanced as an instance of the 'capital-product homogeneity assumption', so that Malthus's observation in his letter of 5 August cannot be thought to refer to it. The fact that with the extension of cultivation to inferior land Ricardo does not revalue capital on inframarginal land in the table from the *Essay* is instead explained by Peach on the basis of his 'tacit assumption of constant prices' (1993: 75).

ROBERTO CICCONE AND PAOLO TRABUCCHI

See also:

Accumulation of Capital; *Essay on Profits*; Land and Rent; Sraffa, Piero, on Ricardo; Surplus.

References

de Vivo, G. (1985), 'Robert Torrens and Ricardo's "corn-ratio" theory of profits', *Cambridge Journal of Economics*, **9**(1), 89–92.
de Vivo, G. (1994), '(Mis)interpreting Ricardo', *Contributions to Political Economy*, **13**(1), 29–43.
de Vivo, G. (1996), 'Ricardo, Torrens and Sraffa: a summing up', *Cambridge Journal of Economics*, **20**(3), 387–91.
Eatwell, J. (1975), 'The interpretation of Ricardo's *Essay on Profits*', *Economica* (New Series), **42**(166), 182–7.
Garegnani, P. (1982), 'On Hollander's interpretation of Ricardo's early theory of profits', *Cambridge Journal of Economics*, **6**(1), 65–77.
Garegnani, P. (1983), 'Ricardo's early theory of profits and its "rational foundation": a reply to Professor Hollander', *Cambridge Journal of Economics*, **7**(2), 175–8.
Garegnani, P. (1984), 'Value and distribution in the classical economists and Marx', *Oxford Economic Papers*, **36**(2), 291–325.
Garegnani, P. (2002), 'Misunderstanding classical economics? A reply to Blaug', *History of Political Economy*, **34**(1), 241–54.
Hollander, S. (1973), 'Ricardo's analysis of the profit rate, 1813–15', *Economica* (New Series), **40**(159), 260–82.
Hollander, S. (1975), 'Ricardo and the corn profit model: reply to Eatwell', *Economica* (New Series), **42**(166), 188–202.
Hollander, S. (1979), *The Economics of David Ricardo*, Toronto: University of Toronto Press.
Hollander, S. (1983), 'Professor Garegnani's defence of Sraffa on the material rate of profit', *Cambridge Journal of Economics*, **7**(2), 167–74.
Hollander, S. (1995), 'Sraffa's rational reconstruction of Ricardo: on three contributions to the *Cambridge Journal of Economics*', *Cambridge Journal of Economics*, **19**(3), 483–89.
Kurz, H.D. (1994), 'Review of Peach (1993)', *European Journal of the History of Economic Thought*, **1**(2), 411–20.
Langer, G.F. (1982), 'Further evidence for Sraffa's interpretation of Ricardo', *Cambridge Journal of Economics*, **6**(4), 397–400.
Malthus, T.R. ([1814] 1986), 'Observations on the effects of the Corn Laws, and of a rise or fall in the price of corn on the agriculture and general wealth of the country', in E.A. Wrigley and D. Souden (eds), *The Works of Thomas Robert Malthus, Vol. VII*, London: William Pickering, pp. 87–109.
Mongiovi, G. (1994), 'Misinterpreting Ricardo: a review essay', *Journal of the History of Economic Thought*, **16**(2), 248–69.

Peach, T. (1984), 'David Ricardo's early treatment of profitability: a new interpretation', *The Economic Journal*, **94**(376), 733–51.

Peach, T. (1993), *Interpreting Ricardo*, Cambridge, UK: Cambridge University Press.

Peach, T. (1998), 'On *Interpreting Ricardo*: a reply to Sraffians', *Cambridge Journal of Economics*, **22**(5), 597–616.

Peach, T. (2002), 'Interpreting Ricardo: a further reply to Sraffians', *Cambridge Journal of Economics*, **26**(3), 381–91.

Prendergast, R. (1986), 'A comment on "David Ricardo's early treatment of profitability: a new interpretation"', *The Economic Journal*, **96**, 1098–104.

Smith, A. ([1776] 1979), *An Inquiry into the Nature and Causes of the Wealth of Nations*, in *The Glasgow Edition of the Works and Correspondence of Adam Smith*, reprint, (eds) R.H. Campbell, A.S. Skinner and W.B. Todd, Oxford: Oxford University Press.

Vianello, F. (2011), 'The Smithian origin of Ricardo's corn-ratio theory of profits. A suggested interpretation', in R. Ciccone, C. Gehrke and G. Mongiovi (eds), *Sraffa and Modern Economics, Vol. I*, Oxford and New York: Routledge.

Demand and Supply

'I confess it fills me with astonishment – wrote Ricardo to Malthus in 1818 – 'to find that you think . . . that natural price, as well as market price, is determined by the demand and supply' (letter of 30 January 1818, *Works*, VII: 250). Ricardo was highly critical of the doctrine according to which the natural price of commodities is determined by demand and supply. In Chapter XXX of the *Principles*, entirely devoted to the question, he states: 'The opinion that the price of commodities depends solely on the proportion of supply to demand, or demand to supply, has become almost an axiom in political economy, and has been the source of much error in that science' (ibid.: 382).

In basing his own theory of value on Smith's theory of natural price as determined by the cost of production, which Ricardo understood as the quantity of inputs that are technically necessary to obtain a unit of the commodity and not as determined by the sum of the natural rates of wages, profit and rent, and on Smith's analysis of gravitation of market price towards natural price, he regarded demand and supply as influencing only market price. Natural price, which prevails when competition has had its full effect by directing capitals to the most profitable trades, cannot be influenced by the temporary scarcity or abundance of supply with respect to demand that is at the basis of the movement of market prices, but is regulated by more fundamental forces:

> It is the cost of production which must ultimately regulate the price of commodities, and not, as has been often said, the proportion between the supply and demand: the proportion between supply and demand may, indeed, for a time, affect the market value of a commodity, until it is supplied in greater or less abundance, according as the demand may have increased or diminished; but this effect will be only of temporary duration. (*Works*, I: 382)

Early formulations of the demand-and-supply principle

Like the majority of his contemporaries, Ricardo did not regard 'demand' and 'supply' as functions relating quantities demanded and supplied to price, as in modern neoclassical theories, but rather as single quantities (see Garegnani, 1983). The demand-and-supply principle that he criticizes finds its standard exposition, in his time, in Lauderdale's *An Inquiry into the Nature and Origin of Public Wealth* (1804), one of the authors who Ricardo quotes in Chapter XXX of the *Principles*. Lauderdale connects value to two characteristics of goods: utility and scarcity. Utility, however, cannot in itself confer value to a commodity: it has in fact to be understood in the sense of use value, that is, a quality or a number of qualities that render a good capable of satisfying human needs or wants. It was, in the theories of the time, a qualitative prerequisite rather than a quantitative determinant of value (Bharadwaj, 1978), as is shown by the famous paradox by which very useful goods may have null or negligible value. What really confers value according to Lauderdale is 'scarcity', the circumstance for which there is less of a useful good than would be necessary to fully satisfy human needs and wants: 'Experience shews us' – he states – 'that every thing is uniformly considered as valuable, which, to the possession of qualities, that make it the object of the desire of man, adds the circumstance of existing in scarcity' (Lauderdale, 1804: 12). If the available quantity of the commodity is a fundamental determinant of value, it follows that any variations in value 'must depend upon the alteration of the proportion betwixt the demand for, and the quantity of, the commodity' (ibid.: 15), that is, upon any of four different causes: 'a diminution of its quantity', 'an augmentation of its quantity', 'an increased demand', 'a failure of demand' (ibid.: 13–14), or on the same causes applied to the commodity used as a standard (ibid.: 14–15).

In Lauderdale's formulation, the price of a good appears to be determined by the simple ratio between two quantities (the quantity demanded and the quantity of it available), and its variations by the variations of this ratio. In order for this to be a sufficient principle for the determination of price, the quantity demanded and the quantity available must be determined by independent causes; the former being an expression of the needs or desires of the buyers, the latter being limited either by the natural scarcity of the good or by the difficulty of producing it. It is worth noting that Lauderdale's formulation closely echoes earlier formulations of the demand-and-supply principle, and that a similar simple formula for the determination of price can be traced back at least to John Locke, who in the essay 'Some considerations of the consequences of lowering of interest, and raising the value of money' ([1691] 1727) maintains: 'He that will justly estimate the value of any Thing, must consider its Quantity in proportion to its Vent, for this alone regulates the Price' (ibid.: 20), or, with an analogous meaning: 'the Price of any Commodity rises or falls, by the proportion of the number of Buyers and Sellers' (ibid.: 16).

Thus, these early formulations of the demand-and-supply theory of price not only rely strongly on the notion of scarcity, but propose a simple formula for the determination of price, which results as the outright ratio between two quantities (see also Stirati, 2011a: 351). In case only two commodities were involved in exchange, the demand for the commodity would be the quantity of the other commodity offered in exchange for it.

The demand-and-supply principle for the determination of the value can be found, in a more complex form, in the analysis of Jean-Baptiste Say, also mentioned by Ricardo along with Lauderdale in Chapter XXX of the *Principles*. It is worth noting that Say's theory of value underwent some modifications in the course of time, as appears from the comparison between the different editions of his *Traité d'Economie Politique* (see the introduction in Say [1803] 2006). While in the first edition (1803; only the fourth edition has been translated into English) Say's analysis of value closely echoes Smith's analysis of gravitation of market price towards natural price and the role of demand and supply is confined to the determination of the market price (*prix courant*, in Say's terminology), in the subsequent editions he progressively elaborates a general demand-and-supply theory of value in which the notion of natural price plays no relevant role. In the fourth edition ([1819] 1821) this demand-and-supply theory is already developed. In the first edition the relationship between current price (*prix courant*) and natural price (*prix naturel*) is analysed in the following terms:

> The *current price* of a commodity always tends to set itself at the level of its *natural price*. For, whenever it rises above the natural price, the production of this commodity, better paid for than the other productions, will attract on its side land, capitals, industry; the quantity supplied will increase relative to the quantity demanded, and price will decrease. On the other hand, when the *current price* falls below the *natural price*, that is the price which is necessary to pay for the productive services, the services which find themselves insufficiently paid for will withdraw; production stops, and the quantity supplied becomes smaller relative to the quantity demanded, price rises until it reaches a level where it is possible to pay conveniently for productive services. (Say, 1803, II: 60; my translation, original emphasis)

Demand and supply appear as the determinants of the *prix courant*:

> When speaking of the price of a thing, with no other specifications, we mean its current price and not its natural price. Price is established according to the ratio that occurs between the quantity of the commodity that is offered for exchange or for sale, and the quantity of the same *commodity* that people are prepared to buy. (Ibid.: 57–8; my translation, original emphasis)

That Say regards demand and supply as specific quantities, and defines the price as the simple ratio between the two quantities, appears clearly in the following passage:

> A variation in the quantities supplied and demanded brings about no changes in price, provided that the variation is the same on both sides. It is the ratio of the two quantities that determines price; when the ratio stays the same, also price stays the same. (Ibid.: 58; my translation)

Since the first edition of the *Traité*, however, some elements of Say's analysis of value are different from Smith's. In opposition to Smith, Say tries to state a theory in which utility, and not the cost of production, is the cause of value. He regards the exchange value of a commodity as a measure of its utility (Say, 1803, I: 24–5). Moreover, he introduces the idea of a decreasing relationship between natural price and quantity demanded (such that an increase in price reduces the number of buyers who can afford to buy the commodity and thus reduces the demand for it, while a reduction of price makes it increase; see Say, 1803, II: 72), which in the subsequent editions of the *Traité* will be employed to found a demand-and-supply analysis aimed at determining not only the current price but price in general. The analysis of gravitation is still referred to, although briefly, in the second edition (1814) – the one quoted by Ricardo in the *Principles* – where Say maintains that current price always tends to natural price (1814, II: 464). At the same time, however, in other passages he seems to regard the cost of production not as the regulator of price, but only as setting the lowest limit below which price cannot fall without causing a commodity to be withdrawn from the market by potential sellers. It is on these passages that Ricardo focuses his critical attention: "'We have seen," says M. Say, "that the cost of production determines the lowest price to which things can fall: the price below which they cannot remain for any length of time, because production would then be either entirely stopped or diminished"' (*Works*, I: 383).

The possibility of a permanent divergence of price from cost of production is explained by Say, in a passage dealing with the price of precious metals (quoted and commented on by Ricardo), by means of the interaction of demand and supply:

> He afterwards says, that the demand for gold having increased in a still greater proportion than the supply, since the discovery of the mines, 'its price in goods, instead of falling in the proportion of ten to one, fell only in the proportion of four to one' [Say, 1814, II: 18]; that is to say, instead of falling in proportion as its natural price had fallen, fell in proportion as the supply exceeded the demand. (*Works*, I: 383)

It is worth noting that, in regarding the balance between demand and supply as the general principle of value, Say (1814, II: 430–31) also applies it to the determination of the price of productive services.

In the fourth edition of the *Traité*, Say ([1819] 1821) states that it is the value of products (i.e., utility) that confers value to productive services, criticizing Ricardo for maintaining the opposite (Say [1819] 1821, II: 6); and regards the demand for productive services as a derivation of the demand for goods, an idea that will be fully developed in later neoclassical theories.

The contradictions of the second edition, where the dependence of natural price on cost of production seems to coexist with a general analysis of value in terms of demand and supply, tend to disappear in the subsequent editions given that Say progressively focuses his attention on the *prix courant*, while the notion of natural price loses importance. In the fourth edition he states:

> The cost of production is what Smith calls the natural price of products, as contrasted with their current or market price, as he terms it. But it results from what has been said above, that every act of barter or exchange, among the rest even that implied in the act of production, is conducted with reference to current price. (Ibid.: 23–4)

Apart from the multiple and sometimes contradictory elements that are to be found in Say's analysis of value, it is worth noting that when he resorts to the demand-and-supply principle, he necessarily refers to some causes that limit the quantity available of the commodity with respect to its demand (the physical capacity of mines, in the case of gold and silver) or necessarily increases the difficulty of obtaining it.

It is to this notion of commodities as fundamentally characterized by scarcity (either of the commodity itself or of the means for obtaining it) that Ricardo's critique to the demand-and-supply principle is directed.

Ricardo's critique to the scarcity principle

At the basis of Ricardo's critique to the demand-and-supply principle for the determination of natural price there lies the idea that reproducibility, and not scarcity, is the essential characteristic of commodities. This implies the long-period elasticity of their supply in response to changes in demand. As Smith ([1776] 1976, I: 74) had noted:

> The quantity of every commodity brought to market naturally suits itself to the effectual demand. It is the interest of all those who employ their land, labour, or stock, in bringing any commodity to market, that the quantity never should exceed the effectual demand; and it is the interest of all other people that it never should fall short of that demand.

Following Smith, Ricardo draws attention to the fact that, under unrestricted competition, capitals will accrue to trades where temporary scarcity of supply has brought about increases of price and higher-than-normal profits, thus adjusting supply to effectual demand (the latter being the quantity of the commodity that the market is prepared to absorb at the natural price).

The reason why the interaction between demand and supply is not sufficient, according to Ricardo, to determine value lies thus in the dependence of the quantity supplied, in the long period, on the quantity demanded. Though there are goods of a particular kind whose quantity cannot be increased by labour, yet the 'greatest part of those goods which are the objects of desire' may be multiplied, by means of labour, 'almost without any assignable limit' (*Works*, I: 12). It is the operation of competition, in ensuring gravitation of market prices towards their natural level, which ensures that adjustment between supply and demand occurs through changes in the quantity supplied, and not through changes in price aimed at restricting demand. Any temporary discrepancy between demand and supply of a commodity – caused, for example, by an increase in demand (ibid.: IV and VI) – will in fact produce a temporary divergence of its market price from the natural price and an excess of profits, in that particular trade, with respect to the 'general and adjusted rate of profits'; capitals will be attracted to the production of that commodity where higher-than-normal profits may be earned, supply will increase, the market price will converge to the natural one and the excess profits disappear.

Ricardo's critique is thus a critique of the idea that scarcity is such a general characteristic of commodities as to represent the basis of a general theory of value. Only in some very peculiar circumstances, he maintains, may demand and supply be seen as determining long-period prices. This applies to those goods that for natural reasons cannot be reproduced and are thus in fixed supply ('rare statues and pictures, scarce books and coins, wines of a peculiar quality'), which, however, 'form a very small part of the mass of commodities daily exchanged in the market' (ibid.: 12), and also applies to the cases in which scarcity is artificially induced by some restrictions to competition, that is, for commodities 'which are monopolized, either by an individual, or by a company', so that prices 'fall in proportion as the sellers augment their quantity, and rise in proportion to the eagerness of the buyers to purchase them' (ibid. 385). In the general case when competition operates, price depends 'not on the state of demand and supply, but on the increased or diminished cost of their production'.

It is hardly necessary to note that the 'competition' Ricardo refers to is the competition of capitals, that is, the possibility of capitalists to freely move their capitals from one trade to another in search of a better profit. Competition among buyers has no role in determining natural price:

> [T]he buyers have the least in the world to do in regulating price – it is all done by the competition of sellers, and however the buyers might be really willing to give more for iron, than for gold, they could not, because the supply would be regulated by the cost of production. (Letter to Malthus of 9 October 1820, *Works*, VIII: 277)

Competition among buyers is indeed among the causes that influence market prices, the 'accidental and temporary deviations' from natural prices (*Works*, I: 88). As Smith had remarked, such deviations may be greater or smaller as the temporary divergence between demand and supply and its specific cause, combined with the greater or lesser necessity for buyers of securing the commodity or for sellers of getting rid of it, 'happen to animate more or less the eagerness of the competition' (*WN*, I.vii.10). Besides being subject to a great number of possible influences and accidental circumstances, market prices are temporary in nature: their tendency to be above or below natural price, which alone is fully determined by the sign of the divergence between demand and supply, is sufficient to induce the adjustment of the quantity supplied that will eventually eliminate the deviation. This explains why in searching for the general causes of value Ricardo abstracts from 'any temporary or accidental cause' and focuses his attention exclusively on natural prices (*Works*, I: 92; see Vianello, 1989).

Ricardo's conception of natural price as depending on the difficulty of production, and not on the interaction between demand and supply, seems to be already present, in its essential lines, in the *Essay on Profits* (1815), where he states: 'Wherever competition can have its full effect, and the production of the commodity be not limited by nature, as in the case with some wines, the difficulty or facility of their production will ultimately regulate their exchangeable value' (*Works*, IV: 19–20) and in a footnote he added: 'Though the price of all commodities is ultimately regulated by, and is always tending to, the cost of their production, including the general profit of stock, they are all subject, and perhaps corn more than most others, to an accidental price, proceeding from temporary causes' (ibid.: 20).

As regards the determination of wage, Ricardo's analysis rests on a very similar principle and an analogous contrast between the natural price and the market price of labour, the former being 'that price which is necessary to enable the labourers, one with another, to subsist and to perpetuate their race, without increase or diminution' (*Works*, I: 93), the latter being 'the price which is really paid for [labour], from the natural operation of the proportion of the supply to the demand' (ibid.: 94). According to Ricardo, labour 'like all other things which are purchased and sold' is reproducible, so that it 'may be increased or diminished in quantity' (ibid.); this implies that the natural wage will be exclusively influenced by the cost of reproduction of labour. It is the incorrect application of the demand-and-supply principle to the determination of natural wage that in Ricardo's opinion brings D. Buchanan, in commenting on the *Wealth of Nations*, to neglect the necessary influence on wages of a change in the price of provisions or in taxes (*Works*, I: 216 and 382).

As for the mechanism ensuring that labour supply adjusts to demand and market wage gravitates towards natural wage, Ricardo identifies it with the law of population (see especially ibid. V), although admitting that natural wage contains an institutional element that sets it apart from physiological subsistence (ibid.: 96–8; see Stirati, 2011a, for a critique of the idea that the natural wage is in Ricardo only compatible with stationary population, and Levrero, 2011, for an analysis of alternative mechanisms ensuring adjustment of labour supply to demand especially referred to Marx's analysis but also applicable to Ricardo's).

In the *Notes on Malthus* (1820) commenting on Malthus's *Principles* (1820), Ricardo seems to propose a broader definition of natural wage as a 'price as is necessary to supply constantly a given demand' (*Works*, II: 227 and 228), not necessarily implying that demand for labour must be stationary; confirming, however, his main point, that is, the definition of natural wage as the cost of reproduction of labour (albeit socially determined; see Bharadwaj, 1987) and its independence of the demand-and-supply principle.

Malthus's objections and Ricardo's reply
The just quoted *Notes on Malthus* gave Ricardo the opportunity to deal systematically with Malthus's (1820) objections to his own theory of value and Malthus's attempt at restating the demand-and-supply principle for the determination of natural price (both of commodities and of labour). Though recognizing the validity of Ricardo's critique of the simple formulation of the demand-and-supply theory (ibid.: 65), Malthus tries, however, to reformulate the principle in a different way and introduces to this end the concept of 'intensity' of demand, defined as 'the will and power to make a greater sacrifice in order to obtain the object wanted' (ibid.: 72), in order to show that changes in prices, although they cannot depend on autonomous changes in the proportion between the extent of supply and demand, do, however, depend on changes in their relative strength.

In observing that an increase in the intensity of demand (an increase, that is to say, in the price that at least some of the buyers are prepared to pay) is a necessary condition if a reduction of the quantity supplied or an increase in the cost of production is actually to cause an increase in price, Malthus (ibid.: 67ff) concludes that each change in price is determined by changes in the intensity of demand. This, however, far from providing a theory of natural values, amounts to describing in greater detail the movements of market prices and the role of supply and demand in affecting them, as well as in the process of adjustment of natural price to a new level following a change in its determinants.

But according to Malthus 'the great principle of demand and supply is called into action to determine what Adam Smith calls natural prices as well as market prices' (ibid.: 75). To give substance to this statement he lists a number of cases in which price permanently diverges from cost of production, thus maintaining that the latter cannot be considered as the general principle determining it. The cases Malthus mentions are monopolized commodities (ibid.: 73); raw products (which have widely different prices according to the different seasons even if their cost of production has remained the same, ibid.: 73–4); or, as regards the price of labour, the effect of poor rates in England, which, by inducing a greater supply of labourers than would be induced by the real cost of rearing a family, imply that real wage can diverge for long periods from the cost of production of labour (ibid.: 77). He also mentions as a case in point the artificial value of bank notes, which is totally independent of their cost of production (ibid.: 78). 'The principle of demand and supply' – Malthus concludes – 'is the paramount regulator of the prices of labour as well as of commodities, not only temporarily but permanently' (ibid.: 241).

In his comments Ricardo notes the peculiar nature of Malthus's examples, which implies that no general theory of value can be derived from them. He restates the fundamental principle of reproducibility that holds for the generality of commodities as well as for labour. This principle obviously cannot apply to such particular cases as paper money, nor to monopolized commodities for which scarcity may be artificially induced, but only to the circumstances when 'every one is free to supply the commodities in such quantity as he chuses' (*Works*, II: 48–9; see the whole passage for a detailed critique of Malthus's examples). Once the limitations supposed by Malthus are removed, and the general case considered, Malthus's analysis proves unable to provide a solid basis for the demand-and-supply principle as determining natural prices.

On the 'neoclassical' interpretation of Ricardo

Given Ricardo's uncompromising critique of the demand-and-supply principle and of the underlying idea that scarcity is a general attribute of economic goods and of labour, it seems particularly difficult to contend, following some interpreters (Hicks and Hollander, 1977; Samuelson, 1978; Hollander, 1979 and 2011), that his analysis was an (albeit primitive and incomplete) attempt at founding a demand-and-supply theory of value and distribution, and to regard him as a sort of early neoclassical economist.

In neoclassical theories the principle of scarcity is the founding principle for the determination of value and distribution by means of demand and supply. This has been achieved, once reproducibility is recognized as a general attribute of commodities, by conferring the quality of scarcity to resources: in the words of Cassel: 'That a commodity is reproducible only means, of course, that its scarcity can be ascribed to the absolute scarcity, from the viewpoint of production, of other commodities. These absolutely scarce commodities we call the primary factors of production' (Cassel, 1918: 147). The dependence of demand of commodities on price has been restated on the firmer basis of the analysis of individual preferences and the maximizing behaviour of agents, thus giving rise to the construction of definite decreasing demand functions for goods; while the non-horizontality of the supply curves for goods, which is necessarily required if demand and supply are to determine price, reflects the influence that the changes in the quantities produced of the commodities exert on the demand of scarce factors of production and thus on distribution (Garegnani, 1983: 310). This implies that the demand-and-supply determination of prices of commodities necessarily rests on the demand-and-supply determination of prices of factors (Garegnani, 1990b: 288). In such a framework, the possibility of substitution among factors of production – either direct or indirect – is essential to the attainment of equilibrium. In fact, if consumers' tastes were such as to imply fixed proportions of the various goods in consumption regardless of price changes, and if at the same time the production of the various goods required fixed proportions of factors of production regardless of changes in distribution, no equilibrium would ever be possible except by chance, because no mechanism would ensure the existence of a set of prices bringing demand and supply to equality. As Cassel ([1918] 1932: 144) synthesizes:

> The demand for a product represents an attempt to attract certain factors of production to a particular use. Conflicting with this attempt are similar attempts in the form of demands for the other products. There arises in this way a struggle for the relatively scarce factors of production, which is decided in the exchange economy by placing uniform prices on the factors, which prices in turn determine the prices of the products and thus form a means of effecting the necessary restriction of demand.

The interpretation of Ricardian economics in neoclassical terms is carried out by Samuelson and Hollander by superimposing on Ricardo's analysis some elements that seem to be profoundly extraneous to it: Samuelson (1978) maintains that Ricardo's lack of consideration of the influence of demand on prices is a fallacy in his analysis and that some form of substitution between factors must exist, as would allegedly be proven by the hypothesis of diminishing returns to land. Hollander (1979), on the other hand, tries to convey the idea that in Ricardo there is simultaneous determination of prices, distribution and quantities by means of demand and supply by interpreting the process of profit rate equalization among sectors as entailing change in factor proportions at the level of the economy thus affecting distribution. When trying to make explicit Ricardo's determination of wage by means of demand and supply, however, Hollander refers to 'secular tendencies', that is, the interaction between accumulation, changes in population and wage which he interprets in terms of definite functional relationships of the neoclassical type (see Hollander, 1983 and 2011). In this respect, Stirati (2011b) notes that a proper demand-and-supply determination of wage would require identifying demand and supply functions of the static type, that is, referring to given population and given stage of capital accumulation, which are not to be found in Ricardo owing to the absence in his analysis of the neoclassical mechanisms of substitution, while the dynamic equilibrium would not guarantee the tendency to full employment (see especially p. 321).

Both Samuelson and Hollander seem to regard the simultaneous determination of prices and quantities through the demand and supply functions as the only possible way of studying the relationships between demand, quantity and price, and thus fail to recognize the characteristic Ricardian method of separating the determination of relative prices and the rate of profit from that of the real wage and outputs, the latter being taken as given when determining the former variables (Garegnani, 1990a). Such a method does not imply excluding an indirect influence of demand on prices, through its effects on the quantity produced and thus, possibly, on the difficulty of production: given the complexity of the relations involved and the impossibility of representing them through definite quantitative functions, however, Ricardo and the classical economists typically used a two-stage procedure for analysing these kinds of influences (see Garegnani, 1990b).

What 'neoclassical' interpreters of Ricardo reveal, in general, is the difficulty of envisaging the structure of classical theory as distinct from, and alternative to, neoclassical theories (Garegnani, 1990a). Classical economists, and Ricardo among them, in analysing the central question of the production and distribution of the economy's surplus, did not regard prices and wage as expression of the scarcity of commodities and of labour relative to their demand, but rather as establishing the conditions of their reproducibility.

ANTONELLA PALUMBO

See also:

Comparative Advantage; Competition; Exchange Value and Utility; Malthus–Ricardo Debate; Natural and Market Prices; Ricardo's Four Magic Numbers; Say, Jean-Baptiste, and Ricardo.

References

Bharadwaj, K. (1978), 'The subversion of classical analysis: Alfred Marshall's early writing on value', *Cambridge Journal of Economics*, **2**(3), 253–71.

Bharadwaj, K. (1987), 'Wages in classical economics', in J. Eatwell, M. Milgate and P. Newman (eds), *The New Palgrave Dictionary of Economics*, London: Macmillan.

Cassel, G. ([1918] 1932), *The Theory of Social Economy*, revised translation of 5th German edition, 1932, New York: Harcourt, Brace & Company; reprinted 1967 by A.M. Kelley.

Garegnani, P. (1983), 'The classical theory of wages and the role of demand schedules in the determination of relative prices', *American Economic Review*, **73**(2), 309–13.

Garegnani, P. (1990a), 'Sraffa: classical versus marginalist analysis', in K. Bharadwaj and B. Schefold (eds), *Essays on Piero Sraffa*, London: Routledge.

Garegnani, P. (1990b), 'Revisionist findings on Sraffa. Comment', in K. Bharadwaj and B. Schefold (eds), *Essays on Piero Sraffa*, London: Routledge.

Hicks, J. and S. Hollander (1977), 'Mr. Ricardo and the moderns', *Quarterly Journal of Economics*, **91**(3), 351–69.

Hollander, S. (1979), *The Economics of David Ricardo*, Toronto: University of Toronto Press.

Hollander, S. (1983), 'On the interpretation of Ricardian economics: the assumptions regarding wages', *American Economic Review*, **73**(2), 314–18.

Hollander, S. (2011), 'Sraffa and the interpretation of Ricardo. The Marxian dimension', in R. Ciccone, C. Gehrke and G. Mongiovi (eds), *Sraffa and Modern Economics, Vol. I*, London: Routledge.

Lauderdale, J. Maitland, Earl of (1804), *An Inquiry into the Nature and Origin of Public Wealth*, Edinburgh: Longman, Hurst, Rees, Orme and Brown.

Levrero, E.S. (2011), 'Marx on absolute and relative wages and the modern theory of distribution', *Review of Political Economy*, **25**(1), 91–116.

Locke, J. ([1691] 1727), 'Some considerations of the consequences of lowering of interest, and raising the value of money. In a letter sent to a Member of Parliament', *The Works, of John Locke, Volume II*, London: Rivington.

Malthus, T.R. (1820), *Principles of Political Economy*, London: John Murray.

Samuelson, P.A. (1978), 'The canonical classical model of political economy', *Journal of Economic Literature*, **16**(4), 1415–34.

Say, J.-B. (1803). *Traité d'économie politique ou simple exposition de la manière dont se forment, se distribuent et se consomment les richesses*, 1st edition, Paris: Deterville.

Say, J.-B. ([1803] 2006), *Traité d'économie politique ou simple exposition de la manière dont se forment, se distribuent et se consomment les richesses*, variorum edition, (ed.) C. Mouchot, Introduction and Notes by J.-P. Potier, J.-M. Servet, P. Steiner and A. Tiran, Paris: Economica.

Say, J.-B. (1814), *Traité d'économie politique ou simple exposition de la manière dont se forment, se distribuent et se consomment les richesses*, 2nd edition, Paris: Renouard.

Say, J.-B. ([1819] 1821), *A Treatise on Political Economy, or the Production, Distribution, and Consumption of Wealth*, translated by C.R. Prinsep from the 4th (1819) French edition, Boston, MA: Wells and Lilly.

Smith, A. ([1776] 1976), *An Inquiry into the Nature and Causes of the Wealth of Nations*, in *The Glasgow Edition of the Works and Correspondence of Adam Smith*, (eds) R.H. Campbell, A.S. Skinner and W.B. Todd, Oxford: Clarendon Press.

Stirati, A. (2011a), 'Interpretations of the classics. The theory of wages', in R. Ciccone, C. Gehrke and G. Mongiovi (eds), *Sraffa and Modern Economics, Vol. I*, London: Routledge.

Stirati, A. (2011b), 'A comment on Hollander on Sraffa and the "Marxian dimension"', in R. Ciccone, C. Gehrke and G. Mongiovi (eds), *Sraffa and Modern Economics, Vol. I*, London: Routledge.

Vianello, F. (1989), 'Natural (or normal) prices: some pointers', *Political Economy. Studies in the Surplus Approach*, **5**(2), 89–105.

Dmitriev, Vladimir Karpovich, on Ricardo

The Russian mathematical economist Vladimir Karpovich Dmitriev (1868–1913) was a private scholar who wrote several survey articles and book reviews as well as three major essays on economic theory. Born near Smolensk, Dmitriev studied medicine and political economy at the University of Moscow. In 1898 he published an essay (in Russian) on Ricardo's theory of value, followed in 1902 by two further essays on Cournot's theory of competition and on the theory of marginal utility. In 1904 the three essays were published together in a book entitled *Economic Essays. First Series: Attempt at an Organic Synthesis of the Labour Theory of Value and the Theory of Marginal Utility*. A French translation of this collection of essays was published in 1968 and an English translation in 1974; subsequently, the three essays were also translated into Italian, Spanish and German (see Schütte, 2003).

In his first essay of 1898, entitled 'The theory of value of David Ricardo. An attempt at a rigorous analysis', Dmitriev made important contributions to classical economic theory. In particular, he demonstrated that (a) prices can be decomposed into wages and profits via a 'reduction to dated quantities of labour'; (b) relative prices are proportional to relative labour values only with zero profits or with 'equal organic composition'; (c) Ricardo's concept of the inverse relationship between the general rate of profits and the real wage rate, given the technical conditions of production, that is, the wage–profit relationship, can be given a precise analytical expression; and (d) the data of Ricardo's approach (i.e., the real wage rate and the technical conditions of production in the wages goods industry) suffice to determine simultaneously relative prices and the general rate of profits.

Reduction to dated quantities of labour

Dmitriev investigated first how the total amount of labour expended in the production of a commodity can be ascertained. He considered a single product system that can be represented, in matrix notation, as:

$$\mathbf{v} = \mathbf{l} + \mathbf{A}\mathbf{v}, \tag{1}$$

where **A** is the $n \times n$ matrix of commodity inputs, **l** is the n-vector of direct labour inputs, and **v** is the n-vector of direct and indirect labour inputs. Then:

$$\mathbf{v} = \mathbf{l} + \mathbf{Al} + \mathbf{A}^2 \mathbf{l} + \ldots + \mathbf{A}^t \mathbf{l} + \ldots, \tag{2}$$

or

$$\mathbf{v} = \mathbf{l}_0 + \mathbf{l}_1 + \mathbf{l}_2 + \ldots + \mathbf{l}_t + \ldots,$$

where $\mathbf{l}_t = \mathbf{A}^t \mathbf{l}$. Dmitriev set out the simultaneous equation system (1) and concluded that since there are as many equations as unknowns **v** is determined, given **A** and **l**. He thus disposed of the common misconception that a 'historical digression' would be required in order to ascertain the total labour contents of commodities: 'We can always find the total sum of the labour directly and indirectly expended on the production of any product *under present-day production conditions . . .* the fact that all capital under *present-day* conditions is itself produced with the assistance of other capital in no way hinders a precise solution of the problem' (Dmitriev, [1904] 1974: 44; original emphasis).

However, in the following, Dmitriev then assumed for simplicity that the series of dated quantities of labour in (2) is finite. He thus implicitly adopted what has been called an 'Austrian' perspective: Dmitriev's representation of production processes in terms of finite series of dated quantities of labour corresponds to Austrian processes of the 'flow-input/point-output' type, and presupposes the non-existence of basic commodities (Kurz and Salvadori, 1995: 176–8). Within this framework, Dmitriev then confirmed a proposition that had originally been suggested by Smith and then had been advanced also by Ricardo, and that had been emphatically rejected by Marx: namely, that the price of every commodity can be entirely resolved into wages and profits without leaving a commodity residue. Following the classical authors, wages are assumed to be paid *ante factum* and prices are explained in terms of a reduction to (a finite stream of) dated quantities of labour, that is:

$$\mathbf{p} = (1+r)\, w\, [\mathbf{l} + (1+r)\mathbf{Al} + (1+r)^2\mathbf{A}^2\mathbf{l} + \ldots + (1+r)^k\mathbf{A}^k\mathbf{l}], \tag{3}$$

or:

$$\mathbf{p} = (1+r)\, w\, [\mathbf{l}_0 + (1+r)\, \mathbf{l}_1 + (1+r)^2\, \mathbf{l}_2 + \ldots + (1+r)^k\, \mathbf{l}_k].$$

With this proof Dmitriev initiated a widespread misunderstanding of the precise nature of Marx's objection, which concerns the fact that Ricardo's (and Smith's) implicit adoption of an 'Austrian' production framework implies the non-existence of a finite maximum rate of profits. As Marx pointed out, Ricardo's adoption of the simplifying assumption he typically entertained in his observations on wages and profits that the advanced capital consists only of, or can be entirely reduced to, past and present wages, misled him into contending erroneously that the rate of profits depends only on proportional wages (see Gehrke and Kurz, 2006 for a more detailed discussion of this point).

Proportionality of prices and labour values

Dmitriev next turned to the investigation of relative prices, which in his framework are given by:

$$\frac{p_i}{p_j} = \frac{(1+r)w e_i^T [1 + (1+r)\mathbf{A}\mathbf{l} + (1+r)^2\mathbf{A}^2\mathbf{l} + \ldots + (1+r)^k\mathbf{A}^k\mathbf{l}]}{(1+r)w e_j^T [1 + (1+r)\mathbf{A}\mathbf{l} + (1+r)^2\mathbf{A}^2\mathbf{l} + \ldots + (1+r)^k\mathbf{A}^k\mathbf{l}]},$$
(4)

or:

$$\frac{p_i}{p_j} = \frac{l_{i0} + (1+r)l_{i1} + (1+r)^2 l_{i2} + \ldots + (1+r)^k l_{ik}}{l_{j0} + (1+r)l_{j1} + (1+r)^2 l_{j2} + \ldots + (1+r)^k l_{jk}},$$

where $l_{it} = e_i^T l_t$. Dmitriev's analysis confirmed Ricardo's finding that relative prices are proportional to relative labour values in two special cases only: (a) when the series of dated quantities of labour are linearly dependent pairwise, that is, when the commodities exhibit 'identical organic composition'; and (b) when the rate of profits is zero.

Wage–profit relationship

Dmitriev next turned to the analysis of the general rate of profits and natural prices. He praised Ricardo for having clearly specified the factors that determine the general rate of profits, that is, (a) the real wage rate and (b) the technical conditions of production in the industries producing wage goods or means of production used (directly or indirectly) in the production of wage goods: 'Ricardo's immortal contribution was his brilliant solution of this seemingly insoluble problem' ([1904] 1974: 58). Dmitriev suggested that Ricardo had accomplished the solution of this problem because he recognized 'that there is one production equation by means of which we may determine the magnitude of r directly (i.e., without having recourse for assistance to the other equations)' (ibid.: 59). In Dmitriev's reading, Ricardo had adopted the simplifying assumption that the real wage basket consists only of corn, that is:

$$w = p_c c,$$
(5)

where c is the amount and p_c the price of corn, respectively. In this case the rate of profits was determined from the price equation of the corn industry alone, without recourse to the price system, since:

$$p_c = (1+r)\, p_c c e_c^T [1 + (1+r)\mathbf{A}\mathbf{l} + (1+r)^2\mathbf{A}^2\mathbf{l} + \ldots + (1+r)^k\mathbf{A}^k\mathbf{l}],$$
(6)

or:

$$\frac{1}{c} = (1+r)e_c^T\,[\mathbf{l}_0 + (1+r)\,\mathbf{l}_1 + (1+r)^2\,\mathbf{l}_2 + \ldots + (1+r)^k\,\mathbf{l}_k],$$

and therefore:

$$r = f\,(l_{c0}, l_{c1}, l_{c2}, \ldots, l_{ck};\, c),$$

where $l_{ct} = e_c^T l_t$. Dmitriev thus anticipated the so-called 'corn-ratio' interpretation, which was later suggested by Piero Sraffa as providing the rational foundation of Ricardo's early theory of profits (*Works*, I: xxxiii):

> The essence of Ricardo's views of the profit rate may be briefly summarized: given an industry where production costs may be reduced *ultimately* to the same product *A* obtained as a result of the production process, the *profit rate* in that industry is determined *independently of the price of the product*. Now, if the costs of all other industries are also reducible *ultimately* to product *A*, the profit rate established in that industry will also prevail (because entrepreneurs move from less profitable to more profitable industries) in all other branches of industry, so that the profit embodied in the price of all products will itself be determined independently of market conditions. (Dmitriev, [1904] 1974: 213–14; original emphasis)

In the following, Dmitriev then considered the case of many wage goods and vindicated Ricardo's proposition – which had been disputed by Marx – that the general rate of profits is not affected by changes in the conditions of production of the 'non-basic' industries, that is, industries that produced neither wage goods nor means of production used directly or indirectly in the wage goods industries. Moreover, he demonstrated that Ricardo's concept of the inverse relationship between the general rate of profits and the real wage rate, given the technical conditions of production, that is, the wage–profit relationship, could be given a precise analytical expression within his framework.

Simultaneous determination of prices and distribution
Dmitriev then turned to the refutation of an objection that had been raised, amongst others, by Léon Walras against Ricardo's theory of prices and distribution. According to Walras ([1874] 1954, Lesson 40: §368), the number of unknowns exceeds the number of equations in the classical approach to value and distribution, and Ricardo's 'cost of production explanation of prices' therefore involved circular reasoning, 'defining prices from prices' (ibid.). Dmitriev deserves the credit for having demonstrated that the data of Ricardo's approach, that is, the real wage rate and the technical conditions of production, suffice to determine relative prices and the general rate of profits simultaneously.

Dmitriev's formalization of Ricardo's theory of prices and distribution was a major source of inspiration for Ladislaus von Bortkiewicz, who praised his essay of 1898 as a 'remarkable work', which 'bears evidence of an exceptional theoretical talent and presents something really new' (Bortkiewicz [1906–7] 1952: 20, 31n). As von Bortkiewicz pointed out, Dmitriev introduced the idea of solving systems of simultaneous equations into the classical analysis of prices and distribution and greatly contributed to the clarification of the analytical structure of classical economic theory.

However, while Dmitriev praised Ricardo for a number of theoretical achievements, he also considered his analysis of prices and distribution incomplete and in part unsatisfactory. This concerns in particular Ricardo's theory of competition and his neglect of the role of demand in the determination of prices. The starting point of Dmitriev's criticism is the (correct) observation that Ricardo had failed to provide a theory of the 'price determination of products under monopoly' ([1904] 1974: 214) – a lacuna that he suggested could be filled by having recourse to Cournot's analysis of monopoly. However, in Dmitriev's view Ricardo's analysis cannot be considered fully satisfactory even for commodities produced in competitive conditions, because it unduly neglects the role of demand in the determination of prices. With regard to Ricardo's theory of differential rent, Dmitriev rightly observed that it could be generalized from agriculture to all branches in which natural or legal restrictions force some producers to have recourse to more costly production methods than others. In Dmitriev's view:

> Ricardo gives us an impeccable analysis of the law governing the value of products when individual portions of these products are produced with different production costs ... [B]ut this analysis definitely does not prove, as Ricardo assumes, that the value of such products is not ultimately dependent on the conditions of supply and demand and will tend to settle at a level exclusively dependent on production conditions. (Ibid.: 87)

Having established that 'demand matters' in the determination of prices of commodities produced under conditions of monopoly and of non-constant costs, Dmitriev then set out to show, in his second essay, that this also holds true for commodities that can be supplied in unlimited quantities at constant costs in competitive conditions. For this purpose, Dmitriev critically examined Cournot's theory of competition and made some steps towards the development of a theory of competition with strategic interaction. He thereby anticipated some elements of Chamberlin's approach to imperfect competition theory and showed in particular that a homogeneous oligopoly has a determinate solution that corresponds to an implicit collusion (Schütte, 2003: 160–72).

Having argued that the Ricardian theory of prices based on necessary production costs is invalid even with constant production costs, Dmitriev in his third essay turned to the investigation of the influence of the 'conditions of consumption' on prices. This essay is mainly of interest from the perspective of the history of economic thought, because Dmitriev provided a detailed account of the genesis of marginal utility theory and disputed the occurrence of a major break in the development of economic theory in terms of a 'marginal revolution' in the 1870s. He argued that important contributions to marginal utility theory had been made already much earlier by economists such as Gossen, Senior, Rossi, Dupuit, and Molinari, and that, indeed, 'we find *all the information* needed for the construction of a *finished* theory of marginal utility in the work of such an "old" economist as Galiani' ([1904] 1974: 182). He also maintained that '*the Austrian school* as such (Menger, Böhm-Bawerk, Wieser, and others) *added very little* (unless much significance is given to the introduction of new terms) *to what had been done before* them *for the solution of the problem*' (ibid.: 181; original emphasis). Important contributions had only been made by economists who used the mathematical method, including 'Walras (who may justifiably be regarded as the creator of marginal utility theory), Launhardt, Auspitz and Lieben and Jevons' (ibid.: 182). Dmitriev neatly summarized these contributions, but he showed no awareness that utility need not be cardinally measurable and did not contribute to the further development of marginal utility theory.

Although Dmitriev aimed at 'an organic synthesis' of classical and marginal utility theory, he also wanted to retain the fundamental asymmetry in the treatment of the distributive variables that characterizes the classical approach to economic analysis (Skourtos, 1985). He explicitly rejected the view, advocated by authors like von Böhm-Bawerk, that the level of the real wage rate was determined by economic laws, arguing instead for a determination by subsistence requirements or else in terms of a bargaining theory. He insisted that the investigation of the conditions affecting the level of real wages 'falls outside the scope of political economy' ([1904] 1974: 74). He thus sought to integrate demand schedules derived from marginal utility theory into Ricardo's theory of price determination while preserving the fundamental asymmetry of the classical approach to value and distribution: 'factor prices' are not explained in a neoclassical fashion, but in the manner of the surplus approach elaborated by Ricardo.

CHRISTIAN GEHRKE

See also:

Bortkiewicz, Ladislaus von, on Ricardo; Sraffa, Piero, on Ricardo; Tozer, John Edward, on Ricardo; Whewell, William, on Ricardo.

References

Bortkiewicz, L. von ([1906–7] 1952), 'Value and price in the Marxian system', *International Economic Papers*, **2**, 5–60; English translation of Parts 2 and 3 of Ladislaus von Bortkiewicz (1906–07), 'Wertrechnung und Preisrechnung im Marxschen System', *Archiv für Sozialwissenschaften und Sozialpolitik*, **23**(1906): 1–50, **25**(1907): 10–51 and 445–88.

Dmitriev, V.K. ([1904] 1968), *Essais économiques. Esquisse de synthèse organique de la théorie de la valeur-travail et de la théorie de l'utilité marginale*; French translation of a collection of Dmitriev's essays in Russian, (ed.) with an introduction by A. Zauberman and a postface by H. Denis, Paris: Edition du CNRS.

Dmitriev, V.K. ([1904] 1974), *Economic Essays on Value, Competition and Utility*; English translation of a collection of Dmitriev's essays in Russian, (ed.) with an introduction by D.M. Nuti, Cambridge, UK: Cambridge University Press.

Gehrke, C. and H.D. Kurz (2006), 'Sraffa on von Bortkiewicz: reconstructing the classical theory of value and distribution', *History of Political Economy*, **38**(1), 91–149.

Kurz, H.D. and N. Salvadori (1995), *Theory of Production. A Long-Period Analysis*, Cambridge, UK: Cambridge University Press.

Schütte, F. (2003), 'Die ökonomischen Studien V.K. Dmitrievs. Ein Beitrag zur Interpretation und theoriehistorischen Würdigung unter besonderer Berücksichtigung der russischen Volkswirtschaftslehre', doctoral dissertation submitted to the Faculty of Economic Sciences at the Technical University of Chemnitz, accessed 22 December 2014 at http://archiv.tu-chemnitz.de/pub/2003/0110.

Skourtos, M. (1985), *Der 'Neoricardianismus'. V.K. Dmitriev und die Kontinuität in der klassischen Tradition*, Pfaffenweiler: Centaurus Verlagsanstalt.

Walras, L. ([1874] 1954), *Elements of Pure Economics*, London: Allen and Unwin; English translation, (ed.) W. Jaffé, of the definitive edition of L. Walras (1874), *Eléments d'économie politique pure*, Lausanne: Corbaz.

Endogenous Growth

The problem of economic growth was one of David Ricardo's major concerns. Ricardo's argument about what he called the 'natural' course of the economy contemplated an economic system in which capital accumulates, the population grows, but there is no technical progress: the latter is set aside. Hence, the argument is based on the assumption that the set of methods of production from which cost-minimizing producers can choose is given and constant. Profits are viewed as a residual income based on the surplus product left after the used up means of production and the wage goods in the support of workers have been deducted from the social product (net of rents). Assuming that the marginal propensity to accumulate out of profits, s, is given and constant, a 'classical' accumulation function can be formulated:

$$g = \begin{cases} s(r - r_{min}) & \text{if } r \geq r_{min} \\ 0 & \text{if } r \leq r_{min} \end{cases}$$

where $r_{min} \geq 0$ is the minimum level of profitability that, if reached, will arrest accumulation (see *Works*, I: 120).

A given and constant real wage rate
Assuming for simplicity a given and constant real wage rate, Ricardo's view of the long-run relationship between profitability and accumulation and thus growth (in the absence of technical progress) can be illustrated in terms of Figure 6, which is a diagram used by Kaldor (1956). The curve *CEGH* is the marginal productivity of labour-cum-capital; it is decreasing since land is scarce: when labour-cum-capital increases, either less fertile

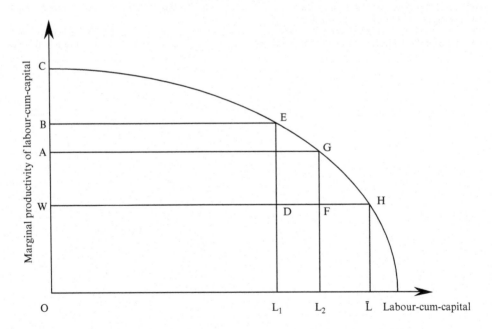

Figure 6   Land as an indispensable resource

qualities of land must be cultivated or the same qualities of land must be cultivated with processes that require less land per unit of product, but are more costly in terms of labour-cum-capital. Let the real wage rate equal OW. Then, if the amount of labour-cum-capital applied is L_1, the area $OCEL_1$ gives the product, $OWDL_1$ gives total capital employed, and BCE total rent. Profit is determined as a residual and corresponds to the rectangular $WBED$. As a consequence, the *rate* of profit can be determined as the ratio of the areas of two rectangles that have the same basis and, therefore, it equals the ratio WB/OW. Let us now consider the case in which the amount of labour-cum-capital is larger, that is, L_2. Then $OCGL_2$ gives the product, $OWFL_2$ the capital, ACG the rent, and $WAGF$ profits. The rate of profit has fallen to WA/OW. Obviously, if a positive profit rate implies a positive growth rate (i.e., $r_{min} = 0$), the economy will expand until labour-cum-capital has reached the level $\bar{L}$ At that point the profit rate is equal to zero and so is the growth rate. The system has arrived at a stationary state. Growth has come to an end because profitability has.

The required size of the workforce is considered to be essentially generated by the accumulation process itself. In other words, labour power is treated as a kind of producible commodity. It differs from other commodities in that it is not produced in a capitalistic way by a special industry on a par with other industries, but is the result of the interplay between the generative behaviour of the working population and socioeconomic conditions. In the most simple conceptualization possible, labour power is seen to be in elastic supply at a given real wage rate (in terms of the number of a given basket of 'necessaries'). Increasing the number of baskets available in the support of workers involves a proportional increase of the workforce. In this view the rate of growth of labour supply adjusts to any given rate of growth of labour demand without necessitating a variation in the real wage rate. Labour can thus put no limit on growth because it is 'generated' within the growth process. The only limit to growth can come from other non-accumulable factors of production: as Ricardo and others made clear, these factors are natural resources in general and land in particular. In other words, in Ricardo, there is only endogenous growth. This growth is bound to lose momentum as the scarcity of natural factors of production makes itself felt in terms of extensive and intensive diminishing returns. (Technical change is, of course, envisaged to counteract these tendencies.)

For the sake of the argument let us discuss Ricardian theory without the problem of land. If land of the best quality was available in abundance, that is, it is a free good, then the graph giving the marginal productivity of labour-cum-capital would be a horizontal line and therefore the rate of profit would be constant whatever the amount of labour-cum-capital. This case is illustrated in Figure 7. As a consequence, the growth rate would also be constant: the system could grow forever at a rate that equals the given rate of profit times the propensity to accumulate. Ricardo was perfectly aware of this implication:

> Accumulation of capital has a tendency to lower profits. Why? Because every accumulation is attended with increased difficulty in obtaining food, unless it is accompanied with improvements in agriculture, in which case it has no tendency to diminish profits. If there were no increased difficulty, profits would never fall, because there are no other limits to the profitable production of manufactures but the rise of wages. *If with every accumulation of capital we could tack a piece of fresh fertile land to our Island, profits would never fall.* (*Works*, VI: 162; emphasis added)

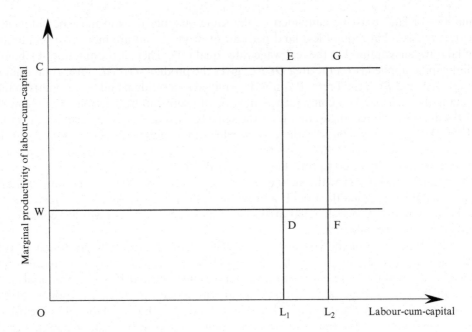

Figure 7   Land as a free good

And again:

> Profits do not necessarily fall with the increase of the quantity of capital because the demand for capital is infinite and is governed by the same law as population itself. They are both checked by the rise in the price of food, and the consequent increase in the price of labour. If there were no such rise, what could prevent population and capital from increasing without limit? (Ibid.: 301)

However, the assumption that land (of the best quality) is available in unlimited quantity cannot be taken too seriously. With the system growing forever, the point will surely come where land of the best quality becomes scarce. This brings us to another constellation in which the rate of profit need not vanish as capital accumulates. The constellation under consideration bears a close resemblance to a case discussed in the economics of 'exhaustible' resources, that is, the case in which there is an ultimate 'backstop technology'. For example, some exhaustible resources are used to produce energy. In addition, there is solar energy that may be considered an undepletable resource. A technology based on the use of solar energy defines the backstop technology mentioned. Let us translate this assumption into the context of a Ricardian model with land.

The case under consideration would correspond to a situation in which 'land', although useful in production, is not indispensable. In other words, there is a technology that allows the production of the commodity without any 'land' input; this is the backstop technology. With continuous substitutability between labour-cum-capital and land, the marginal productivity of labour-cum-capital would be continuously decreasing, but it would be bounded from below. This case is illustrated in Figure 8, with the dashed line giving the lower boundary. In this case the profit rate and thus the growth rate would

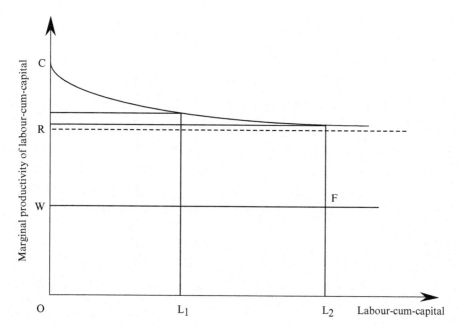

Figure 8 A backstop technology

be falling, but they could never fall below certain levels, which are positive. The system would grow indefinitely at a rate of growth that would asymptotically approach the product of the given saving rate times the value of the (lower) boundary of the profit rate. In Figure 8 the latter is given by *WR/OW*.

Finally, we may illustrate the case of increasing returns to labour-cum-capital (see Figure 9), as it was discussed, following Adam Smith's analysis of the division of labour, by authors such as Allyn Young (1928) and Nicholas Kaldor (1957). For the sake of simplicity, taking the wage rate as given and constant, the rate of profit and the rate of growth are bound to rise as more labour-cum-capital is employed. (In Figure 9 it is assumed that there is an upper boundary to the rise in output per unit of labour-cum-capital given by *OR*.) In order to be able to preserve the notion of a uniform rate of profit, it has to be assumed that the increasing returns are external to the firm and exclusively connected with the expansion of the market as a whole and the social division of labour. This implies that whereas in the case of decreasing returns due to the scarcity of land (see Figures 6 and 8) the product was given by the area under the marginal productivity curve, now the product associated with any given amount of labour-cum-capital is larger than or equal to that amount times the corresponding level of output per unit of labour-cum-capital. It is larger if there is still scarce land; it is equal to it if there is not. In any case, the sum of profits and wages equals the product of the given amount of labour-cum-capital times the corresponding level of output per unit of labour-cum-capital. Let $x = f(L, L^*)$ be the product of the last unit of labour-cum-capital when L represents the amount of labour-cum-capital employed and the division of labour is artificially kept fixed at the level appropriate when the amount of labour-cum-capital employed is L^*. Obviously, $f(L, L^*)$ as a function of L alone is either decreasing as in Figures 6 and 8

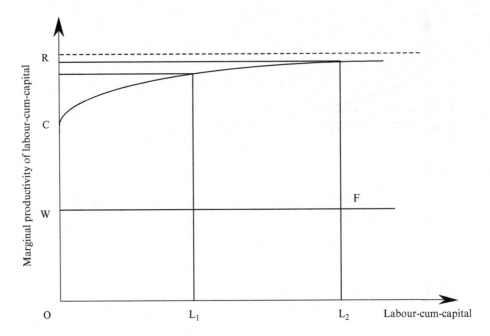

Figure 9   Increasing returns

(if land is scarce) or constant as in Figure 7 (if land is not scarce). The product at L^* equals $\int_0^{L^*} f(L, L^*)\,dL$, that is, the area under the curve $f(L, L^*)$ in the range $[0, L^*]$. If:

$$\frac{\partial f(L, L^*)}{\partial L^*} > -\frac{\partial f(L, L^*)}{\partial L} \text{ for } L = L^*,$$

then the curve $x = f(L, L)$, which is the curve depicted in Figure 9, is increasing, but the product is, as stated above, larger than or equal to the sum of profits and wages, which equals the product of the given amount of labour-cum-capital times the corresponding level of output per unit of labour-cum-capital.

Hence, in the case in which labour-cum-capital is L_2, the product is given by the corresponding rectangle. As a consequence, the product is larger than the area under the marginal productivity curve. The cases of decreasing and increasing returns are therefore not symmetrical. It goes without saying that in this case a rising real wage rate need not involve a falling general rate of profit.

To conclude, it must be stressed again that the 'Ricardesque' patterns of endogenous growth illustrated in Figures 6–9 are intimately related to the fact that labour is envisaged as a commodity that is in some sense 'produced' by using corn and nothing else. The real wage rate is considered 'on the same footing as the fuel for the engines or the feed for the cattle' (Sraffa, 1960: 9). The straight line WF in the above figures can indeed be interpreted as the 'marginal cost function' related to the 'production' of labour. Put in a nutshell, the 'secret' of the endogeneity of growth for classical authors consisted in the assumption of a 'technology'-producing labour.

The real wage rate as a function of the growth rate
The assumption of a given and constant real wage rate that is independent of the rate of growth of the demand for 'hands' can, of course, only be justified as a first step in the analysis. In fact, in some of his discussions with Thomas Robert Malthus, Ricardo appears to have adopted this assumption precisely for the sake of convenience. There is clear evidence that he did not consider it a stylized historical fact of long-term economic development. The relationship between the expansion of the economic system as a whole and the wage and population dynamics is far from simple in Ricardo, and actually is seen to differ both between different countries in the same period and between different periods of the same country, depending on a variety of historical, cultural and institutional factors. For example, Ricardo stressed that 'population may be so little stimulated by ample wages as to increase at the slowest rate – or *it may even go in a retrograde direction*' (*Works*, VIII: 169; emphasis added). And in his *Notes on Malthus* he insisted that 'population and necessaries are not necessarily linked together so intimately'; 'better education and improved habits' may break the population mechanism (*Works*, II: 115).

In this section we want to take account of the idea that higher rates of capital accumulation, which presuppose higher rates of growth of the workforce, correspond to higher levels of the real wage rate. We shall see that the basic logic of the argument that we have illustrated by means of the assumption of a fixed real wage rate remains essentially untouched: in normal conditions the pace at which capital accumulates regulates the pace at which labour grows.

Assume that higher growth rates of the labouring population require higher levels of the corn wage paid to workers. Higher wages, the usual argument goes, give workers and their families access to more abundant and better nutrition and medical services. This reduces infant mortality and increases the average length of life of workers. Let $\bar{w}$ be the wage rate that must be paid in order to keep the labouring population stationary, and let $w = w(g)$ be the wage rate to be paid in order for the labouring population to grow at the rate g. For the sake of simplicity we will assume $w(g):=\bar{w}(1 + g)$. Further, let the marginal productivity of labour-cum-capital (the *CEGH* curve of Figure 6) be the function $f(L)$. Then the rate of profits r turns out to be:

$$r = \frac{f(L) - \bar{w}(1 + g)}{\bar{w}(1 + g)}.$$

Hence:

$$g = s\left[\frac{f(L) - \bar{w}(1 + g)}{\bar{w}(1 + g)} - r_{min}\right],$$

from which we obtain a second degree equation in g:

$$\bar{w}g^2 + [1 + s(1 + r_{min})]\bar{w}g - s[f(L) - (1 + r_{min})\bar{w}] = 0,$$

which, for $f(L) > \bar{w}(1 + r_{min})$, has a positive and a negative solution. The negative solution is insignificant from an economic point of view because it is less than -1 and would thus be associated with a negative real wage rate. The positive solution is:

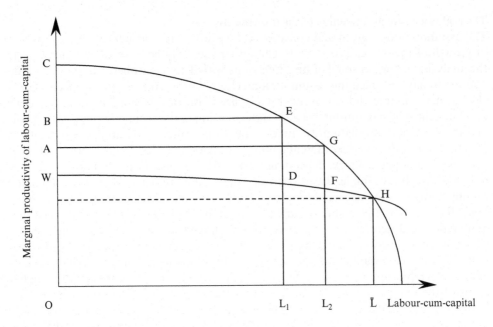

Figure 10   The wage rate as function of the growth rate

$$g = \frac{\sqrt{[1 - s(1 + r_{min})]^2 \overline{w}^2 + 4sf(L)\overline{w}} - [1 + s(1 + r_{min})]\overline{w}}{2\overline{w}}.$$

The result of this simple exercise is that the WDFH curve (see Figure 10 where, for simplicity, $r_{min} = 0$), which in Figure 6 was a horizontal straight line, becomes a decreasing curve:

$$\overline{w}(1 + g) = \frac{\sqrt{[1 - s(1 + r_{min})]^2 \overline{w}^2 + 4sf(L)\overline{w}} + [1 - s(1 + r_{min})]\overline{w}}{2}.$$

Note that if $f(L) > \overline{w}(1 + r_{min})$, then $\overline{w}(1 + g) > \overline{w}$, whereas if $f(L) = \overline{w}(1 + r_{min})$, then $\overline{w}(1 + g) = \overline{w}$. To conclude, the resulting modifications of Figure 10 with respect to Figure 6 do not change the substance of the view expounded above. They can also easily be replicated in Figures 8–9 (Figure 7 does not require any change).

Workers do not consume the agricultural product

In a quotation above (*Works*, VI: 162) Ricardo was fully aware of the fact that the 'accumulation of capital has a tendency to lower profits' because 'accumulation is attended with increased difficulty in obtaining food'. Therefore, there is another possible interpretation of Figure 7: workers consume only non-agricultural commodities, which are produced without using land either directly or indirectly. D'Alessandro and Salvadori (2008) analyse such a situation within a closed economy. In the model the products of the agricultural sector are taken to be consumed by capitalists and landlords. The rate of profit is determined only by the conditions of production of the industrial commodity, whereas the conditions of production of the agricultural commodity play a role only in the determination of the price of the agricultural commodity in terms of the industrial commodity.

A different situation is analysed by Salvadori and Signorino (forthcoming), who assume a small open economy confronted with given international prices in which workers consume only the agricultural commodity. They determine two thresholds in the course of the accumulation process. Only the agricultural commodity is produced prior to the lower threshold and the industrial commodity is obtained by international trade; the rate of profit and the rate of growth are declining over time. When the accumulation process takes place between the two thresholds, both agricultural and industrial commodities are produced but only the agricultural commodity is exported, nevertheless the quantity of the agricultural commodity produced is constant over time and any increase in the pace of the accumulation process is obtained through an increase in the production of the industrial commodity; both the rate of profit and the rate of growth are constant over time above the lower threshold. There is only one difference above the higher threshold: only the industrial commodity is exported.

These analyses belong to a strand of literature begun by a number of papers by Kurz and Salvadori (1998, 1999, 2006), who have argued that the structure of some of the models developed within the so-called new growth theory is substantially 'classical' rather than 'neoclassical' since it does not determine the rate of profit in terms of the demand and supply of capital, but in terms of a 'technology' producing, in the different approaches, 'human capital' or 'knowledge'. This procedure is analytically equivalent to the assumption adopted by classical economists, most notably Adam Smith and David Ricardo, of a real wage rate determined by the social conditions prevailing in the economy.

HEINZ D. KURZ AND NERI SALVADORI

See also:

Accumulation of Capital; Corn Model; Kaldor, Nicholas, on Ricardo; Mathematical Formulations of Ricardian Economics; Pasinetti, Luigi Lodovico, on Ricardo; Ricardian Dynamics; Technical Change.

References

D'Alessandro, S. and N. Salvadori (2008), 'Pasinetti versus Rebelo: two different models or just one?' *Journal of Economic Behavior & Organization*, **65**(3–4), 547–54.

Kaldor, N. (1956), 'Alternative theories of distribution', *Review of Economic Studies*, **23**(2), 83–100.

Kaldor, N. (1957), 'A model of economic growth', *Economic Journal*, **67**(268), 591–624.

Kurz, H.D. and N. Salvadori (1998), 'Endogenous growth models and the "classical" tradition', in H.D. Kurz and N. Salvadori (eds), *Understanding 'Classical' Economics. Studies in Long-Period Theory*, London and New York: Routledge, pp. 66–89.

Kurz, H.D. and N. Salvadori (1999), 'Theories of "endogenous" growth in historical perspective', in M.R. Sertel (ed.), *Contemporary Economic Issues. Proceedings of the Eleventh World Congress of the International Economic Association, Vol. 4, Economic Behaviour and Design*, London: Macmillan, pp. 225–61.

Kurz, H.D. and N. Salvadori (2006), 'Endogenous growth in a stylised "classical" model', in G. Stathakis and G. Vaggi (eds), *Economic Development and Social Change*, London: Routledge, pp. 106–24.

Salvadori, N. and R. Signorino (forthcoming), 'From stationary state to endogenous growth: international trade in a mathematical formulation of the Ricardian system', *Cambridge Journal of Economics*.

Sraffa, P. (1960), *Production of Commodities by Means of Commodities*, Cambridge, UK: Cambridge University Press.

Young, A. (1928), 'Increasing returns and economic progress', *Economic Journal*, **38**(152), 527–42.

Essay on Profits

In the aftermath of the Napoleonic Wars, the political debate in Great Britain was largely dominated by three hot topics: (1) the repeal of the Bank Restriction Act of 1797 and the resumption of specie payments, (2) the management of the huge war-induced public debt and (3) the expediency of new Corn Laws to protect British agriculturists against their lower-cost foreign competitors. Up to his untimely death in 1823, David Ricardo extensively contributed to all these issues through a whole panoply of literary products ranging from newspaper articles and letters to pamphlets and encyclopaedic articles, not to mention his Parliamentary speeches and, obviously, his magnum opus, *The Principles of Political Economy and Taxation*. From this perspective, it may be argued that the pamphlet *Essay on Profits* (1815) was the natural outcome of Ricardo's live interest in the main policy issues of his times. As noted by Piero Sraffa, Ricardo's *Essay on Profits* belongs to the rich pamphlet literature that blossomed 'in anticipation of the debates in the House of Commons on the question of the Corn Laws' (*Works*, IV: 4) and has aptly been described as '"an essay in persuasion", an appeal for a substantial degree of freedom for the corn trade' (Hollander, 1979: 118).

To fully appreciate the message of Ricardo's *Essay on Profits* his intellectual relationship with Malthus must be briefly recollected. Malthus and Ricardo became personal acquaintances, at Malthus's initiative, only in June 1811, after a controversy on the bullion question conducted exclusively on the press (*Works*, III: 11). In the summer of 1813 the focus of the Malthus–Ricardo correspondence begins to shift from monetary issues towards a theme, the relationship between capital accumulation and the rate of profits, closer to those subsequently dealt with in their 1815 essays. Exactly one year before the *Essay on Profits*, in February 1814 Ricardo wrote some (now missing) papers on the profits of capital in which, for the first time, the famous principle of the determining role of the agricultural rate of profits is explicitly stated – 'it is the profits of the farmer that regulate the profits of all other trades' (*Works*, IV: 3–4; see also Ricardo to Trower, 8 March 1814, *Works*, VI: 104) – a principle that looms large in the *Essay on Profits*, to which Malthus strongly objected ever since its first formulation and that finally disappeared in the mature version of Ricardo's theory of profits developed in the *Principles* (*Works*, I: xxxi).

Sraffa conjectures that the *Essay on Profits* may ideally be divided into two parts: the first part was probably written by Ricardo before the appearance in print in February 1815 of two pamphlet essays by Malthus; while the second part develops Ricardo's own comments and criticisms of the latter (see *Works*, IV: 4, 3fn). Malthus's 1815 pamphlet essays extensively commented on by Ricardo are: *An Inquiry into the Nature and Progress of Rent, and the Principles by Which it is Regulated* (printed on 3 February) and *The Grounds of an Opinion on the Policy of Restricting the Importation of Foreign Corn: Intended as an Appendix to 'Observations on the Corn Laws'* (printed on 10 February). It is remarkable that Ricardo's *Essay on Profits* had been published on 24 February (ibid.: 5), that is, only a few days after Malthus's two works. This fact gives weight to the conjecture advanced by many commentators that Malthus's rent theory was not received by Ricardo as a path-breaking theoretical innovation that called for a thorough reconsideration of his economic doctrines but, rather, as a piece nicely fitting his already established system of thought (see Patten, 1893: 329 and Hollander, 1979: 134).

What was entirely new (and shocking) for Ricardo in the moment he was drafting his *Essay on Profits* was Malthus's *volte-face* on the issue of the free importation of cheap foreign corn. In fact, in 1814 Malthus had published another pamphlet on the corn trade, *Observations on the Effects of the Corn Laws, and of a Rise or Fall in the Price of Corn on the Agriculture and General Wealth of the Country*. Though Malthus describes his 1814 essay as a detached attempt to evaluate 'with the strictest impartiality' (Malthus [1814] 1986: 88) the pros and cons of the two corn trade policy options under scrutiny (free versus restricted importation of cheap foreign corn), it is fair to say that, on balance, Malthus's analysis ends up on the side of free trade (for a similar appraisal see Hollander, 1997: 820–24). By contrast, in the 1815 essay, *The Grounds of an Opinion*, Malthus undresses the clothes of an impartial observer to wear those of a committed protectionist:

> I firmly believe that, *in the actual state of Europe*, and under the *actual circumstances of our present situation*, it is our wisest policy to grow our own average supply of corn; and, in so doing, I feel persuaded that the country has ample resources for a great and continued increase of population, of power, of wealth, and of happiness. (Malthus [1815] 1986: 174; emphasis added)

Malthus's unexpected protectionist turn upset Ricardo. After reading Malthus's *Rent* essay, Ricardo expresses his warm admiration to his friend in a letter dated 6 February 1815:

> I have now read with very great attention your essay on the rise and progress of rent [Ricardo refers to *An Inquiry into the Nature and Progress of Rent*] with a view of selecting every passage which might afford us subject for future discussion. *It is no praise to say that all the leading principles in it meet with my perfect assent*, and that I consider it as containing many original views, which are not only important as connected with rent, but with many other difficult points, such as taxation &ca. &ca. (*Works*, VI: 172; emphasis added)

But just a week later, after reading Malthus's protectionist essay, Ricardo exposes what, in his view, appears to be a chasm between Malthus as the pure theorist of *An Inquiry into the Nature and Progress of Rent* and Malthus as the supporter of a protectionist policy in *The Grounds of an Opinion*:

> I have read the Appendix [Ricardo refers to *The Grounds of an Opinion*] also with great attention and cannot help thinking that you have quite thrown off the character of impartiality to which in the observations [Ricardo refers to *Observations on the Effects of the Corn Laws*] I thought you fairly entitled. You are avowedly for restrictions on importation; of that I do not complain. It is not easy to estimate justly the dangers to which we may be exposed. Those who are for an open trade in corn may underrate them, and it is possible that you may overrate them. It is a most difficult point to calculate these dangers at their fair value, – but in an economical view, altho' you have here and there allowed that we might be benefited by importing cheap, rather than by growing dear – you point out many inconveniences which we should suffer from the loss of agricultural capital, and from other causes; which would make it appear as if even economically you thought we ought [not] to import corn, – such is the approbation with which you quote from Adam Smith of the benefits of agriculture over commerce in increasing production, and which *I cannot help thinking is at variance with all your general doctrines*. (Ibid.: 177–8; emphasis added)

As I show above, the critical strategy adopted by Ricardo in the *Essay on Profits* consists in making use of the analytical results obtained by Malthus in his *Rent* essay concerning the relationship between rent and profits and a few arguments taken from Malthus's 'objective' essay, *Observations on the Effects of the Corn Laws*, to counter the arguments used by Malthus to support protectionism in the 'committed' essay, *The Grounds of an Opinion*.

In this entry I concentrate on this aspect of Ricardo's *Essay on Profits* that Ricardo develops in the second part of his pamphlet. For a more complete analysis of the first part of the *Essay on Profits* and its famous 'Table, shewing the Progress of Rent and Profit under an assumed Augmentation of Capital' the reader can consult the entry 'Corn Model'. Here the following remarks must suffice.

In the first part of the *Essay on Profits* Ricardo assumes constant agricultural technology and given real wages, explicitly (*Works*, IV: 12) and perfect mobility of agricultural capital and a demand for corn as an increasing function of population size only, implicitly. In the first stages of the growth process, thanks to the abundance of fertile plots of land, the profits of capital absorb the whole of the net product:

> In the first settling of a country rich in fertile land, and which may be had by any one who chooses to take it, the whole produce, after deducting the outgoings belonging to cultivation, will be the profits of capital, and will belong to the owner of such capital, without any deduction whatever for rent. (Ibid.: 10)

The growth of population and the progressive extension of tillage to less fertile or favourably situated plots of lands provoke a decrease in the rate of profits and the raise of a (differential) rent on the more fertile or favourably situated plots of lands. By means of his table – wilfully built on data that Ricardo plainly acknowledges to be 'probably very far from the truth' (ibid.: 15n) – Ricardo intends to provide his readers with a straightforward numerical example that elucidates what Ricardo holds to be his basic *and* innovative contribution:

> [D]uring the progress of a country the whole produce raised on its land will increase, and for a certain time that part of the produce which belongs to the profits of stock, as well as that part which belongs to rent will increase; but that at a later period, every accumulation of capital will be attended with an absolute, as well as a proportionate diminution of profits, – though rents will uniformly increase ... This is a view of the effects of accumulation which is exceedingly curious, and has, I believe, never before been noticed. (Ibid.: 15–16)

To put it briefly, Ricardo would have most likely approved the diagrammatic representation of his thought provided by Kaldor (1955–56): the only difference is that the product per unit of capital-cum-labour is constant at the very beginning of the curve. Since corn (a catch-all word for agricultural products) is the main component of workers' wage basket, the forces of free competition will, in the long run, align the dynamics of the agricultural rate of profits with the dynamics of the general rate of profits:

> Wherever competition can have its full effect, and the production of the commodity be not limited by nature, as in the case with some wines, the difficulty or facility of their production will ultimately regulate their exchangeable value. The sole effect then of the progress of wealth on prices, independently of all improvements, either in agriculture or manufactures, appears to be to raise the price of raw produce and of labour, leaving all other commodities at their

original prices, and to lower general profits in consequence of the general rise of wages. (*Works,* IV: 19–20)

Yet, for Ricardo, the main interest of rent theory is not purely theoretical but consists in its policy implications:

> It follows then, that the interest of the landlord is always opposed to the interest of every other class in the community. His situation is never so prosperous, as when food is scarce and dear: whereas, all other persons are greatly benefited by procuring food cheap. High rent and low profits, for they invariably accompany each other, ought never to be the subject of complaint, if they are the effect of the natural course of things. (Ibid.: 21)

The basic goal pursued by Ricardo in the second part of the *Essay on Profits* is to demonstrate that 'high rent and low profits' in the post-war Great Britain would be the effect not of a 'natural course of things' but, rather, of an ill-conceived policy of corn trade restraint. In fact, as concerns rent theory and its logical implications, Ricardo stresses: (1) the inverse relationship between rent and profits, given real wages and agricultural technology:

> [B]y bringing successively land of a worse quality, or less favourably situated into cultivation, rent would rise on the land previously cultivated, and precisely in the same degree would profits fall; and if the smallness of profits do not check accumulation, there are hardly any limits to the rise of rent, and the fall of profit. (Ibid.: 14)

And (2) the nature of rent as a transfer payment so that whatever cause reduces aggregate rent increases aggregate profits *pari passu*, such a redistribution of purchasing power from landlords to farmers leaving aggregate expenditure unaffected:

> The general profits of stock depend wholly on the profits of the last portion of capital employed on the land; if, therefore, landlords were to relinquish the whole of their rents, they would neither raise the general profits of stock, nor lower the price of corn to the consumer. It would have no other effect, as Mr. Malthus has observed, than to enable those farmers, whose lands now pay a rent, to live like gentlemen, and they would have to expend that portion of the general revenue, which now falls to the share of the landlord. (Ibid.: 21–2)

Rent theory and its logical implications are the bedrock on which Ricardo anchors his endorsement of a free-trade policy: 'The consideration of those principles [which regulate the rise and fall of rent], together with those which regulate the profit of stock, have convinced me of the policy of leaving the importation of corn unrestricted by law' (ibid.: 9).

Accordingly, Ricardo's challenge in the *Essay on Profits* is to demonstrate that Malthus's 1815 endorsement of protectionism derives uniquely from his overvaluation of the political risks arising from foreign corn dependence in times of war or poor harvest abroad:

> From the general principle set forth in all Mr. Malthus's publications, I am persuaded that he holds the same opinion as far as profit and wealth are concerned with the question; but, viewing, as he does, the danger as formidable of depending on foreign supply for a large portion of our food, he considers it wise, on the whole, to restrict importation. Not participating with him in those fears, and perhaps estimating the advantages of a cheap price of corn at a higher value,

I have come to a different conclusion. Some of the objections urged in his last publication, 'Grounds of an Opinion' &c. I have endeavoured to answer; they appear to me unconnected with the political danger he apprehends, and to be inconsistent with the general doctrines of the advantages of a free trade, which he has himself, by his writings, so ably contributed to establish ... *It is, then, the dangers of dependence on foreign supply for any considerable quantity of our food, which can alone be opposed to the many advantages which, circumstanced as we are, would attend the importation of corn.* These dangers do not admit of being very correctly estimated, they are in some degree, matters of opinion and cannot like the advantages on the other side, be reduced to accurate calculation. (Ibid.: 9 and 27; emphasis added)

Ricardo's counter-argument develops through the following chain of reasoning. Malthus assumed that France, Britain's traditional enemy, would become by far the largest corn supplier to Great Britain, once the latter were to allow the free import of cheap foreign corn. By contrast, Great Britain could, Ricardo maintained, avail itself of a plurality of trading partners, besides France. Implicit in Ricardo's argument was the assumption that many corn-producing countries had at that time few incentives to cultivate intensively the whole of their fertile lands and no incentive to invest additional capital into their agricultural sectors. The main culprit of such a lack of incentives, Ricardo argued, was precisely the British Corn Laws since they made British demand for foreign corn almost unpredictable and thus discouraged corn-producing countries from investing additional resources into their agricultural sectors. Conversely, should Great Britain enact legislation allowing the free importation of foreign corn whenever its domestic market price exceeds the international market price – and not only in times of poor domestic harvest and abnormally high domestic market prices – then Great Britain would certainly become a large net corn-importing country:

If we became a regularly importing country, and foreigners could confidently rely on the demand of our market, *much more land would be cultivated in the corn countries with a view to exportation* ... In contemplating a trade in corn, unshackled by restrictions on importation, and a consequent supply from France, and other countries, where it can be brought to market, at a price not much above half that at which we can ourselves produce it on some of our poorer lands, *Mr Malthus does not sufficiently allow for the greater quantity of corn, which would be grown abroad, if importation was to become the settled policy of this country.* There cannot be the least doubt that if the corn countries could depend on the markets of England for a regular demand, if they could be perfectly secure that our laws, respecting the corn trade, would not be repeatedly vacillating between bounties, restrictions, and prohibitions, a much larger supply would be grown, and the danger of a greatly diminished exportation, in consequence of bad seasons, would be less likely to occur. *Countries which have never yet supplied us, might, if our policy was fixed, afford us a considerable quantity.* (Ibid.: 27–8 and 30; emphasis added)

The increase in the number of British trading partners and, therefore, the diversification of Britain's sources of corn supply would drastically reduce the likelihood of an international production of corn insufficient to match British food requirements: in Ricardo's view, the worldwide variance of corn harvests is a decreasing function of the number of corn-producing countries tied by trade relations (ibid.: 31).

Then Ricardo turns to an analysis of the political danger of too heavy a dependence on foreign corn supply, raised by Malthus in the protectionist essay, *The Grounds of an Opinion.* Ricardo's argument to downplay Malthus's natural security issue is based on the following three assumptions. First, agricultural investment is largely a sunk cost. Second, Great Britain would become a quasi-monopsonist in the international corn market, if it were to adopt a free corn trade policy. Third, in every country, the domestic market price of corn is highly sensitive with respect to (positive or negative) market excess demand. A small excess (deficiency) in the quantity produced causes a sharp fall (rise) in the market price of corn:

> When we consider the value of even a few weeks consumption of corn in England, no interruption could be given to the export trade, if the continent supplied us with any considerable quantity of corn, without the most extensively ruinous commercial distress -distress which no sovereign, or combination of sovereigns, would be willing to inflict on their people; and, if willing, it would be a measure to which probably no people would submit. It was the endeavour of Bonaparte to prevent the exportation of the raw produce of Russia, more than [any] other cause which produced the astonishing efforts of the people of that country against the most powerful force perhaps ever assembled to subjugate a nation. *The immense capital which would be employed on the land, could not be withdrawn suddenly, and under such circumstances, without immense loss; besides which, the glut of corn in their markets, which would affect their whole supply, and lower its value beyond calculation*; the failure of those returns, which are essential in all commercial adventures, would occasion a scene of wide spreading ruin, which if a country would patiently endure, would render it unfit to wage war with any prospect of success. (Ibid.: 28; emphasis added)

And again: even 'Bonaparte, when he was most hostile to us, permitted the exportation of corn to England by licenses, when our prices were high from a bad harvest, even when all other commerce was prohibited' (ibid.: 29). Hence, Ricardo's chain of reasoning implies that it is very unlikely that foreign corn-producing countries, once they have largely invested into their agricultural sectors in order to increase their corn producing capacity to match British demand for corn, will reduce or even halt their corn export towards Great Britain in case of a war or a deficient domestic harvest. Ricardo's plea to the British Parliament not to enact a protectionist legislation derives from his reasoned guess on the equilibrium trade strategy of foreign corn-producing countries: 'Would it be wise then to legislate with the view of preventing an evil which might never occur; and to ward off a *most improbable* danger, sacrifice annually a revenue of some millions?' (ibid.: 29–30; emphasis added).

While Ricardo disagreed with Malthus on the likelihood of the adoption of corn export restrictions by foreign countries, he concurred with him that a sudden abolition of the Corn Laws would lead to the financial bankruptcy of those British farmers who, by growing corn on marginal, less fertile, plots of lands, could not withstand the competition with cheap foreign corn producers. Accordingly, Ricardo proposed a temporary tariff protection to be withdrawn as soon as existing agricultural lease contracts expired (ibid.: 33). Yet, he ridiculed any attempt to ground a protectionist argument on the bankruptcy of those British farmers:

> [Malthus] dwells with much stress on the losses of agricultural capital, which the country would sustain, by allowing an unrestricted importation. He laments the loss of that which by the course of events has become of no use to us, and by the employment of which we actually lose. We might just as fairly have been told, when the steam-engine, or Mr. Arkwright's cotton-machine, was brought to perfection, that it would be wrong to adopt the use of them, because the value of the old clumsy machinery would be lost to us. (Ibid.)

As noted by King (2013), Ricardo was fond of such a rhetorical device that may be considered as 'a variant of the *classical reductio ad absurdum* principle: if you are prepared to accept policy X, he would ask his opponents, why not also endorse the (much more obviously obnoxious) policy Y, which could be defended by the same argument?' (King, 2013: 68). It is not a mere coincidence, in fact, that exactly the same argument is restated by Ricardo right at the conclusion of the *Essay on Profits* so to imprint it firmly into his readers' memory:

> I shall only further observe, that I shall greatly regret that considerations for any particular class, are allowed to check the progress of the wealth and population of the country. If the interests of the landlord be of sufficient consequence, to determine us not to avail ourselves of all the benefits which would follow from importing corn at a cheap price, they should also influence us in rejecting all improvements in agriculture, and in the implements of husbandry; for it is as certain that corn is rendered cheap, rents are lowered, and the ability of the landlord to pay taxes, is for a time, at least, as much impaired by such improvements, as by the importation of corn. To be consistent then, let us by the same act arrest improvement, and prohibit importation. (*Works*, IV: 41)

To sum up, from a strictly theoretical point of view, both Malthus in the *Observations on the Effects of the Corn Laws* and Ricardo in the *Essay on Profits* were alive to the substantial and mutual gains engendered by a free trade policy between an agricultural manufacturing countries, but Malthus opted for protectionism in *The Grounds of an Opinion* because he attached to the national security issue a greater value than trade-induced prosperity. Malthus ([1815] 1986) endorses food autarky for Great Britain since he fears that foreign corn-producing countries (particularly France) might adopt a restrictive corn export policy in case of war or poor domestic harvest. In his view, it is safer for the manufacturing country to keep on growing its own corn to match its average food requirements. By contrast, for Ricardo, agricultural investments lock foreign countries into their trade relationship with Great Britain, given the sunk cost nature of agricultural investment and the role of quasi-monopsonist that Great Britain would have played in the international corn market. Accordingly, Ricardo holds that the potential threat of a corn export cut in times of war or poor domestic harvests turns out to be a non-credible one, once foreign countries were induced to invest into their agricultural sectors to match a British demand for corn permanently increased by Great Britain's irreversible adoption of a free corn trade policy.

RODOLFO SIGNORINO

See also:

Corn Model; Malthus–Ricardo Debate; *Notes on Malthus*; *Principles of Political Economy, and Taxation*; Sraffa, Piero, on Ricardo.

References

Hollander, S. (1979), *The Economics of David Ricardo*, Toronto: University of Toronto Press.
Hollander, S. (1997), *The Economics of Thomas Robert Malthus*, Toronto: University of Toronto Press.
Kaldor, N. (1955–56), 'Alternative theories of distribution', *Review of Economic Studies*, **23**(2), 83–100.
King, J.E. (2013), *David Ricardo*, Basingstoke, UK and New York: Palgrave Macmillan.
Malthus, T.R. ([1814] 1986), 'Observations on the effects of the Corn Laws, and of a rise or fall in the price of corn on the agriculture and general wealth of the country', in *The Works of Thomas Robert Malthus, Vol. 7*, (ed.) E.A. Wrigley and D. Souden, London: W. Pickering, pp. 87–109.
Malthus, T.R. ([1815] 1986), 'The grounds of an opinion on the policy of restricting the importation of foreign corn: intended as an appendix to "Observations on the Corn Laws"', in *The Works of Thomas Robert Malthus, Vol. 7*, (ed.) E.A. Wrigley and D. Souden, London: W. Pickering, pp. 151–74.

Patten, S.N. (1893), 'The interpretation of Ricardo', *Quarterly Journal of Economics*, 7(3), 322–52.

Exchange Value and Utility

Ricardo resisted incorporating utility magnitudes into the determination of value in exchange despite repeated challenges, primarily from Jean-Baptiste Say, to do so. Ricardo had two reasons for his stance. First, he held that utility was superfluous to explaining the magnitude of value. Since value was explained by the cost of production, it was for Ricardo basically attributable to labour. This is the superfluity argument. The second, less familiar point is that Ricardo did not agree that different commodities could be compared on a single scale of utility. Since value for him was something common to commodities, utility could not be a gauge of exchange value. This incommensurability argument is important. In contrast to the superfluity argument, it is a direct objection to utility as a basis for value.

Interpreting Ricardo's views along these lines means there is good reason why he would abjure utility notions in the determination of exchange value. It was not that he was unsophisticated about utility notions or that he simply overlooked the application of marginal analysis to them, yet such a suggestion is made in influential writings on the development of utility theory. Thus, we find George Stigler claiming that:

> Bentham had indeed planted the tree of utility. No reader could overlook the concept of utility as a numerical magnitude; and the implications for economic analysis were not obscure. But they were overlooked . . . The economists of Bentham's time did not follow the approach he had opened. One may conjecture that this failure is due to the fact that Ricardo, who gave the economics of the period much of its slant and direction, was not a Benthamite. It is true that he was the friend of Bentham and the close friend of James Mill, Bentham's leading disciple. Yet there is no evidence that he was a devout utilitarian and much evidence that he was unphilosophical – essentially a pragmatic reformer. (Stigler, 1950: 311)

Similar remarks are made by Joseph Schumpeter (1954) and Terence Hutchison (1956). However, there is dispute about Stigler's last point. Many authors contend that Ricardo was under James Mill's sway to such an extent that he was indeed a 'devout utilitarian'. In this matter Stigler, on the evidence cited in this entry, is correct: Ricardo was not a utilitarian. However, the evidence also shows that Ricardo was hardly indifferent to philosophical writing. Indeed, he had a considered position on utility, one that did not see 'utility as a numerical magnitude'. If Bentham planted the tree of utility, Ricardo was not taken by it. He did not find it a specimen worth nurturing.

The superfluity argument

Adam Smith influenced Ricardo's views on the basis of exchange value. Ricardo uses Smith's ideas early on to distinguish his own from Bentham's. In his 'Notes on Bentham' (*Works*, III: 267–341), which date from 25 December 1810 to 11 January 1811, Ricardo refers to a passage where Bentham appears to equate value and utility: 'I like the distinction which Adam Smith makes between value in use and value in exchange. According to that opinion utility is not the measure of value' (ibid.: 284). This passage marks the beginning of a long-held position of Ricardo's, expanded on later in the *Principles* and elsewhere. While the passage shows he had no trouble distinguishing himself from Bentham on the topic of utility, Ricardo's main opponent on the role of utility in value theory was Say. It is in exchanges with him that we can trace the evolution of Ricardo's ideas. Ricardo objects to Say's position in a letter written two years before his *Principles* appeared (18 August 1815):

> You have I perceive a little modified the definition of the word value as far as it is dependent on utility, but with great diffidence, I observe, that I do not think you have mastered the difficulties which attach to the explanation of that difficult word. Utility is certainly the foundation of value, but the degree of utility can never be the measure by which to estimate value. A commodity of difficult production will always be more valuable . . . A commodity must be useful to have value but the difficulty of its production is the true measure of its value. For this reason iron though more useful is of less value than gold. (*Works*, VI: 247–8)

Here we see Ricardo expanding on the comment on Bentham. The typical classical distinction of use and exchange value is made, the latter depending on the cost of production. The reason for not employing utility as a measure of value is that it is superfluous (even while utility is needed 'as a foundation' for there to be exchange value at all). Since the magnitude of value is explained by cost of production, there is no role left to play for utility. Ricardo never seems to have abandoned this view. He writes to Malthus (9 October 1820) five years later saying much the same. Commodities cannot be valuable in proportion to utility since value is not dependent on demand factors: 'it is all done by the competition of the sellers' (*Works*, VIII: 276–7). Within the confines of the superfluity argument, the main thrust of Ricardo's argument is that utility, though it is a prerequisite for a commodity to have exchange value, cannot indicate its magnitude, since it is redundant.

Ricardo buttressed the superfluity argument with a more direct criticism of utility as a basis for value. Utility, being multifaceted, could not be measured along a single scale. This obviated the use of utility since value was to be measured by a common substance. There are hints of this view in the first two editions of the *Principles* (1817 and 1819), but this idea becomes more prominent in the third edition (1821) as well as in late correspondence with James Mill. Before turning to this argument, it is important to establish that Ricardo would have been familiar with philosophical considerations on utility as it was found in contemporary treatises.

Ricardo's reading
Stigler held, as we have seen, that Ricardo was 'unphilosophical'. A variant of this theme, noted and thoroughly documented by Milgate and Stimson (1991: 3–4, 3n), is that any philosophy Ricardo may have had was identical to James Mill's, whose puppet he was. This amazing and long-lived assessment is reinforced by many commentators and was started by Bentham and the Mills. John Stuart Mill claimed that his father 'induced' Ricardo to enter Parliament where he functioned to render service 'to his and my father's opinions on political economy and on other subjects' ([1873] 1924: 19). This image is repeated in Leslie Stephen's sketch of Ricardo as a 'defender' of established utilitarian ideas (Stephen, 1950, 2: 27); in Toynbee's statement that 'Ricardo's political opinions in fact merely reflect those of James Mill' ([1852–83] 1884: 127); and in Halévy's view that 'All the actions in Ricardo's life, after 1811, were willed by James Mill'

(1949: 266). No doubt this approach was also inspired by Bentham's claim that he was the 'spiritual' father of James Mill, and Mill was Ricardo's, 'so that Ricardo was my spiritual grandson' (Bentham, 1843: 498). Finally, we have James Mill's communication to McCulloch, immediately following Ricardo's death, that Ricardo had 'hardly a thought or a purpose, respecting either public, or his private affairs, in which I was not his confidant and adviser' (James Mill to McCulloch, 19 September 1823, *Works*, IX: 390).

Other than the bombastic claims made by Bentham and Mill historians might be given to think that Ricardo's views on philosophical topics derived entirely from the views of Bentham or James Mill for two reasons. First, Ricardo did not have a typical education based on the standard classical and contemporary texts. He came to read important texts only later in life. Ricardo felt this lack deeply, and complained of 'all the disadvantages, too, of a neglected education, which it is now in vain to seek to repair' (12 September 1817, *Works*, VII: 190; see also Ricardo to Mill, 29 September 1818, ibid.: 305). This situation came to pass because during his early years Ricardo had no time for studies. He worked at the Stock Exchange from the age of 14 until he was 25 years old and financially secure. Only at this time did he have leisure to study. The second issue is that while he originally turned to studying 'mathematics chemistry, geology, and mineralogy' and, of course, political economy (*Works*, X: 4–7), in 1817 and 1818 Ricardo did considerable reading on philosophy, religion, history and government under Mill's supervision. From this circumstance someone might conclude that Ricardo was Mill's disciple on matters relating to philosophical topics, including utility. Certainly, Ricardo read widely at this time. His notebooks (*Works*, X, Appendix C) and comments in correspondence indicate that he read Bacon, Berkeley, Locke's *Essay* ('twice', while he did 'not take much pleasure in such subjects as that Essay treats of' – Ricardo to Mill, 9 November 1817, *Works*, VII: 205–6), Hume's *Natural History of Religion*, Millar, Rousseau, Burke, Montesquieu, James Mackintosh's *Vindiciae Gallicae* (1791), Stewart, Beattie, Reid and Warburton, in addition to Mill's *History of British India* (1817–29). He became acquainted, in other words, with the promoters and precursors of utilitarian ideas as well as their Scottish critics. Much of this literature turned on how to relate utility to the association of ideas in the mind, a topic that cannot be covered in this entry (see Halévy, 1949; Daston, 1988; Rizvi, 1992).

However, while it is clear that James Mill did have an influence on Ricardo, who often looked to Mill for intellectual guidance, it does not make sense to claim either that he was philosophically untutored or that he was a clone of Bentham and Mill. We shall see that he was an independent, informed, knowledgeable and clear thinker, who came to differ with Mill on important issues and, in particular, on utility. He raised important questions to James Mill, who did not, so far as we can tell, provide him with answers.

The incommensurability argument

Ricardo's writings establish that he had direct objections to the use of utility as a measure of value. Indeed, he registers some of these objections even before the reading programme guided by James Mill. Ricardo may have been familiar with the controversies on establishing utility as a basis for political theorizing earlier than we have been able to determine from his works and correspondence; or he may have come to these arguments independently. In any case, the specificity of Ricardo's objections to utility as a basis for value becomes greater after his reading programme; and the terms in which he then addresses the issue borrow from the debates in the readings.

In a passage appearing in all editions of the *Principles* (and which therefore predates the reading programme just described) Ricardo writes, when discussing the possibility of gluts that: 'One set of necessaries and conveniences admits of no comparison with another set; value in use cannot be measured by any known standard; it is differently estimated by different persons' (*Works*, I: 429). Here, to use modern terms, he rejects the ideas that different baskets of goods are comparable (a requirement for the existence of a utility function), that utility is measurable, and that utility is interpersonally comparable. About five months after the publication of the first edition of the *Principles*, Ricardo wrote to Malthus on 4 September 1817 (again on gluts), employing similar language. The objection, to again use modern terms, is that not everyone will have the same preferences – thus, an approach based on them has no predictive power, as regards luxury consumption:

> Happiness is the object to be desired, and we cannot be quite sure that provided he is equally well fed, a man may not be happier in the enjoyment of the luxury of idleness than in the enjoyment of the luxuries of a neat cottage, and good clothes. (*Works*, VII: 185)

Ricardo's responses to Say are illuminating. Ricardo devoted much of Chapter XX of the first edition of the *Principles* to controverting Say's views on utility, value and riches. But Say challenged Ricardo explicitly following the publication of the fourth edition of his *Traité* (*Treatise* [1819] 1821). In response Ricardo altered Chapter XX in the third edition of the *Principles* (*Works*, VIII: 228, 279–88, 298–9, 315). The added text in the third edition of the *Principles* retains the superfluity argument, but now also contains typical elements of the incommensurability argument, specifically, the importance of a common substance to permit measurement of the magnitude of value:

> To conclude, I cannot agree with M. Say, in estimating the value of a commodity, by the abundance of other commodities for which it will exchange; I am of the opinion of a very distinguished writer, M. Destutt de Tracy, who says, that 'To measure any one thing is to compare it with a determinate quantity of the same thing which we take for a standard of comparison, for unity' ... labour is a common measure, by which their real as well as their relative value may be estimated. (*Works*, I: 284)

However, he does not refer here to utility as such. Additional and more precise insight into Ricardo's thoughts on utility is provided in his correspondence with James Mill, in reaction to Mill's *History of British India*, which, despite its title, employs utility ideas to judge cultures (Stokes, 1959 and Thomas, 1979: 3). On 6 January 1818, by the time he had got to the third volume of the *History*, Ricardo transmitted to Mill his objection to utility theory in more direct terms:

> The difficulty of the doctrine of expediency or utility is to know how to balance one object of utility against another – there being no standard in nature, it must vary with the tastes, the passions and the habits of mankind. This is one of the subjects on which I require to be enlightened. (*Works*, VII: 240–44)

The language here is reminiscent of the passage from the *Principles* (*Works*, I: 249) cited above. James Mill, in the extant correspondence, does not reply directly to Ricardo's request, which seems never to have been satisfied. There is a rather odd declamation James Mill makes later in 1818: 'This is the plain rule of utility, which will always guide you right, and in which there is no mystery' (*Works*, VIII: 302). It seems rather a *non sequitur* as it comes in the middle of Mill's advice, in a letter of 23 September 1818, to Ricardo on how to be an efficient Member of Parliament. After a gap of many years, James Mill, on 8 August 1823, offers to send Ricardo a manuscript, which is 'something considerable towards the exposition of all the phenomena classed under the title of Thought' (*Works*, IX: 331–5). Ricardo replies on 30 August 1823:

> I am rejoiced to know that you . . . have actually got upon paper all that has been long floating in your mind on the difficult subject of Thought, Sensation, Association &c . . . I shall be greatly indebted to you if you make all these matters clear to me, for hitherto though I have occasionally paid a little attention to them, I have never been sure that I have accurately understood what the authors whose works I have read have wished to express. I believe the subject to be very difficult, but if any one can place it in a clear point of view, I am sure it is you. I beg to see what you have done, and to profit by your labours. (Ibid.: 373–9)

Ricardo died the following month and never seems to have seen Mill's manuscript, which was not finished until 1829 (Mill [1829] 1869). To the extent we can take the lack of Mill's replies to these repeated inquiries by his 'pupil' to be real, and not just to be gaps in the correspondence, Mill's silence is hardly worthy of someone who had boasted that he intended to make the 'human mind as plain as the road from Charing Cross to St. Paul's' (James Mill to Francis Place, 6 December 1817, cited in Halévy, 1949: 451).

Ricardo, then, had two objections for basing the measurement of value in exchange by utility. He argued that exchange value, being determined by cost of production, was redundant or superfluous. He also was familiar with controversies surrounding the use of utility in political economy. With this background in mind we can also see in his writings a more direct objection to utility as a measure. For him, this required a standard, or common measure, and utility, given that is was valued differently by different people, could not serve that purpose.

S. Abu turab Rizvi

See also:

Bentham, Jeremy, and Ricardo; Competition; Demand and Supply; Natural and Market Prices.

References

Bentham, J. (1843), *The Works of Jeremy Bentham*, (ed.) J. Bowring, Edinburgh: William Tait.
Daston, L. (1988), *Classical Probability and the Enlightenment*, Princeton, NJ: Princeton University Press.
Halévy, E. (1949), *The Growth of Philosophic Radicalism*, translated by M. Morris, London: Faber and Faber.
Hutchison, T.W. (1956), 'Bentham as an economist', *Economic Journal*, 66(2), 288–306.
Milgate, M. and S.C. Stimson (1991), *Ricardian Politics*, Princeton, NJ: Princeton University Press.
Mill, J. ([1829] 1869), *Analysis of the Phenomena of the Human Mind*, 2 vols, London: Longmans, Green, Reader and Dyer.
Mill, J.S. ([1873] 1924), *Autobiography of John Stuart Mill*, reprint, New York: Columbia University Press.
Rizvi, S.A.T. (1992), 'Ricardo's resistance to utility and the association of ideas debate', paper presented to the History of Economics Society, Eastern Economic Association, and Duke University Economic Thought Workshop.
Say, J.-B. ([1819] 1821), *A Treatise on Political Economy, or the Production, Distribution, and Consumption of Wealth*, translated by C.R. Prinsep from the 4th (1819) French edition, Boston, MA: Wells and Lilly.
Schumpeter, J. (1954), *History of Economic Analysis*, New York: Oxford University Press.

Stephen, L. (1950), *The English Utilitarians*, 3 vols, New York: P. Smith.
Stigler, G.J. (1950), 'The development of utility theory I', *Journal of Political Economy*, **58**(4), 307–27.
Stokes, E. (1959), *The English Utilitarians and India*, Oxford: Oxford University Press.
Thomas, W. (1979), *The Philosophic Radicals: Nine Studies in Theory and Practice, 1817–1841*, Oxford: Clarendon Press.
Toynbee, A. ([1852–83] 1884), *Lectures on the Industrial Revolution of the 18th Century in England*, London: Rivingtons.

Exhaustible Resources and Mines

Ricardo develops an analysis of exhaustible resources in the context of a discussion of the difference between rent and profits. In the *Principles* Ricardo defines rent rigorously in the following way:

> Rent is that portion of the produce of the earth, *which is paid to the landlord for the use of the original and indestructible powers of the soil*. It is often, however, confounded with the interest and profit of capital, and, in popular language, the term is applied to whatever is annually paid by a farmer to his landlord. (*Works*, I: 67; emphasis added)

Adam Smith, Ricardo goes on to argue, did not stick to a rigorously defined concept when using the word 'rent':

> He [Smith] tells us, that the demand for timber, and its consequent high price, in the more southern countries of Europe, caused a rent to be paid for forests in Norway, which could before afford no rent. Is it not, however, evident, that the person who paid what he thus calls rent, paid it in consideration of the valuable commodity which was then standing on the land, and that he actually repaid himself with a profit, by the sale of the timber? If, indeed, after the timber was removed, any compensation were paid to the landlord for the use of the land, for the purpose of growing timber or any other produce, with a view to future demand, such compensation might justly be called rent, because it would be paid for the productive powers of the land; *but in the case stated by Adam Smith, the compensation was paid for the liberty of removing and selling the timber, and not for the liberty of growing it*. (Ibid.: 68; emphasis added)

The Smith reference is clearly to *WN*, I.xi.c.5. Ricardo's criticism extends to Smith's dicussion of coal mines and stone quarries:

> He [Smith] speaks also of the rent of coal mines, and of stone quarries, to which the same observation applies – that the compensation given for the mine or quarry, is paid for the value of the coal or stone which can be removed from them, and has no connection with the original and indestructible powers of the land. (*Works*, I: 68)

In Ricardo's view the distinction between profits and rent is crucial, because as capital accumulates and the population grows the two component parts of the social surplus are typically affected differently:

> This is a distinction of great importance, in an enquiry concerning rent and profits; for it is found, that *the laws which regulate the progress of rent, are widely different from those which regulate the progress of profits, and seldom operate in the same direction*. In all improved countries, that which is annually paid to the landlord, partaking of both characters, rent and profit, is sometimes kept stationary by the effects of opposing causes; at other times advances or recedes, as one or the other of these causes preponderates. In the future pages of this work,

then, whenever I speak of the rent of land, I wish to be understood as speaking of that compensation, which is paid to the owner of land for the use of its original and indestructible powers. (Ibid.: 68–9; emphasis added)

Hence what Smith called 'rent' of coal mines or stone quarries is to Ricardo profits and not rent. But does Ricardo not contradict himself by giving Chapter 3 of the *Principles* the title 'On the Rent of Mines'? Scrutiny shows that this is not so. Chapter 3 is actually devoted to the rent of mines precisely in the sense Ricardo intended. Each mine is typically subject to a capacity constraint that limits the amount of the coal or ore that can be extracted per unit of time. This constraint itself depends typically also on the amount already extracted. Effectual demand cannot be satisfied in the given circumstances by operating exclusively the most 'fertile' mine, because the required rate of output in order to meet effectual demand cannot be generated in this way. Hence mines possessed of different 'fertilities' are operated simultaneously. In such circumstances, Ricardo stresses, it is the 'relative fertility of mines [which] determines the portion of their produce, which shall be paid for the rent of mines' (ibid.: 330). Ricardo concludes that 'the whole principle of rent is here . . . as applicable to land as it is to mines' (ibid.). When mines of different fertilities need to be wrought simultaneously, then this makes room for the emergence of (extensive) rents, exactly as in the case of the cultivation of different qualities of land. This is rent in the true sense of the word and has nothing whatsoever to do with what we nowadays call 'royalties'. What we call 'royalties', Ricardo actually calls 'profits'.

Ricardo's use of the concept of profits for 'the compensation . . . paid for the liberty of removing and selling the timber' is not surprising: timber can be sown and grown again, it is clearly not an exhaustible resource, but a reproducible good, and to the extent to which it is used as a produced means of production it is capital. But the use of the word 'profits' for the compensation paid for the liberty of removing and selling coal or stones may be surprising: coal cannot be reproduced by men, neither can stones. However, new coal pits can always be expected to be discovered and the cost of the search is equal to the value of the mine, a value that decreases with the amount of the resource that has been removed. In other words, Ricardo did not consider minerals and ores and so on as such as fully exhaustible in the foreseeable future. Both in Ricardo and in Smith we encounter time and again references to the finding of new deposits with no serious consideration given to the fact that such deposits, taken as a whole, are limited:

In this search [for new mines] there seem to be no certain limits either to the possible success, or to the possible disappointment of human industry. In the course of a century or two, it is possible that new mines may be discovered more fertile than any that have ever yet been known; and it is just equally possible that the most fertile mine then known may be more barren than any that was wrought before the discovery of the mines of America. (*WN*, I.xi.m.21)

Modern theory has emphasized what is now called the 'Hotelling Rule' (Hotelling, 1931). As it is typically presented, it concerns the fact that the prices of resouces in situ need to increase over time at a rate that is equal to the competitive rate of profits. This rule is obviously related to the fact that royalties are a form of profit. Indeed, it follows from the requirement that the conservation of a resource is an economic activity that ought to yield to the proprietors of deposits of the resource the same rate of profits as is obtained from any productive activity. Ricardo did not elaborate on what is now the

Hotelling Rule, but this seems mainly because the total exhaustion of certain resources was not yet considered a possibility worth studying.

The Hotelling Rule seems to imply that *all* prices need to change over time. But this is not obvious at all. Indeed, the increases in the prices of resouces in situ over time according to the Hotelling Rule are entirely passed on to the prices of the extracted resouces and, consequently, to the other prices, if the following assumptions hold:

(A1)   *The resource is available in a homogeneous quality and in an overall quantity that is limited and that at any moment of time is known with certainty.*

(A2)   *The amount of the resource that can be extracted in a given period of time, a year, for example, is only constrained by the amount of it left over from the preceding period.*

As mentioned above, Ricardo is concerned with the fact that each mine has a limited capacity of extraction and it is this fact that creates the rent that owners of mines can obtain. As clarified by Kurz and Salvadori (2009, 2011) even if (A1) holds, the price of the extracted resouce may be constant. The owners of deposits obtain both royalties and rents, in the course of time rents fall and royalties rise, and the sum of both may remain constant. If this condition is met, then the price changes of resources in situ will not affect any other prices in the economic system.

But there is something more. As usual, Ricardo is 'desirous only to elucidate the principle' at work (*Works*, I: 121), as he stresses in another context, and therefore bases his argument on strong assumptions. These assumptions imply that the exhaustion of each and every single deposit of an exhaustible resource will nevertheless leave the prices of all produced commodities unaffected over time. We might go to the opposite extreme and postulate instead of assumptions (A1) and (A2) the following:

(A3)   *For each exhausted deposit of the resource another one with exactly the same characteristics is discovered and the cost of the search, in terms of labour and commodities, is always the same.*

(A4)   *The working of each deposit is subject to a capacity constraint that limits the amount of the resource that can be extracted in a given period of time.*

If assumption (A3) held true, even if assumption (A2) holds, while each deposit would be exhaustible, the resource as such would not; and each deposit could in fact be treated as if it was a (reproducible) machine – the price of the new machine equals the cost of the search and the price of an old machine of age t equals the value of the deposit after t periods of utilization (see Kurz and Salvadori [1995] 1997: 359–60). The price of the resource in situ would change as predicted by the Hotelling Rule, but the price of the extracted mineral would be constant over time. As mentioned above, if (A1) and (A4) apply, the changes of the prices of the resources in situ do not imply changes in the other prices.

Ricardo's approach to the problem of exhaustible resources and mines in terms of differential rents highlights the empirically important fact that the working of each single deposit of a resource is typically subject to a capacity constraint. Hence, several deposits will have to be worked side by side, and if they are differently 'fertile' differential rents will obtain. Ricardo's approach can easily be cross-bred with Hotelling's, giving rise to the familiar result that the prices of the resources in situ will rise at the competitive rate of profits, which in Ricardo is determined endogenously (whereas in Hotelling's original contribution it was given from the outside). This rise in these prices need not, however, affect the prices of the resources that have been extracted and thus the prices of commodities in whose production they enter.

HEINZ D. KURZ AND NERI SALVADORI

See also:

Capital and Profits; Land and Rent; *Principles of Political Economy, and Taxation*; Ricardo on Adam Smith.

References

Hotelling, H. (1931), 'The economics of exhaustible resources', *Journal of Political Economy*, **39**(2), 137–75.
Kurz, H.D. and N. Salvadori ([1995] 1997), *Theory of Production. A Long-Period Analysis*, revised paperback edition, Cambridge, UK: Cambridge University Press.
Kurz, H.D. and N. Salvadori (2009), 'Ricardo on exhaustible resources, and the Hotelling Rule', in A. Ikeo and H.D. Kurz (eds), *A History of Economic Theory. Essays in Honour of Takashi Negishi*, London: Routledge, pp.68–79.
Kurz, H.D. and N. Salvadori (2011), 'Exhaustible resources: rents, profits, royalties and prices', in V. Caspari (ed.), *The Evolution of Economic Theory. Essays in Honour of Bertram Schefold*, London: Routledge, pp.39–52.
Smith, A. ([1776] 1976), *An Inquiry into the Nature and Causes of the Wealth of Nations*, in *The Glasgow Edition of the Works and Correspondence of Adam Smith*, (eds) R.H. Campbell, A.S. Skinner and W.B. Todd, Oxford: Clarendon Press.

Foreign Trade

> All of them [the tailor, the shoemaker, the farmer] find it for their interest to employ their whole industry in a way in which they have some advantage over their neighbours, and to purchase with a part of its produce, or what is the same thing, with the price of a part of it, whatever else they have occasion for.
>
> (*WN*, IV.ii.11)

Before Ricardo's *Principles*, the theoretical arguments on the benefits and the determinants of foreign trade did not go much beyond this explanation of domestic specialization and exchange, with only a few exceptions. It has been debated (Seligman and Hollander, 1911) whether the argument of the 'territorial division of labour' in Torrens (1815) also remains a theory of domestic trade, based on absolute advantage, or is it already a theory of international trade in terms of comparative advantage?

It is also an open question whether Ricardo's theory of foreign trade is a special, although seminal, case of the neoclassical theory of international trade or also possesses general features that the latter has concealed and superseded. We note that his is a theory of trade and costs of production, whereas the neoclassical approach explains, in simple terms, the trade among individuals in the absence of production, on the basis of different endowments and preferences. Second, in Ricardo, as in Smith, a normative and a positive theory of trade are merged together; conversely, the modern theory maintains a distinction between the two. Third, and most importantly, his principle of comparative advantage is also applicable to economies in a state of unemployment equilibria.

Foreign trade and comparative advantage

In Chapter 7 'On Foreign Trade' in the *Principles*, an example explains the gains from trade by means of four numbers: the number of workers whose labour is required for one year in order to produce the same quantity of a commodity (cloth, wine) in each country (Portugal, England). The numbers are tabulated as follows in Table 3.

For instance, 80 and 120 are the numbers of workers required to produce the same quantity of wine in Portugal and in England respectively. Let X_c denote the quantity of cloth and X_w the quantity of wine. X_c, X_w are arbitrary exchangeable absolute amounts. Ricardo 'simply' observes that, if England produces and exchanges $X_{ec} = X_c$ units of cloth for $X_{pw} = X_w$ units of wine, this country *saves* the work of 20 English workers, in comparison to the alternative in which the same amount X_w is made at home. If Portugal produces and exchanges $X_{pw} = X_w$ units of wine for $X_{ec} = X_c$ units of cloth, this country *saves* the work of ten Portuguese workers, in comparison to home-made X_c. The condition for mutual gains from trade is:

$$100/120 < X_{pw}/X_{ec} < 90/80 \qquad (1)$$

Table 3   Numbers of workers required to produce a given quantity of each commodity

	Cloth	Wine
Portugal	90	80
England	100	120

The terms of trade are equal to the ratio X_{pw}/X_{ec} whose numerical value is not specified. The 'gains' from trade in the example are self-contained in a voluntary exchange, compared with no exchange, and are measured by increments of labour productivities, which are equivalent to a labour-saving technical change. Other effects of trade are not dealt with by the example, because they need the assumptions of a more complete model. In particular, the argument does not depend on the assumption of quantities associated with full capacity utilization of the trading countries. Condition (1) explains, from a normative viewpoint, Ricardo's sentence 'Thus England would give the produce of the labour of 100 men, for the produce of the labour of 80' (*Works*, I: 135). Another condition in terms of prices corresponds to (1) and explains the pattern of trade between the two economies under free competition. We shall expand on this correspondence between the normative and the positive interpretation of the theory.

The prices in a competitive equilibrium satisfy the conditions of absence of extra profits in each activated industry, and this must explain (a) why two countries that initially are in a state of autarky equilibrium move to a trading equilibrium and (b) why they do not move to an autarky equilibrium, if initially they are in a state of free trade equilibrium. Therefore, a double check of profitability has to be satisfied as in the choice of techniques within a closed economy: at the pre-trade autarky prices *and* at the post-trade world prices. It is useful to look at the problem from the point of view of a single country facing given terms of trade. Let us adopt the symbols:

X_j = the output of industry $j = 1, 2$;
L_j = the input of labour in the industry $j = 1, 2$;
w = the autarky nominal wage;
W = the nominal wage with free trade;
p_j = the autarky nominal price of good $j = 1, 2$;
P_j = the nominal world price of good $j = 1, 2$;
$T = P_1/P_2$ the international price of good 1 in terms of good 2 (the terms of trade).

Assume T as given. The conditions that make it profitable to move from autarky to free trade and to export, say, commodity 1 in exchange for commodity 2, at the autarky prices are:

$$L_1 w = X_1 p_1$$

$$L_2 w = X_2 p_2$$

$$p_1 < T p_2$$

The latter inequality is inconsistent with a competitive equilibrium: commodity 2 would be produced at a price equal to its labour costs and also imported from abroad with extra profits. Instead, the conditions that preserve this pattern of trade at the world prices are:

$$L_1 W = X_1 P_1$$

$$L_2 W > X_2 P_2$$

$$P_1 = T P_2$$

In this system the inequality is consistent with a competitive equilibrium in which commodity 2 is not produced at home. The two sets of conditions above imply:

$$\frac{p_1}{p_2} < T$$

For another country with an opposite pattern of relative costs we have:

$$\frac{p_1}{p_2} > T$$

Therefore, the condition for the existence of trade between England and Portugal is:

$$\frac{p_{ec}}{p_{ew}} < T < \frac{p_{pc}}{p_{pw}} \tag{2}$$

Condition (2), corresponds to Ricardo's condition (1) in terms of relative labour costs. (1) is a condition for the gains from trade (normative theory); instead (2) is a condition for the existence of trade under free competition (positive theory). This correspondence breaks down if the markets are non-competitive or condition (2) may become a post-trade property of international equilibrium and misses its explanatory role.

Foreign trade and analogies
Two achievements of Ricardo's theory of foreign trade have been mostly celebrated. He proved that the prices of the goods traded among nations and within a closed economy are ruled by different principles; in particular, the labour theory of value cannot be applied to the international exchange. Furthermore, he explained that the absolute (dis)advantage does not prevent mutually advantageous trade, performed according to the comparative advantage.

This basic property is often explained by the analogy between the specialization of nations and the specialization of individuals. We resort to the stock example of the absolutely capable lawyer and the absolutely less capable secretary to show why comparative advantage prevails over absolute advantage. Yet, the analogy with foreign trade is only partial. In a sense, the trade of commodities between two nations can be interpreted as a second-best solution, in comparison with a full integration where capital and labour can move across them; no such kind of integration is possible in the lawyer–secretary example and the exchange between them is a first-best solution. Next, the absolute advantage of the lawyer depends on his or her intrinsic skills; instead in the Portugal–England example the similar advantage of Portugal may depend on different factors (skills, climate, institutions and, in the short period, given endowments of capital goods). The latter feature becomes important if we want to assess the additional advantage from full integration.

Two other analogies have been adopted in order to facilitate the grasp of the causes and the effects of trade. The analogy between the choice of techniques and the choice of the pattern of trade has already been mentioned above. Another analogy is that between the opening of trade and a technical innovation. We shall deal with this issue later when discussing the connection of the chapter 'On Foreign Trade' with the chapter 'On Machinery' in *Principles*.

The need for generalizations

Ricardo explains that the basic explanation of international exchange, based on comparative advantage, does not change if the assumption of barter is replaced with that of a medium of exchange, like gold–money, adopted in the transactions. Movements of gold among nations and corresponding changes in the levels of money prices of the traded commodities will be the mechanism through which the pattern of trade satisfying the basic principle emerges.

Still, the following limitations of Ricardo's contribution to the pure theory of foreign trade under free competition remain: (a) the terms of trade are left undetermined; (b) the distinction between aggregate (or national) gains and individual (or class) gains is treated only in passing; (c) there is a dimensionality restriction in his argument: the assumption of only two commodities and homogeneous labour performed over a uniform period of production. The recognition of such limitations has stimulated the development of different models of international trade both in the mainstream and in alternative traditions (see Steedman, 1979). We shall limit ourselves to compare the textbook Ricardian model of international trade, called here 'Ricardian model' for short, with the argument on foreign trade discussed so far.

The Ricardian model

The 'Ricardian model' is a formalization of Ricardo's argument supplemented by the apparatus of supply and demand schedules, as suggested by John Stuart Mill ([1844] 1948) and applied to the markets of two produced commodities and to the labour market. The model adopts the assumption of constant returns to scale. The coefficients Table 4 replace the figures in Table 3 not only because symbols are used instead of numbers, but also for this additional assumption about the technology.

The coefficient a_{ij} denotes a fixed labour coefficient: the input of labour per unit of output j produced in country i. Let X_{ij} be the output of good j and L_i a fixed supply of labour in country i. The national (autarky) full-employment equation:

$$a_{ic} X_{ic} + a_{iw} X_{iw} = L_i, i = p, e$$

is represented by a linear production possibility frontier and the world (two-country) transformation schedule is reported in Figure 11. The gains from trade for the two-country world economy are described in the figure by a comparison between the world production frontier ABC and the internal point D associated with full employment without trade. The autarky relative costs are represented by the slope of the line AB for Portugal, of BC for England.

Table 4   Fixed labour coefficients

	Cloth	Wine
Portugal	a_{pc}	a_{pw}
England	a_{ec}	a_{ew}

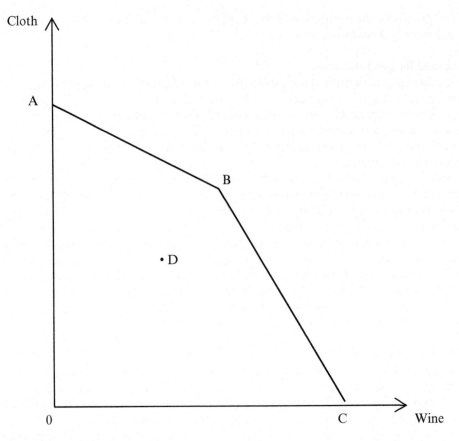

Figure 11   The efficiency frontier and the autarky point

The model fills the gap of the undetermined terms of trade, T, by assuming the existence of a market clearing equilibrium. The determination of T is represented in Figure 12 as an equilibrium on the world market for cloth in the two-country economy: the intersection between a stepwise rising aggregate supply curve and an aggregate downward-sloping demand curve.

This Ricardian model seems to establish a theoretical continuity between the classical and the neoclassical approaches applied to the theory of international values. The equilibrium relative prices before and after trade are equal to full-employment opportunity costs. Therefore, such a model might convey the idea that Ricardo's principle of comparative advantage is confined to a full-employment equilibrium. This is an unduly restrictive interpretation (Parrinello, 1988). In fact, the conditions for trade (1), (2) do not change, if we allow for an unlimited supply of labour in the trading countries at given positive wages. The gains from trade are measured by a decrease of labour employed per unit output or by an increase of the output/labour ratio. The principle does not determine to what extent the change of these ratios in a definite direction is due to the change in the numerator or to the change of opposite sign in the denominator. In particular, the re-employment and the additional product of labour that is saved by moving from

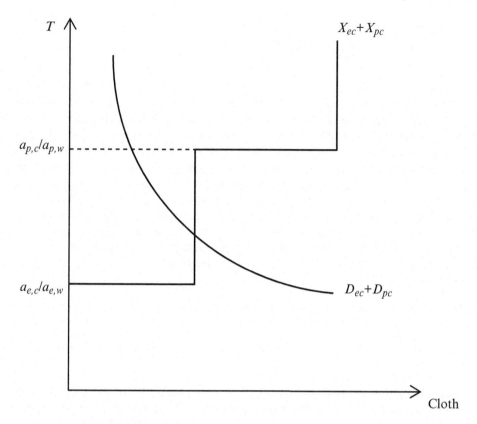

Figure 12 Free trade equilibrium

autarky to free trade is not required by whatever positive theory of trade. Furthermore, it does not exclude losses for some class of individuals (workers in particular). This possibility is implicitly admitted by Ricardo in Chapter 31 'On Machinery' in *Principles*.

'On Foreign Trade' in the light of 'On Machinery'

Suppose that initially Portugal is a closed country that produces only cloth for its domestic consumption. It could also produce wine, but this good is not in demand. Such an autarky model shares all the characteristics of Ricardo's corn model. Part of the total amount of cloth available is used as circulating capital for the subsistence of the labour force and part is consumed by capitalists and landlords. On the other side, England can be initially a closed economy with opposite characteristics and would be described by a wine model, although it might be capable of also producing cloth that it is not in home demand. Now suppose that free trade between the two countries becomes possible. For each country this occurrence is equivalent to a technical innovation as suggested by Schumpeter ([1942] 1975: 83): 'The opening up of new markets, foreign or domestic, and the organizational development from the craft shop and factory to such concerns as U.S. Steel illustrate the same process of industrial mutation.'

The opening of trade in Ricardo's example can be assimilated to the introduction of a new machinery, specific for each country. The new machinery in Portugal is 'wine', which procures to this country the same amount of cloth with less labour. For similar reasons the new machinery in England is 'cloth'. Such 'new products' can be interpreted as different types of new intermediate goods that 'produce', through a process of exchange, the commodity desired for consumption and should be replaced at the end of the year to allow for a new cycle of production. The exchange is simultaneous, but workers must be employed for one year to produce wine in Portugal in order to get cloth for this country at the end of the year, on the same basis as the direct production of cloth in Portugal would require the labour of 90 workers performed over one year. A similar remark applies to England. It may happen that the labour productivities in the industries of a country are such that the opening of foreign trade increases its net national income (net of the subsistence wages, according the classical definition) but decreases its gross national income (gross of the subsistence wages) in comparison to the autarky state. The recognition of this possibility suggests a connection between Ricardo's argument on 'new machinery' and his 'foreign trade', as widely acknowledged in Jeck and Kurz (1983) and resumed, in passing, by Parrinello (1988). It legitimates the following interpolation in Ricardo's passage:

> All I wish to prove, is, that the discovery and use of machinery [*or the opening of foreign trade*] may be attended with a diminution of gross produce; and whenever that is the case, it will be injurious to the labouring class, as some of their number will be thrown out of employment, and population will become redundant, compared with the funds which are to employ it. (*Works,* I: 390; emphasis added)

We also note that the analogy between the opening of free trade and a technical innovation has limited scope if the two events are conceived as recurrent factors of growth. An opening sequence of trade among nations has its own limit when a state of world integration is achieved; instead, technical progress does not seem to have any point of saturation.

Foreign trade in a global economy

Ricardo has stressed the difference between the principles that govern international trade and those underlying domestic trade by the comparison of the trade between England and Portugal with that between the London area and Yorkshire. The principle of comparative advantage must be applied to the former, and the principle of absolute advantage to the latter. Ricardo traces the difference between the two principles back to the different mobility of resources: the high mobility of produced commodities and the low mobility of capital (financial capital as distinct from tradable capital goods) and labour among nations versus the mobility of products, labour and capital among regions of the same nation. We now ask whether one of these polar cases can describe the trade relations among nations in the contemporary stage of globalization.

In Parrinello (2009) it is argued that an intermediate model of international trade should be adopted for this purpose, instead of the two polar cases envisaged by Ricardo. A contemporary global economy is not a fully integrated economy like two regions of the same country or a group of nations that form an economic union. A model of such an economy should recognize the contrast existing between the high international mobility of products and of financial capital and the specific national characteristics of the labour markets. The latter may depend on a limited international mobility of labour or on national norms that regulate labour and wages in the different countries. This asymmetry is revealed by the observation of persistently wide differentials among national wages for the same type of labour versus the small difference in the rates of return on financial capital invested in different countries, after allowing for risk compensations. It follows that a more useful model of a global economy should assume the full mobility of products and capital and two alternative or joint restrictions on labour across countries: (a) labour immobility and (b) different national institutional wage settings. Under such assumptions, the determination of the pattern of international trade departs from the principle of comparative advantage and conforms to that of absolute advantage. Some variants of the Portugal–England and London–Yorkshire examples have to be taken into account. For the sake of argument let us imagine Europe and China as the two partners in a global market. Two modelling approaches should be considered. In both of them the pattern of trade in a long-period competitive equilibrium is associated with a uniform rate of profit for the global economy and is consistent with different wage rates in Europe and in China.

In the neoclassical approach a market clearing equilibrium pertains to each national labour market, under the assumptions of a given supply of labour, flexible wages and a sufficient technical substitutability between labour and capital goods. This case is equivalent to that of a single fully integrated Europe–China economy endowed with two distinct types of labour, which can be fully employed before and after trade, although differently allocated among industries. The possible absolute technical advantage of one of the two countries would be compensated by higher equilibrium wages and, therefore, as in the case of comparative advantage, neither China nor Europe would undersell the other.

Alternatively, and perhaps more realistically, a competitive equilibrium before and after trade is consistent with unemployment and not fully flexible wages. The competitive choice of the pattern of trade is equivalent to a choice of techniques that maximizes the rate of profit, with different types of labour that receive given real wages. Then, as in the example of free trade between London and Yorkshire, it is possible that all capital and capitalist production flows, say, to China and leaves Europe. Complete delocalization is a synthetic word that describes this possibility.

SERGIO PARRINELLO

See also:

Comparative Advantage; Competition; Corn Laws; *Essay on Profits*; Ricardo's Four Magic Numbers.

References

Jeck, A. and H.D. Kurz (1983), 'David Ricardo: Ansichten zur Maschinerie', in H. Hagemann and P. Kalmbach (eds), *Technischer Fortschritt und Arbeitslosigkeit*, Frankfurt: Campus, pp. 38–166.
Mill, J.S. ([1844] 1948), *Essays on Some Unsettled Questions of Political Economy*, London: London School of Economics.
Parrinello, S. (1988), 'On foreign trade and the Ricardian model of trade', *Journal of Post Keynesian Economics*, **10**(4), 585–601.
Parrinello, S. (2009), 'The notion of national competitiveness in a global economy', in J. Vint. J.S. Metcalfe, H.D. Kurz, N. Salvadori and P. Samuelson (eds), *Economic Theory and Economic Thought: Essays in Honour of Ian Steedman*, London: Routledge.
Schumpeter, J. ([1942] 1975), *Capitalism, Socialism and Democracy*, New York: Harper, pp. 82–8.

Seligman, E.R.A. and J.H. Hollander (1911), 'Ricardo and Torrens', *The Economic Journal*, **21**(83), 448–68.
Smith, A. ([1776] 1976), *An Inquiry into the Nature and Causes of the Wealth of Nations*, in *The Glasgow Edition of the Works and Correspondence of Adam Smith*, (eds) R.H. Campbell, A.S. Skinner and W.B. Todd, Oxford: Clarendon Press.
Steedman, I. (ed.) (1979), *Fundamental Issues in Trade Theory*, London: Macmillan.
Torrens, R. (1815), *An Essay on the External Corn Trade*, London, Hatchard.

Funding System

The Napoleonic Wars bequeathed a public debt of about £840 million (almost three times its pre-war level) to Great Britain. More than half of British government expenditure was devoted to servicing debt charges (Churchman, 2001: 129–35 and Dome, 2004: 8–10). No surprise that the defrayal of the public debt and its likely consequences on future economic prospects were burning issues that raised vast public concern and a rich pamphlet literature in the 1810s and 1820s (Hargreaves [1930] 1966: Chapter 9).

Like David Hume in his 1752 essay 'Of Public Credit' and Adam Smith in Book V, Chapter 3, 'Of Public Debts', of the *Wealth of Nations* before him, David Ricardo was alive to the economic and political dangers engendered by an increasing public debt. In the *Principles of Political Economy, and Taxation* he contemplates the possibility that some future war could drive Great Britain towards a national bankruptcy (*Works*, I: 173). In various Parliamentary speeches he defines public debt as a national evil 'which almost any sacrifice would not be too great to get rid of' since it 'destroyed the equilibrium of prices, occasioned many persons to emigrate to other countries, in order to avoid the burthen of taxation which it entailed, and hung like a mill-stone round the exertion and industry of the country' ('On Budget', 9 June 1819, *Works*, V: 21). Public debt and the Corn Laws are singled out by Ricardo as the twin evils that exert a momentous growth-retarding effect on the British economy: 'This would be the happiest country in the world, and its progress in prosperity would be beyond the power of imagination to conceive, if we got rid of two great evils – the national debt and the corn laws' ('Agricultural Distress', 30 May 1820, ibid.: 55).

Yet, unlike Smith's *Wealth of Nations*, Ricardo's *Principles* do not include a specific chapter on the public debt issue. Ricardo's neglect of the public debt issue in the *Principles* may help explain why 'while there is no aspect of Ricardo's work that has not been subject to scrutiny, his views on the public debt have received little attention of a comprehensive nature' (Churchman, 2001: 12). Churchman's remark is far from being an overstatement: a quick search on Jstor and Google Scholar databases reveals that, for a long time, the only journal paper explicitly devoted to this issue has been Roberts (1942); while a chapter on public debt within Sam Hollander's 1979 lengthy book on the economics of David Ricardo is notable by its absence (O'Brien, 1981: 381). Before Churchman's 2001 monograph, a renewal of interest on 'Ricardo on public debt' had been ignited, in the mid-1970s, by the debate on the alleged Ricardian origins of Robert Barro's 1974 debt taxation equivalence proposition: see Barro (1976), Buchanan (1976), O'Driscoll (1977) and, more recently, Ahiakpor (2013). Though it cannot be denied that the emergence of the new classical macroeconomics in the 1970s has largely contributed to rescue from oblivion Ricardo's contribution to fiscal theory (King, 2013: Chapter 6), yet the alleged Ricardian pedigree of the Ricardian equivalence proposition has been questioned by many historians of economic analysis: for example, Mark Blaug (1996: 132), summarizing the content of Chapter XVII of Ricardo's *Principles* claims that 'there is no real equivalence between paying for government expenditures by taxation or by borrowing, so that the modern "Ricardo equivalence theorem" that some commentators have read into this chapter is yet another misnomer associated with the name of Ricardo'. Nonetheless, Barro insists that 'David Ricardo (. . .) was the first to articulate this theory. Therefore, the attribution of the equivalence theorem to Ricardo is appropriate *even if he had doubts about some of the theorem's assumptions*' (1989: 39n; emphasis added). By the same token, a strictly related issue, the 'sinking fund', receives only a very cursory treatment in the *Principles*: Ricardo just mentions it in Chapters XXI, 'Effects of Accumulation on Profits and Interest' (*Works*, I: 197) and XXVII, 'On Currency and Banks' (ibid.: 231) and devotes a few lines in Chapter XVII, 'Taxes on other Commodities than Raw Produce'. Here Ricardo endorses (without mentioning) Robert Hamilton's thesis according to which 'no sinking fund can be efficient for the purpose of diminishing the debt, if it be not derived from the excess of the public revenue over the public expenditure' and regrets that 'the sinking fund in this country is only such in name; for there is no excess of revenue above expenditure. It ought, by economy, to be made what it is professed to be, a really efficient fund for the payment of the debt' (ibid.: 173). By contrast, Ricardo pays tribute to Hamilton, the author of *An Inquiry Concerning the Rise and Progress, the Redemption and Present State, and the Management of the National Debt of Great Britain and Ireland* (first edition, 1812; third edition, 1818) in his article in the *Supplement to the Fourth, Fifth and Sixth Editions of the Encyclopaedia Britannica*, the 'Funding System' (1820). In this latter work, expressly devoted to an investigation of 'the rise, progress, and modifications of the Sinking Fund, accompanied with some observations as to the probability of its accomplishing the object for which it was instituted' (*Works*, IV: 149), Ricardo plainly acknowledges that 'it has been shown by Dr Hamilton that no fund can be efficient for the reduction of debt but such as arises from an excess of revenue above expenditure' (ibid.: 167).

The story of the composition of the 'Funding System' has been reconstructed in detail by Piero Sraffa: Macvey Napier, the editor of the *Supplement*, asked James Mill to persuade Ricardo to contribute the article at the beginning of September 1819. After some hesitation, Ricardo eventually accepted the proposal and completed the manuscript in the final days of the same month; while the article was actually published exactly one year later, in September 1820 (ibid.: 145–7). As his September 1819 correspondence reveals, Ricardo was flattered by Macvey Napier's invitation to contribute the 'Funding System' article. Yet, he was initially hesitant to accept it since he thought to have nothing original to say on the subject, after Hamilton's book (see Ricardo to Mill, 6 and 9 September 1819, Ricardo to Place, 18 September 1819, Ricardo to Malthus, 21 September 1819 and Ricardo to Trower, 25 September 1819, *Works*, VIII: 54, 60–61, 69, 72–3 and 78 respectively). It appears that it was Mill who finally persuaded Ricardo that the effort was worthwhile:

> The mode in which a sinking fund, when real, operates to pay debts, is one – the mode in which a sinking fund, when no longer real, may be made to appear real, is another – and a third is (*what you have not been anticipated in by anybody*) the utter absurdity of trusting a government like ours with a sinking fund at all. The last topic is original, *and if worked in your best manner will be striking.* (Mill to Ricardo, 11 September, 1819, ibid., VIII: 67; emphasis added)

It is probably not a mere coincidence that the political argument – 'the utter absurdity of trusting a government like ours with a sinking fund' – stressed by Mill in the letter quoted above, enjoyed pride of place in the 'Funding System'. For Ricardo, in fact, it is just the lack of a credible commitment by the government not to misapply the sinking fund and the ready compliance of the Parliament to any violation (overt or in disguise) of it proposed by the Chancellor of the Exchequer that constitute the basic reasons why '*in the present constitution of Parliament*, the superintending authority, the sinking fund is pernicious, and that it cannot be too soon abolished' (*Works*, IV: 199; emphasis added).

Though this is not the right place to investigate James Mill's influence on Ricardo's thought, yet, what was quoted above should not be misinterpreted as implying that it was Mill who dictated the agenda to Ricardo when he finally accepted Napier's invitation to contribute the 'Funding System' article in mid-September 1819. Ricardo had already elaborated and forcefully expressed the 'political' argument in a couple of Parliamentary speeches of June 1819:

> Mr. Ricardo said, he had already opposed the grant of 3 millions towards a sinking fund, because he did not wish to place such a fund at the mercy of ministers, who would take it whenever they thought that urgent necessity required it. He did not mean to say that it would be better with one set of ministers than another; for he looked upon it that all ministers would be anxious, on cases of what they conceived emergency, to appropriate it to the public use. He thought the whole thing a delusion upon the public, and on that account he would never support a tax to maintain it ... He therefore never would give a vote in support of any tax which went to continue a sinking fund; for if that fund were to amount to 8 millions, ministers would on any emergency give the same account of it as they did at present. The delusion of it had been seen long ago by all those who were acquainted with the subject; and it would have been but fair and sound policy to have exposed it. ('The Budget', 9 June 1819, *Works*, V: 20–21)

Similarly:

> A sinking fund was only useful – was only what it pretended to be – when a surplus of income was strictly applied to the purposes for which it was established – the extinction of debt. No appropriation of money under the name of sinking fund ever had, and, in his [Ricardo's] opinion, ever would be constantly applied to this purpose; it would always be considered by ministers as a resource of which they might avail themselves when they were under any difficulty, in raising money by new taxes ... He [Ricardo] had a jealous distrust of raising money beyond immediate necessity, and placing it in the hands of ministers; not the present ministers only, but any ministers responsible to a House of Commons constituted like ours. ('Excise Duties Bill', 18 June 1819, ibid.: 24 and 25)

Moreover, it has to be remarked that Ricardo's interest in the sinking fund issue predates his entry into Parliament, representing the Irish 'pocket' borough of Portarlington in February 1819. Ricardo was long aware of the frequent misapplications of the sinking fund by the government. As early as the 1815, in the final pages of his *Essay on Profits* Ricardo reports Nicholas Vansittart's 1813 'Plan of Finance' as a subversion of Mr. Pitt's original system (the reference is to the sinking fund established by William Pitt the Younger in 1786 that Ricardo analyses in detail in the 'Funding System'):

> They [the stockholders] have suffered too from the inroads lately made on the sinking fund, and which, it is supposed, will be still further extended – a measure of the greatest injustice – in direct violation of solemn contracts; for the sinking fund is as much a part of the contract as the

dividend, and, as a source of revenue, utterly at variance with all sound principles . . . To meddle with the sinking fund, is to obtain a little temporary aid at the sacrifice of a great future advantage. It is reversing the whole system of Mr. Pitt, in the creation of that fund. (*Works*, IV: 40)

Notwithstanding such awareness, before 1819 Ricardo appears not to be prejudicially opposed to the sinking fund as an effective fiscal policy instrument targeted at debt reduction and tax burden relief. Still, in 1816 he is willing to give government a chance to demonstrate its good faith in respecting the sinking fund, as the following letter to Trower shows:

I hope the minister will not now touch the sinking fund – I hope he will never touch it. It is the general saving bank of the Nation and should be encouraged on the same principles as encouragement is given to those institutions. I am sorry to observe that amongst those who have the power to decide on these matters there does not appear any reluctance to meddle with the sinking fund. I am told that Lord Grenville is not averse to such a measure. (Ricardo to Trower, 4 February 1816, *Works*, VII: 17; see also Ricardo to McCulloch, 9 June 1816, ibid.: 37–8)

By contrast, in 1819 Ricardo reaches the unwavering conclusion that no further confidence can be bestowed on government's good faith with regard to the inviolability of the sinking fund:

Our sinking fund is gone, and I am not disposed to raise a new one, for the purpose of placing it again at the disposal of ministers. Do what you will, they will not respect it, and after a few years we should be as much in debt as ever. I am for a vigorous system of taxation, if it is for the purpose of paying off debt once for all, but I am sure that ministers will never respect any fund, which is to accumulate at compound interest. With the slightest pressure on the finances such a fund would be diverted from the employment to which it had been destined. (Ricardo to Trower, 28 May 1819, *Works*, VIII: 33)

Till his untimely death four years later, Ricardo does not change his mind on this issue any further. Such a change of mind as to government's reliability leads Ricardo to emphasize a substantial difference between his (new) position, championed in the 'Funding System', and that endorsed by Hamilton with regard the expediency of keeping a sinking fund. Three days before the manuscript of the 'Funding System' was mailed to Mill and Place, Ricardo writes to Trower that:

[The] only point of difference between Dr. H[amilton] and me is this, – he would I believe support the Sinking Fund, I would get rid of it entirely, or leave it at that small amount as to give security that if the revenue suffered any unexpected defalcation there was this surplus to apply to.

And adds:

I am equally impressed with Dr. Hamilton with the importance of diminishing our enormous debt, the *question with me is, will the Sinking Fund effect it? I am persuaded that it never will, for it will never be safe from the gripe of ministers*. (Ricardo to Trower, 25 September 1819, *Works*, VIII: 78–9; emphasis added)

The 'Funding System' may be described as Ricardo's passionate plea for the repeal of the sinking fund and the introduction of a capital levy to redeem British public debt.

In this entry I concentrate on Ricardo's views of the sinking fund issue. For a more complete analysis of Ricardo's views of the public debt the reader can consult the entry 'National Debt' in this volume.

As concerns the sinking fund issue, Ricardo grounds his argument on a sharp distinction between lessons from pure theory and lessons from actual practice (Roberts, 1942: 263–4). On the one hand, Ricardo holds the view that 'in point of economy there is no real difference' in either of the three alternative fiscal options to defray wartime expenditure, that is, war taxes, loans-cum-taxes covering mere interest charges and loans-cum-sinking-fund, that is, loans-cum-taxes higher than mere interest charges (see *Works*, IV: 186). Accordingly, for Ricardo, the sinking fund, if it helps the government persuade the public to bear a higher level of taxation and is rigorously applied to its original target, that is, if it may be placed in a safe harbour, away from government's fiscal discretion, may turn out to be an effective policy instrument for public debt redemption and tax-burden relief:

> The sinking fund was established with a view to diminish the national debt during peace, and to prevent its rapid increase during war. The only wise and good object of war-taxes is also to prevent the accumulation of debt. A sinking fund and war-taxes are only useful while they are strictly applied to the objects for which they are raised; they become instruments of mischief and delusion when they are made use of for the purpose of providing the interest on a new debt . . . The sinking fund is, therefore, useful as an engine of taxation; and, *if the country could depend on ministers*, that it would be faithfully devoted to the purposes for which it was established, namely, to afford at the termination of war a clear additional surplus revenue beyond expenditure, in proportion to the addition made to the debt, it would be wise and expedient to keep it as a separate fund, *subject to fixed rules and regulations*. (Ibid.: 157 and 172; emphasis added)

On the other hand, Ricardo warns his readers that facts tell a radically different story. Following Hamilton, Ricardo devotes the first 20 pages of the 'Funding System' to detail how the sinking fund has been repeatedly encroached upon to defray current deficits ever since 1733 when, for the first time '500,000*l*. [£500 000] was taken from that fund, and applied to the services of the year' (ibid.: 150). The paradoxical consequence of such a recurrent misuse of the sums stored in the sinking fund has been that the latter 'has, instead of diminishing the debt, greatly increased it. The sinking fund has encouraged expenditure' (ibid.: 195). Hence, the sinking fund, considered from the perspective of public debt redemption and tax burden relief, has actually displayed a very dismal performance.

Ricardo is perfectly aware that the crux of the question is the (in)ability of the Parliament to bind the government to a strict observance of the rules that pledges the progressive discharge of the various loans to which the respective sinking funds are attached. Ricardo has no hesitation in locating the root of the problem in (what may dubbed as) an insufficient fiscal commitment by the government (Churchman, 2001: 107–8). As aptly noted by King (2013: 135), 'in the political climate of the time, [Ricardo] believed, increased tax revenues would simply increase wasteful government spending and encourage rent-seeking by powerful interest groups. His objection to the Sinking Fund was based on these political considerations, to which he attributed great significance.' For Ricardo, the temptation to violate the sinking fund proves an irresistible one for the Chancellor of the Exchequer and, by the same token, any promise to keep it inviolate turns out to be a non-credible one. That is the basic reason why Ricardo ridiculed

Mr. Pitt's belief that entrusting a few selected Commissioners to the management of the sinking fund would have solved the problem. The relevant passages are worthy of a full quotation:

> When Mr. Pitt, in 1786, established the sinking fund, he was aware of the danger of entrusting it to ministers and parliament; and, therefore, provided that the sums applicable to the sinking fund should be paid by the Exchequer into the hands of commissioners, by quarterly payments, who should be required to invest equal sums of money in the purchase of stock, on four days in each week, or about fifty days in each quarter. The commissioners named were, the Speaker of the House of Commons, the Chancellor of the Exchequer, the Master of the Rolls, the Accountant General of the Court of Chancery, and the Governor and Deputy-Governor of the Bank. He thought, that, under such management, there could be no misapplication of the funds, and he thought correctly, for the commissioners have faithfully fulfilled the trust reposed in them ... Mr. Pitt flattered himself most strangely, that he had found a remedy for the difficulty which 'had hitherto been the bane of this country'; he thought he had discovered means for preventing 'ministers, when it suited their convenience, from getting hold of this sum, which ought to be regarded as most sacred.' With the knowledge of Parliament which he had, it is surprising that he should have relied so firmly on the resistance which the House of Commons would offer to any plan of ministers for violating the sinking fund. Ministers have never desired the partial repeal of this law, without obtaining a ready compliance from Parliament ... It is true that the measures of Mr. Pitt locked it up from their immediate seizure, but they knew it was in the hands of the commissioners, and presumed as much upon it, and justly, with the knowledge they had of Parliament, as if it had been in their own. They considered the commissioners as their trustees, accumulating money for their benefit, and of which they knew that they might dispose whenever they should consider that the urgency of the case required it. (*Works*, IV: 190–91, 192–3 and 194)

To persuade his readers of 'the utter absurdity of trusting a government like ours with a sinking fund' Ricardo employs a second element, besides the past history of the sinking fund. Ricardo refers to an argument 'now common in the mouths of ministers when they wish to lay on new taxes, for the purpose of creating a new sinking fund, in lieu of one which they have just spent' (ibid.: 197), that is, the national security argument: the sinking fund 'will make foreign countries respect us; they will be afraid to insult or provoke us, when they know that we are possessed of so powerful a resource' (ibid.: 197–8). Ricardo is ready to seize the opportunity to highlight the inherent contradiction between the sinking fund as a means for debt redemption and the sinking fund as a means to defray current expenditure in times of war:

> [The sinking fund] cannot, at one and the same time, be employed in the annoyance of an enemy, and in the payment of debt. If taxes are, as they ought to be, raised for the expences of a war, what facility will a sinking fund give to the raising of them? None whatever. It is not because the possession of a sinking fund will enable them to raise new and additional taxes that ministers prize it; for they know it will have no such effect; but because they know that they will be enabled to substitute the sinking fund in lieu of taxes, and employ it, as they have always done, in war, and providing interest for fresh debt. (Ibid.: 198)

Hence, for Ricardo, his previous conclusion – that the sinking fund encourages fiscal profligacy – also holds to its new role as a war fund. Accordingly, if peace-keeping is the target, Ricardo claims that such a target may be more easily hit if the government is not endowed with the financial means to start a war rather than by the fear of foreign countries that the sinking fund may be turned into a war fund:

There cannot be a greater security for the continuance of peace than the imposing on ministers the necessity of applying to the people for taxes to support a war. Suffer the sinking fund to accumulate during peace to any considerable sum, and very little provocation would induce them to enter into a new contest. They would know that, by a little management, they could make the sinking fund available to the raising of a new supply, instead of being available to the payment of the debt. (Ibid.: 197)

What is quoted above is not an extemporaneous outburst but an argument Ricardo was deeply persuaded of. In several Parliamentary speeches, both before and after the publication of the 'Funding System', Ricardo denounces the subversion of the sinking fund as a war fund by the government: see, for example, 'Excise Duties Bill', 18 June 1819, 'Motion for a Committee on the Agricultural Distress', 18 February 1822 and 'Financial Situation of the Country', 21 February 1823 (*Works*, V: 25, 130 and 251, respectively). Similarly, in a letter to Trower in Spring 1822 he writes:

I should be neglecting my duty if with my opinions of the Sinking Fund I did not do everything in my power to get rid of it. Of what use can it be to diminish the debt in time of peace, if you leave in the hands of ministers a fund which experience shews will be used only for the purpose of ultimately further increasing the debt? *While ministers have this fund virtually at their disposal they will on the slightest occasion be disposed for war. To keep them peaceable you must keep them poor.* (Ricardo to Trower, 25 March 1822, *Works*, IX: 180; emphasis added)

To sum up. Whenever the sinking fund was the issue both in his Parliamentary speeches or private correspondence Ricardo reiterated the conclusion he reached in the 'Funding System', that is, that 'no securities can be given by ministers that the sinking fund shall be faithfully devoted to the payment of debt, and without such securities we should be much better without such a fund' (*Works*, IV: 196). The lack of a credible commitment by the government not to misapply any sinking fund is the basic reason why Ricardo, in the course of his entire public life, was an outspoken opponent to any tax proposal intended to support the sinking fund and why he supported the capital levy proposal for public debt redemption, though he was perfectly aware of its unpopularity and of the heavy damages it entailed to his reputation as an economist.

RODOLFO SIGNORINO

See also:

Member of Parliament; National Debt; Ricardian Equivalence; Taxation.

References

Ahiakpor, J. (2013), 'The modern Ricardian equivalence theorem: drawing the wrong conclusions from David Ricardo's analysis', *Journal of the History of Economic Thought*, **35**(1), 77–92.
Barro, R.J. (1974), 'Are government bonds net wealth?', *Journal of Political Economy*, **82**(6), 1095–117.
Barro, R.J. (1976), 'Perceived wealth in bonds and social security and the Ricardian equivalence theorem: reply to Feldstein and Buchanan', *Journal of Political Economy*, **84**(2), 343–50.
Barro, R.J. (1989), 'The Ricardian approach to budget deficits', *The Journal of Economic Perspectives*, **3**(2), 37–54.
Blaug, M. (1996), *Economic Theory in Retrospect*, 5th edition, Cambridge, UK: Cambridge University Press.
Buchanan, J.M. (1976), 'Barro on the Ricardian equivalence theorem', *Journal of Political Economy*, **84**(2), 337–42.
Churchman, N. (2001), *David Ricardo on Public Debt*, Basingstoke, UK and New York: Palgrave Macmillan.
Dome, T. (2004), *The Political Economy of Public Finance in Britain, 1767–1873*, London: Routledge.
Hargreaves, E.L. ([1930] 1966), *The National Debt*, London: Frank Cass & Co. Ltd.

Hollander, S. (1979), *The Economics of David Ricardo*, Toronto: University of Toronto Press.

King, J.E. (2013), *David Ricardo*, Basingstoke, UK and New York: Palgrave Macmillan.

O'Brien, D.P. (1981), 'Ricardian economics and the economics of David Ricardo', *Oxford Economic Papers*, **33**(3), 352–86.

O'Driscoll, G.P. (1977), 'The Ricardian nonequivalence theorem', *Journal of Political Economy*, **85**(1), 207–10.

Roberts, R. (1942), 'Ricardo's theory of public debts', *Economica*, New Series, **9**(35), 257–66.

General Glut

The controversy that developed around Say's Law revolves mainly around the question of general gluts. The term 'general glut', although hardly found in modern textbooks of economics, was a familiar concept to classical economists. In the early nineteenth century the role of savings was one of the most controversial issues in political economics. Debates on over-production were closely linked to the debate on over-saving or under-consumption. The controversy reached its peak with the famous debate between Ricardo and Malthus on the possibility of general gluts at the end of the Napoleonic Wars and subsequent controversies in which every major economist was involved. Classical economists like Ricardo rejected the concept of a general glut. Ricardo pointed out that demand does not constitute a decisive barrier to economic growth. Identifying decisions to save with decisions to invest and thus the connection between production and income, Ricardo came to the conclusion 'that there is no amount of capital which may not be employed in a country, because demand is only limited by production' (*Works*, I: 290). Whereas over-production may exist in certain sectors of the economy, it can never exist for all sectors simultaneously.

Controversy has never ceased since the early debate on a general glut between Ricardo, James Mill and Say on the one hand, and on the other, Sismondi, Malthus and, earlier, Lauderdale (1804), who held a theory of excess saving or general glut of capital and emphasized that public spending was required to offset private thrift if stagnation was to be avoided. Indeed, the history of economic theory from the classical period to Keynes can be regarded as a shift from a paradigm where Say's Law holds to one where it does not (Morishima and Catephores, 1988: 23). However, there are elements of continuity but also substantial differences in the meaning and understanding of Say's Law over time. Whereas a closer adherence to Say's Law and the quantity theory of money (at least in the long run) characterizes an orthodox position or supply-side economist, emphasis on the possibility and empirical recurrence of a general glut is one of the hallmarks of a 'heterodox' economist. The historical context of the origin and rise of the general glut controversy should not be overlooked (see also Davis, 2003). Emphasizing that saving and investment are decisive for the growth of the wealth of nations and opposing the view that a general shortage of demand would be the prime impediment to prosperity, James Mill, Say and Ricardo were following Adam Smith and his emphasis on the role of capital accumulation. Smith as well as Turgot fought against crude under-consumptionist views, as represented, for example, by Mandeville in his famous *Fable of the Bees* ([1714/1729] 1924), according to which an increase in saving automatically leads to an economic crisis since consumption was considered as the only form of expenditure: Mandeville held the view that spending of necessity would benefit the community whereas saving injures it. Furthermore, Smith's analysis was directed against mercantilist doctrines when emphasizing that the growth in the wealth of nations depends on capital accumulation and the ability to produce and generate income instead of on the property of precious metals, and so on. This argumentation implied putting more emphasis on the production or real side of the economy than on the monetary side.

According to his closest associate Richard Kahn (1984), Keynes, in the *General Theory*, attacked the two main pillars on which classical economics was built: Say's Law and the quantity theory of money. Against the classical doctrine 'that supply creates its own demand' (Keynes [1936] 1973, *Collected Writings*, VII: 18), which requires the underlying assumption that saving promotes the accumulation of national wealth and thereby the identity of saving and net investment, Keynes directed his antithetical 'principle of effective demand' and considered Malthus the most important precursor of his own approach. Whereas Keynes's rejection of Say's Law is the most crucial of the many differences between Keynes and Ricardo – and also a main difference between Marx and Ricardo – it is important to analyse how economists from Ricardo to Keynes formulated Say's Law and how they interpreted it. For example, Ricardo identified decisions to save with decisions to invest, whereas Keynes did not.

Since in the general glut debate the great majority of economists followed the classical doctrine of savings and investment and the approach that had been shaped by Adam Smith, we begin our analysis with a discussion of Smith's contribution. Smith's analysis of the process of capital accumulation, and of productive and unproductive labour plays a major role in the dispute between Ricardo and Malthus. Emphasis will be on the distinction between a partial and a general glut, and on the role of money in alternative approaches, particularly the emphasis on the consequences of money as a store of value, first pointed out by John Stuart Mill and Wilhelm Roscher, and later taken up as a decisive argument against the validity of Say's Law by all leading critics as diverse as Marx and Keynes. Two other major topics deserve closer attention. The first is the role of the time dimension, especially the difference between Ricardo's long-run perspective and the concern with the short run by, for example, Malthus and Keynes. This affects the question of whether general over-production is regarded as a temporary or as a permanent problem. The second issue refers to the (non-)integration of the labour market, that is, the question of whether the acceptance of Say's Law implies full employment or not. Whereas Keynes, with a view to the orthodox neoclassical interpretation, took Say's Law to imply being 'equivalent to the proposition that there is no obstacle to full employment' (*Collected Writings*, VII: 26), such a staunch defender of Say's Law as Ricardo was the first major economist who pointed out the importance of the 'machinery problem', that is, the possibility of technological unemployment.

Smith: the 'Adam of Say's Law'
There has been a long and controversial debate on the question of who really discovered Say's Law, in particular whether priority has to be given to James Mill or Jean-Baptiste Say. Even in recent assessments, leading economists still come to different conclusions. While Baumol (1999: 202–4) and Schoorl (2013) join the Mill camp, Hollander (2005: 219–22) sides with the view that Say had indeed preceded Mill. However, there can be no doubt that Mill as well as Say based their argument strongly on Smith's approach who had shaped the classical doctrine of saving and investment. In a key passage of the *Wealth of Nations* he had stated:

> Whatever a person saves from his revenue he adds to his capital, and either employs it himself in maintaining an additional number of productive hands, or enables some other person to do so, by lending it to him for an interest, that is for a share of the profits ... What is annually saved is as regularly consumed as what is annually spent, and nearly in the same time too; but it is consumed by a different set of people. (*WN*, I.iii.15 and I.iii.18)

The text makes clear that either decisions to save are automatically identified with decisions to invest or that the interest rate mechanism functions as the equalizer. As a consequence the circular flow of income is maintained and a general glut cannot occur. Savings, for Smith, are a precondition of economic growth and thus for an increase in the wealth of nations. Of course, it is not savings per se but their investive employment that increases the wealth of an economy. Like other classical economists after him Smith presupposes the 'savings-equals-investment' axiom. Ricardo, for whom savings also determine capital accumulation, argues: 'There cannot, then, be accumulated in a country any amount of capital which cannot be employed productively' (*Works*, I: 290). For Smith the production and employment possibilities of an economy are limited by the available capital:

> The general industry of the society never can exceed what the capital of the society can employ. As the number of workmen that can be kept in employment by any particular person must bear a certain proportion to his capital, so the number of those that can be continually employed by all the members of a great society, must bear a certain proportion to the whole capital of that society, and never can exceed that proportion. No regulation of commerce can increase the quantity of industry in any society beyond what its capital can maintain. (*WN*, IV.ii.3)

This idea runs through classical political economics as indicated by the first of John Stuart Mill's fundamental propositions respecting capital: '[t]hat industry is limited by capital' (J.S. Mill [1871] 1965: 63). Capital accumulation thus holds a key position in the process of economic growth that is accentuated by the positive correlation with productivity growth. However, capital formation is not an exogenous variable but determined by the size of the surplus product and the propensity to accumulate. In the key passage quoted earlier, Smith understands capital accumulation as an increase of consumption by productive workers at the expense of unproductive consumption. The limits for capital formation are thus set by the propensity to luxury consumption by recipients of profit and rent incomes. Furthermore, Smith emphasizes that in advanced countries that are governed by the rule of law, 'a man must be perfectly crazy, who . . . does not employ all the stock which he commands, whether it be his own or borrowed of other people' (*WN*, II.i.30). The Smithian statement includes full capacity utilization as 'a vital component of Say's Law' (Eltis, 1984: 75).

The Smithian system excludes the possibility that an excess of savings can cause cyclical disturbances that lead to Keynesian unemployment. The economy is in a dynamic equilibrium in which growing productivity induces a rise in employment and income and thereby creates its own demand. It is therefore justified to perceive of Smith as 'the father of the Say's Law discussion' (Thweatt, 1979: 93) or the 'Adam of Say's Law' (Streissler, 1981: 51).

General versus partial over-production

'It will be recollected, that the question of a glut is exclusively whether it may be general, as well as particular, and not whether it may be permanent as well as temporary', Malthus ([1827] 1986: 62) writes after the death of Ricardo with whom he had been involved in the controversy on a general glut. Clearly, the issue at stake had never been the possibility of partial over-production. The preclusion of a general glut for Ricardo,

Say and James Mill never did imply questioning the existence of partial gluts. Ricardo, who excluded a permanent effect of product demand on profits, was well aware that for single commodities discrepancies between the quantity supplied and effective demand can exist and lead to profit rate differentials. 'Too much of a particular commodity may be produced, of which there may be such a glut in the market, as not to repay the capital expended on it; but this cannot be the case with respect to all commodities' (*Works*, I: 292). In the case of partial gluts causing profit rates differentials, competition, intersectoral capital mobility and the resulting resource reallocation via gross investment would restore production capacities and a structural composition of output better adapted to the pattern of demand and re-establish a uniform rate of profits. This argument, which could be traced back to the first 1803 edition of Say's *Traité* (*Treatise*) and to James Mill's *Commerce Defended* (1808), is clearly made by the latter in his *Elements of Political Economy*:

> The commodity, which happens to be in superabundance, declines in price; the commodity, which is defective in quantity, rises . . . The lowness of the price, in the article which is superabundant, soon removes, by the diminution of profits, a portion of capital from that line of production: The highness of price, in the article which is scarce, invites a quantity of capital to that branch of production, till profits are equalized, that is till the demand and supply are adapted to one another. (J. Mill [1821] 1965: 235)

However, like his friend Ricardo, James Mill considered a discrepancy between aggregate output and aggregate demand for the economy as the whole as impossible and insisted 'that there can be no glut of commodities in the aggregate, though there may be in particular instances' (ibid.: 238).

The controversy between Ricardo and Malthus

Keynes was full of praise for Malthus and his position in the dispute with Ricardo on the question of a general glut and the effects of the accumulation of capital on the general rate of profits and thus on the incentive to further accumulation. In particular, Keynes appreciated that Malthus had recognized the possibility that demand could set a limit to aggregate production and had 'a complete comprehension of the effects of excessive saving on output via its effects on profit' (1972, *Collected Writings*, X: 99). Malthus's *Principles of Political Economy*, which was first published in April 1820, was mainly a critical discussion of Ricardo's *Principles*. Ricardo reacted immediately and found Section III of Chapter VII 'Of Accumulation, or the Saving from Revenue to add to Capital, considered as a Stimulus to the Increase of Wealth' most unsound (see *Works*, II: 301–31). Thus, he wrote in a letter to McCulloch: 'The most objectionable chapter in Mr. Malthus' book is that perhaps on the bad effects from too great accumulation of capital, and the consequent want of demand for the goods produced' (*Works*, VIII: 181). In particular, Ricardo had difficulties in making sense of Malthus's proposal that luxury consumption could be beneficial to an economy.

Malthus had directly attacked the doctrine held by Say, James Mill and Ricardo that 'there cannot possibly be a glut of commodities in general', which he considered 'as utterly unfounded, and completely to contradict the great principles which regulate supply and demand' (Malthus [1820] 1989: 353). Ricardo, on the other hand, always had been a strong defender of Say's law of markets. For example, after receiving the second 1814 French edition of Say's *Treatise* he wrote to Malthus that 'Mr. Say . . . supports, I think, very ably the doctrine that demand is regulated by production' (*Works*, VI: 163–4). In the Appendix to *The High Price of Bullion*, Ricardo in 1811 had already argued:

> [No] country ever possessed a general glut of commodities. It is evidently impossible. If a country possesses every thing necessary for the maintenance and comfort of man, and these articles be divided in the proportions in which they are usually consumed, they are sure, however abundant, to find a market to sell them off. (*Works*, III: 108)

Any interpretation of the controversy between Ricardo and Malthus must begin by analysing their different views on two propositions on the effects of capital accumulation on the rate of profits formulated by Adam Smith. The starting point of Malthus's disquisition was the opinion shared by Smith and Ricardo 'that capitals are increased by parsimony, that every frugal man is a public benefactor and that the increase of wealth depends upon the balance of produce above consumption' (Malthus [1820] 1989: 8). According to Malthus, this proposition is true to a great extent but not indefinitely: 'the principle of saving, pushed to excess, would destroy the motive to production' (ibid.). Too great an accumulation of capital imposes levels of aggregate demand too low to utilize production capacity at normal level. The result would be a general overproduction of commodities with prices falling relatively to money wages and a consequential fall in profitability. 'I cannot agree with Mr. Mill . . . that, with reference to a nation, supply can never exceed demand', Malthus had already written to Ricardo in September 1814 (*Works*, VI: 132).

Malthus thus accepted the second of Smith's propositions that states that capital accumulation reduces the general rate of profits, due to the merchants' intensified competition, but he rejected the first one that asserts that the growth of the wealth of a nation depends on the proportion of productive to unproductive workers; the larger this ratio the more rapidly the economy expands. Ricardo held exactly the opposite view. He denied any tendency of the profit rate to fall and criticized Smith for erroneously extending the case of a limit that the market poses to the expansion of output in a single industry to the economy as a whole. However, the overall rate of profits does not change unless the real wage or the technical conditions of production in the wage-goods industries change, as is the case if the output of means of subsistence for a growing population can be increased only at increasing labour costs due to decreasing returns in agricultural production. While discrepancies between supply and effective demand may cause temporarily differential profit rates between the sectors of the economy, Ricardo denied that aggregate output would permanently affect the rate of profits. Accelerated accumulation and an increased ratio of productive to unproductive workers cannot cause a discrepancy between aggregate output and aggregate demand. Ricardo's approval of Say's proposition that 'demand is only limited by production' is based on his identifying decisions to save with decisions to invest. However, the Keynesian problem of coordinating saving and investment decisions and the potentially explosive effects of coordination failures is rather alien to him. We also cannot find in Ricardo's works an elaboration of the 'notion that the rate of interest is the balancing factor which brings the demand for saving in the shape of new investment . . . into equality with the supply of saving' (*Collected Writings*, VII: 165). One may therefore 'conclude that in Ricardo "Say's Law" was not the result of an analysis of the investment-saving process but rather the result of the *lack* of any such analysis' (Garegnani, 1978: 340; original emphasis).

Malthus shared Ricardo's view that savings, that is, income not spent for consumption purposes, are entirely converted into investment, and that by saving one either employs productive workers, or lends to someone who does. Malthus conceived of saving as 'the conversion of revenué into capital' (Malthus [1820] 1989: 369). Hence no discrepancy between productive capacity and aggregate demand could arise. Malthus failed to see that to perceive of parsimony as implying a reallocation from unproductive to productive workers, that is, an investive employment of the financial means, does not cause a discrepancy between saving and investment, as later conceived by Keynes in his theory of effective demand. Identifying investment with saving is equivalent to accepting Say's Law.

But how does Malthus then explain the existence of a general glut and the resulting danger of unemployment due to a shortage of aggregate demand? His argument, based on the 'effect of a preference of indolence to luxuries' (ibid.: 358), could be easily dismissed by Ricardo, who pointed out that if people would enjoy more leisure, then an over-production of luxury goods could not come into being, against Malthus's emphasis that 'it is absolutely necessary that a country with great powers of production should possess a body of unproductive consumers' (ibid.: 463). Against this reasoning, which could be interpreted as providing a rationale for the feudal lifestyle of the landowning class, Ricardo soberly responded: 'A body of unproductive labourers are just as necessary and as useful with a view to future production, as a fire, which should consume in the manufacturers warehouse the goods which those unproductive labourers would otherwise consume' (*Works*, II: 421).

Ricardo was no longer able to respond to passages in the second edition of Malthus's *Principles*, in which the author pointed out a general diminution of demand compared with supply, as, for example, in a longer transition period to a peace economy after the end of the Napoleonic Wars (Malthus [1836] 1986: 420–21).

Clearly Malthus had an intuition that Say's law of markets could not claim universal validity and that a shortage of aggregate effective demand is a real possibility. However, he did not coherently support his case. Despite Keynes's praise, Malthus therefore cannot be considered a genuine precursor of the theory of effective demand.

It is evident that Malthus put more emphasis on short-run disturbances whereas Ricardo had a much greater interest in long-run trends and centres of gravitation. Malthus also did not elaborate his critique of Ricardo in the context of a genuine monetary economy but developed his argument for a barter-type economy in which the neutrality postulate of money holds.

Money as a store of value: the consequences

'Say, like practically all the theorists of that age, neglected the store-of-value function of money and therefore the fact that there is an element in the 'demand' for it that is not accounted for by his theory' (Schumpeter, 1954: 620). Ricardo's famous statement that 'Productions are always bought by productions, or by services, money is only the medium by which the exchange is effected' (*Works*, I: 291–2) could be considered as characteristic of the idea that holding cash balances rather than spending them on goods was quite alien to classical economists.

The consequence of the role of money as a store of value is the separation of the act of purchase and the act of sale. Sellers are now not automatically buyers any more as in the barter economy or as in Ricardo's 'monetary' economy, where money only functions as a medium of exchange. This argument is at the centre of all later critique of Say's Law, such as, for example, in Marx and Keynes. John Stuart Mill was the first economist to point out this decisive difference between a monetary and a barter economy and connect commercial crises to the ability of money to function as a store of value, in the second essay 'Of the Influence of Consumption on Production' in *Essays on Some Unsettled Questions of Political Economy*:

> If, however, we suppose that money is used . . . there is this difference – that in the case of barter, the selling and the buying are simultaneously confounded in one operation; you sell what you have, and buy what you want, by one indivisible act, and you cannot do the one without doing the other. Now the effect of the employment of money, and even the utility of it, is, that it enables this one act of interchange to be divided into two separate acts or operations; one of which may be performed now, and the other a year hence, or whenever it shall be most convenient. Although he who sells, really sells only to buy, he needs not buy at the same moment when he sells; and he does not therefore necessarily add to the *immediate* demand for one commodity when he adds to the supply of another. The buying and selling being now separated, it may very well occur, that there may be, at some given time, a very general inclination to sell with as little delay as possible, accompanied with an equally general inclination to defer all purchases as long as possible. This is always actually the case, in those periods which are described as periods of general excess. And no one, after sufficient explanation, will contest the possibility of general excess, in this sense of the word. The state of things which we have just described, and which is of no uncommon occurrence, amounts to it. (J.S. Mill [1844] 1974: 69–70; original emphasis)

'Is this the voice of a classical economist, or . . . the voice of Keynes?' John Hicks (1983: 62) asked, who considered the *Essays on Some Unsettled Questions of Political Economy* as 'perhaps the freshest of Mill's economic writings' (ibid.: 60). The essays were written in 1829–30 against the historical background of the first of a series of credit crises in England in 1825, two years after Ricardo's death. Although Mill's *Essays* were only published in 1844 they clearly show John Stuart Mill, a competent follower of the doctrines of Ricardo and his father James Mill, to be the first economist who had pointed out the consequences of money as a store of value in the context of the general glut debate. As in his second essay, Mill later emphasized in his *Principles* that at times of a commercial crisis 'there is really an excess of all commodities above the money demand: in other words, there is an under-supply of money' (J.S. Mill [1871] 1965: 574). In both works Mill makes it very clear that the occurrence of a general glut is a temporary phenomenon, arising only in periods of financial crises, and that the excess demand for money in the crises is not caused by a general over-production of commodities but the consequence of excessive speculation and a lack of commercial confidence. Furthermore, the quoted passage from his *Principles* as well as his earlier statement in the *Essays* that 'undoubtedly . . . there cannot be an excess of all other commodities, and an excess of money at the same time' (ibid.: 71) shows Mill to have anticipated Walras's Law.

A similar argument of the consequences of money as a store of value was developed independently by Wilhelm Roscher in a 1849 essay, which was only amended slightly in the later 1861 book version in which the term 'production crisis' was substituted by the term 'sales crisis' to characterize the essence of the disease: a lack of aggregate demand (see Hagemann, 1995). Roscher pointed out that 'the mediation of money enables the seller to buy only after some time, that is, to delay the second half of the exchange as much as he likes' (Roscher [1849] 1861: 297), and he acknowledged the existence of general crises.

The argument put forward by Mill and Roscher that the store-of-value function of money constitutes a crucial difference between a monetary and a barter economy in allowing the separation of the two acts to sell and to buy and thereby the possibility of a general glut was taken up by Marx as well as by Keynes in their critique of Say's Law. Marx knew the writings of Mill and Roscher very well. His analysis of the distinction between the possibility and the reality of the crisis in Chapter 17 of Volume II of his *Theories of Surplus Value*, in particular his positive argument in Section 10, clearly indicates how much it has been shaped by Mill. This cannot be argued away by dialectical skill, a procedure that Marx attests to Ricardo concerning the possibility of a general glut. Marx made great efforts to demonstrate that capitalist economies are inevitably crisis prone and focused on the realization problem and a breakdown in the circuit of money capital, $M - C \ldots P \ldots C' - M'$. Over-production crises proceed from the pressures within competitive capitalism, including an insufficient aggregate demand and also elements of disproportionality.

Interestingly, Keynes, who in general was rather critical of the Marxian doctrine, in his attack against Say's Law came rather close to the argument of Marx, to whom he attested a 'pregnant observation' (1979, *Collected Writings*, XXIX: 81). Keynes even took up the Marxian notation when he confronted the Marxian formula $M - C - M'$ for a monetary economy with the formula $C - M - C'$ of the classical theory, which corresponds to a real exchange economy. However, in contrast to Mill and Roscher, who neither developed an asset motive to hold money nor made the resulting problem from the store-of-value function of money a regression line of their thought, Keynes elaborated the speculative demand for money into his liquidity preference theory. He strongly rejected the idea that the interest mechanism would equilibrate savings and investment.

General glut: a temporary or a permanent problem?

'When a classical economist asserted the impossibility of "gluts", he had in mind not periodic crises but secular stagnation' (Blaug, 1985: 157). This is best indicated by Mill's innovative second essay 'On the Influence of Consumption on Production', in which Mill points out the problems resulting from the store-of-value function of money but also makes it very clear in the final three pages that he adheres to Say's law of markets and the quantity theory of money in the long run. Thus, Mill emphasizes that it is 'of the utmost importance to observe that excess of all commodities . . . means only a temporary fall in their value relatively to money' and that the 'argument against the possibility of general over-production is quite conclusive, so far as it applies to the doctrine that a country may accumulate capital too fast' (J.S. Mill [1844] 1974: 72–3). The recognition that at times of financial or commercial crises, such as 1825, there is a motive for holding money beyond the immediate need for transaction purposes, and a general glut appears as a temporary phenomenon, does not imply a permanent discrepancy between aggregate demand and aggregate supply. Mill therefore concludes his essay with the statement that the admittance that a general glut may exist in a crisis, although not caused by over-production but by a want of commercial confidence, does not endanger the preservation of the Ricardo-Mill-Say doctrine 'that there cannot be permanent excess of production, or of accumulation' (ibid.: 74). Mill adhered to this flexible Ricardian position and the long-run implications of the quantity theory throughout his life (see also Laidler, 1991: 26).

Parts of the controversy between Malthus and Ricardo resulted from the fact that while Ricardo tackled the long-run problems of capital accumulation, income distribution and cost-minimizing systems of production, he left the problem of crises or business cycles unsolved. Malthus put more but not exclusive emphasis on short-run disturbances. Like Sismondi, the other great opponent of the *Pax Ricardiana* who was concerned with the impoverishment of the masses in the rising factory system and the inequality in the distribution of income creating an under-consumption problem due to a too high propensity to save, he focused on the problem of insufficient aggregate demand. However, a major difference between Malthus and Keynes exists in the fact that for Malthus the origin of over-production lies in a too high investment demand whereas for Keynes investment demand is too low.

For Ricardo, recessions were not caused by deficient demand but by misdirected production. In the debates over the recession following the Napoleonic Wars, Say agreed more with Malthus than Ricardo that spending for public infrastructure could be helpful to offset the decline in aggregate demand and the rise in unemployment (see Hollander, 2005). Thus, it may be said that Say himself recognized that his 'law of markets' only holds in the long run but not in the short run. Ricardo, on the other hand, did not consider aggregate demand problems as a cause of a general glut but only as its accompaniment.

The (non-)integration of the labour market

For Keynes, the acceptance of Say's law of markets implied the full-employment assumption. Unfortunately, in the attack against Say's Law in his *General Theory*, Keynes lumped together as 'classical economics' the orthodox neoclassical version of Say's Law implying that changes in the interest rate ensure equality between savings and investment and that the economy achieves full employment, with the understanding of Say's Law by classical economists, of whom he explicitly refers to John Stuart Mill. However, no classical economist who denied the possibility of a general glut in the long run ever made use of Say's Law to derive conclusions about the performance of the labour market, least of all making a proposition of achieving full employment. Ricardo could easily combine the denial of a general glut, that is, that there could be no permanent surplus or under-utilization of capital, with the existence of the machinery problem, that is, technological unemployment, which could be eliminated by further accumulation of capital. Thus, the classical approach allows for unemployment despite Say's Law.

This also holds for John Stuart Mill who, like Ricardo, held the view that aggregate demand could not create a barrier for demand in the long run. Among Mill's four fundamental propositions respecting capital, are not only the second one that 'capital is the result of saving' but also the fourth one that 'demand for commodities is not demand for labour'. Following Ricardo's argument Mill emphasizes time and again that the employment level is a direct function of capital formation. Mill clearly distinguishes between 'employment of capital' and 'employment of labour'.

That, in classical understanding, Say's Law did not comprise the full-employment assumption, is also indicated by the writings of one of the fiercest critics. Karl Marx, who held a theory of a permanent industrial reserve army, when criticizing Smith's explanation of a permanent fall in the rate of profit due to an over-accumulation of capital, pointed out: 'Permanent crises do not exist' (Marx, [1863] 1969: 497n). Thus, there could be no permanent under-utilization of capital. Nothing is said about the situation on the labour market.

HARALD HAGEMANN

See also:

Demand and Supply; Keynes, John Maynard, on Ricardo; Limiting and Regulating Principles; Say's Law.

References

Baumol, W.J. (1999), 'Retrospectives: Say's Law', *Journal of Economic Perspectives*, **13**(1), 195–204.

Blaug, M. (1985), *Economic Theory in Retrospect*, Cambridge, UK: Cambridge University Press.

Davis, T. (2003), 'The historical context of the general glut controversy', in S. Kates (ed.), *Two Hundred Years of Say's Law*, Cheltenham, UK and Northampton, MA: Edward Elgar Publishing.

Eltis, W. (1984), *The Classical Theory of Economic Growth*, London: Macmillan.

Garegnani, P. (1978), 'Notes on consumption, investment and effective demand. I', *Cambridge Journal of Economics*, **2**(2), 335–53.

Hagemann, H. (1995), 'Roscher and the theory of crisis', *Journal of Economic Studies*, **22**(3–5): 171–86.

Hicks, J.R. (1983), 'From classical to post-classical: the work of J.S. Mill', in J. Hicks, *Classics and Moderns, Collected Essays on Economic Theory, Vol. III*, Oxford: Basil Blackwell, pp. 60–70.

Hollander, S. (2005), *Jean-Baptiste Say and the Classical Canon in Economics. The British Connection in French Classicism*, London and New York: Routledge.

Kahn, R.F. (1984), *The Making of Keynes 'General Theory'*, Cambridge, UK: Cambridge University Press.

Keynes, J.M. ([1936] 1971–89), *The Collected Writings of John Maynard Keynes, Vols I–XXX*, London: Macmillan.

Laidler, D. (1991), *The Golden Age of the Quantity Theory*, New York and London: Philip Allan.

Lauderdale, Lord (1804), *An Inquiry into the Nature and Origin of Public Wealth and into the Means and Causes of its Increase*, Edinburgh: Constable.

Malthus, T.R. ([1820] 1989), *Principles of Political Economy*, variorum edition, (ed.) J. Pullen, Cambridge, UK: Cambridge University Press.

Malthus, T.R. ([1827] 1986), *Definitions in Political Economy*, London: John Murray, reprinted 1986, Fairfield, NJ: Augustus M. Kelley.

Mandeville, B. ([1714/1729] 1924). *The Fable of the Bees: or Private Vices, Publick Benefits*, 2 vols, Oxford: Clarendon Press.

Marx, Karl ([1863] 1969), *Theories of Surplus Value, Vol. II*, reprint, London: Lawrence & Wishart.

Mill, J. (1808), *Commerce Defended*, London: C. and R. Baldwin.

Mill, J. ([1821] 1965), *Elements of Political Economy*, London: Henry G. Bohn; reprint of 1844 3rd edition, New York: Augustus M. Kelley.

Mill, J.S. ([1844] 1974), *Essays on Some Unsettled Questions of Political Economy*, London: John W. Parker; reprint of 1874 2nd edition, Clifton, NJ: Augustus M. Kelley.

Mill, J.S. ([1871] 1965), *Principles of Political Economy with Some of Their Applications to Social Philosophy*, 2 vols, 7th edition, London: Longmans, Green, Reader and Dyer, in J.M. Robson (ed.), *Principles of Political Economy with Some of Their Applications in Social Philosophy by John Stuart Mill* (*Collected Works of John Stuart Mill, Vols 2–3*), Toronto: University of Toronto Press.

Morishima, M. and C. Catephores (1988), 'Anti-Say's Law versus Say's Law: a change in paradigm', in H. Hanusch (ed.), *Evolutionary Economics. Applications of Schumpeter's Ideas*, Cambridge, UK: Cambridge University Press, pp. 23–70.

Roscher, W. ([1849] 1861), 'Die Productionskrisen mit besonderer Rücksicht auf die letzten Jahrzehnte', in *Die Gegenwart. Eine encyklopädische Darstellung der neusten Zeitgeschichte für alle Stände, Vol. 3*, Leipzig: Duncker & Humblot, pp. 721–58; republished as Chapter VI 'Zur Lehre von den Absatzkrisen' in W. Roscher, *Ansichten der Volkswirthschaft aus dem geschichtlichen Standpunkte*, Leipzig and Heidelberg: C.F. Winter.

Say, J.-B. ([1803], 1971), *Traité d'économie politique ou simple exposition de la manière dont se forment, se distibuent et se consomment les richesses*, Paris: Deterville; 4th edition translated under the title *A Treatise on Political Economy*, 1834, Philadelphia: G.R. Elliott; reprint, New York: Augustus M. Kelley.

Schoorl, E. (2013), *Jean-Baptiste Say. Revolutionary, Entrepreneur, Economist*, London: Routledge.

Schumpeter, J.A. (1954), *A History of Economic Analysis*, London: Oxford University Press.

Sismondi, J.-C.-L. de ([1819] 1827), *Nouveaux principes d'économie politique, Vol. I, Books 1, 4; Vol. II, Appendix*, 2nd edition, Paris: Delaunay.

Smith, A. ([1776] 1979), *An Inquiry into the Nature and Causes of the Wealth of Nations*, in *The Glasgow Edition of the Works and Correspondence of Adam Smith*, reprint, (eds) R.H. Campbell, A.S. Skinner and W. B. Todd, Oxford: Oxford University Press.

Streissler, E.W. (1981), 'Adam Smith – Der Adam oder nur Wachstum? Paradoxa einer wissenschaftlichen Revolution', in F. Neumark (ed.), *Studien zur Entwicklung der ökonomischen Theorie I*, Berlin: Duncker & Humblot, pp. 43–52.

Thweatt, W.O. (1979), 'Early formulators of Say's Law', *Quarterly Review of Economics and Business*, **19**, 79–94.

Gold

Ricardo's analysis on gold was and is very important but not simple. His keen interest in it was heightened by his activities as a dealer and when the Bank of England suspended the convertibility of its bank notes to gold in 1797, caused by the inflationary pressure during the Napoleonic Wars. Moses, his brother, said that Ricardo was led to reflect upon the subject of currency also by 'the immense transactions . . . which he had with the Bank of England, in the course of his business' (*Works*, III: 3).

In 1809, Ricardo anonymously published his first article 'The Price of Gold' in the *Morning Chronicle*. The following year he published the pamphlet *The High Price of Bullion, a Proof of the Depreciation of Bank Notes* (from now on referred to as *Bullion*) and in subsequent years he intervened again on this theme with several letters to the *Morning Chronicle* and with his *Reply to Mr. Bosanquet's Practical Observations on the Report of the Bullion Committee* (from now on referred to as *Observations*). In 1816, he published his *Proposals for an Economical and Secure Currency* (from now on referred to as *Proposals*) in which he defined his 'Ingot Plan' already outlined in an Appendix of the 1811 edition of *Bullion*. Besides these publications, there are considerable signs that illustrate Ricardo's thoughts, until the very end of his life, about the role of gold as the standard with which to measure value. This is confirmed by the 1823 draft manuscript on 'Absolute Value and Exchangeable Value'.

In the present entry – whose content relies also on many previous works of Quadrio Curzio – on Ricardo's contribution on the role of gold, this precious metal is considered as a homogeneous, historically accepted value of reserve as well as a scarce raw material with its own inherent costs. Such properties induced Ricardo (and other economists) to consider gold as a good approximation of the 'standard numéraire' and to underline its role as a link between real factors (productive aspects) and monetary factors (liquidity and reserve value aspects). For these reasons, gold throughout history has taken on the role of a monetary function. When this function was removed and gold became merely a commodity, only an institutional profile remained, gold being included in the official reserves of Central Banks (Quadrio Curzio 1982b: 8).

The value of gold and the value of money

Ricardo made a fundamental distinction between the value of gold, obeying the general law of value, and the value of money, dependent on its quantity and measured by the purchasing power of money over gold, with gold as the standard of money. In his *Principles of Political Economy, and Taxation* (1817) (from now on referred to as *Principles*) Ricardo affirmed that:

> The Nations of the world must have been early convinced, that there was no standard of value in nature, to which they might unerringly refer, and therefore chose a medium, which on the whole appeared to them less variable than any other commodity. To this standard we must conform till the law is changed, and till some other commodity is discovered, by the use of which we shall obtain a more perfect standard, than that which we have established. (*Works*, I: 149)

The reasons to choose gold as a standard of money was explained in *Bullion*. Ricardo wrote that gold (and other precious metals) 'have an intrinsic value which is not arbitrary, but is dependent on their scarcity, the quantity of labour bestowed in procuring them, and the value of the capital employed in the mines which produce them' (*Works*, III: 52).

Quoting Smith, Ricardo underlined that the value of precious metals 'was antecedent to, and independent of their being employed as coin, and was the quality which fitted them for that employment' (ibid.: 53):

> Ricardo affirmed that there is a 'natural' quantity of money when the market price of the standard does not deviate from the official price and the rate of exchange is close to the official par (i.e. the ratio between the foreign and the domestic official prices of gold). Hence, the quantity of money was at its natural level whenever the purchasing power of the currency over gold was kept constant at home and abroad. (Marcuzzo and Rosselli, 1991: 335)

Price signal was the mechanism used to ascertain if the quantity of money was not at its natural level. The signals were the discrepancy between the market price and the mint price of gold bullion, and the difference between the market exchange rate between currencies and the official par. An excess of money affected the exchange rate, causing its depreciation: liquidity pushed up prices for foreign currencies and assets and brought down the price of the domestic currency.

For Ricardo, a variation in the quantity of money from its natural level would provoke a change in the value of money, but not in the value of gold, which depended on the conditions for its production. He firmly believed that an excess in the supply of money was a necessary but not sufficient condition for gold outflows, as any amount of imports could be paid by offsetting the exports of British goods. Ricardo wrote in *Bullion*:

> Strictly speaking, there can no be permanent measure of value. A measure of value should itself be invariable; but this is not the case with either gold or silver, they being subject to fluctuations as well as other commodities. Experience has indeed taught us, that though the variations in the *value* of gold or silver may be considerable, on a comparison of distant periods, yet for short spaces of time their value is tolerably fixed. It is this property, among their other excellencies, which fits them better than any other commodity for the uses of money. Either gold or silver may therefore, in the point of view in which we are considering them, be called a measure of value. (*Works*, III: 65n; original emphasis)

Thus, if the price of gold was kept fixed, changes in the price of commodities would depend only on changes in the relative value of commodities in terms of the standard. For Ricardo, the importance of having a standard was not linked to preventing price instability but to preventing variations in the measure of money prices. Ricardo wanted to prevent this possible abuse by the monetary authority. He evidently had more faith in markets, believing that if monetary authorities wanted to accelerate adjustment processes and keep down inflation they must look at the excess market price of gold rather than to gold's inherent value.

Gold as a proxy to the standard commodity

From a different but complementary viewpoint, David Ricardo treated the problem of gold as a standard in a series of extremely subtle analyses concerning the theory of value and of income distribution. Isolating 'an invariable measure of value' was one of his most troubling problems because by finding the 'absolute value' of a commodity he would obtain an invariable standard with which to compare values. As with income distribution, the invariable standard would allow the ascertainment of the effects of a unitary wage change on the rate of profit without disturbances from the associated shifts in prices (Quadrio Curzio 1982b: 2).

In his search for an invariable measure of value, gold played a key role. In the third edition of *Principles* (1821) Ricardo admitted that the same differences faced in determining relative prices also conditioned his attempt to define the essential properties of a correct standard. Even if:

> the same quantity or labour . . . would . . . be always required to obtain the same quantity of gold, still gold would not be a perfect measure of value, by which we could accurately ascertain the variations in all other things, because it would not be produced with precisely the same combinations of fixed and circulating capital as all other things; nor with fixed capital of the same durability; nor would it require precisely the same length of time before it could be brought to market. (*Works*, I: 44–5)

He now searched for a 'medium standard', a commodity produced with proportions that are 'so nearly equally distant from the two extremes, the one where little fixed capital is used, the other were little labour is employed, as to form a just mean between them' (ibid.: 45–6). This problem became a real dilemma that occupied Ricardo till the last months of his life, when he was working on his 'Absolute Value and Exchangeable Value' manuscript. He recognized that in nature a perfect measure of value does not exist since any commodity used as a standard would be invariant to changes in distribution only if 'precisely the same length of time and neither more nor less were necessary to the production of all commodities. Commodities would then have an absolute value directly in proportion to the quantity of labour bestowed upon them' (*Works*, IV: 382). But commodities are not produced and brought to the market at precisely the same time and:

> difficulty or facility of production is not absolutely the only cause of variation in value, there is one other, the rise or fall of wages . . . It appears then that we should have no difficulty in fixing on a measure of value, or at least in determining on what constituted a good measure of value, if all commodities were produced exactly under the same circumstances . . . The difficulty then under which we labour in finding a measure of value applicable to all commodities proceeds from the variety of circumstances under which commodities are actually produced. (Ibid.: 368)

Even if not satisfied with this solution.

This issue was also a central feature of Sraffa's analysis: the standard commodity produced under 'average' conditions of production, provided a tool that allows one to say both when Ricardo's problem is solvable (and when it is not), and to construct the solution whenever it exists (Kurz and Salvadori, 1993).

Gold and the quantity theory of money: the Bullion Controversy

Ricardo's quantity theory analysis of inconvertible bank notes played a central role in the debate that took place after the 1797 Bank Restriction Act that followed the war against Napoleonic France. At that time, the gold reserves were not sufficient to cover the Bank of England's notes in circulation (and indirectly those of the regional country banks). In 1797 the banking system was severely tested by bank runs. Consequently, Parliament in 1797 decided to suspend specie payments of pound notes. The Bank of England – a private institution founded in 1694 – in that period had the monopoly on issuing notes in London and the surrounding area, thereby becoming the pivot of the monetary and banking systems. The circulation of Bank of England notes increased and the British balance of payments fell into a permanent deficit.

Gold's market price increased significantly and overtook the mint price of gold. The domestic and foreign value of the paper pound fell and, according to Gresham's law, 'bad' paper currency ousted 'good' metallic currency. The 'Bullionist Controversy', in which Ricardo played a relevant part, got its name from the discussions, namely on the reasons for the fluctuating market price of gold. 'Bullionists' were critical of the Bank of England and supported a return to convertibility while the 'Anti-Bullionists' defended the Bank and accepted an inconvertible system.

Ricardo entered the debate in 1809, after the 'first round' (1801–4) animated by Boyd, Thornton, Wheatley and King for the Bullionists and by Baring for the Anti-Bullionists. Close to Wheatley's position, Ricardo maintained that a rise in the price of gold and a depreciation of the pound in the foreign exchanges was caused by monetary expansion – provoked by an overissuing of bank notes by the Bank of England – and could be solved by a return to convertibility. For the Anti-Bullionists this was due to real (i.e., war expenditures) rather than monetary factors.

Ricardo first stated in an anonymous article in the *Morning Chronicle* in 1809 (*Works*, III, 15–21) that there had been an excess supply of inconvertible bank notes. Then in 1810 he published the pamphlet *Bullion* (ibid.: 47–127 where he elaborated on the same argument, affirming that:

> Parliament, by restricting the Bank from paying in specie, have enabled the conductors of that concern to increase or decrease at pleasure the quantity and amount of their notes; and the previously existing checks against an over-issue having been thereby removed, those conductors have acquired the power of increasing or decreasing the value of the paper currency. (Ibid.: 75)

He argued that:

> If the Bank directors had kept the amount of their notes within reasonable bounds; if they had acted up to the principle which they have avowed to have been that which regulated their issues when they were obliged to pay their notes in specie, namely, to limit their notes to that amount which should prevent the excess of the market above the mint price of gold, we should not have been now exposed to all the evils of a depreciated, and perpetually varying currency. (Ibid.: 95)

Ricardo concluded that the Bank Restriction Act needed to be revoked (ibid.: 98–9) and that the Bank should be obliged to pay the notes on demand in specie, reducing the amount of bank notes in circulation:

> The remedy I propose for all the evils in our currency, is that the Bank should gradually decrease the amount of their notes in circulation until they shall have rendered the remainder of equal value with the coins which they represent, or, in other words, till the prices of gold and silver bullion shall be brought down to their mint price. (Ibid.: 94)

From these quotations we see how clear Ricardo's position is concerning the relation between the sum of transactions and the amount of currency.

For Ricardo the two significant issues of the period – foreign allowances to finance war expenses and a series of bad harvests – were linked to the gold movement in a peculiar way. Besides the common conviction that these factors caused a change in the price of gold in different countries, resulting in an immediate shift of gold prices to restore a new and again uniform price, Ricardo affirmed that the price of gold in different countries would not change as a consequence of bad harvests in England. If unfavourable exchanges existed, England would export more. The shifts needed to restore balance were not of gold but of other commodities, especially those whose value was low. Consider what Ricardo wrote to Thornton: 'The exportation of the coin is caused by its cheapness, and is not the effect, but the cause of an unfavourable balance' (ibid.: 61). Ricardo concludes that if gold flows out of England, this does mean that its value is lower than elsewhere. For Ricardo there is only one answer: an excess of currency, and – since England has no gold mines – there can be only one responsible for this: the Bank of England, as it is the only bank capable of increasing the money supply.

In 1809, the price of gold rose again. The implication of the higher price and the conclusion of the Bullionist Committee (a Parliamentary Committee appointed by the House of Commons on 18 February 1810 to enquire into the cause of the high price of gold bullion), published in its 1810 *Bullion Report* that a correct money supply policy by the Bank of England could restore the exchange rate. Parliament in 1811 rejected the steps – in which we can find much of Ricardo's quantity theory analysis – recommended by the Committee.

The core of the Anti-Bullionists' position (supported by the directors of the Bank of England), was that the price of gold and the level of exchange rates were determined independently of the notes in circulation; the decline in the value of money was due to the poor balance of payments caused by the war and the bad harvests. Ricardo, in reply to these arguments, strongly defended his quantity theory conclusions in 1810 in the pamphlet *Three Letters to the Morning Chronicle on the Bullion Report* (ibid.: 129–53) and in 1811 with his *Reply to Mr. Bosanquet's 'Practical Observations on the Report of the Bullion Committee'* (ibid.: 155–256). However, over the following ten years there was a shift in the Parliamentary position and the influence of the Bullionist position grew, also thanks to the role played by David Ricardo, who in 1819 became a Member of Parliament by buying the Portarlington, Ireland seat. That same year, Parliament decided to return to the gold standard.

Nonetheless a point remained unclear, should convertible bank notes be considered as 'real' money or merely circulating credit mediums, and did they have an influence on the value of money? This debate emerged a few years after Ricardo's death, but even then his theories had a relevant part in influencing the so-called Currency School (Overstone, Torrens et al.) – that ended with the Bank Charter Act of 1844 – supporting the quantity theory as opposed to the Anti-Bullionist and anti-quantity theory positions led by Thomas Tooke.

The historical reconstruction of the debate shows that Ricardo did not limit the validity of the quantity theory only to inconvertible paper money, but extended it to convertible bank notes and even to metallic money, as he believed that any change in the money supply would entail a proportional change in the level of prices (see Rieter, 1998: 245). In his words, examining the relative situation of countries that have abundant commerce with each other:

> If a mine of gold were discovered in either of these countries, the currency of that country would be lowered in value in consequence of the increased quantity of the precious metals brought in circulation, and would therefore no longer be of the same value as that of other countries. Gold and silver, whether in coin or in bullion, obeying the law which regulates all other commodities, would immediately become articles of exportation; they would leave the country where they were cheap, for those countries where they were dear, and would continue to do so, as long as the mine should prove productive, and till the proportion existing between capital and money in each country before the discovery of the mine, were again established, and gold and silver restored everywhere to one value. (*Works*, III: 54)
> If instead of a mine being discovered in any country, a bank were established, such as the Bank of England, with the power of issuing its notes for a circulating medium; after a large amount had been issued either by way of loan to merchants, or by advances to government, thereby adding considerably the sum of the currency, the same effect would follow as in the case of the mine. The circulating medium would be lowered in value, and [the prices of] goods would experience a proportionate rise. The equilibrium between that and other nations would only be restored by the exportation of part of the coin. (Ibid.: 54–5).

From these considerations Ricardo concluded that a depreciation in the circulating medium was the necessary consequence of its excess supply.

Towards the gold exchange standard
This part has to do with the so-called 'Ingot Plan' published by Ricardo in his 1816 *Proposals*. This 'plan' was already outlined in an Appendix of the 1810 edition of *Bullion* (*Works*, III: 99–127) and contained many elements of the gold exchange standard as recognized by other great economists such as Keynes and Hawtrey.

According to what Sraffa wrote in his 'Note on Economical and Secure Currency', Ricardo worked on *Proposals* at the suggestion of Pascoe Grenfell, a Member of Parliament who demanded that Parliament adopt measures to limit the Bank of England's profits made through its transactions with government. Ricardo had various meetings with Grenfell and the latter supplied him with relevant sources: Parliamentary papers and accounts, his own calculations and some of Allardyce's pamphlets on the Bank (*Works*, IV: 45).

While elaborating his proposal, Ricardo asked advice from Malthus, and particularly Mill who revised the text. Sraffa underlined how Mill's encouragement was decisive for the publication of the Ingot Plan (ibid.: 47). The plan was based on the principle that a country needs money to develop its economy, and paper money presents some advantages with regards to specie but needs to be linked to gold. In presenting his plan, Ricardo underlined that he did not think 'that a more economical mode of effecting our payments might be advantageously adopted' (ibid.: 51). Therefore, he shaped a plan for the circulation of paper money, based on the gold standard by making bank notes convertible into gold 'ingots' rather than coins:

> To secure the public against any other variations in the value of the currency than those to which the standard itself is subject, and, at the same time, to carry on the circulation with a medium the least expensive, is to attain the most perfect state to which a currency can be brought, and we should possess all these advantages by subjecting the Bank to the delivery of uncoined gold or silver at the mint standard and price, in exchange for their notes, instead of the delivery of guineas; by which means paper would never fall below the value of bullion without being followed by a reduction of its quantity. (Ibid.: 66)

Gold was not to be used in circulation but would remain the basis of the system, and determined the value of the notes. In Ricardo's words:

> If foreign nations are not sufficiently enlightened to adopt this liberal system, and should continue their prohibitions and excessive duties on the importation of our commodities and manufactures, let England set them a good example by benefiting herself; and instead of meeting their prohibitions by similar exclusion, let her get rid, as soon as she can, of every vestige of so absurd and hurtful a policy. The pecuniary advantage which would be the result of such a system would soon incline other states to adopt the same course, and no long period would elapse before the general prosperity would be seen to be best promoted by each country falling naturally into the most advantageous employment of its capital, talents, and industry. (Ibid.: 71)

Ricardo's plan was effectively implemented in 1821 on the basis of Peel's Bill for the Resumption of Cash Payments, the so-called 'Resumption Act' adopted in 1819, which imposed on the Bank of England the return to convertibility of bank notes in gold bullion. By doing so, Britain continued to use paper as means of payment and restrained the great profits of the Bank of England that remained a private institution until 1946.

Some conclusions

Ricardo's quantity approach stated the existence of a causal and direct relation between money supply and the level of prices, and denied that money could have real effects. A limit to this theory was the belief that gold flows were only signs of monetary problems and not real problems. There was in fact the conviction that it was impossible to have a general glut of commodities within a country or among countries (i.e., clear acceptance of 'Say's Identity').

Ricardo was convinced that rules could be effective in checking abuses and in maintaining monetary order. He undervalued the need for an active monetary policy, because of his strong belief in a self-regulating monetary economy without considering, for example, the possibility of a confidence crises underlined by Thornton. Ricardo was a winner in the theoretical approach even post-mortem with the Bank Charter Act of 1844. However, in practice, the Bank of England in the nineteenth century played an increasingly active role.

Even in a paper money system, there could not be uncontrolled inflation if the system guaranteed full convertibility of bank notes in bullion, and complete freedom to export and import it. If these conditions – known as the gold standard conditions – were respected, the exchange rates between the currencies of countries adhering to this system would remain fixed, apart from little fluctuations around the 'gold points' (due to transportation and the insurance costs of gold).

According to certain streams of thought, the history of monetary systems based on facts and political choices and not on theory, pushed gold out of the international (and domestic) monetary systems. This debate went on for centuries but rarely with the degree of sophistication found in the Ricardian analysis.

ALBERTO QUADRIO CURZIO AND CLAUDIA ROTONDI

See also:

Bullionist Controversy; Monetary Theory; Natural Quantity of Money.

Bibliography

Arnon, A. (1998), 'Bullionist debate', in H.D. Kurz and N. Salvadori (eds), *The Elgar Companion to Classical Economics*, Cheltenham, UK and Lyme, NH: Edward Elgar Publishing, pp. 50–56.
de Vivo, G. (1987), 'Ricardo, David, 1772–1823', in J. Eatwell, M. Milgate and P. Newman (eds), *The New Palgrave: A Dictionary of Economics, Vol. 4*, London: Macmillan, pp. 183–98.
Hollander, S. (1979), *The Economics of David Ricardo*, Toronto: University of Toronto Press.
Kurz, H.D. and N. Salvadori (1993), 'The "standard commodity" and Ricardo's search for an "invariable measure of value"', in M. Baranzini and G.C. Harcourt (eds), *The Dynamics of the Wealth of Nations: Growth, Distribution, and Structural Change: Essays in Honour of Luigi Pasinetti*, New York: St. Martin's Press, pp. 95–123.
Kurz, H.D. and N. Salvadori (1998), *The Elgar Companion to Classical Economics*, Cheltenham, UK and Lyme, NH: Edward Elgar Publishing.
Marcuzzo, M.C. and A. Rosselli (1991), *Ricardo and the Gold Standard. The Foundations of the International Monetary Order*, London: Macmillan.
Pasinetti, L.L. (1960), 'A mathematical formulation of the Ricardian system', *Review of Economic Studies*, **27**, 78–98.
Quadrio Curzio, A. (1981), 'Un diagramma dell'oro tra demonetizzazione e rimonetizzazione', *Rivista Internazionale di Scienze Economiche e Commerciali*, **10–11**, 915–40.
Quadrio Curzio, A. (ed.) (1982a), *The Gold Problem: Economic Perspectives*, Oxford: Oxford University Press.
Quadrio Curzio, A. (1982b), 'Introduction. Gold problems and conference on gold', in A. Quadrio Curzio (ed.) (1982a): 1–17.
Rieter, H. (1998), 'Quantity theory of money', in H.D. Kurz and N. Salvadori (eds), *The Elgar Companion to Classical Economics*, Cheltenham, UK and Lyme, NH: Edward Elgar Publishing, pp. 239–48.
Rotelli, C. (1983), *Le origini della controversia monetaria (1797–1844)*, Bologna: Il Mulino.
Schumpeter, J.A. (1954), *History of Economic Analysis*, New York: Oxford University Press.

Hayek, Friedrich von, on Ricardo

Although the most widely known contributions by Friedrich von Hayek have been to the theories of money, capital and the cycle and to the evolution of patterns of spontaneous orders, he was also a prolific writer in the history of ideas. His contributions to this field include not only collections of essays, but also attempts at clarifying the prehistory of topics with which he was currently dealing. In particular, in Hayek's early work on money, theoretical innovation and investigations into the history of the subject were closely related.

Thus, one would expect that an author as important to our discipline as David Ricardo would occupy a prominent place in Hayek's writings in this regard. However, looking at the instances when Hayek referred to Ricardo, we find that – although there are numerous citations – most references are not to the core of Ricardo's theoretical works, but rather to more peripheral issues. (This is also true for the short article on Ricardo – Hayek, 1955.) These references concern, first, the role Ricardo played in the evolution of monetary thought at the time of the Bullion Controversy, where the focus is on those points where Ricardo is seen as 'anticipating' later developments; and second, the famous 'Ricardo effect' – an idea that Hayek took from Ricardo but used, in his own idiosyncratic way, as a mechanism of the business cycle. These will also be the two main areas dealt with in the following.

Hayek on Ricardo, the monetary theorist

Hayek's early work on money evolved in two directions. Besides his well-known attempts at the integration of money into equilibrium theory, he turned to monetary policy, investigating such subjects as neutral money, the (misguided) goal of price stabilization, international monetary systems and so on. According to Hayek, any investigation into monetary policy had to be accompanied by thorough historical studies. In this vein, he started in 1930 (see Hayek [undated] 1991) a venture into the history of money, which he continued updating in the following years (see Hayek, [1931] 2012; [1933] 2012; [1939] 2012; [1941] 2007).

Although the hero of Hayek's studies of the monetary writings at the turn of the eighteenth century and beyond is Henry Thornton, with regard to the development of monetary theory Ricardo is approvingly acknowledged for two vital insights (see Hayek, 1991: 200 and 208) – first, for specifying the 'indirect mechanism' of the propagation of changes in the quantity of money, that is, by means of deviations of the market rate of interest from its 'natural' level; second, for accepting – in his discussion with Malthus – a version of the forced saving doctrine, that is, the influence exercised by the excessive issue of credit on the interest rate and the structure of production (see *Works*, III: 91 and 122). In Hayek's view ([1931] 2012: 200–10), these insights mark two important stages in the development of monetary theory, leading ultimately to the theory of money and the cycle he himself expounded.

As concerns monetary policy, Ricardo is portrayed as a strict (yet in comparison with Thornton too rigid) adherent to the Bullionist party in nineteenth-century debates (see Hayek, 1991: Chapters 11 and 12). In the Bullion Controversy, Ricardo with *The High Price of Bullion* in 1811 (*Works*, III: 47–127) sided with the Bullionists in identifying the excessive issue of notes during the period of the restriction of cash (that is, gold) payments and thus in effect a period of paper money as crucial. Subsequently, with regard to the restoration of gold, in another influential pamphlet of 1816 *Proposals for an Economical and Secure Currency* (*Works*, IV: 43–141), Ricardo opted for a gold bullion standard, that is, a currency fixed in its value to gold, but using paper notes convertible into gold bullion instead of gold coins as the means of payment. This is, indeed, how the gold standard worked in Great Britain, albeit for a very short period, 1821–23. Finally, in 1824 the posthumously published *Plan for the Establishment of a National Bank* (*Works*, IV: 271–300) propagated a solution for the innate conflicts emanating from the unique position of the Bank of England by separating the task of note issue from the other banking functions, and by creating a new entity, a National Bank, for the supervision of the note issue – a solution foreshadowing the position of the Currency School. In this account, Hayek characterized Ricardo as a not very innovative but stern defender of what was to become British monetary orthodoxy, a position that was to inspire the thinking of both Hayek and (already earlier) Mises. In fact, Hayek found only one major shortcoming in the orthodox position ascribed to Ricardo, namely the neglect of the extent to which bank notes could be substituted in their function as means of payment by deposits created by commercial banks. This deficiency both made the execution of monetary policy less straightforward than it might have been regarded by Ricardo (and the Currency School) and via the existence of 'circulation credit' it opened up a source for bringing about booms and depressions (see Hayek [1933] 2012: Chapter 4, especially 125, 19n).

Finally, considering the restoration of the gold standard, Ricardo recommended the return to gold at the old parity, yet not in any circumstance. Specifically, he would have advised against such a return, had it involved a revaluation of the pound of, say, 30 per cent (letter to John Wheatley, 18 September 1821, in *Works*, IX: 71–4). In his writings Hayek repeatedly quoted Ricardo in this respect as an authority. Had Great Britain learned his lesson it would have abstained from the ill-conceived return to gold at the pre-war parity in 1925 (see e.g., Hayek, 1991: 215, 72n).

Hayek's 'Ricardo effect'
What Hayek ([1939] 2012, 1942) introduced as the 'Ricardo effect' is nothing more than the application of the idea that (relative) factor prices act as a determinant of the structure of production, in particular of the relative use of labour and capital, that is, what the Austrians called 'roundaboutness' or 'capital intensity'. For example, it has been a long-standing idea of Austrian capital theory from Böhm-Bawerk onwards that a lower rate of interest will be associated with a higher capital intensity. Correspondingly, Hayek's Ricardo effect examined the impact of changes in real wages: drawing on a numerical example in Ricardo's *Principles* (*Works*, I: 39–43 and 395), Hayek maintained that in general a fall in the real wage is bound to bring about the adoption of less capital-intensive methods of production.

There has been much debate as to the extent to which the Ricardo effect indeed descends from Ricardo. Yet, at least there appears to be agreement that the gist of Ricardo's analysis pointed to the effects of changes in technology brought about by technical progress on overall employment and not to the response of technology to factor price changes. Similarly, although Hayek was able to find some precedents in Ricardo's writings (Hayek, [1941] 2007: Appendix 2) Ricardo used it as a device for explaining the effects of the introduction of new technology and not like Hayek (and others before him) as an element of the business cycle. Thus, to appreciate the role of the Ricardo effect for the purpose for which Hayek had destined it, a closer look at Hayek's theory of the cycle is needed.

In Hayek's view the boom phase of the business cycle induced by too low a rate of interest and by excessive credit creation is characterized by over-investment. Each dose of inflation will distort relative prices, with prices of capital goods too high, and of consumption goods too low, relative to wages. Now the crucial question in this scenario is how to explain the upper turning point. In the early versions of Hayek's theory ([1931] 1935), the boom is brought to an end and the crisis starts with an increase in the rate of interest and the cessation of credit creation; thereby the relation between relative prices is reversed, resources are redirected towards consumption, and it is the restricted mobility of some capital goods that is responsible for both unemployment and idle capacity in the economy. Yet, apart from questioning the logical consistency of Hayek's approach (most prominently by Sraffa, 1932), another strand of criticism, implicit in the novel Keynesian framework, maintained that his assumptions were unrealistic: there existed unused resources from the outset, with a paper currency credit creation at a low interest rate might go on almost indefinitely, and wages were not as flexible as supposed, but rigid. With the Ricardo effect, Hayek tried to show that even in these circumstances (in particular, assuming fixed money wages) there was a built-in tendency for the boom to eventually lead to a crisis.

Specifically, Hayek ([1939] 2012) assumed an economy in the midst of a boom phase, with the money wage and the rate of interest given, the volume of credit demand-determined, rising incomes, a capacity constraint in the production of consumption goods but excess capacity and demand-determined production in the capital goods sector. Thus, an increase in its demand would increase the price of consumption goods, yet leave money wages (and prices of capital goods) unchanged. This means that wages in terms of consumption goods will fall and, according to the Ricardo effect, production should become less capital intensive, so that even if there is a kind of accelerator effect on investment demand, eventually investment demand, and thereby aggregate demand, must decrease. Thus, apparently it should be possible to derive the upper turning point even under this more realistic set of assumptions.

Yet, there is something wrong with Hayek's Ricardo effect. The most devastating critique came from Kaldor ([1942] 2012), echoing an earlier one by Wilson (1940). Kaldor concluded that the Ricardo effect either cannot fulfil the task it has been set to accomplish or, if so, then only by taking recourse to Hayek's original mechanism for the upper turning point. Put in a nutshell, Kaldor argued that Hayek misconstrued the results of neoclassical production theory. The structure of production will change only with a change in *relative* factor prices. In this case, these are, on the one hand, the money wage and, on the other, the rental price of capital, determined by the rate of interest and the price of capital goods. With all these assumed constant, a rise in the price of consumption goods will *not* change relative factor prices, but will only increase the profitability of producing consumption goods and thus stimulate a proportional increase in planned production, so that there is no incentive to use less capital and more labour. Such a change in the structure of production could only result when – in the course of the boom – due to capacity constraints eventually a rise in prices of capital goods would precede a rise in wages. Then, with capital goods becoming more expensive relative to labour, the structure of production would indeed be redirected towards labour. However, this outcome would not be due to the Ricardo effect as perceived by Hayek, but simply mirror the reaction to a rise in the rate of interest as in his earlier version.

Thus, eventually, although Hayek ([1969] 2012) undertook a belated attempt to salvage it, the Ricardo effect has neither survived as an ingredient of business cycle theory nor as an enrichment of the interpretation of Ricardo's thought. It might be remembered only as an idea that brilliantly failed.

As an afterthought it should be noted that just from the time when Hayek lost the debate with Kaldor and henceforth withdrew from most of current discussions in economic theory, his perception of contemporary economics became quite selective. So it might not come as a surprise that he remained rather ignorant of post- or neo-Ricardian strands of thought, and especially of the results of the famous Cambridge controversies on capital theory. Although in the 1930s, and definitely in his own capital theory ([1941] 2007), Hayek must have been aware of the problems inherent in the quest for a scalar indicator of capital (or of the capital intensity of production), that is, of the price and real Wicksell effects involved in any such attempts, he never grasped the full power of these (negative) results. In the end, Hayek's Ricardo effect proved not only open to criticisms concerning its use in business cycle theory, but also as being based on a doctrine regarding the effects of relative factor prices on the choice of technique that cannot be sustained as generally valid.

Conclusion: what is missing?

Summarizing, one wonders why the work of Ricardo has not left more traces in Hayek's own. Almost all instances where Hayek dealt with Ricardo refer to peripheral parts of his work. There is scarcely any discussion of Ricardo on methodology, scant references to Ricardo as the adherent to the classical surplus approach, to his 'objective' approach to value theory, even to the theory of comparative costs and the effects of the (international) division of labour, which the Austrians might have appreciated. In this respect, Hayek, the subjectivist Austrian, and Ricardo, the classical economist, appear like the inhabitants of two separate worlds.

HANSJOERG KLAUSINGER

See also:

Böhm-Bawerk, Eugen von, on Ricardo; Bullionist Controversy; Capital and Profits; Kaldor, Nicholas, on Ricardo; Monetary Theory; Papers on Money and Banking; Rate of Interest; Technical Change.

References

Hayek, F.A. von ([undated] 1991), 'Währungsgeschichte', unpublished typescript, translated and reprinted in *Collected Works, Vol. 3*, Chs 9–12.

Hayek, F.A. von ([1931] 2012), *Prices and Production*, London: Routledge, 2nd revised edition 1935; reprinted in 2012 in *Collected Works, Vol. 7*.

Hayek, F.A. von ([1933] 2012), *Monetary Theory and the Trade Cycle*, London: Jonathan Cape; reprinted in 2012 in *Collected Works, Vol. 7*.

Hayek, F.A. von ([1939] 2012), 'Profits, interest, and investment', in *Profits, Interest, and Investment*, London: Routledge; reprinted in 2012 in *Collected Works, Vol. 8*, Ch. 8.

Hayek, F.A. von ([1941] 2007), *The Pure Theory of Capital*, London: Routledge; reprinted in 2007 in *Collected Works, Vol. 12*.

Hayek, F.A. von (1942), 'The Ricardo effect', *Economica* (New Series), **9**; reprinted in 2012 in *Collected Works, Vol. 3*, Ch. 9.

Hayek, F.A. von (1955), 'Ricardo, David', in *Chamber's Encyclopaedia, Vol. 9*, new edition, London: George Newnes, pp. 680–81.

Hayek, F.A. von ([1969] 2012), 'Three elucidations of the Ricardo effect', *Journal of Political Economy*, **77**; reprinted in 2012 in *Collected Works, Vol. 8*, Ch. 11.

Hayek, F.A. von (1988–), *The Collected Works of F.A. Hayek* [*Collected Works*], 19 vols, various editors, Chicago, IL: University of Chicago Press and London: Routledge.

Kaldor, N. ([1942] 2012), 'Professor Hayek and the concertina effect', *Economica* (New Series), **9**; reprinted in 2012 in *Collected Works, Vol. 8*, Ch. 10.

Sraffa, P. (1932), 'Dr. Hayek on money and capital', *Economic Journal*, **42** (165), 42–53.

Wilson, T. (1940), 'Capital theory and the trade cycle', *Review of Economic Studies*, **7**, 169–79.

Hicks, John R., on Ricardo

Hicks's interest in classical economics arose in the 1960s in the context of his work on growth theory and, more generally, on the methods of dynamic economics. In fact, Hicks considered the theories of growth of Smith and Ricardo as outstanding examples of the use of the static method in dynamic economics. In the following years the Oxford economist widened his interests in classical theory to monetary topics and to other economists, like Cantillon, the Physiocrats and Mill. However, Ricardo's theory of distribution and growth remained Hicks's main concern in classical economics.

Appraisal of the static method used by Smith and Ricardo

According to Hicks (1965: 30) 'every method of analysis of a process of change can be exhibited . . . as a sequence analysis'. The particular characteristic of the static method in economic dynamics is that static theory is used as a single-period theory of the dynamic process. In each single period the economic system is taken to be in static equilibrium, where the variables are determined by current parameters only. The single period is self-contained and the dynamic process is reduced to a sequence of static equilibria. In Hick's view both Smith and Ricardo adopted this framework and met similar difficulties. Moreover, Ricardo's early growth model overlaps with Smith's basic model to some extent. Therefore, it is instructive to consider Hick's methodological appraisal of Smith's work before moving to Ricardo.

In his basic model Smith makes the single period, the agricultural year, self-contained by the assumption that all capital is circulating capital and that capital is homogeneous. In the economy there is only one commodity, corn. The corn output of one year is employed, in the following year, either to pay wages to non-productive labourers, or to pay wages to the labourers employed in the production of corn. Therefore, the growth rate of the economy is:

$$g = q\,(p/w) - 1 \tag{1}$$

where g is the rate of growth of corn output, q the proportion of previous year's output that is used to employ labourers in the production of corn, p the productivity of labour and w the wage rate. From equation (1) it follows that growth is slowed down by unproductive consumption. This is the fundamental message Smith wanted to give.

It should be noticed that, if we assume that q, p and w are constant over time, the value of g in equation (1) becomes the steady state rate of growth of the economy. But, in Hicks's view, it is not necessary to interpret Smith in this way. Actually, Smith believed that the division of labour would generate increasing returns and that growth would bring about an increase in wages, so that p and w would increase over time, not necessarily at the same rate. Therefore, equation (1) should be used in a more flexible way to explain the growth rate of the economy, year by year. So far so good. However, Smith did not want to confine productive labour to agriculture and therefore went on to consider a system with many commodities, agricultural and otherwise, many kinds of capital, fixed and variable, and different periods of production. But by doing so he lost the homogeneity of capital and output and the natural period of agriculture, which in his basic model had made the single period self-contained. In fact, Hicks shows that in Smith's general model, whatever the definition of the single period, a consistent measure of the initial capital and output requires that the equilibrium rate of profit and the equilibrium prices of the present period and of the previous periods are the same. But this would be possible only if all production was conducted under constant returns to scale, while Smith insists all along that the division of labour would bring about increasing returns. Therefore, Hicks concludes that in Smith's general model there is a fatal contradiction between the static method and the hypothesis of increasing returns.

According to Hicks, Ricardo's early growth model, presented in the pamphlet *Essay on Profits*, has a lot in common with Smith's basic model. Since the central topic of the *Essay* is the Corn Laws, Ricardo cannot take agriculture as representative of the whole economy and is obliged to distinguish between the agricultural sector and the rest of the economy. However, Ricardo's model of the agricultural sector is very similar to Smith's basic model, the only important difference being the introduction of diminishing returns in agriculture. In fact, Ricardo assumes that labourers consume only agricultural products, namely corn, and that in the agricultural sector there is only circulating capital, the corn output of the previous year, as in Smith's basic model. What happens in the agricultural sector is independent from what happens in the rest of the economy and therefore Ricardo can concentrate himself on what happens in agriculture in the self-contained agricultural period.

In terms of equation (1) the hypothesis of decreasing returns in agriculture implies that, as the agricultural sector expands, p decreases and therefore the rate of growth of the agricultural product falls; this until p becomes equal to w and the agricultural sector becomes stationary. However, the model of the agricultural sector of the *Essay* is somewhat richer than Smith's basic model, since Ricardo is interested not only in the rate of growth of the sector, but also in the distribution of the agricultural product between wages, rent and profits. Hicks describes Ricardo's model of the *Essay* and derives from it the well-known results: as employment in agriculture increases, the rate of profit falls and rent increases; improvements in agriculture and importation of corn raise the rate of profit and reduce rent; sooner or later agriculture falls into a stationary state. So far so good. But what about the rest of the economy? In the *Essay* Ricardo thought it sufficient to point out that competition would maintain the same rate of profit in all sectors. However, the rest of the economy could not be fitted into the scheme of a self-contained single period unless we assume that all products take a year to produce. More generally, if we abandon the assumption that in agriculture there is no fixed capital and that all commodities have the same period of production, we lose the self-containedness of the single period, which is crucial for the static method. In Ricardo, as in Smith, equilibrium cannot be confined to the single period, however defined; the economy must have been in static equilibrium much longer than that. But this long-run equilibrium is not possible in Ricardo, since Ricardo assumes diminishing returns in agriculture, which imply a diminishing rate of profit and, hence, changes in relative prices. Therefore, Hicks concludes that in Ricardo we find the same inconsistency as in Smith, between the use of the static method in economic dynamics and the assumption of non-constant returns.

In my view, Hicks's criticism of Ricardo goes a bit too far since it depends on the assumption that in Ricardo the marginal product of labour in agriculture falls continuously. In fact, as we shall see in the third section of this entry, it is legitimate to assume that in Ricardo the marginal productivity of labour falls in steps and that the steps are long enough to allow the economy to be in steady state for a long period of time. When the marginal productivity of labour decreases, the economy moves towards a new steady state and so on. From this perspective the growth path of the economy could be described as a sequence of steady states – steady states that can be treated with the static method. However, even if we accept this view, it remains true that Ricardo's static method shows its limits since it cannot describe the transition of the economic system from one steady state to the next. Therefore, in the end, Hicks is right in saying that, while the static method is very convenient and allows us to understand several aspects of a growing economy, there are important or even crucial problems of dynamics that cannot be treated with such a method. Something else is needed (Hicks, 1965: 47; 1985: 42–3).

Hicks's discussion of Ricardo's theory of distribution in the traditional fix-wage Ricardian model

A few years after the methodological discussion of the classical growth model, Hicks ([1972] 1983) went back to Ricardo to discuss his theory of distribution, in the wake of a renewed criticism of Ricardo's conclusions and, in particular, of Ricardo's statement about the necessary increase of the share of rent. In the first part of the paper Hicks deals with the conventional problem of the three-way distribution of income and shows that, while the share of wages in total product is necessarily an increasing function of employment in agriculture (since the supply of labour can be taken to be perfectly elastic at a given real wage) and the share of profit a decreasing function, the share of rent does not necessarily rise with employment, as stated by Ricardo. However, Hicks points out that, if we assume that when land is abundant relatively to labour, the marginal product of land is zero, and that at some level of employment in agriculture the marginal product of labour becomes zero, we can state that the share of rent necessarily rises both at the beginning and at the end of the process of economic growth. In between the share of rent might fall, but under Ricardo's assumptions such a possibility should be considered 'abnormal', since it depends on the possibility that at some point the elasticity of substitution between land and labour becomes greater than one, while at the beginning and at the end of growth it is less than one. Therefore, in Hicks's view, in his statement about the rise of the share of rent during the process of economic growth 'Ricardo is guilty of no more than the omission of a qualification' (ibid.: 36).

In any case, according to the Oxford economist, Ricardo's main concern was not the three-way distribution of gross revenue, but the distribution of net revenue, which is saveable revenue, between profits and rents. In fact, since the rate of capital accumulation depends both on the rate of profit and on the aggregate propensity to save and invest, for Ricardo's theory of the 'retardation' of growth it is important to show that, as growth proceeds, the rate of profit falls *and* net revenue is transferred 'from a class which looks like having a high propensity to save and to invest to one that looks like having a much lower propensity' (ibid.: 37). Hicks shows that, under Ricardo's assumptions, as the economy grows, the rate of profit declines without exception, while the possibility of a fall of the share of rent in net revenue is very remote indeed. In fact, since the ratio between net revenue and gross revenue necessarily falls with the increase of employment in agriculture, the share of rent in net revenue would rise even if rent was a constant proportion of gross revenue and could rise even if its share in gross revenue was falling. Therefore, Hicks concludes that in Ricardo 'the retardation of growth is established: securely on the side of incentive, sufficiently on the other' (ibid.).

Hicks's contribution to the new variable wage interpretation of Ricardo's theory of distribution and economic growth

As we have seen, in his discussion of Ricardo's theory of distribution Hicks accepts the traditional fix-wage interpretation of Ricardo. However, in the paper 'Mr Ricardo and the Moderns', written with S. Hollander (Hicks and Hollander 1977), Hicks abandons such interpretation and presents a Ricardian model in which the wage rate is determined by the interplay between the rate of capital accumulation and the rate of growth of labour supply. The model is built on the following assumptions, which are derived from the *Principles*:

(A1)   *The returns to labour are a monotonically decreasing function of the amount of labour employed on land.*

(A2)   *The rate of growth of labour supply is an increasing function of the difference between the market wage rate and the natural wage rate.*

(A3)   *Capital accumulation is an increasing function of the difference between the market rate of profit and the minimum rate of profit required by capitalists.*

(A4)   *The wage rate rises or falls, from one period to the next, as the rate of capital accumulation is higher or lower than the rate of increase of labour supply.*

From the working of the model Hicks derives the following propositions:

(P1)   *During the process of growth the wage rate is, most of the time (possibly all the time), above the natural level and the rate of profit is above the minimum.*

(P2)   *The economic system converges to the stationary state.*

(P3)   *During the process of growth the wage rate and the rate of profit may rise or fall from one period to the next, but in the neighbourhood of the stationary state they necessarily fall.*

According to Hicks, this model is closer to Ricardo's thought than the traditional fix-wage model, since it allows us to derive a higher number of Ricardo's conclusions. In particular, it confirms Ricardo's statement that workers benefit for a long period of time from the process of growth, since the market wage rate remains above the natural level most of the time, while in the traditional model these benefits are ephemeral, since it is assumed that market equilibrium converges very rapidly to natural equilibrium. However, there is an important point on which Hicks's Ricardian model differs from Ricardo. In fact, while the latter states that during the process of economic growth both the wage rate and the rate of profit fall, Hicks's model justifies only the much weaker proposition (P3).

A few months after the publication of the Hicks–Hollander paper, Casarosa (1978) formulated, quite independently, a Ricardian model that is free from the partial inconsistency just mentioned. The model is similar to Hicks's model and differs from it mainly in the assumption that returns to labour decrease by steps and that the steps are rather long. Along each step the economic system converges towards a dynamic equilibrium position, characterized by the equality between the rate of capital accumulation and the rate of growth of labour supply. Therefore, it is suggested that the evolution of the economy over time should be described in terms of dynamic equilibrium rather than in terms of natural equilibrium. As for the evolution over time of the dynamic equilibrium of the economy, it is shown that the dynamic equilibrium values of the wage rate, the rate of profit and the rate of growth are increasing functions of the marginal productivity of labour in agriculture. Therefore, as decreasing returns set in, the wage rate and the rate of profit fall and go on falling until the system reaches the stationary state.

Hicks welcomed the dynamic equilibrium interpretation of Ricardo, stressing the similarities with his own interpretation: 'the main thing which is said in each paper is the same. Both are attacking the "fix-wage" interpretation of Ricardo, which has become conventional; in both it is shown . . . that "fix-wage" is a travesty of Ricardo's meaning' (Hicks, 1979a: 133). As for the differences between the two approaches, Hicks considered them quite interesting: 'The reader can take his choice between these two presentations; it may well be that there are separate lessons to be derived from each. But the main lesson from each . . . is the same' (ibid.: 134). However, on further reflection (Hicks, 1979b: 54n; 1985: 42n) the Oxford economist became somewhat critical of the dynamic equilibrium model on the ground that the assumption that returns fall by (long) steps, on which the model is built, is not to be found in Ricardo. Hicks admitted that this assumption is necessary to guarantee the consistency between Ricardo's static method and decreasing returns and in fact Hicks himself had made the same assumption in *Capital and Time* (1973: 147). However, he came to the conclusion that on the whole it is 'more illuminating to recognize that the static equilibrium and the diminishing returns do not fit' (Hicks, 1985: 42n).

For what it matters, I have no question with Hicks's conclusion. However, I would like to point out that the relevance of the dynamic equilibrium path is not tied to the assumption that, in agriculture, returns fall by (long) steps. In fact, if we consider the dynamic equilibrium path in the framework of the Hicks–Hollander model, as I have done (Casarosa, 1982), we can state the following propositions:

(P4)   If the market wage rate is below the dynamic equilibrium value (which guarantees the equality between the rate of growth of capital and the rate of growth of population), the wage rate rises, while if it is above the dynamic equilibrium value it falls.

(P5)   Sooner or later, during the process of growth, the market wage rate rises above the dynamic equilibrium value.

(P6)   From the moment the market wage rate has risen above the dynamic equilibrium value the wage rate, the rate of profit and the rate of growth will fall continuously until the economy reaches the stationary state.

Therefore, the reference to the dynamic equilibrium path allows us to obtain all Ricardo's results, independently from the form of the production function in agriculture and independently from the static method.

Appraisal of Ricardo's machinery analysis

Given Hicks's increasing scepticism about the static method, it is easy to understand the Oxford economist's theoretical interest in Ricardo's analysis of the effects of machinery, although this interest arose at first in the context of his attempt to explain the impact of industrialization on the labour market (Hicks, 1969). In fact, Hicks see Ricardo's machinery question as a typical example of what he calls the 'traverse', that is, the transition path from one steady state to another.

As is well known, in the chapter 'On Machinery' of the *Principles* Ricardo states that, while in the long run improved machinery is beneficial to all classes of society (labourers, capitalists and landlords), during the process of adjustment of the economy to a new technology it may happen, and very often it does happen, that the conditions of the workers get worse for a significant span of time. In the third section of 'Explanations and Revisions' (1977) Hicks points out that Ricardo's machinery problem can be approached in neoclassical terms, by considering the short- and long-run effects of a strongly labour-saving invention that diminishes the marginal product of labour. However, the Oxford economist thinks that the neoclassical approach (which, as we know, he pioneered in Chapter VI of the his *Theory of Wages*, 1932) makes it difficult to assess whether the strongly labour-saving case is important or not and therefore he prefers to deal with Ricardo's problem in the framework of a simplified version of the 'Austrian' model of *Capital and Time*. The simplified model is the following: the production process has a constructional stage in which a 'machine' is produced, and a utilizational stage, in which the machine is used to produce a given amount of consumption goods. The amount of time taken by the two stages is the same with any technique so that, if we assume that there are only two inputs, machines and labour, we can identify any technique by the labour coefficients of the two stages of its production process.

Let us now assume that the economy is initially in steady state and suppose that a new technique becomes available that is more profitable than the old one. The higher profitability of the new technique may arise in three different ways: (a) both coefficients are lower on the new technique; (b) the construction coefficient is higher, but the utilizational coefficient is so much lower as to more than compensate; (c) the utilizational coefficient is higher, but the construction coefficient is so much lower as to more than compensate.

In cases (a) and (c) both the short- and the long-run effects of the new technology are favourable to the workers as well to the other classes of society, while in case (b) we have Ricardo's machinery effect. In fact, since the construction coefficient is higher with the new technology, there is at least one period in which the production of consumption goods must fall below its initial level; actually, if the comparative advantage of the new technology is not too large, the production of consumption goods remains below the initial level for several periods. It follows that, if the level of consumption of the capitalists, of the landlords and of the state is not reduced at the necessary extent, and there is no reason for this to happen, the workers suffer from the change of technology. More precisely, if the real wage rate is kept constant, the level of employment falls, while, if the wage rate is flexible, full employment is maintained, but the real wage rate falls. However, at some point of the process of substitution of the new machines to the old ones the production of consumption goods and the demand for labour start rising and go on rising until the system reaches the new steady state.

We can therefore conclude that Hicks's analysis confirms and clarifies Ricardo's idea that during the transition from one technology to another the workers may suffer for a considerable amount of time. However, while Ricardo seems to think that the 'machinery effect' is very frequent (*Works*, I: 388 and 392), Hicks shows that it emerges only if the technological improvement is of a particular type and, more precisely, if it has 'a very strong forward bias' (Hicks, 1973: 98). Actually, according to Hicks, the technical change that gives rise to the 'machinery effect' is most likely to take place in the early phases of the processes of rapid industrialization, when we have '*introduction* [original emphasis] of machinery' rather than '*improvement* [my emphasis] of machinery' (ibid.: 99).

In a recent paper Samuelson (1994) has shown that in an economy with a fixed amount of land there are many ways other than Ricardo's (and Hicks's) machinery effect in which a technological change may harm the workers in any run. However, it seems to me that Ricardo's (and Hicks's) machinery effect is much more relevant (than the other cases pointed out by Samuelson) for the understanding of the effects of technological change both in the initial phases of the processes of industrialization and in the normal working of a fully industrialized economy. Actually, I wonder whether something like the machinery effect might not have contributed to the rise of the rate of unemployment in Europe and to the slowdown of the growth of real wages in the USA during the 1980s of last century.

CARLO CASAROSA

See also:

Accumulation of Capital; Endogenous Growth; Labour and Wages; Mathematical Formulations of Ricardian Economics; Pasinetti, Luigi Lodovico, on Ricardo; Ricardian Dynamics.

References

Casarosa, C. (1978), 'A new formulation of the Ricardian system', *Oxford Economic Papers*, **30**(1), 38–63.
Casarosa, C. (1982), 'The new view of the Ricardian theory of distribution and economic growth', in M. Baranzini (ed.), *Advances in Economic Theory*, Oxford: Basil Blackwell.
Hicks, J.R. (1932), *The Theory of Wages*, London: Macmillan.
Hicks, J.R. (1965), *Capital and Growth*, Oxford: Clarendon Press.
Hicks, J.R. (1969), *A Theory of Economic History*, Oxford: Oxford University Press.

Hicks, J.R. ([1972] 1983), 'Ricardo's theory of distribution', in M. Peston and B. Corry (eds), *Essays in Honour of Lord Robbins*, London: Weidenfeld and Nicholson, pp.160–67; reprinted in J.R. Hicks (1983), *Classics and Moderns, Collected Essays on Economic Theory, Vol. III*, Oxford: Basil Blackwell, pp.32–8.
Hicks, J.R. (1973), *Capital and Time*, Oxford: Clarendon Press.
Hicks, J.R. (1977), 'Explanations and revisions', in J.R. Hicks, *Economic Perspectives*, Oxford: Clarendon Press, pp.177–95.
Hicks, J.R. (1979a), 'The Ricardian system: a comment', *Oxford Economic Papers*, **31**(1), 133–4.
Hicks, J.R. (1979b), *Causality in Economics*, Oxford: Basil Blackwell.
Hicks, J.R. (1985), *Methods of Dynamic Economics*, Oxford: Clarendon Press.
Hicks, J.R. and S. Hollander (1977), 'Mr. Ricardo and the moderns', *Quarterly Journal of Economics*, **XCI**, 351–69; reprinted in J.R. Hicks (1983), *Classics and Moderns, Collected Essays on Economic Theory, Vol. III*, Oxford: Basil Blackwell, pp.39–59.
Samuelson, P. (1994), 'The classical classical fallacy', *The Journal of Economic Literature*, **32**(2), 620–39.

Historical Schools on Ricardo

Anti-classical economics, which for the sake of simplicity we will put under the label of the Historical School(s) – where the 's' suggests some heterogeneity of the economists included – was critical of David Ricardo throughout the whole of the nineteenth century. This unfavourable judgement represented a further accretion to the disapproval expressed by many representatives of the mainstream (classical) school, which centred above all on two aspects: the excessive use of the abstract-deductive method that had led Ricardo for having 'pushed [economics] in a vacuum' (*'poussée dans le vide*': Say [1803] 2006: 47; also cited by Marx [1861–63] 1968, Vol. 2: 525) and, above all, for the 'socialist' implications of the theory of rent (Carey [1847] 1967: 74–5; Ferrara [1856] 1956: 460; Foxwell [1899] 1952: 277).

The criticisms advanced by the exponents of the Historical Schools, were, however, of a rather different type. While Smith had upheld the distinction/contradiction between 'benevolence', dominant in the *Theory of Moral Sentiments*, and the 'self-love' that is dominant in *The Wealth of Nations* – herein the so-called 'Adam Smith problem' consisted – Ricardo had thoroughly pursued the implications of self-love without taking benevolence into account. As the pupil of Bentham that he was, Ricardo had built up a morally indifferent political economy, in contrast with historical experience and with human nature itself.

This interpretation may seem to be convergent with that put forward by the young Marx, who had defined Ricardo's language as *'cynique'* (cynical) because it went to the heart of the capitalist system, presenting it as it really was (Marx, 1847: 27; see also Faucci, 1998). In actual fact, the two critical approaches start out from opposing visions, because the anti-Ricardian economists ascribed a character to Ricardo that Marx regarded as intrinsic to the bourgeois economy.

In this entry we will focus on the major non-mainstream authors who addressed Ricardo's work from a critical perspective. Such criticisms concerned almost all aspects of Ricardianism. They focused not only on his general vision of economic science, with its clear-cut separation between economics and morals, but also on the main assumptions of Ricardian theory, especially as regards the inverse relationship between profits and wages. Finally, these criticisms additionally concerned the long-term trend of the economy according to Ricardo, a trend that, in absence of technological improvements and free imports of corn, would inevitably lead to increasing rents, decreasing profits and wages at a subsistence level and that had been disproved by the empirical evidence of the European countries after 1850.

France

In the multifaceted landscape of the French-speaking economists in the nineteenth century, Ricardo does not take centre stage, as this position was occupied by Jean-Baptiste Say, an opponent of the Ricardian theory of value (cf. Breton and Lutfalla, 1991). Jean-Charles-Léonard de Sismondi, on the other hand, is a case apart, since he opposed both Say and Ricardo.

It is difficult to place Sismondi appropriately within the strands of early nineteenth-century economic thought. Although Marx included him among the classical economists from the point of view of his analysis of the capitalist process, some elements of his vision – his idealization of the medieval corporative economy as well as his somewhat anachronistic predilection for the hierarchical relations between landowners and share-croppers – characterize him as a Romantic and anti-capitalist thinker of a conservative inclination, and implicitly as a 'historicist' economist.

In his *Nouveaux principes d'économie politique* (1819) Sismondi criticizes the conclusions reached by Ricardo in Chapter XXI of his *Principles*, 'Effects of Accumulation on Profits and Interest', according to which, under the premise that the aim of any production is consumption, there cannot exist a situation in which one deliberately refuses to consume despite being able to do so. This is due to the fact, as Say also teaches, that 'productions are always bought by productions . . . money is only the medium by which exchange is effected' (*Works*, I: 291; see the quotation by Sismondi, 1819: 341). Ricardo believes that the road to follow is not that of support for demand, but rather that of an improvement in the conditions of production, in particular a decrease in the cost of wage commodities. In this manner the growth of profits will be assured, increased profits will create an increase in income and, finally, greater demand will be obtained. Sismondi counters Ricardo's (and Say's) argument by objecting that the capital accumulated by setting aside profits is not automatically transformed into income. The lesson of the periodic crises that succeeded one another after 1815, Sismondi points out, is that a growing quantity of capital can be accumulated for speculative purposes and then be lost due to insolvencies, bankruptcies or other events, without giving rise to the increase in demand that Ricardo believed to be automatically assured by the mere fact of accumulation.

Sismondi's article 'Sur la balance des consommations avec les productions' (1824) was reprinted as an Appendix to the second edition of his *Nouveaux principes* (in 1827), and was definitively included in his *Etudes sur l'économie politique* (1837). Here, Sismondi dedicated a lengthy footnote to criticize Ricardo's position, he considered entirely favourable to technical progress. Sismondi tried to show that a technological unemployment in agriculture could hardly be absorbed by an increased employment in the '*manufacture des pauvres*' (Sismondi [1824] 1837: 60), as Ricardo maintained, and would rely only on an expansion of the industry of luxuries, as Malthus rightly argued. Incidentally, we have to note that Sismondi neglected Ricardo's chapter 'On Machinery'.

Adolphe Blanqui was an eclectic economist with a penchant for philanthropy. He esteemed many Italian economists, who he felt to be close to French thinkers and quite distinct from English authors. Nevertheless, in Chapter XL of his *Histoire de l'économie politique en Europe* Blanqui portrays Ricardo as a shrewd monetary economist whose writings on the price of gold, the exchange rate and the circulation of paper money showed he had considerable insight. On the other hand, Blanqui rejects the inverse relation between wages and profits that constitutes the central assumption of *Principles*; for him it represents no more than a far-fetched hypothesis (Blanqui [1837] 1882: 415).

Italy

In Italy throughout the eighteenth century were economists like Ferdinando Galiani, Pietro Verri and Cesare Beccaria, who excluded morals and history from their approach and concentrated on a set of policy proposals in order to improve the state of the economy. Their writings were collected in Baron Pietro Custodi's edition of *Scrittori classici italiani di economia politica* in 50 volumes (1803–16). Custodi didn't provide a general introduction to this editorial enterprise. His junior colleague, Giuseppe Pecchio, an *émigré* patriot living in England, published a slim book in 1829, *Storia della economia pubblica in Italia*, which aimed to illustrate the Italian economic tradition as shown by the Custodi collection. We can consider Pecchio as something more than an amateur economist. He was the author of an essay on the financial administration of the Napoleonic Kingdom of Italy (1820) and of a book on the economic crisis in Britain in 1826. Moreover, he was a careful observer of English society, which he admired very much (see his *Osservazioni semiserie di un esule sull'Inghilterra*, 1831).

Pecchio terminated his *Storia* with a comparison between Italian and English economists. He said that both English and Italian economists in the eighteenth century had realized that political economy bore a close relation to political science, in particular to legislative measures. This inductive and empirical approach had been followed by Hume and Smith exactly, as well as by their Italian fellow economists, but this method had been forsaken in England at the outset of the new century. 'Through overuse of ideas that are too general and complex, sometimes the modern English thinkers have fallen into obscurity and unintelligible jargon. Who always understands Riccardo [sic]?' (Pecchio [1829] 1949: 253). On the other hand, the statesmen governing England, Pecchio argued, adopted a diametrically opposite style. Sir Robert Peel's speeches on the awkward question of the paper currency and paper circulation were characterized by great clarity and equally by great depth of perception. 'What a difference between these speeches which are intelligible to all persons and the hieroglyphic pages of Riccardo [sic], understandable only by those who have been initiated into his mysteries!' (ibid.). Pecchio felt there was a gulf between the language of active politics and that of political economy, and that the gulf was strongly tipped towards the former.

As far as the content of political economy were concerned, Pecchio noted that while modern English economists concentrated on production, the corresponding figures in Italy preferentially dwelt on welfare and collective happiness. It follows that development factors occupied a central position in political economy investigations undertaken by English economists, while Italian authors devised systems that tended towards rest and quietude (ibid., 257–8). But, at the same time, it could not be denied that from the point of view of presentation of the arguments the Italians tended to err on the side of 'verboseness' and literary preciousness in comparison to the mathematical terseness of economists on the opposite side of the English Channel. Pecchio thus felt that ideally there should be a blending of the two styles, which would temper the excesses of both.

The Milanese exile was a good prophet, since mid-nineteenth century Italian economists abandoned the Galiani-Verri-Beccaria theoretical approach to embark on a historicist-moralist reconstruction of the discipline (see Faucci, 2014: 67–8), which caused a severe gap between the remaining European economics – a gap destined to last until 1890 (see Schumpeter [1954] 1994: 855).

Great Britain
In Great Britain, essayists addressing a broader public charged economists with professing a science devoid of history, institutions or morality. In 1843 the Scot Thomas Carlyle published his book *Past and Present*, in which a number of references to the political economy of the era may be found. Carlyle contended that political economy was based on the 'law of demand and supply' and on application of the Mandevillian principle of 'private vices, publick benefits', updated with Benthamian utilitarianism. Although Ricardo is not mentioned, the object of the attack is post-Smithian classical economics, the secular arm of which, according to Carlyle, was the free trade approach embodied in the Anti-Corn Law League. To mitigate the social conflict that inevitably ensued from the classical theories, Carlyle glorified a vision of a corporative and strongly homogeneous society, at the tip of which he placed a 'chivalry of labour', a phrase that seems to foreshadow Alfred Marshall's 'economic chivalry'.

In 1862 John Ruskin brought out *Unto this Last*, a sort of manifesto of an economy with a human dimension. In Ruskin's view, wealth does not depend on the quantity of goods, but on the quantity and quality of human labour. Ruskin moves into the field of theory when he charges Ricardo with having led John Stuart Mill into error concerning the fact that the 'demand for products is not demand for labour' (Ruskin [1862] 1908: 161). Here what Ruskin seeks to emphasize is that for mainstream – hence, Ricardian – economics the final goal of production is individual consumption, whereas in a humanistic view of economics – which was the perspective Ruskin advocated – consumption is but a means of 'production of life' (ibid.: 163).

Within the heterogeneous body of those who were critical of political economy one also finds Arnold Toynbee, the author of a single book, *Lectures on the Industrial Revolution*, which came out posthumously in 1884. This work had the merit of introducing into English professional literature a significant expression, namely 'Industrial Revolution', which had arisen in the French cultural milieu (see Fohlen, 1971). Inspired by a strong religious fervour, and deeply committed to the Christian Social Union, which sought to usher in a reform of the Anglican Church, Toynbee was consistently regarded by his contemporaries as a passionate figure. This implied that he was a person whose qualities allowed him not so much to shed light on theories as, rather, to raise dramatic questions concerning the impact of theories on human behaviour, indeed on man himself.

Accordingly, instead of addressing theoretical and methodological issues, his battle dealt with the practical conclusions Ricardo had reached, given that such conclusions appeared to be refuted by the actual course of events. Toynbee's arguments highlighted the realization that a number of improvements that had been achieved – reduction in transport costs, technical progress in manufacturing and agriculture, the responsible behaviour shown by the trades unions, and above all the adoption of free trade – didn't corroborate, but rather disprove the income distribution trends emerging from Ricardo's theory (see Toynbee [1884] 1956: Chapters 11–13). But if the 'laws' of economics did not give a full account of the underlying tendencies of the system, inasmuch as they do not sufficiently take into consideration the transformations affecting the structure of the economy, then the door is opened for social reform. Thus, proposals for reform would no longer be subject to the demographic and productive constraints posited by the classics, such as the Malthusian population doctrine and the related wage-fund theory. Cooperative societies, industrial and wage legislation, public services funded by more extensive state and local expenditure (municipalized services) are elements of a programme in line with political economy in the amended form proposed by Toynbee.

Furthermore, it was important for the reforms to be compatible with the existing social order, which in Toynbee's view could be improved but did not deserve to be destroyed. His fundamental concern was that the reforms should avoid jumping out of the frying pan into the fire, a risk that could ensue if credence were given to modes of thought that were not only deficient on the plane of theory but also pernicious from the social point of view. This explains his polemical attitude towards Henry George, the American essayist who was the author of a bestseller of the time, *Progress and Poverty* (1879). In his book and in a series of talks Toynbee gave in London in early 1883, he voiced his critical stance towards George, who, basing his argument on the Ricardian approach, invoked nationalization of the land for the purpose of expropriation of rents. Finally, Toynbee expressed his strong opposition to any hypothesis of agricultural socialism.

Partly in the wake of Toynbee's publication, in the closing years of the nineteenth century there arose an English school of economists-historians, featuring interesting figures such as William Cunningham, William Ashley, Thomas Cliffe Leslie and others (see Koot, 1987), whose distinctive characteristic was their support for the imperialist and protectionist ideas of Joseph Chamberlain. The two versions of British imperialism – the approach that drew its inspiration from free trade under the teachings of Ricardo and Cobden, and the tendency towards protectionism – stood sharply in opposition to each other on the occasion of the 1903 elections, which saw the defeat of Chamberlain (see Semmel, 1960).

Germany

It may seem surprising that the exponents of the German Historical School devoted only scanty attention to Ricardo. For instance, Ricardo is ignored by Friedrich List, even though the latter was an adversary of both the Smithian and the Ricardian theory of international trade. Wilhelm Roscher in his 1843 manual displayed a generically respectful attitude to Ricardo, defining Ricardo's method as close to that of Rau, the main German liberal economist (Tribe, 1988: 206). Gustav Schmoller, in a passing observation, considered him as a follower of natural law-based political economy (!) (Alcouffe and Diebolt, 2009: 123). Karl Knies took the trouble to criticize the value theory presented by Ricardo in the very first pages of *Principles*. Knies objects that even the goods that cannot be reproduced at will, such as paintings, can have a differentiated value, which is clearly not dependent on scarcity (Knies [1883] 1930: 65). Thus, Knies reproached Ricardo for not taking demand into account.

The German writer on economic subjects who showed the greatest familiarity with Ricardo – to the point of earning a charge of plagiarism advanced by Engels – proves to have been Johann Karl Rodbertus-Jagetzow, who can hardly be included on the list of historicist economists, being more plausibly classifiable among social reformers working on classical Ricardian bases (Alcouffe and Diebolt, 2009: 318–22).

Turning to the anti-historicist front, the presence of Ricardo in the debate among German-speaking economists was likewise sidelined. In fact, the founding figure of Austrian economics, Carl Menger, showed no special Ricardian leanings in his *Grundsätze* (1871), and the *Methodestreit* wrangle that saw Menger pitted against Schmoller in the subsequent decade in no way featured the English economist as a pivotal element of the polemic (see Shionoya, 2001).

RICCARDO FAUCCI

See also:

Bentham, Jeremy, and Ricardo; Ricardo on Adam Smith; Riches and Value.

References

Alcouffe, A. and C. Diebolt (eds) (2009), *La pensée économique allemande*, Paris: Economica.
Blanqui, A. ([1837] 1882), *Histoire de l'économie politique en Europe depuis les anciens jusqu'à nos jours*, Paris: Guillaumin.
Breton Y. and M. Lutfalla (eds) (1991), *L'économie politique en France au XIXe siècle*, Paris: Economica.
Carey, H. ([1847] 1967), *The Past, the Present and the Future*, New York: Kelley.
Carlyle, T. (1843), *Past and Present*, London: Chapman and Hall.
Custodi, P. (1803–16), *Scrittori classici italiani di economia politica*, 50 vols, Milan: G.G. Destefanis.
Faucci, R. (1998), 'Marx, Karl, as an interpreter of the classical economists', in H.D. Kurz and N. Salvadori (eds), *The Elgar Companion to Classical Economics, Vol. 2*, Cheltenham, UK and Lyme, NH: Edward Elgar Publishing.
Faucci, R. (2014), *A History of Italian Economic Thought*, London and New York: Routledge.
Ferrara, F. ([1856] 1956), 'Introduzione a Torrens, Bailey, Whately, Ricardo, Rae', in B.R. Ragazzi (ed.), *Opere complete, Vol. 3*, Rome: De Luca.
Fohlen, C. (1971), *Qu'est-ce que la révolution industrielle?*, Paris: Laffont.
Foxwell, H.S. ([1899] 1952), 'Introduction to A. Menger's *Right to the Whole Produce of Labour*', reprinted in H.W. Spiegel (ed.), *The Development of Economic Thought. Great Economists in Perspective*, New York and London: Wiley and Sons.
George, H. (1879), *Progress and Poverty*, Garden City, NY: Doubleday.
Knies, K. ([1883] 1930), *Die politische Oekonomie vom geschichtlichen Standpunkte*, Leipzig: Hans Buske.
Koot, G. (1987), *English Historical Economics, 1870–1926. The Rise of Economic History and Neomercantilism*, Cambridge/New York/Melbourne: Cambridge University Press.
Marx, K. (1847), *Misère de la philosophie, Réponse à la philosophie de M. Proudhon*, Paris: Frank/Brussels: Vogler.
Marx, K. (1861–63] 1968), *Theories of Surplus Value*, 3 vols, London: Lawrence and Wishart.
Pecchio, G. ([1829] 1849), 'Confronto fra gli scrittori italiani e gli scrittori inglesi', in G. Pecchio, *Storia della economia pubblica in Italia*, Lugano: Tip. della Svizzera italiana.
Pecchio, G. ([1831] 1976), *Osservazioni semiserie di un esule sull'Inghilterra*, in G. Nicoletti (ed.), Milan: Longanesi.
Ruskin, J. ([1862] 1908), *Unto this Last. Four Essays on the First Principles of Political Economy*, New York: Wiley.
Say, J.-B. ([1803] 2006), *Traité d'économie politique*, (ed.) A. Tiran, Paris: Economica.
Schumpeter, J.A. ([1954] 1994), *History of Economic Analysis*, with a new introduction by M. Perlman, London: Routledge.
Semmel, B. (1960), *Imperialism and Social Reform: English Social-Imperial Thought, 1895–1914*, Cambridge, MA: Harvard University Press.
Shionoya, Y. (ed.) (2001), *The German Historical School. The Historical and Ethical Approach to Economics*, London and New York: Routledge.
Sismondi, J.-C.-L. de (1819), *Nouveaux principes de l'économie politique, ou de la richesse dans ses rapports avec la population*, Paris: Delaunay.
Sismondi, J.-C.-L. de ([1824] 1837), 'Sur la balance des consommations avec les productions', in *Etudes sur l'économie politique, Vol. 1*, Brussels: Société typographique belge.
Toynbee, A. ([1884] 1956), *Lectures on the Industrial Revolution in England*, preface by A.J. Toynbee, Boston, MA: Beacon Press.
Tribe, K. (1988), *Governing Economy. The Reformation of German Economic Discourse 1750–1840*, Cambridge, UK: Cambridge University Press.

Hollander, Jacob Harry, on Ricardo

In the first half of the twentieth century Jacob H. Hollander (1871–1940) was a leading authority on Ricardo. He not only discovered and edited several Ricardo letters and man-uscripts (see Hollander, 1895a, 1903, 1931, 1932; Bonar and Hollander, 1899; Hollander and Gregory, 1928), but also provided an influential interpretation of the development of Ricardo's theory of value (1904), an appraisal of the 'Ricardian' theory of differential rent and its relation to the concept of 'marginal rent' (1895b), an assessment of Ricardo's contributions to monetary theory (1911a), and a book-length *A Centenary Estimate* of David Ricardo's life, work and influence (1910; see also Hollander, 1911b). Moreover, he engaged in a vigorous debate with Edwin R. Seligman over the question of Ricardo's versus Torrens's priority in the exposition of the theory of comparative costs and the principle of differential rent (1910, 1911c).

With regard to the theory of value and distribution, Hollander interpreted Ricardo as having advocated essentially a cost of production theory along Smithian lines, in which the price of a commodity is arrived at by adding up its independent cost components:

> Interest and ... rent enter into cost of production, co-ordinate with wages, when production has become capitalistic, ... and the real prices of commodities [are] increased or diminished by every corresponding change in the ordinary rate of profits, the rate of wages and the rent of land. (1904: 461 and 473)

However, Hollander maintained that Ricardo's advocacy of such a cost of production theory underwent considerable change over time and that it is possible to distinguish 'three clearly defined phases in Ricardo's treatment of value' (ibid.: 456). In the first phase, which extended from his first reading of the *Wealth of Nations* in 1799 to the end of 1814, Ricardo adopted and 'remained mentally content with the general outline of Adam Smith's concept of value' (ibid.: 463). The second phase, which started with the writing of the pamphlet *Essay on Profits* in 1815 and ended with the publication of the first edition of the *Principles* in 1817, was characterized by a partial dissociation of Ricardo from Smith's value theory and in particular from the latter's idea that a rise in wages must raise all prices. In addition, it also involved the rejection of Smith's 'labour commanded' measure in favour of a 'labour embodied' measure of value. The third phase, which comprised the period from 1817 up to Ricardo's death in 1823, involved a gradual retreat from the principle of embodied labour as regulator of exchangeable value, prompted by the objections raised by Torrens, Malthus and others as to 'the adequacy of labor as a measure of value' (ibid.: 457).

In his 'Introduction' to the *Principles* Sraffa (*Works*, I: xxx–xlix) has conclusively shown that Hollander's interpretation cannot be sustained. Whereas Hollander ascribed to Ricardo a theory of value from his first acquaintance with economic literature, Ricardo's correspondence (not all of which had been available to Hollander) shows that he only began to concern himself with the problem of value in late 1815, when he first became aware that his 'dealing with the difficulties of price piecemeal' (ibid.: xxxiv) was insufficient, and that he arrived at the formulation of a proper theory of value at the earliest in 1816. Up to this time, Ricardo had developed his theory of profits without finding it necessary to enter into a discussion of prices at all, because his reasoning was conducted in terms of physical quantities. In a letter to Malthus, dated 26 June 1814,

Ricardo wrote: 'The rate of profits and of interest must depend on the proportion of production to the consumption necessary to such production' (*Works*, VI: 108). From this theory of profits based on a physical surplus produce, Ricardo then derived the principle that 'it is the profits of the farmer which regulate the profits of all other trades' (ibid.: 104). By focusing attention on the agricultural sector, where both 'production' and 'necessary consumption' could be conceived of as physically homogeneous (i.e., as quantities of 'corn'), Ricardo was able to determine the rate of profits without any recourse to prices. Given his physical conceptualization of the rate of profits, it comes as no surprise that, at this time, Ricardo perceived no contradiction between his profit theory and the Smithian proposition that 'the prices of all commodities must increase if the price of corn be increased' (ibid.: 114). It was only when Malthus, in spring 1815, insisted that the advanced capital ('necessary consumption'), in both manufactures and agriculture alike, in general also consists of necessaries other than corn, that Ricardo first recognized the need for a systematic theory of prices. Soon afterwards he then adopted the labour theory of value, because he believed that it would enable him to determine the rate of profits in a non-circular fashion in multi-commodity economic systems, where both the capital and the surplus produce consist of heterogeneous commodities. For Ricardo, then, the concern with value theory was clearly subordinated to the distribution problem.

According to Hollander, the sole and dominating theme in the second phase of Ricardo's treatment of value was 'the disproof of the dictum that high wages necessarily meant high prices' (1904: 470). But Hollander neglects the important point that by means of his 'corn-ratio' reasoning Ricardo had been able to perceive the constraint binding changes in the distributive variables: for a given technique a higher real wage rate must imply a lower rate of profits and vice versa. Hollander therefore also fails to see that Ricardo criticized Smith not merely for the 'dictum' mentioned above, but also for determining the price of a commodity by adding up wages, profits and rents, so that all three components appear as independent parts of it. On the basis of this component parts theory it seemed natural to conclude, as 'Adam Smith and all the writers after him' had in fact done, that higher wages must lead to higher prices. Ricardo escaped from this fallacy by treating money (or gold) as a commodity like any other. By treating gold or money *as if* it were an invariable measure of value, he then arrived at the conclusion that in terms of the money commodity some prices must rise and others must fall with an increase in wages. This 'curious effect', announced to Mill in a letter of 14 October 1816 (*Works*, VII: 82), was used by Ricardo not only to disprove the particular 'dictum' mentioned by Hollander, but also, and more importantly, to demonstrate the erroneousness of the cost of production or component parts theory of value advocated by Smith.

In Hollander's account, Ricardo in the third phase is supposed to have steadily retreated in subsequent editions of the *Principles*, under pressure from his critics, from the theory of value presented in the first edition. But Sraffa (*Works*, I: xxxviii–xlix) has shown that this reading entails conceptual misunderstandings on Hollander's part in his interpretation of the textual changes introduced by Ricardo in the second and third editions of the *Principles*, and that the only substantial change from the first to the third edition concerned the choice of an invariable measure of value, while 'no essential change was made in successive editions about the rule which determines value' (ibid.: xl). In all three editions Ricardo assumed gold to be invariable in value. However, in the first two editions of the *Principles*, Ricardo assumed gold to be produced by unassisted labour for a year, and utilized it to refute Smith's component parts theory. Upon his recognition that such a specification of the production conditions of gold would not render it an invariable measure of value when there are distributional changes, Ricardo in the third edition assumed gold to be produced under average technical conditions.

In view of Hollander's misunderstandings with regard to Ricardo's theory of value, it is not surprising to find him advocating the view, in his *Centenary Estimate*, that 'the effective contribution of Ricardo to economic science was not content but method' (1910: 129). According to Hollander, Ricardo 'established the title of economic inquiry to the rank of positive science, capable of pursuit by the logical method of deduction'; he therefore should be considered as 'the true founder of the science of economics' (ibid.: 130 and 1934: 379). As regards the content of Ricardo's economics, Hollander maintained that 'our present-day wisdom with respect to (a) currency, (b) taxation and (c) international trade is based upon Ricardo's analyses' (1910: 123; see also 1934: 379). With respect to currency issues, he depicted Ricardo as an orthodox monetary theorist, whose 'service was not merely to confirm and amplify . . . earlier doctrines, but to coordinate them with monetary practice to a degree that removed the questions involved from the arena of debate and established them as positive monetary canons' (1910: 123). According to Hollander, Ricardo's early currency pamphlets:

> represent a discriminating acceptance of prevailing monetary theories, made precise by faultless logic and intimate knowledge of monetary affairs, and made forcible by an effective literary manner. There was little in the positive content of the 'High Price of Bullion' that had not been said before and even said better. (1911b: 469)

Ricardo is said to have 'established the territorial distribution of the precious metals as the theoretical basis of the international price level' and to have 'laid the groundwork of modern monometallism' (1910: 123). In his appraisal of Ricardo's chapters on taxation Hollander pointed out that tax incidence analysis was placed at the centre of modern fiscal discussion by Ricardo:

> We owe to Ricardo acceptance of the principles, first that the social utility of any tax is determined not by its productivity but by its ultimate incidence; and second, that this 'influence of taxation on different classes of the community' is traceable by scientific enquiry, being governed by the laws of economic distribution. (Ibid.: 124)

But Hollander also emphasized that Ricardo's theory of value and distribution provided no adequate basis for tax incidence analyses, and that Ricardo himself had maintained (in a letter to Trower) that 'on the subject of taxation a wide field is open for those, who will patiently think, to give instruction to the Public' (*Works*, VIII: 79). With respect to foreign trade, Hollander's main concern is with showing that Ricardo, and not Torrens, deserves to be credited with the first consistent exposition of the theory of comparative costs. His overall conclusion is that 'the theory of international trade, as it was left by Ricardo, and expounded, but not substantially altered by Mill, has furnished the scientific basis for the practical rule of free trade' (1910: 125).

Unlike Marshall, Hollander made no attempt to depict Ricardo as an early precursor of a supply-and-demand theory in price determination, with the demand side still in its infancy. But Hollander also sought to gloss over the differences between the classical and the neoclassical approach to economic analysis, for instance in his paper on rent, where he suggested that the apparent contradiction between the neoclassical concept of 'marginal rent' and the classical concept of 'differential rent' 'rests upon the curious neglect of a fundamental element in the law of differential costs' (1895b: 175). The two concepts are reconcilable with one another, he asserted, when it is recognized that the classical authors, and in particular Ricardo, knew not only extensively, but also intensively diminishing returns, and that 'the cultivation of any piece of land, marginal or intramarginal, is always pushed intensively to that point where the final application of labor and capital yields bare wages and interest' (ibid.: 186). Hollander thus emphasized the existence of a line of development from Ricardo's theory of rent to marginal productivity theory. At the same time, he rejected 'the tendency of modern social history to speak of the economic radicalism of the nineteenth century as an emanation of the Ricardian economics' (1910: 126), thereby dissociating Ricardo from the later attempts to elaborate on the surplus approach by writers like Rodbertus or Marx.

Among doctrinal historians Jacob H. Hollander is also remembered for the magnificent library of rare economics books, tracts, and autographs that he had privately collected. However, his scholarly reputation has suffered a serious blow through some documents that came to light with the opening of Piero Sraffa's unpublished papers at Trinity College, Cambridge. These documents show that Hollander for several years obstructed the preparation of the definitive edition of Ricardo's *Works and Correspondence* by not disclosing to Sraffa that he was in the possession of additional manuscripts and letters that he had obtained from Frank Ricardo, Ricardo's great-grandson, together with the *Notes on Malthus*, in 1919, and by holding back others that he had purchased privately. For a more detailed account of this affair, see Gehrke and Kurz (2002).

CHRISTIAN GEHRKE

See also:

Biaujeaud, Huguette, on Ricardo; Marshall, Alfred, on Ricardo; Ricardo on Adam Smith; Sraffa, Piero, on Ricardo.

References

In the writing of this entry extensive use has been made of the entry 'Hollander, Jacob Harry, as an interpreter of classical economics' by Heino Klingen (1998), to which the interested reader is also referred for further details on the critique of Hollander's interpretation of Ricardo's theory of value.

Bonar, J. and J.H. Hollander (eds) (1899), *Letters of David Ricardo to Hughes Trower and Others, 1811–1823*, Oxford: Clarendon Press.

Gehrke, C. and H.D. Kurz (2002), 'Keynes and Sraffa's difficulties with J.H. Hollander: a note on the history of the RES edition of *The Works and Correspondence of David Ricardo*', *The European Journal of the History of Economic Thought*, **9**(4), 513–37.

Hollander, J.H. (ed.) (1895a), *Letters of David Ricardo to John Ramsay McCulloch 1816–1823*, New York: Macmillan.

Hollander, J.H. (1895b), 'The concept of marginal rent', *Quarterly Journal of Economics*, **9**(2), 175–87.

Hollander, J.H. (ed.) (1903), *Three Letters on The Price of Gold Contributed to The Morning Chronicle (London) in August–November, 1809, by David Ricardo*, Baltimore, MD: Johns Hopkins University Press.

Hollander, J.H. (1904), 'The development of Ricardo's theory of value', *Quarterly Journal of Economics*, **18**(4), 455–91.

Hollander, J.H. (1910), *David Ricardo. A Centenary Estimate*, Baltimore, MD: Johns Hopkins University Press.

Hollander, J.H. (1911a), 'The development of the theory of money from Adam Smith to David Ricardo', *Quarterly Journal of Economics*, **25**(3), 429–70.

Hollander, J.H. (1911b), 'The work and influence of Ricardo', *American Economic Review*, **1**(2), 71–84.

Hollander, J.H. (1911c), 'Ricardo and Torrens: a reply', *Economic Journal*, **21**(83), 455–68.

Hollander, J.H. (ed.) (1931), *Letters of John Ramsay McCulloch to David Ricardo (1818–1823)*, Baltimore, MD: Johns Hopkins University Press.

Hollander, J.H. (ed.) (1932), *Minor Papers on the Currency Question 1809–1823 by David Ricardo*, Baltimore, MD: Johns Hopkins University Press.

Hollander, J.H. (1934), 'David Ricardo', in E.R. Seligman (ed.), *Encyclopedia of the Social Sciences, Vol. 13*, New York: Macmillan.

Hollander, J.H. and T.E. Gregory (eds) (1928), *Notes on Malthus's Principles of Political Economy by David Ricardo*, Baltimore, MD: Johns Hopkins University Press.

Klingen, H. (1998), 'Hollander, Jacob Harry, as an interpreter of classical economics', in H.D. Kurz and N. Salvadori (eds), *The Elgar Companion to Classical Economics, Vol. 1*, Cheltenham, UK and Lyme, NH: Edward Elgar Publishing, pp. 372–6.

Improvements in Production

For Ricardo, improvements in production must invariably lower the relative values of commodities, because 'it is the essential quality of an improvement to diminish the quantity of labour before required to produce a commodity' (*Works*, I: 80; see also IV: 374). However, improvements need not necessarily lower the natural prices of commodities, because the latter depend not only on production conditions but also on the value of money. Accordingly, an improvement can lead to a general rise in prices, including the price of the commodity to which it is applied, if it brings about an inflow of precious metals and thus causes the value of money to fall. Of course, a general rise in prices (and money wages) can also emanate from improvements in the mining of gold and silver, that is, from a reduction in the amount of labour that is needed in the production of the commodities that serve as the monetary standard. As Ricardo succinctly put it his pamphlet *Essay on Profits*:

> Improvements in agriculture, or in the implements of husbandry, lower the exchangeable value of corn; improvements in the machinery connected with the manufacture of cotton, lower the exchangeable value of cotton goods; and improvements in mining . . . lower the value of gold and silver, or which is the same thing, raise the price of all other commodities. (*Works*, IV: 19)

While all improvements lower the exchangeable value of the commodity to which they are applied, the effects on income distribution and on the prices of other commodities depend crucially on the type of commodity under consideration, that is, whether the improved production method concerns a necessary or a luxury commodity. Because he tended to identify the agricultural sector with the production of necessaries (supplying food or 'corn' as a basic means of subsistence), Ricardo distinguished sharply between improvements in agriculture and improvements in manufacturing, trade and transport.

Agricultural improvements
The origin of Ricardo's analysis of the effects of agricultural improvements, which he only set out systematically in Chapter II of the *Principles*, can be found in his Anti-Corn Law pamphlet of 1815, the *Essay on Profits*, which concluded with the well-known statement:

> If the interests of the landlords be of sufficient consequence, to determine us not to avail ourselves of all the benefits which would follow from importing corn at a cheap price, they should also influence us in rejecting all improvements in agriculture, and in the implements of husbandry; for it is as certain that corn is rendered cheap, rents are lowered, and the ability of the landlord to pay taxes, is for a time, at least, as much impaired by such improvements, as by the importation of corn. To be consistent then, let us by the same act arrest improvement, and prohibit importation. (*Works*, IV: 41)

Ricardo noticed that foreign trade gives rise to a choice of technique problem and that whenever it is cheaper to import a commodity than to produce it at home, importation can be regarded as an improved production method. Accordingly, he maintained that there is a strict analogy, as regards the impact on income distribution, between importing and improving the production conditions of necessaries and between importing and improving the production methods of commodities that do not enter into the wage basket as strict necessities:

> There are two ways in which a country may be benefited by trade – one by the increase of the general rate of profits, which, according to my opinion, can never take place but in consequence of cheap food, which is beneficial only to those who derive a revenue from the employment of their capital, either as farmers, manufacturers, merchants, or capitalists, lending their money at interest – the other by the abundance of commodities, and by a fall in their exchangeable value, in which the whole community participate. In the first case, the revenue of the country is augmented – in the second the same revenue becomes efficient in procuring a greater amount of the necessaries and luxuries of life. It is in this latter mode only that nations are benefited by the extension of commerce, by the division of labour in manufactures, and by the discovery of machinery, – they all augment the amount of commodities, and contribute very much to the ease and happiness of mankind; but, they have no effect on the rate of profits, because they do not augment the produce compared with the cost of production on the land. (Ibid.: 25–6)

According to Ricardo, the 'immediate' effects of improvements in corn production and of corn imports are similar: with a given demand for corn, both diminish the price of corn, lower rents and increase the general rate of profits. He acknowledged that ultimately rents would rise again, because 'the low price of corn, caused by improvements in agriculture, would give a stimulus to population, by increasing profits and encouraging accumulation, which would again raise the price of corn and lower profits' (ibid.: 19n). But the 'immediate' effects of agricultural improvements would be effective at least for an entire generation and thus would be much more important for the landowners than the more remote ones associated with them, on which Malthus had focused attention in his *Inquiry into the Nature and Progress of Rent* (1815). In the well-known table in the *Essay on Profits* (see *Works*, IV: 17), Ricardo conducted his analysis of the impact of the accumulation of capital on profits and rents by explicitly setting aside technical progress. The resulting tendency of a falling rate of profits, he asserted, could be retarded but not permanently prevented by agricultural improvements:

> That great improvements have been made in agriculture, and that much capital has been expended on the land, it is not attempted to deny; but with all those improvements, we have not overcome the natural impediments resulting from our increasing wealth and prosperity, which obliges us to cultivate at a disadvantage our poor lands, if the importation of corn is restricted or prohibited. (Ibid.: 32)

The more systematic analysis of agricultural improvements Ricardo presented in the *Principles* was probably prompted by James Mill, who in December 1815 set him the following 'school exercise': 'You have stated repeatedly this proposition, That improvements in agriculture . . . raise the profits of stock, and produce immediately no other effects. But you have nowhere stated the proof. You have left it to be inferred from your general doctrine, as to rent' (ibid.: 339). Ricardo sought to provide such an explicit 'proof' in the latter part of the chapter 'On Rent', but the purpose of his analysis of the effects of improvements there seems to be also that of providing examples that demonstrate clearly the nature of differential rent, in that 'whatever diminishes the inequality in the produce obtained from successive portions of capital employed on the same or on new land, tends to lower rent; and that whatever increases that inequality, necessarily produces an opposite effect, and tends to raise it' (*Works*, I: 83). In order to prove his proposition that the immediate effect of improvements is to raise the rate of profits and to lower rents, Ricardo produced two numerical examples, in both of which he assumed 'the inequality in the produce obtained from successive portions of capital' to remain unaffected by the improvement. He produced two examples, because:

> improvements in agriculture are of two kinds: those which increase the productive powers of the land, and those which enable us, by improving our machinery, to obtain its produce with less labour. They both lead to a fall in the price of raw produce; they both affect rent, but they do not affect it equally. (Ibid.: 80)

Ricardo thus distinguished between what may be called 'land saving' and 'capital (alias labour) saving' improvements. He mentioned as examples of the land-saving kind a more skilful rotation of crops and a better choice of manure, and concluded: 'These improvements absolutely enable us to obtain the same produce from a smaller quantity of land' (ibid.). On the contrary, agricultural improvements of the second kind:

> do not increase the productive powers of the land; but they enable us to obtain its produce with less labour. They are rather directed to the formation of the capital applied to the land, than to the cultivation of the land itself . . . Less capital, which is the same thing as less labour, will be employed on the land; but to obtain the same produce, less land cannot be cultivated. (Ibid.: 82)

Ricardo's analysis of agricultural improvements in Chapter II of the *Principles* attracted the attention of major economists, including John Stuart Mill, Marx, Marshall and Wicksell. Malthus's view that rents are increased rather than lowered by agricultural improvements was rejected by Ricardo in his *Notes on Malthus* (*Works*, II: 134–7) and in Chapter XXXII of the *Principles* (*Works*, I: 412–13). In the post-Ricardian period, authors like Perronet Thompson, Richard Jones and William Whewell also sought to disprove Ricardo's theory of agricultural improvements, but based their reasoning on premises that differed from Ricardo's. John Stuart Mill ([1848] 1987: 717–18) endorsed Ricardo's analysis, but in his numerical illustration of land-saving improvements by inadvertence constructed an example in which the post-improvement marginal land is fully employed. In this case competition amongst landlords need not suffice to make the rent on this quality of land vanish.

Marx was critical of Ricardo's analysis of agricultural improvements, to which he put forward three main objections. First, he pointed out that the reduced prices that result from agricultural improvements could raise the demand for agricultural products, and thus cause rents to rise ([1861–63] 1989: 533). Second, he dismissed Ricardo's distinction between 'land saving' and 'capital (alias) labour saving' agricultural improvements, because it 'does not touch upon the real question at all', which in Marx's view is how the 'organic composition of capital' (and, thereby, the maximum rate of profits) is affected by an improvement (ibid.: 535). Third, Marx pointed out that agricultural improvements that consist chiefly in the substitution of fixed for circulating capital could be associated with 'a decrease in the absolute mass of products' ([1894] 1959: 767). This is so because fixed capital, as opposed to circulating capital, only requires replacement of the annual wear and tear plus normal profits on the advanced capital, and therefore can be profitably employed on the land even if the annual output per unit of land is smaller than that of the method already in use. This possibility was indeed overlooked by Ricardo, who conducted his analysis on the implicit assumption of circulating capital only.

A fierce criticism of Ricardo's theory of agricultural improvements, and particularly of his numerical examples, was put forward by Edwin Cannan, who maintained that Ricardo 'is absolutely and almost obviously wrong' with regard to the second kind of improvements, and his reasoning is said to end 'in complete and hopeless failure' ([1893] 1967: 259–60). Essentially the same criticism was reiterated some 50 years later by Harry G. Johnson (1948); it was also shared by modern interpreters like Blaug, O'Brien, Samuelson and others. However, it can be shown that Ricardo was not wrong in any substantive sense and that the two examples can be interpreted in such a way that they emerge as a fully correct illustration of the respective case under consideration (Gehrke et al., 2003). The key to understanding this is to recognize that Ricardo employed different definitions of rent in his two numerical examples, which imply different assumptions with regard to the timing of the payment of rent. In fact, in order to be coherent, in the first example one has to assume that rent is paid *post factum*, whereas in the second example it has to be taken as paid *ante factum*.

Improvements in manufactures

In the *Principles*, Ricardo reiterated his proposition from the *Essay on Profits* that the tendency of the rate of profits to fall, which arises from the need to have recourse to less and less productive soils or methods of land cultivation, could be checked temporarily by improvements in the production of necessaries:

> The natural tendency of profits then is to fall; for, in the progress of society and wealth, the additional quantity of food required is obtained by the sacrifice of more and more labour. This tendency, this gravitation as it were of profits, is happily checked at repeated intervals by the *improvements in machinery, connected with the production of necessaries*, as well as by discoveries in the science of agriculture which enable us to relinquish a portion of labour before required, and therefore to lower the price of the prime necessary of the labourer. (*Works*, I: 120; emphasis added; see also VI: 194)

He also reiterated his proposition that improvements in manufacturing, trade and transport, unless they are connected, directly or indirectly, with the production of necessaries, increase the quantity and variety of commodities and lower relative values, but leave the rate of profits unaffected:

> The rate of profits is never increased by a better distribution of labour, by the invention of machinery, by the establishment of roads and canals, or by any means of abridging labour either in the manufacture or the conveyance of goods. These are causes which operate on price, and never fail to be highly beneficial to consumers, since they enable them with the same labour, to obtain in exchange a greater quantity of the commodity to which the improvement is applied; but they have no effect whatever on profit. (Ibid.: 133)

It needs to be stressed that in the carefully worded passage above it is *not* claimed that improvements must always lower the money prices of the commodities to which they are applied. This would be the case only if gold or money were supposed to be invariable in value and 'all alterations in price to be occasioned by some alteration in the value of the commodity' under consideration (ibid.: 46) – as Ricardo in fact supposed up to Chapter

VII of the *Principles*. However, in the chapter 'On Foreign Trade' he dispensed with this simplifying assumption and addressed the problem of changes in the value of money caused by alterations in the international distribution of the precious metals (see ibid.: 137–41). He maintained:

> that the improvement of a manufacture in any country tends to alter the distribution of the precious metals amongst the nations of the world: it tends to increase the quantity of commodities, at the same time that it raises general prices in the country where the improvement takes place. (Ibid.: 141)

Starting from a situation of balanced trade, an improvement in the production of an export commodity raises all prices (including money wages) in the country in which it has been introduced, because it leads to a trade surplus, an inflow of precious metals, and a fall in the value of money. According to Ricardo, it is only:

> in the early stages of society, when manufactures have made little progress . . . [that] the value of money in different countries will be chiefly regulated by their distance from the mines which supply the precious metals; but as the arts and improvements of society advance, and different nations excel in particular manufactures, . . . the value of the precious metals will be chiefly regulated by those manufactures. (Ibid.: 143–4)

A problem that can arise in connection with the introduction of improvements, both in agriculture and in manufacturing, is the obsolescence of previously installed fixed capital items. Ricardo noted that whether or not such items remain in use is a cost-minimization problem that is decided by calculating the 'quasi-rents' that can still be earned. With reference to fixed capital that has been invested on the land (e.g., for fencing, draining or amelioration), Ricardo observed:

> If . . . capital can be withdrawn . . . it will only be withdrawn, when it will yield more to the owner by being withdrawn than by being suffered to remain where it was; it will only be withdrawn then, when it can elsewhere be employed more productively both for the owner and the public. [The farmer] consents to sink that part of his capital which cannot be separated from the land, because with that part which he can take away, he can obtain a greater value, and a greater quantity of raw produce, than by not sinking this part of his capital. His case is precisely similar to that of a man who has erected machinery in his manufactory at a great expense, machinery which is afterwards so much improved upon by more modern inventions, that the commodities manufactured by him very much sink in value. It would be entirely a matter of calculation with him whether he should abandon the old machinery, and erect the more perfect, losing all the value of the old, or continue to avail himself of its comparatively feeble powers. (Ibid.: 270–71)

Finally, it is interesting to note that Ricardo, in a letter of 29 March 1820, disputed McCulloch's claim 'that the great discoveries and improvements made by us in machinery and manufactures have been particularly favourable to this country' (*Works*, VIII: 171). In Ricardo's view, improvements in production, by increasing the quantity and variety of commodities and lowering their exchangeable values, are 'equally advantageous to every other country, even if they are retained in this country only' (ibid.: 171–2). For Ricardo, improvements in production, although not necessarily freely available, are a general good.

CHRISTIAN GEHRKE

See also:
Accumulation of Capital; Endogenous Growth; Technical Change.

References
Cannan, E. ([1893] 1967), *A History of the Theories of Production and Distribution in English Political Economy from 1776–1848*, London: P.S. King; reprint, New York: Augustus M. Kelley.
Gehrke, C., H.D. Kurz and N. Salvadori (2003), 'Ricardo on agricultural improvements: a note', *Scottish Journal of Political Economy*, **50**(3), 291–6.
Johnson, H.G. (1948), 'An error in Ricardo's exposition of his theory of rent', *Quarterly Journal of Economics*, **62**(5), 792–3.
Marx, K. ([1861–63] 1989), *Economic Manuscript of 1861–63. A Contribution to the Critique of Political Economy [Theories of Surplus Value]*, in *Karl Marx, Frederick Engels: Collected Works, Vol. 32*, New York: International Publishers.
Marx, K. ([1894] 1959), *Capital, Vol. III*, Moscow: Progress Publishers; English translation of *Das Kapital, Vol. III*, Hamburg: Meissner.
Mill, J.S. ([1848] 1987), *Principles of Political Economy*, reprint of 1909 edition, Fairfield, NJ: Augustus M. Kelley.

Invariable Measure of Value

As has been pointed out by Sraffa in his 'Introduction' to Ricardo's *Works*, the search for an invariable measure of value 'preoccupied Ricardo to the end of his life' (*Works*, I: xl). However, in the course of time Ricardo's view as to the function such a standard would have to perform and the characteristic features it would have to exhibit underwent considerable change (for the following, see also Kurz and Salvadori [1993] 1998).

Intertemporal and interspatial comparisons
The first time we encounter in Ricardo's writings the problem of an invariable standard of value is in his contribution to the Bullionist Controversy in 1810 (see Marcuzzo and Rosselli, 1994). There Ricardo opposed the popular view that the value of a currency should be measured in terms of its purchasing power over the 'mass of commodities' (*Works*, III: 59); it should rather be measured by the purchasing power over the commodity, which was used as the standard. The choice of a monetary regime would have to comply with the task of keeping the purchasing power of money over the standard fairly constant. Changes in money prices of commodities (other than the standard) could then be unambiguously traced back to 'real' causes (see ibid.: 64n). Here Ricardo is concerned with a standard that would measure the value of commodities at different times and places, that is, he is interested in intertemporal and interspatial comparisons, a concern that is closely related to the time-honoured problem of distinguishing between 'value' and 'riches' (see *Works*, I, XX) that had already worried authors such as Petty and Smith: in this regard Ricardo's contribution is largely in accord with the discussion of his time. While no single commodity can be considered a perfect and thus 'permanent' measure, it is Ricardo's contention that gold and silver are least subject to fluctuations and hence, for comparisons of periods, which are not too distant from one another, may reasonably be used as measures of value.

The problem of an invariable measure of value is dealt with in greater detail in Ricardo's *Principles*. In the first and second editions he maintained that in order to be invariable in value a commodity should require 'at all times, and under all circumstances, precisely the same quantity of labour to obtain it' (*Works*, I: 27n). Here again the criterion of invariability is defined in terms of the intertemporal and interspatial constancy of the total amount of labour needed to produce one unit of the respective commodity. If such a commodity could be found and were used as a standard of value, any variation in the value of other commodities expressed in terms of this standard would unequivocally point towards changes in the conditions of production of these commodities. Value measured in the invariable standard Ricardo called 'absolute value'. (In the third edition of his *Principles* he also used the term 'real value'.) Ricardo's early approach to the problem under consideration is neatly summarized in the following passage:

> If any one commodity could be found, which now and at all times required precisely the same quantity of labour to produce it, that commodity would be of an unvarying value, and would be eminently useful as a standard by which the variations of other things might be measured.

The passage continues:

> Of such a commodity we have no knowledge, and consequently are unable to fix on any standard of value. It is, however, of considerable use towards attaining a correct theory, to ascertain what the essential qualities of a standard are, that we may know the causes of the variation in the relative value of commodities, and that we may be enabled to calculate the degree in which they are likely to operate. (ibid.: 17, 3n)

Basically the same opinion as to the 'essential qualities' of the invariable measure of value is expressed in several other places. For example, in his *Notes on Malthus*, completed in November 1820, Ricardo emphasized that (1) '[l]ength can only be measured by length, capacity by capacity, and value by value'; (2) 'invariability is the essential quality of a measure of value'; and (3) invariability means 'that precisely the same quantity of labour was required' at different times for the production of the standard (see *Works*, II: 29–33).

The impact of changes in distribution
Although Ricardo in the first and second editions was clearly aware of the modifications necessary to the labour embodied rule of relative value, he apparently did not think that these modifications rendered his original definition of the invariable measure of value or his approach to the theory of profit obsolete. In the third edition, however, he conceded that the same difficulties encountered in determining relative prices also carried over to his attempt in defining the essential properties of a correct standard. He argued that even if:

> the same quantity of labour [would] be always required to obtain the same quantity of gold, still gold would not be a perfect measure of value, by which we could accurately ascertain the variations in all other things, because it would not be produced with precisely the same combinations of fixed and circulating capital as all other things; nor with fixed capital of the same durability; nor would it require precisely the same length of time, before it could be brought to market ... Neither gold then, nor any other commodity, can ever be a perfect measure of value for all things. (*Works*, I: 44–5)

Whereas in his original approach to the problem of the standard of value Ricardo was exclusively concerned with intertemporal and interspatial comparisons, that is, measurement with respect to different technical environments, he is now in addition concerned with the different problem of measurement with respect to the same technical environment, but changing distributions of income.

Indeed, Ricardo considered both the problem of interspatial and intertemporal comparisons and the problem of price changes due to changes in distribution as theoretical issues (ibid.: 45). Yet it is a common feature of all approaches to the theory of value and distribution, including Ricardo's, that the socio-technical environment is taken as given. Therefore, the first aspect of Ricardo's concept of an 'invariable measure of value' simply cannot in general be treated within this context.

McCulloch put forward a similar criticism in his letter to Ricardo of 11 August 1823:

> There is a radical and essential difference between the circumstances which determine the exchangeable value of commodities, and a measure of that value, which I am afraid is not always kept sufficiently in view. If you are to measure value, you must measure it by the agency of some one commodity or other possessed of value . . .; and as the circumstances under which every commodity is produced must always be liable to vary none can be an invariable measure, though some are certainly much less variable than others and may, therefore, be used as approximations. It is evident I think that there neither is nor can be any real and invariable standard of value; and if so it must be very idle to seek for that which can never be found.

McCulloch continues: 'The real inquiry is to ascertain what are the circumstances which determine the exchangeable value of commodities *at any given period*' (*Works*, IX: 344; emphasis added). And in his reply of 24 August to Ricardo's answer three days earlier McCulloch put his view on what he called 'the vexata questio of value' even more succinctly. He expressed anew his conviction that the problem of the invariable measure of value, as stated by Ricardo, 'is quite insoluble' and that he himself did not want to enter 'this transcendental part of Pol Economy': 'before I attempt to get a measure of the value of cloth and wine in the reign of Augustus and George IV, I must obtain a measure of their value in the same market' (ibid.: 369).

Ricardo in his answer to the first of the two letters insisted that despite their disagreement even McCulloch 'will still contend for the mathematical accuracy of the measure'. He continued:

> I do not see the great difference you mention between the circumstances which determine the exchangeable value of commodities, and the medium of that value . . . Is it not clear . . . that as soon as we are in possession of the knowledge of the circumstances which determine the value of commodities, we are enabled to say what is necessary to give us an invariable measure of value? (Ibid.: 358)

A similar passage is to be found in his letter to Trower of 31 August 1823, in which his dispute with McCulloch is touched upon. Ricardo criticizes the latter for not seeing 'that if we were in possession of the knowledge of the law which regulates the exchangeable value of commodities, we should be only one step from the discovery of a measure of absolute value' (ibid.: 377). According to Sraffa 'this came close to identifying the problem of a measure with that of the law of value' (*Works*, I: xli).

'Absolute Value and Exchangeable Value'

As is well known, two most important documents of Ricardo's search for an invariable measure of value are a complete draft and an unfinished later version of his paper

'Absolute Value and Exchangeable Value', which must have been written shortly before Ricardo fell ill in early September 1823 (see Sraffa's note in *Works*, IV: 359–60). In the two manuscripts Ricardo attempted to render precise his own concept of the standard of value and confront it with those advocated by Malthus, Torrens, Mill and McCulloch. Here a brief summary of Ricardo's argument must suffice.

To begin with, it is important to notice that Ricardo's main concern was still with intertemporal and interspatial comparisons. This is expressed in various passages (see, for instance, *Works*, IV: 396). Next it deserves to be mentioned that Ricardo's own efforts were explicitly directed at establishing a straightforward analogy between measurement in natural sciences and in economics. In one place he writes:

> There can be no unerring measure either of length, of weight, of time or of value *unless there be some object in nature* to which the standard itself can be referred and by which we are enabled to ascertain whether it preserves its character of invariability. (*Works*, IV: 401; emphasis added)

Referring implicitly to his earlier views on the subject he continues:

> It has been said that we are not without a *standard in nature* to which we may refer for the correction of errors and deviations in our measure of value, *in the same way as in the other measures which I have noticed*, and that such a standard is to be found in the *labour of men*. (Ibid.; emphasis added)

However, this opinion has turned out to be erroneous, the reason being that commodities:

> will not vary only on account of the greater or less quantity of labour necessary to produce them but also on account of the greater or less proportion of the finished commodity which may be paid to the workman . . . It must then be confessed that *there is no such thing in nature as a perfect measure of value*. (Ibid.: 404; emphasis added)

The study of the impact of distribution on relative prices is frequently couched in terms of intertemporal comparisons of situations before and after a change in the real wage rate. However, the real point at issue is not what may cause real wages to rise or fall, but rather that there are *two* circumstances affecting relative value at any point in time, that is, the technical conditions of production and the division of the product between wages and profits. The impact of the second factor on 'natural' prices is best studied by carrying out some thought experiments. This is what Ricardo does in a couple of simple numerical examples, where he hypothetically varies the wage rate, taking into account that with given technical conditions of production the rate of profits is bound to vary in the opposite direction, and then tries to ascertain the involved movement of relative prices (cf., for example, *Works*, IV: 373–8).

After having disposed of the idea that there might exist such a thing as a perfect standard of value, fulfilling both criteria enunciated by him Ricardo asks: 'But as it is desirable that we should have one measure of value . . . to which shall we give the preference [?]' (ibid.: 389). On the premise that the criterion of technological invariability is met, what does invariability with respect to variations in income distribution mean? Since 'the value of all commodities resolves itself into wages and profits' (ibid.: 392), the proximate answer to be given is: that commodity is invariable in value, in which the fall in the profit component is equal to the rise in the wage component (consequent upon a rise in the real wage rate and a corresponding fall in the general rate of profits). This is, in fact, the answer implicit in Ricardo's argument (cf., e.g., ibid.: 372–3, 404, 407). The conclusion is close at hand that the commodity under consideration should 'require capital as well as labour to produce [it]' (ibid.: 371): 'To me it appears most clear that we should chuse a measure produced by labour employed for a certain period, and which always supposes an advance of capital' (ibid.: 405). Accordingly, the standard advocated by Ricardo is different from Malthus's:

> It is not like Mr. Malthus's measure one of the extremes[,] it is not a commodity produced by labour alone which he proposes, nor a commodity whose value consists of profits alone, but one which may fairly be considered as the *medium between these two extremes*, and as agreeing more nearly with the circumstances under which the greater number of commodities are produced than any other which can be proposed. (Ibid.: 372; emphasis added)

Elsewhere Ricardo is more explicit about what he thinks the 'medium' actually is:

> That a commodity produced by labour employed for a year is a mean between the extremes of commodities produced on one side by labour and advances for much more than a year, and on the other by labour employed for a day only without any advances, and the mean will in most cases give a much less deviation from truth than if either of the extremes were used as a measure. (Ibid.: 405)

As can already be seen from the last few quotations, Ricardo was not content with the proximate answer referred to above. His concern was with rendering as precise as possible the causes that account for the dependence of relative prices on income distribution. Clearly, the major cause is 'the variety of circumstances under which commodities are actually produced' (ibid.: 368). This, in conjunction with the fact that 'profits [are] increasing at a compound rate[,] . . . makes a great part of the difficulty' (*Works*, IX: 387; similarly IV: 388). Hence, an important part of Ricardo's efforts was directed at describing more carefully the 'variety of circumstances' under which commodities are produced.

This Ricardo tried to effectuate in various terms. We have already seen that one way of differentiating between these circumstances was in terms 'of the different proportions in which the whole result of labour is distributed, between master and workers' (*Works*, IV: 385). However, since these proportions are themselves but a reflection of differences in the underlying conditions of production, it is desirable to conceive of these differences more directly. As we have seen in the above, the most general distinction of the circumstances under discussion given by Ricardo is in terms of different proportions of fixed and circulating capital, where circulating capital includes the wages of labour, different durabilities of fixed capital, and different durabilities of circulating capital (see also *Works*, I: xlii).

In addition, Ricardo used more compact formulae to express these differences. For example, he talks of the 'proportions in which immediate labour and accumulated labour enter into different commodities' (*Works*, IV: 379), or the proportions in which 'labour and capital' are employed in their production. Apparently, Ricardo was aware that since the means of production are heterogeneous the concept of 'capital' is an intricate one.

Therefore, it comes as no surprise that Ricardo was in search of a description of the differences under consideration, which is less assailable. In his letter to McCulloch of 13 June 1820 he had already hinted at what appeared to him to be the most abstract denomination of the circumstances that account for the deviation of relative prices from relative quantities of labour embodied in the various commodities: 'All the exceptions to the general rule come under this one of time'; and 'there are such a variety of cases in which the time of completing a commodity may differ' (*Works*, VIII: 193). This idea is taken up again in his manuscript essay 'Absolute Value and Exchangeable Value', in which he stresses: 'In this then consists the difficulty of the subject that the circumstances of time for which advances are made are so various' (*Works*, IV: 370). Finally, it deserves mention that the reduction of all differences to one of time complies with Ricardo's preconception that the standard of value should ultimately be referred back to some 'object in nature'.

The 'medium between the extremes' standard

Let us now turn briefly to Ricardo's choice of a 'medium between the extremes'. According to Ricardo 'it is evident that by chusing a mean the variations in commodities on account of a rise or fall in wages would be much less than if we took either of the extremes' (*Works*, IV: 373). The motivation for this choice comes out somewhat more clearly in the above-quoted letter to McCulloch of 13 June 1820:

> The medium . . . is perhaps the best adapted to the general mass of commodities; those commodities on one side of this medium, would rise in comparative value with it, with a rise in the price of labour, and a fall in the rate of profits; and those on the other side might fall from the same cause. (*Works*, VIII: 193)

However, Ricardo did not take the composite commodity 'social product', or, in his terms, the 'mass of commodities', as the standard of value. He considered this possibility, but rejected it on the grounds that '[i]f it be admitted that one commodity may alter in absolute value, it must be admitted that 2, 3, 100, a million may do so, and how shall I be able with certainty to say whether the one or the million had varied' (*Works*, IV: 401). The same opinion is expressed elsewhere. Ricardo there declines the proposed measure, which was taken into consideration in the context of a discussion of the impact of distribution on relative value, given the technical conditions of production, with the argument that it does not meet with the criterion of technological invariability:

> In our own times great improvements have been made in the mode of manufacturing cloth, linen and cotton goods, iron, steel, copper, stockings – great improvements have been made in husbandry all which tend to lower the value of these goods and of the produce of the soil and yet these are made a part of the measure by which you would measure the value of other things. (Ibid.: 374)

The basic idea underlying the concept of the 'medium between the extremes' seems to be that the processes of production of the different commodities can somehow be expressed in terms of a single variable, that is, the time that elapses between an initial expenditure of labour and the completion of the product. In other words, Ricardo's approach appears to start from the supposition that commodities can somehow be distinguished in terms of the length of their production periods. With some circularity of production this idea necessarily breaks down, while with unidirectional processes of production it is applicable in very special cases only. There is ample evidence that Ricardo was aware of the fact that most commodities are produced by means of commodities.

However, he did not succeed in grasping fully the implication of the inter-industry relationships for his specification of the standard of value.

A further remark concerns the fact that even though Ricardo refrained from taking the aggregate of commodities as his measure of value, he nevertheless invoked 'the circumstances under which the greater number of commodities are produced' to rationalize his own choice. The measure is supposed to reflect to some extent the conditions of production of 'the generality of commodities which are the objects of the traffic of mankind', 'the greatest number of commodities which are the objects of exchange' (*Works*, IV: 389 and 405). Interestingly, whenever Ricardo gives examples of which particular commodities should by all means be taken into consideration in defining the properties of the standard, he always refers to necessaries (as opposed to luxuries). In one place he writes: 'The circumstance of this measure being produced in the same length of time as corn and most other vegetable food which forms by far the most valuable article of daily consumption would decide me in giving it a preference' (ibid.: 405–6).

HEINZ D. KURZ AND NERI SALVADORI

See also:

Exchange Value and Utility; Gold; Malthus–Ricardo Debate; McCulloch, John Ramsay, and Ricardo; Natural and Market Prices; *Principles of Political Economy, and Taxation*; Sraffa, Piero, on Ricardo; Technical Change.

References

Kurz, H.D. and N. Salvadori ([1993] 1998), 'The "standard commodity" and Ricardo's search for an "invariable measure of value"', in M. Baranzini and G.C. Harcourt (eds), *The Dynamics of the Wealth of Nations. Growth, Distribution and Structural Change*, London: Macmillan, pp.95–123; reprinted in H.D. Kurz and N. Salvadori, *Understanding 'Classical' Economics. Studies in Long-Period Theory*, London and New York: Routledge, pp.123–47.
Marcuzzo, C. and A. Roselli (1994), 'The standard commodity and the standard of money', *Cahiers d'Economie Politique*, **23**(1), 19–31.

Jevons, William Stanley, on Ricardo

A great disruption in the history of economic thought is commonly associated with William Stanley Jevons (1835–82). The so-called 'marginal revolution' is said to have begun with the publication of three books: Jevons's *Theory of Political Economy* (1871), Menger's *Grundsätze der Volkswirthschaftslehre* (1871) and Walras's *Eléments d'économie politique pure* (1874). Despite some important differences both in substance and context, this trilogy of dissident thinkers shared an ambitious aim – a total reconstruction of political economy – and the means by which it can be accomplished: simultaneously but independently of one another, they developed a group of ideas connected to the term 'marginal utility', significantly breaking with the classical approach to value. Early marginalism is said to have established the basis for a new, more exact economic science, launching a fundamental change in ideas and method, both far-reaching and long-lasting.

Some authors such as Dobb (1973) and Hutchison (1978) put aside the coupling of Menger, Jevons and Walras and limit the scope of 'the Jevonian revolution' to Britain. Hutchison argues that in the 1860s and 1870s Ricardian economics 'underwent a remarkably sudden and rapid collapse of credibility and confidence' (1978: 58), as central pillars of 'the Ricardo-Mill School' were deemed inadequate and deficient. According to Dobb, Jevons 'completed that reaction against Ricardo' (1973: 166). Indeed, a prominent and well-known feature of Jevons's *Theory of Political Economy* is his harsh critique of classical writers, in particular of David Ricardo, who is said to have 'shunted the car of Economic science on to a wrong line' (Jevons [1871] 1965: li). Thus, in order to intellectually advance in economics one has to break with the classical approach to value and distribution: the cost of production theory of value, Mill's wages fund theory and Ricardo's natural wage concept in particular should be overthrown. He felt sure that 'the only hope of attaining a true system of Economics is to fling aside, once and for ever, the mazy and preposterous assumptions of the Ricardian School' (ibid.: xliv). To Jevons the then prevailing orthodox thinking seemed to be a wavering theoretical edifice, soon to be replaced: 'It is evident, then, that a spirit of very active criticism is spreading, which can hardly fail to overcome in the end the prestige of the false old doctrines. But what is to be put in place of them?' (ibid.: xvi). The *Theory of Political Economy* is intended to provide the answer.

To assess the content of the Jevonian revolution, the results of Jevons's endeavour to reconstruct political economy are summed up. His redesign of the theory of value and distribution rests on three related pillars: the vision of an exact mathematical science of economics, utility as the central concept and a marginal productivity theory of distribution.

Method

Jevons is well known as a promoter of the mathematization of economic analysis. He argues that economics must necessarily be treated in mathematical terms, simply because it is fundamentally involved with quantities. In his view differential ('fluxional') calculus is the proper method to express economic relationships. Moreover, Jevons considered mathematics as the means of improving the scientific status of economics: 'It is clear that Economics, if it is to be a science at all, must be a mathematical science' (ibid.: 3)

His enthusiasm for the mathematic method led Jevons to compile a bibliographic list of 'mathematico-economic' writings, appended to later editions of the *Theory of Political Economy*. As a by-product of his eager search for precursors of his own theory, Jevons had to accept that 'novelty can no longer be attributed to the leading features of the theory' (ibid.: xxxviii).

A further element of Jevons's vision of an exact mathematical science concerns Ricardo's abstract deductive method, which should not be overthrown but redefined: to ensure the usefulness of purely analytical reasoning, an inductive, statistical complement is needed. 'In the absence of complete statistics, the science will not be less mathematical, though it will be immensely less useful than if it were, comparatively speaking, exact' (ibid.: 12). Therefore, the 'deductive science of Economics must be verified and rendered useful by the purely empirical science of Statistics' (ibid.: 22). What Jevons called the 'complete method' is intended to ensure that both the presumed and the derived are in harmony with facts. Logical consistency and empirical validity serve both as guidelines for Jevons's own theoretic inquiry and as criteria for evaluating previous economic theories (Signorino, 2004).

Value

Jevons's approach to value is based on the psychological laws of utility, which rest on the hedonistic proposition that the individual pursues positive feelings and avoids negative ones to gain a maximum of happiness. Already in his 'Notice of a general mathematical theory of political economy' (1863) Jevons argued that the general laws acting in the economic sphere emanate from the deliberations of the human mind: 'A true theory of economy can only be attained by going back to the great springs of human action – *the feelings of pleasure and pain*' (Jevons [1871] 1965, Appendix III: 304; original emphasis). He thus devoted the *Theory of Political Economy* to the study of the 'mechanics of self-interest and utility' (ibid.: xviii).

Jevons's simplified version of Benthamite utilitarianism (see Sigot, 2002) implied a major shift in emphasis regarding the origins of value: not the cost incurred in production but consumer needs and desires guide the valuation of an object. 'Value,' Jevons stressed at the outset, 'depends entirely upon utility' (Jevons [1871] 1965: 1). Central to his subjectivist theory of value is the 'law of variation of utility', which states that 'the degree of utility varies with the quantity of commodity, and ultimately decreases as that quantity increases' (ibid.: 53). Therefore, not total utility but the 'final degree of utility' (Jevons's term for marginal utility) is the effective magnitude that guides human action.

It is important to note that Jevons did not limit his treatment of economics in terms of pleasure and pain to the market-period analysis of pure exchange with given endowments of consumables (on Jevons's exchange model see Creedy, forthcoming). The human habit of optimizing also governs the individual's supply of labour. As labour is generally assumed as an activity implying pain and as continuously adjustable, the 'free' working decision involves the balancing of the 'the amount of painful exertion' and the 'amount of utility gained'. Hence the individual ultimately ceases to work at the point where the marginal disutility of labour equals the marginal utility of the produce (Jevons [1871] 1965: 170–77). Further, capital is regarded as a source of disutility. In his capital theory Jevons emphasized that capital is essentially time and allows for lengthening the production period. And those who provide capital suffer from pain due to a 'temporary sacrifice of enjoyment'. Thus, the interest rate rewards the capitalist's abstinence (ibid.: 233–47).

Chapter V of the *Theory of Political Economy* is devoted to the analysis of production and cost of production. Here and in the subsequent chapters, Jevons, just like all neoclassical writers of the first generation, adopted the classical method of long-period ('equilibrium') position to determine normal prices and the normal income distribution (Kurz and Salvadori, 2003). In the long-run equilibrium 'there can be no motive for altering or regretting the distribution of labour, and the utility produced is at its maximum' (Jevons [1871] 1965: 185). Thus, both the amount and the composition of the produce are seen as regulated by utility considerations. But because Jevons intended to recast the classical approach to value by stressing the all-pervading influence of (marginal) utility, his long-run equilibrium analysis yields a somewhat surprising result: defining marginal labour costs as the sole costs of production Jevons concluded that in equilibrium the ratio of marginal utilities of commodities exchanged is equal to the respective ratio of the marginal labour costs. Jevons seemed willing to accept that once production is taken into account, costs influence prices. He states: 'It may tend to give the reader confidence in the preceding theories when he finds that they lead directly to the well-known law, as stated in the ordinary language of economists, that value is proportional to the cost of production' (ibid.: 186).

Steedman (1997) comments that:

> Unless one attaches great significance to Jevons's differentiations between origins, causes and determinants of value it must seem that his bold opening declaration '*value depends entirely upon utility*' . . . was, to say the least, overenthusiastic. Jevons knew full well that 'utility' was *not* the only factor affecting ratios of exchange *even within his own theory*. (Steedman, 1997: 59; original emphasis)

One can add that not only Jevons but also other major early exponents of marginal utility theory, such as Eugen von Böhm-Bawerk, Friedrich von Wieser, Philip Wicksteed and John Bates Clark, held the 'view that with regard to reproducible goods the then novel (marginal) utility theory of value amounted to materially the same thing as the pure labor theory of value' (Kurz and Salvadori, 2002a: 233).

Distribution

The third element of Jevons's attempt to push economic science back on the rails concerns his view on distribution. In the preface to the second edition of the *Theory of Political Economy* Jevons articulated the vision that a general law is applicable to determine the remuneration of all factors of production: he stressed that labour, land and capital are 'conjoint conditions of the whole produce' (Jevons [1871] 1965: xlvi), that productive resources cannot be the cause of value and thus have to be linked to value symmetrically by the same relationship. In particular, 'the parallelism between the theories of rent and wages is seen to be perfect in theory . . . Precisely the same view may be applied, *mutatis mutandis*, to the rent yielded by fixed capital, and to the interest of free capital' (ibid.: l). Though Jevons never completed a systematic new distribution theory, Steedman (1997: 61) concludes that 'Jevons did in effect proclaim a ramified marginal productivity theory of rents, wages, quasi-rents and the rate of interest' and that he relied on the classical theory of rent to develop his argument.

A mathematical statement of Jevons's marginal productivity theory of wages can be found in the short Chapter VI on rent. Here, Jevons assumes that different qualities of land are available and labour spent on a certain piece of land is subject to diminishing marginal returns. Again, hedonistic calculations at the margin are all-important: the representative labourer allocates his working time in such a manner that the marginal productivities of labour across all qualities of land are equal to one another and specifies the amount of labour devoted to a certain piece of land by maximizing net pleasure. As no capital is explicitly used in cultivating land – the produce is a function of labour only – the amount of the produce is also thus specified. Concerning remuneration of production services, Jevons then assumes that the last increment of labour is compensated in the amount of its marginal productiveness, and that this real wage rate applies to the whole amount of labour spent (Jevons [1871] 1965: 215–19).

Jevons's attempt to explain all sorts of factor incomes symmetrically based on marginal contribution to production diverges substantially from the classical theory of distribution: an established school of interpreters of Ricardo identifies the distinct characteristic of 'the classical approach' with the non-symmetric treatment of distributive variables. In the classical surplus-based approach the real wage rate is amongst the given set of data, whereas the profit rate is explained residually. In contrast, neoclassical authors rejected the asymmetric treatment of distributive variables and tried to explain shares of wages, profits and rent in terms of a single principle – scarcity (Kurz and Salvadori, 2003).

This divergence in substance is also related to the 'indeterminate system charge' raised by early marginalist writers, who blamed Ricardo for attempting to determine two unknowns from one single equation. This charge was raised inter alia by Walras ([1874–77] 1954), Wicksteed (1894) and Jevons and has been rightly refuted.

Jevons's accusation that Ricardo provided an indeterminate system can be found in Chapter VIII, 'Concluding Remarks' of the *Theory of Political Economy*. It reads:

> We thus arrive at the simple equation – Produce = profit + wages. A plain result also is drawn from the formula; for we are told that if wages rise profits must fall, and *vice versâ*. But such a doctrine is radically fallacious; *it involves the attempt to determine two unknown quantities from one equation*. I grant that if the produce be a fixed amount, then if wages rise profits must fall, and *vice versâ*. Something might perhaps be made of this doctrine if Ricardo's theory of a natural rate of wages, that which is just sufficient to support the labourer, held true. But I altogether question the existence of any such rate. (Jevons [1871] 1965: 268–9; original emphasis)

Jevons's assessment of Ricardo involves both a logical and an empirical criticism: first, the inverse relationship between wages and profits only holds true when the output level is given – a presumption Jevons rejected. Second, the determination of the profit rate is based on the assumption of a given wage level. But to Jevons Ricardo's fixed wage theory cannot be sustained, because the underlying assumptions are not consonant with facts; it is not possible to define the subsistence level and a thus given fixed wage rate ignores the evident heterogeneity of skills and wage rewards.

Steedman (1972: 125) notes that Jevons's criticism of Ricardo's treatment of wages actually misses the point. For Ricardo, the given wage rate is neither necessarily equal to a physiological subsistence level, it may be determined on historical and institutional grounds, nor does Ricardo assume away differences in skill level, as the wage of each skill level may be taken as given fact. Concerning the logical critique, Kurz and

Salvadori (2002b) argue that the classical equation 'Produce = Wages + Profit' is set out by Ricardo to determine profits as a residual. Since in the classical theory of value and distribution the given set of data consists of (1) the technical conditions of production, (2) the size and composition of the social product and (3) the ruling wage rate, these data suffice to determine the unknown, the rate of profit. Thus, Ricardo cannot be blamed for having committed an elementary error. Thus, Signorino (2004) maintains that Jevons does not fully understand the analytical structure of the classical theory but points out that he was actually aware of the fact that Ricardo took both 'produce' and 'wages' as given. Nevertheless, as Jevons's judgement of Ricardo's theory was heavily influenced by his own theoretical beliefs, he regarded taking 'produce' as given as a theoretical mistake, whereas it was only the reflection of a different approach to the problem of value and distribution.

DAVID HAAS

See also:

Marshall, Alfred, on Ricardo; Walras, Marie-Esprit-Léon, on Ricardo; Wicksell, Knut, on Ricardo.

References

Creedy, J. (forthcoming), 'William Stanley Jevons', in G. Faccarello and H.D. Kurz (eds), *Handbook of the History of Economic Thought*, Cheltenham, UK and Northampton, MA: Edward Elgar Publishing.
Dobb, M.H. (1973), *Theories of Value and Distribution since Adam Smith. Ideology and Economic Theory*, Cambridge, UK: Cambridge University Press.
Hutchison, T.W. (1978), *On Revolutions and Progress in Economic Knowledge*, Cambridge/Melbourne/New York: Cambridge University Press.
Jevons, W.S. (1863), 'Notice of a general mathematical theory of political economy', *Report of the British Association for the Advancement of Science*, Cambridge, UK, pp. 158–9.
Jevons, W.S. ([1871] 1965), *The Theory of Political Economy*, reprint of 5th edition of 1957, (ed.) H.S. Jevons, New York: Kelley.
Kurz, H.D. and N. Salvadori (2002a), 'Mark Blaug on the "Sraffian interpretation of the surplus approach"', *History of Political Economy*, **34**(1), 225–36.
Kurz, H.D. and N. Salvadori (2002b), 'One theory or two? Walras's critique of Ricardo', *History of Political Economy*, **34**(2), 365–98.
Kurz, H.D. and N. Salvadori (2003), '"Classical" vs. "neoclassical" theories of value and distribution and the long-period method', in F. Petri and F. Hahn (eds), *General Equilibrium: Problems and Prospects*, London: Routledge, pp. 216–45.
Menger, C. (1871), *Grundsätze der Volkswirthschaftslehre*, Vienna: Wilhelm Braumüller.
Signorino, R. (2004), 'Jevons on the Ricardian theory of distribution: an interpretation', *Studi Economici*, **59**(84), pp. 29–42.
Sigot, N. (2002), 'Jevons's debt to Bentham: mathematical economy, morals and psychology', *Manchester School*, **70**(2), 262–78.
Steedman, I. (1972), 'Jevons's theory of capital and interest', *Manchester School*, **40**(1), 31–52.
Steedman, I. (1997), 'Jevons's theory of political economy and the "marginalist revolution"', *European Journal of the History of Economic Thought*, **4**(1), 43–64.
Walras, L. ([1874–77] 1954), *Elements of Pure Economics*, translated by W. Jaffé, London: Allen and Unwin.
Wicksteed, P.H. (1894), *An Essay on the Co-ordination of the Laws of Distribution*, London: Macmillan.

Jewish Background

The Jewish heritage of David Ricardo can be followed back through five generations. All that can be said in general is that the family came from Portugal, probably around 1593, when Jews were invited by the Grand Duke of Tuscany to settle in the free port of

Livorno (Leghorn). In the seventeenth century, Leghorn developed into a centre of the coral industry, in which Jews played an important role (Roth, 1946: 343–50).

Around 1680, Samuel Israel, the great-great grandfather of David Ricardo came with his family from Leghorn to Amsterdam. He is the earliest ancestor we know anything about for certain. Samuel Israel joined the great Sephardic community of Amsterdam, for which the famous synagogue, or *snoge*, was built in 1675. His death on 28 October 1691 is registered in the archives of the Sephardic cemetery at Ouderkerk, near Amsterdam. Behind his name is written the word '*ger*' (Hebrew, meaning convert to Judaism or circumcised later in life). This does not necessarily mean that originally he was not Jewish. It may simply refer to his being circumcised later in life and taking on the name Israel in order to be accepted by the Portuguese-Jewish community in Amsterdam, as his ancestors were out of touch with the Jewish orthodoxy when in Portugal. They kept the name Israel in the Jewish community till around 1800, adding the Italian name Ricardo.

Samuel Israel Ricardo's wife Dina lived until 1722. According to the municipal archives three sons, David Israel (1652–1709), Benjamin Israel (1667–1733) and Raphael Israel (1672–1752), are referred to as 'of Livorno' on the occasion of their respective marriages in 1692, 1694 and 1697, all three in Amsterdam. David is a '*koopman*' (merchant), and Benjamin and Raphael are both recorded as '*koraal maker*' (coral worker). In view of the importance of Leghorn as a centre of the coral industry and trade (Yogew, 1978: 103–9) and the intensive commercial relationship between Leghorn and Amsterdam at the time, it is highly probable that Samuel was either also a coral worker or involved in the coral trade. When in Leghorn, in 1822, David Ricardo visited a manufactory of coral beads (Ricardo, 1891: 88; *Works*, X: 322).

David Israel, the eldest son of Samuel, was born in Leghorn in 1652. On 29 August 1692, he married Estrellia Amadios in Amsterdam. They were the great-grandparents of David Ricardo, and lived in Batavierenstraat in the Jewish quarter. David Israel died on 11 February 1709. Joseph Israel Ricardo, the son of David Israel, was the grandfather of David Ricardo, the economist. He was born in 1699, and died in Amsterdam on 11 June 1762. On 31 January 1721, he married Hannah Abaz in a civil ceremony, and on 8 Sjewat 5481 (4 February) in the synagogue. Sraffa writes that Joseph married twice: the first marriage was in 1721 to Hannah Israel, and the second in 1727 to Hannah Abaz (*Works*, X: 19). This is an error. The marriage certificate of Joseph Israel Ricardo and Hannah Abaz in the municipal archives is dated 31 January 1721, and in the Portuguese archives it is dated 8 Sjewat 5481; the error is understandable. In the archives of the Portuguese Synagogue Hannah Abaz is named Hannah Israel. After her name was written '*Gijoret*', which means 'Christian converted to Judaism'. As a result of the old Dutch style of writing, the year 1721 must have been misinterpreted as 1727. Sraffa corrected the mistake at my suggestion in Volume XI of *Works* (*Works*, XI: xxxix). Hannah Israel died on 21 November 1781. The marriage contract stipulated that Joseph brought with him all his goods and that Hannah brought with her 1000 guilders. They had four sons: David Hizkiau (1725–78), Abraham (1734–1812), Samuel (1736–95), and Moses (1738–1800). Abraham was David Ricardo's father. The grandparents of David Ricardo were buried in the Portuguese-Jewish cemetery at Ouderkerk.

At the time of his marriage, Joseph Israel Ricardo lived on the Keizersgracht. After the death, in 1715, of Abraham Abaz, Hannah's father, a house in the Weesperkerkstraat was part of the legacy. Hannah was entitled to a quarter of the house. In 1737, Joseph bought the remaining three-quarters of the house for 3000 guilders from the other heirs. Joseph and his wife lived in this home for the rest of their lives. Joseph Israel Ricardo became a non-official broker in funds and stocks, what is known as a '*beunhaas*', somebody who has no official nomination on the stock exchange.

Joseph Israel Ricardo was a man of substance when he died in 1762. According to his will, the beneficiaries were his wife, his four sons, his daughters Ribca and Sara, and his grandchild Rachel da Silva Curiel, daughter of his deceased daughter Rachel. There were also two legacies of 200 guilders to the *Sedaca* (fund for poor members of the Jewish community), with the stipulation that every year, on the Day of Atonement and on the Sabbath following the anniversary of his wife's death, the prayer *Ascabah* should be read for him and his wife; and the other of 100 guilders to the *Abi Yetomin* (aid for orphans). After the death of the executor Moses Raphael Hisquia da Vega, the new executors were Abraham da Vega and the uncles of the economist Samuel Israel Ricardo and Moses Israel Ricardo. His daughter Ribca received a legacy that had to be paid after the death of Hannah Abaz. As, however, Ribca died in 1770 and Hannah in 1781, the legacy had to be paid to Ribca's children in 1781. According to the will of Joseph Israel Ricardo, the executors would have to be the guardians of his underage heirs. The guardians of Ribca's children bought half of the house in the Weesperkerkstraat. Rehuel Lobatto, Ribca's widower, bought the other half. He lived in the house with his children. When Lobatto died in 1789, the executors of the will of Joseph Israel Ricardo and the executors of Lobatto's will sold the house to Salvador Bonaguetti Fano for 5012 guilders. Since this house was in the possession of the family when David Ricardo was in Amsterdam from 1783 till 1785, it is possible that he paid a visit to his cousins.

Abraham Israel Ricardo was born in Amsterdam in the year 1734 as the second son of Joseph Israel Ricardo. Like two of his brothers, Abraham became a stockbroker. He spent his youth in Amsterdam and, also like his brothers, gave financial support to the Talmud Torah and Ets Haim Jewish library. On the occasion of Abraham's death on 21 March 1812, an obituary announced that he died in his eightieth year, which establishes his date of birth as about 1733 (*Works*, X: 20). I am able to reveal his exact date of birth. I came across a circumcision booklet of the *mohel* Salomo ben Isaac Curiel Abaz (1724–61). It appears that he circumcised Abraham, son of Joseph Israel Ricardo, on 19 March 1734. Assuming no health problems, I conclude that Abraham's date of birth was 11 March 1734 (given that circumcision customarily takes place on the eighth day following the day of birth). When he died on 21 March 1812, he was just over 78 years old. The same *mohel* circumcised Abraham's brother Samuel Ricardo on 25 June 1736 and Moses Ricardo, the youngest brother, on 16 September 1738. This new information fixes the Samuel's date of birth (17 June 1736) and Moses's (8 September 1738).

During the Seven Years War, the Dutch invested enormous amounts in English funds. Many firms had agents in London to manage their investments, and one of the agents in 1760 was Abraham Israel Ricardo. On behalf of his father, he went to London in the spring of 1760. According to a notarized document dated 16 May 1760, his father authorized Abraham Ricardo 'of London' to buy and sell South Sea Company stocks. He started as an agent for his father, but he soon began business on the London stock market in his own right. His name appears as Abraham Ricardo for the first time in the stock ledgers of English funds on 27 February 1761 as a holder of 4 per cent annuities of 1760. As Abraham Israel Ricardo he submitted himself on 15 October 1760 for assessment at the Bevis Marks Synagogue (*Works*, X: 20). He was still a Dutch citizen, though living in London, when on 30 April 1769 he married Abigail Delvalle, the daughter of a Sephardic family who had been living in England for three generations. Then, in 1770, he became a British citizen, and in 1773 was appointed to one of the 12 brokerships allotted to Jews in the City of London.

When David Ricardo was born, his father was thus an Englishman, and, when Ricardo was a boy, an established London stockbroker, but he was also a prominent figure in the Sephardic community of London. He was elected to serve as *parnas* (religious leader and administrator) in 1785, 1789 and 1802 (Hyamson, 1951: 437–9). At the time of his death on 21 March 1812, 11 years after his wife, he left a fortune of about £45 000.

Intellectual background

David Ricardo, Abraham's third son, was born on 18 April 1772. He was circumcised on 25 April, with Joseph de Isaac Capadose as *padrinho* (godfather) and his aunt, Leah de Abraham del Valle, as *madrinha* (godmother). After him, six girls and eight more boys were born. The family lived in the City until 1792 and in that year they moved to Bow. Of Ricardo's youth very little is known. In 1824, his brother Moses published a memoir of David Ricardo. From this we quote the following:

> When very young, he was sent to Holland. His father, who had designed him to follow the same business in which he was engaged, and whose transactions lay chiefly in that country, sent him there not only with a view to his becoming acquainted with it, but also that he might be placed at a school of which he entertained a very high opinion. After two years' absence he returned home, and continued the common school-education till his father took him into business. At his intervals of leisure, he was allowed any masters for private instruction whom he chose to have, but he had not the benefit of what is called a classical education. (*Works*, X: 3)

From 1783 to 1785, David lived in Amsterdam in the house of one of his uncles. The question is, which uncle? Sraffa assumes it must be Samuel Israel Ricardo's house, because 'he was married and had children'. David Israel Ricardo Jr had died already in 1778 and Moses Israel Ricardo did not marry and had no children (ibid.: 30). On the basis of research in the archives and looking at the facts from a different perspective, I come to another conclusion. First of all, Samuel only married in 1791, when he was 55, to Rachel Pereira, who was 56. In 1778 a young child of Samuel's was buried at Ouderkerk, but there is no evidence of any marriage before 1791. Samuel went bankrupt in 1770, with a total debt of around 10 000 guilders, his biggest debt of almost 4000 guilders being to his brother David Israel Ricardo Jr. Samuel died in 1795, one month after his wife Rachel.

David Israel Ricardo Jr bought a house in 1775 on the Keizersgracht, between Weesperstraat and Amstel. This house is still in existence, the address nowadays being Nieuwe Keizersgracht 70. Although David died in 1778, the house remained in the family until 1798. His wife, who died in 1800, and his children lived there. One of the daughters is Rebecca Ricardo (1769–1841), the mother of Isaac Da Costa, the Dutch poet (1798–1860) – in 1797 she married Daniel Haim Da Costa (1761–1822).

Moses Israel Ricardo was registered as a Jewish trader, living 'in the Rapenburgerstr' up to 1783, 'op de Keizersgraft by Brands Hofje' (ibid.). As no other house was registered under the name of Ricardo on this part of the canal, it is certain that Moses

Ricardo went to his brother David's house. In fact, it appears from a list of documents in the Da Costa archive that Moses Israel Ricardo sold the house in the Rapenburgerstraat, which he partly rented, as executor of the will of two older brothers, who each owned half of the house and died, respectively in 1781 and 1782. In other words, Moses Israel Ricardo moved 1783 to his brother David's house on the Keizersgracht to live there with his sister-in-law, her children and perhaps also with Samuel, who is not registered as a Jewish trader.

According to the archives, it is Moses who was a very active stockbroker acting on behalf of his brother David before his death and who had the financial contacts with London, and also without any doubt with his brother Abraham. From Abraham's point of view, it was important to ally Moses with his son David Ricardo and enable him 'to follow the same business in which he [Abraham] was engaged' (ibid.: 1). I assume, therefore, that Ricardo the economist lived in this house as a boy. There he met his cousin Rebecca Ricardo, not only during 1783 to 1785, but also in 1788, when he came over from London with his younger brothers Moses and Jacob, and again in 1792. In the letter to his son Osman on the Continental tour, David Ricardo wrote on 27 July 1822 from Amsterdam:

> From the age of 11 to 13 I resided in Amsterdam in the house of my uncle and this cousin was then an inmate of his home – I had seen her in one or two visits which I paid to the family after that time, the last of which was about 30 years ago. Since that time both she and I had married. (Ricardo, 1891: 19; *Works*, X: 207)

Although from a legal point of view the house belonged to the heirs of David Israel Ricardo Jr, it is natural that David as a young boy considered the house to belong to his uncle Moses. Presumably David learned a lot about the financial profession of his uncle, filling in the blank spot in his education, if we view informal learning as part of the intellectual and professional development of an intelligent youngster.

Sraffa and Henderson suggested that David Ricardo was sent to the great Amsterdam Talmud Torah school (Sraffa, *Works*, X: 31; Henderson and Davis, 1997: 150) but there is no evidence in favour of this in the Amsterdam archives. It is a fact that one of the managers of the Talmud Torah in 1784 was Dr Immanuel Capadose who was described by David Ricardo in 1822 as 'a very friendly man, whom I knew when I was in Holland'. But the Ricardo and Capadose families had had business relations for generations, and this fact alone is inconclusive. Furthermore, Capadose may have been a guest of the house on the Nieuwe Keizersgracht and Ricardo may be referring to his stay in Holland in 1788. The possibility that Ricardo did attend the Talmud Torah is very remote. In the memoir of his brother, Moses perhaps refers to this possibility, but in the sense that it was something that his father had only considered. As Ricardo himself does not even mention a school, it is highly probable that he received some education at the house on the Nieuwe Keizersgracht 70 in the form of reading, writing and arithmetic, French and Spanish from a private tutor. There is no doubt that he went every Saturday with his uncle Moses to the nearby synagogue in Amsterdam. But there is no indication that he received any particular Jewish education as Cremaschi and Dascal suggest (Cremaschi and Dascal, 1996: 490). To strengthen my position on this issue, I would like to point out that his father was a respected figure in the Bevis Marks Synagogue in London. Associated with that synagogue is the Medrash of Heshaim, often referred to as the

Talmud Torah, a school for boys, originally intended solely for instruction in Hebrew and Judaism. In 1736 the teaching of English subjects and of arithmetic was added to the school curriculum and in 1758 the institution was again reorganized (Hyamson, 1951: 94–5). Why should Abraham send his son David to the Amsterdam Talmud Torah if there was one in London? On the other hand, it is almost certain that he prepared himself in Amsterdam for his *bar mitzvah* in London in April 1785. The new evidence on the role of Moses Israel Ricardo as his financial coach, makes it even less probable that he went to the Talmud Torah. Let us not forget that he joined his father's firm at the age of 14.

David Ricardo kept in contact with Amsterdam during his entire life. After his visits in the years 1783–85, he came over to Amsterdam to accompany his younger brother Moses, born in 1776, and his brother Jacob, born in 1780, both destined for the stock market (*Works*, X: 4). During the tour on the Continent he visited several cities in Holland. In Amsterdam, he called on several family members, not only his cousin Rebecca Ricardo but also her son Isaac Da Costa, who was baptized in 1822. While visiting Amsterdam, Ricardo, his wife and two daughters stayed in the Doelen Hotel. He still understood Dutch, spoke a few words and knew his way around (Ricardo, 1891: 18–22; *Works*, X: 205–12).

Ricardo paid several visits to members of the Portuguese Synagogue in Amsterdam and The Hague in 1822. Ricardo supported several family members financially, as well as Portuguese Jews outside his family (*Works*, X: 133). He also supported the foundation of a Jewish School in The Hague in 1820, as can be learned from a letter by Abraham Suasso of 24 November 1820 in the Ricardo Papers in Cambridge. In 1822 he had not belonged to the Jewish community for 30 years (Ricardo, 1891: 16; *Works*, X: 205). This change in attitude is expressed openly by his marriage in December 1793 to Priscilla Ann Wilkinson, a Quaker. This marriage led to a breach with his parents. He never saw his mother again. After the death of his mother in 1801, his father repaired the breach. It follows from a codicil that, in March 1807, David became the executor of his father's will. Despite his formal departure of the Jewish community, in his day Cobbett referred to him as 'Ricardo the Jew' (Weatherall, 1976: 58) and Lady Holland used the phrase 'that little Jew Ricardo' in a letter of May 1819 (ibid.: 152).

Ricardo and religion

According to Lord Hardwick's Act of 1753 all marriages in England had to be performed in the established Church, except for Jews and Quakers; and since David Ricardo had renounced his Jewish faith and Priscilla Wilkinson had been disowned by the Quakers, they were married in their parish church of St Mary's, Lambeth. But this did not mean that Ricardo was baptised as a member of the Church of England; and though the births of all his children were registered with the Society of Friends, he never was a Quaker. For several years after the marriage he seems occasionally to have attended Quaker Meetings (compare the anonymous note in the *Sunday Times* of 21 September 1823) and then he was drawn to the Unitarians. As is well known, the Unitarians do not accept the dogma of the Trinity. In 1809 he became a 'hearer' at 'Mr. Aspland's Chapel in Hackney' (*Works*, X: 40).

With the established Church his relations were always less clearly defined. In 1808, when he was living at Bromley St. Leonard's, he was elected churchwarden; but though the churchwarden had to take an oath on the whole Bible, the office was of more secular than religious significance. The position of High Sheriff of Gloucestershire, to which he was nominated in 1817, was, however, more difficult for him. It was customary for the High Sheriff to take Corporate Communion and Ricardo showed very clearly that he did not want to take Corporate Communion. He was protected by the Indemnity Bill. Then, in 1819, he entered Parliament, and took the oath on 'the true faith of a Christian'. A Unitarian, of course, considers himself a Christian, although he denies the divinity of Christ; and there can be no doubt that David Ricardo felt himself to be a Unitarian. Certainly he was buried with the rites of the established Church.

His attitude towards matters of religion may be illustrated by the following quotation, taken from his speech in Parliament on 26 March 1823:

> All religious opinions, however absurd and extravagant, might be conscientiously believed by some individuals. Why, then, was one man to set up his ideas on the subject as the criterion from which no other was to be allowed to differ with impunity? Why was one man to be considered infallible, and all his fellow-men as frail and erring creatures? Such a doctrine ought not to be tolerated: It savoured too much of the Inquisition to be received as genuine in a free country like England. A fair and free discussion ought to be allowed on all religious topics. (*Works*, V: 280)

William Wilberforce, who spoke after Ricardo, made the following entry in his diary: 'I had hoped that Ricardo had become a Christian; I see now that he has only ceased to be a Jew'.

Defining a Jew as a man who professes the Jewish religion, David Ricardo had, of course, 'ceased to be a Jew'. But there was also his Jewish heritage. In October 1822 he went to Leghorn where, together with his wife and daughters, he visited the synagogue, 'which is a very beautiful one; – we saw a manufactory of coral beads, and polishing pieces of coral and fitting them for necklaces' (*Works*, X: 322). I cannot avoid thinking that Ricardo's feelings dwelt for some time on his great-grandfather Samuel van Mozes Israel, the necklace-maker, who around 1660 went from Leghorn to Amsterdam.

Portuguese-Jewish community

Where does Ricardo's scientific approach come from? There is no question of higher education or of formal teachers. There is no sign of knowledge of economic literature or of erudition in general. Ricardo earned his living as a trader in stocks and funds. Can we explain how a financial businessman came to develop economic models? The Ricardo family exemplifies the history of the Portuguese Jews in Amsterdam. From generation to generation, they are amidst a network of family, religious, commercial and scientific contacts. These four aspects of human activity influence and complement each other and bring unity in pluriformity. In all this, the still impressive Synagogue in the centre of Amsterdam and the Talmud played a crucial role.

David Ricardo went to this Synagogue with his uncle Moses Israel Ricardo. The Portuguese Synagogue has been a weekly meeting point since 1675. It is a religious place, business is done and intellectual disputes are carried out. Elderly people try to broaden and deepen their insights, youngsters informally receive a broad education that competes with regular schooling. And there is the study of the *Talmud* and the *Torah*. The concentrated attention, the reduction of many-sided phenomena to a few basic principles, the unravelling description, analysis and normative judgement are building blocks in the sharpening of minds that request structure. In order to judge Ricardo as a deductive economist, one cannot circumvent the study of the *Talmud* according to an age-long tradition. On the one hand, he learned to think within a dogmatic system of strict rules and, on the other, he developed a talent for thinking independently.

The Ricardos from Amsterdam first lived in Leghorn and earlier in Lisbon. Again and again, they left an established order, often being forced to leave. Again and again, not only the Ricardos, but also other Sephardic Jews looked for the unorthodox way out. It is not surprising that such a community from time to time produces remarkable thinkers. I mention Baruch Spinoza (1632–77), who grew up in the neighbourhood of the *snoge*. Spinoza developed into a great axiomatic thinker, into a defender of tolerance and freedom of expression and remained a trader (*koopman*) and a cutter of lenses. His progressive ideas, I gather, must have been discussed many years later in the *snoge*, even though he had been excommunicated.

Another remarkable figure in the Sephardic community was Isaac De Pinto (1717–87) (Nijenhuis, 1992). In his youth he lived in the De Pinto House (named after his family), in the Sint Antoniebreestraat. Isaac De Pinto was circumcised in 1717 by the same *mohel*, Aboab, who in 1725 also circumcised David Ricardo's uncle, the eldest son of Joseph Israel Ricardo. This illustrates how tight connections were. De Pinto grew up as an active member of the Sephardic community and must have had weekly contact in the *snoge* until 1760 with the grandfather and father of David Ricardo.

As a banker, De Pinto was active in international financial transactions. He wrote on philosophical topics and differed in opinion with Spinoza. In 1761, De Pinto started to write his most important economic publication on circulation and credit. The book appeared in 1771 when De Pinto was living with his family in The Hague (De Pinto, 1771). His great work on the significance of credit, future transactions of the stock exchange and, in particular, public debt for economic growth, shows his vision and insight and, above all, his international orientation. David Ricardo never mentions De Pinto, although he must have heard about him from his father.

A further consideration may be added that diminishes the gap between business and a deductive approach in economics and also brings us nearer to Ricardo. Portuguese Jews were sophisticated men of business, stockbrokers and entrepreneurs. Their activity was to decide at a time (t) to buy goods with a view of selling at time ($t + 1$) at a profit. In fact, this behaviour implies the ability to introduce assumptions on endogenous and exogenous factors, to reason from assumptions, to deduce conclusions, and to act. Briefly, a businessman of standing uses a model, which he adapts in the light of new facts and disappointments. The deductive attitude with respect to trade has been pointed out in the famous book by Joseph Penso de la Vega, written in dialogue form on the financial operations of the stock market in Amsterdam, *Confusion de Confusiones* (de la Vega, 1688; Smith, 1939). In the recent literature a penetrating analysis of this book has been given by De Marchi and Harrison and by Cardoso (De Marchi and Harrison, 1994; Cardoso, 2002). De la Vega also belonged to the Portuguese Jewish Community of Amsterdam.

But, if all this is so, Ricardo the stockbroker and Ricardo the great theorist are 'two sides of the same coin'. At first, implicitly for many years, he used models in his dealings on the stock exchange, and later travelled this road explicitly, but without a commercial connection and at a higher level of abstraction. Somebody who nowadays applies game theory to doing business seems to be more successful than somebody who does not. Let me quote in full a passage written by Bagehot in his chapter on Ricardo:

> The writings of Ricardo are unique in literature, so far as I know, as a representative on paper of the special faculties by which the Jews have grown rich for ages. The works of Spinoza, and many others, have shown the power of the race in dealing with other kinds of abstraction: but I know none of but Ricardo's which can awaken a book-student to a sense of the Jewish genius for the mathematics of money-dealing. His mastery over the abstractions of Political Economy is of a kind almost exactly identical. (Bagehot, 1880: 133)

Alfred Marshall also referred to Ricardo's Jewish background and did not consider him to be an Englishman (Marshall [1890] 1961: 60). In his inaugural lecture of 1885, Marshall observed: 'The faults and virtues of Ricardo's mind are traceable to his Semitic origin; no English economist has had a mind similar to his' (Marshall, 1885: 12).

Summing up, the basis for Ricardo's remarkable achievements is the combination of the Portuguese-Jewish background, which Ricardo confronted from his birth onwards, with international orientation and the study of the *Talmud*, and the business activity passed on from father to son, the successful outcome of which calls for the implicit use of models. The scientific approach and opinions of Ricardo do coincide to a large extent with Spinoza's. In general, one does not encounter Jews among the institutional, descriptive economists, but rather in great numbers among the abstract, deductive thinkers. That seems to be related in one way or another to their often forced movements in space, the permanent crossing of borders and the necessity of linking the past with the future.

ARNOLD HEERTJE

See also:

Belsham, Thomas, and Ricardo; Life and Activities.

References

Bagehot, W. (1880), *Economic Studies*, London: Longman Green.

Cardoso, J.L. (2002), 'Confusion de confusions: ethics and options on seventeenth-century stock exchange markets', *Financial History Review*, **9**(2), 109–23.

Cremaschi, S. and M. Dascal (1996), 'Malthus and Ricardo on economic methodology', *History of Political Economy*, **28**(3), 475–511.

de la Vega, J.P. (1688), *Confusion de Confusiones*, Amsterdam.

De Marchi, N. and P. Harrison (1994), 'Trading "in the wind" and with guile: the troublesome matter of the short-selling of shares in seventeenth-century Holland', *History of Political Economy*, Supplement, **26**(0), 47–65.

De Pinto, I. (1771), *Traité de la Circulation et du Crédit*, Amsterdam: Michel Rey.

Henderson, J.P. and J.B. Davis (1997), *The Life and Economics of David Ricardo*, Boston, MA: Kluwer Academic Publishers.

Hyamson, A.M. (1951), *The Sephardim of England*, London: Methuen.

Marshall, A. (1885), *The Present Position of Economics*, London: Macmillan.

Marshall, A. ([1890] 1961), *Principles of Economics*, 9th edition, annotated by G.W. Guillebaud, London: Macmillan.

Nijenhuis, I. (1992), *Een Joodse Philosophe*, Amsterdam: NEHA.

Ricardo, D. (1891), *Letters Written by David Ricardo During a Tour on the Continent*, London: privately printed.

Roth, C. (1946), *The History of the Jews of Italy*, Philadelphia, PA: The Jewish Publication Society of America.

Smith, M.F.J. (ed.) (1939), *Verwarring der verwarring*, The Hague: Martinus Nijhoff.

Weatherall, D. (1976), *David Ricardo, A Biography*, The Hague: Nijhoff.

Yogew, C. (1978), *Diamonds and Coral, Anglo-Dutch Jews and Eighteenth Century Traders*, Leicester, UK: Leicester University Press.

Kaldor, Nicholas, on Ricardo

Nicholas Kaldor (1908–86) belonged to a generation – almost the last generation – in which a deep knowledge of the classic texts was regarded as an essential part of the education of all economists. His most inspiring teacher, as he often recalled, was Allyn Young, an enthusiastic disciple of Adam Smith who will certainly have encouraged his students to read the *Wealth of Nations*. Precisely when Kaldor first read Ricardo's *Principles* is not known. As a young lecturer at the London School of Economics in the 1930s he came under the influence of his professors, Friedrich von Hayek and Lionel Robbins, both with research interests in the history of economic thought. In Cambridge, where the LSE had relocated for the duration of the war, Kaldor lectured on 'Distribution' (later on 'Value and Distribution'). Here, too, he became a friend of Piero Sraffa, the editor of Ricardo's *Collected Works*. The secretive Italian was never willing to discuss his own theoretical system with Kaldor, but this inhibition did not extend to his ideas on Ricardo. Kaldor even stood in for him when he 'suffered stage fright at the prospect of giving a promised lecture on Ricardo', and to do so he borrowed Sraffa's notes (Thirlwall, 1987: 78). As Kaldor later recalled, this was one of the rare occasions where Sraffa was prepared to discuss economics with him (Marcuzzo, 1986: 50). By 1945 he was lecturing on 'General Principles of Economic Analysis', with both Ricardo's and Marshall's *Principles* as set texts, together with Keynes's *General Theory* and books by Knut Wicksell, Kenneth Boulding and George Stigler (ibid.: 100). Thus, when Kaldor cited Ricardo in his own published work he knew exactly what he was talking about.

His first reference to Ricardo came in the course of a brief but acrimonious controversy in 1942 with Hayek, with whom his personal relations had become increasingly strained. In the 1930s Hayek had published two book-length explanations of the trade cycle, which Kaldor believed to contradict each other. In the second, the 1939 *Profits, Interest and Investment*, Hayek argued that an increase in the demand for consumer goods would lead to an increase in their price, a fall in real wages, and the adoption of less capital-intensive methods of production by entrepreneurs who would react to the decline in the cost of labour, relative to capital. Higher spending on consumption would thus lead to a decline in investment expenditure, and not to an increase. Hayek had thus replaced the well-known acceleration principle with what Kaldor described as a 'deceleration principle' (Kaldor, 1942: 361). This was not only incredible, Kaldor maintained, but it also contradicted Hayek's own previous analysis of the cycle (see also Thirlwall, 1987: 41–7).

Hayek had given the name 'the Ricardo effect' to the reduction in the capital–labour ratio that resulted from a relative fall in the real wage rate, referring to a brief passage in Chapter 1, §V of the *Principles* and to the numerical example used there (see also Hayek, 1942a, 1942b). Kaldor claimed that Ricardo had been misrepresented by Hayek: 'the assumptions are different, the mode of operation is different, and the conditions of validity are quite different', so that 'any criticism made against Professor Hayek's "Ricardo effect" would not necessarily apply to Ricardo' (Kaldor, 1942: 364; see Zamagni, 1987 for a defence of Hayek on these matters). In his brief reply Hayek denied any inconsistency with his earlier work, but made no mention of Ricardo, who was indeed somewhat peripheral to the controversy. Neither Hayek nor Kaldor offered any detailed discussion of Ricardo's views on the trade cycle, his denial of the possibility of 'general gluts', or his relationship with Malthus, and Hayek's own deceleration theory of the cycle was never anything more than a historical curiosity.

Kaldor's second reference to Ricardo – indeed, his first major reference – came in 1950. He had been commissioned to write the entry on 'Distribution, theory of' for *Chambers's Encyclopaedia*, and drew on his lecture notes to do so. He devoted almost half of his four-page essay to the classical theory of distribution, describing Ricardo's statement in the preface to the *Principles* as the '*locus classicus* of this theory' and endorsing his three-class model of society and the related threefold division of total output into rent, profit and wages. Kaldor included a beautifully simple, lucid diagram, possibly adapted from Marshall ([1920] 1962: 687–8, Figures 40 and 41), which summarized his interpretation of Ricardo's theory of distribution. Figure 13 in this entry is a slightly amended version of Kaldor's diagram, in which agricultural output per unit of labour-and-capital is measured on the vertical axis and the quantity of labour-and-capital employed on the horizontal axis. Capital and labour are assumed to be applied in fixed proportions, and can be varied continuously, so that the average product (AP) and marginal product (MP) curves are also continuous. Total output is shown by the area under the MP curve; there are diminishing returns, so that both AP and MP fall as more units of labour-and-capital are applied to a given area of land. Kaldor assumes that AP falls at an increasing rate, so that MP falls even faster. When OL_1 units of labour-and-capital are employed, the average product is OK (= AL_1). On the classical assumption

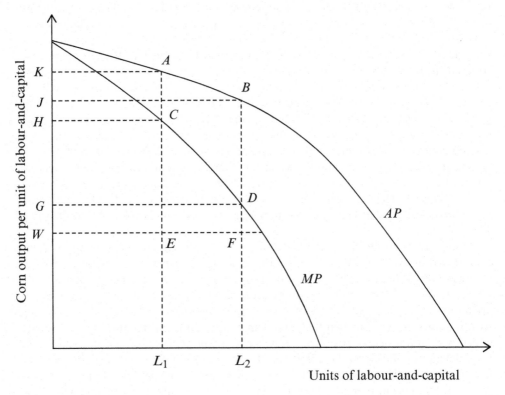

Figure 13　Kaldor's Ricardian diagram

of a fixed real wage (the 'natural rate of wages'), the wage is $OW (= EL_1)$ and the total wage bill is shown by the rectangle $OWE\,L_1$. Rent is the difference between the average product and the marginal product (which, as Kaldor points out, depends on the elasticity of the AP curve): total rent payments are therefore equal to the area $HKAC$. Profit is a 'residue', and is shown by the area $HWEC$. The shares of rent, profit and wages can be read off the y-axis: they are $HK (= AC)$, $WH (= CE)$ and $OW (= EL_1)$ respectively, each divided by $OK (= AL_1)$.

Capital accumulation proceeds, and employment increases, up to OL_2. At this point profit has fallen to DF per unit, which is the minimum required to compensate the capitalists for their time and trouble (including the necessary risk premium), and accumulation ceases. In the resulting Ricardian 'stationary state', the shares of rent, profit and wages are equal to $JG (= BD)$, $GW (= DF)$ and $OW (= OL_2)$ respectively, all divided by $OJ (= BL_2)$. The wage share must increase as the economy approaches the stationary state, since the real wage is constant and therefore takes up an increasing proportion of the declining average product. The shares of land and capital, taken together, must decline, but the course followed by the individual shares of rent and profit over time will depend on the precise shape of the AP and MP functions (see Davidson, 1959).

Note that this does *not* identify Ricardo as a forerunner of the marginal productivity theory of distribution, as argued (for example) by Alfred Marshall. On the contrary – Kaldor was very clear that this was not legitimate. Although the marginal productivity principle 'was already implicit in Ricardo', the classical economists had assumed that both 'labour and capital have definite long-run supply prices. Only the remuneration of the third factor, land, was derived from the operation of the marginal principle' (Kaldor, 1950: 555). Kaldor himself was a strong critic of neoclassical capital theory, and there is no suggestion that his figure is derived from an aggregate production function. It is – typically for Kaldor – an informal construction, which is best construed as applying to a one-commodity, 'corn model' economy in which the insoluble problems posed for neoclassical theory by heterogeneous capital goods simply do not arise.

The *Chambers's* entry formed the basis for Kaldor's 1956 paper on 'Alternative theories of distribution', one of the most widely read of all his articles (between 1960 and 1993 it was reprinted, in whole or in part, in at least seven anthologies of economics articles). Both in the encyclopaedia entry and in the 1956 article, Kaldor was clear that, although Ricardo's model was a major intellectual achievement, it was not relevant to twentieth-century industrial capitalism. In the *Chambers's* entry, he concluded that 'the problem posed by Ricardo, the discovery of "the laws which regulate distribution", still eludes the grasp of economists' (Kaldor, 1950: 556). By 1956 this verdict had been revised, since Kaldor now claimed that he himself had provided the basis for a solution with his own macroeconomic (or 'Keynesian') model of distribution, in which there was neither land, nor landlords, nor rent. He now had the advantage of access to Sraffa's edition of the *Principles*, with its masterly editorial introduction. Kaldor referred to it at several points in his article, most significantly to emphasize the distinction between agricultural and industrial production and the difficulties that this poses for Ricardo's theory (Kaldor, 1956: 86–7).

Kaldor's own interests had shifted towards growth theory and the analysis of taxation, both of which now receive some attention. There is more discussion of the Ricardian steady state, though oddly enough this feature is missing from the simplified version of his figure presented there (ibid.: 85), and on the implications of classical distribution theory for the incidence of taxation. Since Marx had taken his theory of surplus value from Ricardo, and the neoclassicals had extended the marginal productivity principle from land to all factors of production, 'both Marx and Marshall are able to claim Ricardo as their precursor' (ibid.: 89). Neither, however, had succeeded in formulating an acceptable theory of distribution. Kaldor notes that his own theory is in a sense the polar opposite of Ricardo's. The real wage is now determined by the investment ratio and the capitalist propensity to save; it is not (as in Ricardo) the basic datum of the system. Thus, it is the share of wages, rather than the profit share, that is a residual in Kaldor's model, and all taxes fall on wages, not on rent (ibid.: 96).

Kaldor was still showing interest in Ricardo two years later, when he presented a paper at a conference on the theory of capital. Indeed, his was the only one of the 13 papers to cite Ricardo (Kaldor, 1961: 179–82, 188–9), and according to the transcript he was one of only two participants – the other being Paul Samuelson – to refer to him in the conference discussion. Somewhat anachronistically, Kaldor claimed that Ricardo (along with Marx and von Neumann) had 'thought neo-classical theory nonsense' (Hague, 1961: 294–5). Presumably he meant that they would have done, given the chance. Kaldor later observed that the classical stationary state 'has never materialised', and the proportion of the labour force in most developed countries that was employed in agriculture had fallen to '5 per cent or less'. This demonstrated that 'the improvement in the "arts of cultivation" (to use Ricardo's own expression) was more "land-saving" than "labour-saving" in character' (Kaldor [1981] 1985: 220). At the very end of his life, however, Kaldor still found it useful to compare Ricardo's ideas on growth and distribution with the analyses of Hicks, Wicksell and Keynes (ibid.: 190).

In the 1970s, as his own interests shifted to the theory of international trade, Kaldor began to criticize the theory of comparative advantage. The context in which he wrote was both economic and political. Kaldor was trying to explain the relatively slow growth of the British economy after 1945, which he attributed to the poor performance of manufacturing industry, and was also engaged in the controversy over British membership of the European Common Market (the forerunner of the European Union), which he opposed. Ricardo's case for free trade, he maintained, rested on the assumption that there were constant returns to scale in all activities. But this was true neither of agriculture, where diminishing returns prevailed, nor – crucially – of manufacturing, which was subject to both static and dynamic increasing returns. This had fatal consequences for Ricardo's theory of comparative advantage: 'under these conditions it can be demonstrated that free trade may lead to stunted growth, or even impoverishment of some regions (or countries) to the greater benefit of others' (Kaldor, 1978: 237). Kaldor also objected to the implicit assumption of full employment that he believed Ricardo to have made, which he regarded as illegitimate in a model in which the real wage had a lower bound (the 'natural rate of wages'). Many scholars would, of course, deny that Ricardo did assume full employment in this (or any other) context.

Kaldor believed that Ricardo had presented a strong case against protecting British agriculture, a case that was still powerful when directed against the Common Agricultural Policy of the European Common Market (Kaldor [1970] 1978: 183). For Britain, in 1846, the repeal of the Corn Laws 'could bring nothing but advantages: (1) lower food prices; (2) lower wages in terms of manufactured goods; (3) higher profits and faster capital accumulation in industry; (4) enlarged markets for British manufactured goods, on account of higher imports'. It was less clear, he suggested, that the overseas countries that had exported food and raw materials to Britain had gained to the same extent. Indeed, there had been a reduction in both employment and output in small-scale industries in Europe and Asia due to competition from cheaper imported goods. Thus, 'Ricardo's later formulations of the doctrine of "comparative costs" insinuated further assumptions into the argument with the unfortunate consequence that more was claimed for "free trade" than was in fact justified' (Kaldor, 1978: 238). Free trade had been good for Britain at first, allowing the share of UK manufactures in the world market to increase. When France, Germany, Japan and the USA began to develop their own industries behind the shelter offered by protective tariffs, Britain's insistence on maintaining free trade proved to be a costly error, since new industries failed to emerge and the benefits of increasing returns to scale were lost. Free trade was equally inappropriate for underdeveloped countries that wished to industrialize; here Friedrich List had scored an important intellectual victory over Ricardo (Kaldor [1970] 1978: 183).

Kaldor himself was once compared directly to Ricardo. Reviewing the third and fourth volumes of his collected essays, Arthur Smithies commented that:

> he observes the economic scene with the cold detachment of a Ricardo . . . Like Ricardo also, great intellectual power is exhibited with an absence of wit, a solemnity of purpose, and hasty drafting. Spectacular conclusions emerge from the 'stylising' (to use Kaldor's word) of facts and premises. (Smithies, 1966: 881)

The reference to 'hasty drafting' was fair comment, at least as applied to Kaldor; 'cold detachment' and 'absence of wit' would be less easy to justify. Kaldor himself always had a very high opinion of Ricardo as an economic theorist, once describing Ricardo's *Principles* as being 'generally regarded as the basis of modern economics' (Kaldor [1970] 1978: 183). As he wrote in 1982, in a lecture on Keynes's *General Theory*: 'It will rank as one of the top 5 classics in the field – of comparable importance to Adam Smith's *Wealth of Nations*, Ricardo's *Principles*, Marx's *Das Kapital* and Alfred Marshall's *Principles of Economics*' (Kaldor, 1982: 259). But Kaldor himself was never, in any sense, a Ricardian.

JOHN E. KING

See also:

Accumulation of Capital; Endogenous Growth; Keynes, John Maynard, on Ricardo; Pasinetti, Luigi Lodovico, on Ricardo.

References

Davidson, P. (1959), 'A clarification of the Ricardian rent share', *Canadian Journal of Economics and Political Science*, **25**(2), 190–95.
Hague, D.C. (1961), 'Summary record of the debate', in F.A. Lutz and D.C. Hague (eds), *The Theory of Capital: Proceedings of a Conference Held by the International Economic Association*, London: Macmillan, pp. 295–403.
Hayek, F.A. von (1942a), 'The Ricardo effect', *Economica* (New Series), **9**(34), 127–52.
Hayek, F.A. von (1942b), 'A comment', *Economica* (New Series), **9**(36), 383–5.
Kaldor, N. (1942), 'Professor Hayek and the concertina effect', *Economica* (New Series), **9**(36), 359–82.
Kaldor, N. (1950), 'Distribution, theory of', *Chambers's Encyclopaedia*, 6th edition, Edinburgh: Chambers, pp. 553–6.
Kaldor, N. (1956), 'Alternative theories of distribution', *Review of Economic Studies*, **23**(2), 83–100.

Kaldor, N. (1961), 'Capital accumulation and economic growth', in F.A. Lutz and D.C. Hague (eds), *The Theory of Capital: Proceedings of a Conference Held by the International Economic Association*, London: Macmillan, pp. 177–222.

Kaldor, N. ([1970] 1978), 'Europe's agricultural disarray', *New Statesman*, 3 April, reprinted in N. Kaldor, *Further Essays on Applied Economics*, London: Duckworth, pp. 175–86.

Kaldor, N. (1978), 'The nemesis of free trade', in N. Kaldor, *Further Essays on Applied Economics*, London: Duckworth, pp. 234–41.

Kaldor, N. ([1981] 1985), 'The role of increasing returns, technical progress and cumulative causation in the theory of international trade and economic growth', *Economie Appliquée*, **34**(4), pp. 593–617, cited in N. Kaldor, *Further Essays on Economic Theory and Policy*, (eds) F. Targetti and A.P. Thirlwall, London: Duckworth, pp. 201–23.

Kaldor, N. (1982), 'Limitations of the *General Theory*', *Proceedings of the British Academy*, **68**, 259–73.

Kaldor, N. (1986), 'Limits on growth', *Oxford Economic Papers*, **38**(2), 187–98.

Marcuzzo, M.C. (1986), *Nicholas Kaldor: Ricordi di un Economista*, Bologna: Garzanti.

Marshall, A. ([1920] 1962), *Principles of Economics*, 8th edition, London: Macmillan.

Smithies, A.J. (1966), 'Review of N. Kaldor, *Essays on Economic Policy, Volumes III and IV*', *American Economic Review*, **56**(4), 881–5.

Thirlwall, A.P. (1987), *Nicholas Kaldor*, Brighton: Wheatsheaf.

Zamagni, S. (1987), 'Ricardo-Hayek effect', in J. Eatwell, M. Milgate and P. Newman (eds), *The New Palgrave: A Dictionary of Economics, Vol. IV*, London: Macmillan, pp. 198–9.

Keynes, John Maynard, on Ricardo

Keynes's comments on Ricardo and his economic theory come in two distinct varieties. There are some short, mostly affirmative statements either giving Ricardo credit for the quantity theory (Keynes, 1971–89, *Collected Writings* [*CW*], X: 88), the gold exchange standard (Ingot Plan) (*CW*, I: 22, 51; V: 296; XIX: 357, 377–8) and the purchasing power parity theory (*CW*, IV) or pointing out the lack of a discussion of bank rate policy in Ricardo's writings (*CW*, V: 167). These statements predominantly stem from the time up to 1930.

However, after the publication of his *Treatise on Money* (*CW*, V and VI) in 1930 the tone changes completely and Keynes becomes extremely critical of Ricardo. These critical remarks can be found in his biographical essay on Malthus (*CW*, X: 71–108), his book *The General Theory of Employment, Interest and Money* published in 1936 (*CW*, VII) and some material written in preparation of the *General Theory* (*CW*, XIII and XXIX).

According to Keynes it was extremely unfortunate for the development of economic theory that 'Ricardo conquered England as completely as the Holy Inquisition conquered Spain' (*CW*, VII: 32; a somewhat misplaced remark, one should add, directed, as it is, against a descendant of Sephardic Jews; see Kurz, 2008, on this biographical detail and for a qualification of Keynes's statement about Ricardo's influence). Because of his 'pseudo-arithmetical doctrines' (*CW*, X: 88), Ricardo 'constrained the subject [of economics] for a full hundred years in an artificial groove' (ibid.: 97) because '[t]he great puzzle of effective demand . . . vanished from economic literature' (*CW*, VII: 32). Therefore, the 'complete domination of Ricardo's for a period of a hundred years has been a disaster to the progress of economics' (*CW*, X: 98; see also VII: 3; this indictment of Ricardo is similar to the one pronounced by Jevons some six decades earlier – see *CW*, X: 136).

This 'disaster' spawned 'envelopes of . . . misguided education' obscuring 'what should never have ceased to be obvious' (ibid.: 101) and had adverse effects on the welfare of economies – but could have been avoided, if Malthus, whom Keynes considered to be his predecessor, had prevailed in the great debate with Ricardo on the possibility of 'general gluts' or, more specifically, the role of aggregate demand in the determination of the rate of profits: 'If only Malthus, instead of Ricardo, had been the parent stem from which nineteenth-century economics proceeded, what a much wiser and richer place the world would be to-day!' (ibid.)

But before entering into a discussion of Keynes's critical assessment of Ricardo, attention should be drawn to a glimpse of Ricardo's 'invariable standard of value' (at least similar to Sraffa's later version) flashing up in the *General Theory* entirely unexpectedly. In Chapter 4 ('The Choice of Units', written in 1934 and drawing on ideas first presented in Keynes's Michaelmas lectures for 1933) of the *General Theory* Keynes discussed various possibilities of aggregating the 'non-homogeneous complex' of 'the community's output of goods and services' (*CW*, VII: 38) into one variable that would allow for general statements about changes in demand, income and employment, because he had moved from the Marshallian analysis of a single market to the analysis of output as a whole. As he did not take recourse to the analytical trick of modern times of simply assuming away the heterogeneity of goods and labour, Keynes pointed out that under such circumstances income cannot be measured in physical terms, 'except in certain special cases, as for example when all the items of one output are included in the same proportions in another output' (ibid.). This can be compared with a note by Sraffa, written in 1931, contemplating ' the case in which "the value of total capital in terms of total goods produced cannot vary [as income distribution changes], since the goods are composed exactly in the same proportions as the capitals which have produced them" (D3/12/7: 157(3))' (Kurz and Salvadori, 2008: 263).

In order to understand the reasons for Keynes's damning verdict against Ricardo, and assess their validity, some preparatory remarks are necessary concerning on the one hand, Keynes's view of the relation between the economic theories of Ricardo (or classical economics proper) and Marshall (neoclassical or marginalist economics), and on the other hand, his growing disenchantment with the economic doctrines of Marshall, Pigou and others starting after the publication of his *Treatise on Money*.

Keynes accepted Marshall's claim of continuity of economic analysis from Ricardo to Marshall and, adding Pigou and other contemporary economists, spoke of a single school (or tradition) of 'classical economists' (sometimes 'orthodox economists') as the object of his criticism after 1930 (*CW*, VII: 3, 33). He expressed this view as follows: 'It is generally recognised that the Ricardian analysis was concerned with what we now call long-period equilibrium. Marshall's contribution mainly consisted in grafting on to this the marginal principle and the principle of substitution' (*CW*, XIV: 112; for similar statements see the forewords to the *General Theory*). Because of this perceived continuity Keynes, as will become clear in what follows, always tended to ascribe theoretical results of marginalist economists (like Pigou), especially concerning the equilibrium level of output and employment, to Ricardo as well.

Soon after the publication of his *Treatise on Money* Keynes realized that the analysis he had developed was flawed because the full-employment long-period position serving as the reference for his discussion of monetary theory and monetary policy ran the danger of being unstable. His solution to this problem, leading to the notion of the investment multiplier, was the assumption of a marginal propensity to consume with a value of less than one (Barens, 1989) together with the notion that savings and invest-ment were two distinct entities brought into equality by changes in output and employ-ment. But this implied, according to Keynes, that Say's Law was invalid and that the long-period position of the economy could entail any level of output and employment, depending on the propensity to consume vis-à-vis the level of investment demand, which in turn depended on the rate of interest. The possibility that the economy could, and in general would, gravitate towards a level of employment below full employment because of excessive savings (compared to the level of investment as determined by marginal effi-ciency of capital and the rate of interest) turned Keynes into a heretic who would fight orthodox, that is, marginalist economic theory because of its notion of a self-adjusting economic system from within its citadel (*CW*, XIII: 489). As a by-product, the Ricardian foundations of Marxism would be pushed away (ibid.: 488 and XXVIII: 42).

Keynes was convinced that the invalidity of Say's Law, which he interpreted as equal-ity of aggregate demand (price) and aggregate supply (price) at any level of output and employment (*CW*, VII: 25 and 29), was caused by money as it was used in the economy 'in which we happen to live' (*CW*, X: 97). This money was not neutral but due to some 'essential properties' opened up the possibility of leakages from the circular flow of incomes and aggregate demand (price) and aggregate supply (price) being equal at only one level of output and employment. If, instead, Say's Law was valid, there would be no barrier that could keep 'the forces of competition between entrepreneurs' from pushing employment to its maximum (or optimum), that is, full employment level (*CW*, VII: 26 and 29; for the many interpretations of the meaning of Say's Law see Baumol, 1977 and Clower and Leijonhufvud, 1973).

Because Keynes was convinced that the orthodox theory of his days, that is, marginal-ist theory, was free of logical flaws in its analysis he searched for 'its tacit assumptions' that 'are seldom or never satisfied, with the result that it cannot solve the economic prob-lems of the actual world' (*CW*, VII: 378; see also ibid.: xxi and XXIX: 79). Attempting to pin down these crucial but implicit assumptions, he sketched out a taxonomy of model economies: in a barter economy without use of money and a cooperative (real-wage) economy using 'money merely as a temporary convenience, with a view to spending the whole of it forthwith on ... current output' (*CW*, XXIX: 76–7) no involuntary unem-ployment could arise. An entrepreneur economy (money-wage or monetary economy), when left to its own devices, could, and in general would, gravitate towards involuntary unemployment. In addition, he conceived of a neutral entrepreneur economy (neutral money economy), in which the non-neutrality of money was sterilized by appropriate means and full employment would prevail (ibid.: 66–101: see Barens, 1990 for a discus-sion of these various model economies).

With this mind-set Keynes, in 1933, prepared his biographical essay on Thomas Robert Malthus for publication. In the years before he had already read this essay to the Political Economy Club at Cambridge on various occasions, but now he had access to Malthus's letters to Ricardo that had recently been discovered by the editor of the works and letters of Ricardo, Sraffa, 'from whom nothing is hid', as Keynes famously put it (*CW*, X: 97; see the editorial note at the beginning of the essay for details of the changes in the final version due to this new material). In this correspondence he saw Malthus struggling to convince Ricardo that aggregate demand, effective demand in Malthus's parlance (ibid.: 99), must not be neglected in economic analysis and stressing the possibility of savings becoming excessive, while Ricardo was 'stone-deaf' to Malthus's arguments (*CW*, VII: 364), instead defending Say's Law and, while indeed assuming the use of money in his reasoning, only allowing for its passive role as a medium of exchange (*Works*, I: 291–2; see also VII: 32–3).

There were no doubts in the mind of Keynes that in their great debate about the relevance of aggregate demand Malthus had been right and Ricardo had been wrong. He expressed this verdict in terms of his model economies: 'Malthus is dealing with the *monetary economy* in which we happen to live; Ricardo with the abstraction of a *neutral money economy*' (*CW*, X: 97; emphasis added; see also XXIX: 67 where Marshall is added to Ricardo). And elsewhere Keynes conjectures that 'the classical theory is, in effect, assuming either a co-operative or neutral economy' (*CW*, XXIX: 101; for an argument to the same effect, but without reference to model economies, see *CW*, VII: 243–4). The upshot of this is evident: Keynes was convinced that Ricardo held the view of the economy gravitating towards a long-period full-employment position, and this was the ultimate reason for his disapproval; Malthus, on the contrary, by allegedly dealing with a monetary or entrepreneur economy allowed, so Keynes thought, for the possibility that 'the volume of employment, the marginal disutility of which is equal to the utility of its marginal product, may be "unprofitable" in terms of money' (*CW*, XXIX: 79). In the *General Theory*, Keynes repeats this allegation concerning Ricardo's stance on full employment, now explicitly within the framework of long-period positions:

> Ricardo and his successors overlook the fact that even in the long period the volume of employment is not necessarily full . . . and that to every banking policy there corresponds a different long-period level of employment; so that there are a number of positions of long-period equilibrium corresponding to different conceivable interest policies on the part of the monetary authority. (*CW*, VII: 191; see also XIII: 408 and XXIX: 57 for earlier versions of this argument)

It is striking that Keynes never did supply direct textual evidence verifying that Ricardo indeed was of the opinion that the economy would be gravitating towards full employment. He only arrived at his conjecture by way of a very precarious line of reasoning:

1. Ricardo accepted Say's Law.
2. According to his understanding this implies equality of aggregate demand (price) and aggregate supply (price) at any level of output and employment.
3. This, in turn, implies that no barrier could inhibit the 'natural tendency' (*CW*, VII: 33) towards full employment.
4. Therefore Ricardo must have held the view that the long-period position of the economy would necessarily entail full employment; Q.E.D.

Before the validity of this reasoning will be assessed, attention should be drawn to a striking similarity between the form of Malthus's critique of Ricardo and Keynes's critique of orthodox theory. Malthus conceded that Ricardo did give a valid account of the factors determining the upper limit or maximum level of the rate of profits but insisted that 'limitation is essentially different from regulation' (Malthus, 1836: 275–6), that is, that the actual level of the rate of profits was determined quite differently, with aggregate demand playing a decisive role (Kurz, 1998). Keynes accepted that orthodox theory determined the maximum level of output and employment quite correctly but insisted that it failed to determined their actual levels. Thus, on the very first page of the *General Theory*, Keynes framed his disagreement with marginalist economic theory just like Malthus did concerning his disagreement with Ricardo:

> I shall argue that the postulates of the classical theory are applicable to a special case only and not to the general case, the situation which it assumes being a *limiting point* of the possible positions of equilibrium. Moreover, the characteristics of the special case assumed by the classical theory happen not to be those of the economic society in which we *actually* live. (*CW*, VII: 3; emphasis added)

With the benefit of hindsight, it is possible to recognize where Keynes went astray in his interpretation of Ricardo and the 'classical economists'. He did not recognize that despite the methodological continuity from Ricardo to Marshall and Pigou (and the author of the *Treatise on Money* as well!), that is, long-period positions being the object of economic analysis, a decisive discontinuity had occurred with the advent of marginalist (or neoclassical) economic theory, which proceeded to determine the characteristics of long-period positions (prices of commodities, rates of remuneration of factors of production) in terms of demand and supply (Garegnani, 1976). Determining the real wage at the equilibrium of demand for and supply of labour necessarily implied that the economy gravitates towards or around full employment of labour. But this does not seem to have been Ricardo's position (see below). Instead, the 'natural tendency', referred to above, hinged on what Keynes had labelled the 'postulates of the classical economics' (*CW*, VII: 4–7) and these were nothing but a paraphrase of marginalist labour market equilibrium conditions.

Thus, Keynes was barking up the wrong tree when he chastised Ricardo for his alleged belief in a long-period full-employment equilibrium position. But maybe Keynes could have been warned. He was quite aware that Ricardo did not adhere to a marginalist explanation of commodity prices (*CW*, XIII: 516); he suspected that he 'was overlooking' the inverse relation between the rate of interest and the demand for capital derived by marginalist economists (*CW*, VII: 192); he emphasized that Ricardo considered the distribution of income and not its level to be the object of economic analysis (*CW*, X: 97). Finally, and most importantly, on the second page of his *General Theory* he even quoted from a letter of Ricardo to Malthus (9 October 1820) (*CW*, VII: 4), in which Ricardo explicitly states that: '[n]o law can be laid down respecting quantity, but a tolerably correct one can be laid down respecting proportions. Every day I am more satisfied that the former enquiry is vain and delusive, and the latter only the true objects of the science' (*Works*, VIII: 279). But, unfortunately, Keynes did not realize that inferring that Ricardo saw the economy with necessity gravitating towards full employment from his acceptance of Say's Law amounted to tacitly assuming and falsely attributing to Ricardo a quite specific 'law respecting quantity', that is, the one developed by marginalist economists. Therefore, in the end, one has to realize that everything that Keynes said about Ricardo after 1930 is not very reliable, to say the least, but, instead, very informative about Keynes himself.

It is ironic that Malthus, to whom Keynes gave so much praise, did not share Keynes's view of savings and investment – and therefore would not have Keynes's 'monetary economy' in mind (his attack on Say's Law being rejected by Ricardo for good reason, see Kalmbach and Kurz, 2009), while Ricardo had no need to take recourse to Keynes's 'neutral money economy' because of his scepticism concerning a 'law respecting quantity'. The irony is amplified by the fact that Ricardo's approach, so scornfully dismissed by Keynes, would, in the hands of Sraffa and others (Garegnani, 1978, 1979), become the foundation for a critique of the notion of capital as a factor of production and, by implication, for a critique of the object of Keynes's endeavour (*CW*, XIII: 486): the marginalist notion of an self-adjusting economy system.

INGO BARENS

See also:

Kaldor, Nicholas, on Ricardo; Malthus–Ricardo Debate; Say's Law.

References

Barens, I. (1989), 'From the "banana parable" to the principle of effective demand. Some reflections on the origin, development and structure of Keynes' *General Theory*', in D.A. Walker (ed.), *Perspectives on the History of Economic Thought, Vol. II: Twentieth-Century Economic Thought. Selected Papers from the History of Economics Society Conference 1987*, Aldershot, UK and Brookfield, VT: Edward Elgar Publishing, pp. 111–32.

Barens, I. (1990), 'The rise and fall of the "entrepreneur economy": some remarks on Keynes's taxonomy of economies', in D.E. Moggridge (ed.), *Perspectives on the History of Economic Thought, Vol. IV: Keynes, Macroeconomics and Method. Selected Papers from the History of Economics Society Conference 1988*, Aldershot, UK and Brookfield, VT: Edward Elgar Publishing, pp. 85–102.

Baumol, W. (1977), 'Say's (at least) eight laws, or what say and James Mill may really have meant', *Economica*, **44**(174), 145–61.

Clower, R.W. and A. Leijonhufvud (1973), 'Say's principle, what it means and doesn't mean', *Intermountain Economic Review*, **4**, 1–16.

Garegnani, P. (1976), 'On a change in the notion of equilibrium in recent work on value and distribution. A comment on Samuelson', in M. Brown, K. Sato and P. Zarembka (eds), *Essays in Modern Capital Theory*, Amsterdam/New York: North-Holland, pp. 25–45.

Garegnani, P. (1978), 'Notes on consumption, investment and effective demand: I', *Cambridge Journal of Economics*, **2**(4), 335–53.

Garegnani, P. (1979), 'Notes on consumption, investment and effective demand: II', *Cambridge Journal of Economics*, **3**(1), 63–82.

Kalmbach, P. and H.D. Kurz (2009), 'Malthus: Vorgänger von Keynes?', in H. Hagemann, G. Horn and H.-J. Krupp (eds), *Aus gesamtwirtschaftlicher Sicht*, Marburg: Metropolis-Verlag, pp. 163–83.

Keynes, J.M. (1971–89), *The Collected Writings of John Maynard Keynes*, 30 vols, (eds) E. Johnson and D. Moggridge, London: Macmillan; citation given as *CW* followed by volume number and page number.

Kurz, H.D. (1998), 'Limiting and regulating principles', in H.D. Kurz and N. Salvadori (eds), *The Elgar Companion to Classical Economics, Vol. 2*, Cheltenham, UK und Lyme, NH: Edward Elgar Publishing, pp. 45–50.

Kurz, H.D. (2008), 'David Ricardo (1772–1823)', in H.D. Kurz (ed.), *Klassiker des ökonomischen Denkens, Vol. 1: Von Adam Smith bis Alfred Marshall*, Munich: C.H. Beck, pp. 120–39.

Kurz, H.D. and N. Salvadori (2008), 'On the collaboration between Sraffa and Besicovitch: the "proof of gradient"', in G. Chiodi and L. Ditta (eds), *Sraffa or an Alternative Economics*, New York: Palgrave Macmillan, pp. 260–74.

Malthus, T.R. (1836), *Principles in Political Economy*, 2nd edition, London: W. Pickering.

Labour and Wages

The revival of the surplus approach to economic analysis and the critique of the marginalist theory of distribution based on factor demand functions, both originating in the contributions by Piero Sraffa (1960 and his introduction to *Works*, I), brought about a renewed interest for the classical theory of distribution. However, the interpretation of Ricardo's wage theory has proved very controversial. It has often been portrayed either as very similar to the marginalist theory, or essentially based on population adjustment following a departure of wages from the subsistence minimum – a mechanism that could hardly be of interest for current economic analysis.

The following will provide an overview of the main contents of Ricardo's writings on wages and their interpretations offering a somewhat unusual perspective, that is, that there are major similarities between the two interpretations that have been usually regarded as the main contenders, the so-called 'new view' and 'fix-wage' interpretations. Owing to these similarities, the controversy has tended to neglect a decisive point for the interpretation of the theory of wages in Ricardo, namely, what exactly is the meaning of the expression 'demand for labour' – whether a given number of labourers, a 'wages fund' or a demand function. It will also be maintained that there is a third point of view concerning the interpretation of wage theory in the classical economists, which has not always been accurately understood and discussed in earlier surveys of the controversy on the interpretation of Ricardo. Unlike the others, this 'alternative interpretation', as I shall label it for brevity, centres on the absence of a systematic decreasing relation between real wage and employment levels in Ricardo and other classical economists. Viewed in this perspective then, the classical approach to income distribution would appear as quite distinct from subsequent theoretical developments in this field, and a viable alternative to the explanation of distribution based on supply and demand curves. The alternative interpretation will be presented in some detail, and subsequently some questions arising from Ricardo's definitions of market and natural wages will be assessed.

Ricardo's definitions of the natural and market price of labour

The enduring controversy on the interpretation of Ricardo's wage theory, and by implication on classical wage theory, has undoubtedly been favoured by the existence of some difficulties in Ricardo's own writings on wages. We can thus proceed to examine Ricardo's main definitions and propositions concerning wages, so as to understand some of the problems underlying the controversy. In reading Ricardo, it must be kept in mind that the natural wage is a money wage, but the value of money is assumed constant through the analysis (*Works*, I: 97).

Ricardo provides definitions of the natural and market price of labour that match those of the natural and market price of any other commodity. The natural price thus reflects the costs of subsistence of the labourer and his family. As understood by the classical tradition, however, these costs are determined by habit and therefore subject to change in different historical and social circumstances:

> Labour, like all other things which are purchased and sold, and which may be increased or
> diminished in quantity, has its natural and its market price. The natural price of labour is that

price which is necessary to enable the labourers, one with another, to subsist and perpetuate their race, without either increase or diminution.

The power of the labourer to support himself and the family which may be necessary to keep up the number of labourers ... depend on ... the quantity of food, necessaries and conveniences *become essential to him from habit* ... The natural price of labour, therefore, depends on the price of food, necessaries and conveniences required for the support of the labourer and his family. (Ibid.: 93; emphasis added)

The above definition of the natural price allows Ricardo to make a point that is very much at the centre of his concerns as an economist: the effect of increased costs of production in agriculture, causing an increase in the relative price of necessaries, will bring about an increase in wages, and hence a fall in the rate of profit:

With a rise in the price of food and necessaries, the natural price of labour will rise ... With the progress of society the natural price of labour has always a tendency to rise, because one of the principal commodities by which its natural price is regulated, has a tendency to become dearer, from the greater difficulty to produce it. (Ibid.)

It is admitted, however, that improvements in agriculture or imports from other countries 'may for a time counteract the tendency to a rise in the price of necessaries' (ibid.).

The market price of labour is the actual price, which reflects the proportion of supply to demand, but has a tendency to converge to the natural price owing to the tendency of supply to adjust to the quantity demanded. In the case of labour, it is the population that tends to adjust when the market wage differs from the natural wage:

The market price of labour is the price which is really paid for it, from the natural operation of the proportion of the supply to the demand; labour is dear when it is scarce, and cheap when it is plentiful. However much the market price of labour may deviate from the natural price, it has, like commodities, a tendency to conform to it.

It is when the market price of labour exceeds its natural price that the condition of the labourer is flourishing and happy ... however, by the encouragement which high wages give to the increase of population, the number of labourers is increased, wages again fall to their natural price ...

When the market price of labour is below its natural price, the condition of the labourers is most wretched ... after their privations have reduced their number, or the demand for labour has increased, the market price for labour will rise to its natural price. (Ibid.: 94)

These definitions involve a difficulty that has fuelled the controversy. Ricardo generally regards market prices as transitory deviations from the natural price, and tending to converge to or around the latter. But in the case of labour the mechanism that should bring about this adjustment is much slower and even uncertain in its operation, very much unlike any other produced commodity, and Ricardo is very well aware of this difference:

Notwithstanding the tendency of wages to conform to their natural rate, their market rate may, in an improving society, for an indefinite period, be constantly above it; for no sooner may the impulse, which an increased capital gives to a new demand for labour be obeyed, that another increase of capital may produce the same effect; and thus, if the increase of capital be gradual and constant, the demand for labour may give a continuous stimulus to an increase of people. (Ibid.: 95)

Actually, the process described above might, to some extent, occur for any commodity the demand for which should be ever increasing as accumulation proceeds. But in the case of labour the adjustment of supply requires much more time:

> [L]abour is a commodity which cannot be increased and diminished at pleasure. If there are too few hats in the market for the demand, the price will rise, but only for a short time; for in the course of one year, by employing more capital in that trade, any reasonable addition may be made to the quantity of hats, and therefore their market price cannot long very much exceed their natural price; but it is not so with men; you cannot increase their number in one or two years when there is an increase of capital, nor can you rapidly decrease their numbers when capital is in a retrograde state . . . therefore . . . *there must be a considerable interval before the price of labour be exactly regulated by the price of corn and necessaries.* (Ibid.: 165–6; emphasis added)

In addition to this, Ricardo in some instances expresses doubts even on the existence and direction of the effect of high wages on population: 'The increase of population . . . will generally be the effect, but not the necessary effect of high wages' (ibid.: 406–7); 'population may be so little stimulated by ample wages as to increase at the slowest rate – or it may even go in a retrograde direction' (Letter to McCulloch, 29 March 1820, *Works*, VIII: 169); 'population and necessaries are not necessarily linked so intimately . . . It is not difficult to conceive that with better education and improved habits, a day's labour may become much more valuable estimated even in what are now called the necessaries of the labourer' (*Works*, II: 115).

Ricardo summarizes his discussion of wages by stating that wages are subject to change from two causes: '1st. The supply and demand of labourers. 2dly. The price of commodities on which the wages of labour are expended' (*Works*, I: 97).It is clear from his definitions of market and natural price of labour that Ricardo envisages a hierarchy between these two causes, whereby the second has a more persistent and structural nature than the first. But this may appear inconsistent with his statements concerning the possibility for market wages to diverge from the natural wage even for long time spans. However, it will be maintained below that these difficulties in Ricardo wage theory may, after all, carry less weight than is usually believed.

The interpretations of Ricardo's wage theory

The 'new view' interpretation is generally associated with the work of Samuelson (1978), Casarosa (1978) and Hicks and Hollander (1977). On the basis of the definitions seen above, and particularly of the statement that in a growing economy the market wage may be persistently above the natural one, this interpretation defines the natural wage as the wage just sufficient to support a stationary population, and maintains that it will only prevail in the final stationary state, towards which the economy tends in the very long run as a consequence of decreasing returns in agriculture. According to the new view, before reaching this state, what we may label (on the basis of the generally accepted use in economics) the *normal* wage rate is what Ricardo calls the market price of labour, determined by 'supply and demand'. The wage thus determined may be regarded as the normal wage (or long period wage, according to Marshall's classification) because it is the wage determined in a given state of the economy by the data of the system, ignoring both short-term accidental and transitory factors and secular changes such as those determined by capital accumulation and demographic change. For some representatives of the new view, the normal 'equilibrium' wage is that particular level of the market wage that equalizes the growth rates of population and capital, these being an increasing and a decreasing function of the wage rate, respectively. The proponents of this interpretation claim interdependence among economic variables and similarity between classical and neoclassical theories. According to Casarosa, for example, there is interdependence between 'the wage rate, the rate of profit and the rates of growth of population and capital', which are 'simultaneously determined' (Casarosa, 1982: 228). For Samuelson, the claimed interdependence is one between distribution, relative prices and outputs, implicitly of the same nature as that found in marginalist theory (Samuelson, 1978: 1420). This view has been regarded as inconsistent with, and indeed opposed to, Sraffa's interpretation of Ricardo. In the latter, the real wage and the quantities produced are taken as given when determining the rate of profits and relative prices. For example, Peach has written: 'acceptance of the *New view* would dissolve the perception of Ricardo as a "surplus theorist" in any meaningful sense' (Peach, 1988: 111; original emphasis).

The other main contender in the controversy is the fix-wage interpretation, mainly associated with Kaldor (1955–66) and Pasinetti (1960). According to this view, wages tend to be at their natural subsistence level in Ricardo owing to the response of population to a divergence between market wages and subsistence. The real wage accordingly should be taken as given at its natural level when determining relative prices and the rate of profits. This is consistent with Ricardo's analogy between labour and any other commodity and with his analysis of the effects of increased costs of production in agriculture on the rate of profit. Such analysis is a central concern in Ricardo's work, and is based on the tendency of wages to be at their natural level. This interpretation is also regarded as consistent with Sraffa's interpretation of Ricardo, and with the procedure of determining relative prices and the rate of profit, taking the real wage as given (as in Pasinetti, 1960). This point will be taken up again in the next section.

New view and fix-wage interpretations are similar in one specific but very important respect: the economic forces determining wages in any given period, that is, given population size and capital stock (the normal wage according to the definition provided above). In both streams of interpretation, the real wage is determined on the basis of the wages-fund theory (or, in the case of Hicks and Hollander, 1977, of 'factor substitution') and a given labour supply.

Thus if, for example, the wage is higher than the natural wage, population grows and the ratio between the wages-fund and population falls until the equilibrium wage equals the natural wage. This is made clear by the following: 'the feature which the modern mind may find most difficult to swallow is not that capital accumulation should lead to a rise in population but that the reaction should be taken as something so swift as to ignore the intervening stage, *where the increase in the wages fund should raise the rate of wages rather than the numbers employed*' (Kaldor, 1955–56: 86fn; emphasis added). In Pasinetti, the current real wage is similarly determined by the ratio of the given wages-fund to the population and the tendency towards the natural wage depends on the reaction of population to the difference between current and natural wage: in his representation of Ricardo's system, the equation that determines the 'scale' of the economy is $W = xN$ (1960: 83). In the market equilibrium, W (the wages fund, which also represents total advanced capital) and N (the level of employment equal to the given labour supply) are given variables and x (the real wage) is endogenously determined as the 'market' full-employment equilibrium wage (ibid.: 83 and 86, see also 81, 84). In the natural equilibrium, x has reached its natural level through population adjustment. In new view contributions such as Casarosa (1978: 43) we find the same view. Hicks and Hollander (1977) attribute to Ricardo a decreasing demand schedule for labour based on decreasing marginal product. In the first part of his 'classical canonical model', Samuelson assumes neither a given wages fund nor substitution between labour and capital, hence ruling out a decreasing demand schedule for labour, and draws from this rather extreme conclusions (see next section), only to later state that: 'Ricardo and Marx were not so naïve observers as to believe literally in fixed proportions between capital goods and labour. Their . . . commentaries presuppose recognition that at certain price and profit rates, substitutions will be made' (Samuelson, 1978: 1423). Thus, the two views are not really so far apart in the interpretation of what forces determine the normal wage rate in a given period, given population and capital stock. This is regarded as determined by the interaction of a decreasing demand function (based either on the wages-fund theory or on factor substitution) and a given labour supply (population) and is a *full-employment equilibrium wage*. Accordingly, the tendency of this equilibrium wage to coincide with the subsistence natural wage or to be very close to it simply depends on the assumptions made concerning the reaction of population growth to the difference between it and the subsistence minimum. The similarity of the views concerning the 'demand side' of the labour market on both sides of the controversy has placed the focus on the speed of population adjustment as the ultimate determinant of the correctness of either interpretation.

Finally, the wages-fund interpretation of Ricardo's theory in fix-wage contributions casts some doubts on the consistency of the latter with Sraffa's reading of Ricardo and the meaning he attributed to the return to the classical approach. There is evidence in his manuscripts that Sraffa saw the advantage of this approach as being the absence of a mechanical or 'natural' determination of distribution, a determination that is independent of the actions undertaken by the parties (see Pivetti, 1999, for discussion of this point and quotations from Sraffa's unpublished papers); by contrast, the emergence of the wages-fund doctrine brought with it precisely such a notion of a 'natural' determination of distribution.

In the literature there is a third line of interpretation of the theory of wages in Ricardo, consistent with the reading of Ricardo as a 'surplus theorist' (Garegnani, 1984, 1990; Stirati, 1992, 1994; before the controversy developed, also see Napoleoni, 1974: 65–6; 68–70; a similar perspective, albeit with a different focus, is in Picchio, 1992). According to this 'alternative interpretation', in the classical economists up to and including Ricardo (but with the exception of Malthus), there was no notion of a systematic inverse relation between wages and employment level. The demand for labour is rather a given quantity, associated with the productive capacity existing in the system and the technologies embodied in it. In the chapter on wages of the *Principles* Ricardo maintains that capital is that part of the wealth of a nation consisting of 'food, clothing, *tools*, *raw materials*, *machinery*, etc., necessary to give effect to labour' (*Works*, I: 95; emphasis added) and states that 'in proportion to the increase of capital will be the demand for labour; in proportion to the work to be done will be the demand for those who are to do it' (ibid.). Hence the demand for labour depends on the existing capital, and the latter is clearly defined as 'productive capacity' including fixed capital – that is, is not defined as a 'wages fund'. The full utilization of the existing productive capacity, reflecting the existing technology and output composition, will require a certain amount of employed labour ('in proportion to the work to be done will be the demand'). Thus, the proportion between supply and demand for labour is simply the ratio of the number of workers required by employers and the working class population, that is, what we now call the employment rate, an indicator of labour market conditions.

There is an obvious analogy with the definition of effectual demand for a commodity (*WN*, I.vii.7–8, fully accepted by Ricardo, *Works*, I: 91). In the case of commodities, the 'proportion of demand to supply' is the ratio between two given quantities: effectual demand and 'quantity brought to market'. Actually, the contemporary critics of J.S. Mill's wages-fund doctrine opposed the just described notion of demand to that proposed in the wages-fund theory: Longe wrote: 'a ratio between demand and supply is only intelligible if by demand we mean the quantity demanded . . . The demand for a commodity then is not the quantity of money wherewith it is to be purchased, but the quantity of the commodity itself wanted by purchasers' ([1866] 1903: 34; see also Thornton, [1870] 1971: 49–50, 87). Hence, the notion of 'effectual demand' as a given quantity was widespread at the time, and the wages-fund theory introduced a different notion of demand for labour that was regarded as incorrect and inconsistent with the common use of the term.

Thus, according to the alternative interpretation, in Ricardo we do not find a tendency towards full employment of labour, since there is no demand curve for labour inversely related to the wage. This is consistent with the conclusions of Ricardo's chapter 'On Machinery', where he maintains that the introduction of the latter may 'be injurious to the labouring class, as some of their number will be thrown out of employment, and population will become redundant' (*Works*, I: 390). In that same chapter Ricardo writes that a 'redundant population' and 'competition for employment' 'will sink the value of wages and very materially deteriorate the condition of the labouring class' (ibid.: 394), but nowhere regarding this as causing a re-employment of the workers made redundant by the introduction of machinery. The latter, according to Ricardo, *may* only gradually come about by means of additional investments and capital accumulation. These conclusions have often puzzled modern interpreters, who could not reconcile them with the notion of an inverse relation between wage level and employment: Wicksell ([1924] 1981) and Schumpeter ([1954] 1982: 683), for example, were much perplexed by Ricardo's conclusions, and pointed out that the workers made redundant by the introduction of machinery, according to 'fundamental economic principles' (i.e., to marginalist theory), would compete for employment, cause a fall in wages, and hence render more profitable the adoption of processes with a higher labour intensity, leading to a return to full employment.

The alternative interpretation also claims consistency with another aspect in the interpretation of Ricardo that has often been found 'puzzling' – his analysis of the incidence of taxation (on both taxation and machinery see Stirati, 1999: 205–6, 218–22). In the case of taxation of wages or necessaries, Ricardo thought that money wages would rise so as to leave workers' after-tax purchasing power unaltered: 'in the case of a tax on corn, there is not necessarily any excess in the supply of labour, nor any abatement of demand, and therefore there can be no reason why the labourer should sustain a real diminution of wages' (*Works*, I: 165–6). According to Ricardo, in sharp contrast with what was later maintained on the basis of the wages-fund theory by J.S. Mill (among others), wages would adjust rapidly, and the adjustment would *not* require any change in population: 'no interval which could bear oppressively on the labourer, would elapse between the rise in the price of raw produce, and the rise in the wages of the labourer' (ibid.; see also 161 and VIII: 196). Such conclusion, it may be noted, is also inconsistent with the interpretation of Ricardo as a precursor of Marshallian theory (Stirati, 2011: 328), however, it is consistent with a reading based on the absence of a decreasing demand function for labour. In the terms Ricardo himself uses, since the tax has not altered the proportion between the quantity of labour demanded and its supply, and since, it may be added, the historical factors determining the subsistence of the workers are also unchanged, the forces determining the real wages that the workers can obtain are unaltered. In other words, the relative bargaining position of the workers is not affected, and they will be able to obtain the increase in money wages that is required to preserve their purchasing power.

Indeed, if demand for labour means a given quantity, then the proportion of labour demand (that is, employment) to labouring population must be regarded as one of the factors affecting the bargaining position of the parties when they establish the wage rate. It should be emphasized that the term 'bargaining position' is meant here to refer to the ability of the parties to impose favourable conditions of the labour contract in processes of collective or individual bargaining, but does not *necessarily* refer to situations in which there exist forms of monopoly or monopsony in the labour market. For example, the 'disputes' between the master and his employees referred to by Smith (*WN*, I.viii.2), suggest forms of collective bargaining in situations in which, however, there are no well-organized 'combinations' of workers (see also Garegnani, 2007: 217–19).

Although labour market conditions, described by the proportion of the employed population, play a prominent part in Ricardo's analysis of the causes of changes in wages, he did not rule out the role of other institutional factors (which had been emphasized by Adam Smith). For example, he believed that workers' combinations could bring about a permanent increase in workers' income share, and criticized Malthus's opinion that a wage increase brought about by workers' combinations would cause unemployment: 'A combination among the workmen would increase the amount of money to be divided among the labouring class' (Letter to Malthus, 21 October 1817, *Works*, VII: 202–3).

Following this interpretation, the two sets of circumstances listed by Ricardo as the causes of changes in wages (see above) can be described as follows: (1) economic and institutional factors affecting the bargaining position of the parties – among these, Ricardo gave prominence to the ratio between the quantity of labour demanded and population; and (2) the living standards of the workers, determined by historical circumstances – accordingly, Ricardo maintains that the natural price (cost of production) of the subsistence basket of commodities determines the natural wage in money terms (with an assumed constant value of money). The first set of conditions affect the wage level in relation to and within boundaries determined by the latter.

Thus, according to this reading of Ricardo's wage theory, its distinctive character with respect to both wages-fund and marginalist theories rests essentially on the differences between the forces determining normal wages in a given period (i.e., given the size of population and the stage reached by capital accumulation), that is, on the absence of a systematic decreasing relation between wages and employment level and hence of the tendency to full employment.

The absence of a systematic decreasing relation between wages and employment level in turn imposes a non-mechanical analysis of the forces determining the wage rate. In this light it can be argued that a separate analysis of wage rate determination and the determination of relative prices in the classical approach is associated with the necessarily different levels of abstraction and generality of their explanations. In the case of wages, institutional and historical analysis is an essential aspect of the enquiry.

The problems arising from Ricardo's definitions
As seen above, the focus of the new view has been on the fact that various passages in Ricardo suggest that what he defines as the market wage can be persistently above subsistence in a growing economy. This, according to various contributions to the debate: (1) would deny convergence of wages towards the natural wage except in the stationary state; and (2) would deny the possibility of taking wages as given at their subsistence levels when determining relative prices, and would create an interdependence between the wage actually prevailing, the rate of profit and the rate of accumulation that can only be solved by simultaneous determination. This, as we have seen above, is considered to conflict with the possibility of describing the analytical structure of Ricardo's theory as a 'surplus approach'.

Concerning problem (1), two comments can be made. On one hand, the claim that the natural wage would prevail only in the stationary state does not appear well-founded and contrasts with several important aspects of Ricardo's analysis. As emphasized in fix-wage contributions, Ricardo regarded the stationary state as a remote possibility, while the notion that wages tend to be at their natural level is central in his analysis of changes in the rate of profits *before* the stationary state is reached by the economy. On the other hand, it is true that in Ricardo there are some contradictions that derive from a definition of the natural wage in analogy with the natural price of a commodity that is too restrictive for it to characterize the normal wage actually prevailing in the economy in any given period (which might be influenced, for example – as recognized by Smith – by persistently tight labour market conditions, or persistently high unemployment). As maintained in Stirati (1995) this might be due to Ricardo's willingness to make his conclusions concerning the effects of increasing costs in agriculture on the rate of profits more clear-cut, by playing down the possible countervailing effect on wages deriving from a declining growth rate of the economy (and hence of employment) as the rate of profits falls, which had been advocated by Malthus.

Yet these problems do not have the implications claimed with respect to point (2). Even conceding the new view's mechanical interpretation of the relationship between the wage and the rate of growth of capital and population, this, by itself, would not be in contrast with taking the normal wage as given in any period (that is, given population size and capital stock). The relations between wage and growth rates of population and capital emphasized by the new view concern the secular movement of the normal wage, and cannot substitute an explanation of the latter in a given period. One may recall here, for example, that in marginalist theory the secular changes of the equilibrium wage depend on the relative growth of capital and population, and the former depends on the rate of interest. However, inquiry into these relations is left to growth theory, and equilibrium wages in any given period are simply determined, irrespective of those relations, by the interaction of supply and demand schedules, which are constructed under the assumption of given capital and given population. In a similar way from the point of view of the *method* of analysis, in classical theory the very long-run interaction between rate of profit, wages and accumulation is not inconsistent with taking the normal wage as given in the determination of relative prices and the rate of profits. Nor is there any analytical problem in regarding such a given normal rate of wages as determined by the historically determined living standards, institutional circumstances and persistent conditions of the labour market – the latter described by the classical economists with reference to the proportion between employment and population.

Thus, what is really at stake between the different interpretations of Ricardo is not whether there is a very long-run interdependence between normal wages, growth and the rate of profit in classical theory. What is at stake is how normal wages are determined in a given period, with a given capital stock and population. What indeed establishes a similarity between classical theory as interpreted in the new view and marginalist theory is the fact that wages in every period are determined by the interplay of a 'static' decreasing demand function for labour and labour supply.

When modelling the relationship between growth rates and distributive variables the new view must explicitly or implicitly use a 'static' labour demand function in order to avoid unacceptable results. Without such a function, what would happen if at any given period the labour demanded exceeded supply? Would wages keep rising for all the time required to raise population to the level of demand? And then fall to bring the rate of increase of population to equality with the rate of employment growth? And what if population exceeded demand? Would wages fall to zero by the effects of unlimited competition, and population 'dye like flies' in order to bring population to a level with employment? Indeed, this is what is supposed to take place in Samuelson's canonical classical model when fixed proportions between labour and capital are assumed, but it is definitely at odds with anything we can find in Ricardo or any other classical economist (for a critical discussion of Samuelson's interpretation see Garegnani, 2007: 212–26).

This takes us back to the central point in the controversy: either textual evidence can be found indicating that a 'static' decreasing demand function for labour can be attributed to the classical economists, which brings labour demand to equality with labour supply in each period; or alternatively one must necessarily think in terms of a competitive process in the labour market that is bounded by conventional and institutional factors such as the habitual living standards of the workers, while the ratio of the quantities of labour demanded and supplied (which will normally differ in any period) is a factor affecting normal wages through its influence on the 'bargaining position' of the parties.

The distinctive character of Ricardian and classical wage theory according to the alternative interpretation is not in the role played by institutional factors as opposed to market forces, but rather in a different view of what market forces actually are.

ANTONELLA STIRATI

See also:

Capital and Profits; Endogenous Growth; Hicks, John R., on Ricardo; Poor Laws; Population.

References

Casarosa, C. (1978), 'A new formulation of the Ricardian system', *Oxford Economic Papers*, **30**(1), 38–63.

Casarosa, C. (1982), 'The new view of the Ricardian theory of distribution and economic growth', in M. Baranzini (ed.), *Advances in Economic Theory*, Oxford: Basil Blackwell.

Garegnani, P. (1984), 'Value and distribution in the classical economists and Marx', *Oxford Economic Papers*, **36**(2), 291–325.

Garegnani, P. (1990), 'Sraffa: classical versus marginalist analysis', in K. Bharadwaj and B. Schefold (eds), *Essays on Piero Sraffa. Critical Perspectives on the Revival of Classical Theory*, London: Unwin Hyman.

Garegnani, P. (2007), 'Professor Samuelson on Sraffa and the classical economists', *European Journal of the History of Economic Thought*, **14**(2), 181–242.

Hicks, J. and S. Hollander (1977), 'Mr. Ricardo and the moderns', *Quarterly Journal of Economics*, **91**(3), 351–69.

Kaldor, N. (1955–56), 'Alternative theories of distribution', *Review of Economic Studies*, **23**(2), 83–100.

Knight, F.H. ([1956] 1963), *On the History and Method of Economics*, Chicago, IL: Chicago University Press.

Longe, F. ([1866] 1903), *The Wage-Fund Theory*, reprinted in J. Hollander (ed.), *Economic Tracts*, Baltimore, MD: Johns Hopkins University Press.

Napoleoni, C. (1974), *Smith, Ricardo, Marx*, Torino: Boringhieri.

Pasinetti, L. (1960), 'A mathematical formulation of the Ricardian system', *Review of Economic Studies*, **27**, 77–88.

Peach, T. (1988), 'David Ricardo: a review of some interpretative issues', in W.O. Thweatt (ed.), *Classical Political Economy*, Boston, MA: Kluwer.

Picchio, A. (1992), *The Political Economy of Social Reproduction of Labour: Analytical and Historical Aspects of Labour Supply*, Cambridge, UK: Cambridge University Press.

Pivetti, M. (1999), 'On Sraffa's "cost & surplus" concept of wages and its policy implications', *Rivista italiana degli economisti*, **4**(2), 279–300.

Samuelson, P.A. (1978), 'The canonical classical model of political economy', *Journal of Economic Literature*, **16**(4), 1415–35.

Schumpeter, J. ([1954] 1982), *History of Economic Analysis*, London: Allen and Unwin.

Smith, A. ([1776] 1976), *An Inquiry into the Nature and Causes of the Wealth of Nations*, in *The Glasgow Edition of the Works and Correspondence of Adam Smith*, (eds) R.H. Campbell, A.S. Skinner and W.B. Todd, Oxford: Clarendon Press.

Sraffa, P. (1960), *Production of Commodities by Means of Commodities. Prelude to a Critique of Economic Theory*, Cambridge, UK: Cambridge University Press.

Stirati, A. (1992), 'Institutions, unemployment and the living standard in the classical theory of wages', *Contributions to Political Economy*, **11**(0), 41–66.

Stirati, A. (1994), *The Theory of Wages in Classical Economics: A Study of Adam Smith, David Ricardo and Their Contemporaries*, Aldershot, UK and Brookfield, VT: Edward Elgar Publishing.

Stirati, A. (1995), 'Smith's legacy and the definitions of natural wages in Ricardo', *Journal of the History of Economic Thought*, **17**(1), 106–32.

Stirati, A. (1999), 'Ricardo and the wages fund', in F. Petri and G. Mongiovi (eds), *Value, Distribution and Capital, Essays in Honour of Pierangelo Garegnani*, London: Routledge.

Stirati, A. (2011), 'On Hollander on Sraffa and the "Marxian dimension"', in C. Gherke, G. Mongiovi and R. Ciccone (eds), *Sraffa and Modern Economics*, London: Routledge.

Thornton, W.T. ([1870] 1971), *On Labour, Its Wrongful Claims And Rightful Dues, Its Actual Present and Possible Future*, 2nd edition, reprinted Shannon: Irish University Press.

Wicksell, K ([1924] 1981), 'Ricardo on machinery and the present unemployment: an unpublished manuscript by Knut Wicksell', *Economic Journal*, **91**(361), 195–205.

Labour Theory of Value

Ricardo first stated his labour theory of value in print in the first edition of his *Principles of Political Economy, and Taxation* (1817, *Works*, I). This theory was, in his opinion, 'a doctrine of the utmost importance in political economy; for from no source do so many errors, and so much difference of opinion in that science proceed, as from the vague ideas which are attached to the word value' (ibid.: 13). Since then, the theory attracted much attention and generated lively controversies, mainly for three reasons. First, this theory was openly opposing what Adam Smith had stated in his *Inquiry into the Nature and*

Causes of the Wealth of Nations ([1776] 1976), especially because Ricardo was maintaining that Smith's assertion that all prices vary with a change in wages, and in the same direction, was erroneous. Second, some commentators – Torrens in particular – stressed the fact that Ricardo's developments on the subject were flawed. Third, subsequent to the publications of Karl Marx's *Zur Kritik der politischen Ökonomie* (1859), the first and third volumes of *Das Kapital. Kritik der politischen Ökonomie* (1867 and 1894) and Kautsky's edition of *Theorien über den Mehrwert* (1905–10), Ricardo's theory of value was typically read through a Marxian lens. This, however, conferred a special theoretical and political bias to the debates until the edition by Piero Sraffa, with the collaboration of Maurice Herbert Dobb, of *The Works and Correspondence of David Ricardo*, from 1951 onwards.

The first debates involved, for instance, in correspondence as well as in print, Thomas Robert Malthus (1820, 1823), James Mill (1821), Robert Torrens (1818, 1821), John Ramsey McCulloch (1818, 1825), Samuel Bailey (1825) and John Stuart Mill ([1823] 1986; 1848). After Marx, the most interesting contributions were certainly published by Vladimir Karpovitch Dmitriev ([1904] 1974) and Laudislaus von Bortkiewicz ([1906–7] 1971). But the literature is immense and cannot obviously be summarized here (for contrasting views on value, see, for example, J. Hollander, 1910; Biaujeaud [1933] 1988; Sraffa in *Works*, I: xiii–xliv; S. Hollander, 1979; Caravale and Tosato, 1980; Garegnani 1984; Caravale, 1985; Peach, 1993; de Vivo 1994; Mongiovi 1994; Henderson and Davis, 1997; Kurz and Salvadori, 2007, 2013; Kurz, 2011; King, 2013, and the references quoted in all these studies). In the following, we concentrate on the main features of Ricardo's texts as they can be interpreted today and synthetically presented.

A quest for standards
From the beginning of his reflections as an economist, Ricardo had been confronted with the problem of finding standards in order to understand economic phenomena properly. As is well known, the first confrontation was with monetary questions during the Bullionist Controversy. One of the problems then was to analyse the evolution of prices. But prices are expressed in monetary units, for example, the pound sterling. When the price of a commodity increases or decreases, what is the origin of this change? Is it a real cause, which takes place in the production process of the commodity, or a monetary cause, that is, a variation of the value of the currency – or a mix of the two? Now, how to assess the variation of the value of the currency unit? This unit being defined as a definite amount of gold, its value is expressed in terms of this standard. In a gold standard regime with perfect convertibility, the value of the currency, that is, the inverse of the price of gold in the gold market, is stable and approximately equal to that given by the mint price. In a regime of inconvertibility, the value of the currency depends on its quantity and the difference between the price of gold in the market and its mint price is the principal sign of a depreciation or appreciation of the currency. This analysis is, of course, only possible, Ricardo stressed, because the currency and the monetary standard have been carefully distinguished.

If the value of money is stable, the evolution of a money price is thus only due to a real cause. But which one: a cause modifying the value of the commodity or the value of gold (the monetary standard)? Hence, the first problem Ricardo had to face and tried to solve was to find a measure of value that would allow one to assess, when relative prices change, the cause of this variation. Would it not be desirable, he asks, to find a commodity that would itself be invariable in value and to adopt it as the monetary standard? In Ricardo's view, this question was fundamental and he tried to answer it in his subsequent writings.

Ricardo was still debating the question of an adequate measure of value in 1823 in his last drafts of 'Absolute Value and Exchangeable Value' (*Works*, IV: 361–412), critically scrutinizing the opinions of Malthus, Torrens, James Mill and McCulloch. It is, however, important to note that, from the outset, Ricardo was perfectly aware that the search for a perfectly invariable (monetary) standard in terms of a real commodity amounts to looking for a will-o'-the-wisp: no commodity is invariable in value. The real problem was instead to find a commodity that could form the best approximation to an ideal standard. In 1810–11, in *The High Price of Bullion, a Proof of the Depreciation of Bank Notes*, he justified the choice of the precious metals, gold and silver, on an empirical basis:

> Strictly speaking, there can be no permanent measure of value. A measure of value should itself be invariable; but this is not the case with either gold or silver, they being subject to fluctuations as well as other commodities. Experience has indeed taught us, that though the variations in the *value* of gold or silver may be considerable, on a comparison of distant periods, yet for short spaces of time their value is tolerably fixed. It is this property, among their other excellencies, which fits them better than any other commodity for the uses of money. Either gold or silver may therefore, in the point of view in which we are considering them, be called a measure of value. (*Works*, III: 65n; original emphasis)

Ricardo thus had to face a second problem. The search for a good monetary standard led him to search for another standard, an invariable standard of value. But in what does the value of a commodity consist; how is it determined? Ricardo's views on these questions evolved over time. Broadly speaking, he first accepted Smith's ideas on the matter but then changed his opinion during the controversy about the renewal of the Corn Laws and in the course of the writing his 1815 pamphlet *Essay on the Influence of a Low Price of Corn on the Profits of Stock* (*Works*, IV: 9–41). However, in spite of this evolution, his general approach was well defined from the outset and remained unchanged afterwards. He clearly had in mind the idea that the natural value of a commodity depends on the difficulty of its production, and that while utility is an essential aspect for a commodity, this utility is not the measure of value.

In 1810–11, again in *The High Price of Bullion*, he spoke of gold and silver having 'like other commodities, an intrinsic value which is not arbitrary but is dependent on their scarcity, the quantity of labour bestowed in procuring them, and the value of the capital employed in the mines which produce them' (*Works*, III: 52). In the same period, in his 'Notes on Bentham's "Sur les prix"', he declared: 'I like the distinction which Adam Smith makes between value in use and value in exchange. According to that opinion utility is not the measure of value' (ibid.: 284). The same words are again to be found in the different editions of the *Principles* in the opening chapter 'On Value' (*Works*, I: 11–12). There Ricardo specified that the theory of value does not concern the two extreme cases of free or non-reproducible goods, and monopolized commodities. The term 'scarcity' used in 1810 as well as in 1817 simply means that the commodity is not a free good: 'In speaking then of commodities, of their exchangeable value, and of the laws which regulate their relative prices, we mean always such commodities only as can be increased in quantity by the exertion of human industry, and on the production of which competition operates without restraint' (ibid.: 12). It is to be noted, moreover, that, like Smith, Ricardo admitted that demand could influence prices, but market prices, which in the end gravitate around natural prices (ibid.: 88–92).

Finally a third important problem arises when dealing with the question of value. It is clear that Ricardo's main interest lay in the determination of 'exchangeable value', 'relative value', 'comparative value' or 'proportional value' of commodities – which are all interchangeable phrases Ricardo used more or less frequently. But does not an exchange ratio presuppose a quantitative comparability of the commodities, their 'intrinsic value' as Ricardo wrote in 1810, a phrase that is again to be found in the *Principles*, especially in passages on money, but that is also replaced, in the same *Principles*, with 'absolute value'? This last appellation was to be almost exclusively used later in 1823 in the drafts on 'Absolute Value and Exchangeable Value' – where 'real value' also appeared with the same meaning, as in Ricardo's correspondence, with Hutches Trower in particular, together with 'positive value'. This question of an intrinsic, real or absolute value of commodities, first intimately linked to the determination of their exchange ratios and expressing value in terms of an invariable standard, was still important in Ricardo's last thoughts.

Towards a labour theory of value
After the Bullionist Controversy Ricardo had another occasion to develop his views on value. He actively participated in the debates around the renewal of the Corn Laws and fought in favour of a free external grain trade. His views were stated in his 1815 *Essay on Profits* and in the correspondence that preceded and followed its publication. As is well known, his arguments involved his views on the distribution of income between rents, profits and wages and his aim was to show that 'the interest of the landlord is always opposed to the interest of every other class in the community' (*Works*, IV: 21). More specifically, supposing an increasing population and the consequent extension of the cultivation of agricultural products – 'corn' – to land of always poorer quality, the value of corn was bound to rise, entailing a rise in sum total and rates of rent, in the value of the real wages and a fall in the rate of profits in agriculture and in all other activities: 'I am only desirous of proving that the profits on agricultural capital cannot materially vary, without occasioning a similar variation in the profits on capital, employed on manufactures and commerce' (ibid.: 12n).

It is at this point that Ricardo felt again the necessity to tackle the problem of value. To prove his assertions, he not only had to make use of Malthus's theory of rent, but he also had to ascertain that the values of all other commodities outside agriculture would not follow the price of corn – or only in a moderate way to take into account the variations in the prices of raw products. 'It has been thought that the price of corn regulates the prices of all other things. This appears to me to be a mistake' (ibid.: 21n). This is the reason why, once more, he referred to a value based on the conditions of production. In competitive markets and for reproducible commodities, 'the difficulty or facility of their production will ultimately regulate their exchangeable value' (ibid.: 20), that is, prices gravitate around the costs of production, 'the general profits of stock' included (ibid.: 20n).

Ricardo, however, did not develop the theory of value in the *Essay* further. When analysing what was happening in agriculture and developing the theory of rent he supposed that corn was the standard of value and in the two famous tables (ibid.: 17) showing the progress of rent and the evolution of profits, all data are expressed in terms of quantities of corn: the capital invested on each piece of land is 'of the value' of a certain amount of corn (ibid.: 14), and the cost of production is 'estimated in corn' (ibid.: 21n). This circumstance, together with the absence of any clear and widely used theory of value in the *Essay*, gave rise to the statement by Piero Sraffa that underlying Ricardo's reasoning was a 'corn model' based on the hypothesis that, in agriculture, the inputs and the outputs were homogeneous and consisted of 'corn' (*Works*, I: xxxi–xxxii). It was thus possible 'at the cost of considerable simplification' to determine the rate of profit in agriculture in real terms, 'without the need of a method for reducing to a common standard a heterogeneous collection of commodities' (ibid.: xxxii) – this rate imposing itself in turn on all other activities. By contrast, the adoption of a labour theory of value in the *Principles* could allow a determination of the profit rate 'in society as a whole instead of through the microcosm of one special branch of production' (ibid.). While the hypothesis of a homogeneity between inputs and output could be found in some authors more or less at the same period and could implicitly refer to the Physiocrats, the effective presence of this hypothesis in Ricardo's *Essay on Profits* is questionable and gave rise to some lively debates (see, for example, S. Hollander, 1979, 1995; Faccarello, 1982; Garegnani 1982; Skourtos, 1991; Kurz 2011; Kurz and Salvadori 2013, and the references quoted in these studies). But it is certainly true that a 'corn model' can form a possible logical framework – among others – to interpret statements like 'it is the profits of the farmer which regulate the profits of all other trades' (Ricardo to Hutches Trower, 8 March 1814, *Works*, VI: 104) and express Ricardo's underlying and lasting conviction that the distribution of income could be explained in purely physical terms (Kurz, 2011).

The final step towards the adoption of a labour theory of value was made by Ricardo when, encouraged by James Mill and developing the ideas set out in the *Essay on Profits*, he was working on his *Principles of Political Economy, and Taxation* (1817). Here, he eventually found an unambiguous expression for the 'difficulty of production', 'the real foundation of exchangeable value' (*Works*, I: 25): the total amount of labour directly and indirectly necessary to produce a commodity. Whatever the state of the society and the degree of the division of labour:

> still the same principle would hold true, that the exchangeable value of the commodities produced would be in proportion to the labour bestowed on their production; not on their immediate production only, but on all those implements or machines required to give effect to the particular labour to which they were applied. (Ibid.: 24)

Of course, labour itself is not homogeneous, and an hour's work in one profession is difficult to compare with an hour's work in another because of the difference of skills and intensity. But, for Ricardo, the problem was easy to solve – as it had been for Smith before him. The scale of remunerations 'adjusted in the market with sufficient precision for all practical purposes' could be a good guide, and, 'once formed, is liable to little variation' (ibid.: 20) – Marx later reconsidered the problem and made a clear distinction between what he called 'abstract labour', the homogeneous 'substance of value', and different kinds of non-comparable 'concrete labour'; but as regards the scale to be established between 'simple' or unskilled and 'complex' or skilled labour, he 'solved' the problem in the same way as Ricardo did. Ricardo supposed, moreover, that the average skill and intensity is always approximately the same in one profession, thus allowing a comparison of the value of a commodity across time – especially if the periods are not too distant: 'at least . . . the variation is very inconsiderable from year to year, and therefore, can have little effect, for short periods, on the relative value of commodities' (ibid.: 22). And at this point Ricardo asserted that only the analysis of relative values and their possible evolution matters:

> As the inquiry to which I wish do draw the reader's attention, relates to the effect of the variations in the relative value of commodities, and not in their absolute value, it will be of little importance to examine into the comparative degree of estimation in which the different kinds of human labour are held. (Ibid.: 21–2)

Absolute value, relative value and the measure of value

It seems that Ricardo had found what he was looking for: the total labour 'bestowed' on a commodity is the measure of its value and the exchange ratios between commodities are determined by the relative amounts of labour expended to produce them and bring them to market. This is the reason why the search for an invariable measure of value could logically somewhat vanish here: to see the cause of a variation in relative prices, it was enough to look at the amounts of labour bestowed. But, of course, it could still be useful to find a commodity the production of which would always require the same total quantity of labour. Once this commodity was adopted as standard of value, any change in prices could immediately and unambiguously be interpreted as originating in the conditions of production of the commodity under consideration.

Ricardo, however, remarked immediately that things are not so simple. In conditions of free competition, as Turgot and Smith had already insisted, the principle of the uniformity of the profit rate – or of a stable scale of rates according to the different degrees of risk and so on inherent in the various activities – is essential. Normal or natural prices must reflect this profit rate. As a consequence, the total quantities of labour bestowed on commodities no longer determine the relative prices of commodities alone and the labour theory of value, only just formulated, had to be amended. As a consequence, too, the search for an invariable measure of value is rekindled: variations in relative prices may be also caused by changes in distribution and not only by changes in quantities of embodied labour.

Ricardo was, from the outset, perfectly conscious of the problem. In the first edition of the *Principles*, 1817, he stressed this fact and tried to tackle it thoroughly. While, on the one hand, he asserted many times that 'labour is the foundation of all value' and the relative quantities of labour 'determine' the relative prices, he recognized on the other hand that the accumulation of capital necessarily 'introduces a considerable modification to the rule' dictated by the labour theory of value, which was true 'in the early states of society' (*Works*, I: 66). 'Besides the alteration in the relative value of commodities, occasioned by more or less labour being required to produce them, they are also subject to fluctuations from a rise in wages, and consequent fall of profits' (ibid.: 53). The explanation of this effect of the distribution of income on the exchange ratios is due to the fact, Ricardo stressed, that (1) capitals invested in different sectors exhibit different proportions of fixed and circulating capital and (2) the fixed capitals are of 'unequal duration'.

In this context, whenever wages are modified and the rate of profit changes as a consequence – all other things being equal, in particular the quantities of labour bestowed upon commodities – the relative prices of commodities must vary in order to restore the uniformity of the profit rate in all activities.

While clear and unambiguous, the analysis of the first edition of the *Principles* presents two features that somewhat limit its generality. The first is that Ricardo felt that the division of capital between fixed and circulating is 'not essential' and that 'the line of demarcation cannot be accurately drawn' (ibid.: 31, 52n). And in fact, in the numerical examples he advanced in order to study the effects of a change in the distribution of income on relative prices, he supposed that the entire circulating capital consists solely in wages: the influence of the proportions of fixed and circulating capital and of the durability of the fixed capital was thus easier to illustrate.

The second feature is that Ricardo chose a peculiar measure of value: he supposed the monetary standard being always produced with the same quantity of labour but without any 'fixed' capital: 'I am supposing money to be of an invariable value; in other words, to be always the produce of the same quantity of unassisted labour' (ibid.: 63). This is precisely the measure of value Malthus would have proposed later and that Ricardo would have rejected. But this choice allowed Ricardo to establish a result 'of such importance to the science of political economy' (ibid.: 61) that reinforced his anti-Smithian position: when wages rise, all money prices fall (!):

> It appears, then, that in proportion to the quantity and the durability of the fixed capital employed in any kind of production, the relative prices of those commodities on which such capital is employed, will vary inversely as wages; they will fall as wages rise. It appears too that no commodities whatever are raised in absolute price, merely because wages rise . . . but that all commodities in the production of which fixed capital enters, not only do not rise with a rise of wages, but absolutely fall. (Ibid.: 62–3)

The discussions that followed the publication of the first edition of the *Principles* – especially with Malthus and Torrens – induced Ricardo to rework his first chapter on value. In the third and final edition, 1821, three main points are to be noted.

First of all, Ricardo, while sticking to the idea that the labour bestowed 'is really the foundation of the exchangeable value of all things' (ibid.: 13), stressed again the fact that the existence of fixed capital 'introduces a considerable modification to the rule' (ibid.: 38; cf. also 30). As before, the causes were the different proportions between fixed and circulating capital and the different durability of fixed capital: to which he added a third, namely, 'the unequal rapidity with which it is returned to its employer' (ibid.: 38).

But Ricardo showed some hesitation: he was keen to minimize the quantitative aspects of the problem and noted that the relative quantities of labour still 'almost exclusively' determine the exchange ratios and their variations (e.g., ibid.: 12, 20). While these ratios are 'not exactly' given by the labour bestowed (ibid.: 34), the deviation is supposed to be 'minor' (ibid.: 42) and it would thus be 'incorrect to attach much importance to it' (ibid.: 36). He justifies his point of view first on the basis of some numerical examples that, in his opinion, show that 'this cause of the variation of commodities is comparatively slight in its effects . . . Not so with the other great cause . . . namely, the increase or diminution in the quantity of labour necessary to produce them' (ibid.: 36; cf. also 45). Second, he also remarked that the causes that modify the rate of profit are not permanently in action and act on the long period while those who change the quantities of labour bestowed 'are of daily occurrence' (ibid.: 36). He reiterated his points subsequently (cf., for example, *Works*, IV: 368). The labour theory of value could thus be considered as an approximate solution to the problem of relative prices and their variations. But Ricardo honestly always considered this problem as not fully settled, as becomes clear in his correspondence with James Mill, McCulloch, Malthus and Torrens and in his manuscript fragments on 'Absolute Value and Exchangeable Value'.

The second point to be stressed is that, in the second and third editions of the *Principles*, as noted above, Ricardo was still struggling with the definitions of fixed and circulating capital (*Works*, I: 31). Here too, the numerical examples mainly suppose that circulating capital consists solely of wages. In a fragment on Torrens, however, dated 1818, he tried to solve the problem and, in a way, to put the definition in accordance with his examples: it appears, Ricardo wrote, 'that every thing is fixed capital which is employed on production except that which resolves itself into wages' (*Works*, IV: 312). In the manuscript, the sentence is deleted, nevertheless, had he maintained it, Marx's definition of constant and variable capital would have been identical to Ricardo's distinction between fixed and circulating capital (cf. Sraffa in *Works*, IV: 306). But Ricardo never fully abandoned this idea. In his 1823 manuscript, he was still writing of the various 'proportions in which immediate labour and accumulated labour enter into different commodities' (Works IV: 379), thus opposing again labour to the material means of production.

This problem of definition notwithstanding, the consequences of the existence of the different kinds of capital on the relative values of commodities are now better analysed and in a more general way. This is also due to the fact that Ricardo abandoned his previous simplifying definition of a monetary standard produced with a constant quantity of unassisted labour. As a result, relative prices could be said to vary in both directions as a result of a change in wages and the profit rate:

> The degree of alteration in the relative value of goods, on account of a rise . . . of labour, would depend on the proportion which the fixed capital bore to the whole capital employed. All commodities which are produced by very valuable machinery, or in very valuable buildings, or which require a great length of time before they can be brought to market, would fall in relative value, while all those which are chiefly produced by labour, or which would be speedily brought to market would rise in relative value. (*Works*, I: 35)

Finally the third point to note regards the measure of value. The invariable standard of value must not only be produced with an unchanged quantity of labour, it must also be invariable when the wage and the profit rates vary: these conditions of course 'disqualify any commodity that can be thought of from being a perfectly accurate measure of value' (ibid.: 44). If by some unlikely chance a commodity could be found that satisfies the first requirement, it would nevertheless be a perfect measure of value only 'for all things produced under the same circumstances precisely as itself, but for no others' (ibid.: 45), that is, for commodities produced with the same proportion of labour to the different kinds of capital. In another words, the neutralization of the influence of the distribution of income amounts to say that the relative price of those commodities is simply equal to their relative labour value.

Now it is possible to find out a more precise meaning for Ricardo's phrase: 'under the same circumstances precisely as itself'. Using a decomposition in dated quantities of labour – utilized by Ricardo in an elementary way but specified later by Dmitriev, Bortkiewicz and Sraffa – suppose two commodities a and b produced in m and n periods respectively, p_i being the money price, L_τ a dated quantity of labour, r the rate of profit and w the money wage rate ($i = a, b$ and $\tau = m, n$):

$$p_i = (1 + r)L_{1i}w + (1 + r)^2 L_{2i}w + \ldots + (1 + r)^\tau L_{\tau i}w$$

The relative price of the commodities is thus given by:

$$\frac{p_a}{p_b} = \frac{(1 + r)L_{1a}w + (1 + r)^2 L_{2a}w + \ldots + (1 + r)^m L_{ma}w}{(1 + r)L_{1b}w + (1 + r)^2 L_{2b}w + \ldots + (1 + r)^n L_{nb}w} = \frac{L_{1a} + (1 + r)L_{2a} + \ldots + (1 + r)^{m-1}L_{ma}}{L_{1b} + (1 + r)L_{2b} + \ldots + (1 + r)^{n-1}L_{nb}}$$

Let $\lambda_i = L_{1i} + L_{2i} + \ldots + L_{\tau i}$ be the labour value of commodity i. It is easy to see that $\frac{p_a}{p_b} = \frac{\lambda_a}{\lambda_b}$ if and only if (i) $r = 0$ or (ii) the following conditions are realized simultaneously: $m = n$ and $\frac{L_{1a}}{L_{1b}} = \frac{L_{2a}}{L_{2b}} = \ldots = \frac{L_{ma}}{L_{nb}} = \alpha$ ($\alpha > 0$). Condition (i) is trivial and irrelevant; condition (ii), extremely restrictive, expresses Ricardo's statement.

Ricardo asserted again, however, that the situation was not without a way out. In the first place, as the effects of a change in the distribution on relative prices are supposed to be quantitatively slight, and if it is supposed further that gold is approximately produced over time with the same difficulty of production, gold would constitute 'as near an approximation to a standard measure of value as can be theoretically conceived' (ibid.). In the second place Ricardo stressed the fact that this would be all the more true if gold could be considered as produced with an 'average' proportion of capital 'so nearly equally distant from the two extremes, the one where little fixed capital is used, the other where little labour is employed, as to form a just mean between them' (ibid.: 45–6). In this way the variations of wages and profits could possibly compensate each other and gold be 'a standard so nearly approaching to an invariable one'. This is what Ricardo supposed as an openly simplifying device – 'I fully allow that money made of gold is subject to most of the variations of other things' – in order to facilitate his enquiry: 'the advantage is, that I shall be enabled to speak of the variation of other things, without embarrassing myself on every occasion with the consideration of the possible alteration in the value of the medium in which price and value are estimated' (ibid.: 46). Significantly enough Marx, confronted with an analogous problem in his theory of prices of production in Book III of *Capital*, adopted a similar solution, imagining an 'average branch of production' where the labour value of the commodity could equal its price. Later on, Sraffa (1960: Chapters IV and V) reconsidered the question and imagined a composite 'standard commodity' the price of which is invariable with respect to changes in the distribution of income.

To conclude, it is worth noting again that, at the end of his life, Ricardo was still struggling with the concept of real or absolute or positive value. On the one hand, he almost gave a physiological flavour to it when, in his 1823 drafts, he asked: 'Have we no standard in nature by which we can ascertain the uniformity in the value of a measure?' His answer was positive: 'labour is that standard. The average strength of 1000 or 10,000 men it is said is nearly the same at all times' (*Works*, IV: 381). On the other hand, and as a consequence, some expressions could be interpreted as a tendency to strictly separate the two concepts of absolute and exchangeable value. On 4 July 1821, he wrote to Trower that 'I do not, I think, say that the labour expended on a commodity is a measure of its exchangeable value, but of its positive value' (*Works*, IX: 1). He went on:

> You say if there were no exchange of commodities they could have no value, and I agree with you, if you mean exchangeable value, but if I am obliged to devote one month's labour to make me a coat, and only one weeks labour to make a hat, although I should never exchange either of them, the coat would be four times the value of the hat; and if a robber were to break into my house and take part of my property, I would rather that he took 3 hats than one coat. (Ibid.: 2)

Ricardo did not develop this idea further, however. He returned to his discussions with Malthus, Torrens, J. Mill and McCulloch. His sudden death left the debated questions unsolved.

GILBERT FACCARELLO

See also:

Demand and Supply; Invariable Measure of Value; Labour and Wages; Natural and Market Prices; Ricardo's Emancipation from Smith's Theory of Prices; Surplus.

References

Bailey, S. (1825), *A Critical Dissertation on the Nature, Measures, and Causes of Value, Chiefly in Reference to the Writings of Mr Ricardo and his Followers*, London: Hunter.

Biaujeaud, H. ([1933] 1988), *Essai sur la théorie ricardienne de la valeur*, Paris: Sirey; reprint, Paris: Economica.

Bortkiewicz, L. von ([1906–7] 1971), 'Wertrechnung und Preisrechnung im Marxschen System', *Archiv für Sozialwissenschaft und Sozialpolitik*; 1906, **XXIII**(1), 1–50; July 1907, **XXV**(1), 10–51; September 1907, **XXV**(2), 445–88; reprint in L. von Bortkiewicz, *La teoria economica di Marx e altri saggi su Böhm-Bawerk, Walras e Pareto*, Turin: Einaudi, pp. 5–104.

Caravale, G. (ed.) (1985), *The Legacy of Ricardo*, Oxford: Basil Blackwell.

Caravale, G. and D. Tosato (1980), *Ricardo and the Theory of Value, Distribution and Growth*, London: Routledge.

De Vivo, G. (1994), '(Mis)interpreting Ricardo', *Contributions to Political Economy*, **13**, 29–43.

Dmitriev, V.K. ([1904] 1974), Экономические очерки [*Economic Essays*]; English translation D.M. Nuti (ed.), *Economic Essays on Value, Competition and Utility*, Cambridge, UK: Cambridge University Press.

Faccarello, G. (1982), 'Sraffa versus Ricardo: the historical irrelevance of the "corn-profit" model', *Economy and Society*, **11**(2), 122–37.

Garegnani, P. (1982), 'On Hollander's interpretation of Ricardo's early theory of profits', *Cambridge Journal of Economics*, **6**(1), 65–77.

Garegnani, P. (1984), 'Value and distribution in the classical economists and Marx', *Oxford Economic Papers*, **36**(2), 291–325.

Henderson, J. and J.B. Davis (1997), *The Life and Economics of David Ricardo*, Dordrecht: Kluwer Academic Publishers.

Hollander, J.H. (1910), *David Ricardo: A Centenary Estimate*, Baltimore, MD: Johns Hopkins University Press.

Hollander, S. (1979), *The Economics of David Ricardo*, Toronto: The University of Toronto Press.

Hollander, S. (1995), 'Sraffa's rational reconstruction of Ricardo: on three contributions to the *Cambridge Journal of Economics*', *Cambridge Journal of Economics*, **19**(3), 483–9.

King, J.E. (2013), *David Ricardo*, London: Palgrave Macmillan.

Kurz, H. D. (2011), 'On David Ricardo's theory of profits: the laws of distribution are "not essentially connected with the doctrine of value"', *The History of Economic Thought*, **53**(1), 1–20.

Kurz, H.D. and N. Salvadori (2007), *Interpreting Classical Economics. Studies in Long-Period Analysis*, London: Routledge.

Kurz, H.D. and N. Salvadori (2013), 'On the "*vexata questio* of value". Ricardo, Marx and Sraffa', in L. Taylor, Z. Rezai and T. Michl (eds), *Social Fairness and Economics. Economic Essays in the Spirit of Duncan Foley*, London: Routledge, 213–227.

Malthus, T.R. (1820), *Principles of Political Economy, Considered with a View to their Practical Application*, London: John Murray.

Malthus, T.R. (1823), *The Measure of Value Stated and Illustrated, with an Application of it to the Alterations in the Value of the English Currency Since 1790*, London: John Murray.

McCulloch, J.R. (1818), 'Mr Ricardo's theory of exchangeable value vindicated from the objections of R. [paper signed M.]', *The Edinburgh Magazine and Literary Miscellany*, **III**, November, 429–31.

McCulloch, J.R. (1825), *The Principles of Political Economy, with a Sketch of the Rise and Progress of the Science*, Edinburgh: William and Charles Tait/London: Longman and Co.

Mill, J. (1821), *Elements of Political Economy*, London: Baldwin, Cradock and Joy.

Mill, J.S. ([1823] 1986), 'Malthus's measure of value', *Morning Chronicle*, 5 September, in A. and J. Robson (eds) (1986), *Collected Works of John Stuart Mill, Vol. XXII: Newspaper Writings, December 1822–July 1831*, Toronto: University of Toronto Press/London: Routledge and Kegan Paul, pp. 51–60.

Mill, J.S. (1848), *Principles of Political Economy, with Some of their Applications to Social Philosophy*, London: John W. Parker.

Mongiovi, G. (1994), 'Misinterpreting Ricardo. A review essay', *Journal of the History of Economic Thought*, **16**(2), 248–69.

Peach, T. (1993), *Interpreting Ricardo*, Cambridge, UK: Cambridge University Press.

Smith, A. ([1776] 1976), *An Inquiry into the Nature and Causes of the Wealth of Nations*, in *The Glasgow Edition of the Works and Correspondence of Adam Smith*, (eds) R.H. Campbell, A.S. Skinner and W.B. Todd, Oxford: Clarendon Press.

Skourtos, M. (1991), 'Corn models in the classical tradition: P. Sraffa considered historically', *Cambridge Journal of Economics*, **15**(2), 215–28.

Sraffa, P. (1960), *Production of Commodities by Means of Commodities. Prelude to a Critique of Economic Theory*, Cambridge, UK: Cambridge University Press.

Torrens, R. (1818), 'Strictures on Mr Ricardo's doctrine respecting exchangeable value [paper signed R.]', *The Edinburgh Magazine and Literary Miscellany*, **III**, October, 335–8.

Torrens, R. (1821), *An Essay on the Production of Wealth. With an Appendix, in Which the Principles of Political Economy are Applied to the Actual Circumstances of this Country*, London: Longman, Hurst, Rees, Orme and Brown.

Land and Rent

In *The Principles of Political Economy, and Taxation* (1817) David Ricardo defined rent as 'that portion of the produce of the earth, which is paid to the landlord for the use of the original and indestructible powers of the soil' (*Works*, I: 67). He saw the determination of the laws of distribution – that is, of the division of the net product between wages, profits and rents – as the main task of political economy. As observed by Piero Sraffa in his introduction to the *Principles* (*Works*, I: xxiii), Ricardo deviated from the structure he had more or less copied from Adam Smith's *Wealth of Nations* by treating rent at a very early stage of the book, in Chapters 2 and 3. That decision was motivated by Ricardo's strategy to put rent aside (in a letter to John Ramsay McCulloch of 13 June 1820 he used the expression 'getting rid of rent' – *Works*, VIII: 194) in order to simplify the analysis of the distribution between wages and profit. For Ricardo it was clearly of great importance to establish what he called the 'true doctrine of rent; without a knowledge of which, it is impossible to understand the effect of the progress of wealth on profits and wages' (*Works*, I: 5). This also explains why he returned to the question of rent towards the end of the book, devoting two chapters to a critical analysis of what he considered to be erroneous views on the subject: Chapter 24 dealing with Smith and Chapter 32 dealing with Thomas Robert Malthus.

Ricardo had laid the foundations of his theory of differential rent two years before the publication of the *Principles*, in the pamphlet *An Essay on the Influence of a Low Price of Corn on the Profits of Stock* (1815). Spurred by the debates on the Corn Laws in the

British Parliament, in the span of a few weeks several authors expounded their views on rent. In the preface of the *Principles* Ricardo referred explicitly to the works of Malthus ([1815] 1986) and Edward West ([1815] 1903), but Robert Torrens (1815) also published a book that touched upon the subject. Apparently at that time no one was aware of the fact that James Anderson (1777) had anticipated all of them.

In this entry we begin by explaining Ricardo's theory of rent. We present the different varieties of rent, examine the consistency of Ricardo's reasoning, and explore the intimate connection between the evolution of rent and the tendency of the rate of profits to fall. Then we look briefly at the influence of Ricardo's theory on Marxist and neoclassical thought. Sraffa's *Production of Commodities by Means of Commodities* (1960) provides a fertile framework for the analysis of the formal aspects of Ricardian rent theory; we end by looking at some of its limits and at the results obtained in the Sraffian literature on rent.

Ricardo's theory of extensive rent

In the chapter of the *Principles* devoted to Smith's theory of rent, Ricardo criticized Smith's idea that rent is one of the components that determines the price of goods. That is not the case, Ricardo maintained, because 'price is everywhere regulated by the return obtained by this last portion of capital, for which no rent whatever is paid' (*Works*, I: 329). This reveals the baseline of Ricardo's reasoning: rent always has to do with differences in productivity (returns), and land at the margin of cultivation never pays rent.

Ricardo first formulated his theory in the *Essay*. The basic assumptions of the model presented there can be summarized as follows: (a) land exists of different qualities; (b) of each quality of land, the available area is limited and fixed; (c) a quality of land where the available area is not entirely used for cultivation does not pay rent; and (d) the rate of profit is the same in all sectors of the economy. Ricardo furthermore assumed implicitly that corn is the only agricultural product. When the demand for corn is low and there is more than enough land of the best quality available to satisfy demand, no rent is paid. But as soon as the area of land of the best quality needs to be fully occupied, that is, as soon as land of the best quality becomes scarce and part of the land of the second-best quality must be put into cultivation, the price of corn rises up to a level that makes the cultivation of that type of land profitable. The owners of land of the best quality earn a positive rent, equal to the difference in the cost of production of corn on the second-best quality of land and the cost of production of corn on the best quality of land. (The cost of production is defined as the sum of capital costs, which include wages, and normal profits.)

When the demand rises even further and land of the second-best quality also becomes fully occupied, there is again a sudden increase of the price of corn and the creation of rent on land of the second-best quality. The fundamental principles of Ricardian rent theory are that the price of corn is equal to the cost of production of corn on the type of land that is partly in use (we shall refer to it as the 'marginal land') and that positive rents are paid for those types of land that are fully used, such that the differences in the cost of production of corn are levelled out. When the demand for corn gradually rises, less and less fertile lands have to be brought into cultivation one after another, and the price of corn as well as the rents of land increase spasmodically.

Ricardo's exposition of the theory of rent in the *Essay* presupposes that the corn values of the capital required for a given output of corn on the different types of land remain constant throughout the process of extension of cultivation. Let $k_1, k_2, \ldots$ with $k_1 < k_2 < \ldots$ be the corn values of the capital required to produce one quarter of corn. The order $1, 2, \ldots$ in which the different lands are cultivated coincides with the rent order of the different lands. When land i is marginal, the rent (per unit of corn produced) associated to land j is equal to $z_j(i) = 1 - (k_j/k_i)$, and it is easy to see that whatever may be i, we always have $z_1(i) > z_2(i) > \ldots$ The assumption of constant corn values of capital is, however, most unlikely, since every time the marginal land switches, relative prices change. Hence, the corn values of capital depend upon the marginal land i, and should be denoted as $k_1(i), k_2(i), \ldots$ In general, it cannot be maintained that we always have $k_1(i) < k_2(i) < \ldots$, and so the order of cultivation may be different from the rent order for a particular marginal land. In principle, it could even occur that the order of cultivation is not uniquely defined. It has been shown, however, that under certain conditions the order of cultivation is unique for a given real wage or a given rate of profits (Quadrio Curzio, 1967; Montani, 1975).

In the *Principles* Ricardo presented his theory of rent in a slightly different way. He classified the different types $1, 2, \ldots$ of land according to the corn output $q_1, q_2, \ldots$ obtained by employing a given dose of capital and labour, with $q_1 > q_2 > \ldots$ The hypothesis makes the order of cultivation $1, 2, \ldots$ independent of prices, and the same for the order of rents: since the corn rent of land j when land i is marginal is equal to $z_j(i) = q_j - q_i$, we have $z_1(i) > z_2(i) > \ldots$ This effectively solves the difficulty encountered by Ricardo in the *Essay*, but then another problem appears. In the *Principles* Ricardo presumed that the labour theory of value applies. This implies that there must be equal organic composition of capital. In itself this is an extremely strong assumption to make, but in the extensive rent case it must hold whatever the marginal land may be. It has been shown that this requires another strong assumption: the corn inputs of the different production processes must be proportional to the labour inputs (Erreygers, 1991; Klimovsky, 1993).

Other aspects of Ricardo's rent theory
The extensive rent case is based on the assumption that every type of land has its own specific constant-returns-to-scale method of production. But Ricardo also referred to another case: the one where successive doses of capital and labour are used on the same piece of land, yielding less and less corn (*Works*, I: 71; see also IV: 14). This can be interpreted as if a method of production exists characterized by a fixed factor (the land) and decreasing returns to scale with respect to a variable factor (doses of capital and labour). According to Ricardo, the same principle also applies in this case: the last dose of capital invested on the land generates no rent. That property is essential for Ricardo's construction: since prices are determined by the marginal methods of production, rent can be ignored to begin with.

An increase in the demand for corn may therefore be met by a more intensive use of land rather than by an extension of the area of cultivation. The rent created by this process is usually designated as intensive rent. Being more productive, the previously invested doses of capital and labour give rise to rent, 'for rent invariably proceeds from the employment of an additional quantity of labour with a proportionally less return' (*Works*, I: 72).

Ricardo stressed that the price of corn increases not because rents increase, but because it becomes more difficult to produce corn. Therefore, high rents are the effect of high prices, and Smith was mistaken when he asserted that rent is a component part of the price of commodities (ibid.: 79–80).

In the part of the *Principles* devoted to taxation Ricardo pointed out that a tax on rent affects only the landowners who earn rents. Since prices are determined by the methods of production that do not pay rents, a tax on rent has no effect on prices. Hence, landowners cannot shift taxes to consumers by increasing prices (ibid.: 173–5). He also explored the effects of tithes (ibid.: 176–80) and land taxes (ibid.: 181–90).

The tendency of the rate of profit to fall

In the theory of distribution Ricardo saw a methodological simplification in the possibility of getting rid of rent in order to deal with the more specific subject of the division of the net product between profits and wages. He was especially interested in the evolution of the rate of profits.

In any given period, the net product is distributed over rents, wages and profits. Ricardo used the theory of rent to construct a two-stage distribution theory: in the first stage the rents are determined, and in the second is the division of what is left of the net product between wages and profits. The division between wages and profits is governed by the evolution of the value of the real wage. By assumption, the average wage basket consists predominantly of corn (or corn-related products, such as bread) and is close to subsistence level, so that its composition hardly changes over time. This means that the value of the real wage tends to be determined by the value of corn. In particular, if it becomes more difficult to produce corn, the value of the real wage will increase and a greater share of the net product must be allocated to wages.

Ricardo's elimination of rent is a device to simplify economic analysis. What Ricardo tried to show (albeit perhaps not always coherently; see Erreygers, 1991) is that the development of the economic system tends to be to the advantage of the landowners and to the disadvantage of the capital owners. When the demand for food increases – as a result of population growth, not of rising real wages – the production of corn requires the cultivation of ever worse qualities of land, which raises the price of corn and the rents earned by landowners. In terms of labour value, a greater share of labour is devoted to the production of food, and landowners and labourers increase their shares in the economy's net product (yet without individual labourers being able to buy more). The share of capital owners, by contrast, erodes, which translates itself into a tendency of the rate of profits to fall. Since capital owners are in charge of investments, and a declining rate of return reduces their incentives to invest, there is a real danger that the economic system comes to a standstill in the future.

According to Ricardo, for a country like England the main answer to this threat is to open up the borders to foreign grain imports and to specialize in industrial products. He saw the outside world as an immense reservoir of land where corn can be produced relatively cheaply at a more or less constant cost. With these arguments, Ricardo intervened in the debates on the British Corn Laws. The issue at stake was whether the existing limitations and taxes on imports and exports of corn should be maintained (which in general benefited landowners, by keeping their rents high) or be abolished (which would benefit capital owners, by reducing the tendency of the rate of profits to fall).

Influence of Ricardo's theory of rent

The Ricardian theory of rent had a profound influence on a wide range of economists of the nineteenth and twentieth centuries (see Valassina, 1976; Guigou, 1982; Vidonne, 1986). We limit ourselves here to three remarkable examples.

Marx struggled for a long time with the (Ricardian) theory of rent; in a letter to Engels of June 1862 he even referred to it as 'rent shit' (*Grundrentscheiße*) ([1862] 1964: 248). In the end Marx departed partly from Ricardo: he accepted the existence of differential rent, but wanted to show that the labour theory of value was also compatible with a non-Ricardian type of rent, which he called absolute rent. He presented this theory both in the second volume of the *Theorien über den Mehrwert* ([1905–10] 1985) and in the third volume of *Das Kapital* ([1894] 1983), with minor differences between the two versions.

For Marx, profits and rents can only be the result of the exploitation of labour: they are different forms of surplus value. Marx realized at an early stage that the pure labour theory of value, according to which all commodities are sold at their labour values, presents serious difficulties. Given that the organic composition of capital differs widely across sectors, the pure labour theory of value would lead to higher rates of profits in labour-intensive sectors. The non-uniformity of the rates of profits across sectors would be in conflict with the hypothesis of competitive free markets. He therefore put forward a theory of prices of production, which are derived from labour values through a process of transformation. This transformation process is seen as a manifestation of the law of competition: it equalizes all rates of profits and brings about an average rate of profits in the economic system. It has the effect of transferring surplus value from labour-intensive sectors to capital-intensive sectors. Since agriculture is a labour-intensive sector, the law of competition would imply that agriculture is forced to transfer part of the surplus value it creates to the capital-intensive industrial sectors. But according to Marx this need not happen. Landowners are in fact in a position to resist the law of competition: as owners of indispensable natural resources, they have the power to shield agriculture from the competitive process. Hence, the agricultural sector does not have to transfer any of the surplus value that it creates. But since the profit rate in agriculture must be the same as in any other sector, the landowners are able to reap part of the surplus value created in agriculture as absolute rent.

The notion of absolute rent can be understood only in the context of Marx's labour theory of value and the transformation process. It becomes problematic as soon as one tries to elaborate a coherent theory of prices of production. The point was made already a long time ago by Ladislaus von Bortkiewicz (1911: 425).

Rent theory plays a central role in the discussions concerning the relationships between the marginalist theory, which was elaborated in the last quarter of the nineteenth century, and classical political economy. Widely different views on these relationships have been put forward, depending on whether the emphasis is laid on similarity or on divergence. The first approach is illustrated in the *Principles of Economics* by Alfred Marshall, who considered that marginalist theory extends the Ricardian rent theory to all commodities: even if most commodities can be reproduced, which is the basis of the classical theory of value, they are scarce at any time since their available amount at a given date is finite. Rents or quasi-rents are therefore attached to all commodities. According to this view, 'the rent of land is seen, not as a thing by itself, but as the leading species of a large genus' (Marshall [1890] 1920: viii).

The notion of rent has been adapted and extended in modern approaches to explain incomes linked to the holding of privileged positions in the economic system. It is then associated with the idea of a monopoly (such a link was not made by Ricardo but is either implicit or explicit in Marx's, Walras's and many other works), as well as with the idea of a distribution of national income adverse to common interest, which is indeed an adaptation of Ricardo's argument.

Sraffa and neo-Ricardian rent theory

The modern formalization of Ricardo's ideas on rent is due to Sraffa (1960). Sraffa started by studying single-product systems without land, where the net product is entirely distributed between wages and profits. He proved the existence of a trade-off between the general rate of profits and the level of the real wage. The brief Chapter 11 on land comes at the end of the second part of the book, devoted to multiple-product systems. The reason for this is that land can be considered as both an input and an output of an agricultural process, giving rise to joint production of an agricultural commodity and land. The particular structure of the technical coefficients relative to land (in every process, the amount of land utilized is identical to the amount produced) allowed Sraffa to assert that lands are non-basic goods, thereby providing an analytical foundation to Ricardo's proposition with regard to the effects of a tax on land. Other peculiarities of systems of production with land (such as the non-existence of a positive standard commodity, for instance) are also related to the joint production nature of these systems.

When writing down the price equations, Sraffa used an alternative representation where lands appear on the input side only, and land prices are replaced by rents. In formal terms, Sraffa's price equations can be written in a compact way as follows:

$$\mathbf{Bp} = (1 + r)\mathbf{Ap} + \Lambda\rho + \boldsymbol{\ell}w \qquad (1)$$

where $\mathbf{A}$ is the input matrix (lands excluded), $\mathbf{B}$ the output matrix, Λ the land input matrix, $\boldsymbol{\ell}$ the labour input vector, $\mathbf{p}$ the price vector, ρ the rent vector, w the wage rate and r the rate of profits. In the extensive rent case where one agricultural commodity (corn) is produced by m different lands, the Ricardian idea of zero rent on the marginal land is translated by Sraffa as:

$$\rho_1\rho_2 \cdots \rho_m = 0 \qquad (2)$$

In his study of rent, Sraffa followed Ricardo's methodology and, even if he avoided any explicit reference to demand, studied how a 'progressive increase of production' (1960: 76) modifies the existing equilibrium and leads to the choice of a new marginal method. It is that faithfulness to Ricardo's approach which explains why he departed here from the explicit warning of the preface, where he wrote 'that no changes in output . . . are considered' (ibid.: v). Sraffa stressed that the incoming marginal method is determined by a profitability criterion: it is a matter of comparing relative costs. He (ibid.: 75) therefore criticized Ricardo's reference to the notion of fertility as a physical characteristic of land: the order in which lands are brought into cultivation depends on costs and, as a consequence, may vary with the distribution variable taken as exogenous (the rate of profits for Sraffa, the real wage for Ricardo). Likewise, the order of the rents for a given level of demand need not coincide with the order in which the lands are brought into cultivation.

It must be said, however, that Ricardo did take the value criterion explicitly into account in some passages of the *Principles*, as exemplified by the numerical example attached to the final note of Chapter 2. In that respect, Sraffa's critique may be reinterpreted as mainly addressed to Ricardo's reference to the labour theory of value, which implies that the relative costs and prices are independent of distribution and, therefore, may sustain an economic interpretation in physical terms.

Sraffa (1925) had already considered the issue of the intensification of cultivation as a rational alternative to its extension. Sraffa's (1960) explanation of intensive rent is different from Ricardo's: he assumed that a choice can be made between several methods of cultivation on the same homogenous land. As long as the demand for corn is low, only one method of production, the cheapest, is operated and no rent is paid. When land has become fully cultivated, a more productive method must be operated (productivity being defined as net output of corn per unit of land used). Sraffa introduced the idea of the coexistence of both methods on the same land. The occurrence of intensive rent is then explained as the result of the need to combine the previous method, which was used because of its relative cheapness, with the new one, which is more expensive, but also more productive. The price of corn must be high enough to cover the cost of production of the second method of production. An adequate choice of the intensive rent allows one to level out the overall costs of production of both methods, which are then equally profitable and may be operated side by side. Further increases in production will be met by expanding the more productive method at the expense of the other, with no change in prices and rents, until the previous method is totally eliminated.

On the whole, Sraffa's analysis of rent leads to rather optimistic conclusions as to the existence of prices and rents able to sustain a high level of production, whether it be through extensive or intensive cultivation. Moreover, if Sraffa mentioned that complications may arise from the multiplicity of agricultural products, he considered them as inessential, so that the general analysis can be reduced to combinations of the above simple cases (ibid.: 76–7).

The post-Sraffian literature on rent, initiated by Quadrio Curzio (1967), has first dealt with the two basic cases of extensive cultivation proper and intensive cultivation proper. Extensive cultivation proper corresponds to the hypotheses of a unique agricultural good, a unique method of production on each land and a unique method for every industrial product. Under these stringent assumptions, Montani (1975) showed that the order of cultivation for a given rate of profits then coincides with that of the decreasing wages that the lands would pay for a zero rent. But that simple law can hardly be extended outside its initial framework.

The development of the analysis beyond these basic cases led to the adoption of a more general framework and, simultaneously, a more precise formalization of the rent problem. That formalization takes explicitly into account the demand vector and the physical limits given by the scarcity of lands. A long-term equilibrium is then characterized as a solution to a system of inequalities with complementarity relationships: for instance, the condition that the rent on the marginal land must be zero, which was written as (2) in Sraffa's formalization, is now written as the inequality $\rho_i \geq 0$ for every land, which becomes the equality $\rho_i = 0$ if land i is not fully cultivated (Salvadori, 1986). Since the 1980s, several phenomena that Ricardo and Sraffa had not foreseen have been identified and analysed (see the collection of essays edited by Bidard, 1987). One of these is the multiplicity of long-term equilibria for a given demand basket (for instance, D'Agata, 1983), each with its own set of prices, rents and activity levels. This may happen even in the case of extensive cultivation (only one method of cultivation per type of land) or intensive cultivation (only one homogeneous land) with one agricultural product, and suggests that Sraffa's analysis was incomplete.

However interesting these results are, the approach developed these last fifty years is mainly based on the study of a system of equations for a given level of demand, and the methodology followed differs significantly from that used by Ricardo and Sraffa, which was centred on the transformations of equilibrium with demand: Ricardo and Sraffa stressed that the economic answer to a physical scarcity consists in introducing one new method and, therefore, their reflections concern the law governing the succession of methods. That law plays no role in the static approach. Let us show how a return to dynamics helps us understand the phenomena at stake.

A first example concerns the possible emergence of non-Ricardian equilibria (Saucier, 1981). When a scarcity constraint is met on a land, the price of corn rises and the non-operated corn methods become more profitable. The price of iron also increases as soon as the presently operated iron method makes use of corn. Consider an alternative iron method, which is not yet operated but is corn-saving with regard to the present method. Its profitability suffers from the rise of corn (but only slightly since, by hypothesis, the corn input is small) and benefits from that of iron. On the whole, it may happen that its profitability rises and reaches the normal level before any alternative corn method. In the next equilibrium, two iron methods are operated, with the corn-saving method being progressively substituted for the other when the demand for corn increases. Such a non-Ricardian equilibrium is characterized by the coexistence of two methods of production of iron, while corn is produced on one type of land that is fully cultivated by one method of production only. Prices are determined by the two industrial methods, and rent by the agricultural method. Then Ricardo's general strategy fails: even if all methods are of the single-product type (lands apart), the standard economic laws do not hold because the methods that determine prices do not constitute a single-product system.

More generally, let us start from a given equilibrium and consider the effects of an increasing demand for corn. In a first step, no change in prices and rents occurs and the adaptation of the economy is merely in physical terms: cultivation is extended on some quality of land, or a more productive method is progressively substituted for another. A limit is reached when the corresponding quality of land is fully cultivated or the previous method completely eliminated. Then corn becomes scarce: its price increases, as explained by Ricardo, but also the prices of all goods in the production of which corn enters directly or indirectly. The changes of prices affect the profitability of all non-marginal methods. The next method that will be introduced is the first that did not yield the normal rate of profits in the previous state but becomes profitable after the changes. If that method does provide a solution to the scarcity problem, either because it produces more corn or saves on its use, a new equilibrium is reached. However, even in the case of intensive rent proper, it may be the case that the incoming method does not solve the physical problem, because it is less productive per unit of land than the method it replaces. In other words, the origin of the difficulties comes from the fact that the loss of the previous equilibrium is due to a physical reason, whereas the choice of the incoming method is entirely determined on the basis of its profitability. The fault in Sraffa's reasoning is to admit that the expensiveness of the incoming method guarantees its higher productivity (Sraffa may have been aware of that point but, contrary to his opinion [1960: 87], the positivity of rent does not suffice to ensure that property). As the debates on capital theory initiated by Sraffa's book itself have shown, that identity is a hypothesis that does not hold automatically. If the hypothesis is met (that condition can be written in algebraic terms), the Ricardian dynamics work (Bidard, 2014) and the uniqueness of the solution for a given demand is ensured (Erreygers, 1990). If it is not met, a contradiction is found between the physical side and the value side of the land problem. The possible existence of multiple equilibria for a given level of demand, a phenomenon pointed at by the static approach, reveals indirectly the failure of the dynamics at some stage when demand grows from a low to a high level.

Exhaustible resources

Ricardo mostly talked about the rent of lands, but he was convinced that the same principles apply to the rent of mines, and he lambasted Smith for making a distinction between the two (*Works*, I: 329). At the beginning of the chapter on the rent of lands he explicitly mentioned that rent is paid 'for the use of the original and indestructible powers of the soil' (ibid.: 67). When talking about the rent of mines, however, Ricardo focused mainly on the differences in the qualities of mines, neglecting the fact that mines are not indestructible: since mines can be exhausted, they have a limited lifetime. Taking into account this aspect leads to a specific theory of exhaustible resources and to the notion of royalty, which differs from the Ricardian notion of differential rent. No hints of such a theory can be found in Sraffa, who followed Ricardo in assimilating mineral deposits with lands (1960: 74), and only proposed to extend the theory of rent to the case of 'machines of an obsolete type which are still in use' (ibid.: 78), somewhat analogous to Marshall's notion of quasi-rent. The pioneering (neoclassical) contribution to the theory of exhaustible resources is Hotelling (1931). In recent years, attempts have been made to develop a neo-Ricardian theory of exhaustible resources with original features (see *Metroeconomica*, 2001), but not everyone agrees on the necessity to introduce the Hotelling Rule.

CHRISTIAN BIDARD AND GUIDO ERREYGERS

See also:

Capital and Profits; Exhaustible Resources and Mines; Foreign Trade; Labour and Wages; Marshall, Alfred, on Ricardo; Marx, Karl Heinrich, on Ricardo; *Principles of Political Economy, and Taxation*.

References

Anderson, J. (1777), *Observations on the Means of Exciting a Spirit of National Industry*, London: T. Cadell/ Edinburgh: C. Elliot.
Bidard, C. (ed.) (1987), *La Rente: Actualité de l'Approche Classique*, Paris: Economica.
Bidard, C. (2014), 'The Ricardian rent theory: an overview', Centro Sraffa Working Paper No. 8.
Bortkiewicz, L. von (1911), 'Die Rodbertus'sche Grundrententheorie und die Marx'sche Lehre von der absoluten Grundrente', *Archiv für die Geschichte des Sozialismus und der Arbeiterbewegung*, 1, 1–40, 391–434.

D'Agata, A. (1983), 'The existence and unicity of cost-minimizing systems in intensive rent theory', *Metroeconomica*, **35**(1–2), 147–58.

Erreygers, G. (1990), *Terre, Rente et Choix de Techniques. Une Etude sur la Théorie Néo-Ricardienne*, PhD dissertation, Université Paris X – Nanterre.

Erreygers, G. (1991), 'Production of commodities without commodities: Ricardo on profit and rent in the *Principles*', *Recherches Economiques de Louvain*, **57**(4), 349–60.

Guigou, J.-L. (1982), *La Rente Foncière. Les Théories et leur Evolution depuis 1650*, Paris: Economica.

Hotelling, H. (1931), 'The economics of exhaustible resources', *Journal of Political Economy*, **39**(2), 137–75.

Klimovsky, E. (1993), 'L'ambiguïté de la notion de composition du capital dans les *Principes* de Ricardo', *Cahiers d'Economie Politique*, **22**, 111–24.

Malthus, T.R. ([1815] 1986), *An Inquiry into the Nature and Progress of Rent, and the Principles by which it is Regulated, Vol. 7*, in E.A. Wrigley and D. Souden (eds), *The Works, of Thomas Robert Malthus*, London: Pickering & Chatto, pp. 115–45.

Marshall, A. ([1890] 1920), *Principles of Economics*, London: Macmillan.

Marx, K. ([1894] 1983), *Das Kapital. Kritik der politischen Ökonomie. Dritter Band* in *Marx-Engels-Werke, Vol. 25*, Berlin: Dietz.

Marx, K. ([1905–10] 1985), *Theorien über den Mehrwert* in *Marx-Engels-Werke, Vol. 26*, 26.2, Berlin: Dietz.

Marx, K. ([1862] 1964), 'Letter to Engels', in *Marx-Engels-Werke, Vol. 30*, letter 141, Berlin: Dietz p. 248.

Metroeconomica (2001), 'Special issue: symposium on exhaustible natural resources and Sraffian analysis', *Metroeconomica*, **52**(3), 239–328.

Montani, G. (1975), 'Scarce natural resources and income distribution', *Metroeconomica*, **27**(1), 68–101.

Quadrio Curzio, A. (1967), *Rendita e Distribuzione in un Modello Economico Plurisettoriale*, Milan: Giuffrè.

Salvadori, N. (1986), 'Lands and choice of techniques within the Sraffa framework', *Australian Economic Papers*, **25**(46), 94–105.

Saucier, P. (1981), *Le Choix des Techniques en Situation de Limitation des Ressources*, PhD dissertation, Université Paris II.

Sraffa, P. (1925), 'Sulle relazioni tra costo e quantità prodotta', *Annali di Economia*, **2**, 277–328.

Sraffa, P. (1960), *Production of Commodities by Means of Commodities*, Cambridge, UK: Cambridge University Press.

Torrens, R. (1815), *An Essay on the External Corn Trade*, London: J. Hatchard.

Valassina, G. (1976), *La Teoria della Rendita nella Storia del Pensiero Economico*, Milan: Vita e Pensiero.

Vidonne, P. (1986), *La Formation de la Pensée Economique*, Paris: Economica.

West, E. ([1815] 1903), *Essay on the Application of Capital to Land*, a reprint of J.H. Hollander (ed.), *Economic Tracts*, Baltimore, MD: Johns Hopkins University Press.

Life and Activities

Early life

David Ricardo was born on 18 April 1772 in London as the third child of Abraham Ricardo and Abigail Delvalle. Abraham lived until 1812, having been born in Amsterdam on 11 March 1734. Abraham Ricardo was a stockbroker, just like his father Joseph Israel Ricardo (1699–1762). In the spring of 1760, Abraham went to London as an agent for his father, and married there on 30 April 1769. He was elected '*Parnas*', or warden, of the Portuguese-Jewish community of London in 1785, 1789, 1793, 1798 and 1802, and was also a very successful stockbroker for this community. David Ricardo's grandfather, Joseph Israel Ricardo, had died in 1762 and was buried in Ouderkerk, the famous cemetery of the Portuguese-Jewish community, near Amsterdam. In 1721, he had married Hanna Abaz, a Christian woman who converted to Judaism (a '*Gijoret*'). In the municipal archives of Amsterdam, the father of Joseph Israel Ricardo is referred to as David Israel of Livorno. His brothers did not use the name Ricardo either but just the name Israel, mostly 'of Livorno'. Often the profession of 'coral maker' is mentioned in the archives, but perhaps coral trader is meant. It seems probable that the Ricardos had left Spain for Livorno around 1650.

When arriving in Amsterdam, the Ricardos became active members of the Portuguese-Jewish community. Abraham and most of his family gave financial support to the Talmud Tora and Ets Haim (Jewish religious educational establishments). But the Ricardos were not entirely based in Amsterdam. Apart from The Hague and London, they went to North and South America and Curaçao. For example, the son of David Hizkiau Ricardo (Abraham's brother), Mordechay Ricardo (1771–1842), went to Curaçao and there he became the patron of military and political leader Simon Bolivar. Abraham's sister Rebecca was the mother of Isaac Da Costa, the Dutch poet (1798–1860).

Little is known about David Ricardo's youth. In 1824, *A Memoir of David Ricardo* appeared anonymously, in which it was said that his father wanted him to go into business, in particular in the stock exchange. We now know that his brother Moses (1776–1866) wrote the memoir. In a letter of 10 January 1824 James Mill wrote to John Ramsay McCulloch on David Ricardo: 'You have probably seen the account of him in the Annual Obituary which has been written by his brother Moses'. This confirms Piero Sraffa's suggestion of 1951 (*Works*, X: 14).

From the memoir we learn that to this end Abraham sent his son David to Amsterdam from 1783 until 1785, where he stayed in the house of his uncle David Israel Ricardo Jr's widow on the Nieuwe Keizersgracht 70, where his uncle Moses Israel Ricardo (1738–1800), registered as a Jewish trader, also lived (Heertje, 2004, 2005). It is highly probable that he received some education at the house on the Nieuwe Keizersgracht in the form of reading, writing and arithmetic, as well as the French and Spanish languages from a private tutor. There is no doubt that he and his uncle Moses went to the nearby Portuguese synagogue in Amsterdam every Saturday. Presumably, David learned a lot about his uncle's financial profession and the blank spot in his education seems to be complete if we look at informal learning as part of the intellectual and professional development of an intelligent youngster. After his return to London in 1785, he followed a normal school education 'till his father took him into business' (*Works*, X: 3). From his 14th year, he helped his father on the stock exchange.

In a letter to her mother, dated 14 November 1821, writer Maria Edgeworth wrote that Ricardo told her:

> We were 15 children. My father gave me but little education. He thought reading, writing and arithmetic sufficient because he doomed me to be nothing but a man of business. He sent me at eleven to Amsterdam to learn Dutch, French, Spanish but I was so unhappy at being separated from my brothers and sisters and family that I learned nothing in 2 years but Dutch which I could not help learning. (Colvin, 1971: 266)

Sraffa suggests that Ricardo was sent to the religious school of the Portuguese-Jewish community in Amsterdam, the Talmud Tora (*Works*, X: 210). However, I have come to the conclusion that this is highly improbable – I did not find Ricardo's name in the list of pupils of the Talmud Tora. Moses, in his memoir, does not refer to the Talmud Tora, and Ricardo did not mention to Maria Edgeworth that he had ever received a religious education. That his stay in Holland during 1783–85 made a big impression on him follows from a letter written from Amsterdam to his eldest son Osman in 1822. 'Although I had not been in this town for more than 30 years I had no difficulty in finding my way, alone, about those places which had formerly been familiar to me' (ibid.: 208). This letter is part of a set of letters written to describe his tour on the Continent with his wife and two daughters. His personal visits to Amsterdam in 1822 concern Portuguese Jews.

On 20 December 1793, David Ricardo married Priscilla Ann Wilkinson, an English Quaker. This marriage led to a breach with his parents. He never saw his mother again. After the death of his mother in 1801, his father repaired the breach. He left his father's firm and with the help of friends he established himself as stockbroker in the City of London. Within the space of only a few years, he managed to become far richer than his father. His prestige on the stock exchange was high. Around 1819, he retired from the financial world in London to live at his country house Gatcombe Park in Minchinhampton, which he acquired in 1814, and is currently the house of Princess Anne. The Society of Friends of the Quakers formally disowned Priscilla Ricardo-Wilkinson, nevertheless, the birth of all their children was registered at the Society.

Ricardo on the stock exchange
Ricardo was employed on the stock exchange by his father at the age of 14 in 1786, and by the beginning of 1793 he was doing some business there on his own. He was what was called a stockjobber, one of those who dealt on his own account. The stockjobber phase was crucial in his development. It led directly to his becoming a loan contractor and an economist, and it arose directly from his ancestral tradition.

Government expenditure is partly financed by means of loans. In Ricardo's days these loans were raised by contractors operating on the stock exchange who competed for providing the loan. Each contractor formed a list of subscribers who were associated with him and who took a share in the loan. It was in 1806 that the names of John Barnes, James Steers and David Ricardo were first found among the would-be contractors, bidding on behalf of their list from the stock exchange (*Works*, X: 79). There were then loans every year until the end of the Napoleonic Wars, and the biggest of the loans was raised on 14 June, just four days before the Battle of Waterloo in 1815. Among the four contractors was the stock exchange list of Barnes, Steers and Ricardo. The terms were very favourable to the lenders, and Ricardo, who invested a large amount in the loan, made a large profit after the victory. In all, he was a successful contractor in seven loans. It is noteworthy, however, and illustrative of his detached scientific reasoning that while his grandfather, his father, and he had enriched themselves on the stock exchange, he held a negative view of the existence of any public debt at all.

During the reign of George III (1760–1820) the Jewish community held a less alien position than before, although the influx of Jews from the Continent tended to maintain their foreign character. But Jews such as Benjamin and Abraham Goldsmid became important financiers and especially after Waterloo the Jewish community had improved its economic position, which also led to a higher ranking in social and cultural life. Thus, during Ricardo's lifetime the position of the Jews rose steadily, notwithstanding the absence of legislative actions. This environment helped, and perhaps his heredity helped more.

Ricardo's public life
From an intellectual point of view, Ricardo was a late-flowering individual, although already in his youth he showed 'a taste for abstract and general reasoning' (*Works*, X: 4). Ricardo had no systematic education, and his natural gifts blossomed only after his

financial activities and success. From his 25th year onwards, Ricardo's financial success enabled him to study mathematics, chemistry, geology and mineralogy. In 1808 he became a member of the Geological Society (ibid.: 49). His inclination for the exact sciences changed direction when, almost by accident, he came across a copy of the *Wealth of Nations* in 1799 (McCulloch, 1846: xvii). He then fell in love with economics, although it took another ten years before he wrote, anonymously in the *Morning Chronicle*, an article the 'Price of Gold' (*Works*, III: 30), which provoked many reactions. After this first article, he wrote several pamphlets, and eventually his magnum opus in 1817. In 1814, James Mill (1773–1836), father of the famous John Stuart Mill (1806–73), not only had more or less forced Ricardo to begin writing his *Principles* but also urged him to take up a seat in Parliament (*Works*, VI: 138). At first, Ricardo was not inclined to act on either of Mill's suggestions on account of his innate modesty and apparent lack of eloquence, both orally and in writing. Ricardo himself made the prospect of a career in Parliament depend on the success of his book. This can be concluded from his letter to Mill of December 20th, 1815:

> I do not readily fall in with your suggestions respecting a seat in Parliament. I fear I should be mere lumber there. From the trials which I have already made I am sure I should never be able to deliver my sentiments on any subject in debate, and I cannot perceive in what other way I could be in the least useful. If my book succeeds, as you promise me, perhaps my ambition may be awakened, and I may aspire to rank with senators, but at present I have the greatest awe for the distinguished persons who figure in St. Stephens. If you are indeed right in your prognostications, if I am really to be the author of a book of merit, I shall bow to your superior discernment. Let me however first be convinced that you are not a partial judge, and do not view my performance through the medium of a too friendly bias. (*Works*, VII: 113–14)

Nevertheless, in the spring of 1819, Ricardo became a member of the House of Commons where he remained until his death in 1823. Before entering Parliament, complicated negotiations took place during almost two years behind the scenes on the borough of Portarlington, the seat in Ireland for which Ricardo applied in 1819. Once in the House of Commons, he aligned with neither the Whigs nor the Tories. Later, he was described as a 'moderate oppositionist' and as somebody who 'voted on the side of the people' (*Works*, V: xix). Ricardo made several speeches in Parliament, in particular on economic topics. Time and again, Ricardo defended the interests of the poor and in doing so revealed his social concerns. His attitude towards matters of religion can be illustrated by the following quotation, taken from his speech in Parliament on 26 March 1823:

> All religious opinions, however absurd and extravagant, might be conscientiously believed by some individuals. Why, then, was one man to set up his ideas on the subject as the criterion from which no other was to be allowed to differ with impunity? Why was one man to be considered infallible, and all his fellow-men as frail and erring creatures? Such a doctrine ought not to be tolerated. It savoured too much of the Inquisition to be received as genuine in a free country like England. A fair and free discussion ought to be allowed on all religious topics. (Ibid.: 280)

William Wilberforce, who spoke after Ricardo, made the following entry in his diary: 'I had hoped that Ricardo had become a Christian; I see now that he has only ceased to be a Jew' (ibid.).

While Ricardo was a member of the House of Commons, he took part in several Select Committees. I mention just a few. On 9 February 1819 the Select Committee on the Poor Law was appointed. David Ricardo was added on 1 March 1819. On 7 March 1821 the Select Committee on Petitions complaining of the Depressed State of Agriculture was appointed. Ricardo played an important role in this Agricultural Committee. He called two merchants as witnesses, Thomas Tooke and Edward Solly, the latter a London merchant formerly of Danzig (ibid.: xxiv). Ricardo examined the agricultural witnesses with great competence. In a letter to John Ramsay McCulloch of 25 April 1821, Ricardo refers to the two men he called, commenting first on Tooke, and then he writes:

> Mr Solly, the other merchant I called, gave some valuable information respecting the price of corn in Poland, and in the Prussian Ports, and also regarding the expense of conveying corn from the interior, to the Ports of Embarkation, and from these ports in London. (*Works*, VIII: 374)

This letter makes it clear that Ricardo is prepared to collect information from acquaintances with knowledge about data that he does not possess himself (Heertje, 2007: 546). This evidence supports the view of Timothy Davis that Ricardo is not only an outstanding theoretical but also an empirical economist (Davis, 2005: 100ff). A year later the Select Committee on the Allegations of the Several Petitions presented to the House in the last and present Sessions of Parliament complaining of the Distressed State of Agriculture was appointed, of which again Ricardo was a member. This time the report was strongly protectionist, in contrast with that of the Committee of 1821. Ricardo comments on the report in the publication *On Protection to Agriculture* (Ricardo, 1822). Other important committees were the Committee on Public Accounts, appointed on 18 April 1822 and the Committee on the Labouring Poor in Ireland, appointed on 20 June 1823. Ricardo was added to this Committee on 23 June 1823. The Committee reported on 16 July 1823, just two months before Ricardo's untimely death (*Works*, VIII: 374).

In November 1817 Ricardo was nominated High Sheriff of Gloucestershire for the year 1818. The duties of the High Sheriff, who is the chief officer of the king in every shire or county, were mainly ceremonial (Weatherall, 1976: 96). However, in 1818 Ricardo's duties appeared to be rather heavy. First of all, in view of three Assizes in 1818, he had to meet with the Judges, escort them into the city, preside at a dinner and to escort them next morning to Divine Service at the cathedral. Then in 1818 a General Election took place that had to be organized by the High Sheriff. Finally, in December 1818 Queen Charlotte died, and the High Sheriff was requested to convene a County Meeting. In a letter to Trower he described his experience with the high office:

> I thank you for your congratulations on the occasion of the high honours which I have attained. The hour is fast approaching when I shall have to appear before the Judges, arrayed in the masquerade suit which I have been obliged to provide. The Assizes for our County commence on the 1st of April. I hope I shall sustain my high office with becoming dignity – the difficulty is much increased by my being so much a stranger in the county, never having been present on any public occasion whatever. From this moment however I may date my public life; as the ice once broken, I shall not fail to meet my neighbours 2 or 3 times a year in Gloucester.
>
> The expense of the office in our county does not exceed £ 450, so that on that score I shall be better off than you. You may depend on having all the advantage which my experience can give you in the way of instruction previous to your election. (*Works*, VII: 258–9)

In a letter of 5 May 1819 to an unknown clergyman, Ricardo comes back to his role as High Sheriff in 1818. He writes:

> Having served the office of Sheriff last year, I have been as usual appointed steward of the ensuring annual meeting of the Governors of the Hospital, this year, and it becomes my duty to request a Clergyman to preach the sermons for the benefit of the Institution at the Cathedral on the Sunday preceding the summer Assizes. Under these circumstances I venture to request you to be so obliging as to undertake the duty of preaching the sermon on that occasion. (Letter, private collection, A.H.)

Ricardo, the economic thinker

His publications in the years 1809–15 mainly dealt with monetary and financial topics. In these writings, Ricardo reacted to the problems of the day, and made use of his experience as a man of financial business. But even in these contributions he showed a high degree of independent thinking and originality. An interesting illustration of this was his proposal to substitute the gold standard for a gold bullion standard, which saves gold in relation to the quantity of bank notes. In his more theoretical publications after 1815, his sense for abstract reasoning and deduction came to the fore. This development culminated in the publication of his major book *On the Principles of Political Economy, and Taxation* in 1817. The printing of the first edition of the *Principles* began at the end of February 1817 and 750 copies were printed. A second edition was printed in 1819, a third in 1821, both consisting of 1000 copies. These numbers indicate that Ricardo's book became a success within a rather short time. The book, however, is by no means a popular publication. It is difficult both with regard to composition and style and to economic theory. Ricardo did not plan the *Principles* in the sense that he had a framework in his mind before he started writing, but, as Sraffa puts it: 'he wrote according to the sequence of his own ideas' (*Works*, I: xxii). Ricardo was a far better thinker than writer on economics. On 22 December 1815 James Mill wrote to Ricardo: 'For as you are already the best *thinker* on political economy, I am resolved you shall also be the best writer' (*Works*, VI: 340; original emphasis). His treatment of economics is less descriptive than, for example, Adam Smith's treatment in the *Wealth of Nations*.

Ricardo's book illustrates the deductive method. The use of the word 'suppose' is characteristic. Although Ricardo did not make use of mathematics himself, he laid down the foundations of the modern approach in economics, in particular the introduction of models in economic analysis. In Ricardo's hands economics is less a subject with absolute statements and becomes more relativistic. With a change in assumptions, the conclusions also change.

When Ricardo published his *Principles of Political Economy* he was already a well-known author. Thus, the publication of the *Principles* did not happen suddenly or accidentally – it was the culmination of a long series of events, the earlier writings on economics and the dazzling career on the stock exchange, which are not independent of his Jewish environment and background. He was led to write on currency, his brother Moses said, because of the great number of transactions he had had with the Bank of England as a loan contractor. In particular, he studied the difference that existed between the value of the coin and the bank note and he wanted to 'ascertain from what cause the depreciation of the latter arose' (*Works*, X: 7).

In our time economics has developed partly into a set of economic models. It is interesting to note that Ricardo has been reproached for his use of the deductive method, which was criticized as being impracticable and non-social. Both reproaches are unfounded and can be ascribed to an insufficient understanding of exact reasoning in the study of social relationships. Ricardo's method has the advantage of bringing into the open his assumptions and of making explicit the relationship between assumptions and conclusions. This is the basis for the continuing improvement of the theory. Schumpeter referred to the habit of applying results of pure theory to the solution of practical problems as the 'Ricardian Vice' (Schumpeter, 1954: 473). Moreover, Ricardo's speeches in Parliament and his social behaviour only reflect his deep concern for the weak and the poor. His coolness as a theorist must be distinguished from his warmth as a person. His conclusion that in the course of economic development wages will just cover the cost of living springs from his analysis of a decentralized economy in which the economic role of the state is modest. It does not imply that he considered the level of wages ideal or socially justified.

This brings us to a very important aspect of Ricardo's position in economics. The fact is that the interpretation of his work is still under debate. On the one hand, we recognize the Sraffian, and on the other hand, the neoclassical interpretation of Ricardo. According to the neoclassical interpretation, Ricardo belongs to the Classical School of Adam Smith, Thomas Robert Malthus and John Stuart Mill. As such, he is part of the harmony model in economics. In this model everybody aims at the maximization of individual welfare as consumer and producer, which leads to the best of all possible worlds. In modern economic theory, this is structured in terms of general equilibrium and Pareto optimality. Political liberalism is based on it, and Ricardo was a liberal. He was neither dogmatic nor intolerant, knew how to separate personal feelings from business and preferred individual freedom to collective governance. He was a defender of free trade and in favour of small government (Hollander, 1979, 1995).

At the same time, Ricardo's work opens up the possibility to regard him as a forerunner of Karl Marx, the founder of the conflict model in economics, that is, the conflict between the proletariat and the capitalists. In the hands of Karl Marx, Ricardo's labour theory of value became an absolute doctrine. Ricardo restricted his analysis of prices to the case of reproducible goods. Marx exploited this theory to make labour the source of value.

Ricardo also paved the way for Karl Marx in another respect. While in the 1817 and 1819 editions of his *Principles*, Ricardo did not expect serious consequences for the labourers of introducing machinery, he changed his mind on this issue in the third edition of his book in 1821. He added a new chapter 'On Machinery', in which he explained that labourers might suffer from the introduction of machinery. Later, Marx quoted with approval Ricardo's famous phrase: 'Machinery and labour are in constant competition' (*Works*, I: 395). The essence is that technical change may cause a conflict between the proletariat and the capitalists. On the one hand the introduction of machinery raises the quantity of consumer goods, on the other hand its labour-saving character raises the level of unemployment. Again, in Marx's hands, a more or less incidental observation by Ricardo became the cornerstone of his theory on the breakdown of capitalism (Cozzi and Marchionatti, 2001).

Let me add a further note on Ricardo's distinction between reproducible and non-reproducible goods. Natural prices, reflecting reproduction costs of (reproducible) goods, have to be distinguished from market prices in Ricardo's theory. Market prices are a short-run phenomenon. They are a result of demand and supply. The Sraffians (Kurz, 2000 and Kurz and Salvadori, 2003) put all the emphasis on Ricardo's long-run price theory. The neoclassical economists neglect the long-run approach in Ricardo, and refer to market prices and the market mechanism in Ricardo. As a member of the Classical School, Ricardo adhered to the notion of a one-way avenue of production to consumption. But, as a Sraffian, he would look at the economic process as a cyclical process, based on reproduction (Caravale, 1985). He would be at ease with the title of Sraffa's book, *Production of Commodities by Means of Commodities* (Sraffa, 1960). On this major theoretical theme, Ricardo, Marx and Sraffa would be in full agreement.

While Ricardo put aside the case of non-reproducible goods like paintings and historical monuments, as they are the exception rather than the rule, these days these goods are becoming more and more relevant. From the point of view of price theory, there is still the problem of Ricardo's day. Nothing more can be said about such goods than what Ricardo himself already asserted in 1817, that is, their value 'varies with the varying wealth and inclinations of those who are desirous to possess them' (*Works*, I: 12). In my view the distinction between reproducible and non-reproducible goods is a lasting contribution by David Ricardo to economic theory. The analysis of this distinction and its consequences for value and price theory is a challenge for present-day economic theory.

Tour on the Continent

In July 1822, near the end of his life, Ricardo went on a tour on the Continent with his wife, their two youngest daughters, Mary and Birtha, the governess Miss Lancey and Mrs Ricardo's maid Mrs Cleaver. They were joined by Shuman the courier. The tour with their own carriage brought them to Belgium, Holland, Germany, Switzerland, Italy and France. By 8 December 1822 they were back in London. In a certain sense the tour was a replica of the six-week excursion Ricardo made in 1817 with his brother Ralph. While in Amsterdam, the party visited Ricardo's family members of the Portuguese-Jewish community. A few months later they visited the synagogue in Leghorn, Italy.

It was James Mill who had suggested that Ricardo should write a day-to-day account of his journey on the Continent. This idea took the form of a journal. The letters were written on folio sheets and were meant to be sent to James Mill who would circulate them to Ricardo's children. But after the first letter Ricardo decided otherwise. The remaining letters were sent to his eldest son Osman (1795–1881) and his wife Harriet (1799–1875). The letters were preserved by Osman and after his death passed into the hands of Frank Ricardo (1850–97), the fifth son of Ricardo's youngest son Mortimer Ricardo (1807–76).

In 1891 the journal was privately printed for the family under the title *Letters Written by David Ricardo During a Tour on the Continent* (*Works*, X: 180). The question arises, which member of the family is responsible for the initiative to publish the letters in a book for private circulation? In August 2008 I was able to buy a copy of the book. In fact, it is a presentation copy of Frank Ricardo to his cousin Henrietta Louisa, great-grandchild of Henrietta, Ricardo's daughter (1796–1839). A letter is tipped in, written by Frank's wife Alice Henrietta Monckton (1849–1930). The letter, dated 21 April 1891 reads as follows:

My dearest Nettie,

We are sending you a copy of some letters written by your great-grandfather to Uncle Osman and which we have printed thinking they would interest the family. I copied them out, so I feel almost an authoress. Should you be in London next week and if so may I come to tea one day? In great haste and with love from us both.

Yours affectionately Alice H. Ricardo.

The letter makes clear that Frank Ricardo decided to make the journal available for living descendants of David Ricardo and that his wife took on the burden to copy all the material.

Ricardo's death

Ricardo's tour on the Continent was his farewell tour as he died in the following year. As if Ricardo intuitively felt the end of his life was approaching he wrote his last letter to Thomas Robert Malthus (1766–1834) on Sunday 31 August 1823. The correspondence between Thomas Robert Malthus and David Ricardo in the preceding years belongs to the most impressive debates in the history of economic thought. However, in his final letter, Ricardo wrote to Malthus the following amazing and moving statement:

And now my dear Malthus I have done. Like other disputants after much discussion we each retain our own opinions. These discussions however never influence our friendship; I should not like you more than I do if you agreed in opinion with me. (*Works*, IX: 382)

Eleven days later, on 11 September 1823, David Ricardo died at his estate Gatcombe Park due to an inflammation of the ear.

ARNOLD HEERTJE

See also:

Belsham, Thomas, and Ricardo; Jewish Background; Member of Parliament; Porter, Sarah Ricardo.

References

Caravale, G.A. (ed.) (1985), *The Legacy of Ricardo*, Oxford: Basil Blackwell.
Colvin, C. (ed.) (1971), *Maria Edgeworth, Letters from England 1813–1844*, Oxford: Clarendon Press.
Cozzi, T. and R. Marchionatti (eds) (2001), *Piero Sraffa's Political Economy*, London: Routledge.
Davis, T. (2005), *Ricardo's Macroeconomics, Money, Trade Cycle and Growth*, New York: Cambridge University Press.
Heertje, A. (2004), 'The Dutch and Portuguese-Jewish background of David Ricardo', *The European Journal of the History of Economic Thought*, **11**(2), 281–94.
Heertje, A. (2005), 'The Dutch and Portuguese-Jewish background of David Ricardo', *The European Journal of the History of Economic Thought*, **12**(1), 183–4.
Heertje, A. (2007), 'An unpublished letter by David Ricardo', *History of Political Economy*, **39**(3), 545–50.
Hollander, S. (1979), *The Economics of David Ricardo*, London: University of Toronto Press.
Hollander, S. (1995), *Ricardo – The New View, Collected Essays I*, London: Routledge.
Kurz, H. (ed.) (2000), *Critical Essays on Piero Sraffa's Legacy in Economics*, Cambridge, UK: Cambridge University Press.
Kurz, H. and N. Salvadori (eds) (2003), *The Legacy of Piero Sraffa, I and II*, Cheltenham, UK and Northampton, MA: Edward Elgar Publishing.
McCulloch, J.R. (ed.) (1846), *The Works of David Ricardo, Esq-MP*, London: John Murray.
Schumpeter, J.A. (1954), *History of Economic Analysis*, New York: Oxford University Press.
Sraffa, P. (1960), *Production of Commodities by Means of Commodities, Prelude to a Critique of Economic Theory*, Cambridge, UK: Cambridge University Press.
Weatherall, D. (1976), *David Ricardo, A Biography*, The Hague: Martinus Nijhoff.

Limiting and Regulating Principles

Thomas Robert Malthus's distinction between two principles – one 'limiting' the general rate of profits and the other one 'regulating' it – emerged in a controversy between him and David Ricardo on the possibility, or otherwise, of a 'general glut' of commodities. This controversy may be considered the first systematic expression of the opposite views that aggregate effective demand may, or may not, exert a lasting influence on the distribution of income. More recent expressions of it are to be found in the debate about the validity, or otherwise, of Keynes's 'principle of effective demand' and in attempts to generalize that principle to the long period (see Kurz, 1994).

Ricardo, as is well known, advocated 'Say's Law', while Malthus criticized it. The point in dispute between the two concerns the effects of the accumulation of capital on the general rate of profits and thus on the incentive to further accumulation. More specifically, they differed with regard to two propositions put forward by Adam Smith. According to the first one, the growth of wealth of a nation depends on the proportion of 'productive' to 'unproductive' workers: the larger this proportion the more rapidly the economy grows (Smith [1776] 1976, *WN*, I.iii). According to the second proposition the accumulation of capital causes the general rate of profits to fall. Smith had argued:

> When the stocks of many rich merchants are turned into the same trade, their mutual competition naturally tends to lower its profit; and when there is a like increase of stock in all the different trades carried on in the same society, the same competition must produce the same effect in them all. (*WN*, I.ix.2)

While Malthus (1820) accepted the second proposition and rejected the first one, Ricardo (1817, *Principles*) was of the opposite opinion.

Ricardo: profits depend on wages and on nothing else

Ricardo criticized Smith's view as to the falling tendency of the 'normal' or 'ordinary' rate of profits by pointing out that Smith erroneously applied an argument to the economy as a whole that is correct only with regard to a single industry. For the economy as a whole the normal rate of profits does not need to change as long as the real wage rate and the technical conditions of production in the industries, which directly or indirectly produce wage-goods, remain the same (*Works*, I, XXI). Ricardo distinguished two cases in which the rate of profits tends to fall: (1) if, with unchanged technical conditions of production, the rate of capital accumulation exceeds the rate of growth of the workforce and capitalists start bidding up the real wage rate; (2) if, with a constant real wage rate, an increase in the production of necessaries to feed a growing population can only be brought about at increasing labour and material costs due to decreasing returns in the production of corn.

The two cases may be illustrated by means of the constraint binding changes in the real wage rate, w, and the general rate of profits, r, discovered (though not consistently demonstrated) by Ricardo (see Figure 14). As is well known, the w–r relationship refers to the conditions of production on the marginal land, whereas on intramarginal plots of land a rent is yielded by the landlords, which is higher the higher is the difference in unit costs between the marginal land and intramarginal qualities of land.

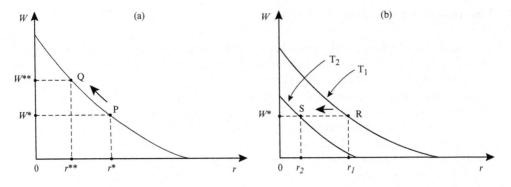

Figure 14a, b   The w–r relationship

In case (1) above the *w–r* relationship remains the same (Figure 14a). The change in income distribution contemplated (from P to Q) involves a movement *on* the curve. As Ricardo pointed out, the tendency of the real wage to rise due to rapid capital accumulation may contain the germs of its own destruction. For, with a falling rate of profits, capital accumulation may decelerate, and with the corresponding rise in real wages the growth of the workforce may accelerate. In case (2) a movement *of* the curve is involved (Figure 14b). Since the process of capital accumulation and growth necessitates the extension of cultivation to lands of lower 'fertility' (extensive diminishing returns) or the more intensive cultivation of land of given qualities (intensive diminishing returns), the *w–r* relationship shifts towards the origin. For a given real wage rate this entails a fall in the rate of profits (see the movement from R to S). It is obvious that with regard to both cases Ricardo sets aside technical progress, that is, improvements (see Kurz, 2010). Improvements tend to shift the *w–r* relationship outwards or oppose and overcome its shift inwards. In the case of technical progress in the production of wage-goods or in industries supplying the wage-goods industries with inputs, Ricardo insisted, the rate of profits need not fall: technical and organizational improvements are a counteracting factor of the 'niggardliness' of nature (given a constant or moderately rising level of the real wage rate).

Ricardo referred to the two cases in various places in his *Notes on Malthus* (*Works*, II). In one place we read that case (1) is characterized by an 'increase in the price of labour' (that is, the real wage rate) due to a 'scarcity of labour', while case (2) is the consequence of a 'diminution in the productive powers of land' (ibid.: 321). In both cases the money wage rate rises – in the first case relative to the price level of necessaries, in the second case in line with it. Ricardo emphasized: 'These two causes may both be classed under the name of high or low wages. Profits in fact depend on high or low wages, and on nothing else' (ibid.: 252; similarly 264–5). (This view Karl Marx rightly criticized, because in a circular flow framework in which commodities are produced by means of commodities, as, for example, in the *Tableau économique*, an economic model first described by Quesnay in 1758, the rate of profits depends also on what Marx called 'constant capital'. In such a framework the maximum rate of profits, corresponding to zero wages, would be finite and not infinite as in the framework chosen by Ricardo in his respective analysis in order to simplify matters: in it production is conceived of as a one-way avenue leading from original factors of production, especially 'unassisted' labour, to the final product in a finite number of steps.)

According to Ricardo a permanent impact of product demand on profits is to be excluded. Discrepancies between the quantity brought to the market and effectual demand may play a role with regard to single commodities and will lead to differences in profit rates. With free competition, that is, the absence of notable barriers to entry into or exit from markets (an ideal situation Ricardo and Malthus assumed in much of their analyses), capital and labour will move between industries and thus tend to restore the equality of supply and demand at 'natural' prices, characterized by a uniform rate of profits and uniform rates of remuneration for all units of a given quality of labour or land. For the economy as a whole, a discrepancy between aggregate output and aggregate demand with respect to commodities is thus considered impossible thanks to Say's Law. Therefore, Ricardo maintained that an acceleration of accumulation and the corresponding increase in the proportion of productive to unproductive labourers cannot lead to a deficiency of effective demand, because any additional saving will be exactly matched by an additional investment of the same magnitude: 'there is no amount of capital which may not be employed in a country, because demand is only limited by production' (*Works*, I: 290). It is important to emphasize that reference is to the employment of *capital*, not labour. In fact, Ricardo and the classical authors more generally envisaged Say's Law to apply only to capitalistically produced commodities. Since labour, while a commodity, is not produced and reproduced in a capitalistic way, Say's Law did not apply. (It was only later, in marginalist theory, that the so-called 'law of markets' was generalized to include the labour market: with flexible prices and sufficient substitutability between goods in consumption or factors in production, all markets, including the markets for 'factors of production' [labour, capital and land], were taken to clear. Hence, the forces of supply and demand were seen to establish a tendency to the full employment of labour and the full utilization of productive equipment.)

In short, according to Ricardo the principle that limited the rate of profits in terms of the real wage rate and the given technical conditions of production at the same time tended to regulate it. There was essentially only a single principle. As we have heard: 'Profits in fact depend on high or low wages, *and on nothing else*' (*Works*, II: 252; emphasis added) (given, of course, technical conditions of production). Malthus took issue with this view. He did not dispute the fact that the maximum rate of return on capital was constrained by the given level of real wages – this was Ricardo's 'limiting principle'. But he insisted that there was a second factor at work: aggregate effective demand. We may thus express Malthus's 'regulating principle' as follows, picking up and extending Ricardo's formula: 'Profits in fact depend on high or low wages, and on aggregate effective demand.'

Malthus: profits depend on wages and on aggregate effective demand

Malthus started from a view that Smith had expressed and Ricardo had endorsed, namely 'that capitals are increased by parsimony, that every frugal man is a public benefactor, and that the increase of wealth depends upon the balance of produce above consumption' (cf. Malthus in *Works*, II: 7). Malthus commented on this:

> That these propositions are true to a great extent is perfectly unquestionable. No considerable and continued increase of wealth could possibly take place without that degree of frugality

which occasions, annually, the conversion of some revenue into capital, and creates a balance of produce above consumption; but it is quite obvious that they are not true to an indefinite extent, and that the principle of saving, pushed to excess, would destroy the motive to production. (Ibid.: 7–8)

This would be the case, Malthus continued, because capital accumulation presupposes a reduction of 'unproductive consumption' of the propertied classes. Too large an accumulation of capital would involve levels of aggregate demand too low to fully utilize productive capacity. There would be a general overproduction of commodities, a 'general glut', with prices falling relative to money wages and a consequent fall in profitability. Malthus concluded: 'both capital and population may be at the same time, and for a period of great length, redundant, compared with the effective demand for produce' (ibid.: 427).

The difference between his theory of profits and that of Ricardo Malthus expressed in terms of the two principles. While Ricardo's limiting principle is concerned with identifying the factors affecting the maximum rate of profits, that is, (a) the state of the productive powers of labour and land and (b) the real wage rate, Malthus's regulating principle is concerned with identifying the factors affecting the actual rate of profit, which include the two factors mentioned plus (c) the level of effective demand:

> We can know little of the laws which determine profits, unless, in addition to the causes which increase the price of necessaries, we explain the causes which award a larger or smaller share of these necessaries to each labourer. And here it is obvious that we must have recourse to the great principles of demand and supply, or to that very principle of competition brought forward by Adam Smith, which Mr Ricardo expressly rejects, or at least considers as of so temporary a nature as not to require attention in a general theory of profits. (Malthus, ibid.: 269)

Factors (b) and (c) are, however interrelated: the lower (higher) is effective demand, the lower (higher) are money prices and, given the money wage rate, the higher (lower) is the real wage rate and, *a fortiori*, the lower (higher) is the actual rate of profits.

Hence, in Malthus's view Ricardo determines only an upper constraint of profitability, but not actual profitability, whereas his own, Malthus's principle, allows one to explain the current level of profits. In this explanation, effective demand is envisaged to be a major factor affecting profitability, whose impact cannot be restricted to the short period and to single industries only.

While, as was pointed out by Ricardo, Malthus's various statements are not without contradictions and therefore pose difficult problems of interpretation, it seems to be clear that in his view the modern economy tends to forgo production possibilities because of deficient levels of effective demand. This deficiency of demand is reflected in a 'redundancy' of capital and labour, which may be interpreted as involving a less than 'full' or 'normal' utilization of plant and equipment and unemployed workers. We might illustrate the constellation under consideration in a schematic way in terms of Figure 15. For the purpose of the comparison, taking the level of the real wage rate as given at $w = w^*$, the regulating principle may imply an (average) rate of profit actually realized, ρ, which falls short of the 'normal' rate of profits, r^*, $\rho < r^*$; here r^* expresses Ricardo's limiting principle.

Malthus did not succeed in convincing Ricardo of the correctness of his doctrine. This is hardly surprising since Malthus, like Ricardo, saw factors at work that tended to bring

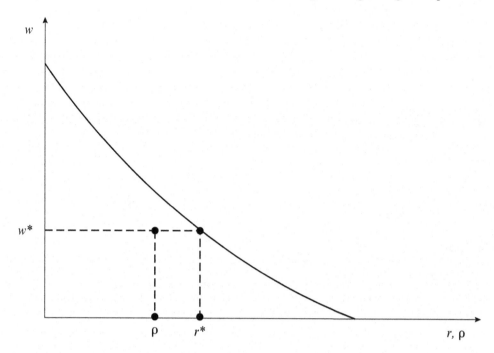

Figure 15   Limiting and regulating principle

about a volume of investment that equalled any given volume of savings. This, however, meant that any reduction in aggregate effective demand (savings) was compensated by an additional effective demand of the same magnitude (investment). How could there ever be a lack of effective demand with respect to the system as a whole? Keynes, who esteemed Malthus a good deal higher than Ricardo, had to admit:

> since Malthus was unable to explain clearly (apart from an appeal to the facts of common observation) how and why effective demand could be deficient or excessive, he failed to furnish an alternative construction; and Ricardo conquered England as completely as the Holy Inquisition conquered Spain . . . The *great puzzle of effective demand* with which Malthus had wrestled vanished from economic literature. (Keynes [1936] 1978, *Collected Writings*, VII: 32; emphasis added)

Later authors
As Keynes acknowledged, this is put too strongly, since during the century that elapsed between the Ricardo–Malthus debate and the publication of the *General Theory*, the puzzle lived on 'furtively, below the surface in the underworlds of Karl Marx, Silvio Gesell or Major Douglas' (*Collected Writings*, VII: 32). As Steindl (1952: Chapter XIV) stressed, in Marx we have a short-run and a long-run relationship between the real wage rate and the rate of accumulation that are entirely contrary to one another. While in the short run the rate of accumulation depends negatively on the real wage rate, which in turn depends negatively on the degree of unemployment, in the long run – in Marx's own words – 'The magnitude of accumulation is the independent variable, that of the wage

is the dependent one, not the other way round' (quoted in Steindl, 1952: 231). The idea that the development of effective demand and thus the pace at which capital is accumulated has an effect on the average degree of capacity utilization and as a consequence on income distribution was expressed prior to Keynes by the Polish economist Michal Kalecki. In more recent times the problem under consideration has been dealt with in various attempts to combine the classical surplus approach to the theory of value and distribution, as reformulated by Sraffa (1960), with the Keynesian-Kaleckian principle of effective demand (see, for example, Kurz, 1994).

HEINZ D. KURZ

See also:

Accumulation of Capital; Capital and Profits; Endogenous Growth; Keynes, John Maynard, on Ricardo; Malthus–Ricardo Debate.

References

Keynes, J.M. (1973–88), *The Collected Writings of John Maynard Keynes*, 32 vols, (eds) A. Robinson and D. Moggridge, London: Macmillan.

Kurz, H.D. (1994), 'Growth and distribution', *Review of Political Economy*, **6**, 393–420.

Kurz, H.D. (2010), 'Technical change, growth and income distribution in the classical economists: Adam Smith, David Ricardo and Karl Marx', *European Journal of the History of Economic Thought*, **17**(5), 1183–222.

Malthus, T.R. (1820), *The Principles of Political Economy Considered with a View to Their Practical Application*, London: John Murray.

Smith, A. ([1776] 1976), *An Inquiry into the Nature and Causes of the Wealth of Nations*, in *The Glasgow Edition of the Works and Correspondence of Adam Smith*, (eds) R.H. Campbell, A.S. Skinner and W.B. Todd, Oxford: Clarendon Press.

Sraffa, P. (1960). *Production of Commodities by Means of Commodities. Prelude to a Critique of Economic Theory*, Cambridge, UK: Cambridge University Press.

Steindl, J. (1952), *Maturity and Stagnation in American Capitalism*, New York: Monthly Review Press.

Malthus–Ricardo Debate

The debate between Malthus and Ricardo is documented by a bulky correspondence that lasted over 12 years, and luckily enough is preserved to a remarkable extent, as well as by direct or indirect echoes in published works by both. Keynes believed it to be 'the most famous literary correspondence in the whole development of Political Economy' ([1933] 1972: 90) and indeed he was the first to make it the subject of some discussion, followed by a few others (Pancoast, 1943), even if systematic discussion may be said to have begun in the 1970s (Porta, 1978; Dorfman, 1989; Cremaschi and Dascal, 1996, 1998a, 1998b; Dascal and Cremaschi, 1999).

The controversy's development

Malthus and Ricardo first met in June 1811, at a time when Malthus already was the famous author of the *Essay on Population*, while Ricardo had just started publishing on topics of monetary policy in the *Morning Chronicle*. All we know is that they met in London, where Malthus used to come regularly from Haileybury College. After 1814, when Ricardo began to spend half of the year on his estate at Gatcombe Park, Malthus visited there just three times, but Ricardo apparently spent a number of weekends with the Malthuses at Haileybury, and also, after the Political Economy Club was founded, they started meeting regularly at its monthly dinners (Henderson, 1997: 286–336).

A correspondence between them began that lasted until Ricardo's death. In the first two letters both expressed the wish to settle 'by an amicable discussion in private' (Malthus to Ricardo, 18 June 1811, *Works*, VI: 21) those that appeared to be 'the very few objections' that prevented them 'from being precisely of the same opinion' (Ricardo to Malthus, 18 June 1811, ibid.: 23–4). Correspondence became more frequent between 1817 and 1820 after Ricardo's *Principles*. Malthus responded in his own *Principles* (1820) while trying to avoid giving the work 'a too controversial air' (Malthus to Ricardo, 3 December 1817, *Works*, VII: 215). Ricardo in turn responded with his *Notes on Malthus*. After this phase the flow of letters slowed down, but it is as well to note that they enjoyed rather frequent occasions to meet, among others the Political Economy Club monthly dinners. In the third edition of the *Principles* Ricardo introduced important qualifications to his own value theory, mostly reacting to Malthus's objections. In 1823 there was again an intensified flow of letters concentrating on the issue of the 'measure of value'.

The controversy ended without any real 'closure', for it was brought to a sudden end by Ricardo's death in 1823. In the very last letter Ricardo wrote, as if he had some premonition, an epitaph to the whole controversy: 'Like other disputants after much discussion we each retain our own opinions. These discussions however never influence our friendship' (Ricardo to Malthus, 31 August 1823, *Works*, IX: 382). Yet, there was an aftermath in Malthus's later publications, where he kept on defending his own approach vis-à-vis the so-called 'New School', the alleged Ricardo-Mill-McCulloch orthodoxy.

Positive contents

Henderson (1997: 509) singled out three 'rounds': the first around the *Grounds* and the *Essay on Profits*, the second around the two volumes of *Principles*, the third around the theme of the measure of value. A more detailed subdivision may be into nine rounds.

Such rounds or cycles may be identified in terms of their main topics, and accordingly at least two of them may be thought to be overlapping:

1. On the influence of the currency upon foreign exchanges, the possibility of a 'general glut' and the nature and function of effective demand (June 1811–February 1812).
2. The Corn Laws and rent and profit, that is, the prospective effect of the proposed corn duties upon economic classes and upon their respective incomes (August 1813–January 1815).
3. On rent (February–April 1815).
4. On the growth of wealth, multi-causality, temporary and permanent effects (April 1815–January 1817).
5. On the relationship of wages and profits or the wage-fund doctrine (1817–20).
6. On the determinants of value, its distinction from wealth, and its relationship to exchange value (1817–20).
7. On language and definitions, theory and practice, and the 'value-free' character of political economy (May–November 1820).
8. On the determinants of value in a pre-capitalist economy and on machinery (1821).
9. On the possibility of an invariable measure of value and on various proposals for the best measure, either gold or a mean between corn and labour (April–August 1823).

Each cycle starts with discussion of one topic, mostly a policy issue, and tends to follow a recurrent pattern of intensification in the frequency of the letters exchanged and in the number of topics discussed in the various phases (Dascal and Cremaschi, 1999). Although each is typically under the aegis of one point of positive doctrine, most of the time the discussion of positive claims trespasses into that of methodological topics.

Methodological themes

It is noteworthy that a number of methodological divergences show up over and over again and are invoked in order to support individual positive claims. It is worth noting also that allegiance to one methodological claim by either Malthus or Ricardo does not imply that he will consistently have recourse to the same claim in the following. Nevertheless, there are at least some family resemblances among the methodological claims advanced by each, although occasionally the same claim is used for opposite purposes. What cannot be found is a ready-made methodology that each of them could have learned beforehand and applied consistently in the discussion. The methodological issues discussed may be summarized as follows:

The definition of political economy

For Ricardo, it is the science of the 'laws' regulating distribution, for Malthus, the science of the 'causes' of the growth of wealth. Presumably, Malthus wants to be true to Adam Smith, a choice that is probably associated with the Scottish-Cantabrigian methodology he had been taught (Cremaschi, 2010). Ricardo probably had in mind an idea of laws as opposed to causes deriving from the Priestly-Hartley-Belsham methodological tradition, as means for expressing relations between phenomena, provided that the true essence of things and ultimate causes are unknowable.

Mono-causality vs multi-causality

Malthus stresses the importance of multiple interacting causes as well as of temporary causes, as contrasted with permanent ones; Ricardo contends that there is generally one prevailing cause and other causes may be ignored since permanent causes constantly at work will sooner or later bring about permanent states, the only ones for which we may try to account. He writes:

> There are so many combinations –, so many operating causes in Political Economy, that there is a great danger in appealing to experience in favor of a particular doctrine, unless we are sure that all the causes of variation are seen and their effects duly estimated. (Ricardo to Malthus, 7 October 1815, *Works*, VI: 295)

And he later adds:

> one great cause of our difference in opinion . . . is that you have always in your mind the immediate and temporary effects of particular changes – whereas I put these immediate and temporary effects quite aside, and fix my whole attention on the permanent state of things which will result from them. (Ricardo to Malthus, 24 January 1817, *Works*, VII: 120)

The distinction between questions of fact and questions of principle

Ricardo sees economic science as the construction of abstract models depicting ideal or permanent states, the 'strong cases'; Malthus believes in a semi-historical character of the science of political economy, since the phenomena it explains are located within processes, and disequilibrium is the rule, not an exception.

Simplicity in theories

Malthus insists on the need to keep complexity in mind. He believes he has detected in Ricardo the same flaw that Adam Smith and Dugald Stewart used to reproach to Cartesianism, namely a 'desire to simplify'. He writes:

> [A] desire to simplify, which has often led away the most scientific men, has induced you to ascribe to one cause phenomena that properly belong to two, and not to give sufficient weight to the facts which . . . appear to make against your doctrine. (Malthus to Ricardo, 23 Februry 1812, *Works*, VI: 82)

Ricardo favours instead simplification, abstraction and mono-causality in the name of an alleged impossibility to know all the causes at work behind phenomena.

Vagueness or precision of language

Each of them occasionally blames the other for inconsistency in his use of terminology. Presumably both appeal to shared standards of linguistic propriety and yet, whereas Ricardo constantly presumes proper use of language to be tantamount to precision and univocity, Malthus always presumes that propriety is tantamount to explicit definitions and conformity to the usage of 'the best educated part' of society.

The controversy's impact on Ricardo's work

A few tentative conclusions on the role the debate played in Ricardo's development may be the following.

First, facing the fact that two classical political economists went on disagreeing in a systematic and sustained way, some commentators have been seduced into thinking that after all they lacked a shared ground or paradigm (Würgler, 1957). Instead, Malthus and Ricardo were typically classical economists, that is, they shared a paradigm in Kuhn's senses: a pre-comprehension of the field of social phenomena they set about studying, a body of positive claims, an exemplar of economic theorizing, a basic model of the economy (Samuelson, 1978), and a disciplinary matrix, including a set of basic metaphors. Accordingly, they may be said to share a scientific style in the sense of an general attitude of an age that allows for formulation and treatment of certain questions while ruling out questions of a different kind (Cremaschi and Dascal, 1998b). Second, even within this broad shared background, there was room for deep differences: in the choice of emphasizing either states of equilibrium or processes of social change, in the methodological claims professed, in the strategies adopted. These factors, when taken together, amount to a difference in the specific scientific 'style' practised by each. Third, a scientific controversy is a kind of affair that cannot be settled by any well-defined decision procedure for it involves, among other things, questioning the opponent's standards of problem-solving. Fourth, although scientific controversies have no decision procedure, they are not just a matter of taste or arbitrariness. To be sure, different styles lead to emphasizing opposite aspects of a shared paradigm, but the resulting emphasis cannot go as far as one likes, since it is under constraints posed by the controversy's 'demands'. Fifth, the controversy was no deplorable accident, as Ricardians believed. Take, for example, Torrens's assessment:

> A few years ago, when the brilliant discoveries in chymistry began to supersede the ancient doctrine of phlogiston, controversies analogous to those which now exist amongst Political Economists, divided the professors of natural knowledge; and Dr. Priestley, like Mr. Malthus, appeared as the pertinacious champion of the theories which the facts established by himself had so largely contributed to overthrow ... With respect to Political Economy the period of controversy is passing away, and that of unanimity rapidly approaching. Twenty years hence there will scarcely exist a doubt respecting any of its fundamental principles. (Torrens, [1821] 2000: xiii)

Almost two hundred years have elapsed since then and there is still, to say the least, scarcely any certainty respecting the fundamental principles of economic theory.

The main intellectual 'influence' on Ricardo's work came – unsurprisingly – from Malthus himself. In the third edition of the *Principles*, Ricardo changed substantially his previous claims on the determinants of relative values in a pre-capitalist economy; he also introduced drastic changes on salaries and technical innovation. In the famous chapter on machines in fact, he endorsed the claim that replacement of human labour by machinery often runs against the interests of the working class, insofar as it may raise the net revenue of a society while diminishing its gross revenue, and it is well known how Mill's and McCulloch's reactions to such changes were far from enthusiastic insofar as these were perceived as a surrender to Malthus.

The circumstances that the most weighty influence on Ricardo's work came from his main opponent and that the way this influence was exerted was obviously no kind of top-down process (from methodology to positive theory) may help in understanding better Ricardo's path of enquiry and the shaping of his own 'cast of mind'. The relevant points are that: (1) Ricardo, before his first meeting with Mill, was clearly enough something more than 'an unlettered *pater familias*' and had been exposed instead, at least to some minimal extent, to philosophical ideas neither identical with nor totally alien to those shared by either Mill or Malthus; (2) direct influence by Mill in matters of philosophy and methodology amounted to nothing or near to nothing; (3) speculations about the true Ricardian philosophy and its influence on his work in political economy are, more than mistaken answers, answers to the wrong kind of questions; (4) what emerges from both the correspondence and printed sources proves that methodological considerations were worked out by Ricardo at some stage in his career with a view to self-clarification, as a way of spelling out what had been his own 'scientific style', and such a self-clarification was born out of a dialogue with his friend/opponent Malthus.

SERGIO CREMASCHI

See also:

Comparative Advantage; Demand and Supply; Foreign Trade; *Essay on Profits*; Limiting and Regulating Principles.

References

Cremaschi, S. (2010), 'Malthus's idea of a moral and political science', *The Journal of Philosophical Economics*, **3**(2), 5–57.

Cremaschi, S. and M. Dascal (1996), 'Malthus and Ricardo on economic methodology', *History of Political Economy*, **28**(3), 475–511.

Cremaschi, S. and M. Dascal (1998a), 'Persuasion and argument in the Malthus–Ricardo correspondence', in W.J. Samuels and J.E. Biddle (eds), *Research in the History of Economic Thought and Methodology, Vol. XVI*, Stamford, CONN: JAI Press, pp. 1–63.

Cremaschi, S. and M. Dascal (1998b), 'Malthus and Ricardo: two styles for economic theory', *Science in Context*, **11**(2), 229–54.

Dascal, M. and S. Cremaschi (1999), 'The Malthus–Ricardo correspondence: sequential structure, argumentative patterns, and rationality', *Journal of Pragmatics*, **31**(9), 1129–72.

Dorfman, R. (1989), 'Thomas Robert Malthus and David Ricardo', *Journal of Economic Perspectives*, **3**(3), 153–64.

Henderson, J.P. (1997), *The Life and Economics of David Ricardo*, with supplemental chapters by J.B. Davis, Boston, MA: Kluwer.

Keynes, J.M. ([1933] 1972), 'Robert Malthus. The first of the Cambridge economists', in J.M. Keynes, *Essays in Biography*, London: Macmillan, pp. 95–149.

Malthus T.R. (1820 [1989]), *Principles of Political Economy*, variorum edition, (ed.) J. Pullen, Cambridge, UK: Cambridge University Press.

Pancoast, O. Jr (1943), 'Malthus versus Ricardo: the effects of distribution on production', *Political Science Quarterly*, **58**(1), 47–66.

Porta, P.L. (1978), 'Il dibattito tra Ricardo e Malthus: aspetti di teoria del valore e della distribuzione', *Giornale degli economisti*, **37**(5–6 and 7–8), 317–43 and 454–68.

Samuelson, P.A. (1978), 'The canonical classical model of political economy', *Journal of Economic Literature*, **16**(4), 1415–34.

Torrens, R. ([1821] 2000), '*An Essay on the Production of Wealth*', in *Collected Works, Vol. 3*, (ed.) G. De Vivo, London: Thoemmes.

Würgler, H. (1957), *Malthus als Kritiker der Klassik. Ein Beitrag zur Geschichte der klassischen Wirtschaftstheorie*, Winterthur: Keller.

Marshall, Alfred, on Ricardo

A story of 'astonishing claims'

The phrase in quotes in the title of this section comes from Denis O'Brien's study of the relation between Marshall and the classical economists (O'Brien, 1990: 136 and *passim*).

The gist of O'Brien's reconstruction is that Marshall, in trying to plug the new marginal analysis into the body of the pre-existing theory, 'was led to make claims about the nature of classical analysis . . . which are difficult to interpret as anything other than an exaggerated "pietas" with rhetorical undertones' (ibid.: 156). Ricardo stands out among the classical economists as the author who benefited – or suffered, depending on the perspective – most from this tendency of Marshall's. Praises that were poured on him reached disconcerting levels – a fact that was noted from the very beginning by readers of the *Principles of Economics* (1890) and has since remained one of the many puzzles surrounding Marshall's peculiar ways of dealing with his sources and predecessors. While authors to whom he might have been indebted – such as Jevons – received no or scarcely any acknowledgement, Ricardo was credited with ideas that he had not entertained and that Marshall could in no way have derived from him. Indeed, the *Principles* had scarcely left the printing press when the economic historian William Ashley pointed out the existence of a problem in this respect (Ashley, 1891). Marshall's 'rehabilitation' of Ricardo could not be passed off as simply a 'generous interpretation', according to Ashley, because it was twisted to the point of rendering an entirely unfaithful portrait of the historical figure. This episode marked the beginning of a minor stream of literature, references to which can be found in O'Brien (1990) and Groenewegen (1993). Although he did not contribute to this particular literature, Piero Sraffa, surely the greatest interpreter of Ricardo during the course of the twentieth century, also seems to have been intrigued by the curious bond between the two characters, as we shall see.

This chapter attempts to make sense of the story by highlighting a number of points that seem to establish a logical connection between Marshall's views of Ricardo, other opinions concerning the latter and circulating in Britain in the course of the nineteenth century, and Marshall's entrenched political beliefs. Briefly, the steps of the argument are the following:

1.   During his formative years, Marshall did not derive from Ricardo as much inspiration as he did from other authors. Yet he admired him, apparently because he felt that Ricardo was the first British economist to show the full force of a mathematical style of reasoning, based on rigorous deductions from well-defined and aptly chosen hypotheses.

2.   Ricardo's theory had been the object of a sensational attack by Jevons in 1871, an attack that in the latter's intentions was to serve as a prelude to a phase of reconstruction of the entire science of economics upon radically new foundations. As a participant in the same 'new economics' programme as Jevons, however, Marshall abhorred the idea of discontinuities in the progress of knowledge, which he thought of as an incremental process consisting of series of small changes added to the pre-existing body of ideas and practices.

3.   Although he was a supporter of free trade and an icon of Manchesterism, Ricardo was also perceived of as an author who had unwittingly provided ammunition for the 'scientific' line of socialist thought, a notion that was shared by socialists and by opponents to socialism alike. Among the latter there were interlocutors who Marshall respected, such as Ashley himself, and especially the long-time (at least until 1908) friend and colleague Herbert Foxwell.

4.   Given these premises, it seems perfectly consequential that, having achieved emi-

nence among the British economists of his generation, and in the process of preparing what aspired to be the bible of the new economics, Marshall decided to bring all his authority to bear in an attempt to re-establish Ricardo's reputation along the two lines that concerned him most, the scientific and the political. In the *Principles* he praised Ricardo immoderately for allegedly anticipating the new doctrines based on utility, margins and the equilibrium of supply and demand, and remonstrated against those – primarily Marx and Rodbertus – who, by attributing to Ricardo a labour theory of value, tried to enlist him as an originator of scientific socialism. In arguing his case, Marshall was led to make unsupported claims, for some of which Ashley immediately upbraided him. In spite of this, he never recanted. It seems as if his interest for the 'historical' Ricardo was overwhelmed by a concern with, on the one hand, defending the idea of continuity in the progress of economic science and, on the other, denying to the socialists any title to Ricardo's legacy. On both accounts, we may conclude that Marshall's aim in orchestrating his defence of Ricardo was, in a broad sense, political.

Marshall's admiration for Ricardo as a monetary theorist is a separate and less problematic aspect of the relationship between the two that will not be examined here. The reader may refer to O'Brien (1990: 127–8, 144–7 and 155–6).

Ricardo: a genius, not a guide
Point (1) in the above summary is borne out by the relatively scanty occurrence of direct references to Ricardo in Marshall's early papers and lecture notes. It is true that, during the years (from 1865 to 1870) in which he moved from being a part-time mathematics coach with interests mainly in philosophy and psychology to embracing political economy as a professional field, Marshall picked the typically Ricardian themes of rent and international trade as training grounds for his own mathematical skills. As argued by Whitaker (1975: 50–51) and Groenewegen (1993: 46–8), however, his direct source for these 'mathematical translations' was not Ricardo, but the *Principles of Political Economy* by John Stuart Mill. Except for a single reference, in all the autobiographical recollections scattered throughout his correspondence, Marshall consistently indicated Mill as the author through whom he had come in contact with Ricardo's (and Smith's) doctrines. This is confirmed by his personal copy of Mill's *Principles*, which is interspersed with pages and pages of annotations and exercises (Groenewegen, 1995: 145–9).

The early exercises reveal that, from the very beginning, Marshall regarded the Ricardian doctrines as little more than profound intuitions, rigorously but incompletely argued owing to Ricardo's inclination for extreme hypotheses, and as such only starting points that needed to be developed and rounded off in order to become operative. While he himself was working out such developments, Marshall drew inspiration from various sources, but never from Ricardo himself. The case of rent provides perhaps the best illustration of his using a Ricardian concept simply as raw material to be combined with other components and eventually transformed into something barely recognizable. In manuscripts of the early 1870s (Marshall, 1975, I: 224ff), he reset the basic principle of Ricardian rent theory – the value of the produce determined by the costs in the most unfavourable conditions – inside a Millian supply and demand framework, within which he went on to explore its implications in alternative hypothetical cases. In the light of his later achievements, we can see that Marshall was already striving to turn the principle into a universal rule of imputation that applied in all cases of (temporarily or permanently) non-reproducible resources utilized by competing producers, whatever the form of ownership of these resources might have been. As he wrote to Foxwell as early as 1878, the law of rent 'in just that form in which Ricardo laid it down' was a particular case due to the co-existence of decreasing returns along with inequality of fertility:

> but it seems to me that this is an accident & not essential to the nature of rent . . . When these conditions are not present, we have I think Rent still: ie the owner of any natural monopoly is able to obtain payment for the use of it & this payment is regulated by economic laws; These Laws may be called Laws of Rent; but they would differ in form from Ricardos Law, because of the difference in kind of the limitations of supply. (Marshall, 1996, I: 93)

In another letter to Foxwell of 1881, in commenting on the Ricardian device (which he himself, together with Mary Paley Marshall, had adopted in the *Economics of Industry* in 1879) of analysing the wage–profits distribution by placing the point of observation at the no-rent margin, Marshall was even more explicit as to the direction of his moving away from Ricardo: 'In Mill's sense, we think Land Tenure belongs to Distribution, but the Ricardian theory of rent – a mere dry algebraical formula – to the "Mechanism of Exchange"' (ibid.: 147). Marshall was clearly making his way, on the one hand, towards the theory of equilibrium prices with generalized quasi-rents that he would expound in Book V of the *Principles*; on the other, towards the universalization of the Ricardian principle as an explanatory scheme applicable also to social and institutional settings that were quite different from the British system of his day, as he would argue in the *Principles* and in controversies with Cunningham and the Duke of Argyll in two papers of 1892 and 1893 (reproduced in Marshall [1890] 1961, II: 735–50 and 492–512).

The other great Ricardian theme that Marshall developed in the early years, that is, international trade, followed a similar pattern. Here again, Ricardo came to Marshall through the mediation of John Stuart Mill, who in Book III, Chapter XVIII of his *Principles* had already gone well beyond Ricardo. But there were other influences, of course, especially Cournot (see Creedy, 2006). And the manuscript chapters on foreign trade and domestic values that constitute Marshall's first large-scale attempt at an original theoretical treatise (Marshall, 1975, II) show clearly that, for him, Ricardo's and Mill's propositions were no more than raw materials for an innovative construction that brought all his familiarity with classical mechanics to bear in an analysis of equilibrium positions that emphasized multiplicity and stability in relation to the shapes of the curves. Other seminal but (in these chapters) less developed themes, such as the blurring of the dividing line between foreign and domestic trade in consideration of the obstacles to free movements of capital and labour inside a country, drew inspiration from Smith's 'circumspect inductions', from Mill's concern for the 'conventional barriers' of custom, even from suggestions contained in empirically oriented works by Thomas Cliffe Leslie (ibid.: 119–23; see also Marshall, 1925: 122ff) – all sources that Marshall invoked to counteract Ricardo's overly narrow predilection for deductive reasoning in sharply defined cases. This was a rebuke, the only rebuke that Marshall made to Ricardo, which would later resurface and become the central point in the critical tribute paid to Ricardo in the inaugural lecture of 1885 (Marshall, 1925: 153ff): Ricardo's brilliant achievements were obtained at the cost of focusing on extreme hypotheses that inevitably did away with the mixture of stickiness and variability that characterizes human morality and cognition, and that for Marshall was the ultimate substance of social phenomena. That economics is only a part of a (virtual) all-encompassing science of society is a teaching that Marshall attributes primarily to Mill, often also to Adam Smith, never to Ricardo.

Marshall's relative lack of attention, in his formative years, to Ricardo's theory of value completes the general picture. The important manuscript essay on value of the early 1870s (Marshall, 1975, I: 119ff) contained only passing references to him. In lecture notes from the same years (reproduced in Cook and Foresti, 2010), mention was made of Ricardo's doctrine according to which relative values may change with changes in wages, depending on the ratios between direct and embodied labour. But Ricardo's search for an invariable standard of value was dismissed as unclear ('I don't see the use of his position', ibid.: 27–28); and Marshall did not fail to remark that the necessity for determining the relative values of different kinds of labour as a precondition for determining labour values showed that 'Ricardo's position is not as has been said entirely independent of the principle of supply & demand' (ibid.: 28). He also noted that, with reference to value, Mill 'adds nothing to the substance [of Ricardo], but expresses a few things [concerning the market/natural values dichotomy] more clearly' (ibid.: 29); and, later on, even Bastiat was mentioned as saying 'nothing that Mill or Ricardo does not' (ibid.: 32). From these scarce references we can conclude that, at this stage, Marshall did not know what to make of Ricardo's attempt to ground value on amounts of labour variously spent in production, and that the recasting of this theory in a supply and demand framework was for him the only way to make sense of it.

Throughout this period Marshall never missed an occasion to emphasize Ricardo's unique skill in casting his arguments in the shape of rigorous deductions from exactly circumscribed hypotheses, in contrast with Mill's blunders 'whenever he ventured far beyond Ricardo's track' (manuscript note, quoted by Whitaker, 1975: 50, 48n). Even Smith was unfavourably compared with Ricardo in this regard: 'The distinction between Adam Smith and Ricardo is that Ricardo knew clearly what he was assuming: and Smith did not' (from early lecture notes, Marshall, 1975, II: 253). Admittedly, for Marshall both Ricardo and Mill were mathematically naive to the point of being unaware of the difference between a demonstration and a numerical illustration (ibid.: 132–3). Yet the former knew how to choose his numbers and to what extent these supported an argument, thanks to the instincts that enabled him 'to tread his way safely through the most slippery paths of mathematical reasoning' (Marshall, 1925: 99; see also [1890] 1961, I: 836). Ricardo founded one of 'the two great schools of abstract economics' – the other one was the school of Quesnay in France (Marshall, 1975, II: 85) – and was perhaps the sole exception to the rule that economic thought is 'the product of the age' and not of single individuals (from an 1892 letter to L.L. Price, Marshall, 1996, II: 80). But, as recalled above, Marshall was alert to what he considered the main flaw in this unique genius, the intellectual one-sidedness that rendered him an unreliable guide in trying to get to the core of social phenomena. In the spirit of the distinction made in the aforementioned letter to Price, the admiration for Ricardo that Marshall developed in his youth may well be said to concern 'the form of his thought rather than the substance'.

Rescuing Ricardo from enemies and false friends

The *Principles* contain further elaborations of some of the early themes that we met in the previous section, the most important of which was, of course, the bringing to completion of the plan of extending Ricardian rent into the more general category of quasi-rent. In Book VI, Chapters II and III of the first edition, Marshall traces the single steps of this generalization – the no-rent land turned into a locus of indifference, the incomes not clearly partaking of the nature of wages or interest revealed as pure rents, quasi-rents or profits, depending on the time horizon of the analysis – in much clearer detail than in the corresponding Book V, Chapters VIII–X of the eighth edition (see Marshall [1890] 1961, II: 440ff). What is definitely new in the *Principles* as compared with the selective interests of the 1870s is, instead, Marshall's zooming in on Ricardo's theory of value. This was the object of a long 'Note on Ricardo's Theory of Cost of Production in Relation to Value' in the first edition, which was to become, with few changes, Appendix I on 'Ricardo's Theory of Value' in the eighth edition. Here for the first time, we find the extravagant attributions 'verging on apologetics' noted by O'Brien (1990: 131). Ricardo is depicted as being so convinced of the relevance of utility and demand to value that he omitted to explain their influence, because it was too obvious; as 'feeling his way towards the distinction between marginal and total utility' and being blocked only by his ignorance of the language of differential calculus; as being aware of the classification of commodities according to the three laws of returns and assuming constant returns only provisionally (Marshall [1890] 1961, I: 814; see also 503, 817). To defend this strained interpretation, Marshall uses the argument that Ricardo did not intend to publish his *Principles* but wrote them only for friends who were already familiar with his ideas and did not need to be reminded of all the details – a justification that Piero Sraffa dismissed as being totally groundless (*Works*, I: xx). But apart from these curiosities, the most remarkable aspect of Appendix I is the fact that it sets Ricardo in perspective between two diametrically opposite characters: Jevons, who in his *Theory of Political Economy* had drastically criticized Ricardo, and Marx, a self-appointed theoretical heir. Against the former, Marshall purports to reconstruct the theory of value-cost of production in such a way that Ricardo's and Jevons's theories appear to complement each other in a coherent whole; against the latter, he formulates the notion of cost of production so as to show that there is no possible thread linking Ricardo to Marx's surplus labour and exploitation. Here as follows, I shall examine these two aspects in sequence. A possible connection is discussed in the conclusions.

For the most part, Appendix I appears to be a follow up to Marshall's 1872 review of Jevons's *Theory*. In a later manuscript note attached to that review (Marshall, 1925: 99–100), Marshall remarked that his reaction to Jevons's book was triggered by 'youthful loyalty' boiling over at the sight of Ricardo, the natural mathematical genius he admired, being under attack. And indeed, in a sort of act of revenge, the most vicious blows in the review were aimed at Jevons's clumsiness in the handling of mathematics, revealed by both his small use of calculus and his blunders in simple mathematical expressions (ibid.: 98–9). A first line of defence of Ricardo on value is set up here when, while claiming that value depends entirely upon utility, Jevons concedes that it may depend on labour only as far as labour, by affecting supply, affects also the degree of utility of a commodity. '[I]t is almost startling to find that [Jevons] regards the Ricardian theory as maintaining labour to be the origin of value in a sense inconsistent with this last position' (ibid.: 93),

Marshall retorts. And in Appendix I, he develops this argument by reversing Jevons's proposition and claiming that the doctrines of Ricardo (and Mill) 'imply that what is true of supply, is true *mutatis mutandis* of demand', that is, utility affects value only as far as it affects costs by changing 'the amount which purchasers took off the market' (Marshall [1890] 1961, I: 817). The stage is thus set for Marshall's final resolution, which consists of a synthesis of the two opposite propositions. While each is true 'as far as it goes', the synthesis is achieved by turning the two corresponding causal chains, from cost to utility to value or from utility to cost to value, into a system of mutually interacting forces. The well-known metaphors of the three balls in a bowl, and of the blades of the scissors, are conjured up at this point in order to underline the general truth that emerges from Jevons's and Ricardo's one-sided, partial truths (ibid.: 818–20). The picture is completed by inserting it within the frame of Marshall's own period analysis in order to show how each author can be placed at the one or the other end of it, with Ricardo's half-truth finding its home near the long-run extremity and Jevons's near the short one. This device, as Marshall wrote to the Dutch economist Nicolaas Pierson in 1891, 'holds the key of all the paradoxes which this long controversy has raised', and makes it possible 'to work all existing knowledge on the subject of value into one Continuous & harmonious whole' (Marshall, 1996, II: 29–30). A non-secondary effect of this deft handling of the controversy is the establishing of a parallelism between the two main antagonists, who are both depicted as extremely brilliant but one-sided intelligences and guilty of the same bad habit of carelessness in expressing themselves. Insistence on the intellectual symmetry between Ricardo and Jevons recurs also in Marshall's correspondence of previous years (ibid., I: 164, 176).

Before we go any further, it may be interesting to consider how Marshall's claim to having reconciled old and new doctrines was questioned by Sraffa in private papers and lecture notes of the late 1920s, now available at Trinity College Library, Cambridge (see Garegnani, 2005 for a detailed reconstruction from archive materials of the points mentioned below). One of the objects of Sraffa's prolonged meditation on the Marshall–Ricardo relationship was the precise nature of the break that he saw hidden behind the alleged reconciliation. In order to encompass Jevons's utility and Ricardo's costs within the same analytical scheme, according to Sraffa, Marshall had to interpret costs as regulators of the producers' supply decisions, in the same way as utility was the regulator of the buyers' demand decisions through demand prices, so that costs had to shed the original Ricardian characterization as objective measures of labour spent in production and to take up a new meaning as measures of all the subjective motivations lying behind the act of bringing a commodity to the market. Consequently, far from achieving a reconciliation Marshall operated a shift in the analytical plane, from the level of objective phenomena to that of all the basically psychological motivations that are related to production. This is how Sraffa saw things. However, in Appendix I Marshall seems to have pre-empted his point, for here he is careful to point out that the object of his reconciliation is not the relation of utility and cost to value, as Jevons misleadingly put it, but how the latter is determined by an equilibrium between demand and supply marginal prices (Marshall [1890] 1961, I: 818–20). Following a distinction that he had already put forward as early as 1876, one thing is seeing a commodity as the embodiment of pleasures and pains measured by its exchange value, as the modern theory tends to do, and quite another thing, once this market measure is given, to reason on the mechanics of exchange values without taking into further account the underlying feelings, as the branch of economic theory that Marshall calls 'pure' or 'abstract' economics tends to do (Marshall, 1925: 125–8). Since Ricardo was for Marshall, as recalled above, the founder of abstract economics in England, there was no need to attribute a concern for human motives to him and, in particular, to interpret his costs as anything else than, in Marshall's own terminology, 'expenses of production' (ibid.: 126–7). In §3 of Appendix I, Marshall seems to be content with this minimalist interpretation. At a certain point he even observes that the supposed antagonism between Ricardo and modern theory would be reduced if one thought of the latter not as founded on utility, as Jevons had done, but as founded simply on the interaction between supply and demand, in the fashion of Cournot (Marshall [1890] 1961, I: 820). This point is reinforced by a parallel drawn by Marshall, in a few lines of the third edition of the *Principles* (later suppressed), between his own extension of Ricardian rent theory to all kinds of competing resources and Cournot's derivation of a theory of competitive markets from a generalization of the theory of monopoly (ibid., II: 450).

Yet Sraffa did have a point, as we can see from §2 of the same Appendix and from a passage related to it in Book VI, Chapter VI, §3 of the *Principles*. Somewhat contradicting his interpretation of Ricardo as the prototypal pure economist interested only in the machinery of exchange, here Marshall credits him with a two-factor theory of the cost of production that implies that 'Time or Waiting as well as Labour' (ibid., I: 816) has to be paid for in order to bring a commodity to market – as if Ricardo had held that waiting and labour can be treated as two kinds of discomfort that only the expectation of a reward is able to elicit. Going into this matter was clearly not needed for the Ricardo–Jevons reconciliation. The purpose, as Ashley argued in the above-mentioned 1891 article, and as Marshall was willing to admit, was rather to exculpate Ricardo from all suspicions of involuntary connivance with the Marxian theory of surplus value, an allegation that rested precisely on 'the statement that has been made by many of Ricardo's friends and enemies, and has been turned to good account for their own uses by Rodbertus, Marx and others, that the value of a thing depends entirely on labour'. This sentence is taken from the manuscript draft of a reply to Ashley that Marshall never published (Marshall Papers 5/5/4, Marshall Library of Economics, Cambridge), in which we also find the following revelation: 'the fact that [Ricardo] had [been] commonly and by competent persons understood to hold [the doctrine that the value of a thing depends entirely on labour] was the avowed and the only cause of my going out of the way to argue that he did not hold it'. Here then was the second task that Marshall undertook in Appendix I. Although the part of the text that he devoted to it takes up less space than his confutation of Jevons, we must not be tempted to conclude that for him this was a secondary issue. His argument with socialism in all the versions he met, including the Marxian version from the late 1860s, was a life-long concern. According to Marshall's recollections and other evidence, he read the first volume of *Das Kapital* in German at approximately the same time that he was studying Mill, in 1867–70 (see Groenewegen, 1995: 577–8). Add to this the closeness, which lasted for many years before the final cooling down of their friendship, to Herbert Foxwell, whose position on Ricardo's (and Mill's) responsibility in providing theoretical props for Marxian socialism fuelled a recurrent dispute between the two (on the relationship between Marshall and Foxwell, see Groenewegen, 1995: 670–79;

Winch, 2009, Chapter 9). Appendix I was just an episode, and not the last one as we shall see, in this long story.

While taking Marx seriously, especially as a source for the history of the factory system, Marshall deemed his theory of surplus value to be entirely based on what he considered to be a '*petitio principii*', that is, the claim that value was the product of labour alone, and not of labour joined to other factors, in particular waiting (Marshall, 1996, I: 302–3; [1890] 1961, I: 586–8). In countering Marx's attempt to invoke the authority of Ricardo in support of his position, Marshall relied on the discussion of the influence of wages and profits on the relative values of commodities employing capitals of unequal durability in §§IV and V of the chapter 'On Value' in Ricardo's *Principles*. In these sections, the argument implied that time, intended as a modifier of labour productivity through the construction of durable implements, needs to be paid for – a statement that Ricardo put forward as a matter of fact without any attempt at an explanation or a justification. That this payment could not be explained except as an outcome of the existing relations of force between social classes, which allowed one class to exploit the surplus labour of another in the form of interest, was the thesis that Marx attached to it. Marshall could not fail to understand that the only way to prevent Marx from taking advantage of Ricardo's reticence was to fill in the gap left by the latter with an alternative justification of interest. And it was only consistent on his part to suggest that Ricardo was implicitly thinking of interest as being a reward that was necessary in order to induce the supply of waiting. In separating Ricardo from Marx, he was in fact using the same tactics that he used in establishing a link of continuity between Ricardo and Jevons: he did not contradict what Ricardo had said, but suggested that Ricardo had also intended something that he had not said. As Marshall wrote to Foxwell in 1893: 'I don't think Ricardo anticipated all modern work. What I say is that his analysis is consistent with modern work' (Marshall, 1996, II: 88).

A secondary issue raised in the discussion of the alleged Ricardian origins of scientific socialism concerned the attributing of an 'iron law of wages' to Ricardo. Marshall had admitted in his early manuscripts that Ricardo might have held such a view; therefore, an analogous willy-nilly admission in the *Principles* ([1890] 1961, I: 508–9), surrounded by plenty of Marshall's habitual caveats, is not surprising. An elaborate argument of Ashley's (1891: 481–8) on this point received only a noncommittal comment from Marshall in the third edition (see [1890] 1961, I: 509, 2n). When Ashley's criticism extended to Marshall's own reconstruction of the Ricardian theory of value, however, the reaction was more vigorous. Ashley had pointed out that 'Ricardo did not think [that the modifications of labour value discussed in §§IV and V of his first chapter] touched the essence of his doctrine' (Ashley, 1891: 477). In the above-mentioned draft of his reply to Ashley, Marshall started with what looks like an implicit admission of having somehow distorted Ricardo's meaning:

'Rehabilitation' may mean 'clothing anew'. I admit that Ricardo's doctrines were offered to the world sadly naked, and wanted a good deal of clothing. I dont altogether deny the charge of having tried in a humble way to do a little tailoring and outfitting for him. It has been a work of love for his results, more than for himself.

But then he went on to quibble about 'the essence' to which Ashley referred ('the "modifications" did not *touch* the essence of his doctrine, only because they were themselves that very essence itself'; original emphasis), and concluded that all that his argument really needed was the fact that Ricardo had taken the payment of interest on capital 'as a matter of course' – a claim that Ashley himself had conceded. Only bits of this manuscript resurface in the third edition of the *Principles*, especially in footnote 1 on p. 816. While reaffirming the just-mentioned weak claim in the footnote, however, in the main text Marshall introduced a new and much bolder claim that amounted to attributing to Ricardo a full-blown theory of waiting: 'it seems difficult to imagine how [Ricardo] could more strongly have emphasized the fact that Time or Waiting as well as Labour is an element of cost of production' ([1890] 1961, I: 816). In the first edition Marshall had not been so explicitly assertive. Evidently, the dispute with Ashley had reinforced his beliefs, and judging from the fact that the text of Appendix I remained practically unchanged from the third to the eighth and final edition, these had now reached their definitive form. Evidence of how deeply convinced he was that this was the right way of interpreting Ricardo is supplied by his private reaction to a rekindling of the controversy a few years later, when Foxwell wrote an introduction to the 1899 English translation of Anton Menger's treatise on the juridical postulates of socialism, *The Right to the Whole Produce of Labour*. Both Foxwell and Menger had emphasized the supposed role of Ricardo in providing economic underpinnings for a line of English socialism from which, according to them, Marx and Lassalle had drawn their inspiration. Comments pencilled in his personal copy of Menger's book (preserved at the Marshall Library of Economics, Cambridge) show Marshall repeating for his own use the lessons that he had established in the *Principles*. 'Mengers [sic] blunder about Ricardo is conspicuous', he jots down on the title page with reference to a later page on which Menger traces the sources of the labour theory of value in the first chapter of Ricardo's *Principles*. 'The doctrine is not in ch[apter] I. It is only started in ch I § 1' Marshall annotates at the bottom of the page. And at the margin of one of Foxwell's tirades about the perverse implications of Ricardian doctrines, we find the comment: 'This is fair when interpreted generously, as Ricardo is *not* interpreted here or by most other critics' (original emphasis).

Conclusions
In view of the fact that Marshall's admiration for Ricardo derived more from the latter's intellectual powers than from the specific contents of his economic theory, and given that leaving Jevons's rejection of Ricardo unchallenged would have meant letting the socialists boast scientific credentials that they did not deserve, the two operations that Marshall carried out in the note on Ricardo in the *Principles* appear to be two stages of a perhaps unintentional but strategically coherent unique plan. By refuting both Jevons's and Marx's somewhat convergent allegations, Marshall managed to anchor Ricardo firmly in the economic mainstream that culminated in his own theory, although at the cost of stretching the historical record as Ashley had pointed out. This is not the only case in which Marshall forgoes historical accuracy for the sake of affirming the continuity of scientific progress; and his reaction to Ashley shows clearly enough that, in the case of Ricardo, accuracy was the last of his concerns. He seemed to admit as much in the unpublished draft of his reply to Ashley: 'I have not any very strong personal interest in Ricardo'. Rather, there is reason to believe that the main concern underlying the whole operation was of a political kind. A free trader, a source of inspiration of Manchesterism (Marshall, 1996, II: 385), neither a disguised socialist nor a 'partisan of

capital' – 'Ricardo had very little sympathy one way or the other', Marshall remarks in 1885 ([1890] 1961, II: 599): this powerful reasoner was worthy to become a member of that continuous line of descent to which Marshall wanted to connect his own economics, imbued as it was with moderately progressive liberalism.

MARCO DARDI

See also:

Exchange Value and Utility; Jevons, William Stanley, on Ricardo; Marx, Karl Heinrich, on Ricardo; Walras, Marie-Esprit-Léon, on Ricardo; Wicksell, Knut, on Ricardo.

References

Ashley, W.J. (1891), 'The rehabilitation of Ricardo', *Economic Journal*, 1(3), 474–89.
Cook, S. and T. Foresti (eds) (2010), 'Marshall's notes for his advanced course in political economy', *Marshall Studies Bulletin*, 11, accessed 23 February 2014 at www.disei.unifi.it/cmpro-v-p-96.html.
Creedy, J. (2006), 'The theory of international trade', in T. Raffaelli, G. Becattini and M. Dardi (eds), *The Elgar Companion to Alfred Marshall*, Cheltenham, UK and Northampton, MA: Edward Elgar Publishing, pp.453–8.
Garegnani, P. (2005), 'On a turning point in Sraffa's theoretical and interpretative position in the late 1920s', *European Journal of the History of Economic Thought*, 12(3), 453–92.
Groenewegen, P. (1993), 'Marshall on Ricardo', in M. Baranzini and G.C. Harcourt (eds), *The Dynamics of the Wealth of Nations*, London: Macmillan, pp.45–70.
Groenewegen, P.D. (1995), *A Soaring Eagle: Alfred Marshall 1842–1924*, Aldershot, UK and Brookfield, VT: Edward Elgar Publishing.
Marshall, A. ([1890] 1961), *Principles of Economics*, 9th (variorum) edition, 2 vols, (ed.) C.W. Guillebaud, London: Macmillan.
Marshall, A. (1925), *Memorials of Alfred Marshall*, (ed.) A.C. Pigou, London: Macmillan.
Marshall, A. (1975), *The Early Economic Writings of Alfred Marshall*, 2 vols, (ed.) J.K. Whitaker, London: Macmillan.
Marshall, A. (1996), *The Correspondence of Alfred Marshall, Economist*, 3 vols, (ed.) J.K. Whitaker, Cambridge, UK: Cambridge University Press.
O'Brien, D.P. (1990), 'Marshall's works in relation to classical economics', in J.K. Whitaker (ed.), *Centenary Essays on Alfred Marshall*, Cambridge, UK: Cambridge University Press, pp.127–63.
Whitaker, J.K. (1975), 'The evolution of Alfred Marshall's economic thought and writings over the years 1867–90', in A. Marshall, *The Early Economic Writings of Alfred Marshall, Vol. I*, (ed.) J.K. Whitaker, London: Macmillan, pp.3–113.
Winch, D. (2009), *Wealth and Life*, Cambridge, UK/New York: Cambridge University Press.

Marx, Karl Heinrich, on Ricardo

Marx had great respect for Ricardo as a theorist and a man of integrity. Marx argued that Ricardo firmly placed bourgeois economics on the foundation of the labour theory of value, and that he emphasized the inverse relation between wages and profit, which follows from the labour theory of value, thereby implying the class conflict between workers and capitalists that is inherent in capitalism. Marx stated in the *Contribution to a Critique of Political Economy*:

> Although encompassed by his bourgeois horizons, Ricardo analyses the bourgeois economy, whose deeper layers differ essentially from its surface appearances, with such theoretical acumen that Lord Brougham could say of him: 'Mr. Ricardo seemed as if he had dropped from another planet'. (Marx [1859] 1970, *Critique [CR]*: 60–61)

On the other hand, Marx argued that Ricardo's labour theory of value was still crude and incomplete, and had many weaknesses: it did not clearly distinguish between abstract labour and concrete labour; it did not derive the necessary connection between abstract labour and money; it did not present an explicit theory of profit, nor of the rate of profit, nor of prices of production based on the rate of profit; and its theory of the falling rate of profit was overly simplistic.

This entry reviews Marx's evaluation of Ricardo's theory. Marx's longest and most thorough discussion of Ricardo's theory (by far) is in *Theories of Surplus Value*, Volume II (i.e., in the *Manuscripts of 1861–63*), there are also many brief discussions in *The Grundrisse, A Contribution to a Critique of Political Economy* and Volume 1 of *Capital*.

Value and money

Marx praised Ricardo for insisting that the starting point of an analysis of capitalism is the determination of value by labour time: 'The determination of exchange-value by labour-time has been formulated and expounded in the clearest manner by Ricardo' (*CR*: 60). Marx commented that Smith vacillated between theory and empirical observations, and his successors continued to 'jumble up' the two:

> But at last Ricardo steps in and calls to science: Halt! The basis, the starting point for the physiology of the bourgeois system . . . is the determination of *value by labour-time* . . . This then is Ricardo's great historical significance for science. (Marx [1861–63] 1968, *Theories of Surplus Value II* [*TSV.II*]: 166; original emphasis)

Marx considered Ricardo's theory of the magnitude of value 'by far the best', but it also had its 'insufficiencies', mainly the failure to clearly distinguish between abstract labour as the producer of value and concrete labour as the producer of use values: 'But it does not occur to the economists [including Ricardo] that a purely quantitative distinction between the kinds of labour presupposes their qualitative unity of equality, and therefore their reduction to abstract human labour' (Marx [1867] 1977, *Capital*, I [*C.I*]: 173).

But Marx's main criticism of Ricardo's labour theory of value is that it is concerned *only* with the magnitude of value, and does not consider the necessary form of appearance of value, which is money. Marx derived money as the necessary form of appearance of value in the very important §3 of Chapter 1 of *Capital*. Because abstract labour is not directly observable as such, it must acquire the objective form of appearance of money, in order to make possible the unconscious and indirect regulation of social labour in a commodity-producing society. This is the 'necessary intrinsic connection' between commodity-producing abstract labour and money. However, because Ricardo and the other classical economists tended to view capitalism as the natural form of social production, they did not recognize this necessary and intrinsic connection; they just took it for granted that labour is expressed in money and prices, as a 'nature imposed necessity'. Marx argued that the necessity of money is not imposed by nature, but is instead imposed by the way labour is regulated in a commodity society (indirectly and unconsciously through the exchange of the products of labour):

> But *Ricardo does not examine* the form – the peculiar characteristic of labour that creates exchange-value or manifests itself in exchange-values – the *nature* of this labour. Hence he does not grasp the connection of *this labour* with *money* or that it must assume the form of *money*. Hence he completely fails to grasp the connection between the determination of the exchange-

value of the commodity by labour-time and the fact that the development of commodities necessarily leads to the formation of money. Hence his erroneous theory of money. Right from the start he is only concerned with the *magnitude of value*. (*TSV.II*: 164; emphasis original; see also *C.I*: 173–4)

With respect to Ricardo's theory of the quantity of money, Marx argued that Ricardo started out on the right track, and determined the quantity of money in circulation by the 'needs of circulation', that is, by the sum total of the prices of all commodities, adjusted for the velocity of money. However, Ricardo confused the laws that govern commodity money with the laws that govern inconvertible paper money (as in England during the Napoleonic Wars), and as a result he switched over to the quantity theory of money, according to which the price level is determined by the quantity of money. Ricardo only considered money in its function of means of circulation and ignored the other functions of money, such as hoarding, which is the means by which the quantity of commodity money adjusts to the 'needs of circulation' (*CR*: 170–79).

Surplus value
Marx also criticized Ricardo for failing to present an explicit theory of profit or surplus value, and thus for failing to clearly demonstrate that the source of profit is surplus labour. There is, of course, a theory of profit implicit in Ricardo's labour theory of value, but he did not explicitly present this theory. Marx argued in the *Grundrisse* that Ricardo could not fully comprehend the origin of profit because of his 'bourgeois horizon'; an understanding of the origin of profit would lead to a recognition of the exploitation of workers in capitalism (Marx [1857–58] 1973, *Grundrisse* [*G*], 551 and 595–6).

The one element of a theory of profit that Ricardo emphasized is that the rate of profit varies inversely with wages, which, of course, follows from the labour theory of value. This inverse relation between wages and profit reveals the inherent conflict between workers and capitalists in capitalism, which led other classical economists such as the American 'harmonizer' Carey to denounce Ricardo as the 'father of communism' (*TSV. II*: 166).

However, Ricardo did not go further, and he failed to show the division of the working day into necessary labour and surplus labour, which 'obscures the understanding' (ibid.: 405). As a result, Ricardo did not recognize capital's 'compulsion to expand surplus labour', which explains both the conflict over the working day (absolute surplus value) and inherent technological change (relative surplus value). Instead, Ricardo took the working day as a given length, and thus did not explain the conflict over the working day. On the other hand, even though Ricardo did not explain capitalism's inherent tendency toward technological change, he did understand that wages depend on the labour-time required to produce the workers' means of subsistence, and thus that profit varies inversely with the labour-time required to produce the means of subsistence; that is, he understood relative surplus value. Marx considered Ricardo's emphasis on relative surplus value to be one of his scientific achievements (ibid.: 417–19).

A related criticism is that Ricardo was not able to explain the exchange between capital and labour on the basis of the labour theory of value (ibid.: 395–404). Marx argued that the reason Ricardo was not able to explain this exchange is that he conceived it as an exchange of labour rather than an exchange of labour power, and 'the quantity of labour required to produce a quantity of labour' is an 'absurd tautology' (*C.I*: 675). Marx argued that, in his discussion of the 'value of labour', Ricardo unconsciously substituted the worker for labour, and determined the 'value of labour' by the labour time required to produce the worker (i.e., to produce the workers' wage goods), and thus in effect substituted labour power for labour. But because he continued to use the irrational concept of the value of labour, Ricardo was not able to clearly explain wages on the basis of the labour theory of value, and this was one of the two main factors that led to the decline of his school (Marx [1861–63] 1971, *Theories of Surplus Value* III [*TSV.III*]: 237).

Rate of profit and prices of production (cost prices)
Marx also argued that Ricardo did not present a theory of the rate of profit, or a theory of prices of production based on the rate of profit. In Ricardo's very first chapter 'On Value' (*Works*, I: 30–43), he introduced the rate of profit 'out of nowhere', and assumed it to be 10 per cent, without a theory of what determines this rate. Then he assumed (again arbitrarily) that the rate of profit declines to 9 per cent, due to an increase of wages (of an unspecified amount), and analysed the effects of these changes on relative prices. But nowhere did he explain how the rate of profit is determined. Marx argued that, instead of presupposing the rate of profit at the beginning of his theory, he first should have abstracted from the rate of profit, and then explained it later on the basis of the conclusions derived in earlier stages of the theory. A theory of the rate of profit is especially important in the case of the labour theory of value, because a general rate of profit (equal across industries) appears to contradict the labour theory of value. Therefore, it is incumbent on any proponent of the labour theory of value to explain how equal rates of profit are consistent with the labour theory of value and how the general rate of profit is determined by the labour theory of value. Ricardo could not provide this explanation, but Marx did. Ricardo's inability to answer this fundamental question was one of the two main reasons the labour theory of value was rejected in the decades that followed (*TSV.III*: 237).

As with surplus value, the one element of a theory of the rate of profit that Ricardo emphasized is that the rate of profit varies inversely with wages, and thus an increase of wages causes the rate of profit to fall. Ricardo's theory of the falling rate of profit will be considered in the next section.

Marx also criticized Ricardo for failing to present a theory of prices of production (i.e., long-run equilibrium prices with equal rates of profit). Ricardo was only interested in analysing the effect of an increase of wages on prices of production; he was not interested in the more fundamental question of how prices of production are determined. Marx argued that Ricardo should have used the labour theory of value to explain how prices of production differ from values (throughout *Theories of Surplus Value* Marx used the term 'cost price' to mean what he later called prices of production):

> Ricardo, instead of deriving the difference between cost prices and value from the determination of value itself, admits that 'values' themselves . . . are determined by influences that are independent of labour-time and that the law of value is sporadically invalidated by these influences . . .
>
> Ricardo does not dwell on the conclusion which follows from his own illustration, namely, that – quite apart from the rise or fall of wages – on the assumption of constant wages, the cost prices of commodities must differ from their values, if cost prices are determined by the same percentage of profit.

This illustration in itself already assumes cost prices regulated by an average profit of 10 per cent and differing from the values of commodities. The question is, how are these cost prices affected by the rise or fall in profit, when the capitals employed contain different proportion of fixed and circulating capital. This illustration . . . has nothing to do with the essential question of the transformation of values into cost prices. (*TSV.II*: 191–2; see also 189–215 and 384–6)

Absolute rent

Marx also argued that, because Ricardo did not clearly understand the difference between values and prices of production, he came to the erroneous conclusion that absolute rent (rent on the least fertile land that is not due to a monopoly price) is not possible. Marx argued, to the contrary, that absolute rent is possible, precisely because of the difference between values and prices of production. If the composition of capital in agriculture is less than the social average composition (which, in fact, it was at that time in England and other countries), then the value of agricultural goods will be greater than the price of production of agricultural goods, which means that the surplus value produced in agriculture will be greater than the average profit in the economy as a whole. Landlords (because of their monopoly of the land) are able to prevent the transformation of the value of agricultural goods into their price of production, and thus prevent the transformation of the surplus value produced in agriculture into average profit (i.e., to prevent the 'sharing' of this extra surplus value in agriculture with capitalists in non-agricultural industries). Instead, the landlords appropriate this extra surplus value in agriculture for themselves as absolute rent. Ricardo could not understand the possibility of absolute rent because he did not clearly understand the difference between values and prices of production.

Falling rate of profit

Marx also criticized Ricardo's theory of the falling rate of profit as being overly simplistic (*TSV.II*: 438–69). Marx argued that the only cause of a falling rate of profit considered by Ricardo was rising money wages (due to declining productivity in agriculture and higher prices of food, which is itself a dubious assumption). In Marx's terms, the only cause of a falling rate of profit was a falling rate of surplus value. Thus, Marx argued that Ricardo tended to treat the rate of profit and the rate of surplus value as 'identical'. Marx acknowledged that Ricardo also mentioned in a few places that an increase in the price of raw materials could also cause the rate of profit to fall, but Ricardo's overwhelming emphasis was on rising wages. In Chapter 15 of *Theories of Surplus Value*, Marx discussed different ways in which changes in the composition of capital might affect the rate of profit (especially due to technological change), with the rate of surplus value (or wages) constant (*TSV.II*: 379–84). Marx argued that Ricardo ignored all these possible causes of a falling rate of profit, with his narrow focus on rising money wages.

Say's Law and the possibility of crises

Ricardo accepted Say's Law, according to which a 'general glut' of commodities is not possible. Marx presented a critique of Say's Law in Chapter 3 of Volume 1 of *Capital* – that this 'law' presumes either barter exchange or that sales are always followed immediately by purchases (i.e., assumes no hoarding; the only function of money considered is means of circulation). Marx briefly discussed Ricardo's acceptance of Say's Law in Chapter 17 (§§8–9) of *Theories of Surplus Value*. He quoted several passages from

Ricardo (e.g., 'productions are always bought by productions'; 'no man produces, but with a view to consume or sell, and never sells, but with an intention to purchase some other commodity') and commented that: 'This is the childish babble of a Say, but it is not worthy of Ricardo' (*TSV.II*: 502).

Effect of machinery on employment

This is an issue about which Ricardo changed his mind, and Marx praised Ricardo for his scientific integrity. In Chapter 31 of Ricardo's *Principles* (added to the third edition), Ricardo explained that he had previously held the view that any time machinery replaces labour in one industry, it would set free an equivalent amount of capital that could be used to employ workers in other industries. Employment would remain the same and wages would remain the same. The only difference is that workers would be employed in other industries, perhaps the machine-building industry. Marx called this the 'compensation theory'. However, on further reflection, Ricardo changed his mind and instead concluded that the introduction of machinery could cause the reduction of both employment and wages. Marx commented: 'This section, which Ricardo added to the 3rd edition, bears witness to his *honesty*, which so essentially distinguishes him from the vulgar economists' (*TSV.II*: 555; original emphasis).

However, Marx also commented that Ricardo's views remained somewhat 'apologetic', in the sense that he argued that the negative effects of machinery on employment and wages could be offset by increased demand for menial servants (because machinery reduces the price of luxury goods, which leaves more profit and rent left over to hire servants!) and by cheaper wages goods (ibid.: 571–3).

In summary, Marx applauded Ricardo for insisting that the starting point of a theory of capitalism is the determination of value by labour time, and for using the labour theory of value to derive the inverse relation between wages and profit, and thus implicitly reveal the conflict of interests between workers and capitalists. However, this is as far as Ricardo got, and there were other important aspects of a theory of capitalism that Ricardo was not able to explain – a theory of money, of profit, of the rate of profit, and of prices of production. It was left to Marx to further develop the labour theory of value to explain these important phenomena of capitalism.

FRED MOSELEY

See also:

Bortkiewicz, Ladislaus von, on Ricardo; Dmitriev, Vladimir Karpovich, on Ricardo; Ricardian Socialists; Sraffa, Piero, on Ricardo.

References

Marx, K. ([1857–58] 1973), *The Grundrisse*, Harmondsworth, UK: Penguin Books. In the text referred to as *G*.
Marx, K. ([1859] 1970), *A Contribution to the Critique of Political Economy*, New York: International Publishers. In the text referred to as *CR*.
Marx, K. ([1861–63] 1968), *Theories of Surplus Value, Vol. 2*, Moscow: Progress Publishers. In the text referred to as *TSV.II*.
Marx, K. ([1861–63] 1971), *Theories of Surplus Value, Vol. 3*, Moscow: Progress Publishers. In the text referred to as *TSV.III*.
Marx, K. ([1867] 1977), *Capital, Vol. 1*, New York: Random House. In the text referred to as *C.I*.

Mathematical Formulations of Ricardian Economics

Although the first mathematical exposition of some elements of the Ricardian system appeared ten years after the last edition of the *Principles* (Whewell, 1831), modern mathematical formulations are much later as they are contemporary to modern growth theory and follow Sraffa's complete edition of Ricardo's *Works*. The purpose of this entry is to introduce the reader to the Ricardian dynamical models developed since the 1950s. We organize the exposition around what seems to represent the basic ingredients of the Ricardian system: (a) decreasing returns, (b) theory of distribution, (c) wage and luxury goods, (d) Malthusian law of population, (e) capital accumulation and distribution. The labour theory of value does hold under the assumptions made in the following exposition and the value problems arising in more general models are not even mentioned.

Decreasing returns

Constant returns are often assumed in presenting both Ricardo's trade theory and the Ricardian theory of value, but decreasing returns in the wage-goods sector is a fundamental element of any dynamical Ricardian model. With land in fixed supply, additional units of labour increase the output of this sector, but with a diminishing rate of increase. This generates the 'production function' for the wage-goods as a whole elaborated in what follows. The distribution effects of decreasing returns (i.e., rent theory) are, however, relegated to the second section. The general formulation contained in Samuelson (1959) will be used in the exposition. Then the assumptions underlying the most usual formulations will be assessed.

Consider the wage-goods industries of an economy producing $n \geq 1$ commodities and assume that at least one of the wage-goods is agricultural (this means that land is an essential input into the production function of the good). If the composition of the output in the sector is given (it can be hypothesized, for example, that all wage-goods are demanded in given proportions), then total output is proportional to a given positive vector, **d**, whose dimension is equal to n, the number of existing wage-goods. If it is assumed in addition that in the economy capital consists of the wage-goods advanced by capitalists (this assumption is common to almost all full-fledged dynamical Ricardian models), and that the set of known methods of productions is finite, then the technology of the sector can be represented by means of the labour input vector $\mathbf{l} \geq \mathbf{0}$, the land input matrix $\mathbf{C} \geq \mathbf{0}$, and the output matrix $\mathbf{B} \geq \mathbf{0}$. The number of rows of **l**, **C** and **B** is equal to the number of known processes of production. While the number of columns of **C** is equal to the number of the different qualities of land available, and the number of columns of **B** is equal to the number of wage-goods.

Assume now that all the different qualities of land are in fixed supply, $\mathbf{h} > \mathbf{0}$. Then production cannot be expanded without facing decreasing returns. Thus, the problem is to determine how labour is allocated to the various qualities of land under free competition. Samuelson proved that in equilibrium the system minimizes the labour employed in the production of a given output (see Samuelson, 1959: 29), and this under our technological assumptions leads to the following linear programming problem:

$$\min x^T \mathbf{1}$$

$$\begin{cases} x^T \mathbf{B} \geq \theta d^T \\ x^T \mathbf{C} \leq h^T \\ x \geq \mathbf{0}, \end{cases} \tag{1}$$

where x is the intensity vector and $\theta \geq 0$ is the number of wage-goods baskets to be produced.

Problem (1) is a linear programme whose dual (i.e., the price system with which we shall deal in the second section) has always a feasible solution. Hence, by the duality theorem, it has an optimal solution if and only if it has a feasible solution. Then programme (1) has an optimal solution for $\theta_M \geq \theta \geq 0$, where θ_M is the maximum number of baskets that can be produced in the system. Furthermore, the theory of linear parametric programming can be used to investigate the family of problems obtained by varying θ in the interval $[0, \theta_M]$. In particular, if N_W is the minimum value of problem (1), then the increasing function:

$$N_W = g^{-1}(\theta) \tag{2}$$

is continuous, piecewise linear, and convex as shown in Figure 16 (see e.g., Franklin, 1980: 69–72). We can therefore take the concave function:

$$\theta = g(N_W) \tag{3}$$

as the 'production function' of the wage-goods sector as a whole.

The 'production function' commonly found in Ricardian models (see Kaldor, 1955–56; Pasinetti, 1960; Findlay, 1974; Hicks and Hollander, 1977; Costa, 1977, 1985; Samuelson, 1978; Casarosa, 1978, 1985; Caravale and Tosato, 1980; Gordon, 1983; Bhaduri and Harris, 1987; Freni, 1989):

$$X = f(N_W) \tag{4}$$

differs from (3) essentially in two respects. First, it refers only to one agricultural product (X), called 'corn'. Second, it is smooth (exceptions are e.g., Pasinetti, 1981 and Freni, 1994). Since we are not interested in the analysis of land specialization and gave away *ab initio* substitution among wage-goods, the first difference is not an important one. The second difference highlights the fact that the existence of a dense spectrum of processes and/or of qualities of land is often assumed and that when it is not then we should be cautious as regards the use of the derivative of the production function. Developing (4) from (3), however, points out that the extension of cultivation (hence extensive rent theory) can be subsumed under the usual treatment of decreasing returns by means of the production function (4). A simple example will illustrate how to adapt the tools developed above to the analysis of extensive rent theory with a continuum of lands.

Assume there is a single agricultural product and a continuum of qualities of land and assume that the technology can be described as follows: one unit of land of quality

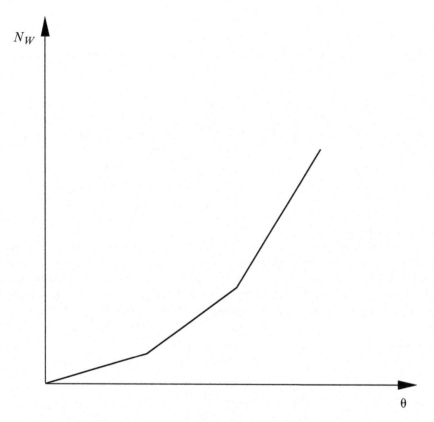

Figure 16   The 'inverse production function' of the wage-goods sector

$s \geq 0$ and $1 + s$ units of labour produce one unit of output. Suppose in addition there is not a finite mass of land of any quality s, so that if at a given time any land of quality s is in use, then all of it is. Finally, to simplify, assume that $h(s) = 1$ for each $s \geq 0$ (i.e., the distribution of land quality is a linear function). Of course, we can still determine the equilibrium allocation of labour over the available lands by finding the minimum amount of labour that is needed to produce a given output. So we have to solve the analogue of problem (1) that under the new assumptions is the (infinite dimensional) linear programming:

$$Min \int_0^{+\infty} x(s)\,(1 + s)\, ds$$

$$\begin{cases} \int_0^{+\infty} x(s)\, ds \geq \theta \\ \\ 0 \leq x(s) \leq 1 \quad s \geq 0. \end{cases} \tag{5}$$

Since the labour coefficient increases with the index s, the optimal solution of problem (5) is very simple: $x(s) = 1$ for $s \leq \bar{s}$ and $x(s) = 0$ for $s > \bar{s}$, where $\bar{s}$ solves the equation:

$$\int_0^{\bar{s}} ds = \theta. \tag{6}$$

Clearly, indeed, optimality requires to cultivate first the best land, then the next best land and so on until the required output is reached. Then we have:

$$N_W = \int_0^{\bar{s}} (1 + s)\, ds = \bar{s} + \frac{\bar{s}^2}{2}, \tag{7}$$

from which, using equation (6), we obtain the 'inverse production function'

$$N_W = \theta + \frac{\theta^2}{2}. \tag{8}$$

Theory of distribution

The solution of problem (1) in the section above is associated with the pricing of both wage-goods and land services. The wage-goods pricing problem and a part of the distributional problem (i.e., the determination of rent) are therefore implicitly solved in the course of the minimization process leading to competitive equilibrium. This can be seen most clearly by considering the dual of problem (1) that takes the form:

$$\max (\theta \mathbf{d}^T \mathbf{p} - \mathbf{h}^T \mathbf{q})$$
$$\begin{cases} \mathbf{Bp} - \mathbf{Cq} \leq \mathbf{l} \\ \mathbf{p} \geq 0 \\ \mathbf{q} \geq 0, \end{cases} \tag{9}$$

where $\mathbf{p}$ is the price vector of wage-goods and $\mathbf{q}$ is the vector of rent rates.

In equilibrium, $\mathbf{p}$, $\mathbf{q}$ and $\mathbf{x}$ satisfy the conditions:

$$\begin{cases} \mathbf{x}^T \mathbf{B} \geq \theta \mathbf{d}^T \\ \mathbf{x}^T \mathbf{Bp} = \theta \mathbf{d}^T \mathbf{p} \\ \mathbf{x}^T \mathbf{C} \leq \mathbf{h}^T \\ \\ \mathbf{x}^T \mathbf{Cq} = \mathbf{h}^T \mathbf{q} \\ \mathbf{Bp} - \mathbf{Cq} \leq \mathbf{l} \\ \mathbf{x}^T \mathbf{Bp} - \mathbf{x}^T \mathbf{Cq} = \mathbf{x}^T \mathbf{l}. \end{cases}$$

Moreover, since by duality:

$$N_W = \theta \mathbf{d}^T \mathbf{p} - \mathbf{h}^T \mathbf{q}, \tag{10}$$

we have:

$$g'(N_W) \mathbf{d}^T \mathbf{p} = 1 \tag{11}$$

for each point in which $g(N_W)$ is differentiable. Therefore, the rent in terms of output is simply given by:

$$\frac{\mathbf{h}^T\mathbf{q}}{\mathbf{d}^T\mathbf{p}} = g(N_W) - g'(N_W)N_W. \tag{12}$$

(Note that where the production function has a kink the rent is indeterminate and can assume any value in an interval.) The same relation can obviously be found in all the versions of the Ricardian system with only one agricultural good and smooth 'production function' mentioned at the end of the first section above. In these models, using function (4), total rent R is given by:

$$R = f(N_W) - f'(N_W)N_W. \tag{13}$$

By eliminating the rent, the distribution problem reduces to the theory of wage rate determination (Kaldor, 1955–56). Indeed, since $g'(N_W)$ (or $f'(N_W)$ in the single-good case) is the amount of wage-goods a worker produces at the margin, we have:

$$w + wr_W = g'(N_W)\,(or\,f'(N_W)), \tag{14}$$

where $w\mathbf{d}$ is the real wage rate and r_w is the rate of profit of the wage-goods sector. Therefore, the rate of profit can be obtained residually once the wage rate is given. Note that $w\mathbf{d}^T\mathbf{p}$, the 'monetary' wage, depends both on w and, given (11), on the marginal conditions of production of wage-goods.

Two theories of wages often coexist in Ricardian models. Sometimes the focus is on the short-run market wage that is given by the market equilibrium condition:

$$w = \frac{W}{N}, \tag{15}$$

where W is a given wage-fund and N is the labour supply (see e.g., Pasinetti, 1960; Hicks and Hollander, 1977; Costa, 1977). Sometimes the 'natural' wage rate $\overline{w}$ (the wage rate that keeps labour supply constant, see 'Malthusian law of population' below) is assumed to prevail (in this case, given the wage-fund, the labour supply is endogenous) (see e.g., Pasinetti, 1960; Findlay, 1974; Samuelson, 1978):

$$w = \overline{w}. \tag{16}$$

In any case, a consistent theory of wage-goods pricing and distribution is obtained conditional upon the value of $g'(N_W)$. A theory of demand is therefore necessary to close the model.

Wage and luxury goods
Not surprising, perhaps, the demand theory we encounter in Ricardian models is limited to what is required by the bare necessities of consistency and completeness. Its importance, however, is raised by the connection with the problem of the independence of the general rate of profit of the no-wage-goods conditions of production, a theme that is of some relevance in Ricardian economics.

The key assumption of the simple demand theory suitable to the purposes mentioned above is the following: capitalists demand only wage-goods (in the given proportion), while rentiers do not consume wage-goods at all (Pasinetti, 1960; Findlay, 1974). The set of markets comprising all rentiers' consumption goods does not comprise, therefore, 'necessaries' and can be identified with the luxury-goods sector. Once the existence of these two disjoint sets of goods is granted, rent given in equation (12) (or (13)) can be interpreted as the net supply of the wage-goods sector, whose net demand is given by the sum of wages and profits earned outside the sector. Therefore, in equilibrium, we have:

$$g(N_W) - g'(N_W)N_W = w(1 + r_l)N_l \tag{17}$$

$$r_l = r_W (= r), \tag{18}$$

where r_l is the rate of profit earned in the luxury-goods sector and N_l is the sector's employment (as before $f()$, takes the place of $g()$ in the case of a single wage good). Thus, from equations (17), (18) and (14):

$$N = \frac{g(N_W)}{g'(N_W)}, \tag{19}$$

where $N = N_W + N_l$ (full employment is assumed).

Since equation (19) implicitly defines the non-decreasing function $N_W = m(N)$ and the non-increasing function $g'(N_W) = n(N)$, sectorial employments, all the equilibrium values of all wage-sector unknowns, and the general rate of profit are univocally determined given the labour supply. Note that the condition of production of the luxury-goods are nowhere mentioned. The equilibrium value of the profit rate r is, therefore, independent of these conditions. More precisely, each of the two specified Ricardian models descending from the endorsement of one of the wage theories mentioned in the second section above has a unique momentary equilibrium. Indeed, given the two state variables N and W, the market equilibrium is the unique solution of system (3), (12), (14), (15), (19). On the other hand, given the single state variable W, the natural equilibrium is the solution of the enlarged system (3), (12), (14), (15), (19), (16).

We can now examine the forces governing the evolution of the system over time, and the reasons at the root of the shrinkage in the state space implicit in natural equilibrium dynamics.

Malthusian law of population

In most Ricardian models (an exception is the model in Caravale and Tosato, 1980), the natural wage is linked to the evolution of labour supply by means of the Malthusian law: the growth rate of labour supply is an increasing function of the difference between the (real) market wage rate and the (real) natural wage rate. Furthermore, since the labour supply is assumed to be constant when the market wage is at the natural level, this function is zero for $w = \bar{w}$. Mathematically:

$$\varepsilon \frac{\dot{N}}{N} = h(w - \overline{w}), \tag{20}$$

where $h(0) = 0$, $h' > 0$, and $\varepsilon \geq 0$ is a parameter inversely related to the speed at which population changes in reaction to differences between the market and the natural wage rate.

Equation (20) suggests a very natural way to justify the continuous prevalence of the natural wage. If the population adjusts very quickly (i.e., ε is close to zero), then most of the time the market wage rate virtually stays at the natural level. In the 'short-circuited case' $\varepsilon = 0$ (Samuelson, 1978), equation (20) dissolves as a dynamic relation, becoming the static wage determining equation (16).

Finally, in order to have a complete dynamic system, we need to add a saving rule to equation (20), and to the corresponding set of momentary equilibrium determining equations.

Capital accumulation and distribution
The assumed behaviour of rentiers and the hypothesis that wages are payed *ante factum* imply that neither workers nor landowners contribute to the accumulation of capital. All we are left with are capitalists. Capitalists are, indeed, the saving class in most of the Ricardian models (but see Burgstaller, 1989).

In the simplest case, capitalists save (and accumulate) the whole amount of profits when the profit rate is above the natural level, $\overline{r}$, $\overline{r} \geq 0$. The accumulation of capital is, therefore, ruled by the following equation:

$$\frac{\dot{W}}{W} = r - \overline{r}. \tag{21}$$

In the natural wage scenario, it follows from equations (14), (16) and (19) that the profit rate r is a non-decreasing function of the state variable W. Thus, if some viability conditions hold, equation (20) has, excluding singular cases, a single non-zero equilibrium that is asymptotically stable (Figure 17) (cf. Pasinetti, 1960).

Market dynamics can be analysed in a similar way. By substituting the market profit rate obtained from equations (14), (15) and (19) in equation (21) and the market equilibrium wage obtained from equation (15) in equation (20), we have the system:

$$\dot{W} = g(m(N)) - (1 + \overline{r})W \tag{22}$$

$$\varepsilon \frac{\dot{N}}{N} = h\left(\frac{W}{N} - \overline{w}\right), \tag{23}$$

whose phase portrait is depicted in Figure 18 for the case of a smooth technology (the phase portrait for the case of a discrete technology is structurally similar; the only difference is that the nullcline $\dot{W} = 0$ contains flats)

Since there is a one to one correspondence between the set of equilibria of the planar system (22)–(23) and that of the natural system, the above qualifications about existence and uniqueness apply. Asymptotic stability of the non-zero stationary state under

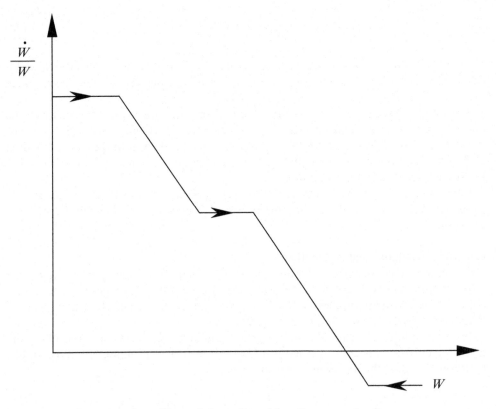

Figure 17   The 'natural equilibrium' dynamics with a discrete technology

market dynamics can be analysed by means of the nullicline configuration and the phase portrait in Figure 18 (see, e.g., Costa, 1985). All solutions in Region I with $N > 0$ (solutions with $N = 0$ tend to unstable equilibrium $(0,0)$) head downward and to the right and all solutions in Region II head upward and to the left. Thus they either enter one of the two regions labelled III and IV or tend directly to the non-zero equilibrium point. If solutions enter Regions III (IV) they then head upward and to the right (downward and to the left), but they cannot leave the region. Thus they too tend to the stationary state. We therefore conclude that all solutions starting with a positive population tend to the positive long-run equilibrium.

The simple market dynamics displayed in Figure 18 depends on the sharp distinction between wage and luxury goods that the assumptions of the third section imply. Without this distinction, indeed, the the nullcline $\dot{W} = 0$ is not necessarily non-decreasing and the market equilibrium behaviour can become more complex. A case that has been discussed in the literature is that of the simple aggregative Ricardian system with a smooth technology whose dynamics is given by the following differential equations (see e.g., Hicks and Hollander, 1977; Gordon, 1983):

$$\dot{W} = f'(N)N - (1 + \bar{r})W \qquad (24)$$

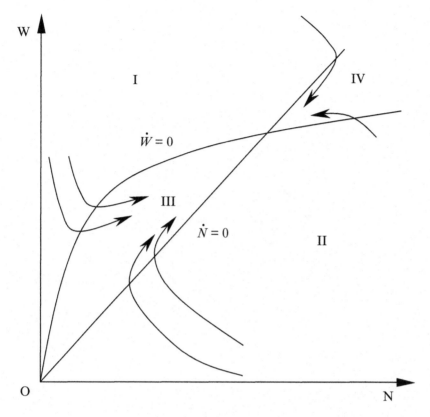

W

I

IV

$\dot{W} = 0$

III

$\dot{N} = 0$

II

O

N

Figure 18   The 'market equilibrium' dynamics with a smooth technology

$$\varepsilon \frac{\dot{N}}{N} = h\left(\frac{W}{N} - \overline{w}\right), \tag{25}$$

where, as before, gross investment is the part of gross profits $f'(N)N$ that exceeds $\overline{r}W$.

We consider the case in which $\dot{W} = 0$ is not monotone as shown in Figure 19. Local asymptotic stability of the non-zero stationary state can be established by linearizazion, but global asymptotic stability cannot be studied with the methods used above. Nevertheless, it can be obtained by using the Poincaré-Bendixson theorem (see Hirsch and Smale, 1974: 248–9) and the Bendixson negative criterion (see Guckenheimer and Holmes, 1983: 44). We give a brief sketch of the proof. Consider the rectangle $OABC$ whose corners are $(0,0)$, $(0, \max f'(N)N)$, $(\frac{\max f'(N)N}{\overline{w}}, \max f'(N)N$, and $(\frac{\max f'(N)N}{\overline{w}}, 0)$. Every solution at a boundary point of $OABC$ either enters the rectangle or slides along the boundary. Therefore the rectangle is positively invariant. Then by the Poincaré-Bendixson theorem the ω limit set of any point in $OABC$ with $N > 0$ is the non-zero stationary state or a limit cycle in the rectangle. However, the existence of a limit cycle can be excluded by means of the Bendixson negative criterion. Hence, given that $OABC$ is absorbing, the basin of attraction of the positive equilibrium is the whole first quadrant with exclusion of the halfline $N = 0$.

GIUSEPPE FRENI

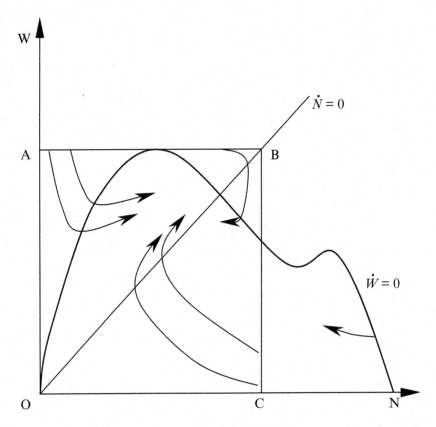

Figure 19   The 'market equilibrium' dynamics with a smooth technology for the one sector Ricardian model

See also:

Accumulation of Capital; Corn Model; Endogenous Growth; Kaldor, Nicholas, on Ricardo; Pasinetti, Luigi Lodovico, on Ricardo; Recent Interpretations; Ricardian Dynamics; Samuelson, Paul Anthony, on Ricardo.

References

Bhaduri, A. and D. Harris (1987), 'The complex dynamics of the simple Ricardian system', *Quarterly Journal of Economics*, **102**(4), 893–901.
Burgstaller, A. (1989), 'A classical model of growth, expectations and general equilibrium', *Economica*, **56**(223), 373–93.
Caravale, G. and D. Tosato (1980), *Ricardo and the Theory of Value, Distribution and Growth*, London: Routledge and Kegan Paul.
Casarosa, C. (1978), 'A new formulation of the Ricardian system', *Oxford Economic Papers*, **30**(1), 38–63.
Casarosa, C. (1985), 'The new view of the Ricardian theory of distribution and economic growth', in G. Caravale (ed.), *The Legacy of Ricardo*, Oxford and New York: Blackwell.
Costa, G. (1977), 'La convergenza allo stato stazionario di un'economia di tipo ricardiano', in F. De Cindio and P. Sylos Labini (eds), *Saggi di economia in onore di Antonio Pesenti*, Milan: Giuffrè, pp. 57–76.
Costa, G. (1985), 'Time in Ricardian models: some critical observations and some new results', in G. Caravale (ed.), *The Legacy of Ricardo*, Oxford and New York: Blackwell, pp. 59–83.
Findlay, R. (1974), 'Relative prices, growth and trade in a simple Ricardian system', *Economica*, **41**(161), 1–13.
Franklin, J. (1980), *Methods of Mathematical Economics*, New York: Springer Verlag.

Freni, G. (1989), 'Pluralità di equilibri ed instabilità dello stato stazionario in un semplice modello dinamico ricardiano', *Economia Politica*, **6**, 363–79.

Freni, G. (1994), 'The complex dynamics of the simple Ricardian system: a note', *Metroeconomica*, **45**(1), 89–95.

Gordon, K. (1983), 'Hicks and Hollander on Ricardo: a mathematical note', *Quarterly Journal of Economics*, **97**(2), 721–6.

Guckenheimer, J and P. Holmes (1983), *Nonlinear Oscillations, Dynamical Systems, and Bifurcations of Vector Fields*, New York: Springer-Verlag.

Hicks, J.R. and S. Hollander (1977), 'Mr. Ricardo and the moderns', *Quarterly Journal of Economics*, **91**(3), pp. 351–69.

Hirsch, M.W. and S. Smale (1974), *Differential Equations, Dynamical Systems and Linear Algebra*, New York: Academic Press.

Kaldor, N. (1955–6), 'Alternative theories of distribution', *Review of Economic Studies*, **23**(2), 83–100.

Pasinetti, L.L. (1960), 'A mathematical formulation of the Ricardian system', *Review of Economic Studies*, **27**(2), 78–98.

Pasinetti, L.L. (1981), 'On the Ricardian theory of value: a note', *Review of Economic Studies*, **48**(4), 673–5.

Samuelson, P.A. (1959), 'A modern treatment of the Ricardian theory', *Quarterly Journal of Economics*, **53**(1–2), 1–35, 217–31.

Samuelson, P.A. (1978), 'The canonical classical model of political economy', *Journal of Economic Literature*, **16**(4), 1415–34.

Whewell, W. (1831), 'Mathematical exposition of some of the leading doctrines in Mr. Ricardo's "Principles of Political Economy, and Taxation"', *Transactions of the Cambridge Philosophical Society*, pp. 1–44.

McCulloch, John Ramsay, and Ricardo

John Ramsay McCulloch was one of David Ricardo's main correspondents on various topics in economics. It is well known that McCulloch was the first economist who published a favourable view of Ricardo's *Principles* when it appeared in 1817. Although it is often said that McCulloch did not make original theoretical contributions to the political economy, he contributed to various economic policy issues such as the Corn Laws, the Poor Laws, taxation, national debt, the sinking fund, foreign trade and money.

McCulloch was born in Scotland in 1789 and died in London in 1864. He studied at Edinburgh University, but did not graduate from it. He wrote many articles on economic issues in *The Scotsman* and the *Edinburgh Review*, and books such as *The Principles of Political Economy; with a sketch of the rise and progress of the science* ([1825] 1995), and *A Treatise on the Principles and Practical Influence of Taxation and the Funding System* ([1845] 1995). In addition, he edited dictionaries of economics and commerce, compiled statistical data and collected early English tracts on money and commerce. He played an important role in disseminating Ricardo's economics by writing textbooks and giving lectures on economics in Edinburgh and London. McCulloch can also be regarded as the first historian of economics in Britain (O'Brien, 1970).

The correspondence between Ricardo and McCulloch began in June of 1816 when McCulloch sent to Ricardo his first pamphlet in which he proposed interest rate reduction on national debt with decline in prices (McCulloch, 1816a), and continued until about three weeks before Ricardo's sudden death on 11 September 1823. Since 1816, through their correspondence, they discussed various topics in economics for a long time, but their first meeting seems to have occurred in mid-May 1823, only a few months before Ricardo's death (*Works*, IX: 284, 291, 300–302). After Ricardo's death, McCulloch edited and published the collected writings of David Ricardo with a note on his life and writings (McCulloch, 1846).

Before Ricardo's *Principles*

Before the appearance of Ricardo's *Principles*, McCulloch had already read Ricardo's pamphlets on money and gold (1810–11) and the Corn Laws (1815). It is likely that Ricardo influenced McCulloch to a certain extent when he formed his views on money, finance and trade. His first pamphlet on national debt, entitled *An Essay on the Reduction of the Interest of the National Debt* (McCulloch, 1816a), argued that the interest rate on public debt issued during a period of inflation should be reduced with an overall fall in prices.

In the first edition of the pamphlet, McCulloch expressed his view on the depression after the Napoleonic Wars. In his view, the main causes of that depression were the heavy taxation and the restriction on the importation of corn. The heavy taxation and the restriction of corn importation by the Corn Laws of 1804 and 1815 raised the corn price, by which the money-wage rate and the prices of necessaries were increased. In his arguments on the post-war depression, McCulloch emphasized the close connection between agriculture and manufactures. The development of manufactures increases the demand for agricultural products, for which the agriculture develops. He cited the authority of Malthus to explain the connection between agriculture and manufactures, calling Malthus 'the great political economist' (ibid.: 6).

McCulloch regarded the price of corn as the principal regulator of the prices of commodities in general, including the necessary goods, although its regulation is neither instantaneous nor proportionate. An increase of corn price, for example, increases the prices of other necessary goods, especially food for labourers, which in turn increases the money-wage rate and the cost of production. The increase of the cost of production weakens the competitiveness of the domestic industries in the international markets, thereby lowering their rates of profits. The increase in the money-wage rate is not in proportion to the increase of the price of corn or other necessary goods. Therefore, the higher cost of living due to a rise of corn price induces people to emigrate abroad, which will in turn reduce demands for domestic products. This fall in the profits rates causes the capital flight abroad, resulting in the decline of domestic industries (ibid.: 8–14).

Falling corn price results in decline of the wage rate, but it takes time. According to McCulloch, the price of corn is not the sole regulator of the wage rates; prices of other necessaries also have a considerable effect on wages (ibid.: 26). In addition, the effect of declining corn price on the prices of the other commodities also takes time and not in proportion (ibid.: 28–30). A fall in the price of corn and other commodities diminishes the revenues of the landlords and farmers, without increasing their demands for commodities (ibid.: 27–8). When heavy taxes and the Corn Laws are removed, the wage rate and the cost of production will be diminished, which in turn strengthens the competitive position of domestic manufacturing industries (ibid.: 32–3).

In general, a fall in the commodity prices results in an increase in the real burden of debts, which will depress industries and increase the burden of the state to pay the interest on national debt. McCulloch observed that the value of money in Britain fell from 1797 to 1813, but rose thereafter (ibid.: 41–2). He took into consideration change in corn price when he discussed prices in general (that is, the value of money). He saw that the reduction in the nominal price of corn lowered the prices of manufactures.

McCulloch contended for a reduction in taxation and a retrenchment of public expenditures. Of the public expenditures the most important were those relating to the maintenance of the military forces and the payment of interest on national debt. The military expenditures should and could be reduced in peace time. As to the national debt, McCulloch proposed the reduction of the interest rate on the national debt contracted during an inflationary period, when prices fell and the real burden of the state increased. He maintained that the reduction of the interest rate does not violate the principle of justice, because it does not diminish the real value of the interest paid to creditors of the state. This reduction of the interest rate benefits holders of the national debt, by reducing the taxes that the holders will have to pay. An interest rate reduction on national debt also increases the security of holders' properties, because it can contribute to preventing the bankruptcy of the state (ibid.: 52–3). When he proposed a reduction in the interest rate on national debt, McCulloch quoted Malthus as being 'the highest authority' (ibid.: 44):

If the price of corn were now to fall to 50s. a quarter, and labour and other commodities nearly in proportion, there can be no doubt that *the stockholders would be benefited unfairly*, at the expense of the industrious classes of society, and consequently at the expense of the wealth and prosperity of the whole country. (Malthus [1815] 1986: 38; original emphasis)

In the second edition of the *Essay* (McCulloch [1816b] 1995), McCulloch expanded his arguments on the effects of changes in the value of money. He adopted Ricardo's ideas on the determination and changes of the value of money and the exchange rates. The resumption of cash payment was deemed necessary to deprive the directors of the Bank of England of their power to change at will the value of properties by changing the quantity of notes in circulation under the system of inconvertibility. A closed system would enable the Bank to change the issue of notes without limits or without fearing of changing of the exchange rates. McCulloch was of the opinion that virtually the same thing happened under the system of inconvertibility after 1797 (ibid.: 185–8).

In McCulloch's view, the resumption of cash payment by the Bank of England diminishes prices of commodities in general (that is, an increase in the value of money). This increase in the value of money does not diminish proportionally the prices of commodities (of the necessary goods, in particular) and the money-wage rates at the same time. Rather, the prices of necessaries are deemed to fall faster than the money-wage rates, therefore causing the profits rates to decline, which in turn diminishes the capital accumulation and growth of labour employment. A fall of prices also enhances the real burden of debts, particularly the national debt for the state, and hence the burden for the state's citizens.

At that time, McCulloch accepted Smith's theory of prices according to which a rise in the price of corn increases the prices of all the other products by way of an increase in the money-wage rates of labour. However, by observing that the price of corn was fictitiously kept high by the Corn Laws, he proposed a remedy to diminish the duties on corn importation according to a gradually diminishing scale, for example by 4s or 5s per year until the corn price reached 50s per quarter. McCulloch supported free trade in general: 'A free and unfettered intercourse, is alike productive of general and local advantage' (ibid.: 146). The repeal of the Corn Laws would reduce the money-wage rates and the cost of production. In this case, lowering money-wage rates does not diminish the welfare of the labour classes, because the fall in the prices of necessaries consequent to the fall in corn price increases the demands for their products and labour (ibid.: 137).

Regarding the security of food supply, he expressed the same view as Ricardo. In fact, McCulloch said:

> When one nation has been for a series of years in the habit of importing corn from another, she has exported some more acceptable produce as an equivalent: The benefits are, therefore, reciprocal, and foreigners will be equally with ourselves interested in a continuance of the traffic. (Ibid.: 140)

To support his contention of the necessity to repeal the Corn Laws, McCulloch quoted a passage from Ricardo's *Essay on Profits* (1815) (ibid.: 140–41). At the same time, he quoted Malthus's *Grounds of an Opinion* ([1815] 1986) to support his proposal to reduce the rate of interest on national debt as a precondition for the resumption of cash payment by the Bank of England and the repeal of the Corn Laws (ibid.: 198–201).

Ricardo opposed McCulloch's proposal of reducing the rate of interest on national debt, on the grounds that one cannot know for certain which holders of national debt bought it before the fall of prices. This also applies to private contracts. If contracts have to be revised every time there is a change in prices, chaos and confusion will arise in commercial transactions. McCulloch quoted several long passages from Malthus's *Grounds of an Opinion*. In one of the passages quoted, Malthus criticized stockholders for getting unfair benefits when the corn price fell, by reasoning that the money-wage rate and prices of commodities in general fell nearly in proportion to the corn price. Ricardo criticized this passage as erroneous (his letter to McCulloch 1816, *Works*, VII: 105). He had already publicly denied Smith's theory of prices in his *Essay on Profits* in 1815.

Later, McCulloch seems to have abandoned his idea of reducing the interest rate on national debt when the corn price and prices of commodities in general fell. Ricardo, in a note in the *Principles*, referred to the McCulloch's pamphlet of 1816 (McCulloch, 1816a) as an 'able publication' (*Works*, I: 426n). McCulloch omitted this reference when he published Ricardo's *Principles* in the collected writings of David Ricardo he edited in 1846 (*Works*, I: 426, editor's note). For example, in the review article of Ricardo's *Proposals for an Economical and Secure Currency* (1816) published in 1818 (McCulloch, [1818b] 1995), he did not touch on his proposal to reduce the interest rate on the national debt, when the pernicious effects of a rapid rise of the value of money (that is, a fall of prices in general) occur (ibid.: 79). However, when Ricardo proposed in Parliament to pay off the national debt at a reduced value, McCulloch supported that proposal (his letter to Ricardo, on 28 February 1820, *Works*, VIII: 157–8 and the editor's footnote 2).

On the *Principles of Political Economy, and Taxation*

When Ricardo's *Principles* first appeared in the April of 1817, an unfavourable and very harsh review by an anonymous author appeared in the *British Review* (Anon [1817] 2003). The anonymous author provided a general assessment of the work:

> The work before us, however, seems to afford but too strong evidence that his [Ricardo's] mind is better suited for conducting an argument on an insulated question than for taking extended views of his subject, or for establishing general doctrines – that he is, in short, one of that numerous class of writers, who succeed in a pamphlet and fail in a volume. (In Peach, 2003, I: 42)

As to Ricardo's labour theory of value and the inverse relationship between the wage rate and the profit rate, the author told readers, 'It is true only in a certain very limited acceptance of language, and a very particular combination of circumstances' (ibid.: 43). He further observed, 'It would be waste of time to state or analyse the argument by which Mr. Ricardo labours to make out his favourite point, that the price of all commodities is regulated by the cost of their production in the most unfavourable circumstances' (ibid.: 49).

In addition, the anonymous author ridiculed the 'curious effect' discovered by Ricardo when he was struggling to make his own theory of value, by referring to it as 'this remarkable effect', and as 'but too fair and true a specimen of that absurd kind of hypothetical reasoning with which this volume is filled, and which, as we have already remarked, leads us so frequently to conclusions at complete variance with the actual state of things around us' (ibid.: 43–4). He criticized Ricardo's assumption, when explaining the 'curious effect', that a machine can be durable for 100 years as absurd and unrealistic. Regarding rent, he criticized Ricardo's theory as 'this strange doctrine', contending that there is no land that pays no rent and regulates the price of corn (ibid.: 47).

McCulloch reacted critically to that review. He had previously published a review in *The Scotsman* (3 May 1817; McCulloch [1817a] 2003), where he recognized the validity of Ricardo's labour theory of value, stating that the relative quantities of labour bestowed are the only foundation of exchangeable values of such commodities, 'which can be increased to any extent in quantity by the exertion of industry, and on the production of which competition operates without restraint' (ibid.: 39). He also recognized that a change in the wage rate affects only the rate of profits, without changing the relative prices of commodities (ibid.: 40–41).

McCulloch had a keen interest in the 'curious effect' that a rise of wage rate lowers the prices of products produced with a higher ratio of fixed capital than the standard of value. He also admitted the inverse relationship between the wage rate and the profit rate to be true, and he applied this proposition to the case of an open economy, pointing out the limits of the rise of wages and taxation in that case (ibid.: 39–41).

McCulloch's response to the anonymous writer in the *British Review* was harsh. He said, 'The (British) Reviewer does not indeed, and in so far he certainly acts very wisely, venture to controvert any of the fundamental principles on which the doctrine rests' (McCulloch [1817b] 2003: 73). McCulloch gave a high valuation to Ricardo's labour theory of value, 'in point of originality, perspicuity, and simplicity, [it] has no parallel in this science' (ibid.: 73). He admitted that Ricardo's assumption of the machine being durable for 100 years was unrealistic, but he defended that assumption as a valid method to theoretically elucidate and to establish principles. On the reviewer's criticism of Ricardo's rent theory, McCulloch remarked that the reviewer showed 'a still more deplorable ignorance' (ibid.).

McCulloch presented his own detailed review of Ricardo's *Principles* in the *Edinburgh Review* in 1818 (McCulloch, 1818a). In that review article, he expressed his full support for Ricardo's theory as a whole. McCulloch refuted the composition theory of prices advanced by Smith and others (ibid.: 64, 68), and called Ricardo's labour theory of value 'this new and important doctrine'. At the same time, he remarked that Ricardo 'has given too mathematical a cast to his reasoning, to make it perfectly intelligible to the generality of readers'. He tried to explain the theory in a more familiar and plain manner (ibid.: 64–8). Then, he proceeded to illustrate the inverse relationship between the wage rate and the profit rate (ibid.: 68–9, 72), and also recognized the truth of the 'curious effect', even though it seemed paradoxical, emphasizing its importance in refuting Adam Smith's theory of prices. He concluded that these theories had a revolutionary meaning for political economy (ibid.: 70–72).

McCulloch tried to provide his own explanation of the 'curious effect' (ibid.). In the case of a rise in money-wage rate:

> If he [a producer with machines] did not voluntarily reduce his price, there would be influx of capital to his particular department of industry; and as others could furnish themselves with machines at the same price they had cost him, they would soon so multiplied, that he would unavoidably be obliged to sink the price of his goods, till they afforded only the usual and general rate of profits. (Ibid.: 70)

That is, if a producer with machines is affected less by a rise of the wage rate compared with a producer without machines and does not change his price, the former gets a higher rate of profits. This increase of profit rate attracts others with machines into that branch of industry, which in turn intensifies the competition in that industry and reduces the price of the product. In contrast, even if there is a general rise in the money-wage rate, a producer without machines cannot raise his price, because a general rise of the wage rate does not give any reason to raise prices in particular industries.

Ricardo's theory of rent was most severely criticized by the *British Review* article (Anon [1817] 2003). McCulloch illustrated in detail Ricardo's differential theory of rent and the determination of the price of agricultural product, contrasting with prices of manufactured commodities. In his view, Ricardo was not as original on the subject of rent as in other parts of his theory, however, 'he [Ricardo] has given a much better exposition of the principles which regulate the rise and fall of rent, than any other writer' (McCulloch, 1818a: 72). McCulloch showed an accurate understanding of the nature of rent as payment for 'the use of the *natural and inherent* powers of the soil' (ibid.: 73; original emphasis), clearly distinguishing rent from profits of capital. Ricardo's explanation of rent was criticized by the anonymous author in the *British Review* for his assumption of the existence of zero rent land. McCulloch justified that assumption by reasoning that there should be some land that pays no rent and that the price of agricultural products is determined by 'the sum barely necessary to cover the cost of production on the lands last taken into cultivation, or to yield the ordinary rate of profit on the capital last applied to the old land'. 'It is the same thing if there be any capital employed on land which yields only the return of stock with its ordinary profits, whether that capital be employed on new or old land' (ibid.: 78). McCulloch also recognized that 'rent does not, under any circumstances whatever, enter into, or constitute a part of the price of raw produce, or of any species of commodities' (ibid.: 79). He also agreed with Ricardo on the landlords' interest opposed to all the other classes of society.

Ricardo repeatedly stated the idea that the long-run tendency of the profit rate was to fall during the process of economic growth in a closed system without technical progress. That was Ricardo's theoretical basic model that theorized his original vision he had from very early times. McCulloch appreciated that Ricardo ascribes the long-run fall of the general profit rate to the diminishing returns in agriculture rather than to more intense competition among capitals as claimed by Smith, Malthus and Say (ibid.: 79).

McCulloch further appreciated the role of rent in the Ricardo's system. According to him, a proper understanding of rent is a step, though a very material one, towards ascertaining the laws by which the profits of stock are regulated. However, he was unable to present an accurate explanation of the determination of the profit rate in agriculture.

Ricardo explained the determination of the profit rate in agriculture as follows. The price of corn (measured in money of invariable value) is determined according to the necessary quantity of labour on the land of the least productivity cultivated or on the last dose of capital employed on the old land, where the value of the product per unit of labour is constant, because when the labour theory of value holds the price of corn rises precisely in proportion to the increase of labour input at the margin but at the same time the product per unit of labour decreases in the same proportion. Therefore, if the wage rate is given in some way, the profit rate in agriculture is determined. If, the marginal productivity in agriculture declines and the price of corn rises during the process of economic growth, the money-wage rate (measured always in money of invariable value) rises and the profit rate declines, because the value of the product per unit of labour at the margin is constant. McCulloch was unable to explain the constancy of the value of the product per unit of labour at the margin in agriculture. He could explain only the profit rate determination in manufactures (ibid.: 79–80).

Regarding the chapter on the foreign trade, McCulloch said:

> This is one of the most valuable and original parts of the work before us; and affords a striking example of Mr. Ricardo's uncommon sagacity in investigating and tracing the operation of fixed and general principles, and in disentangling and separating them from those of a second-ary and accidental nature. (Ibid.: 83)

On taxes, he briefly summarized the Ricardo's conclusions on the ultimate effects (incidence) of taxes on wages, on necessaries, and luxury commodities. A tax on wages does not raise prices. It raises the wage rate, which reduces the rate of profits. A tax on necessaries raises their prices, which in turn raises the wage rate. Therefore, it falls partly on profits and partly on consumers. A tax on a necessary good raises its price to the extent of the tax only, but it raises the wage rate, by the rise of which the profit rate falls. A tax on luxuries will fall almost entirely on consumers, because it does not raise the wage rate (ibid.: 84–6).

McCulloch pointed out that these are the general and ultimate effects of taxation. A tax on wages, for example, does not raise the money-wage rate instantaneously except in the stationary state in which the real wage rate is at the subsistence level, or in the case where capital and population are increasing at the same rate. In the latter case, a tax on necessaries cannot raise the wage rate to the same extent at once; the extent of the rise of the wage rate becomes equal to the tax only after the rate of population increase declines (ibid.: 86). Population takes time to change. In the mean time, a tax on necessaries falls partly on employers and partly on labourers.

After referring to Ricardo's main writings before *Principles*, McCulloch assessed Ricardo as follows: 'He has done more for its [of political economy] improvement than any other writer, with perhaps the single exception of Dr Smith' (ibid.: 60). He called Ricardo's *Principles* 'his great work' (ibid.: 83), and concluded that 'It is to Mr Ricardo's own work, however, that such of our readers as wish to acquire a thorough knowledge of the subject, must have recourse' (ibid.: 87).

McCulloch sent his review to Ricardo in July 1818, before it appeared in the *Edinburgh Review* in August. In a letter to Ricardo, he stated that he had 'the most profound admiration' for Ricardo's work. But at the same time, he remarked that he had the impression that Ricardo was reluctant to show 'the impolicy and ruinous effects of a heavy taxation', and hoped that Ricardo would revise that part in the next edition (his letter to Ricardo, 15 July 1818, *Works*, VII: 281). The heavy taxation during and after the Napoleonic Wars was, in McCulloch's view, one of the main causes of the depression. Ricardo agreed with that remark, and promised to revise those passages that might give such an impression (his letter to McCulloch, 22 August 1818, ibid.: 286). McCulloch was also opposed to the statement regarding, 'the impossibility of improving the condition of a country by diminishing its public debt' (his letter to Ricardo, 6 December 1818, ibid.: 351). Ricardo contended that a country's economic burden of an expenditure of the state is the same whether it is financed by taxation or by national debt. Saving of income is necessary to improve the condition of the country. Ricardo remarked that McCulloch thought 'so lightly of the extinction of our national debt' (his letter to McCulloch, 3 January 1819, *Works*, VIII: 4).

After Ricardo's *Principles* appeared, McCulloch expressed his views about Ricardo's ideas and writings mainly in the *Edinburgh Review*. McCulloch changed his basic position in economics and became a supporter of Ricardo's economics.

On Ricardo's *Economical and Secure Currency* (1816)

McCulloch published a review article in the *Edinburgh Review* in 1818 on Ricardo's *Proposals for an Economical and Secure Currency* published in 1816 (McCulloch, 1818b). McCulloch outlined two principles of determination of the value of money: the production cost principle and the limitation principle. The former is based on Ricardo's labour theory of value, which is the principle of determination of value for ordinary commodities produced under competition that can be increased without limits. The latter is a monopoly theory of value, in which the value of money can vary to any extent inversely to the relative quantity with the need of circulation, whatever it may consists of (gold, silver, paper, etc.) (ibid.: 54–7). He examined Ricardo's proposal for the resumption of cash payment by the Bank of England: that is, to convert bank notes into ingots of gold, not into specie (Ricardo, *Proposals*: 25–7, *Works*, IV: 65–7).

In Ricardo's Ingot Plan, the minimum quantity of metal (gold or silver) convertible from bank notes is 20oz. McCulloch ardently supported Ricardo's plan, but he pointed out at the same time that the minimum quantity of metal convertible from bank notes should be larger than that proposed by Ricardo. An important characteristic of Ricardo's plan was the reduction of the quantity of the reserve of gold the Bank had to maintain and the security against panics. Ricardo did not mention the security against panics. In McCulloch's view, panics are caused by a mass of people demanding the conversion of small sums of bank notes into metal or specie. Therefore, by limiting convertibility to large amounts of metal (for example, more than 500 or 1000oz), only people with large sums of bank notes can demand such conversion into bullion (McCulloch, 1818b: 70–72). There was a fear of note forgery, but he contended that the issue of forgeries had nothing to do with the circulation of paper currency. Rather, it only meant that notes should be made in a sufficiently fine state to prevent forgeries. Even if coins circulate, there will still be forgeries (ibid.: 73).

McCulloch contended that Ricardo's plan of circulation of paper money convertible into bullion over a certain minimum quantity is preferable to the system of mixed currency that existed before the restriction in 1797 for stability of the value of currency. 'As a device for preserving paper on a par with gold, Mr. Ricardo's plan is, in some material respects, infinitely preferable to the old method of exchanging notes for coins' (ibid.: 70).

Ricardo's idea of paper currency convertible into bullion was first presented in the Appendix of the fourth edition of *The High Price of Bullion* (1811). This was pointed out in *Memoir of the Life and Writings of Ricardo, Esq, M.P.* written by McCulloch in 1825 (McCulloch [1825] 1846).

On the Corn Laws

McCulloch published a review article entitled 'Taxation and the Corn-Laws' in the *Edinburgh Review* (McCulloch, 1820), in which he illustrated his basic ideas on important issues such as the Corn Laws, the Poor Laws, taxation, capital levy and machinery. Ricardo made detailed comments on this article in the correspondence, and they discussed several points to clear their differences.

As explained above, in McCulloch's view, the depression after the Napoleonic Wars was caused mainly by the heavy taxation and the Corn Laws. McCulloch had repeatedly emphasized the pernicious effects of the Corn Laws. The Corn Laws raised the price of corn by restricting the importation of corn. The rise in the price of corn raised the wage rate, which diminished the profit rate and slowed down the rate of capital accumulation, causing unemployment. In addition, the Corn Laws forced 'a very large proportion of the capital and industry of the country into a comparatively disadvantageous employment' (ibid.: 185).

McCulloch contended that the restriction on importation of corn has the same effects as taxation. He called the Corn Laws 'the most oppressive and ruinous of all possible taxes' (ibid.: 185). In his estimation, the burden of the Corn Laws was equal to approximately £25 million, which was '*nearly double the whole expenditures of the Government*, including the interest of the public debt at that epoch' (ibid.: 174–5; original emphasis).

McCulloch believed that the Corn Laws should be abolished, but he emphasized, 'we think the abolition ought to be cautiously and carefully brought about, Time ought to be given gradually to withdraw capital from the poor soils now under cultivation' (ibid.: 185). The repeal of the Corn Laws proposed by McCulloch was a plan to reduce the duties on importation gradually according to a scale. Ricardo had presented a similar idea for the repeal of the Corn Laws in the first edition of the *Principles*, and he added a footnote in its second edition, in which he regarded McCulloch's ideas as 'excellent suggestions' (*Works*, I: 267n). Ricardo proposed a permanent tax to compensate for the 'peculiar taxes' imposed only on agriculture as 'the wisest policy'. In the letter to McCulloch of 28 February 1820, Ricardo stated:

> A permanent tax on importation, to the amount only of the peculiar taxes to which the growth of corn is subject, would be I think the wisest policy, but it is probable that such a limited tax would be far from satisfying the landed interest. We should then have to chuse between a higher permanent tax, or tax varying with the price. (*Works*, VIII: 158)

McCulloch had a stronger conviction to abolish the Corn Laws than Ricardo, but in the end he agreed with Ricardo's proposal. 'I agree with you in thinking that if there were no other alternative a permanent tax on the importation of corn, or even a tax varying with the price, might on the whole be preferable to the present system' (his letter to Ricardo, 19 March 1820, ibid.: 166). Later, Ricardo, in his pamphlet, *On Protection to Agriculture* (1822), discussed his idea in more detail (*Works*, IV: 217–18, 264).

On the Poor Laws
McCulloch admitted that the Poor Laws had pernicious effects 'to weaken the motives stimulating to industry and economy, and to strengthen those of an opposite character' (McCulloch, 1820: 158). Nevertheless, he contended that the Poor Laws were unable to explain the rapid increase in the amount of expenditures to provide relief for the poor since the end of the eighteenth century. It was not chiefly due to the nature of the Poor Laws. 'Neither are we disposed to agree with the Committee of the House of Commons, and those who contend that it is chiefly, if not entirely, owing to the pernicious operation of the Poor Laws' (ibid.). In McCulloch's view, the increase in the poor and the expenditures for the poor relief were the result of the economic depression caused by the heavy taxation during and after the Napoleonic Wars and the restriction on the importation of corn intensified by the Corn Laws of 1804 and 1815.

McCulloch observed that Great Britain was the only country that was faced with a general depression in all of its industries after the Napoleonic Wars. During the depression, pauperism rapidly increased, and a general decline of the conditions of workers was felt in every sector of employment. He maintained that the main cause of general decline of people's conditions was not the loss of Britain's monopoly in world commerce after the restoration of peace, because that decline had already begun before the war ended (ibid.: 155–6). The poor rates increased rapidly from the end of the eighteenth century to the first decade of the nineteenth century. Malthus attributed this rapid increase of poor relief expenditures to the nature of the Poor Laws, which, he saw, operated to increase the population by weakening the preventive checks and the motive to work of the labour classes. Ricardo, following Malthus, showed a very strong abolitionist view of the Poor Laws. He even expressed in the *Principles* a fear that the poor rates might ultimately absorb the whole economic surplus. The Parliamentary Committee of the House of Commons on the Poor Laws (1817) expressed the same fear.

McCulloch observed that the pernicious effects of the Poor Laws were exaggerated (ibid.: 159). 'But, however pernicious the Poor Laws may be supposed to be – and we believe them to have been most pernicious – there is no ground for supposing that they have operated more injuriously during the last twenty years, than in any former period' (ibid.: 158). The recent rapid increase of the poor rates must have been caused by factors other than the Poor Laws. Of these factors, '*Taxation*, and the *restrictions on trade in corn*, have been decidedly the most powerful' (ibid.: 159; original emphasis). In their correspondence, Ricardo simply remarked that if the population growth was higher than the capital growth poverty would follow (his letter to McCulloch, 29 March 1820, *Works*, VIII: 170–71), without denying McCulloch's analysis. It may have been because Ricardo had weakened his position of abolitionism of the Poor Laws after reading *A Second Letter to the Right Hon. Robert Peel for the University of Oxford on the Increase of Pauperism and the Poor Laws* by Edward Copleston (1819) of the University of Oxford. In the letter, Copleston estimated the real burden of the poor rates by taking into account the population growth and the rise of prices and concluded that the real burden of the poor rates did not have the tendency to increase from the mid-eighteenth century to the first decade of the nineteenth century in England.

On the effects of heavy taxation

According to McCulloch, a heavy tax on the necessaries of life is prejudicial to both labourers and employers (he believed that it has the same effect with a direct tax on wages). However, its effects are different in different conditions. In a new country with uncultivated fertile lands such as the United States, a tax on necessaries is not accompanied by very injurious effects. In such a country, the real wage rate and the rate of profits are high, and labourers can save the amount of the tax to be paid from their wages. The money-wage rate will rise very little, without diminishing much the profit rate. In an old country such as Britain, 'taxation is infinitely more injurious' (McCulloch, 1820: 160). The real wage rate is low and near the subsistence level; there is very little room to save out of the wages; and, the labourers are unable to increase the money-wage rate to the extent of the tax imposed on necessaries they consume. The labour supply cannot change immediately with variations of the prices of necessaries. Population takes time to change. Therefore, the conditions of labourers' lives will be reduced to a lower level.

McCulloch also emphasized that the effects of taxation can vary with differences of the rapidity of tax increase too. A rapid increase of taxation on necessaries is very injurious to the labour classes, because such a tax increase does not give labourers time to adjust their life habits to the decline in the real wages; in other words, labourers cannot have time to form moral restraint, in Malthus's term, and change the rate of increase of population. In contrast, a slow and gradual increase of taxation will give some relief of the burden of the increase of taxation, by making the principle of moral restraint more efficient:

> Taxation, by increasing the cost of commodities, operates in precisely the same way as a deterioration of the powers of the soil, or as any other cause which has the effect of rendering it more difficult to procure a comfortable subsistence; and therefore, its *slow and gradual* increase, by adding to the efficacy of the principle of moral restraint, has a tendency to relieve society of some part of the evils of which it is always productive. But a sudden increase of taxation is unaccompanied by any alleviating circumstance. The mischiefs which it occasions are pure and unmixed. It precludes the possibility of previously changing or modifying the habits of those subjected to its operation. (Ibid.: 163–4; original emphasis)

McCulloch also pointed out that the effects of taxation are different for different goods. In the case of a necessary good, a tax reduction increases the demand and consumption for the good and, by increasing the production and employment of labour, it may also have the effect of increasing the revenue of the government. On the other hand, an increase in a tax on a necessary good may result in a decline in the demand and consumption of the good, thereby diminishing the employment of labour and the revenue of the government. That is, a tax increase on necessary goods deteriorates the conditions of labourers. In contrast, in the case of a luxurious good that only the rich can purchase, any reduction of taxes cannot greatly increase its demand, and will not have any effect of increasing the revenue of the government (ibid.: 186). Thus, McCulloch emphasized the pernicious effects of a tax increase on necessary goods, not only for labourers but also for employers of labour, because it will increase the cost of production of goods by raising the wage rate and lowering the rate of profits. In addition, such a tax increase may even decrease the revenue of the government.

In his correspondence with McCulloch, Ricardo contended that taxes in the hands of the government give employment of labour almost to the same extent as when they remain in the hands of the people. In Ricardo's view, taxes are pernicious to the labour classes only when they retard the capital accumulation and the growth of demand for labour (his letter to McCulloch, 29 March 1820, *Works*, VIII: 169–70). McCulloch reasoned that taxes in the hands of the government can give only less employment of labour than when such revenues remain in the hands of people, because the additional revenue by an increase of taxes may be spent for subsidies to foreign countries and there is usually more wastage in the government expenditures (his letter to Ricardo, 2 April 1820, ibid.: 174–5). McCulloch considered the injurious effects of a heavy taxation more serious that Ricardo.

On capital levy

McCulloch opposed Ricardo's proposal of capital levy to pay off the national debt in a short time and to finance by the tax enormous expenditures such as war-related expenditures (*Works*, IV: 196–7). McCulloch called the plan 'this bold and decisive measure', and regarded the capital levy proposed by Ricardo as the last resort ('*le dernier resort*') (McCulloch, 1820: 180). McCulloch's idea for the reconstruction of public finance was first to reduce public expenditures, second to reduce taxation. For the reduction of public expenditures, he proposed the reduction of military expenditures, for example. He maintained that there was no need to maintain the army and navy at wartime levels when the peace returned (ibid.: 185–6). As for tax reduction, the prices of necessaries should be diminished by the reduction of taxes, which would in turn increase the demands and production of the necessaries and the tax revenues would be augmented. McCulloch repeatedly emphasized the effect of falling prices of necessary goods on increasing demands.

Ricardo's reply to McCulloch's criticism was that it is important to finance a heavy expenditure, not by loans, but by taxation within the year. Finance by taxes is less injurious than by loans (his letter to McCulloch, 29 March 1820, *Works*, VIII: 172). Loans weaken people's motive to save, because they are unaware that the amount of expenditure is the same whether financed by loans or by taxes (*Works*, I: 244–6).

On machinery

McCulloch stated his view on the effects of introducing machinery on the conditions of labour classes. In the long run, machinery has advantageous effects of increasing productivity and production, because increase in productivity diminishes prices, which in turn increases consumption of goods. In the case of luxury goods, a fall in prices may not increase their consumption, but in the case of necessary goods, a fall in prices increases their consumption, for which the production of necessary goods increases. Therefore, McCulloch argued, the comforts and welfare of labourers are augmented by the introduction of machinery. However, under the influence of John Barton, he admitted that introduction of machinery may have some pernicious effects on the labour classes in the short run, because it may cause unemployment by changing the circulating capital into fixed capital, and employment of labour depends on circulating capital (McCulloch, 1820: 171).

Ricardo's reply to McCulloch on the effects of the introduction of machinery was that it never diminishes the demand for labour, and that machinery never causes the wage rate to fall; the introduction of machinery is the effect of a rise in the wage rate (his letter to McCulloch, 29 March 1820, *Works*, VIII: 171). McCulloch subsequently changed his idea on the effect of machinery, accepting Ricardo's comment in the correspondence. In the article, 'Effects of Machinery and Accumulation', in the *Edinburgh Review* in March 1821 (McCulloch [1821] 1995), McCulloch denied the pernicious effects of the introduction of machinery. There, he concluded:

> It appears, then, that no improvement of machinery can possibly diminish the demand for labour, or reduce the rate of wages. The introduction of machinery into one employment, *necessarily occasions an equal or greater demand for the disengaged labourers in some other employment*. The only hardship which it ever imposes on the labourer, is, that in some cases it forces him to change his business. This, however, is not material one. (Ibid.: 182; original emphasis)

As is well known, Ricardo added a new chapter in the third edition of the *Principles* (1821), in which he admitted the unfavourable effects of the introduction of machinery for labourers in the short run on the grounds that it can diminish the gross product of the economy, including funds for employing labour, even if it augments the net revenue. He changed his mind under the influence of the arguments of John Barton. To that change of position McCulloch furiously reacted and criticized Ricardo's change of mind (his letter to Ricardo, 5 June 1821, *Works*, VIII: 381–5).

Position of McCulloch
McCulloch changed his basic position of economics after Ricardo's *Principles* appeared in 1817. In his first publications in 1816, McCulloch appreciated Malthus, who followed Smith's theory of prices, more than Ricardo, and called Malthus 'the highest authority'. But after Ricardo's *Principles* was published, he became a passionate supporter of Ricardo's economics, and he began to criticize Malthus, incorporating Ricardo's theories in his arguments. James Mill wrote to McCulloch when Ricardo died: 'you and I are his two only genuine disciples' (his letter to McCulloch, 19 September 1823, *Works*, IX: 391). In 1824, McCulloch was nominated the first lecturer of the course of lectures under Ricardo's name (The Ricardo Memorial Lectures) established by Ricardo's friends (Bain [1882] 1966: 213–14; *Works*, IX: 301, editor's note; O'Brien, 1970: 48–57). McCulloch edited *The Works, of David Ricardo, Esq, M.P.* in 1846. In the biography of Ricardo, 'Life and Writings of Ricardo' (a slightly revised version of *Memoir* of 1825) attached to the collected works, McCulloch expressed his deep respect for him. Ricardo highly appreciated McCulloch as an able writer who could explain principles and theories in a more understandable and convincing manner than he. After Ricardo's death, McCulloch wrote textbooks of economics, in which he explained Ricardo's theories in a plain and intelligible manner for general readers.

KATSUYOSHI WATARAI

See also:

Mill, James, and Ricardo; Tooke, Thomas, and Ricardo; Torrens, Robert, and Ricardo; Trower, Hutches, and Ricardo.

References

Anon ([1817] 2003), 'Ricardo and Say on political economy', *British Review*, 1817, 309–33; reprint in T. Peach (ed.), *David Ricardo: Critical Reponses, Vol. 1*, London: Routledge, pp. 42–64.

Bain, A. ([1882] 1966), *James Mill: A Biography*, London: Longman, Green, and Co; reprint, New York: A.M. Kelley.

Copleston, E. (1819), *A Second Letter to The Right Hon. Robert Peel M.P. for the University of Oxford on the Causes on the Increase of Pauperism and the Poor Laws*, Oxford: John Murray. A summary by Ricardo in the Ricardo Papers at the University Library of Cambridge, is printed in J.H. Hollander (ed.) (1932), *Minor Papers on the Currency Question 1809–1823 by David Ricardo*, Baltimore, MD: Johns Hopkins University Press, pp. 135–45.

Malthus, T.R. ([1815] 1986), *The Grounds of an Opinion on the Policy of Restricting the Importation of Foreign Corn: intended as an Appendix to 'Observations on the Corn Laws'*; reprint in E.A. Wrigley and D. Souden (eds), *The Works, of Thomas Robert Malthus, Vol. 7*, London: Pickering, pp. 151–74.

McCulloch, J.R. (1816a), *An Essay on the Reduction of the Interest of the National Debt, proving, that this is the only possible means of relieving the distresses of the commercial and agricultural interests; and establishing the justice of that measure on the surest principles of Political Economy*, 1st edition, London: Joseph Mawman and David Brown.

McCulloch, J.R. ([1816b] 1995), *An Essay on the Reduction of the Interest of the National Debt; to which the justice and expediency of that measure are fully established*, Edinburgh: David Brown and Adam Black; reprint of the 2nd edition in D.P. O'Brien (ed.), *The Collected Works, of J.R. McCulloch, Vol. 1*, London: Routledge/Thoemmes Press.

McCulloch, J.R. ([1817a] 2003), 'Review of *On the Principles of Political Economy and Taxation*', *The Scotsman*, 3 May 1817, 119–20; reprint in T. Peach (ed.), *David Ricardo: Critical Reponses, Vol. 1*, London: Routledge, pp. 39–41.

McCulloch, J.R. ([1817b] 2003), 'Mr. Ricardo and the *British Review*', *The Scotsman*, 15 November 1817, 34; reprint in T. Peach (ed.), *David Ricardo: Critical Reponses, Vol. 1*, London: Routledge, pp. 71–3.

McCulloch, J.R. (1818a), 'Ricardo's *Principles of Political Economy*', *Edinburgh Review*, **XXX**(59), Article II, 59–87.

McCulloch, J.R. (1818b), 'Economical and secure currency', *Edinburgh Review*, **XXXI**(61), Article III, 53–80.

McCulloch, J.R. (1820), 'Taxation and the Corn-Laws', *Edinburgh Review*, **XXXIII**(65), Article IX, 155–87.

McCulloch, J.R. ([1821] 1995), 'Effects of machinery and accumulation', *Edinburgh Review*, **XXXV**(69), 102–23; reprint in D.P. O'Brien (ed.), *The Collected Works, of J.R. McCulloch, Vol. 8*, London: Routledge/Thoemmes Press.

McCulloch, J.R. ([1825] 1846), *Memoir of the Life and Writings of David Ricardo, Esq. M.P.*, London: Richard Taylor; revised version in J.R. McCulloch, *The Works, of David Ricardo, Esq. M.P.*, London: John Murray, pp. xv–xxxiii.

McCulloch, J.R. ([1825] 1995), *The Principles of Political Economy; with a sketch of the rise and progress of the science*, Edinburgh: Adam and Charles Black; reprint of the 4th edition in D.P. O'Brien (ed.), *The Collected Works, of J.R. McCulloch, Vol. 2*, London: Routledge/Thoemmes Press.

McCulloch, J.R. ([1845] 1995), *A Treatise on the Principles and Practical Influence of Taxation and the Funding System*, London: Longman, Brown, Green, and Longmans; reprint in D.P. O'Brien (ed.), *The Collected Works, of J.R. McCulloch, Vol. 4*, London: Routledge/Thoemmes Press.

McCulloch, J.R. (1846), *The Works, of David Ricardo, Esq. M.P.*, London: John Murray.

O'Brien, D.P. (1970), *J.R. McCulloch: A Study in Classic Economics*, New York: Barnes & Noble.

Peach, T. (ed.) (2003), *David Ricardo: Critical Reponses*, 4 vols, London: Routledge.

Member of Parliament

At the General Election of 1818, Richard Sharp (a wealthy merchant and 'conversationalist') was returned as the Member of Parliament for the Irish pocket borough of Portarlington – where there were just 12 registered voters. When Sharp vacated the seat in February 1819, David Ricardo was returned in consideration for a loan of £25 000 (at 6 per cent) and a payment of £4000 to Lord Portarlington who controlled the borough corporation. As Elie Halévy put it, Portarlington was one of 18 Irish boroughs 'where the franchise belonged to a close corporation . . . [and] the right to elect the member was the private property of the landlord, who had succeeded in making himself the "patron" of the corporation' (Halévy [1913–46] 1949–52: 119, *Works*, I: 119 and n1). The *History of Parliament* wryly records that 'it was on this principle of political economy that Ricardo held the seat for the rest of his life and [Lord] Portarlington obtained the freedom to ruin himself' (Thorne, 1986: 682).

Notwithstanding their democratic credentials, the radical reformers often quipped that this practice was not all bad. James Mill, for example, wrote in 1827 that the 'men who most frequently open their way to Parliament by the direct instead of the indirect use of the purse are men of mercantile wealth'; and he enquired rhetorically of existing representatives: 'Are they a class of men whom their country has less cause to trust than it has to trust you?' (Mill, 1827: 342). Then there was Bentham's famous remark that if he had £10 million or £20 million he would 'buy liberty with it for the people' (Bentham, 1838–43, III: 486). The suggestion that Ricardo should enter Parliament came from James Mill. He had proposed it first in 1815 and, towards the end of 1816, when Ricardo had declined to run in a contested election for the seat of Worcester, Mill offered the following advice: 'If I were in your situation, the rottenest borough I could find would be my market, with nothing to do but part with a sum of money' (*Works*, VII: 101–2).

Reform of the electoral franchise

As a rule, in addressing the question of who should vote, or, what amounts to the same thing, the question of political citizenship, Ricardo's contemporary philosophical radicals spoke in voices that they adjusted to suit the circumstances. Ricardo was no exception to this rule. Although he did declare himself against any piecemeal approach to reform on the floor of the House of Commons in 1823, when he was faced with the charge that democracy was an avatar of the end of civilization Ricardo spoke in an accommodating voice. Thus, one can find him talking of securing 'unbiased good sense' among electors (letter to Trower, 22 March 1818, *Works*, VII: 260; see also a letter to McCulloch, 17 January 1821, *Works*, VIII: 336), of enfranchising only 'the reasonable part of the country' (letter to Trower, 2 November 1818, *Works*, VII: 320, of getting 'all the wisdom and virtue of the country to act in Government', and of taking 'precautions' in 'bestowing the elective franchise' (letter to Trower, 20 December 1818, ibid.: 366 and 368). In his speech to the House of Commons on Lord Russell's motion for a reform of Parliament, Ricardo even invoked the authority of Montesquieu to support his faith in 'the people' and to bolster his main conclusion 'that instead of selecting demagogues and disturbers of the peace, as was unjustly apprehended, the people, if left to the unrestricted exercise of their choice, would act wisely and prudently' (*Works*, V: 289).

But it is one thing to have to meet the scare-mongering of political adversaries head on in Parliamentary debate (and the direct involvement of the philosophical radicals in daily politics helps to explain why they devoted so much attention to the moral character of electors in that particular context); it is quite another to settle the issue of the extent of the franchise on principle. What is decisive about Ricardo's contribution to that more theoretical project is that he seems to have resolved the matter of principle in a way that sets him apart not only from James Mill, but also from John Stuart Mill (whose best-known intervention in the debate came some 40 years after Ricardo's death).

The idea that the general question of political organization could be analysed from an economic point of view was stated quite explicitly by Ricardo in the first of his two discourses on politics, *Observations on Parliamentary Reform*: 'although it may be true that the country has flourished with a House of Commons constituted as ours has been, it must be shown that such a constitution of it is favourable to the prosperity of the country' (*Works*, V: 499).

In setting himself the task of producing an argument for a democratic polity on the grounds that it tended to promote material prosperity, Ricardo stands in contrast to James Mill, who, as we have seen, made the extent of the franchise turn on the relationship between his more directly individualistic premises of democratic participation and rising individual 'mental qualities' or improved 'levels' of personal development.

Ricardo did claim that an extension of the electoral franchise might act to forestall any actual or practical possibility of social revolution. He set out the idea in a letter to Mill in 1819:

> Reform is the most efficacious preventative of Revolution, and may in my opinion at all times be safely conceded. The argument against reform now is that people ask for too much, and that a Revolution is really meant. Would they be better able to bring about a Revolution, if reform was conceded? . . . Reform may be granted too late, but it can never be given too soon. (Letter to Mill, 10 August 1819, *Works*, VIII: 49–50)

Gender, religion and the franchise

In recommendations concerning the appropriate organization of a democratic polity the demand for universal suffrage is never meant to be taken literally. Except, perhaps, in the most pure of cases, there is always a qualification to be met. Ricardo is no exception, and he never endorsed universality (for his specific reservations about universal suffrage, see *Works*, V: 29, 45, 502; *Works*, VII: 270, 360, 369–70; *Works*, VIII: 99, 107, 129; and on his qualified support for a plan of household suffrage see *Works*, V: 473, 485; *Works*, VII: 273, 273n). In this sense, 'The People', in whose name political authority is exercised, and upon whose sanction its continued legitimacy is made to depend, is an artificial entity. Some are always excluded. Leaving aside the question of the enfranchisement of women, a subject on which Ricardo said nothing, the most familiar exclusionary principle other than gender – namely, social class – was openly rejected by Ricardo in the context of his delineation of the reasonable part of the country. However, these were not the only grounds on which exclusion from the political nation was mandated in Britain at the time. Another was religion.

In the early decades of the nineteenth century the debate over religious toleration was played out largely in the context of the Catholic Question. With the Roman Catholic community deprived of political liberties, enjoying neither the franchise nor the right to occupy a seat in either House of Parliament, and being severely disadvantaged in the civil sphere as well, the issue of Catholic emancipation was high on the agenda of Parliamentary reformers. Although non-conforming and dissenting Protestant sects had originally laboured under many of the same civil disabilities, the eighteenth century had witnessed a gradual relaxation in both the letter and the application of the laws that curtailed their civil liberties.

The newer evangelical Protestant sects, for example, had found ways around the Corporation and Test Acts, under which a whole array of military, civil and political offices were closed to those who refused to swear an oath rejecting the authority of the See of Rome and to take the Sacrament according to the rites of the Church of England. The expedient of occasional conformity, of taking communion in the Anglican form only to return to one's own congregation thereafter (outlawed in 1719), was sufficiently wide-spread by the end of the eighteenth century as to have seen Parliament adopt the convention of passing yearly Indemnity Bills that issued a blanket pardon for all breaches of the 1719 Act that had taken place in the previous year. Ricardo himself had a direct encounter with the Test Act when (late in 1817) he found his name to be second on the list of nominees for the office of High Sheriff of Gloucestershire for 1818. As he wrote to Malthus: 'as Col. Berkeley, the first named, will in all probability be excused on account of his intended application to the House of Lords for the Peerage . . . I shall no doubt be selected' (letter to Malthus, 16 December 1817, *Works*, VII: 223–4). This office was subject to the provisions of the Test Act, and Ricardo instructed his lawyers to seek an opinion as to what course of action should be followed. The options were two: to seek exemption under the Toleration Act, or to rely on the annual Act of Indemnity for violations against the Test Act. The lawyers favoured the first as the safest course, but were confident that the annual Act of Indemnity would be sufficient. (See the account given by Sraffa in *Works*, X: 42–3.)

Although such a deception may have weighed heavily on the conscience of many a dissenter who was forced to adopt it, it did not amount to apostasy as it would have done for practising Catholics. Furthermore, the Toleration Act of 1689 had already formally expanded the civil rights of dissenting Protestants by legalizing all assemblies at which the form of worship did not follow the liturgy of the Church of England provided only that a declaratory oath be signed affirming the participant's Protestantism, his repudiation of Papal authority, including a denial of the doctrine of transubstantiation.

For Roman Catholics, as will be perfectly clear, the case was quite different. For them, the Toleration Act was not tolerant, and there were no practical expedients by which the Corporation and Test Acts could be circumvented (save conversion) in order to facilitate political participation. Even the proposal issuing from some of their own number, that British Catholics would agree to limit the domain of Papal authority to spiritual matters in return for political and civil emancipation, fell on deaf ears – and this only partly because the dividing line between matters spiritual and matters temporal was difficult to draw. No other single religious community, with the exception of the Jews, was similarly disadvantaged. Church of Englandism, as Bentham dubbed it, ruled the roost.

At the most general level, Ricardo's views on religious toleration seem to have been the standard fare of philosophical radicalism. Though articulated in less colourful language than anything employed by Bentham, who had grown up as a child of David Hume, Ricardo objected to all forms of discrimination grounded on religious affiliation. He voiced such opinions repeatedly in the House of Commons, speaking in support of a petition for the release of Mary Ann Carlile who had been gaoled for blasphemous libel for selling works by Thomas Paine. Her sentence had been for a year's imprisonment and a fine of £500. If on the expiry of the year the fine remained unpaid, the guilty party was to remain in prison until the fine was discharged. The year had been served, but the fine remained unpaid, and a petition had come before the House of Commons for her release (see Sraffa's editorial annotations in *Works*, V: 277). Ricardo had argued that since all 'religious opinions, however absurd and extravagant, might be conscientiously believed by some individuals' it was unacceptable that one man should by law be permitted 'to set up his ideas on the subject as the criterion from which no other was to be allowed to differ with impunity'. Instead, Ricardo maintained that a 'fair and free discussion ought to be allowed on all religious topics' (*Works*, V: 280).

Indeed, it would seem to have been the case that, for Ricardo, even the complete absence of any religious belief whatsoever provided no ground for disqualification from political citizenship. Just such an argument appears to lie behind his speech to the House of Commons in July 1823 in support of a petition for free discussion introduced by Joseph Hume. *Hansard* reported that Ricardo 'firmly believed in the possibility of a man's being very honest for all social purposes and essential obligations of the community in which he lived, and still not assenting to the belief of a future state' (ibid.: 327). A little incident surrounding this speech bears recording. In this speech Ricardo had gone on to cite the case of Robert Owen, asking: 'Why, then, was such a man (for by the law he was) to be excluded from the pale of legal credibility' (ibid.: 328). This led another member (Mr Money) to chide Ricardo, saying that Owen had communicated to him the falsity of Ricardo's claim. Ricardo's defence against the charge on the floor of the House was rather feeble. He was not amused. It seems that Ricardo had himself obtained Owen's consent to the remark before he had made it, and was understandably annoyed at his subsequent disavowal of it; but he refused to reveal the exchange in his reply (see the editorial annotations in *Works*, V: 331, n1, for more of the details).

Privately, however, Ricardo was prepared to be much more explicit on the matter. In a letter to Isaac Goldsmid, the campaigner for Jewish emancipation who had registered his admiration of Ricardo's speech on the Mary Ann Carlile petition, Ricardo stated that he was quite prepared to 'carry my principles of toleration very far'; so far, indeed, that on the question of political exclusion he did not 'know how, or why any line should be drawn, and am prepared to maintain that we have no more justifiable ground for shutting the mouth of an Atheist than that of any other man' (letter to Goldsmid, 4 April 1823, *Works*, IX: 278).

On the specific question of Catholic emancipation Ricardo did not speak in Parliament but was very clear in his correspondence. In 1820 he wrote to Trower that while he did not expect much reform from the new ministry, he was at least confident that 'we may probably find men who will remove the disabilities from the Roman catholics' (letter to Trower, 26 November 1820, *Works*, VIII: 304). In 1821, again to Trower, he reported that William Plunkett (the member for Trinity College, Dublin) had made a 'very fine' speech in support of a motion for the establishment of a committee to examine the claims of Irish Catholics, adding that he 'should not see much to regret if Ireland had a catholic establishment, in the same way as Scotland has a presbyterian one' (letter to Trower, 2 March 1821, ibid.: 350–51). Plunkett's motion passed the Commons but was defeated in the Lords, at which time Ricardo wrote again to Trower: '[t]he catholic bill is lost. I am sorry for it, though I cannot but think it is only delayed' (letter to Trower, 21 April 1821, ibid.: 369). The curious absence of Ricardo's name from the published list of the division on Plunkett's motion, which prompted Edwin Cannan to speculate that perhaps Ricardo had abstained under pressure from Lord Portarlington (at whose pleasure Ricardo occupied his Parliamentary seat), seems rather to have been an error (see Sraffa's editorial remarks on this subject, *Works*, V: xxii–xxiii).

There is an addendum to be made to the above account of Ricardo's radical opinions on the subject of religion. William Wilberforce, who also spoke in the debate over the petition on behalf of Mary Ann Carlile to which Ricardo had contributed (and with whom, on the subject of toleration, Ricardo was again to cross swords in the House of Commons in July 1823), sarcastically remarked that Ricardo had 'seemed to carry into more weighty matters those principles of free trade which he had so successfully expounded'. Furthermore, after this debate Wilberforce made an entry in his diary (in reference to Ricardo) to the effect that while he 'had hoped that Ricardo had become a Christian', he could now see that 'he has only ceased to be a Jew' (*Works*, V: 280, n1). This episode merits attention because it highlights an important, and not always unspoken, consequence for the reception of Ricardo's views of his family background as the son of a Sephardic Jew. An anti-Semitic theme in commentary on Ricardo has not been the exclusive preserve of his political opponents. Walter Bagehot, as we have already seen, indulged in it. Even Alfred Marshall, no small admirer of Ricardo, remarked on his un-Englishness, and attributed an alleged 'bias towards the abstract calculations connected with the trade of money dealing' to Ricardo's 'Semitic origin' (Marshall [1890] 1920: 629, n1; Marshall also cites Bagehot's opinion in this passage).

We mention these comments, because they speak quite directly to the question of the reception of those opinions. What the prevalence of this kind of stereotyping confirms (apart, of course, from the particular prejudices of its propagators), is Ricardo's status as an outsider. This was something Ricardo was well aware of:

> It appears to me a disgrace to the age we live in, that a part of the inhabitants of this country are still suffering under disabilities imposed upon them in a less enlightened time. The jews have most reason to complain, for they are frequently reproached for the dishonesty, which is the natural effect of the political degradation in which they are kept. (Letter to Goldsmid, 4 April 1823, *Works*, IX: 278)

What all of this makes very clear is that one must look beyond the qualifications of religion, property or gender to understand Ricardo's principle of exclusion.

Economic matters

It is not the purpose here to outline Ricardo's economics, but his opinions on economic matters as expressed as an MP are interesting. Ricardo had voted against the 'Six Acts' that were promulgated after the massacre at Peterloo. In speaking against one of them (the Seditious Meetings Prevention Bill) on the floor of the House of Commons on 6 December 1819 he made it perfectly clear that he was not for prohibiting such opinions, but rather for having them better represented in that very House (*Works*, V: 28–9).

He had made a very similar argument in correspondence to Trower two months before, which renders visible the basis of this earlier argument (letter to Trower, 25 September 1819, *Works*, VIII: 80). The argument rests on a direct correspondence between genuine representation and political freedom. It did not matter whether the complaints were real or imagined – inadequate representation precluded the opinions from being registered as they should be registered if freedom was to be secured as justice mandated. Once Ricardo had availed himself of his new-found theoretical principle on the effects of machinery, which confirmed the grievance to be real and not imagined, the result was only to strengthen the basis of his support for the representation of common opinion by giving it an additional grounding in his economics in a manner it had not enjoyed before.

Another striking example of his confidence in the opinion of workers came in his opposition to a proposed act (in 1823) to increase by statute the number of apprentices taken on board all vessels of the Merchant Marine. Ricardo spoke against this measure in the House of Commons on three separate occasions (13 and 24 March, and 18 April 1823; *Works*, V: 273, 276–7), each time making the point that the proposed act was drafted only in the interests of employers; and that they sought only to lower wages. He urged the Honourable Members to consult the seamen, who would be able to acquaint them with the real motive and the true effect. None of this sounds like the voice of the friend of the bourgeoisie.

It is worth noticing that there is a striking passage in a letter to James Brown, written during the stagnation of 1819, which seems at once to reinforce the very opposite opinion (namely that Ricardo was very much concerned over the condition of the working class) and to place in a clearer light his alleged tendency to focus exclusively on long-run rather than short-run effects. The remark, it should be noted, is made in the context of a discussion of the effects of introducing one of Ricardo's favourite policies, a freer trade in corn:

> We all have to lament the present distressed state of the labouring classes in this country, but the remedy is not very apparent to me. The correcting of our errors of legislation with regard to trade would ultimately be of considerable service to all classes of the community, but it would afford no immediate relief . . . the derangement which such measures would occasion in the actual employment of capital, and the changes which would become necessary, would rather aggravate than relieve the distress under which we are now labouring. (Letter to Brown, 13 October 1819, *Works*, VIII: 103; emphasis added)

Furthermore, the relative frequency with which Ricardo cites instances like these, where workers came to form the correct opinion (that is, an opinion conformable to the interest of the nation), suggests that they were not necessarily a special or limited class of cases. In *Parliamentary Reform*, for example, Ricardo spoke of an unjustified 'presumption of mistaken views of interest' entertained by the ruling classes with respect to their inferiors (*Works*, V: 502).

The one notable exception to this rule seems to have been Ricardo's position on the old Poor Laws, to which he was fervently opposed. One other case where Ricardo berated the opinions of workers, namely the Spitalfields silk weavers (whose employment contract was underwritten by special legislation), does not seem to stand as a glaring exception to the rule. Ricardo's argument here was that the Spitalfield weavers enjoyed their local privileges at the expense of weavers in other parts of the country. That is, what Ricardo opposed was the idea that the interests of a faction of a class should be allowed to dominate the interests of the class as a whole. The problem here, of course, is not so much that this opposition diminishes his credentials as being a 'friend to the poor' (*Works*, I: 106–7). It would be difficult to prosecute that case, given that Ricardo was the first to admit the misery labourers experienced in times of depression, and that he insisted that any project for the removal of existing legislation had to be slow and gradual. Rather, the problem is that Ricardo spoke with a such conviction of the need to 'teach the labouring classes that they must themselves provide for those casualties to which they are exposed' (letter to Trower, 26 January 1818, *Works*, VII: 248) that one is led to wonder why it was that the poor themselves did not learn that the Poor Laws ran directly counter to the principles of political economy (at least, that is, in the version they were enunciated by Ricardo), and so to their own (and the nation's) interests.

Ricardo does, however, provide us with a clue as to the resolution of this paradox.

As it turns out, it is a clue that might be just as helpful in explaining the rule, as it is in explaining the exception. According to Ricardo, the failure of the poor to comprehend the 'pernicious tendency of these laws' was the direct consequence of their having lived for too long within a culture, itself the immediate product of those laws, where social norms and values were such as to render it impossible for them even to begin to do so. The Poor Laws had 'been so long established', argued Ricardo, that 'the habits of the poor' had been 'formed upon their operation' (*Works*, I: 106). This idea, that character and culture were closely related in this way, differed hardly at all from that of a much more famous friend of the poor, Robert Owen. Nevertheless, it must be said that on the general question of the poor, Ricardo advanced not far beyond the opinions of other reformers. Here the influence of Malthus's principle of population seems to have been the decisive factor in shaping his views. So wedded was he to this, that he proposed no policies that might alleviate the sufferings of the poor if, on that principle, they would contribute to further population increase.

Exemplary of his use of an economic argument for democratic participation is Ricardo's sustained assault on the conduct of monetary policy by successive Tory governments. Commencing with the Bullionist Controversy of 1809–10, Ricardo had consistently maintained that bankers and, more especially, the directors of the Bank of England, had been pursuing their own interests in direct opposition to, and at the expense of, the national interest. According to Ricardo, the actual space for the exercise of these sinister interests had been opened up by a complex combination of circumstances; the precondition for which had been Parliament's act to suspend specie payments in 1797. By removing this legislative restriction on the Bank of England's ability to issue paper currency, but while still allowing it to enjoy a monopoly of note issue, this act had set in motion a sort of self-reinforcing vicious cycle. Remembering that it was always open to the Bank's directors to augment their profits by issuing paper currency (in the form of loans at interest or the discounting of bills) in excess of the underlying monetary base (gold stocks), and remembering too that these overissues, as they were called, were (according to standard quantity theory conclusions) inflationary, a situation had arisen whereby the interest of the community (price stability) was opposed to the interests of the monetary authorities (bank profits); and the problem was that the monetary authorities had the power to act on their interests, while the community was powerless to stop them.

Against the above-mentioned (and other) illiberal practices, Ricardo mustered a number of arguments. In the first place, he mounted a moral crusade (one that had been suggested to him by James Mill) against the Bank being allowed to appropriate to itself the profits derived from the use of deposits of public funds. The public, on Ricardo's thinking, were in 'justice' entitled to remuneration, while the Bank was in 'gratitude' bound 'voluntarily to relinquish to the state, the whole benefit' (*Works*, IV: 93). Writing to Malthus in the period leading up to the publication of this pamphlet, Ricardo stated: 'I think the Bank an *unnecessary* establishment getting rich by those profits which fairly belong to the public' (letter to Malthus, 10 September 1815, *Works*, VI: 268; emphasis added).

Ricardo calculated that from deposits of public funds, the Bank had secured to its own benefit (between 1806 and 1816) some £3.8 million in profits; and this, directly at the expense of the public. He was especially outraged that the Bank (that is, the owners of Bank stock) was actually claiming a right to these purloined profits under their Charter:

'Is it not lamentable to view a great and opulent body like the Bank of England, exhibiting a wish to augment their hoards by undue gains wrested from the hands of an over-burthened people?' (*Works*, IV: 93).

Ricardo repeated essentially the same argument in Parliament years later; although he does appear to have toned it down a little by attributing the conduct of the directors of the Bank rather more to their 'error' of 'not knowing how to manage [their own concerns] upon true principles' (*Works*, V: 143). He added that 'the directors had convinced him by their conduct that they did not know what they were about' (ibid.: 144). *Hansard* reported him as follows: 'With regard to the directors, he was willing, at all times, to give them full credit for honesty of intention; but he could not help thinking, that they had at different times involved the country in considerable difficulties' (ibid.: 143).

Ricardo's second line of attack saw him deploy an argument bringing forward the value of free information as a check to what he saw as existing abuses of the Bank: 'But the public attention has been lately called to the affairs of the Bank; and the subject of their profits is generally canvassed and understood' (*Works*, IV: 114).

While both of these challenges were not without their own force, it is well to note that they had both been suggested to Ricardo by James Mill. Ricardo's third avenue of attack, however, appears to have been utterly original to him. In it, he maintained that popular sovereignty, not just a change of economic policy, nor a sacking of the Bank's current directors, nor even threats to remove its existing Charter, was the ultimate channel through which such abuses could permanently be checked. *Hansard* reported the speech in which Ricardo made this argument as follows: '[Mr Ricardo] did not think this a question only between the Bank and ministers . . . but rather between ministers and the Bank on the one side, and the country on the other' (*Works*, V: 9–10).

With this argument, of course, Ricardo immediately distanced himself from both the Whigs and the Tory liberals (like William Huskisson); and this, despite the fact that all three of these groups favoured roughly the same change of policy (control over excessive note issue). Unlike Ricardo, the two existing parties (and here one should also include the majority of Tories who had sided with Nicholas Vansittart against the *Bullion Report* in 1811) seem to have seen the underlying issue as exclusively one about the appropriate design of monetary policy. Whatever their position on that score then, they uniformly saw the question entirely as a matter 'between ministers and the Bank'. For Whigs, who regularly criticized the Tory government's lax financial policies, a sufficient solution was that Tory ministers be replaced by Whig ministers. For the Tory liberals, the solution was the resumption of specie payments; a measure they succeeded in carrying out in 1819. But Ricardo had introduced an entirely novel idea concerning the ultimate check on the conduct of monetary policy – for that check was to be exercised by the country itself (or, more accurately, 'the reasonable part' of it), and not just by the theories of the political economists as imbibed by the legislators. The idea of this kind of direct public involvement in politics was (and is) remarkable. It contrasts sharply with both the traditional Benthamite confidence in professional expertise in government, and the more modern Schumpeterian theory of democracy that gives similar primacy to elites in policy-making and relegates the people to simply choosing among elites.

This, of course, is not to say that Ricardo depreciated the value of expert advice in the formulation of government policy. His own contributions in that regard are sufficient to dispel that inference. What appears rather to have been the case, is that the requisite knowledge for useful inputs into politics was not seen by Ricardo to have been the exclusive preserve of experts.

MURRAY MILGATE

See also:

Corn Laws; Life and Activities; Mill, James, and Ricardo.

References

Bentham, J. (1838–43), *The Works, of Jeremy Bentham, Vol. 3: Usury, Political Economy, Equity, Parliamentary Reform*, published under the Superintendence of his Executor, J. Bowring, Edinburgh: William Tait.

Halévy E. ([1913–46] 1949–52), *History of the English People in the Nineteenth Century*, translated by E.I. Watkin, London: Ernest Benn, Ltd.

Marshall, A. (1890] 1920), *Principles of Economics*, 8th edition, London: Macmillan.

Mill, J. (1827), *Constitutional Legislation, Parliamentary Review, Sessions of 1826–1827 and 1827–1828*, London: Baldwin & Credock, pp. 335–74.

Thorne, R.G. (1986), *The House of Commons: 1790–1820*, London: Secker and Warburg.

Mill, James, and Ricardo

James Mill (1773–1836) was educated at Edinburgh University where Dugald Stewart was his professor. He moved to London and tried to earn a living as a journalist, was adopted by Jeremy Bentham as a secretary, became the Philosophical Radicals' main organizer, and finally obtained a prestigious position at the East India Company. Besides a large number of reviews, he published tracts on political economy such as *Commerce Defended* (1808), politics, such as the *Essay on Government* (1820), ethics, such as the *Fragment on Mackintosh* (1835), and a bulky historical work, the *History of British India* (1818), and a no less cumbersome treatise on the theory of knowledge, the *Analysis of the Phenomena of Human Mind* (1829) (Ball, 2010).

Mill and Ricardo on political economy

James Mill and Ricardo first met in 1810, at a time when the latter had already published his first articles on monetary issues in newspapers, while the former was already an established essayist on political and economic issues (Henderson, 1997: 274–86). The relationship between them started as some kind of master–disciple relationship and soon evolved into a warm friendship, and then, as Ricardo won more and more intellectual independence, into a more complex and dialectical relationship.

It is far from clear whether Ricardo owed Mill any single idea in economic theory. It is beyond any doubt, though, that without the latter's practical help the former's intellectual career would have been much less successful. Mill provided decisive moral support in making the writing of everything Ricardo published up to 1817 possible, and his role in the gestation of Ricardo's *Principles* was very important. He encouraged Ricardo, gave him advice about organization of ideas and writing technique, and kept promising help in terms of editing and revisions (Cremaschi, 2004). However, as Sraffa remarks:

> Mill's contribution to the making of the *Principles* was less than might have been expected from his promises and encouragement. On the theory there is little doubt that his influence was negligible . . . Mill's letters of the period are full of advice relating to 'the art of laying down

your thoughts, in the way most easy to apprehension'. But despite his repeated assurance that he would see to the order and arrangement . . . in the main the sequence of topics has been left as Ricardo had originally worked through them. (*Works*, I: xx–xxi)

In fact, in 1817, Mill had been out of touch with political economy for several years, and Ricardo's evident intellectual superiority placed him at a level where only Malthus could compete with him.

Mill's *Elements of Political Economy* (1821) corroborates well his renown as 'an egregious simplifier of complex issues' (Ball, 2010) as it was a popularization of Ricardo's *Principles*, trying to establish a new Ricardian orthodoxy alternative to Malthus by offering simple answers where Ricardo had given highly qualified ones, for example, by simply identifying the determinants of value with labour.

Mill and Ricardo on the science of legislation and philosophy

After the *Principles* were published and before Ricardo was elected to Parliament, he undertook a massive programme of philosophical and political reading, following Mill's suggestions. If one looks at the works mentioned it seems that the latter just handed over to him his own reading lists from Edinburgh University. Among authors mentioned in the correspondence between October 1817 and December 1818 are Bayle, Locke, Hume, Millar, Bacon, Dugald Stewart, Reid, Berkeley, Warburton and Beattie. Mill also wanted to initiate him to the 'science of legislation', to which his own *History of British India* could be 'no bad introduction' (*Works*, VI: 195).

A reference to the Benthamite School in the correspondence has been mistaken by Halévy and followers for a profession of faith in Benthamite methodology. Ricardo wrote to the writer Maria Edgeworth: 'I like the formal method, after the manner of Bentham and Mill' (*Works*, IX: 259), but, from the context, the formal method turns out to be the expository technique Mill had taught him. Two more references to the school's ethical doctrine need be taken more seriously. On two occasions, with reference to the principle of utility, he expressed apparent support for 'the Bentham and Mill school' (ibid.: 52 and 239). The first time, he was writing to Francis Place and defending Malthus's use of the words 'right' and 'law of nature' by arguing that it meant actually something close to 'utility' or 'the good of the whole'; the second time, he was writing to Maria Edgeworth and delivering a semi-serious statement in favour of cultivation of potatoes if it could be proved that it would be a remedy to famines, concluding that he would fight 'till death in favor of the potatoe, for my motto, after Mr. Bentham, is "the greatest happiness to the greatest number"' (ibid.: 238–9). In fact, in the former case he was arguing that differences in theory between utilitarianism and natural law were irrelevant in practice, and in the latter he was poking fun at Bentham.

Ricardo, when Mill's *History of British India* was published, expressed admiration for such a performance, but once he started reading he also started raising objections, precisely on utility as a mark of rational action, challenging the possibility of measuring and comparing utility of different goals for action (*Works*, VII: 242).

Halévy's and Hutchinson's mythology

In Mill's dreams, Ricardo should have been in charge of the Utilitarian School's economic branch. Hollander rightly writes that 'James Mill was interested in economic theory as a weapon in the service of his political program' (Hollander, 1985: 28). The dream, albeit unfulfilled, turned into legend in Halévy's hands (1901–4, II: 246). In reaction, Schumpeter ([1954] 1994: 473) and Samuel Hollander (1979: 109–13, 593–7) adopted the opposite strategy of trying to detect in Ricardo some purely 'scientific' contribution, free from any philosophy. Sraffa shared basically the same attitude, but at least pointed at Ricardo's acquaintance with natural science as a possible source of methodological inspiration (*Works*, I: xxi).

Hutchinson staged an attempt at resurrecting Halévy, but with a difference, namely he tried to have it both ways by arguing that Mill was, more than a Benthamite, the performer of a Millian 'scientific revolution' yielding an 'economic science' more abstract and more scientific than Adam Smith's (Hutchinson, 1995: 50–83). De Marchi (1983) elegantly dismantled the argument. Hollander argued that 'a sharp distinction must be made between the methodological orientations of James Mill and David Ricardo. It is James Mill who was guilty of what has been termed by Professor Schumpeter "The Ricardian Vice"' (Hollander, 1985, I: 1), and that Ricardo 'was unhappy on empirical grounds with James Mill's oversimplified behavioural assumptions' and felt that the latter 'went too far by adopting simplifications which yielded positively misleading conclusions' (ibid.: 24). Dascal and the present writer have elaborated on De Marchi's and Hollander's conclusions by reconstructing the philosophical context in some more detail (Cremaschi and Dascal, 1996, 1998). Last of all, Depoortère resurrected Hutchinson's thesis of a Millian-Scottish (as contrasted with a Millian-Benthamite) methodological legacy (Depoortère, 2008).

SERGIO CREMASCHI

See also:

McCulloch, John Ramsay, and Ricardo; Tooke, Thomas, and Ricardo; Torrens, Robert, and Ricardo; Trower, Hutches, and Ricardo.

References

Ball, T. (2010), 'James Mill', in E.N. Zalta (ed.), *The Stanford Encyclopedia of Philosophy* (summer 2010 edition), accessed 30 December 2014 at http://plato.stanford.edu/archives/sum2010/entries/james-mill/.

Cremaschi, S. (2004), 'Ricardo and the utilitarians', *The European Journal of the History of Economic Thought*, 11(3), 377–404.

Cremaschi, S. and M. Dascal (1996), 'Malthus and Ricardo on economic methodology', *History of Political Economy*, 28(3), 475–511.

Cremaschi, S. and M. Dascal (1998), 'Persuasion and argument in the Malthus–Ricardo correspondence', in W.J. Samuels and J.E. Biddle (eds), *Research in the History of Economic Thought and Methodology, Vol. XVI*, Stamford, CT: JAI Press, pp. 1–63.

De Marchi, N.B. (1983), 'The case for James Mill', in A.W. Coats (ed.), *Methodological Controversy in Economics*, London: JAI Press, pp. 155–84.

Depoortère C. (2008), 'On Ricardo's method: the Scottish connection considered', *History of Political Economy*, 40(1), 73–110.

Halévy E. (1901–4), *La formation du radicalisme philosophique*, 3 vols, Paris: Alcan.

Henderson, J.P. (1997), *The Life and Economics of David Ricardo*, with supplemental chapters by J.B. Davis, Boston, MA: Kluwer.

Hollander, S. (1979), *The Economics of David Ricardo*, Toronto: University of Toronto Press.

Hollander, S. (1985), *The Economics of John Stuart Mill*, Toronto: University of Toronto Press.

Hutchinson, T. (1995), *Uses and Abuses of Economics*, London: Routledge.

Mill, J. ([1808] 1992), *Commerce Defended*, in *The Collected Works of James Mill*, 7 vols, London: Routledge and Thoemmes.

Mill, J. ([1817] 1997), *History of British India*, 10 vols, London: Routledge/Thoemmes.

Mill, J. ([1820] 1992), *An Essay on Government*, in *The Collected Works of James Mill*, 7 vols, London: Routledge and Thoemmes.

Mill, J. ([1829] 1992), *An Analysis of the Phenomena of Human Mind*, 2 vols, in *The Collected Works of James Mill*, 7 vols, London: Routledge and Thoemmes.

Mill, J. ([1835] 1992), *A Fragment on Mackintosh*, in *The Collected Works of James Mill*, 7 vols, London: Routledge and Thoemmes.

Schumpeter, J. ([1954] 1994), *A History of Economic Analysis*, London: Routledge.

Mill, John Stuart, on Ricardo

It is a commonly accepted prejudice among economists to see John Stuart Mill by and large as 'a synthesizer of Ricardian economics' (Ekelund and Tollison [1976] 1987: 106), 'a flabby echo of Ricardo' (Stigler, 1955: 296), 'a guardian of Ricardianism' (De Vivo [1981] 1987: 201) or at best as a transition figure between classical and neoclassical period in economic theorizing. Mill is widely considered to be just an administrator of Ricardian doctrine, a kind of steward, maintaining the heritage of Ricardian and his father's thoughts (Schwartz, 1972: 1–2). Although it is debatable whether this interpretation is true in all its particulars, it must be stated that at least for the early years of John Stuart Mill we can find sound arguments supporting this interpretation. Even George Stigler, although defending the 'originality' in Mill's economic writings, confesses that '[o]ne must search carefully in Mill's Principles to discover his own ideas' (Stigler, 1955: 296) and that it not has been Mill's primary intention 'to build a new system but only to add improvements here and there to the Ricardian system' (ibid.: 299). Analysing Mill's economic writings, for Schwartz it remains quite unclear why 'John Stuart [Mill] could not or would not complete his intellectual emancipation' (Schwartz, 1972: 49). One reason for this eclecticism in Mill's economic contribution might be found in his understanding of science. He believed that progress in science is advanced by the contribution of a lot of scholars, and he understands his economic research exactly in this sense – as just a contribution to a centenary project. Therefore, his aim was not to replace Ricardian economics but just to make some improvements (Mill [1963] 2006: 149–50). But, on the other hand, it is questionable whether John Stuart Mill ever had the choice of emancipating from Ricardian doctrine. Undergoing an intellectual education that was largely determined by the spirit of Ricardian doctrine and utilitarian philosophy (Schwartz, 1972: 235–7) his economic thinking was influenced by his father from early childhood. This might, at least to some extent, explain his fidelity to Ricardian economics.

John Stuart Mill's lessons in economic started in 1819, shortly after Ricardo had published his *Principles of Political Economy, and Taxation*. The educational programme of the 13-year-old boy consisted of lectures in Ricardian economy, declaimed daily by his father:

> He expounded to me each day a part of the subject, and I gave him next day a written account of it, which he made me write over and over again until it was clear, precise and tolerably complete. In this manner I went through the whole extent of the science; and the written outline of it . . . served him afterwards as notes from which to write his Elements of Political Economy. (Mill [1981] 2006: 31)

After having read Ricardo's *Principles* and other writings himself, John Stuart Mill proceeded with the economic writings of Adam Smith. During this reading 'it was one of my father's main objects to make me apply to Smith's more superficial view of political economy, the superior lights of Ricardo, and detect what was fallacious in Smith's arguments, or erroneous in any of his conclusions' (ibid.). Mill concludes that such intellectual education 'was excellently calculated to form a thinker' (ibid.). Later on, young John Stuart Mill became acquainted with David Ricardo during one of his visits in his father's house. Now, Ricardo himself completed James Mill's educational programme by giving additional lectures to John Stuart Mill and debating with him on economic questions (ibid.: 55). Thus, it might be said, that Ricardian political economy became a kind of reference point for the 'exactness' in economic thinking for young John Stuart Mill. Years later, when John Stuart Mill met twice a week with some friends to proceed in their studies of social sciences, the 'systematic' approach of Ricardo – especially as depicted in James Mill's 'Elements' – became central to their discussions. Nevertheless, these discussions also became the starting point for Mill's own considerations, which led to his improvements and modifications of Ricardian doctrine (ibid.: 123–5).

It is difficult, however, to decide whether the improvements John Stuart Mill mentions in his autobiography really concern the original Ricardian doctrine or merely what his father taught him as Ricardian. Although Mill had read Ricardo's writings himself his view on Ricardo was heavily shaped by his father's interpretation (Schwartz, 1972: 20–21). However, it is hard to distinguish whether in his later years John Stuart Mill really emancipated from Ricardian doctrine or from what his father considered to be Ricardian economics.

It is worth noting at this point that Mill's improvements have never been mentioned as a critique of the Ricardian system itself. His aim was to defend Ricardian economics against various allegations (Hollander, 1985: xiii). Symptomatic of this discussion was the dispute between the representatives of the so-called 'old school' and the representatives of a new methodology in economics primarily based on the Ricardian approach of deducing from a priori axioms. Mill defended this new approach by either pointing out that critics have misunderstood Ricardian theory or showing that the sources of the dissent lay in methodological differences:

> Mill did not want openly to attack as false the views held by his fellow economists . . . His strategy . . . was to look for what was useful, or at least not incompatible with Ricardo's doctrines, in the opinion they held, and to acknowledge this, while at the same time stating positively the true (Ricardian) position. (De Marchi [1974] 1987: 135)

But Mill's efforts went beyond solely to defend the 'true' Ricardian doctrine. Because political economy in general and the positive method of Ricardo in particular had been widely criticized as a radical and hard-hearted point of view, his defence of political economy aimed at establishing 'the legitimacy and good intentions of the subject as a whole' (ibid.: 125). By and large, one must conclude that the project was successful. Especially Mill's discussions concerning the futurity of labouring class, although criticized in detail, contributed to the acceptance of the Ricardian point of view. None of the critics 'questioned the relevance of Ricardo's conceptual framework to the question of wages' and in the following this question occupied a 'central . . . place in social and economic discussion in the late 1840's, and the two decades following' (ibid.: 145).

The 'positive' methodology of political economy – between defence and concession

Major concerns of contemporary scholars rose from the deductive method of Ricardian economy. Basically, this critique was twofold: first, contemporary economists accused the representatives of the Ricardian doctrine of setting off from imaginary, a priori assumptions, ignoring the historical facts and variations in society and which therefore, second, could not be applied to national economies without making certain allowances for factual historical economic circumstances (De Marchi [1974] 1987: 125–6). In fact, Ricardian economy, thus the allegation, while true in itself, could not be applied to reality because of the taken-for-grantedness of its speculative first principles. As a consequence, the recommendations for practical policy, as traced out from such theory, would lead logically to consequences that are of at least marginal match with the factual conditions of mankind (Bagehot [1848] 1987: 8). For Bagehot economists differ in two ways: while, what he calls, 'common-sense thinkers', like Adam Smith, consider 'extraneous influences' in their theories as important phenomena that should be respected when concluding from pure theoretical assumptions, the 'abstract thinkers', like Ricardo, set out 'from certain primitive assumptions' and than proceed 'to evolve all … results by mere deduction' (ibid.). Taking this interpretation widely, Bagehot asserts a kind of '*Methodenstreit*' concerning the right methodology in political economics (Hollander [1983a] 1987: 569–71). While inductivists claim that only the examination of historical and social development allows for universal generalizations in political economy, deductivists believe in general abstractions and the possibility to conclude from a priori axioms and evidences about human behaviour or capital accumulation to factual development of nation economies. Thus, inductivists criticized not only the 'wrong methodology' in general but also the wrong assumptions and illegitimate generalizations in Ricardian economy, a position held especially by the so-called 'Cambridge inductivists' (Hollander, 1985: 149–58). Even if deductive economics were possible on the base of inductively generated universal laws, Ricardian doctrine would be far from completing an axiomatic system that would allow for deductive methodology (Hollander [1983a] 1987: 581).

Mill tries to overcome this difficulty. Although estimating high the Ricardian positivist methodology, he is aware that in every deductive procedure 'there must be a direct induction as the basis of the whole' (Mill [1973] 2006: 454), stating that this 'inductive operation' is the first step in deduction:

> Mr. Mill has substantially expressed his intention of conciliating the two modes of dealing with the subject; that is, of combining the abstract deduction and logical accuracy which are exemplified in Ricardo with the largeness of view and thorough acquaintance with diversified matters of fact for which the 'Wealth of Nations' is so eminently remarkable. (Bagehot [1848] 1987: 9)

By and large Mill sees the differences between the schools. But one of his aims is to defend the whole subject of the 'new science' of political economy. Therefore, he tries to bridge the differences and to draw a positive picture; although some critical remarks on Ricardian doctrine, brought forward by the Cambridge inductivist school, without doubt have been legitimate, Mill's first intention was to avoid such '*Methodenstreit*' (Hollander [1983a] 1987: 593; 1985: 158). Nevertheless, he believes in the accurateness of Ricardian economy and considers this to be a basic requirement to establish economy as a science. In one of his early writings, a survey in the *Westminster Review* of 1825, Mill summarizes the basic elements of the 'new school' he wants to defend:

> We have been accustomed to believe that political economy, which was left, even by Adam Smith, in a state of great vagueness and uncertainty, had been raised to the rank of a science chiefly by three discoveries: the principle of population, the theory of rent, and Mr. Ricardo's theory of foreign commerce. (Mill [1967a] 2006: 30)

And in his essay *On the Definition of Political Economy* he summarizes:

> Political Economy, therefore, reasons from assumed premises – from premises which might be totally without foundation in fact, and which are not pretended to be universally in accordance with it. The conclusions of Political Economy, consequently, like those of geometry, are only true, as the common phrase is, in the abstract; that is, they are only true under certain suppositions, in which none but general causes – causes common to the whole class of cases under consideration – are taken into the account. The à priori method ... is ... the only method by which truth can possibly be attained in any department of the social science' (Mill [1967b] 2006: 326)

Impractical theorists and the question of applied economy

An additional contemporary discussion between the representatives of the 'old school' and the 'new school' concentrated on the social consequences of the Ricardian doctrine. By focusing on theoretical questions of production and capital accumulation Ricardo, thus a commonly accepted impeachment has taken stand against the legitimate interests of the labouring class. Questions of moral and social justice thus have been excluded from economic theory (De Marchi [1974] 1987: 126–7). In an open letter 'To the Heads of the University of Oxford' David Robinson, one of the representatives of the 'old school' as he explicitly mentions at the end of his letter, criticizes this lack of social awareness of Ricardian doctrine by drawing a gloomy picture of the expected outcome of the application of such theory: 'the mass of our countrymen cannot produce a sufficiency of the necessaries of life; and I conscientiously believe the great cause is to be found in the application of these principles' (Robinson, 1829: 510). In Ricardian doctrine he sees a relapse into 'barbarism': 'By making high profits, the sine qua non of national wealth, and low wages that of high profits, it in reality makes it the grant principle of civil government, to keep the mass of the human race in the lowest stages of indigence and suffering' (ibid.: 511). And, touching on the political consequences of such a view, he adds: 'Of course, according to them, profits must be at the highest, when wages are at the lowest. They thus place wages and labourers in fierce and eternal conflict with profits and capitalists' (ibid.: 513). Consequently, the humanitarians argued that moral considerations have to be ranked before pure economic doctrines, especially if such doctrines are used to advise governments, and that statistical knowledge should not override humanitarian sentiment.

When writing his principles based on Ricardian doctrine Mill thus tried to avoid the image of hard-heartedness by including humanitarian considerations about the 'probable futurity of the labouring classes' (Mill [1965] 2006: 758–96) but, at the same time, refused humanitarian sentimentalities by holding consequently to the Malthusian and Ricardian position strictly underpinning the causality of growth in population and the production of wealth (De Marchi [1974] 1987: 132; Hollander, 1985: 185). In this respect he made clear changes to Malthus's pessimistic view as well as to Ricardo's theoretical assumptions. This 'synthesis' is quite respected by other contemporary economists. Thus, for example, right after publication of Mill's *Principles*, Walter Bagehot praises Mill's new perspective, pointing out that he was the first among the English economists who believes that the present division of classes into capitalists and labourers is of temporarily limited relevance and that the distribution of wealth is more important than its production (Bagehot [1848] 1987: 7).

Furthermore, Mill in his economic writings tries to avoid another Ricardian 'vice'. While Ricardo based his theories solely on theoretical assumptions Mill endeavours to connect theoretical and practical considerations. As he points out in his essay concerning the method of political economy from 1836, theoretical considerations and practical experiences have to be combined if misleading conclusions should be avoided:

> [W]hile the philosopher and the practical man bandy half-truths with one another, we may seek far without finding one who, placed on a higher eminence of thought, comprehends as a whole what they see only in separate parts; who can make the anticipations of the philosopher guide the observation of the practical man, and the specific experience of the practical man warn the philosopher where something is to be added to his theory. (Mill [1967b] 2006: 334–5)

Thus, Mill strives more to use practical examples and to show the overall relations of political economy with social sciences. By making these concessions he does not turn away from 'Ricardian orthodoxy' but tries to make the new science more popular.

Between science and art

Another point where Mill clearly takes a position for the accurate methodology of Ricardian economics against the critics of the 'old school' concerns his distinction between science and art. While science aims at discovering the laws of nature, art gives precepts and looks for means to reach a given end. Mill concludes:

> Rules therefore, for making a nation increase in wealth, are not a science, but they are the results of science. Political economy does not of itself instruct how to make a nation rich; but whoever would be qualified to judge of the means of making a nation rich, must first be a political economist. (Mill [1967b] 2006: 312)

In a review of Mill's *Essays on some Unsettled Questions of Political Economy* (1844) and his *Principles of Political Economy* (1848), Nassau William Senior analyses the different understandings of political economy as science or art at different British economists. While Adam Smith – and thus, may be added, most representatives of the 'old school' – perceive political economy as an art (*WN*, IV.i) that aims first at providing sufficient subsistence for all people and second at supplying the nation state with revenue sufficient for offering essential public services (Senior [1848] 1987: 38), this perception is not shared by later economists of the 'new school'. In opposition to Smith, John Ramsay McCulloch, well known among his contemporaries for his article on political economy in the Supplement of the *Encyclopaedia Britannica*, for instance, defines the target of political economy as searching for the laws that regulate production, accumulation, distribution and consumption, and thus sees political economy as a science aiming at the improvement of theoretical knowledge. Nevertheless, McCulloch also sees an additional task of political economy in the development of means for increasing the wealth of nations, and thus treats political economy also as an art (McCulloch, 1870: 9–10; Senior [1848] 1987: 39). Similarly, following Ricardo's traces, Mill defines political economy as a 'science which treats of the production and distribution of wealth, so far as they depend upon the laws of human nature' (Mill [1967b] 2006: 318, see also Ricardo, *Works*, I: 5–6). Thus, with respect to his scientific approach to political economy, Senior sees John Stuart Mill as a clear representative of the Ricardian School (Senior [1848] 1987: 56). On the other hand, Ricardo himself, for Senior, remains an exception: while less scientific in his writings than other contemporary political economists he waives giving precepts or using illustrations drawn from known facts and common experiences (ibid.: 39). Nevertheless, Ricardo is seen as the first representative of a new (scientific) methodology in political sciences, based not on observation but on assumed premises, and Mill is perceived as one as his most prominent successors:

> Among the writers who have taken this view of Political Economy, the most remarkable is Mr. Ricardo. His treatment of it, indeed, is more abstract than that proposed by Mr. Mill. He adds to Mr. Mill's hypothesis other assumptions equally arbitrary. And he draws all his illustrations not from real life, but from hypothetical cases. Out of these materials he has framed a theory as to the distribution of wealth possessing almost mathematical precision. (Ibid.: 43)

Such hypothetical reasoning remains doubtful for Senior for at least three reasons (ibid.: 43–4), First, such considerations are obviously unattractive because no one wants to know what might be the case under given restrictions. Second, writers basing their theories on arbitrarily chosen assumptions tend to forget the arbitrariness of these assumptions when drawing their conclusion, which, as Senior states, 'has been the source of much error in Ricardo'. Third, pure theorists using pure deduction tend to overlook facts and to omit important influences when establishing their principles. Thus, the conclusions of such theorists might be right in a formal manner but unrealistic from the practical point of view. Also, Whewell criticizes the arbitrariness of Ricardo's assumptions; especially in the case of the 'iron law of wages' (*Works*, I: 101–5) he believes that 'there is not the slightest ground for asserting this to be the law of such changes, any more than any other law arbitrarily assumed' (quoted in Hollander [1983a] 1987: 585). Whewell adds that an economic science relying solely on an underdeveloped axiomatic basis ignoring the different causes at work in reality is in danger of deviating far from the facts (ibid.: 582).

In this context it is interesting to see how Mill extends the Ricardian position to deal with its critics. He accepts the inability of economic models to serve as predictive instrument and concedes that the axiomatic base of political economy must be proofed on empirical facts, which allows for improvements of the basic assumptions as well as correcting logical errors (ibid.: 588). Thus, Mill, on the one hand, insists on the Ricardian deduction as basic methodology for his new science but, on the other hand, makes allowances for the concrete historic situation as it is demanded from Ricardian critics. As a science, political economy strives for exploring 'the moral or psychological laws of the production and distribution of wealth' and analyses 'what effects follow from these mental laws acting in concurrence with those physical ones' (Mill [1967b] 2006: 318). In this context Mill's distinction between 'laws of matter' and 'laws of mind' (ibid.: 316–17) is important; it allows for extenuating the ferociousness of the 'iron law' and additionally gives room for adjusting economic laws to national peculiarities. In this sense, the production of wealth was determined by 'natural' economic laws, operating inexorably, but the distribution of wealth could follow social and humanitarian considerations and enable society for necessary adjustments (Schapiro [1943] 1987: 89).

The *Principles of Political Economy*

With the publication of the *Principles of Political Economy*, as De Marchi points out, Mill pursued three specific goals: it was first thought of as a summary of the state of the art of the new science 'political economy'; it was second taken as an occasion to promote the 'Ricardian' positive method as the correct scientific approach to political economy; and finally, it served Mill as an opportunity to express his personal (moral) point of view on the economic development of society (De Marchi [1974] 1987: 124). Thus, although based on Ricardian thinking, the *Principles* follow the tradition of Adam Smith and focus also on the social implications of economic development (Bladen [1948] 1987: 100; [1965] 1987: xxii; Schapiro [1943] 1987: 80–81). And though Mill believes that 'Political Economy ... has grown up almost from infancy since the time of Adam Smith' (Mill [1965] 2006: xcii) – not at least due to the works of Thomas Malthus, David Ricardo and James Mill – his aim is not to replace the 'old school' but to incorporate 'the results of these speculations, and bringing them into harmony with the principles previously laid down by the best thinkers on the subject' (ibid.: xci). As he writes in a letter to Henry S. Chapman, dated from November 1844, he plans to write on political economy 'not in the abstract manner of Ricardo and my father, but in the practical and popular manner of Adam Smith'. He expresses his belief that the 'whole science requires extremely to be recast, incorporating, of course, ... all the ... new doctrines and shewing how they do not contradict but fit into the others'. Additionally, for study purposes, the book should be 'at once free from gross error and teaching the applications along with the principles, which it is the beauty of Adam Smith's book that he did' (Mill [1963] 2006: 642). Nevertheless, Mill's own positioning as 'Ricardian' is undeniable. In a review on 'De Quincey's logic of political economy' in the *Westminster Review* from 1845 he states:

> One of his merits is his early and consistent appreciation of Ricardo, the true founder of the abstract science of political economy, and whose writings are still, after all that has been since written, its purest source. What has been added to the science since Ricardo, does not need to be substituted for his doctrines, but to be incorporated with them. They do not require alteration or correction, so much as fuller exposition and comment. (Mill [1967c] 2006: 394)

And because Ricardian doctrine 'is still far from being admitted by the common herd of political economists' (Mill [1963] 2006: 659) Mill makes it his task to make Ricardian doctrine popular. His intention is to recast Ricardian economics in a more positive and optimistic manner (Capaldi, 2004: 205).

Wage fund theory

Based on the 'iron law of wages' (*Works*, I: 101–5) Mill draws a general negative picture on the long-term development of wages and, by this, in principle follows the ideas of Ricardo and Malthus (Senior [1848] 1987: 59, 65). In the long run the remuneration of workers has the tendency to fall to the physical minimum, which allows the existence of the labouring class. Following the Ricardian doctrine Mill believes that every law or regulation aimed at improving the wage level at a given stage of production will disadvantage instead of benefit the labouring class because this either leads to an increase of the prices of wage-paying commodities that would annihilate the wage effects, or to a decrease of production that leads to a decrease in the employment rate. Nevertheless, Mill, in opposition to Ricardo and Malthus, sees a 'moral obligation' of the rich not to reduce wages to the absolute minimum and to create work places for those willing to work (Mill [1965] 2006: 356–7) and, thus, as Bagehot sums up, 'the benevolence on the higher classes answers all the purposes of an extra demand for labour' (Bagehot [1848] 1987: 26). Thus, for Mill the 'iron law' is not a prediction of future development, or, as Hollander states: 'It had less a descriptive than an exhortatory purpose' (Hollander [1984] 1987: 622). For Mill the prediction was valid only in the case that the unskilled workers would be not willing to change their habits. As a consequence Mill stresses the moral and intellectual development of the working class by education and positive incentives (Ekelund and Tollison [1976] 1987: 112). Although Mill considers himself to be 'Malthusian' he is less pessimistic concerning the future of the labouring class and the moral and social development of industrial workers than Ricardo and Malthus. It might go too far to conclude with Bagehot that 'Mr. Mill does not believe the doctrine of Malthus and Ricardo, that an increase of the comforts or a decrease in the misery of the labouring classes is invariably followed by an accelerated increase of population' (Bagehot [1848] 1987: 17). Nevertheless, Mill sees the opportunity that education, enlightenment and increasing standards of living will lead to changes in the attitude of their behaviour and might retard the increase of population.

Theory of rent

A typical example of Mill's trial to reconcile 'old school' thinkers with Ricardian doctrine by reinterpreting the differences as a simple misunderstanding or pointing out that some of the assumptions of Ricardian critics are wrong is his essay on *The Nature, Origin, and Progress of Rent* from 1828. On the question of rent Mill strictly follows the Ricardian position. Following Ricardo, rent results from different fertility of land. Given an increasing population and therefore an increasing demand for agricultural products, land of inferior quality has to be brought under tillage, which requires more labour for cultivation. In this case the owner of the superior land yields a rent of the amount of labour he is able to save on his land due to the superior quality of the soil (*Works*, I: 69–71). In fact this theoretical analysis seems to be self-evident. Nevertheless, in practice, land of the first quality is no always brought under tillage first. One argument for this is that farmland often consists of different qualities of soil; another is that most fertile soil is no always the easiest to cultivate (Mill [1967d] 2006: 171–2). Mill responds to the critics not by showing that the concrete observations they had made were wrong but by arguing that they had mistaken the meaning of 'fertility'. Fertility, he argues, must not be seen as absolute crop yield but has to be put in relation to the efforts made for cultivation. In this sense land that yields 100 quarters of wheat but requires an outlay equal to 50 quarters for capital and labour is more fertile than land that produces an absolute amount of wheat of 150 quarters but requires an outlay equal to 80 quarters (ibid.: 173). What Mill, as well as Ricardo, completely ignores is the possibility of different use of land, the basic of this critique (in detail see Haney [1910] 1987: 86–97), and the question whether inferior or superior product qualities should be produced. In another review in the *Westminster Review* from October 1851, concerning 'Newman's political economy'

(Mill [1967e] 2006), Mill reacts on the same critique as Newman's, on Ricardo's theory of rent. Also here, Mill simply ignores Newman's argumentation, who comments on the Ricardian theory of rent:

> This may be not uninstructive, as illustrating how the successive suppressing of the average gains in an agricultural community tends to generate and increase rent; but it is very untrue as a representation of the real state of an advanced country. In fact it assumes that wheat is the only agricultural product, and that the value of land is to be measured by capacity of producing it. But this is an entire fiction. There are such things as dairy farms; there are market gardens, orchards, vineyards, copses, and shooting grounds; there are mulberry-trees for the silkworm, there is flax, barley, oats, and in hotter climates an infinity of other products. It is incorrect to call land absolutely best. (Newman, 1851: 153–4)

Thus, in principle, the critique of the 'old school' was not that the theory of rent was wrong per se, but that it was built upon an oversimplification of agricultural production. Mill defends what he sees as orthodoxy by becoming impolite and repeating the same arguments as before. Stating that Newman in principle follows the best ideas of contemporary writers Mill continues that his 'deviations from them in our opinion are seldom improvements' (Mill [1967e] 2006: 447). Quoting the above-mentioned paragraph in Newman he sees this as a 'complete misapprehension', pointing out that Ricardo just wants to illustrate his theory by using the wheat example and that the same also could be done by using other agricultural products. Only in cases where farmers cultivate land for subsistence and not for profit do some allowances have to be made (ibid.: 447–8). But again Mill misses (or wants to miss) the point of Newman's critique on Ricardo. He is either not willing or unable to reconsider Ricardian doctrine.

Conclusion

'Both James and J. S. Mill presented themselves as followers, indeed they felt they were followers. But feeling does not make it so. J. S. Mill's achievement was so great and so clear that he was not taken at his own valuation while James's achievement quickly became invisible and his own valuation has stood' (Aldrich, 2004: 397). While assessing the relation between John Stuart Mill's and the Ricardian conception of political economy one should keep in mind that Mill, despite all 'filial respect', found Ricardian doctrine a useful tool for analysing economical problems (Hollander [1976] 2000: 55). 'In his economics, J. S. Mill remained faithful to the Ricardian doctrines as he understood them – and, to some extent, improved upon them in the process of interpreting them' (Viner, [1949] 1987: 155). When Mill in his later years turned his focus more and more towards the social question, he followed – maybe influenced by Harriet Taylor – his philanthropic ideals more than, as often presumed, socialistic ideas. And maybe his writings concerning the futurity of the labouring classes and his sympathy for workers' cooperatives have been built more on hope than on clear analysis or sound expectation. Nevertheless, in his economical analyses he remained a strong 'Ricardian', and he used Ricardian methodology also as 'a powerful weapon in the battle for social reform' (Hollander [1983b] 2000: 64). The differences between Ricardian and Mill's economy therefore result from Mill's broader view on society but not from systematic differences.

MICHAEL S. AßLÄNDER

See also:

Marx, Karl Heinrich, on Ricardo; Mill, James, and Ricardo.

References

Aldrich, J. (2004), 'The discovery of comparative advantage', *Journal of the History of Economic Thought*, **26**(3), 279–399.

Bagehot, W. ([1848] 1987), 'Principles of political economy', *The Prospective Review*, **VI**(16), 460–502; reprint in J.C. Wood (ed.), *John Stuart Mill: Critical Assessments, Vol. 2*, London: Croom Helm, pp. 7–35.

Bladen, V.W. ([1948] 1987), 'John Stuart Mill's *Principles*: a centenary estimate', *American Economic Review*, **39**(2), 1–12; reprint in J.C. Wood (ed.), *John Stuart Mill: Critical Assessments, Vol. 2*, London: Croom Helm, pp. 98–108.

Bladen, V.W. ([1965] 2006), 'Introduction', in *Mill, John Stuart: Principles of Political Economy*, in *Collected Works, Vol. 2–3*, Toronto: University of Toronto Press; reprint, Indianapolis: Liberty Fund.

Capaldi, N. (2004), *John Stuart Mill – A Biography*, Cambridge, UK: Cambridge University Press.

De Marchi, N.B. ([1974] 1987), 'The success of J.S. Mill's *Principles*', *History of Political Economy*, **VI**(Summer), 119–57; reprint in J.C. Wood (ed.), *John Stuart Mill: Critical Assessments, Vol. 2*, London: Croom Helm, pp. 122–54.

De Vivo, G. ([1981] 1987), 'John Stuart Mill on value', *Cambridge Journal of Economics*, **5**(1), 67–9; reprint in J.C. Wood (ed.), *John Stuart Mill: Critical Assessments, Vol. 2*, London: Croom Helm, pp. 201–4.

Ekelund, R.B. and R.D. Tollison ([1976] 1987), 'The new political economy of J.S. Mill: the means to social justice', *London Journal of Economics*, **9**(2), 213–231; reprint in J.C. Wood (ed.), *John Stuart Mill: Critical Assessments, Vol. 3*, London: Croom Helm, pp. 106–23.

Haney, L.H. ([1910] 1987), 'Rent and price: "alternative use" and "scarcity value"', *Quarterly Journal of Economics*, **25**(1), 119–38; reprint in J.C. Wood (ed.), *John Stuart Mill: Critical Assessments, Vol. 1*, London: Croom Helm, pp. 86–97.

Hollander, S. ([1976] 2000), 'Ricardianism, J. S. Mill and the neo-classical challenge', in J.M. Robson and M. Laine (eds), *James and J. S. Mill: Papers of the Centenary Conference*, Toronto: University of Toronto Press, pp. 67–85; reprint in S. Hollander, *Collected Essays, Vol 3: John Stuart Mill on Economic Theory and Method*, London: Routledge, pp. 41–61.

Hollander, S. ([1983a] 1987), 'William Whewell and John Stuart Mill on the methodology of political economy', *Studies in the History and Philosophy of Science*, **14**(2), 127–68; reprint in J.C. Wood (ed.), *John Stuart Mill: Critical Assessments, Vol. 1*, London: Croom Helm, pp. 567–608.

Hollander, S. ([1983b] 2000), 'On John Stuart Mill's defence of Ricardian economics', *Revue d'Economie Politique*, **93**(6), 894–99; reprint in S. Hollander, *Collected Essays, Vol 3: John Stuart Mill on Economic Theory and Method*, London: Routledge, pp. 63–8.

Hollander, S. ([1984] 1987), '"Dynamic equilibrium" with constant wages: J.S. Mill's Malthusian analysis of the secular wage path', *Kyklos*, **37**(2), 247–65; reprint in J.W. Wood (ed.), *John Stuart Mill: Critical Assessments, Vol. 1*, London: Croom Helm, pp. 609–24.

Hollander, S. (1985), *The Economics of John Stuart Mill, Vol. 1: Theory and Method*, Oxford: Blackwell.

McCulloch, J.R. (1870), *Political Economy – With Sketch of the Rise and Progress of the Science*, London: Murray and Son.

Mill, J.S. ([1963] 2006), *The Earlier Letters of John Stuart Mill*, in *Collected Works, Vol. 12–13*, Toronto: University of Toronto Press; reprint, Indianapolis: Liberty Fund.

Mill, J.S. ([1965] 2006), *Principles of Political Economy*, in *Collected Works, Vol. 2–3*, Toronto: University of Toronto Press; reprint, Indianapolis: Liberty Fund.

Mill, J.S. ([1967a] 2006), *The Quarterly Review on Political Economy*, in *Collected Works, Vol. 4–5: Essays on Economics and Society*, Toronto: University of Toronto Press; reprint, Indianapolis: Liberty Fund.

Mill, J.S. ([1967b] 2006), *On the Definition of Political Economy*, in *Collected Works, Vol. 4–5: Essays on Economics and Society*, Toronto: University of Toronto Press; reprint, Indianapolis: Liberty Fund.

Mill, J.S. ([1967c] 2006), 'De Quincey's logic of political economy', in *Collected Works, Vol. 4–5: Essays on Economics and Society*, Toronto: University of Toronto Press; reprint, Indianapolis: Liberty Fund.

Mill, J.S. (1967d), *The Nature, Origin, and Progress of Rent*, in *Collected Works, Vol. 4–5: Essays on Economics and Society*, Toronto: University of Toronto Press; reprint Indianapolis: Liberty Fund.

Mill, J.S. ([1967e] 2006), 'Newman's political economy', in *Collected Works, Vol. 4–5: Essays on Economics and Society*, Toronto: University of Toronto Press; reprint Indianapolis: Liberty Fund.

Mill, J.S. ([1973] 2006), *A System of Logic Ratiocinative and Inductive*, in *Collected Works, Vol. 7–8*, Toronto: University of Toronto Press; reprint Indianapolis: Liberty Fund.

Mill, J.S. ([1981] 2006), *Autobiography*, in *Collected Works, Vol. 1: Autobiography and Literary Essays*, Toronto: University of Toronto Press; reprint, Indianapolis: Liberty Fund.

Newman, F.W. (1851), *Lectures on Political Economy*, London: John Chapman.

Robinson, D. (1829), 'Political economy no. 1 – to the Heads of the University of Oxford', *Blackwood's Magazine*, **26**(September), 510–23.

Schapiro, J.S. ([1943] 1987), 'John Stuart Mill, pioneer of democratic liberalism in England', *Journal of the Histories of Ideas*, **4**(2), 127–60; reprint in J.C. Wood (ed.), *John Stuart Mill: Critical Assessments, Vol. 1*, London: Croom Helm, pp. 78–103.

Schwartz, P. (1972), *The New Political Economy of John Stuart Mill*, London: Weidenfeld & Nicolson.

Senior, N.W. ([1848] 1987), 'Mill, *The Principles of Political Economy*', *Edinburgh Review*, **LXXXVIII**(October), 293–339; reprint in J.C. Wood (ed.), *John Stuart Mill: Critical Assessments, Vol. 2*, London: Croom Helm, pp. 36–75.

Smith, A. ([1776] 1981), *An Inquiry into the Nature and Causes of the Wealth of Nations*, (eds) R.H. Campbell, A.S. Skinner and W.B. Todd, Indianapolis: Liberty Fund.

Stigler, G.J. (1955), 'The nature and role of originality in scientific progress', *Economica* (New Series), **22**(88), 293–302.

Viner, J. ([1949] 1987), 'Bentham and J.S. Mill: the utilitarian background', *American Economic Review*, **39**(2), 360–82; reprint in J.C. Wood (ed.), *John Stuart Mill: Critical Assessments, Vol. 1*, London: Croom Helm, pp. 145–64.

Monetary Theory

David Ricardo is most often considered by historians of economic thought as being representative of monetary orthodoxy, if not the father and the most typical proponent of that doctrine. For example, he adopted the quantity theory of money 'in [a] strict sense' (Schumpeter, 1954: 703), 'espousing a hard-line version of it' (Blaug, 1995: 31); in the debates of 1809–11 on the depreciation of the pound sterling, he defended an 'extreme Bullionist' position (Viner, 1937: 106). No doubt he promoted the use of the bank note as a cheaper currency than specie, but this was simply 'an argument which harked back to Adam Smith's defence of paper money in the *Wealth of Nations*' (Laidler, 1987: 293).

This story that plays down Ricardo's theoretical contribution and overemphasizes his doctrinal extremism in monetary matters is inaccurate. Ricardo's views on money build a theory of their own, which is neither a simple development of Hume or Smith's, nor a systematization of the Bullionist approach, nor a preliminary version of the Currency Principle. Further, this singularity, having been misunderstood in the debates of the time and overlooked by most of modern commentators (favourable or hostile), the orthodoxy of Ricardo became a prejudice. The present entry aims to show that the singularity of Ricardo's monetary theory makes him unorthodox on money.

Ricardo started and ended his writing of books in economics with two pamphlets on the issuing of bank notes, stressing respectively the consequences of their inconvertibility (*The High Price of Bullion, a Proof of the Depreciation of Bank Notes*, 1810–11; *Works*, III: 47–127) and the advantages of their public issue (*Plan for the Establishment of a National Bank*, 1823, published posthumously in 1824; *Works*, IV: 275–300). In between, the theoretical foundations of his ideas on money, together with their practical implications, were published in the essay *Proposals for an Economical and Secure Currency* (1816; *Works*, IV: 49–141) and in Chapter XXVII 'On Currency and Banks' of his economic treatise *On the Principles of Political Economy, and Taxation* (1817–21).

Ricardo's monetary theory may be summed up by the following extract from his 1816 essay:

> The only use of a standard is to regulate the quantity, and by the quantity the value of a currency. . . without a standard it would be exposed to all the fluctuations to which the ignorance or the interests of the issuers might subject it. (*Works*, IV: 59)

In modern language, this sentence illustrates the way Ricardo integrates money in his theory of value: the theory of the value of commodities does *not* apply to money – which consequently is *not* a commodity – but to a standard that 'regulates' the quantity of money, hence its value. Thus, the concept of monetary standard is central in Ricardo's theory of money, since it is that concept that ensures the consistency between the theory of the value of commodities and the theory of the value of money.

This has two consequences. First, a full-fledged theory of money could only be found after Ricardo had built his own theory of value, that is, in *Principles*. This does not imply the existence of a break in Ricardo's views on money: on the contrary, they show a high degree of permanence from his early monetary writings to his last ones: the main practical scheme designed by Ricardo to improve the monetary system appeared as early as 1811, six years before *Principles*. But these permanent views on money could only be theoretically grounded in *Principles*, where the concept of standard shows up in Chapter I ('On Value') and Chapter XXVII ('On Currency and Banks'). This is the reason why, in this entry, I will concentrate on Ricardo's analysis starting with his 1816 pamphlet (partly reprinted by Ricardo himself in *Principles*).

The second consequence is that, strictly speaking, Ricardo's theory of money only applies to a monetary system regulated by a standard. Again, the statement that the value of money depends on its quantity is permanent in Ricardo, from 1809 to 1823. But, when note convertibility was suspended, and although the measure of the depreciation of the currency still required the use of the standard, the latter no longer regulated the quantity of the currency. As a consequence, the monetary system could not work properly. Hence, Ricardo's positive and normative approach to money relied on the concept of monetary standard. I will consequently leave aside here Ricardo's views about an inconvertible currency.

If the above quotation sums up Ricardo's theory of money, the following one (from *Principles*) indicates the type of ideal monetary system to which this theory leads:

> A currency is in its most perfect state when it consists wholly of paper money, but of paper money of an equal value with the gold which it professes to represent. (*Works*, I: 361)

Both quotations illustrate the logical structure of Ricardo's argument: (a) the value of a currency depends on its quantity; (b) that quantity may only be regulated when the currency is linked to a standard; and (c) this regulation should operate through the use of paper money alone, issued in such a way that its value equals that of the standard. Ricardo's monetary theory may then be understood by distinguishing four successive logical steps:

1. The relation between the quantity and the value of money.
2. The theory of the monetary standard.
3. The theory of the monetary system.
4. The conception of international adjustment consistent with this approach.

The 'principle of limitation of quantity'

The principle of limitation of quantity is exposed in the first pages of Chapter XXVII of *Principles*. Here Ricardo intends to 'take only a brief survey of some of the general laws which regulate its [currency] quantity and value' since 'none but the prejudiced are ignorant of its true principles' (ibid.: 352). As we will see, things are not that simple.

The starting point is reminiscent of the theory of value put forward in Chapter I, and leads to a first relation between the quantity and the value of money when its function of circulating medium is performed by gold or silver as commodity:

> Gold and silver, like all other commodities, are valuable only in proportion to the quantity of labour necessary to produce them, and bring them to market. Gold is about fifteen times dearer than silver . . . solely because fifteen times the quantity of labour is necessary to procure a given quantity of it. The quantity of money that can be employed in a country must depend on its value: if gold alone were employed for the circulation of commodities, a quantity would be required, one fifteenth only of what would be necessary, if silver were made use of for the same purpose. A circulation can never be so abundant as to overflow; for by diminishing its value, in the same proportion you will increase its quantity, and by increasing its value, diminish its quantity. (Ibid.)

This extract may be a surprise to anyone accustomed to the quantity theory of money, since it exhibits a causal relation from the value of money to its quantity, not the other way round as expected. The reason is simple: the circulating medium here is a commodity (gold or silver) produced in competitive conditions, as testified by the fact that the labour theory of value applies to it, in the same way that it applies to commodities defined in Chapter I of *Principles*. In the next paragraph, Ricardo considers what happens 'while the State coins money' (ibid.: 353): the (say, gold) coin will now have the same value as any piece of the same weight in gold whenever the State does not charge a seigniorage for coinage, and a higher value if the seigniorage reflects the labour cost of fabricating the coin. The causal relation from value to quantity remains the same, since State coins only replace commodity gold as means of circulation, without altering the competitive determination of their value.

Things change with metallic coinage being subject to a monopoly: 'While the State alone coins, there can be no limit to this charge of seignorage; for by limiting the quantity of coin, it can be raised to any conceivable value' (ibid.). The causal relation is here reversed: if the State monopolist of coined money restricts its quantity, it may increase its value above the value of gold it contains, without limit. This is what Ricardo labels 'the principle of limitation of quantity [of money]' (ibid.) – hereafter PLQ.

The two preliminary steps of the analysis, referring to a currency competitively produced, without or with State coinage, have only a pedagogical character: there is no indication, here or elsewhere, that Ricardo had historical situations in mind. And it is worthwhile noting that PLQ logically emerges, not because money is metallic but because its production (of money, not gold) is monopolized. In other words, PLQ in Ricardo is neither the consequence of a commodity theory of money (commodity being understood in Ricardo's sense of a competitive product) nor of a State theory of money; it has to do with a monopoly on money creation. This is the reason why, according to Ricardo, PLQ may be applied to paper money:

> It is on this principle that paper money circulates: the whole charge for paper money may be considered as seignorage. Though it has no intrinsic value, yet, by limiting its quantity, its value in exchange is as great as an equal denomination of coin, or of bullion in that coin ... There is no point more important in issuing paper money, than to be fully impressed with the effects which follow from the principle of limitation of quantity. (Ibid.)

PLQ implies that the value of bank notes is neither determined by its material content ('intrinsic') nor fixed by the State, but entirely depends on the existence of a monopoly of issue. The equivalence of a £1 bank note with a £1 metallic coin can then be obtained through the issuance of an appropriate quantity of notes.

It is worthwhile noting that PLQ applies to publicly minted coins and privately issued notes as well, provided the creation of each type of circulating medium is monopolized. A consequence is that, in a mixed monetary system like the one in England, where metallic coins and bank notes circulated side by side, the policy of the Bank of England – which had a monopoly on the note issue within a radius of 65 miles around London – not only influenced the value of notes but also the circulating value of the metallic coins, since it affected the aggregate quantity of money:

> After the establishment of Banks, the State has not the sole power of coining or issuing money. The currency may as effectually be increased by paper as by coin; so that if a State were to debase its money, and limit its quantity, it could not support its value, because the Banks would have an equal power of adding to the whole quantity of circulation. (Ibid.: 354)

Thus, it is the stability of the value of the currency itself – and not only of the paper part of the circulating medium – that requires an adequate note issue, hence the necessity for stating the right principles on which it should be based. The previous quotation continues:

> On these principles, it will be seen that it is not necessary that paper money should be payable in specie to secure its value; it is only necessary that its quantity should be regulated according to the value of the metal which is declared to be the standard. (Ibid.)

The first (negative) sentence refers to convertibility and should not be misunderstood: convertibility of bank notes *is* necessary – otherwise, its quantity not being regulated by a standard, the inconvertible currency 'would be exposed to all the fluctuations' (see the first quotation above from *Works*, IV: 59). What is *not* necessary is convertibility *in specie* (coins). The second (affirmative) sentence states that the value of the standard should regulate the quantity of notes, a recollection of the above 1816 extract. I will first analyse the influence of the standard on the value of money and then I will examine how it regulates the quantity of notes.

The theory of the monetary standard

During the 1822–23 debates in Parliament about the consequences of the resumption of note convertibility, Ricardo defended himself against the accusation of having in 1819 promoted a plan now responsible for the observed deflation:

> He [Ricardo] had undoubtedly given an opinion in 1819, that, by the measure then proposed, the prices of commodities would not be altered more than 5 per cent; but, let it be explained under what circumstances that opinion had been given. The difference in 1819, between paper

and gold, was 5 per cent, and the paper being brought, by the bill of 1819, up to the gold standard, he had considered that, as the value of the currency was only altered 5 per cent, there could be no greater variation than 5 per cent, in the result as to prices. But this calculation had always been subject to a supposition, that no change was to take place in the value of gold . . . [However, since then] No doubt, gold had altered in value, and why? Why, because the Bank [of England], from the moment of the passing of the bill in 1819, set their faces against the due execution of it . . . By their measures they [the Bank] occasioned a demand for gold, which was, in no way, necessarily consequent upon the bill of 1819; and so raising the value of gold in the general market of the world, they changed the value of the standard with reference to which our currency had been calculated, in a manner which had not been presumed upon . . . By increasing the value of gold 5 per cent, it had become necessary to raise the value of paper 10 per cent, instead of 5 per cent, to make it conform to the enhanced value of gold. (*Works*, V: 311–12)

Ricardo thus stated that, gold being the standard, the change in the value of money in terms of commodities in general was equal to the change in the value of gold plus the change in the value of money in terms of gold. Since the value of money in terms of gold is the reciprocal of the money price of gold, the following relation holds:

$$\dot{v}_M = \dot{v}_G - \dot{p}_G \qquad (1)$$

with $\dot{v}_M$ the rate of change of the value of money in terms of commodities, $\dot{v}_G$ the rate of change of the value of gold in terms of all other commodities, and $\dot{p}_G$ the rate of change of the money price of gold. In the case observed by Ricardo: $10\% = 5\% - (-5\%)$.

The value of gold is determined at the world level, and, as for any commodity produced in competitive conditions, reflects its difficulty of production, which increases when production has to be increased. The variation in the value of gold is thus not only influenced by changes in mining and in the demand for luxury uses, but also by the characteristics of the monetary systems operative in various parts of the world: the more reserves they required to secure issuing banks, the more the value of gold tended to increase, *ceteris paribus*. This is why Ricardo held the Bank of England responsible for half the 10 per cent deflation that occurred after the resumption of cash payments, since its behaviour of building excess reserves had provoked an increased demand in the world market for gold, resulting in an estimated 5 per cent increase in the value of that metal.

The second factor of variation in the value of money, as shown in equation (1), was changes in the market price of gold: a change in the quantity of money was translated into a change in the value of money (with an opposite sign) through a change in the money price of gold (with the same sign). In a gold standard monetary system, this was the meaning attached by Ricardo to 'the principle of limitation of quantity': *ceteris paribus*, an increase in the quantity of convertible bank notes diminished the value of money (in terms of commodities) since it increased in the same proportion the money price of the standard (gold). The focus was then on the relation between the quantity of money and the price of gold, *not* the relation between the quantity of money and the general price level, as would later be emphasized by the quantity theory of money. The charges levelled against Ricardo, of having postulated a strict proportionality between the quantity of money and the general price level and neglected the adjustment process by which the latter responds to a change in the former, are consequently groundless: proportionality and adjustment concern the market price of gold, not the general price level (for a detailed analysis of the relation between the quantity of money and the market price of the standard, see Deleplace, 2013).

This fundamental difference between Ricardo's 'principle of limitation of quantity [of money]' and the usual quantity theory of money is testified by Ricardo's repeated insistence on dispelling the confusion between a fall in the value of money and a depreciation of money. The previous quotation was immediately preceded by the warning:

> The hon. gentleman, and those who supported his opinions, were always confounding the terms 'depreciation', and '[diminution in] value'. A currency might be depreciated, without falling in value; it might fall in value, without being depreciated, because depreciation is estimated only by reference to a standard. (*Works*, V: 310–11)

Thus for Ricardo the price of gold was not a proxy of the general price level:

> With reference to the currency, he [Ricardo] had said and he now repeated it, that the price of gold was the index of the depreciation of the currency, not the index of the value of the currency, and it was in this that he had been misunderstood. (Speech in Parliament, 12 June 1822, ibid.: 203–4)

The sentence 'A currency might be depreciated, without falling in value' does not contradict equation (1): *ceteris paribus*, a fall in the value of money is a necessary consequence of depreciation, but it does not happen if the depreciation of the currency is exactly compensated by an increase in the value of gold.

Equation (1) shows that the value of money might be stabilized if: (a) the monetary standard was selected on the basis of its manifesting small variations in value, and (b) the price of the monetary standard was prevented from varying. The first requirement implied an appropriate choice of the standard, the second one an appropriate design of the monetary system, the latter being the proper object of the Ingot Plan. I will now examine the first requirement before studying the second one in details.

The issue of how to minimize the variability of the value of the monetary standard raises two questions. The first one concerns the uniqueness of the monetary standard. As early as 1810, Ricardo had opposed the double standard (gold and silver), on the grounds of the unavoidable change in the effective standard that it would entail: 'No permanent measure of value can be said to exist in any nation while the circulating medium consists of two metals, because they are constantly subject to vary in value with respect to each other' (*Works*, III: 65). It was so because the market ratio of the price of gold to that of silver was subject to changes due to the respective conditions of production of the two metals, as for every commodity, whereas the relative value of gold to silver in the coins was legally fixed. Whenever the market ratio fell below the legal ratio, no one would bring silver to the mint to be coined, because it was more advantageous to sell it in the market for gold coins or notes convertible into gold coins; gold became the de facto standard. Therefore, even if it was legally proclaimed (as before 1797), there could never be practically a double standard, except by chance when the market ratio happened to coincide with the legal ratio. Ricardo's opposition to the double standard would be reiterated in *Proposals* (p. 63), in *Principles* (pp. 366–71), and as late as 1823 when financier Alexander Baring launched a campaign favouring its reintroduction (see Ricardo's hitherto unpublished letter dated 19 January 1823 in Deleplace, Depoortère, and Rieucau, 2013).

The second question concerns the selection of the metal that should be chosen as sole standard. Consistently with the requirement of the smallest variations in value, the selected metal had to be the one the least affected by changes in the conditions of production. This is the reason why, after having favoured silver in *Proposals* (p. 63) because of its use as standard by most foreign countries, Ricardo changed his view in favour of gold in 1819, when he learnt that machinery was 'particularly applicable to the silver mines', a factor that could 'conduce to an increased quantity of that metal and an alteration of its value' (*Works*, V: 391). Gold being then chosen as standard, silver had to be used as token currency, with a seigniorage raising its legal value above its intrinsic one and restrictions about access to coinage and legal tender.

One remark is important here. The criterion of the smallest variations in value to select the standard faced, in Ricardo's view, logical difficulties. The fact that gold was less exposed than silver (or other commodities like corn) to changes in the conditions of production was not enough to assert that it was less variable in value than other commodities. The value of gold in equation (1) is expressed in terms of all other commodities; hence, as Ricardo recognized in the sixth section of Chapter I introduced in the third edition of *Principles* (1821), it cannot be 'invariable' since changes in the distribution between wages and profits affect the value of gold in terms of the commodities produced with a ratio of fixed capital to labour different from what it is in the production of gold. To rule out this other cause of variability (the distribution of income, and not only the difficulty of production), Ricardo assumes that the above ratio in the gold industry is the average of what it is in the production of all other commodities:

> May not gold be considered as a commodity produced with such proportions of the two kinds of capital as approach nearest to the average quantity employed in the production of most commodities? May not these proportions be so nearly equally distant from the two extremes, the one where little fixed capital is used, the other where little labour is employed, as to form a just mean between them? (*Works*, I: 45–6)

To put it briefly, in order to be more eligible than any other commodity as monetary standard, gold should not only have a less variable difficulty of production, but it should also be produced with a capitalistic structure being the average of that of the economy as a whole. The first assumption might be debated as a matter of fact, but the second was merely a postulate. This is probably the reason why Ricardo felt it necessary to explore this question in his last manuscript before his death, entitled 'Absolute Value and Exchangeable Value'. As is well-known, this draft manuscript (*Works*, IV: 361–412) was discovered and published by Sraffa, who underlined that Ricardo's search for an invariable measure of value was the basis of his own 'conception of a standard measure of value as a medium between two extremes' (Sraffa, 1960: 94). The postulate about the conditions of production of gold remains, however, the weak point of Ricardo's integration of money in his theory of value.

Now it is time to look at the plan designed by Ricardo to ensure the stability of the price of gold and, still more importantly, the security of the monetary system.

The regulation of the note issue by the standard: the Ingot Plan
Ricardo had entitled his 1816 pamphlet *Proposals for an Economical and Secure Currency*. The two aims of his plan announced in this title were summarized in the

sentence that opens the long passage of the pamphlet quoted in the second and third editions of *Principles*:

> To secure the public against any other variations in the value of the currency than those to which the standard itself is subject, and, at the same time, to carry on the circulation with a medium the least expensive, is to attain the most perfect state to which a currency can be brought. (*Works*, IV: 66; see also *Works*, I: 356–7)

This quotation continues with the following passage, which embodies the main technical provisions of the plan:

> and we should possess all these advantages by subjecting the Bank [of England] to the delivery of uncoined gold or silver at the Mint standard and price, in exchange for their notes, instead of the delivery of guineas; by which means paper would never fall below the value of bullion, without being followed by a reduction of its quantity. To prevent the rise of paper above the value of bullion, the Bank should be also obliged to give their paper in exchange for standard gold at the price of 3*l*. [£3] 17*s*. per ounce . . . The most perfect liberty should be given, at the same time, to export or import every description of bullion. These transactions in bullion would be very few in number, if the Bank regulated their loans and issues of paper by the criterion which I have so often mentioned, namely, the price of standard bullion, without attending to the absolute quantity of paper in circulation. (*Works*, IV: 66–7; see also *Works*, I: 357–8)

These provisions reflect the two principles on which the plan was founded. First, there is what may be called the 'ingot principle': the Bank of England notes had to be convertible into bullion (bars), instead of specie (coins) as they were prior to 1797. Symmetrically, these notes could be obtained from the Bank against bullion at a fixed legal price, slightly below the mint price of £3.17.10½ per standard ounce at which they were convertible. Second, the quantity of bank notes issued had to vary inversely with changes in the observed market price of bullion, instead of being left to the discretion of the Bank, as before. This provision constituted a 'judicious management of the quantity' of paper money (*Proposals*: 57) and may thus be called the 'management principle'.

The specificity of both principles should be underlined. The ingot principle makes sense of the above-quoted sentence in *Principles* (*Works*, I: 354), that 'it is not necessary that paper money should be payable in specie to secure its value': Ricardo was against the inconvertibility of notes, but he favoured another kind of convertibility than the one usually put forward before (and also after) him. The management principle meant that the issue of notes had to be modified according to an objective criterion – the market price of bullion – which in no way implied any judgement on an appropriate level of the stock of circulating notes or of the metallic reserves of the Bank (as would later be the case with the Currency Principle). The object of these two principles was twofold: stabilizing the market price of bullion, thus preventing the currency from being depreciated or appreciated; and increasing the security of the monetary system. Let us look successively at these two goals.

With convertibility of notes into bullion as into specie, arbitrage makes the market price of bullion fluctuate with supply and demand between two fixed limits depending on the monetary regime, but the width of this margin is consequently not the same. Let us call P_G the market price of an ounce of gold bullion and P_L its legal price. With convertibility of notes into freely exportable bullion, the cost of fraudulently melting the coins obtained from the Bank disappeared, so that arbitrage ensured that the market price of gold could not be higher than its legal price. Symmetrically, the charge of interest while waiting for the delivery of coins by the mint was eliminated, so that arbitrage ensured that the market price of gold could not be lower than its legal price minus the commission b of the Bank, which could be made as little as desirable. As a consequence:

$$P_L \geq P_G \geq P_L(1 - b) \tag{2}$$

In Ricardo's terms:

> That regulation is merely suggested, to prevent the value of money from varying from the value of bullion more than the trifling difference between the prices at which the Bank should buy and sell, and which would be an approximation to that uniformity in its value, which is acknowledged to be so desirable. (*Works*, IV: 67; see also *Works*, I: 358)

One object of the Ingot Plan was then to ensure a higher stabilization of the market price of bullion, hence, for a given value of the commodity chosen as standard, a higher stabilization of the value of money itself (because of equation (1)). But there was another object, still more important. Inequalities (2) were ruling in the normal course of events, but when the pressure on the currency became hard, the two sides of the inequalities were exposed to different threats. Whenever the Bank remained open to the public, it could absorb all the bullion that depressed the market and consequently appreciated the currency; the only drawback imposed on the Bank by the Ingot Plan was to force it to accumulate a sterile asset. On the other hand when, for any reason, the market price of bullion increased, signalling a depreciation of the currency, this movement was hindered by arbitrage as long as the Bank had enough reserves to ensure the convertibility of its notes. The suspension of cash payments decided in 1797 had shown that this could not always be guaranteed. The issue at stake here was no longer the range of variation of the value of the currency in normal times, but the security of the monetary system, which could be jeopardized by a drain of the Bank reserves. As the title of the 1816 pamphlet made explicit, convertibility into bullion was supposed to increase the security of the currency, as compared with convertibility into specie. How precisely was it so?

With convertibility into specie, one had to distinguish between three types of drain. The first one was caused by a panic, when notes were brought back to the Bank, not to substitute a circulating medium for another, but to hoard the metal itself as a store of value:

> Against such panics, banks have no security, *on any system*; from their very nature they are subject to them, as at no time can there be in a Bank, or in a country, so much specie or bullion as the monied individuals of such country have a right to demand. (*Works*, IV: 68; original emphasis; see also *Works*, I: 358)

This kind of run could then jeopardize the monetary system because notes issued through discounting of commercial bills were not backed by corresponding metallic reserves. This was the price to pay for issuing money to the benefit of owners of commercial capital and not only of precious metals. For this kind of drain the Ingot Plan could not improve upon convertibility into specie because the threat to security was consubstantial with banking activity itself.

The second type of drain was caused by the coexistence of coins and notes in the domestic monetary system; it was thus an internal drain. Old coins becoming light through debasement in one way or another while keeping their nominal legal value, the market price of bullion increased, and new full-bodied coins were demanded from the Bank (against notes) to be melted and sold in the market to pocket the difference. Facing a drain of its reserves, the Bank had to purchase bullion in the market to have it coined, then sustaining the market price above the legal price; this process could go on indefinitely, imposing losses on the Bank. In the Ingot Plan, notes convertible into bullion did not aim at complementing coins but at eliminating them altogether (as quoted above: 'A currency is in its most perfect state when it consists wholly of paper money'). The elimination of the metallic currency radically prevented this internal drain from occurring, by suppressing the defects that were attached to that kind of currency and caused that drain.

There was an additional advantage: having no longer to guard itself against an internal drain, the Bank could hold a smaller reserve. The system was then more 'economical' *because* it was more 'secure'. This 'economy' contributed in turn to the stabilization of the value of money: as long as the market price of bullion remained equal to its legal level, the circulation of notes could increase (to accommodate the needs of trade) without the size of the reserve having to increase (as quoted above, the Bank would not have to bother about 'attending to the absolute quantity of paper in circulation'). Consequently, the working of the monetary system did not alter the world demand for gold. The changes in the value of the standard were then limited to real causes; in equation (1), the Ingot Plan not only reduced $\dot{p}_G$ to zero but also eliminated domestic monetary causes of $\dot{v}_G$.

A third type of drain remained: the external one, when gold was obtained from the Bank to be exported. To understand how this external drain could be handled in the Ingot Plan, one needs to consider international adjustment.

The consequences of the stabilization of the price of gold for international adjustment
The analysis of international adjustment rests on the relation between changes in the internal value of money, as given by equation (1), and changes in the external value of money, that is, the exchange rate of the domestic currency in terms of foreign ones. In Ricardo's time, the literature on this question was grounded in two accepted views: the gold-points mechanism and the price-specie flow mechanism. To sum up Ricardo's contribution, it amounted to specifying the conditions under which the stabilization of the exchange rate by the gold-points mechanism could be more effective and to substitute a policy rule for the price-specie flow mechanism.

As early as his first writings during the debates of 1809–11, Ricardo explicitly mentioned what is known as the gold-points mechanism. For example:

> While the circulating medium consists, therefore, of coin undebased, or of paper-money immediately exchangeable for undebased coin, the exchange can never be more above, or more below, par, than the expenses attending the transportation of the precious metals. But when it consists of a depreciated paper-money, it necessarily will fall according to the degree of the depreciation. (*Works*, III: 72)

Based on international arbitrage by the bullion traders, this mechanism operated whatever the monetary regimes in the various countries (for a detailed study of gold standard international adjustment with stable and unstable monetary regimes, see Marcuzzo and Rosselli, 1991). But the range of variation of the exchange rate that it allowed did depend on these regimes. This is why the Ingot Plan also had consequences for the stabilization of the exchange rate, because of the gold-points mechanism.

Let e be the exchange rate of the pound £ in the foreign currency f, and $P_L^f/P_L^£$ the legal par of exchange between the two currencies. For the sake of simplicity, let us suppose that gold could be purchased and sold in the foreign country at the legal price P_L^f, so as to concentrate on the influence of the monetary regime in England. International arbitrage ensured that e was constrained around $P_L^f/P_L^£$ by limits that depended on the various costs associated with the import of gold to or its export from England. One was the transportation cost, which we may suppose identical at the import and export (equal to c as a proportion of the value transported). The other was the difference between the price $P_G^£$ at which gold could be sold and purchased for notes in the London market and its legal price $P_L^£$, this difference being constrained by inequalities (2).

As a consequence, the range of variation of the exchange rate was given by:

$$\frac{P_L^f}{P_L^£}\frac{1+c}{1-b} \geq e \geq \frac{P_L^f}{P_L^£}(1-c) \tag{3}$$

Thus the stabilization of the market price of bullion not only produced domestic monetary stability but also contributed to the international one.

One should now make the same observation about (3) as about (2): this stabilization occurred in normal times, when the Bank could accommodate the demand for gold against notes. The security of the monetary system required that an external drain (demand for gold for export) could not threaten its metallic reserves. During the debates of 1809–11, Ricardo had stated that an external drain could *only* be caused by an excess issue of notes: an unfavourable exchange was the consequence of the market price of gold being above the legal price – signalling a depreciation of the currency – not the other way round. Consequently, any external drain would be avoided if the Bank reduced its issuing of notes when the market price of bullion tended to increase. As stated in a quotation above, the management principle would ensure that 'these transactions in bullion [at the export or import] would be very few in number' (*Works*, IV: 67; *Works*, I: 357).

It is worthwhile noting that this international adjustment rested only on the stabilization of the price of gold, not on the adjustment of domestic price levels and corresponding changes in the balance of commerce (as in the price-specie flow mechanism). Further, if the same gold standard system à la Ricardo were adopted in every trading nation, the stability of the international monetary system could be achieved without any international movement of gold. Not only would gold stop circulating inside each nation, but it would also stop moving from one nation to another, since the respective domestic quantities of paper money would endogenously adjust, without having to be corrected by the actual export or import of gold. In that sense, Ricardo's Ingot Plan not only rendered the price-specie flow mechanism useless but the price-bullion flow mechanism also.

Concluding remarks

A careful examination of Ricardo's theory of money leads to one main conclusion: the concept of monetary standard played a central role in that theory. This conclusion may look trivial, since Ricardo is commonly considered as an advocate of the gold standard. But, as compared with monetary orthodoxy that would rule in Britain until the end of the classical gold standard (in 1914), Ricardo's concept of monetary standard – hence his theory of money, as embodied in the 1816 Ingot Plan – had a revolutionary content, which put it far ahead of its time.

In Ricardo's system, the standard is a commodity, which provides an anchor for the currency defined in terms of it, but it is a very specific commodity. It has a world value, determined, like the value of all competitively produced commodities, by its difficulty of production, but its domestic market price is not governed by the gravitation process of supply and demand, for two reasons. First, being the standard in which the unit of account is defined by the State, it is the only commodity that has a legal price, in addition to its market price. Second, the positive (or negative) difference between its market price and its legal price reflects the excess (or deficiency) of the quantity of money in respect to 'the wants of commerce', hence the depreciation (or appreciation) of the currency. Consequently, 'in a sound state of the currency the value of gold may vary, but its price cannot' (evidence before a committee of Parliament, 4 March 1819, *Works*, V: 392). On the basis of equation (1), a corollary of this statement reads as follows: 'in a sound state of the currency', the value of money may vary, but money cannot depreciate or appreciate. The 'most perfect state' of the currency would be achieved if the monetary system were designed in such a way as to prevent depreciation or appreciation, leaving changes in the value of the standard as the sole possible cause of variation in the value of money. In addition, this cause could be restricted to the real factor of change in the value of the standard (its difficulty of production) if the monetary system minimized the pressure on the world production of the commodity (gold) acting as monetary standard: the currency was all the more 'secure' since it was 'economical'.

How to achieve this 'sound' (i.e., 'secure') state of the currency? Two conditions were necessary and sufficient: convertibility of bank notes into bullion (ingot principle) and regulation of their issue so as to maintain the market price of bullion equal to its legal price (management principle). The first principle prevented an internal drain of the gold reserves of the issuing bank (except in the case of a panic, which no monetary system could prevent; see above); the second principle prevented an external drain. These two principles ensured that the currency conformed to the standard (to prevent monetary causes of instability in its value), although it was not issued through the monetization of the standard but of circulating capital (to ensure the fulfilment of the needs of trade). They testified to the fact that money was not subject to physical constraints: in Ricardo's system, the monetary standard is a specific commodity, but money is no commodity at all. No natural laws explain changes in the value of money: they apply in equation (1) to one of their determinants (changes in the value of the standard), but not to the other (changes in the price of the standard, which entirely depends on the institutions ruling the monetary system). The quantity of money is not restricted by the available quantity of gold (whether at the level of the world as a whole or in the reserves of the issuing bank) but is adjusted to 'the wants of commerce'. The soundness of money only depends on the soundness of the plan designed for it.

The standard and the paper currency were then two complementary but distinct features of Ricardo's ideal monetary system, and this distinction is in no way trivial in the history of monetary thought and in the history of money as well. On the one hand, the Ingot Plan led to a demonetization of gold in domestic circulation: gold was the standard of money but no longer money. As Bonar (1923: 298) would put it one century later: 'His [Ricardo's] complete Plan was to be the euthanasia of metal currency.' On the other hand, Ricardo was the first to theorize the gold-exchange standard, by separating domestic circulation (of convertible notes) and foreign payments (in bullion), though preserving a link through gold (which acted as domestic monetary standard and international means of settlement).

About Ricardo there is a double paradox. Although he was no doubt the greatest monetary author in the nineteenth century, his unorthodox ideas had to wait until the twentieth century to be applied. Nevertheless, most historians of economic thought considered and still consider him as an obsolete orthodox. Reading him again shows that he was not only a giant on value, distribution, and accumulation, but on money too.

GHISLAIN DELEPLACE

See also:

Bullionist Controversy; Gold; Natural Quantity of Money; Papers on Money and Banking; Rate of Interest.

References

Blaug, M. (1995), 'Why is the quantity theory of money the oldest surviving theory in economics?' in M. Blaug et al. *The Quantity Theory of Money. From Locke to Keynes and Friedman*, Aldershot, UK and Brookfield, VT: Edward Elgar Publishing, pp. 27–49.

Bonar, J. (1923), 'Ricardo's Ingot Plan: a centenary estimate', *The Economic Journal*, **33**: 281–304; reprinted in J.C. Wood (ed.), *David Ricardo. Critical Assessments, Vol. IV*, London: Routledge, 1991, pp. 25–43.

Deleplace, G. (2013), 'The role of the standard in Ricardo's theory of money', in Y. Sato and S. Takenaga (eds), *Ricardo on Money and Finance*, Abingdon, UK: Routledge, pp. 115–23.

Deleplace, G., C. Depoortère and N. Rieucau (2013), 'An unpublished letter of David Ricardo on the double standard of money', *The European Journal of the History of Economic Thought*, **20**(1), 1–28.

Laidler, D. (1987), 'Bullionist Controversy', in J. Eatwell, M. Milgate and P. Newman (eds), *The New Palgrave: A Dictionary of Economics, Vol. I*, London: Macmillan, pp. 289–94.

Marcuzzo, M.C. and A. Rosselli (1991), *Ricardo and the Gold Standard. The Foundations of the International Monetary Order*, London: Macmillan.

Schumpeter, J.A. (1954), *History of Economic Analysis*, New York: Oxford University Press.

Sraffa, P. (1960), *Production of Commodities by Means of Commodities. Prelude to a Critique of Economic Theory*, Cambridge, UK: Cambridge University Press.

Viner, J. (1937), *Studies in the Theory of International Trade*, New York: Harper.

National Debt

Ricardo's contribution to the debate on national debt has to be seen within the context of a substantial literature, especially that accompanying the increase in public borrowing during the extraordinarily long period of wars with France from 1792 to 1815 (O'Brien, 1999, III). At first glance the problem was not too serious. The total debt charge in 1792 was 55 per cent of government expenditure (50 per cent of tax revenue); in 1817 the corresponding figures were 46 and 48, and in 1821 they were 55 and 53. However, the jump between 1817 and 1821, following the abolition of the income tax in 1816 (final receipts were in 1820) was very marked. Even more significant was the rise in the debt charge, and the debt itself, in relation to GDP. In 1801 the debt charge was 7.2 per cent of GDP; in 1821 it was 11 per cent. Most strikingly of all was the huge size of the debt itself in relation to GDP. In 1801 the debt was 197 per cent of GDP; the figure for 1821 was 288 per cent. Even allowing for the fact that contemporaries would have had little information on GDP, and the possible criticism of modern estimates based on census figures, this is remarkable. The war had been, to a remarkable extent, debt financed. (Data are from Mitchell, 1962: 366, 388, 391–2, 396, 402.) To contemporaries, the abolition of the income tax was a particular concern (O'Brien, 1999, IV). As Preston ([1816] 1999: 83–4) and D. Buchanan ([1817] 1999: 153–4) pointed out, by 1814 the income tax was vital; indeed, it had been yielding about half the annual debt service charge (see also Shoup, 1960: 144–8, 234–5). Ricardo himself was not in favour of the income tax – indeed, astonishingly for a matter of great economic controversy during his lifetime, he largely ignored it. Rather than raise taxes to service the debt, Ricardo wished to see the debt wiped out.

Ricardo's views on national debt are apparent from a number of sources. The main one is the 1820 article that he wrote for the Supplement to the fourth to sixth editions of *Encyclopaedia Britannica*, entitled 'Funding System'. He also made a number of references to the debt in Parliamentary speeches, discussed the matter in correspondence, and alluded to it briefly in his *Principles*. All of these are included in the Sraffa (1951–73) edition of Ricardo, which will be referred to here by volume and page number.

He had himself become enormously wealthy through operations as a contractor for national debt. Despite claiming publicly that he had no particular personal interest in the debt (*Works*, V: 86), he bid for every loan from March 1806; from 1811 to the end of the war in 1815 he was a contractor (albeit usually in partnership) for every loan, and he was an unsuccessful bidder in 1819; and he is widely believed to have made £1 million (more than £69 million at 2010 prices) on the news of the victory of Waterloo alone (*Works*, X: 75–91). He was a contractor for loans totalling £73.5 million. Taking 1810 as the mid-point for indexation purposes, this would now be about £4500 million. If, conservatively (because the government also borrowed at 5 per cent in which case the contractor's charge was also 5 per cent) we take the figure of 2 per cent, which Ricardo gives as the contractor's charge on an issue of debt with a 3 per cent coupon (*Works*, IV: 184), this would yield £90 million yield at today's prices. In addition, there were substantial profits accruing to the contractor from the emergence of a premium on new issue of debt, as exemplified by the Waterloo episode. Indeed, the estimates of Ricardo's estate, given these figures, seem extraordinarily low. Sraffa (*Works*, X: 103) puts the figure at between £675000 and £775000. At today's prices that would amount to between £63 million and

£72 million. Even allowing for the fall in land values after 1815, this seems a very low figure given the profit on Waterloo alone.

The evils of national debt

According to Ricardo there were three methods of financing a war – an increase in taxation, increased public borrowing, and increased public borrowing together with extra taxes to finance a 'sinking fund'. Ricardo was satisfied that the present value of all three methods was the same (*Works*, IV: 185–7). His strong preference was for tax as war finance. It would, he believed, discourage war, an argument previously advanced by Robert Hamilton ([1818] 1995: 457–8) on whose work concerning the sinking fund Ricardo leant heavily. He made remarkable claims about the ease of paying sufficient taxes to finance a war (*Works*, I: 245; IV: 188), believing that those faced with large tax demands could simply sell property, or borrow at interest to meet the demands. He believed that war taxes would produce 'little permanent derangement' (*Works*, IV: 189). Of course, the interest rate would be higher for private individuals, though Ricardo assumed that they would borrow at the same rate as government (presumably because both were ostensibly constrained by the upper limit of the usury laws at 5 per cent). Even if in the event individuals would have had to pay a higher rate, Ricardo's argument implies that they would have to borrow less than the state if it resorted to war finance through debt (Roberts, 1942: 259). The total interest charge would thus be lower. They would, however, have to write down the value of private capital, in the way that Ricardo assumed taxpayers, faced with a future stream of tax payments, did, so that there was a loss of wealth in both cases, a matter that he neglected.

Behind all this lay a remarkably crude savings function, where the choice between consumption and saving (equated with investment) was a function of the tax demand (ibid.: 258). Indeed, this enabled Ricardo to assume that a tax would fall on private consumption, while public borrowing would soak up capital. The national capital stock would thus be protected by tax finance rather than debt creation. Saving for investment is apparently autonomous, and unaffected by changes in the level of tax demanded. Yet any individual required to pay extra tax would normally cut back on saving rather than sell property or borrow. There was thus no basis for the clear distinction that Ricardo made between tax and debt creation in their effect on national capital (*Works*, I: 247; IV: 187–8).

At all events a national debt existed. Ricardo's aversion to it was so strong that, as Shoup (1960: 156) observed, 'Ricardo allowed his tone to become uncharacteristically shrill'. Ricardo described the debt as a 'one of the most terrible scourges which was ever invented to afflict a nation' (*Works*, IV: 197). It was an even greater evil than the Corn Laws (*Works*, V: 38, 187). It was 'an evil which almost any sacrifice would not be too great to get rid of' (ibid.: 34) and was 'the most oppressive burden on the industry of the country' (ibid.: 472). Taxes raised to service the debt brought about capital emigration (*Works*, I: 247–8; V: 21, 33). As deflation increased the weight of fixed taxes, their real burden increased. Even national bankruptcy was a possibility, as the weight of service taxes rose with each outbreak of war (*Works*, I: 248–9; Shoup, 1960: 156–7), though it was not clear why this should be more onerous than greatly increasing taxation at that point in order to pay for the war directly.

It was not that the debt had been incurred incompetently; Ricardo was dismissive of the argument that borrowing in the 3 per cents at 60 left the country with a larger nominal debt than borrowing in 5 per cents (the 3 per cents would rise to par after the war) when interest rates fell (Hamilton [1818] 1995: 608–18). As a market professional, Ricardo knew that it was harder to borrow in 5 per cents than 3 per cents – there was a limited demand for the former. In 1798 the 3 per cents had been at 50, implying a market rate of 6 per cent, which would have put the 5 per cents at £83 6s 8d but they were at 73 (*Works*, IV: 184, but see *Works*, VIII: 320, 322 for Trower's cogent objections). Ricardo, locked into his model, did not see the interest rate falling to around 3 per cent on the return of peace, though this did happen in the 1830s (Mitchell, 1962: 455, 460). There was thus no possibility, Ricardo believed, of the 3 per cents rising to par, and he had for long no intention of paying off the debt at par, but at what he anticipated would be the market values, given that he expected wartime interest rates to persist post-war.

Ricardo was not prepared to countenance alternative views of the debt. He ignored the possibility that economic growth would reduce the burden of a given tax charge – constancy of such a burden was central to his argument for a capital levy (*Works*, IV: 187). He dismissed the sensible view of Malthus and McCulloch that the existence of a readily purchasable security like public debt could both benefit saving and widen the distribution of wealth (*Works*, II: 444–5; McCulloch [1863] 1975: 405). Malthus's argument was perfectly reasonable; the debt provided both secure investment and, as Ricardo knew, profit opportunities for the non-landed middle class who might later, like Ricardo, invest in land. This was a dynamic argument but Ricardo responded with the purely static idea that there was a *stock* of capital, before the creation of the debt, which remained unaltered. Wider considerations, such as J.S. Mill's later idea ([1848] 1923: 877) that public goods could legitimately be funded by debt, did not enter into Ricardo's discussion. He was instead concerned that debt allowed government to expand with little check. He had an extraordinarily narrow view of the role of government (Churchman, 2001: 57) and, as Shoup (1960: 249) has pointed out, was opposed to all taxation (see also Roberts, 1942: 257). He voted against all tax increases in Parliament, and in favour of all tax reductions (Cannan, 1894, II: 420). He even envisaged the possibility of getting rid of the customs and excise if the national debt were repaid (*Works*, IV: 190; V: 268). Oddly, despite all his concern about the burden of debt service taxes, Ricardo seems to have been untroubled by the distributional consequences (*Works*, I: 244–6). Given the 1800–15 tax base, and the narrow ownership of public debt, such consequences would have been highly regressive. But Ricardo, locked into his model, and telescoping the long run and the short run, believed all taxes paid by the labourers were passed on (*Works*, I: 159–61; V: 26–7). It was because of the long-run effect on economic activity that Ricardo wished to get rid of debt service taxes, though he rejected the idea of short-run effects (*Works*, VIII: 145) as inconsistent with his model. As Shoup (1960: 249) has put it, Ricardo's passages on taxation 'leave the impression each time that he had just come from rereading some part of the *Principles*'. In summary, then, Ricardo's concern was with the effect of debt creation on the capital stock and with the possibility of bankruptcy through a rise in the real burden of taxation as a result of deflation, itself partially brought about by a loss of precious metal as a result of uncompetitive prices due to taxation.

Ricardo had subsidiary objections to the debt. In particular he was extremely hostile to the Bank of England, which he believed to have profited from debt management (*Works*, IV: 51–4, 81–99) about which he was extremely indignant (*Works*, V: 100;

VI: 333, 347). (Why management was more objectionable than contracting remained unclear.) He proposed that management of the debt should be taken away from the Bank and placed in the hands of commissioners (*Works*, IV: 289–91; VI: 268). It is, however, implausible that, as has been suggested (Anderson and Tollison, 1986), he sought to abolish the debt in order to transfer the burden of tax, by imposing a capital levy on all classes of property while the landed classes would enjoy a reduction in the land and assessed taxes. For in practise it is inconceivable that the vast majority of a capital levy would fall anywhere else than on land (though Ricardo also proposed a substantial levy on the holders of national debt – Asso and Barucci, 1988: 28), and Ricardo had become a major land-holder.

Debt and sinking fund

Ricardo accepted that a sinking fund, used to buy back debt, and then employing the interest on such debt to make further purchases, would be valuable if it really worked (*Works*, I: 248–9; V: 268–9). (It would not, however, actually permit any reduction in tax until the debt was paid off, as debt owned by the fund would still have to be serviced.) As late as 1816 he still held that government should not meddle with the fund (*Works*, VII: 37–8, 106). But Robert Hamilton, to whose work Ricardo's attention seems to have been drawn by Francis Place (*Works*, IV: 145; VIII: 66n), exposed the fund as a sham ([1818] 1995: 602–7), and Ricardo accepted this. Hamilton's work was much more substantial and systematic than Ricardo's *Encyclopaedia* article, and Ricardo acknowledged its value (*Works*, VIII: 78–9). Not only did he follow Hamilton on the futility of the fund, but also on its history in the war years, and he may also have been influenced by Hamilton's advocacy of greater use of taxation to finance war. Above all, he accepted that the fund, instead of diminishing debt had actually increased it, through increasing government revenue requirements. Having read Hamilton, the only one of the books sent by Place (apart from that of Price – *Works*, IV: 151, 184; VIII: 64, 66) to which he seems to have paid any attention, Ricardo viewed the fund as simply a device for raising government expenditure. He refused to support taxes destined for the fund, on the grounds that government would always raid it (*Works*, IV: 190–95; V: 20–21; VIII: 33).

Given that a sinking fund was ruled out, Ricardo's solution to the burden of debt was a capital levy to pay it off. His plan first appeared in his *Principles* (*Works*, I: 247–8; see also *Works*, V: 21, 34–5, 38–9) and Ricardo believed this to be his own special contribution to the issue (*Works*, IV: 145, 196–7; VIII: 78) to such an extent that he seems to have been touchy about priority (*Works*, VIII: 144). However, he was forced to accept that the plan was entirely unoriginal (*Works*, V: 37) and indeed, as Brougham pointed out to Ricardo, it was one that had regularly surfaced since its first appearance from the pen of one Archibald Hutcheson in 1721 (Hutcheson [1714] 1721). (See also Shoup, 1960: 161n on earlier schemes.) Given such a long history, it is not surprising that a great many difficulties with it had previously been pointed out, as Brougham emphasized (*Works*, V: 40–41), and it was a radical step beyond recognizing the burden of debt. Hutcheson's priority was also emphasized by McCulloch (1829; [1863] 1975: 461). The core of Ricardo's argument was that the present value of £20 million payable now as a levy was the same as £1 million per annum in perpetuity, as the prospective flow of debt service taxes (or £1.2 million per annum with a debt sinking fund of £200 000 per annum over 45 years) (*Works*, IV: 187–8; see also *Works*, I: 247). Ricardo persisted with this claim, without exploring its sensitivity to the underlying assumptions (*Works*, VIII: 187, 238–9). The most crucial assumption was that of discounting the tax flow to infinity. This involved a degree of unrealism, which it is hard to defend and that was much criticized by later writers, notably in Italy (D.H. Buchanan, 1958: 114–22). More realistic time periods yield rather different results. If we compare an individual faced with a tax charge of £1000 per annum, or a capital levy of £20000, then discounted over 20 years (probably quite as far as it was reasonable to look forward, particularly given life expectancies) the present value of the tax stream is £12462 not £20000. Over 12 years, which his friend Trower seems to have envisaged when putting forward his own scheme, the sum is only £8863. The neat equivalence is also upset by different interest rates. As noted above, Ricardo was strangely confident that the rate of interest would remain at 5 per cent because, as ever, he was fixed in his model (*Works*, VIII: 145) in which the rate of interest was determined by the marginal rate of profit in agriculture. If, however, we consider the rate of interest ruling in the 1830s, which was about 3.5 per cent, we find that over 20 years the corresponding present value is £14212 and over 12 years it is £9663. So equality of present values is simply a special case.

Ricardo's claim concerning present values has become embedded in the literature under the name 'Ricardian equivalence' (though in the different context of the argument that deficit spending by government will not raise demand as taxpayers will capitalize future debt service taxes – Barro, 1974). However, it has been argued that such 'equivalence' was not Ricardo's idea, and that Ricardo thought that tax was *better* than debt (Churchman, 2001: 38) while taxpayers preferred debt and a debt service charge. O'Driscoll (1977) sees this as 'fiscal illusion' and adds there is a net wealth effect – people feel better off with the existence of a debt. However, Edgeworth had explained long before that this was not necessarily an illusion; satisfaction levels were not captured by comparison of present values (1915: 76).

Ricardo, however, *did* believe that there was equivalence, to the extent of equality of present values, and used this as the argument for a capital levy – this would, he argued, leave taxpayers no worse off on the basis of present value. The question then arises of the price at which the debt should be redeemed. In general, Ricardo seems to have thought that payment should be at market rather than par values (*Works*, VIII: 144, 147, 157–8). As Cannan pointed out, this involved partial repudiation of the debt (Cannan, 1894, II: 421, 423n – a second repudiation, in addition to charging debt holders a capital levy). Shoup (1960: 161) has also pointed out that Ricardo never explained how, legally, the debt could be retired at market price. Perhaps because of such considerations, Ricardo later advocated repayment at par (*Works*, IX: 173–4). Having changed his position, he now declared that paying off at less than par would be 'a breach of national faith'. It is not clear how long he thought that paying off the debt would take; in 1819 he seems to have thought four to five years (*Works*, V: 39; Asso and Barucci, 1988: 28). In 1820 it two to three years (*Works*, IV: 197). In March 1823 he even suggested two to 12 months (*Works*, V: 270–71).

Ricardo envisaged a puzzling payment mechanism. Government would apparently issue exchequer bills to pay off the debt. These could then be used in payments to government. The money supply would then, he believed, be unaffected (*Works*, V: 39; VIII: 239) though this is odd since whatever would have been used to pay government would then be freed for other purposes. But the real puzzle is the sequence. On the face of it, those paying the capital levy would sell property to pay the levy and government would then use the proceeds to purchase the debt. But it is very difficult to make out from what Ricardo actually wrote that what he must have envisaged is that government would issue the exchequer bills before any receipts from the capital levy, for he argued that those selling property would be able to sell to those who had parted with government securities (*Works*, I: 247–8; V: 34–5; see also IV: 197).

The problems with such a drastic approach to national debt were legion, and evident to his contemporaries. Ricardo was dismissive of the idea of capital market disruption (*Works*, IV: 175–80) and only reluctantly acknowledged the effect on inventory values of repealing debt service taxes (ibid.: 181–2), though Hamilton ([1818] 1995: 607) had recognized this. There were serious valuation problems for a capital levy, since Ricardo intended the levy to cover merchants and manufacturers' capital (*Works*, V: 86, 472) as well as land and national debt holdings themselves (Asso and Barucci, 1988: 28). There was the likelihood of a capital flight when a levy plan was made public, and Ricardo apparently had in mind draconian measures to prevent this (*Works*, V: 38; VIII: 239) though he never explained what they were. Perhaps most remarkably, the professions would escape such a levy – as J.S. Mill was later to point out, this involved a switch in the burden of taxation. The point was not new; David Hume had made the same criticisms of Hutcheson's plan a century earlier (Hume [1752] 1999: 184). Ricardo's astonishing response to this was that subsequent entry into the professions would lower earnings until they were at the previous level relative to other sectors of the economy (*Works*, IV: 188–9; VIII: 238–9).

Nor did the repayment of an existing national debt guarantee that a new one would not be created. This raised the possibility of a series of capital levies, and Ricardo privately admitted the danger of creating a new debt if the old one were paid off (*Works*, VIII: 148). The Duke of Gloucester, not widely regarded as an intellectual, also pointed out to Ricardo that, if a country were debt free, this might encourage war (*Works*, X: 187n). Ricardo would brook no opposition.

When Brougham, who was, after all, a lawyer, pointed out that there were problems over legal titles, which would make a fortune for lawyers in the event of asset sales to meet a levy (*Works*, V: 40–41), Ricardo simply suggested overriding titles (*Works*, V: 268–9; VIII: 239). According to Ricardo, if A held a property but B really owned it, B would have had to sell it anyway to meet the levy. It was an extraordinarily static argument; B would not be given the choice of which property to sell from his possessions.

Ricardo also suggested that the landowners would not mind parting with property to fund a levy, if the levy left them all in the same relative position as before, an argument that ignored critical valuation problems and assumed that relative rather than absolute wealth was the only consideration (*Works*, VIII: 238; Roberts, 1942: 265). Just how large a proportion of property might be involved Ricardo never made public, but the remarkable document discovered by Asso and Barucci (1988) shows that he envisaged a figure as high as 25 per cent (Asso and Barucci date the manuscript at 1819). The nominal debt in 1819 was £844.3 million. Ricardo uses a figure of £650 million, suggesting that £100 of debt in 3 per cent consols would be paid at £77. This value implies a yield on consols of 3.9 per cent, which is indeed the figure for 1818, while that for 1819 of 4.2 per cent (Mitchell, 1962: 455) implies a value of £71 for consols. Holders of debt faced two repudiations: a capital levy on their holdings of 25 per cent, and a reduction from face value of 23 per cent. Thus, holders of debt would pay £162 million, on a value of the debt that Ricardo gave as £650 million, the remaining £488 million to be paid by landowners, farmers, manufacturers and merchants, whose capital Ricardo estimated, presumably on the basis of income tax data (Asso and Barucci, 1988: 20n), at £1952 million. In addition, the intrusion involved in the assessments, a highly contentious issue in relation to the income tax, and one to which Ricardo himself was sensitive, referring to 'the obnoxious measure of prying into every man's concerns, and arming commissioners with powers repugnant to the habits and feelings of a free country' (*Works*, I: 161) was not even considered by him in the capital levy context.

Contemporaries had no hesitation in making clear their view that Ricardo's plan was ridiculous. Baring used the word 'absurd' (*Works*, V: 270) and according to Grenfell it was the wildest of all plans (ibid.: 271). Ricardo had to recognize that his plan was regarded as 'chimerical' (ibid.: 39, see also *Works*, VIII: 144, 147n, 197). Yet he remained impervious to criticism. In the House of Commons he stated that 'he had heard no argument to show that the measure he would recommend was not the best policy' (*Works*, V: 55). Indeed, it was clear to his contemporaries that his mind was closed on the subject. According to the diarist J.L. Mallet, Ricardo 'meets you upon every subject that he has studied *with a mind made up*, and opinions in the nature of mathematical truths'. Mallet wrote further 'It is this very quality of the man's mind, his entire disregard of experience and practise, which makes me doubtful of his opinions on political economy. His speech on paying off the national debt has very much damaged him in the House of Commons' (*Works*, VIII: 152n; see also Mallet's comment, ibid.: 147n).

The irony is that there were more sensible and temperate plans for dealing with the debt. McCulloch had suggested reducing the interest paid on the debt, in line with deflation (1816a, 1816b), foreshadowing later conversion operations. Parnell proposed using the sinking fund to compensate holders of perpetuities by replacing them with terminable annuities (*Works*, V: 270; IX: 175; Parnell, 1823: 536, 548; 1831: 285–8, 323), a process that would take 35 to 45 years, in contrast to Ricardo's own drastic timetable. Even Heathfield (1819; [1833] 1999: 198–9), who like Ricardo offered a drastic plan for repayment, would repay the debt at par (*Works*, VIII: 143–5). Ricardo's friend Hutches Trower, more realistic than Ricardo about the foresight of wealth owners as already noted, proposed paying off the 4 per cent debt (McCulloch [1863] 1975: 440–41) at par, by allowing those liable to assessed taxes to compound them over 12 years at 5 per cent (Bonar and Hollander, 1899: 183–5). Trower's remarkably ingenious plan would have involved no new taxation at all; revenue lost through capitalization of annual assessed taxes, less the interest saved by redeeming the 4 per cents, would come from existing taxes destined for the sinking fund.

Conclusion
Ricardo's treatment of national debt has to be seen in the context of a large literature. What distinguishes his own contribution was his conviction that the debt was such a serious problem that the cogent criticisms of his proposals offered by his contemporaries should be disregarded.

D.P. O'BRIEN

See also:

Funding System; Member of Parliament; Ricardian Equivalence; Taxation.

References

Anderson, G.M. and R.D. Tollison (1986), 'Ricardo on the public debt: principle versus practise', *History of Economics Society Bulletin*, **8**, 49–58.

Asso, P.F. and E. Barucci (1988), 'Ricardo on the national debt and its redemption: some notes on an unpublished manuscript', *Economic Notes*, **1**(2), 5–36.

Barro, R.J. (1974), 'Are government bonds net wealth?', *Journal of Political Economy*, **82**(6), 1095–117.

Bonar, J. and J.H. Hollander (eds) (1899), *Letters of David Ricardo to Hutches Trower and Others 1811–1823*, Oxford: Clarendon Press.

Buchanan, D. ([1817] 1999), *Observations on the Subjects Treated of in Dr. Smith's Inquiry into the Nature and Causes of the Wealth of Nations*, in O'Brien, *The History of Taxation, Vol. III*, pp. 121–56.

Buchanan, D.H. (1958), *Public Principles of Public Debt*, Homewood, IL: Irwin.

Cannan, E. (1894), 'David Ricardo in Parliament, I and II', *Economic Journal*, **4**, 249–61 and 409–23.

Churchman, N. (2001), *David Ricardo on Public Debt*, Basingstoke, UK: Palgrave Macmillan.

Edgeworth, F.Y. (1915), *The Cost of War*, Oxford: Clarendon Press.

Hamilton, R. ([1818] 1995), *An Inquiry Concerning the Rise, Progress, Redemption, Present State, and Management of the National Debt of Great Britain and Ireland*, 3rd edition, Edinburgh: Oliphaunt, Waugh and Innes; reprinted in J.R. McCulloch (ed.) (1857), *A Select Collection of Valuable Tracts and Other Publications on the National Debt and the Sinking Fund*, pp. 421–688; reprint, London: Pickering & Chatto.

Heathfield, R. (1819), *Elements of a Plan for the Liquidation of the Public Debt of the United Kingdom*, London: Longman.

Heathfield, R. ([1833] 1999), *Observations Occasioned by a Motion in the House of Commons*, in D.P. O'Brien, *The History of Taxation, Vol. IV*, London: Pickering & Chatto, pp. 189–206.

Hume, D. ([1752] 1999), *Of Public Credit*, in D.P. O'Brien, *The History of Taxation, Vol. I*, London: Pickering & Chatto, pp. 171–89.

Hutcheson, A. ([1714] 1721), *A Proposal for Payment of the Publick Debts*, in *A Collection of Treatises Relating to the National Debts and Funds*, London.

McCulloch, J.R. (1816a), *An Essay on a Reduction of the Interest of the National Debt, Proving that this is the only Possible Means of Relieving the Distresses of the Commercial and Agricultural Interests; and Establishing the Justice of that Measure on the Surest Principles of Political Economy*, London: Mawman/Edinburgh: Brown.

McCulloch, J.R. (1816b), *Essay on the Question of Reducing the Interest of the National Debt; in which the Justice and Expediency of that Measure are Fully Established*, Edinburgh: Brown and Black.

McCulloch, J.R. (1829), 'Saddler on Ireland', *Edinburgh Review*, **49**, 300–317.

McCulloch, J.R. ([1863] 1975), *A Treatise on the Principles and Practical Influence of Taxation and the Funding System*, 3rd edition, London: Longmans; reprint edited by D.P. O'Brien, Edinburgh: Scottish Academic Press.

Mill, J.S. ([1848] 1923), *Principles of Political Economy with Some of their Applications to Social Philosophy*, reprint edited by W.J. Ashley, London: Longman.

Mitchell, B.R. with P. Deane (1962), *An Abstract of British Historical Statistics*, Cambridge, UK: Cambridge University Press.

O'Brien, D.P. (1999), *The History of Taxation*, 9 vols, London: Pickering & Chatto.

O'Driscoll, G.P. (1977), 'The Ricardian nonequivalence theorem', *Journal of Political Economy*, **85**(1), 207–10.

Parnell, H. (1823), 'Speeches in the House of Commons', *Hansard*, **8**, cols. 536–8, 548–50.

Parnell, H. (1831), *On Financial Reform*, 3rd edition, London: Murray.

Preston, R. ([1816] 1999), *A Review of the Present Ruined Condition of the Landed and Agricultural Interests*, in D.P. O'Brien, *The History of Taxation, Vol. III*, London: Pickering & Chatto, pp. 57–120.

Roberts, R.O. (1942), 'Ricardo's theory of public debts', *Economica*, **9**, 257–66.

Shoup, C. (1960), *Ricardo on Taxation*, New York: Columbia University Press.

Natural and Market Prices

The distinction between the natural and market prices of commodities is one of the hallmarks of classical economic theory. As is well-known, the distinction refers to the sharply different nature of the forces involved: unlike their market counterparts, natural prices were taken by classical authors to reflect the permanent and systematic forces at work whenever competition operates without restraint. In modern rational reconstructions of classical economics, natural prices are those prices that obtain in a cost-minimizing system of production, given (1) the technical conditions of production of the various commodities, (2) the size and composition of the social product, (3) one of the distributive variables (either the real rate of wages as in classical authors or the rate of profits as in Sraffa, 1960: §44) and (4) the quantities of the different qualities of land available and the known stocks of depletable resources: see Kurz and Salvadori (1995: 14ff) and Steedman (1998). As a consequence, natural and market prices have quite a different analytical status and relevance within classical economics: classical economists devoted their best analytical energies to the study of the former, leaving the analysis of the latter somewhat in the background (Ciccone, 1999; Salvadori and Signorino, 2013).

In an oft-quoted passage of Chapter 4, 'On Natural and Market Price', of his *Principles of Political Economy, and Taxation* Ricardo plainly acknowledged Adam Smith's authority on the subject:

> In the 7th Chapter of the *Wealth of Nations*, all that concerns this question is most ably treated. Having fully acknowledged the temporary effects which, in particular employments of capital, may be produced on the prices of commodities, as well as on the wages of labour, and the profits of stock, by accidental causes, without influencing the general price of commodities, wages, or profits, since these effects are equally operative in all stages of society, we will leave them entirely out of our consideration, whilst we are treating of the laws which regulate natural prices, natural wages and natural profits, effects totally independent of these accidental causes. (*Works*, I: 91–2)

Yet, in the mature stage of his thought in economics, Ricardo was no strict follower of Smith on the subject of price theory and in several places in the *Principles* he put emphasis on what he considered to be Smith's theoretical blunders. While a thorough comparison of Smith's and Ricardo's price theories is obviously beyond the scope of this entry, a few differences will be hinted at in what follows.

As far as natural price determination is concerned, Smith endorsed what may be called an adding-up theory of natural prices since he claimed that the natural prices of the various commodities derive from the summation of the natural rates of wages, profits *and* rents:

> When the price of any commodity is neither more nor less than what is sufficient to pay the rent of the land, the wages of the labour, and the profits of the stock employed in raising, preparing, and bringing it to market, according to their natural rates, the commodity is then sold for what may be called its natural price. (*WN*, I.vii.4)

The latter three magnitudes are to be understood as the average rates 'at the time and place in which they commonly prevail' (ibid.: 3). By contrast, as emerges from an oft-quoted letter to McCulloch dated 13 June 1820 (*Works*, VIII: 194), Ricardo was eager to 'get rid of rent' to simplify the problem of income distribution between capitalists and workers. As is well known, in the preface of his *Principles* Ricardo plainly pointed out that many of the theoretical deficiencies he detected in *The Wealth of Nations* derive just from Smith's imperfect comprehension of the 'true doctrine of rent'. For Ricardo, rent, due to its differential nature, does not enter into the cost of production of the various commodities. Rent is price determined and not price determining:

> The value of corn is regulated by the quantity of labour bestowed on its production on that quality of land, or with that portion of capital, which pays no rent. Corn is not high because a rent is paid, but a rent is paid because corn is high. (*Works*, I: 74)

Moreover, Ricardo strongly criticized the Smithian view according to which a rise in wages, due to a rise in the price of corn, causes a proportional rise of all commodity prices, regardless of existing differences in the fixed to working capital ratio of each commodity:

> Adam Smith, and all the writers who have followed him, have, without one exception that I know of, maintained that a rise in the price of labour would be uniformly followed by a rise in the price of all commodities. I hope I have succeeded in showing, that there are no grounds for such an opinion, and that only those commodities would rise which had less fixed capital employed upon them than the medium in which price was estimated, and that all those which had more, would positively fall in price when wages rose. (Ibid.: 46)

As noted by Sraffa (*Works*, I: xiii–lvii), Ricardo had initially subscribed to this view, which he eventually rejected as soon as he realized that it was inconsistent with his own theory of distribution based on the inverse relationship between wages and profits. Finally, in Chapter I, 'On Value', of his *Principles* Ricardo criticized Smith for limiting the labour theory of value to a primitive a-capitalistic economy since:

> [e]ven in that early state to which Adam Smith refers, some capital, though possibly made and accumulated by the hunter himself, would be necessary to enable him to kill his game. Without some weapon, neither the beaver nor the deer could be destroyed, and therefore the value of these animals would be regulated, not solely by the time and labour necessary to their destruction, but also by the time and labour necessary for providing the hunter's capital, the weapon, by the aid of which their destruction was effected. (Ibid.: 22–3)

As is well known, Ricardo struggled with the problem of value till the end of his life. Yet, his final view on the subject was that, *pace* Smith, in an advanced economy as well as in a primitive one, the ratio between the direct and indirect labour requirements of two commodities determines their relative value, the only significant exception being due to the different time structures of the capital goods involved in their production.

As far as market price determination is concerned, in several places in the *Principles* Ricardo clarified that the interplay of supply and demand determines the following:

1. The market price of commodities whose available quantity is given (such as rare statues and pictures, scarce books and coins) or which are produced by means of a non-human factor of production whose quantity is given (such as wines of a peculiar quality, which can be made only from grapes grown on a particular soil).
2. The market price of commodities produced under a regime of monopoly or where competition is somehow restrained.
3. The market prices of those commodities that 'can be increased in quantity by the exertion of human industry, and on the production of which competition operates without restraint' (ibid.: 12).

By contrast, for Ricardo, cost of production determines the natural price of commodities *sub* (3). Supply and demand have no role to play in the circumstances:

> When a commodity is at a monopoly price, it is at the very highest price at which the consumers are willing to purchase it. Commodities are only at a monopoly price, when by no possible device their quantity can be augmented; and when therefore, the competition is wholly on one side – amongst the buyers . . . Those peculiar wines, which are produced in very limited quantity, and those works of art, which from their excellence or rarity, have acquired a fanciful value, will be exchanged for a very different quantity of the produce of ordinary labour, according as the society is rich or poor, as it possesses an abundance or scarcity of such produce, or as it may be in a rude or polished state. The exchangeable value therefore of a commodity which is at a monopoly price, is nowhere regulated by the cost of production. (Ibid.: 249–50)

> [T]he proportion between supply and demand may, indeed, for a time, affect the market value of a commodity, until it is supplied in greater or less abundance, according as the demand may have increased or diminished; but this effect will be only of temporary duration . . . Commodities which are monopolized, either by an individual, or by a company, vary according to the law which Lord Lauderdale has laid down: they fall in proportion as the sellers augment their quantity, and rise in proportion to the eagerness of the buyers to purchase them; their price has no necessary connexion with their natural value: but the prices of commodities, which are subject to competition, and whose quantity may be increased in any moderate degree, will ultimately depend, not on the state of demand and supply, but on the increased or diminished cost of their production. (Ibid.: 382 and 385)

See also Ricardo's letters to Malthus dated 9 October and 24 November 1820 (*Works*, VIII: 279 and 302).

A few historians of economic analysis, following the lead of the famous Appendix I of Alfred Marshall's *Principles of Economics* ([1890] 1920), have elaborated rational reconstructions of Ricardo's long-run competitive price theory in which supply and demand do play a significant role: see Hollander (1979) and Rankin (1980). Peach (1993: Chapter 6) and Caravale (1998) provide a brief discussion of the literature on the subject. Whether or not Ricardo implicitly assumed constant returns in value theory is the *vexata questio* in the long-lasting controversies on what 'Ricardo really meant'. Ricardo was perfectly aware that, in the course of time, relative natural prices (typically, the relative price of agricultural to manufactured commodities) do change. Nonetheless, he insisted that 'It is the cost of production which must ultimately regulate the price of commodities, and not, as has been often said, the proportion between the supply and demand' (*Works*, I: 382), a statement that, translated into a Marshallian framework, would naturally amount to an implicit and generalized assumption of constant returns. A possible explanation to this theoretical puzzle is provided by the young Sraffa in his 1925 Italian contribution on Marshallian value theory. Sraffa ([1925] 2003: 324–5) stressed that classical authors treated the phenomena of decreasing and increasing productivity in relation to the theory of rent, a chapter of distribution theory, and in relation to the process of division of labour, a chapter of production theory, respectively. To put it briefly, for Sraffa, no classical economist ever thought to coordinate the two phenomena in one single law of non-constant productivity and to make such a law the cornerstone of the explanation of the equilibrium price of a given commodity produced under competitive conditions. This point of view was further elaborated upon by Sraffa, once moved to Cambridge, in his 1928–1931 *Lectures on the Advanced Theory of Value*: see Signorino (2005: 363ff).

Anyway, Ricardo's treatment of the competition process has an unmistakable Smithian flavour. Perhaps the single important element of novelty is Ricardo's analysis of the role of financial capital in the gravitation process of market prices towards their natural levels (Kurz and Salvadori, 1995: 7–8; Steedman, 1998: 148). Ricardo pointed out as a fact beyond dispute that real world markets are seldom if ever in a situation of (what may be called) natural, or long-run, equilibrium, that is, in a situation in which (1) the quantities produced of the various commodities match their respective Smithian effectual demands and (2) a uniform rate of profits and a uniform rate of wages obtain. As a consequence, actually observable magnitudes (market prices) seldom if ever coincide with their theoretical counterparts (natural prices):

> In the ordinary course of events, there is no commodity which continues for any length of time to be supplied precisely in that degree of abundance, which the wants and wishes of mankind require, and therefore there is none which is not subject to accidental and temporary variations of price. (*Works*, I: 88)

How to justify then the privileged role accorded by Ricardo to natural values within his own economic analysis? The answer is that market prices may be safely assumed as gravitating towards their natural levels. (Smith and Ricardo took for granted, and thus did not bother to demonstrate formally, that market and natural prices coincide on average. For a critical discussion of the literature on gravitation in classical economics see Bellino, 2011.) Obviously, such an assumption is warranted provided that in all markets where competition operates without restraint a very powerful mechanism is at work to adjust the quantities produced of the various commodities to their respective Smithian effectual demands. And this was just Ricardo's opinion:

> When we look to the markets of a large town, and observe how regularly they are supplied both with home and foreign commodities, in the quantity in which they are required, under all the circumstances of varying demand, arising from the caprice of taste, or a change in the amount of population, without often producing either the effects of a glut from a too abundant supply, or an enormously high price from the supply being unequal to the demand, we must confess that the principle which apportions capital to each trade in the precise amount that it is required, is more active than is generally supposed. (*Works*, I: 89–90)

To put it in a nutshell, for Ricardo, unrestrained competition is very effective at dampening the variance of market prices around their average, or natural, levels. In Ricardo's view the main actors behind such adjustment mechanism were the rich manufacturers and the financial capitalists, 'the monied class' as Ricardo called them, that is, those who 'live on the interest of their money, which is employed in discounting bills, or in loans to the more industrious part of the community'. Ricardo depicted entrepreneurs as economic agents endowed with a peculiar alertness towards the profits differentials that continually emerge out from the ebb and flow of supply and demand in the various markets. At the aggregate level, the individual choices prompted by the search of the highest available rate of return for one's own capital are supposed to enforce (a tendency to) a uniform rate of profits:

> Whilst every man is free to employ his capital where he pleases, he will naturally seek for it that employment which is most advantageous; he will naturally be dissatisfied with a profit of 10 per

cent, if by removing his capital he can obtain a profit of 15 per cent. This restless desire on the part of all the employers of stock, to quit a less profitable for a more advantageous business, has a strong tendency to equalize the rate of profits of all. (Ibid.: 88)

(The alleged long-run tendency to a uniform rate of profits and a uniform rate of wages does not imply that classical economists ignored persistent inequalities in the rate of profits or wages due to the existence of non-pecuniary differences among sectors: see Kurz and Salvadori, 1995: Chapter 11.) As clarified by Ricardo's example from the textile sector, in his view the specific role of financial capitalists is to assist entrepreneurs in the process of reorganization of the material conditions of production to keep pace with ever-changing market opportunities:

> When the demand for silks increases, and that for cloth diminishes, the clothier does not remove with his capital to the silk trade, but he dismisses some of his workmen, he discontinues his demand for the loan from bankers and monied men; while the case of the silk manufacturer is the reverse: he wishes to employ more workmen, and thus his motive for borrowing is increased: he borrows more, and thus capital is transferred from one employment to another, without the necessity of a manufacturer discontinuing his usual occupation. (*Works*, I: 89)

Stockbroker Ricardo knew quite well that financial capital is endowed with a much higher intersectoral mobility than physical capital, particularly the fixed part of it, and thus the former, unlike the latter, may be assumed as not being tied to a given productive sector. As a consequence, fixed capital ends up playing the role of the slackening element in the adjustment process sketched above: the higher the share of fixed capital on total capital, the higher the share of sunk costs on total costs of production and thus the stronger the unwillingness of entrepreneurs to quit their sector whenever market conditions are altered by a technological breakthrough, a change of fashion, the introduction of a new tax or the repeal of an old one, the start or the end of wartime and so on. That is particularly evident in Chapter 19 of the *Principles* where Ricardo compared the different effects of 'sudden changes in the channels of trade' in rich and poor countries:

> The commencement of war after a long peace, or of peace after a long war, generally produces considerable distress in trade. It changes in a great degree the nature of the employments to which the respective capitals of countries were before devoted; and during the interval while they are settling in the situations which new circumstances have made the most beneficial, much fixed capital is unemployed, perhaps wholly lost, and labourers are without full employment. The duration of this distress will be longer or shorter according to the strength of that disinclination which most men feel to abandon that employment of their capital to which they have long been accustomed. (Ibid.: 265)

Though the high price of agricultural products is, in Ricardo's view, the main culprit of high wages and thus low profits and low rate of capital accumulation, Ricardo was aware that an abrupt removal of the obstacles to the free importation of cheap foreign corn in England, in the aftermath of Napoleonic Wars, would have destroyed much of the value of the capital invested in domestic agriculture. In the circumstances, he invoked an active government policy to compensate for the negative effects of free trade:

> The best policy of the State would be, to lay a tax, decreasing in amount from time to time, on the importation of foreign corn, for a limited number of years, in order to afford to the home-grower an opportunity to withdraw his capital gradually from the land. (Ibid.: 266–7)

Hence, at least on this occasion, Ricardo cannot be found guilty of what Schumpeter (1954) famously christened the 'Ricardian Vice', that is, the (bad) habit to apply crudely the conclusions derived from a highly simplified model to real-world problems, turning a blind eye to short-term frictions and maladjustments!

RODOLFO SIGNORINO

See also:

Competition; Demand and Supply; Exchange Value and Utility; Labour Theory of Value; Riches and Value.

References

Bellino, E. (2011), 'Gravitation of market prices towards natural prices', in R. Ciccone, C. Gehrke and G. Mongiovi (eds), *Sraffa and Modern Economics*, London and New York: Routledge.
Caravale, G. (1998), 'Supply and demand', in H.D. Kurz and N. Salvadori (eds), *The Elgar Companion to Classical Economics, Vol. II: L–Z*, Cheltenham, UK and Lyme, NH: Edward Elgar Publishing, pp. 434–9.
Ciccone, R. (1999), 'Classical and neoclassical short-run prices. A comparative analysis of their intended empirical content', in G. Mongiovi and F. Petri (eds), *Value, Distribution and Capital. Essays in Honour of Pierangelo Garegnani*, London: Routledge, pp. 69–92.
Hollander, S. (1979), *The Economics of David Ricardo*, London: Heinemann.
Kurz, H.D. and N. Salvadori (1995), *Theory of Production. A Long-Period Analysis*, Cambridge, UK: Cambridge University Press.
Marshall, A. ([1890] 1920), *Principles of Economics*, 8th edition, London: Macmillan.
Peach, T. (1993), *Interpreting Ricardo*, Cambridge, UK: Cambridge University Press.
Rankin, S.C. (1980), 'Supply and demand in Ricardian price theory: a re-interpretation', *Oxford Economic Papers*, **32**(2), 241–62.
Salvadori, N. and R. Signorino (2013), 'The classical notion of competition revisited', *History of Political Economy*, **45**(1), 149–75.
Schumpeter, J.A. (1954), *History of Economic Analysis*, London: George Allen & Unwin.
Signorino, R. (2005), 'Piero Sraffa's *Lectures on the Advanced Theory of Value 1928–31* and the rediscovery of the classical approach', *Review of Political Economy*, **17**(3), 359–80.
Smith, A. ([1776] 1976), *An Inquiry into the Nature and Causes of the Wealth of Nations*, in *The Glasgow Edition of the Works and Correspondence of Adam Smith*, (eds) R.H. Campbell, A.S. Skinner and W.B. Todd, Oxford: Clarendon Press.
Sraffa, P. ([1925] 2003), 'On the relation between cost and quantity produced', in L.L. Pasinetti (ed.) (1998), *Italian Economic Papers, Vol. III*, Bologna: Il Mulino and Oxford: Oxford University Press, pp. 323–63; reprinted in H.D. Kurz and N. Salvadori (eds), *The Legacy of Piero Sraffa, Vol. I*, Cheltenham, UK and Northampton, MA: Edward Elgar Publishing; English translation of Sraffa, P. (1925), 'Sulle relazioni fra costo e quantità prodotta', *Annali di Economia*, **2**, pp. 277–328.
Sraffa, P. (1960), *Production of Commodities by Means of Commodities. Prelude to a Critique of Economic Theory*, Cambridge, UK: Cambridge University Press.
Steedman, I. (1998), 'Natural and market price', in H.D. Kurz and N. Salvadori (eds), *The Elgar Companion to Classical Economics. Vol. II: L–Z*, Cheltenham, UK and Lyme, NH: Edward Elgar Publishing, pp. 146–9.

Natural Quantity of Money

The concept of the 'natural' quantity of money plays a pivotal role in Ricardo's monetary theory, which is concerned with monetary regimes with convertible or inconvertible paper money, with or without coins in circulation, where gold is always the standard of money. The role of this standard is to measure the deviations of the quantity of money from its natural level; the price at which the currency can be legally converted into gold, domestically and internationally, determines the ratio that must exist between the currency and its standard. When the market price of gold is equal to the mint price, the quantity of money is, by definition, at its natural level; when it deviates from it, the quantity of money differs from the natural level in exactly the same proportion, since the price of the standard on the domestic and international market depends entirely and exclusively on the amount of the currency (*Works*, III: 239). The natural quantity of money (ibid.: 105, 193; VI: 75) is a benchmark signalled by the purchasing power of the currency over gold.

Deviations of the quantity of money from its natural level are automatically corrected only in some monetary regimes, where gold can be obtained at a fixed price (and at a small cost) at home and can be freely exported and imported. The mechanism that ensures that the quantity of money adjusts to its 'natural level' relies on individuals' responses to profitability conditions for arbitraging in gold in the domestic and foreign markets. If the price of gold bullion on the domestic market rises above the mint price, bullion is bought at the Bank or coins are melted and sold on the market, thereby lowering its price and decreasing the quantity of money in circulation. If the market rate of exchange falls (rises) relatively to the mint par (given by the ratio between the mint prices of the standard in the two countries) and it reaches the so called 'gold points', which bound the profitability conditions for shipping gold, gold is exported (imported), the quantity of money is reduced (increased) to its 'natural' level and the market rate of exchange is once again brought back to level with par.

In other regimes, where the convertibility of the currency into gold is suspended and there are no longer gold coins in circulation, the quantity of money is no longer self-adjusting, but the price of gold bullion and the market rate of exchange still measure the deviation of the quantity of money from the 'natural' level. In these cases, however, the 'uniformity in the value of money' cannot be maintained (*Works*, IV: 69), rather, its 'value must be constantly vacillating' (*Works*, III: 139), which, for Ricardo, is a most undesirable state of affairs:

> In the present state of the law [Bank of England's notes were no longer convertible into gold at an official price] they [Bank's directors] have the power, without any control whatever, of increasing or reducing the circulation in any degree they may think proper: a power which should neither be intrusted to the State itself, nor to any body in it; as there can be no security for the uniformity in the value of the currency, when its augmentation or diminution depends solely on the will of the issuers. (*Works*, IV: 69 and quoted in I: 359)

Ricardo's 'natural' quantity of money does not require the value of gold to be constant in terms of commodities. This value need neither be calculated by relating the cost of production of gold to the cost of production of commodities, nor is it determined as the equilibrium condition given by the equality of supply and demand of money. Ricardo explicitly denied that one could know precisely what the quantity of money ought to be at a given moment of time and his policy recommendations were always consistent with this premise:

> ... the demand for circulating medium is subject to continual fluctuations, proceeding from an increase or decrease in the amount of capital and commerce; from a greater or less facility which at one period may be afforded to payments by a varying degree of confidence and credit; and ... the same commerce and payments may require very different amounts of circulating medium. (*Works*, III: 247)

If the 'natural' level of money is interpreted as an equilibrium level, then a gratuitous inference is drawn from Ricardo's monetary theory: the attainment of the purchasing power parity of gold in terms of commodities among countries (Arnon, 2011: 128).

To clarify the argument, let us suppose that in each country adopting a gold standard the money supply depends on the stock of gold for monetary use, according to some proportionality factor. Furthermore, let us suppose that the demand for money is a proportion of the amount of commodities exchanged, expressed in money terms. From the equilibrium condition – demand of money equals the supply of money – a unique relation is established between the prices of commodities, the stock of gold held for monetary purposes (and hence with the quantity of money) and the purchasing power of gold in terms of commodities. When gold can be freely exported and imported, the equilibrium quantity of gold is determined by the further condition that equal purchasing power in terms of commodities is attained by gold at home and abroad. The equilibrium quantity of gold (and hence of money) is thus made self-adjusting by response to either a change in the relative price levels (price-specie flow mechanism) or in the demand for money (monetary approach; see Humphrey and Keleher, 1982: 154, 322).

In the price-specie flow mechanism, gold outflows are the effect of a negative balance of trade, when exports decrease and imports increase in response to a rise in the domestic relative to the foreign prices. The outflow of gold, by reducing the quantity of money at home and increasing it abroad, provides the adjusting mechanism. Gold movements come to a halt when the purchasing power parity of gold in terms of commodities is attained at home and abroad.

On the other hand, the monetary approach denies that prices of international traded commodities may diverge, since they are determined in a world market where the law of one price prevails. Gold movements respond not to a disequilibrium in the balance of trade, but to a disequilibrium in the money market. If there is an excess of supply of money (relatively to the domestic demand), individuals will turn directly to the foreign markets to buy goods and assets until the equality of demand and supply of money is re-established. In the monetary approach the equality of the purchasing power of gold in terms of commodities is the presupposition rather than the outcome of the adjustment process. Both theories rely on an equilibrium quantity of money (hence gold) to study the self-adjusting property of the system.

On the contrary, in our interpretation (Marcuzzo and Rosselli, 1991, 1994; Marcuzzo, 2002; Rosselli, 2008) the 'natural' level associates the quantity of money not to an equilibrium quantity of gold and to the relative value of gold in terms of commodities constant across countries, but to the equality of the purchasing power of gold relative to the currency at home and abroad. This means that the relative value of gold in terms of commodities may differ, while arbitrage on the international gold market equalizes the price of gold across countries. Furthermore, in our interpretation the enforcement of the law of one (international) price is required only for gold, not for all tradable commodities as is implied by the purchasing power parity condition that is imposed in order to close the gold-standard type of models attributed to Ricardo. This was clearly stated by Ricardo in a letter to James Mill in 1811:

> You say . . . 'the value of the precious metals throughout the globe is uniform', – or rather 'the only difference which can exist is the difference constituted by the expense of carriage'. I should

have agreed with you if you had said 'price' instead of 'value'. If a bill on London for £100 will sell in Hamburgh for £98 or as much of the money of Hamburgh as is equal to the bullion in £98 of our's then I should say that the price of bullion differed 2 pct in the two countries. But when we speak of the value of bullion we mean a very different thing – we mean, I apprehend, to measure it by some other commodity – corn, coffee, hardware or any amongst the thousands of commodities which may be exported. Estimated in either of these commodities money or bullion may differ in value in any two countries, not only all the expenses attending its exportation, but also all the expenses attending the importation of the commodity to be given in exchange for it. (*Works*, VI: 54–5)

Ricardo was firmly persuaded that, whatever the composition of the circulating medium, the quantity of money that should circulate within a given country, ought to be equal to the quantity that would circulate if the entire circulation were made up of gold, but this does not imply that this quantity is determined by the gold/commodities ratio nor that it must be defined as a determined quantity. The point of having a standard is precisely this: the price signal bypasses the need for a quantity target. Ricardo defined the 'right' quantity as the 'natural' level, but he did not specify what this level was nor did he try to calculate it from the gold/commodities ratio.

In conclusion, there is a profound misunderstanding of Ricardo's thought to attribute him with a naive monetary theory that runs thus: money is only gold, its value depending on its labour content, the price level being the ratio between gold and commodities, internationally equalized through international gold movements, and the quantity of money being adjusted so as to conform to the labour theory of value. Only because of this interpretation does there appear to be a contradiction between the theory of the value of gold and monetary theory, as if Ricardo had two distinct monetary theories: one for the short run, where the stock of gold determines prices according to some form of quantity theory, and one for the long run, where the price of gold determines the equilibrium quantity of money (Laidler, 1975: 217; Blaug, 1985: 198–9; 1995: 31; de Vivo, 1987: 186). It can be shown that this need not be the case.

When Ricardo argues that the value assumed by certain variables is at its natural level, as opposed to market level, he means to draw a distinction between 'permanent' and 'temporary' causes, a distinction that cannot be assimilated to the distinction between short-run and long-run analysis. While the former pertains to the question of which causes are eligible to become part of a theory, the latter pertains to the question of which effects come sooner or are more short-lived than others. This distinction pertains to the nature of the forces involved and not to the time sequence in which they are assumed to operate. A 'permanent' cause should be interpreted as a sufficient condition for something to happen: its effects are certain regardless of the time interval necessary for their implementation. Permanent causes are sufficient but not necessary conditions, since the same effects could be brought about by other causes that Ricardo labels as 'temporary': neither necessary nor sufficient. 'Temporary' causes are not sufficient because either their effects are not certain and may well be offset by the working of more permanent forces or they are not necessary because a given effect cannot be unambiguously imputed to them.

For instance, a change in the conditions of production of a given commodity is a 'permanent' cause of a change in its price, which means that the price will certainly change, although not every variation in commodity prices can be imputed to variations in the conditions of production. On the contrary, a change in demand is a 'temporary' cause of a change in prices, not because its effect does not last long enough, but because it is not certain. Similarly, when discussing natural wages, Ricardo granted that money wages can be pushed downwards when the supply of labour grows faster than demand but that if there is at the same time a change in the conditions of production of wage goods, making them more difficult to produce, their money prices rise and the overall effect is an increase, not a decrease, in money wages. The former, the depressing effect on wages of a large supply of labour, can be taken as an example of a temporary cause, while the latter – an increase in the price of wage goods – is a permanent cause of wage increases.

It is our contention that the definition of the natural quantity of money in Ricardo is given by analogy with the definition of natural wages and natural prices. First of all, the natural quantity of money, like other natural magnitudes, puts to rest the forces that determine its changes. When the price of a commodity is at its natural level (it reflects the condition of production and the uniformity of the rate of profit in all industries) there is no incentive to modify the quantity produced. Similarly, when the quantity of money is at its natural level, the market price of gold is equal to the mint price and the quantity of the currency is not changed by the convertibility of the currency into gold. When observing variations in the price of a commodity it is necessary to distinguish between permanent causes that may have generated it – which modify the natural price – and temporary causes, which affect the market price: the uniformity of the rate of profit is the signal that makes the distinction possible. When observing variations in the quantity of money, we know that they may be permanent, that is, reflecting changes in the structure of the economy that requires a different natural level for the quantity of money, or temporary. The conformity of the price of gold to the mint price allows us to make this distinction.

The natural quantity of money does not serve the purpose of providing the target to the monetary authority, which should react only to the signal coming from the price of the standard:

> The issuers of paper money should regulate their issues solely by the price of bullion, and never by the quantity of their paper in circulation. The quantity can never be too great nor too little, while it preserves the same value as the standard. (*Works*, IV: 64)

It is thus ironic that Ricardo, who placed importance on a price rather than a quantity, ended up by being interpreted as the inspirer of the 1844 reform of the British monetary system that fixed the precise amount of currency that could be issued by the Bank, thus giving birth to the first monetary recommendation that identified in a given amount of money the target for the monetary policy.

MARIA CRISTINA MARCUZZO AND ANNALISA ROSSELLI

See also:

Bullionist Controversy; Gold; Monetary Theory; Papers on Money and Banking; Rate of Interest.

References

Arnon, A. (2011), *Monetary Theory and Policy from Hume and Smith to Wicksell: Money, Credit, and the Economy*, Cambridge, UK: Cambridge University Press.

Blaug, M. (1985), *Economic Theory in Retrospect*, 4th edition, Cambridge, UK: Cambridge University Press.

Blaug, M. (1995), 'Why is the quantity theory of money the oldest surviving theory in economics?', in M. Blaug (ed.), *The Quantity Theory of Money. From Locke to Keynes and Friedman*, Aldershot, UK and Brookfield, VT: Edward Elgar Publishing.

de Vivo, G. (1987), 'Ricardo, David', in J. Eatwell, M. Milgate and P. Newman (eds), *The New Palgrave: A Dictionary of Economics*, London, Macmillan.

Humphrey, T.H. and R.E. Keleher (1982), *The Monetary Approach to the Balance of Payments, Exchange Rates, and World Inflation*, New York: Praeger.

Laidler, D. (1975), *Essays on Money and Inflation*, Manchester, UK: Manchester University Press.

Marcuzzo, M.C. (2002), 'David Ricardo and the "natural" level of the quantity of money', in B. Schefold (ed.), *Exogenität und Endogenität. Die Geldmenge in der Geschichte des ökonomischen Denkens und in der modernen Politik*, Marburg: Metropolis, pp.171–85.

Marcuzzo, M.C. and A. Rosselli (1991), *Ricardo and the Gold Standard. The Foundations of the International Monetary Order*, London: Macmillan.

Marcuzzo, M.C. and A. Rosselli (1994), 'Ricardo's theory of money matters', *Revue Economique*, **45**(5), 1251–68.

Rosselli, A. (2008), 'Ricardo and Thornton on an "unfavourable" balance of trade', *Cahiers d'économie politique*, **55**, 65–79.

Non-English Editions of Ricardo's *Works*

A full bibliography of non-English editions of Ricardo's works up to 1932 was compiled by Piero Sraffa (see *Works*, X: 374–85). The purpose of this entry is to complement this list with regard to more recent non-English editions and to note some anomalies, shortcomings and specific characteristics of non-English editions that have been important for the reception of Ricardo's ideas by readers from the non-English-speaking world. The attention focuses on the more important languages; no attempt has been made to provide a complete list of non-English editions in the twentieth and early twenty-first centuries.

French editions

French editions of Ricardo's writings were published early. A French translation of the third edition of *The High Price of Bullion* was published already in September 1810 in the *Gazette nationale, ou Le moniteur universel*, and some excerpts from Chapter 1 of the *Principles* in French were published in 1817–18 in Geneva as part of the *Bibliothèque Universelle*. F.S. Constâncio then published a complete translation of the first edition of the *Principles* in 1819, appended with 'explanatory and critical notes' by Jean-Baptiste Say. This edition was very important for the reception and dissemination of Ricardo's ideas among non-English readers, because it was used widely not only in the French-speaking countries, but also in other parts of Continental Europe, including the German-speaking countries and Spain, Italy, Portugal and Russia. Say's critical notes were translated and then also appended to other non-English editions of the *Principles*, including the first German one. Moreover:

> Constâncio's translation . . . revised in 1847 by Alcide Fonteyraud . . . formed the basis for most subsequent editions and remained the main reference in France . . . until the new 1992 translation published by Flammarion . . . It was, however, defective, with many errors and approximations that obscured the meaning of some chapters – the chapter on rent in particular. (Béraud and Faccarello, 2014: 19)

For some 25 years, Constâncio's edition of 1819, which was reprinted twice in 1835, remained the most important source for the dissemination of Ricardo's ideas on the

Continent. Thereafter, the French translation of McCulloch's edition of the *Works of David Ricardo*, which was published by Alcide Fonteyraud in 1847, 'has provided for nearly a century the standard introduction to Ricardo for a large part of the non-English-speaking world' (*Works*, X: 375). Unfortunately, this edition also exhibited some grave shortcomings. As Sraffa noted:

> the version of the *Principles* . . . is no better than a pastiche of the first and third original editions. It is based on Constancio's translation of ed. 1, revised (e.g. substituting 'rente' for 'fermage') by Fonteyraud who has also translated the most obvious passages added by Ricardo in ed. 3, including the new chapter On Machinery: the revision however is far from complete and much of the resulting text is still that of ed. 1. (Ibid.: 375–6)

Fonteyraud's edition of Ricardo's *Oeuvres complètes* was reprinted in 1882 with a newly added preface by Maurice Block. Sraffa has drawn attention to a curious build-up of mistakes in the successive French editions of the *Principles*, which concerns a passage in the chapter 'On Machinery':

> A build-up of mistakes in successive French editions of Ricardo's *Principles* resulted in a total travesty of his original statement on the effects of machinery. He had written: 'the opinion entertained by the laboring class, that the employment of machinery is frequently detrimental to their interests, is not founded on prejudice and error, but is conformable to the correct principles of political economy.' (I, 392.) The chapter on Machinery (which was added in ed. 3 of the *Principles*, 1821) was first translated into French in the Paris edition of 1847, and the above passage read as follows: 'l'opinion des classes ouvrières sur les machines qu'ils croient fatales à leurs intérêts, ne repose pas *seulement* sur l'erreur et les préjugés, mais sur les principes les plus fermes, les plus nets de l'Économie politique.' (Editor's italics.) The intrusion of the word 'seulement' made nonsense of the whole statement. The editor of the next French edition (1882) tried to put it right without referring to the original English; and taking it for granted that Ricardo must have held the orthodox view, amended the passage to read: 'l'opinion des classes ouvrières sur les machines qu'ils croient fatales à leurs intérêts, ne repose pas *seulement* sur l'erreur et les préjugés, mais sur *l'ignorance* des principes les plus fermes, les plus nets, de l'Économie politique.' (Editor's italics.) Thus the revised version represented Ricardo as saying precisely the opposite of what he had actually said. This travesty held the field for half a century. The correct version was first given in C. Debyser's translation of the *Principles*, Paris, Costes, 1933–4, p. 217. (*Works*, XI: xxix–xxx)

Debyser's translation (see Ricardo, 1933–34) was announced as being based on the English edition by E.C.K. Gonner of 1891, but 'borrowed in fact a lot from the former translations, even reproducing some of their mistranslations and errors' (Béraud and Faccarello, 2014: 66). In the twentieth century there were several re-editions of the earlier French editions of the *Principles* and of the 1847 Fonteyraud edition of Ricardo's *Oeuvres complètes*, as well as new French editions of the *Essay on Profits* in 1988 and of Ricardo's monetary writings in 1991. Flammarion published a new French translation of the *Principles* by Cécile Soudan, under the editorship of François R. Mahieu in 1992 (see Ricardo, 1992). A full list of French editions of Ricardo's writings in the twentieth century is provided in Béraud and Faccarello (2014: 66–7).

German editions
C.A. Schmidt published the first German edition of Ricardo's *Principles* in 1821 in Weimar. Schmidt's translation of the first English edition was complemented by a

German translation of some of Say's critical notes, which had been appended to the first French edition. In 1837, Eduard Baumstark published a new German translation of Ricardo's *Principles*, based on the second English edition, under the title *David Ricardo's Grundsätze der Volkswirthschaft und der Besteuerung*. In the following year, Baumstark supplemented his translation of the *Principles* with a companion volume with explanatory notes of just over 800 pages (see Baumstark, 1838). Baumstark's commentaries are partly unrelated Ricardo's text and also exhibit a number of serious misunderstandings of Ricardo's theoretical propositions (for details, see Gehrke, 2014: 77–9). A German translation of the third edition of Ricardo's *Principles* was not available until 1877, when Baumstark published a 'second edition' of his earlier translation, which incorporated the changes and alterations that Ricardo had introduced in his text in the third English edition. Baumstark's companion volume was not republished on this occasion.

In 1905, Heinrich Waentig of the University of Halle published a new German translation of the third edition – translated by O. Thiele. Waentig's edition, entitled *Grundsätze der Volkswirtschaft und Besteuerung*, was supplemented by Karl Diehl's companion volume *Sozialwissenschaftliche Erläuterungen zu David Ricardos Grundgesetzen der Volkswirtschaft und Besteuerung* (in two volumes, 1905), which show a much better understanding of Ricardo's principal propositions on value and distribution than Baumstark's commentaries of 1838. Waentig's edition of the *Grundsätze* went through two further editions in 1921 and in 1923.

The next German edition, entitled *Über die Grundsätze der Politischen Ökonomie und der Besteuerung*, was published in 1959 in the German Democratic Republic (Ricardo, 1959) under the editorship of Peter Thal. It was based on a new translation of the original third edition by Gerhard Bondi. In West Germany, Fritz Neumark edited an abbreviated new German edition of the *Principles* in 1972, which was based on a slightly revised version of Waentig's text. The Neumark edition (Ricardo, 1972) also contained a German translation of *The High Price of Bullion*. The most recent German edition of Ricardo's *Principles* was published in 1994 under the editorship of Heinz D. Kurz (Ricardo, 1994). It is based on a revised version of Bondi's translation, and the volume also contains an introduction by the editor and a new German translation of Ricardo's *Essay on Profits*, of Sraffa's editorial notes, and of his 'Introduction' in Volume I of the *Works and Correspondence of David Ricardo*. A revised and amended second edition, edited by Christian Gehrke and Heinz D. Kurz, was published in 2006.

Italian editions

The first Italian translation of the *Principles* was published only in 1856, as a volume in the series *Biblioteca dell'economista*, with an introduction by the editor of the series, Francesco Ferrara. A selection of Ricardo's monetary writings was published in 1857, together with essays on banking by other writers, and in 1860 and 1866 there were first Italian translations of the *Essay on Profits* and of *Protection to Agriculture*.

In the twentieth century, a selection of Ricardo's essays and an Italian edition of the *Principles* was published by UTET in 1947, with an introduction by Achille Loria. A new Italian edition of the *Principles*, edited and introduced by Fernando Vianello, was published in 1976, and a selection of Ricardo's monetary writings, entitled *Scritti monetari*, was edited and introduced by Bernard Schmitt in 1985. In the following year, UTET then published a new Italian edition of the *Principles*, which was based on the Sraffa edition and was edited and introduced by Pier Luigi Porta as Volume 1 of *Opere di David Ricardo*; this was followed in 1987 by a second volume, which contained Ricardo's *Notes on Malthus* and a selection of his pamphlets (see Ricardo, 1986–87).

Spanish editions

The first Spanish translation of some extracts from the *Principles* was made in 1848. However, it was ignored and forgotten for a century until Piero Sraffa recovered a reference made by L. Cossa in 1895 to this translation, but reported that 'no copy of such a translation has been traced, and its existence is extremely doubtful' (*Works*, X: 355–6). In the meantime, a Spanish translation of the first seven chapters of the third English edition made by Juan Antonio Seoane has been found. It was published in 1848 in two instalments in the journal *El Amigo del Pais*, directed by Seoane and published by the Real Sociedad Económica de Madrid. A second part of the translation, which covers Chapters 8 to (the beginning of) 20 of the *Principles*, translated by Fernando Cos-Gayón and published in the same journal, has also been traced. Thereafter, however, the translation was interrupted, because the journal ceased publication in 1850 due to financial problems. Ricardo's *Principles* were thus never published completely and in book form in Spanish in the nineteenth century (see Almenar, 2014: 167).

Three full Spanish translations of the *Principles* were published in the 1930s; the first two (Ricardo, 1932, 1936) in Spain and the third one (Ricardo, 1937) in Argentina. All three translations were reprinted or re-edited on numerous occasions. A Spanish translation of Sraffa's edition of the *Works and Correspondence of David Ricardo* (covering Volumes I–IX only) was published from 1958 to 1965 in Mexico, under the editorship of Manuel Sánchez Sarto. From this edition, the text of the *Principles* was later reprinted several times, partly with new introductions. A full list of twentieth-century translations of David Ricardo's writings in Spanish can be found in Almenar (2014: 171–2).

Portuguese editions

The first Portuguese translation of Chapters 1 and 2 of the *Principles*, based on the text of Gonner's 1891 edition, appeared as late as 1938 (see Ricardo, 1938a, 1938b), and a complete edition of the *Principles* in Portuguese, based on the text of Fogarty's edition, was only published for the first time in 1975 (Ricardo, 1975). On the reception of Ricardo in Portugal and Brazil, see Cardoso (2014).

Russian editions

The first Russian edition of Ricardo's *Principles*, based on McCulloch's edition of Ricardo's *Works*, was edited and translated by Nikolai Sieber and published in 1873 as *Works*, Volume I. Sieber had also planned to publish a second volume containing Ricardo's pamphlets, but this did not materialize. Instead, a second edition of the *Principles* appeared in 1882. New Russian editions appeared in 1908 and 1910, edited by David Riazanov. In the 1920s, Riazanov, as director of the Marx-Engels Institute in Moscow, initiated a project on the translation and editing of Ricardo's collected works in Russian, with Isaak I. Rubin as a major collaborator. As part of this project the 1908 edition was reprinted in 1929 and the forthcoming *Collected Writings* were announced. In 1935, a new Russian edition of the *Principles*, which was apparently the result of Riazanov's and his wife's efforts to refine the earlier translation, was published as Volume 2 of Ricardo's *Collected Writings*. However, both Rubin and Riazanov became victims of Stalin's cleansing operations, and the editorial project was interrupted.

The most complete Russian edition of Ricardo's *Collected Writings* was edited by M.N. Smith in five volumes and published from 1955 to 1961. While Smith made use of Sraffa's edition for the editorial work on Ricardo's papers and correspondence, she left entirely unnoticed the interpretation proposed by Sraffa in his 'Introduction' (see Bogomazov and Melnik, 2013: 297). After the collapse of the Soviet Union, a new Russian edition of the *Principles* was published in 2008, which was edited and introduced by Peter Klyukin (see Ricardo, 2008). On the diffusion of Ricardo's theories in Russia, see Melnik (2014).

Japanese editions

Japanese translations of Ricardo's writings appeared relatively late. Abridged editions of the *Principles* were first published in 1921, followed in 1928 by an unabridged edition of the third English edition and by a variorum edition. Editions of Ricardo's pamphlets and correspondence followed in the 1930s and 1940s, first of his monetary writings (in 1931) and a selection of his pamphlets, including the *Essay on Profits* and *Protection to Agriculture* (in 1938), then of Bonar's edition of his letters to Malthus (in 1942–43) and of J.H. Hollander's edition of Ricardo's letters to McCulloch (in 1949). Since then, apart from several reprints and re-editions of the *Principles*, all 11 volumes of Sraffa's edition have been translated into Japanese, by different translators and various editors, in the period from 1969 to 1999 (see Ricardo, 1969–99). For a complete list of Japanese translations of Ricardo's writings see Izumo and Sato (2014: 239–40).

Apart from the non-English editions of Ricardo's works referred to above, there have also been translations of Ricardo's *Principles* in Polish, Danish, Hungarian, Indian (Bengali) and Chinese.

CHRISTIAN GEHRKE

See also:

Principles of Political Economy, and Taxation; Ricardo Editions; Say, Jean-Baptiste, and Ricardo; Sraffa, Piero, on Ricardo.

References

(Bibliographical information on non-English editions of Ricardo's works published before 1932 can be found in the compilation provided by Sraffa in *Works*, X: 374–85. In order to save space, these editions have not been included here.)

Almenar, S. (2014), 'The reception of Ricardo in Spain', in G. Faccarello and M. Izumo (eds), *The Reception of David Ricardo in Continental Europe and Japan*, London and New York: Routledge.

Baumstark, E. (1838), *Volkswirtschaftliche Erläuterungen, vorzüglich über David Ricardo's System*, Leipzig: Verlag von Wilhelm Engelmann.

Béraud, A. and G. Faccarello (2014), '"Nous marchons sur un autre terrain." The reception of Ricardo in the French language: episodes from a complex history', in G. Faccarello and M. Izumo (eds), *The Reception of David Ricardo in Continental Europe and Japan*, London and New York: Routledge.

Bogomazov, G. and D. Melnik (2013), 'Ricardo's writings in Russia: influence and interpretations', in E.S. Levrero, A. Palumbo and A. Stirati (eds), *Sraffa and the Reconstruction of Economic Theory, Vol. III, Sraffa's Legacy: Interpretations and Historical Perspectives*, Basingstoke, UK and New York: Palgrave Macmillan.

Cardoso, J.L. (2014), 'The diffusion of Ricardo in Portugal', in G. Faccarello and M. Izumo (eds), *The Reception of David Ricardo in Continental Europe and Japan*, London and New York: Routledge.

Diehl, K. (1905), *Sozialwissenschaftliche Erläuterungen zu David Ricardos Grundgesetzen der Volkswirtschaft und Besteuerung*, 2 vols, Leipzig: Verlag von Wilhelm Engelmann.

Gehrke, C. (2014), 'The reception and further elaboration of Ricardo's theory of value and distribution in the German-speaking countries, 1817–1914', in G. Faccarello and M. Izumo (eds), *The Reception of David Ricardo in Continental Europe and Japan*, London and New York: Routledge.

Izumo, M. and S. Sato (2014), 'The reception of Ricardo in Japan', in G. Faccarello and M. Izumo (eds), *The Reception of David Ricardo in Continental Europe and Japan*, London and New York: Routledge.

Melnik, D. (2014), 'Diffusion of Ricardo's theory in Russia', in G. Faccarello and M. Izumo (eds), *The Reception of David Ricardo in Continental Europe and Japan*, London and New York: Routledge.

Ricardo, D. (1932), *Principios de economia politica e imposición fiscal*, 2 vols, introduction, notes and appendix by Sir E.C.K. Gonner, translated by E. Hazera, Barcelona: El Consultor Bibliográfico.

Ricardo, D. (1933–34), *Principes de l'économie politique et de l'impôt*, 2 vols, with introduction, notes and appendices by E.C.K. Gonner, translated by C. Debyser, Paris: A. Costes.

Ricardo, D. (1936), *Principios de economia politica y de tributación*, prologue and translated by V.A. Álvarez, Madrid: Aguilar.

Ricardo, D. (1937), *Principios de economia politica y de tributación*, introduction by F.W. Kolthammer, translated by Dr. E. Pepe, Buenos Aires: Claridad.

Ricardo, D. (1938a), *Sobre a Teoria do Valor*, Lisbon: Editorial Inquérito, translated by E. Salgueiro from Gonner's edition, 1919.

Ricardo, D. (1938b), *Sobre a Teoria da Renda*, Lisbon: Editorial Inquérito, translated by E. Salgueiro from Gonner's edition, 1919.

Ricardo, D. (1955–61), *Works*, Russian edition in five vols, (ed.) M.N. Smith, Moscow: Politizdat.

Ricardo, D. (1958–65), *Obras y correspondencia de David Ricardo*, (eds) P. Sraffa and M.H. Dobb, Mexico: Fondo de Cultura Económica.

Ricardo, D. (1959), *Über die Grundsätze der Politischen Ökonomie und der Besteuerung*, translated and introduced by G. Bondi, (ed.) P. Thal, Vol. 1 of the series *Ökonomische Studientexte*, Berlin: Akademie Verlag.

Ricardo, D. (1969–99), *Japanese Translation of: The Works and Correspondence of David Ricardo, edited by P. Sraffa with the collaboration of M.H. Dobb*, Tokyo: Yushodo Shoten; Vol. I: 1972, (ed.) T. Hori; Vol. II: 1971, (ed.) K. Suzuki; Vol. III: 1969, (ed.) S. Suenaga et al.; Vol. IV: 1970, (ed.) Y. Tamanoi; Vol. V: 1978, (ed.) T. Sugimoto et al.; Vols VI–IX: 1970–1975, (ed.) T. Nakano et al.; Vol. X: 1970, (ed.) T. Hori; Vol. XI: 1999, (ed.) T. Sugimoto et al.

Ricardo, D. (1972), *Grundsätze der Politischen Ökonomie und der Besteuerung*, from the translation of H. Waentig, edited and introduced by F. Neumark, Stuttgart: Gustav Fischer.

Ricardo, D. (1975), *Principios de Economia Política e de Tributação*, Lisbon: Fundação Calouste Gulbenkian, translated by M.A. Fereira from Fogarty's edition, 1965.

Ricardo, D. (1976), *Sui principi dell'economia politica e delle tassazione*, edited and introduced by F. Vianello, Milan: Isedi.

Ricardo, D. (1986–87), *Opere di David Ricardo, Vol. I: Principi di economia politica e dell'imposta; Vol. II: Note a Malthus e Saggi*, edited and introduced by P.L. Porta, Turin: UTET ('Classici dell'economia').

Ricardo, D. (1992), *Principes de l'économie politique et de l'impôt*, translated by C. Soudan in collaboration with B. Delmas, T. Demals, F.-R. Mahieu, H. Philipson and F. Vandervelde, Paris: Flammarion.

Ricardo, D. (1994), *Über die Grundsätze der Politischen Ökonomie und der Besteuerung*, translated by G. Bondi, (ed.) H.D. Kurz with the collaboration of C. Gehrke and O. Kotheimer, Marburg: Metropolis.

Ricardo, D. (2008), *Russian Translation of: Principles of Political Economy, and Taxation. Selected Works*, edited with an introduction by P.N. Klyukin, Moscow: ECSMO.

Notes on Malthus

The title *Notes on Malthus* properly refers to the contents of Volume II, first printed in 1951, of the Royal Economic Society Edition of the *Works and Correspondence of David Ricardo*, edited by Piero Sraffa. The volume reproduces the first edition (1820) of T.R. Malthus's *Principles of Political Economy* together with the 'Notes on Mr. Malthus work "Principles of Political Economy, considered with a view to their practical application" By David Ricardo' inscribed (in Ricardo's own hand) on the front page of the original manuscript now preserved in Cambridge at the University Library.

In a more general way the name can be extended to include Ricardo's further *Notes on Malthus's 'Measure of Value'*, which are described by Sraffa as 'the only considerable item' not included in the Royal Economic Society edition (*Works*, X: 392). They should in fact have been included in Volume IV (*Pamphlets and Papers, 1815–23*) published four years earlier. This omission is probably the only relatively serious oversight in a critical edition otherwise close to perfection. They were published more recently (see Ricardo [1823] 1992) by Cambridge University Press as a 'companion volume' to the Ricardo edition.

Besides the extant *Notes*, it should be observed that the debates between Ricardo and Malthus, at that stage, were also in parallel with the criticisms of J.-B. Say on Malthus, in Say's *Lettres à M. Malthus*, of 1820 (Say, 1820). Ricardo also wrote notes on Say's *Lettres*, as he states in a letter to Malthus (see *Works*, VIII: 301). Ricardo was 'by no means pleased' with the quality of Say's rebuttal of Malthus: in Say's works – Ricardo observed – 'there is a great mixture of profound thinking, and of egregious blundering' (ibid.: 302) but Ricardo's notes on Say have not been found.

The *Notes on Malthus*, properly speaking, were the result of a remarkable episode in 1820 among the continuing exchanges between the two authors, which had so much influence in shaping Ricardo's political economy. While Malthus had risen to fame as the author of the *Essay on Population* well in advance of his acquaintance and first exchanges with Ricardo in 1811, he only had occasion to put forward his own views on political economy, vis-à-vis Ricardo's views, through journal articles or in pamphlets and, of course, in correspondence. It was only after the first appearance of Ricardo's own *Principles* in 1817 that Malthus became determined to outline his own position in the more comprehensive form of a full treatise on political economy. 'I want to answer you' – he wrote to Ricardo – without giving my work a controversial air' (quoted by Sraffa, *Works*, II: vii).

Malthus's book of *Principles* appeared in print in April 1820. As soon as the book came out Ricardo felt immediately attracted by it. He found it easy and enjoyable to restate his own views in writing in opposition to Malthus's. This course of action was probably suggested to him by the French edition of his own *Principles*, edited and annotated by J.-B. Say, published the year before. He must have imagined giving Malthus's book the same treatment. He proceeded by quoting a few words from Malthus's text and adding his own comments.

While the idea of a publication was certainly present in Ricardo's mind during the process of drafting the *Notes* at least as a possibility, once they had been laid down, he ended up changing his mind on the matter. He was torn between considering that an annotated edition could in fact attract a good deal of interest toward Malthus's book (which by itself appeared to sell poorly), while at the same time realizing that the *Notes* did not have a sufficiently inviting form for the public to warrant publication. On the other side, Malthus, far from encouraging an annotated edition, made it immediately clear to Ricardo that he was himself working on a new edition of the book.

Ricardo having given up any project of publication of the *Notes*, the manuscript (which, of course, was known to exist among Ricardo's disciples) disappeared from sight for almost a century, only to return to light in 1919, when it was found by a great-grandson of David Ricardo at one of David's country residences. The discovery was later communicated to Jacob H. Hollander, the greatest Ricardian scholar at the time, who published the *Notes* with T.E. Gregory as co-editor in 1928 (see Ricardo [1820]

1928). The Hollander-Gregory edition, however, was criticized for failing to fulfil Ricardo's own original plan of printing Malthus's text with Ricardo's *Notes* distributed at the bottom of the page. The Sraffa edition comes much closer to that model, though it is not itself entirely satisfactory, as Malthus's text is not given in full, being cut to approximately two-thirds of the original size.

Instead of producing a second edition of his book (that would in fact only appear post-humously in 1834), Malthus soon brought out a much smaller pamphlet, *The Measure of Value Stated and Illustrated*, published in 1823 (see Ricardo [1823] 1992). That pamphlet too immediately came to be the object of a further set of *Notes* by Ricardo (as mentioned above, this set of *Notes* was first published only in 1992), which are in fact a short sequel to the main *Notes* of 1820.

Ricardo was evidently amused reading Malthus's books and, particularly in the main *Notes* of 1820, he let his pen run riot with comments and remarks. He considered that 'if I do send it forth it will want a great deal of lopping' (quoted by Sraffa, *Works*, II: ix). What Ricardo's *Notes* can offer a reader today is a relaxed, though constantly control-led and rigorous, restatement of various parts of Ricardo's system in interesting and perceptive ways. At the same time the *Notes* give evidence of a number of developments of Ricardo's political economy. In what follows we shall try to highlight some of the relevant issues discussed in the *Notes*.

The main object of discussion between Malthus and Ricardo in the *Notes on Malthus* is twofold. On the one side we have a debate on value, which has more space in the first half of the book. After that, especially in the second part, we find the discussion on the possibility of a 'general glut'. What we call here the 'first part' of Malthus's book (over 300 pages out of 522 in the original: *Works*, II gives the original paging of Malthus's first edition) is largely devoted to value, followed by distribution. The sequence of the chapters is as follows: (1) Wealth and productive labour (definitions), (2) Value, (3) Rent, (3) Wages, (5) Profits. The clash of ideas is explicit. From the start Ricardo readily remarks that Malthus appears to be self-contradictory on value. 'Mr Malthus justly complains' – Ricardo argues – 'of gold and silver as being variable commodities, and therefore not fit for a measure of real value . . . What we want is a standard . . . which shall be itself invariable' (Note 11, *Works*, II: 29). On that premise Malthus proceeds, altogether incoherently (in Ricardo's view), to choose labour or corn – despite their obvious variability – as the standard and he ends up declaring (obviously an empty dec-laration, in Ricardo's view) that both of them are invariable. Here, a general character of Malthus's book is surfacing, namely the inclination to return to Adam Smith in opposi-tion to Ricardo. Value is a case in point: Ricardo had already emphasized his difference from Adam Smith very clearly, right through the opening pages of his *Principles*. In those pages Smith is accused of wavering between two entirely different standard measures of the value of a commodity, that is, between 'labour bestowed on their production' and 'quantity [of labour] which it can command in the market' (*Works*, I: 13–14). The former standard is – Ricardo adds (ibid.) – 'under many circumstances an invariable standard', while 'the latter is subject to as many fluctuations as the commodities compared with it'. Malthus, in his *Principles*, thus appears to Ricardo to passively follow suit and fall into the same error.

It should be recalled that Ricardo's work on the *Notes on Malthus* was done in parallel with the revision of his own *Principles* for the third edition, which would appear in print the year after. With the exception of the insertion of a new chapter (the famous Chapter 31, 'On Machinery'), as far as the rest of the book is concerned it is well-known that most of Ricardo's revisions concerned the first chapter ('On Value'). One of Ricardo's aims was to show that increases in wages are *not* passed on to prices: an increase of wages simply reduces profits (this fact is at the root of his 'language about proportions'; see below). To achieve the result, of course, it was enough to rely on the labour theory of value. In trying to go beyond the, avowedly imperfect, labour-embodied principle, Ricardo discovered the extraordinary conclusion that in many cases an increase of wages, far from leading to increased prices, is in fact bound to produce a surprising *decrease* of prices.

Malthus, in his own chapter on the 'Measures of Value', observed (see *Works*, II: 60) – with reference to Ricardo's measure of value – that the 'proposition of Mr. Ricardo, which shews that a *rise* in the price of labour *lowers* the price of a large class of commodities, has undoubtedly a very paradoxical air; but it is nevertheless true' (emphasis added). Ricardo had himself stressed the significance of this counterintuitive result (see the famous discussion by Sraffa in his 'Introduction' to *Works*, I: xxxv). In the *Notes* – as Malthus appeared now ready to approve – Ricardo's first reaction was to rebuke Malthus (Note 24, *Works*, II: 60–61) for his past concessions to the popular contrary view, that a rise of wages is inflationary, while readily congratulating him for a healthy change of mind on the issue. At the same time, however, Malthus was able to carry the argument one step further by making the case of those commodities ('a large class' he writes) 'where the proportion of labour is very great compared with the capital which employs it' (ibid.: 63, 64). These commodities – Malthus argues – will definitely *have* to rise in price when wages rise (and profits fall), so that it cannot be correct (Malthus concludes) to say, as Ricardo had done in his second edition, that 'no commodities whatever are raised in exchangeable value merely because wages rise' (*Works*, I: 63n). The iconic case here is Malthus's 'silver . . . found by a day's search on the sea-shore' (*Works*, II: 81).

Confronted with Malthus's comment, Ricardo readily acknowledged (Note 25, ibid.: 64) that 'I inadvertently omitted to consider the converse of my first proposition'. He thereby introduced the necessary amendments to the choice of the standard. Concerning the standard of value, the solution he would adopt in the third edition of his *Principles* (in the new Section 6 of the first chapter on the 'invariable measure': see *Works*, I: 45), was in fact anticipated in Note 24 (*Works*, II: 61), where the concession was introduced that:

> [i]n all cases where the rise in the price of corn, is followed by a rise in the money price of wages, and a fall of profits, so far from it being true that all other commodities would also rise in price, there will be a large class which will absolutely fall – some which will not vary at all, and another large class which will rise.

The concession is, indeed, made rather grudgingly ('The last class will rise only in a trifling degree', ibid.: 63). At any rate the result is, as Sraffa observes (*Works*, I: xliv), that '[t]his concession in the *Notes on Malthus* marks the transition between ed. 2 and ed. 3' of Ricardo's *Principles*. In the third edition a standard commodity is chosen that may be 'so nearly equally distant from the two extremes' (ibid.: 45).

This is a case where an insight by Malthus prompted Ricardo to refine his own views significantly. Other similar instances had concerned rent theory or the corn-ratio theory of profits. In the relationship Malthus was probably attracted by Ricardo's unfailing rigour, while Ricardo must have appreciated Malthus's imaginative insights, while he felt at ease on the logical ground.

In 1823 it was the reading of Malthus's pamphlet on value, that induced Ricardo to return to the issue after over two years' interval: the measure of value was thus brought back in place as the dominant problem in his letters during the last months of his life (he died on September 11). In his *Notes* on Malthus's 1823 pamphlet, Ricardo insisted on criticizing the arbitrary character of Malthus's choice of a standard. Both here and in the ensuing correspondence, however, Ricardo, by increasingly emphasizing the *impossibility* of attaining a perfect standard, admitted that a choice was open among avowedly imperfect 'special cases'. In that context, Malthus's standard (labour commanded or silver picked up on the seashore in a day) could take its place as one such case: though in principle no more subject to criticism than any other special case, Ricardo (in line with his *Notes* of 1820) came to regard it as an extreme case.

Through the chapters on distribution Malthus takes Ricardo to task on rent, which he calls 'that specific surplus so much under-rated by Mr Ricardo' (in *Works*, II: 210; see also Note 59, ibid.: 123). In a typical reaction: 'Perhaps in no part of his book has Mr Malthus so much mistaken me as on this subject', Ricardo writes. Malthus 'represents me as supporting the doctrine that the interests of landlords are constantly opposed to those of every other class of the community, and one would suppose from his language that I consider them as enemies of the state'. Ricardo disclaims the indictment completely (Note 58, ibid.: 117). He insists that 'Mr Malthus's great mistake' is that of identifying surplus with rent (see in particular, Note 73, ibid.: 134; see also 122 and 128). He also defends his own 'language about proportions' (Note 115, ibid.: 196), but he concedes to Malthus that rent 'is not a proportion of the produce obtained – it is not governed like wages and profits by proportions' (ibid., 196: n1, a deleted passage). Ricardo's 'language about proportions', or value measured by proportions, looms large in the *Notes* of 1820: Notes 161 (ibid.: 252ff) and 171 (ibid.: 264ff) offer clear and neat examples. Ricardo argues that there are cases where '[t]he portion paid to the labourers is less, but the proportion of the whole produce obtained by their labour is greater . . . I contend then that a greater proportion and a greater value mean the same thing' (ibid.: 254), for 'value is measured by proportions, and a high value means a large proportion of the whole produce'. On the contrary 'Mr Malthus says value is not measured by proportions it is measured by quantity' (ibid.: 267).

It is interesting that in at least two of Ricardo's comments to the chapter on wages we can read an anticipation of his revolutionary change of mind on machinery, which is further evidence of how the drafting of the *Notes* went hand in hand with the preparation of the third edition of the *Principles*, as already noted above in the case of the measure of value. In Note 149 (ibid.: 235–6) Ricardo wrote:

> It appears that to a person saving capital, it can be of no importance whether it be employed as fixed or as circulating . . . The country, which is enriched only by the net income, and not by the gross income, will be equally powerful in both cases . . . but it is of the greatest importance to those who live by the wages of labour . . . If capital is realized in machinery, there will be little demand for an increased quantity of labour.

In Note 153 (ibid.: 239) Ricardo further argues that 'it might happen with a cheaper mode of cultivation the demand for labour might diminish'; and he makes the case of the substitution of horses for men in agricultural production. Ricardo's change of mind would give rise to the new Chapter 31 of the third edition of *Principles*, 1821.

Keynes's well-known opinion on the devastating success of Ricardian economics was, of course, essentially based on the question of the role of demand and on the validity of Say's Law. Other sides of the question, concerning the overall significance of Ricardo's economics, are left aside by him. As he quotes a sentence where Malthus states, in a letter to Ricardo, the 'opinion that practically the actual check to produce and population arises more from want of stimulus than want of power to produce', Keynes is led to exclaim:

> One cannot rise from a perusal of this correspondence [between Malthus and Ricardo] without a feeling that the almost total obliteration of Malthus's line of approach and the complete domination of Ricardo's for a period of a hundred years has been a disaster to the progress of economics. (Keynes [1933] 1972: 98)

The possibility of a general glut, upheld by Malthus and denied by Ricardo, is perhaps the single issue for which their controversy is famous. Let us see how far and why Ricardo's *Notes* of 1820 are to be rated a *locus classicus* in that respect: 'The part of your book to which I most object,' Ricardo wrote in one of his letters to Malthus 'is the last. I can see no soundness in the reasons you give for the usefulness of demand, on the part of unproductive consumers. How their consuming, without reproducing, can be beneficial to a country, in any possible state of it, I confess I cannot discover' (see *Works*, VIII: 301).

As Malthus puts the question 'how is it possible to suppose that the increased quantity of commodities, obtained by the increased number of productive labourers should find purchasers', Ricardo's answer is that:

> if the commodities produced be suited to the wants of the purchasers, they cannot exist in such abundance as not to find a market. Mistakes may be made . . . but then this is owing to the mistake, and not to the want of demand for productions. (Note 196, *Works*, II: 303–5)

> Mr Malthus talks of 'an economy of consumption, and a discouragement to the indulgence of those tastes and wants which are the very elements of demand'. The whole matter in dispute is centered in these few words. Mr Say, Mr Mill and I say that there will be no economy of consumption no cessation of demand . . . The will to consume exists wherever the power to consume is. (Note 201, ibid.: 311)

'[D]emand depends only on supply' (Note 243, ibid.: 365). '[C]ommodities' – Ricardo contends – 'are purchased with commodities' (Note 263, ibid.: 395).

When it comes to argue of a 'body of unproductive consumers' to make up for an excessive and rapid accumulation, Ricardo retrieves his own theory of savings, investment and growth (e.g., ibid.: 417) and he concludes: 'A body of unproductive labourers are just as necessary and as useful with a view to future production, as a fire, which should consume in the manufacturers warehouse the goods which those unproductive labourers would otherwise consume' (Note 284, ibid.: 421).

PIER LUIGI PORTA

See also:

Essay on Profits; General Glut; Malthus–Ricardo Debate; Say's Law.

References

Keynes, J.M. ([1933] 1972), *Essays in Biography*, in *The Collected Writings of John Maynard Keynes, Vol. X*, London: Macmillan.

Ricardo, D. ([1820] 1928), *Notes on Mr. Malthus' 'Principles of Political Economy'*, (eds) J.H. Hollander and T.E. Gregory, Baltimore, MD: Johns Hopkins University Press.

Ricardo, D. ([1823] 1992), *David Ricardo: Notes on Malthus's 'Measure of Value'*, (ed.) P.L. Porta, Cambridge UK: Cambridge University Press, accessed 5 December 2014 at http://igamo.free.fr/maltuval.pdf.

Say, J.-B. (1820), *Lettres à M. Malthus sur différens sujets d'économie politique*, Paris/London: Bossange et Co.

Papers on Money and Banking

Money is what made Ricardo become an economist. As Piero Sraffa wrote in 1951 in his 'Note on the Bullion Essays':

> Ricardo's first appearance in print marked the beginning of what came to be known as the Bullion Controversy. It took the shape of an anonymous article on The Price of Gold published in the *Morning Chronicle* of 29 August 1809. (*Works*, III: 3)

This sentence emphasizes two striking aspects of Ricardo's first monetary writing. On the one hand, it was the first time Ricardo expressed himself publicly (albeit anonymously), although he was at the time already aged 37 and had engaged for a long time in extensive business transactions as a jobber and a loan contractor, that is, a financial intermediary specialized in government funds. On the other hand, this article, together with two further published letters and Ricardo's 1810 pamphlet *The High Price of Bullion, a Proof of the Depreciation of Bank Notes* (*Works*, III: 47–99), launched the so-called Bullionist Controversy, which culminated with the report of the Bullion Committee, appointed in 1810 by the House of Commons. Thus, Ricardo's first publications on money gained him immediate recognition as a major figure in the economic debates of the time.

What Sraffa calls 'the Bullion Essays' of 1809–11 would remain the only works by Ricardo during four more years, until he published in 1815 *An Essay on the Influence of a Low Price of Corn on the Profits of Stock*. Again, during the interval that separated this essay from his 1817 masterpiece *On the Principles of Political Economy, and Taxation*, Ricardo published (in 1816) a new monetary pamphlet, *Proposals for an Economical and Secure Currency* (*Works*, IV: 49–141), where he suggested a plan that he would later defend in Parliament. His last pamphlet, *Plan for the Establishment of a National Bank*, published posthumously in 1824 (*Works*, IV: 275–300), was also a monetary publication. All in all, around one half of Ricardo's published writings are on money, and they all aimed at influencing, in a controversial but also constructive tone, the debates of his time. Not only was Ricardo a great monetary economist but he also battled to criticize others' views on currency and banks and to persuade his contemporaries of the beneficial practical consequences of his own views.

During the 14 years of Ricardo's writings on money, two main periods may be distinguished. The first covers the 'Bullion Essays' of 1809–11. The issue was then the working of a monetary system in which the Bank of England note had become inconvertible (in 1797), and the explanation of why this had resulted in a fall in the value of the pound sterling. Ricardo's tone was mainly critical (particularly of the Bank of England – BoE hereafter), although the last writing of that period contained a scheme for a new monetary system. The second period runs from 1816 to Ricardo's death in 1823. The end of the Napoleonic Wars opened up the possibility of a return to a normal (i.e., with convertibility of the BoE note) monetary system, and Ricardo's aim was to show that the pre-1797 situation should not just be reverted to, but changed substantially. He successively advocated two plans, one based on convertibility of the BoE note into bullion (the so-called 'Ingot Plan') and one based on the substitution of a public bank for the BoE as sole issuer of bank notes (the plan for a national bank). Although Ricardo won the Parliament's approval for his first plan in 1819, the return to convertibility at pre-war parity actually took place in 1821 along pre-1797 lines, and this led Ricardo to develop his second plan, which remained unsuccessful because of his death in 1823.

Ricardo and the Bullionist Controversy (1809–11)

The main writing by Ricardo during that period was *The High Price of Bullion, a Proof of the Depreciation of Bank Notes*, published in early January 1810 and republished three times, the fourth edition of April 1811 with an Appendix. Together with three letters previously published in the *Morning Chronicle* in 1809, this pamphlet launched the debate that led to the *Bullion Report*. Three other letters published in the same newspaper in 1810, and the pamphlet *Reply to Mr. Bosanquet's Practical Observations on the Report of the Bullion Committee* of January in 1811 (*Works*, III: 155–256), were a defence of that report.

The focus of the Bullionist Controversy was on the causes of the fall in the value of the pound. Ricardo's starting point was the established fact of a high price of gold bullion in pound sterling, that is, a market price higher than the legal price of gold in coin (£3 17s 10½d an ounce of standard gold). In other words, the current value of the pound in terms of gold taken as the standard was below its legal one. What did that fact reflect? In Ricardo's terms, of what was it 'a proof'? The market price of bullion being a money price, its high level could mean that gold was 'high' or that money was 'low'. In the first case, it was a proof of something happening on the side of gold and affecting the relation between the supply of and the demand for gold in the market, independently of money. In the second case, it was a proof of something happening on the side of money: its depreciation, measured by the spread between the market price of gold in bullion and the legal price of gold in coin. Then Ricardo's first task was to distinguish between these two cases. According to Ricardo, the distinction between them was usually obscured by two related confusions: between a fall in the value of the currency and a depreciation of the currency, and between the value and the price of gold: 'The error of this [Thornton's] reasoning proceeds from not distinguishing between an increase in the value of gold, and an increase in its money price' (*Works*, III: 60). These confusions would always be a matter of recurrent complaint by Ricardo, and he tried to dispel them in his later writings.

The distinction between two possible causes of the high price of gold bullion was at the heart of the Bullionist Controversy and of Ricardo's contributions to it. First, Ricardo rejected the explanation by an adverse foreign balance; second he explained the high price of bullion by the depreciation of the inconvertible bank notes. In the case of a diagnosis that gold was 'high', one had to look for the (real) factors affecting the relation between the supply of and the demand for it. Here another established fact should be considered: the fall in the exchange rate of the pound. A large part of the *Reply* was devoted to a discussion of the amount of this fall. In contrast with the internal depreciation of the currency, which may be precisely measured by the spread between two observable magnitudes (the market price of gold bullion and the legal price of gold in coin), the external depreciation (the amount by which the exchange was 'against' England) is harder to compute, because it is measured by the spread between an observed magnitude (the quoted exchange rate of the pound in terms of a chosen foreign currency) and a computed one (the par of exchange on the coins). In the case of the exchange with Hamburg – the other important centre in Europe in addition to Paris – the computation of the par was all the more complicated since the pound was on a de facto gold standard and the mark banco was on a de jure silver standard.

The fall in the exchange rate of the pound excluded a factor operating at world level (e.g., a decline in gold production), since in that case the exchange rate would have been left unchanged. In the absence of an observed increase in the domestic demand for gold, there remained one candidate only: the demand for export, generated by England's adverse foreign balance. This had been well-known for a long time: in such a case (whatever the reason for the adverse balance) the demand for bills of exchange denominated in foreign currencies was higher than the demand for bills denominated in pounds, and the exchange rate of the pound declined. When it reached the export bullion point, gold was demanded in London for export and its price moved upward.

The first question raised by Ricardo was thus: did the adverse foreign balance, independently of any monetary disorder, account for the high price of bullion? Thornton, in his 1802 book, *An Enquiry into the Nature and Effects of the Paper Credit of Great Britain*, had recognized this possibility, which, according to him, explained the 1793–97 crisis and the fall of the exchange rate in 1800–2. Was it happening again? Ricardo's answer, as early as his first 1809 article and in all his subsequent writings, was that not only did this not happen in the circumstances of the time, but it could *never* happen.

The reason was the following. In normal conditions (i.e., a monetary system with metallic coins and convertible bank notes, as pre-1797), the fall of the exchange rate would stop at the export bullion point, computed on the basis of the legal price of gold (obtained from the BoE against notes) and the cost of its transportation abroad – this was the so-called 'gold-points mechanism'. The export of gold would then correct the balance, since gold was a commodity like any other, and its export would continue until it stopped the fall of the exchange rate. In the conditions of the time, however, when bank notes had ceased to be convertible and consequently gold could not be obtained from the BoE at the legal price, exportable gold was only to be found in the market, and the cost of its export now also included the spread between the market price of gold in bullion and the legal price of gold in coin, that is, the depreciation of the currency. The gold-points mechanism still operated (as in normal conditions), but the depreciation of the currency opened a greater margin of fall of the exchange rate:

> While the circulating medium consists, therefore, of coin undebased, or of paper-money immediately exchangeable for undebased coin, the exchange can never be more above, or more below, par, than the expenses attending the transportation of the precious metals. But when it consists of a depreciated paper-money, it necessarily will fall according to the degree of the depreciation. (*Works*, III: 72)

The conclusion was clear-cut: the fall in the exchange rate of the pound was the consequence of the high price of gold bullion, not its cause. This disqualified the explanation of the fall in the value of the pound by autonomous real factors causing an adverse foreign balance; on the contrary the balance (gold excluded) was against England because its currency was depreciated. The explanation had to be found on the side of money.

Turning to money, a second question arose: which money was responsible for the high price of gold bullion? It could be metallic money (specie) or paper money (bank notes). In the first case, the state of the gold and/or silver coinage was at fault. Such a possibility had been debated at the end of the seventeenth century (at the time of the 1696 silver recoinage) and again in the 1760s (leading to the gold recoinage of 1774). Was it happening again? In the second case, bank notes were depreciated, and their excess issue was at fault. The suspension of convertibility and the behaviour of the issuing banks (the BoE and country banks) were then placed centre-stage.

On this question Ricardo's answer was again clear-cut: although he admitted that the state of the coinage could in general be responsible for the depreciation of the currency (this was the reason why Ricardo would advocate the complete substitution of bank notes for metallic coins; see below), he denied it was the case in the conditions of the time. The general case was the following:

> An excess in the market above the mint price of gold or silver bullion, may, whilst the coins of both metals are legal tender, and there is no prohibition against the coinage of either metal, be caused by a variation in the relative value of those metals; but an excess of the market above the mint price proceeding from this cause will be at once perceived by its affecting only the price of one of the metals. Thus, gold would be at or below, while silver was above, its mint price, or silver at or below its mint price, whilst gold was above. (Ibid.: 77)

This general possibility of the market price of one metal being above its legal one (signalling a depreciation of the currency in terms of that metal) explained why Ricardo was against bimetallism (ibid.: 65–6). But, as shown in the quotation, it required specific conditions to be verified. Two possible situations consistent with a high price of gold bullion might be considered. The first one, with coins of both metals being undebased (i.e., their actual intrinsic content in each precious metal being the legal one), happened when, for whatever reason, the market ratio between the price of gold and the price of silver rose above the legal ratio. Nobody would then bring gold to the mint to be coined, because it was more advantageous to sell it in the market; as a consequence silver became the de facto standard. This situation, however, was contradicted by the conditions of the time, where the mint was closed to private agents for silver and the observed market price was above the legal one for both metals (and not only gold). This latter observation was consistent with a second situation, in which coins of one metal (or both) were debased; but this possibility was contradicted by the fact that debased coins were then restricted legal tender (up to £25). In the end, the depreciation of the currency could not be explained by the state of the coinage.

Therefore, as stated in the title of Ricardo's 1810 pamphlet, 'the high price of bullion' was entirely 'a proof of the depreciation of bank notes'. More precisely, the BoE, no longer constrained by the convertibility of its notes, had overissued; it alone was at fault, because the circulation of its notes regulated that of the country banks:

> The writer [Ricardo] proposes, from the admitted principles of political economy, to advance reasons, which, in his opinion, prove, that the paper-currency of this country has long been, and now is, at a considerable discount, proceeding from a superabundance in its quantity, and not from any want of confidence in the Bank of England, or from any doubts of their ability to fulfil their engagements. (Ibid.: 51)

One should observe that, according to Ricardo, the ultimate cause of the observed monetary disorders was not the loss of confidence in the BoE note (a subjective element), but the excess of its quantity issued (an objective one). In the absence of convertibility, the issuing of notes could not be regulated; there was still a standard of the currency (gold) but it could not play its role of regulator of the quantity of money – hence of its value. This statement would be central in Ricardo's later monetary theory.

Having diagnosed that the disease of the pound was a monetary one, caused by an 'excess issue of BoE notes permitted by inconvertibility, Ricardo deduced the appropriate remedy: an immediate contraction of the note issue by the BoE:

> The remedy which I propose for all the evils in our currency, is that the Bank [of England] should gradually decrease the amount of their notes in circulation until they shall have rendered the remainder of equal value with the coins which they represent, or, in other words, till the prices of gold and silver bullion shall be brought down to their mint price. (Ibid.: 94)

This reduction in the market price of bullion would then allow resuming convertibility, without jeopardizing the security of the BoE. The argument put forward by the opponents to such resumption, namely that it should be delayed until the foreign balance ceased to be against England, was then turned upside down. As Ricardo had already written ironically in one of his 1809 letters:

> What becomes then of the argument which has so often been urged in Parliament, that whilst the rate of exchange continued against us, it would not be safe for the Bank to pay in specie; when it is evident that their not paying in specie is the cause of the present low exchange. (Ibid.: 20–21)

These conclusions were in agreement with the *Bullion Report*. But Ricardo went further: the return to convertibility should not be done along pre-1797 lines; the monetary system had to be adapted to increase its security against future disorders. This was the aim of a plan sketched out as early as 1811 (in the Appendix to the fourth edition of *High Price*) and which would be at the heart of all his later monetary proposals.

Ricardo and the return to convertibility (1816–23)

After the end of the Napoleonic Wars in 1815, the debates around the return to convertibility led Ricardo to design two plans, contained in two pamphlets written in 1816 and 1823 respectively (the latter being published posthumously in 1824). The link between these two writings is Chapter XXVII, 'On Currency and Banks' of *On the Principles of Political Economy, and Taxation*, which, in its second (1819) and third (1821) editions, quoted the 1816 essay extensively, and, as early as the first edition (1817), put forward the idea, developed in the 1823 essay, of an independent public bank.

The pamphlet *Proposals for an Economical and Secure Currency* was published in 1816. It introduced two main novelties for BoE notes: they were to be convertible into bullion (ingots bearing the legal price of gold but deprived of legal tender in domestic circulation, hence the name Ingot Plan) instead of specie (as before 1797), and their quantity issued was to vary inversely with the sign of the spread between the market price of gold bullion and the legal price at which it could be obtained (against notes) from the BoE. As for the notes issued by country banks, Ricardo suggested either making them also convertible into bullion, or making BoE notes legal tender, so that country banks' notes would be convertible into them.

The note-issuing rule constituted a radical change with the liberty left until then to the BoE directors to decide at will on an increase or a contraction in the note circulation. This liberty was unrestrained since the suspension of convertibility, but it was already dangerous when (before 1797) they knew that notes issued in excess could be returned to them. The reason was that, as for any banker, they were only interested in the quality of the bills they discounted, but, disregarding the market price of gold or the exchange rate, they were not in a position to vary the overall note circulation in an appropriate way:

> Though I am fully assured, that it is both against the interest and the wish of the Bank [of England] to exercise this power to the detriment of the public, yet, when I contemplate the evil consequences which might ensue from a sudden and great reduction of the circulation, as well as from a great addition to it, I cannot but deprecate the facility with which the State has armed the Bank with so formidable a prerogative. (*Works*, IV, 69; I: 359–60)

The management principle of the note issue suggested by Ricardo was to eliminate these 'evil consequences'. As for the first provision of the plan – the ingot principle, that is, note convertibility into bullion – it introduced a revolutionary change in the monetary system: the circulation would be composed of bank notes *only*, and the elimination of metallic coins amounted to demonetizing gold as domestic means of payment. Gold remained solely the standard regulating the value of money in a more economical but above all more secure way:

> To secure the public against any other variations in the value of the currency than those to which the standard itself is subject, and, at the same time, to carry on the circulation with a medium the least expensive, is to attain the most perfect state to which a currency can be brought. (*Works*, IV: 66; *Works*, I: 356–7)

Ricardo, in the sentence immediately following the four pages of *Proposals* inserted in *Principles*, stated that the object of the plan was to substitute (convertible) paper money for specie: 'A currency is in its most perfect state when it consists wholly of paper money, but of paper money of an equal value with the gold which it professes to represent' (*Works*, I: 361).

When the debates on the return to convertibility resumed in 1819, Ricardo defended his Ingot Plan successfully in the House of Commons (where he had been elected), which adopted it as the basis of the return to convertibility anticipated for 1821. He described this episode in a letter as 'the triumph of science and truth in the great councils of the Nation' (*Works*, VIII: 44). Unfortunately, this 'triumph' did not last. During the 1819 legislative process an amendment had been introduced according to which, starting on 1 May 1822, the BoE would have the choice to pay its notes in coin or bullion (*Works*, V: 8, n1); knowing the hostility of the BoE to note convertibility into bullion, this implied shortening the Ingot Plan experiment. When the date of the return to pre-war parity (1 May 1821) arrived, a new act anticipated this possibility of choice. Finally, Ricardo's plan was legal only from 1 February 1820 till 1 May 1821; this was purely formal, since during that period the market price of gold was below the legal price, so that only 13 'Ricardoes' (the popular name for the stamped ingots) were demanded as collectors' pieces out of the 2028 delivered in 1820 by the mint to the BoE (cf. the 'Notes on the evidence on the resumption of cash payments' written by Sraffa in 1952, *Works*, V: 368–70).

In spite of his plan having been dropped, Ricardo was accused of being responsible for the deflation that followed the resumption of cash payments. In a controversy with Charles Western that covered two Parliamentary sessions (1822–23), Ricardo maintained that the resumption of cash payments could only explain an increase in the value of money up to 10 per cent, half as a consequence of the return to the pre-1797 mint price of gold, the other half as a consequence of an increase in the world value of gold, provoked by the purchases of the BoE in the perspective of a return to convertibility into coin. In Ricardo's view, his Ingot Plan could not be held responsible for that outcome, since, by economizing on the gold reserves of the BoE, convertibility into bullion, if adopted, would have avoided half of the deflation having a monetary origin.

There was more: Ricardo was convinced that the BoE, who, from the very beginning, had opposed it, had torpedoed his plan. Another plan was found in his papers after his death on 11 September 1823; it developed an idea already present in *Principles*: the transfer of the note issue from the Bank of England to an independent public bank (for an analysis of the controversy between Western and Ricardo and a comparison between the two plans, see Deleplace, 2008).

Besides the Ingot Plan, a large part of the 1816 pamphlet had been devoted to a critique of the excessive profits made by the BoE in its lending activity to the government (an activity that had been the initial reason for its establishment in 1694). This cost incurred by the management of the national debt was an inconvenience that added up to the incompetence of the BoE in the management of the note issue. Both defects could be eradicated if the monopoly of the note issue was transferred from the BoE to a public bank, whose independent commissioners would also manage the national debt. This idea appeared in a letter to Malthus as early as 1815:

> I cannot help considering the issuing of paper money as a privilege which belongs exclusively to the state. – I regard it as a sort of seignorage, and I am convinced, if the principles of currency were rightly understood, that Commissioners might be appointed independent of all ministerial controul who should be the sole issuers of paper money. (*Works*, VI: 268)

The idea was introduced publicly in the first edition of *Principles* (1817), and preserved for the two later editions in addition to the Ingot Plan. It was only when it became clear in 1821 that the BoE had torpedoed the Ingot Plan that Ricardo developed his other idea in a proper plan.

The *Plan for the Establishment of a National Bank* was written by Ricardo in July and August 1823, shortly before his death, and was published by his brother Moses Ricardo in February 1824. It had been anticipated in Chapter XXVII of *Principles*, where the proposal of an independent public bank included the ingot and management principles, which in this case were transferred from the existing BoE note to a new public note. Its advantage was to do away with the interest paid by the State on the money borrowed from the BoE, and consequently to save individuals the taxes necessary to pay for that charge of interest. Ricardo discarded two objections that could be raised to that proposal. The first objection was that a public note issue would soon become beyond control. Ricardo responded as follows:

> Under an arbitrary Government, this objection would have great force; but, in a free country, with an enlightened legislature, the power of issuing paper money, under the requisite checks of convertibility at the will of the holder, might be safely lodged in the hands of commissioners appointed for that special purpose, and they might be made totally independent of the control of ministers. (*Works*, I: 362)

The second objection was that, by removing the possibility of issuing notes through the discounting of bills, the proposal would reduce the availability of borrowed funds to merchants and slow down their activity. Ricardo was straightforward: referring to his theory of value and rent, he maintained that the rate of interest at which the BoE lent to some of the merchants had no influence on the overall accumulation of capital, which would remain the same under the proposed banking system:

> In another part of this work, I have endeavoured to show, that the real value of a commodity is regulated, not by the accidental advantages which may be enjoyed by some of its producers, but by the real difficulties encountered by that producer who is least favoured. It is so with respect to the interest for money; it is not regulated by the rate at which the Bank will lend, whether it be 5, 4, or 3 per cent, but by the rate of profits which can be made by the employment of capital, and which is totally independent of the quantity, or of the value of money. (Ibid.: 363)

In his 1823 plan, Ricardo again advocated that the issuing of notes and discount lending, linked in the BoE, could and should be separated. He stated that: 'Five Commissioners shall be appointed, in whom the full power of issuing all the paper money of the country shall be exclusively vested' (*Works*, IV: 285). This had three consequences. First, the BoE would remain solely a discount bank, like any other. Second, since the new bank got the monopoly of the note issue for the whole country – and not only for the London area, as was the case previously for the BoE – country banks were also deprived of their issuing power. Third, after his Ingot Plan had been abandoned in 1821, Ricardo stepped back to a mixed monetary system (coins and notes) and to note convertibility into specie; he nevertheless suggested obliging the new bank to sell gold bullion at a fixed price, which amounted to separate convertibility for domestic and foreign payments. Moreover, Ricardo stood firmly on the management principle of varying the note issue with the observed market price of gold bullion ('Regulating their issues by the price of gold, the commissioners could never err'; ibid.: 293). This variation would be obtained through purchases or sales by the bank, either on the gold bullion market or on the government securities market. The bank was, however, forbidden to lend directly to the State:

> I propose also to prevent all intercourse between these Commissioners and ministers, by forbidding every species of money transaction between them. The Commissioners should never, on any pretence, lend money to Government, nor be in the slightest degree under its control or influence. (Ibid.: 282)

Published five months after the death of Ricardo, the plan did not arouse much attention, then or in 1838 when another of his brothers, Samson, republished it as an Appendix to a pamphlet.

The legacy of Ricardo's monetary battles
The usual – albeit incorrect – assimilation of Ricardo with monetary orthodoxy manifests itself in an overemphasis, in much of the literature since, on what that doctrine inherited from him. I will limit myself to mentioning the supposed link with the Currency School, through which Ricardo's orthodoxy is usually acknowledged. Although this current of thought used the posthumous patronage of Ricardo, the orthodox model of central banking it implemented was in fact at odds with his explicit principles, and Ricardo's

most important monetary proposals – note convertibility into bullion, management and public monopoly of the note issue – did not find their way until the twentieth century.

The division of the BoE into an issue department and a banking department, which was embodied in the Bank Charter Act of 1844, is often presented as deriving from Ricardo's conception of central banking. This is misleading for two reasons. First, this division maintained the note issue in the hands of (to use Ricardo's words) 'a company of merchants' (the BoE), instead of nationalizing it. Second, it did put an end to the liberty of the directors of the BoE to vary the issue at will, but replaced it by a rule that linked the change in the quantity of notes issued to the variation of the metallic reserves of the issue department. This was at odds with Ricardo's statement that the note issue should be *managed*, irrespective of the amount of the metallic reserves of the issuer and of the absolute volume of the outstanding circulation, but solely in reference to the market price of the standard.

This discrepancy between Ricardo's proposed regulation of the note issue and the 'Currency Principle' was not just the outcome of circumstances. They were rooted in different conceptions of the monetary system. The Currency School maintained a mixed monetary system of coins and notes, which contrasted with Ricardo's proposal of an exclusive circulation of paper convertible into gold bullion. It also applied the two main aspects of the Hume-Smith price-specie flow mechanism: its automaticity and the interdependence between domestic circulation and international payments. The metallic reserve of the BoE that constrained the note issue varied with the foreign balance, which in turn depended on the volume of domestic circulation; this automatic adjustment – which was unable to prevent the crises of 1847, 1857 and 1866, when the Bank Charter Act had to be suspended – contrasted with Ricardo's attempt, thanks to convertibility into bullion, to separate domestic note circulation and international bullion payments.

Ricardo's concept of convertibility de facto restricted to foreign payments, as it was embodied in the ingot principle, was his belated but lasting legacy. Later known as the gold-exchange standard, it was resurrected as a practical device by Alfred Marshall in 1887 and Alexander Lindsay in 1892, with explicit reference in both cases to Ricardo (for a comparison between Ricardo's Ingot Plan and Marshall's bimetallic scheme, see Deleplace, 2013). The 'Lindsay scheme' was implemented in India in the very first years of the twentieth century, and in 1913 John Maynard Keynes observed approvingly that 'in the last ten years the gold-exchange standard has become the prevailing monetary system of Asia' (Keynes [1913] 1971: 25), also crediting Ricardo for this breakthrough: 'Its theoretical advantages [of the gold-exchange standard] were first set forth by Ricardo at the time of the bullionist controversy . . . He suggested . . . that gold might be available for purposes of export only, and would be prevented from entering into the internal circulation of the country' (ibid.: 22). As is well known, this system was extended to other countries in inter-war years, and later institutionalized, with qualifications, at Bretton Woods.

GHISLAIN DELEPLACE

See also:

Bullionist Controversy; Gold; Monetary Theory; Natural Quantity of Money; Rate of Interest.

References

Deleplace, G. (2008), 'Les deux plans monétaires de Ricardo', *Cahiers d'économie politique*, **55**, 13–33.

Deleplace, G. (2013), 'Marshall and Ricardo on note convertibility and bimetallism', *The European Journal of the History of Economic Thought*, **20**(6), 982–99.

Keynes, J.M. ([1913] 1971), *Indian Currency and Finance*, in *The Collected Writings of John Maynard Keynes, Vol. 1*, London: Macmillan.

Lindsay, A.M. (1892), *Ricardo's Exchange Remedy: A Proposal to Regulate the Indian Currency by Making it Expand and Contract Automatically at Fixed Sterling Rates, with the Aid of the Silver Clause of the Bank Act*, London: Effingham Wilson & Co.

Marshall, A. ([1887] 1925), 'Remedies for fluctuations of general prices', *Contemporary Review*, **51**, 355–75; reprinted in A.C. Pigou (ed.), *Memorials of Alfred Marshall*, London: Macmillan, pp.188–211.

Thornton, H. ([1802] 1991), *An Enquiry into the Nature and Effects of the Paper Credit of Great Britain*, 1939 edition, edited with an introduction by F.A. von Hayek, London: George Allen and Unwin; reprint: Fairfield, NJ: A.M. Kelley.

Pasinetti, Luigi Lodovico, on Ricardo

Luigi Pasinetti is one of the leading scholars of the classical Keynesian approach. He has a degree in Economics from Università Cattolica del Sacro Cuore, Milan, and a PhD in Economics from Cambridge University, UK. He also studied at Harvard and Oxford. He became a lecturer in economics at the University of Cambridge and a full Professor of Economic Analysis (now Emeritus) at the Università Cattolica del Sacro Cuore. His research spans from production theory, capital theory, value theory, structural change to the history of economic analysis.

In 1960, in the *Review of Economic Studies*, he published an article containing a mathematical formulation of the Ricardian system, which has become the primary reference for all scholars interested in Ricardian economics ever since. It was written in the academic year 1957–58 when Pasinetti was at Harvard University attending a series of seminars for graduate students organized by Franco Modigliani, who was at Harvard that year on leave from Northwestern University. Modigliani asked his students to choose their favourite economist and express his theory in mathematical terms. Pasinetti chose Ricardo (I obtained these details in private conversations with Luigi Pasinetti, who is gratefully acknowledged). His interest in Ricardo had arisen from his previous academic year spent at Cambridge where he had the opportunity to read the Kaldor (1955–56) paper, attend his lectures and read the 'Introduction' to *Works*. Pasinetti recalls that in its first formulation, his paper dealt separately with first the case of just one commodity ('corn'), naturally following Kaldor's diagrams which were put into equations, and then with the case of two commodities ('corn' and 'gold'). When the work was later submitted to Sraffa for discussion, the latter expressed strong disagreement with such a distinction and convinced Pasinetti to immediately start with the case of two commodities (later on, in his *Lectures* – see Pasinetti, 1977: Chapter 1 – he re-proposed this distinction, essentially as a didactic device).

The mathematical formulation

Consider an economic system composed of three classes: landowners, capitalists and workers. Capitalists organize the production process by employing workers and the lands rented by landowners. Two categories of goods are produced, which in the mathematical formulation are reduced to one good for each category: 'necessary' goods (say 'corn') used as wage-goods for workers, and 'luxury' goods (say 'gold'). Both production cycles take exactly one year and capital is constituted just by the wage-good advanced to workers. Lands used in corn production may differ in fertility. Capitalists behave rationally and organize the production of corn on the various plots of land in order of decreasing fertility: lower-quality land is used as the production of corn is increased. This technology can be represented by the function:

$$Q_c = f(N_c), \tag{1}$$

where Q_c is the output of corn and N_c are the workers employed in corn production. Let us suppose that:

$$f(0) \geq 0, \tag{1a}$$

$$f'(N_c) > 0, \tag{1b}$$

$$f''(N_c) < 0, \tag{1c}$$

$$f'(1) > \bar{x}. \tag{1d}$$

Assumption (1a) is trivial; assumptions (1b) and (1c) together reflect the fact that as corn production is extended the additional product decreases as additional workers are employed on less and less fertile plots of land (assumption (1b) was not explicitly intro-duced by Pasinetti). We thus have decreasing returns to scale due to an extensive use of lands of varying quality. From the formal point of view, conditions (1b) and (1c) can also be interpreted in intensive terms, according to the usual assumption of decreasing mar-ginal returns of factors (see Pasinetti, 1977: 10, fn8); this interpretation of conditions (1b) and (1c) is not, however, very relevant for Ricardian analysis. Morishima (1989: 50–51) objected that a unique corn production function, summarizing the input–output relation of *all* lands, could be used 'to explain the rent of a land as the surplus which it yields'; Kurz and Salvadori (1992: §3) proved that Morishima's claim is wrong by showing that, under Pasinetti's assumptions, it is always possible to build a production function of the corn industry as a whole.

Assumption (1d) is a 'viability' condition: 'at least when the economic system begins to operate and workers are employed on the most fertile piece of land, they must produce more than what is strictly necessary for their support' (Pasinetti, 1960: 82; in this original article assumption (1d) takes the form $f'(0) > \bar{x}$; the formulation here adopted is bor-rowed from Pasinetti, 1977, equation (I.3.8–*b*)).

Given the different qualities of lands, the owners of cultivated lands will be able to claim payment from capitalists: the rent. On each plot rent will at most be equal to the difference between the corn produced on that plot and the corn produced on the least productive cultivated plot – called 'marginal land' – given by $f'(N_c)$. Capitalists would have, in fact, the alternative of cultivating on the marginal land or worse lands, where cultivation is free. Total rents (R) are thus given by the difference between the total quantity of corn produced, $f(N_c)$, and the corn that would be produced if all lands had the same fertility as that of the marginal land, $N_c f'(N_c)$:

$$R = f(N_c) - N_c f'(N_c). \tag{2}$$

Gold is produced by labour under constant returns to scale; its technology is described by:

$$Q_g = \alpha N_g, \tag{3}$$

where Q_g is the output of gold, N_g are the workers employed in gold production and α is the quantity of gold produced by one worker. Also, the unit wage x is fixed at the subsistence level $\bar{x}$ on the basis of the Malthusian principle:

$$x = \bar{x}; \tag{4}$$

$\bar{x}$ is not what is physiologically considered as the necessary minimum needed to support workers. It is the level that in a given country and in a specific stage of society keeps the population constant. Total wages (W) are:

$$W = (N_c + N_g)x. \tag{5}$$

Capital (K) consists just in wages advanced to workers:

$$K = W; \tag{6}$$

the total amount of corn that can be advanced to workers is given:

$$K = \bar{K}. \tag{7}$$

Profits are determined as a surplus, that is, as the difference between the gross product (net of rents) and the 'necessary consumption' needed to repeat the production process year after year at least at an unchanged scale. In both industries, necessary consumption consists just of wages. Profits in the corn industry (P_c) are determined in physical terms, as the difference between homogeneous quantities of the same commodity (corn):

$$P_c = (Q_c - R) - N_c x. \tag{8}$$

On the contrary, profits in the gold industry (P_g) must be calculated in value, being the difference between amounts of heterogeneous commodities:

$$P_g = p_g Q_g - p_c N_g x, \tag{9}$$

where p_c and p_g are the prices of corn and of gold. To explain what determines p_c and p_g, we must elaborate a theory of value. Coherently with the analysis developed in the *Principles*, Pasinetti resorts to a pure labour theory of value, according to which the value of each commodity (net of rent, if any) is equal to the quantity of labour required to produce it:

$$p_c(Q_c - R) = N_c, \tag{10}$$

$$p_g Q_g = N_g. \tag{11}$$

However, there is no necessity to introduce explicitly the pure labour theory of value. We will return later to this point. For the moment observe that in Pasinetti (1977) value theory in the Ricardian system is introduced in a different way. We read: 'Ricardo argues that what fundamentally determines the "value" or "natural price" of produced commodities is their cost of production', that is, 'wages plus profits at the ruling rate of profit' (see Pasinetti, 1977: 14). In formal terms this means:

$$p_c(Q_c - R) = p_c x N_c(1 + r) \tag{10$'$}$$

$$p_g Q_g = p_c x N_g(1 + r). \tag{11$'$}$$

Given these conditions, Pasinetti just writes:

$$p_g Q_g / N_g = p_c(Q_c - R)/N_c,$$

which is easily obtained by (10$'$) and (11$'$). This equation (which equalizes the value of the product per worker – net of rents – of the two industries) together with $p_g \alpha = 1$ (which coincides with equation (11) after substituting (3)), replace equations (10) and (11).

The rate of profits of the system (r) is given by:

$$r = \frac{p_c P_c + pg \, Pg}{p_c K}. \tag{12}$$

We thus have 12 equations in 13 unknowns: $Q_c, Q_g, N_c, N_g, R, x, W, K, P_c, P_g, p_c, p_g, r$. The remaining degree of freedom is closed by formulating a theory of expenditure. Like Ricardo, Pasinetti supposes that rents are entirely spent on luxuries (with the exception of a negligible part, not considered here). Hence:

$$p_g Q_g = p_c R. \tag{13}$$

This equation implicitly entails that the output of corn equals the incomes of the other two classes taken together, that is, profits plus wages. In fact, after substitution of equations (8) and (9) into (12) we obtain:

$$r p_c K = p_c(Q_c - R - x N_c) + p_g Q_g - p_c x N_g,$$

and thanks to (5) and (13) one gets:

$$p_c Q_c = r p_c K + p_c W.$$

The configuration described by equations (1)–(13) is called by Pasinetti the 'natural' equilibrium of the Ricardian system. This configuration is actually a 'moving' equilibrium. In fact, besides a theory of distribution, a theory of value and a theory of demand, it is quite easy to enucleate a theory of growth from the economy described by this model. As capitalists save (the main part of) their profits and accumulate them into the stock of corn K available at the beginning of each period, an even higher number of workers can be employed in both industries as time goes by. This entails the cultivation of more and more plots of land of increasingly lower quality. Rents thus augment, squeezing profits from a certain point on, till they are zeroed out (or below that level that induces capital accumulation), with total wages increasing proportionally. The capital accumulation process thus stops and the system reaches the (Ricardian) stationary state. A simple way to study this process is to study the sign of the derivatives of the natural equilibrium value of the endogenous variables of the model with respect to K. More in general, Pasinetti points out that there are at least four dynamic processes at work in Ricardo's system: (i) capital mobility, which tends to equalize the rates of profits of the industries by channelling capital towards the more profitable industries; (ii) a demographic dynamics, determined by the Malthusian mechanism, which pushes the wage rate to its natural level; (iii) capital accumulation, as just described above, and (iv) technical progress, which delays – without subverting – the convergence to the stationary state through shifts of the corn production function. In Pasinetti we do not find an explicit analysis of dynamics (i) and (iv): beyond temporary oscillations, a uniform rate of profits is supposed as permanently achieved on average, while technical progress is supposed by Ricardo to not alter the main conclusions of his analysis. More emphasis is devoted to processes (ii) and (iii), which require the setting of a truly dynamic system that is presented by Pasinetti in the Appendix of his article. The convergence to the stationary state characterized by a rate of profits equal to zero and a wage rate equal to its natural level is formally proved there. But an analysis of process (iii) separated from process (ii) is more interesting from the economic point of view:

> Ricardo, however, investigates the properties of his system at a very particular stage of the whole movement, which he considers the relevant one. Most of the analysis is carried on *as if* the demographic mechanism has already fully worked through, while the capital accumulation process has not yet been completed. (Pasinetti, 1960: 87; original emphasis)

For this reason, the rough analysis based on the sign of partial derivatives of the natural equilibrium value of the endogenous variables of the model with respect to K proves to be more informative than the analysis in the Appendix. Pasinetti obtains thus that all these magnitudes increase as a consequence of capital accumulation with just two exceptions: the rate of profits that decreases, and total profits that increase at the beginning of the process of capital accumulation and decrease when the system approaches the stationary state.

Principles versus *Essay* and the 'early writings'

System (1)–(13) is a stylized version of a Ricardian economy suitably simplified in such a way as to present the core of Ricardo's *Principles* while avoiding all those complications that prevent him from providing univocal and rigorous results. The crucial assumption that makes this experiment possible is the supposition that just one commodity ('corn') is used as capital good. Not surprisingly, but quite interestingly, this simplification coincides with that adopted by Ricardo in the *Essay* (*Works*, IV: 1–41) and in some other early writings that Sraffa (1960; see also the introduction to *Works*) has allowed us to reappraise for their theoretical content and insight. The crucial device of these works is the substantial homogeneity between outputs and inputs (wage-goods or, simply, 'corn') due to the primacy of agriculture. This homogeneity makes it possible to determine the rate of profits of agriculture in *physical* terms with the consequence that competition among capitalists will induce other industries to align their rates of profits to that obtained in agriculture. A simple restyling of the model presented by Pasinetti (1960) provides us with an analytical formulation of this distribution and value theory contained in Ricardo's early writings that seems even more effective than the one provided by Pasinetti of Ricardo's *Principles*. Let us replace the five equations (8)–(12) with the following four equations:

$$r_c := \frac{Q_c - R - xN_c}{xN_c}, \tag{8E}$$

$$r_g = \frac{p_g Q_g - p_c xN_g}{p_c xN_g}, \tag{9E}$$

$$r_g = r_c, \tag{10E}$$

$$p_g \alpha = 1 \tag{11E}$$

(the letter E following the equation numbers stands for *Essay* and Early writings). Equations (8E) and (9E) define the rates of profits of the two industries. The physical nature of the rate of profits of the corn industry emerges immediately: it is a ratio between quantities of corn, Q_g, R, and xN_c; after substituting (1) and (2) r_c can be re-expressed as:

$$r_c = \frac{f'(N_c) - x}{x}.$$

The rate of profits of the corn industry can thus be known *before* the determination of prices. On the other hand, the rate of profits of the gold industry depends on prices. Capital mobility will tend to align the rate of profits of gold to the rate of profits of corn, as stated by equation (10E). Thus, the rate of profits of the entire system is:

$$r = \frac{f'(N_c) - x}{x} \equiv \frac{1 - x/f'(N_c)}{x/f'(N_c)}, \tag{14}$$

where $x/f'(N_c)$ is the quantity of corn paid as wage to the amount of labour required to produce one unit of corn on the marginal land. This result echoes the famous 'basic principle' that 'it is the profits of the farmer that regulate the profits of all other trades' contained both in Ricardo (*Works*, IV: 1–41) and in his correspondence in 1814 and early 1815 with other economists (see *Works*, I: xxxi). This equalization takes place through suitable changes of the relative price of gold in terms of corn: after substituting (8E) and (9E) into (10E) and using (1), (2) and (3) one obtains:

$$\frac{p_g}{p_c} = \frac{1/\alpha}{1/f'(N_c)}. \tag{15}$$

Last, equation (11E) fixes the quantity of gold produced by one worker (α) as the unit of account. Observe that $1/\alpha$ and $1/f'(N_c)$ express the quantities of labour required to produce one unit of gold and one unit of corn on the marginal land, respectively. A pure labour theory of value re-emerges but here it does not enter as an assumption, like in equations (10) and (11), nor does it play a particular role in the theory here considered. It is just a consequence of the assumption that the capital of both industries is constituted by a single commodity; capital intensity is thus uniform between industries, $xN_c/N_c = xN_g/N_g = x$, and the labour theory of value holds (curiously enough, the assumption that capital consists of corn anticipated to workers only leads us also to the opposite extreme, that is, the pure capital theory of value: multiplying both the numerator and the denominator of the right-hand side of (15) by $\bar{x}$ allows us to see the relative price of gold in terms of corn as regulated by the ratio of the quantities of capital-wage required to produce one unit of the two goods). For further reference let us denote by (E) the model constituted by equations (1)–(7), (8E)–(11E) and (13). It contains 12 equations in 12 unknowns: Q_c, Q_g, N_c, N_g, R, x, W, K, p_c, p_g, r_c, r_g.

The direct connection with Sraffa (1960)
Model (E) constitutes the crucial link in the chain from Ricardo's early writings to Sraffa (1960; see also the introduction to *Works*). Sraffa's works appear thus as the generalization of Ricardo's distribution and value theory contained in his early writings:

> It should . . . be stated that it was only when the Standard system and the distinction between basics and non-basics had emerged in the course of the present investigation that the above interpretation of Ricardo's theory [presented here in the above section on '*Principles* versus *Essay* and the "early writings"'] suggested itself as a natural consequence. (Sraffa, 1960: 93; a criticism of this Sraffian 'interpretation' of Ricardo's theory is expressed by Porta, 1986)

The unacceptable restriction that corn was the only commodity required for its own production as well as for the production of all other commodities is now totally removed. By introducing some additional assumptions in the Sraffa system we can see its direct connection with system (E).

(A1)   Wages are paid ex ante

The price system become thus:

$$\mathbf{p}^T = (1 + r)(\mathbf{p}^T\mathbf{A} + w\mathbf{l}^T), \tag{16}$$

where $\mathbf{p}$ is the price vector, $\mathbf{A}$ is the input coefficient matrix, $\mathbf{l}$ is the direct labour coefficient vector and w is the money wage rate.

(A2)   Wages are constituted by a composite commodity represented by vector $\mathbf{x}$

Then:

$$w = \mathbf{p}^{\mathrm{T}}\mathbf{x}. \tag{17}$$

Thanks to (17) the price system (16) can be rewritten as:

$$\mathbf{p}^{\mathrm{T}} = (1 + r)(\mathbf{p}^{\mathrm{T}}\mathbf{A} + \mathbf{p}^{\mathrm{T}}\mathbf{x}\mathbf{l}^{\mathrm{T}}) = (1 + r)\mathbf{p}^{\mathrm{T}}\mathbf{S}, \tag{18'}$$

where $\mathbf{S} = \mathbf{A} + \mathbf{x}\mathbf{l}^{\mathrm{T}}$ is the socio-technical matrix. In this case the ensuing rate of profit is:

$$r = \frac{1 - \lambda_S^*}{\lambda_S^*}, \tag{19}$$

where λ_S^* is the dominant eigenvalue of $\mathbf{S}$.

(A3)   Commodities are just required as wage-goods and not as capital goods

Hence, $\mathbf{A} = \mathbf{O}$.

(A4)   Wages are constituted by just one commodity, say commodity 1

Then $\mathbf{x} = [x_1, 0, \ldots, 0]^{\mathrm{T}}$, matrix $\mathbf{S}$ is reduced to a matrix having all zero entries except for in the first row, which has components $x_1 l_m$, $m = 1, \ldots, M$, where M is the number of commodities. Then $\lambda_S^* = x_1 l_1$, and (19) collapses into:

$$r = \frac{1 - x_1 l_1}{x_1 l_1} \tag{19'}$$

which coincides with equation (14), as $x_1 l_1$ still represents the quantity of commodity 1 paid as wage to the amount of labour required to produce one unit of commodity 1. In this way the correspondence between the Sraffa system and the model presented in the section on '*Principles* versus *Essay* and the "early writings"' above is complete. If some of the above assumptions – in particular (A2), (A3) and (A4) – are relaxed and we allow that commodities are also employed as capital goods and that wages enter as generalized purchasing power and are expressed in terms of the Sraffa Standard commodity, then relation (19') finds its correspondent in:

$$r = \frac{1 - w}{w + 1/R}, \tag{20}$$

where R is the uniform physical rate of surplus of basic commodities (see, for example, Bellino, 2004). Hence, relation (20) extends to the general case of $C \, (\leq M)$ basic commodities the idea (conveyed by (14)) that the rate of profits of a system can be expressed in purely physical terms as the surplus of the production process of basic commodities only.

Concluding remarks
Pasinetti's formulation of the Ricardian system was originally conceived as a mathematical presentation of the basic structure of Ricardo's *Principles*. But the assumption that

capital is constituted just by one commodity has two consequences: on the one hand, it establishes a direct connection of the model with the logical structure described by Ricardo in his *Essay*, rather than in its *Principles*; on the other hand, it renders unnecessary the introduction of the labour theory of value as an assumption, as we have no necessity to measure aggregates of commodities with different compositions in order to calculate the rate of profits. This rate emerges as a ratio of physical quantities of corn for the entire economic system. This result is the point of departure of Sraffa's generalization to any number of basic commodities.

ENRICO BELLINO

See also:

Accumulation of Capital; Corn Model; Endogenous Growth; Hicks, John R., on Ricardo; Kaldor, Nicholas, on Ricardo; Mathematical Formulations of Ricardian Economics; Ricardian Dynamics; Sraffa, Piero, on Ricardo; Technical Change.

References

Bellino, E. (2004), 'On Sraffa's Standard commodity', *Cambridge Journal of Economics*, **28**(1), 121–32.
Kaldor, N. (1955–6), 'Alternative theories of distribution', *The Review of Economic Studies*, **23**(2), 83–100.
Kurz, H.D. and N. Salvadori (1992), 'Review article – Morishima on Ricardo', *Cambridge Journal of Economics*, **16**(2), 227–47.
Morishima, M. (1989), *Ricardo's Economics. A General Equilibrium Theory of Distribution and Growth*, Cambridge, UK: Cambridge University Press.
Pasinetti, L.L. (1960), 'A mathematical formulation of the Ricardian system', *The Review of Economic Studies*, **27**(2), 78–98.
Pasinetti, L.L. (1977), *Lectures on the Theory of Production*, London: Macmillan.
Porta, P. (1986), 'Understanding the significance of Piero Sraffa's Standard commodity: a note on the Marxian notion of surplus', *History of Political Economy*, **18**(3), 443–54.
Sraffa, P. (1960), *Production of Commodities by means of Commodities. Prelude to a Critique of Economic Theory*, Cambridge, UK: Cambridge University Press.

Poor Laws

After the English Reformation, the old monastic protection of the poor was replaced by a complex system of public relief in which the parishes of England and Wales were required to offer aid to their own poor and to raise ad hoc taxes. The system began in 1597–1601 with two Acts of Queen Elizabeth and was shaped over two centuries by central law as well as by local practice. For a long time it evolved slowly, until the end of the eighteenth century; at that time, the total amount of relief dramatically increased, more persons – notably the 'labouring poor' – became eligible and a wider range of provisions were established. This sudden evolution stressed the traditional mode of administration, whose effectiveness was much questioned for some decades in public opinion, in the writings of economists and social reformers and in a series of Parliamentary Reports. Despite many attempts at improvement, it was not until 1834 (Poor Law Amendment Act) that a fully fledged reform radically modified the administration of the poor.

According to Solar (1995), poor relief under the English (old) Poor Laws had three distinctive features. As compared to Continental Europe, it was (1) more uniform and comprehensive; (2) more certain and generous; and (3) its source of finance was a specific tax (the 'poor rate'), levied on property income (mainly from land and buildings), rather than general taxation or voluntary donations as in most continental countries.

By uniformity and comprehensiveness it is not meant, of course, that it was a centralized system. To the contrary, every year some administrators (the 'magistrates' or 'overseers') were selected in each parish (frequently among the leading property owners) and they were responsible for determining poor rates, as well as the quality and quantity of aid to the deserving poor legally settled in their territory; since there were about 15000 parishes, there was a minute decentralization in practical administration, and the overseers frequently had a detailed knowledge of personal circumstances (Blaug, 1963: 160). Conversely, by the Settlement Law, the poor were not free to move from one parish to another and each 'belonged' to his or her parish. This was especially true of rural districts, whereas in industrial areas 'non-resident' relief was occasionally admitted upon repayment from the parish of settlement (Solar, 1995: 7). The system was 'uniform' in the sense that it was established by law that *every* English man and woman under specified conditions had the right to relief: for this reason, every parish was responsible for taking care of the poor and had the authority to raise ad hoc taxes.

As to certainty and generosity, the fundamental question was who were the 'deserving poor'? Old age, widowhood, illness or disability were the traditional entitlements of the poor to claim aid. Even seasonal unemployment in agriculture became a non-controversial entitlement. In this respect, it is agreed that the system worked like a sort of social insurance or 'welfare state in miniature' (cf. Blaug, 1964: 229; Solar, 1995: 7; Winch, 1996: 259–60). By contrast, the rights of the unemployed and those of the 'labouring poor' were open to controversy and were a matter of local judgement and historical circumstances. According to Blaug (1963: 151), 'until late in the eighteenth century, public relief was largely confined to those too young, too old, or too sick to work'; until that time, a strict minority of 'able bodied' were sent to workhouses (indoor relief), but, as Blaug remarks, 'magistrates were frequently reluctant to "offer the house" which was invariably an unsanitary and disorderly institution' (ibid.: 157); besides, there were only some 400 workhouses in the whole country. At the turn of the eighteenth century the inadequacy of real wages, the condition of being unemployed and a large family became entitlements. The French Revolutionary Wars (1792–1801), the 1794 bad harvest, the 1795 famine and the consequent food scarcity and high price of corn depressed real wages greatly. This added to the general distress of the agricultural workers and to the destruction of the handicraft industry that characterized the first phase of the Industrial Revolution in England.

A turning point in the administration of the (old) Poor Laws occurred in 1795, with the institution of the so-called 'Speenhamland system'. In a series of agricultural counties in South-Eastern England, the poor rates started to be used as a subsidy to wages up to a minimum level of subsistence; the (money) subsidy was indexed to the price of bread (the 'bread scale') and included child allowances. Along similar lines, the unemployed were also granted a minimum income. The subsidy was in money or in kind according to the use of the different parishes. This allowance system was almost invariably supplemented by the 'Roundsman system' by which the parish 'sold' to farmers the labour of the unemployed poor at a very low wage, giving to the worker the difference up to the minimum wage. Also, allotments of small portions of free land were used to some extent. The exceptional depression of wages and the corresponding increase in expenditures for poor relief called for urgent Parliamentary intervention. All attempts in that period, however, were rather unfortunate (see Poynter, 1969: 55–76). The agricultural crisis was not confined to the exceptional circumstances of the 1790s, however, and the expenditure for poor relief increased steadily in the following decades especially in the 'Speenhamland counties'. Moreover, it should not be forgotten that poor relief was also given in industrial towns where expenditure increased during downturns in the form of unemployment benefits (cf. Boyer, 1990: Chapter 8). According to Porter (1836: 84), 'the weight of pauper expenditure, in proportion to the population . . . was as 7 in 1831 to 4 in 1801'; a peak was reached in 1817–18 (cf. Porter, 1836: 79 and Blaug, 1963: 163–4).

The increase in poor rates became a matter of serious concern and it is important to clarify who bore the tax. Nominally, the poor rates were levied on income from local property. In agriculture it was paid by the farmer in relation to the rental value of the land that he occupied; in industry it was paid by the manufacturer in relation to the value of the buildings where his plants were placed. Ricardo offered a very clear analysis of incidence in Chapter XVIII of his *Principles*, based on the difference between the rent that a farmer actually paid to his landlord and the annual value of the land occupied by him. Even though the tax was 'professed to be levied in proportion to [the former]' (*Works*, I: 258), it was in fact levied in proportion to the latter. This had an important consequence for incidence, because the rental value, and not the actual rent, included the prospective income from the capital invested on land by the tenant. If the tax were levied on the actual rent, Ricardo argues, then the landlord would bear the full burden, because profits and food prices would be regulated by the land on which no rent and no tax was paid. But the marginal land normally had a positive rental value and did pay a tax, because the tenant invested some capital on it. For this reason the farmers bore part or all of the tax. The incidence on 'the consumer of raw produce' depended on poor rates in agriculture relative to those in manufacturing. According to Ricardo, 'a much larger amount falls on the farmer than on the manufacturer' and therefore 'the farmer will be enabled to raise the price of his produce by this whole difference' (ibid.: 260). The 1834 Report of the Royal Poor Laws Commission held that the poor rates fell both on rents and profits. It estimated that in many parishes 'the pressure of the poor rate reduced the rent to half, or to less than half, of what it would have been if the land had been situated in an unpauperised district' (quoted by Boyer, 1990: 200). However, the farmers' profits also fell, and this determined some abandonment of farming in 'pauperised' districts.

It is worth noting that the administration of the poor had a negative impact on profits *notwithstanding* the fact that wages were partially paid out of the poor rates, because the productivity of the subsidized workers had a tendency to fall: according to the Report, the farmer 'can reap the immediate benefit of the fall of wages, and when . . . the apparently cheap labour has become really dear, he can either quit [the farm] at the expiration of his lease, or demand on its renewal a diminution of rent' (ibid.).

The increasing burden of the poor rates did not help in improving the condition of the agricultural workers and had the tendency to set the different classes of society against each other and to dry up the sources of the tax itself (cf. Porter, 1836: 84). It is not surprising, therefore, that an abolitionist view, which had been first proposed by Rev. Thomas Alcock (1752) and Rev. Joseph Townsend (1786), gathered momentum at the turn of the century.

The pre-1834 debate on the Poor Laws had many facets, involving as it did philosophic, ethical, religious as well as strictly economic arguments and we find on the abolitionist side intellectuals of different orientation such as Burke and Bentham. For the general debate in the framework of the English intellectual history of this period the reader is referred to Poynter (1969), Himmelfarb (1985) and Winch (1996). Put briefly, the abolitionists considered the certainty of support as a pernicious interference with the natural order: by artificially modifying the interplay of punishment and reward, pain and happiness with human action, such a certainty was allegedly responsible for favouring idleness and improvidence among the lower classes and hindering prudence, industry and self-reliance. Even worse, these bad habits had a demoralizing effect and made an increasing number of workers dependent upon aid. As Burke wrote in an often-quoted passage: 'Hitherto the name of poor . . . has not been used for those who can, but for those who cannot labour . . . but when we affect to pity, as poor, those who must labour or the world cannot exist, we are trifling with the condition of mankind' (E. Burke, *Letters on a Regicide Peace*, 1797, quoted in Winch, 1996: 198). From a strictly economic point of view, the violation of the principles of free competition in labour and commodity markets was considered detrimental to the condition of all ranks of society, including the working classes, and it is not coincidental that the economic arguments against the Poor Laws were to some extent interwoven with those against the Corn Laws.

Adam Smith, even though he cannot be assigned to the abolitionist camp, condemned the Settlement Law on the ground that it was a serious obstacle to labour mobility, and obstructed a natural remedy to low local wages:

> The very unequal price of labour which we frequently find in England in places at no great distance from one another, is probably owing to the obstruction which the law of settlements gives to a poor man who would carry his industry from one parish to another . . . The scarcity of hands in one parish, therefore, cannot always be relieved by their super-abundance in another, as it is constantly in Scotland. (*WN*, I.x.c.58)

Malthus, who was with Ricardo the leading economist on the abolitionist side, fully endorsed Smith's criticism:

> The whole system of settlement . . . is contradictory to all ideas of freedom . . . And the obstructions continually occasioned in the market of labour, by these laws, have a constant tendency to add to the difficulties of those who are struggling to support themselves without assistance. (Malthus [1803] 1992: 102)

But he added a series of other arguments, based on his theory of wages and population. In the short run, he argued, wages depended on the available supply of food as compared with the number of workers. An artificial increase in the wages of some categories of workers (the subsidized labouring poor and the unemployed) had the fatal effect of diminishing the wages of the other workers, especially in great towns (cf. ibid.: 118): it followed that 'it is to be feared that though [the Poor Laws] may have alleviated a little the intensity of individual misfortune, it has spread the evil over a much larger surface' (ibid.: 89). The adverse effect on real wages worked via an increasing price of food, stimulated by the higher demand for it (in the absence of free foreign trade). The acute food scarcity in the last decade of the eighteenth century, when Malthus wrote his *Essay*, contributed to shape this view. In the long run, according to Malthus, the certainty of relief would stimulate population growth, thereby determining a lasting downward pressure on wages (cf. ibid.: 100).

Ricardo served as a member of the Poor Law Select Committee of Parliament in 1819. The Report, on which he agreed, recommended that the impediments to the free circulation of labour should be immediately removed, and that in due time the parishes should be freed from the obligation of finding employment for those who need it, and should confine aid to those unable to work (see *Works*, V: xxiv). Even though Ricardo had a direct knowledge of the problems involved, his criticism of the Poor Laws basically followed in Malthus's footsteps, as he explicitly recognized (see *Works*, I: 106). Ricardo borrowed the population argument from Malthus, but, in comparison with him, perhaps put more emphasis on the potential effects concerning economic growth and overall prosperity. The legal principle that 'every human being wanting support could be sure to obtain it . . . in such a degree as to make life tolerably comfortable' (ibid.: 108) was bound to absorb, according to Ricardo, all the net output of the country, which was the source of capital accumulation and of the increase in wages above mere subsistence in periods of prosperity. It therefore accelerated the tendency towards the stationary state, as did diminishing returns in agriculture and protection from foreign trade; but, unlike them, it would also absorb rents: for this reason, he claimed that 'the clear and direct tendency of the poor laws . . . [is] to deteriorate the condition of both poor and rich' (ibid.: 105–6). Ricardo praised, in comparative terms, the system of local poor rates, as opposed to proposals for a general tax, but did not fail to remark that taxation on land rental value hinders technical improvements in agriculture (see ibid.: 259), thereby accelerating, once again, the attainment of the stationary state. Both Malthus and Ricardo advocated a complete repeal of the Poor Laws, but it must be stressed that both of them also recommended the utmost gradualness (see Malthus, [1803] 1992: 118; *Works*, I: 106).

It is difficult to speculate on whether low wages and unemployment merely determined high poor rates or were also determined by them, as Malthus and Ricardo feared. Twentieth-century historiography (e.g., Blaug, 1963) tended to downplay a direct effect of the Poor Laws in depressing wages and promoting population growth; rather, increasing poor relief, demoralization of the labouring poor and distress of farming were considered as different aspects of an overall milieu that characterized the English early phase of industrialization. The end of the old Poor Laws coincides with the beginning of the Victorian era, in which this milieu progressively changed and so did the capacity of the working classes to gain a share of the increasing prosperity.

ARRIGO OPOCHER

See also:

Malthus–Ricardo Debate; Member of Parliament.

References

Alcock, T. (1752), *Observations on the Defects of the Poor Laws*, London: R. Baldwin.
Blaug, M. (1963), 'The myth of the old Poor Law and the making of the new', *The Journal of Economic History*, **23**(2), 151–84.
Blaug, M. (1964), 'The Poor Law Report reexamined', *Journal of Economic History*, **24**(2), 229–45.
Boyer, G.R. (1990), *An Economic History of the English Poor Law 1750–1850*, Cambridge, UK: Cambridge University Press.
Himmelfarb, G. (1985), *The Idea of Poverty*, New York: Vintage Books.

Malthus, T.R. ([1803] 1992), *An Essay on the Principle of Population*, based on the 1803 edition, selected and introduced by D. Winch, Cambridge, UK: Cambridge University Press.
Porter, G.R. (1836), *The Progress of the Nation, Vol. 1*, London: Charles Knight & Co.
Poynter, J.R. (1969), *Society and Pauperism. English Ideas on Poor Relief, 1795–1834*, London: Routledge & Kegan Paul.
Smith, A. ([1776] 1976), *An Inquiry into the Nature and Causes of the Wealth of Nations*, in *The Glasgow Edition of the Works and Correspondence of Adam Smith*, (eds) R.H. Campbell, A.S. Skinner and W.B. Todd, Oxford: Clarendon Press.
Solar, P.M. (1995), 'Poor relief and English economic development before the industrial revolution', *The Economic History Review*, **48**(1), 1–22.
Townsend, J. ([1786] 1971), *A Dissertation on the Poor Laws*, reprinted 1971, Berkeley, CA: University of California Press.
Winch, D. (1996), *Riches and Poverty. An Intellectual History of Political Economy in Britain, 1750–1834*, Cambridge, UK: Cambridge University Press.

Population

The adequacy or inadequacy of population numbers to meet circumstances is a multi-faceted theme of perpetual interest, and each age has had its own fears of either a 'too small' or 'too great' population. Broadly speaking, in the sixteenth and early seventeenth centuries the dominant sentiment was that of the superfluity of the people, as witnessed by the number of paupers, whereas the mercantilist period was characterized by the opposite fear that population was insufficient to meet taxes for war. In the course of the eighteenth century, the pendulum swung again towards the fear of an excessive population. This sentiment established itself very firmly in Ricardo's time and lasted until the middle of the nineteenth century, when it softened gradually.

The host of conceptual elaborations and policy actions prompted by these alternating fears reached its climax in the 50 years or so after the publication of the first edition of Malthus's *Essay on the Principle of Population* in 1798: by that time the fundamental arithmetic of population change was reasonably clear, proper censuses were being established in many countries, and the 'new' economic science was able to provide a nuanced understanding of the many linkages between population growth and the economy. Most importantly, the tendency to overpopulation in Europe was at that time more widely and more strongly perceived than in any other age.

Ricardo first read Malthus's *Essay* in the second (1803) edition and presumably soon after its publication. He writes that is 'many years since [he] read it' in January 1816 (see *Works*, VIII: 2, n1). In the latter, as well as in other places, Ricardo expressed a great admiration for Malthus's book; in October 1817 he wrote of the fifth edition in the following terms:

> I have it now here, and I have been reading all the new matter again, and I am surprised at the little that I can discover with the utmost ingenuity to differ from. In every part you are exceedingly clear, and time only is wanted to carry conviction to every mind. (Ibid.: 201)

We also find explicit praise in the *Principles* (see *Works*, I: 398).

Malthus's book offered (in the various editions) a masterly coordination and implementation of previous knowledge and has been more influential than any other single work on population. The 'Malthusian age' is generally seen, therefore, both as a culmination of developments of precedent and as a time of comparison for later periods.

Thus, we may consider the population problem from an historical perspective under three headings: the pre-Malthusian period, the Malthusian age and the post-Malthusian period.

The pre-Malthusian period

A clear link between population, means of subsistence and poverty was established in the sixteenth and early seventeenth centuries both by regulators and thinkers. The population was decidedly on the increase and price of food had a marked tendency to rise, while employment opportunities were falling (see Marshall, 1920: 174; Slack, 1990: 3); as a consequence, the number of paupers expanded beyond what society was prepared to tolerate and new institutions of poor relief were introduced throughout Europe.

The broad idea that a population increase in a certain territory is limited by the latter's capacity to supply food was expressed in the modern tones of the writers of that time. The Italian diplomat and thinker Giovanni Botero (1540–1617) opposed the current opinion that population increase was simply checked by plagues, wars, famine and other similar causes. In his *Delle cause della grandezza delle città* (1588), he stressed the importance of the interplay between human fecundity (*virtù generativa*), soil fertility (*virtù nutritiva*) and the ability to bring food from distant places (*virtù attrativa*). An excess of the former source relative to the latter was bound to determine emigration until people were no longer capable of a further increase due to starvation (*inopia*) and lack of space (*strettezza dei confini*). Similar concerns about the prospects of the world population were expressed by the English poet, explorer and writer Sir Walter Raleigh (1552–1612) in his *History of the World* (1614).

The seventeenth century saw the first scientific attempts at calculating the prospective increase in population both in the proximate future and over long periods of time. On the main basis of systematic records of mortality (notably in the city of London), John Graunt (*Natural and Political Observations Upon the Bills of Mortality*, 1662) and William Petty (*Essay in Political Arithmetick*, 1683) calculated by inference the numbers and the prospective progression of population. In so doing, they adopted the central concept of 'doubling time', thus implying a tendency to a geometrical increase. Such a time was *not* fixed, however, and they did not fail to stress its wide variability in different places and historical periods.

During the eighteenth century the records of baptisms, marriages and burials were available (in parishes) on a more systematic basis than previously and a more accurate study of the sources of population change was possible. The contribution of the German theologian and statistician Johann Peter Süssmilch (*Die Göttliche Ordnung*, 1741) is considered the most complete early treatise on population. In England, nearly one century after Graunt and Petty, the dissenting minister and moral philosopher Richard Price (1723–91) was able to infer from the bills of mortality valuable information on the age structure of the population, life expectancy and past migration flows in his *Observations on the Nature of Civil Liberty* (1773).

These early authors did not fail to stress the impossibility of an indefinite expansion of population, but placed it far in the future. They could fully adhere, therefore, to the pro-population mercantilist spirit. Not that the paupers had disappeared, nor that the expenses for their relief had diminished, but the concern with individuals and their happiness, which characterized the Renaissance, had been overcome by a stronger concern with the state and its ambition of becoming superior, in the nation's interest, to other competing states. There was then a change in priorities: a large population was considered as a sign of, and a condition for, national prosperity, and its growth in numbers was encouraged by all possible means (see Stagenland, 1904: 118–22 for details).

By the second half of the eighteenth century there was a renewed interest in the well-being of the people and a shift of emphasis towards the means for supporting it. It is at this time and chiefly through the works of Quesnay and Turgot that the population problem comes to be reconsidered under a proper economic point of view. In the words of Quesnay:

> One would imagine that the great wealth of a state is obtained through an abundance of men; but men can obtain and perpetuate wealth only by means of wealth, and to the extent that there is a *proper proportion between men and wealth*. (Quesnay [1759] 1972: 19–20, n(a); emphasis added)

Such a 'proper proportion' and the mechanisms by which it is attained are in fact at the heart of the population theories to come.

Adam Smith elaborated on such a mechanism. An excess population would determine a downward adjustment, more by increasing mortality (notably of infants) among the 'inferior ranks of people' than by diminishing fecundity (see *WN*, I.viii.38–39). Conversely, an excess of necessaries would determine an increase of population, *both* by encouraging early marriages (thereby increasing fecundity) and by better rearing of children (thereby diminishing mortality) (ibid.: viii: 40; and IV, vii, b: 2). The equilibrating mechanism consisted of wage setting. Competition in the labour market forced wages to diminish in periods in which the market was 'over-stocked', and to increase in periods in which it was 'under-stocked'. Smith could conclude, then, that:

> the demand for men, like that for any other commodity, necessarily regulates the production of men; quickens it when it goes on too slowly, and stops it when it advances too fast. It is this demand which regulates and determines the state of propagation in all the different countries of the world. (Ibid.: 40)

The Malthusian age

At the turn of the eighteenth century, population started increasing at unprecedented rates in Europe, the price of food increased and the number of paupers under relief dramatically increased. The rising tide of the British population began around the middle of the eighteenth century and it accelerated in the first 30 years of the nineteenth century. According to G.R. Porter, Ricardo's brother-in-law, it ranged from an average annual increase of about 0.3 per cent in the first half of the eighteenth century to about 0.8 per cent in the second half (as calculated from the bills of mortality), to about 1.5 per cent in the 30 years between 1801 and 1831 (as calculated from census data). Such a rate was almost twice as much as that of France (see Porter, 1836: 14–15 and 18; consistent figures are reported by Malthus [1803] 1992: 149).

In the traditional interpretation, such a demographic explosion was accounted for by falling mortality, due to better medical assistance, vaccinations, greater general healthiness of the country, superiority and cheapness of clothing and so on (see Marshall, 1935: 67–8; Porter, 1836: 19), but there is no conclusive assessment concerning the relative importance of fecundity and mortality (migrations being of minor importance in that period), because registration at birth was not instituted till 1837. The issue therefore remains somewhat controversial (for instance, Krause, 1958, challenged the traditional view).

Population records mirrored social and economic evidence of overpopulation in England. The able-bodied poor increased in number and were subsidized in many different ways, so that the real expenditure for poor relief almost doubled (as deflated by the price of wheat) in the 30 years from 1801 to 1831 (see 'Poor Laws' in this *Companion*). More generally, the early phase of the Industrial Revolution until the 1830s is known to have been characterized by low and fluctuating wages and uncertainty of work (see Opocher, 2010). The food scarcity at the end of the eighteenth century, due to the Napoleonic Wars and the 1794 bad harvest, made this state of distress particularly severe.

The widespread perception of overpopulation, the increasing burden of taxation under the Poor Laws, the demoralizing effects of poor relief, the inability of workers to take permanent advantage of technological progress – as opposed to the post-revolutionary hopes of human perfectibility, theorized by political philosophers like Godwin and Condorcet – are the background against which Malthus's *Essay* must be placed. Different from the social philosophers of the former generation like Hume and Wallace, Malthus stressed the imminent nature of population pressure (see Winch, 1992: xii): its effects were visible 'in the present state of society', and required urgent understanding and action. He posed very neatly the question of why the bulk of the people were subject to alternating fortunes in which a 'tolerably comfortable' situation was incapable of lasting and gave way to a 'season of distress'.

The relation between living standards and population involved what Malthus called a 'positive check' to population growth: better living standards relaxed such a check by reducing mortality; periods of distress tightened it for the opposite reason. But also a 'preventive check', via postponement of marriages and reduction of births ('moral restraint'), cooperated in reducing a tendency to overpopulation, and Malthus believed that the progress of civilization would change the relative weights of the two checks in favour of the second (see Malthus [1803] 1992: 25 and 43). Likewise, Ricardo distinctly understood that comfortable and refined lives made for fewer births than unruly and miserable lives (see *Works*, I: 100); this was to soon become a common understanding (see Porter, 1836: 22). Better living standards therefore had opposite effects on the two checks, relaxing the former, and reinforcing the latter. If a taste for comfortable living were to spread through the working classes, overpopulation could be prevented, thus avoiding the most ruinous phases of distress mentioned above, but this was not yet in sight at the time of Malthus and Ricardo, the latter observing that 'in practice it is invariably found that an increase of population follows the amended condition of the labourer' (*Works*, I: 407).

As a conscientious and pious clergyman, Malthus abhorred the methods of birth control that were practised in France and were advocated, among others, by Condorcet, Bentham and Place; he considered them as a source of vice, no less than he did concerning some effects of overpopulation. Moreover, in an Appendix to the 1817 fifth edition, he maintained that 'if it were possible for each married couple to limit by a wish the number of their children, there is certainly reason to fear that the indolence of the human race would be very greatly increased . . . the restraints which I have recommended are quite of a different character' (Malthus [1803] 1992: 369). Ricardo's opinion on the 'artificial checks' was less explicit than that of Malthus, but he seemed to broadly agree with him. In a letter of 10 September 1821 to Malthus he wrote: 'Place speaks of one of Owen's preventives to an excessive population – he does not dwell upon it, but I have a little doubt whether it is right *even to mention it*' (*Works*, IX: 62; emphasis added). In 1822, Francis Place would publish a book (*Illustrations and Proofs of the Principle of Population*) that is credited with being the first work on population in the English language recommending birth control. However, it was not until 1823 – the year of Ricardo's death – that 'the English Neo-Malthusianism movement began in earnest' (Himes, 1928: 627).

Key to the success of Malthus's *Principle of Population* was his connection between population and economic processes. The proportion of cultivated land to population was subject to economic forces, so that population pressure on the means of subsistence may be well felt before a hypothetical limit to food production is reached. The theoretical basis of his analysis of the interplay between 'the constant effort towards population', the extension of cultivated land and the labour market, consisted in the broad vision of Adam Smith and was reinforced by the current developments on the theory of value and distribution put forward by his contemporaries, whose leading authority was David Ricardo. Malthus embarked upon writing a separate treatise of political economy as a reaction to Ricardo's *Principles* (see *Works*, I: vii). In turn, Ricardo's *Notes* on Malthus's *Principles* vindicated the former's doctrines.

We cannot enter here into the many details of the Ricardo–Malthus debate and must restrict ourselves to some selected aspects. First, in Ricardo's opinion, Malthus was 'too much inclined to think that population is only increased by the previous provision of food'. Rather, 'the general progress of population is affected by the increase of capital'. (ibid.: 406). And capital consisted not only of food but also of 'clothing, tools, raw materials, machinery &c. necessary to give effect to labour' (ibid.: 95). The wage found was to be considered as variable and dependent on the drivers of capital accumulation and a prosperous industry would make for high wages as much as a prosperous agriculture.

The oscillations in the fortunes of the working classes were part of a wider process of convergence towards a stationary state, in which both population and food production gradually and progressively slowed down, due to diminishing returns in agriculture. Not only did the cultivation of less and less fertile lands retard the adjustment of food to population (an aspect particularly stressed by Malthus); it also brought about a change in income distribution adverse to profits (and wages) and in favour of rents (on the more fertile lands), thus discouraging capital accumulation (as Ricardo particularly stressed). Technical improvements in agriculture and international trade could only delay the attainment of the stationary state; Ricardo challenged Malthus's view that technical improvements in agriculture increased rents and were beneficial to the landlords (see ibid.: 412). Moreover, he totally disagreed on Malthus's defence of the Corn Laws. Since manufacturing was *not* subject to diminishing returns, the importation of food in exchange for manufactured goods could in principle accelerate the provision of necessaries to an increasing population. Here 'Malthus found himself at odds with the new orthodoxy that was forming around Ricardo's ideas' (Winch, 1992: xx). Malthus believed that a secure country must rely by and large on its own sources of food production, and that the importation of food should meet only exceptional needs arising from a deficient crop (cf. Malthus [1803] 1992: 154–5). By contrast, Ricardo maintained that it was in the natural course of things that population increase in an old settled country should raise the price of domestically produced food, by diminishing returns, 'and give encouragement to its importation' (*Works*, I: 373). His theory of foreign trade was entirely in support of the beneficial effects of liberalizing imports of food in exchange for manufactured goods, which would promote both the well-being of labourers and the prospects of capital accumulation in the same way as would technical improvements.

Both Malthus and Ricardo advocated a gradual but complete repeal of the Poor Laws (see Malthus [1803] 1992: 118; *Works*, I: 106). Malthus took it for granted that the Poor Laws encouraged improvident marriages, thus increasing population pressure (Malthus [1803] 1992: 100 and 101). Ricardo's criticism of the Poor Laws followed in Malthus's footsteps, as he explicitly recognized (see *Works*, I: 106), placing a special emphasis on the fact that Poor Law provisions were bound to absorb all the net output of the country, rents included (by taxation), so that 'the clear and direct tendency of the poor laws . . . [was] to deteriorate the condition of both poor and rich' (ibid.: 105–6).

A generation after Malthus and Ricardo, the hardest effects of the Industrial Revolution on the condition of the working classes softened (not least in consequence of the new labour legislation), the trend of the real wages started to increase, and the social context around working-class families improved (in terms of better education, establishment of friendly societies, etc.). What Ricardo considered as an abstract possibility (self-restraint by labouring classes), became a reasonable hope for the proximate future. In J.S. Mill's words:

> A well educated labouring class could, and we believe would keep up its condition to a high standard of comfort, or at least at a great distance from physical destitution, by the exercise of the same degree of habitual prudence practiced by the middle class. (Mill [1845] 1967: 379)

The post-Malthusian period

Neither Malthus nor Ricardo could predict two major historical developments that reshaped the population problems in the course of the nineteenth century: the large-scale importation of food and emigration. Giffen (1882: 535) calculated that 'about 12 millions at least of the people of the United Kingdom live on imported food, and a certain part of the populations of Germany, France, Belgium, and Holland also live on imported food – the importations being mainly from the United States'. In Marshall's time, then, the main issue became the quality, not the quantity of the population, that is, their skills and character.

There had also been a spectacular increase in the number of emigrants from the UK to America and Australasia in the 1830s and 1840s, up to an average of 170 000 per year, and the emigration flows remained at that level in the second half of the century; according to Giffen (ibid.), about eight million Britons emigrated as of 1880, of which about five million were to the USA.

The capacity of the USA to attract European immigrants and supply food to Western Europe gave a quietus to the fears of overpopulation in Europe, but 'Malthusianism' remained real to some extent. Assuming demographic expansion to continue at the same rates, Giffen calculated that 'the present economic circumstances of the European family of nations . . . [were] not likely to continue for more than a generation or two' (ibid.: 537).

However, demographic expansion did *not* continue at the same rates. As Galor (2005) recently stressed, precisely during the 1870s the birth rates in England and Western Europe began a precipitous decline, leading to what has been called a 'demographic transition' towards a regime in which, over long periods of time, sustained economic growth was associated with declining rates of population growth. The 'Malthusian devil' was so to speak, 'in chains' in the wealthier countries of Europe, precisely thanks to that 'taste for comfort and enjoyment' that, according to Ricardo, was the best 'security against a superabundant population' (*Works*, I: 100).

ARRIGO OPOCHER

See also:

Accumulation of Capital; Endogenous Growth; Labour and Wages; Malthus–Ricardo Debate; Ricardian Dynamics.

References

Galor, O. (2005), 'The demographic transition and the emergence of sustained economic growth', *Journal of the European Economic Association*, **3**(2–3), 494–504.
Giffen, R. (1882), 'The utility of common statistics. The inaugural address of Robert Giffen, Esq., President of the Statistical Society, delivered of Tuesday 21st November 1882', *Journal of the Statistical Society of London*, **45**(4), 519–46.
Himes, N.E. (1928), 'The place of John Stuart Mill and of Robert Owen in the history of English Neo-Malthusianism', *Quarterly Journal of Economics*, **42**(4), 627–40.
Krause, J.T. (1958), 'Changes in English fertility and mortality', *The Economic History Review*, **11**(1), 52–70.
Malthus, T.R. ([1798, 1803] 1992], *An Essay on the Principle of Population*, 2nd edition, selected and introduced by R. Winch, Cambridge, UK: Cambridge University Press.
Marshall, A. (1920), *Principles of Economics*, 8th edition, London: Macmillan.
Marshall, T.H. (1935), 'The population of England and Wales from the industrial revolution to the World War', *The Economic History Review*, **5**(2), 65–78.
Mill, J.S. ([1845] 1967), 'The claims of labour', in J.S. Mill, *Collected Works of John Stuart Mill, Vol. IV*, (ed.) J.M. Robson, Toronto: University of Toronto Press, pp. 631–68.
Opocher, A. (2010), 'The future of the working classes: a comparison between J.S. Mill and A. Marshall', *European Journal of the History of Economic Thought*, **17**(2), 229–53.
Porter, G.R. (1836), *The Progress of the Nation, Vol. 1*, 1st edition, London: Charles Knight & Co.
Quesnay, F. ([1759] 1972), *Quesnay's Tableau Economique*, with new materials, translations and notes, (eds) M. Kuczynski and R.L. Meek, London: Macmillan.
Slack P. (1990), *The English Poor Law*, Cambridge, UK: Cambridge University Press.
Smith, A. ([1776] 1976), *An Inquiry into the Nature and Causes of the Wealth of Nations*, in *The Glasgow Edition of the Works and Correspondence of Adam Smith*, (eds) R.H. Campbell, A.S. Skinner and W.B. Todd, Oxford: Clarendon Press.
Stagenland, C.E. (1904), *Pre-Malthusian Doctrines of Population: A Study in the History of Economic Theory*, New York: Columbia University Press.
Winch, R. (1992), 'Introduction', in T.R. Malthus, *An Essay of the Principle of Population*, Cambridge, UK: Cambridge University Press.

Porter, Sarah Ricardo

Sarah Ricardo was born on 22 December 1790 to Abraham Ricardo and Abigail Delvalle, the youngest in a family of 15 and 20 years younger than David. Sraffa writes that she married George Richardson Porter and she is known as a writer on educational subjects (*Works*, X: 60). If this sounds disappointing, wait to see what Henderson has to say in 675 pages, namely just that she married outside the Jewish community and we ignore where she was buried (Henderson, 1997: 140–41).

No details about her education or other circumstances in her life before marriage are known apart from that Abraham Ricardo left, at his death in 1812, a remarkable fortune that he allotted in his will in equal share to both sons and daughters, that he established that the daughters' share should be left in trust until they married, with an annual allowance of £90, that David offered further financial support and Sarah kindly declined the offer (Esther and Sarah Ricardo to their brother David, in *Works*, X: 133).

Sarah married George Richardson Porter in 1814 or earlier (ibid.: 60) and appears to have become a Christian by marriage, like several other siblings (Henderson, 1997: 140). Her husband was born in London in 1792, the son of a merchant, was employed in the statistical department of the board of trade and in 1841 became one of the secretaries of the railway department. He published two books on colonial agriculture and the massive statistical report *The Progress of the Nation* 1836–38. The *Gentleman's Magazine* tells us that Sarah died on 13 September 1862, at her residence, West Hill, Wandsworth, aged 71 (Anon, 1862).

Sarah, while living the life of a middle-class married woman, became one of those literary women – ranging from Jane Marcet, the author of a series of renowned introductory books for children to various branches of learning, to Sarah's cousin Delvalle Varley *née* Lowry, the author of an introduction to mineralogy – who were remarkable novelties from the 1830s onwards. Her first publication was *Alfred Dudley, or the Australian Settlers* (1830), mentioned here and there in histories of literature as a work possibly by an unidentified Sarah Porter (Wilde et al., 1994: 2; Hunt, 1995: 323). The author was first identified as Ricardo's sister in the new *Oxford Dictionary of Biography* (Drain, 2004). The plot is as follows: loss of land and wealth by a member of the gentry due to the sinister influence of a dishonest speculator; emigration to Australia; hard choice faced by the eldest son between either return to England in order to inherit an estate from an uncle and a seat in the House of the Lords or loyalty to his family and the new homeland; choice of wealth without status and virtuous use of inherited wealth in a development project that will offer land and home for destitute-but-honest members of their original English community.

The circumstance of having been the wife of the most famous British statistician and the sister of the most famous political economist of her times clearly played an important role in shaping Sarah's concerns, and yet the novel's message sounds more original than repetition of her brother's and husband's ideas, namely that: (1) manual labour is as dignified as any activity; (2) cultivation of intellect is a necessity for every rank; (3) relationships between different races may prove peaceful, friendly and useful; and (4) becoming a philanthropist is the greatest calling for a human being and the only source of additional happiness once the need for basic comfort has been satisfied. She writes that, living 'in comparative affluence and comfort, his wealth could but little increase the enjoyments of his family and himself, except by being expended in the blessed office of doing good to others' (Porter, 1830: 178).

Five years afterward, she published a textbook, *Conversations in Arithmetic*, conceived along the lines of Jane Marcet's series of *Conversations* (on Chemistry, on Political Economy, and other subjects) and Delvalle Varley's *Conversations on Mineralogy*. The exposition is in the form of a dialogue between teacher and pupil, and here the pupil's name is also Alfred Dudley, the novel's main character. The preface explains that 'the form of conversation has been chosen, since it affords a greater facility for explanation and familiar illustration than any other . . . avoiding all terms or even words, but those which it might be supposed a young child can well understand' (Porter, 1835: vii).

The book was restyled as a textbook for classwork under the title *Rational Arithmetic*, abandoning the dialogical structure. The preface explains that 'to rescue arithmetic from the degraded rank it at present occupies among intellectual pursuits is a principal object of the following work' (Porter, 1852: v) and that it may provide the main tool for turning children not into mathematicians but rather into reasoning beings, for no other subject is 'so admirably adapted to call forth and strengthen the reasoning powers' (ibid.).

Sarah contributed two essays to volumes published by the Central Society for Education, a recently founded society (among whose members there were four Ricardo siblings) committed to the cause of a non-Church-based system of education. In 'On infant schools for the upper and middle classes' she quotes Locke to the effect that virtue and control over the passions cannot be taught by speeches but need be learned through habit and example (Porter, 1838: 238). She pleads for the extension of school education to children of all classes and argues for due place to be conceded to imagination, for 'the teaching of facts is made too much an all-important feature . . . Children should be rather encouraged to show their own ingenuity and contrivance in different games, than be always led from one occupation to another' (ibid.: 236).

Similar topics are discussed in 'The expediency and the means of elevating the profession of the educator in public estimation'. She quotes Johann Heinrich Pestalozzi and Philipp Emanuel von Fellenberg to the effect that systems alone do not suffice in order to shape the character, but what is required is the educator as a living personality. She contends that obstacles to the growth of a body of competent and dedicated educators lie, first, in 'want of respect' for teachers on the part of society as a whole, second, in 'want of independence of character and of high moral dignity on the part of the educator' (Porter, 1839: 450). Finally, she addresses the issue of religious education. She had argued in the previous essay that children from families belonging to different confessions may attend the same school and yet the Christian religion be 'taught to all the children in a manner approved of by all the parents. There is, then, a common ground on which children of all denominations may meet, and learn Christianity and brotherly love at the same time' (ibid.: 238).

In the second essay she clarifies that a choice should be made upon reflection among three competing hypotheses, namely, separate denominational religious education, no religious education, and the one she favours, that is, religious education on an interdenominational Christian basis. It may be remarked that, albeit a Jew by birth, she does not consider children from non-Christian families.

Apart from the interest the overlooked story of this educational writer and novelist has in its own right, there are lessons for Ricardo scholars too (Cremaschi, forthcoming). One is that the ideas that Ricardo 'had his mind to form, he had even his education to commence and to conduct' (Mill [1823] 1995: 212), or that he was a 'modest, unlettered paterfamilias' (Hutchison, 1995: 51) are not so plausible. If we keep in mind that brother Moses was a physician (Henderson, 1997: 138–9) and Sarah the author of several publications, the statements that it is 'not true . . . as has been insinuated, that Mr. Ricardo was of a very low origin, and that he had been wholly denied the advantages of education' for his father was 'both able and willing to afford his children all the advantages which the line of life for which they were destined appeared to require' (*Works*, X: 4) may be taken at face value. One implication is that Ricardo was probably no self-made pure scientist vaccinated forever against 'metaphysics', and another is that James Mill's intellectual influence on Ricardo was not so overwhelming as some literature has implied. One further consideration is that, if his younger sister was committed to the causes of a general system of education and war on poverty, perhaps also her older brother was not a wholehearted apologist for the status quo as some literature has implied, albeit in more respectful terms, for example, than those employed by Leslie Stephen while writing that Ricardo 'was a Jew ... Now Jews, in spite of Shylock's assertions ... are naturally without human feeling' (Stephen, 1900, II: 222). On the whole, apart from undesirable effects of firm belief in iron laws and especially so at the beginning of his career, Ricardo was one more friend of humankind who hoped that political economy, as scientifically worked out as possible, would finally contribute in singling out the cause of poverty as well as possible remedies.

SERGIO CREMASCHI

See also:

Jewish Background; Life and Activities.

References

Anon (1862), 'Obituary: Porter Sarah', *Gentleman's Magazine*, **213**, October, p. 509.

Cremaschi, S. (forthcoming), 'Sarah Ricardo's tale of wealth and virtue', *History of Economics Review*.

Drain, S. (2004), 'Porter, Sarah Ricardo', in H.C.G. Matthew and B. Harrison (eds), *Oxford Dictionary of National Biography, Vol. XLIV*, Oxford: Oxford University Press, p. 973.

Henderson, J.P. (1997), *The Life and Economics of David Ricardo*, with supplemental chapters by J.B. Davis, Boston, MA: Kluwer.

Hunt, P. (ed.) (1995), *Children's Literature: An Illustrated History*, Oxford: Oxford University Press.

Hutchinson, T. (1995), *Uses and Abuses of Economics*, London: Routledge.

Mill, J. ([1823] 1995), 'Letter to the editor of the *Morning Chronicle*', in *The Collected Works, of James Mill, Vol. VII*, London: Routledge and Thoemmes Press, pp. 212–13.

Porter, G.R. (1836–38), *The Progress of the Nation, in its Various Social and Economical Relations, from the Beginning of the Nineteenth Century to the Present Time*, 2 vols, London: Knight.

Porter, S. *née* Ricardo [Anonymous] (1830), *Alfred Dudley, or the Australian Settlers*, London: Murray.

Porter, S. *née* Ricardo [Mrs G.R. Porter] (1835), *Conversations in Arithmetic*, London: Murray.

Porter, S. *née* Ricardo [Mrs G.R. Porter] (1838), 'On infant schools for the upper and middle classes', in *The Second Publication of the Central Society of Education*, London: Central Society of Education, pp. 229–42.

Porter, S. *née* Ricardo [Mrs G.R. Porter] (1839), 'The expediency and the means of elevating the profession of the educator in public estimation', in *The Educator. Prize Essays on The Expediency and the Means of Elevating the Profession of the Educator in Public Estimation*, London: Central Society of Education, pp. 435–535.

Porter, S. *née* Ricardo [Mrs G.R. Porter] (1852), *Rational Arithmetic*, London: Murray.

Stephen, L. (1900), *The English Utilitarians*, 3 vols, London: Duckworth.

Wilde, W.H., J. Horton and B. Andrews (eds) (1994), *Oxford Companion to Australian Literature*, Melbourne: Oxford University Press.

Principles of Political Economy, and Taxation

In the following we provide a summary account of Piero Sraffa's Introduction to Volume I of *The Works and Correspondence of David Ricardo* (*Works*, I: xiii–lxii). In our view the Introduction provides the best account of the making, publication and changes of contents across the three editions of the *Principles* (1817, 1819, 1821). The text below follows closely Sraffa's argument and consists in fact to a large extent of passages taken from it. We felt that it would make little sense to change Sraffa's meticulous text. We shortened it, connected the parts quoted by us, and cut details concerning the invariable measure of value and the corn model that are largely treated in other parts of this *Companion*. We ask the reader to look up Sraffa's Introduction in order to get the full picture. In order not to clutter the text we refrained from giving the details of the passages from the *Works* Sraffa cited in his Introduction and the page numbers of the parts of Sraffa's Introduction we quote. To avoid confusion we printed our words in italics and Sraffa's in roman.

The Writing of the *Principles*
'The plan from which the *Principles of Political Economy, and Taxation* originated had taken shape soon after the publication of the *Essay on the Influence of a Low Price of Corn on the Profits of Stock* in February 1815. At first Ricardo's intention (at James Mill's suggestion) had been merely to produce an enlarged version of the *Essay*'. *However, Ricardo encountered serious difficulties of composition.* 'It is remarkable that in [his] letters of October and November 1815 which give the main headings of the proposed work (Rent, Profit, Wages) there is no reference to Value. This is mentioned for the first time, as a separate subject with which it occurred to Ricardo that he would have to deal, in a letter to Mill of 30 December . . . From this time onwards the problem of Value increasingly troubled him. On 7 February 1816 he writes to Malthus: "If I could overcome the obstacles in the way of giving a clear insight into the origin and law of relative or exchangeable value I should have gained half the battle".'

In February 1816 Ricardo moved to London, bringing with him his papers, some of which he read to Mill. Alas, the work made no progress. In July he resumed work back at Gatcombe. On 14 October 1816 he sent Mill a manuscript, covering the ground of the first seven chapters. He wrote to Mill that he was now going to consider taxation. 'The real reason for the delay was that he had "been very much impeded by the question of price and value" (as he wrote to Malthus), and that (as he informed Mill) he had "been beyond measure puzzled to find out the law of price".' *By 17 November 1816 Ricardo had completed and sent to Mill the 'inquiry into the subject of Taxation' (as Mill described it).* 'This part, Mill thought, would require more work than the first one before it was ready for the press: "you have followed the order of your own thoughts", and the matter would need re-arrangement so as "to facilitate introduction into the minds of your readers".'

'Up to this point what Ricardo had done was (as he wrote to Malthus) "rather a statement of my own opinions, than an attempt at the refutation of the opinions of others". Having finished taxation, he proceeded "to read Adam Smith once more, to take note of all passages which very much favor, or are directly opposed to my peculiar opinions"; he also re-read Say's *Traité d'Économie politique* and Buchanan's commentary on the *Wealth of Nations* and made notes of his own criticisms. These criticisms formed the basis of the group of controversial chapters which follows the chapters on taxation. Finally, at the end of January he read again Malthus's pamphlets on rent and corn, and early in March, while printing was in progress, he sent to Malthus the MS of his last chapter, which contains his comments upon them.'

The printing of the Principles *began towards the end of February 1817. On 26 March, Ricardo handed over to the printer the last part of his manuscript, but complained about the irregular pace at which the latter proceeded. The book was probably published on 19 April 1817.*

James Mill's contribution
Sraffa stressed 'that Mill's contribution to the making of the *Principles* was less than might have been expected from his promises and encouragement. On the theory there is little doubt that his influence was negligible; he had been out of touch with Political Economy for some time and his letters to Ricardo contain little discussion of theoretical issues. Mill's letters of this period are full of advice relating to "the art of laying down your thoughts, in the way most easy of apprehension". But despite his repeated assurances that he would see to the order and arrangement ("if you entrust the inspection of it to me") it seems likely that in the main the sequence of topics was left as Ricardo had originally worked through them. In detail however Mill probably did a good deal of work. Here and there a phrase unmistakeably characteristic of Mill . . . provides evidence of his hand. His touch can also be recognized in the polished wording of the Preface and in the long passage on the "pernicious tendency" of the poor laws'.

'Among Mill's more humble tasks was probably the compilation of the Index, which in method and clarity of expression is strikingly similar to the Index of his *History of British India*, published later in 1817. It is noticeable that several entries exhibit misunderstanding of the text or radical change of emphasis such as to suggest that they cannot be by the author of the book. At any rate contemporary critics of Ricardo seized upon the contrast between the language of the text and that of the Index, to the disadvantage of the former'. 'The accurate yet free translation of the passages quoted from Say is probably also due to Mill, who had advised against quotation in French.'

Arrangement and subdivision
Mill's promises that he himself would attend to the proper arrangement of Ricardo's thoughts apparently did not materialize. 'This arrangement was the direct result of the manner in which Ricardo proceeded in his work. As his letters show, he wrote according to the sequence of his own ideas, without any more elaborate plan than was implied in the heading, "Rent, Profit and Wages". Mill, indeed, had instructed him to "proceed, without loss of time . . . thinking nothing of order, thinking nothing of repetitions, thinking nothing of stile – regarding nothing, in short, but to get all the thoughts blurred upon paper some how or another". "When we have the whole before us, we will then lay our heads together, to see how it may be sorted and shaped to the best advantage". The three parts in which Ricardo composed it and which he sent separately to Mill correspond to the three groups into which the chapters of the published work naturally fall: the Political Economy, Taxation and the polemical chapters at the end. The arrangement would have been less open to criticism if this division had been made explicitly by means of separate headings.'

It deserves to be remarked that within each of the first two parts the order of the chapters coincides largely with the order in which the topics are treated in the Wealth of Nations. *There is only a single important difference, which concerns the place given to Rent. This was dictated by the necessity for Ricardo of 'getting rid of rent', in order to simplify the problem of the distribution between wages and profits. Unlike Adam Smith, Ricardo thus deals with Rent immediately after Value and before Wages and Profits.*

The parallel applies also to Taxation. 'This group of chapters on taxation is followed by Chapter XVII, On Sudden Changes in the Channels of Trade (numbered XIX in ed. 3), the position of which is determined by its arising immediately out of the subject of the removal of capital from one employment to another, discussed at the end of the chapter on Poor Rates. The third, and last, group consists of the chapters commenting upon various doctrines of Adam Smith and other writers, forming "the appendix" or a series of critical excursuses, with little connection each with the other.'

'It was only after the whole was written that thought was given to the question of subdivision. As late as 16 December 1816, after receiving the MS both of the Political Economy and of Taxation, Mill asks: "And how would you arrange it in Chapters and Sections? Think of your Chapters and Sections; and when you have made out a list send it to me". To this Ricardo replies: "as for the division into chapters, and sections, I am greatly afraid that I shall be unequal to it". Thus the process of cutting up the undivided work into chapters began after writing was completed; indeed, it went on while the printing was in progress, and the last cut was made after the book had actually been printed off.'

The correspondence with Mill and the make-up of the book enable us to follow the process of dividing the work into chapters up to the last moment before publication. This process continued even later, in the form of the subdivision of Chapter I into sections, which was only done in the second edition, and carried further in the third edition.

The chapter 'On Value' in the first edition

'By far the most perplexing as well as most extensive changes in successive editions of the *Principles* occur in the first chapter. A necessary preliminary to a study of these changes is a survey of the formation of the new theory of value out of the fragmentary elements of such a theory which are to be found in the *Essay on the Influence of a low Price of Corn on the Profits of Stock.*'

'At first, both in the *Essay* and in Ricardo's letters of 1814 and early 1815, a basic principle had been that "it is the profits of the farmer that regulate the profits of all other trades". Malthus opposed him in this view, asserting that "the profits of the farmer no more regulate the profits of other trades, than the profits of other trades regulate the profits of the farmer". After the *Essay* this principle disappears from view, and is not to be found in the *Principles.*'

'The rational foundation of the principle of the determining role of the profits of agriculture, which is never explicitly stated by Ricardo, is that in agriculture the same commodity, namely corn, forms both the capital (conceived as composed of the subsistence necessary for workers) and the product; so that the determination of profit by the difference between total product and capital advanced, and also the determination of the ratio of this profit to the capital, is done directly between quantities of corn without any question of valuation.' *Sraffa then provides the textual evidence that led him to the corn-ratio theory of profits, also known as the 'corn model'. We do not mention it here.*

'In the *Principles*, however, with the adoption of a general theory of value, it became possible for Ricardo to demonstrate the determination of the rate of profit in society as a whole instead of through the microcosm of one special branch of production. At the same time he was enabled to abandon the simplification that wages consist only of corn, which had been under frequent attack from Malthus, and to treat wages as composed of a variety of products (including manufactures), although food was still predominant among them. It was now labour, instead of corn, that appeared on both sides of the account – in modern terms, both as input and output: as a result, the rate of profits was no longer determined by the ratio of the corn produced to the corn used up in production, but, instead, by the ratio of the total labour of the country to the labour required to produce the necessaries for that labour. (But while the theory that the profits of the farmer determine all other profits disappears in the *Principles*, the more general proposition that the productivity of labour on land which pays no rent is fundamental in determining general profits continues to occupy a central position.)'

'Many years later, an echo of the old corn-ratio theory (which rendered distribution independent of value) can perhaps be recognised when Ricardo in a moment of discouragement with the difficulties of value writes to McCulloch: "After all, the great questions of Rent, Wages, and Profits must be explained by the proportions in which the whole produce is divided between landlords, capitalists, and labourers, and which are not essentially connected with the doctrine of value".'

'Parallel with this ran another theme in the development of Ricardo's thought. At first he had subscribed to the generally accepted view that a rise in corn prices, through its effect upon wages, would be followed by a rise of all other prices. He had not regarded this view as inconsistent with his theory of profit so long as the latter had been expressed in its primitive "agricultural" form. The conflict between the two however was bound to become apparent in the degree to which he groped towards a more general form of his theory; since the supposed general rise of prices obscured the simple relation of the rise of wages to the fall of profits. Already in the *Essay on Profits*, although his general presentation is still in the "agricultural" form, he repudiates the accepted view in a footnote: "It has been thought that the price of corn regulates the prices of all other things. This appears to me to be a mistake". Elsewhere in the *Essay*, in connection with this question, there are passages which foreshadow his full theory of value and already link it with the theory of profits: "The exchangeable value of all commodities rises as the difficulties of their production increase. If then new difficulties occur in the production of corn, from more labour being necessary, whilst no more labour is required to produce gold, silver, cloth, linen &c. the exchangeable value of corn will necessarily rise, as compared with those things". Further on in the *Essay* he states: "A fall in the price of corn, in consequence of improvements in agriculture or of importation, will lower the exchangeable value of corn only, – the price of no other commodity will be affected. If, then, the price of labour falls, which it must do when the price of corn is lowered, the real profits of all descriptions must rise".'

'All these elements of the *Essay* are taken over into the chapter On Value in the *Principles* with the addition of several new ones, some of which have come to be regarded as the most characteristic of Ricardo's theory, and are there built into a systematic theory of Value, on which are now based the theories of Rent, Wages and Profit.'

'The turning point in this transition from the *Essay* to the *Principles* was reached at the end of 1815, when Ricardo faces the necessity for a general solution of the problem, instead of being content with dealing with the difficulties of price piece-meal as they arise in particular problems. At once a proper understanding of the matter appears to him as involving: (*a*) the distinction between causes which affect the value of money and causes which affect the value of commodities; (*b*) the supposition of the invariability of the precious metals as a standard of value; (*c*) the opposition to the view that the price of corn regulates the prices of all other commodities. These three things, which are so closely connected in his mind as to be almost identified, are what he calls "the sheet anchor on which all my propositions are built".'

'The distinction between the two types of influences upon value (on the side of money and on the side of commodities) is made possible by Ricardo's treatment of money as a commodity like any other. Thus a change in wages could not alter the prices of commodities, since (if the gold mine from which money was obtained were in the same country) a rise of wages would affect the owner of the gold mine as much as the other industries. Hence it was the relative conditions of production of gold and of other commodities that determined prices, and not the remuneration of labour'.

'The attempt to weave into his general theory the proposition which he had established that a rise of wages does not raise prices, led immediately to his discovery of "the curious effect which the rise of wages produces on the prices of those commodities which are chiefly obtained by the aid of machinery and fixed capital". It yielded the triumphant conclusion that, not only was it false that a rise of wages would raise the price of every commodity (as "Adam Smith, and all the writers who have followed him" had maintained that it would do), but on the contrary, it caused the prices of many commodities to fall: a result of which he stressed the "importance to the science of political economy", although it accorded so little "with some of its received doctrines".'

'The importance which Ricardo came to attach to the principle that the value of a thing was regulated by the quantity of labour required for its production, and not by the remuneration of that labour, reflected his recognition that what his new theory was opposed to was not merely the popular view of the effect of wages on prices but another and more general theory of Adam Smith (of which that effect came to appear as a particular case) – what Ricardo referred to in writing to Mill as Adam Smith's "original error respecting value". This latter theory, in brief, was that "as soon as stock has accumulated in the hands of particular persons" and "as soon as the land of any country has all become private property", the price of commodities is arrived at by a process of *adding up* the wages, profit and rent: "in every improved society, all the three enter more or less, as component parts, into the price of the far greater part of commodities". In other words, "wages, profit, and rent, are the three original sources . . . of all exchangeable value". Adam Smith speaks also of the natural price varying "with the natural rate of each of its component parts, of wages, profit, and rent".'

'In the chapter On Value, Ricardo criticises Adam Smith for limiting the rule that commodities exchange according to the amount of labour required for their production to "that early and rude state of society, which precedes both the accumulation of stock and the appropriation of land"; "as if when profits and rent were to be paid, they would have some influence on the relative value of commodities, independent of the mere quantity of labour that was necessary to their production". But, Ricardo adds, Adam Smith "has no where analysed the effects of the accumulation of capital, and the appropriation of land, on relative value". (The effect of "the appropriation of land" is left by Ricardo for later consideration in the chapter On Rent, and in the chapter On Value he deals only with the accumulation of capital.) This passage in which he criticises Adam Smith has puzzled readers, since it appears to be "flatly contradicted" (as Cannan put it) by the following sections of the chapter.'

It is not until 1818 in a letter to Mill that Ricardo states precisely why he finds Smith's respective doctrine erroneous. 'This he does by contrasting his own reading of the matter with that of Torrens. "He [Torrens] makes it appear that Smith says that after capital accumulates and industrious people are set to work the quantity of labour employed is not the only circumstance that determines the value of commodities, and that I oppose this opinion. Now I want to shew that I do not oppose this opinion in the way that he represents me to do so, but Adam Smith thought, that as in the early stages of society, all the produce of labour belonged to the labourer, and as after stock was accumulated, a part went to profits, that accumulation, necessarily, without any regard to the different degrees of durability of capital, or any other circumstance whatever, raised the prices or exchangeable value of commodities, and consequently that their value was no longer regulated by the quantity of labour necessary to their production. In opposition to him, I maintain that it is not because of this division into profits and wages, – it is not because capital accumulates, that exchangeable value varies, but it is in all stages of society, owing only to two causes: one the more or less quantity of labour required, the other the greater or less durability of capital: – that the former is never superseded by the latter, but is only modified by it".'

Principal changes in the chapter 'On Value' in the second and the third editions

'It has come to be a widely accepted opinion about Ricardo that in subsequent editions he steadily retreated under pressure of his critics from the theory of value presented in edition 1 . . . All the evidence in favour of a "weakening" of Ricardo is based on the current misunderstanding of certain changes in the text which the letter to Mill quoted [above] enables us to rectify.'

'The alterations were certainly extensive; little more than half of the final version (edition 3) of the chapter On Value being found in the same form in edition 1. Although the changes made in edition 2 were small and there was little rearrangement of the matter, the subdivision into sections was first introduced in that edition; this only emphasized the repetition and lack of order in the treatment and rendered necessary the complete rearrangement and rewriting of edition 3. Thus the statement of the exceptions to the law of value due to different proportions of capital (or, as Ricardo put it, to the rise or fall of wages), which was repeated in edition 1 in different places (and is still scattered under several sections in edition 2) is mostly collected in edition 3 under Sections IV and V.'

Although no essential change was made in successive editions about the rule that determines value, Sraffa notes two considerable alterations were made in connection with the choice of an invariable measure of value. We do not mention them here.

Second edition

'Only 750 copies of edition 1 of the *Principles* had been printed, and within two months of publication Murray told Ricardo that a second edition would "most assuredly be required". Ricardo, however, heard no more of this until after the appearance of McCulloch's review in the number of the *Edinburgh Review* for June 1818 (actually published in August) by which the sale was "much accelerated". On 8 November 1818 Ricardo wrote to Mill: "I hear from various quarters that my book is selling very fast, and that a new edition will soon be required"; adding, "I think in the last conversation we had together we agreed that there would not be very great advantage in making any new arrangement of the contents, as it appears to have made the impression I could wish on those who have well considered it". On 17 November 1818 he received a request from Murray to prepare a second edition; and within a week Ricardo had the book ready for the press. In sending the revised copy to Murray, he mentioned that it contained "a few very trifling alterations" and asked that the proposed division into sections of the first chapter should be sent by messenger to Mill for his approval. However, the second edition was not published until 27 February 1819.'

'In the intervening period he received the French translation of his own *Principles*, with Say's notes; and in reply to one of these notes he added a passage referring to the question whether the theory of rent depended upon the existence of land which paid no rent. This point had also been the subject of discussion during a visit of Malthus to Gatcomb in December 1818. At one time he thought of having Say's notes translated and published as an appendix of his own ed. 2; but he referred the matter to Murray, who evidently decided against it.'

With a single exception, the alterations in the second edition were unimportant. The only prominent change concerned the chapter 'On Value', which was subdivided into sections each carrying its own heading. It was on these that Ricardo had consulted Mill. This subdivision required the rewriting of certain passages. On the whole very little rearrangement was made.

Third edition

'Before Ricardo left London for the country in July 1820 Murray told him that "he should soon wish to publish a new edition" of the *Principles*; and during the next six months (which, after a few weeks at Brighton, he spent at Gatcomb) he revised his book for edition 3. This was done in the intervals of what was to become his main preoccupation during this period: re-reading, and writing his Notes on, Malthus's *Principles of Political Economy*. At first he had intended to include in edition 3 his defence against Malthus's attacks. But he afterwards gave up this project; Mill (who in August and September was on a visit to Gatcomb) had "strongly dissuaded" him from it, and advised him not to notice any attacks for fear of "giving too controversial a character" to the book.'

The changes in this edition were much more extensive than those made in edition 2. Yet Ricardo seems to have regarded them as mostly unimportant. The main changes in the first chapter have already been mentioned. Many of the Notes on Malthus's Principles *are reflected in the alterations made in the new edition.* 'On the advantages of free importation of corn Ricardo was even more emphatic than he had been in previous editions. In the "Advertisement to the Third Edition" he directs the attention of the reader to the changes which he has introduced into the last chapter, in order to throw into sharper relief the doctrine of the increased ability of a country to pay taxes as a result of a diminished cost of food.'

'The most revolutionary change in edition 3 is the new chapter On Machinery, in which Ricardo retracts his previous opinion that the introduction of machinery is beneficial to all the different classes of society. "My mistake", he explains, "arose from the supposition, that whenever the net income of a society increased, its gross income would also increase; I now, however, see reason to be satisfied that the one fund, from which landlords and capitalists derive their revenue, may increase, while the other, that upon which the labouring class mainly depend, may diminish". His conclusion must have shocked his friends even more than the change of principle itself: "That the opinion entertained by the labouring class, that the employment of machinery is frequently detrimental to their interests, is not founded on prejudice and error, but is conformable to the correct principles of political economy".'

'Previously Ricardo had held the view that, since machinery made it possible to produce commodities at a lower cost, it must lead to an increase in their quantity and accordingly be beneficial to all classes of society. He had not expressed this view in the earlier editions of the *Principles*, and the only place where he had stated in print an opinion as to the effect of machinery upon labour was an incidental reference in the *Essay on Profits* where he alluded to "the effects of improved machinery, which it is now no longer questioned, has a decided tendency to raise the real wages of labour". But as he says at the beginning of the new chapter he had "in other ways" given support to those doctrines. He probably had in mind a speech in Parliament in 1819 on Robert Owen's plan in which he had declared that "it could not be denied, on the whole view of the subject, that machinery did not lessen the demand for labour". Barton's pamphlet of 1817, *Observations on the Condition of the Labouring Classes*, with its view as to the adverse effects of machinery on labour, does not seem to have influenced Ricardo at the time of its publication; although he quotes it with approval in the new chapter in edition 3. When McCulloch, in an article on "Taxation and the Corn Laws" in the *Edinburgh Review* of January 1820, had approved the ideas of Barton (of whose pamphlet the article was ostensibly a review), Ricardo wrote to McCulloch contesting this opinion. McCulloch had stated that "the fixed capital invested in a machine, must always displace a considerably greater quantity of circulating capital, – for otherwise there could be no motive to its erection; and hence its first effect is to sink, rather than increase, the rate of wages". In reply Ricardo had said: "the employment of machinery I think never diminishes the demand for labour – it is never a cause of a fall in the price of labour, but the effect of its rise". McCulloch became a convert to this view, and in an article in the *Edinburgh Review* of March 1821 maintained that "no improvement of machinery can possibly diminish the demand for labour, or reduce the rate of wages". It is scarcely surprising that he should have taken strong exception to Ricardo's sudden change of front on the matter, and that on seeing the new edition he should have bitterly complained of "the extreme erroneousness of the principles to which you have incautiously lent the sanction of your name".'

HEINZ D. KURZ AND NERI SALVADORI

See also:

Biaujeaud, Huguette, on Ricardo, Corn Model; *Essay on Profits*; Invariable Measure of Value; Labour Theory of Value; Malthus–Ricardo debate; Mill, James, and Ricardo; *Notes on Malthus*; Sraffa, Piero, on Ricardo.

Rate of Interest

Interest is the price for the use of capital in production – the 'pure' remuneration of capital whatever the form of its employment, whether financial or real. If production is carried out with the firm's own capital, interest constitutes its opportunity cost and as such will enter into that normal cost that in the long run tends to be equated with the unit price. Firms would not continue to replace plant that is wearing out unless the prices for their commodities were such that they could not do better for themselves by investing their depreciation funds in gilt-edged securities; conversely, commodity prices could not permanently involve rates of return on the firms' funds exceeding the relevant rates of interest – those to be earned in the market on long-term fixed-interest securities in which there is no element of risk – by more than a normal remuneration for the 'risk and trouble' of productively employing capital. The case of share capital does not alter the fundamentals of this picture. It may be presumed that the nearest competing alternative to shares is long-term bonds, and that ordinary shares will be held only if the expected yield on them exceeds the yield on long-term bonds. As there is a significant section of the investing public ready to switch from one kind of investment to the other, this tends to maintain their respective yields at a steady level. That is to say, at any given time there will be a certain relationship between the prices of the various classes of securities: a shift in the price of one large class must be followed by a general shift in the whole range of prices. Thus, a rise in prices for long-term government bonds – a fall in the long-term rate of interest resulting from the pursuing of a cheap-money policy – will be followed by a rise in prices of securities generally. But a higher quotation for existing equities implies that companies can raise capital by issuing shares on more favourable terms; in the words of Keynes, a high quotation for existing equities has 'the same effect as if (companies) could borrow at a low rate of interest' ([1936] 1964: 151n). So the issue of common stocks, as a method of financing investment available to joint-stock companies, will also become cheaper (or dearer) in the face of a persistent fall (or rise) in interest rates.

We may conclude, therefore, that quite irrespective of the kind of capital employed in production a lasting lowering (or raising) of interest rates tends to make normal costs stand lower (or higher) than they would otherwise have done, and thus, by the competition among firms within each industry, to affect prices correspondingly. Given the level of money wages, any such change in the price level brought about by a lasting change in interest rates would then be accompanied by a change in the same direction in the level of prices in relation to the level of money wages, thereby causing changes in income distribution. A prolonged fall in interest rates should cause a fall in prices relative to the wage level and thereby bring about a lower rate of profit and a higher real wage, while a prolonged rise in interest rates should raise the rate of profits, and thus reduce the real wage.

Although economic theory has always looked at interest as the price for the use of capital in production, it has, however, also generally regarded it as a subordinate phenomenon. In the words of Ricardo: '[t]he rate of interest depends on the rate of profit . . . [o]ne is the cause, the other the effect, and it is impossible for any circumstances to make them change places' (*Works*, I: 300n), and in the words of Joan Robinson: '[o]ver the long run, the interest rate rentiers can exact is dominated by the profits that entrepreneurs can earn, not the other way round' (1979: xxii). In fact, according to both classical and neoclassical economists there is, between the normal rate of profit and the money rate of interest, a long-run causal relationship going from the former to the latter, so that the rate of interest is ultimately determined by those real forces that explain the course of the normal rate of profit: the real wage rate and production techniques, in the classical theory of distribution up to David Ricardo; the 'fundamental phenomena' of productivity and thrift, as far as the neoclassical theory is concerned. An important implication of this way of conceiving the relation between interest and profit is the denial of any substantial power on the part of the monetary authorities. Given the state of the real forces governing normal profit – the 'natural real rate' – the impact on the price level or on real output and accumulation of any lasting discrepancy between the courses of the two rates would force the monetary authorities to act so as to make the rate of interest move in sympathy with the normal rate of profit. An autonomous lowering of the lending rate by the monetary authorities would drive the price level up, contrary to what has been outlined above; this is because overall monetary expenditure would expand as a consequence of the difference that would be created between the lending rate and the 'natural real rate'. In actual experience, however, rising prices very rarely coincide with low or falling interest rates and the opposite is the general rule (the so-called 'Gibson Paradox' or 'price puzzle'). Instead of assuming a lowering of interest rates by the monetary authorities, other things being equal, one would then simply have to make the alternative assumption that a difference between the natural real rate and the actual money rate generally arises because it is *the former* that rises or falls, while the latter remains unchanged and only belatedly follows (see Wicksell [1906] 1962: 204–5). The 'natural rate' notion permeates also the so-called 'new consensus monetary policy model'. Indeed, inflation targeting (IT) postulates the existence of a long-run equilibrium real rate of interest, to which the interest rate policy instrument must be adjusted in order to check fluctuations in inflation and keep output at potential (see Pivetti, 2010 for a critical discussion of the IT framework).

On the commonly accepted notion of the rate of interest as a subordinate phenomenon, somewhat dissenting views can be found both before and after the inception of marginalism. The two most outstanding cases are those represented by Marx and Keynes. Marx did not share Ricardo's view that lasting changes in the rate of interest must reflect changes in the normal rate of profit. He regarded 'the average rate of interest prevailing in a certain country' as a magnitude determined by socioeconomic and institutional circumstances unrelated to the real forces that, in his analysis, govern the normal rate of profit. From a consideration of the role played by the monetary authorities and the credit system, by the world market and domestic customs (see Marx [1894] 1977: 425, 427, 431–2), he was led to regard the money rate of interest as 'independently determined', and to maintain that 'there is no such thing as a "natural" rate of interest' – 'no general law by which the average rate of interest may be determined' (ibid.: 428; see also 426). The point is, however, that Marx's 'autonomous determination' of the rate of interest is accompanied by a marked weakening of the connection between this variable and the normal rate of profit, because the latter still depends in his analysis, as in that of Ricardo, on the real wage. The only connection between interest and profit acknowledged by Marx is that the normal rate of profit would constitute 'the maximum limit of interest', while within that limit the average rate of interest prevailing in a certain country ('as differentiated from the continually fluctuating market rates') could take any level whatsoever (ibid.: 423–6). To a very large extent, then, in Marx's analysis both rates appear capable of being determined independently of each other – hardly an acceptable view in the light of the interpretation, shared by Marx himself, of a positive profit of enterprise as a normal phenomenon (since 'to represent functioning capital is not a sine-cure, like representing interest-bearing capital'; ibid.: 446).

As to Keynes's views on interest, an unprejudiced observation of concrete reality clearly played a significant part in his interpretation of the rate of interest as a 'monetary phenomenon'. The fact that Keynes was far from being entirely happy with his monetary explanation of interest (see Keynes [1937] 1973: 213) did not shake his conviction that the rate of interest is *not* determined by the real forces envisaged by the neoclassical theory. Unfortunately, the persistence in Keynes's analysis of some traditional neoclassical premises seriously weakens his concept of the rate of interest as a magnitude determined by monetary factors. In particular, the idea of an investment demand schedule constitutes an obstacle that a monetary theory of interest cannot easily overcome. Notwithstanding the statement in the *General Theory* that he 'no longer' regards Wicksell's notion of a 'natural real rate' as 'a most promising idea' (ibid.: 234), the natural rate is still there, as the rate that would ensure equality between full-employment saving and investment decisions. Keynes's underemployment equilibrium is ultimately the result of the presence in the economic system of factors that hinder the possibility of bringing the actual rate of interest down to its 'natural' or full-employment level. It is, in other words, the result of a limited flexibility of the money rate of interest.

This limited flexibility is actually all that Keynes has to offer as a basis for his non-orthodox concept of interest as a monetary phenomenon. But if one takes into account the fact that even in Wicksell there is no automatic gravitation of the money rate towards the level of the natural real rate (banking policy having to perform the task), then the difference between the two authors will not appear that marked. They both share the idea of an inverse relation between the rate of interest and investment decisions, while the conflict of opinions is essentially centred upon the degree of the (non-automatic) flexibility of the rate of interest, in the face of discrepancies between full-employment savings and investment decisions. One can say that it was largely in the light of this comparison that the neoclassical synthesis could argue, successfully and with foundation, that the determination of the current rate of interest by the intersection of the supply schedule of money and the demand schedule for money, while adequate for showing that the flexibility of the rate of interest is not of an automatic nature, is, however, insufficient to sustain the thesis of a limited flexibility of the rate of interest. And if current money interest can normally be brought to, and kept at, its 'natural' level – provided the monetary authority applies to its action 'a modest measure of persistence and consistency of purpose' (Keynes [1936] 1964: 204) – then the neoclassical real forces of productivity and thrift may still be regarded as the ultimate determinants of the equilibrium rate of interest.

Things are quite different if there is no such thing as a 'natural' rate of interest – a normal rate of profit, that is to say, determined independently by real forces and that can be taken as the *primum movens*. We would be back in this case to the picture outlined at the beginning of this entry, that is, it would be difficult not to acknowledge that, given money wages and production techniques, a lowering (raising) of interest rates by the monetary authorities would actually drive the price level down (up), owing to the adaptation of prices to normal costs caused by competition. There would thus be nothing 'paradoxical' in the positive correlation between interest and prices one generally finds in actual experience. And at a given level of real output, the rate of interest would also regulate the quantity of money in active circulation – a quantity that adapts itself to the needs of trade – via its influence on the price level: interest, prices and the quantity of money would all move in the same direction, with the policy-determined interest rate acting as the *primum movens* of the process.

The 'monetary' explanation of distribution that I started to develop in the early 1990s (see Pivetti, 1991) is precisely an attempt to emancipate us from any real explanation of the rate of interest – an attempt prompted by Sraffa's suggestion that in the necessary long-run connection between normal profit and money interest it is the latter that is susceptible to setting the pace (see Sraffa, 1960: 33). By focusing on the actual mechanism whereby the rate of interest is likely to set the pace in its connection with normal profit, eventually I got hold of the notion of money interest as an autonomous determinant of normal money production costs that governs the ratio of prices to money wages. As pointed out earlier, this interpretation of interest does not require any particular assumption as to the kind of capital employed in production: borrowed, in the forms of shares or a firm's own capital. For any given situation of technique, there is a price level that depends on the money wage and on the money rate of interest, with the latter acting as the regulator of the ratio of the price level to the money wage. This ratio is thus seen as the connecting link between the rate of interest and the rate of profit: by the competition among firms within each industry, a persistent change in the rate of interest causes a change in the same direction in the level of prices in relation to the level of money wages, thereby generating a corresponding change in the rate of profits and an inverse change in the real wage. Wage bargaining and monetary policy come out of this analysis as the main channels through which class relations act in determining distribution. Class relations are seen as tending to act primarily upon the profit rate, via the money rate of interest, rather than upon the real wage as maintained by both the English classical economists and Marx. Indeed, the level of the real wage prevailing in any given situation is viewed as the final result of the whole process by which distribution of income between workers and capitalists is actually derived. Interest rate determination is thus not seen as constrained by some natural, technical or accidental circumstances – be they the relative scarcity of capital and labour, a 'subsistence' real wage, or the rate of growth of the economic system. Rather, the rate of interest is regarded as a policy-determined variable, a conventional monetary phenomenon 'determined from outside the system of production' (ibid.: 33) and not subject to any general law. One can describe interest rate determination in terms of sets of objectives and constraints, on the action of the monetary authorities, which have different weights both among the various countries and for a particular country at different times (see Pivetti, 1991: 11–17, 33–6), and with which, to a very large extent, the parties' relative strength is ultimately intertwined.

MASSIMO PIVETTI

See also:

Capital and Profits; Monetary Theory; National Debt.

References

Keynes, J.M. ([1936] 1964), *The General Theory of Employment, Interest and Money*, London: Macmillan.
Keynes, J.M. ([1937] 1973), 'Alternative theories of the rate of interest', in D. Moggridge (ed.), *The Collected*

Writings of John Maynard Keynes, Vol. XIV: The General Theory and After Defence and Development, London: Macmillan and Cambridge University Press for the Royal Economic Society, pp. 201–15.

Marx, K. ([1894] 1977), *Capital: A Critique of Political Economy, Vol. III*, London: Lawrence & Wishart.

Pivetti, M. (1991), *An Essay on Money and Distribution*, London: Macmillan.

Pivetti, M. (2010), 'Interest and the general price level: some critical notes on "the new consensus monetary policy model"', in A. Birolo, D.K. Foley, H.D. Kurz, B. Schefold and I. Steedman (eds), *Production, Distribution and Trade: Alternative Perspectives. Essays in Honour of Sergio Parrinello*, London and New York: Routledge, pp. 216–32.

Robinson, J. (1979), *The Generalisation of the General Theory and other Essays*, London: Macmillan.

Sraffa, P. (1960), *Production of Commodities by Means of Commodities*, Cambridge, UK: Cambridge University Press.

Wicksell, K. ([1906] 1962), *Lectures on Political Economy. Vol. II: Money and Credit*, London: Routledge & Kegan Paul.

Recent Interpretations

A recurring theme in modern debates over the interpretation of Ricardo concerns the degree to which he had anticipated or was groping toward the marginalist supply-and-demand theory that emerged in the closing decades of the nineteenth century, or had instead been elaborating an altogether different theory of value and distribution. This theme is neatly reflected in the conflicting views of Ricardo held by Alfred Marshall and William Stanley Jevons. In his famous Appendix I to the *Principles of Economics* (1890), Marshall, who wanted to buttress the standing of the then new marginalist theory by tracing its pedigree to a highly respected classical predecessor, characterized Ricardo's value theory as an underdeveloped version of the theory of supply and demand. Ricardo, according to Marshall, had downplayed the role of demand in determining price, partly on the basis of an implicit constant returns assumption. Jevons ([1871] 1879: xliii), on the other hand, saw Ricardo's theory as a disastrous detour that had 'shunted the car of Economic science on to a wrong line' – the right line being, of course, the utility-based approach hinted at, but not rigorously expounded, in the writings of Thomas Robert Malthus and Jean-Baptiste Say. By the late 1920s the marginalist view that prices and income distribution are regulated by the forces of supply and demand had acquired the status of orthodoxy, and the basic elements of the theory had been largely worked out. Most economists had come to regard the supply-and-demand theory as obvious common sense, and Marshall's historiography, which posits a clear line of descent running from Ricardo through John Stuart Mill to the marginalists, became the standard reading.

Sraffa's interpretation
In 1951, Piero Sraffa put forth an alternative interpretation in his Introduction to the first volume of *The Works and Correspondence of David Ricardo*. According to this interpretation, some time in 1813, that is, shortly before the 1815 publication of the *Essay on Profits* (*Works*, IV), Ricardo had abandoned the competition of capitals theory of the profit rate, to which he had previously adhered. That theory, which Adam Smith had put forward in the *Wealth of Nations* and that Malthus accepted, contends that as a market economy accumulates capital, competition among ever more numerous units of capital drives down market prices and hence the normal rate of profit. In the *Essay on Profits*, Sraffa argued, Ricardo put forth an entirely different theory that explained the profit rate in terms of the material conditions of production – the technological requirements

of the system – and the real wages paid to labour. This alternative explanation of profits underpinned Ricardo's well-known claim that 'the profits of the farmer . . . regulate the profits of all other trades' (Ricardo to Trower, 8 March 1814, *Works*, VI: 104). Sraffa suggested that the 'rational foundation' for this claim was the supposition that in agriculture the output, the material inputs and the real wages of labour all consist of the same commodity, corn. On this supposition, the profit rate *r* can be conceptualized as a ratio of physical quantities of grain. Assuming that wages are advanced, we may express this mathematically as follows:

$$r = \frac{Q - (M + W)}{(M + W)}$$

where Q is the output of grain, M is the amount of seed-corn capital required to produce Q, and W is the amount of corn paid as real wages to the labour employed in the production of Q. Since under conditions of free competition, profit rates will tend to converge toward one another across different sectors, the market prices of non-agricultural goods must adjust to bring the rates of return in those sectors into line with the materially determined agricultural profit rate.

As is well known, Malthus objected that 'In no case of production, is the produce exactly of the same nature as the capital advanced' (*Works*, VI: 117). Ricardo accepted this criticism, and when he came to write his book *On the Principles of Political Economy, and Taxation* (*Works*, I, first edition 1817) he realized that the components of the ratio that defines the profit rate need to be reckoned in terms of their long-period normal prices, and that, incidentally, the agricultural sector could no longer occupy the anchoring role he had assigned to it in the *Essay on Profits*. Here the difficulty arose that long-period prices themselves depend upon the profit rate. There was a problem of mutual determination: Ricardo needed to know prices before he could determine the profit rate, but he also needed to know the profit rate before he could determine prices. His way round the problem was to suppose that commodities exchange roughly in proportion to the amounts of labour that enter directly and indirectly into their production. Then the elements of the ratio that explains the profit rate could be expressed as commensurable quantities of labour time. Ricardo fully grasped the provisional nature of this solution: he knew that commodities don't in fact exchange in proportion to the labour embodied in them except in highly special circumstances, and that the impact of a change in distribution on relative prices depends in a systematic way on the proportions in which labour and produced inputs are utilized in production (though he did not fully appreciate the complexity of the relationship; see Sraffa, 1960).

Ricardo's approach to the theory of value and distribution, in the Sraffian view, has the following features that distinguish it from the neoclassical supply-and-demand theory (see Garegnani, 1984 for a thorough elaboration). First, relative prices are determined by material conditions, notably the technology of production and the distribution of the social product between wages and profits. Second, the explanation of relative prices and the profit rate is conducted separately from the determination of outputs. That is to say, unlike the marginalist theory, which determines outputs simultaneously with prices and distribution via the interaction of price-elastic supply and demand functions, Ricardo's theory takes the social product as given in its explanation of prices and the profit rate.

Finally, and perhaps most crucially, Ricardo treated the real wage as parametric in his account of prices and the profit rate. In particular, and again in contrast with the marginalist theory, he did not view the normal wage as a factor price determined by the forces of supply and demand in the market for labour; he understood it to be a historically determined social norm whose magnitude depends upon the institutional conditions prevailing in the economic system under consideration.

It would be fair to say that Sraffa's account of Ricardo's thought elicited little controversy for two decades. That interpretation posed no obvious direct challenge to neoclassical economics. Economists could, and by and large did, continue to regard the Ricardian system as an underdeveloped, and in some respects wrong-headed, engine of analysis, mainly on account of its failure to assign to demand a role co-equal with cost in determining price (see, for example, Schumpeter, 1954: 588–95). On neoclassical reasoning, the absence of demand functions deprived the theory of an explanation of outputs, and impaired its ability to take account of non-constant returns since, if unit costs vary with output, price cannot be determined independently of output. When George Stigler (1958) hypothesized that Ricardo had a 93 per cent labour theory of value – that Ricardo was making the empirical assumption that changes in labour input requirements account for nearly all observed variation in relative prices – he saw no reason to take issue with Sraffa's interpretation.

In *Production of Commodities by Means of Commodities* (1960), Sraffa showed that the theoretical framework described above could be rigorously grounded. The theory could explain relative prices and the profit rate on the basis of the data from which Ricardo started – the size and composition of the social product, the technical conditions of production, and the real wage – without relying upon the problematic assumption that prices are proportional to embodied labour time. Starting from Sraffa's interpretation, and drawing also on Nicholas Kaldor's (1955–56) sketch of Ricardo's approach to the analysis of distribution, Luigi L. Pasinetti (1960) considered Ricardo's account of the dynamics of a capitalist economy. Ricardo's main interest was to understand how the distributive shares – profits, wages, rents – are affected by the process of growth, and how growth-induced changes in distribution might influence the accumulation process itself. Ricardo believed that as an economy expanded, increased demand for food (to maintain a growing labour force) and raw materials (to support an expanding industrial sector) would require successively less fertile tracts of land and successively less productive mines to be brought into use. Rising rents on the more productive land and mines would squeeze profits, since real wages are more or less parametric, that is, set at the level necessary to enable the working class to reproduce itself at its normal standard of living.

In the *Principles*, Ricardo (*Works*, I: 93) defines the natural wage as the real wage that would keep the working population constant. Once this natural wage and the economy's capital stock are specified, Pasinetti's Ricardian model determines prices, sectoral outputs and sectoral employment levels (in this respect Pasinetti diverges from Ricardo, who provided no formal theory of output determination), and the profit rate. Ricardo acknowledged that the market wage might not coincide with the natural wage, but he argued that population adjustments would push the actual real wage toward the natural wage. When the market wage exceeds the natural wage, population will expand and cause the actual wage to move toward the natural wage; the opposite occurs if, at the given population level, the actual wage is below the natural wage. Pasinetti stresses that the mechanism that causes population to adjust in response to deviations of the market wage from the natural wage does not itself determine the natural wage: it serves merely to ensure that the actual wage gravitates toward the natural wage, which is conceived as a physiological and social norm. Operating in parallel with this population mechanism is a second one in which a profit rate above a certain minimum threshold induces investment in excess of what is required to replace circulating capital and depreciated plant and equipment. As this second mechanism plays out and the economy's capital stock and output expand, rents rise, causing the profit rate to fall until it reaches a point at which net capital accumulation is zero. These two mechanisms move the economy toward a stationary state – a stable position in which labour is remunerated at its natural rate, so that there is zero population growth, and the profit rate is low enough to remove any inducement to accumulate capital. It must be noted, however, that Ricardo was not especially preoccupied with the stationary state, which is a minor theme in his writings. He was confident that productivity-enhancing technical change and the abandonment of the Corn Laws, which restricted grain imports, would retard the decline of the profit rate sufficiently to push the eventual stationary state into the very remote future (see Roncaglia, 1985; Kurz, 2010).

Post-1960 neoclassical interpretations of Ricardo

Sraffa's *Production of Commodities*, in addition to establishing the robustness of Ricardo's theoretical framework as an alternative to the marginalist theory, also provided the grounding for a powerful capital theoretic critique of the latter theory. That critique called into question the foundations of the neoclassical theory of distribution in terms of price-elastic factor demand and supply functions (see Symposium, 1966). It is perhaps not a coincidence that the Ricardo debates, dormant for decades, were reactivated in the aftermath of the publication of *Production of Commodities*, which brought to light a serious defect in the neoclassical theory of distribution while simultaneously showing that an alternative approach with roots in the work of the classical economists was viable. One of the fronts on which neoclassical theory sought to defend itself was intellectual history.

The opening shot was fired by Samuel Hollander in a 1973 paper that challenged Sraffa's corn-ratio interpretation of the profit rate theory Ricardo had put forward in the *Essay on Profits*. Hollander argued that Ricardo arrived at his conclusions about the connections among wages, the profit rate and rents by supposing that the money wage rises in reaction to the increases in the prices of wage goods that ensue as the economy is compelled to bring less fertile tracts of land into cultivation. The higher money wage in the face of unchanging prices for non-wage goods is what accounts for the fall in the profit rate, according to Hollander. Hence, in Hollander's view, Ricardo never explained the profit rate in material terms as Sraffa maintained.

Forceful and persuasive critiques of Hollander's position were advanced by Eatwell (1975) and Garegnani (1982). The byzantine subtleties of the debate cannot be entered into here; a few remarks will have to suffice. Eatwell (1975: 183) noted that Hollander's position is impossible to reconcile with Ricardo's insistence, from 1813 onwards, that 'the rate of profit could not be permanently affected by circumstances outside the conditions of production, such as variations in demand'. Garegnani pointed out, first, that Ricardo had arrived at his new theory of the profit rate *before* abandoning the idea (which he had earlier taken on board from Smith) that an increase in the money wage causes all prices to rise; and, second, that this latter idea is not compatible with the mechanism that Hollander attributes to Ricardo (for Hollander's interpretation requires the prices of final goods to remain unchanged when the money wage rises). Hollander also seems to have been troubled by the fact that in the *Essay on Profits*, Ricardo expresses his accounts in units of money, not quantities of grain. But as Garegnani (1982: 71) explains:

> To the extent to which the argument in terms of 'material rate of produce' allowed Ricardo to determine the rate of profit, it also allowed him to determine the ratio between value of the product and value of capital (whether the two quantities were to be expressed in corn or money). This being so, we should expect Ricardo's explicit statements to be generally in terms of value quantities. He was, in fact, concerned with conclusions applicable to reality and not, merely, with correct deductions from an assumption – that of wages consisting entirely of corn – the realism of which could, and would, be immediately disputed. Given the decisive importance of agricultural capital, he would feel confident that conclusions reached by adopting the simplification of wages consisting entirely of 'corn' would be of general validity: and he would argue these conclusions with reference to a reality where agricultural capital consisted entirely, though not exclusively, of corn.

In subsequent writings Hollander (1979, 1985) has contended that Ricardo's theoretical system is in substance a variant of the neoclassical general equilibrium model:

> Ricardian economics . . . comprises in its essentials an exchange system fully consistent with the marginalist elaborations. In particular [Ricardo's] cost-price analysis is pre-eminently an analysis of the allocation of scarce resources, proceeding in terms of general equilibrium, with allowance for final demand and the interdependence of factor and commodity markets . . . Ricardo's cost prices make no sense except within a demand-supply framework allowing for alternative uses of resources. (Hollander, 1979: 17, 23)

Morishima (1989) and Samuelson (1978) interpret Ricardo in a similar vein, though Samuelson is more inclined than Morishima or Hollander to fault Ricardo for not articulating his theory in rigorous neoclassical terms. (For a critique of Morishima, see Kurz and Salvadori, 1992.) As Samuelson (1978: 1415) puts it:

> within every classical economist there is to be discerned a modern economist trying to be born. A Ricardo or Mill did not so much replace supply and demand theory by quite different mechanisms but rather sought to be able to say something significant and limiting about their properties, quite in the same way that we moderns endeavor to do.

One direction in which this view has been developed focuses on Ricardo's treatment of wages. In his discussion of the dynamics of the economy, Ricardo, as noted above, allows that accumulation may cause the market wage to diverge from the natural wage, but that population adjustments will over time tend to push the actual wage back toward the natural wage. Some neoclassical writers have interpreted this argument as a supply-and-demand mechanism that in effect determines the natural wage. In an often-cited contribution Casarosa (1978) takes issue with Pasinetti's view of Ricardo's wage theory. In Pasinetti's formulation of the Ricardian system, the natural equilibrium is unstable outside of the stationary state: growth entails a declining profit rate until the system settles into a stable stationary state. Hence, Casarosa argues, in a growing economy, the natural equilibrium is not a centre of gravitation for the wage and profit rates. He attributes this view to Ricardo, partly on the basis of the latter's acknowledgment that the market wage:

> may, in an improving society, for an indefinite period, be constantly above [the natural wage]; for no sooner may the impulse, which an increased capital gives to a new demand for labour be obeyed, than another increase of capital may produce the same effect; and thus, if the increase of capital be gradual and constant, the demand for labour may give a continued stimulus to an increase of people. (*Works*, I: 94–5)

Furthermore, Casarosa (1978: 39) writes: 'Ricardo maintains that, because of diminishing returns in agriculture, the process of economic growth brings about a continuous fall of the real wage and of the rate of profit, until the economic system falls into the stationary state and the wage rate settles down to the natural level.'

The interpretative problem for Casarosa is that the conventional view, since it treats the natural real wage as an exogenous constant unaffected by diminishing returns in agriculture cannot explain Ricardo's contention that the real wage declines with economic growth. Hence:

> either Ricardo considered natural equilibrium as the 'attraction' point of market equilibrium, as Pasinetti maintains, but in this case Ricardo's statement that in the process of economic growth the real wage tends to fall does not make any sense; or this latter statement is correct, but then we cannot say that Ricardo examines the behaviour of the economic variables in terms of natural equilibrium. (Ibid.: 40–41)

Casarosa favours the latter option, arguing that Ricardo does not depict the economy in terms of natural equilibrium, but in terms of dynamic equilibrium in which the real wage and the profit rate take values that make the rate of population growth equal to the rate of capital accumulation. (In the *Essay on Profits*, Ricardo defines the natural wage not as the wage that ensures zero population growth – the approach he would take in the *Principles* – but as the wage that equalizes the rate of population growth to the rate of growth of demand for labour, that is, to the needs of accumulation; for a detailed discussion, see Kurz and Salvadori, 2006.) Casarosa's reading presumes that productivity growth due to technical change is nil. A significant implication of Casarosa's interpretation is that the profit rate cannot be conceptualized as a residual, since it is determined simultaneously with the dynamic equilibrium value of the real wage.

This general outlook, which has come to be termed the 'new view' of Ricardo's wage theory, can be found, inter alia, in Hollander (1979), Hicks and Hollander (1977) and Samuelson (1978). A number of persuasive criticisms have been levelled against this reading. Rosselli (1985) provides a superb overview, from a Sraffian perspective, of the interpretative issues surrounding Ricardo's treatment of wages; see also Roncaglia (1985) and Caravale (1985). Peach (1993: Chapter 3) makes a convincing argument against the 'new view' from a non-Sraffian angle. These critiques point out that in various respects the 'new view' does not mesh well with overwhelming textual evidence that Ricardo understood the profit rate as a residual share, and that he did not conceive of the natural wage as determined by the population mechanism. Roncaglia (1985: 118–19) argues that Hollander '[confuses] the classical adjustment process with the marginalist allocation problem' wherein the wage and the profit rate must take values that maximize allocative efficiency – a role they do not play in the classical theory. He also notes that Ricardo posited no formal 'functional relationship between the real wage and population growth' and recognized that a change in wages 'has a small and very delayed bearing on the labour supply' (ibid.: 114).

Among writers who interpret Ricardo as a nascent neoclassical economist, S.C. Rankin (1980) has gone so far as to suggest that Ricardo had a fully articulated supply-and-demand theory differing in no significant respect from what is found in neoclassical economics – notwithstanding the fact that Ricardo (*Works*, I: XXX) explicitly renounced Malthus's contention that prices are regulated by the forces of demand and supply. Ricardo (*Works*, I: 119–20) understood, of course, that the level of demand has a bearing on natural price when production is characterized by non-constant returns. This does not entail, however, that price must be explained in terms of the interaction of price-elastic demand and supply functions. According to Rankin, Ricardo's objections to supply and demand as determinants of natural price rest upon a narrow and idiosyncratic understanding of the supply-and-demand mechanism. What Ricardo criticizes, Rankin contends, is the idea of a price-elastic demand function confronting a perfectly inelastic supply of output to determine price, without reference to cost of production and without recognition of the fact that if market price diverges from cost of production an adjustment of supply must occur in the long run. Ricardo, in other words, understood the term 'supply and demand' to refer only to the short-period situation in which output is fixed. It was this restricted definition of supply-and-demand theory that Ricardo rejected; but his own account of price determination is in essence no different from the neoclassical theory.

Rankin's interpretation, which is shared by Hollander (1979: 273–93), is problematic. Malthus attempted in at least one instance to develop a supply-and-demand argument in terms of price-elastic output adjustments. To this, Ricardo (*Works*, II: 40–41) responded that 'Mr Malthus here substantially admits, that it is not the relation of demand to supply, which finally and permanently regulates the price of commodities, but the cost of their production'. Thus, Ricardo rejected the supply-and-demand theory even when it explicitly allows for output adjustments. As noted, Ricardo was fully aware that when costs are not constant, the level of demand is relevant to price determination. But his writings contain no trace at all of the idea that the forces of supply and demand, represented by two independent functional relationships, interact to determine both price and output simultaneously. When, in discussing the influence of demand on price, Ricardo refers to an 'increased demand for corn' Rankin interprets him to mean a rightward shift of a price-elastic demand schedule, though there is no textual evidence that Ricardo was thinking in these terms. Given the state of demand theory at the time, and Ricardo's well-known scepticism about the possibility of isolating a definite relationship between price and quantity demanded – 'no general rule can be laid down for the variations of price in proportion to quantity' (*Works*, IV: 220) – it is unlikely that Ricardo had such a notion in mind (for a fuller discussion, see Mongiovi, 1988).

Summing up

The literature on Ricardo is vast and cannot be distilled into a simple story. Instead of consensus there are several broad outlooks. One view holds that Ricardo's work constitutes a foundational contribution in a more or less well-defined surplus-approach tradition that runs through Marx to Sraffa, which is distinct from neoclassical theory and that constitutes a robust and viable alternative to the theory of supply and demand. This view seems to me to align most closely with the textual record. A second view follows Marshall in considering Ricardo to be a nascent neoclassical economist, or in some formulations, a modern neoclassical economist *avant la lettre*. Still other interpreters, echoing Jevons, see Ricardo's theory as differing in important ways from the neoclassical theory, and on that account consider it to be deficient. Samuelson (1959, 1978), for example, insists that the absence of a satisfactory (i.e., an essentially neoclassical) treatment of demand constitutes a serious defect of Ricardo's model, since the magnitude of rents, and hence of the other distribution variables, cannot be determined independently of demand (see also Arrow, 1991). Peach (1993) falls into yet another category, for he rejects both the neoclassical interpretations and the Sraffian interpretation. His critique of Hollander and the 'new view' is generally convincing. He is less persuasive when he fails to find any coherence at all in Ricardo's value theory; for assessments of Peach's reading of Ricardo see Kurz (1994), Mongiovi (1994) and Kurz and Mongiovi (2002). John King's *David Ricardo* (2013) provides an excellent overview of Ricardo's life and work, including, in Chapter 8, a balanced discussion of the various interpretative approaches to Ricardo.

GARY MONGIOVI

See also:

Hicks, John R., on Ricardo; Kaldor, Nicholas, on Ricardo; Pasinetti, Luigi Lodovico, on Ricardo; Sraffa, Piero, on Ricardo.

References

Arrow, K. (1991), 'Ricardo's work as viewed by later economists', *Journal of the History of Economics Thought*, **13**(1), 70–77.
Caravale, G.A. (1985), 'Diminishing returns and accumulation in Ricardo', in G.A. Caravale (ed.), *The Legacy of Ricardo*, Oxford: Basil Blackwell, pp. 127–88.
Casarosa, C. (1978), 'A new formulation of the Ricardian system', *Oxford Economic Papers*, **30**(1), 38–63.
Eatwell, J. (1975), 'The interpretation of Ricardo's *Essay on Profits*', *Economica*, **42**(166), 182–7.
Garegnani, P. (1982), 'On Hollander's interpretation of Ricardo's early theory of profits', *Cambridge Journal of Economics*, **6**(1), 65–77.
Garegnani, P. (1984), 'Value and distribution in the classical economists and Marx', *Oxford Economic Papers*, **36**(2), 291–325.
Hicks, J.R. and S. Hollander (1977), 'Mr Ricardo and the moderns', *Quarterly Journal of Economics*, **91**(3), 351–9.
Hollander, S. (1973), 'Ricardo's analysis of the profit rate, 1813–15', *Economica*, **40**(159), 260–82.
Hollander, S. (1979), *The Economics of David Ricardo*, Toronto: University of Toronto Press.
Hollander, S. (1985), 'On the substantive identity of the Ricardian and neoclassical conceptions of economic organization: the French connection in British classicism', in G.A. Caravale (ed.), *The Legacy of Ricardo*, Oxford: Basil Blackwell, pp. 3–44.
Jevons, W.S. ([1871] 1879), *The Theory of Political Economy*, 2nd edition, London: Macmillan.
Kaldor, N. (1955–56), 'Alternative theories of distribution', *Review of Economic Studies*, **23**(2), 83–100.
King, J.E. (2013), *David Ricardo*, London: Palgrave Macmillan.
Kurz, H.D. (1994), 'Review of T. Peach, *Interpreting Ricardo*', *European Journal of the History of Economic Thought*, **1**, 411–20.
Kurz, H.D. (2010), 'Technical progress, capital accumulation and income distribution in classical economics: Adam Smith, David Ricardo and Karl Marx', *European Journal of the History of Economic Thought*, **17**(5), 1183–222.
Kurz, H.D. and G. Mongiovi (2002), 'Interpreting Ricardo: a rejoinder to Peach', *Cambridge Journal of Economics*, **26**(3), 371–80.
Kurz, H.D. and N. Salvadori (1992), 'Morishima on Ricardo', *Cambridge Journal of Economics*, **16**(2), 227–47.
Kurz, H.D. and N. Salvadori (2006), 'Endogenous growth in a stylised "classical" model', in G. Stathakis and G. Vaggi (eds), *Economic Development and Social Change*, London: Routledge, pp. 106–24.

Marshall, A. (1890), *Principles of Economics*, London: Macmillan.

Mongiovi, G. (1988), 'The role of demand in the classical theory of price', in D.A. Walker (ed.), *Perspectives on the History of Economic Thought, Vol. 1*, Aldershot, UK and Brookfield, VT: Edward Elgar Publishing, pp. 114–30.

Mongiovi, G. (1994), 'Misinterpreting Ricardo: a review essay', *Journal of the History of Economic Thought*, **16**(2), 248–69.

Morishima, M. (1989), *Ricardo's Economics: A General Equilibrium Theory of Distribution and Growth*, Cambridge, UK: Cambridge University Press.

Pasinetti, L.L. (1960), 'A mathematical formulation of the Ricardian system', *Review of Economic Studies*, **27**(2): 78–98.

Peach, T. (1993), *Interpreting Ricardo*, Oxford: Oxford University Press.

Rankin, S.C. (1980), 'Supply and demand in Ricardian price theory: a re-interpretation', *Oxford Economic Papers*, **32**(2), 241–62.

Roncaglia, A. (1985), 'Hollander's Ricardo', in G.A. Caravale (ed.), *The Legacy of Ricardo*, Oxford: Basil Blackwell, pp. 105–23.

Rosselli, A. (1985), 'The theory of the natural wage', in G.A. Caravale (ed.), *The Legacy of Ricardo*, Oxford: Basil Blackwell, pp. 239–54.

Samuelson, P.A. (1959), 'A modern treatment of the Ricardian economy: I. The pricing of goods and of labor and land services', *Quarterly Journal of Economics*, **73**(1), 1–35.

Samuelson, P.A. (1978), 'The canonical classical model of political economy', *Journal of Economic Literature*, **16**(4), 1415–34.

Schumpeter, J.A. (1954), *History of Economic Analysis*, New York: Oxford University Press.

Sraffa, P. (1960), *Production of Commodities by Means of Commodities*, Cambridge, UK: Cambridge University Press.

Stigler, G.J. (1958), 'Ricardo and the 93% labor theory of value', *American Economic Review*, **48**(3), 357–67.

Symposium (1966), 'Paradoxes in capital theory: a symposium', *Quarterly Journal of Economics*, **80**(4), 503–83.

Revenue

The term 'revenue' was once used as equivalent to the modern term 'income', which has now replaced it. Both the concept and the word came from France, where *revenu* is the past principle of *revenir*, to return. In Ricardo's writings we find both words, revenue and income, used with exactly the same meaning (see the *Notes on Malthus*, where the two words are interchangeably used in the same note, *Works*, II: 149).

The distinction between gross and net revenue is one of the issues that originated modern economic science. The classical definitions are those offered by Adam Smith. As he writes in the *Wealth of Nations* (*WN*, I.ii.5):

> The gross revenue of all the inhabitants of a great country comprehends, the whole annual produce of the land and labour; the neat revenue, what remains free to them after deducting the expence of maintaining; first their fixed; and, secondly, their circulating capital; or what, without encroaching upon their capital, they can place in their stock reserved for immediate consumption.

The ambiguities of the Smithian definition of net revenue have generated a 200-year-old discussion: should we consider the subsistence fund of the wage earners as circulating capital, therefore excluding it from the net revenue, or as final consumption, and then as a part of it?

Smith's eighteenth-century French predecessors had offered a clear-cut answer. Having in mind a specific picture of the circular process of production, they defined net revenue (the physiocratic *produit net*) as the annually produced wealth (*reproduction totale*) minus the advances required to repeat the process on the same scale. Workers' subsistence, to which wages were strictly limited, were an obvious part of the advances, on the same footing as cattle feed. Net revenue was then the value of the surplus product, which remained available to be – in the words of Achille Nicolas Isnard, a French civil engineer – 'nobly enjoyed by the proprietors' (Isnard, 1781, I: 37). This clear-cut distinction faded away with Smith because he was tried to take into account workers' consumption (and the employment level) in assessing the prosperity of a nation. Therefore, he was sometimes led to include wages in the net revenue and sometimes to consider gross (instead of net) revenue as the crucial indicator for the evaluation of prosperity.

Ricardo raised three main points about the distinction between gross and net revenue. First of all he reverted unambiguously to the original meaning of net revenue (*Works*, I, XXVI) identifying it with the sum of rents and profits alone. He criticized Smith for his preference for 'a large gross, rather than a large net income'. The rationale of this attitude was that taxes are paid from net revenue only and that therefore the power of a country 'of supporting fleets and army, and all species of unproductive labour' (*Works*, I: 347–8) is in proportion to its net revenue only. It is remarkable how similar this argument is to that advanced, almost 60 years before, by Quesnay ([1759] 1972: 20), an author who was familiar to Smith, but definitely not to Ricardo.

Curiously enough, as noted by Vianello (1999), it is Smith himself who emphasized that the 'real wealth' of the inhabitants 'is in proportion, not to their gross, but to their neat [sic] revenue' (*WN*, I.ii.5). It may be that Ricardo failed to notice such a clear statement, but it appears more likely that he chose to overlook it, being aware that the 'neat revenue' Smith refers to does not coincide with the sum of profits and rents.

Ricardo raised his second point on the distinction between gross and net revenue in the third edition of his *Principles* (*Works*, I, XXXI). With the employment of machinery in production (and with the simple substitution of horses for men) 'an increase of the net produce of a country is compatible with a diminution of the gross produce' and therefore 'the opinion entertained by the labouring class, that the employment of machinery is frequently detrimental to their interests, is not founded on prejudice and error, but is conformable to the correct principles of political economy' (ibid.: 392).

Later on, Tugan-Baranowsky (1905) maintained the symmetrical opinion that capitalists could choose a reduction of the 'net revenue' before an increase of the gross product. But this bizarre conclusion depended on his misleading identification of the net product with social consumption (by workers as well as by capitalists). The aim was to show the abstract possibility of an economy in which machines are automatically produced by machines and the labour force is paradoxically reduced to only one worker.

Ricardo also raised the third point on net revenue in the third edition of the *Principles* (*Works*, I, XXVI). After having stated that 'the whole produce of the land and labour of every country is divided into three portions', that 'of these, one portion is devoted to wages, another to profits, and the other to rent' and that 'it is from the two last portions only, that any deductions can be made for taxes, or for savings; the former, if moderate, constituting always the necessary expenses of production', he adds a note, as follows:

Perhaps this is expressed too strongly, as more is generally allotted to the labourer under the name of wages, than the absolutely necessary expenses of production. In that case a part of the net produce of the country is received by the labourer, and may be saved or expended by him; or it may enable him to contribute to the defence of the country. (Ibid.: 347–8)

The same occurrence is evoked again in Chapter XXXII. Suppose, he writes, a part of the landlord's rent is shifted to additional wages for labourers: it will only prove:

that the situation of another class, and by far the most important class in society, is chiefly benefited by the new distribution. All that they receive . . . forms part of the net income of the country, and it cannot be expended without adding to its revenue, its happiness, or its power. (*Works*, I: 425)

This means that wages should be theoretically treated as composing two different parts. The part consisting of the necessary subsistence of the workers belongs to the means of production and therefore has to be advanced as circulating capital. But the second part is a share of the surplus product. This last part can therefore be paid only at the end of the production process, when the surplus is realized. The first part is in principle given and determined by the methods of production, while the second part (if existent) is variable and depends on the distribution of net revenue.

In more recent times, the current notion of national income (inclusive of the totality of wages) definitely prevailed in applied economics, but the theoretical question remained unsettled. See, for instance, Edgeworth quoting, and criticizing, a remark advanced by Jevons (and others) as an argument in favour of the exclusion of necessary consumption from the net income: 'as the horse has to be clothed and stabled, so the productive labourer has to be clothed and housed' (Edgeworth, 1896). (But, as Sraffa later noted [Sraffa Papers, Trinity College, Cambridge], criticizing Edgeworth, the tax exemption limit meant that the subsistence part of wages did not enter into net income.)

Leontief emphasizes the arbitrary nature of the very definition of net income, a definition depending on the type and level of the input–output scheme (a completely consolidated table, reduced to a single box, would show no net income: see Leontief, 1941: 16). The theoretical notions of surplus and of net income are simply discarded by him as meaningless.

Eventually, Sraffa reverts to the original notion of national income as the gross product minus the value of the commodities used up in all industries, while, à la Ricardo, workers' subsistence 'continue to appear with the fuel, etc. among the means of production' (1960: §8). A difficulty, however, persists: how can we operationally determine the subsistence level (and therefore define the 'surplus' part of the wage)?

The Italian economist Zangheri raised the question in a letter to Sraffa dated 29 January 1969: 'By which criterion can we distinguish between what is "necessary" to the worker and what the worker actually gets? . . . After all, from the point of view of the capitalist, all he has to pay in order to obtain the labour services is "necessary", isn't it?' Sraffa's comment, on this occasion, was somewhat cursory: 'Historic, not physiological, but it does not become tautological, as it would be if identified with all that he gets' (see Finzi and Gilibert, 2011: 365–7). Nevertheless, Sraffa had devoted much attention to this question at the end of the 1920s, when exploring the notion of 'real costs' (Sraffa Papers, D3/12/3).

A few quotations about horses, slaves and machines
In the fourth edition of his *Principles* ([1898] 1920) Marshall opens Book VI ('The Distribution of the National Income') with the following sentence: 'The keynote of this book is in the fact that free human beings are not brought up to their work on the same principles as a machine, a horse or a slave.' Now, though it is undoubtedly true that slaves (and horses and machines) are not free by definition, it is also true that the abstract comparison between a slave society and a society based on wage-earning workers can be useful to clarify important theoretical points, and specifically the determination of subsistence level.

Marshall is well aware of the subsistence component of wages. He quotes Turgot as saying that *l'ouvrier ne gagne que sa vie* (Marshall [1898] 1920, I: 505). In the first two editions of the *Principles*, this sentence was translated as: 'the worker gains nothing but his life'. In the following editions, the translation was changed to: 'the worker earns no more than his living'. (Marshall used to credit this correction, which points to a better understanding of the notion of subsistence wage, to the excellent proofreaders at Cambridge University Press.)

At the end of the 1920s, Sraffa devotes much consideration to the working of a slave economy (his note commenting Marshall's opening sentence of Book IV is significantly titled 'Why slavery assumed'). The first quotation might seem rather surprising:

> The with-surplus equations must be introduced with the assumption of a community in which all the human work (including supervision etc.) is done by slaves.

> The advantage of this assumption is that it rids us of the question: how are wages determined? Because of course our equations assume that they are constants. The food and other necessaries for efficiency of slaves are determined in the same way as the amount of fodder given to horses, the amount of fuel given to a machine, the amount of manure given to land: they are not determined outside economics, but for the present purpose they are regarded as given constants. (D/3/12/7, Piero Sraffa Papers, Catalogue, ed. J. Smith, Wren Library, Trinity College, Cambridge)

In the same year, Edwin Cannan wrote in a similar vein:

> We cannot estimate or form any definite idea of the supposed two parts of income, the part derived from the 'source' of current labour and the part derived from the source of personal qualities, whether these are natural or acquired.

> We could do so if the completest chattel slavery existed so that the workers occupied the same position towards owners that horses occupy at present. The workers would then have an income from the human slave point of view just like that which horses have at present from their equine point of view. It would amount (except in the case of a few kept as pets) to a subsistence or maintenance just sufficient for efficiency . . . This would be the income which the labourers would derive from their labour. (Cannan, 1929: 328)

Returning to Sraffa:

> This is a convenient way of positing the question of value and distribution in its simplest form: it eliminates the (supposed) puzzles connected with the freedom of the workers in working more or less or not at all. It shows clearly that the 'wages' (i.e. maintenance) of the slave worker are not to be regarded as a share in the product but as a part of the initial stock, i.e. that they are

paid in connection with a work that has not yielded a product, before and not after production; that their significance is not 'to induce' the worker (which is superfluous, since he is not free) but to 'enable' him to work. It also shows that the sort of 'cost' which determines values is the collection of material things used up in production and not a sum of 'efforts and sacrifices'. (D/3/12/7)

After all, Sraffa observes, the difficulty of distinguishing in wages the real cost from the surplus element may be great in practice, but not greater than that of distinguishing 'in the total sum paid for the hire of a horse, what is food, shelter and depreciation of the horse and what is interest on capital' (D/3/12/42):

There appears to be no objective difference between the labour of a wage earner and that of a slave; of a slave and of a horse; of a horse and of a machine; of a machine and of an element of nature (? this does not eat). It is a purely mystical conception that attributes to human labour a special gift of determining value. Does the capitalist entrepreneur, who is the real 'subject' of valuation and exchange, make a great difference whether he employs men or animals? Does the slave-owner? (D/3/12/9)

The question had been answered, some years before, by Tugan-Baranowsky:

Our imaginary slave owner can decide that a work can be exerted more efficiently by horses than by workers: he will therefore substitute horses for a part of his workers. He will assign a part of his land to horses instead of cultivating rye for men. The slave economy will support a smaller number of men, but more horses. The slave owner will become not poorer, but richer, because the cultivation of his land will result in a disposable surplus product resulting in a greater amount of consumption means. Thus we have an increase in owner's consumption together with a reduction in human productive consumption. This last reduction can be so significant as to reduce total consumption (i.e. the consumption of the owner and of his slaves). The economy will achieve its final end, the satisfaction of the slave owner, employing means of production, which are different from labour-force. Physical production will increase and will be used up, without residue, as productive consumption (but in a new way: horses will take the place of a part of the men). The amount of the surplus product will increase, while total human consumption will decrease, a fact which cannot disturb in any way the equilibrium of the slave economy. (Tugan-Baranowsky, 1905: 222–3)

GIORGIO GILIBERT

See also:

Capital and Profits; Labour and Wages; Land and Rent; Surplus; Taxation; Wealth.

References

Cannan, E. (1929), *A Review of Economic Theory*, London: King and Son.
Edgeworth, F.Y. (1896), 'Income', *Palgrave's Dictionary of Political Economy*, London: Macmillan.
Finzi, R. and G. Gilibert (2011), 'Sviluppo distorto, merci di lusso, salario di sussistenza in uno scambio epistolare fra Renato Zangheri e Piero Sraffa', *Studi storici*, **LII**(2), 357–73.
Isnard, A.N. (1781), *Traité des richesses*, Lausanne: Grasset.
Leontief, W. (1941), *The Structure of American Economy*, New York: Oxford University Press.
Marshall, A. ([1898] 1920), *Principles of Economics*, 4th (variorum) edition, (ed.) C.W. Guillebaud, London: Macmillan.
Quesnay, F. ([1759] 1972), *Tableau économique*, (eds) M. Kuczynsky and R. Meek, London: Macmillan.
Smith, A. ([1776] 1976), *An Inquiry into the Nature and Causes of the Wealth of Nations*, in *The Glasgow Edition of the Works and Correspondence of Adam Smith*, (eds) R.H. Campbell, A.S. Skinner and W.B. Todd, Oxford: Clarendon Press.

Sraffa, P. (1960), *Production of Commodities by Means of Commodities*, Cambridge, UK: Cambridge University Press.
Tugan-Baranowsky, M. (1905), *Theoretische Grundlagen des Marxismus*, Leipzig: Duncker & Humblot.
Vianello, F. (1999), 'Social accounting with Adam Smith', *Value, Distribution and Capital*, (eds) G. Mongiovi and F. Petri, London and New York: Routledge, pp. 165–80.

Ricardian Dynamics

In *The Wealth of Nations* Adam Smith repeatedly pointed out that capital accumulation is one of the key factors of strong economic growth. Economists of Ricardo's generation wondered whether the capitalist system would continue to provide sufficient stimuli for capital accumulation and be capable of maintaining economic growth in the long run. Ricardo adopted a rather pessimistic view: he believed that the scarcity of lands would pose an insurmountable obstacle to sustained economic growth. In the long run, this physical constraint would be translated into a change of the division of the net product favouring the landowners at the expense of the capital owners. Confronted with decreasing returns on investment, capital owners would lose the incentive to invest and capital accumulation would come to a standstill. But Ricardo also admitted that two factors might alter this pessimistic outlook: on the one hand, free trade and, on the other, technical progress. Both of these can push the spectre of a stationary state to a more distant future.

Growth and distribution

There is an extensive literature on the interpretation of Ricardo's growth model, with diverging and sometimes opposing views. Among the main contributions we can mention Pasinetti (1974), Samuelson (1978), Casarosa (1985) and Morishima (1989). In this entry we do not engage with that literature, but refer directly to Ricardo's own writings.

Although growth is at the heart of Ricardo's analysis, it can be studied properly only if its effects on distribution are taken into account. This explains why Ricardo in the preface to *On the Principles of Political Economy, and Taxation* wrote: 'To determine the laws which regulate this distribution, is the principal problem in Political Economy' (*Works*, I: 5). Ricardo was referring to the distribution of the net product between the three classes of society: capital owners, who invest their capital in industry or in agriculture; labourers, who supply their labour force; and landowners, who rent out their lands. These three classes share the national product, earning respectively profits, wages and rents. When the share of one class rises, what remains for the other two diminishes. Ricardo focused both on the opposition between profits and wages, and on the opposition between profits and rents. One of the basic tenets of Ricardo's theory of rent is that the values of agricultural goods are determined by the conditions of production at the margin. Since marginal lands do not pay rent, the analysis can in a first stage be limited to the relation between profits and wages. In the long run, however, the expansion of agricultural output shifts the focus of attention to the evolution of profits and rents, and to what, according to Ricardo, constitutes the main menace to the future of the capitalist system.

Short-run dynamics

Let us imagine a capitalist society where no rent is paid because there is plenty of land, and where the net product consists entirely of profits and wages. How is the division between wage earners and profit earners determined? Ricardo's answer is to explain first the level of wages, and then to derive the level of profits as a residual category. It is the movement of the rate of profits that plays a central role in Ricardo's dynamic analysis.

Labour, like all commodities, has a natural and a market price. The natural price is determined by the conditions of its reproduction. This means that the natural level of the wage corresponds to 'the price of the food, necessaries, and conveniences required for the support of the labourer and his family' (*Works*, I: 93). Since corn may be considered as the staple food of the labouring classes, any increase in the difficulty of production of corn (and hence of its value) will be reflected in an increase of the share of labour in the net product, even though the real wage remains constant. The market price of labour, by contrast, depends upon the supply and demand of labour. Consequently, changes in the supply and demand of labour may produce fluctuations of the market wage around its natural level. When it exceeds the natural level, 'the condition of the labourer is flourishing and happy', but such a state will not last forever, since 'by the encouragement which high wages give to the increase of population, the number of labourers is increased, [and] wages again fall to their natural price' (ibid.: 94). In the opposite case 'the condition of the labourers is most wretched', and a long and painful process may be needed to restore the natural order: 'It is only after their privations have reduced their number, or the demand for labour has increased, that the market price of labour will rise to its natural price, and that the labourer will have the moderate comforts which the natural rate of wages will afford' (ibid.).

Undoubtedly Ricardo was aware of the fact that these changes in supply and demand may be caused by short-term phenomena such as the trade cycle, and therefore have only temporary effects on the market wage. However, he seemed more interested in the structural tendencies of the supply and demand for labour and the possibility that the market wage deviates for longer periods of time from the natural wage. With regard to the supply of labour, he referred explicitly to Thomas Robert Malthus's writings on the principle of population. He observed that even in circumstances where the population grows very fast (e.g., doubling in a period of 25 years), it can be outpaced by the amount of capital. That could lead to a situation in which the demand for labour increases more rapidly than the supply, and to the market wage exceeding the natural wage for a very long period of time (ibid.: 98). The normal state of things, however, would be the opposite:

> In the natural advance of society, the wages of labour will have a tendency to fall, as far as they are regulated by supply and demand; for the supply of labourers will continue to increase at the same rate, whilst the demand for them will increase at a slower rate. (Ibid.: 101)

It should be noted that the natural wage itself is also liable to change, since the basket of goods determining the natural wage 'essentially depends on the habits and customs of the people' (ibid.: 96–7). Therefore, the composition of the basket may change over time and differ between countries. Ricardo seemed rather confident that economic growth would eventually lead to a gradual improvement of the living standard of the labouring population.

The crucial variable of interest for capitalists is the rate of profits. It is calculated as the ratio of profits to the value of capital, which includes fixed and circulating capital goods as well as wages (in Sraffa's analysis wages are not part of capital, but this assumption does not lead to different qualitative conclusions). In Ricardo's view the average (or normal) rate of profits is the outcome of an economic mechanism based on competition. Since every capitalist seeks the most profitable employment of his funds, he will move his capital from less profitable to more profitable sectors. This flow of capital exerts a downward pressure on prices and hence on the rate of profits in the more profitable sectors, while the opposite occurs in the less profitable sectors. The movement stops when prices are equal to their natural values and the rates of profits in all sectors are equal to the natural rate of profits. This aspect of Ricardian dynamics, usually designated by the term of gravitation, will not be analysed here.

In given conditions of production, an increase of wages will lead to a greater share of wages in the net product and hence to a smaller share for profits and to a reduced natural rate of profits. However, this trade-off between wages and profits does not constitute in itself a threat to the capitalist system because of the existence of strong mechanisms to keep the wage close to its natural level. But then the working of these mechanisms must not be hampered, and it is for this reason that Ricardo condemned attempts by the state to regulate the determination of wages. He objected in particular to the Poor Laws and their 'pernicious tendency' (ibid.: 106).

The conclusion with regard to the trade-off between wages and profits also remains valid when rent is paid, provided that its level is given. In the long run, however, the increase of demand will lead to a change in rents, the consequences of which require an extension of the analysis.

Long-run dynamics
For Ricardo, capital accumulation is the engine of economic development. It is in the interest of society as a whole that capital accumulation is strong, and since it is the expectation of profits that incites investment the rate of profits must be high. The argument is once again of a dynamic nature – in fact, a transfer of income to the expense of capitalists and in favour of landowners is not innocuous, because the economic behaviour of the two classes is different. Capitalists typically save and invest, while landowners devote a large part of their income to domestic servants and unproductive activities. It is therefore necessary to analyse the origin and the level of rent.

The increase in the number of workers, due to the development of capitalism, requires an increase in the quantity of agricultural products, which are the labourers' staple diet. More and more lands must be cultivated. The most fertile lands are first cultivated, as the costs of production are lower. When the best lands are fully exploited, any further increase of agricultural production requires the use of less fertile lands (extensive cultivation) or of more capital-intensive methods on best-quality lands (intensive cultivation). The analysis of both cases being similar, we only consider an extension of cultivation. In terms of labour values, the fact that the newly cultivated lands are less fertile means that more and more labour is devoted to the production of additional quantities of food. As a consequence, the overall quantity that society bestows on the workers' consumption increases more rapidly than the number of workers. Even if the real wage remains constant and rent is ignored, the part of net production accruing to capital decreases: 'The natural tendency of profits then is to fall' (*Works*, I: 120).

This phenomenon is reinforced when the economic conditions allowing for an extension of cultivation are analysed, taking into account the private ownership of land. Let us rank the lands according to decreasing fertility: 1, 2, . . ., *m*. The most fertile lands, those of quality type 1, are first cultivated. As long as the demand is low, they suffice to meet society's requirements and no landowner is able to reap rent because other lands of the same quality are still free. Cultivation is progressively extended on lands of type 1 until they are fully exploited. When demand continues to increase, the cultivation must be extended to lands of type 2. This requires a sudden rise in the price of corn in order to cover the higher cost of production on these lands, including the normal remuneration of capital. As the price of corn, be it produced on one or the other land, is unique, the owners of land of quality type 1 are in a position to extract a positive rent from their farmers. The level of that rent is such that it exactly compensates the difference in the costs of production on both qualities of land: it is a 'differential' rent. The farmers on the best lands are obliged to pay that rent, as they have no economic alternative. These rules are general: in a given state, the price of corn is determined by the condition of production on the marginal land, that is, the last one taken into cultivation. That quality is easily recognized: it is the only one to be partly cultivated, the better lands being fully exploited and the worse left fallow. The rent on the marginal land is zero, while those on the better lands are positive and reflect the differences in the conditions of production with the marginal land. It turns out that, when demand increases, the price of corn increases spasmodically, and the same for rents. On the one hand, the quantity of labour required for the production of the wage goods consumed by workers increases, so that the part of the net product that goes to non-workers decreases; on the other, the rents themselves increase. The profits are therefore doubly hit in that evolution.

To sum up, the principal threat to capitalism is rooted in its very development, which leads to the fall of the normal rate of profits. At the beginning of the nineteenth century, when the workers were not yet organized, the antagonism between capitalists and landowners underpinned many of the political discussions in Great Britain. It is from that perspective that one can understand Ricardo's views on the Corn Laws (see his *Essay on Profits* of 1815, *Works*, IV: 9–42) and on foreign trade (*Works*, I: 128–49).

Free trade and technical progress

The tendency of the rate of profits to fall entails the prospect of a stationary state in the long run. Is that evolution inescapable? Free trade, and in particular the importation of cheap foreign grain, is one way of reversing the tendency. If a foreign country has an absolute advantage in the production of agricultural goods, the importation of grain without taxes from that country amounts to replacing local production by foreign production, which is done in more favourable conditions. As a result, both the price of corn and rents will be lower, and the rate of profits will remain high. Ricardo reinforced the case for free trade by arguing that even if the home country had an absolute advantage in the production of agricultural goods, it would still benefit from the importation of those goods provided that it has a relative advantage in the production of industrial goods. This could be seen as a plea for an international division of labour in which the more developed countries would specialize in industrial production and less advanced countries in agricultural activities.

Another way to prevent the rate of profits from falling is to implement technical progress. Whether technical progress occurs in agriculture or in industry, it leads to a reduction of the direct or indirect amount of labour required for the production of the real wage basket, and as a result the share of the net product going to the subsistence of the labouring class becomes smaller. Moreover, the greater facility of production by means of new machines or new methods also leads to a lesser direct or indirect demand of lands, therefore to a stability or reduction of rents, which may explain why landowners are often opposed to technical improvements in agriculture. For both reasons, technical progress leads to a rise in the rate of profits, therefore to a higher rate of accumulation, and to the prosperity of capitalism. This explains the coexistence of two seemingly opposite messages in Ricardo's works: the main lesson on dynamics of the *Principles* is that capitalism evolves towards a stationary state, because the rate of profits tends to fall. The stress on that tendency can be understood as an argument in the political fights of Ricardo's times between capitalists and landowners, where Ricardo showed himself as the theoretical champion of the rising capitalist class. In other private documents, however, Ricardo appeared to be much more optimistic on the long-run future of capitalism: for instance, in a letter to Hutches Trower dated 5 February 1816, Ricardo confided that we 'may look forward with confidence to a long course of prosperity' (*Works*, VII: 17), as if technical progress was sufficient to counterbalance the threat of a falling rate of profits and to push away indefinitely the prospect of a stationary state.

In comparison to Smith, who stressed the division of labour, Ricardo seemed more cautious about the link between capitalism and social progress. For Ricardo, the real wage is determined by social and historical conditions and we have already noticed that economic growth would lead to a slow rise in the real wage. But the path towards that ultimate result appears to be much more chaotic than Ricardo first thought. In his famous chapter entitled 'On Machinery', which Ricardo inserted into the third edition of the *Principles* (*Works*, I: 386–97), he changed his previous views on the topic and admitted that the introduction of new machines might be harmful to the labouring class, both in the short run (technical unemployment, in modern language, partly compensated by the transfer of workers from one employment to another) and in the long run, when an increase in the net product (i.e., profits and wages) goes together with a reduction in the gross product (profits, rents and wages).

Conclusion

Dynamic aspects occupied a central place in Ricardo's analysis. He paid special attention to the relations between distribution and dynamics, because rising rents and wages tend to lower the rate of profits, which could pose a threat to the survival of capitalism. The focus on this issue in his theoretical works can be explained by the historical context of Great Britain at the beginning of the nineteenth century and the political debates opposing landowners and capitalists. But in some writings Ricardo appeared to be optimistic about the possibilities of technical progress to reverse the tendency of the rate of profits to fall. As a matter of fact, his fears did not materialize: the rate of profits did not fall to a level at which investment would come to a standstill, and the part of profits in the national income has remained remarkably stable.

CHRISTIAN BIDARD AND GUIDO ERREYGERS

See also:

Accumulation of Capital; Endogenous Growth; Foreign Trade; Land and Rent; Mathematical Formulations of Ricardian Economics; Natural and Market Prices; Technical Change.

References

Casarosa, C. (1985), 'The "new view" of the Ricardian theory of distribution and economic growth', in G.A. Caravale (ed.), *The Legacy of Ricardo*, Oxford: Basil Blackwell, pp.45–58.
Morishima, M. (1989), *Ricardo's Economics: A General Equilibrium Theory of Distribution and Growth*, Cambridge, UK: Cambridge University Press.
Pasinetti, L.L. (1974), *Growth and Income Distribution. Essays in Economic Theory*, Cambridge, UK: Cambridge University Press.
Samuelson, P.A. (1978), 'The canonical classical model of political economy', *Journal of Economic Literature*, **16**(4), 1415–34.

Ricardian Equivalence

The Ricardian equivalence proposition is based on economic models where private households perceive debts as postponed taxes: forward-looking private households fully anticipate future tax increases triggered by additional public debt. They will rationally adjust their spending/saving behaviour to foreseeable changes in taxation, irrespective of the expected timing of a tax change (whether it is expected to occur tomorrow or in 20 years). Put another way, the budget constraint of the government is immediately translated to the level of individual budgets and individual consumer choices, notably regarding consumption, saving and borrowing: as it were, consumers 'internalize' the government's budget constraint. In the terminology of modern macroeconomics, government bonds held by the public must not be counted as part of the aggregate wealth in the consumption function because the public anticipates the future tax liabilities implied. In models where Ricardian equivalence holds good, the level of consumption in any period is driven by the level of wealth or net earnings in the long run: as consumers should not feel either richer or poorer merely on the grounds of the timing of tax changes, the equivalence proposition implies that the spending behaviour of households should not be affected by the temporal pattern of changes in tax obligations. More generally, increasing the level of public debt instead of an equivalent tax increase neither should have an effect in terms of enhancing aggregate demand nor should it be regarded as a drag on accumulation. Briefly summarized, the choice between the two methods of finance has no impact on aggregate demand, output, the price level, interest rate, accumulation and the exchange rate.

Ricardo's argument on the neutrality of the method of financing public expenditures (tax vs debt) is a fine example of Ricardo's analytical gifts and his ability to disentangle complex issues, including various kinds and levels of argument. At the same time, the way in which Ricardo dealt with the 'result' of that argument (i.e., the neutrality proposition) sheds serious doubt on the claim that Ricardo generally suffered from what has been called the 'Ricardian Vice': that is, giving abstract models based on bold or patently unrealistic assumptions too much weight in terms of immediate conclusions purportedly relevant for the real world.

The empirical and political relevance of Ricardo's neutrality proposition as such has been disputed ever since it was put forward. Yet such discussions sometimes tend to obscure the nature of his achievement as a theorist. Ricardo himself did not believe that his neutrality proposition was suitable as immediate guidance for policy. Viewing together all pertinent passages in the *Principles* (*Works*, I), and even more so considering his later article on the 'Funding System' in the *Encyclopaedia Britannica* (*Works*, IV), it is fairly obvious that Ricardo was perfectly aware of the limitations of his model-like reasoning on debt and the neutrality of financing methods. And he certainly did not fail to express that awareness by contextualizing his argument, directly or indirectly referring to the real world as well as what could be called the classical tradition on public debt. That tradition by and large used to be highly critical of debt as a method of financing the public household.

Ricardo's more encompassing considerations regarding the politico-economic dimension of the problem notwithstanding, it is somewhat beside the point to claim that Ricardo in fact 'enunciated a non-equivalence theorem' while the term '"Ricardian Equivalence Theorem" is, consequently, a misnomer', as is claimed by O'Driscoll (1977). It is beside the point for the following reason: first, the conclusions supported by a 'non-equivalence theorem' are hardly new in the classical context in which Ricardo wrote. With regard to his policy conclusions in the light of likely real-world circumstances, Ricardo is, by and large, in keeping with this tradition as far as the critical view of debt as a regular method of government finance is concerned. He succinctly paraphrased the classical policy advice concerning public debt: 'That which is wise in an individual, is also wise in a nation' (*Works*, I: 248). For the classical economists, the main focus of the discussion on public debt was its impact on capital accumulation. Considering authors such as David Hume, Adam Smith and David Ricardo, one can trace the evolution of a critical stance vis-à-vis public debt. According to the classics, debt-financed purchases by the government tend to impair accumulation. A country that has accumulated a large debt is placed in an unnatural (Hume [1752] 1993: 209) or even a 'most artificial' (*Works*, I: 247) state. Some authors of the late classical period, such as John Stuart Mill and McCulloch, tended to be slightly less gloomy about the effects of debts.

Yet regarding the theoretical analysis of public debt, the outstanding achievement of classical economics *is* Ricardo's contribution. An attentive reader of Ricardo's pertinent passages in the *Principles* and 'Funding System' may get more out of them than just the argument supporting the neutrality proposition: a sense for the status and the great virtues of abstract modelling in economics, given that due attention is paid to the dangers of drawing unwarranted practical/political conclusions. This virtue is displayed in the context of an attempt to answer a question regarding public finance, which can be put sufficiently clearly in non-technical terms to be understandable by almost anybody. Its status could be summarized as follows: the Ricardian equivalence theorem is likely to be empirically false in the real world. Indeed, the pertinent propositions seem to be far off the mark: the design of fiscal policy, particularly the temporal structure of some given amount of public revenues, is for various reasons *not* in general irrelevant in the real world. Nonetheless, the equivalence theorem may be highly useful in the context of an advanced discussion of real-world problems of public debt. Ricardo's neutrality proposition allows for the neat conceptual distinction between the effects of government expenditures per se and the effects of the method of financing them. It is the benchmark for the proper identification of the reasons for non-neutrality of the method of financing. It may help clarify the precise reasons why the temporal structure of tax revenues does indeed matter, the structure of expenditures remaining the same: it may be helpful in shedding critical light on sloppy reasoning regarding the causes of non-neutrality of the fiscal design.

Put succinctly and more generally: Ricardo's pertinent passages reveal his acute sense for the value of abstract (or 'unrealistic') models for purposes of criticism and the development of better theories, while realizing that immediate political conclusions are a non sequitur. In that respect, Ricardian equivalence may well be the *first* theorem in the history of economic analysis focusing on the neutrality (or 'equivalence', 'invariance', 'irrelevance') of some aspect of a socioeconomic arrangement that was believed to matter a lot, but can be shown to play no role in some model setting. The invariance thesis of the Coase theorem, the Modigliani-Miller theorem and Samuelson's observation that economic outcomes are independent of whether capital hires labour or labour hires capital are further examples showing that such critical results typically are (or at any rate should be) rather the starting point than the final word of a more rigorous scholarly debate.

The historical context
The classical view itself has an extended pre-history. Adam Smith's passages on public debt (e.g., *WN*, V.iii) suggest that it evolved in attempts to refute two arguments that are ascribed to Jean-François Melon, a French civil servant and collaborator of John Law. Both arguments are couched by Melon in terms of a critical response to an even older common-sense view according to which the shift of burdens to future generations is the unavoidable feature of *any* kind of debt financing. Melon's first argument became common currency much later in what James Buchanan (1958) called the 'new orthodox' position on public debt. It established a crucial asymmetry between private debt and public debt, which is challenged in Hume's essay 'Of public credit' ([1752] 1993: 208):

> We have indeed been told, that the public is no weaker on account of its debts, since they are mostly due among ourselves, and bring as much property to one as they take from another. It is like transferring the money from the right hand to the left, which leaves the person neither richer nor poorer than before. Such loose reasoning and specious comparisons will always pass where we judge not upon principles.

Hume comes up with several counter-arguments. Apart from raising points such as distributional effects, price effects or the case of foreign debt that make the argument break down, Hume shows by means of a thought experiment that public indebtedness cannot be increased without limits. Public bankruptcy would be the only way out.

In a lengthy chapter on public debt in the *Wealth of Nations* (*WN*, V.iii.47), Adam Smith combats a second argument also ascribed to Melon, according to which debt financing enhances accumulation: 'The publick funds . . . have by one author been represented as the accumulation of a great capital superadded to the other capital of the country, by means of which its trade is extended, its manufactures multiplied.' Similar reasoning was to play a role in Keynesian macroeconomics. When assessing Smith's counter-arguments, two issues must be kept apart. According to Smith, government expenses, whether tax financed or debt financed, generally imply a shift from the productive sector to the unproductive sector of the economy and hence diminish the part of the annual produce that functions as capital. It is turned away from 'maintaining productive labourers to maintain unproductive ones'. The question now is whether the method of financing may be the source of any additional effect. According to Smith (ibid.: 49), the first-order effects of public debts (called 'funding' by Smith) and taxes differ: 'If the method of funding destroys more old capital, it at the same time hinders less the accumulation or acquisition of new capital, than that of defraying the publick expense by a revenue raised within a year.' But Smith does not provide any direct conjectures about the relative magnitudes of the different effects. Do they perhaps just offset each other? This question is left open by Smith, who hastens ahead with providing empirical reasons why debt financing must be expected to be worse: debt financing causes fiscal illusion that prevents individuals from realizing how costly state activity, most notably a war, really is. Notice that, while Smith locates the myopia-related causes of the detrimental effects of debt financing in political decision-making, Ricardo (*Works*, I: 247) argues that individual economic decisions will be distorted: 'debt-financing is a system that tends to make us less thrifty – to blind us to our real situation'.

Moreover, distributional effects must be expected. In this context, Smith (like Hume) implicitly uses the idea that plays a crucial role in the systematic accounts from Ricardo to Barro: public debts are postponed taxes. Different time patterns of financing imply different incidence of taxes. Differences in tax incidence may be accompanied by systematically different incentive effects. Smith and Hume raise the concern that a class of idle and extremely mobile wealth owners is created. The reason why this is detrimental to the economy is most clearly expressed in the following passage (ibid.: 56): 'But a creditor of the publick, considered merely as such, has no interest in the good condition of any particular portion of the Land, or in the good management of any particular portion of the capital stock.' Hence the pace of accumulation and improvement may be affected.

From David Ricardo to Robert Barro

Here is the core of the argument as developed by Ricardo. For any given pattern of government spending programmes, tax and debt finance is equivalent. The basic logic of this neutrality is given by David Ricardo. In Chapter XVII of the *Principles*, he expands on the equivalence of financing £20 million of expenses for a war by a public loan:

> Whether the interest [for public loans] be paid or not paid, the country will be neither richer nor poorer. Government might at once have required the twenty millions in the shape of taxes; in which case it would not have been necessary to raise annual taxes to the amount of a million. This, however, would not have changed the nature of the transaction. An individual instead of being called upon to pay 100*l*. [£100] per annum, might have been obliged to pay 2000*l*. once for all. It might also have suited his convenience rather to borrow this 2000*l*. and to pay 100*l*. per annum for interest to the lender, than to spare the larger sum from his own funds. (*Works*, I: 244–5)

But this reasoning is eventually used in a context of arguments jointly supporting the conclusion that even the extraordinary financial requirements of a war could be best met by tax increases: 'Of these three modes [tax finance of war expenses, borrowing, borrowing *cum* tax financed sinking fund], we are decidedly of opinion that preference should be given to the first' (*Works*, IV: 186) Subsequent passages support that opinion by a suitable combination of equivalence logic ('In point of economy, there is no real difference in either of the modes . . .'), fiscal illusion ('We are apt to think, that war is burdensome only in proportion to what we are at the moment called to pay for it in taxes, without reflecting on the probable duration of such taxes'), and ensuing allocation effects. In the case of a tax increase, 'an effort is made to save to the amount of the whole expenditure of the war, leaving the national capital undiminished' and causing 'little permanent derangement' to the industry of the country. The following answer to a specific counter-argument (invoking the case that some taxpayers may be unable to save the required amount) nicely illustrates that the logic of neutrality is not necessarily at odds with the policy conclusions of pre-Ricardian classical arguments on public debt – and that Ricardo's concern really was putting that tradition on a sound logical basis (ibid.: 188):

> The usual objection made to the payment of a larger tax is, that it could not be conveniently paid by manufacturers and landholders, for they have not large sums of money at their command . . . That there are persons disposed to lend to individuals is evident from the facil-ity with which government raises its loans. Withdraw this great borrower from the market, and private borrowers would readily be accommodated. By wise regulations, and good laws, the greatest facilities and security might be afforded to individuals in such transactions. In the case of a loan, A. advances the money, and B. pays the interest, and everything else remains as before. In the case of a war tax, A. would still advance the money, and B. pay the interest, only with this difference, he would pay it directly to A.; now he pays it to government, and govern-ment pays it to A.

As indicated in the above, it would be unfair to say that the literature before Ricardo, particularly *Wealth of Nations*, was generally characterized by a confusion concerning the effects of the method of government finance (debt or tax) on the one hand and of government spending programmes on the other. Yet Ricardo disentangled pertinent issues with unprecedented clarity. The 'Ricardian equivalence theorem' was formally stated as a theorem in a paper by Robert Barro (1974) – which had a considerable impact on new classical macroeconomics (for a more encompassing perspective on its implica-tions, see Barro, 1989) – and was so christened by James Buchanan (1976). As a scholar who is renowned for contributions on excessive public indebtedness caused by the logic of democratic decision-making, Buchanan stresses the dangers of taking the equivalence theorem as guidance for policy. As a connoisseur of Italian public finance, Buchanan (1976: 337), moreover, points out that a leading protagonist of the important Italian tradition in public finance, Antonio de Viti de Marco (1893 and 1936), 'elaborated the Ricardian thesis in a somewhat modified setting'. Indeed, in the fifth Book (on 'extraor-dinary revenues') of his textbook, de Viti de Marco (1936) provides an impressive range of casuistic and complementary considerations, for example distinguishing between dif-ferent kinds of taxes and stressing differences between private borrowing and state bor-rowing. For instance, government bonds can be easily traded and hence may be expected to be held by those investors who find them most attractive, whereas trade of private debt titles is not so 'easy and secure', says de Viti de Marco. He was not the only theorist to discuss the issue in Italy. One discussion amongst Italian economists is interesting insofar as the usual arguments referring to the realism or lack of realism of the under-lying assumptions is complemented by more far-reaching considerations pertinent to research strategies. It involves Pareto and two of his disciples who pursued the research programme of 'fiscal sociology' advocated by Pareto (see McLure, 2003). Pareto dis-missed the equivalence reasoning along the lines of Ricardo and de Viti de Marco out of court, as it is based on the presumption that economic logic may be employed to gain an understanding of what is going on in the public sector. According to Pareto, this approach is fundamentally flawed. The public realm is governed by illogical influences such as power, patron–client relations, and so forth.

Be that as it may, the equivalence theorem depends on a number of very strong assumptions. First of all, individuals are assumed to be fully rational and informed, in that they are aware of the government's budget constraint. Moreover, individuals consume/save according to the permanent income/life-cycle hypothesis and have infinite horizons. (If not, they would count only the fraction of public debt for which they are liable within their planning horizon.) In order to lend some credibility to the infinite horizon assumption, Robert Barro introduces a further assumption, the extended (or dynastic) family: individuals live in families and are linked to each other by intergenerational altruism. Children are the extension of oneself, as it were. (Ricardo was well aware that myopic behaviour destroys 'Ricardian equivalence'.) In addition, capital markets are assumed to be perfect, that is, there are no borrowing constraints for individuals. That this condition is needed for Ricardian equivalence is alluded to in the above quote from Ricardo and was pointed out by McCulloch (1863: 628) who considered it implausible. Borrowing constraints (liquidity constraints) are also a major element of the Keynesian view of public debt that is sharply opposed to the Ricardian *and* the neoclassical tradition. Furthermore, no systematic redistributive effects may occur between classes of individuals with different marginal propensities to save or consume. (Passages by Smith and Hume may be interpreted as conjectures postulating that this condition is unrealistic.) Finally, it is assumed that taxes be non-distortionary (which applies to lump sum taxes only; notice that McCulloch [ibid.] also stressed that differential incentive effects should be expected to accompany different patterns of tax increases) and that the method of financing exhibits no systematic interdependences with the political process. (As was seen above, this was doubted by Smith, who conjectured that public debts have a tendency to distort political decision-making. Similar doubts are articulated by James Buchanan and the public choice school, according to which budget deficits and surpluses are asymmetric in terms of political feasibility.) There is a quasi-consensus in the literature that this set of conditions is altogether unrealistic, yet there is nothing coming close to a consensus on what this means for theory and policy.

Public choice theorists, adherents of the neoclassical crowding-out model as well as Keynesians consider Ricardian equivalence as difficult to sustain – but in the context of different perspectives. The scope of its practical relevance is, indeed, contingent upon a host of empirical and conceptual questions that are hard to answer. Anyway, those ambiguities should not blind us to the main merits of Ricardo's model-like argument: it forces us clearly to distinguish the effects of public debt and of government purchases. It enables us to identify the effective causes of non-neutrality of the method of financing. Like the somehow related theorem by Modigliani and Miller, claiming neutrality of the structure of corporate finance, it is 'unrealistic', but a useful benchmark. Finally, Barro's model directs our attention to an interdependence that is theoretically interesting, which may be empirically relevant and that did not receive much attention in either conventional neoclassical or Keynesian economics: the interdependence between planning horizons, family structures and macroeconomic developments. (Interestingly, Adam Smith argued that family structure may affect the choice between different methods of debt financing government purchases.)

There is hardly another area in public economics where the main issues, political and theoretical, continue to be as controversial as they appear to have been in the early days of economics. The much more advanced state of empirical research has not brought decisive clarity. To be sure, there is agreement on the logical side of the models. It has become possible to discuss the implications of variations of assumptions. There seems, however, to be little hope that economics will be able to deliver much more than this in the foreseeable future.

RICHARD STURN

See also:

Funding System; National Debt; Taxation.

References

Barro, R.J. (1974), 'Are government bonds net wealth?' *Journal of Political Economy*, **82**(6), 1095–117.
Barro, R.J. (1989), 'The Ricardian approach to budget deficits', *Journal of Economic Perspectives*, **3**(2), 37–54.
Buchanan, J.M. (1958), *Public Principles of Public Debt*, Homewood, IL: Irwin.
Buchanan, J.M. (1976), 'Barro on the Ricardian equivalence theorem', *Journal of Political Economy*, **84**(2), 337–42.
de Viti de Marco, A. (1893), 'La pressione tributaria dell'imposta e del prestito', *Giornale degli economisti*, **1**, 216–31.
de Viti de Marco, A. (1936), *First Principles of Public Finance*, translated by E.P. Marget, New York: Harcourt Brace.
Hume, D. ([1752] 1993), *Selected Essays*, Oxford: Oxford University Press.
McCulloch, J.R. (1863), 'Funding system', in *An Inquiry into The Wealth of Nations by Adam Smith, LL.D., with a life of the author, introductory discourse, notes, and supplemental dissertations, by J.R. McCulloch Esq.*, Edinburgh: Adam and Charles Black.
McLure, M. (2003), 'An Italian foundation for a new fiscal sociology: a reflection on the Pareto–Griziotti and Pareto–Sensini letters on Ricardian equivalence and fiscal theory', Conference Paper at the 16th HETSA Conference, Australian Catholic University, 15–18 July, accessed 5 January 2015 at www.biz.uwa.edu.au/home/research/discussionworking_papers/economics/2003?f=151063.
O'Driscoll, G.P. (1977), 'The Ricardian nonequivalence theorem', *Journal of Political Economy*, **85**(1), 207–10.
Smith, A. ([1776] 1976), *An Inquiry into the Nature and Causes of the Wealth of Nations, Vol. 11*, in *The Glasgow Edition of the Works and Correspondence of Adam Smith*, (eds) R.H. Campbell, A.S. Skinner and W.B. Todd, Oxford: Clarendon Press.

Ricardian Socialists

The term 'Ricardian socialists' was first used by Herbert Foxwell (1899) to describe a loose grouping of radical writers who, in the 1820s and 1830s, asserted the labourer's 'right to the whole produce of labour', the title of an important critique of their ideas by Anton Menger (1899). Consistently critical of the established order for violating this right, the Ricardian socialists never constituted a school in any formal sense. Sometimes drawing on Smith, Ricardo and other classical economists to substantiate their critique, they were part of a vibrant intellectual milieu that included Jacobins, Owenites, monetary reformers, opponents of 'Old Corruption' and early advocates of the People's Charter in an environment characterized by great economic and political discontent. Disputes raged over the fundamental causes of the deeply felt economic, political and social grievances of the working population and the appropriate remedies to be pursued (Claeys, 1987, 1988; N. Thompson 1984, 1988, 1998).

The most important Ricardian socialists were John Francis Bray (1809–97), John Gray

(1799–1883), Thomas Hodgskin (1787–1869) and William Thompson (1775–1833). A notable forerunner was Charles Hall (c.1738–c.1825), with significant contributions also coming from Thomas Rowe Edmonds (1803–89), the pseudonymous Piercy Ravenstone and the anonymous author of an 1821 pamphlet entitled *The Source and Remedy of the National Difficulties*. All but two were English: Thompson was an Irishman, and Bray was born and died in the United States but lived in England between 1822 and 1842. To what extent these writers were 'Ricardian', and how far they can be described as 'socialists', remain matters of contention, along with the extent of their influence on Karl Marx.

The first and most serious defect of the existing order, the Ricardian socialists maintained, was an extreme and quite indefensible degree of inequality, which they often attributed to the unjust and artificial system of property rights. Since, as John Locke had demonstrated, every producer was entitled to the full fruits of his own labour, the working man was clearly receiving much less than his due. Agitators like William Cobbett, the scourge of 'Old Corruption', attributed this to the operation of an undemocratic political system that taxed the poor to provide lucrative sinecures for the rich. The Ricardian socialists saw this as a secondary problem, instead explaining the grossly unjust distribution of income and wealth as the result of inequality in economic relations. Several of them also criticized the capitalist system on efficiency grounds, since periodic industrial crises threw millions of working people into utter destitution and forced the economy to operate well below its potential capacity; this phenomenon was linked to the inequality of income, which was held responsible for a chronic tendency to underconsumption (King, 1980). All these writers denied the Malthusian claim that nature placed severe limits on material progress; instead it was capitalism that stood condemned for perpetuating poverty in the midst of potential plenty. Social, political and (above all) economic institutions were to blame for the continuing misery of the mass of the population, not divine displeasure or the niggardliness of nature.

Many of the fundamental arguments of the Ricardian socialists were anticipated by Charles Hall, a Devon doctor whose only major work, *The Effects of Civilization*, was published in 1805. Hall regarded agriculture and 'coarse manufactures' as the only truly productive activities. 'Refined' or luxury manufactured goods, consumed by the rich, were the products of unproductive labour. Poverty was not a natural phenomenon, Hall maintained in opposition to Malthus, but rather the result of social injustice, which denied the working man and his family the ability to consume more than a small proportion – Hall estimated it at one-eighth – of the produce of his own labour. He dismissed capital, in the words of one anonymous contemporary critic, as 'a mere instrument of tyranny in the hands of the possessors' (cited by Dinwiddy, [1976] 1992: 98). This was not the only Marxian notion that Hall anticipated: 'expressions such as expropriation, surplus value, class antagonisms, proletarianization and imperialism are not to be found in his work; but the concepts are definitely there, in a more or less developed form' (ibid.: 105). He also foreshadowed Marx's critique of the fetishism of commodities, arguing with respect to capitalist production that 'the exploitative nature of the whole process was not transparent. Rather, "money covers and conceals the action, as the case of a watch does the motion"' (Cunliffe, 1994: 541, citing Hall [1805] 1965: 103).

The identity of 'Piercy Ravenstone' is disputed: Joseph Dorfman claimed that it was the pseudonym of an Anglican clergyman, Edward Edwards, while Piero Sraffa believed him to be Richard Puller (fl. 1789–1831). The first 150 pages of Ravenstone's *A Few*

Doubts ([1821] 1966) were devoted to a survey of the evidence on population growth, ancient and modern, in Europe and the United States. He concluded that population had increased everywhere without 'any inconvenience', except recently in England. This was sufficient to refute Malthus: 'What is peculiar to one country cannot have arisen from causes common to all' (ibid.: 77). Like Hall, Ravenstone was convinced that poverty was due not to 'Providence' but to 'our own institutions' (ibid.: 150), in particular to class relations in a situation of relative abundance. 'When the labour of one half of the members of society suffices to procure subsistence for the whole', he maintained, 'the other half will live in idleness' (ibid.: 174), and later in the book he refers to 'the surplus produce' as the source of non-wage incomes (ibid.: 242). 'Both rent and profit, both property and capital equally arise from the surplus produce of the cultivator's labour . . . The only difference between them is, that one shares directly, the other indirectly, in the earnings of the productive labourer' (ibid.: 311). Thus, capital was not itself productive, as its defenders claimed. On the contrary, 'so far from being to be dreaded, the loss of our capital would be the happiest event that could possibly take place' (ibid.: 352). The solution that Ravenstone proposed was, however, much less radical than these statements might suggest. He defended the Poor Laws (ibid.: 460–61), and called for the repeal of all taxes on consumption and their replacement by 'impositions solely on property' (ibid.: 441). Evidently Ravenstone was not in any sense a socialist.

The Marxian notion of 'surplus labour', implicit in the works of both Hall and Ravenstone, became explicit in an anonymous pamphlet published in 1821 and rediscovered by Karl Marx several decades later: 'Whatever may be *due* to the capitalist, he *can only receive the surplus labour* of the labourer . . . the interest paid to the capitalists, whether in the nature of rents, interests of money, or profits of trade, is paid out of the *labour of others*' (Anon, 1821: 23, cited by Marx [1861–63] 1972: 239; original emphasis). The same principle underpinned Thomas Hodgskin's *Labour Defended*, written in defence of trade unions during the debate over the repeal of the Combination Acts (Stack, 1998; Milgate and Stimson, 2009). Despite a tenfold increase in productivity in Britain over the previous two centuries, Hodgskin claimed, real wages had remained constant. 'All the advantages of our improvements go to the capitalist and the landlord' ([1825] 1969: 23). But capital was nothing more than the 'co-existing labour' of other labourers (ibid.: 45). Any worker in one trade relied on the simultaneous production of necessary materials by those employed in other trades; that was the true meaning of circulating capital (ibid.). Similarly, the 'instruments and tools' that were termed 'fixed capital' were 'merely the result of *previous* labour' (ibid.: 54; original emphasis). Thus, Hodgskin endorsed 'the admirable maxim that "he who sows shall reap"' (ibid.: 104). His short book ended with a ringing call 'to do justice, and allow labour to possess and enjoy the whole of its produce' (ibid.: 109), without offering any specific proposals for far-reaching social and economic reform.

The much longer *Popular Political Economy* ([1827] 1966) added relatively little to this, though Hodgskin was now much more critical of the law of diminishing returns, which he attacked as both factually incorrect and inconsistent with 'the progress of society' (ibid.: 226). Contrary to the beliefs of the 'Political Economists', he maintained, poverty was neither natural nor inevitable. 'All the arguments they have urged in justification of their views, seem to be founded on the effects of some social institutions, which they assume to be natural laws' (ibid.: 268). These themes also dominated Hodgskin's third book, *The Natural and Artificial Rights of Property Contrasted* ([1832] 1973). Here he quoted John Locke at some length, defending the individual's natural right to property, which was derived from labour. In Hodgskin's own words, 'nature gives to each individual his body and his labour; and what he can make or obtain by his labour naturally belongs to him' (ibid.: 26). Property rights established by law were artificial, and when they conflicted with this natural right they were also unjust. The artificial right to property 'severs the natural connection between labour and its rewards', and encourages idleness, luxury and crime (ibid.: 155).

William Thompson was born in Cork into a wealthy Protestant family (Lane, 2009). Like all the Ricardian socialists, Thompson was self-taught. He was an eclectic, who read widely in British political economy and was also familiar with the contemporary French literature, including the work of Sismondi and the Saint-Simonians. Thompson seems to have been the only Ricardian socialist who was personally acquainted with David Ricardo (Pankhurst [1954] 1994: 11). In his *Inquiry*, which had a great influence on the British Owenites, Thompson drew on both utilitarianism and the labour theory of value to criticize the injustice of the existing distribution of income and wealth. The book was 'perhaps the first sustained attack on competition produced in the English language' (ibid.: 38). Thompson's theory of value closely followed Ricardo's own account in the *Principles*, starting from the premise that labour was the sole source of wealth. Thompson drew what appeared to him to be the unavoidable consequence, which Ricardo had not: capitalists and landlords obtained profit and rent by exploiting the real producers. 'Wealth is produced by labour,' he wrote. 'Labour is the sole universal measure, as well as the characteristic distinction of wealth . . . All the products of labour ought to be secured to the producers of them' ([1824] 1963: 4–6).

Thompson also took Malthus seriously, but (like Hall and Ravenstone) refused to accept that population growth was an insuperable obstacle to social progress. A convinced feminist, he was also a strong advocate of birth control. In *Labour Rewarded* ([1827] 1969) Thompson took issue with Hodgskin on the specific issue of the productive nature of non-manual labour, which Hodgskin had denied, but he did so from a perspective that was broadly similar. As in the *Inquiry*, Thompson attacked the political economists and denied the benefits of free trade, describing capital as 'the mere creature of labour and materials' (ibid.: 90). While he supported trade unionism, tax reform, currency stabilization and voluntary unemployment insurance, Thompson regarded these measures as mere palliatives. Only the establishment of socialist communities could secure the rights of working men and women, he maintained. He committed both his energies and his personal fortune to the socialist movement, spending his last 17 years as a non-smoker, vegetarian and teetotaller, and leaving a large bequest to further the cause.

Like Thompson, John Gray was initially a convinced Owenite. His *Lecture on Human Happiness* asserted the same underlying principle, that 'labour is the sole foundation of property, and that, in fact, all property is nothing more than accumulated labour' ([1825] 1971: 28). 'Every unproductive member of society is a DIRECT TAX upon the productive classes. Every unproductive member of society is also an [sic] USELESS member of society, unless he gives an EQUIVALENT for that which he consumes' (ibid.: 11; original emphasis). In particular, interest and rent were fundamentally unjust (ibid.: 30–33). Gray used Patrick Colquhoun's pioneering national income estimates from 1814 to calculate the proportion of total output that accrued to the unproductive classes. He painstakingly distinguished 51 categories of people, from 'Nos. 1, 2 and 3. The King, and others of the Royal Family', to 'No. 51. Paupers' (ibid.: 18–23). Gray concluded that, 'by the present arrangements of society, the productive classes are deprived of very nearly four-fifths of the produce of their labour' (ibid.: 47). In addition, this produce itself was much smaller than it could be under more suitable social arrangements. 'In the present state of society', he argued, 'production is limited by *demand*' (ibid.: 51; original emphasis), and demand was limited by competition, in particular by 'the increased struggle to obtain employment' (ibid.: 54). This was a version of the low-wage under-consumption theory advocated by the French writer J.C.L. Simonde de Sismondi. Gray had a very clear remedy for these social ills, which he set out in his draft constitution for a 'Friendly Association for Mutual Interests'. This was a proposed Owenite community, guaranteeing equal rights for women and the socialization of housework, with an initial maximum eight-hour day that could be considerably reduced in the near future. In his *Social System* ([1831] 1973) Gray moved away from his earlier communitarianism to advocate a centrally controlled, technocratic socialist economy that owed more to Saint-Simon than to Owen. By 1848 he was instead focusing on a much more narrow reform of the monetary system.

Thomas Rowe Edmonds, a Cornish actuary who settled in London, 'came within a hair's breath of Marx's concept of surplus value' (Perelman, 1980: 83) in his *Practical, Moral and Political Economy* ([1828] 1969), and was also very close to anticipating the Marxian analysis of the transformation of values into competitive prices of production. In addition, Edmonds set out a three-stage typology of human history, in which '[t]he slave system has been succeeded by the money system, and the money system will be succeeded by the social system, one system following the other, perhaps in a necessary order'. The driving force was the development of human productivity:

> By means of the money system, the useful arts have advanced ten times more rapidly than they could have done under the slave system. By means of the social system, the useful arts will advance ten times more rapidly than they have done under the money system. The perfection of the money system is the commencement of the social system. (Ibid.: 58–9)

Much the same would be argued by Marx and Engels, 20 years later, in the *Communist Manifesto*. Edmonds's typology was very similar to Thompson's earlier distinction between three 'modes of human labour . . . first, labour by force, or compulsion direct or indirect; second, labour by unrestricted individual competition; third, labour by mutual cooperation'. Like Edmonds, Thompson had concluded that the third mode of labour, by mutual cooperation, would prove to be 'as superior in production and happiness to the second, or that by individual competition, as the second is superior to the first' ([1824] 1963: xviii).

John Francis Bray was the last of the Ricardian socialists (Henderson, 1985; King, 1988). He added little to the arguments of earlier writers, but he did state their case with exceptional clarity in his *Labour's Wrongs and Labour's Remedy*, fighting the political economists 'on their own ground, with their own weapons' ([1839] 1968: 41). Bray treated 'the capitalists and economists' as identical throughout the book (ibid.: 130), but did not hesitate to cite their authority in support of his proposals for social reform, quoting at length from the works of (unnamed) economists whom, he believed, had unwittingly demonstrated the truth of his own arguments (ibid.: 195–208). It was labour alone that created wealth, Bray insisted. Equality of labour should bring equality of reward, but instead a 'most unequal system of exchanges' had benefited the capitalist at the expense of the labourer (ibid.: 48). The interests of 'the capitalists and the employers' were thus opposed to those of 'the producers at large' (ibid.: 61). Whatever the form of government, class relations would prevent justice without far-reaching social change. Bray therefore called for 'the subversion of the present social system' and its replacement by a 'system of communities' based on the principle of equal exchange (ibid.: 107).

It was necessary, Bray believed, for both capital and land to be in the possession of the labourers, and for there to be fundamental monetary reform. He set out both a very lucid theory of exploitation, and also an unusually explicit refutation of Say's Law of markets. 'Under the present system', he wrote:

> every working man gives to an employer at least six days' labour for an equivalent worth only four or five days' labour ... It all amounts to this, that the working class perform *their own labour, and support themselves, and likewise perform the labour of the capitalist, and maintain him into the bargain!* (Ibid.: 56, 153; original emphasis)

And again:

> Thousands now starve in unproductive inaction because the capitalist cannot employ them – the capitalist cannot give them work because he cannot find a market for his produce – there is no market for the produce because those who want the produce have nothing but their labour to give in exchange for it – and their labour is unemployed because the capitalist does not know how to set them to work – and thus the evils of the present system run round in a circle, one connected with and dependent upon another, and every one individually incurable. (Ibid.: 156)

In the 'social system' that Bray proposed, production would be undertaken by worker-owned joint-stock companies, which would acquire the means of production peacefully, through purchase. Compensation would be paid to the former owners, and output would be planned 'by means of general and local boards of trade' (ibid.: 162). The resulting increase in production, Bray claimed, would allow the debts incurred in the purchase of capital and land to be paid off within 20 years, and for a five-hour day to replace the eight-to-ten-hour day that would at first be necessary (ibid.: 160, 172). Under the new system, free trade would at last benefit the producers, and 'unlimited machinery' could be used to their advantage (ibid.: 184, 186). Reason would soon triumph, Bray concluded. 'The light of mind is beaming through the gloomy boundaries of the Age of Might, and ushering in the Age of Right!' (ibid.: 216). This is the final sentence of his book.

The Ricardian socialists had a considerable influence on working-class radicalism in Britain and Ireland in the second quarter of the nineteenth century, their writings providing the basis for a vigorous and coherent 'popular political economy' (N. Thompson, 1984). Respectable middle-class economists reacted with horror (Dobb, 1973), so much so that 'Thomas Hodgskin was a name to frighten children with in the days following the repeal of the Combination Laws in 1824' (Meek [1956] 1973: 124). The reputation of Ricardo himself seems to have suffered through a process of guilt by association (Hollander, 1980; Winch, 2009: 257). Only John Stuart Mill responded at all sympathetically to socialist arguments, most strongly in the third edition of his *Principles*, where he rejected the Malthusian critique of socialism and came out in favour of self-managed workers' cooperatives rather than Owenite communities or state-owned enterprises. For their part Marx and Engels criticized what they described as 'Utopian Socialism' (Engels [1892] 1962), but their objections applied principally to French writers (especially Proudhon), and Marx especially was much more sympathetic to early British critics of capitalism, above all to Bray (Marx [1861–63] 1972; King, 1983). As we have seen, several of them, beginning with Hall, had anticipated some of his own most important ideas. The rediscovery of the Ricardian socialists in the 1890s owed much to the contemporary resurgence of socialist ideas, and their second rediscovery in the 1970s and 1980s must again be viewed in the context of a powerful (if short-lived) student movement attracted to radical political economy (Hunt, 1977, 1979).

Just how Ricardian were these authors, then, and how far can they be described as socialists? With the exception of Hall, they all wrote after the publication of the *Principles* and would thus have been aware of Ricardo's ideas at least in broad outline, either at first or second hand. That said, the references to Ricardo in their works are relatively few, and seldom very complimentary. There are numerous references to 'our political economists', most of them critical, together with attempts (like that of Bray) to invoke the arguments of – unnamed – contemporary economists to support their own position. If anything in their attitude to political economy united the Ricardian socialists, it was their unqualified hostility to Malthus. Several of them also made repeated use of Adam Smith, citing the *Wealth of Nations* in support of their own arguments and comparing him favourably with later economists, especially Malthus. But they drew on Locke no less than on Smith, and neither of these authorities would have accepted either their fundamental critique of capitalism or their broadly socialist remedies.

Hall, the first of the Ricardian socialists, 'appears to have taken a certain amount from the English [sic] classical economists, especially Adam Smith' (Dinwiddy, [1976] 1992: 101), together with Malthus, Lauderdale and possibly Bentham. He owed more, however, to radical political thinkers like William Ogilvie, Thomas Spence and Tom Paine. Ravenstone attacked Malthus in several places, cited Adam Smith a couple of times, and made some slighting references to the errors of 'our political economists', but there is no mention of Ricardo anywhere in his 474 page book. Neither is Ricardo cited in Thompson's 600-page *Inquiry*. After a brief mention of Godwin, Malthus and Mill in the preface, Thompson confines himself to a few brief references to Bentham and a very occasional disparaging comment on (unnamed) 'political economists', for example because they 'too often slavishly or ignorantly worshiped' capitalist property relations ([1824] 1963: 585).

After Thompson, Hodgskin was the best read of the Ricardian socialists, and *Labour Defended* has many references to Smith, Malthus, McCulloch and James Mill, in addition to Ricardo. The allusions to Ricardo are either neutral, as when Hodgskin cited the three distributional categories and the subsistence theory of wages ([1825] 1969: 29–30) or favourable, when he invoked Ricardo's theory of profits and rent to support his own conclusion that the exactions of capital are responsible for the poverty of the labourer (ibid.: 78–82). *Popular Political Economy* was a sustained critique of 'the errors of the great Masters of the science of political economy' ([1827] 1966: xxi), from which Adam Smith was largely exempted. The only significant reference to Ricardo came towards the end of the book, where he was attacked (along with Malthus) for advocating the law of diminishing returns and thereby denying the ability of society to progress (ibid.:

231–2). There was no mention of Ricardo in *The Natural and Artificial Rights of Property Contrasted*, which defended Locke and Smith (along with Bacon and Burke) against Bentham, Malthus and Mill. On the evidence of this volume, Hodgskin was a Lockean, or perhaps a Smithian, but not a Ricardian.

John Gray, in contrast, made no reference to any economist other than Colquhoun in his 1825 *Lecture*, and then only for his statistics. In his later works, however, Gray quoted extensively from James Mill, McCulloch, Smith and Malthus, devoting a whole chapter of his *Social System* to 'the political economists' ([1831] 1973: Chapter 11). He was especially critical of Mill's defence of Say's Law, which he described as 'the *Monster error* of the political economists' ([1848] 1972: 49n; original emphasis). The only authority cited in Edmonds's 300-page book was the French mathematician Abraham de Moivre (Edmonds, [1828] 1969: 46–8); there is no reference to any economist. Finally, Bray was 'indebted to Colquhoun, Volney, Hodgskin, Adam Smith, Ricardo, Charles Knight and Harriet Martineau, and he quotes extensively from their works either for the purpose of refuting the orthodox economists or to make his own points clear' (Lloyd-Prichard, 1957: 14).

Politically, the Ricardian socialists drew on conservative (Hall, Ravenstone) and liberal ideas (Hodgskin), in addition to Owenite and Saint-Simonian socialism (Bray, Edmonds, Gray, Thompson). It is probably best to treat Hodgskin, the one self-proclaimed liberal among them, as an outlier, since he was the only one who argued that free competition with unregulated markets would redress the grievances of the working class. Not surprisingly, perhaps, Hodgskin eventually moved into the mainstream of mid-Victorian intellectual life (as did Edmonds and Gray). Hall was exceptional in a different way, his essentially Physiocratic vision of a better society being 'resolutely agrarian' (Cunliffe, 1994: 545). In fact, the tension between conservatism and socialism in early nineteenth-century radical thought was not confined to economic issues, but pervaded contemporary debates on political reform, culture, religion and family life. As the career of William Cobbett demonstrated very clearly, it was both a strength and a weakness, allowing the radicals to tap into powerful sentiments of tradition, betrayal and usurpation, but also generating deeply contradictory beliefs and attitudes towards the future. At their best, the Ricardian socialists overcame these problems to articulate a clear and compelling vision of a more just and more efficient society based on cooperation rather than competition. The most consistent and most successful in this regard were Bray and Thompson, who remained faithful to their socialist vision until the end.

JOHN E. KING

See also:

Marx, Karl Heinrich, on Ricardo.

Primary bibliography

*Reissued by Routledge/Thoemmes Press in 1997 as part of a seven-volume set, which also contained a lengthy (but not always accurate) introductory essay by T.A. Kenyon (1997). The Kelley and Routledge/Thoemmes reissues of these works are all exact photographic copies of the first editions, with the original pagination preserved. Only the anonymous 1821 pamphlet, *The Source and Remedy of the National Difficulties, Deduced from Principles of Political Economy, in a Letter to Lord John Russell*, has not been reprinted; there is a copy in the British Library.

Bray, J.F. ([1839] 1968), *Labour's Wrongs and Labour's Remedy*, New York: A.M. Kelley.*

Bray, J.F. ([1842] 1957), *Voyage from Utopia*, London: Lawrence & Wishart.
Edmonds, T.R. ([1828] 1969), *Practical, Moral and Political Economy*, New York: A.M. Kelley.
Gray, J. ([1825] 1971), *A Lecture on Human Happiness*, New York: A.M. Kelley.*
Gray, J. ([1831] 1973), *Social System*, New York: A.M. Kelley.
Gray, J. ([1848] 1972), *Lectures on the Nature and Use of Money*, New York: A.M. Kelley.
Hall, C. ([1805] 1965), *The Effects of Civilization on the People in European States*, New York: A.M. Kelley.
Hodgskin, T. ([1825] 1969), *Labour Defended Against the Claims of Capital*, New York: A.M. Kelley.*
Hodgskin, T. ([1827] 1966), *Popular Political Economy*, New York: A.M. Kelley.*
Hodgskin, T. ([1832] 1973), *The Natural and Artificial Rights of Property Contrasted*, New York: A.M. Kelley.*
Ravenstone, P. ([1821] 1966), *A Few Doubts as to the Correctness of Some Opinions Generally Entertained on the Subjects of Population and Political Economy*, New York: A.M. Kelley.*
Ravenstone, P. ([1824] 1966), *Thoughts on the Funding System and Its Effects*, New York: A.M. Kelley.
Thompson, W. ([1824] 1963), *Inquiry into the Principles of Wealth Most Conducive to Human Happiness*, New York: A.M. Kelley.
Thompson, W. ([1827] 1969), *Labour Rewarded: The Claims of Labour and Capital Conciliated*, New York: A.M. Kelley.*

Secondary bibliography

Claeys, G. (1987), *Machinery, Money and the Millennium: From Moral Economy to Socialism, 1815–1860*, Princeton, NJ: Princeton University Press.
Claeys, G. (1988), *Citizens and Saints: Politics and Anti-Politics in Early British Socialism*, Cambridge, UK: Cambridge University Press.
Cunliffe, J. (1994), 'Charles Hall: exploitation, commercial society and political economy', *History of Political Thought*, **15**(4), 535–53.
Dinwiddy, J.R. ([1976] 1992), 'Charles Hall, early English socialist', *International Review of Social History*, **21**(2), 256–76, cited from J.R. Dinwiddy, *Radicalism and Reform in Britain 1780–1850*, London: Hambledon Press, pp. 87–107.
Dobb, M.H. (1973), *Theories of Value and Distribution since Adam Smith: Ideology and Economic Theory*, Cambridge, UK: Cambridge University Press.
Engels, F. ([1892] 1962), *Socialism, Utopian and Scientific*, in K. Marx and F. Engels, *Selected Works, Volume II*, Moscow: Foreign Languages Publishing House, pp. 93–155.
Foxwell, H.S. ([1899] 1970), 'Introduction', in A. Menger, *The Right to the Whole Produce of Labour*, New York: A.M. Kelley, pp. v–cxvi.
Henderson, J.P. (1985), 'An English communist, Mr. Bray [and] his remarkable work', *History of Political Economy*, **17**(1), 73–95.
Hollander, S. (1980), 'The post-Ricardian dissensions: a study in economics and theology', *Oxford Economic Papers*, **22**(3), 370–410.
Hunt, E.K. (1977), 'Value theory in the writings of the classical economists, Thomas Hodgskin and Karl Marx', *History of Political Economy*, **9**(3), 322–45.
Hunt, E.K. (1979), 'Utilitarianism and the labor theory: a critique of the ideas of William Thompson', *History of Political Economy* **11**(4), 545–71.
Kenyon, T.A. (1997), 'Introduction: interpreting the thought of the Ricardian Socialists', in P. Ravenstone (1821), *A Few Doubts*, London: Routledge/Thoemmes, pp. v–xlviii.
King, J.E. (1980), 'Perish commerce! Free trade and underconsumptionism in early British radical economics', *Australian Economic Papers*, **20**(37), 235–57.
King, J.E. (1983), 'A reconsideration of the Ricardian socialists', *History of Political Economy*, **15**(3), 345–73.
King, J.E. (1988), *Economic Exiles*, London: Macmillan.
Lane, F. (2009), 'William Thompson, class and his Irish context, 1775–1833', in F. Lane (ed.), *Politics, Society and the Middle Class in Modern Ireland*, Basingstoke, UK: Palgrave Macmillan, pp. 21–47.
Lloyd-Prichard, M.F. (1957), 'Introduction' to J.F. Bray (1842), *A Voyage to Utopia*, London: Lawrence & Wishart, pp. 7–30.
Marx, K. ([1861–63] 1972), *Theories of Surplus Value, Part III*, London: Lawrence & Wishart.
Meek, R.L. ([1956] 1973), *Studies in the Labour Theory of Value*, 2nd edition, London: Lawrence & Wishart.
Menger, A. ([1899] 1970), *The Right to the Whole Produce of Labour*, New York: Kelley.
Milgate, M. and S.C. Stimson (2009), *After Adam Smith: A Century of Transformation in Politics and Political Economy*, Princeton, NJ: Princeton University Press.
Pankhurst, R.K.P. ([1954] 1994), *William Thompson (1775–1833): Pioneer Socialist, Feminist, and Co-operator*, 2nd edition, London: Pluto.
Perelman, M. (1980), 'Edmonds, Ricardo, and what might have been', *Science and Society*, **44**(1), 82–5.

Stack, D. (1998), *Nature and Artifice: The Life and Thought of Thomas Hodgskin (1787–1869)*, Woodbridge, UK: Royal Historical Society/Boydell Press.

Thompson, N. (1984), *The People's Science: The Popular Political Economy of Exploitation and Crisis, 1816–1834*, Cambridge, UK: Cambridge University Press.

Thompson, N. (1988), *The Market and its Critics: Socialist Political Economy in Nineteenth Century Britain*, London: Routledge.

Thompson, N. (1998), *The Real Rights of Man: Political Economies for the Working Class 1775–1850*, London: Pluto.

Winch, D. (2009), *Wealth and Life: Essays on the Intellectual History of Political Economy in Britain, 1848–1914*, Cambridge, UK: Cambridge University Press.

Ricardo Editions

A complete bibliography of the editions of Ricardo's writings up to 1932 was compiled by Piero Sraffa in Volume X, Appendix A, of his edition of *The Works and Correspondence of David Ricardo* (see *Works*, X: 356–74). The purpose of this entry is to complement this list with regard to later editions of Ricardo's writings in English (for non-English editions, see the separate entry 'Non-English Editions of Ricardo's *Works*'), the main focus being on the editions of Ricardo's *Principles*. Summary accounts of the content of the editorial introductions to Ricardo's *Principles* by McCulloch (1846), Gonner (1891), Ashley (1895), Kolthammer (1911), Sraffa (1951), Fellner (1963), Fogarty (1965), Hartwell (1971), Winch (1973), Wright (2005) and Gosh (2010) are provided in King (2013, Chapter 7).

John R. McCulloch published the first posthumous edition of Ricardo's *Principles* in 1846 in his edition of *The Works of David Ricardo*. In addition to reprinting the text of the third edition of the *Principles* McCulloch's edition contained some 320 pages of additional material, including *The High Price of Bullion, Reply to Mr. Bosanquet, Essay on Profits, Proposals for an Economical and Secure Currency, Protection to Agriculture, Plan for a National Bank*, the essays *Funding System* and *Observations on Parliamentary Reform*, and the *Speech on the Plan of Voting by Ballot*, as well as a greatly expanded 20-page index. The edition was introduced by McCulloch with a brief sketch of Ricardo's life and work, and over the next 40 years was reprinted seven times; it went out of print in 1913. The McCulloch edition also formed the basis of the French edition of Ricardo's *Oeuvres complètes*, edited by Alcide Fonteyraud in 1847, which 'has provided for nearly a century the standard introduction to Ricardo for a large part of the non-English speaking world' (*Works*, X: 375).

The next edition of the *Principles* was published in 1891 by George Bell & Sons as a volume in 'Bohn's Economic Library' under the editorship of Edward Carter Kersey Gonner. The Gonner edition was highly successful; between 1895 and 1929 it went through 11 reprints, totalling some 10000 copies (*Works*, X: 365). In 1923, Gonner supplemented his edition of the *Principles* with a companion volume, in which he reprinted five of Ricardo's pamphlets (*The High Price of Bullion, Reply to Mr. Bosanquet, Proposals for an Economical and Secure Currency, Essay on Profits, Protection to Agriculture*) with a substantial editorial introduction (Gonner, 1923). In 1911, Frederick William Kolthammer edited Ricardo's *Principles* for J.M. Dent's 'Everyman's Library' series; the first printing of 10000 copies was followed by four reprints, of 4000 copies each, in 1917, 1923, 1926 and 1929. The first American edition of the *Principles* was published in

1819. It was a reprint of the first English edition of 1817 and was published by Joseph Milligan. An abbreviated version of the *Principles*, comprising only the first six chapters, was published in 1895 as part of the 'Economic Classics' series by the New York branch of Macmillan under the editorship of William James Ashley.

Publication of Ricardo's correspondence began relatively late, although some of the letters Ricardo had received from Jean-Baptiste Say were published by Charles Comte in Say's posthumous *Mélanges et correspondance d'économie politique* already in 1833. After James Bonar had published some letters of Ricardo to Malthus in 1887, Jacob H. Hollander followed in 1895 with the publication of the *Letters of David Ricardo to John Ramsay McCulloch (1816–1823)*. In 1899, Bonar and Hollander jointly edited a collection of Ricardo's letters to Hughes Trower and others, and in 1931 Hollander published a series of letters from McCulloch to Ricardo. A few Ricardo letters were also published separately in various journals.

As regards the publication of manuscripts that had remained unpublished in Ricardo's lifetime, the first of these was the *Plan for the Establishment of a National Bank*, which was published posthumously by Moses Ricardo in 1824 (*Works*, V: 273), and was then also included in McCulloch's edition of the *Works*. The 'Three Letters on the Price of Gold' that Ricardo had contributed to the *Morning Chronicle* in August–November 1809 were first edited by Jacob H. Hollander (1903), who also edited (jointly with T.E. Gregory) Ricardo's *Notes on Malthus's Principles* (1928) as well as 'some notes and jottings' of Ricardo on monetary issues, which he published under the title *Minor Papers on the Currency Question 1809–1823* in 1932.

The definitive edition of Ricardo's *Works and Correspondence* was prepared by Piero Sraffa, with the collaboration of Maurice H. Dobb, under the auspices of the Royal Economic Society, and published in 11 volumes from 1951 to 1973. Since the concluding volume appeared in 1973 there have been only a few additions, mostly of newly found letters by Ricardo. Such letters were discovered and published by Heertje and Weatherall (1978), Heertje et al. (1985), and Heertje (1991, 2007). Recently, Deleplace et al. published a further letter by Ricardo on monetary theory (2012), and another one was recently discovered by Depoortère (2014). Asso and Barucci (1988) published a brief manuscript fragment by Ricardo with some calculations on a capital levy, probably dating from late 1819 or early 1820, which was discovered in the Gratz collection at the Historical Society of Pennsylvania in Philadelphia. The only full manuscript of Ricardo that was published after the completion of Sraffa's edition is the *Notes on Malthus's 'Measure of Value'*, which was edited by Pier Luigi Porta in 1992. This 'series of rough notes', made by Ricardo while reading Malthus's pamphlet, were found with the 'Mill-Ricardo papers' in 1943. Sraffa had drawn attention to the existence of these notes, but had refrained from including them in his edition, because 'the notes in question were largely used in writing the letters to Malthus of 29 April and 28 March 1823 (above, IX, 280, 297), which are devoted to a criticism of that pamphlet' (*Works*, X: 392).

Since Volume I of Sraffa's definitive edition appeared in 1951 there have been six further English-language editions of Ricardo's *Principles*. In 1963, the educational publishing company Irwin under the editorship of William J. Fellner brought out a new American edition. Two years later, the 'Everyman's Library' edition by Kolthammer of 1911 was replaced by a new one, with an 11-page introduction by the new editor Michael Patrick Fogarty, and in 1971 Penguin Books published a further edition of the

Principles under the editorship of Ronald Max Hartwell. A third Dent edition of the *Principles* appeared in 1977; it was now edited and introduced by Donald N. Winch. In 2005, Robert E. Wright edited and introduced a new edition of the *Principles* for the 'Barnes & Noble Library of Essential Reading', and in 2010 the first English-language edition of Ricardo's *Principles* was produced for the Indian market under the editorship of R.N. Gosh.

Finally, it deserves to be mentioned that Piero Sraffa's definitive edition of Ricardo's *Works and Correspondence* has been made freely available in electronic form (and almost freely available in paperback as well) by Liberty Fund Org.

CHRISTIAN GEHRKE

See also:

Non-English Editions of Ricardo's *Works*; Sraffa, Piero, on Ricardo.

References

Asso, P.F. and E. Barucci (1988), 'Ricardo on the national debt and its redemption: some notes on an unpublished Ricardian manuscript', *Economic Notes*, **1**(2), 5–36.
Bonar, J. (ed.) (1887), *Letters of David Ricardo to Thomas Robert Malthus 1810–1823*, Oxford: Clarendon Press.
Bonar, J. and J.H. Hollander (eds) (1899), *Letters of David Ricardo to Hughes Trower and Others 1811–1823*, Oxford: Clarendon Press.
Deleplace, G., C. Depoortère and N. Rieucau (2013), 'An unpublished letter of David Ricardo on the double standard of value', *European Journal of the History of Economic Thought*, **20**(1), 1–28.
Depoortère, C. (2014), 'Two unpublished letters of David Ricardo on a monetary pamphlet by Samuel Tertius Galton', paper presented at the 18th Annual ESHET Conference in Lausanne, Switzerland, 29–31 May.
Gonner, E.C.K. (1923), *Economic Essays by David Ricardo*, London: George Bell & Sons.
Heertje, A. (1991), 'Three unpublished letters by David Ricardo', *History of Political Economy*, **23**(3), 519–26.
Heertje, A. (2007), 'An unpublished letter by David Ricardo', *History of Political Economy*, **39**(3), 545–50.
Heertje, A. and D. Weatherall (1978), 'An unpublished letter of David Ricardo to Thomas Smith of Easton Grey', *Economic Journal*, **88**(351), 569–71.
Heertje, A., R.W. Polak and D. Weatherall (1985), 'An unpublished letter of David Ricardo to Francis Finch, 24 February 1823', *Economic Journal*, **95**(380), 1091–2.
Hollander, J.H. (ed.) (1931), *Letters of John Ramsay McCulloch to David Ricardo (1818–1823)*, Baltimore, MD: Johns Hopkins University Press.
Hollander, J.H. (ed.) (1932), *Minor Papers on the Currency Question 1809–1823 by David Ricardo*, edited with an introduction and notes by Jacob H. Hollander, Baltimore, MD: Johns Hopkins University Press.
Hollander, J.H. and T.E. Gregory (eds) (1928), *Notes on Malthus's 'Principles of Political Economy' by David Ricardo*, Baltimore, MD: Johns Hopkins University Press.
King, J.E. (2013), *David Ricardo, Great Thinkers in Economics Series*, (ed.) A.P. Thirlwall, Basingstoke, UK and New York: Macmillan.
Ricardo, D. (1992), *Notes on Malthus's 'Measure of Value'*, edited with an introduction by P.L. Porta, Cambridge, UK: Cambridge University Press.
Say, J.-B. (1833), *Mélanges et correspondance d'économie politique, ouvrage posthume de J.-B. Say publié par Charles Comte, son gendre*, Paris: Chamerot.

Ricardo on Adam Smith

As it happens, the initial stimulus for Ricardo's intellectual engagement with political economy was his chancing upon a copy of the *Wealth of Nations* (Smith [1776] 1976; hereafter *WN*) in 1799. The story is recounted in a memoir by his brother, Moses Ricardo (*Works*, X: 7, 14, 35) and in the diary of John Cam Hobhouse (Lord Broughton), the latter writing:

Ricardo . . . told me he never thought of political economy till happening one day, during an illness of his wife, to be at Bath, he saw an Adam Smith in a circulating library, and turning over a page or two ordered it to be sent to his house. He liked it so much as to acquire a taste for the study. (*Works*, X: 36)

Ricardo would then have been 26 or 27 years old.

His high regard for Smith is later frequently expressed in his writings. In the process of drafting his *Principles*, Ricardo, writing to James Mill, resolves to reread *WN*, and to note both the passages that accord with his own views and those that are 'directly opposed' (17 November 1816, *Works*, VII: 88–9; cf. III: 7; X: 390–91). Here, discussing his draft manuscript, Ricardo also expresses a considerable deference to Smith:

I have dwelt very little on the effect of those taxes on which there can be no difference of opinion, and have not mentioned many which have been ably handled by Adam Smith. His language is so clear, and his explanations so satisfactory, that I feel a reluctance to weaken the effect of it by using my words instead of his, and always feel a propensity to quote him without a word of comment. (*Works*, VII: 88)

Nevertheless, two weeks later he tells Mill that, rereading *WN*, he has found 'many opinions to question, all I believe founded on his [Smith's] original error respecting value' (2 December 1816, ibid.: 100; also 115). In the preface to the *Principles* Ricardo indicates that 'in combating received opinions', he will particularly refer to his differences with Smith, but this should not be read as Ricardo's not sharing 'the admiration which the profound work of this celebrated author so justly excites', though similar sentiments are there also expressed toward Jean-Baptiste Say (*Works*, I: 6).

In letters to Thomas Robert Malthus and Hutches Trower there are similar strong expressions of Ricardo's regard for Smith's work (2 January 1816, *Works*, VII: 2; 26 January 1818, ibid.: 246). Note, however, that Ricardo nowhere refers to Smith's other book, *The Theory of Moral Sentiments* (1759), though it appears that he possessed a copy of the 1797 eighth edition (*Works*, X: 399). It is impossible to reconstruct anything like a complete catalogue of Ricardo's library. He certainly owned and used a copy of the 1814 edition of *WN*, edited by David Buchanan (ibid.). But it is hardly believable that Ricardo would have possessed no copy of the book prior to that date, in light of the evident impact upon him of his 1799 encounter with it. This judgement is further considerably supported by the fact that *WN* is quoted quite a few times in Ricardo's 1810 essay on *The High Price of Bullion* (e.g., *Works*, III: 52–3), and cited specifically by book and chapter, and quoted, elsewhere in 1810 Ricardo publications (*Works*, III: 143, 151). The *WN* page reference he cites in a 23 October 1814 letter to Malthus indicates that Ricardo was at that time using one or other of the third to ninth editions (1784–99) of the book (*Works*, VI: 148; *WN*, V.i.e.26). In his 'Introduction' to the *Principles* Piero Sraffa draws attention to the parallels between the ordering of the subject matter of the first two of the three parts of Ricardo's book ('the Political Economy' and 'Taxation') and the order in which the same topics are treated in *WN*, the third and final part being 'the polemical chapters at the end' (*Works*, I: xxii–xxv).

There are five subjects in particular on which Ricardo self-consciously departs from Smith's political economy: the theory of value or relative commodity prices, from which flows criticism concerning choice of a standard for measuring value and the effect of wages changes on commodity prices; the theory of functional income distribution, with particular regard to the relation between rates of wages and profits and between land rents and agricultural prices; the significance of gross versus net revenue; tax incidence; and finally, aspects of monetary analysis and policy. (Hereafter, unless otherwise indicated, 'rent' is employed as shorthand for land rents.)

Exchange value

Mention was made above of Ricardo's December 1816 comment, after rereading *WN*, that many of Smith's views that Ricardo then found questionable as a result of that reading were all derivative from Smith's 'original error' concerning value. Smith is much mentioned in the early pages of the first chapter of the *Principles*, 'On Value' (*Works*, I: 11–22). In affirming the labour-embodied theory of value – for commodities that are subject to competition and whose production can be varied practically without limit, so long as sufficient labour is applied to their production – Ricardo appeals to Smith's allowing a labour-embodied theory of relative prices to apply to primitive exchange (*WN*, I.vi.1–4), and to his rather different idea of 'toil and trouble' as the 'real price' of commodities (*WN*, I.v.2). Smith's text clearly enough implies that production in the primitive state is by direct labour alone – 'that early and rude state of society which precedes both the accumulation of stock and the appropriation of land' (*WN*, I.vi.1) – but Ricardo takes the view that 'some capital' would also have been employed in such primitive production (*Works*, I: 22–3).

In the third edition of the *Principles* Ricardo in these opening pages of Chapter I nowhere mentions that Smith *limits* the labour-embodied theory to such primitive exchange. Smith immediately goes on to deny its application to relative natural prices in social economies in which profits on capital and rent become 'component parts of price' (*WN*, I.vi.5–14). In the first and second editions of the *Principles*, at the beginning of the following §III of Chapter I, the section in which Ricardo addresses incorporation of indirect labour into his theory of value (*Works*, I: 22n–23n), he did make explicit Smith's restricting the labour-embodied theory to primitive exchange. In the third edition, rather than explicitly criticizing Smith's restriction of the labour-embodied theory, Ricardo turns to the question of a 'standard' or measure of value and of variations in value, rejecting Smith's recourse to corn and labour commanded as candidates for this function (*Works*, I: 13–20; also 273–5, 373–8, 416; IV: 409; V: 210–12; IX: 2, 380; *WN*, I.v.1–22). They are not invariable standards, any more than gold and silver (though Ricardo subsequently assumes, for expository purposes, that gold *is* such a standard: *Works*, I: 44–6). To the extent that value is determined by labour embodied for Ricardo (at least, 'almost exclusively': ibid.: 20), there is no reason to expect in general that the labour time required to produce corn, real wages, gold or silver, will be any more invariant than the labour time required to produce other commodities. (In a strange twist, in the framework of Sraffa's modern formulation of the classical approach to the theory of distribution and prices, a certain vindication of a labour-commanded numéraire emerges – Sraffa, 1960: 18, 31–3, 94.)

What then *is* the 'original error' that Ricardo regarded as the root of so much of his differences with Smith (*Works*, VII: 100)? There, Ricardo does not make it explicit. Sraffa plausibly argues that it is the adding-up theory of natural prices, whereby natural price is understood as explained by the sum of the wages, profits and rents of the labour, capital and land that enter into a commodity's production, when those remunerations are paid at their 'natural' rates (*Works*, I: xxxv–xxxvii; *WN*, I.vi.1–vii.6), drawing attention to a 28 December 1818 letter of Ricardo to Mill:

> Adam Smith thought, that . . . accumulation, necessarily, without any regard to the different degrees of durability of capital . . . raised the prices or exchangeable value of commodities, and consequently that their value was no longer regulated by the quantity of labour necessary to their production. In opposition to him, I maintain that it is not because of this division into profits and wages, – it is not because capital accumulates, that exchangeable value varies, but it is in all stages of society, owing only to 2 causes: one the more or less quantity of labour required, the other the greater or less durability of capital: – that the former is never superseded by the latter, but is only modified by it. (*Works*, VII: 377)

Just as Ricardo's rejection of corn and labour commanded as invariable standards for measuring value and its variations derives from his rejection of the adding-up theory, so also does his rejection of the Smithian proposition that a general rise in wages raises the prices of all commodities – and therefore also, his rejection of the Smithian doctrine that a rise in the price of corn, to the extent that it raises wages in general, will also raise the prices of all commodities (*Works*, I: 46, 302, 307–9, 315; IV: 21n; VII: 105; *WN*, IV.v.a.10–14). Ricardo is certainly right on this. In a world with a commodity money, a general rise in money-wages causes no general rise in money prices of commodities; and this is the kind of monetary regime Smith theorizes in *WN*. (On the evolution of Ricardo's position on this, away from that of Smith, see Garegnani, 1982: 67–8, 72–5.) In such a world there is no absolute price level, distinct from commodity relative prices. Under the notion of such a money-commodity world one may include, as well, a world with also paper money but a fixed monetary standard in the sense that the value of the commodity money is strictly fixed in terms of the conventional unit of account (e.g., pounds, shillings and pence) and the paper money is fully convertible.

In Ricardo's system, money-wage rises do not raise commodity prices in general, not because wages are irrelevant to prices, but because wages are *equally* relevant to all commodity costs and prices (including the cost of production of gold: *Works*, I: xxxv, 55, 104–5), so long as the labour-embodied theory is valid. Ricardo also disputes Smith's view that the British-monopolized colony trade increases profit rates both in that trade and generally. But even if there were such a general rise in profit rates, analogously to the case he makes with regard to a general rise in wages, Ricardo argues that this will not raise commodity prices in general, 'prices being regulated neither by wages nor profits' (ibid.: 344–6; VII: 100, 202).

Ricardo's repudiation of the doctrine that the price of corn, via its influence upon money-wages, regulates all other commodity prices, also informs his rejection of Smith's diagnosis of the effect of export bounties and import duties placed on corn. For Ricardo, a corn export bounty can have no impact on the domestic natural price of corn unless the consequent higher production of domestic corn alters its 'real cost of production' or 'a different quantity of labour becomes necessary to [corn] production'. If the domestic natural price of corn does not rise, then there is no possibility of an influence from a higher domestic corn price to higher wages, so the question of whether or not higher wages increase all prices is irrelevant. But in any case, Ricardo rejects both Smith's suppositions, that an export bounty will increase the domestic natural corn price, and that if it does so, this will increase domestic wages in the same proportion, also making the point that a general increase in wages, if it *were* to occur, would 'equally' affect all commodities.

Ricardo goes on to dissect Smith's notion that, because of a supposed peculiarly unalterable (labour-commanded) 'real value' of corn, landowners cannot benefit from a higher commodity price due to trade protection, in the manner in which manufacturers can. On the contrary, under competitive conditions neither manufacturers nor farmers can benefit from protection, in terms of higher profit rates. But to the extent that protection increases domestic production of corn, and therefore 'land of a worse quality must be taken into cultivation, on which more labour will be required to produce a given quantity', it is precisely the landowners who will gain a 'permanent' benefit, a conclusion reliant upon Ricardo's theory of rents (*Works*, I: 301–17; *WN*, IV.v.a.1–25). He also questions Smith's claim that a colonial power can gain no benefit from restrictions on a colony's trade (*Works*, I: 338–40).

In contemplating Ricardo's differences with Smith on exchange value one should not overlook a deeper fundamental accord between them, particularly vis-à-vis later marginalist theory, insofar as they both regard use value as irrelevant to the magnitude of exchange value. The very first sentence of the *Principles* defers to Smith on this, Ricardo agreeing with him that '[u]tility . . . is not the measure of exchangeable value' (*Works*, I: 11; also III: 284), even if Smith is not quite entirely consistent on this. Later in the *Principles*, in relation to Smith's recourse to corn as an invariable standard of value, Ricardo chides him:

> Corn, according to him, is always of the same value, because it will always feed the same number of people. In the same manner it might be said, that cloth is always of the same value, because it will always make the same number of coats. What can value have to do with the power of feeding and clothing? (*Works*, I: 374)

Human usefulness is merely a prerequisite for exchange value (ibid.: 11). Ricardo allows a class of exceptions to this, exceptions to the (qualified) rule that labour embodied explains exchange value: 'scarce' commodities whose supply cannot be adapted to demand by application of labour. Among other examples, he here instances wines made from grapes that grow only on 'a particular soil, of . . . very limited quantity' (ibid.: 12), an example Smith also uses to illustrate exceptions to the rule of natural prices under conditions of free competition (*WN*, I.xi.b.29–31).

Consistent with the irrelevance of use value to exchange value, Ricardo affirms that demand can only influence exchange value by influencing the relative cost of production of commodities (*Works*, VI: 148). And like Smith, Ricardo rejects the possibility of a determinate theory of demand-prices (thereby implicitly denying the possibility of latter-day demand schedules): 'no general rule can be laid down for the variations of price in proportion to quantity' (*Works*, IV: 220; Aspromourgos, 2009: 87–90) – the context indicating that by 'quantity' Ricardo here means imbalance between actual commodity supply and 'ordinary demand'. So, also, in his notes on Malthus's *Principles of Political Economy* (1820) Ricardo writes: 'The author forgets Adam Smith's definition of natural price, or he would not say that demand and supply could determine natural price' (*Works*, II: 46; also 38, 52).

Ricardo's distinction between value and 'riches' or 'wealth' is similarly an expression of his objective theory of exchange value. Concurring with Smith's notion of riches as command over necessaries and luxuries, Ricardo adds: 'Value, then, essentially differs from riches, for value depends . . . on the difficulty or facility of production'. But Smith and others have confused the two by also identifying riches with the value of commodities – the quantities of necessaries and luxuries produced in a society – measured in money, or corn, or labour commanded. Technical progress enables wealth or riches to increase, without either labour embodied or labour commanded increasing (*Works*, I: 273–8; also 285–7, 314, 429; *WN*, I.v.1). Hence in Parliamentary argument against corn as a standard of value, Ricardo comments:

> It was a part of Adam Smith's argument that corn was a steadier criterion, because it generally took the same quantity to furnish one man's sustenance. That might be; but still the cost of production did not the less vary, and, that must regulate the price. Its power of sustaining life was one thing: its value was another. (*Works*, V: 210–12)

Functional income distribution

It is in the context of discussing export bounties that Ricardo draws an analytical connection between Smith's error concerning the influence of corn prices, via wages, on all commodity prices and his failure to recognize, or at least his neglect of, the negative influence of money-wage levels upon profit rates. The latter failure or neglect may also be attributed, at least partly, to Smith's 'original error': the adding-up theory blinds him to the dependence of the general level of profit rates upon real wages (whether wages are expressed in money or other commodities), or more generally, upon the labour time required to produce those wages. Ricardo comments (following a quotation from *WN*, IV.v.a.11–14):

> In considering a rise in the price of commodities as a necessary consequence of a rise in the price of corn, he [Smith] reasons as though there were no other fund from which the increased charge could be paid. He has *wholly neglected* the consideration of profits, the diminution of which forms that fund, without raising the price of commodities. If this opinion of Dr. Smith were well founded, profits could never really fall, whatever accumulation of capital there might be. (*Works*, I: 308; emphasis added; also 303)

One point remains unclear from this, turning on the ambiguity of the term 'neglect'. Ricardo does not here explicitly and clearly state that Smith has *no* recognition of the inverse relation between real wages (or the labour time required to produce real wages) and profit rates; but nor does Ricardo anywhere state that Smith *does* have any degree of recognition of it. However, earlier in the *Principles* Ricardo, reiterating the inverse relation, comments:

> Adam Smith . . . *uniformly* ascribes the fall of profits to accumulation of capital, and to the competition which will result from it, without ever adverting to the increasing difficulty of providing food for the additional number of labourers which the additional capital will employ. (*Works*, I: 289–91; emphasis added; *WN*, I.ix.1–2; also *Works*, VIII: 380)

This quite clearly implies that Smith has no grasp of the inverse relation, supporting the same implication from Ricardo's characterization of Smith's theory of natural prices as an adding-up theory. This is essentially a correct judgement, partly a consequence of Smith's unsatisfactory treatment of rents. However, Ricardo here imposes upon Smith's text (*WN*, I.ix.2) the supposition that the increase of wages considered by Smith there can only be temporary (*Works*, I: 289), which is not at all necessarily Smith's view (Aspromourgos, 2009: 205–14). Related to this, see Stirati (1994: 147–52, 156–7) concerning the somewhat different conceptions of natural wages in Smith and Ricardo.

By removing one degree of freedom, Ricardo's inverse relation renders redundant Smith's attempt to formulate separately a theory of the general level of real wages (notably, in *WN*, I.viii and I.x) and a theory of the general level of profit rates (notably, in *WN*, I.ix and I.x). With regard to profits, Ricardo elsewhere also approvingly cites Smith on the difficulty of ascertaining profit rates and the use of market interest rates as a proxy for profit rates (*Works*, I: 296–7); the rate of interest being regulated by profit rates, not by the quantity of money (*Works*, III: 25–6, 88–9, 143–5, 150, 194n; V: 12); and the determinants of natural profit rate differentials (*Works*, IV: 12n).

Ricardo's own treatment of rents as a function of the prices of agricultural produce (in particular, 'food') leads him to repudiate Smith's idea of rent as an expression of a bounty of nature in agriculture, in contrast to manufacture. On the contrary, high or rising rent is a consequence of the niggardliness of nature, which causes the labour required to produce food, and hence the price of food, to be high or rising. This is a rejection of Smith's notion of rent as 'a component part of the price of commodities', in the sense of a determinant of prices (*Works*, I: 76–8; *WN*, II.v.12; also *Works*, II: 42–5). In a chapter devoted to Smith on land rent, Ricardo pursues this criticism systematically, indicating inconsistencies in Smith's treatment of rents, as to whether they are price determining or price determined (*Works*, I: 327–37). Earlier there is also criticism of Smith for commonly not employing the term 'rent' in its strict sense, as payment 'for the use of the original and indestructible powers of the soil' (*Works*, I: 67–8; *WN*, I.xi.c.5, 16–19; cf. *Works*, I: 201–3; *WN*, V.ii.e.1–6; Kurz and Salvadori, 2009: 72–4).

Gross versus net revenue

Ricardo's criticism of Smith in relation to gross and net revenue takes its bearings from the peculiar, and certainly flawed, doctrine of *WN*, Book II, Chapter v, concerning a supposed hierarchy of direct labour to capital ratios, and of revenue per unit of capital ratios, descending from agriculture, to manufacture, to commodity distribution (i.e., wholesaling, retailing and international transportation). Ricardo particularly quotes Smith's proposition that per unit of capital advanced, both direct labour employment and revenue (gross sales revenue presumably) are higher in agriculture than manufacture, and higher in manufacture than 'the trade of exportation' (*Works*, I: 347; *WN*, II.v.19). Ricardo's prime target here is not the labour intensity and revenue hierarchy (on the latter, see also *Works*, II: 20; IV: 37–8; VI: 178; IX: 193). Rather, it is Smith's apparent supposition of the desirability of maximizing gross employment and gross revenue rather than net revenue. It is 'net revenue', 'net income' or 'net produce' that is of interest to the owner of capital and to the nation:

> Its [i.e., the nation's] power of supporting fleets and armies, and all species of unproductive labour, must be in proportion to its net, and not in proportion to its gross income ... [T]he power of paying taxes, is in proportion to the net, and not in proportion to the gross, revenue. (*Works*, I: 347–9, with *WN*, II.v.31; also *Works*, II: 381–3; VII: 379)

Subsequently, Ricardo seems to allow that capital employed on infra-marginal land is associated with higher labour employment (and implicitly, higher revenue) than other capital. The proposition with respect to employment is difficult to make sense of in Ricardo's framework (for an interpretation, see Gehrke, 2012: 59–61). Ricardo rightly rejects the further Smith proposition concerning differences in employment and revenue per unit of capital employed in manufacture versus international transportation (*Works*, I: 350–51; also 129). To the extent that the labour theory of value holds (exactly or approximately), gross revenue at natural prices is proportional to the total quantity of labour directly and indirectly employed, as well as proportional to capital advanced. (In Ricardo's system, for agriculture this applies only to revenue from no-rent land.) But an assumption of uniform capital–labour ratios – which, together with all production reduced to a uniform, discrete time period, ensures the exact validity of the labour theory – entails also proportionality between gross revenue and direct labour employed.

Judging the validity of Ricardo's criticism on the gross versus net revenue issue is somewhat complicated by its not being entirely clear in *WN*, Book II, Chapter v whether Smith intends precisely gross revenue. Probably he does; though elsewhere he is clear that wages, insofar as they are necessary costs of production, cannot bear the incidence of taxation – either of wages directly, or of the commodities that form part of the necessary consumption of labour (*WN*, V.ii.i.1–7 and k.1–9). In fact, Smith is considerably more willing than Ricardo to allow that wages include an element of above necessary consumption, certainly in liberal capitalist societies with high accumulation (Aspromourgos, 2009: 199–201, 205–12). In the third edition of the *Principles*, but not the first two editions, Ricardo concedes this possibility in the context of his criticism of Smith on gross versus net revenue, though merely in an added footnote (*Works*, I: 348n; also II: 380–81). But as he indicates in that note, Ricardo's argument concerning net revenue stands, whether or not wages share in the social net product. It may be also noted that Smith rather unsatisfactorily conceptualizes net revenue elsewhere in *WN*, drawing the distinction between gross and net revenue, so as to include most wages, even of productive labour, in the latter (*WN*, II.ii.1–25; Aspromourgos, 2009: 150–52, 196–7). Ricardo's definition, which includes, along with profits and rents, only that part of wages over and above 'absolutely necessary expenses' (*Works*, I: 348n), is more coherent.

In Book II, Chapter v, Smith's notion of a labour intensity and revenue hierarchy, combined with his supposition of the desirability of maximizing gross employment and gross revenue, points to the desirability of ordering the allocation of a society's capital in favour of agriculture first, then manufacture, then foreign commerce. Those two doctrines are logically separable from Smith's Book III argument (which immediately follows Book II, Chapter v) that 'the natural Progress of Opulence' entails priority for agricultural development over manufacture and manufacture over foreign commerce (*WN*, III.i.1); but the two sets of arguments support and reinforce each other (*WN*, II.v.19–20 and 36–7). The Book III, Chapter i argument – for agriculture naturally developing first, then manufacture, then foreign commerce, in the course of historical economic development – cannot rest on the peculiar Book II, Chapter v doctrines.

Smith is entirely conscious of this: maximizing employment or revenue cannot motivate the allocation decisions of owners of capital (*WN*, II.v.37). Other factors are introduced to explain motivation consistent with 'natural' economic development in Book III, Chapter i. In the course of Book II, Chapter v Smith also argues that foreign commerce in a sense is forced upon nations by domestic demand constraints (*WN*, II.v.33–6). Ricardo rejects this element of the argument also, appealing to Say's principle that 'there is no amount of capital which may not be employed in a country, because demand is only limited by production' (*Works*, I: 290–96). A rather similar notion is actually expressed in Smith's saving-is-spending doctrine (*WN*, II.iii.18); but his political economy as a whole is more equivocal concerning the possibility of demand constraining activity levels (Aspromourgos, 2009: 192–6). It is possible to regard as preferable Smith's equivocation as to whether activity levels and growth are demand led or supply led, as half right, over Ricardo's consistency on the issue, as wholly wrong.

Policy
Ricardo endorses four norms enunciated by Smith as the criteria for justifiable and equitable taxation, providing the standard by which actual taxation policies should be judged. It is Smith's mistaken descriptive theory, not his tax norms, that lead him into error on tax policy from Ricardo's point of view. Smith's 'peculiar view . . . of rent, from his not having observed that much capital is expended in every country, on the land for which no rent is paid' leads him wrongly to conclude that the incidence of all taxes on land ultimately falls on rents, and as a result, to err in his assessment of the equity of land taxation (*Works*, I: 181–6; *WN*, V.ii.b.1–6, c.1–2 and d.1; also *Works*, I: 199; IV, 33n–34n, 239). Ricardo points to a contradiction between this view of Smith's that leads to the conclusion that taxes on agricultural products do not raise their prices, and Smith elsewhere arguing that a tax on malt falls on beer consumers not on rents (*Works*, I: 183–4, 252–4; *WN*, V.ii.d.1 and k.52–5; also *Works*, VII: 115). Ricardo does acquiesce, in principle, in Smith's proposition that land rents are the particular income category that can be taxed without detriment to the level of annual national product, but rejects such an exclusive tax on equity grounds, appealing to the first of Smith's four maxims (*Works*, I: 203–4; *WN*, V.ii.b.3 and e.10–11).

On taxation of wages, Ricardo approvingly quotes Smith's formulation of money-wages as depending on the real commodity wage in terms of a consumption bundle (determined by the state of labour demand) and the money prices of those commodities, with Ricardo taking this given real wage to be equivalent to necessary consumption. But he parts company with regard to Smith's further argument, that a direct tax on wages is backward or forward shifted by owners of capital in such a manner that the incidence falls entirely upon rents and (non-labour or surplus) final consumption, the latter captured in Ricardo's phrase, 'rich consumers'. In Ricardo's framework, with real wages regulated by a given subsistence, a rise in money-wages due to taxation, whether via direct taxation or taxation of subsistence commodities, will cause profit rates to fall not rents – just as any other source of a permanent rise in money-wages will – the only difference being that taxation of subsistence commodities will also cause their prices to rise, and thereby falls also upon 'rich consumers': 'a tax on wages is in fact a tax on profits' (*Works*, I: 215–29; *WN*, V.ii.i.1–3; also *Works*, I: 232–6).

There is one Ricardo proposition here that is particularly questionable: 'Dr. Smith *uniformly*, and I think justly, contends, that the labouring classes cannot materially contribute to the burdens of the State. A tax on necessaries, or on wages, will therefore be shifted from the poor to the rich' (*Works*, I: 235; emphasis added). Smith is actually rather more equivocal than that, just as he is far more willing than Ricardo to allow that real wages can settle at levels above necessary subsistence (*WN*, V.ii.i.1–7 and k.1–9). Elsewhere, Smith is quoted approvingly on the incidence of property transfer taxes, and on the capacity of private 'frugality' and accumulation to more than offset tax-financed unproductive government expenditure (*Works*, I: 153–4; VI: 120).

There are also a fairly considerable number of comments on Smith in Ricardo's discussions of monetary theory and policy, mostly not involving any very substantial criticisms. Smith is defended against Buchanan, his 1814 editor, in relation to the significance of excess paper currency issue, although Ricardo perceives some inconsistency with respect to Smith's views on American colonial currency (*Works*, I: 354–6; *WN*, II.ii.52–4, 100). There are comments on Smith and paper currency in earlier Ricardo writings as well, in one instance again defending Smith, who 'could never have anticipated' inconvertibility of paper currency, against Henry Thornton (*Works*, III: 76–7; also 58, 96–7, 148–51, 236–7, 327–8). There is also a passing reference to Smith's underestimating the use of paper instruments, vis-à-vis bullion, in international exchange (ibid.: 112).

A more substantial difference occurs with respect to Smith's proposition that banking and credit arrangements that enable enterprises to operate with less currency balances thereby enables them to expand capital employed in production and hence the aggregate level of economic activity (*WN*, II.ii.46). Ricardo rejects this on the basis that '[t]he whole business, which the whole community can carry on, depends on the quantity of its capital', which 'can neither be increased nor diminished by the operations of banking' (ibid.: 365–6). It is significant also that in his 1811 *Reply* to Charles Bosanquet, Ricardo notes his appeal to the authority of Smith (quoting *WN*, II.ii.58–9) in support of Bosanquet's view that banks' discounting only 'bills . . . for *bonâ fide* transactions' is a sufficient principle for appropriately limiting the quantity of money in circulation, which Ricardo rejects (*Works*, III: 219–20). He downplays Smith's statement, appealing to Smith's frequently enunciated view that:

> [t]he whole paper money of every kind which can easily circulate in any country never can exceed the value of the gold and silver, of which it supplies the place, or which (the commerce being supposed the same) would circulate there, if there was no paper money. (*WN*, II.ii.48; this is the Smith quotation as it appears in the text of the Glasgow Edition; Ricardo's quotation of it involves four slight variants)

But Smith evidently believes that, at least in a system with paper money fully convertible at a fixed standard, the discounting-of-bills principle, in ensuring that paper money or credit are not issued for speculative purposes, ensures that the quantity of paper money issued is limited to the value of the quantity of commodity money it replaces in circulation (ibid.: 26–106). This 'real bills' doctrine did indeed provide some inspiration for the Banking School's opposition to Ricardo and others on monetary issues (Green, 1992: 114–27). There are also references to Smith in relation to endorsement of free trade in the precious metals (*Works*, I: 228–9; III: 55, 81, 188), the relative value of gold and silver (*Works*, I: 366, 369–70; III: 253), exchange rates (*Works*, III: 163) and seigniorage (ibid.: 179–81, 222).

Conclusion

In contemplating Ricardo's criticisms of Smith's political economy, in their particulars and their totality, one should not lose sight of the forest for the trees. Behind those criticisms lies a larger agreement, a good part of it silent. Some major explicit substantive agreements have been indicated above (see also the opening paragraphs). There are others as well. The last paragraph of the chapter of the *Principles* 'On Natural and Market Price' opens with the comment: 'In the 7th chap. of the Wealth of Nations, all that concerns this question is most ably treated' – and that natural/market price framework is, of course, fundamental to the *Principles* (*Works*, I: 91). In this regard, Ricardo's theory operates within a conceptual framework first systematized in *WN*. For another example, in an 1822 Parliamentary speech on protection, Ricardo approvingly quotes one of the most fundamental normative principles of *WN* (IV.viii.49):

> Consumption is the sole end and purpose of all production; and the interest of the producer ought to be attended to, only so far as it may be necessary for promoting that of the consumer. The maxim is so perfectly self-evident, that it would be absurd to attempt to prove it. But in the mercantile system, the interest of the consumer is almost constantly sacrificed to that of the producer; and it seems to consider production, and not consumption, as the ultimate end and object of all industry and commerce. (*Works*, V: 219; correcting the *Hansard* record, Sraffa quotes Edwin Cannan's edition, which ends: 'as if production and not consumption were the end of all industry and commerce'; see also *Works*, V: 43; III: 145)

Nevertheless Smith's iconic if not canonical status, already in 1817, just four decades after publication of *WN*, evidently caused adverse sentiment towards Ricardo's criticisms. John Ramsay McCulloch writes to Ricardo that because Smith is 'worshipped as a demigod' in Edinburgh, Ricardo's book was regarded as 'petty treason' there (3 September 1818, *Works*, VII: 295). On the editorial commentary of Germain Garnier's translation of *WN*, Ricardo writes: 'Garnier is in every instance opposed to me when I attack his favorite author' (14 December 1822, *Works*, IX: 245), adding in a letter to Malthus: 'Neither he [Garnier] nor M. Say have succeeded in at all understanding what my opinions are' (16 December 1822, ibid.: 249; also VII: 219).

As against the sense of Ricardo as primarily a critic or opponent of Smith's political economy, it is possible to perceive him as first and foremost a genuine Smithian, standing on the shoulders of that giant, and thereby seeing further than Smith on just certain particular (albeit in some instances, fundamental) issues. This view can be supported by supposing – on the basis of Ricardo's deference to Smith in the *Principles* preface and elsewhere – that beyond his own relatively narrow frame of reference in the *Principles*, Ricardo must tacitly agree with 'the big picture' of Smith's political economy. On the other hand, and quite apart from Ricardo's specific and particular criticisms of Smith's theoretical views, some have perceived a deeper and more fundamental methodological gulf, with Ricardo treated as a key figure in the creation of a narrow, deductive, mechanical economics that is a distinctly post-Smithian creation. The truth surely lies somewhere between these two extremes. There is considerable literature on various aspects of this issue; for example, Hollander (1979: 652–60), Winch (1983, 1996), Skinner (1996: 178–9, 252), Walsh (2000), Haakonssen and Winch (2006) and Milgate and Stimson (2009).

In the preface to the *Principles* Ricardo famously declares that '[t]o determine the laws which regulate . . . distribution, is the principal problem in Political Economy' (*Works*, I: 5). This commonly has been interpreted as a prescriptive statement concerning what should be the primary purpose of the science. But it might better be read as a descriptive statement concerning what, in Ricardo's view, remains, in 1817, the key unsatisfactorily treated part of the science, and hence the principal *remaining* problem. This reading is supported by the comment Ricardo immediately adds: 'much as the science has been improved by the writings of Turgot, St[e]uart, Smith, Say, Sismondi, and others, they afford very little satisfactory information respecting the natural course of rent, profit, and wages' (ibid.). On 29 October 1815, as he was struggling with the idea of writing the *Principles*, Ricardo writes to Trower:

> Mr. Malthus and I continue to differ in our views of the principles of Rent, Profit and Wages. These principles are so linked and connected with every thing belonging to the science of Political Economy that I consider the just view of them as of the first importance. *It is on this subject*, where my opinions differ from the great authority of Adam Smith Malthus, &c^a. *that I should wish to concentrate* all the talent I possess, not only for the purpose of establishing what I think correct principles but of drawing important deductions from them. For my own satisfaction I shall certainly make the attempt, and perhaps with repeated revisions during a year or two I shall at last produce something that may be understood. (*Works*, VI: 315–16; emphasis added)

TONY ASPROMOURGOS

See also:

Capital and Profits; Exchange Value and Utility; Exhaustible Resources and Mines; Labour and Wages; Land and Rent; Natural and Market Prices; Revenue; Ricardo's Emancipation from Smith's Theory of Prices; Surplus.

References

Aspromourgos, T. (2009), *The Science of Wealth: Adam Smith and the Framing of Political Economy*, London: Routledge.
Garegnani, P. (1982), 'On Hollander's interpretation of Ricardo's early theory of profits', *Cambridge Journal of Economics*, **6**(1), 65–77.
Gehrke, C. (2012), 'Ricardo on gross and net revenue', in H.M. Kraemer, H.D. Kurz and H.-M. Trautwein (eds), *Macroeconomics and the History of Economic Thought: Festschrift in Honour of Harald Hagemann*, London: Routledge, pp. 47–63.
Green, R. (1992), *Classical Theories of Money, Output and Inflation: A Study in Historical Economics*, London: Macmillan.
Haakonssen, K. and D. Winch (2006), 'The legacy of Adam Smith', in K. Haakonssen (ed.), *The Cambridge Companion to Adam Smith*, Cambridge, UK: Cambridge University Press, pp. 366–94.
Hollander, S. (1979), *The Economics of David Ricardo*, London: Heinemann.
Kurz, H.D. and N. Salvadori (2009), 'Ricardo on exhaustible resources, and the Hotelling Rule', in A. Ikeo and H.D. Kurz (eds), *A History of Economic Theory: Essays in Honour of Takashi Negishi*, London: Routledge, pp. 68–79.
Milgate, M. and S.C. Stimson (2009), *After Adam Smith: A Century of Transformation in Politics and Political Economy*, Princeton, NJ: Princeton University Press.
Skinner, A.S. (1996), *A System of Social Science: Papers Relating to Adam Smith*, 2nd edition, Oxford: Clarendon Press.
Smith, A. (1759), *The Theory of Moral Sentiments*, London: Millar; Edinburgh: Kincaid and Bell.
Smith, A. ([1776] 1976), *An Inquiry into the Nature and Causes of the Wealth of Nations*, in *The Glasgow Edition of the Works and Correspondence of Adam Smith*, (eds) R.H. Campbell, A.S. Skinner and W.B. Todd, Oxford: Clarendon Press.
Sraffa, P. (1960), *Production of Commodities by Means of Commodities: Prelude to a Critique of Economic Theory*, Cambridge, UK: Cambridge University Press.
Stirati, A. (1994), *The Theory of Wages in Classical Economics: A Study of Adam Smith, David Ricardo and their Contemporaries*, Aldershot, UK and Brookfield, VT: Edward Elgar Publishing.
Walsh, V. (2000), 'Smith after Sen', *Review of Political Economy*, **12**(1), 5–25.
Winch, D. (1983), 'Science and the legislator: Adam Smith and after', *Economic Journal*, **93** (September), 501–20.
Winch, D. (1996), *Riches and Poverty: An Intellectual History of Political Economy in Britain, 1750–1834*, Cambridge, UK: Cambridge University Press.

Ricardo's Emancipation from Smith's Theory of Prices

Ricardo began his studies in economics after reading Smith's *Wealth of Nations* while he was staying in Bath in 1799, and during his early period he followed Smith's theory of prices. According to his understanding, in Smith's theory, a price is formed by adding wages, profits and rents per unit of product ('adding-up theory'), therefore, when the wage rate rises, all the prices should rise, because labour is necessary to produce all the products.

On the other hand, Ricardo had his own vision or basic idea: as the population increases in the process of capital accumulation and economic growth, the demand for food increases and the production of agriculture increases. Agricultural production increasingly becomes more difficult and the price of the agricultural product (corn) will rise, which will raise the rate of money-wages, which lowers the rate of profits of the economy. The core of Ricardo's vision can be expressed by the proposition that when the productivity of food production diminishes in the process of economic growth, the rate of profits declines.

The ultimate cause of the decline of the profit rate is the decrease of the productivity in agriculture. Accounts that show such a vision can be found in many of Ricardo's writings, but we quote as an example a passage from his main work, *On the Principles of Political Economy, and Taxation*:

> However abundant capital may become, there is no other adequate reason for a fall of profit but a rise of wages, and further it may be added, that the only adequate and permanent cause for the rise of wages is the increasing difficulty of providing food and necessaries for the increasing number of workmen. (*Works*, I: 296)

Ricardo seemed to have established this vision before his letter to Malthus of 17 August 1813, in which he says, 'My conclusion is that there has been a rapid increase of Capital which has been prevented from shewing itself in a low rate of interest by new facilities in the production of food' (*Works*, VI: 95).

Ricardo tried to explain his vision, but while he followed Smith's theory of prices he could not prove the fall of the profit rate by the rise of the rate of money-wages. Smith's theory of prices was not compatible with Ricardo's vision, but Ricardo maintained it long after he had established his own, without recognizing that incompatibility. Although he could not explain his own vision convincingly, he was quite confident of its truth.

In the *Principles* Ricardo repeatedly emphasizes that Smith's theory of prices is definitively wrong. In Chapter 1, for example, he says:

> Adam Smith, and all the writers who have followed him, have, without one exception that I know of, maintained that a rise of the price of labour would be uniformly followed by a rise in the price of all commodities. *I hope I have succeeded in showing, that there are no grounds for such an opinion.* (*Works*, I: 46; emphasis added)

In the *Essays on Profits* Ricardo had also pointed out quite clearly that it is wrong. There must have been a decisive change of mind at some point before the *Essay*.

Ricardo apparently maintained Smith's theory of prices until after his letter to

Malthus of 11 August 1814 at the latest. There he explains the decline of the profit rate in manufacturing industries when the corn price rises, as a consequence of the restriction of the importation:

> It is true that the Woolen or Cotton manufacturer will not be able to work up the same quantity of goods with the same capital if he is obliged to pay more for the labour which he employs, but his profits will depend on the price at which his goods when manufactured will sell. If every person is determined to live on his revenue or income, without infringing on his capital, the rise of his goods will not be in the same proportion as the rise of labour, and consequently his percentage of profit will be diminished if he values his capital, which he must do, in money *at the increased value to which all goods would rise in consequence of the rise of the wages of labour.* (*Works*, VI: 119–20; emphasis added)

It is obvious that Ricardo was trying to persuade Malthus of the validity of his vision using Smith's price theory, but in vain. After that letter, we cannot find any illustration based on Smith's theory of prices. At the same time, we cannot find any reference to it that denies its validity.

Ricardo's letter to Malthus dated 23 October 1814 is very important to Ricardo's emancipation from Smith's price theory. There he distinguishes various causes of the rise of agricultural product, and examines the effects of each cause:

> It appears to me important to ascertain what the causes are which may occasion a rise in the price of raw produce, because the effects of a rise, on profits, may be diametrically opposite. *A rise in the price of raw produce may be occasioned by a gradual accumulation of capital which by creating new demands for labour may give a stimulus to population and consequently promote the cultivation or improvement of inferior lands, – but this will not cause profits to rise but to fall, because not only will the rate of wages rise, but more labourers will be employed without affording a proportional return of raw produce.* The whole value of the wages paid will be greater compared with the whole value of the raw produce obtained . . . An advanced price of raw produce may also proceed from a fall in the value of currency, which would raise the price of produce, for a time, more than it would wages, and would therefore raise profits. Both these [bad seasons and the fall of the value of currency] you will allow are *temporary causes, no way affecting the principle itself, but merely disturbing it in its progress.* (Ibid.: 146; emphasis added)

It is particularly important that in the above passage he made a distinction between the cultivation of inferior lands and the fall of the value of money. If there is a rise in the rate of money-wages caused by the fall in the money value, all products other than the commodity money will rise in value, measured in terms of the commodity money. But if the wage rate rises due to the rise of the price of corn caused by the increase of difficulty in its production, that price rise is peculiar to the corn; therefore, in this case the corn price measured in terms of the commodity money should rise, because the corn has an additional factor raising price – decrease in productivity. However, the prices of all the other products do not necessarily rise in terms of the commodity money, because there are no other additional factors with regard to products other than corn. It should be emphasized that Ricardo's problem is the effects of the rise of the money-wage rate caused by the rise of corn price due to the increase of difficulty in its production.

The earliest evidence that clearly shows Ricardo's emancipation from Smith's theory of prices can be found in his letter to Malthus dated 18 December 1814:

If the mass of commodities be increased we diminish their exchangeable value as compared with those things whose quantity is not augmented. If we double the quantity, or rather double the facility of making, stockings, we diminish their value one half, as compared with *all* other commodities. If we do the same with regard to hats and shoes, we restore the accustomed relations between stockings, hats, and shoes, but not with respect to other things. It is here I think, that our difference rests and I hope soon to hear all that you have to advance in favor of your view of the question. (Ibid.: 163; original emphasis)

In the above passage, Ricardo's idea is not obvious, but it is evident that he is no longer following Smith's price theory. In his *Essay on Profits* (published probably on 24 February 1815), Ricardo definitively denies Smith's theory of prices:

> *It has been thought that the price of corn regulates the prices of other things. This appears to me to be a mistake.* If the price of corn is affected by the rise or fall of the value of the precious metals themselves, then indeed will the price of commodities be also affected, but they vary, because the value of money varies, not because the value of corn is altered. Commodities, I think, cannot materially rise or fall, whilst money and commodities continue in the same proportion, or rather whilst the cost of production of both estimated in corn continues the same. (*Works*, IV: 21n; emphasis added)

Here Ricardo made public for the first time his denial of Smith's theory of prices. It is noteworthy that he distinguishes the rise of corn price caused by the fall of money value from 'the change of the value of corn', and that, in the latter case, Smith's theory of prices is wrong.

The clue to Ricardo's emancipation from Smith's economic theory was the recognition that the money is also a commodity produced by labour following the same law of value variation as the other commodities. If the money is a commodity produced, it requires labour for its production; in this case, the rise of the rate of money-wages does not necessarily raise the prices of products other than money, because the rise of the wage rate influences not only the other products but also the money itself. Ricardo seemed already aware in his letter to Malthus of 18 December 1814 that the crucial difference between them was in the difference in their recognition of the value of money. Malthus did not take into consideration the influence of the rise of the wage rate on the commodity money, so that for him the rise of the wage rate influences only the prices of the products measured in money, for which the rate of profits may not diminish or may rise with the rise of the wage rate. This point can be corroborated by the following explanation in Ricardo's letter to Malthus dated 27 March 1815:

> I have observed in the bullion pamphlet that many who say they consider money only as a commodity, and subject to the same laws of variation in value from demand and supply as other commodities, seldom proceed far in their reasoning about money without shewing that they really consider money as something peculiar, – varying from causes totally different from those which affect other commodities. Do you not fall into this error when you say 'In the first place all depends upon the relation between corn and other commodities, and as labour and corn enter into the prices of all commodities the difference between corn and other commodities cannot possibly increase in any proportion to the increase in the money price of corn'? *If money be a commodity does not corn and labour enter into its price or value? and if they do, why should not money vary as compared with corn and labour by the same law as all other commodities do?* (*Works*, VI: 203; emphasis added)

If 'the difference between corn and other commodities cannot possibly increase' with the rise of the price of corn, the prices of all other commodities should rise with the rise of the price of corn measured in the commodity money.

The recognition that money is also subject to the same law of value variation as other commodities already exists in Ricardo's early writings. For example, he stated clearly in the Appendix to the fourth edition of *The High Price of Bullion* in 1811:

> It is particularly worthy of observation that so deep-rooted is the prejudice which considers coin and bullion as things essentially differing in all their operations from other commodities, that writers greatly enlightened upon the general truth of political economy seldom fail, after having requested their readers to consider money and bullion merely as commodities subject to 'the same general principle of supply and demand which are unquestionably the foundation on which the whole superstructure of political economy is built;' to forget this recommendation themselves, and to argue upon the subject of money, and the laws which regulate the export and import, as quite distinct and different from those which regulate the export and import of other commodities. (*Works*, III: 103–4)

From the above considerations, we may conclude that Ricardo emancipated himself from Smith's theory of prices sometime between 11 August and 18 December 1814, and very possibly between 23 October and 18 December 1814. The clue was in his reconsideration of the idea that the commodity money also follows the same law of value variation, which he had already recognized in 1811.

Ricardo could begin to proceed to make his own theory of prices only when he denied the validity of Smith's theory of prices. After various attempts to explain price variation, he finally determined the labour theory of value as valid in the capitalist economy, and he adopts it in the *Principles* to theorize his vision. In the process of the making of his labour theory of value, he discovers a 'curious effect' that a decline of price follows a rise in the money-wage rate. In the case of different capital–labour ratios, the price of a product produced with a higher capital–labour ratio than the commodity money should decline with a rise in the money-wage rate, because the influence pulling down the price derived from the decline in the profit rate caused by the rise of wage rate is greater than the influence of raising the price due to the rise of wage rate. He was delighted with that discovery, because it is a complete counter-example to Smith's theory of prices as Ricardo understood it. In the *Principles*, he emphasized the importance of the 'curious effect'.

By adopting the labour theory of value, Ricardo could theorize his own vision as follows. When the labour theory of value holds, the relative prices are proportional to the relative labour inputs per unit of product. Therefore, a rise of the money-wage rate influences both the commodities measured and the money that measures them in the same proportion, so that no change arises in prices measured in money (gold). But an increase in labour input in the production of corn will raise only the price of corn relative to the other products only to the degree of the increase of labour input, so the rise of the money-wage rate lowers the rate of profit in the production of corn and in other industries. The corn price tends to rise due to diminishing returns in agriculture and the profit rate has a tendency to decline in the long run due to the rise of the money-wage rate caused by the rise of corn price.

When he theorized his vision, he searched for an invariable measure of value. If the value of the measure that measures the values or prices of the products other than the measure is kept invariable, the variation of prices that may occur are all non-monetary, and a rise of corn price should not raise prices of the other products even if the wage rate rises. By adopting the commodity money (gold) as the invariable measure of value in the case in which the labour theory of value holds, Ricardo could analyse the pure effects of decrease of productivity in agriculture, refuting Smith's theory of prices at the same time. As Sraffa pointed out, money as a commodity, invariable measure of value, and criticism of Smith's theory of prices, were closely connected in Ricardo's mind (*Works*, I: xxxiv).

KATSUYOSHI WATARAI

See also:

Labour Theory of Value; Natural and Market Prices; Ricardo on Adam Smith; Surplus.

Ricardo's Four Magic Numbers

After noting that 'Almost every great name in the field of economics turns out to be represented in the international field as well', Paul Samuelson ([1969] 1972: 678) referred to David Ricardo's 'four magic numbers that constitute the core of the doctrine of comparative advantage theory'. Of Ricardo's contributions to economic theory, Samuelson had earlier observed that 'His greatest tour de force was the theory of comparative advantage' (1962: 9). His numerical example can be said to mark the birth of the theory of international trade as the first applied field of economics. The purpose of this entry is to throw new light on Ricardo's celebrated principle of comparative advantage. At the same time, absolute advantage is shown to retain an important role in determining the after-trade relative standards of living in the two trading countries, England and Portugal. Both absolute and comparative advantage can be illustrated in terms of the four numbers that appear in Chapter 7 of the *Principles of Political Economy, and Taxation* of 1817.

On the basis of the well-known passages of Ricardo's *Principles* that relate to comparative advantage in foreign trade, Ricardo's four numbers are presented below in tabular form in order to facilitate their analysis. They yield two propositions concerning the 'eighteenth-century rule for the gains from trade' and comparative advantage itself. The four numbers are then used to determine the 'factorial terms of trade' between England and Portugal, defined as their relative per worker incomes. The relationship between the factorial terms of trade and the commodity terms of trade is illustrated in Figure 20, which shows that the after-trade income of Portuguese workers is 25 per cent higher than that of English workers.

The often-quoted paragraphs of Chapter 7 where Ricardo formulates the principle of comparative advantage are:

> The quantity of wine which she [Portugal] shall give in exchange for the cloth of England, is not determined by the respective quantities of labour devoted to the production of each, as it would be, if both commodities were manufactured in England, or both in Portugal.
>
> England may be so circumstanced, that to produce the cloth may require the labour of 100 men for one year; and if she attempted to make the wine, it might require the labour of 120 men for the same time. England would therefore find it her interest to import wine, and to purchase it by the exportation of cloth.

To produce the wine in Portugal, might require only the labour of 80 men for one year, and to produce the cloth in the same country, might require the labour of 90 men for the same time. It would therefore be advantageous for her to export wine in exchange for cloth. This exchange might even take place, notwithstanding that the commodity imported by Portugal could be produced there with less labour than in England. Though she could make the cloth with the labour of 90 men, she would import it from a country where it required the labour of 100 men to produce it, because it would be advantageous to her rather to employ her capital in the production of wine, for which she would obtain more cloth from England, than she could produce by diverting a portion of her capital from the cultivation of vines to the manufacture of cloth.

Thus England would give the produce of the labour of 100 men, for the produce of the labour of 80. (*Works*, I: 135)

To express Ricardo's principle in simple algebraic terms, assume that England (country E) trades X of cloth (commodity C) for Y of wine (commodity W) with Portugal (country P), so that Portugal's terms of trade (defined as the price of wine in terms of cloth) are X/Y. My interpretation of Ricardo's numbers follows that of Piero Sraffa (1930) and Roy Ruffin (2002). Citing Sraffa, Ruffin interprets the four numbers as representing the quantities of labour needed to produce the amounts of wine and cloth actually traded by England and Portugal. As Maneschi (2004) points out, they therefore do not represent labour input–output coefficients, as claimed by many textbooks of international trade. Ricardo did not assign numbers to X and Y, so that these remain in algebraic form.

The numbers chosen by Ricardo in the above passage for the workers L_{Xi} and L_{Yi} needed to produce X of C and Y of W in country i (i = E, P) are given in Table 5.

Since $L_{YP} < L_{XP}$ and $L_{XE} < L_{YE}$, each country uses less labour to produce its exports than it would have needed to produce the imports it receives in exchange, from which it follows that both countries gain from trade. This outcome is consistent with what Jacob Viner refers to as the 'eighteenth-century rule' for gains from trade, which stipulates that 'it pays to import commodities from abroad whenever they can be obtained in exchange for exports at a smaller real cost than their production at home would entail' (Viner, 1937: 440). According to the eighteenth-century rule, Portugal gains from trade since 80 < 90, while England gains since 100 < 120. Each country's gains from trade are expressed as the difference between the labour needed to produce X and Y, equal to the amount of labour it saves by trading. Ricardo's numbers show that by trading Portugal saves ten workers annually while England saves 20.

The inequalities that express the eighteenth-century rule for trade gains, $L_{YP} < L_{XP}$ and $L_{XE} < L_{YE}$, can be rewritten as $L_{YP}/L_{XP} < 1$ and $1 < L_{YE}/L_{XE}$ respectively, and combined to yield the proposition:

(P1) (*Eighteenth-century rule for the gains from trade*): $L_{YP}/L_{XP} < 1 < L_{YE}/L_{XE}$. *The labour contained in each country's export bundle is smaller than the labour it would need to produce its import bundle.*

Table 5   Workers needed annually to produce X units of cloth and Y units of wine

	X of C	Y of W
Portugal	L_{XP} (= 90)	L_{YP} (= 80)
England	L_{XE} (= 100)	L_{YE} (= 120)

Multiplying all terms of the double inequality of (P1) by X/Y, and substituting the values shown in Table 5, yields:

$$(L_{YP}/L_{XP})(X/Y) = 0.89(X/Y) < X/Y < (L_{YE}/L_{XE})(X/Y) = 1.2(X/Y). \tag{1}$$

Assume now that the production of the two commodities is subject to constant unit costs, shown in Table 6 as the unit labour costs of producing X and Y in each country, where a_{ji} is the amount of labour needed to produce one unit of j in country i ($i = E, P; j = C, W$). From Table 6, equation (1) can be rewritten as:

$$a_{WP}/a_{CP} < X/Y < a_{WE}/a_{CE}. \tag{2}$$

According to the labour theory of value that Ricardo postulated throughout most of the *Principles*, in autarky (or the absence of trade) relative prices are equal in each country to the ratio between the amounts of labour needed to produce one unit of each good, which is given by a_{WP}/a_{CP} in Portugal and a_{WE}/a_{CE} in England. Hence equation (2) shows that the autarky price ratios lie on either side of the terms of trade X/Y, which implies that when trade opens each country imports the commodity that costs less abroad than at home. We thus obtain the proposition:

(P2)   (Comparative advantage): $a_{WP}/a_{CP} < X/Y < a_{WE}/a_{CE}$. *The terms of trade X/Y are intermediate between the autarky price ratios of Portugal and England, so that each country has a comparative advantage in, and exports, the commodity that is cheaper under autarky.*

(P1) implies (P2) and vice versa. Hence the gains from trade according to the eighteenth-century rule result from a specific pattern of comparative advantage, and trade according to this pattern leads each country to gain from trade.

The division of the gains from trade between England and Portugal

John Stuart Mill and other classical economists pointed out that the gains from trade are not shared equally among trading countries. The closer the terms of trade are to a country's autarky price ratio, the smaller its gains from trade and the larger the gains accruing to the other country. In his numerical and algebraic examples of trade between England and Germany, Mill illustrated extreme cases where 'the whole advantage will be on the side of England' and 'the whole advantage will be on the side of Germany' (Mill [1871] 1920: 600). The force of reciprocal demand determines the position of the terms of trade in the interval contained between the two countries' autarky price ratios. The greater a country's demand for its import good, the higher its price and hence

Table 6   Workers needed annually to produce one unit of cloth (C) and wine (W)

	1 unit of C	1 unit of W
Portugal	$a_{CP} = L_{XP}/X = 90/X$	$a_{WP} = L_{YP}/Y = 80/Y$
England	$a_{CE} = L_{XE}/X = 100/X$	$a_{WE} = L_{YE}/Y = 120/Y$

the lower the country's terms of trade defined as the price of its exports in terms of its imports.

One can relate the share of the overall gains from trade accruing to a country to the deviation between the terms of trade and its autarky price ratio. Assume in Ricardo's example that each country's terms of trade are defined as the price of its export good divided by that of its import good. In Portugal's case, its terms of trade X/Y are one-ninth or 11 per cent above its autarky price ratio of wine in terms of cloth given by (8/9) (X/Y). In England's case, its terms of trade Y/X are 20 per cent above its autarky price ratio of cloth in terms of wine given by (5/6)(Y/X). The ratio between the percentages by which the terms of trade deviate from the autarky price ratio in England and Portugal, or (20 per cent)/(11 per cent), is approximately two to one, and therefore matches closely the ratio between the gains from trade calculated above for each country, or $20/10 = 2$.

This allows a specific conclusion to be attached to Ricardo's numerical example: that England gains twice as much as Portugal, in terms of the number of workers that trade sets free for other pursuits. In welfare terms, however, British gains from trade are not twice as great as Portugal's since, as shown in the next section, Portuguese workers are more productive than British ones.

Implications of absolute advantage for countries' relative standards of living

Although absolute advantage is independent of comparative advantage and does not indicate the direction of trade, it is vital for determining the relative standards of living that countries achieve in their trading equilibrium. Table 6 implies that Portugal uses less labour than England to produce one unit of each traded good, or that it holds an absolute advantage over England in producing both wine and cloth. The consequence is that after trade Portuguese workers have a higher income (and hence are better off) than English workers.

To show this, assume that the two countries share a common currency, that each country specializes in its export good, and that w_i is labour's wage in country i, r_i the profit rate it pays on circulating capital in the form of advanced wages, and p_j is the price of commodity j. The inverse of a_{ji}, or $\pi_{ji} = 1/a_{ji}$ is the productivity of labour in producing commodity j in country i ($i = E, P; j = C, W$). The cost of producing commodity j in country i is the sum $a_{ji}w_i(1 + r_i)$ of the cost of labour $a_{ji}w_i$ and the profits $r_i a_{ji}w_i$ earned on circulating capital $a_{ji}w_i$.

Since competition equates price and unit cost in each country, we obtain:

$$a_{WP}w_P(1 + r_P) = p_W \text{ and } a_{CE}w_E(1 + r_E) = p_C. \tag{3}$$

Income per worker in country i, y_i, is the sum of the wage rate and profit per worker, or:

$$y_i = w_i(1 + r_i). \tag{4}$$

Hence equation (3) can be rewritten as:

$$a_{WP}y_P = p_W \text{ and } a_{CE}y_E = p_C, \tag{5}$$

which yields:

$$y_P/y_E = (a_{CE}/a_{WP})(p_W/p_C) = (\pi_{WP}/\pi_{CE})(p_W/p_C). \tag{6}$$

Hence, as compared to England, relative income per worker in Portugal is higher, the higher is Portuguese labour productivity in wine compared to English productivity in cloth, and the more favourable to Portugal are its commodity terms of trade p_W/p_C.

The relationship between relative income per worker (or 'factorial terms of trade') in the two countries and Portugal's commodity terms of trade is depicted by segment BC of the broken line ABCD in Figure 20. Point B corresponds to terms of trade equal to Portugal's autarky price ratio $0.89(X/Y)$, which would lead England to specialize fully in cloth while Portugal may produce both goods. In that case the price of cloth is given by $p_C = a_{CP}y_P = a_{CE}y_E$, so that the ratio of per worker incomes in Portugal and England is given by:

$$y_P/y_E = \pi_{CP}/\pi_{CE} = 100/90 = 1.11. \tag{7}$$

Relative income per worker is thus equal to the two countries' relative labour productivity in cloth. If $p_W/p_C < 0.89(X/Y)$, trade ceases since both countries specialize in cloth. Equation (7) continues to hold and y_P/y_E corresponds to segment AB of Figure 20.

Point C corresponds to terms of trade equal to England's autarky price ratio $1.2(X/Y)$, with Portugal specializing fully in wine while England may produce both goods. In that case p_W is given by $p_W = a_{WP}y_P = a_{WE}y_E$, which yields:

$$y_P/y_E = \pi_{WP}/\pi_{WE} = 120/80 = 1.5. \tag{8}$$

Relative income per worker reaches its maximum value of 1.5 when it equals the two countries' relative labour productivity in wine, the commodity in which Portugal holds a comparative as well as an absolute advantage. If $p_W/p_C > 1.2(X/Y)$, trade ceases since both countries specialize in wine, in which case y_P/y_E is given again by equation (8) and shown by segment CD of Figure 20. The upper and lower bounds of relative income per worker are thus reached at the two countries' autarky price ratios when only one country specializes in its export good, or in the unlikely case where both countries specialize in the same good.

Returning to the case where England and Portugal specialize fully in their export commodities, cloth and wine, and assuming as before that labour productivity in both countries is constant at any level of output, we have $\pi_{WP} = Y/80$ and $\pi_{CE} = X/100$. Substituting these values into equation (6), we obtain:

$$y_P/y_E = 1.25 \, (Y/X)(p_W/p_C). \tag{9}$$

When p_W/p_C is equal to the terms of trade X/Y, equation (9) yields $y_P/y_E = 1.25$ as shown by point E in Figure 20.

We conclude that Portugal's absolute advantage in both wine and cloth allows its workers to earn an income per capita that is 25 per cent higher than England's. Economists have often wondered why Ricardo postulated that Portugal was more productive than England in both sectors, given that England is where the Industrial Revolution began. Samuelson notes that Ricardo's numbers imply that Portugal had

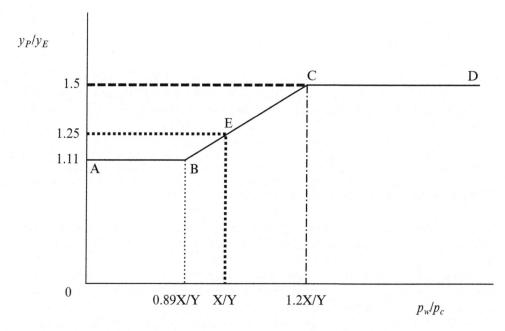

Figure 20   Relative per worker incomes in the Ricardian model

'a real per capita G.N.P. in Colin Clark units that is somewhere between one-ninth and one-half greater [than England's] depending upon whether you are a drunkard or a dandy'. He ascribes 'this odd economic geography' to the fact that Ricardo's reader was 'in need of being reassured that another country could not undersell him in everything even if it were *more* productive in everything' (Samuelson [1969] 1972: 679; original emphasis).

Although comparative advantage is Ricardo's signal contribution to the theory of international trade, absolute advantage is thus shown to retain a fundamental role in his trade model since it determines the relative standards of living in the two countries. Ricardo himself was fully aware of the power of absolute advantage in setting Portugal's standard of living relative to England's. In the last sentence of the passage from Chapter 7 of the *Principles* quoted above, he stated, 'Thus England would give the produce of the labour of 100 men, for the produce of the labour of 80'. When the produce of 100 Englishmen is exchanged for the produce of 80 Portuguese workers, it follows that the ratio of their per worker incomes is indeed 100/80 = 1.25, as shown by point E in Figure 20.

Comparative advantage, the rate of profits, and the dynamic gains from trade
In Chapter 7 of the *Principles*, before his paragraphs on comparative advantage, Ricardo claimed that international trade yields another type of gain besides that associated with reallocating the labour force toward the export sector:

It is quite as important to the happiness of mankind, that our enjoyments should be increased by the better distribution of labour, by each country producing those commodities for which by its situation, its climate, and its other natural or artificial advantages, it is adapted, and by their exchanging them for the commodities of other countries, as that they should be augmented by a rise in the rate of profits. (*Works*, I: 132)

The second gain he mentions, a rise in the profit rate, is unrelated to and incommensurable with the first. Since a rise in the profit rate implies a fall in the money wage, this gain is observed only when the commodities imported enter into workers' consumption:

It has been my endeavour to shew throughout this work, that the rate of profits can never be increased but by a fall in wages, and that there can be no permanent fall of wages but in consequence of a fall of the necessaries on which wages are expended. If, therefore, by the extension of foreign trade, or by improvements in machinery, the food and necessaries of the labourer can be brought to market at a reduced price, profits will rise. (Ibid.)

Because of the special nature of the imported commodities if this second gain is to eventuate, they cannot consist of luxury goods that do not enter the workers' consumption basket.

The increase in the profit rate achievable through trade was important for Ricardo since he had argued in previous chapters of the *Principles* that the pressure of population on land leads to diminishing returns at both the extensive and intensive margins of cultivation. Diminishing returns in turn imply an increase in the price of 'corn' (grains), a rise in the money wage, and hence a fall in the rates of profit and of capital accumulation. In the absence of trade or of technical change, the economy heads toward the stationary state. A trade-induced rise in the profit rate, resulting from the fall in the money wage when cheaper corn is imported, reverses this trend by boosting the rate of capital accumulation. This 'dynamic' gain from trade is additional to the 'static' gain resulting from a reallocation of resources in line with comparative advantage.

The cloth–wine model analysed above is not suitable for portraying this second gain from trade since it assumes constant unit labour coefficients in both sectors. For an attempt to broaden this model by casting it in terms of an agricultural sector subject to diminishing returns to labour on a given stock of land, and a manufacturing sector that enjoys constant returns to labour as in the model sketched above, see Maneschi (2008). A model of this type was originally pioneered by Ronald Findlay (1974) when he integrated Ricardian comparative advantage with economic growth. Growth in the labour force expands employment in both sectors, and the diminishing returns manifested in agriculture cause the price of corn to rise in terms of manufactures if the economy remains closed to trade. As Ricardo describes in Chapters 5 and 6 of the *Principles*, this causes the money wage to rise and the profit rate to fall.

The assumption of diminishing returns in the corn sector can be illustrated by a concave production function and yields a concave production possibility frontier, rather than the linear one used in most textbooks to depict the Ricardian trade model. As a consequence, specialization in the export commodity is incomplete rather than complete. The resulting diagram can be used to illustrate both the 'static' gains from trade postulated by the eighteenth-century rule and the 'dynamic' gains arising from a rise in rate of profits. If the foreign price of corn is lower than the domestic one when the economy opens to trade, the output of corn falls and that of manufactures rises. This raises both the marginal product of labour in the corn sector and the profit rate in agriculture, which competition equalizes to that in the manufacturing sector. In addition to reallocating resources in favour of a sector more in line with Britain's vocation as the 'workshop of the world', trade would cause a pronounced redistribution of income from landlords to capitalists, which Ricardo viewed as an important supplementary boon resulting from a less protectionist British economy.

Ricardo and the classical economists who followed him associated trade with higher economic growth, so that trade affects the economy's trajectory over time. From the frequency with which Ricardo referred throughout the *Principles* to the need for England to repeal the Corn Laws that held the price of grain artificially high, this second gain from trade held for him an even greater significance than the saving of labour associated with the principle of comparative advantage (Maneschi, 1992). It served to ward off the approach toward the stationary state that was otherwise foreshadowed by him and his fellow classical economists.

ANDREA MANESCHI

See also:
Comparative Advantage; Competition; Corn Laws; Foreign Trade.

References
Findlay, R. (1974), 'Relative prices, growth and trade in a simple Ricardian system', *Economica*, **41**(161), 1–13.
Maneschi, A. (1992), 'Ricardo's international trade theory: beyond the comparative cost example', *Cambridge Journal of Economics*, **16**(4), 421–37.
Maneschi, A. (2004), 'The true meaning of David Ricardo's four magic numbers', *Journal of International Economics*, **62**(2), 433–43.
Maneschi, A. (2008), 'How would David Ricardo have taught the principle of comparative advantage?', *Southern Economic Journal*, **74**(4), 1167–76.
Mill, J.S. ([1871] 1920), *Principles of Political Economy*, 7th edition, (ed.) W.J. Ashley, London: Longman, Green and Co.
Ruffin, R.J. (2002), 'David Ricardo's discovery of comparative advantage', *History of Political Economy*, **34**(4), 727–48.
Samuelson, P.A. (1962), 'Economists and the history of ideas', *American Economic Review*, **52**(1), 1–18.
Samuelson, P.A. ([1969] 1972), 'The way of an economist', reprinted in R.C. Merton (ed.), *The Collected Scientific Papers of Paul A. Samuelson, Vol. 3*, Cambridge, MA: MIT Press.
Sraffa, P. (1930), 'An alleged correction of Ricardo', *Quarterly Journal of Economics*, **44**(3), 539–44.
Viner, J. (1937), *Studies in the Theory of International Trade*, New York: Harper.

Riches and Value

Ricardo devoted Chapter 20 of his *Principles* to the subject 'Value and Riches, their Distinctive Properties'. The chapter sets out to show, in contrast to the confusion of Smith and J.-B. Say, that value and wealth are totally different concepts. Wealth, as Smith himself says, is made up of all the goods that provide for our needs, comfort and luxury. Value, on the other hand, expresses the effort that is required to procure these goods, that is, to produce them. It is measured by the working time needed for the production of the good. 'Every thing rises or falls in proportion to the facility or difficulty of producing it, or, in other words, in proportion to the quantity of labour employed in its production' (*Works*, I: 273).

If labour productivity increases, the value of goods decreases, and this – says Ricardo – brings down the value of goods of the same kind that had already been produced (ibid.: 273–4). As accumulation goes ahead, wealth and value diverge in opposite directions, contrary to what Malthus maintains (see *Works*, II: 375). Ricardo writes: 'By constantly increasing the facility of production, we constantly diminish the value of some of the commodities before produced, though by the same means we not only add to the national riches, but also to the power of future production' (*Principles*, Chapter 20, *Works*, I: 274). Thus, 'value depends on the cost of production, riches on the abundance of productions' (*Works*, II: 207, n125; see also ibid., 33–4, n11).

Therefore, if the quantity of goods is lower, in contrast to Lauderdale's claim, wealth does not increase, but declines (*Principles*, Chapter 20, *Works*, I: 276–7). In actual fact, adds Ricardo, Smith gives two definitions of wealth. On the one hand he correctly states that a man is rich or poor according to the goods he owns; on the other hand, that he is rich or poor according to the amount of labour he is able to buy (or command) on the market by exchanging it for his goods (ibid.: 277–9). This is Smith's well-known concept of labour 'commanded' (see *WN*, I.vi), which Ricardo again confutes as he did in the first chapter.

Ricardo writes: 'the wealth of a country may be increased in two ways'. One is by expanding productive labour, that is, by channelling part of the wealth previously spent on luxury consumption into investment. This increases both the quantity and the value of commodities as a whole. The other way is by increasing labour productivity. In this case there would be an increase in the quantity but not in the overall value of goods. The latter method is preferable to the former because it expands wealth without reducing satisfaction (*Works*, I: 278).

Then Ricardo confutes J.-B. Say (ibid.: 279–87), who in fact seems to use the concepts of wealth (use value) and value as if they were interchangeable. What's more, Say uses both concepts of labour value and utility value (as we call them today) at the same time, while for Ricardo they are clearly incompatible (see on this S. Hollander, 2005: 145–65).

This is briefly what Chapter 20 of the *Principles* is about. As usual, Ricardo's logical rigour eliminates the confusion found in the concepts of other authors (see Cannan, 1893, I: 3). But at times this same rigour also eliminates the complexity of the problems. It is up to historians to reconstruct such a complexity. This is actually present in Ricardo's thought, but its different elements are scattered through his work. In our case, the criticism of Smith's concept of labour 'commanded' (or of Say's confusion of wealth and value) makes us forget how increase in productivity, increase in wealth and variations of value are related to the driving force of economic development, that is, the advantage of the more productive productions.

Let us follow Ricardo's reasoning. He writes that if the labour that produced gold and silver or that which produced velvet were to double their productivity, this would not mean that their producers could hire workers for twice as long as before. It would merely mean that, to buy one day's work, they would have to pay twice as much silver and velvet as they paid before (*Works*, I: 278). In Chapter I, devoted to value, Ricardo criticizes Smith, who argues 'as if because a man's labour had become doubly efficient, and he could therefore produce twice the quantity of a commodity, he would necessarily receive twice the former quantity in exchange for it' (ibid.: 14).

Shortly afterwards Ricardo adds that wage changes have a direct impact on variations of profits, and vice versa. But neither of these variations has any effect on the value of the good produced. The latter depends purely on labour productivity. Greater productivity in sock manufacturing means that the socks can command a smaller quantity of other goods (ibid.: 24–5). The same applied in trading fish for game: 'If with the same quantity of labour a less quantity of fish, or a greater quantity of game were obtained, the value of fish would rise in comparison with that of game' (ibid.: 27).

In the view of the labour theory of value, these statements cannot be challenged. But taken in themselves, without considering other factors, they give the impression that Ricardo believes that technical progress, which is responsible for the increase in productivity, is of no benefit to the more dynamic sectors (where it occurs), but does benefit backward sectors (where it does not occur). In his examples, with the increase in productivity, goods from backward sectors are exchanged for a larger quantity of goods from the more dynamic sectors.

Of course, Ricardo did not see it in these terms. Like Smith, he clearly saw that a society's accumulation of wealth was due to the increase in productivity, and that the underlying logic of the variations in exchange value reflected this process. However, this vision needs to be reset by examining other parts of his book, but first by positioning his analysis in its historical framework.

Value and wealth in the previous economic culture

Wealth and value are among the oldest economic concepts, but it is only in modern times that they were gradually linked. This was in the analysis of capitalist accumulation. The pre-modern culture regarded wealth with mistrust from the very beginning. A Greek myth tells that out of greed, King Midas asked for and received the gift of transforming everything he touched into gold. Because of this he could no longer eat, and he died of hunger. This myth has a double meaning: on the one hand, wealth does not consist of money or gold, but in the goods useful for life; on the other hand, there is no point in accumulating money as an end in itself. This vision dominated the whole pre-modern era. Aristotle stressed the two senses of the Midas myth and handed them down to posterity.

In antiquity only a few authors held a favourable view of wealth (the Sophists, Aristotle, Epicurus and some of the Stoics). All of them, however – apart from Epicureans – condemned the desire to get rich: from the myth of Prometheus to the seventeenth-century Catholic moralists. The basic economic canon of the pre-modern era was: the enrichment of someone is the impoverishment of another. This maxim, expressed by Aristotle, was repeated time and again up to Montaigne (and even to Galiani in the eighteenth century). It is typical of static economies, where wealth does not increase. In fact, in a static context it is true that if wealth increases somewhere it must diminish elsewhere.

So, the pre-modern authors saw the desire to get rich as a threat to the established order of society. However, in the fifteenth and sixteenth centuries some humanists, influenced by the works of Epicurus, put forward a positive view of wealth. In the end this gave rise to the seventeenth-century free-thinkers, who argued against the religious canon of renunciation and legitimized the desire to get rich (e.g., Bayle and Mandeville).

Meanwhile, two other groups helped to change the attitude to wealth. The Protestants saw enrichment as a sign of divine grace. On the other hand, Mercantilists put forward new policies to make their country rich. These early economists took an empirical approach, which, however, implied the new values (dignity of work, freedom of economic activity, legitimacy of wealth-getting and self-interest). Naturally the Mercantilists, too, knew that wealth does not consist of money, but of goods (despite what is said by the great majority of successive economists, who for 250 years have been talking about these authors without ever reading them). Based on this, they outlined a strategy for development. It envisaged an important role for money, as financial capital, and for exports; but these were only means to increase production, employment and productivity.

The philosophers and economists of this phase changed the very concept of wealth. Instead of being a gift of nature, it came to be the product of human intelligence and labour. This was the premise needed for a modern analysis of value.

Unlike wealth, value is not an intuitive concept. Aristotle was the first to use it, showing its two fundamental aspects. First of all, he distinguished between use value and exchange value. Second, he looked for the common element that allowed the exchange of two goods with different use values. The answer to this question – which he was unable to find – would have explained why two goods are exchanged in a certain proportion and in no other (exchange value).

The problem was taken up again by the scholastics, who investigated what the just price of goods is. They identified some objective components of the price – those that make up the cost of production (raw materials, labour, transport, storage) – and other subjective components (rarity, social esteem).

In the modern age Davanzati and Montanari based value on rarity. But Petty took up Aristotle's analysis, seeking the par, the element shared by the two goods being exchanged, and he found it in the cost of labour. This gave rise to two lines of approach: that of Cantillon, who measured the cost of labour in terms of the land needed to produce the wage-goods required; and that of (among others) Carmichael, Hutcheson and Adam Smith, who – amidst great uncertainty – measured exchange value in terms of the working time needed to produce the goods (see Perrotta, 2004: Chapters 2–5, 8).

Increase in wealth and in value not deriving from labour

The gradual emergence of exchange value in terms of quantity of labour is consistent with the modern cultural revolution. Labour, despised in antiquity and regarded with distrust in the Middle Ages, became for the humanists the basis of the dignity of man. This gave legitimacy to self-interest, the pursuit of riches, and development. Here is the link that connects the concepts of wealth and value.

Smith knew that accumulation, that is, society's continual growth of wealth, was based on labour. But he noticed that the increase in wealth was not due to labour only. It was also due to the capitalist organization of production and to the entrepreneurial spirit. This gave rise to new incomes not generated directly by labour: profit and rent. The concept of 'labour commanded', which includes the new incomes, although it is defective in logical terms, expressed precisely the capitalist increase in wealth.

Thus, it is true, as Ricardo writes, that Smith seems uncertain as to whether value is measured by wages (labour cost) or by working time (*Works*, I: 16–17); and that he confuses labour 'contained' with labour 'commanded' (ibid.: 12–17, 277–9). But despite this he appropriately outlines the links between technical progress and accumulation, which is the real essence of economic development.

However, Ricardo supports accumulation too strongly. In Chapter 31, 'On Machinery', which was added in the last edition, he deals with the question of innovation. On the one hand, in a famous self-criticism, he acknowledges that replacing labour with machines is not always good for the workers. In the short run it creates a difference between net product (profit), which rises, and gross product (capital invested), within which the wage fund is reduced (ibid.: 388–92). On the other hand, Ricardo defends technical progress. It increases profits and social wealth, and therefore – in the long run – expands the demand for labour and employment (ibid.: 395–6). Besides, he says, the innovator has an 'additional advantage' (ibid.: 387). And he warns: unless we adapt to the technical progress that takes place in other countries, we risk an unfavourable exchange in international trade. 'You might give a commodity which cost [sic] two days labour for a commodity which cost one' (ibid.: 397).

Here, then, the strict rule stated before does not hold. In Chapter 20 the increase in productivity has no influence on profits; it confines itself to depreciating the product that results from innovation. But in Chapter 31, in order to defend accumulation, Ricardo forgets that approach. He implicitly acknowledges an exchange similar to that put in motion by Smith's labour 'commanded'; that is, an exchange that benefits the more productive production (as it seems natural). This exchange is not based on labour 'contained', but on the advantage the more productive sector obtains when its production costs are lowered. But if this advantage exists in foreign trade, why shouldn't it exist in the exchange between different sectors?

This might be seen as an empirical observation, which has no impact on the author's general theory. However, this alternative approach is confirmed by another famous derogation of Ricardo to the principle of labour value, concerning the 'curious effect'. The introduction of machines, that is, of durable capital, keeps a part of capital bound beyond the cycle of production. Such a capital has to generate a profit greater than that produced by circulating capital, which runs out in one cycle of production. This makes the value of the final product higher than the mere labour added to it, 'on account of the time which must elapse before one set of commodities can be brought to market' (ibid.: 34; see also the whole section: 30–38). This effect holds as well for the time it takes to an oak tree to grow, or the time needed for wine mellowed by age (see *Works*, IV: 369, 377). But it is clear that durable capital is mainly due to the mechanization of production.

Ricardo very often maintains that such a derogation from the principle of labour value produces only a secondary and 'comparatively slight' effect (for example, see *Works*, I: 45). But the effect does not seem so negligible, if he spent his last years in search of the invariable measure of value, which in his mind should have solved the problem (ibid.: 43–7). In fact, the effects of that derogation are enormous for accumulation. Moreover, from this analysis Ricardo arrived at the conclusion that the value of the final product is determined by the composition of the investment; that is, by the proportion between fixed and circulating capital, and the proportion between the parts of fixed capital with different durability.

Therefore, mechanization and the increase in productivity do not generate just an increase in social wealth. They also act on the value of final goods, but do so in two different directions. On the one hand, they lower absolute value, in proportion to the reduction of the necessary labour time; on the other, they tend to raise relative value, that is, exchangeable value, in relation to the duration of capital employment.

Because of these contrasting effects, different interpretations arose among historians. Some have maintained that in Ricardo, rather than a labour theory of value, we find a theory of value based on the cost of production (e.g., Stigler, [1958] 1985; see also the comments to Stigler in Wood, 1985; see also Blaug, 1958: 33–7). Others have stressed

Ricardo's insistence in believing (coherently, or despite all things) in the labour theory of value (Sraffa, *Works*, I: xxxvii–xl; St. Clair [1957] 1965: Chapter 3). Finally, others have stressed the contradiction between the two theories (J. Hollander [1904] 1985; Napoleoni, 1973: 97–110).

In the final analysis this increase in value of the final product, which does not derive from the working time but from the fixed capital, is not very different from the Smithian concept of labour 'commanded'. The latter, in fact, does not derive from trade, but from production, since the additional incomes are a part of the cost of production (*WN*, I.vi.24, and, above all, *WN*, I.vii.1–7).

COSIMO PERROTTA

See also:

Exchange Value and Utility; Labour Theory of Value; Natural and Market Prices; Ricardo on Adam Smith; Wealth.

References

Blaug, M. (1958), *Ricardian Economics. A Historical Study*, Westport, CT: Greenwood.
Cannan, E. (1893), *A History of the Theories of Production and Distribution in English Political Economy from 1776 to 1848*, London: Percival.
Hollander, J. ([1904] 1985), 'The development of Ricardo's theory of value', *Quarterly Journal of Economics*, **18**(4), 455–91, reprinted in J.C. Wood (ed.), *David Ricardo. Critical Assessments, Vol. II*, London/Sydney: Croom Helm, pp. 21–43.
Hollander, S. (2005), *Jean-Baptiste Say and the Classical Canon in Economics*, London/New York: Routledge.
Napoleoni, C. (1973), *Smith, Ricardo, Marx*, Milan: Il Saggiatore.
Perrotta, C. (2004), *Consumption as an Investment*, New York/London: Routledge.
Smith, A. ([1776] 1976), *An Inquiry into the Nature and Causes of the Wealth of Nations*, in *The Glasgow Edition of the Works and Correspondence of Adam Smith*, (eds) R.H. Campbell, A.S. Skinner and W.B. Todd, Oxford: Clarendon Press.
St. Clair, O. ([1957] 1965), *A Key to Ricardo*, reprint New York: A.M. Kelley.
Stigler, G.J. ([1958] 1985), 'Ricardo and the 93% labor theory of value', *American Economic Review*, reprinted in J.C. Wood (ed.), *David Ricardo. Critical Assessments, Vol. II*, London/Sydney: Croom Helm, pp. 57–66.

Samuelson, Paul Anthony, on Ricardo

Paul Anthony Samuelson (1915–2009) was, in Adam Smith's words, a most impressive exemplar of those 'philosophers or men of speculation, whose trade it is, not to do any thing, but to observe every thing; and who, upon that account, are often capable of combining together the powers of the most distant and dissimilar objects' (*WN*, I.i.9). He contributed to almost all the fields of economics including consumer theory, capital theory, international trade, general equilibrium, welfare economics, public economics and economic dynamics among others. He contributed important papers on major economists, including Adam Smith, Ricardo, Johann Heinrich von Thünen (who was one of his all-time favourites), Karl Marx, Eugen von Böhm-Bawerk, Knut Wicksell, Irving Fisher and many more. He was keen to put their arguments into mathematical form, which served him as a device to assess their consistency.

When we edited the *Elgar Companion to Classical Economics* (Kurz and Salvadori, 1998), Paul Anthony Samuelson was still with us. At that time we thought that an entry on 'Samuelson, Paul Anthony, as an Interpreter of Classical Economists' was needed despite the fact that entries of such a format were designed for scholars who were no longer alive. Paul Samuelson would have been the exception that proves the rule. We asked several of his previous pupils to write the entry and some of them accepted at first, but then declined with the observation: 'Paul has written so much on this topic!' So we eventually decided to ask Paul Samuelson himself to contribute the entry. He accepted by fax overnight and sent us a beautiful piece in a very short while.

In the following we reprint his entry with a few changes that do not affect the substance of his argument: we delete parts that do not refer to Ricardo and provide information concerning Volumes VI and VII of the *Collected Scientific Papers of Paul A. Samuelson*, which at the time when Paul Samuelson composed his entry were not yet available. Before we do so we recall an episode Samuelson related in his Presidential Address to the International Economic Association in 1969 (see Samuelson 1966–2011, III: Chapter 186), which expresses the admiration Samuelson had for Ricardo. Samuelson and the mathematician Stanislaw Ulam were both members of the Society of Fellows at Harvard (before 1940, when Samuelson became Assistant Professor at MIT) and Ulam used to tease Samuelson by saying 'Name one proposition in all of the social sciences which is both true and nontrivial'. Samuelson remarked:

> This was a test that I always failed. But now, some thirty years later . . . an appropriate answer occurs to me: the Ricardian theory of comparative advantage . . . That it is logically true need not be argued before a mathematician; that it is not trivial is attested by the thousands of important and intelligent men who have never been able to grasp the doctrine for themselves or to believe it after it was explained to them. (Ibid.: 683)

Paul Anthony Samuelson on Paul Anthony Samuelson

Paul Samuelson, having been the student of Jacob Viner and Frank Knight at the University of Chicago and of Joseph Schumpeter at Harvard, was in that first post-1930 generation of economists no longer required to study the history of economic doctrines. However, he soon became critical of the then orthodox commentators on classical and post-classical economics. Alfred Marshall and David Ricardo were worshipped gods back in 1930, but in the next two-thirds of a century some basic trends of evaluation were discernible, to which Samuelson assented and towards which his writings contributed.

Where pre-1870 classical economics is concerned, Samuelson perceived a need to audit objectively the claims for David Ricardo generated and augmented by Piero Sraffa's magnificent complete edition of his works and correspondence; and by comparison to dispel the Schumpeterian and others' disparaging of Smith as an uninspired theorist who happened to speak for the ideology of the market just at the time when the objective winds of history were blowing Britain and Europe towards bourgeois harbours.

Himself a pioneer in twentieth-century mathematical economics, Samuelson might perhaps have been expected to champion Pareto over Walras, and the analytic Ricardo over the encyclopaedic Smith and over the influential Malthus, who convinced the Manchester School of the impotence of do-good reform to raise the living standards of the procreating masses. Samuelson's interest, and perceived comparative advantage, was in history of analysis from a viewpoint within economics. As stated in his American Economics Association 1962 Presidential Address, insider giants like Marshall and Ricardo never cut much ice in outsiders' intellectual history as compared to, say, Smith, Marx or Keynes.

Ricardo's tergiversations on the labour theory of value provide an illuminating case study on analytic history. He pilloried Smith for lack of fervour for the labour theory. But Smith is nearer to the following simple truth: the shared long-run classical system was a three-factor scenario involving (1) labour (freely suppliable in the long run at, and supposedly only at, a specifiable real subsistence wage rate); (2) land(s) (in allegedly fixed supply); and (3) time-phased heterogeneous produced inputs (capital goods). In its easiest case of a limited homogeneous supply of land, Ricardo's alleged trade-off between the profit and real wage rate lacks invariant existence! Instead, for known single-product technologies, there is a three-way trade-off among (real wage, real rent rate, profit rate) = (w, R, i). Both w and i can be moved in the same direction by taste changes that induce a compensating R move in the opposite direction; and, when new knowledge of viable techniques arises, at an unchanged subsistence wage rate, one at least of profit and rent rates must rise. Save for singular improbabilities about measurable identical (wage/profit, rent/wage) intensities, there are no 'natural prices' invariant to taste and consumer-demand changes.

Ricardo begrudgingly admitted how goods' different 'time intensities' vitiated the existence of wheat/cloth price ratios invariant to demand shifts. But he never understood that, time aside (as when i remains zero), the existence of scarce land(s) did qualitatively invalidate the labour theory of value also. A crude land theory of value would be no worse for the classical scenario than his labour theory would be. His blunder is the greater inasmuch as he did recognize that, in the presence of fixed land, a good's cost in terms of labour was rising rather than constant as its q^i rose. (On these obvious Ricardian non-optimalities editor Sraffa chose to remain surprisingly silent.) As soon as Quesnay–Marx–Leontief–Sraffa technologies involved goods that directly or indirectly need themselves as inputs, the Stigler–Ricardo approximate 93 per cent labour theory of value can easily unravel into a 1 per cent labour theory of value.

Worse still, suppose you grant David Ricardo exactly uniform 'organic' compositions of input intensities (or of wage: rent: interest compositions), the pseudo Stigler–Ricardo labour theory of value is then 100 per cent correct – but only in that all

(p^i/p^j)s are unaffected by taste changes. Yet still the Ricardo who asserts that the laws of distribution are the all-important laws of economies gets nothing from this pseudo labour theory of value to help describe, explain and understand how growth in labour/ land intensities and in accumulation of vectors of produced-input endowments can affect and change fractional (wage, rent, interest) shares. The 100 per cent pseudo labour theory of value is no labour theory of value at all! Child Samuelson had to point this out to the Emperor's Court. And, in Hans Christian Andersen, no one paid any attention to the child.

Samuelson himself considers his deepest contributions to the understanding of the classical economic system to be two. One is his 1978 canonical classical growth model, which fits well with the hazy visions of pre-Smith writers, with Smith himself and with the shared economies specified by Malthus, Ricardo, J.S. Mill and Karl Marx too. This is a prosaic paradigm of supply and demand, differing from post-1870 schemata only in elaborations and in the special classical insistences on fixity of land and endogenous reproducibility of population. It covers both the classicals' long-run steady-state analysis and their shorter-run models in which factor stocks' movements generate transient factor prices movements.

His other major novelty was to discern the jewel in the classical crown. Hidden there in clear sight is the (dated) land contents system of natural land prices invariant to taste changes. Thus, for the interest rate at zero, corn and cloth each have their embodied land requirements (embodied directly and indirectly and inclusive of the embodied land needed to produce the subsistence wage market basket) that suffice to set the unique real ($P^{corn}/Rent$, $P^{cloth}/Rent$) vector. This physiocratic jewel, perhaps somewhat sensed by Richard Cantillon, escaped Quesnay and followers and seems to have escaped the Smith-to-Mill-to-Marx writers and the top circles of twentieth-century commentators on doctrinal history.

Miscellaneous Samuelson contributions to David Ricardo history include the following:

1. Defending Ricardo's late chapter (on how invention could hurt workers) from the scathing criticisms of Wicksell, Kaldor, Schumpeter, Stigler and other twentieth-century commentators who wrongly accused Ricardo of abandoning Say's Law and of claiming that perfect competition could be (in later parlance) Pareto-non-optimal. Ricardo was merely rediscovering the obvious – that invention can hurt any sub-set of factors – and was doing that with an over-special circulating–fixed capital distinction that is neither necessary nor sufficient for a cogent 1820 analysis of technical change.
2. The Ricardo–Torrens classical theory of comparative costs presents a perfect example of Samuelson's kind of analytical history. That theory, with its four cost coefficients for wine and cloth in Portugal and England, was itself a precocious leap in the early nineteenth century into the post-1870 world. Already in 1829, the young Mill added the reciprocal demand functions that 1817 Ricardo had still lacked; also Mangoldt and Edgeworth generalized this analysis to multiple commodities, along with a chain of writers (Marshall, Frank Graham, McKenzie and, above all, John Chipman). Samuelson himself joined the parade, culminating with the elegant Dornbusch–Fischer–Samuelson continuum model that is so manageable for

teaching purposes and insights. The nineteenth century lives on, into the twenty-first and beyond.

For crude contrast, history of a scholarly discourse can be strung between the poles of antiquarian history and Whig history. Samuelson, because of his focus on doctrines and paradigms, veered towards the Whig side. But there are many variants of whiggery, not all equally pejorative. Both Viner and Samuelson criticize attempts to read into Ricardo 1820 formalisms that are not there. But using later tools to deduce what had to be the properties of Ricardo's specified scenarios, and dramatizing where Ricardo missed his mark, these are characteristic of Samuelson's explication of Ricardo-like, Marx-like, Quesnay-like and Thünen-like systems.

It is idle to castigate eighteenth-century writers for not being twentieth-century virtuosi, but it is mandatory to point out their errors in describing their own systems and scenarios; and especially to do so when top modern commentators (Schumpeter, Sraffa, Stigler, Blaug, S. Hollander, Kaldor, Wicksell etc.) sometimes share their errors of omission and commission.

The real objects of Samuelson's more heated criticisms were his own time's contemporaneous historians of economic science rather than ancient heroic scholars with their understandable limitations inseparable from the times they lived in. In scope, method and results, Samuelson felt himself to be nearest to Jacob Viner, Joseph Schumpeter, George Stigler, John Chipman and Jürg Niehans as twentieth-century commentators on classical economists.

In the *Collected Scientific Papers of Paul A. Samuelson*, Volumes I–V, (1965 [2 vols], 1972, 1978, 1986), see Chapter 29 (1957); 31 and 32 (1959); 15 (1960); 113 (1962); 125 (1963); 183 (1967); 176 (1968); 186, 189 and 191 (1969); 311 (1970); 278 (1972); 208 (1974); 274 (1975); 252 and 278 (1976); 298, 316 and 342 (1977); 340 (1978); 315 (1980); 296, 312 and 343 (1982); 304, 305, 313 and 339 (1983).

Volumes VI and VII of the *Collected Scientific Papers of Paul A. Samuelson*
The first two parts of Volume VI are devoted to 'Classical economics' (Chapters 389–405) and to 'Neoclassical, Marxian and Sraffian economics' (Chapters 406–427). Among these at least three chapters are explicitly devoted to Ricardo: Chapters 393 (1988) and 394 (1989), defending (in Samuelson's terminology 'mathematically vindicating') Ricardo's chapter 'On Machinery', and Chapter 422 (2001), devoted to the gains from trade in inputs and finished goods in what Samuelson called Ricardo–Sraffa paradigm. Volume VII includes the entry 'David Ricardo (1772–1823)' that Samuelson wrote for the *International Encyclopedia of the Social & Behavioral Sciences* in 2001 (Chapter 558).

HEINZ D. KURZ AND NERI SALVADORI

See also:
Mathematical Formulations of Ricardian Economics; Pasinetti, Luigi Lodovico, on Ricardo; Sraffa, Piero, on Ricardo; Technical Change.

References
Kurz, H.D. and N. Salvadori (1998), *The Elgar Companion to Classical Economics*, Cheltenham, UK and Lyme, NH: Edward Elgar Publishing.

Samuelson, P.A. (1966–2011), *Collected Scientific Papers of Paul A. Samuelson*, 7 vols, Cambridge, MA: MIT Press.

Smith, A. ([1776] 1976), *An Inquiry into the Nature and Causes of the Wealth of Nations*, in *The Glasgow Edition of the Works and Correspondence of Adam Smith*, (eds) R.H. Campbell, A.S. Skinner and W.B. Todd, Oxford: Clarendon Press.

Say, Jean-Baptiste, and Ricardo

Jean-Baptiste Say strongly influenced the reception and dissemination of classical political economy in France and Continental Europe, both through his own writings and through his critical comments on the writings of the British economists. With his 'explanatory and critical notes', which were appended to the first French edition of the *Principles* by Constâncio (1819), Say shaped the assessment of Ricardo's economic theories in France and major parts of Continental Europe, including the German-speaking countries and Russia, for several decades (see Béraud and Faccarello, 2014; Gehrke, 2014). With his own writings, and in particular with his highly influential *Traité d'économie politique* (first edition, 1803) and his *Catéchisme d'économie politique* (first edition, 1815), Say furnished the dissemination and popularization of Adam Smith's economic doctrines and liberal economic ideas on the Continent. In his books, Say proposed a 'neo-Smithian economics', that is, he advocated a modified version of Adam Smith's theory of value and distribution, in which the role of demand and supply and of subjective utility was particularly emphasized.

Ricardo and Say first met in December 1814 when during his stay in England Say visited Ricardo at Gatcombe Park and the two together went to see Mill and Bentham at Ford Abbey (*Works*, VI: 161). There were further meetings between the two economists, first in 1817 in London, and then again in 1822, when Ricardo, during his stay in Paris on the occasion of his Continental tour, 'saw Say several times' (*Works*, IX: 248–9). In 1815, immediately after his return from England, Say sent Ricardo a plan for the reform of the French currency system inspired by the Appendix to the *High Price of Bullion*. Shortly later, Ricardo was to receive Say's newly published *Catéchisme d'économie politique* and a correspondence started between them, which was mainly devoted to debates over Say's theory of value, his distinction between value and riches, and the problem of the measure of value (see Gehrke and Kurz, 2001 for a summary account).

At the beginning of their intellectual encounter the relationship between Ricardo and Say was characterized by mutual respect. In the preface of his *Principles* Ricardo paid tribute to:

> the excellent works of M. Say, who not only was the first, or among the first, of continental writers, who justly appreciated and applied the principles of Smith, and who has done more than all other continental writers taken together, to recommend the principles of that enlightened and beneficial system to the nations of Europe; but who has succeeded in placing the science in a more logical, and more instructive order; and has enriched it by several discussions, original, accurate, and profound. (*Works*, I: 7)

While Ricardo considered certain aspects of Say's analysis, and in particular his exposition of the '*loi des débouchés*' (law of markets), as an advance on Smith, from the beginning he was critical of other aspects and especially of Say's theory of value and distribution. His letters show that Say, ever since they had first met in 1814, felt the need to respond to the objections Ricardo had raised against his doctrines and in the successive revisions of his *Traité* he explicitly sought to bring his own exposition into conformity with Ricardo's ideas. This process began in 1815, before Ricardo had published his *Principles*, and it continued until Ricardo's death in 1823. However, in Ricardo's view Say did not succeed in removing the inconsistencies. This led to a growing disenchantment on Ricardo's part, which seems to have been caused mainly by the fact that he felt that his opponent was unwilling to concede the erroneousness of some of his own views – even when the logical flaws in his argument had been clearly exposed.

More importantly, after the publication of the *Principles* Ricardo also realized that Say failed to understand some of the more important analytical points of his own theory of value and distribution. After he had read Say's 'explanatory and critical notes' in Constâncio's French translation of the *Principles*, Ricardo observed in a letter to James Mill of December 1818: 'M. Say does not appear to me to have clearly seen the doctrine which I wish to establish' (*Works*, VII: 371). For a time Ricardo had even contemplated the idea of having Say's notes translated and published as an Appendix in the second edition of his *Principles*, together with his comments on them, but he then decided to make 'no other answer to M. Say's observations but that of remarking that he has left my main position respecting the regulator of rent unanswered' (ibid.: 379). (For a discussion of the passage that Ricardo inserted in the second edition of the *Principles* [*Works*, I: 73–4n] to this effect, see below.)

It is immediately obvious that the two economists held very different views with regard to the scope and proper method of economic analysis. In their disputes over the theory of value, Ricardo's abstract, analytical approach clashed with Say's realism and anti-deductivism. Say opted for a political economy that was practically useful and this aim, he thought, necessitated the employment of the inductive method. Say was of the opinion that mathematics had no role to play in the study of economic phenomena and that mathematical calculation was 'the most dangerous of all abstractions' ([1821] 1971: xxviii n). Say's writings abound with practical observations and superficial wisdom, which makes them 'easily accessible' for the layperson. This contrasted sharply with Ricardo's abstract theoretical approach to economic problems. It is therefore ironic to note that Ricardo's success as a stockjobber and financier also stood in sharp contrast to Say's poor entrepreneurial capacities.

Say and Ricardo also had different views of society and its stratification. Although he was aware of conflicts and social unrest, Say expressed an essentially harmonious view. He was convinced that political economy could alleviate, and eventually dissolve, such conflicts of interest. In fact, he contended that political economy 'satisfactorily proves that the interest[s] of the rich and poor, and of different nations, are not opposed to each other, and that all rival-ships are mere folly' (ibid.: lix).

The differences of opinion between Ricardo and Say concerned the core fields of political economy: the theory of value, including the problem of the measure of value and the distinction between 'value' and 'riches', and the theory of income distribution, especially the explanation of rent and of profits. Ricardo indeed did not endorse the central 'principles' Say advocated, that is, doctrines that the latter had adopted with some adaptations from Smith's *Wealth of Nations*, and which Ricardo had already criticized in Smith. In Ricardo's view, Say's overall economic analysis was contradictory and incoherent. The disagreements were there right at the beginning of their intellectual encounter and did not go away over time, notwithstanding Say's repeated affirmations that he had absorbed Ricardo's doctrine and made use of it in the numerous changes between the different editions of the *Traité*. Ricardo's letters show that he became more and more disenchanted, and after the conversations he had with Say in Paris he observed in a letter to Malthus of December 1822: 'M. Say has not succeeded in at all understanding what my opinions are' (*Works*, IX: 249).

Before entering into a more detailed discussion of Ricardo's criticisms of Say's theory of value and distribution, we should notice two areas in which they agreed – or in which their disagreements were at least less pronounced. With regard to monetary theory the two authors were largely in agreement, and throughout his writings Say unreservedly acknowledged Ricardo's achievements in this field. In 1814, during his stay in England, Say wrote a plan for the reorganization of the banking system in France, which he afterwards sent to Ricardo, who replied that in its essential points it was similar to the proposals he himself had made for the Bank of England in the 1811 Appendix to *The High Price of Bullion* (*Works*, VI: 165). The main difference was that in Say's plan the note issue was to be entrusted to the government. At the time, Ricardo considered this to be too dangerous, because he believed that governments could not be trusted not to misuse their power (ibid.: 164–5). However, he subsequently changed his mind, because in his *Proposals for an Economical and Secure Currency* of 1816 Ricardo then suggested that after the expiration of the Bank's charter in 1833 the right to issue notes might be vested exclusively in 'commissioners responsible to parliament only' (*Works*, IV: 114). Accordingly, it has been suggested that Say influenced Ricardo in recommending government issue of banknotes (see Sayers [1953] 1971: 50–51). It should be noted, however, that Ricardo still mistrusted governments and particularly stressed the role of Parliamentary control in his proposal. Subsequently, Say also fully approved of Ricardo's Ingot Plan and adopted it in the third edition of his *Traité*. He reiterated his approval of Ricardo's views on monetary questions in his notes to the French translation of the *Principles* (Say, in Ricardo, 1819: 236–7), and after Ricardo's death singled out the latter's contributions to monetary theory as his main title to fame ([1825] 1848: 278).

Another topic on which the two authors were also largely in agreement, at least at first sight, was the 'law of markets' (now known as 'Say's Law'). In his preface to the *Principles* Ricardo specifically drew attention to the chapter on the '*loi des débouchés*' in Say's *Traité*, which was said to contain 'some very important principles, which I believe were first explained by this distinguished writer' (*Works*, I: 7). And when Ricardo expounded his own understanding of the law of markets in Chapter 21 of the *Principles*, he again acknowledged Say's earlier exposition of it:

> M. Say has ... most satisfactorily shewn, that there is no amount of capital which may not be employed in a country, because demand is only limited by production. No man produces, but with a view to consume or sell, and he never sells, but with an intention to purchase some other commodity, which may be immediately useful to him, or which may contribute to future production. By producing, then, he necessarily becomes the consumer of his own goods, or the purchaser and consumer of the goods of some other person. (Ibid.: 290)

Ricardo and Say both insisted that acts of saving do not involve a reduction in effective demand for consumption goods, but rather a change from 'unproductive' to 'reproductive' consumption. Hence they concluded that there cannot be a general glut of commodities, as was maintained by authors such as Malthus and Simonde de Sismondi. But in spite of their general agreement on the impossibility of general gluts there were in fact important differences of opinion between them also with regard to this issue.

In Chapter 21 of the *Principles* Ricardo concluded that 'there cannot . . . be accumulated in a country any amount of capital which cannot be employed productively, until wages rise so high in consequence of the rise of necessaries, and so little consequently remains for the profits of stock, that the motive for accumulation ceases' (ibid.: 290). To this statement Ricardo appended a footnote, in which he asked:

> Is the following quite consistent with M. Say's principle? 'The more disposable capitals are abundant in proportion to the extent of employment for them, the more will the rate of interest on loans of capital fall'– Vol. ii p. 108. If capital to any extent can be employed by a country, how can it be said to be abundant, compared with the extent of employment for it? (Ibid.: 290n)

This criticism of Say anticipated a central element of Ricardo's argument in his later controversy with Malthus, in which he used Say's Law in support of his theory of profits against Malthus's competition of capitals theory. The differences between Ricardo and Say's understanding of the 'law of markets' became even more apparent when Say presented Ricardo with a copy of his *Lettres à M. Malthus* (1820). In the *Letters*, Say conceded to Malthus that countries could indeed suffer from a stagnation in commerce, and in a long footnote he criticized Ricardo, reiterating his view that a lack in total effective demand can be caused by wrong policies adopted by governments or central banks:

> Mr. Ricardo insists that, notwithstanding taxes and other charges, there is always as much industry as capital employed; and that all capital saved is always employed, because the interest is not suffered to be lost. On the contrary many savings are not invested, when it is difficult to find employment for them, and many which are employed are dissipated in ill calculated undertakings. Besides, Mr. Ricardo is completely refuted, not only by what happened to us in 1813, when the errors of Government ruined all commerce, and when the interest of money fell very low, for want of good opportunities of employing it; but by our present circumstances when capitals are quietly sleeping in the coffers of their proprietors. (Say [1821] 1967: 49n)

In a letter to Malthus, Ricardo wrote that he was 'by no means pleased' with Say's *Lettres*, and that 'for the opinions we hold in common, he does not give such satisfactory reasons as might I think be advanced' (*Works*, VIII: 301). And in one of his notes on Cazenove's 'A reply to Mr. Say's letter to Malthus' Ricardo observed: 'I am as much dissatisfied as the author with M. Say's defence of the principle which both he and I maintain to be true' (*Works*, X: 410). Ricardo defended his position in a further letter to Malthus, where he commented on Say's note as follows:

> In the note . . . he [Say] concedes too much. The difficulty of finding employment for Capital in the countries you [Malthus] mention proceeds from the prejudices and obstinacy with which men persevere in their old employments,– they expect daily a change for the better, and therefore continue to produce commodities for which there is no adequate demand. With abundance of capital and a low price of labour there cannot fail to be some employments which would yield good profits, and if a superior genius had the arrangement of the capital of the country under his controul [sic], he might, in a very little time, make trade as active as ever. *Men err in their productions, there is no deficiency of demand . . . I cannot conceive it possible, without the*

grossest miscalculation, that there should be a redundancy of capital, and of labour, at the same time. (Works, VIII: 277–8; emphasis added)

In another letter to Malthus Ricardo pointed out a further disagreement with Say, which concerned the immediate cause of a commercial crisis:

I think he [Say] falls into the same error as Torrens . . . They both appear to think that stagnation in commerce arises from a counter set of commodities not being produced with which the commodities on sale are to be purchased, and they seem to infer that the evil will not be removed till such other commodities are in the market. But surely the true remedy is in regulating future production,– if there is a glut of one commodity produce less of that and more of another but do not let the glut continue. (Ibid.: 227–8)

According to Ricardo, it is the lack of foresight on the part of the producers rather than the lack of a counter set of commodities that is the immediate cause of stagnation: 'It is at all times the bad adaptation of the commodities produced to the wants of mankind which is the specific evil, and not the abundance of commodities' (*Works*, II: 306, n196; see also IX: 132). Ricardo also provided a brief account of the mechanism by which the supply of commodities is adapted to an increase in the propensity to save:

If every man was intent on saving, more food and necessaries . . . would be produced than could be consumed. The supply above the demand would produce such a glut, that with the increased quantity you could command no more labour than before. All motive to save would cease, for it could not be accomplished, but the precise reason for this is, that . . . the labourers would be in a condition to command a very great quantity of the net produce. This could only last till the population was increased, when labour would again fall, and the net produce be more advantageously distributed for the capitalist. During the period of very high wages, food and necessaries would not be produced in such quantities as to occasion a glut, for it would be the interest of the producer to produce such things as were in demand, and suited to the tastes of those who had high wages to expend. (*Works*, IX: 131)

To conclude, while Say and Ricardo both advocated the law of markets, they by no means agreed on the economic mechanisms at work.

Controversial issues in the theory of value and distribution

Say emphasized the importance of utility for prices and argued that the latter were determined by demand and supply. According to Ricardo, these propositions were either wrong or vacuous, because the notions of 'demand' and 'supply' had little or no analytical content. As regards income distribution, Say mixed Smithian ideas, such as the one concerning the conflict between masters and workmen over wage bargaining, with his own demand-and-supply approach, yielding a compromise that Ricardo found unsound. He criticized Say especially for not having understood the principle of differential rent and, once rent is set aside by focusing attention on marginal (i.e., no rent) land, that the rate of profits is determined once the real wage rate is known. According to Ricardo, Say's attempt to provide separate explanations for the determination of the levels of real wages and of (the rate of) profits was ill founded.

Say had difficulty in understanding the role of the concept of an 'invariable measure of value' in the context of Ricardo's theory of value and distribution. In particular, he failed to perceive that for Ricardo the concept of a measure that was invariable with respect to changes in income distribution was essentially an analytical device that was meant to allow him to see through the complexities of the dependence of relative prices on the rate of profits. Say objected to the very idea of searching for such a measure, arguing that 'an invariable measure of value is a pure *chimera*, because one cannot measure values other than in terms of values, that is, by a quantity essentially variable' (Say in Ricardo, 1819, I: 12; original emphasis). He thus anticipated Samuel Bailey's relativistic critique of the concept.

An important topic of the debates between Ricardo and Say in their correspondence was Say's inconsistent definitions of 'value' and 'riches'. In the final passages of Chapter 20 of the *Principles* Ricardo accused Say of having 'confounded two things which ought always to be kept separate, and which are called by Adam Smith, value in use and value in exchange' (*Works*, I: 280n). Say responded to Ricardo's criticisms in several lengthy notes that he inserted in the French edition of the *Principles* (see Say in Ricardo, 1819, II: 89–102) as well as by introducing some changes in the fourth edition of his *Traité*. This forced Ricardo to alter the relevant passage in the third edition of the *Principles*, because the quotations from Say's *Traité* had to be adapted to the latest edition. But the substance of Ricardo's criticism remained unaltered; in his view, Say had not succeeded in removing the inconsistency by his reformulation.

With regard to the distinction between net and gross revenue, Ricardo saw Say committing essentially the same error as Smith – an error that derived from the defective theory of value the two authors advocated. According to that theory the price of a commodity equals the added-up payments of 'factor services' employed in its production. By this 'adding-up of components' theory of price they were misled into contending that all prices would rise or fall when wages rose or fell. The two authors thus missed the constraint binding changes in the distributive variables, given the technical conditions of production, demonstrated by Ricardo. Say failed to notice the inconsistency in Smith's social accounting when the latter reckoned the wages of productive labourers as both part of the advanced capital and of the net income. Accordingly, Say's own definition of the terms 'gross' and 'net produce' (or revenue) was also to suffer from an inconsistency, because the gross produce was defined as 'the total revenue of the community' (or 'total value-added'), consisting of wages, profits and rents, but the remunerations of the factor services were then also taken to form the costs of production that must be deducted from the gross produce in order to obtain the net revenue. Ricardo pointed out this inconsistency in the third edition of his *Principles*:

> Of net produce and gross produce, M. Say speaks as follows: 'The whole value produced is the gross produce; this value, after deducting from it the cost of production, is the net produce.' . . . There can then be no net produce, because the cost of production, according to M. Say, consists of rent, wages, and profits . . . Take a whole from a whole, and nothing remains. (*Works*, I: 421n)

Say maintained that the problems of value and of distribution were essentially of the same nature, and therefore had to be dealt with in the same way:

> The causes, which determine the value of things . . . apply without exception to all things possessed of value . . . *amongst others, therefore, to the productive service yielded by industry, capital, and land* . . . [The] relative value . . . rises in direct ratio to the demand, and inverse ratio to the supply. ([1821] 1971: 314–15; emphasis added)

Accordingly, wages, profits and rents are to be explained in terms of demand and supply, where the demand for productive services is to be derived from the demand for products. The link between demand and supply, on the one hand, and cost of production, on the other, Say specified as follows: 'The price paid for every product, at the time of its original attainment or creation, is, the charge of the productive agency exerted, or the cost of its production' (ibid.: 298). The price of each commodity is composed of, and thus can be resolved into, rents, profits and wages, or rather, as Say preferred to call them, into the 'profit of land', the 'profit of capital' and the 'profit of labour' (ibid.: 316–17). Say thus adopted an adding-up concept of value and missed the constraint binding changes in income distribution demonstrated by Ricardo. Let us turn, then, to the explanation given by Say of how each of the three components is determined.

Say's theory of wages is essentially a combination of elements taken over from Smith with a few ideas of his own. Amongst the latter is his much acclaimed discussion of the specific role of the entrepreneur (as opposed to the capitalist) in the process of production, and his conception of the wages of common labour as a particular form of profits. As opposed to Smith, Say did not limit the concept of 'human capital', on which profit accrues in relation to the total costs incurred for education and training, to high-skilled labour only. He argued: 'A full-grown man is an accumulated capital; the sum spent in rearing him is indeed consumed, but consumed in a reproductive way, calculated to yield the product man' (ibid.: 333n). After this remarkable definition one would expect the investors in this kind of capital to obtain the ordinary rate of return, but Say, although he proposed to call wages 'profits of labour', in fact adopted Smith's notion of a historical and cultural subsistence level around which the wages of common labour tend to gravitate. This tendency of wages to conform to the subsistence level is explained along Smithian lines by the advantage that masters are said to have over workers in the conflict over wages and by the working of a kind of Malthusian population mechanism that involves a tendency towards an 'excess of population above the means of subsistence' (ibid.: 339).

Say criticized the scholastic view of usury and the prohibition of interest taking as based on a lack of understanding of 'the functions and utility of capital', and thus of saving. The interest on a loan of (money) capital is considered as a 'rent paid for the utility and use of capital' and taken to depend on the 'aggregate capital' of a nation, which in turn is taken to depend on 'the quantum of previous savings', on the one hand, and on whether there are many or few 'lucrative employments of capital', on the other (ibid.: 348, 349, 366). With regard to the determination of the rate of interest, Say thus enunciated some kind of loanable funds theory.

As regards the profits of productive capital, Say emphasized the difficulty of distinguishing between 'the profit derivable from the employment of capital' on the one hand, and the 'profit of industry' of the entrepreneur, on the other. Smith and the other English economists are accused of having neglected the latter distinction and to have comprised under the head of profits of stock 'many items which evidently belong to the head of profit of industry' (ibid.: 354). According to Say, the rates of profit in different industries are not necessarily uniform; they depend on 'the relative demand and supply for each mode of employment of capital respectively' (ibid.: 356). In Say's view, there is a perfect analogy, also reflected in his peculiar terminology, between the 'profit of capital', the 'profit of land' and the 'profit of labour'. According to him, 'the profit of capital, like that of land and the other natural sources, is the equivalent given for a productive service, which though distinct from that of human industry, is nevertheless its efficient ally in the production of human wealth' (ibid.: 357). In one passage, Say put forward the germs of an explanation of profits in terms of the sacrifices incurred by the saver, his 'forbearance' or, as Nassau W. Senior (1836) was to call it, his 'abstinence'. According to Say, capital is: 'The mere result of human frugality and forbearance to exercise the faculty of consuming ... wherefore, no one else, but he who has practised this self-denial, can claim the result of it with any show of justice' (ibid.: 293). It need hardly be said that Say's view of profit was in strict contrast to Ricardo's, who focused attention on the productive use made of capital and the surplus left over after all necessary costs of production, including the wages of labour, have been deducted from gross outputs.

With regard to Say's explanation of rent, it is apposite to discuss first Say's critical notes on Ricardo's theory of rent in the French edition of the *Principles*, before turning to Say's alternative conceptualization in his *Traité*. In his 'explanatory and critical notes' Say put forward four main objections to Ricardo's proposition that there is no extensive differential rent on the marginal land (or mine). First, he argued that a rent can be claimed for all land, because land is an indispensable factor of production. Second, he maintained that rent is a monopoly price, which cannot be wiped out by competition. Third, some of Say's statements can be interpreted to mean that the reservation price of the land service is generally not zero but positive, because there are alternative uses of land. Fourth, Say argued that whichever plot of land is cultivated is done so because of its peculiar characteristic features that distinguish it from all other plots of land. This could be interpreted to mean that the number of different qualities of land is infinite (and not, as in Ricardo, finite), that is, that there is a continuum of different qualities of land. It should be clear that Ricardo's concept of persistent cost differentials in agricultural production and of differential rent based on them is not affected by any of these criticisms.

In one of his critical notes in the French edition of the *Principles* Say had explicitly maintained that Ricardo's theory of rent depended crucially on the existence of land that pays no rent and that it was contradicted by the empirical observation that a rent was obtained for almost all land in cultivation. Ricardo responded to this criticism by inserting a note in the second edition of his *Principles*, in which he pointed out that Say had failed to show 'that there is not any capital employed on the land for which no rent is paid' (*Works*, I: 413n). This refers, of course, to the theory of intensive differential rent, and Ricardo pointed out that Say had nowhere 'refuted, or even noticed that important doctrine' and, in fact, 'does not appear to be aware that it has even been advanced' (ibid.). The theory of intensive differential rent was indeed only one among several analytical concepts of Ricardo that Say had failed to notice – or, more likely, failed to comprehend. Bloomfield (1989) has shown that even after 1819 Say still embraced the theory of absolute advantage in international trade. Apparently, he had not properly understood, or perceived the importance of, Ricardo's exposition of the theory of comparative costs in Chapter 7 of the *Principles*.

In the exposition of his own theory of rent, Say emphasized the importance of demand: 'The productive power of the soil has no value, unless where its products are objects of demand' ([1821] 1971: 362). According to Say, rent income emanates from the productive power of the soil in conjunction with a high demand for agricultural produce.

Ricardo's theory of differential rent is held to be a muddled way of explaining a fact that can be more easily explained in terms of his own theory: population growth raises the demand for corn, this leads to an increase in price and to increased competition among the farmers, which in turn raises the incomes of the landowners:

> If any circumstance operate to aggravate demand ... the value of agricultural product will exceed, and sometimes very greatly exceed, the ordinary rate of interest upon capital; and this excess it is, which constitutes the profit of land, and enables the actual cultivator, when not himself the proprietor, to pay a rent to the proprietor, after having first retained the full interest upon his own advances, and the full recompense of his own industry. (Ibid.)

Say claimed that 'rent is generally fixed at the highest rate of that profit', because landed proprietors 'are enabled to enforce a kind of monopoly against the farmers' (ibid.: 365–6). This is because 'the bargain between the land-holder and the tenant must always be greatly in favour of the former' (ibid.: 366). This essentially carries over Smith's argument regarding the relative strengths of masters and workers in the conflict over wages to the conflict between landowners and tenants over rent.

Say's posthumous assessment of Ricardo's contributions

After Ricardo's death, Say openly attacked Ricardo and diminished his achievements. In 1825, he maintained: 'Not only has Ricardo's book been given an importance that I feel to be exaggerated; but it was also granted, with as little justification, the merit of originality and novelty' ([1825] 1848: 275). As regards Ricardo's overall achievements in political economy, Say asserted that 'his only title to fame is his doctrine of money' (ibid.: 278). In the fifth edition of his *Traité* (1826) Say inserted several new criticisms of Ricardo, on which he further elaborated in his *Cours complet d'économie politique practique* (1828–29). On Ricardo's proposition of a tendency towards a uniform rate of profits in conditions of free competition Say commented: 'This is what I call *metaphysical political economy*. It has no utility whatsoever, because it cannot provide any guidance in practice' ([1828–29] 1852, II: 68; original emphasis). The reason given for this judgement is that there will never be two pieces of land or two firms absolutely equal to one another. On the 'Ricardian school' as a whole, by which he meant Ricardo, McCulloch and the two Mills, Say remarked: 'The error of this school is to take each principle too absolutely; and, after having presented it in the form of a theorem, to deduce rigorously consequences which very often do not conform to the facts' (ibid.: 400).

CHRISTIAN GEHRKE

See also:

Capital and Profits; Demand and Supply; General Glut; Invariable Measure of Value; Labour and Wages; Labour Theory of Value; Land and Rent; Monetary Theory; Natural and Market Prices; Rate of Interest; Revenue; Riches and Value; Say's Law.

References

Béraud, A. and G. Faccarello (2014), '"Nous marchons sur un autre terrain." The reception of Ricardo in the French language: episodes from a complex history', in G. Faccarello and M. Izumo (eds), *The Reception and Diffusion of David Ricardo in Continental Europe and Japan*, London and New York: Routledge.

Bloomfield, A.I. (1989), 'Aspects of the theory of international trade in France: 1819–1914', *Oxford Economic Papers*, **41**(3), 619–39.

Gehrke, C. (2014), 'The reception and further elaboration of Ricardo's theory of value and distribution in the German-speaking countries: 1817–1914', in G. Faccarello and M. Izumo (eds), *The Reception and Diffusion of David Ricardo in Continental Europe and Japan*, London and New York: Routledge.

Gehrke, C. and H.D. Kurz (2001), 'Say and Ricardo on value and distribution', *European Journal of the History of Economic Thought*, **8**(4), 449–86.

Ricardo, D. (1819), *Des Principes de l'Economie politique, et de l'impôt*, translated by F.S. Constâncio, with explanatory notes and critiques, by M. Jean-Baptiste Say, Paris: Aillaud.

Say, J.-B. (1803), *Traité d'économie politique, ou simple exposition de la manière dont se forment, se distribuent, et se consomment les richesses*, Paris: Deterville.

Say, J.-B. (1815), *Catéchisme d'économie politique, ou Instruction familière qui montre de quelle façon les richesses sont produites, distribuées et consommées dans la société*, Paris: Crapelet.

Say, J.-B. (1820), *Lettres à M. Malthus, sur différents sujets d'économie politique, notamment sur la cause de la stagnation générale du commerce*, Paris: Bossange.

Say, J.-B. ([1821] 1967), *Letters to Mr. Malthus on Several Subjects of Political Economy. And on the Cause of the Stagnation of Commerce. To Which is Added: A Catechism of Political Economy or Familiar Conversations on the Manner in which Wealth is Produced, Distributed, and Consumed in Society*, London: Sherwood, Neely & Jones; reprint, New York: A.M. Kelley.

Say, J.-B. ([1821] 1971), *A Treatise on Political Economy*, translated by C.R. Prinsep from the 4th edition (1819) of *Traité d'économie politique*, Philadelphia: Claxton, Remsen and Haffeldinger; reprint, New York: A.M. Kelley.

Say, J.-B. ([1825] 1848), 'Examen critique du discours de M. MacCulloch sur l'économie politique', *Revue Encyclopédique*, **27**, 694–719; reprinted in Say (1848), *Oeuvres diverses de J.-B. Say*, Paris: Guillaumin, pp. 261–79.

Say, J.-B. ([1828–29] 1852), *Cours complet d'économie politique practique*, 3rd edition, Paris: Guillaumin, Vols X and XI of the *Collection des Principaux Economistes*, in the text referred to as I and II.

Say, J.-B. (1848), *Oeuvres diverses de J.-B. Say*, Paris: Guillaumin.

Sayers, R.S. ([1953] 1971), 'Ricardo's views on monetary questions', *Quarterly Journal of Economics*, **67**(1), 30–49; reprinted in A.W. Coats (ed.), *The Classical Economists and Economic Policy*, London: Methuen, pp. 33–56.

Senior, N.W. (1836), *An Outline of the Science of Political Economy*, London: W. Clowes and Sons.

Say's Law

The expression 'Say's Law' is used in the economics literature to represent the arguments set out by Say in Chapter XV, 'Des Débouchés', Book I, of his *Traité d'Economie Politique* (first edition, 1803; fourth edition, 1819, first English trans. 1821). These arguments, later known and discussed under the different names of *'loi des débouchés'* and 'law of markets', are considered by Ricardo amongst the 'original, accurate, and profound' discussions of an author 'who justly appreciated and applied the principles of Smith' (*Works*, I: 6–7). Ever since Say's exposition and Ricardo's appreciation, the focus and controversies on this law reached two distinct peaks first in the classical and then in the post-Keynesian period. While the classical period, which run between James Mill's explicit draft of the law ([1808] 1965) and J.S. Mill's final qualification of it ([1871] 1929), reached its own peak in Ricardo's outright support, against Malthus's criticisms, of those arguments, the post-Keynesian period was opened by Keynes's outright criticism of Ricardo's system of thought (believed to be based on Say's Law), and corresponding defence of Malthus, in his *General Theory* (Keynes, 1973, *Collected Writings*, VII: 18–21, 32–34, 364).

The different versions, interpretations and misunderstandings that have surrounded the law in the course of time have been so numerous that an entire volume (be it one of those authored by Kates, 1998, Sowell, 1972 and Hutt, 1974, or the one edited by Kates, 2003) may not be enough to account for all of them. This holds even if the law were looked at from the standpoint of a single author, be it Say or Ricardo, or of the interactions within, or between, the systems of thought of these or of many other authors. This entry is intended to single out, amongst these different versions, interpretations and misunderstandings, only those connected, directly or indirectly, with Ricardo's support of the law. Thus the entry is divided into five sections. While the first is focused on the limits of the law from the standpoint of its pure or abstract content and on why it should be more properly referred to as *Say's Principle*, the second section is focused on the split of the law into its two forms known in the literature as 'Say's identity' and 'Say's equality'. The remaining three sections are instead devoted to an analysis of the main endorsements, criticisms and counter-criticisms that have surrounded the law ever since Ricardo came to its support against Malthus, and until Keynes moved against it and, more generally, against Ricardo himself. Some brief conclusions are eventually provided in the final section.

Say's Law or Say's Principle?
Ever since Say proclaimed in his *Traité* that 'it is production which opens a demand for products' so that 'a product is no sooner created than it from that instant affords a market for other products to the full extent of its own value', and even after J.S. Mill provided his final support for what was to be called 'Say's Law' by arguing why 'all sellers are inevitably and *ex vi termini* buyers' ([1871] 1929, III: xiv; see also Skinner, 1967; Thweatt, 1979; Hollander, 2005: Chapter 5), the debate on the true meaning and implications of the law developed in a number of directions. This development was carried out without noticing, to begin with, that the term 'law' is rather a misnomer (Baumol, 1999: 202) for what should more properly be regarded as a 'principle' (a term used sometimes by Ricardo himself) and should accordingly be called 'Say's Principle'. This principle has little to do with the more sophisticated sense in which Clower and Leijonhufvud used this term, in lieu of the old one, and extended its meaning from 'quantities *actually* purchased' and 'prices *actually* paid' to '*expected* purchase prices and *planned* quantities purchased' ([1973] 1984: 149; emphasis added). The essential aim of Say's Principle, as set out by Say himself in his *Traité* as well as in his correspondence with Malthus, was rather to dissolve the appearances, and highlight the substance, of transactions between different individuals, sectors and nations, once looked at in the classical context of the division of labour and of its international trade extensions. These appearances emerge when money comes into the picture as a unit of account or medium of exchange (numéraire) with the only task of facilitating these transactions. When this occurs, the double exchange (of money for commodities, of commodities for money) experienced in everyday transactions must be distinguished from the ultimate exchange between commodities, or between commodities and labour, that lies beyond our practice, or is hidden from our view, of such transactions. This is how and why money was presented as a veil that, necessitated as it is by the division of labour, prevents us from discerning the reality of the production and circulation of national wealth. Say's Principle was therefore formulated, and must be regarded, as a *vérité de raison*, or abstract principle, which is true in theory and, more precisely, in static theory. As such, Say's Principle must be kept apart from all the extensions, deviations and contradictions it undergoes once we move from the realm of *vérité de raison* to the realm of *vérité de fait* (Meacci, 2014), that is, to what is true in practice or, more generally, in dynamic theory or in applied economics.

The issue as to whether Say's Principle is true in practice as well as in theory was tackled by Ricardo and Malthus when they either supported or challenged that principle in the historic contexts of the 'stagnation of trade' experienced after the Napoleonic Wars as well as of the short-term versus long-term policy measures then advocated for coming to grips with that stagnation (Hollander, 1979: 514–35; see also 1997: Chapter 12; and Peach, 1993: 131–43). This adds some extra weight to the conclusion that Say's Principle presents itself, and can be elaborated upon, as something that (in one sense) holds *out* of time as well as something that (in another sense) may fail *in* time (Hicks, 1976).

Say's identity or Say's equality?

The notion of money as a unit of account implies that money has no utility of its own and cannot, therefore, fail to be used but in the purchase of useful commodities, whatever their price. This notion is different from the notion of money as a store of value that was focused upon only much later, sometimes implicitly and sometimes in conjunction with the previous one, as, for instance, in Hayek's view of money as a 'loose joint' (Garrison, 1984). These two notions of money lie behind the two macroeconomic extensions of Say's Principle known in modern literature as 'Say's identity' (turned by Lange, 1942, after including money among the commodities exchanged, into 'Walras's Law') and 'Say's equality' (Becker and Baumol, 1952; Baumol, 1977, 1999; *contra* Lange, see Clower and Leijonhufvud [1973] 1984). Both the identity and the equality refer to what happens to aggregate supply and aggregate demand in a period of time or, more precisely, of historical time; that is, in a period in which ex post (or actual) identities may differ from ex ante (or planned) equalities: while Says' identity implies both the notion of money as a unit of account and an ex post view of the variations of economic magnitudes in a given period, Say's equality implies the notion of money as (also) a store of value along with an ex ante view of these variations. The difference between these notions and views is what makes the equality between aggregate supply and aggregate demand to appear, in the former case, as a logical necessity (in that all useful commodities will inevitably find, in such circumstances, their *débouchés*) and, in the latter case, as a concrete possibility (in that commodities, however useful, may happen to be regarded from time to time as less useful then the storage of money). Moving from Say's identity to Say's equality amounts, therefore, to moving from one assumption, and the resulting conclusion, to another: while, within Say's identity, the conclusion is that no crises due to aggregate supply exceeding aggregate demand would ever occur; the corresponding conclusion, within Say's equality, is that such crises are always possible, regardless of whether they are reversible or not.

Ricardo between Smith and Say

After criticizing both Smith and Say (as well as defending the former from the latter's criticisms) on value and riches in Chapter XX of his *Principles*, Ricardo comes to his famous endorsement of Say's Principle in Chapter XXI where he states that 'productions are always bought by productions, or by services; money is only the medium by which the exchange is effected' (*Works*, I: 291–2; see also *Works*, IV: 17 and VI: 163–4). It is interesting to note, however, that Ricardo's endorsement of Say's Principle goes here hand in hand with his criticisms of some related arguments by Smith in spite of the fact that 'Smith all but enunciated Say's Law' (Baumol, 1977: 157). This 'enunciation' included not only the notion of money as a unit of account (Say's identity) but also the more sophisticated notion (implicitly shared by Ricardo) of saving equal to investment. This notion supports what may be called 'Smith's identity' and leads to what may also be called – in agreement with what was argued above – 'Smith's equality'. The movement from the one to the other proposition reflects a movement from what is a basic assumption of Smith's theory of capital (saving = investment) to the manifold phenomena that may either conform to, or deviate from, this assumption. While the saving = investment assumption is implicitly rendered by Smith's view of the man who would be 'perfectly crazy' if he failed to 'employ all the stock which he commands, in procuring either present enjoyment or future profit' (*WN*, II.i.30) as well as by his even more famous statement that 'what is annually saved is as regularly consumed as what is annually spent, and nearly in the same time too' (ibid., iii: 18), the phenomena that may either conform to, or deviate from, Smith's equality may be assimilated to the discrepancies between changes in the *real* and changes in the *nominal* price of commodities (or in their 'price in labour' and their 'price in money') discussed by Smith himself in one of his previous chapters (ibid., I: v). Accordingly, Smith might here strengthen Ricardo's endorsement of Say's propositions by arguing that, in consistency with the notion of money he starts from, any discrepancy between the annual volumes (as distinct from the concepts) of saving and investment is not to be taken into consideration 'in such a work as this' (ibid.: 22), it being understood that this might well be in a different kind of work. By contrast, Ricardo's criticisms of Smith in the same chapter in which he provides his endorsement of Say's principle are not aimed at what has been called above 'Smith's identity' and 'Smith's equality', but at what Ricardo believes to be the inconsistency between these propositions, on the one hand, and Smith's arguments on the competition of capitals and falling rate of profit, on the other. While interpreting these arguments as envisaging a permanent increase of supply above the increase of demand, Ricardo seems to be misunderstanding the impact of competition of capitals within particular sectors – which would imply the oversupply of particular products – for its different impact in the economy as a whole – which would instead imply an increased demand for labour with the associated increase in wages and corresponding fall of profit (according to an inverse relationship that, however, was intended by Smith in a different sense than by Ricardo) (Meacci, 2006).

Malthus versus Smith, Ricardo and Say
The notion of money as a unit of account or medium of exchange, on which Say's identity and Say's equality are equally based, reappears in Malthus's 'non-monetary' criticisms of these propositions (Sowell, 1972: 96; Cottrell, 1998) in spite of Lange's misleading interpretation (1942: 61) of a note in Malthus's *Principles* (Malthus, 1986, VI: 260–61). For these criticisms are implicitly based on Smith's identity, strengthened as it was both by Malthus's assertion that 'no political economist of the present day can by saving mean mere hoarding' (ibid.: 32) and by Ricardo's equivalent assertion that 'when we say that revenue is saved, and added to capital, what we mean is, that the portion of revenue, so said to be added to capital, is consumed by productive instead of unproductive labourers' (*Works*, I: 151). Malthus, however, parts company with Ricardo (as well as with Smith) when, shifting his analysis to the long run, he focuses on what might be called the second-round effects of an act of saving, that is, on whether the increasing

output resulting from the corresponding investment will be absorbed by an adequate demand. Malthus's negative answer is provided a number of times and in different ways both in his *Principles* and in his vast correspondence with Ricardo (see, for a comprehensive view, Hollander, 1997: Chapter 11). At the roots of his criticisms are, first, his view of demand as the will and power to purchase (Malthus, 1986, V: 51ff) and, second, his idea that the will (and power) to purchase is destined to fall short of the power to sell (ibid., VI: 253ff and 317ff; see also Malthus's letters in Ricardo, *Works*, VI: 131, 168) on the difference between 'necessaries of life' and 'other commodities'. Ricardo's counter-criticisms are developed at length in his correspondence as well as in his *Notes on Malthus*. They reach, however, a unitary climax in Ricardo's *Principles*, Chapter XXI, the aim of which is to deny any pressure towards secular stagnation other than the one contemplated in his own view of the wage–profit inverse relationship in the context of diminishing returns to land.

These counter-criticisms can be summarized in at least three steps. One may be focused on the question, raised by Malthus (1986, VIII: 33) as to whether a glut 'may be general as well as particular, and not whether it may be permanent as well as temporary'. A second step can be traced to Smith's observation (endorsed, albeit partly and for diverging reasons, by Ricardo and Malthus on the desire of food, which is limited by the 'narrow capacity of the human stomach', versus the desire of 'conveniences and ornaments', which 'seems to have no limit or certain boundary' (*Works*, I: 293 and Malthus, 1986, VI: 320, respectively). The third step can in turn be traced to Smith's notions of productive and unproductive labour as distinct (in spite of Malthus's arguments in Book II of his *Principles*) from the notions of productive and unproductive consumption (identified in Malthus's language with unproductive 'consumers').

As for his first counter-criticism, Ricardo's argument was (1) that, in accordance with the coordination failures, miscalculations or disproportionalities admitted by Say himself (Jonsson, 1995) and leading to arguments based on 'Say's equality' rather than on 'Say's identity', 'mistakes may be made and commodities not suited to the demand may be produced' throughout the economy (*Works*, II: 305; see also Torrens on this 'great practical problem' [1821] 1966: 370ff); and (2) that, in the exceptional case of 'a general stagnation of trade', the best thing to do is to adopt the (pre-Keynesian) advice 'to petition the King' and 'to oblige the Government to supply the deficiency of the people' (*Works*, I: 307).

As for the second counter-criticism, this is based on Ricardo's idea that 'the will is very seldom wanting when the power exists' and that the desire of accumulation 'will only change the objects on which the demand will exercise itself' (*Works*, VI: 133). This counter-criticism may be extended by arguing that Malthus's view of the long-run effects of a process of accumulation is anchored to the short-run view of a given wage basket, as if the increasing supply resulting from such a process were to be exclusively confined to the goods (for instance, corn) already existing in it. Ricardo's third counter-criticism can be eventually summarized by objecting that Malthus's arguments are based on a confusion between the motives for accumulation (a question 'not in dispute') and its consequences in the economy as a whole (ibid., 316: n204); or between the origin of an act of saving = investment and its impact on the future blend of productive and unproductive consumption, including the composition of the wage basket (or wages fund) exchanged in the future market for labour (whether productive or unproductive).

Keynes and Malthus versus Ricardo and Say

The assumption of money as a unit of account or medium of exchange, which underlies the classical debate on Say's Principle (including the whole Ricardo–Malthus controversy) along with the quantity theory of money to which it belongs (Hollander, 1979: Chapter 9), was replaced in the literature of the twentieth century by the completely different notion of money as a store of value. The author who produced such a replacement in the context of what was intended to be a new system of thought was J.M. Keynes (1971–89, *Collected Writings*, VII). He summarized the old doctrine as 'supply creates its own demand' and attacked the whole of it as if this expression reflected the true meaning of that principle, and as if this principle were incompatible with any situation of recession or unemployment as well as with any policy aimed at overcoming it (Jonsson, 1997; Kates, 1997, 2005; Eltis, 2005). Thus, Keynes started his overall criticism of Say's Principle and of its implications by stressing not so much the new assumption but the classical saving = investment identity as 'a corollary of the same doctrine' (*Collected Writings*, VII: 18–19), rather than as a starting definition and corollary of the old assumption. As a result, and far from focusing on the compatibilities between the conclusions resulting from those different assumptions, Keynes launched an overall attack on previous authors, starting from Say and, in particular, from Ricardo who was said to be 'stone-deaf to what Malthus was saying' (ibid.: 32–4, 362–4). What Malthus was saying, however, was not without the obscurities denied by Keynes himself when praising Malthus's 'unusual combination' of the 'shifting picture of experience' with the 'principles of formal thought' (*Collected Writings*, X: 108). This combination is required, as argued above, to place Say's Principle in its proper context of *vérité de raison* as distinct from *vérité de fait*. Yet this is what is lacking in Malthus's arguments as well as what escapes Keynes's attention while endorsing those arguments. When arguing, for instance, that Smith's propositions on saving (Smith's identity) are true to 'a great extent' though not to 'an indefinite extent', Malthus (1986, V: 9) seems to imply that Smith's identity, however true in theory, may be untrue in practice, that is, in the context of the 'shifting picture of experience'. Yet, after basing most of his arguments against Say's Principle on the 'great practical question' (*Works*, IX: 10) of 'rapid' or 'sudden' changes of saving, or of an 'inordinate' passion for accumulation, that is, on actual deviations from that principle, Malthus ends up by stressing the necessity for a country to possess a permanent body of unproductive consumers (see, for instance, 1986, VI: 317ff and 329ff; Keynes, *Collected Writings*, X: 99); and by implying, therefore, that Smith's identity is untrue even in theory. Which is what Ricardo objects to when, after admitting the possibility of a general glut, he calls for (in the pre-Keynesian passage quoted above) an ad hoc government intervention rather than Malthus's body of unproductive consumers as such.

Concluding remarks

The different (but compatible) views of Say's Principle (in its two forms of Say's identity and Say's equality) as something that is true in theory but may be untrue in practice, as well as the different (but compatible) notions of money as a unit of account and of money as a store of value, underlie the intertemporal debate that developed on that principle in the context sometimes of static and sometimes of dynamic theory; and, within the latter, sometimes of the theory of growth and sometimes of the theory of fluctuations. This bifurcation of the literature, after ramifying for over two centuries in a variety of different interpretations and extensions, has beclouded the whole debate on Say's Principle to such an extent that it has become harder than ever to disentangle one issue from another, or to trace the different issues to the different systems of thought in which they have been, or should be, framed. Thus, far from coming to an end, the debate has become more far-reaching today than it was in the classical period. An important reason may be detected behind the lines of Schumpeter's final assessment of the debate. After arguing (against Keynes) that it would be more natural not to object to 'Say's Law' 'just as we do not object to the law of gravitation on the ground that the earth does not fall into the sun', Schumpeter (1954: 624) ends up by introducing the most general question resulting from the debate. This is the question as to whether it is the Keynesian theory or (as Keynes believed) the classical theory that represents a special case; or, to put it differently, as to whether it is the study of the obstacles to full employment or the study of the causes of employment as such that must lie at the core of economic analysis. It is unfortunate that Schumpeter, after hinting at this crucial question in a footnote added to the passage quoted above, eventually failed to tackle it at length either at the end, or in the spirit, of his brilliant account of the debate:

> A man of the name of J. B. Say had discovered a theorem of considerable interest from a theoretical point of view that, though rooted in the tradition of Cantillon and Turgot, was novel in the sense that it had never been stated in so many words. He hardly understood his discovery himself and not only expressed it faultily but also misused it for the things that really mattered to him. Another man of the name of Ricardo understood it because it tallied with considerations that had occurred to him in his analysis of international trade, but he also put it to illegitimate use. Most people misunderstood it, some of them liking, others disliking what it was they made of it. And a discussion that reflects little credit on all parties concerned dragged on to this day when people, armed with superior technique still keep chewing the same old cud, each of them opposing his own misunderstanding of the 'law' to the misunderstanding of the other fellow, all of them contributing to make a bogey of it. (Ibid.: 624–5)

FERDINANDO MEACCI

See also:

Accumulation of Capital; Demand and Supply; General Glut; Keynes, John Maynard, on Ricardo; *Notes on Malthus*; Say, Jean-Baptiste, and Ricardo.

References

Baumol, W. (1977), 'Say's (at least) eight laws, or what Say and James Mill may really have meant', *Economica*, **44**(2), 145–61.
Baumol, W. (1999), 'Retrospectives: Say's Law', *Journal of Economic Perspectives*, **13**(1), 195–204.
Becker, G. and W. Baumol (1952), 'The classical monetary theory', *Economica*, **19**(4), 355–76.
Clower, R.W. and A. Leijonhufvud ([1973] 1984), 'Say's Principle, what it means and doesn't mean', in D.A. Walter (ed.), *Money and Markets. Essays by Robert W. Clower*, Cambridge, UK: Cambridge University Press, pp. 145–65.
Cottrell, A. (1998), 'Keynes, Ricardo, Malthus and Say's Law', in J.C.W. Ahiakpor (ed.), *Keynes and the Classics Reconsidered*, Dordrecht: Kluwer, pp. 63–75.
Eltis, W. (2005), 'Money and general gluts: the analysis of Say, Malthus, and Ricardo', *History of Political Economy*, **37**(4), 661–8.
Garrison, R.W. (1984), 'Time and money: the universals of macroeconomic theorizing', *Journal of Macroeconomics*, **6**(2), 197–213.
Hicks, J.R. (1976), 'Some questions of time in economics', in A.M. Tang, F.M. Westfield and J.S. Worley (eds), *Evolution, Welfare, and Time in Economics*, Lexington, MA: Lexington Books, pp. 135–51.
Hollander, S. (1979), *The Economics of David Ricardo*, Toronto: University of Toronto Press.
Hollander, S. (1997), *The Economics of Thomas Robert Malthus*, Toronto: University of Toronto Press.

Hollander, S. (2005), *Jean-Baptiste Say and the Classical Canon in Economics*, London: Routledge.

Hutt, W.H. (1974), *A Rehabilitation of Say's Law*, Athens, OH: Ohio University Press.

Jonsson, P.O. (1995), 'On the economics of Say and Keynes's interpretation of Say's Law', *Eastern Economic Journal*, **21**(2), 147–55.

Jonsson, P.O. (1997), 'On gluts, effective demand, and the true meaning of Say's Law', *Eastern Economic Journal*, **23**(2), 203–18.

Kates, S. (1997), 'On the true meaning of Say's Law', *Eastern Economic Journal*, **23**(2), 191–203.

Kates, S. (1998), *Say's Law and the Keynesian Revolution: How Macroeconomic Theory Lost its Way*, Cheltenham, UK and Lyme, NH: Edward Elgar Publishing.

Kates, S. (ed.) (2003), *Two Hundred Years of Say's Law. Essays on Economic Theory's Most Controversial Principle*, Cheltenham, UK and Northampton, MA: Edward Elgar Publishing.

Kates, S. (2005), '"Supply creates its own demand": a discussion of the origins of the phrase and of its adequacy as an interpretation of Say's law of markets', *History of Economics Review*, **41**, 49–60.

Keynes, J.M. (1971–89), *The Collected Writings of John Maynard Keynes*, 30 vols, (eds) E. Johnson and D. Moggridge, London: Macmillan.

Lange, O. (1942), 'Say's Law: a restatement and criticism', in O. Lange, F. McIntyre and T.O. Matema (eds), *Studies in Mathematical Economics and Econometrics: In Memory of Henry Schultz*, Chicago, IL: University of Chicago Press, pp. 49–68.

Malthus, T.R. (1986), *The Works, of Thomas Robert Malthus*, 8 vols, (eds) E.A. Wrigley and D. Souden, London: Pickering.

Meacci, F. (2006), 'The competition-of-capitals doctrine and the wage–profit relationship', in N. Salvadori (ed.), *Economic Growth and Distribution: On the Nature and Causes of the Wealth of Nations*, Cheltenham, UK and Northampton, MA: Edward Elgar Publishing, pp. 58–74.

Meacci, F. (2014), 'From bounties on exportation to the natural and market price of labour: Smith versus Ricardo', *The European Journal of the History of Economic Thought*, **21**(3), 392–420.

Mill, J. ([1808] 1965), *Commerce Defended*, New York: A.M. Kelley.

Mill, J.S. ([1871] 1929), *Principles of Political Economy with Some of their Applications to Social Philosophy*, (ed.) W.J. Ashley, London: Longmans.

Peach, T. (1993), *Interpreting Ricardo*, Cambridge, UK: Cambridge University Press.

Say, J.-B. (1821), *A Treatise on Political Economy, or the Production, Distribution, and Consumption of Wealth*, translated C.R. Prinsep from the 4th (1819) French edition, Boston, MA: Wells and Lilly.

Schumpeter, J.A. (1954), *History of Economic Analysis*, London: Routledge.

Skinner, A.S. (1967), 'Say's Law: origins and content', *Economica*, **34**(134), 153–66.

Smith, A. ([1776] 1976), *An Inquiry into the Nature and Causes of the Wealth of Nations*, in *The Glasgow Edition of the Works and Correspondence of Adam Smith*, (eds) R.H. Campbell, A.S. Skinner and W.B. Todd, Oxford: Clarendon Press.

Sowell, T. (1972), *Say's Law: An Historical Analysis*, Princeton, NJ: Princeton University Press.

Thweatt, W.O. (1979), 'Early formulators of Say's Law', *Quarterly Review of Economics and Business*, **19**(4), 79–96.

Torrens, R. ([1821] 1966). *An Essay on the Production of Wealth*, New York: A.M. Kelley.

Schumpeter, Joseph Alois, on Ricardo

Joseph A. Schumpeter coined the term 'Ricardian Vice' to chastise David Ricardo's alleged habit of employing highly bold assumptions in an already oversimplified representation of the economy and treating some of the magnitudes involved as givens when in fact they are unknowns. (Interestingly, he levelled the same criticism at John Maynard Keynes.) In Schumpeter's words, Ricardo's 'fundamental problem' was that he 'wanted to solve in terms of an equation between four variables: net output equals rent plus profits plus wages' (Schumpeter, 1954: 569). Operating within this perspective, Ricardo was bound to treat three of the variables as constants. Schumpeter also deplored Ricardo's alleged habit of 'piling a heavy load of practical conclusions upon a tenuous groundwork' (ibid.: 1171).

These criticisms come from Schumpeter's *History of Economic Analysis*, which was published posthumously (Schumpeter died in 1950) by Schumpeter's third wife,

Elizabeth Boody Firuski. In some of his earlier writings he was much less negative about Ricardo's achievements. For example, in his essay on 'Epochen der Dogmen- und Methodengeschichte' (Epochs in the History of Economic Doctrines and Methods), published in 1914, he called Ricardo 'the most important follower of Adam Smith' and Ricardo's *Principles* the 'culminating point' of classical economics (Schumpeter, 1914: 53–4). While he characterized Smith's doctrine as 'relatively superficial' (ibid.: 58, n2), he attested to Ricardo's depth and coherence. Yet compared to Marx's it is said to be 'analytically narrow' and inept to comprehend the 'life and growth of the social body as a whole': Ricardo did not attempt to elaborate a 'universal social science' (ibid.: 60; see also Kurz, 2012: Chapter 3).

It is particularly interesting to note that in his 1914 essay Schumpeter did not adopt Alfred Marshall's (1890) assessment that modern, that is, marginalist economics, which explained relative prices and income distribution in terms of the 'forces' of demand and supply, was a continuation of and elaboration on the analyses of the classical economists. Classical theory and the theory of Marshall, Schumpeter insisted, were only 'connected by a loose tie' (ibid.: 55). Schumpeter's view would change later.

Two examples serve to illustrate what Schumpeter (1954) considered to be Ricardo's inadmissible way of reasoning. The first is Ricardo's famous suggestion, made in 1819, that the whole of the British national debt accumulated during the Napoleonic Wars could be repaid in a few years by means of a lump-sum tax on property (*Works*, V: 21, 34–5). It would be best, he argued, if these debts were paid off as quickly as possible – even at the expense of a one-time reduction in capital. After all, what would happen if the debt burden were still there when the next major emergency happened? Such a tax, Ricardo argued, would not diminish total wealth and would also not unduly hurt the propertied classes, because the capital value of the current taxes levied on them to cover interest charges and amortization was equal to the lump-sum property tax suggested. (This proposal became known as 'Ricardo's equivalence theorem', but in the hands of Robert Barro assumed a rather different meaning.) The second example is Ricardo's view that the burden of a tax on wages or on goods consumed by workers will not be borne by workers (e.g., *Works*, I: 203). Both conclusions are the logical consequence of the underlying premise that workers are paid a given and constant real wage. As Schumpeter opined, Ricardo's theory of wages amounted to taking wages as fixed at the 'subsistence' level (Schumpeter, 1954: 665).

These criticisms elicit the following remarks. The first remark concerns the way Ricardo reasoned. Apparently his critics have not taken seriously his statement that:

> in all these calculations I have been desirous only to elucidate the principle, and it is scarcely necessary to observe, that my whole basis is assumed at random, and merely for the purpose of exemplification. The results though different in degree, would have been the same in principle . . . My object has been to simplify the subject. (*Works*, I: 121–2)

Hence, while it is true that Ricardo frequently employed bold assumptions to 'elucidate' the principle at hand and draw attention to what he considered the most important aspects of the problem under consideration, he certainly did not seek to prevent his readers from trying out less restrictive assumptions and investigating their implications, nor did he abstain from doing so himself. Some later commentators rightly praised him for having heralded an approach in economics that requires a clear statement of the assumptions on the basis of which certain propositions are taken to be valid within a given analytical context. This is now considered an indispensable prerequisite of scientific communication. Therefore, what Schumpeter considered a vice others took to be a virtue.

As regards the analytical core of Ricardo's argument, it would be wrong to take Ricardo as strict follower of the Malthusian concept of a subsistence wage. While he used this concept in some contexts for the sake of simplicity, in others he explicitly stressed the historical and social dimensions of the 'natural wage' and warned that it must not be mistaken for a minimum required for physiological subsistence (see, e.g., *Works*, I: 96–7). He took into account the possibility that workers might receive a share of the social surplus product and maintained that the rate of profits is inversely related to 'the proportion of the annual labour of the country devoted to the support of the labourers' (*Works*, IV: 49). Ricardo's argument applies to any given (feasible) real wage rate – to the minimum 'subsistence' rate no less than to rates above that level. Correspondingly, as the real wage rate is higher, the normal rate of profits will be lower.

Finally, it should be mentioned that after World War I and the collapse of the Habsburg Empire Schumpeter ([1918] 1953) proposed to abolish the huge public debt that Austria had accumulated during the war by means of a property tax not much different from the one Ricardo had advocated.

Let us now turn to the fact that the 'standpoint . . . of the old classical economists from Adam Smith to Ricardo has been submerged and forgotten since the advent of the "marginal" method', as Piero Sraffa remarked perceptively (Sraffa, 1960: v). By the turn of the nineteenth century it was no longer understood that the classical economists had advocated a theory of income distribution that was fundamentally different from the marginalist one. The marginalist approach sought to determine the rate of profits and the wage rate in terms of the relative 'scarcities' of the respective factors of production, capital and labour, and thus on the basis of the economy's given initial endowment of the factors. (With heterogeneous capital goods yielding a uniform rate of profits in competitive conditions, the overall 'amount of capital' in given supply can be expressed only as a sum of value, which spoils the symmetry between the factors with land(s) and labour(s) given in terms of their own natural units.) The classical economists, on the contrary, determined the rate of profits for the system of production in use in terms of the 'social surplus' left over after all used-up means of production and wage goods consumed by workers at a given real wage rate have been deducted from gross output levels. Hence, whereas the marginalist authors treated profits and wages symmetrically, the classicals treated them asymmetrically. This asymmetric treatment was unimaginable to the marginalist authors, including, as we have seen, Schumpeter, who therefore felt entitled to accuse the classical authors of treating as a constant what is a variable – that is, the wage rate. Schumpeter's incomprehension is in fact also encountered in major marginalist authors, such as William Stanley Jevons and Léon Walras, who levelled the same kind of criticism at Smith and Ricardo of treating as givens what are in fact unknowns (see Kurz and Salvadori [2002] 2007: 390–95). However, to treat wages as a given in one part of classical theory is a priori no less admissible than to treat the capital endowment as a given in one part of marginalist theory. Clearly, both magnitudes are variables in other parts of classical or marginalist theory. As Sraffa (1960) has shown, the classical approach to the theory of value and distribution can be formulated in a coherent way that allows one to determine the unknowns (one of the distributive variables and relative prices) in terms of the givens, without depending on bold assumptions, such as the existence of a subsistence wage. Things are different with regard to marginalist theory, because the 'quantity of capital' cannot, in general, be taken as given independently of, and prior to, the determination of the rate of profits and relative prices. It follows that the rate of profits cannot generally be conceived as reflecting the marginal product of capital and the wage rate as reflecting the marginal product of labour.

In his own explanation of profits Schumpeter ([1912] 1934) parted company with all received theories of income distribution by arguing that profits exist only in a dynamic economy, not in the 'circular flow', that is, static conditions. In a stationary economy, he contended, there are no profits and there is no interest at all; there are only wages and rents of land. Profits are the child of innovations: they both emerge and disappear with them (see also Kurz, 2012). This is in striking contrast not only to marginalist, but also to classical economics. In Ricardo (and Smith) there are typically positive (normal) profits even in stationary conditions of the economy as long as wages are smaller than the net productivity of labour on marginal land. What Schumpeter calls 'profits', Ricardo and the classicals called 'extra' or 'surplus profits' reaped by the successful innovator, who introduces, for example, a new method of production, which at the current prices allows them to produce the product at lower unit costs. The extra profits are a temporary monopoly rent. The imitative behaviour of competing firms will eventually lead to the adoption and diffusion of the new method throughout the economy and bring about a new long-period position of the economy, in which all extra profits have disappeared and a uniform normal rate of profits obtains again. Ricardo and the classical economists discuss this process under the heading of the 'gravitation' of 'market' prices and rates of return to their new 'normal' levels. Schumpeter entertains a peculiar variant of this classical concept of gravitation by conceptualizing the process of technical innovation and diffusion as a transition between two circular flows: an innovation upsets the initial circular flow; its absorption by the system leads to a new circular flow. In both, profits (and not just the extra profits of the classical economists) are nil. Schumpeter calls innovations 'new combinations'. The core of his analytical innovation – his 'dynamic' theory of profits – may thus be said to consist in a reconfiguration and recombination of analytical elements he encountered in the classical economists, especially Ricardo, and Marx. Hence, despite Schumpeter's claim to the contrary, his own analysis owes a lot to an author whose groundwork he called 'tenuous'.

In the light of these considerations and granting the fact that Ricardo based some of his arguments on highly simplified analytical constructions, it appears to be problematic for Schumpeter to speak of a 'Ricardian Vice'.

HEINZ D. KURZ

See also:

Böhm-Bawerk, Eugen von, on Ricardo; Capital and Profits; Hayek, Friedrich von, on Ricardo; Jevons, William Stanley, on Ricardo; Marshall, Alfred, on Ricardo; Marx, Karl Heinrich, on Ricardo; Ricardian Equivalence; Walras, Marie-Esprit-Léon, on Ricardo.

References

Kurz, H.D. (2012), *Innovation, Knowledge and Growth. Adam Smith, Schumpeter and the Moderns*, London: Routledge.

Kurz, H.D. and N. Salvadori ([2002] 2007), 'One theory or two? Walras's critique of Ricardo', *History of Political Economy*, **42**(2), 365–98; reprinted in H.D. Kurz and N. Salvadori, *Interpreting Classical Economics: Studies in Long-Period Analysis*, London: Routledge.

Marshall, A. (1890), *Principles of Economics*, London: Macmillan.

Schumpeter, J.A. ([1912] 1934), *Theorie der wirtschaftlichen Entwicklung*, Berlin: Duncker & Humblot; English translation of an abridged and revised version entitled *The Theory of Economic Development. An Inquiry into Profits, Capital, Credit, Interest, and the Business Cycle*, Cambridge, MA: Harvard University Press.

Schumpeter, J.A. (1914), 'Epochen der Dogmen- und Methodengeschichte', in M. Weber et al. (eds), *Grundriss der Sozialökonomik*, I, Tübingen: J.C.B. Mohr, pp. 19–124.

Schumpeter, J.A. ([1918] 1953), 'Die Krise des Steuerstaates', in *Zeitfragen aus dem Gebiet der Soziologie, Vol. 4*, Graz and Leipzig: Leuschner and Lubensky; reprinted in J.A. Schumpeter, *Aufsätze zur Soziologie*, (eds) E. Schneider and A. Spiethoff, Tübingen: J.C.B. Mohr, pp. 1–71.

Schumpeter, J.A. (1954), *History of Economic Analysis*, (ed.) E. Boody Schumpeter, London: Allen and Unwin.

Sraffa, P. (1960), *Production of Commodities by Means of Commodities: Prelude to a Critique of Economic Theory*, Cambridge, UK: Cambridge University Press.

Sraffa, Piero, on Ricardo

Piero Sraffa was born in Turin in 1898. After graduation from the local university he went to the London School of Economics (1921–22) where he attended lectures by Cannan, Foxwell and Gregory. During his first stay in England, Keynes asked him to contribute an article on the Italian banking system for the *Manchester Guardian*. The article was also published in Italian, and provoked fierce reactions by the Fascist government. In November 1923 Sraffa was appointed to a lectureship in Political Economy and Public Finance at the University of Perugia. The preparation of his lectures stimulated him to write 'Sulle relazioni fra costo e quantità prodotta' (1925), which contains an analysis of the foundations of decreasing, constant and increasing returns in Marshall's theory and a critical discussion of the latter's partial equilibrium approach. Not least due to this article Sraffa obtained a full professorship in Political Economy at the University of Cagliari, a post he held *in absentia* until the end of his life, donating his salary to the library. Edgeworth's high opinion of the article led to an invitation to publish a version of it in the *Economic Journal* (see Sraffa, 1926). Moreover, Sraffa was offered a lectureship in Cambridge. In October 1927 he began his teaching in Cambridge, giving courses on the theory of value and on the relationships between banks and industry in Continental Europe. He was to lecture for only three years (apart for a few years during the war), finding the very task increasingly difficult. In 1930 Sraffa was appointed to the position of the librarian of the Marshall Library and was also placed in charge of the Cambridge programme of graduate studies in economics. He gave up lecturing for good.

Shortly after his arrival in Cambridge Sraffa showed Keynes the set of propositions that were to grow into *Production of Commodities by Means of Commodities* (Sraffa, 1960). But his work on the manuscript was overwhelmed both by the intense debate in Cambridge surrounding Keynes's *Treatise on Money*, and later, *The General Theory*, and by Sraffa assuming the editorship of the Royal Economic Society edition of *The Works, and Correspondence of David Ricardo* in 1930. By the late 1940s, the publication of the Ricardo edition had long been delayed. (For the causes of this delay, see Pollit, 1988 and Gehrke and Kurz, 2002.) The first volumes of the *Works and Correspondence of David Ricardo* were finally published in 1951. The edition, for which Sraffa was awarded in 1961 the Söderstrom gold medal by the Swedish Royal Academy, is widely acknowledged to be a scholarly masterpiece. In the late 1950s Sraffa eventually found time to put together, revise and complete his notes on the classical approach to the theory of distribution and value, which were eventually published as *Production of Commodities* in 1960.

Ricardo's 'corn-ratio theory' of profits

In his Introduction to the *Principles* in *Works*, I, published in 1951, Sraffa interpreted Ricardo's 1815 *Essay on Profits* as being based on the idea that there was a trade or sector in the economy that was 'in the special condition of not employing the products of other trades while all the others must employ *its* product as capital' (*Works*, I: xxxi; original emphasis). The sector under consideration was agriculture or, more precisely, the growing of corn. This interpretation Sraffa therefore called the 'corn-ratio theory'. It allowed one to determine the rate of profits in the sector under consideration in purely material terms as the surplus (exclusive of rent) obtained in the sector, a quantity of corn, divided by the capital advanced in the sector, another quantity of corn – without any reference to values. But the rate of profit so determined is also the general rate of profit, since in the case of free competition all other trades or sectors yield to the proprietors of capital the *same* rate of profit:

> [If] there is to be a uniform rate of profit in all trades it is the exchangeable values of the prod-ucts of the *other* trades relatively to their own capitals (*i.e.* relatively to corn) that must be adjusted so as to yield the same rate of profit as has been established in the growing of corn; since in the latter no value changes can alter the ratio of product to capital, both consisting of the same commodity. (Ibid.; original emphasis)

In his 1960 book Sraffa explains when he had arrived at this interpretation. He writes: 'It should perhaps be stated that it was only when the Standard system and the distinc-tion between basics and non-basics had emerged in the course of the present investiga-tion that the [corn-ratio] theory suggested itself as a natural consequence' (Sraffa, 1960: 93). He takes this opportunity to draw the reader's attention to a find he had made in 1927 when reading the French edition of Marx's *Theorien über den Mehrwert*:

> Ricardo's view of the dominant role of the farmer's profits thus appears to have a point of contact with the Physiocratic doctrine of the 'produit net' in so far as the latter is based, as Marx had pointed out [the reference is to Marx, 1969: 46 and to Marx, 1972: 115–16], on the 'physical' nature of the surplus in agriculture which takes the form of an excess of food pro-duced over the food advanced for production; whereas in manufacturing, where food and raw materials must be bought from agriculture, a surplus can only appear as a result of the sale of the product. (Ibid.)

While Sraffa had taken note of Marx's interpretation earlier, it played no role in the systems of equations he elaborated in the first period of his reconstructive work (1927–31). It was only in the second period, starting in 1942, that he introduced the distinction between basic and non-basic commodities, where the former refer to com-modities that enter directly or indirectly into the production of all commodities, while the latter don't. Corn in Marx's interpretation of the Physiocrats is a basic and the only basic commodity, whereas all the other commodities are non-basic. This distinction plays a crucial role in the concepts of the standard system and standard commodity, which Sraffa had succeeded in elaborating (with the help of Abram S. Besicovitch, one of his 'mathematical friends') by May 1944, and in which non-basics have been eliminated (see Kurz and Salvadori, 2008).

With these findings at the back of his mind, Sraffa (with the help of Dobb) then composed his Introduction to Volume I of the *Works*. There he stressed the following:

> The nearest that Ricardo comes to an explicit statement on these lines [i.e., the corn-ratio theory] is in a striking passage in a letter of June 1814: 'The rate of profits and of interest must depend on the proportion of production to the consumption necessary to such production.' [*Works*, VI: 108] The numerical examples in the *Essay* reflect this approach; and particularly in the well-known Table which shows the effects of an increase of capital, both capital and the 'neat produce' are expressed in corn, and thus the profit per cent is calculated without need to mention price. (*Works*, I: xxxii)

In a footnote appended to the word 'Table', Sraffa drew attention to Malthus's criticism of 'the fault of Mr. Ricardo's table', since circulating capital (which includes real wages) did not only consist of corn, but included 'tea sugar cloaths&c for the labourers' (ibid.: xxxii, n4). With the price of corn as the standard of value, the prices of manufactured products were bound to decrease in terms of corn as less and less fertile lands had to be cultivated (and setting aside technical progress). Ricardo did not, of course, need to be convinced by Malthus that capital and wages in agriculture consist of several commodities and not only of corn (a term that, by the way, stood for a composite commodity like 'bread' in the Bible and in Petty). But then, in the *Essay*, after having stated the obvious in the text himself, Ricardo simply ignored it in the table! Indeed, Ricardo stuck unswervingly to his basic vision that the rate of profit could be conceived of in purely physical terms, and that a deeper analysis than Malthus's shallow proposition was both needed and indeed possible, which Ricardo paraphrased, saying that: 'the profits of the farmer no more regulate the profits of other trades, than the profits of other trades regulate the profits of the farmer' (*Works*, VI: 104). This proposition is of no use at all in understanding *how* that regulation is actually meant to work. Ricardo formulated a particularly clear expression of his basic vision some six years later in a letter to McCulloch of 13 June 1820 – to Sraffa (*Works*, I: xxxiii) 'an echo of the old corn-ratio theory'. In it Ricardo insisted: 'After all the great questions of Rent, Wages, and Profits must be explained by the proportions in which the whole produce is divided between landlords, capitalists, and labourers, *and which are not essentially connected with the doctrine of value*' (*Works*, VIII: 194; emphasis added).

As Sraffa stressed, Ricardo's new theory was available only in 'fragmentary terms' in the *Essay*. The two most important fragments were those just mentioned. Let us recall what Ricardo said about his numerical examples, tables, and so on: 'In all these calculations I have been desirous only to elucidate the principle, and it is scarcely necessary to observe, that my whole basis is assumed at random, and merely for the purpose of exemplification' (*Works*, I: 121). The passage, he added, may also be read as a comment on the table in the *Essay*: 'My object has been to simplify the subject, and I have therefore made no allowance for the increasing price of the other necessaries, besides food, of the labourer' (ibid.: 121–2). Ricardo tried to avoid getting entangled in a myriad of complex relationships, whose precise form neither he nor anyone else (including, of course, Malthus) knew at the time. In a letter to Malthus of 17 April 1815 Ricardo spoke of his 'simple doctrine', designed to 'account for all the phenomena in an easy, natural manner' and thus stay away from 'a labyrinth of difficulties' (*Works*, VI: 214). In short, Ricardo upheld his basic vision as to how the rate of profits was determined. He was convinced of the explanatory power of his novel view, although he was not yet possessed of the tools to bring it to full fruition.

On the Principles of Political Economy, and Taxation

According to Sraffa, in the first edition of the *Principles* Ricardo adopted the labour theory as 'a general theory of value' (*Works*, I: xxxii). Indeed, he took the exchange values of commodities to be proportional to the ratios of the quantities of labour needed directly and indirectly in the production of commodities. The labour theory of value involved several analytical advantages compared with the corn-ratio theory in the *Essay*. First, it allowed Ricardo to counter Malthus's criticism effectively by conceiving of real wages as consisting not only of corn, but also of manufactured products (tea, sugar etc.). Possessed of a common measure of value – labour – heterogeneous commodities can be aggregated. Second, this also applies to the determination of the rate of profit for the economic system as a whole with reference to all trades that contributed, directly or indirectly, to the production of wage-goods. Since, physically, the rate of profit is the ratio of two bundles of heterogeneous commodities – with the surplus product in the numerator and the capital advanced in the denominator – the two bundles are made commensurable by assessing them in labour value terms. As Sraffa (*Works*, I: xxxii) put it:

> It was now labour, instead of corn, that appeared on both sides of the account – in modern terms, both as input and output: as a result, the rate of profits was no longer determined by the ratio of corn produced to the corn used up in production, but, instead, by the ratio of the total labour of the country to the labour required to produce the necessaries for that labour.

Sraffa added, however, in parentheses, that while the corn-ratio theory is absent in the *Principles*, 'the more general proposition that the productivity of labour on land which pays no rent is fundamental in determining general profits continues to occupy a central position' (ibid.: xxxiii). The 'turning point' in this transition from the *Essay* to the *Principles* Sraffa sees in a letter to James Mill on 30 December 1815, in which Ricardo wrote: 'I know I shall be soon stopped by the word price' (*Works*, VI: 348), thereby indicating that what was needed was a general theory of value, which Ricardo thought he had found in the labour value-principle.

We may add that there is still another echo of the old corn-ratio theory of profits in the *Principles*, not mentioned by Sraffa. (See, however, the section on Sraffa's reconstructive and interpretive work below, which relates what is being said in the following to Sraffa's reconstructive work in the late 1920s and early 1930s.) In all three editions we encounter a numerical example that satisfies the homogeneity condition between aggregate output and aggregate capital (see *Works*, I: 50 and 64–6). In the example there are three commodities, all of which enter the real wage rate and thus count as 'necessaries' or capital goods needed in the production of the three commodities themselves (and also in the production of other commodities, about which Ricardo does not speak in the context under consideration). The three commodities are hats, coats and corn. Ricardo assumes that of 100 units produced of each of them workers and landlords are paid 25 (or 22) units each. Profits consist accordingly of 50 (or 56) units of each commodity. If capital consists only of the real wages bill, an assumption Ricardo employs in much of his reasoning on profits, the rate of profits can be ascertained independently of values and equals $50/25 = 2$ (or $56/22 = 28/11$). Here we have a case in which the vector of the surplus product and the vector of the capital advanced are linearly dependent and in which, therefore, the rate of profits can be ascertained in purely material terms, confirming Ricardo's dictum that the questions of wages, profits and rent 'are not essentially connected with the doctrine of value'. Here we also have a clear expression of what Ricardo meant by the 'proportions in which the whole produce is divided between landlords, capitalists, and labourers'. Ricardo actually introduced the above example in the following terms:

> It is according to the division of the whole produce of the land and labour of the country, between the three classes of landlords, capitalists, and labourers, that we are to judge of rent, profit, and wages, and *not* according to the *value* at which that produce may be estimated in a medium which is confessedly variable. (*Works*, I: 64; emphasis added)

Last but not least, we also have the inverse relationship between the rate of profits and real wages (and rents), which reflects Ricardo's fundamental theorem of distribution. For example, if wages fell from 25 to 22 units, profits would increase from 50 to 56 units, and the rate of profits would rise from 200 per cent to approximately 254.55 per cent.

Taking into account a multiplicity of wage (or capital) goods, as Malthus had requested, does not spell trouble for Ricardo's grand vision of the factors affecting the general rate of profits and the possibility of conceiving of it in physical terms. As Ricardo made clear on various occasions, the rate depends on the conditions of production in all industries that directly or indirectly contribute to the production of wage-goods, while it does not depend on the conditions of production of luxuries. Ricardo's above example thus could be said to elevate the corn-ratio theory from its previous single (and implicitly composite) commodity conceptualization to an explicitly multi-commodity one. It preserves Ricardo's two fundamental insights, or analytical 'fragments', mentioned above.

These echoes of the old corn-ratio theory notwithstanding, in the *Principles* Ricardo based his argument firmly on the labour theory of value. He attached great importance to it, because it allowed him to dispel two doctrines advocated by Adam Smith. First a rise in real wages did not imply a rise in the prices of all products. This popular doctrine ignores the fact that in given conditions of production a rise in wages is necessarily associated with a fall in the rate of profits, and vice versa; that is, Ricardo's fundamental theorem of income distribution. A rise in wages, therefore, increases only the prices of those commodities whose production exhibits a higher proportion of direct labour to capital goods (or capital goods of a greater durability etc.) than the production of the commodity that is taken as the measure of value. Commodities produced with a lower proportion would instead fall in value relative to the standard. Second, Smith had argued that in an advanced stage of society the prices of all commodities resolve ultimately in three components, wages, profits and rents, and that the natural price varies with the natural rate of each of its component parts, of wages, profits and rents. (It deserves to be mentioned that in other parts of his analysis in the *Wealth of Nations*, Smith comes close to a correct view.) This is what Sraffa dubbed Smith's 'adding-up' theory of value (*Works*, I: xxxv). To this Ricardo objected that the sharing out of the product amongst the different classes of society has no bearing on the relative values of commodities, which are entirely regulated by the 'mere quantity of labour that was necessary to their production' (ibid.: 23n). In addition he insisted in the chapter 'On Rent' (ibid.: Chapter II) that the natural price of corn is determined on the least fertile land cultivated, which pays no rent.

However, it did not escape Ricardo's acuteness for long that relative prices also depend on the proportion of labour to capital in the various trades and the durability of the capital goods employed. This latter influence had to be acknowledged, but in Ricardo's view it only modified the labour-based principle, but did not overturn it. As he stated in a letter to Mill on 28 December 1818: 'exchangeable value varies . . . owing only to two causes: one the more or less quantity of labour required, the other the greater or less durability of capital: – that the former is never superseded by the latter, but is only modified by it' (*Works*, VII: 377).

This position reappears in the second and third editions of the *Principles*, published in 1819 and 1821, respectively, and has been interpreted by some commentators, in particular Jacob Hollander and Edwin Cannan, as a steady 'retreat' from the theory of value presented in the first edition (for evidence cited by Sraffa, see *Works*, I: xxxvii). Sraffa disagrees with this interpretation with reference to the evidence laid out in Ricardo's correspondence (large parts of which had not been available to the commentators). While Sraffa admits that 'the alterations were certainly extensive', he insists that 'an examination of the changes in the text in the light of the new evidence lends no support to this view: the theory of edition 3 appears to be the same, in essence and in emphasis, as that of edition 1' (ibid.: xxxviii). In support of Sraffa's view, it suffices to draw attention to Ricardo's letter of 25 January 1821, in which Ricardo emphasized: 'I am fully persuaded that in fixing on the quantity of labour realised in commodities as a rule which governs their relative value we are in the right course' (*Works*, VIII: 344). There could be no doubt that relative prices also depended on the distribution of the product, but taking it into account, Ricardo surmised, did not change the picture by much.

An invariable standard of value

A theme that preoccupied Ricardo to the end of his life consisted in finding the properties that a commodity is supposed to have in order to be 'invariable' in value. Sraffa interpreted this concern as coming close 'to identifying the problem of a measure with that of the law of value' (*Works*, I: xli).

The problem with which Ricardo originally struggled was, if the exchange value of two commodities changes, what is the source of the change? Is it due to a change in the conditions of production of the first, of the second or of both commodities? In order to decide this it would be good to be possessed of a commodity that would require 'at all times, and under all circumstances, precisely the same quantity of labour' to produce it (ibid.: 27n and 17n). In terms of such a commodity, any change in the price of another commodity could always unambiguously be attributed to a change in the conditions of production of the latter. While Ricardo was convinced that such a commodity did not exist in reality, he felt that it was sufficient to know what its essential properties were.

While in the first and second editions Ricardo retained this specification of the invariable measure of value, in the third edition he noted that a commodity possessed of these properties still 'would not be a perfect standard or invariable measure of value', because 'it would be subject to relative variations from a rise or fall of wages' (ibid.: 44). Hence, the same cause that had made him modify his labour value-principle now forced him to also modify his concept of an invariable measure of value. Such a measure did not only have to be produced with a constant amount of labour, it also had to exhibit proportions of direct labour and capital goods of various durability that would not necessitate a change in its price, because a rise (fall) of wages would increase (decrease) the price by the same amount as the corresponding fall (rise) in the rate of profits would decrease (increase) it. Specifying the proportions under consideration preoccupied Ricardo even after the publication of the third edition of the *Principles*, as his manuscript fragments on 'Absolute Value and Exchangeable Value', written towards the end of his life, show (*Works*, IV). Here we cannot enter into a deeper discussion of this problem; see, therefore, Sraffa (*Works*, I: xli–xlix) and Kurz and Salvadori (1993). It suffices to observe that the two concepts of invariability invoked by Ricardo refer to two different realms of analysis that must not be confounded. A concern with a measure that is always produced with the same amount of labour (while the commodities to be measured are not) belongs to intertemporal and interspatial comparisons, that is, to different technical environments, whereas a concern with a measure that does not react upon changes in income distribution belongs to comparisons given the same technical environment. To be clear, Sraffa's device of the standard commodity (1960: Chapter IV) was exclusively concerned with the latter kind of comparisons. For the latter kind of comparisons, a perfect measure can be constructed (provided it exists) and consists of a composite commodity made up of well-specified amounts of all basic products in the system, whereas non-basics play no role. As regards the former kind of comparisons, a perfect measure can only be found in exceptionally special (and not very interesting) conditions (see Kurz and Salvadori, 1993). In general, one has to have recourse to index numbers.

Foreign trade

In November 1929 the *Quarterly Journal of Economics* published a paper by Luigi Einaudi (1929), who attributed to Ricardo an error in his presentation of the theory of comparative costs. In a note published in the same journal in May 1930, Sraffa showed that Ricardo's alleged error had in fact been committed by James Mill and had already been wrongly attributed to Ricardo by John Stuart Mill. In his reply Einaudi admitted his mistake. Ironically, Sraffa's rectification has not prevented economists at large to see Ricardo's theory of comparative costs through the lens of the two Mills. It was only recently that Sraffa's argument was rediscovered (see Ruffin, 2002), giving rise to a renewed interest in Ricardo's view on foreign trade (see Gehrke, 2014). In the following a brief summary account of Sraffa's argument is given.

The starting point of the debate is the numerical example that James Mill (1821: 86) used to illustrate the principle of comparative cost. He considered the trade of English cloth for Polish corn, and based his reasoning on the following assumptions, shown in Table 7.

He then argued that England, with the quantity of cloth that it produces with 150

Table 7 Days' labour required for producing a unit of cloth and corn

	Cloth	Corn
In Poland	100	100
In England	150	200

days' labour is able to purchase as much corn in Poland that is produced with 100 days' labour. Had this quantity of corn been produced in England, it would have required 200 days' labour. Mill concluded that England gains 50 days' labour from the transaction. Sraffa comments on this:

> So far, we cannot properly speak of an error. To take, as James Mill does, the extreme case in which the ratio of interchange is such that the whole gain is reaped by one of the two trading countries to the exclusion of the other, and use it to illustrate the general theory of foreign trade, is highly misleading; but in itself it does not involve a contradiction. The fallacy comes in with the next step in Mill's argument. (Sraffa, 1930: 539–40)

Mill first says in exchanging corn for cloth, Poland will obtain three pieces for three quarters, but then he says that it will obtain four pieces for three quarters. Obviously, both propositions cannot be true at the same time.

While the error was removed from the third edition of James Mill's *Elements* (1826), John Stuart Mill in his essay 'Of the Laws of Interchange between Nations' (1844: 5–6) made Ricardo 'appear as the villain of the piece' (Sraffa, 1930: 540). Sraffa adds: 'But if we turn to Ricardo's chapter on "Foreign Trade" we find no trace of the error, or even of a mere oversight.' According to the ratio of interchange assumed in Ricardo's famous numerical example, Sraffa continues:

> This ratio of interchange, it may be noticed, involves that the additional product is divided between the two countries, and not that it is gained entirely by one. England gives the cloth produced by 100 Englishmen in exchange for the wine produced by 80 Portuguese; and since this quantity could only have been produced by 120 Englishmen, she gains the labour of 20 Englishmen. Portugal gives the wine produced by 80 Portuguese for the cloth produced by 100 Englishmen; the production of this cloth would have required the labour of 90 Portuguese, and therefore Portugal gains the labour of 10 Portuguese. In no part of this chapter, nor elsewhere so far as I can see, does Ricardo say, or imply, that the ratio of interchange between England and Portugal is inconsistent with the ratio of interchange between Portugal and England – as James Mill does in his first edition. (Ibid.: 541)

Sraffa concludes: 'Thus the account given by J. S. Mill in the Essay of 1844, according to which James Mill made the correction but not the error, must be exactly reversed' (ibid.)

Sraffa's reconstructive and interpretive work
In this section we deal briefly with Sraffa's reconstruction of the classical approach to the theory of value and distribution. This work, which was carried out in three periods of time (1927–31, 1942–46 and 1955–59) and culminated in the publication of *Production of Commodities* (1960), took place partly in parallel with the Ricardo edition, but was also twice interrupted by it, each time for around a decade. In Sraffa's Papers kept at the Wren Library, Trinity College, Cambridge, there is compelling evidence that Sraffa's reconstructive and editorial work benefited from one another and that much of Sraffa's analytical work especially in the first period was inspired by reading Ricardo. The reader interested in a more complete picture of Sraffa's early attempts to come to grips with and reformulate the classical approach is invited to consult Kurz (2003), Kurz and Salvadori (2005), Gehrke and Kurz (2006) and Kurz (2013).

In his papers published in the mid-1920s, Sraffa (1925, 1926) had argued that Marshall's partial equilibrium analysis did not stand up to close scrutiny. However, for a while he still appears to have accepted the idea that Marshall *was* economics and that any new development had to start from him. When in the late 1920s he put himself to the task of making a fresh start, he briefly thought that this required purging Marshall's theory of all subjectivist elements. These were expressed in Marshall's misleading concept of 'real costs', under which he subsumed disutility of labour, sacrifice, abstinence and the like. Sraffa felt that these elements could not possibly be measured, because they are not defined in terms of the method of measuring them, and because they made the theory vulnerable to ideological abuse. And he understood that Marshall's interpretation of the classical economists as early marginalists trying to come out could not be sustained. Alas, their standpoint, Sraffa was to write later 'had been submerged and forgotten since the advent of the "marginal" method' (Sraffa, 1960: v) under thick layers of interpretation. He saw that their approach to an explanation of income distribution and relative prices was very different from the later marginalist authors. But wherein precisely did their approach consist? And could it be revived by means of a reformulation that elaborated on its strengths and shunted its deficiencies?

As regards his reconstructive work, Sraffa in the late 1920s had convinced himself that in the classical authors the value of a commodity reflected the difficulty of producing it. This difficulty was reflected by the amounts of commodities – means of production and means of subsistence – that have to be used up or 'destroyed' in order to bring about the production of the commodity under consideration. In short, what mattered are 'physical real costs' of production, a concept that Sraffa put against Marshall's concept of 'real costs'. The problem was: how does one get from a vector of heterogeneous commodities, physical real costs, to the value of a commodity, a scalar magnitude? Rescuing the standpoint of the classical economists from oblivion required reformulating their theory in terms of simultaneous equations.

In Sraffa's view the classical authors' resort to the labour theory of value was unfortunate and expressed a mismatch between the analytical tools at their disposal and the complexity of the problems they tackled. In his notes composed in the late 1920s Sraffa insisted repeatedly that the labour theory of value involved a 'corruption' of what he considered to be the right concept of cost – physical real cost – which had been advocated by William Petty and the Physiocrats. In November 1927 Sraffa began to study the mathematical properties of what he called his 'first' and 'second equations', that is, systems of equations of production with and without a social surplus. In the former case the economy produces just as much as is being used up of the various commodities as necessary means of production and necessary means of sustenance of workers. It deals with the case of pure necessities. In the latter case the economy produces more of at least some of the products than is being used up of them in the course of production and of no product less than what is being consumed productively. In this case a surplus or net product obtains, which Sraffa then took to be appropriated in terms of a uniform rate of return on the capital invested in the different sectors of the economy. In a third step Sraffa then discussed the implications of a distribution of the surplus away from interest or profits and towards workers. He did so very much like Ricardo in a numerical example in all three editions of the *Principles* (see *Works*, I: 64–5 and the second section above) by contemplating situations in which a growing proportional share of the given surplus is added to subsistence wages and correspondingly taken away from capital income.

Sraffa succeeded in quickly establishing the following facts: first, in a system without a surplus, relative prices are fully determined by the technical conditions of production, that is, real physical costs. Second, in a system with a surplus, this result extends to the determination of the general rate of profits. Third, the rate of profits is inversely related to the share of wages in the surplus product. This reflects Ricardo's fundamental law of income distribution: 'The greater the portion of the result of labour that is given to the labourer, the smaller must be the rate of profits, and vice versa' (*Works*, VIII: 194). Fourth, a change in income distribution affects relative prices: 'It is as clear as sunlight that if wages change values also change' (Sraffa Papers, D3/12/7: 95; our translation from Italian). Fifth, durable or fixed capital can be dealt with in terms of the annuity method, which Ricardo employed in the *Principles* (see Kurz and Salvadori, 2005). The annuity gives that part of the price of a product that is due to the presence of a durable instrument of production and covers the depreciation of the ageing instrument and the profits on it.

In all this there was no need to refer to 'quantities of labour' or 'labour values': the physical data concerning production conditions and real wages were enough to accomplish the task. In fact, it was far from clear what could have been meant by the 'quantities of labour' carried out by different workers or by the 'labour value' of a commodity. As Sraffa stressed repeatedly at the time, what matters are not hours of work performed but the actual advancement of wage-goods to workers. The case of a worker in agriculture whose upkeep and that of his family has to be guaranteed during the entire year and not only during the working seasons underscored the correctness of Petty's concern with 'food' rather than labour. As Petty and the Physiocrats knew well, in agriculture workers have to be fed and sheltered even in periods when natural conditions prevent them from performing at all or at least from performing their normal tasks, such as in winter. (See Sraffa's observations in Sraffa Papers, D3/12/12: 8, composed in summer 1929.) What mattered were the amounts of the means of subsistence in the support of workers and their families. This is why Sraffa in the summer or autumn of 1929 still expressed doubts as to whether 'quantities of labour' are to be taken as 'known' or 'given' in the theory of value (see Sraffa Papers, D3/12/13: 2–5). Seen from the physical real cost point of view, the labour value-based reasoning must indeed have looked like a 'corruption' of the 'true' concept of cost and value.

What Sraffa apparently did not know at the time was that, ironically, in the no-surplus case solving a system of simultaneous equations of the type above arrives at the same exchange ratios between commodities as a consistently formulated labour theory of value. In a system with a circular flow of production, the latter also presupposes solving a system of simultaneous equations, in which 'food' is replaced by the corresponding amounts of concrete labour and different kinds of labour have to be made commensurable by means of the structure of real wages (see Kurz and Salvadori, 2009). This became clear to Sraffa at the latest when in the 1940s he resumed his reconstructive work. He then significantly spoke of the 'Value Theory of Labour'.

Ricardo's deep conviction that the problem of income distribution is not necessarily connected with the theory of value (see the second section above) plays an important role in Sraffa's early manuscripts. At one point he entertained an idea echoing Ricardo's numerical example with three commodities (hats, coats and corn) above. In a document dated February 1931, he wrote: 'it may be said that the value of total capital in terms of total goods produced cannot vary [consequent upon a change in income distribution], since the goods are composed exactly in the same proportions as the capitals which have produced them' – which is precisely the case in Ricardo's example. Sraffa added that this proposition is, of course, 'false, but may contain an element of truth' (Sraffa Papers, D3/12/7: 157(3)). Twelve years later, in November 1943, he stressed that this proposition was based on the assumption of a 'statistical compensation of large numbers' (Sraffa Papers, D3/12/35: 28), and then the proposition recurred under the name 'My Hypothesis' or simply 'Hypothesis', before Sraffa succeeded in elaborating the standard commodity in early 1944. The standard system, Sraffa emphasized, provides 'tangible evidence of the rate of profits as a non-price phenomenon' (Sraffa Papers, D3/12/43: 4), confirming the correctness of Ricardo's conjecture above (see also Kurz, 2011).

In view of these facts, the time, energy and heat devoted to a discussion of the simple 'corn model' in the literature following Sraffa's interpretation of Ricardo in *Works*, I and then in his book (1960: 93) appears to be out of proportion to its importance. Concerned with elaborating a general theory of value and therefore not much interested in special cases, which, suggestive as they may be, Ricardo had already left behind in the *Principles*, the 'basic principle' at work had to be shown to be valid in general. The previous discussion also shows that Ricardo's search for an 'invariable measure of value' as a 'medium between the extremes', prompted Sraffa to elaborate the concept of the standard system and standard commodity. In fact, Sraffa emphasized that the standard commodity 'has been evolved from it' (1960: 94).

This should be enough to see how closely knit Sraffa's reconstructive and editorial works were. From an early time Sraffa tried to understand the classical economists', and especially Ricardo's, approach to the problem of value and distribution by reformulating it in a consistent and general way.

HEINZ D. KURZ AND NERI SALVADORI

See also:

Biaujeaud, Huguette, on Ricardo; Corn Model; *Essay on Profits*; Foreign Trade; Invariable Measure of Value; *Principles of Political Economy, and Taxation*.

References

Einaudi, L. (1929), 'James Pennington or James Mill: an early correction of Ricardo', *Quarterly Journal of Economics*, **43**(1), 164–71.
Gehrke, C. (2014), 'Ricardo's discovery of comparative advantage revisited', manuscript, University of Graz.
Gehrke, C. and H.D. Kurz (2002), 'Keynes and Sraffa's "difficulties with J.H. Hollander." A note on the history of the RES edition of *The Works, and Correspondence of David Ricardo*', *European Journal of the History of Economic Thought*, **9**(4), 644–71.
Gehrke, C. and H.D. Kurz (2006), 'Sraffa on von Bortkiewicz: reconstructing the classical theory of value and distribution', *History of Political Economy*, **38**(1), 91–149.
Kurz, H.D. (2003), 'The surplus interpretation of the classical economists', in W. Samuels, J. Biddle and J. Davis (eds), *The Blackwell Companion to the History of Economic Thought*, Oxford: Blackwell, pp. 167–83.
Kurz, H.D. (2011), 'On David Ricardo's theory of profits: the laws of distribution are "not essentially connected with the doctrine of value"', *History of Economic Thought*, **53**(1), 1–20.
Kurz, H.D. (2013), 'Don't treat too ill my Piero! Interpreting Sraffa's papers', *Cambridge Journal of Economics*, **36**(6), 1535–69.
Kurz, H.D. and N. Salvadori (1993), 'The "standard commodity" and Ricardo's search for an "invariable measure of value"', in M. Baranzini and G.C. Harcourt (eds), *The Dynamics of the Wealth of Nations. Growth, Distribution and Structural Change*, London: Macmillan, pp. 95–123.
Kurz, H.D. and N. Salvadori (2005), 'Removing an "insuperable obstacle" in the way of an objectivist analysis: Sraffa's attempts at fixed capital', *The European Journal of the History of Economic Thought*, **12**(3), 493–523.
Kurz, H.D. and N. Salvadori (2008), 'On the collaboration between Sraffa and Besicovitch: the "proof

of gradient"', in G. Chiodi and L. Ditta (eds), *Sraffa or an Alternative Economics*, New York: Palgrave Macmillan, pp. 260–74.

Kurz, H.D. and N. Salvadori (2009), 'Sraffa and the labour theory of value: a few observations', in J. Vint, S. Metcalfe, H.D. Kurz, N. Salvadori and P.A. Samuelson (eds), *Economic Theory and Economic Thought. Essays in Honour of Ian Steedman*, London: Routledge, pp. 189–215.

Marx, K. (1969), *Theories of Surplus Value, Part I*, London: Lawrence & Wishart.

Marx, K. (1972), *Theories of Surplus Value, Part III*, London: Lawrence & Wishart.

Mill, J. (1821), *Elements of Political Economy*, London: Baldwin, Cradock and Joy.

Mill, J. (1826), *Elements of Political Economy*, 3rd revised and corrected edition, London: Baldwin, Cradock and Joy.

Mill, J.S. (1844), 'Of the laws of interchange between nations: and the distribution of the gains of commerce among the countries of the commercial world', *in Essays on Some Unsettled Questions of Political Economy*, London: Longmans, Green, Reader, and Dyer.

Pollitt, B.H. (1988), 'The collaboration of Maurice Dobb in Sraffa's edition of Ricardo', *Cambridge Journal of Economics*, **12**(1), 55–65.

Ruffin, R.J. (2002), 'David Ricardo's discovery of comparative advantage', *History of Political Economy*, **34**(4), 727–48.

Sraffa, P. (1925), 'Sulle relazioni fra costo e quantità prodotta', *Annali di Economia*, **2**, 277–328.

Sraffa, P. (1926), 'The laws of returns under competitive conditions', *Economic Journal*, **36**(144), 535–50.

Sraffa, P. (1930), 'An alleged correction of Ricardo', *The Quarterly Journal of Economics*, **44**(3), 539–44.

Sraffa, P. (1960), *Production of Commodities by Means of Commodities. Prelude to a Critique of Economic Theory*, Cambridge, UK: Cambridge University Press.

Surplus

The surplus concept plays a key part in the classical theory of distribution, where it is defined as the part of total product left after providing for the replacement of the means of production consumed and the subsistence of the workers employed.

If workers' subsistence, the technical conditions of production and the gross social product of the economy (assumed for simplicity to be in a 'self-replacing state'; see Sraffa, 1960: 11), are taken as known, the latter can be divided into two parts. The first consists of the commodities needed for repetition of the production process, what Ricardo called 'necessary consumption' (*Works*, VI: 108). The second and residual part of the total product is the surplus, an amount of commodities that can be freely disposed of without prejudice to the possibility of repeating the production process on the same scale.

By virtue of its schematic representation of a pre-capitalistic agricultural economy, François Quesnay's *Tableau Economique* (1766) presents one of the simplest forms of the social surplus. This *produit net* is the part of the annual crop remaining after the necessary replacement of the *avances annuel*, which include means of production and subsistence for workers in agriculture. With its physical homogeneity between the commodities produced and those constituting necessary consumption, the particular position of the agricultural sector, at least in the France of Quesnay's day, made it possible to see the surplus without the difficulties connected with value that will be discussed below. Moreover, since the manufacturing sector was not in such a favourable position, Quesnay and the other Physiocrats believed that agriculture alone yielded a surplus, which was viewed as a 'gift' arising from the contribution of land to human activity.

The fundamental feature of Quesnay's *produit net* is its disposability. Normal repetition of the process, with no change in scale, entails no particular use or distribution of that surplus, even though in the society Quesnay was considering it actually went to the *classe des propriétaires*, which included the sovereign, landowners and recipients of tithes (*décimateurs*). In the capitalist economies that Ricardo referred to in his analysis, the division of the surplus then became a more complex phenomenon involving all the different classes into which society is organized.

Surplus and income distribution in Ricardo

Investigation of the circumstances affecting the rate of profit is unquestionably a fundamental aim of economic theory. It is precisely in this respect that we are most indebted to Ricardo, who shed light – first in his *Essay on Profits* (*Works*, IV) and then in the *Principles* (*Works*, I) – both on the relationship between the wage rate and the rate of profit, and on the effect of the cultivation of less fertile soil on the latter.

Although the surplus is a social concept, since it can be determined in general only by referring to the economy as a whole, there are some particular cases in which it is possible to identify the contribution made by a specific sphere of economic activity to the formation of the social surplus. One of the best-known instances of this is unquestionably the agricultural sector in Ricardo's *Essay on Profits*.

As Sraffa remarked (*Works*, I: xxxi), the analysis developed in the *Essay on Profits* contains no explicit statement of the circumstances placing the sector of agriculture – or corn – in such a special position. Sraffa's reconstruction does, however, pinpoint two key assumptions: (a) that subsistence for workers consists of corn; and (b) that the capital employed in agriculture does not include the products of other trades (being essentially conceived as means of subsistence advanced to workers). As in the case of Quesnay's *produit net* considered above (with the noteworthy difference that in Quesnay's analysis the *produit net* was the social surplus and not a sectoral surplus), it is therefore possible to determine in pure physical terms the difference between gross output and necessary consumption for this sector, since both are amounts of corn.

Let P_c and N_c be the amounts of corn constituting respectively the gross output and necessary consumption related to production on the least fertile land under cultivation, which yields no rent since it is free and overabundant. The rate of profit on capital invested in this activity must be:

$$r_c = \frac{P_c - N_c}{N_c} = \frac{P_c}{N_c} - 1 \tag{1}$$

Due to capitalist competition, with its levelling effect on sectoral rates of profit, the rate r_c will correspond to the general rate of profit of the economy as a whole because, as Sraffa pointed out:

> [I]f there is to be a uniform rate of profit in all trades it is the exchangeable values of the products of *other* trades relatively to their own capitals (*i.e.* relatively to corn) that must be adjusted so as to yield the same rate of profit as has been established in the growing of corn; since in the latter no value changes can alter the ratio of product to capital, both consisting of the same commodity. (*Works*, I: xxxi; original emphasis)

Moreover, since the capital invested in the cultivation of land of differing quality must also yield the same rate of profit, the system of differential rent rates for all the qualities of land in use will be determined accordingly. Ricardo was thus able to combine his theory of profit with the theory of differential rent – which had been introduced by Anderson in the eighteenth century but came to his attention only after the publication of Malthus's *Inquiry into Rent* (*Works*, IV: 7) – and then to study the division of the agricultural surplus between profits and rents.

Consequently, according to Ricardo's analysis, a decrease in the ratio P_c/N_c entails a drop in the economy's normal rate of profit. Ricardo attempted to maintain this connection between profits, rents and wages in the *Principles* while at the same time abandoning the idea that the natural rate of profit is determined by the farmers' rate of profit. His attention then moved from the agricultural surplus, which he isolated in the *Essay on Profits* by means of the special assumptions listed above, to focus directly on the social surplus.

The major difficulty Ricardo encountered in this context was the question of value. As he wrote in an often quoted letter to Mill in December 1815, at the beginning of his work on the *Principles*, 'I know I shall soon be stopped by the word price' (*Works*, VI: 348). He was in fact trying to argue that the rate of profit must still 'depend on the proportion of production to the consumption necessary to such production' (ibid.: 108), as maintained in the *Essay on Profits*, but without the aid of the hypotheses that had enabled him to consider them as two quantities of corn and hence to determine their ratio independently of prices. Since the social surplus and necessary consumption are (generally) two aggregates of commodities taken in different proportions, the equation:

$$r = \frac{P - N}{N} \tag{2}$$

can be solved only by considering the quantities P and N – that is, the social product and the necessary consumption – in terms of value (Garegnani, 1984: 300, 301).

When P and N are magnitudes of value instead of physical quantities, the link connecting the distributive variable becomes less clear. If a rise in the wage rate causes an increase in the social product P in terms of value because of the change in the price system, for example, this can cloud our vision of the inverse relation between the profit and the wage rate. Adam Smith himself failed to perceive it, due to his 'adding-up' theory of value, and appears to have believed in the possibility of a situation where the rate of profit and the wage rate are both driven simultaneously to their minimum level by 'competition' (*WN*, I.ix.14).

The idea that the relative prices of commodities could be determined by the ratio of the quantities of labour they embody even in a society in which land and capital are privately owned enabled Ricardo to circumvent this problem. Once the labour theory of value is adopted, P and N become respectively – as Sraffa pointed out (*Works*, I: xxxii) – the 'total labour of the country' and the 'labour required to produce the necessaries for that labour', both of which are quantities independent of the rate of profit.

Ricardo was thus able to arrive at the same conclusion in the *Principles* as in the *Essay on Profits* with two differences: (a) the quantities of corn of the *Essay* were replaced by quantities of labour; (b) the assumption required in the *Essay* to isolate the agricultural surplus could be abandoned. Moreover, the inverse ratio between the rate of profit and the amount of labour embodied in the wage rate emerges very clearly in the *Principles*. If we assume that 'necessary consumption' consists solely of wages paid in advance, as we must in order to make the labour theory of value work, the ratio P/N turns out to be $1/w$, where w is precisely the wage rate in terms of labour value. Therefore:

> a rise of wages, from the circumstance of the labourer being more liberally rewarded, or from a difficulty of procuring the necessaries on which wages are expended, does not, except in some instances, produce the effect of raising price, but has a great effect in lowering profits. (*Works*, I: 48, 49)

The 'core' of the surplus theories

Ricardo considered the wages of labourers as given in his theory of profit. In particular, following Smith's distinction between natural and market level of prices, he claimed that the 'market price of labour' tends to conform to a natural level, understood as the wage 'which is necessary to enable the labourers, one with another, to subsist and perpetuate their race, without either increase or diminution' (*Works*, I: 93). Though set at the 'subsistence level', this wage rate was not, however, understood by Ricardo solely as the commodities necessary for the physiological preservation of a worker, but also as including 'those comforts which custom renders absolute necessaries' (ibid.: 94). We can therefore say in more general terms that the set of commodities forming the real wage rate, which may well be above mere subsistence, depends on elements and forces that cannot be considered without reference to a specific and historically observed social and institutional framework (cf. also Stirati, 1994; Garegnani, 2007; Levrero, 2011). But once this real wage rate is taken as given, as it is in Ricardo's theory of profit, together with the social product and the technical conditions of production, the part of the surplus that takes the form of non-wage income – profits and rents – depends on forces that are sufficiently abstract with respect to the social and institutional context to be treated in general terms.

Once the social product and the technology in use are known, the employment of labour and the quantity of the means of production consumed are determined accordingly. Assuming the economy to be in a self-replacing state, the social net product emerges physically after replacing all the means of production consumed. Non-wage incomes will then be determined ultimately by subtracting the commodities that pay the wages of the workers employed – resulting from the wage rate and the total employment of labour – from the social net product.

The surplus approach can thus be viewed as consisting of two separate stages of analysis that reflect the different nature of the relations to be considered. In what is known as the 'core' stage, the real wage rate, the social product and the technical conditions of production appear as already given (see Garegnani, 1984: 292–9; Kurz and Salvadori, 1995: 14, 15). This makes it possible to study the determination of incomes other than wages, as well as the system of relative prices, on a purely logical basis by means of deductive reasoning, and then to pinpoint these forces, which act essentially in the same way in every capitalist system.

Far more complex relations are considered in the other stage. In particular, the circumstances that appear as data in the 'core' are in fact affected by so many influences capable of combining in so many ways as to make it impossible to address them within a framework of abstract and general analysis. They must instead be considered with reference to the specific form in which these influences actually manifest themselves.

The phenomena typically addressed in this second stage of analysis include those regarding the determination of the wage rate, as briefly mentioned above, capital accumulation (see Ciccone, 1998: 443, 444) and technological change. They are in fact influenced by forces that do not act univocally, and so their effects can hardly be predicted in abstract or general terms. It is therefore necessary to consider them with reference to actual, historically observed situations, and therefore by means of a kind of analysis that is much closer to the inductive approach than the deductive one used in the core (see Garegnani, 2007: 186 and 189, 190).

The modern surplus approach to value and distribution

Even though Ricardo's arguments are strongly based on the hypothesis that commodities are exchanged with one other at a ratio determined by the quantities of labour they embody, his conclusions on the links between distributive variables have been shown to be valid in general, primarily by Sraffa (1960), and the scholars following the trail he blazed.

The attempt made by Ricardo – and Marx – to express the constraint connecting wages and profits in a single equation can, in fact, be maintained despite the fact that the normal prices of commodities are generally different from the ratios of the quantities of labour they embody. As argued by Garegnani (1984), the division of the surplus between profits and wages above the subsistence level (assuming for simplicity that fertile land is free and abundant, as in a newly colonized country) and their resulting rates can be addressed by means of either the 'price-equation method' or the 'surplus-equation method'. While these are basically equivalent, the latter offers some advantages in terms of simplicity and transparency.

The surplus-equation method consists essentially of a generalization of the arguments put forward by Ricardo and discussed above. In particular, as in the *Essay on Profits*, attention will focus on a specific sphere of activity, the one 'which regulates the profits of all other trades' (*Works*, IV: 104): the vertically integrated sector whose physical net output is the amount of the composite wage commodity required for the workers of the economy as a whole.

Let us consider an economy with n commodities, labelled 1, 2, . . ., n. Let us assume that the wage rate is w units of a composite 'wage commodity' and denote by $\lambda_j \geq 0$ the quantity of commodity j entering into the composition of a unit of this wage commodity (with $j = 1, 2, . . ., n$). Finally, let p_j the price of commodity j ($j = 1, 2, . . ., n$) and pl the value of a wage commodity, we have:

$$p_\lambda = \sum_{j=1}^{n} \lambda_j \cdot p_j. \tag{3}$$

If we adopt Smith's 'labour commanded' as the standard of value, which means taking w units of the wage commodity as the numéraire – and therefore $w \cdot p_\lambda = 1$ – the value of net product in this integrated sector is L, that is, the total employment of labour in the economy.

Let us now use L_v and K_j (with $j = 1, 2, . . ., n$) respectively to denote the quantities of labour and commodity j employed in the vertically integrated sector producing the wage commodity, referred to as the 'wage-commodity sector' for brevity.

If there are no extra profits in the wage-commodity sector, as should be the case in every sector in conditions of free competition, the value of its net product must equal the sum of wages and profits. Therefore, since $w \cdot p_\lambda = 1$, we have:

$$L = L_v + r \cdot \sum_{j=1}^{n} K_j \cdot p_j \tag{4}$$

or its equivalent:

$$\frac{L - L_v}{L_v} = r \cdot \sum_{j=1}^{n} \frac{K_j}{L_v} \cdot p_j. \tag{5}$$

In its simplicity, equation (5) gives rise to some interesting observations, which may also shed new light on Ricardo's theory of distribution. First of all, it should be noted that the expression $(L - L_v)/L_v$ coincides numerically with the ratio $(P - N)/N$ found in equation (2) above (the equation encapsulating the theory of profit in Ricardo's *Principles*), since $L = P$ is the total employment of labour of the economy and $L_v = N$ is the quantity of labour directly and indirectly embodied in the wages for L workers. While $(P - N)$ was the surplus value of the whole economy in terms of labour embodied in Ricardo's analysis, however, $(L - L_v)$ is now the surplus value of the wage-goods sector in terms of labour commanded.

Second, since it is not assumed that capital consists exclusively of wages paid in advance for one production cycle (which must instead be assumed in order to make Ricardo's analysis consistent), the ratio $(L - L_v)/L_v$ is not the rate of profit but simply the amount of profit per worker or what Marx called the 'rate of surplus value' (Marx, 1909: 37, 38), which is the same thing. In order to transform this rate of surplus value into the rate of profit, we must also consider the employment of capital per worker in the wage-goods sector, which is the value of the means of production per worker in the case examined here.

The third observation regards the right-hand side of equation (5), which represents the amount of profits per worker allowing remuneration of the capital employed in the wage-goods sector at a rate r. In the form in which the equation is written above, this amount depends explicitly on prices and is therefore not a 'surplus equation' in the strict sense because the rate of profit is not the only unknown appearing in it. As shown in Garegnani (1960 and 1984), however, this obstacle can be overcome by reducing the means of production to 'dated quantities of labour' (Sraffa, 1960: 34–5). Since capital is a produced input, we can list all the quantities of labour employed directly and indirectly in its production and use A_t (with $t = 1, 2, \ldots$) to denote the quantity of labour employed in the production of capital t periods (or stages) before the production process of the final output takes place. Accordingly, with A_0 as the amount of labour directly employed in the production of the final output (which is $w{\times}L$ units of the composite wage commodity), we have $A_0 + A_1 + A_2 + \ldots = L_v$. Recalling that value is expressed in terms of labour commanded and wages are paid *post factum* at the end of each stage of production (this is the only slight difference with the analysis in Garegnani, 1984), we can now rewrite equation (5) as follows:

$$\frac{L - L_v}{L_v} = r \cdot \sum_{t=1}^{\infty} \frac{A_t}{L_v} \cdot (1 + r)^t. \tag{6}$$

We thus finally arrive at an equation in which the rate of profits is the only unknown. The left-hand side of equation (6) shows the amount of surplus value per worker, in terms of labour commanded, in the integrated wage-commodity sector. As stated above, this is also the Marxian 'rate of surplus value' and depends exclusively on the amount of labour directly and indirectly embodied in the real wage rate. The right-hand side instead presents the profits per worker permitting the remuneration of capital at a rate r in the wage-commodity sector.

This amount of profits, expressed in terms of labour commanded, is a monotonically increasing function – called the 'profit function' and denoted by $f(r)$ – of the profit rate whose shape depends solely on the proportional distribution among the various stages of the labour embodied in the wage commodity, that is, on the ratios A_t/L_v with $t = 1, 2,$ ..., which are in turn an expression of the composition of the wage commodity and the technical conditions of its production. As a result, once the physical composition of the wage commodity is fixed, the possible changes in the level of the wage rate do not affect the shape of the profit function.

Plotting the profit function $f(r)$ in a diagram, as in Figure 21, makes it possible to determine the level of the rate of profits that solve the surplus equation (6) graphically. Given the wage rate level, the corresponding rate of surplus value $(L - L_v)/L_v$ is known as well. We can then determine the level of r that makes the profit per worker $f(r)$ equal to the given rate of surplus value. Given that $f(r)$ is a continuous function rising monotonically from the origin without a upper limit – in the case of circular production, $f(r) \to \infty$ as r tends in fact towards a 'maximum rate of profit' (see Garegnani, 1984: 317) – there

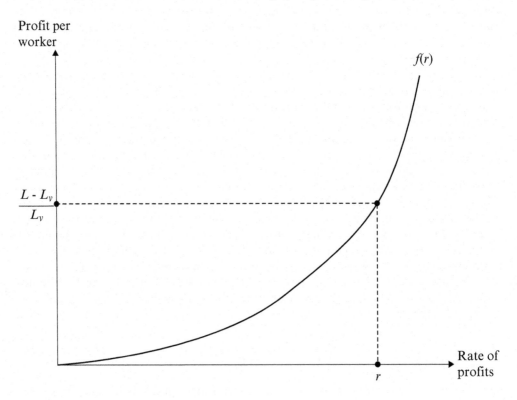

Figure 21   *The profit function*

is one and only one profit rate r solving the surplus equation (6) for a certain wage rate level.

Moreover, since the rate of surplus value $(L - L_v)/L_v$ will decrease with any rise in L_v, an increase of the quantity of the composite wage commodity that constitutes the wage rate (leaving its physical composition unchanged) will cause the rate of profit to decrease, as in Ricardo's analysis. Changes in the composition of the wage commodity must instead be considered case by case, since the only a priori claim that can be made in this connection is that such changes are expected in general to involve both a variation in L_v and a change of the shape of the profit function $f(r)$ (for further analysis, see Garegnani, 1987: 571, 572).

In conclusion, equation (6) makes it possible to address the division of the surplus and the resulting determination of the rate of profit in an extremely transparent way, as Ricardo attempted to do both in the *Essay on Profit* and in the *Principles*. While Ricardo based his analysis, however, on some special assumptions, which Marx himself never succeeded in eliminating completely, the argument developed here is wholly general. The division of the surplus in a particular sector of the economy is, in fact, considered, as in Ricardo's *Essay on Profits*, but without assuming either that wages consist solely of corn or that the net product and capital are physically homogeneous.

SAVERIO M. FRATINI

See also:

Capital and Profits; Corn Model; Invariable Measure of Value; Labour and Wages; Labour Theory of Value; *Principles of Political Economy, and Taxation*; Sraffa, Piero, on Ricardo.

References

Ciccone, R. (1998), 'Surplus', in H.D. Kurz and N. Salvadori (eds), *The Elgar Companion to Classical Economics*, Cheltenham, UK and Lyme, NH: Edward Elgar Publishing.

Garegnani, P. (1960), *Il Capitale nelle Teorie della Distribuzione*, Milan: Giuffrè.

Garegnani, P. (1984), 'Value and distribution in classical economists and Marx', *Oxford Economic Papers*, **36**(2), 291–325.

Garegnani, P. (1987), 'Surplus approach to value and distribution', in J. Eatwell, M. Milgate and P. Newman (eds), *The New Palgrave: A Dictionary of Economics*, London: Macmillan.

Garegnani, P. (2007), 'Professor Samuelson on Sraffa and the classical economists', *The European Journal of the History of Economic Thought*, **14**(2), 181–242.

Kurz, H.D. and N. Salvadori (1995), *Theory of Production*, Cambridge, UK: Cambridge University Press.

Levrero, E.S. (2011), 'Some notes on wages and competition in the labour market', in R. Ciccone, C. Gehrke and G. Mongiovi (eds), *Sraffa and Modern Economics*, London: Routledge.

Marx, K. (1909), *Capital, Vol. 3*, Chicago, IL: Charles H. Kerr and Co.

Quesnay, F. (1766), 'Analyse de la formule arithmétique du Tableau Economique de la distribution des dépenses annuelles d'une Nation agricole', *Journal de l'agriculture, du commerce et des finances*, **5**(3), 11–41.

Smith, A. ([1776] 1976), *An Inquiry into the Nature and Causes of the Wealth of Nations*, in *The Glasgow Edition of the Works and Correspondence of Adam Smith*, (eds) R.H. Campbell, A.S. Skinner and W.B. Todd, Oxford: Clarendon Press.

Sraffa, P. (1960), *Production of Commodities by Means of Commodities*, Cambridge, UK: Cambridge University Press.

Stirati, A. (1994), *The Theory of Wages in Classical Economics*, Aldershot, UK and Brookfield, VT: Edward Elgar Publishing.

Taxation

Ricardo was greatly concerned with taxation, as well as value, distribution and growth. The title of the *Principles of Political Economy, and Taxation* (1817; henceforth *Principles*) is sufficient proof of this. In fact, Ricardo devoted almost one-third of the *Principles* to taxation, examining the effects and incidence of various taxes. From his analysis of taxation, however, Ricardo derived no positive proposals as to how government should raise ordinary revenue. Ricardo's main conclusion was simply that 'taxation under every form presents but a choice of evils' (*Works*, I: 167). Drawing on Dome (2004: 117–43), I will examine why Ricardo reached this conclusion.

Early contributions
Ricardo's early statements on taxation were made in a pamphlet entitled *Reply to Mr. Bosanquet's Practical Observation on the Report of the Bullion Committee* (1811). Criticizing Charles Bosanquet's claim that the sharp rise in the general price level since 1793 could be ascribed to heavy taxes alone, Ricardo declared that taxes would not always raise prices:

> [I]t appears convincingly certain, that neither the income tax, the assessed taxes, nor many others, do in the least affect the prices of commodities. Unfortunate indeed would be the situation of the consumer, if he had to pay additional prices for those commodities which were necessary to his comfort, after his means of purchasing them had been by the tax considerably abridged. The income tax, were it fairly imposed, would leave every member of the community in the same relative situation in which it found him. Each man's expences must be diminished to the amount of his tax. (*Works*, III: 241)

The above quotation displays Ricardo's three concerns with respect to taxation: whether a tax would (1) keep prices unchanged; (2) be paid from consumption or savings; (3) leave the distribution of income unchanged. Let us call these criteria 'the principle of price neutrality', 'the principle of consumption reducibility', and 'the principle of distribution neutrality', respectively.

The principle of distribution neutrality illustrates Ricardo's concept of 'equality' in taxation. The principle of consumption reducibility indicates his concern to minimize impediments to capital accumulation. The principles of price neutrality and consumption reducibility belonged to Smith's maxim of 'economy'. A tax that infringed these two principles would impose a greater burden on the people than the amount of the tax they paid. The above quote indicates that Ricardo thought an income tax observed the principles of distribution neutrality and price neutrality to a greater degree than indirect taxes. Because an income tax was expected to be paid from consumption rather than savings, it would not infringe the principle of consumption reducibility. Ricardo believed that an income tax would satisfy the three criteria.

What opinions did Ricardo hold concerning William Pitt's income tax introduced in 1799? Ricardo was writing the *Principles* when debate heated up in Parliament concerning the continuation or abolition of the income tax. In a letter to Hutches Trower dated 9 March 1816, nine days before the income tax was repealed, Ricardo referred to the Chancellor's final proposal for retention of the tax:

I hope you will bring up a petition with you against the property tax. It is more objectionable I think as a 5 percent than as a 10 percent tax, yet I would willingly submit to it if I thought that it would really end in two years. The machinery of it is too easily worked to allow it to be at the disposal of our extravagant ministers during a period of peace. (*Works*, VII: 27)

This is Ricardo's only reference to Pitt's income tax. It shows that Ricardo preferred an income tax of 10 per cent for two years to 5 per cent over a longer period. Probably Ricardo considered the retention of the income tax for a definite period a measure for redeeming the public debt, but that a long-term income tax would be used for wasteful purposes.

Indirect taxes in the *Principles*
In the chapters on taxation in the *Principles*, Ricardo adopted Smith's maxims of 'certainty' and 'convenience', as well as his own principles of price neutrality, distribution neutrality and consumption reducibility. Ricardo evaluated various taxes on the basis of these maxims and principles. Let us examine first indirect taxes – taxes on raw produce, manufactured necessities and luxuries.

A tax on raw produce would raise its price by the amount of the tax, leaving the prices of other commodities unchanged. Such a tax would increase money wages, and consequently reduce the uniform rate of profit in all industries. This conclusion – as well as conclusions about other taxes – was based on the following assumptions: (1) a differential rent; (2) free movement of capital between all sectors; (3) inelasticity of demand for raw produce; (4) homogeneous units of composite factors for the production of every commodity; (5) a fixed real wage rate; and (6) a constant money supply or the specie-flow price mechanism. Moreover, Ricardo's conclusion required two additional assumptions: that all land in cultivation was taxed, and that no raw produce was imported.

Ricardo assumed diminishing returns with respect to production of raw produce, arguing '[i]t is only ... because land is not unlimited in quantity and uniform in quality, and because in the progress of population, land of an inferior quality, or less advantageously situated, is called into cultivation, that rent is ever paid for the use of it' (*Works*, I: 70). He defined rent as the difference in productivity between lands of superior quality and the least productive land in cultivation – marginal land – where no rent was paid. The natural price of raw produce was regulated by the productivity of marginal land.

The rent of land and the natural price of raw produce would continuously increase with economic growth, because cultivation would extend to poorer-quality land, and the productivity of marginal land would fall. Higher prices for raw produce would raise money wages, and consequently lower profits. Because profits were the main source of economic growth, the economy would slow down and finally reach a stationary state, unless cheaper raw produce could be freely imported from foreign countries. On the basis of the differential rent theory, Ricardo demonstrated that the interests of landlords were in conflict with the national interest.

Ricardo assumed that capital invested in land, as well as capital in manufacturing industries, could freely move between sectors. Consequently, if raw produce was taxed, farmers could increase the price of it by withdrawing their capital and reducing supply. In fact, however, farmers did not have to reduce supply, because demand – for example, for corn – was inelastic:

> Corn being a commodity indispensably necessary to every one, little effect will be produced on the demand for it in consequence of a tax, and therefore the supply would not probably be long excessive, even if the producers had great difficulty in removing their capitals from the land. For this reason, the price of corn will speedily be raised by taxation, and the farmer will be enabled to transfer the tax from himself to the consumer. (Ibid.: 191–2)

Thus, a tax on raw produce would increase its natural price without reducing capital in land.

Ricardo recognized that an increase in the natural price of raw produce would affect the natural price of other commodities: 'The probable effect of a tax on raw produce, would be to raise the price of raw produce, and of all commodities in which raw produce entered' (ibid.: 169). Moreover, Ricardo argued that 'as the value of commodities is very differently made up of raw material and labour . . . it is evident that there would be the greatest variety in the effects produced on the value of commodities, by a tax on raw produce' (ibid.: 171). Through the input–output relationship between commodities, the natural price of all commodities would change. However, Ricardo left the relationship in darkness when discussing the precise effects of various taxes. Ricardo argued as if all commodities had been produced by labour alone, or at least as if all labourers had worked with homogeneous units of composite factors. In other words, Ricardo assumed the case to which his labour theory of value applied. This assumption allowed Ricardo to concentrate on the effect of a tax on the relationship between wages and profits.

Because raw produce, as well as manufactured necessities, was necessary for labourers' subsistence, money wages would rise in line with the increase in the price of raw produce. If money wages had not increased, the growth of the labouring population would have diminished subject to the Malthusian adjustment. Given that demand for labour would remain the same, the price of labour would rise. In order to maintain the balance between supply and demand for labour – namely, maintaining the rate of real wages – money wages had to rise. Because of the reciprocal relationship between wages and profits, the uniform rate of profit would fall. The assumption of homogeneous units of composite factors indicated that relative prices of commodities would not be affected by the change in the relationship between wages and profits.

In contrast to his 1811 pamphlet, Ricardo denied that an increase in money wages because of a tax would raise the general price level. Ricardo argued:

> [C]orn and *all* home commodities could not be materially raised in price without an influx of the precious metals; for the same quantity of money could not circulate the same quantity of commodities, at high as at low prices, and the precious metals never could be purchased with dear commodities. (Ibid.: 168; original emphasis)

Given a constant money supply, the general price level could not rise. However, later, in the third edition of the *Principles*, Ricardo indicated that the general price level could rise because of a tax, even if money supply did not increase. Ricardo explained this by relying on an increase in the velocity of money (ibid.: 213–14).

However, even if the general price level increased because of a tax, such an increase would not last long. The higher price of exports would create a trade deficit. Specie would be exported, and the general price level would fall. Hence, a tax on raw produce 'could not materially interfere with foreign trade, and would not place us under any comparative disadvantage as far as regarded competition in foreign markets' (ibid.: 172).

Thus, a tax on raw produce would increase its price by the amount of the tax, raise money wages, and consequently lower the rate of profit. Given a constant money supply, the general price level would not rise. Even if it rose, the specie-flow price mechanism would bring back it to the pre-tax level. The tax would ultimately fall on capitalists and consumers of raw produce.

Tithes would produce the same effect as a tax on raw produce: 'The only difference between tithes and taxes on raw produce, is, that one is a variable money tax, the other a fixed money tax' (ibid.: 176). However, because in a progressive state of society, the price of corn would rise, 'tithes would be a heavier tax than a permanent money tax' (ibid.: 177).

Taxes on manufactured necessities and manufactured luxuries would also increase their natural prices, towards which market prices would converge. However, in contrast to raw produce, an increase in the natural price of manufactures – particularly manufactured luxuries – would be accompanied with a diminution in demand for them: their supply would have to be adjusted accordingly. Consequently, it would take more time for the market price to become equal to the natural price. If demand for manufactures was elastic, constant returns to scale had to be assumed in order for a tax on manufactures to raise their price exactly by the amount of the tax. In fact, Ricardo assumed constant returns with respect to production of manufactures. For example, when discussing an increase in production of manufactures because of a bounty on their exportation, Ricardo argued:

> A bounty on the exportation of manufactures will . . . raise for a time the market price of manufactures, but it will not raise their natural price. The labour of 200 men will produce double the quantity of these goods that 100 could produce before; and, consequently, when the requisite quantity of capital was employed in supplying the requisite quantity of manufactures, they would again fall to their natural price, and all advantage from a high market price would cease. (Ibid.: 312–13)

With the assumption of constant returns, Ricardo could claim that the price of manufactured necessities would increase by the amount of the tax. The tax would also raise money wages, and lower the uniform rate of profit in all sectors, because manufactured necessities were indispensable for labourers' subsistence, and because real wages were fixed. Lower rates of profit would impede capital accumulation.

Taxes on manufactured necessities – as well as on raw produce – violated the principle of consumption reducibility. Those taxes also violated the principle of price neutrality, because the relative price of the commodity taxed would increase. Finally, they infringed the principle of distribution neutrality: they would fall exclusively on profits, while landlords and stockholders would bear the taxes only as consumers. For this reason, Ricardo thought that taxes on raw produce and manufactured necessities had to be accompanied by direct taxes on the rent of land and on dividends from bonds. If this were done, said Ricardo, 'all the objects of an income tax would be obtained' (ibid.: 161). Thus, taxes on raw produce and manufactured necessities, together with taxes on rent and dividends, could substitute for an income tax.

A tax on manufactured luxuries would not reduce profits: it would simply increase the price of the commodity taxed by the amount of the tax. This result assumed that luxuries were not necessary for labourers' subsistence. From the viewpoint of the principle of consumption reducibility, a tax on luxuries was desirable because it would usually be paid for out of unproductive consumption. However, Ricardo discerned the defect of such a tax; 'there is no certainty as to the amount of the tax' (ibid.: 241), because 'from taxes on expenditure a miser may escape' (ibid.: 167). With respect to certainty, Ricardo acknowledged the advantage of direct taxes. Thus, taxes on luxuries could not be a central pillar of Ricardo's taxation system.

Ricardo discussed a tax on gold as the case in which demand for the commodity taxed was elastic and production was subject to diminishing returns. Ricardo assumed that a country had gold mines, and that gold alone was used as money. With respect to the relationship between supply of money and demand for it, Ricardo stated that '[t]he demand for money is regulated entirely by its value, and its value by its quantity [i.e., supply]' (ibid.: 193). The value of money was indicated by the reciprocal number of the general price level, which was directly influenced by money supply. Thus, Ricardo thought that, given a constant volume of transactions, the money supply regulated demand for money.

A tax on gold would first reduce the profits of capital in the mines. The rate of profit would be lower than that in other sectors. Capital in mines of lower quality would be removed to other sectors in order to obtain the ordinary rate of profit. Consequently, proprietors of mines from which capital was withdrawn would lose all their rent: the rent of other proprietors would also be reduced. The money supply would diminish, and the general price level would fall. The balance of trade would become favourable to this country. However, such a trade surplus would disappear in the long run because of the specie-flow price mechanism. If this country – Ricardo supposed it to be Spain – was the only country in Europe that could produce gold, the general price level in Europe would fall because of the diminution in the circulating quantity of gold. Where was the benefit of a tax on gold to this country? Ricardo answered that it consisted of consumption goods produced by capital removed from the mines to other sectors. Thus, a tax on gold would increase national consumption, while reducing the rent of the mines and the quantity of metallic money circulating in the country and Europe.

A tax on gold was irrelevant to Britain in Ricardo's time. Britain had no great gold mines, and paper money was issued independently of the quantity of gold. However, Ricardo's argument indicated how strongly he was convinced that the quantity of gold as money – as well as the quantity of paper money – had nothing to do with the opulence of a nation.

In contrast to Malthus, Ricardo did not support import duties and export bounties. They would prevent the most efficient use of capital. In particular, protective duties on the importation of raw produce would increase domestic production of raw produce. Poorer-quality land would have to be taken into cultivation, and the natural price of raw produce would rise. Consequently, money wages would rise, and profits would fall: the rent of land would increase. Lower rates of profit would retard economic growth. In order to sustain economic growth as long as possible, Britain had to abolish restrictions on trade, particularly on the importation of foreign corn and raw materials. Ricardo admitted that if agriculture was subject to special taxes – for example, tithes – a countervailing duty could be imposed on foreign corn. However, it would be more desirable without both special taxes on agriculture and countervailing duties. Thus, Ricardo proposed 'to acknowledge the errors which a mistaken policy has induced us to adopt, and immediately to commence gradual recurrence to the sound principles of an universally free trade' (ibid.: 317–18). To Ricardo, an opponent of the Corn Laws, customs duties were not a tax that he could recommend.

Ricardo argued that taxes imposed on transfers of property were taxes on capital rather than revenue, and that they would reduce funds for the maintenance of labour. Those taxes would also prevent productive capital from being distributed in the way most beneficial to the economy. Arguing that '[f]or the general prosperity, there cannot be too much facility given to the conveyance and exchange of all kinds of property' (ibid.: 154), Ricardo refused to consider all taxes on transfers of property – including inheritance taxes.

Direct taxes in the *Principles*
In comparison with indirect taxes, direct taxes on revenue did not violate the principle of price neutrality. No taxes on rent, profits, and wages would change the natural prices of commodities.

Ricardo argued that a tax imposed in proportion to rent would finally fall on landlords. This conclusion was identical to Smith's. However, in contrast to Smith, Ricardo derived it from the theory of differential rent. Landlords could not shift the burden of the tax to the farmers by raising their rent, because they could charge the farmers only for the difference in productivity between their lands and marginal land. A tax on rent could be said to be least harmful to capital accumulation, because it would fall only on the extravagant, namely landlords.

Ricardo thought that a tax on land could be regarded as a tax on rent if it was levied in proportion to the rent of land. However, if, as with the English tithe, a tax on land was imposed in proportion to the produce of land, it would be identical to a tax on raw produce. If, as with the English land tax, a fixed amount of money was imposed per acre of land, it would have the same effect as a tax imposed on profits in the agricultural sector.

Moreover, using numerical examples, Ricardo demonstrated that a land tax proportionate to the productivity of land, tithes, and a tax on raw produce would not change money rents but instead reduce the corn rent (namely, the money rent divided by the price of corn), and that a fixed land tax and a tax on profits in the raw produce sector would increase the money rent, but leave the corn rent intact. Thus, English landlords had no grounds to complain of the land tax.

Following Smith, Ricardo argued that a tax on housing rent would be incurred by the tenant and the landowner, although the proportion of the incidence that fell on each would be indefinite. However, Ricardo did not think that the ground rent was a fit subject for a special tax:

> [I]t would surely be very unjust, to tax exclusively the revenue of any particular class of a community. The burdens of the State should be borne by all in proportion to their means . . . Rent often belongs to those who, after many years of toil, have realised their gains, and expended their fortunes in the purchase of land or houses; and it certainly would be an infringement of that principle which should ever be held sacred, the security of property, to subject it to unequal taxation. (*Works*, I: 204)

Although Ricardo's political economy indicated that the interests of landlords conflicted with the national interest, and that a tax on the rent of land would resolve such a conflict, he never accepted a special tax on rent. Such a tax would violate the security of property, as well as the principle of distribution neutrality.

Ricardo examined David Buchanan's claim that a tax on wages would not always increase money wages. Suppose that the tax would be paid first by labourers, and that the wage fund – namely capitalists' demand for labour – does not change. If the tax revenue was used to employ unproductive labour, the total demand for labour – the government's and capitalists' demand for labour – would increase, and consequently money wages before tax would rise by the amount of the tax: money wages after tax would remain the same as before. However, if the tax revenue was exported as a subsidy to a foreign country, the total demand for labour would not increase. Money wages before tax would not rise. Because money wages after tax would then fall, population growth would be checked by the Malthusian mechanism.

Even if money wages before tax rose because of the increase in demand for labour, the rate of profit would decline. This would retard any accumulation of the wage fund, and consequently money wages would fall in the long run. This argument also applied to an increase in money wages because of taxes on raw produce and manufactured necessities.

Although Ricardo accepted Buchanan's claim, he indicated, as a first approximation, that a tax on wages would raise money wages by a sum equal to the tax. Thus, Ricardo defended Smith's conclusion that 'the labouring classes cannot materially contribute to the burdens of the State' (ibid.: 235). However, in contrast to Smith, Ricardo argued that a tax on wages would fall on profits – not rent. Employers of labour – namely, capitalists – had to incur the burden. Because of homogeneous units of composite factors, a tax on wages would not change the relative prices of commodities.

A tax imposed equally on the profits of all industries would also maintain the relative prices of commodities. Although each capitalist would attempt to shift the burden of the tax by moving their capital to a more advantageous sector, they would fail to find one. Consequently, the tax would fall on capitalists of all industries. Ricardo also indicated that a tax levied on profits in any given sector had the same effect as a tax on the commodity itself. Considering that capitalists finally incurred the burden, a tax on profits in all industries and a tax on wages, as well as taxes on raw produce and manufactured necessities, were equivalent. However, a direct tax on profits had a peculiar fault: it could not be imposed 'without the inconvenience of having recourse to the obnoxious measure of prying into every man's concerns, and arming commissioners with powers repugnant to the habits and feelings of a free country' (ibid.: 161). A direct tax on profits violated the maxim of 'convenience'.

Ricardo applied his conclusions to the incidence of the poor rate:

> The poor rate is a tax which partakes of the nature of all these taxes, and under different circumstances falls on the consumer of raw produce and goods, on the profits of stock, and on the rent of land . . . To know, then, the operation of the poor rate at any particular time, we must ascertain whether at that time it affects in an equal or unequal degree the profits of the farmer and manufacturer; and also whether the circumstances be such as to afford to the farmer the power of raising the price of raw produce. (*Works*, I: 257–8)

According to Ricardo, in the agricultural sector, the poor rate was imposed in proportion to the annual value of land – not the rent that farmers actually paid to the landlords. The annual value of a piece of land was calculated to include all capital that the farmer (or the landlord) had invested in the land – for example, manure, fences and irrigation canals. In contrast, manufacturers paid the poor rate according to the value of the buildings in which they worked, irrespective of the value of the machinery and other productive capital they employed. In reality, the poor rate was a tax on the profits of capital in all sectors, but imposed more heavily in the agricultural sector. The relative price of raw produce would rise by the difference in the burden of the poor rate. It would not fall on the rent of land. Money rents would increase because of a rise in the price of raw produce: hence, 'the tax may, under some circumstances, be even advantageous rather than injurious to landlords' (ibid.: 260). If this was true, landlords had no reason to complain of the poor rate, as well as the fixed land tax.

Although Ricardo did not discuss a general income tax in detail, he believed that a taxation system composed of taxes on the rent of land and dividends of stock and taxes on one or more of raw produce, necessities, wages and profits could substitute for an income tax (ibid.). However, such a system did not strictly satisfy distribution neutrality, because income tax could not be paid by labourers. It would increase their relative share of income compared with the landed and capitalist classes. In contrast to a genuine income tax, Ricardo's system of income tax was not always price neutral. Only a combination of direct taxes on the rent of land, the dividends of bonds, and profits of capital escaped this flaw. However, a tax on profits would bother capitalists with inspections by a tax gatherer. Ricardo's income tax also violated the principle of consumption reducibility because it would fall on profits, and consequently retard capital accumulation.

Ricardo's main conclusions with respect to the effects and incidence of taxes can be summarized as follows: (1) a tax on raw produce (manufactured necessities) would decrease the rate of profit, raising only the price of raw produce (manufactured necessities); (2) a tax on manufactured luxuries would increase their price, but keep the rate of profit and the price of other commodities unchanged; (3) a tax levied in proportion to the rent of land would fall on rent; (4) a tax on the rent of a house would fall on the inhabitant and the landowner, although the proportion of the incidence between them would be indefinite; (5) taxes on wages and on profits would lower the rate of profit, keeping all prices unchanged. Thus, Ricardo decided that most taxes would fall on the profits of capital – rather than the rent of land. This conclusion was produced by Ricardo's system in which rent was excluded from the determination of the price of raw produce, and any increase in the production costs of raw produce and manufactured necessities reduced the uniform rate of profit.

Taxes on raw produce, manufactured necessities, profits and wages violated the principle of consumption reducibility, because they would reduce profits, and retard capital accumulation. Moreover, all indirect taxes would violate the principle of price neutrality, and prevent a natural allocation of resources. Only taxes on the rent of land would be harmless to capital accumulation as well as price neutral. However, a special tax on rent infringed the principle of distribution neutrality. Thus, Ricardo reached the conclusion that 'taxation under every form presents but a choice of evils' (ibid.: 167).

After the first edition of the *Principles*
Ricardo published two revised editions of his *Principles* in 1819 and 1821. Major revisions in the taxation chapters were made to his statements concerning the evil effect of taxes on capital accumulation, the relationship between taxation and the general price level, and ministers' extravagant habits (*Works*, I: 152, 213–14n and 242). However, except these, there were no significant alterations. Ricardo's fundamentally negative attitude towards taxation did not change.

Ricardo held that the main practical purpose of political economy was to indicate right measures of minimizing the preventive effect of taxation on the autonomous development of private economy. However, Ricardo himself did not put forward such measures. For example, with respect to an income tax, Ricardo only continued to ask 'whether you should not tax the profits of trade indirectly, by taxing wages, or necessaries; and other incomes directly, as rent, dividends, annuities' (*Works*, VIII: 154). Ricardo did not answer this question explicitly, and became more negative about a revival of income tax.

In 'Funding System', an article for the *Encyclopaedia Britannica* (1820), Ricardo proposed a capital levy as a means to redeem the outstanding public debt. However, Ricardo proposed a capital levy only as a one-time tax. It was only better than continuous heavy taxes and national bankruptcy. Ricardo's advocacy of the capital levy scheme did not contradict his fundamental opinion that no tax could be positively recommended as a perpetual system of taxation.

Conclusion
Ricardo's political economy demonstrated that no taxation system was completely compatible with both the principles of distribution neutrality, price neutrality and consumption reducibility, and the maxims of certainty and convenience. In particular, Ricardo's theory of tax incidence indicated that most taxes would fall on the profits of capital. Because most taxes would prevent capital accumulation, and no taxes could simultaneously satisfy all his criteria, Ricardo did not make public his overall plan of a fair and efficient system of taxation. What Ricardo achieved in his arguments was to prove rather abstractly that taxation equated to a 'national evil' or 'political diseconomy' caused by any government. If this is true, the title of Ricardo's *Principles* can be changed to *Principles of Political Economy, and Diseconomy*.

Takuo Dome

See also:

Funding System; Member of Parliament; National Debt; Ricardian Equivalence.

Bibliography

Dome, T. (2004), *The Political Economy of Public Finance in Britain 1767–1873*, London and New York: Routledge.
O'Brien, D.P. (2004), *The Classical Economists Revisited*, Princeton, NJ: Princeton University Press.
Shoup, C.S. (1960), *Ricardo on Taxation*, New York: Columbia University Press.

Technical Change

The problem of technical change, its causes, forms and effects, has been high on the agenda of economic analysis ever since its systematic inception in the second half of the seventeenth century and its full blooming at the time of the English classical political economists. This is hardly surprising, since around the same time Western Europe experienced the Industrial Revolution and in its wake the take-off on a path of sustained growth of income per capita. Technical change played an important role in the works of Adam Smith and David Ricardo and an even more important one in that of Karl Marx, who developed his own analysis in no small degree from a critical account of the analyses of Smith and especially Ricardo. Marx, as is well known, saw capitalism as a hotbed whose historical function was to increase productivity 'geometrically'.

However, the prevailing view in the history of economic analysis appears to be that although Smith and Ricardo lived through the Industrial Revolution, they misread its significance and vastly underrated the importance of technical progress for economic development and growth. See, for example, Rostow (1990: 34 and 87), Blaug (2009) and Solow (2010). (See also Eltis, 1984, for a discussion of the classical theory of economic growth. On the concept of 'classical economics', see Garegnani, 1987; Kurz and Salvadori, 1995 and Gehrke and Kurz, 2006.) This assessment is, however, difficult to sustain. While it is true that the role of the manufacturing sector as the engine of growth escaped Smith's attention and that Ricardo in much of his analysis focused on corn production, Smith and especially Ricardo can hardly be accused of having downplayed the importance of technical progress. In particular, Ricardo's respective thinking was not overwhelmed, as is frequently contended, by a concern with diminishing returns in agriculture in combination with Malthus's law of population. Ricardo was no Malthus. In fact, he anticipated, and analysed, with the novel analytical tools he forged, what was not yet to be openly seen – that is, some of the characteristic features and long-term trends of the process of incessant technological and organizational change that had seized the Western European economies. Ricardo deserves to be credited with having elaborated a framework and analytical concepts that allow us to describe and analyse almost *any* form of technical progress and its implications. He has enriched and deepened our understanding of the technological and economic dynamism inherent in capitalism and has forged powerful analytical tools to deal with it (see Schefold, 1976 and Kurz, 2010).

The fundamental law of distribution
The arguably most important analytical tool Ricardo forged formed the basis of what is known as the 'fundamental law of income distribution': the inverse relationship between the general rate of profits and (the share or rate of) wages, given the technical conditions of production. Technical progress would shift this relationship in one way or another and thus affect the level of one or both distributive variables. Different forms of technical progress would shift the relationship in different ways.

Ricardo stated: 'The greater the portion of the result of labour that is given to the labourer, the smaller must be the rate of profits, and vice versa' (*Works*, VIII: 194). He was thus able to dispel the idea that wages and the rate of profits could be determined independently of one another. In much of his analysis of value and distribution, Ricardo assumed a given *real* wage rate, conceived as an inventory of well-specified quantities of certain commodities, reflecting some social and historical level of subsistence, and this is the assumption generally attributed to him in the literature. However, it is frequently overlooked that, depending upon circumstances, a given real wage rate may be reflected in different money wage rates and, correspondingly, in different shares of wages in the

social product. With decreasing returns in agriculture, this is the case of 'a rise of wages
... from a difficulty of procuring the necessaries on which wages are expended' (*Works*,
I: 48). Perhaps even more important, it is also frequently overlooked that Ricardo contemplated the case in which workers are 'more liberally rewarded' (ibid.) and thus participate in the sharing out of the surplus product. In this case, the concepts of a given real or
commodity wage rate and that of subsistence lose much of their former appeal and a new
wage concept is needed, because it can no longer be assumed that workers' consumption
and thus 'wage-goods' could be ascertained independently of income distribution (and
relative prices). Both cases can, however, be dealt with in terms of wages conceived as
'the *proportion* of the annual labour of the country ... devoted to the labourers' (ibid.:
49; emphasis added); that is, in terms of what Sraffa called 'proportional wages' (see
Gehrke, 2003).

Ricardo in fact felt justified to state as a general principle that the rate of profits
depends on wages (whether real or proportional), and on nothing else. This principle,
he thought, covered all cases: the case in which labour productivity decreases due to
diminishing returns in primary production, the case in which it remains constant and the
case in which it increases due to 'improvements' in the methods of production. However,
Ricardo's dictum is only true in very special conditions, which in his observations on the
wage–profit relationship he for the sake of simplicity typically assumed to hold true: that
social capital consists only of wages or can be fully reduced to wages in a finite number
of steps, so that the rate of profits, r, is given by the ratio of profits, P, to the sum total
of (direct and indirect) wages, W:

$$r = \frac{P}{W} = \frac{1 - \omega}{\omega},$$

where ω designates proportional wages or the wage share.

Marx correctly pointed out that this principle is not true in general: within a circular
flow framework the rate of profits depends not only on the share of wages. If Ricardo
had been correct, the rate of profits would go to infinity as wages vanish, whereas with
commodities being produced by means of commodities there would be a finite maximum
rate of profits, R. In the presence of what Marx called 'constant capital' the actual rate of
profits, r, depends on two magnitudes: the share of wages, w, expressing the distribution
side of the problem, and the maximum rate of profits, R, expressing the technology side.

In much of Ricardo's analysis, production is envisaged as a circular flow as, for
example, in François Quesnay's *Tableau Economique*, and several hints indicate that
even in his discussion of the impact of technical change on the system he had that case at
the back of his mind. We therefore feel entitled in the following to start from the premise
that commodities are produced by means of commodities and that any system of production reflecting a given technical knowledge exhibits a maximum rate of profit that is
bounded from above.

Different forms of technical change
Ricardo was clear that technical change was an essential part of the development of
modern society, that different forms of it have to be distinguished and that these typically
have different effects. However, he refrained from speculating, as others did, whether

any particular form will dominate the long-term development. The future was uncertain and open. Like Adam Smith he saw the historical development of an economy as largely shaped by two opposing forces: the 'niggardliness of nature' (that is, the scarcity of natural resources), on the one hand, and man's ingenuity and creativity reflected in new methods of production and new commodities, on the other.

As we have seen in the above, Ricardo is frequently presented as a technological pessimist, who believed in the overwhelming importance of diminishing returns in agriculture in combination with Malthus's law of population and who saw the stationary state around the corner. This interpretation does not do him justice. As early as in the *Essay on Profits* of 1815 he expressed the view that there are no signs pointing in the direction of a falling rate of profits in the foreseeable future: 'we are yet at a great distance from the end of our resources, and . . . we may contemplate an increase of prosperity and wealth, far exceeding that of any country which has preceded us' (see *Works*, IV: 34). This view is confirmed in a letter to Hutches Trower of 5 February 1816, in which he concluded from the fall in grain prices since 1812 that 'we are happily yet in the progressive state, and may look forward with confidence to a long course of prosperity' (*Works*, VII: 17). And in his entry on the 'Funding System' for Volume IV of the Supplements to the *Encyclopaedia Britannica*, published in September 1820, he stressed that 'the richest country in Europe is yet far distant from that degree of improvement' (that is, the stationary state) and that 'it is difficult to say where the limit is at which you would cease to accumulate wealth and to derive profit from its employment' (*Works*, IV: 179).

Ricardo studied various cases and scenarios in order to figure out the range of possible consequences of different forms of technical change. He even contemplated the limiting case of a fully automated production and pointed out: 'If machinery could do all the work that labour now does, there would be no demand for labour. Nobody would be entitled to consume any thing who was not a capitalist, and who could not buy or hire a machine' (*Works*, VIII: 399–400).

He was also aware of the fact that certain forms of technical change met with the stiff opposition of some strata of society, because these forms were seen to be detrimental to their interests. In Chapter 2 of the *Principles* Ricardo discussed both what we may, for short, call 'land saving' and 'capital (alias labour) saving' technical progress, and showed that the former had the effect of reducing the rents of land; no wonder, then, that landlords were often opposed to them. On Ricardo's discussion, see Gehrke et al. (2003). For statements that the landed gentry frequently tried to suppress agricultural improvements, see, inter alia, William Petty ([1899] 1986: 249–50); see also *Works*, IV: 41.

The most important form of technical change, and its varied effects, that is associated with Ricardo's name, is, however, the problem of 'machinery'. This form, and its negative impact on workers, Ricardo analysed in a newly added chapter in the third edition of the *Principles*, published in 1821. There he established the fact that the construction and introduction of improved machines into the production system can frequently be expected to lead to the displacement of workers and thus what was later called 'technological unemployment'. Hicks (1969: Chapter 9) argued that Ricardo's chapter on machinery could be used to explain economic history in England after the Industrial Revolution and especially the delayed increase in real wages. On the debates about 'technological unemployment' triggered by Ricardo's chapter, see Jeck and Kurz (1983) and Hagemann (2009).

Machinery that reduces the gross produce

The discussion in this section focuses attention on this case, not because Ricardo thought that it was the only or most important case to be studied. Rather, we study it for the following reasons. First, because Ricardo originally disputed the possibility of the introduction of machinery that entailed a reduction in gross output and thus employment, but now admitted it. The fact that an authority like him had to change his mind with regard to a crucial question like this deserves to be scrutinized carefully. Second, the progressive replacement of labour by fixed capital is a characteristic feature of modern economic development. Ricardo was one of the first authors to deal with the emerging trend of a growing fixed capital intensity of production and its implications. Third, Ricardo's discussion has met with severe misunderstandings in the literature. Here we attempt to provide a coherent explanation of Ricardo's argument that is faithful to what he wrote. Last, but not least, Marx's idea of a rising organic composition of capital can be shown to consist essentially of an adaptation to Marx's own analytical framework of Ricardo's case. As Rostow (1990: 81) stressed, 'it was the analytic basis for Marx's famous prediction of a reserve army of the unemployed under capitalism'; see also Kurz (1998: 119 and 2010: §4). In order to understand Marx in this regard, one needs first to understand Ricardo. (For a comprehensive study of Ricardo's propositions concerning machinery, see Jeck and Kurz, 1983.)

Technical progress, capital accumulation and income distribution

In the third edition of the *Principles* (1821) Ricardo retracted his former opinion on machinery, according to which 'the application of machinery to any branch of production, as should have the effect of saving labour, was a *general good*, accompanied only with that portion of inconvenience which in most cases attends the removal of capital and labour from one employment to another' (*Works*, I: 386; emphasis added). Ricardo's original position can be summarized as follows. As early as in the *Essay on Profits* of 1815, he had stressed that 'it is no longer questioned' that improved machinery 'has a decided tendency to raise the real wage of labour' (*Works*, IV: 35; see also VIII: 171). This is possible without a fall in the general rate of profits, because improved machinery reduces the quantity of labour needed directly and indirectly in the production of the various commodities: it reduces 'the sacrifices of labour' (*Works*, IV: 397). Hence labour productivity will increase. If the demand for the commodity does not rise in proportion to the increase in labour productivity, some workers will be discharged. However, 'as the capital which employed them was still in being . . . it would be employed in the production of some other commodity, useful to the society, for which there could not fail to be a demand' (*Works*, I: 387). This is, in a nutshell, the theory of automatic compensation of any displacement of workers. It relies on 'Say's Law' in the special form advocated by Ricardo: 'there is no amount of capital which may not be employed in a country, because demand is only limited by production' (ibid.: 290). Technical change will at most lead to (some extra) frictional unemployment.

In the third edition Ricardo qualified his earlier view explicitly as erroneous. Say's Law, he had convinced himself by that time, could not, in each and every case, prevent the net displacement of workers and (extra) unemployment. He concluded: 'I am convinced, that the substitution of machinery for human labour, is often very injurious to the interests of the class of labourers' (ibid.: 388). He expounded:

My mistake arose from the supposition, that whenever the net income [profits and rents] of a society increases, its gross income [net income plus wages] would also increase; I now, however, see reason to be satisfied that the one fund, from which landlords and capitalists derive their revenue, may increase, while the other, that upon which the labouring class mainly depend, may diminish, and therefore it follows . . . that the same cause which may increase the net revenue of the country, may at the same time render the population redundant, and deteriorate the condition of the labourer. (Ibid.)

How does he substantiate his new view?

Cost minimization and extra profits
A newly invented machine will be adopted, Ricardo stressed, if it allows the innovator to reduce the unit cost of the commodity and, given its price in the market, thus reap 'extra profits' (*Works*, I: 387). However, as the new method of production gradually becomes adopted throughout the economic system and replaces the older method, a new system of relative prices will be established and competition will wipe out extra profits. As regards the new level of the general rate of profits, towards which the system can be expected to gravitate, Ricardo was clear that technical progress, taken alone, can never be responsible for any tendency of the rate of profits to fall. For a given real wage rate and given gross output levels, technical change will either increase the rate of profits or leave it unaffected. (Ricardo thus grasped the essence of what was to become known as the Okishio–Shibata theorem. It should be noted, however, that the theorem was anticipated by several authors, including Ladislaus von Bortkiewicz, Georg von Charasoff and Paul Samuelson, 1957.) Profitability will increase if the technological change takes place in industries that directly or indirectly contribute to the production of commodities that enter the real wage rate, so-called 'necessaries', while it will remain constant if the technological change takes place in industries that contribute to the production of 'luxuries'. Ricardo drew a parallel between improved machinery and foreign trade: 'If . . . by the extension of foreign trade, or by improvements in machinery, the food and necessaries of the labourer can be brought to the market at a reduced price, [the rate of] profits will rise' (*Works*, I: 132).

A falling maximum rate of profits
We now look more closely at Ricardo's case for the gross produce-reducing form of technical progress. Comparing the levels of gross income in two subsequent periods (i.e., before and [immediately] after the economy-wide diffusion of improved machinery), the case under consideration is characterized by:

$$Q_1 + P_1 \geq Q_0 + P_0$$

and

$$L_1 = Q_1 + P_1 + W_1 < Q_0 + P_0 + W_0 = L_0,$$

where Q designates the rents of land, W now total wages and L the total amount of direct (or fresh) labour expended in production (total value-added); the subscripts 0 and 1 refer to the period before and after the introduction (and diffusion) of the machine. Hence, while 'neat income' (i.e., the sum total of property incomes [rents and profits]) may be increased, 'gross income' (that is, net income plus wages) may fall. Assuming for simplicity total rents to be unaffected by the change ($Q_1 = Q_0$), and taking (with Ricardo) the value of the capital stock of the system, K, as given and constant ($K_1 = K_0 = K$), it follows that:

$$r_1 = \frac{P_1}{K} \geq r_0 = \frac{P_0}{K}.$$

Obviously, despite a fall in gross produce ($L_1 < L_0$) there are 'motives enough ... to substitute the fixed for the circulating capital' (*Works*, VIII: 389); that is, the machine for wages and thus workers. Competitive conditions will in fact enforce cost-minimizing behaviour. The general rate of profits will rise in the case of a cheapening of wage-goods ($r_1 > r_0$), given the real wage rate (and will remain constant otherwise [$r_1 = r_0$]).

An illustration
We may illustrate the kind of technical change under consideration in the familiar *w–r* diagram. In Figure 22, *T* represents again the 'old' technique and *M* the 'new' one that

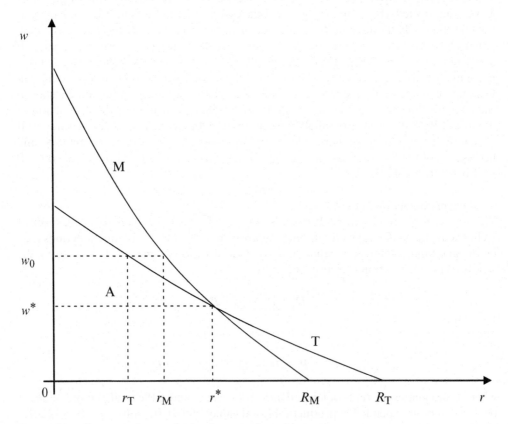

Figure 22   Gross produce-reducing improved machinery

produces and utilizes the machine. The latter exhibits a higher productivity of labour – it has 'the effect of saving labour' – and therefore a higher maximum real wage rate in terms of some given bundle of commodities, illustrated by a higher point of intersection of the wage curve with the ordinate. It also exhibits a lower maximum rate of profits, since with a given value of capital and a lower gross income it follows that:

$$R_M = \frac{L_1}{K} < R_T = \frac{L_0}{K},$$

where subscripts M and T refer to the new and old technology. Translated into the w–r diagram, Ricardo's case involves a movement of the curve away from the origin as regards its point of intersection with the ordinate and towards the origin as regards its point of intersection with the abscissa.

What was perhaps not clear from the outset is now put into sharp relief by the intersection of the two curves at $w = w^*$ ($r = r^*$). This means that the invention of the machine under consideration does not *ipso facto* also involve its automatic adoption, and thus an innovation. The reason is that whether it can profitably be introduced is not independent of the level of real wages and the associated system of relative prices. Cost-minimizing capitalists seeking the largest rate of return on the value of invested capital will adopt technique M if and only if r will be larger at the given wage rate; otherwise they will stick to technique T. If $w > w^*$ the new technique will be introduced and replace the old one, whereas if $w < w^*$ it will not. Hence, whether a new method of production will be adopted depends not only on its own physical characteristics, but also on the characteristics of the world into which it is born. With $w = w_0$, technique M will be adopted and gradually replace technique T until the latter will eventually have been eliminated. At first the innovator will pocket 'supernormal profits', which in the course of the diffusion of the new technique competition will gradually erode. For a given and constant real wage rate, w_0, in the case illustrated the general rate of profits will rise from r_T to r_M. A falling *maximum* rate of profits ($R_M < R_T$) is obviously compatible with a rising *actual* rate. This rise in the actual rate is accompanied by a change in relative ('normal') prices. The price of the commodity in which the technical change has taken place falls relative to the prices of the other commodities. The ratio of any two of the latter will generally also change, depending on the direct and indirect differential cost-reducing effects involved.

The tendency of the rate of profits to fall

Like Adam Smith before and Marx after him, Ricardo held that under certain conditions there is a tendency of the rate of profits to fall. This can most easily be shown in the purely hypothetical case in which there is no technical progress at all. In this case the 'natural course of things' would be the following: as capital accumulates and the population grows, diminishing returns in agriculture shift the w–r frontier towards the origin. The frontier is an expression of the processes of production employed directly or indirectly in the production of necessaries, including the method(s) of production employed on no-rent (or marginal) land. (The above argument applies *cum grano salis* also in the case of intensive diminishing returns. For a discussion of both cases, see Kurz and Salvadori, 1995: Chapter 10.) Intramarginal lands would obtain its proprietors differential rents due to cost differentials between different qualities of land. Since in the course of the development less and less fertile land would have to be cultivated, with the real wage rate taken as given and constant, nominal wages would have to rise, reflecting, as we have heard, the 'difficulty of procuring the necessaries on which wages are expended'. (The money price of corn expressed in gold will rise on the assumption that gold is produced at nearly constant labour cost.) With every inclusion of a less fertile quality of land in the system of production, Ricardo concluded, 'the natural tendency of [the rate of] profits then is to fall', until it reaches a minimum level at which accumulation stops.

Yet the picture changes once technical change is taken into account:

> This tendency, this gravitation as it were of profits, is happily checked at repeated intervals by the improvements in machinery, connected with the production of necessaries, as well as by discoveries in the science of agriculture which enable us to relinquish a portion of labour before required, and therefore to lower the price of the prime necessary of the labourer. (*Works*, I: 120; similarly V: 125–6)

The use of scientific methods may lead to the discovery of improved methods of production that reduce unit costs. In this case the *w–r* frontier will change position and shape. Ricardo stresses that technical change will typically be associated with a reduction of the sum total of the direct and indirect quantity of labour needed to produce the commodity, in which the change takes place, and also of the commodities, in which the former commodity enters directly or indirectly as an input, and so forth. Such technical change may, but need not, be accompanied by an increase in the maximum rate of profits. What, if it is accompanied by a fall in it? This is obviously the case of improved machinery that reduces the gross produce.

Induced technical change
In the above we have pointed out, and illustrated in terms of Figure 22, that the case at hand involves a choice of technique problem that cannot be decided independently of the level wages. A new method of production may not be eligible at the going wage rate (and the corresponding prices) because it is unprofitable: it is born, so to speak, into an inimical habitat. Ricardo was well aware of this possibility. He also saw clearly that the economic system, that is, the habitat, may change from within, endogenously, as capital accumulates and the population grows. As a consequence, the money wage rate and relative prices will have to change, given the real wage rate. Yet such changes may render a new method of production, whose employment at first would have incurred extra costs, eventually profitable. As Ricardo emphasized in a famous passage: 'Machinery and labour are in constant competition and the former can frequently not be employed until labour rises' (*Works*, I: 395). Ricardo's reasoning behind this dictum can be summarized in the following way. According to him, 'The same cause that raises labour [money wages], does not raise the value of machines, and, therefore with every augmentation of capital, a greater proportion of it is employed on machinery' (ibid.). In the course of the development of the economy, the bundle of wage-goods constituting the real wage tends to become more expensive relative to the machine until cost-minimizing producers eventually may have a motive to replace labour power by machine power. A rise in the money wage rate, given the real wage rate, may (but need not) lead to a rise in proportional wages. Whether it will depends on the precise technical specification of the set of methods of production available to producers, the quantities of the different qualities

of land available in the economy and on the inventory of commodities constituting the real wage rate. Here we follow Ricardo in assuming that the share of wages is either constant or rises and the share of rents rises. Accordingly, the share of profits and, given Ricardo's special assumption of a technical progress that, in modern parlance, increases the capital-to-output ratio, the rate of profits are bound to fall.

An illustration
We may illustrate Ricardo's case of induced mechanization again with the help of the $w-r$ relationships associated with different techniques or systems of production. In Figure 23 techniques T_0 and T_3 refer to two different stages in the development of the economy in the purely hypothetical case in which the accumulation of capital is carried out without any further improvements in the methods of production. T_0 relates to an early stage, T_3 to a later one, in which the no-rent quality of land is less fertile than at the previous stage. This is reflected, among other things, in a lower rate of profits: with a given and constant real wage rate, $w = w^*$, the rate of profits will fall from $r = r_{T0}$ to $r = r_{T3}$. This decline will be accompanied by a rise in the money wage rate that is just sufficient to counterbalance the corresponding rise in the money prices of wage-goods.

The question whether it is profitable to introduce a newly invented machine, or a machine that has been invented already some time ago but was not introduced then on grounds of cheapness, will be asked by cost-minimizing producers at any moment of the development of the economy. And at any such moment the technique using the machine can be represented analytically by a $w-r$ relationship that is alternative to the technique that does not use it. In Figure 23, M_0 is the corresponding wage curve in the initial situation (that is, when the machine became available). However, at the given real wage rate w^* it was not profitable to switch over to the new method(s) of production, because whoever would have adopted the novelty would have incurred extra costs and thus obtained an individual rate of profit that is lower than the current general rate, r_{T0}. (The inferiority of the new method at the wage rate and prices the producer faces is also reflected in a lower level of the general rate of profits associated with M_0 compared with that of T_0: $r_{T0} > r_{M0}$). In view of this, Schumpeter's following statement in the context of a discussion of Ricardo's chapter on machinery is a mystery. Schumpeter (1954: 679, n94) contends that none of the major classical authors, including Ricardo, saw the possibility that machines may be introduced 'that are no novelties to producers and, so far as technological knowledge is concerned, could have been introduced but were not introduced before, because it would not have been profitable to do so'. In fact, Ricardo dealt precisely with *this* possibility!

Ricardo's above statement has been severely misunderstood in the secondary literature. 'In this passage,' Ferguson (1973: 6) contended, 'one must interpret "labour rises" as meaning an increase in the real wage rate.' Yet we have just seen that what is at issue is a rise in money (or nominal) wages, with the commodity or real wage rate being constant. As is well-known, marginalist theory faces the problem of distinguishing between factor substitution and technical progress (that is, between movements along a given production function and the setting up of a new function). Apparently, Ferguson took Ricardo to have been concerned with the former problem, whereas in fact he was concerned with a case of induced technical change.

The question remains whether and when will the new machine be introduced into the

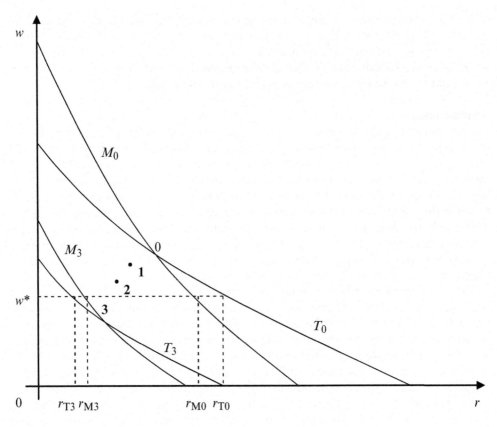

Figure 23   Induced technical change

economic system. In order to answer it we have to trace the switch-point between the *w–r* relationships corresponding to the with-machine and the without-machine techniques, M_i and T_i ($i = 0, 1, 2, \ldots$), across the various stages of economic development, where each stage is characterized, in descending order, by a different quality of land that is marginal and different relative prices, and so forth. The basic idea is illustrated schematically in Figure 23, in which points 0, 1, 2 and 3 give such switch-points. Through each such point pass two wage curves, one that represents the with-machine system and the other that represents the without-machine system of production. Points 0, 1 and 2 lie above the line that is parallel to the abscissa at the level of the given real wage rate $w = w^*$ and thus represent situations in which the machine will not be adopted. However, point 3 lies below the line. The corresponding wage curves are given by M_3 and T_3. In the then prevailing economic conditions, the machine-using technique is superior to its alternative and will be adopted by cost-minimizing producers. The general rate of profits in the new situation will be r_{M3}, which is larger than the rate obtained in the without-machine case, r_{T3}.

With a 'rise in labour' (money wages), the falling tendency of the rate of profits can be decelerated by means of a switch to the technique that produces and employs improved machinery (whether freshly invented or known already for some time). While the switch is beneficial to capital owners, it is prejudicial to the interests of the labouring classes. The rate of profits and the wage rate may even fall together, as Ricardo pointed out with reference to a situation in which some law of population is assumed to hold; see on this Kurz and Salvadori (2006).

Concluding remarks

The above analysis expounds Ricardo's view of technical change and especially his propositions in the chapter on machinery. It shows that Ricardo had a remarkably sophisticated understanding of different forms of technical change and their interaction with the socioeconomic environment. The analytical tools he provided in order to study the phenomenon in a multi-sector economy allowed him to analyse different forms of technical progress and their impact on income distribution, the pace at which the system grows and the structural change that comes with it.

Ricardo's analysis had a considerable impact on the subsequent discussion, especially on Marx. The latter's analysis can in fact be said to consist to a large extent of a critical discussion of Ricardo's views on the matter (Marx, 1959). Marx sought to establish the special form of technical progress Ricardo had contemplated in the chapter on machinery as the dominant form shaping the long-run trend of the capitalist economy. This form is characterized by a growing 'organic composition of capital': the ratio of 'constant capital', C, that is, dead labour incorporated in the produced means of production, to freshly performed, living labour, L. Its inverse gives, of course, in labour value terms the maximum rate of profits, $R = L/C$, associated with zero wages and thus a zero 'variable capital', V. Obviously, if the maximum rate of profits tends to fall towards zero, sooner or later the actual rate will also have to fall. Marx accused Ricardo of having fled 'from political economy into organic chemistry' by explaining a fall in the rate of profits in terms of diminishing returns in agriculture and thus a decreasing productivity of labour. He, Marx, wished on the contrary to show that the rate of profits would fall, 'not because the productivity of labour decreases, but because it increases', it would fall despite technical progress (Marx, 1992: 309; my translation). We now know that in this regard Ricardo was right and Marx wrong: for a given and constant real wage rate (and setting aside the problem of land) technical change would increase the general rate of profits or leave it constant, but does not diminish it.

HEINZ D. KURZ

See also:

Accumulation of Capital: Capital and Profits; Endogenous Growth; Hayek, Friedrich von, on Ricardo; Kaldor, Nicholas, on Ricardo; Land and Rent.

References

Blaug, M. (2009), 'The trade-off between rigor and relevance: Sraffian economics as a case in point', *History of Political Economy*, **41**(2), 219–47.
Eltis, W. (1984), *The Classical Theory of Economic Growth*, London: Macmillan.
Ferguson, C.E. (1973), 'The specialization gap: Barton, Ricardo, and Hollander', *History of Political Economy*, **5**(1), 1–13.
Garegnani, P. (1987), 'Surplus approach to value and distribution', in J. Eatwell, M. Milgate and P. Newman (eds), *The New Palgrave. A Dictionary of Economics, Vol. 4*, 1st edition, London: Macmillan, pp. 560–74.
Gehrke, C. (2003), *Price of Wages. A Curious Phrase*, mimeo, University of Graz.

Gehrke, C. and H.D. Kurz (2006), 'Sraffa on von Bortkiewicz: reconstructing the classical theory of value and distribution', *History of Political Economy*, **38**(1), 91–149.

Gehrke, C., H.D. Kurz and N. Salvadori (2003), 'Ricardo on agricultural improvements: a note', *Scottish Journal of Economics*, **50**(3), 291–6.

Hagemann, H. (2009), 'Capital, growth, and production disequilibria: on the employment consequences of new technologies', in R. Scazzieri, A. Sen and S. Zamagni (eds), *Markets, Money and Capital*, Cambridge, UK: Cambridge University Press, pp. 346–66.

Hicks, J. (1969), *A Theory of Economic History*, Oxford: Clarendon Press.

Jeck, A. and H.D. Kurz (1983), 'David Ricardo: Ansichten zur Maschinerie', in H. Hagemann and P. Kalmbach (eds), *Technischer Fortschritt und Arbeitslosigkeit*, Frankfurt am Main: Campus, pp. 38–166.

Kurz, H.D. (1998), 'Marx on technological change: the Ricardian heritage', in R. Bellofiore (ed.), *Marxian Economics. A Reappraisal, Vol. 2*, Basingstoke and London: Palgrave Macmillan, pp. 119–38.

Kurz, H.D. (2010), 'Technical progress, capital accumulation and income distribution in classical economics: Adam Smith, David Ricardo and Karl Marx', *European Journal of the History of Economic Thought*, **17**(5), 1183–222.

Kurz, H.D. and N. Salvadori (1995), *Theory of Production. A Long-period Analysis*, Cambridge, UK/New York/Melbourne: Cambridge University Press.

Kurz, H.D. and N. Salvadori (2006), 'Endogenous growth in a stylised "classical" model', in G. Stathakis and G. Vaggi (eds), *Economic Development and Social Change*, London and New York: Routledge, pp. 106–24.

Marx, K. (1959), *Capital, Vol. II*, Moscow: Progress Publishers.

Marx, K. (1969), *Theories of Surplus Value, Vol. 2*, Moscow: Progress Publishers.

Marx, K. (1992), *Ökonomisches Manuskript 1863–1865*, in *MarxEngels /Gesamtausgabe, Vol. II/4.2*, Berlin: Dietz.

Petty, W. ([1899] 1986), *The Economic Writings of Sir William Petty*, (ed.) C.H. Hull, New York: Augustus M. Kelley.

Rostow, W.W. (1990), *Theories of Economic Growth from David Hume to the Present*, New York and Oxford: Oxford University Press.

Samuelson, P.A. (1957), 'Wages and interest: a modern dissection of Marxian economic models', *American Economic Review*, **XLVII**(6), 884–912.

Schefold, B. (1976), 'Different forms of technical progress', *Economic Journal*, **86**(344), 806–19.

Schumpeter, J.A. (1954), *History of Economic Analysis*, New York: Oxford University Press.

Solow, R.M. (2010), 'Stories about economics and technology', *European Journal of the History of Economic Thought*, **17**(5), 1113–26.

Tooke, Thomas, and Ricardo

David Ricardo (1772–1823) and Thomas Tooke (1774–1858) were contemporaries in the 'golden era' of classical economics, along with Malthus, Torrens and McCulloch. The central figure in that era was undoubtedly Ricardo with his important contributions to the 'core' theory of value and distribution and it can be claimed that the 'golden era' essentially came to a close with Ricardo's premature death. By contrast, Tooke's important contributions to the theory of money and prices in classical economics came well after Ricardo's demise and they represented an outright rejection of Ricardo's well-established monetary theory. In the golden era, when Tooke first became acquainted with Ricardo, apparently after giving evidence to the Parliamentary committees on the resumption of cash payments in 1819, he had not yet published any economic writings

It is evident though that Ricardo was much impressed with Tooke's grasp of factual economic and financial information as well as his wide knowledge of the workings of the commercial world, which he displayed in evidence to various Parliamentary committees and especially in evidence to the Commons Select Committee on Agricultural Distress in 1821. Indeed, as Tooke (Tooke and Newmarch [1857] 1928, V: 66–7) later recounted, Ricardo was instrumental as a member of the latter committee in summoning him to give evidence before it. In this respect, Tooke not only supported Ricardo on resumption of the gold standard but was also a strong supporter of free trade and the abolition of the Corn Laws. Much of the evidence Tooke gave to the 1821 Committee on Agricultural Distress against the operation of the Corn Laws so impressed Ricardo that he cited it heavily in his 1822 pamphlet *On Protection of Agriculture* (see *Works*, IV: 221, 228, 231, 259). It was advocacy of free trade that in fact became the basis for the inception of the Political Economy Club. As its historian has documented, the Political Economy Club was established in April 1821 with the initial purpose of advancing the principles of the 'Merchants Petition' written by Tooke and signed by most economic writers, including Ricardo (see Higgs, 1921: x–xi).

Whereas Ricardo was considered by his classical contemporaries to be the supreme theorist, a 'deductive thinker' *par excellence*, Tooke was considered to be an empiricist, and, indeed, can be rightfully considered to be the supreme 'inductive thinker' of the English classical economists. A symbiotic relationship of this very sort seems to have been perceived by Ricardo when he encouraged Tooke in his work on prices to write his first publication *Thoughts and Details of High and Low Prices of the Last Thirty Years* published in 1823. In a letter to Malthus dated 16 December 1822 Ricardo wrote:

> I saw Tooke for a few minutes, and was glad to hear from him that he had been writing, and was nearly ready for press. I have a very good opinion of his judgement and of the soundness of his view – he will, I think, from his practical knowledge, throw much light on the question of the influence of an over supply or an increased demand, without a corresponding supply, on price. (*Works*, IX: 250)

In Ricardo's system, the theoretical counterpart of actual prices is 'market prices' determined by a complexity of factors to be explained from empirical evidence by reference to the interaction between quantity demanded and supply brought to market. Who better then to study price fluctuations than an empirically minded intellect like Tooke? This fundamental difference in their methodological approach was well reflected by Ricardo's tendency to interpret factual events consistent a priori with his theory that contrasted with Tooke's approach of establishing the concrete facts in all their complexity by empirical analysis in order to construct a theory. Hence, while Ricardo did not change his monetary theory after 1811, when he had largely worked it out, Tooke progressively altered his position over some 30 years until he had developed his Banking School theory by the 1840s.

The Ricardo and Tooke connection is best known for their opposing monetary theories. As is well known, Ricardo developed his monetary theory in the Bullionist Controversies that raged over the causes of the depreciation of the pound sterling against the pre-1797 mint gold standard during the restriction period of 1797–1821 when the Bank of England was not required to convert its bank notes into gold on demand. Importantly, these controversies took place against the background of the long-running Napoleonic Wars of 1793–1815, with the English economy experiencing high and unstable price inflation. Ricardo was a leading proponent of the Bullionists who argued that the depreciation of the pound and the high inflation was predominantly attributable to the excess of paper money in circulation caused by the Bank of England's overissue of bank notes under the inconvertible currency system of restriction. They argued for the restoration of convertibility and the gold standard, which they believed would prevent the Bank of England from overissuing bank notes. While Tooke was also a Bullionist who argued for an immediate return to convertibility in 1819 he did not agree with Ricardo's monetary theory.

Among English classical economists Ricardo was an exponent of a rigid version of the quantity theory of money. According to Ricardo (*Works*, III: 311) causation ran systematically from the quantity of money (consisting of Bank of England notes and coin) to the price level. In Ricardo's theory (ibid.: 88–90, 276–7, 301; V: 436–8) the velocity of circulation was an institutional datum, essentially fixed by the banking habits of the public, and national income was fixed at full-capacity utilization by Say's Law. On this basis, the quantity of money is conceived to be under the exogenous control of the Bank of England as the central banking authority, so that if it increased (decreased) its issue of notes then, given velocity and income, it would tend to increase (reduce) the price level. An important element in Ricardo's (*Works*, I: 363–4) theory is that in the event of an increase in the quantity of money the rate of interest would decline in relation to the rate of profit to ensure that the excess of money would be absorbed through borrowing to circulate commodities at higher prices. Only in an inconvertible monetary system, which was the case in Britain during the restriction period 1797–1821, did Ricardo's quantity theory apply both to the short and long run. In a gold (or silver) convertible system of currency, Ricardo's quantity theory was confined to the short run because the 'price-specie flow' mechanism operated to effect changes in gold (or silver) reserves to compel the Bank of England to adjust its issues in order to remove any excess (or shortage of) money in circulation. Hence, under a system of gold (or silver) convertibility, the discretionary power of the Bank of England to persistently influence the quantity of money was neutered.

Ricardo's quantity theory of money became the basis for the Currency School's position in the 1840s, which Tooke opposed as the leader of the Banking School. By this time Tooke had developed his Banking School theory of money and prices as an alternative to the classical economist's quantity theory of money that he rejected on both theoretical as well as empirical grounds. The central proposition of Tooke's Banking School theory ([1840] 1928, III: 200; [1844] 1959: 123) was that the quantity of money is determined endogenously by demand so that causation ran from activity and prices to the quantity of money in circulation. An implication of this was that the Bank of England, as the central banking authority, did not have the discretionary power to autonomously regulate the quantity of money in conflict with the requirements of trade. Any attempt by the Bank of England (or the banking sector as a whole) to autonomously expand its bank notes in circulation that was not justified by public demand would be returned to the banking system by way of 'reflux'; while, alternatively, effective measures to withdraw bank notes and coin from active circulation in relation to public demand would result in their substitution by other less convenient monetary instruments (i.e., credit). In this regard Tooke maintained that there was considerable elasticity in the English financial system to accommodate by way of credit finance variations in economic activity and the price level as contingent on the prevailing state of market confidence. Tooke argued ([1844] 1959: 19–20, 71–2; [1848] 1928, IV: 173–218) that the power to autonomously enlarge the quantity of money could only be systematically exercised by a government issuing compulsory fiat money in an inconvertible monetary system to finance its expenditures and, thereby, force it directly into circulation. Otherwise, the power of the Bank of England to influence money in circulation depended on how its temporary influence over interest rates affected activity and prices. However, on this point, Tooke denied a systematic and predictable causal influence of the rate of interest on the inducement to spend. In particular, he denied that the facility to borrow at a low rate of interest on its own provided sufficient inducement to an increase in expenditure on commodities, arguing that the 'error is in supposing the disposition or will to be con-extensive with the power [to purchase]' ([1844] 1959: 79). Hence, Tooke's argument that the banks, in particular the Bank of England, did not have the power to autonomously expand or contract the whole quantity of money in circulation at its discretion is premised on a rejection of any systematic causal influence of the rate of interest on spending.

Another original proposition of Tooke's Banking School theory is that the long-run average money rate of interest constitutes a normal cost of production of commodities so that permanent changes in this rate exert a positive causal influence on the long-run general price level. Hence, Tooke (ibid.: 81, 123–4) argued that a persistent reduction (increase) in the rate of interest would reduce (increase) the cost of production and, through competition, bring about a lasting reduction (increase) in the general price level. It is evident that Tooke ([1838] 1928, II: 346–7) developed this conception from empirical evidence showing a strong correlation between long-run movements of the rate of interest and the general level of prices. Whereas a temporary change in the money rate of interest had no distinct affect on prices, Tooke maintained that a permanent change had a lasting effect on prices 'directly opposite to those which are commonly supposed' ([1840] 1928, III: 166). This conception of money interest as a normal cost of production was essentially the basis of Tooke's unorthodox notion adopted at least from 1838 that the money rate of interest systematically governs the normal rate of profit, the latter determined by the sum of the average money rate of interest plus the remuneration for risk and trouble on the employment of capital in production. In this connection Tooke (1826: 5–31; [1838] 1928, II: 355–64) conceived that in the long run the average rate of interest was determined autonomously and causally prior to the profit rate, by politico-institutional and conventional factors in the financial market that, in conjunction with the process of accumulation, governed the supply of and demand for loan capital (see Smith, 2011: 145–53). This conception by Tooke of the money rate of interest as being determined by forces in the financial system independent of and causally prior to the profit rate was subsequently adopted by J.S. Mill ([1844] 1874: 108–17), Marx ([1894] 1978: 361–5) and, indeed, Keynes ([1936] 1971–89: 203–4; [1937] 1971–89: 123).

The Banking School theory showed that a major problem with the classical economists' quantity theory of money, which Ricardo did much to establish, was that it lacked a plausible transmission mechanism by which a central banking authority could exogenously control the quantity of money. He did this by showing that in classical economics there was no basis for supposing a systematic and predictable causal influence of a change in the money rate of interest in relation to the rate of profit on the inducement to spend. Moreover, from the standpoint of classical economics, Tooke's Banking School theory, with its central conception of endogenous money, is as coherent as Ricardo's monetary theory (Smith, 2011: 197–204). Perhaps it is ironic that Tooke developed his alternative Banking School theory of money and prices on the basis of a great deal of empirical work published in Volumes I–III of his *History of Prices* ([1838] 1928; [1840] 1928) that Ricardo had encouraged from the beginning.

MATTHEW SMITH

See also:

McCulloch, John Ramsay, and Ricardo; Mill, James, and Ricardo; Torrens, Robert, and Ricardo; Trower, Hutches, and Ricardo.

References

Higgs, H. (ed.) (1921), *Political Economy Club Centenary Volume: Minutes of Proceedings, 1899–1920; Roll of Members and Questions Discussed, 1821–1920, Vol. VI*, London: Macmillan.
Keynes, J.M. (1936), *The General Theory of Employment, Interest and Money*, in D. Moggridge and E. Johnson (eds), *The Collected Writings of John Maynard Keynes, Vol. VII*, London: Macmillan for the Royal Economic Society.
Keynes, J.M. ([1937] 1971–89), 'Alternative theories of the rate of interest', in D. Moggridge and E. Johnson (eds), *The Collected Writings of John Maynard Keynes, Vol. XIV*, London: Macmillan for the Royal Economic Society, pp. 201–23.
Marx, K. ([1894] 1978), *Capital: A Critique of Political Economy, Vol. III*, (ed.) F. Engels, reprint, Moscow: Progress Press.
Mill, J.S. ([1844] 1874), 'On profits and interest', in *Essays on Some Unsettled Questions of Political Economy*, 2nd edition, reprint, Clifton, NJ: Augustus M. Kelley, 90–119.
Smith, M. (2011), *Thomas Tooke and the Monetary Thought of Classical Economics*, London: Routledge.
Tooke, T. (1823), *Thoughts and Details of High and Low Prices of the Last Thirty Years, in Four Parts*, London: John Murray.
Tooke, T. (1826), *Considerations on the State of the Currency*, 2nd edition, London: John Murray.
Tooke, T. ([1838] 1928), *A History of Prices and of the State of the Circulation from 1793 to 1837; preceded by a brief sketch of the corn trade in the past two centuries, Vols I and II*, reprint, London: P.S. King and Son.
Tooke, T. ([1840] 1928), *A History of Prices, and of the State of the Circulation in 1838 and 1839, with some remarks of the alterations proposed in our banking system, Vol. III*; reprint, London: P.S. King and Son.
Tooke, T. ([1844] 1959), *An Inquiry into the Currency Principle*, 2nd edition, in *Series of Reprints of Scarce Works, on Political Economy, No. 15*, London: London School of Economics and Political Science.
Tooke, T. ([1848] 1928), *A History of Prices, and of the State of the Circulation, from 1839 to 1847 inclusive: with a general review of the currency question, and remarks on the operation of the Act, 7 & 8 Vict. c32, Vol. IV*, reprint, London: P.S. King and Son.
Tooke, T. and W. Newmarch ([1857] 1928), *A History of Prices and of the State of the Circulation, During the Nine Years 1848–1856, Vols V and VI*, reprint, London: P.S. King and Son.

Torrens, Robert, and Ricardo

Robert Torrens (1780–1864) was not much noticed by historians of economics before the second half of the twentieth century. A favourable assessment by E.R.A. Seligman in a 1903 essay 'On some neglected british economists' did little to elevate Torrens's renown. But in 1958 Lionel Robbins published a lengthy monograph that established Torrens's reputation as a significant participant in the theoretical and policy debates that took place in Britain from 1810 to 1860. Robbins's book appeared at a time of renewed interest in the period, owing to the publication a few years earlier of Sraffa's edition of Ricardo's *Works, and Correspondence*. Though Torrens was a member of Ricardo's circle, the secondary literature on him remains sparse. In the judgment of Robbins (1958: 258), who certainly admired him, Torrens was not an economist of 'the first rank'; he is of interest mainly because 'he was in at the very beginning of the nineteenth-century developments [and] he lived through the main formative phase, himself participating in the process' (ibid.: 3). Schumpeter (1954: 490) wrote of Torrens that he 'was careless in formulation and not a good technician and offers his wheat much mixed with chaff'. Giancarlo de Vivo (1986: 35), however, rates Torrens 'as second only to Ricardo among economists of the Ricardian period'.

Aside from a single letter, which is not concerned with economic matters (see *Works*,

XI: xi–xii), no correspondence between Ricardo and Torrens is known to exist. They knew each other, however, and were on cordial terms, even when they disagreed. Ricardo, Malthus, James Mill and Torrens were all founding members of London's Political Economy Club, where they frequently met one another. What we know of Ricardo's interactions with Torrens comes from Ricardo's correspondence with others, in which Torrens is occasionally mentioned; from remarks in the published writings of the two men; and from some manuscript fragments on value written by Ricardo and Torrens in 1818 (*Works*, IV: 303–18).

Torrens was a prolific and generally lucid writer, but he had a tendency toward long-windedness and pomposity. He is perhaps best known for having formulated, some-what earlier than Ricardo, the theory of comparative advantage (Torrens, 1808, 1815). Ricardo's articulation of the argument is generally deemed to be clearer and more fully developed than Torrens's, and it was, of course, Ricardo's *Principles* (*Works*, I: VII) that gave the theory its initial traction. In later work Torrens (1844) advanced the argument beyond where Ricardo had left it, by noting that the precise terms of trade will depend upon the patterns of demand for traded goods among the trading partners (i.e., the reciprocal demands).

Torrens's writings on value theory intersected with Ricardo's in several ways, and it is on this topic that Torrens is of particular interest to Ricardo scholars. Ricardo's *Essay on Profits* (*Works*, IV) and the first edition of Torrens's *Essay on the External Corn Trade* were published on the same date in 1815. Both authors argued against the Corn Laws, but they reasoned from fundamentally different theoretical perspectives. At this time, Torrens was still thinking in Smithian terms: he believed that a rise in wages would cause the prices of all commodities to rise; and he argued that the profit rate is regulated by the supply of capital relative to the demand for it (the competition of capitals argument). Ricardo had left these ideas behind by 1815. Torrens was profoundly influenced by the arguments of Ricardo's *Essay*, however, and when he next touched upon the topics of value and distribution his views had shifted substantially in Ricardo's direction (de Vivo, 1985, 1986). The second edition of Torrens's *Essay on the External Corn Trade* (1820) put forward an account of the determination of the profit rate that was substantially the same as Ricardo's, with profits conceptualized as a residual share, and the rate of profits determined by the technical conditions of production and the real wages of labour.

A significant feature of the second edition of Torrens's *Essay* is that it explains the profit rate in terms that are essentially identical to Ricardo's corn-ratio theory of the *Essay on Profits*. As de Vivo (1986: 27) notes, Torrens – who liked to build a case by bombarding his readers with arithmetical illustrations – expressed this argument in terms of two types of numerical examples. In the first type of example, Torrens supposed that at the level of the economic system as a whole, commodities appear as outputs and as capital inputs in the same proportions, so that the profit rate can be calculated without reckoning in value terms. Langer (1982) identifies the presence of this argument also in Torrens (1819), and both he and de Vivo (2001) note the conceptual parallel to the Standard commodity of Sraffa's *Production of Commodities by Means of Commodities* (1960). The other sort of example looks at a single sector of the economy, the corn sector, and assumes that capital is comprised of seed-corn and of food in the form of corn. The profit rate in agriculture is then determined in physical terms as a ratio of net output (a quantity of corn) to capital (also a quantity of corn); competition will then ensure that the prices of other goods adjust to bring profit rates in those sectors into line with the physically determined agricultural profit rate.

Both de Vivo and Langer view these instances of physical determination of the profit rate in Torrens's writings as supporting evidence for the corn-ratio interpretation of Ricardo's *Essay on Profits*. Hollander (1995) and Peach (2001) argue, on various grounds, that the presence of corn-ratio reasoning in Torrens provides no support for the attribution of the same reasoning to Ricardo. But de Vivo (1996, 2001) has noted that Torrens himself attests to the influence of Ricardo's *Essay on Profits* on the explanation of the profit rate of the second edition of his *Essay on the External Corn Trade*; while Langer (1982) reminds us that Ricardo had a strongly favourable reaction to Torrens (1819), which advanced a version of the corn-ratio argument, and wrote to McCulloch in February 1820 that he had no substantive objections to anything in it (see *Works*, VIII: 159).

Torrens had reservations about Ricardo's treatment of value in the *Principles*. In 1817, in discussions with Ricardo, he noted that differences in the durability of capital meant that commodities would not exchange in proportion to the amounts of labour required to produce them. Ricardo apparently made some small adjustments to the second edition of the *Principles* in response to this observation (*Works*, VI: 305–15). Then in a short published note on the first edition of Ricardo's *Principles*, Torrens (1818) made the point that unless equal capitals employ the same amount of labour – that is, unless all productive sectors utilize labour and capital in the same proportions – the values of commodities cannot be proportional to the quantities of labour that enter into their production. Reacting to this in his commonplace book, Ricardo (*Works*, IV: 315–18) remarks that in the *Principles* he in fact acknowledged precisely that point and discussed in detail how sectoral differences in capital structure determine the impact on prices of a change in wages. De Vivo (1986: 29–30) calls attention to the close similarity between Torrens's further development of this argument in the *Essay on the Production of Wealth* (1821) and Marx's treatment of the same issue in, for example, *Theories of Surplus Value* ([1862–63] 1969–72, III: 72): like Marx, Torrens made his point by arguing that if the proportions between labour and capital differ across sectors, prices proportional to embodied labour would come into conflict with the uniform profit rate condition for long-period equilibrium.

Torrens was in fact moving toward the idea that the relative values of commodities were regulated not by the quantities of labour required for their production, but by the amounts of capital, both in the form of wages and in the form of produced means of production, needed to produce them. This view Robbins christened the 'capital theory of value'. Torrens developed it at some length in his *Essay on the Production of Wealth* (1821). Ricardo, who continued to grapple with the problem of how to reconcile his labour value analysis with the complications posed by sectoral differences in the proportion in which labour and capital are utilized in production, was not persuaded. In his final essay on value theory, which was left unfinished at the time of his death in 1823, Ricardo (*Works*, IV: 394–6) took a moment to criticize Torrens's capital theory of value, mainly on the ground that when the proportions in which capital and labour are not uniform across sectors, the value of capital cannot be ascertained independently of distribution. 'When Col. Torrens says that equal capitals will produce equal values,' Ricardo (ibid.: 394–5) writes, 'he must then clearly define what he means by equal capitals, and he ought to add "when employed for equal times" for equal capitals do not produce equal results unless they are employed for equal times.' (See de Vivo, 1986: 28–33, for a thorough discussion of the difficulties with Torrens's approach.) The impasse between Torrens and Ricardo on this matter was in part due to the fact that Torrens believed that the only meaningful concept of value was relative value, whereas Ricardo considered the discovery of a practicable measure of absolute value to be central to his theoretical agenda.

Two further points on the relation between Ricardo and Torrens are worth making in conclusion. Torrens was an early expositor of the view that the normal level of wages is a biologically and institutionally determined norm that differs across geographical boundaries and across historical periods. Ricardo (*Works*, I: 96–7) cites the second edition of Torrens's *Essay on the External Corn Trade* (1820), adding, 'The whole of this subject is most ably illustrated by Colonel Torrens'. (But Sraffa tells us in a footnote to this citation that Ricardo added these lines in the second edition of the *Principles* in response to a complaint by Torrens that Ricardo had made no mention of him in the first edition.) Seligman (1903: 342–3) suggests that Torrens was the originator of this conception of the wage, but the idea was already present in the classical literature of his day (Robbins, 1958: 48–9; see also on this topic de Vivo, 2010). Finally, Torrens, in the *Essay on the Production of Wealth* (1821), challenged an argument put forward by Ricardo in his famous chapter 'On Machinery' (*Works*, I: XXXi; added to the third edition) that mechanization can lead to a persistent reduction in the demand for labour. Torrens contended that capitalists introduce new machinery solely with a view to increasing their profits; but the higher profits may be expected in turn to give rise to increased accumulation, which will create sufficient additional demand for labour to bring the displaced workers back into employment (Berg, 1980: 106; see also Karayiannis, 2000).

Gary Mongiovi

See also:

Bentham, Jeremy, and Ricardo; McCulloch, John Ramsay, and Ricardo; Mill, James, and Ricardo; Tooke, Thomas, and Ricardo; Trower, Hutches, and Ricardo.

References

Berg, M. (1980), *The Machinery Question and the Making of Political Economy, 1815–1848*, Cambridge, UK: Cambridge University Press.
de Vivo, G. (1985), 'Robert Torrens and Ricardo's "corn-ratio" theory of profits', *Cambridge Journal of Economics*, 9(1), 89–92.
de Vivo, G. (1986), 'Torrens on value and distribution', *Contributions to Political Economy*, 5, 23–36.
de Vivo, G. (1996), 'Ricardo, Torrens and Sraffa: a summing up', *Cambridge Journal of Economics*, 20(3), 387–91.
de Vivo, G. (2001), 'On Torrens's theory of profits', *Cambridge Journal of Economics*, 25(5), 697–703.
de Vivo, G. (2010), 'Robert Torrens as a "neglected economist"', *Research in the History of Economic Thought and Methodology*, 28-B, 89–110.
Hollander, S. (1995), 'Sraffa's rational reconstruction of Ricardo: on three contributions to the *Cambridge Journal of Economics*', *Cambridge Journal of Economics*, 19(3), 483–9.
Karayiannis, A.D. (2000), 'Robert Torrens on technological progress', *History of Economic Ideas*, 8(2), 63–94.
Langer, G.F. (1982), 'Further evidence for Sraffa's interpretation of Ricardo', *Cambridge Journal of Economics*, 6(4), 397–400.
Marx, K. ([1862–63] 1969–72), *Theories of Surplus Value, Vols I–III*, London: Lawrence & Wishart.
Peach, T. (2001), 'Hollander, de Vivo and the "further evidence" for the corn model interpretation of Ricardo', *Cambridge Journal of Economics*, 25(5), 685–92.

Robbins, L. (1958), *Robert Torrens and the Evolution of Classical Political Economy*, London: Macmillan.
Schumpeter, J.A. (1954), *History of Economic Analysis*, New York: Oxford University Press.
Seligman, E.R.A. (1903), 'On some neglected British economists, I', *Economic Journal*, **13**(51), 335–63.
Sraffa, P. (1960), *Production of Commodities by Means of Commodities*, Cambridge, UK: Cambridge University Press.
Torrens, R. (1808), *The Economists Refuted*, London: S.A. & H. Oddy.
Torrens, R. (1815), *An Essay on the External Corn Trade*, 1st edition, London: J. Hatchard & Son.
Torrens, R. (1818), 'Strictures on Mr Ricardo's doctrine respecting exchangeable value', *Edinburgh Magazine and Literary Miscellany* (October), 335–8.
Torrens, R. (1819), 'Mr. Owen's plans for relieving the national distress', *Edinburgh Review*, **32**(October), 453–77.
Torrens, R. (1820), *An Essay on the External Corn Trade*, 2nd edition with considerable additions, London: J. Hatchard & Son.
Torrens, R. (1821), *An Essay on the Production of Wealth with an Appendix in which the Principles of Political Economy are Applied to the Actual Circumstances of this Country*, London: Longman, Hurst, Rees, Orme & Brown.
Torrens, R. (1844), *The Budget. On Commercial & Colonial Policy*, London: Smith, Elder & Co.

Tozer, John Edward, on Ricardo

In 1838, John Edward Tozer (1806–70), a Cambridge mathematician, published an article 'Mathematical investigation of the effect of machinery on the wealth of a community in which it is employed, and on the fund for the payment of wages', in which he set out to address the following problem: 'A portion of capital, which either has been or would have been employed in the payment of wages, is used in the construction of machinery; to determine the effect on the wealth of the community, and on the fund for the payment of the labourer' (Tozer [1838] 1991: 164).

The question of the effects of machinery on employment was the subject of a hot debate – both theoretical and political – in early nineteenth-century England. Most prominently, Ricardo famously argued that 'the substitution of machinery for human labour, is often very injurious to the interests of the class of labourers' (*Works*, I: 388), and that 'the opinion entertained by the labouring class, that the employment of machinery is frequently detrimental to their interests, is not founded on prejudice and error, but is conformable to the correct principles of political economy' (ibid.: 392). Compensation effects arising from the introduction of machinery, he claimed, would not suffice to offset labour displacement.

With his mathematical background, Tozer could not be content with the numerical examples used by Ricardo and most of his other contemporaries, which he felt were tailored to specific case studies and could hardly be generalized. In an effort to fill this gap, Tozer relied on algebra to build a comprehensive framework for thinking about the effects of machinery; though more abstract, his approach would be more general and logically sounder than numerical examples, and would still be flexible enough to be adapted to the study of individual cases if needed.

As a pioneer in the use of symbols and equations to guide economic thinking, Tozer earned himself a place in the history of mathematical economics. He published some other papers in which he applied mathematics to socioeconomic and even legal problems; his contribution, however, had very limited echo at the time and continued to be largely ignored afterwards, partly because mathematical economics remained a tiny niche in the discipline for long. There is evidence that William S. Jevons, Irving Fisher and Alfred Marshall were familiar with his contribution, but not one of them commented extensively on it. Tozer was rediscovered late, when David A. Collard authored a first painstaking analysis of his contribution, framing it as part of the classical approach to machinery (1968). Few other studies have followed, most of them presenting Tozer as a member of the so-called 'Whewell group' of mathematical economists that was formed in Cambridge at the time, but with little detail on his own work (Theocharis, 1993; Henderson, 1996). In-depth studies of the mathematical arguments and how they contributed to defining Tozer's position with respect to Ricardo came more recently (Gehrke, 2000; Tubaro, 2008).

The purpose of this entry is to show that Tozer's reasoning, in its most basic version, leads to the result that compensating effects prevail so that the introduction of machinery is ultimately beneficial to all social classes including workers; in this sense, his work may seem to challenge Ricardo's more pessimistic opinion. However, when some simplifying assumptions are removed, and more subtle social factors as well as the linkages among them are taken into account, this conclusion no longer holds and Tozer's line of argument tends to broadly support Ricardo's view. Finally, the last section of the entry assesses Tozer's position with respect to Ricardo from a different angle, and points to the emergence of the consumer as a central actor, to be explicitly introduced into economic analysis. Tozer's representation of the consumer is not yet mature, though, and remains in between classical/Ricardian and proto-neoclassical perspectives.

A detailed presentation of Tozer's algebra would be beyond the scope of this entry, all the more so as its clumsy character (by today's standards) and obsolete notation would require extensive comments. Instead, a simpler and modernized presentation of Tozer's argument is adopted here, reducing the formal aspects to a minimum. Focus is on the logical chain of reasoning underpinning Tozer's equations, to illustrate how it constitutes a coherent, cogent whole, enabling us to draw general conclusions. Readers interested in the mathematics are invited to consult Gehrke (2000) and Tubaro (2008) together with the original article, of which reprints are available in Collard's book (1968) and in one of a series of volumes edited by Adrian Darnell (see Tozer [1838] 1991).

The remainder of this entry is organized as follows. First, it discusses Tozer's main line of argument and major findings; it subsequently examines the nuances introduced by Tozer, and finally the role of the consumer in the analysis. The last section sums up and concludes.

A seemingly positive result: compensation effects offset unemployment over time

Tozer distinguished the phase in which the machine is being built from the one in which it is ready and used in production. Beginning with the first, he assumed that a capitalist owns a stock that he uses initially to pay the wages of workers employed to produce some commodity. Suppose the capitalist decides to redirect some of this capital towards a machine-making project; this will be the case if use of this machine in the production of the commodity in question can be expected to lower production costs, and therefore to be more profitable than production of this same commodity with only labour as an input. This decision diverts some of the stock, initially used to pay wages, to machine building and is therefore immediately conducive to unemployment. This remains true even if one takes into account that some labourers will be needed to build the machine and, therefore, the total reduction of the wage-fund is smaller than the total expense needed to build the machine. In all cases at the end of the machine-building phase (which may take several years), the labourers who manufactured it will become redundant, and with respect to the initial state, the wage-fund will be reduced by an amount that is equal to the value of the new machine. This is a form of what the literature usually calls 'technological unemployment', referring to the replacement of workers by machines or other technical devices.

Nevertheless, as soon as the machine is put to use, said Tozer, a gain arises both for the capitalist and for society at large. The former was fully anticipated (and constituted the main reason why the capitalist decided to build the machine in the first place); the latter stems from the fact that for the machine to be profitable, it must lower production costs and, therefore, it must also bring down the price of the final manufactured good, thereby benefiting consumers. Interestingly, Tozer labelled the sum of the two 'community gain', to signify how it integrates into a single indicator the viewpoint of both the producer and consumers: 'the gains of the capitalist are included in those of the community at large' (Tozer [1838] 1991: 169). Tozer then generalized the result of a positive gain to the community, first obtained under the assumption that the general rate of profit remains unchanged, to cases in which the rate of profit varies as a result of the change in production technique. He said:

> If we assume that a capitalist will employ machinery or labour as one or the other will procure for him the highest rate of profit, then the employment of machinery will always increase the wealth of the community. Not only is the capitalist unable to secure his own advantage at the expense of any other class, he cannot even prevent a general participation in the benefit. (Ibid.: 172)

In turn, the (positive) community gain is likely to be used to start new productive processes, which will create new jobs over time. Meanwhile, a new machine will need to be built in order to replace the one that is currently in use at the end of its lifespan: this is also a job-creating process. Combined, these two processes are likely to entirely eliminate the initial technical unemployment so that eventually, total employment may turn out to be even higher than before the introduction of machinery.

Figure 24 (upper panel) summarizes Tozer's argument, with its main steps and the linkages among them. The technological unemployment created at the end of phase 1 (the machine-building process, represented in the left column in the figure) is eventually offset at the end of phase 2 (machine use, right column). One may therefore be tempted to conclude that mechanization, decided solely by the capitalist in self-interested perspective, ultimately yields positive consequences for society as a whole.

In this sense, it may seem that Tozer's result challenges Ricardo's view that the use of machinery in production may harm the labouring class; yet it does so only to a certain, definite extent. Indeed, even in the most favourable cases, technological unemployment is likely to persist for a relatively long time: it is not limited to the transition phase from what we would call today one long-period position (the old, non-machinery-based production technique) to another one (the new, machine-based technique), but may last for a while after the new technique has been adopted. Indeed, it may take time before the compensation effects arising from community gain fully offset the initial labour displacement; in other words, technological unemployment is not a transitional phenomenon only.

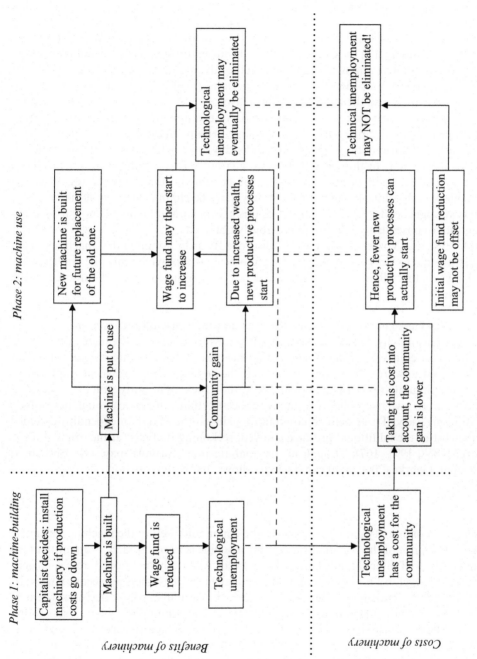

Phase 1: machine-building

Phase 2: machine use

Capitalist decides: install machinery if production costs go down

Machine is built

Wage fund is reduced

Technological unemployment

Machine is put to use

New machine is built for future replacement of the old one.

Wage fund may then start to increase

Community gain

Due to increased wealth, new productive processes start

Technological unemployment may eventually be eliminated

Benefits of machinery

Costs of machinery

Technological unemployment has a cost for the community

Taking this cost into account, the community gain is lower

Hence, fewer new productive processes can actually start

Initial wage fund reduction may not be offset

Technical unemployment may NOT be eliminated!

Figure 24   Tozer's main line of argument (upper panel) and the nuances he subsequently introduces (lower panel)

The social costs of unemployment curb compensation effects
Tozer recognized that his main line of argument, presented above, ignores that the initially created technological unemployment imposes a specific *cost* on society; this simplification must be removed for a more precise account of the effects of machinery on society. Although Tozer himself did not provide details on the nature of this cost, one reason for including it in the calculations may reside in the fact that households are at the same time consumers and workers, therefore the advantage they derive from reductions in the price of the goods they buy may be undermined by the loss of income from which they suffer if they lose their jobs. Another reason, one may argue, is that the community likely has to provide for the unemployed, for example through extra taxes to fund government assistance programmes or through a rise in charitable giving. Be that as it may, the total community gain will be considerably lower when these costs are explicitly taken into account. In this case, there is no guarantee that a lower price for produced goods will free enough wealth to start new job-creating productive processes. Thus, the initially created technical unemployment may *never* be eliminated, even in the long run. The lower panel of Figure 24 summarizes this argument and highlights how it weakens the positive consequences that were previously obtained.

It follows that Tozer's work does not disprove Ricardo's opinion that machinery may be detrimental to workers. Although technological unemployment may be eradicated in the long run, this will not always happen, depending on the cost initially imposed on the community.

An upwards-biased notion of gain and the (partial) emergence of the consumer
Another reason why Tozer's work ultimately fails to invalidate Ricardo's view of the negative consequences of machinery is that his measure of community gain turns out to be biased upwards; therefore, even when the cost of technological unemployment for the community (as defined above) is low, the 'true' community gain may in fact be insufficient to give rise to new productive processes that can create enough new jobs.

More precisely, Tozer defined community gain as 'the saving in expenditure, added to the cost of the additional produce enjoyed, reckoning that cost at the original price' (Tozer [1838] 1991: 167). Though his original algebraic formula may seem obscure at first sight, Gehrke (2000: 489) convincingly shows that it amounts to:

$$G = p_0 q_1 - p_1 q_1 \tag{1}$$

where G = community gain, p_0 = price of the commodity before the machine was introduced, p_1 = price of the commodity after the machine is introduced, q_1 = quantity of the commodity sold after the machine is introduced. As briefly mentioned above, Tozer's idea was to develop a notion of gain that could integrate consumers into economic analysis. Similarly to Ricardo, the key social actor is the capitalist, whose decisions (here, to install new machinery) can affect everybody else in the community; yet to assess collective well-being, consumers' viewpoints also need to be taken into account. Tozer recognized that the fall in prices that mechanization brings about is beneficial for consumers, and can be so in two different ways. On the one hand, it offers the possibility to purchase the same quantity as before, at a lower price; on the other hand, a lower price may enable consumers to buy greater quantities of the good. In other words, there is a shift from p_0q_0 to p_1q_1, where p_0 exceeds p_1, and q_1 may be greater than q_0. That said, Tozer's problem was to determine at which price to value the additional quantity sold $q_1 - q_0$. His solution was simply to value the final quantity q_1 at the initial price p_0 and then at the new price p_1, then to take the difference between the two values p_0q_1 and p_1q_1 (equation (1) above). But because the quantity $q_1 - q_0$ was not bought at the initial price p_0, this measure overestimates gain – except in cases in which the quantity purchased does not change with price, that is, in modern parlance, when demand is vertical in the Cartesian price–quantity coordinate system.

It was only a few years later, with Jules Dupuit ([1844] 1934), that an appropriate solution was devised, equivalent to what is known today as consumer surplus. Having conceptualized demand as a downward-sloping schedule in the price–quantity graph, Dupuit computed the gain of consumers from a price reduction as the area below the demand curve, delimited by the initial and final price levels. With Dupuit's criterion instead of Tozer's, gain is lower (unless, of course, demand is perfectly price inelastic); as a result, mechanization of productive activities appears to be even less favourable to society than Tozer's own account of it suggests.

Admittedly, Tozer was not the only writer who struggled with this problem at the time; examples of other, unsuccessful efforts to define consumer gain or surplus are those of Jean-Baptiste Say ([1803] 1972) and the French engineer Henri Navier (1832). Both were strongly criticized by Dupuit; the latter, in particular, for reasons that would have applied equally well to Tozer. Despite these difficulties, all these writers retain historical interest for their efforts to define a place for the consumer in economic theory. While influenced by the classical school and its focus on production conditions, they all tried to develop a deeper understanding of consumer behaviour and strongly felt the need to incorporate it explicitly in their analyses. As part of this tendency, Tozer's work is profoundly innovative with respect to Ricardo.

Conclusions

Tozer's contribution can be seen as an effort to devise a general, abstract framework for thinking about the causes of technological unemployment, its transformations over time and its social implications. It is meant to overcome the limitations of numerical examples, which concern only particular cases and cannot give rise to universally valid conclusions. It can in principle be applied to many particular cases – indeed, Tozer himself used it to reinterpret some of the numerical examples with which Ricardo and others had illustrated their views, and Gehrke (2000: 500–501) shows that he even managed to bring to the surface an inconsistency in Ricardo's choice of figures.

With his approach, Tozer showed that the existence of a community gain often eradicates unemployment over time – a conclusion that may seem at first sight to disprove Ricardo's view that mechanization may be injurious to the working classes. However, unemployment may persist for long after mechanization; even worse, it may never be reabsorbed if it generates costs that the community must bear, and these costs are high enough to curb the community gain. This more negative conclusion is all the more plausible as Tozer's indicator of community gain is in fact biased upwards, and a more appropriate measure would offer even less scope for compensation effects. In this sense, Tozer's work broadly supports Ricardo's view and should rather be seen as a generalization of the latter's thesis on machines.

Tozer reveals greater originality with respect to Ricardo in his effort to introduce consumers' viewpoint into economic analysis. His attempt is not entirely successful, though, lies halfway between classical and pre-neoclassical perspectives, and is to be superseded by Dupuit's contribution a few years later.

PAOLA TUBARO

See also:

Bortkiewicz, Ladislaus von, on Ricardo; Dmitriev, Vladimir Karpovich, on Ricardo; Whewell, William, on Ricardo.

References

Collard, D.A. (1968), 'Introduction to the work of John Edward Tozer', in D.A. Collard, *J.E. Tozer*, New York: A.M. Kelley, pp. v–xx.
Dupuit, J. ([1844] 1934), 'De la mesure de l'utilité des travaux publics', in J. Dupuit, *De l'utilité et de sa mesure*, (ed.) M. de Bernardi, Torino: La riforma sociale/Paris: Marcel Giard, pp. 29–65.
Gehrke, C. (2000), 'Tozer on machinery', *European Journal of the History of Economic Thought*, **7**(4), 485–506.
Henderson, J.P. (1996), *Early Mathematical Economics: William Whewell and the British Case*, Lanham, MD: Rowman and Littlefield.
Navier, H. (1832), 'De l'exécution des travaux publics et particulièrement des concessions', *Annales des Ponts et Chaussées*, **XXXV**, 1–31.
Say, J.-B. ([1803] 1972), *Traité d'économie politique ou simple exposition de la manière dont se forment, se distribuent et se consomment les richesses*, Paris: Calmann-Lévy.
Theocharis, R.D. (1993), *The Development of Mathematical Economics: The Years of Transition, from Cournot to Jevons*, London, Macmillan.
Tozer, J.E. ([1838] 1991), 'Mathematical investigation of the effect of the machinery on the wealth of a community in which it is employed, and on the fund for the payment of wages', reprinted in *Early Mathematical Economics: Journal Articles and Pamphlets from 1800 to 1900, Vol. II*, (ed.) A.C. Darnell, London: Pickering & Chatto, pp. 163–72.
Tubaro, P. (2008), 'Producer choice and technical unemployment: John E. Tozer's mathematical model (1838)', *European Journal of the History of Economic Thought*, **15**(3), 433–54.

Trower, Hutches, and Ricardo

Hutches Trower (1777–1833) has the claim to fame of being a major correspondent of David Ricardo. One of Trower's four daughters, Frances Trower, was responsible for preserving both Ricardo's letters to Trower and the basic facts relating to her father's life. She mentioned that her mother (Penelope Trower, *née* Slater) had suggested, 'it does an honour to any man to have corresponded with Ricardo' (cited in Bonar and Hollander, 1899: ix). Trower, who survived Ricardo by a decade, became an intimate friend of the whole Ricardo family. Their friendship revealed in their regular correspondence was broadly based. Besides political economy, it embraced politics, social reform, theology, literature, geology, tree planting and comments on affairs of the day.

Trower's friendship with Ricardo began with their daily meetings at the stock exchange where they both worked as stockbrokers. Their friendship was strengthened by their mutual admiration 'of the work of Adam Smith, and of the early articles on Political Economy in the Edinburgh Review' (Ricardo to Trower, 26 January 1818, *Works*, VII: 246). They were subsequently briefly on 'opposite sides' during the Bullionist Controversy. Trower's contribution as 'A Friend of Banknotes, &c', first seemed opposed to Ricardo's doctrines, but not long afterwards, became 'a complete convert to them' ('Memoir of Ricardo', *Works*, X: 7–8). This exchange took place in the pages of the *Morning Chronicle* for the last four months of 1809. Much of it concerned the price of gold – that is, both its market and its mint price – and its relation to the value of bank notes and gold coin (*Works*, III: 22–3). Ricardo (ibid.: 81 and 87–8) cited Trower's piece twice in his 1810 pamphlet, *The High Price of Bullion*, the second citation critical of Trower's acceptance of a monetary explanation of the rate of interest, rather than one based on 'the abundance and scarcity' of real capital. Almost certainly, they would also have discussed these issues in conversation. On their retirement in 1813 to country estates (Ricardo to Gatcombe Park, Trower to Unsted Wood, at Godalming, Surrey), they exchanged letters at roughly monthly intervals until Ricardo's death in 1823.

Following the four correspondence volumes of the works of Ricardo as edited by Sraffa, the extent of their correspondence can be summarized as follows. Volume VI contains nine letters from 8 November 1813 to 21 December 1815, four from Ricardo and five from Trower. Volume VII covers January 1816 to December 1818 with no less than 34 letters, 16 from Ricardo and 18 from Trower. Volume VIII covers January 1819 to the end of June 1821, comprising 31 letters, 17 from Ricardo and 14 from Trower. Volume IX (July 1821 to September 1823) contains 23 letters, 15 from Ricardo and only eight from Trower. Total correspondence between them amounts to 97 letters altogether, 52 from Ricardo and 45 from Trower. Although a substantial exchange of letters, it is considerably less than those between Ricardo and fellow economists, James Mill, Malthus and McCulloch.

Ricardo's first extant letter to Trower (8 November 1813, *Works*, VI: 96) thanked him for a pamphlet, *Christianity in India*, jointly written by Trower. March 1814 sees their first direct exchange of views on economics, namely a draft of Ricardo's paper on the profits of stock. Trower's notes on this draft mentioned in the letter, appear to have been lost. Ricardo's reply sets out his theory of profits, explains his differences with Malthus thereon, indicates the negative association of profits with the diminishing productivity of capital on land, and its positive association with the discovery of new markets in manufacturing, and with cheaper methods of producing food (March 1815, ibid.: 102–5). When Ricardo sent Trower a copy of his *Essay* in 1815, Trower indicated his strong approval. He also praised Ricardo's treatment of rent, but disagreed with Ricardo's scheme of a definite distribution of the surplus to either rent or profit. For Trower (10 March 1815, ibid.: 184), this also depended on the average profits of the farmer. If these were at the same level as profits in general, rent would enjoy the surplus; if below general profits, the surplus went to profits. Ricardo's response to Trower's criticism is not extant.

Trower's next letter to Ricardo (23 July 1815, ibid.: 237–8) commented on retirement, his profits on the sale of omnium (the aggregate value of different stocks in which a loan to government is funded) and the recapture of Napoleon. Two months later, Trower reported the addition of a daughter to his family, his pleasure on learning that Ricardo was still working on political economy, his views on monetary upheavals and his admiration of what he called Ricardo's 'ingenious defence of Bonaparte' (ibid.: 279–81). Ricardo's reply (29 October 1815) particularly commented on his studies of political economy, including preparation of an *Economical and Secure Currency* (1816) and continuing research on rent, profits and wages. Trower's letter in response regretted their limited opportunity to converse on political economy issues, and confessed his life as a country gentleman still enabled him to observe banking issues and variations in the price of bullion (26 November 1815, ibid.: 325–8). Ricardo's reply (25 December 1815, ibid.: 343–5) discussed banking matters, Trower's new mode of life and the decline in rural produce prices. This detailed summary of their 1815 correspondence is a blueprint of their eight years' correspondence until Ricardo's death.

Trower's first letter in 1816 broached banking, asked Ricardo's opinions on savings banks and the poor rates, congratulated him on his daughter Priscilla's wedding and looked forward to frequent meetings when both were in 'town' after Easter (19 January 1816, *Works*, VII: 11–13). Ricardo's response apologized for its lateness (4 February 1816, ibid.: 15–18) and then systematically addressed Trower's questions. He praised savings banks for their contribution to improving the condition and morals of the poor, commented on the price of corn, the 'loss' of another daughter and the scandalous state of his Brook Street house, which he blamed on its former owner. Trower's February letter thanked Ricardo for his 1816 currency pamphlet, raised questions about a proposed silver standard, praised Ricardo's criticism of the Bank of England and recounted his own efforts at creating a local savings bank (ibid.: 21–3). Ricardo's reply stressed his gratitude for both favourable *and* unfavourable criticism, as truth was his only aim when establishing economic principles. He also commented on Trower's savings bank venture (ibid.: 27–9). Trower's next letter invited Ricardo's comments on the role of depositors in governing savings banks, on wanton destruction of farm machinery and on Weyland's book on population. Ricardo replied at some length on all of these topics. Similar issues were pursued in subsequent correspondence. Trower's letter of November 1816 (ibid.: 94–5) expressed pleasure at Ricardo's steady pursuit of political economy, as shown by his preparation of the *Principles*, published in April 1817. Trower promised to read it with 'great eagerness and interest', since it so clearly covered every important aspect of the subject. Unfortunately, Trower's letter with detailed comments on the *Principles* is lost. However, Trower subsequently discussed its theory of value with Ricardo in the light of Torrens's criticism and the views of McCulloch (23 August 1818, ibid.: 288–9) but other 1818 letters mainly addressed constitutional questions. Ricardo's last letter to Trower for 1817 (ibid.: 370) mentioned that the second edition of his *Principles* was 'in the press' and that a French edition had recently appeared.

The letters of 1819 and 1820 pursued similar topics. On 17 January 1819, Trower indicated he had notes to assist Ricardo's second edition, but devoted most of his letter to constitutional problems (*Works*, VIII: 11–16). Ricardo's reply mentioned a Parliamentary inquiry into currency and the exchanges, and the wish to converse when both were in London (ibid.: 18–19). Trower congratulated his friend on his many activities to advance the public good. Ricardo, in reply, sent him the Lords' Report on currency. Correspondence then dealt with bank stock, a topic pursued in several letters; Ricardo's presence on a committee investigating Robert Owen's utopian schemes (ibid.: 42–3), Robert Owen's study of French contraception (ibid.: 71–2), Ricardo's work on the 'sinking fund' (ibid.: 78, 109–10), Trower's work as a country magistrate (ibid.: 111–13), Malthus's *Principles of Political Economy* (ibid.: 132–3, 201–2, 207–8), government borrowing (ibid.: 147–8) and aspects of value theory following Trower's return to active political economy studies. Value also marked the start of their 1820 correspondence (ibid.: 153–6). Other topics were the conduct, and trial, of Queen Caroline (ibid.: 194–200, 206–7, 220–21), Trower's claim that studying Malthus and Ricardo was very time-consuming, particularly on value, profits and rent (ibid.: 217–20, 232–7), and Trower's lengthy discussion on 'necessaries' and 'conveniences' in relation to demand and the theory of value (ibid.: 247–50). Ricardo replied quickly. He suggested the key to the problem was whether 'the supply of corn preceded the demand for it, or does it follow such demand'. Ricardo noted that if supply preceded demand, 'it must be at a lower price than the grower could afford to produce it'. For Ricardo, supply was stimulated when its market price exceeded natural price, the clear indication that supply was less than demand. Similarly, the production of necessities depended on whether the producer had a demand for them, a demand that may arise from the possibility he has of trading necessities for conveniences (ibid.: 255–8). Trower responded at length three days later. This set out his main points of agreement and disagreement with Ricardo:

> I admit most fully, that Commodities will not *continue* to be produced if they do not pay the *costs of production*. I admit there is a sort of *rough level* of profit on productive capital; that *this* directs capital to its most advantageous employment, and, that the *price*, that satisfies these costs, is the *natural price* of Commodities. I admit also, that there is a constant action and reaction, going on, between capital and labor and supply and demand; but what I contend for *is*, that, *in the very nature of things, supply must precede demand*. (Ibid.: 264; original emphasis)

From first principles, Trower elaborated his position in considerable detail. Ricardo's reply (ibid.: 271–6) expressed agreement with Trower on most issues. However, he maintained that his friend erred in assuming that when a given output of corn, iron and cloth doubled, the value of these commodities would stay in the same proportion, even if it affected the division of the total produce between wages and profits. Ricardo claimed this failed to conform to a just application of supply and demand. Doubling corn output, for example, would lower the demand for it and therefore its market price, whereas demand for luxuries does not fall when their output doubles. This argument rested on very special assumptions. Trower's response (ibid.: 287–90) did not pursue the argument further. It discussed general political issues, as did most subsequent letters from Ricardo at the time.

Correspondence then turned to Trower's thanks for Ricardo's *Essay on the Funding System*, and mentioned the best way to deal with Ricardo's *Notes on Malthus* (ibid.: 332). Further correspondence in 1821 discussed their reactions to Malthus's *Principles* (ibid.: 349–50, 361), Godwin's *Population* and Mill's *Elements of Political Economy*. Trower (ibid.: 393–6) indicated he had carefully studied the *Notes on Malthus* and, in addition provided observations on Mill's *Elements*. Ricardo's response is the first letter published in Volume IX of the *Works*. He was very pleased with Trower's very positive response to the *Notes on Malthus*, touched on the meaning of 'exchangeable value', and once again gave his views on market and natural price (*Works*, IX: 1–4). Trower (ibid.: 28–31) elaborated on his problems in understanding exchangeable value, one of the few points in political economy, he confessed, in which he tended to side with Malthus. Ricardo's reply blamed his poor powers of exposition as the cause of Trower's difficulties. He then commented on his work on an Agricultural Committee, tithes, the end of Queen Caroline's troubles and the state of his local economy (ibid.: 37–40). Trower was most impressed with the evidence to the 'Depressed State of Agriculture Committee' that Ricardo had sent him, commented further on the problem of distinguishing real and exchangeable value, expressed his wish for a good book on the practical operation of taxation and replied to Ricardo's remarks on tithes (ibid.: 66–71). Ricardo's next letter (ibid.: 86–90) further commented on these matters, as did Trower (ibid.: 107–11). Ricardo's letter (ibid.: 120–24) contained an account of his presence at a dinner to honour Hume, the radical MP, commented on some recent literature and defended his adherence to gold as the best monetary standard. Trower's reply (ibid.: 144–8) expressed amusement at Ricardo's 'homage to Hume', discussed the Irish questions in terms of 'want of capital and . . . Industry', the merits of Peel as a statesman, taxes on malt and Mill's article on 'Government' for the *Encyclopaedia Britannica*. Ricardo in reply mentioned his imminent return to Parliamentary duties as well as some literary matters (ibid.: 151–5).

Missing letters from Trower then make Ricardo the only 'visible' correspondent for over a year (from January 1822 to March 1823), with letters from Ricardo missing as well. Their final exchange of letters took place in late August/early September 1823, dealing characteristically with political economy, tree planting, Malthus on value, and the relation between profits and production (ibid.: 376–9, 382–4). Trower was informed of Ricardo's sudden death in September 1823, which effectively ended the correspondence.

PETER GROENEWEGEN

See also:

McCulloch, John Ramsay, and Ricardo; Mill, James, and Ricardo; Tooke, Thomas, and Ricardo; Torrens, Robert, and Ricardo.

Reference

Bonar, J. and J.H. Hollander (eds) (1899), *Letters of David Ricardo and Hutches Trower and others 1811–1823*, Oxford: Clarendon Press.

Walras, Marie-Esprit-Léon, on Ricardo

Marie-Esprit-Léon Walras (1834–1910) was Professor of Political Economy at the University of Lausanne, Switzerland. In 1871 he published *Elements of Pure Economics* ([1871] 1954), a work that initiates what has become known as the general equilibrium theory. Most of Part VII of that book is devoted to a critical discussion of some of the views advocated by earlier schools of economic thought. Lessons 38–40 pay special attention to David Ricardo's contribution.

Walras fails to see that the classical approach to the theory of value and distribution is fundamentally different from his own demand-and-supply approach. He treats Ricardo's theory as if it was just an early and crude version of his own elaborate neoclassical general equilibrium theory. This theory attempts to determine quantities, relative prices of goods and income distribution in terms of the following data: (α) technical alternatives; (β) preferences; and (γ) initial endowments of factors of production, including capital, and the distribution of property rights among the members of society. Ricardo in his theory is said to have started essentially from the same sets of data, but to have imposed unnecessary restrictions on them and in addition to have committed logical blunders. Entirely in line with his view of Ricardo, Walras believes he is faithful to the English economist when 'closing' his model of the Ricardian theory of rent in terms of a given 'quantity of capital'. He misses the fact that the data of the classical theory are different: (a) technical alternatives; (b) the size and composition of the social product; (c) the real wage rate; and (d) the quantities of land available. He also misses the fact that in terms of these data, the dependent variables – the rate of profit, the rent rates and relative prices – are fully determinate. There is no need, and indeed no possibility, to add some further givens, such as the capital endowment of the economy or utility. Walras's objection that Ricardo tried 'to determine two unknowns with one equation', meaning that his system is underdetermined, is untenable. In the following we analyse in some detail how Walras criticizes the theories of rent, wages and profits by Ricardo.

Walras on the Ricardian theory of rent

Lesson 39 of the *Elements* is devoted to an 'exposition and refutation' of the Ricardian theory of rent. Walras's algebraic argument can be summarized as follows. Let h_i be the excess product per hectare of land of quality i over the payment of wages, x_i the 'amount of capital' in terms of the numéraire (and exclusive of the wages of labour) employed per acre on land of that quality, and t the 'rate of interest charges expressed in terms of [physical] units of product' (ibid.: 409), then the rent per acre of land of quality i, r_i, is given by:

$$r_i = h_i - x_i t, \qquad (i = 1, 2, \ldots, s) \qquad (1)$$

where s is the number of the different qualities of land available, each of which is in given supply n_i, and where h_i is assumed to depend exclusively on x_i, that is:

$$h_i = F_i(x_i). \qquad (i = 1, 2, \ldots, s) \qquad (2)$$

Walras stresses that in (long-period) equilibrium each quality of cultivated land must earn the same physical return per unit of capital employed, t. In the case in which qualities 1 to m are cultivated ($m \leq s$), we have:

$$t = F_1'(x_1) = F_2'(x_2) = \ldots = F_m'(x_m). \tag{3}$$

Counting the number of equations and unknowns in (1)–(3), Walras observes that there are only $3m$ equations but $3m + 1$ unknowns: the unknowns are $r_1, \ldots, r_m; h_1, \ldots, h_m; x_1, \ldots, x_m;$ and t. Hence there is one degree of freedom. How did Ricardo close the system? Walras's answer is:

> Another equation is needed. We can, *without deviating in any way from a faithful interpretation of Ricardo's theory*, write the following equation, which is analogous to those given in §§242 and 248:

$$n_1x_1 + n_2x_2 + n_3x_3 + \ldots = X. \tag{[(4)]}$$

> According to Ricardo, it seems that in every economy there is a certain amount of capital ... *At any given moment, the amount of capital is determinate*. Let us call such a determinate amount X, and let us distribute it among the different kinds of land in such a way that the rate of yield is the same on all lands. (Ibid.: 410; emphasis added)

Walras thus interprets Ricardo as closing the system in terms of a given 'quantity' of social capital. This interpretation cannot be sustained. In Ricardo's long-period approach to the problem of value and distribution, the amount of capital is not an exogenous given but a magnitude determined endogenously in terms of a particular specification of the set of data (a)–(d). In order for the given output levels to be produced in a cost-minimizing way *and* in order for a uniform rate of return on capital to obtain, the vector of capital goods cannot be given from outside the system of production, but has to be ascertained from within the system in terms of those output levels and the other data of the classical approach.

Walras on the Ricardian theory of wages and profits

In Lesson 40 Walras deals with the classical theory of wages and profits. The lesson is almost exclusively devoted to a criticism of John Stuart Mill and especially his wage-fund doctrine. These parts need not concern us here. There is only one section that is somewhat related to Ricardo's way of thinking and that deserves to be commented upon. We quote §368 in full:

> Let P be the aggregate price received for the products of an enterprise; let S, I and F be respectively the wages, interest charges and rent laid out by the entrepreneurs, in the course of production, to pay for the services of personal faculties, capital and land. Let us recall now that, according to the English School, the selling price of products is determined by their costs of production, that is to say, it is equal to the cost of the productive services employed. Thus we have the equation

$$P = S + I + F, \tag{[(5)]}$$

> and P is determined for us. It remains only to determine S, I and F. Surely, if it is not the price of the products that determines the price of productive services, but the price of productive services that determines the price of the products, we must be told what determines the price of the services. That is precisely what the English economists try to do. To this end, they construct a theory of rent according to which rent is not included in the expenses of production, thus changing the above equation to

$$P = S + I.$$

Having done this, they determine S directly by the theory of wages. Then, finally, they tell us that 'the amount of interest or profit is the excess of the aggregate price received for the products over the wages expended on their production', in other words, that it is determined by the equation

$$I = P - S.$$

It is clear now that the English economists are completely baffled by the problem of price determination; for it is impossible for I to determine P at the same time that P determines I. In the language of mathematics one equation cannot be used to determine two unknowns. This objection is raised without any reference to our position on the manner in which the English School eliminates rent before setting out to determine wages.

Walras's critique misses its target. The critique was explicitly refuted by the Russian mathematical economist Vladimir K. Dmitriev ([1898] 1974: 51ssq). In the following we shall provide an argument that is logically identical to Dmitriev's, but refers also to other parts of the *Elements*. In this way we intend to throw some additional light on certain aspects of Walras's thought, which do not always seem to have been properly understood (see also Kurz and Salvadori, 1995: 25–6; 2002).

Equation (5) is here presented using matrix notation:

$$\mathbf{p} = \mathbf{Cq} + \mathbf{Ew} + \mathbf{Ay},$$

where **p** is the vector of prices of outputs (Walras assumes that the first element of **p** equals unity since the first commodity acts as the numéraire), **C** is the matrix of the production coefficients of land inputs of the operated processes, **q** is the vector of prices of land services (i.e., the rent rates), **E** is the matrix of the production coefficients of labour inputs of the operated processes, **w** is the vector of prices of personal services (i.e., the wage rates), **A** is the matrix of the production coefficients of the inputs of capital goods proper of the operated processes, and **y** is the vector of prices of the services of capital goods proper. (In accordance with Walras, rents and wages are taken to be paid at the end of the uniform period of production.) If, following Ricardo, as mentioned by Walras himself, we take account only of the technology used at the margin (either extensive or intensive; for the intensive margin we have to follow the procedure provided by Guichard, 1982) and if we assume for simplicity that there is only one quality of labour, we obtain the equation:

$$\mathbf{p} = w\mathbf{l} + \mathbf{Ay}. \tag{6}$$

In §238 (similarly §232) Walras asserts that if P_k is the price of a capital good proper, its depreciation charge and its insurance premium are respectively $\mu_k P_k$ and $v_k P_k$. (It deserves to be noted that depreciation charges cannot generally be assumed to be given, as in Walras: they typically depend also on income distribution.) If the mentioned capital good is a circulating one, then $\mu_k = 1$; and if the insurance premium on it is nought, then $v_k = 0$. If, on the contrary, **M** is the diagonal matrix with the exogenously given depreciation charges on the main diagonal and **V** is the diagonal matrix with the given insurance premiums on the main diagonal, then:

$$y = (M + V + iI)p,$$

where i is the 'rate of net income', which, Walras stresses, 'is the same for all capital goods' (§233; see also §§238 and 249; also Walker, 1996: 214). Then equation (6) becomes:

$$p = wl + A(M + V + iI)p, \tag{7}$$

which is a system of n equations in $n + 1$ unknowns, since by definition the first element of p equals unity, where n is the number of products, some (or all) of which could be capital goods proper.

Taking (with Ricardo) the real wage rate as given, we get the $n + 1$ equations needed to determine prices *and* distribution. In fact, if:

$$w = b^T p,$$

where b is a given vector defining the real wage rate, and assuming (with Walras) that wages are paid post factum, equation (7) becomes:

$$p = lb^T p + A(M + V + iI)p.$$

And if the elements of b and the elements on the main diagonal of matrices M and V are small enough, then matrix $I - lb^T - AM - AV$ is invertible with a semipositive inverse and:

$$p = i(I - lb^T - AM - AV)^{-1}Ap.$$

That is, $1/i$ is the Perron-Frobenius eigenvalue of matrix:

$$(I - lb^T - AM - AV)^{-1}A$$

and p is the corresponding eigenvector whose first element equals unity. In this simple exposition we have assumed the existence of a single 'technique', that is, the existence of a single triplet (A, M, V). If there were alternative techniques, the analysis would be more complex, but it is possible to prove that for each alternative a rate of net income i can be determined, and that in conditions of free competition the alternative will be chosen which yields the largest i.

We may thus conclude that Walras's criticism is untenable: Ricardo cannot be accused of having attempted 'to solve two unknowns with one equation'. Ricardo's system is perfectly determinate. The data, or independent variables, from which he started his analysis of the problem of value and distribution suffice to determine the unknowns, or dependent variables, that is, the rate of profit, the rent rates and prices in terms of the given numéraire. No other data, such as utility or demand functions, are needed.

In his reading of Ricardo, Walras was misled by the idea that there is only a single kind of theory in economics: demand-and-supply theory. Assessed in terms of his own theory

Ricardo's was bound to look strange. Had Walras given a closer look to Ricardo's construction he would have found that there is no indeterminacy.

HEINZ D. KURZ AND NERI SALVADORI

See also:

Jevons, William Stanley, on Ricardo; Marshall, Alfred, on Ricardo; Schumpeter, Joseph Alois, on Ricardo; Wicksell, Knut, on Ricardo.

References

Dmitriev, V.K. ([1898] 1974), *Economic Essays on Value, Competition and Utility*, English translation of a collection of Dmitriev's essays published in 1904 in Russian, (ed.) D.M. Nuti, Cambridge, UK: Cambridge University Press; Dmitriev's essay on Ricardo's theory of value was originally published in 1898.
Guichard, J.P. (1982), 'La rente différentielle intensive, expression d'un processus d'intensification de cultures', in R. Arena et al. (eds), *Etudes d'économie classique et néoricardienne*, Paris: PUF, pp. 115–38.
Kurz, H.D. and N. Salvadori (1995), *Theory of Production. A Long-period Analysis*, Cambridge/Melbourne/New York: Cambridge University Press.
Kurz, H.D. and N. Salvadori (2002), 'One theory or two? Walras' critique of Ricardo', *History of Political Economy*, **34**(2), 365–98.
Walker, D. (1996), *Walras's Market Models*, Cambridge, UK: Cambridge University Press.
Walras, L. ([1871] 1954), *Elements of Pure Economics*, London: Allen and Unwin; English translation by W. Jaffé of the definitive edition of *Eléments d'économie politique pure*, first published 1874, Lausanne.

Wealth

The notion of wealth appears and reappears in Ricardo's works within three different sets of arguments. One is concerned with the distinction between wealth and value, another with the causes of the progress of wealth, the third with the consequences of this progress on the trend of natural wages, profits and rents. Ricardo deals with these subjects sometimes in agreement and sometimes in disagreement with Smith. The agreement concerns the notion of wealth as such as well as the causes of its progress, while the disagreement concerns the foundations both of that distinction and of the resulting conclusions on the trend of natural wages, profits and rents.

Ricardo's notion of wealth

Ricardo's notion of wealth coincides with Smith's in the general sense that both of them reject the popular idea that wealth consists in money (gold or silver) along with the associated idea that one nation's gain must be another nation's loss (*WN*, IV.i; *Works*, III: 139–45; see also Meacci, 1998a). It also coincides with that notion, except for some details to be discussed below, in the more specific sense of regarding wealth as the 'annual produce of the land and labour' or, more precisely, as the annual flow of the 'necessaries, conveniences and amusements of human life' (*WN*, I.i and *passim*).

These similarities do not rule out some different meanings in that wealth is intended by both authors sometimes as a flow in a period of time and sometimes as a stock at an instant of time, and in both cases either as a flow or stock sometimes of final goods and sometimes of final and instrumental goods. Thus, while Smith uses the term wealth as synonymous mostly with revenue (a flow) and sometimes with a stock of goods (though never of money), Ricardo uses the same term as synonymous sometimes with riches, sometimes with (the aggregate of) use values, and sometimes with (net and gross) revenue, (net and gross) income and (net and gross) produce (see, for instance, Chapters XXVI and XXXI). Now while the terms 'wealth', 'riches' and 'use values' are different words that may be properly used for the same concept, the terms 'revenue', 'income' and 'produce' convey different concepts depending on whether they are considered from the standpoint either of an individual or of the whole society. When, for instance, it comes to the latter standpoint, the term revenue (which – as noted by Marx [1885] 1978, *Capital*, II: 19 – comes from the French verb *revenir*) rather conveys the idea of final goods that 'return' to life in the current year as a result of the wage goods exchanged for, and consumed by, the labour employed in the process of their reproduction, while the terms 'income' and 'produce' rather convey the different concepts of goods that either 'come in' or are 'produced' in the current year regardless of the labour employed, respectively, in the current or in previous years.

Material vs immaterial objects

However close to Smith's notion of wealth as the 'annual produce of the land and labour of a country' and as the 'necessaries, conveniences and amusements of human life' available in a given period, Ricardo's notion is incidentally different if one looks at his treatment of this issue in his *Notes on Malthus's Principles of Political Economy* (*Works*, II). For in the third of these notes he shares Malthus's attempt to fill the gap left over by Smith by drawing a line between 'material' and 'immaterial' objects and by confining the notion of wealth only to 'those material objects which are necessary, useful, or agreeable to mankind'. This definition, it must be noted, excludes all the services that, though 'necessary, useful, or agreeable to mankind', account for an increasing part of the wealth of a country as this increases from period to period. Moreover, the justification provided by Malthus/Ricardo that only material objects are 'capable of accumulation and definite valuation' denies the existence, stressed by Smith in the first place and shared ever since, of those forms of human capital that are in their turn 'capable of accumulation'. On the other hand, Malthus's further objection, implicitly shared by Ricardo, that Smith's notion of wealth as the 'annual produce of land and labour' is 'not sufficiently discriminate, as it would include all the useless products of the earth, as well as those which are appropriated and enjoyed by man' (*Works*, II, I: i) would be acceptable only if Smith had written 'annual produce of land *or* labour'. However, this never occurs in his work except in a single passage, misquoted by Ricardo as the 'annual produce *either* of land *and* labour' (*Works*, I: 308) where Smith speaks of the produce 'either of land *or* labour' (*WN*, IV.v.14; emphasis added). While Ricardo's use of the term 'and' in the passage just quoted may be viewed as a misprint, Smith's replacement of the term 'or' for the term 'and' used throughout the *Wealth* does not seem to be a misprint if only because Smith is here speaking not of the production and reproduction of national wealth but only of the money price of whatever is produced in relation to a change in the money price of labour.

Yet, in spite of his minor misinterpretation of Smith's famous expression, Ricardo was fairly equipped to enrich rather than, in Malthus's footsteps, to impoverish the notion of national wealth conveyed – and the theory of reproduction introduced – by that expression. For, given the distinction highlighted in *Works*, I, I: §III, Ricardo could have relaunched that notion in the more exact sense of the annual produce of land and labour, whether direct or indirect, rather than in the weaker sense that he seems to share while endorsing Malthus's misleading attempt to criticize Smith's notion of wealth as including 'all the useless products of the earth'. In any case and contrary to this endorsement of Malthus's view, the direct/indirect labour qualification is required in Ricardo's system of thought at least when he comes to the exchangeable value of the annual produce as determined by the total labour embodied in it. Such a qualification is therefore consistent with a notion of wealth that includes, as it does in Smith's system of thought, all the products 'which are appropriated and enjoyed by man' in so far as these products, be they material or immaterial objects, are the exclusive result of the employment of labour.

National wealth vs individual wealth

The common origin of Smith's and Ricardo's notion of wealth is made clear when, right at the beginning of his criticisms of Mercantilism, Smith objects to the popular prejudice that 'a rich country, in the same manner as a rich man, is supposed to be a country abounding in money' (*WN*, IV.i.2). This sentence reveals that the identification of wealth with money (gold or silver) is in turn the result of the more general confusion between the nature and progress of the wealth of an individual ('a rich man') and the nature and progress of the wealth of a nation ('a rich country'). The former kind of wealth is best illustrated by J.S. Mill – and is best distinguished from the other – when he writes that 'to an individual anything is wealth which, though useless in itself, enables him to claim from others a part of their stock of things useful or pleasant' ([1871] 1965: 8). Ricardo's neglect for whatever may be part of the wealth of an individual without being part of the 'annual produce of the land and labour of a country' is justified, however, by Smith's own statement, silently shared by Ricardo, that 'the general stock of any country or society is the same with that of all its inhabitants or members, and therefore naturally divides itself into the same three portions, each of which has a distinct function or office' (*WN*, II.i.11). This statement, which is concerned with the capital stock of a nation as part of its wealth considered at an instant of time, is an assumption that is introduced to simplify – rather than to confuse – the relation between the wealth of an *individual* and the *wealth* of society.

This assumption proves that Ricardo's method of analysis is, at least in this connection, the same as Smith's insofar as both authors look at the progress and distribution of the wealth of nations as two distinct outcomes of the interactions between their different inhabitants. Hence the idea that the component parts of the 'annual produce' of a country cannot be but the property of its individual members along with the idea, partly and incidentally rejected by Ricardo as argued above, that all these parts cannot be but products of their own labour. Hence the importance of keeping apart, while studying together, the concept and theory of exchangeable *value* (i.e., of what is owned by an individual in terms of what is owned by another) from the concept and theory of national *wealth* (i.e., of the flow of the use values annually produced by labour regardless of who owns what).

Wealth vs value

The distinction and connection between the wealth of an individual (which consists of exchangeable values and is based on the concept of property) and the wealth of society (which consists of use values and is unconnected to that concept) comes to the fore in Chapter XX, 'Value and Riches, their Distinctive Properties', of Ricardo's *Principles* (for further details on this issue, see Meacci, 1998b and 2012). Smith's statement on whether 'a man is rich or poor' is here mentioned by Ricardo along with his arguments on whether 'a country is rich or poor' in a manner that reminds of Smith's initial criticisms of Mercantilism, although the whole chapter is intended as a critique of Smith's fundamental theory of value. Here Ricardo lays bare Smith's ambiguity whereby a man is said to be rich or poor depending on the amount of necessaries, conveniences and amusements that 'he can afford to *enjoy*' as well as that 'he can afford to *purchase*' (*WN*, I.v.1; emphasis added) as if these were two equivalent expressions in spite of the cardinal distinction between value in use and value in exchange.

Ricardo then focuses on the resulting confusions by which other authors, such as Lauderdale ([1804] 1962 and Say [1803–19] 1821), deal with this issue in spite of their criticisms of Smith's treatment of the same topic. While Ricardo's criticism of Say is focused on the latter's alleged confusion between value in use and value in exchange, his criticism of Lauderdale is based on the equivalent confusion between the wealth of an individual and the wealth of society. After reconstructing Lauderdale's argument that, if water becomes scarce and is exclusively possessed by an individual, 'you will increase his riches, because water will then have value; and if wealth be the aggregate of individual riches, you will by the same means also increase wealth' (*Works*, I: 276), Ricardo rejects this argument by distinguishing not only between the case of water becoming the object of *monopoly* and the case of water becoming *scarce*, but also between the resulting increase in the wealth of an individual as distinct from the wealth of society:

> You undoubtedly will increase the riches of this individual, but inasmuch as the farmer must sell a part of his corn, the shoemaker a part of his shoes, and all men give up a portion of their possessions for the sole purpose of supplying themselves with water, which they before had for nothing, they are poorer by the whole quantity of commodities which they are obliged to devote to this purpose, and the proprietor of water is benefited precisely by the amount of their loss. The same quantity of water, and the same quantity of commodities, are enjoyed by the whole society, but they are differently distributed. (Ibid.)

In an attempt to strengthen his strictures against Lauderdale's confusion, Ricardo proceeds by arguing that the wealth of a country may increase, unlike the wealth of an individual, only in two ways; that is, either (1) 'by employing a greater portion of revenue in the maintenance of productive labour, – which will not only add to the quantity, but to the value of the mass of commodities'; or (2) 'without employing any additional quantity of labour, by making the same quantity more productive – which will add to the abundance, but not to the value of commodities' (ibid.: 278–9). These arguments reveal some important similarities and differences between Ricardo and Smith. For, Ricardo's conclusion that in the first case 'a country would not only become rich, but the value of its riches would increase' while in the second case 'wealth would increase, but not value' is the same as Smith's with regard to riches (the wealth of nations) but is utterly different with regard to value (the exchangeable value of one commodity in terms of another). Hence the different meanings of the term value and the different variations of its magnitude in the two cases: while the value figured out by Ricardo (as increasing in the first case and remaining unchanged in the latter) is determined by the labour embodied in the 'necessaries, conveniences and amusements of human life' that make up the revenue or wealth of a country, Smith would intend the first part, and would restructure the second part, of Ricardo's sentence above in the sense that not only the quantity but also the value of riches (wealth) would increase in both cases. But while, according to Smith, this quantity would increase for the same reason as Ricardo's, its value would increase in the different sense that the resulting amount of riches would be able to command an increasing amount of labour at a given wage rate (or a constant amount of labour at an increasing wage rate). Hence the more general similarities between Smith and Ricardo as one moves from their common views of wealth to their theory of capital as the main engine for its increase. Thus, in the very chapter on value and riches where he discusses the 'two ways' in which the wealth of a country may increase, Ricardo speaks of capital as 'that part of the wealth of a country which is employed with a view to future production, and may be increased in the same manner as wealth'; that is, again in two ways depending on whether, to use a subsequent terminology, the forms of accumulation are those of 'capital widening' or 'capital deepening'.

Likewise, when in his chapter 'On Wages' he comes to the distinction between the market and natural price of labour as well as to their variations in connection with the accumulation of capital, Ricardo still defines capital as 'that part of the wealth of a country which is employed in production, and consists of food, clothing, tools, raw materials, machinery, &c. necessary to give effect to labour' (*Works*, I: 95). Here capital is regarded in the same sense as wealth, that is, not only as the capital or wealth of a country but also as a stock or a flow, depending on whether capital and wealth are considered at an instant of time (as it happens in the sentence just quoted) or in a period or sequence of periods (when capital and wealth equally appear as two flows of which one corresponds to the 'funds destined to the maintenance of productive labour' while the other corresponds to the 'necessaries, conveniences and amusements of human life' available in a given period).

Wealth vs value and rent

The notions of wealth and value reappear in Ricardo's chapter 'On Rent'. Here, however, he fails to reutilize properly these notions while criticizing the priority assigned by Smith (and others, as he says) to agriculture in the reproduction of national wealth (*WN*, II.v). For, however coherent with the principles of value and rent established in the two initial chapters of his *Principles*, Ricardo's criticisms are here incompatible with the spirit of Book II of the *Wealth* and in particular with its Chapter v. For Smith uses the same term 'rent' with two different meanings depending on whether it comes to the theory of value and distribution developed in Book I (where rent is defined as the 'price paid for the use of land') or to the theory of capital and reproduction developed in Book II (where rent is defined as the 'produce of those powers of nature, the use of which the landlord lends to the farmer'). These different meanings were highlighted by Senior in the sense that the former refers to what 'occasions rent to be demanded' (so that rent in this sense is an 'evil') while 'it is the other which enables it to be paid' (so that rent in this sense is a 'good') ([1836] 1965: 138). Thus, while Ricardo seems to regard rent as an unavoidable 'evil' (hence his view of the interests of landlords as 'always opposed' to those of society), Smith seems to regard it as an 'evil' in Book I and as a 'good' in Book II (hence his view of those interests as 'strictly and inseparably' linked with those of society).

Now Ricardo gets rid of this seeming contradiction by suppressing one of the two terms on which this ambiguity is based. This is the notion of rent as a 'good', that is, as a net product. But, however consistent Ricardo's theory of rent may be with his own theory of value, his interpretation of Smith's ambiguous treatment of the same subject is flawed by his own inability to disentangle the notion of rent as the price that someone pays to someone else for the use of the land as the latter's property (a subject that belongs to the theory of the exchangeable value of commodities) from the notion of rent as the net product that comes to light when the harvest is compared with the advances required to obtain it regardless of who owns the land (a subject that belongs to the theory of wealth as a flow of use values).

It is true, as Ricardo writes at the end of his final chapter on Malthus's opinions on rent, that 'one set of necessaries and conveniences admits of no comparison with another set; value in use cannot be measured by any known standard; it is differently estimated by different persons' (*Works*, I: 429). But here again Ricardo seems to be considering Smith's theory with the eyes of an author whose starting points are very different from those of the author he is criticizing. For the notion of rent as a net product can be accommodated in Smith's system of thought in spite of the heterogeneity of the commodities that mark the beginning and end of their reproduction periods. For the difference between the two flows of use values involved in the 'reproduction of rent' can be overcome if one applies to it the notion of value adopted by Smith and rejected by Ricardo at the very beginning of their systems of thought. This is the notion of value as labour commanded. According to this notion, that difference represents, whatever the heterogeneity of the goods going into and out of the process of reproduction, the power to command, directly or indirectly and inside or outside agriculture, a quantity of labour greater than the quantity spent to obtain this power. It is this, not the other, kind of rent that is in Malthus's mind when he regards rent as a cause of the otherwise impossible origin of cities, armies and fleets, arts, learning, and so on ([1836] 1986, I, 3: i).

A summing up

Except for some minor differences, Ricardo's notion of wealth is the same as Smith's. As such, it is used by Ricardo as synonymous with the notion of the 'annual produce of the land and labour', or of the 'necessaries, conveniences and amusements of human life', available in a country in a period. This coincidence permeates Ricardo's theory of wealth in so far as this theory is focused on the progress, as distinct from the distribution, of wealth. Thus, starting from a similar theory of wealth but from a very different theory of value, Ricardo develops some of his criticisms of Adam Smith's theory on the basis of his distinction between value and riches (wealth) as well as of his exclusive notion of rent as a price paid to the owner of land 'for the use of its original and indestructible powers'. These criticisms are consistent with Ricardo's starting point on value as labour embodied and are in contrast with Smith's different starting point on value as labour commanded.

Ferdinando Meacci

See also:

Capital and Profits; Gold; Land and Rent; Ricardo on Adam Smith; Riches and Value; Taxation.

References

Lauderdale, J.M. ([1804] 1962), *An Inquiry into the Nature and Origin of Public Wealth*, New York: A.M. Kelley.
Malthus, T.R. ([1836] 1986), *Principles of Political Economy*, Vols 5–6, London: Pickering & Chatto.
Marx, K. ([1885] 1978), *Capital*, Vol. 2, London: Penguin.
Meacci, F. (1998a), 'Wealth', in H.D. Kurz and N. Salvadori (eds), *The Elgar Companion to Classical Economics*, Vol. II, Aldershot, UK and Brookfield, VT: Edward Elgar Publishing, pp. 535–41.
Meacci, F. (1998b), 'Value and riches', in H.D. Kurz and N. Salvadori (eds), *The Elgar Companion to Classical Economics*, Vol II, Aldershot, UK and Brookfield, VT: Edward Elgar Publishing, pp. 498–502.
Meacci, F. (2012), 'On Smith's ambiguities on value and wealth', *History of Political Economy*, **44**(4), 663–89.
Mill, J.S. ([1871] 1965), *Principles of Political Economy with Some of Their Applications to Social Philosophy*, Toronto: Toronto University Press.
Say, J.B. ([1803–19] 1821), *A Treatise on Political Economy, or the Production, Distribution, and Consumption of Wealth*, translation by C.R. Prinsep of the 4th (1819) French edition, Boston, MA: Wells and Lilly.
Senior, N. ([1836] 1965), *An Outline of the Science of Political Economy*, New York: A.M. Kelley.
Smith, A. ([1776] 1976), *An Inquiry into the Nature and Causes of the Wealth of Nations*, in *The Glasgow Edition of the Works and Correspondence of Adam Smith*, (eds) R.H. Campbell, A.S. Skinner and W.B. Todd, Oxford: Clarendon Press.

Whewell, William, on Ricardo

William Whewell (1794–1866), a Fellow and Master for many years of Trinity College, Cambridge, was a lecturer in mathematics and a professor of mineralogy (1828–32) and of moral philosophy (1838–52) at the University of Cambridge. In 1825, he was the tutor of David Ricardo's son Mortimer at Trinity College (see *Works*, X: 63). The polymath ventured into political economy in the late 1820s, when he read a paper entitled 'Mathematical exposition of some doctrines in political economy' ([1829] 1971) to the Cambridge Philosophical Society. A second paper, entitled 'Mathematical exposition of some of the leading doctrines in Mr Ricardo's Principles of Political Economy and Taxation' ([1831] 1971), was read in 1831. These two papers, as well as a further one (in two parts) of 1850 (Whewell [1850] 1971), were published in the *Transactions of the Cambridge Philosophical Society*, and later reprinted together in 1971. The first two papers of 1829 and 1831 are concerned with Ricardo's propositions on prices, income distribution, taxes, foreign trade and the rate of exchange, while the third dealt chiefly with John Stuart Mill's theory of foreign trade. In 1862, Whewell also published a booklet entitled *Six Lectures on Political Economy*, which had emanated from a set of lectures he had been asked to deliver to the Prince of Wales, the future King Edward VII, in the preceding year. Some brief discussions, chiefly of methodological issues, pertaining to political economy can also be found in some of his other writings.

Whewell sought to establish and institutionalize an inductive approach to economics as opposed to Ricardo's deductive political economy. His main target was not so much Ricardo, but the Ricardians or 'Ricardoists' (as Whewell put it in a letter to Richard Jones), that is, McCulloch and the two Mills. Whewell was strongly opposed to the philosophical radicalism of the Ricardian Benthamites and also rejected John Stuart Mill's theory of induction. His concern with Ricardian economics was not limited to his own writings but he also encouraged others to scrutinize Ricardo's doctrines. The group of writers he managed to enrol as associates for this campaign included Reverend Richard Jones, Perronet Thompson, Edward R. Rogers, John Edward Tozer, John William

Lubbock and Dionysius Lardner. Malthus, whom he also sought to recruit, maintained a position of reserved approval. The main inductivist critique of Ricardo's doctrines was meant to be delivered by Richard Jones, but the Reverend managed only to publish the first part, on rent, of his *Essay on the Distribution of Wealth* ([1831] 1964). Whewell not only urged Jones to write his *Essay*, but also edited and introduced the latter's *Literary Remains* (see Jones [1859] 1964), which contain some additional material on wages and (very little) on profits. Together with Jones, Whewell was instrumental in the founding of the Statistical Society of London and of the Statistical Section (later relabelled 'Section F') of the British Association for the Advancement of Science.

Methodological issues

Whewell was convinced that 'Political economy ... must be a science of *induction*, not *deduction*. It must *obtain* its principles by reasoning upwards from facts, before it can *apply* them by reasoning downward from axioms' ([1831] 1971: 52, quoted from Henderson, 1996: 61; Whewell's emphasis). Jones was supposed to carry out the task of advancing the fundamental inductivist critique of Ricardian economics, while Whewell would use his considerable mathematical skills in order to demonstrate, by means of mathematical reasoning, that Ricardo had committed errors in his deductions. Accordingly, Whewell started his economic papers with a set of postulates or 'axioms', which he claimed could be attributed to Ricardo, translated them into mathematical symbols and equations, and then compared the algebraically deduced results with Ricardo's statements on prices, income distribution, the incidence of taxes, foreign trade, and so on. In this way he believed he could demonstrate that Ricardo had 'reasoned falsely' and had committed errors 'in the deduction of conclusions from fundamental propositions' (Whewell [1829] 1971: 4 and 5). However, scrutiny shows that what Whewell found could be criticized in Ricardo's analysis was either the premises on which his reasoning was based or the neglect of some further influences or disturbing factors on some specific problem.

The mathematics used in Whewell's economic papers consists mainly of solutions of simultaneous linear equations, with an occasional recourse to sums of infinite series. It has been contended that Whewell 'never exhibited overt concern for convergence or continuity, or for that matter, differentiability', and that he deliberately refrained from employing differential calculus in his economics papers (Henderson, 1996: 135). However, as Kim (2001) has shown, this is not true. In his 1829 essay Whewell implicitly used differential calculus in his comparative static analysis of tax incidence. He set out eight equations that implicitly defined the functional relation between eight endogenous variables and one exogenous variable, then solved the equation system to deduce the implicitly defined functions and calculated their derivatives in order to obtain a quadratic or linear approximation of each function. It must be noted, though, that Whewell never applied differential calculus to the solution of optimization problems.

Whewell's paper of 1829

Whewell's 1829 paper was meant to show the errors in Ricardo's deductive reasoning by assessing his propositions on the incidence of taxes and on the effects of agricultural improvements on profits and rents. Its proclaimed objective was to evaluate the dispute between 'the followers of Mr. Ricardo, &c. [who] maintain that all taxes on the produce of land are ultimately paid by the consumers' and Colonel T. Perronet Thompson who, in his *True Theory of Rent* (1826), 'hold[s] it demonstrable that they fall principally upon the landlord' (Whewell, [1829] 1971: 6).

Whewell analysed the problem of tax incidence in §§13–34 of his 1829 paper (and then again in §13 of his 1831 paper) by focusing attention on five specific taxes: taxes on wages, taxes on agricultural profits, percentage taxes on agricultural produce, taxes on land and taxes on rent. In the first paper he presented a rather confused analysis of taxes on wages, which contained several errors. He suggested, wrongly, that Ricardo had maintained that taxes on wages must fall on the workers (whereas Ricardo had in fact maintained that they must fall on profits) and some of his calculations are erroneous (for details, see Henderson, 1996: 190–92). In his 1831 paper he returned to this question and showed algebraically that when taxes are imposed on wages and the quantity demanded falls in response to increased prices, 'a part falls on the consumer in raised prices, and a part on the capitalist in diminished profits' ([1831] 1971: 28). However, it is the change in the premises underlying his analysis that accounts for Whewell's differing result. The most important difference between Ricardo's treatment of taxes and Whewell's approach lies in his introduction of a demand elasticity concept. Whereas Ricardo had generally premised his tax analysis on a given and unchanging demand for agricultural products, Whewell conducted his analysis of tax incidence by allowing for demand reactions to price changes. In addition, Whewell's analysis of the impact of taxes on prices was somewhat more sophisticated than Ricardo's. Whereas Ricardo for simplicity had assumed prices to be proportional to labour values in his tax analysis, Whewell explicitly took into account that commodities are produced under differing production conditions with regard to the proportions of fixed and circulating capital and/or differing durabilities of fixed capital. However, he failed to take into account production interdependencies, that is, he ignored the fact that commodities whose prices change in consequence of the imposition of a tax could enter as means of production into the production of other commodities, thus causing further commodity prices to change. Nevertheless, with regard to Whewell's tax analysis it would not seem correct to endorse Shoup's overall assessment, according to which 'Whewell casts Ricardo's analysis in the form of algebra, but does not add to it or differ from it' (1960: 109).

It is interesting to note how the notion of demand and the concept of demand elasticity were introduced by Whewell. He employed the following two axioms: 'The increase of price is proportional to the deficiency of supply' and 'The rate of price of any article will be such that the whole price of any portion is equal to the capital employed to produce it together with the usual profits' ([1829] 1971: 11–12). The second axiom clearly related prices to costs of production, which in turn were made to depend on the quantity supplied, while the first one, and notwithstanding Whewell's confusing terminology, concerned in fact the relationship between price and quantity demanded. As Whewell explained, 'supply is a quantity, and offers us no difficulty in measuring it theoretically: but demand is of a more untangible and fugitive nature. It consists originally of moral elements as well as physical: of the vehemence of desire, and the urgency of need which men have, as well as of the extent of their means' (ibid.: 9–10). He therefore proposed to use the observable and measurable 'deficiency of supply' to ascertain the relationship between price and quantity demanded and constructed a table based on the 'King-Davenant law of demand' (ibid.: 10–11). It should be noted that Whewell reversed the usual neoclassical price–quantity relationship by making price the dependent variable and quantity demanded the independent variable.

In the final section (§35) of his 1829 essay Whewell studied the impact of agricultural improvements on profits and rents (ibid.: 34–8). He followed Thompson (1826) in the classification of different types of agricultural improvements, though not in replacing Ricardo's theory of differential rent with a supply-and-demand theory of rent. By means of this analysis Whewell believed to have shown that rents are increased rather than diminished by agricultural improvements, but like Thompson – and unlike Ricardo – did not consider the 'immediate effects' of agricultural improvements with a given population and a given demand for agricultural produce. Instead, he allowed for a rise in the quantity demanded from diminished prices and, consequently, for the possibility of an inferior, not previously utilized quality of land to be brought into cultivation. Moreover, Whewell's reasoning in this section was based on the peculiar assumption that the profit rate remains unaffected by the introduction of agricultural improvements.

In his 1829 paper Whewell erroneously believed to have exposed errors in Ricardo's deductive reasoning, and to have disproved Ricardo's tax theory and his theory of agricultural improvements; he also convinced Malthus, who wrote to him that 'it must be allowed that Ricardo did not always draw correct conclusions from his premises' (quoted in De Marchi and Sturges, 1973: 390).

Whewell's paper of 1831

In his second economic paper Whewell tackled what he considered to be the three main problems studied by Ricardo: (1) the development of the proportional distribution of income in a progressing economy, (2) the 'ultimate incidence and consequences of taxes' and (3) 'some of the questions connected with the subject of foreign trade and the varying value of money' ([1831] 1971: 16). As Whewell's treatment of the second problem was already discussed above in connection with his 1829 paper, the following discussion will focus on points (1) and (3).

Whewell's analysis of the development of the proportional distribution of income, in §§9 and 10 of his 1831 essay, confirmed Ricardo's proposition that with the increased food requirements of a growing population and the extension of cultivation to less and less productive soils the share of rent must rise and the profit share fall. However, according to Whewell it is 'clearly and demonstrably false' that this has been the course of events in England: 'After Mr. Jones's reasonings . . . I do not conceive that any doubt can remain on the subject' ([1831] 1971: 15). In his 1831 *Essay* Richard Jones had argued that the available empirical evidence suggested that the rent income in England, although it had increased in absolute terms, had decreased in relative terms, that is, as a share of income ([1831] 1964: 282). For Whewell, 'it is remarkable that Mr Ricardo's error in this instance is not a mistaken assumption of principles, but it is a defect in his deduction from his principles, a part of his task which is generally supposed to be unexceptionable' ([1831] 1971: 15). However, scrutiny shows that the charge that could be levied at Ricardo again concerns the premises of his analysis: whereas Ricardo had stated explicitly to have set aside technical progress, and in particular improvements in agriculture, Whewell maintained that 'the error resides in his having neglected altogether the effects of an increase in the power of agriculture' (ibid.: 15).

Of more weight is Whewell's next criticism, which concerned Ricardo's treatment of prices. Whewell rightly observed that except in Chapter 1 of the *Principles* Ricardo had generally supposed prices to be proportional to labour values. But this is 'somewhat inaccurate according to his own principles: for in applying the postulate of price, we are to take into account the capital as well as the labour. In consequence of this consideration, the prices of commodities will be affected by the proportion and durability of fixed capital requisite for their production' (ibid.: 19). Accordingly, Whewell introduced a formula for determining the prices of commodities that are produced by means of fixed capital. He proposed to calculate the price of a new machine by means of a reduction series to dated quantities of labour:

$$C = (1 + r)lw + (1 + r)^2l'w + (1 + r)^3l''w + \&c.$$

where C is the price of the new machine, l is the amount of labour employed this year to produce the machine, l' is the amount of labour employed last year, l'' the amount of labour employed two years ago, and so on. By making use of the annuity formula, which Ricardo had implicitly employed in Chapter 1 of the *Principles* (see *Works*, I: 54–5, 56–8, 58–60), Whewell arrived at the equation that gives the production price when fixed capital is used:

$$p = lw(1 + r) + C\frac{r(1 + r)^k}{(1 + r)^k - 1}$$

where k is the number of years over which the machine is utilized (Campanelli, 1982).

Whewell also studied the choice of technique problem that arises when a machine becomes newly available that can replace direct labour in the production process of a commodity. He thus scrutinized a proposition that had been advanced by Ricardo in Section 5 of Chapter 1 and in Chapter 31 of his *Principles*, namely that 'machinery and labour are in constant competition, and the former can frequently not be employed until labour rises' (*Works*, I: 395):

Let a machine have been produced by the labour of l' labourers last year, l'' in the preceding year, l''' in the year before that, and so on. And let l men be employed in working it; then its produce must be worth

$$(1 + r)lw + (1 + r)^2l'w + (1 + r)^3l''w + \&c$$

Let L be the number of men requisite to obtain the same produce without the machine. Then Lw is their wages, and $(1 + r)Lw$ the value of the produce. Therefore, if the machine can be employed without loss,

$$(1 + r)lw + (1 + r)^2l'w + (1 + r)^3l''w + \&c. = \text{ or } < (1 + r)Lw,$$

$$\text{and } l + (1 + r)l' + (1 + r)^2l'' + \&c. = \text{ or } < L.$$

$$\text{Hence } l + l' + l'' + \&c. < L;$$

or, when machinery is employed, it has always cost less labour than would obtain the same produce without machinery. (Whewell [1831] 1971: 20)

This finding confirmed Ricardo's statement that 'these mute agents are always the produce of much less labour than that which they displace' (*Works*, I: 42).

In the final section of his 1831 paper Whewell considered Ricardo's analysis of foreign trade and of the effects of international gold movements on the level of prices. The first part (§§14–16), which is concerned with the restoration of the balance of trade by means of the specie-flow mechanism, seems to consist of no more than an algebraic reformulation of Ricardo's argument. In the second part (§§17–19), Whewell tackled the problem of the determination of the rate of exchange. According to Henderson, this analysis was:

> an oversimplified version of the mechanism of adjustment of international balances. Unfortunately, Whewell's assumptions were so restrictive that this model contributes little to our understanding of that doctrine . . . The international gold flows were assumed to affect only the nation importing gold but to have no influence whatever on either the prices or quantities of exported goods in the nation that exports the gold. (Henderson, 1996: 230)

In the final paragraph, Whewell proposed a simple way to determine the premium over par of the rate of exchange.

Conclusion

The assessments of Whewell's contributions to mathematical economics in the secondary literature differ widely. While Jevons (1879: 303) and Schumpeter (1954: 448n) described his economic papers as 'uninteresting', Whewell has been praised by others for the introduction of the concept of demand elasticity, and depicted as an important precursor of marginalism (Henderson, 1973). Moreover, both Viner (1937: 450n) and Chipman (1965: 492) have pointed to the significance of Whewell's contributions in J.S. Mill's development of the theory of international values. His treatment of Mill's trade theory in 1850 and his use of a rising supply schedule in combination with the demand elasticity concept have also led to conjectures that he might have been an important influence on Alfred Marshall (Henderson, 1996: 291–2).

On the other hand, and although he was decidedly critical of Ricardo's economics in terms of method and content, Whewell can also be said to have made important contributions to the further development of the surplus approach (which, however, went unnoticed by his contemporaries). He elaborated the formula for the reduction of fixed capital to dated quantities of labour, which was independently rediscovered only much later by Ladislaus von Bortkiewicz on the basis of Dmitriev's contribution. In addition, Whewell's treatment of the choice of technique problem in terms of inequalities and his Ricardian model of growth and income distribution in the 1831 paper can also be regarded as significant analytical contributions. Notwithstanding his critical attitude towards Ricardo, Whewell was a very attentive reader of Ricardo's *Principles*, who often noted more clearly than many modern interpreters the set of assumptions on which Ricardo's propositions were based.

CHRISTIAN GEHRKE

See also:

Bortkiewicz, Ladislaus von, on Ricardo; Dmitriev, Vladimir Karpovich, on Ricardo; Foreign Trade; Taxation; Tozer, John Edward, on Ricardo.

References

Campanelli, G. (1982), 'W. Whewell's contribution to economic analysis: the first mathematical formulation of fixed capital in Ricardo's system', *The Manchester School*, **50**(3), 248–65.

Chipman, J.S. (1965), 'A survey of the theory of international trade. Part 1: the classical theory', *Econometrica*, **33**(3), 477–519.

De Marchi, N.B. and R.P. Sturges (1973), 'Malthus and Ricardo's inductivist critics: four letters to William Whewell', *Economica*, **40**(160), 379–93.

Henderson, J.P. (1973), 'William Whewell's mathematical statements of price flexibility, demand elasticity and the Giffen paradox', *The Manchester School*, **41**(3), 329–42.

Henderson, J.P. (1996), *Early Mathematical Economics. William Whewell and the British Case*, Lanham/London: Rowman & Littlefield.

Jevons, W.S. (1879), *The Theory of Political Economy*, 2nd edition, London: Macmillan.

Jones, R. ([1831] 1964), *An Essay on the Distribution of Wealth, and on the Sources of Taxation. Part I. Rent*, London: John Murray; reprint, New York: A.M. Kelley.

Jones, R. ([1859] 1964), *Literary Remains Consisting of Lectures and Tracts on Political Economy of the Late Rev. Richard Jones*, edited with a Prefatory Notice by the Rev. William Whewell, London: John Murray; reprint, New York: A.M. Kelley.

Kim, J. (2001), 'The technique of comparative-static analysis in Whewell's "Mathematical Exposition"', *History of Political Economy*, **33**(4), 843–54.

Schumpeter, J. A. (1954), *History of Economic Analysis*, Oxford: Oxford University Press.

Shoup, C.S. (1960), *Ricardo on Taxation*, New York: Columbia University Press.

Thompson, T.P. (1826), *The True Theory of Rent, in Opposition to Mr. Ricardo and Others*, London: R. Heward.

Viner, J. (1937), *Studies in the Theory of International Trade*, London: Allen & Unwin.

Whewell, W. ([1829] 1971), 'Mathematical exposition of some doctrines of political economy', *Transactions of the Cambridge Philosophical Society*, **3**(1), 192–230; reprinted in W. Whewell, *Mathematical Exposition of Some Doctrines of Political Economy*, New York: A.M. Kelley.

Whewell, W. (1831), 'Jones. On the distribution of wealth and the sources of taxation', *The British Critic. Quarterly Theological Review, and Ecclesiastical Record*, 10 July, No. 19, 41–61.

Whewell, W. ([1831] 1971), 'Mathematical exposition of some of the leading doctrines in Mr Ricardo's Principles of Political Economy, and Taxation', *Transactions of the Cambridge Philosophical Society*, **4**(1), 155–98; reprinted in W. Whewell, *Mathematical Exposition of Some Doctrines of Political Economy*, New York: A.M. Kelley.

Whewell, W. ([1850] 1971), 'Mathematical exposition of some doctrines of political economy. Second memoir' and 'Mathematical exposition of certain doctrines of political economy. Third memoir', *Transactions of the Cambridge Philosophical Society*, **9**(1), 128–49, and **9**(2), 1–7; reprinted in W. Whewell, *Mathematical Exposition of Some Doctrines of Political Economy*, New York: A.M. Kelley.

Whewell, W. ([1862] 1967), *Six Lectures on Political Economy*, Cambridge, UK: Cambridge University Press; reprint, New York: A.M. Kelley.

Wicksell, Knut, on Ricardo

In the summer of 1900 the Swedish economist Knut Wicksell (1851–1926) wrote to his friend Öhrvall that his wife kept 'running wild' whenever she saw him with a book in his hands. She wanted him to spend his time writing instead of reading. 'While she was sleeping, however, I have secretly gone through Ricardo in one go – he is, in a way, the Helmholtz of Political Economy – and this was most refreshing' (quoted in Gårdlund, 1956: 204; my translation). That was no mean compliment for Ricardo, since Helmholtz was one of the greatest scientists of the nineteenth century: a polymath who had used mathematics and physics to find general explanations of phenomena in fields as diverse as chemistry, medicine, psychology, music and philosophy. In a similar fashion, Wicksell insinuated, Ricardo had explored the general principles of political economy. One may add that Wicksell, too, made his major contributions to economic thinking by attempting to develop a unifying framework of analysis, and that he nearly always used Ricardo as the authoritative starting reference.

Another parallel between Ricardo and Wicksell is their central concern with income distribution. Wicksell, who had studied mathematics, came to economics through his reading of Malthusian pamphlets on overpopulation, and through lectures that he subsequently gave on the social question in Sweden (for an account of Wicksell's life and works, see Trautwein, forthcoming). In order to deepen his understanding of political economy, Wicksell travelled to London in the late 1880s, where he studied the classics, and in particular Ricardo's *Principles*, with great intensity. He was less impressed by the progress of economic thinking in England after Ricardo. As he wrote in his first major work, a treatise on *Value, Capital and Rent* (*Über Wert, Kapital und Rente*, 1893): '[N]o general law worthy to be put beside Malthus's *Law of Population* or Ricardo's *Theory of Rent* has been laid down by any of their followers' ([1893] 1954: 29). In Wicksell's view, the sole exception was Jevons who, simultaneously with Walras and Menger, had developed a new theory of value in terms of marginal utility. Wicksell considered this as a transfer of the marginal principle in Ricardo's theory of rent to a more general determination of value that would do away with the shortcomings of Ricardo's labour-based theory of value. In the first volume of his *Lectures on Political Economy*, Wicksell ([1901] 1934: 14) argued that the marginal principle provides the base for a unified framework of economic analysis, as it 'extends far beyond the actual province of the exchange of goods into the fields of production, distribution, and capital. In other words, it governs every part of political economy.'

Wicksell acknowledged that it was an ingenious idea of Ricardo's to argue that 'the exchange values of various goods should stand in more or less direct relation to the quantities of labour required to produce them under the most unfavourable conditions which are necessary for their production, i.e. on the margin of production' (ibid.: 23). Yet he regarded it as 'the fundamental error of the classical theory of value' to assume that the margin of production is 'given *a priori*', whereas it 'is variable and itself depends, among other things, upon the actual exchange value of the goods in question and, to that extent, upon what it has to explain' (ibid.: 24). Even though Wicksell ([1893] 1954: 34–41 and [1901] 1934: 23–9) considered Ricardo's labour theory of value to be flawed in several aspects, he held Ricardo in high esteem: 'In his work the structure of economic theory appears, for the first time, as a coherent, logical system' ([1901] 1934: 23).

While Wicksell appreciated the pioneering work of Jevons and Walras in marginal utility theory, he was dissatisfied with their treatment of capital and interest. In his application of the marginal principle to the determination of factor prices and, hence, the distribution of income, he made use of Böhm-Bawerk's theory of capital and interest with its emphasis on the role of time for productivity and consumption plans. Wicksell (ibid.: 172) argued that 'the time element . . . is the real kernel of the capital concept'. The challenge was to overcome the problem that the capital stock, unlike land and labour, cannot be directly quantified in physical units of area and time, such as acres and hours, as it consists of a variety of incommensurable goods. '[I]t is futile to attempt – with Walras and his followers – to derive the value of capital-goods from their own cost of production or reproduction; for in fact these costs include capital and interest . . . We should, therefore, be arguing in a circle' (ibid.: 149). Wicksell adopted the trick of defining capital as 'saved-up labour and saved-up land' (ibid.: 154), a conglomerate of land and labour services of earlier periods. In this way he considered the rate of interest as being determined by the marginal products of *dated* services of land and labour. In general equilibrium, their marginal products, valued at their prices in the goods markets, correspond to the rent rate and wage rate, multiplied with compound interest. Accordingly, '[i]nterest is the difference between the marginal productivity of saved-up labour and land and of current labour and land' (ibid.). Even so, Wicksell had to assume a given value of the aggregate capital stock – a procedure that he admitted to be valid only under very restrictive conditions ([1911] 1958: 183–4; [1928] 1997: 208). Wicksell thus openly faced a dilemma in his approach to value theory that bears some resemblance to the problems in labour theory of value he had criticized in Ricardo.

Moreover, Wicksell demonstrated in his critique of Ricardo's follower Thünen that, after an increase in aggregate capital, competition for labour and land tends to reduce the marginal product of capital by more than it lowers the rate of interest ([1901] 1934: 148–9). This 'anomaly' of marginal analysis came later to be known as the (real) 'Wicksell effect' (Kurz, 2005). It is closer to Ricardo's insight (*Works*, I: 30–43) that income distribution determines the value of capital goods (and, hence, relative prices) than it is to neoclassical standard postulates that marginal productivity and utility determine income distribution through the system of relative prices. Even though Wicksell hardly referred to Ricardo in the capital-theory context of his *Lectures* (1901), he had pointed out in *Value, Capital and Rent* (1893) that Ricardo had anticipated important aspects of modern interest-rate theory, when he discussed the use of labour-saving machinery in consequence of a wage rise:

> The price of machinery . . . includes profit as well as wages. As this profit, like all the others, must fall when wages rise, the price of machines can consequently never rise in the same proportion as wages. According to the more modern terminology, this means that every increase of wages encourages a lengthening of the period of production, which occupies more time but is more productive, whereby the wage increase is partly compensated. Indeed, in this example of Ricardo's, the fine theories with which Böhm-Bawerk has recently enriched the subject lie enclosed as in the bud. ([1893] 1954: 37–8)

In a later review of Böhm-Bawerk's theory of capital, Wicksell ([1911] 1958: 177) consequently observed that:

> Böhm-Bawerk scarcely does Ricardo justice. It seems to me that however incomplete Ricardo's theory of interest may be, it is quite correct so far as it goes. Its greatest defect is probably that Ricardo, like English economists in general, regards the sole function of capital to be the advancement of wages, whereas it is actually to almost the same extent the advancement of rents as well.

However, Wicksell strongly disagreed with Ricardo's conclusions in the famous 'On Machinery' chapter of the third edition of the *Principles* (*Works*, I, XXXI), according to which the introduction of labour-saving machinery may lead to persistent unemployment and a reduction in aggregate output. In numerous writings, spanning three decades between *Value, Capital and Rent* and an article submitted to the *Economic Journal* in 1923 (but rejected by Keynes; see Wicksell [1923a] 1981), Wicksell argued that, in free competition, the displacement of labour would lead to wage reductions, which in turn would increase the profitability of more labour-intensive, but on average less productive techniques, whereby displaced workers would be reabsorbed into employment. In this way, the introduction of labour-saving machinery would always increase aggregate output. However, Wicksell's hypothesis of factor substitution is based on specific assumptions that have later been critically examined by Neisser, Pasinetti, Samuelson and others (see Hagemann, 2010).

It should be noted that Wicksell, towards the end of his life, became more pessimistic about the reabsorption of displaced labour (Boianovsky and Trautwein, 2003). Moreover, he was never contradicting Ricardo's conclusion that technical change may have detrimental effects on the working class. As Wicksell noted, '[a]n important and most remarkable thing is that the fall of wage ... becomes a necessary condition for the production of the maximum of the aggregate' ([1923a] 1981: 203). Even though he believed that, in many cases, technical progress tends to increase real wages, he was, unlike Ricardo, open to the possibility that it could make wages fall below subsistence level:

> In reality, wages can not only be forced below it for a little, but can remain below it indefinitely, if the labourers and their families can make up the difference by poor relief, as happened in England to a great extent at the end of the eighteenth and the beginning of the nineteenth centuries. ([1901] 1934: 141)

Accordingly, Wicksell advocated wage subsidies, while rejecting minimum wages and working time reductions, as the latter would produce persistent unemployment and impoverishment. He suggested financing wage subsidies out of taxes on the additional social product generated by labour-saving technical progress. Wicksell thus provided a neoclassical justification of employment policies in welfare states.

Wicksell's second book was a treatise on the theory of public finance (*Finanztheoretische Untersuchungen*, 1896). Its first part was based on Wicksell's doctoral dissertation *On the Theory of Tax Incidence*. Comparing the distribution effects of direct and indirect taxes, Wicksell ([1896] 1997: 57–115) showed that, with regard to a maximization of aggregate output and a fair distribution of incomes, a tax on profits is to be preferred. In this context he made numerous references to Ricardo, in particular to Chapters IX and XVI in the *Principles*. Wicksell criticized Ricardo's assertion that a 'tax on labourers, e.g. in the form of higher duties on necessary foodstuffs' would not harm the working class because of 'an immediate wage increase as a consequence of the tax' (ibid.: 108). He found Ricardo's argument self-contradictory and 'disastrous for the working class'. In a later essay on the development of the concept of income, he noted even more harshly: 'Unfortunately the cast-iron logic that characterizes most of Ricardo's writings is absent from these chapters. It is hard to avoid the impression that he had a certain favourite plan concerning the practice of taxation in mind, dimming his critical gaze' (Wicksell [1923b] 1997: 182).

In Wicksell's third major work, *Interest and Prices* (*Geldzins und Güterpreise*, 1898), Ricardo played the more positive role of 'the great master' in whose footsteps Wicksell ([1898] 1936: xxiii–xxiv) wished 'to push on' the development of the quantity theory of money to a theory 'both self-consistent and in full agreement with the facts' of a modern banking system. Wicksell pointed out that Ricardo had demonstrated that an 'excess of money will ... show itself through a rise in all prices, partly through a fall in the rate of interest. But the latter, Ricardo emphasizes, can only be a temporary phenomenon.' It ends when the increase in the quantity of money and the corresponding increase in prices bring the rate of interest back to its original level. In the second volume of his

Lectures, Wicksell praised Ricardo's *High Price of Bullion* (1810) as 'a clear and definite examination' of conflicting views, 'conducted in a language which contrasts favourably by its freshness and directness with his later and much heavier style' and 'for all time a precious pearl in the literature of political economy' ([1915] 1935: 176). Wicksell ([1898] 1936: xxiv–xxv) modified Ricardo's argument by suggesting that a permanent fall in the bank rate of interest would lead to a constant increase in the money supply and a cumulative rise in prices. According to Wicksell, Ricardo had not seen this possibility because credit creation by banks was not yet fully developed in 1810, and because Ricardo tended to interpret the rate of interest in absolute terms. Against this, Wicksell emphasized the systematic occurrence of discrepancies between the market rate of interest (the banks' loan rate) and the 'natural rate of interest'. Wicksell ([1898] 1936: 82, n1) also argued that Ricardo's assertion of the impossibility of 'an invariable measure of value' (e.g., *Works*, I, I: 43–7) 'would to-day be regarded as old-fashioned and is no longer tenable in view of the possibility of employing index numbers'. If the system could be made independent of the restrictions of the gold supply, central banks could eliminate inflation by bringing the market rate of interest in line with the natural rate.

However, when it was pointed out to Wicksell that Ricardo in his *Principles* (Works, I, XXVII, 'On Currency and Banks'), and Henry Thornton before him, had made a distinction between the banks' loan rates and the rate of return on real investment, Wicksell qualified his earlier critique of Ricardo in the second edition of Volume II of his *Lectures* ([1915] 1934: 200). Apparently Wicksell's wife had not slept long enough that night when Wicksell had 'gone through Ricardo in one go'. Yet Wicksell was always willing to give Ricardo the credit he deserved.

HANS-MICHAEL TRAUTWEIN

See also:

Jevons, William Stanley, on Ricardo; Marshall, Alfred, on Ricardo; Walras, Marie-Esprit-Léon, on Ricardo.

References

Boianovsky, M. and H.-M. Trautwein (2003), 'Wicksell, Cassel and the idea of involuntary unemployment', *History of Political Economy*, **35**(3), 385–436.

Gårdlund, T. (1956), *Knut Wicksell. Rebell i det nya riket*, Stockholm: Bonniers.

Hagemann, H. (2010), 'Knut Wicksell über Ricardos Maschinerieproblem', in H. Hagemann (ed.), *Studien zur Entwicklung der ökonomischen Theorie Vol. XXIII*, Berlin: Duncker & Humblot, pp. 173–201.

Kurz, H.D. (2005), 'Wicksell effects', in W.A. Darity (ed.), *International Encyclopedia of the Social Sciences, Vol. 9*, 2nd edition, Detroit: Macmillan Reference USA, pp. 94–6.

Trautwein, H.-M. (forthcoming), 'Knut Wicksell', in G. Faccarello and H.D. Kurz (eds), *Handbook of the History of Economic Analysis*, Cheltenham, UK and Northampton, MA: Edward Elgar Publishing.

Wicksell, K. ([1893] 1954), *Über Wert, Kapital und Rente. Nach den neueren nationalökonomischen Theorien*, Jena: G. Fischer; translation by S.H. Frowein as *On Value, Capital and Rent*, London: Macmillan.

Wicksell, K. ([1896] 1997), *Finanztheoretische Untersuchungen nebst Darstellung und Kritik des Steuerwesens Schwedens*, Jena: G. Fischer; translated as *Part I: On the Theory of Tax Incidence* in B. Sandelin (ed.), *Knut Wicksell – Selected Essays in Economics, Vol. I*, London: Routledge, pp. 57–115.

Wicksell, K. ([1898] 1936), *Geldzins und Güterpreise. Eine Studie über die den Tauschwert des Geldes bestimmenden Ursachen*, Jena: G. Fischer; translated as *Interest and Prices. A Study of the Causes Regulating the Value of Money*, London: Macmillan.

Wicksell, K. ([1901] 1934), *Föreläsningar i nationalekonomi, I: Teoretisk nationalekonomi*, Lund: C.W.K. Gleerups förlag; translated as *Lectures on Political Economy, Vol. I: General Theory*, 1st edition, London: George Routledge & Sons.

Wicksell, K. ([1911] 1958), 'Böhm-Bawerk's theory of capital', in E. Lindahl (ed.), *Knut Wicksell – Selected Papers on Economic Theory*, London: Allen & Unwin, pp. 176–85.

Wicksell, K. ([1915] 1935), *Föreläsningar i nationalekonomi, II: Penningar och kredit*, 2nd edition, Stockholm: Fritzes hofbokhandel; translated as *Lectures on Political Economy, Vol. 2: Money*, London: Routledge.

Wicksell, K. ([1923a] 1981), 'Ricardo on machinery and the present unemployment', reproduced in L. Jonung 'Ricardo on machinery and the present unemployment: an unpublished manuscript by Knut Wicksell', *Economic Journal*, **91**(361), 199–205.

Wicksell, K. ([1923b] 1997), *The Historical Development of the Concept of Income*, in B. Sandelin (ed.), *Knut Wicksell – Selected Essays in Economics, Vol. I*, London: Routledge, pp. 170–212.

Wicksell, K. ([1928] 1997), *On the Theory of Interest (Böhm-Bawerk's 'Third Ground')*, in B. Sandelin (ed.), *Knut Wicksell – Selected Essays in Economics, Vol. I*, London: Routledge, pp. 41–53.

Name index

Ahiakpor, J. 152
Alcock, T. 406
Almenar, S. 378
Anderson, J. 256, 532
Arena, R. 82
Aristotle 491–2
Arnon, A. 41, 50
Ashley, W. 193, 284, 290–92, 464–5
Aspromourgos, T. 470–74
Asso, P.F. 362, 465
Attwood, M. 54
Attwood, T. 54

Bagehot, W. 224, 327, 336, 338, 341
Bailey, S. 246, 504
Bain, A. 18
Baring, A. 54, 173
Baring, F. 47–8
Barro, R.J. 152–3, 453–4, 516
Barton, J. 321
Barucci, E. 362, 465
Baumol, W.J. 161
Baumstark, E. 377
Beccaria, C. 191
Belsham, T. 14–17
Bentham, J. 17–22, 135–7, 323, 331, 407, 412,
    461, 499
Béraud, A. 376
Besicovitch, A.S. 520–21
Biaujeaud, H. 23–5
Bidard, C. 262–3
Blanqui, A. 190–91
Blaug, M. 23–4, 26–9, 153, 405, 547
Block, M. 376
Bloomfield, A.I. 506
Böhm-Bawerk, E. von 30–36, 38, 118, 179,
    214, 495, 594–5
Bonar, J. 355, 379, 465
Bondi, G. 377
Bortkiewicz, L. von 36–40, 117, 246, 253, 259,
    551, 592
Bosanquet, C. 51, 538
Botero, G. 410
Boulding, K. 225
Bowring, J. 21
Boyd, W. 47–8, 49, 173
Bray, J.F. 455–6, 459–62
Buchanan, D. 110, 357, 467, 475, 544

Buchanan, J.M. 152, 451, 453–4
Burke, E. 407

Cannan, E. 24–6, 60, 203, 326, 361, 442, 519,
    524
Cantillon, R. 497
Caravale, G. 367, 436
Cardoso, J.L. 223, 378
Carlyle, T. 192
Casarosa, C. 7–9, 186, 238–40, 435–6, 444
Cassel, G. 111–12
Chamberlain, J. 193
Charasoff, G. von 551
Chipman, J. 497–8, 592
Churchman, N. 152
Clapham, J. 41
Clark, J.B. 36, 214
Cliffe Leslie, T.E. 193, 286
Clower, R.W. 509
Cobbett, W. 456, 462
Collard, D.A. 567
Colquhoun, P. 458
Constâncio, F.S. 375–6, 499, 500
Copleston, E. 318
Cos-Gayón, F. 378
Cossa, L. 378
Cournot, A.A. 114, 117–18, 286, 290
Cremaschi, S. 21
Cunningham, W. 193
Custodi, P. 191

D'Alessandro, S. 126
Darnell, A.C. 567
Davis, J.B. 220, 246
Davis, T. 160, 268
De Marchi, N. 223, 333, 340
De Pinto, I. 223
de Viti de Marco, A. 453
de Vivo, G. 86, 562–4
Debyser, C. 376
Deleplace, G. 22, 465
Depoortère, C. 14, 18, 333, 349, 465
Diehl, K. 377
Dietzel, H. 30
Dmitriev, V.K. 37, 114–19, 246, 253, 579, 592
Dobb, M.H. 212, 246, 465, 521
Dome, T. 538
Dorfman, J. 456